EUROPE

TOP SIGHTS, AUTHENTIC EXPERIENCES

Simon Richmond, Alexis Averbuck, Mark Baker, Oliver
Berry, Abigail Blasi, Cristian Bonetto, Kerry Christiani,
Fionn Davenport, Sally Davies, Peter Dragicevich, Steve
Fallon, Emilie Filou, Duncan Garwood, Bridget Gleeson,
Paula Hardy, Damian Harper, Anna Kaminski, Catherine Le
Nevez, Vi͏   Josephine
Quintero,

Contents

Plan Your Trip

Europe's Top 21 6
Need to Know 26
Hotspots for 28
Local Life 30
Month by Month 32
Get Inspired 35
Itineraries 36
Family Travel 46

Great Britain & Ireland 49

London, Great Britain 50

Westminster Abbey 52
British Museum 58
Buckingham Palace 62
Tower of London 66
A Northern Point of View 72
Sights 74
Tours 85
Shopping 86
Eating 87
Drinking & Nightlife 90
Entertainment 92
Where to Stay 95

Scottish Highlands, Great Britain 96

On the Whisky Trail 98
Loch Ness 100
Inverness 104
Fort William 110

Dublin, Ireland 114

Trinity College 116
Guinness Storehouse 118
Sights 120
Tours 125
Shopping 125
Eating 128
Drinking & Nightlife 129
Entertainment 131
Where to Stay 133

Scandinavia & Northern Europe 135

Copenhagen, Denmark 136

Tivoli Gardens 138
Designmuseum Danmark 140
Sights 142
Tours 146
Shopping 147
Eating 148
Drinking & Nightlife 150
Entertainment 152

Amsterdam, the Netherlands 154

Van Gogh Museum 156
Anne Frank Huis 158
Sights 160
Activities 165
Tours 166

Shopping 166
Eating 167
Drinking & Nightlife 170
Entertainment 172
Where to Stay 175

Reykjavík, Iceland 176

National Museum 178
Blue Lagoon 180
Golden Circle 182
Sights 184
Activities 189
Shopping 190
Eating 191
Drinking & Nightlife 195
Entertainment 197
Where to Stay 199

France, Spain & Portugal 201

Paris, France 202

Eiffel Tower 204
The Louvre 210
Notre Dame 216
Day Trip: Château de Versailles 222
Seine-Side Meander 226
Sights 228
Shopping 236
Eating 239
Drinking & Nightlife 245
Entertainment 248
Where to Stay 251

Provence, France   **252**

Pont du Gard 254
Hilltop Villages 256
Avignon 260
Moustiers
Ste-Marie 266

Barcelona, Spain   **268**

La Sagrada
Família 270
La Rambla 278
Montjuïc 284
Treasures in
the Barri Gòtic 286
Sights 288
Tours 297
Shopping 297
Eating 298
Drinking & Nightlife....301
Entertainment 304
Where to Stay 307

Basque Country,
Spain   **308**

Museo Guggenheim
Bilbao 310
Pintxo Bars 312
Bilbao 316
San Sebastián 323

Lisbon, Portugal   **330**

Mosteiro dos
Jerónimos 332
Lisbon's Trams 334
Sights 336
Activities 341
Tours 342

Shopping 343
Eating 344
Drinking & Nightlife... 346
Entertainment 347
Where to Stay 349

Italy & Croatia   **351**

Rome, Italy   **352**

Colosseum 354
Pantheon 358
St Peter's
Basilica 362
Vatican Museums 366
Roman Forum 372
Centro Storico
Piazzas 378
Sights 380
Shopping 390
Eating 391
Drinking & Nightlife... 394
Entertainment 395
Where to Stay 399

Venice, Italy   **400**

Grand Canal 402
Basilica di
San Marco 404
Palazzo Ducale 406
Venice Gourmet
Crawl 408
Sights 410
Activities 411
Shopping 414
Eating 414
Drinking & Nightlife.... 416
Entertainment 416

Florence, Italy   **418**

Duomo 420
Galleria
dell'Accademia 424
Galleria
degli Uffizi 426
Heart of the City 430
Sights 432
Shopping 438
Eating 440
Drinking & Nightlife... 442

Tuscany, Italy   **444**

Towers of San
Gimignano 446
Leaning Tower
of Pisa 448
Tuscan Road Trip 450
Siena 452
Arezzo 455
Montepulciano 458
Montalcino 460

Ruins of Pompeii,
Italy   **462**

Dubrovnik, Croatia **470**

City Walls & Forts 472
Game of Thrones
Locations 474
Sights 476
Activities 479
Tours 480
Shopping 480
Eating 480
Drinking & Nightlife... 482

Contents

**Germany &
Eastern Europe 485**

Berlin, Germany   486

The Berlin Wall 488
The Reichstag 492
Berlin Nightlife 494
Historical
Highlights 496
Sights 498
Tours 508
Shopping 509
Eating 509
Drinking & Nightlife 513
Entertainment 516
Where to Stay 519

Schloss
Neuschwanstein,
Germany   520

**Prague,
Czech Republic   524**

Prague Castle 526
Prague
River Stroll 530
Sights 532
Tours 539
Shopping 539
Eating 540
Drinking & Nightlife 542
Entertainment 543

**Budapest,
Hungary   546**

Royal Palace 548
Thermal Baths
& Spas 550
Sights 552
Shopping 558
Eating 559
Drinking & Nightlife 561
Entertainment 562

Vienna, Austria   564

Schloss
Schönbrunn 566
Kunsthistorisches
Museum Vienna 568
Sights 570
Activities 578
Shopping 578
Eating 580
Drinking & Nightlife 583
Entertainment 584

**Swiss Alps,
Switzerland   586**

Matterhorn 588
Glacier Express 590
Zermatt 592

CANADASTOCK / SHUTTERSTOCK ©

In Focus

Europe Today 600
History 602
Arts &
Architecture 609
Food & Drink 614

Survival Guide

Directory A–Z 620
Transport 630
Language 635
Index 638
Symbols &
Map Key 646

Left: Cycling past the Reichstag (p492), Berlin;
Top right: Houses in Lisbon (p330); Bottom right: A Tuscan village (p444)

Plan Your Trip
Europe's Top 21

JON ARNOLD / SHUTTERSTOCK ©

London, Britain

Truly one of the world's greatest cities

London is mercurial and endlessly fascinating; you could spend a lifetime getting to know it, then realise it's gone and changed again. Stretching back from the mighty River Thames, its lush parks and historic districts are crammed with extraordinary sights: royal palaces, towering cathedrals and remarkable museums and galleries. Add the pick of the world's theatres, restaurants, sports venues and shops, and you'll be very reluctant to leave. Right: Great Court, British Museum (p58)

1

Venice, Italy

Magical city seemingly floating on water

A sunny winter's day, with far fewer tourists around, is the perfect time to lap up Venice's unique and magical atmosphere. Ditch your map and wander the shadowy backlines of Dorsoduro while imagining secret assignations and whispered conspiracies at every turn. Then visit two of Venice's top galleries, the Gallerie dell'Accademia and the Peggy Guggenheim Collection, which houses works by many of the giants of 20th-century art.

2

Rome, Italy

Classical ruins mixed with contemporary style

From the crumbling Colosseum to the ancient Forum and the Appian Way, few sights are more evocative than the ruins of ancient Rome. Two thousand years ago this city was the centre of the greatest empire of the ancient world, where gladiators battled and emperors lived in unimaginable luxury. Nowadays it's a haunting spot: as you walk the cobbled paths, you can almost sense the ghosts in the air. Top: Roman Forum (p372); Bottom: Colosseum (p354)

ALKPIN / GETTY IMAGES ©

Paris, France

Up close with an architectural icon

Designed as a temporary exhibit for the 1889 Exposition Universelle (World Fair), Paris' elegant art nouveau Eiffel Tower has become the defining fixture of the skyline. Its recent 1st-floor refit adds two glitzy glass pavilions housing interactive exhibits; outside, peer d-o-w-n through the glass floor to the ground below. Visit at dusk for the best day and night views of the City of Light and make a toast at the sparkling champagne bar.

Berlin, Germany

Catch the ever-changing zeitgeist

More than 25 years since the fall of the Berlin Wall, it's hard to believe that this most cosmopolitan of cities once marked the frontier of the Cold War. But reminders of Berlin's divided past still remain: whether you're passing the Brandenburg Gate, gazing at graffiti at the East Side Gallery or soaking up the history at Checkpoint Charlie, it's an essential part of understanding what makes Germany's capital tick. *Drei Mädchen und ein Knabe* (Three Girls and a Boy) by artist Wilfried Fitzenreiter near the Berliner Dom (p503)

5

6

Dubrovnik, Croatia

Spectacular walled city

Dubrovnik's main claim to fame are its historic ramparts, considered among the finest in the world, which surround luminous marble streets and finely ornamented buildings. Built between the 13th and 16th centuries, the walls are still remarkably intact today, and the vistas over the terracotta rooftops and the Adriatic Sea are sublime, especially at dusk, when the fading light makes the hues dramatic and the panoramas unforgettable.

7

Prague, Czech Republic

An architectural central European jewel

The capital of the Czech Republic is one of Europe's most alluring and dynamic places. For all its modern verve, some parts of the city have hardly changed since medieval times – cobbled cul-de-sacs snake through the Old Town, framed by tee-tering townhouses, baroque buildings and graceful bridges. And if castles are your thing, Prague Castle is an absolute beauty: a 1000-year-old fortress covering around 7 hectares – the world's largest.
Charles Bridge (p535)

Vienna, Austria

Grand heart of a former empire

The monumentally graceful Hofburg whisks you back to the age of empires in Vienna as you marvel at the treasury's imperial crowns, the equine ballet of the Spanish Riding School and the chandelier-lit apartments fit for Empress Elisabeth. The palace, a legacy of the 640-year Habsburg era, is rivalled in grandeur only by the 1441-room Schloss Schönbrunn, a Unesco World Heritage Site, and the baroque Schloss Belvedere, both set in exquisite gardens. Schloss Belvedere (p576)

STANDRET / SHUTTERSTOCK ©

CANADASTOCK / SHUTTERSTOCK ©

9

Amsterdam, The Netherlands

World Heritage–listed canals and gabled buildings

To say Amsterdammers love the water is an understatement. Stroll next to the canals and check out some of the thousands of houseboats. Or better still, go for a ride. From boat level you'll see a whole new set of architectural details such as the ornamentation bedecking the bridges. And when you pass the canalside cafe terraces, you can just look up and wave.

MRPHOTOMANIA / SHUTTERSTOCK ©

Budapest, Hungary

Beautiful Hungarian capital straddling the Danube

Straddling both sides of the romantic Danube River, with the Buda Hills to the west and the start of the Great Plain to the east, Budapest is perhaps the most beautiful city in Eastern Europe. Parks brim with attractions, the architecture is second to none, museums are filled with treasures, pleasure boats sail up and down the scenic Danube Bend, Turkish-era thermal baths belch steam and its nightlife throbs till dawn most nights. Széchenyi Baths (p551)

WENDY PAUW PHOTOGRAPHY / GETTY IMAGES ©

Barcelona, Spain

The genius of a visionary architect

Barcelona is famous for its Modernista architecture, much of which was designed by Antoni Gaudí. His masterwork is the mighty cathedral La Sagrada Família, which remains a work in progress close to a century after its creator's death. It's a bizarre combination of crazy and classic: Gothic touches intersect with eccentric experiments and improbable angles. No one is entirely sure when it will be finished; but even half completed, it's a modern-day wonder.
La Sagrada Família (p270)

Lisbon, Portugal

Soulful city armed with Gothic grit

Alfama, with its labyrinthine alleyways, hidden courtyards and curving, shadow-filled lanes, is a magical place to lose all sense of direction and delve into Lisbon's soul. On the journey, you'll pass breadbox-sized grocers, brilliantly tiled buildings and views of steeply pitched rooftops leading down to the glittering Tejo. Pause at cosy taverns filled with easygoing chatter, with the scent of chargrilled sardines and the mournful rhythms of fado drifting in the breeze.

12

SWEN STROOP / SHUTTERSTOCK ©

ANDREW SWINBANK / SHUTTERSTOCK ©

GEORGECLERK / GETTY IMAGES ©

The Scottish Highlands

Scenic grandeur and echoes of the past

Breathtaking views abound in the Highlands. From the regal charm of Royal Deeside, via the brooding majesty of Glen Coe, to the mysterious waters of sweeping Loch Ness – these are landscapes that inspire awe. The region is scattered with fairy-tale castles and the hiking is suitably glorious. Add the nooks of warm Highland hospitality found in classic rural pubs and romantic hotels, and you have an unforgettable corner of the country.

13

Dublin, Ireland

Pints of Guinness and literary connections

Whether you're wandering the leafy Georgian terraces of St Stephen's Green or getting acquainted with the past at Kilmainham Gaol, in Dublin you're never far from a literary or historic sight. And then there are the city's pubs: there are few better places to down a pint than Dublin, and you can even make a pilgrimage to the original Guinness brewery on the city's outskirts. Either way, you'll make a few Irish friends along the way.

14

15

Tuscany, Italy

Italy's most romanticised region

The gently rolling hills of Tuscany, bathed in golden light and dotted with vineyards, sum up Italy's attractions in a nutshell. Battalions of books, postcards and lifestyle TV shows try to do this region justice, but nothing beats a visit. Here picture-perfect hilltop towns vie with magnificent scenery and some of Italy's best food and wine – creating a tourist hotspot. Visit in spring or autumn to see it at its calmest.

16

Pompeii, Italy

Ancient city destroyed and preserved by Vesuvius

Frozen in its death throes, the sprawling, time-warped ruins of Pompeii hurtle you 2000 years into the past. Wander through chariot-grooved Roman streets, lavishly frescoed villas and bathhouses, food stores and markets, theatres and even an ancient brothel. Then, in the eerie stillness, with your eye on ominous Mt Vesuvius, ponder the town's final hours when the skies grew dark and heavy with volcanic ashes.

17

Basque Country, Spain

Home to fabulous food and architecture

This is where mountain peaks reach for the sky and sublime rocky coves are battered by mighty Atlantic swells. Food is an obsession, whether it's the Michelin-starred restaurants of San Sebastián or the fabulous *pintxo* (Basque tapas) bars in the same city or in Bilbao. And the Basque Country has reinvented itself as one of Spain's style and culture capitals, with Bilbao's stunning Museo Guggenheim leading the way.

Reykjavík, Iceland

The world's most northerly capital

Most Icelanders live in Reykjavík and even on the shortest visit you'll be struck by how quirky and creative a population this is. Despite being on the northern margin of Europe, the locals have crafted a town packed with captivating art, rich cuisine and an epic music scene. Learn about a history stretching back to the Vikings and use the city as a base for trips to Iceland's amazing natural wonders.

Far left: Blue Lagoon (p180); Left: Hallgrímskirkja (p184)

LAMIAFOTOGRAFIA / SHUTTERSTOCK ©

JOSE ANTONIO SANCHEZ / SHUTTERSTOCK ©

MASKOT / GETTY IMAGES ©

Copenhagen, Denmark

Coolest kid on the Nordic block

Scandivania is all about paired-back contemporary style – something that the Danish capital has in spades. Home to a thriving design scene, Copenhagen sports Michelin-starred restaurants, hipster cafes and bars and swoon-worthy boutiques around every corner. Add in top-class museums and galleries and a thousand-year-old harbour town area with handsome historic architecture and you have the perfect Scandi city. Top: Nyhavn (p142); Above Left: Royal Danish Library, designed by Schmidt Hammer Lassen Architects; Above Right: Barista making coffee

19

PATHARA BURANADILOK / SHUTTERSTOCK ©

Matterhorn, Switzerland

Hike, ski and admire this Swiss peak

It graces chocolate-bar wrappers and evokes stereotypical Heidi scenes, but nothing prepares you for the allure of the Matterhorn. This mesmerising peak looms above the timber-chalet-filled Swiss village of Zermatt. Gaze at it from a tranquil cafe, hike in its shadow along the tangle of alpine paths above town, with cowbells clinking in the distance, or pause on a ski slope and admire its craggy, chiselled outline.

20

ROXANA BASHYROVA / SHUTTERSTOCK ©

Florence, Italy

Tailor-made for fastidious aesthetes

Home to Brunelleschi's Duomo and Masaccio's Cappella Brancacci frescoes, Florence, according to Unesco, contains 'the greatest concentration of universally renowned works of art in the world'. Florence is where the Renaissance kicked off and artists such as Michelangelo, Brunelleschi and Botticelli rewrote the rules of creative expression. The result is a city packed with artistic treasures, blockbuster museums, elegant churches and flawless Renaissance streetscapes. Galleria degli Uffizi (p426)

21

Plan Your Trip
Need to Know

When to Go?

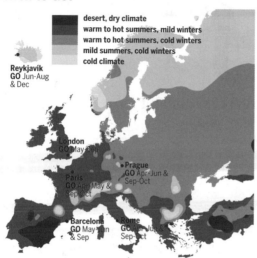

desert, dry climate
warm to hot summers, mild winters
warm to hot summers, cold winters
mild summers, cold winters
cold climate

Reykjavík
GO Jun-Aug
& Dec

London
GO May-Sep

Paris
GO Apr-May &
Sep-Oct

Prague
GO Apr-Jun &
Sep-Oct

Barcelona
GO May-Jun
& Sep

Rome
GO Apr-Jun &
Sep-Oct

High Season (Jun–Aug)

o Everybody comes to Europe and all of Europe hits the road.

o Hotel prices and temperatures are their highest.

Shoulder (Apr–May & Sep–Oct)

o Crowds and prices drop, except in Italy where it's still busy.

o Temperatures are comfortable but it can be hot in southern Europe.

o Overall these are the best months to travel in Europe.

Low Season (Nov–Mar)

o Outside ski resorts, hotels drop their prices or close down.

o The weather can be cold and days short, especially in northern Europe.

Currency

Euro (€), Pound (£), Swiss franc (Sfr), Danish krone (Dkr), Hungarian Forint (Ft), Icelandic króna (kr), Czech crown (Koruna česká; Kč), Croatian Kuna (KN)

Language

English, French, German, Italian, Spanish

Visas

EU citizens don't need visas for other EU countries. Australians, Canadians, New Zealanders and Americans don't need visas for visits of less than 90 days.

Money

ATMs are common; credit and debit cards are widely accepted.

Mobile Phones

Europe uses the GSM 900 network. If you're coming from outside Europe it's worth buying a prepaid local SIM.

Time

Britain, Ireland and Portugal (GMT), Central Europe (GMT plus one hour), Greece, Turkey and Eastern Europe (GMT plus two hours).

Daily Costs

Budget: Less than €60

- Dorm beds: €10–20

- Admission to museums: €5–15

- Pizza or pasta: €8–12

Midrange: €60–200

- Double room in a small hotel. €50–100

- Short taxi trip: €10–20

- Meals in good restaurants: around €20 per person

Top end: More than €200

- Stay at iconic hotels: from €150

- Car hire: from around €30 per day

- Theatre tickets: €15–150

Useful Websites

Lonely Planet (www.lonelyplanet.com/europe) Destination information, hotel bookings, traveller forum and more.

The Man in Seat Sixty-One (www.seat61.com) Encyclopedic site dedicated to train travel plus plenty of other tips.

Hidden Europe (www.hiddeneurope.co.uk) Fascinating magazine and online dispatches from all the continent's corners.

VisitEurope (www.visiteurope.com) With information about travel in 33 member countries.

Spotted by Locals (www.spottedbylocals.com) Insider tips for cities across Europe.

Where to Stay

Europe offers the fullest possible range of accommodation for all budgets. Book up to two months in advance for a July visit, or for ski resorts over Christmas and New Year.

Hotels Range from the local pub to restored castles.

B&Bs Small, family-run houses generally provide good value.

Hostels Enormous variety, from backpacker palaces to real dumps.

Homestays and farmstays A great way to really find out how locals live.

Arriving in Europe

Schiphol Airport, Amsterdam (p174) Trains to the centre (20 minutes).

Heathrow Airport, London (p94) Trains (15 minutes) and Tube (one hour) to the centre.

Aéroport de Charles de Gaulle, Paris (p250) Many buses (one hour) and trains (30 minutes) to the centre.

Tegel Airport, Berlin (p517) Buses (40 minutes) and taxis (30 to 45 minutes) to the centre.

Leonardo da Vinci Airport, Rome (p397) Buses (one hour) and trains (30 minutes) to the centre.

El Prat Airport, Barcelona (p306) Buses (35 minutes) to the centre.

Getting Around

In most European countries, the train is the best option for internal transport.

Train Europe's train network is fast and efficient but rarely a bargain unless you book well in advance or use a rail pass wisely.

Bus Usually taken for short trips in remoter areas, though long-distance intercity buses can be cheap.

Car You can hire a car or drive your own through Europe. Roads are excellent but petrol is expensive.

Ferry Boats connect Britain and Ireland with mainland Europe and criss-cross the Mediterranean.

Air Speed things up by flying from one end of the continent to the other.

Bicycle Slow things down on a two-wheeler, a great way to get around just about anywhere.

For more on **getting around**, see p631

Plan Your Trip
Hotspots for...

History

Europe's epic history is writ large across the continent with headline sights that bring it vividly to life – from Rome's majestic ruins to grand palaces and parliaments.

CRISTIAN PUSCASU / SHUTTERSTOCK ©

Rome (p352)
History reverberates all over the Eternal City, from the gladiatorial Colosseum to the Vatican.

Birth of an Empire
Romulus supposedly founded Rome in Palatino (p380).

London (p50)
Indomitable London has seen it all from the Romans and the Great Fire to the Blitz and the Swinging Sixties.

Royal History
Monarchs were crowned in Westminster Abbey (p52).

Berlin (p486)
Reminders of the German capital's glorious and troubled past await you around every corner.

WWII Icon
Brandenburger Tor (p498) is a symbol of the Cold War.

The Great Outdoors

From magnificent mountains and rolling hills covered in flowers and vines to sandy-beach coasts with vistas of charming islands, Europe's landscapes are a visual treat.

COLIN DEWAR / SHUTTERSTOCK ©

Switzerland (p586)
Switzerland's majestic landscapes soaring to the heights of the Alps will make your knees go weak.

Alpine Vistas
Marvel at the iconic Matterhorn (p588) from Zermatt.

Dubrovnik (p470)
An ancient walled town overlooks sapphire waters speckled with countless forested islands.

Coastal Enclaves
Admire the Adriatic from the walls of Dubrovnik (p473).

Scottish Highlands (p96)
Big skies, sweeping landscapes, mysterious lochs (lakes) and spectacular wildlife.

Big Skies
Highland's primary city, Inverness (p104), is on River Ness.

Arts & Architecture

World-class museums and galleries, thriving theatres and concert halls, ancient castles and ornate public buildings: Europe's cultural treasures are guaranteed to excite and delight.

CHAOSS / SHUTTERSTOCK ©

Florence (p418)
Florence is home to a magnificent array of Renaissance art and architecture.

Renaissance Treasures
Swoon over the art at Galleria degli Uffizi (p427).

Vienna (p564)
Grand imperial palaces, revered opera houses and superb art museums can be found in Vienna.

Empire of Art
Kunsthistorisches Museum (p569) brims with works.

Amsterdam (p154)
Ground zero for European art during the Golden Age, fostering the likes of Rembrandt and Vermeer.

Golden Age
Rijksmuseum (p160) is the city's premier art trove.

Food & Drink

Europe's culinary diversity and quality is almost unrivalled; whether you like Michelin-starred restaurants or casual cafes, you'll be treated to delicious local produce.

IRINA MELIUKH / SHUTTERSTOCK ©

Paris (p202)
Food is not fuel here – it's a religion and the reason you get up in the morning.

Artistic Food
Enjoy art-like masterpieces at Restaurant AT (p242).

Barcelona (p268)
This Catalan city has a celebrated food scene fuelled by world-class chefs and imaginative recipes.

Avant Garde
Expect the unexpected at Disfrutar (p300).

Copenhagen (p136)
One of the hottest culinary destinations, with more Michelin stars than any other Scandinavian city.

New Nordic
Geranium (p150) transforms local ingredients into art.

Plan Your Trip
Local Life

K13 ART / SHUTTERSTOCK ©

Activities

Europe is just one great playground for lovers of the great outdoors. Hiking and biking trails criss-cross mountains, hills, fields, forests and coastlines. Among the huge range of activities you can take part in are fishing, horse riding, skiing, climbing, kayaking and sailing. And if outdoor pursuits are not your thing, then Europe's urban centres are well set up for those interested in learning to cook a local dish, learn a new language or follow a guided specialist tour.

Shopping

You've no doubt heard about the European Union's 'single market'. The reality is infinitely better: a multiplicity of markets and other varied retail options are to found from the highlands of Scotland to the streets of Lisbon. Be it in the grand department stores and fashion houses of Paris, London and Rome, the craft stalls and artists' ateliers of Venice or Prague, or

farmers markets everywhere, there are a million and one ways to find that perfect souvenir to bring home.

Entertainment

When it comes to mass entertainment, Europe practically wrote the book. Rome's Colosseum may no longer be a functioning arena, but there are countless other giant stadiums and storied venues across the continent. The sheer range of performing arts is impressive, spanning classical music to grunge rock, Shakespeare to contemporary dance. Europeans also love their sporting events with soccer being a major preoccupation.

Eating

Europe's delicious cuisine reflects the multitude of different countries and regions spread across the continent. The Mediterranean diet is listed as an 'Intangible Cultural Heritage' by Unesco and has a number of variants, including

Italian, Spanish and Greek. French food is practically a religion. Nordic food is the trendy new upstart of the culinary world. The UK excels in cosmopolitan Asian flavours and has invented its own brand of spicy Anglo-Indian cuisine. Wherever you go in Europe, eating is not just a pleasure but a valuable insight into the local history and culture.

Drinking & Nightlife

Whatever your tipple or taste in nightlife, Europe is sure to deliver. Whether you're pounding the streets of Reykjavík, Paris or Barcelona, you're sure to find pumping dance clubs with cutting edge DJs and designer cocktail bars, as well as cosy pubs and third-wave coffee shops. Slip into a local pub in Scotland to sample Highland whiskies, or a bar in Prague to sip on craft beers. And let's not even start on the wonderful wines of France, Spain and Italy – visiting vineyards could keep you occupied the whole trip.

★ Best Restaurants

Dinner by Heston Blumenthal (p89)
Restaurant Guy Savoy (p244)
Cafe Jacques (p461)
Tapas 24 (p300)
Pizzarium (p392)

From left: Market in Prague (p524); Royal Albert Hall (p93), London

Plan Your Trip
Month by Month

February

Carnival, in all its manic glory, sweeps the Catholic regions. Cold temperatures are forgotten amid masquerades, street festivals and general bacchanalia.

✺ Carnevale, Italy

In the period before Ash Wednesday, Venice goes mad for masks (www.venice-carnival-italy.com). Costume balls, many with traditions centuries old, enliven the social calendar in this storied old city.

March

Spring arrives in southern Europe. It's colder further north, though days are often bright.

✺ St Patrick's Day, Ireland

Parades and celebrations with friends and family are held on 17 March across Ireland to honour the country's beloved patron saint.

☆ Budapest Spring Festival, Hungary

This two-week festival in March/April is one of Europe's top classical-music events (www.springfestival.hu). Concerts are held in a number of beautiful venues, including stunning churches, the opera house and the national theatre.

April

Spring arrives with a burst of colour, from the glorious bulb fields of Holland to the blooming orchards of Spain.

✺ Settimana Santa, Italy

Italy celebrates Holy Week with processions and passion plays. By Holy Thursday Rome is thronged with the faithful as hundreds of thousands converge on the Vatican and St Peter's Basilica.

✺ Koninginnedag (Queen's Day), Netherlands

The nationwide celebration on 27 April is especially fervent in Amsterdam, awash

with orange costumes and fake Afros, beer, dope, leather boys, temporary roller coasters, clogs and general craziness.

May

May is usually sunny and warm and full of things to do – an excellent time to visit.

🍺 Beer Festival, Czech Republic

This Prague beer festival (www.ceskypivni festival.cz) offers lots of food, music and – most importantly – around 70 beers from around the country from mid to late May.

June

The sun has broken through the clouds and the weather is generally gorgeous across the continent.

🎊 Karneval der Kulturen, Germany

This joyous street carnival (www.karneval-berlin.de) celebrates Berlin's multicultural tapestry with parties, global nosh and a fun parade of flamboyantly costumed dancers, DJs, artists and musicians.

★ Best Festivals

Carnevale, February

St Patrick's Day, March

Bastille Day, July

Notting Hill Carnival, August

Festes de la Mercè, October

🎊 Festa de Santo António, Portugal

Feasting, drinking and dancing in Lisbon's Alfama in honour of St Anthony (12 to 13 June) top the even grander three-week Festas de Lisboa (http://festasdelisboa. com), which features processions and dozens of street parties.

July

One of the busiest months for travel across the continent with outdoor cafes, beer gardens and beach clubs all hopping.

From left: *Correfoc* during Festes de la Mercè (p34), Barcelona; Dancers at Karneval der Kulturen, Berlin

✳ Sanfermines (Running of the Bulls), Spain

Fiesta de San Fermín (Sanfermines) is the week-long nonstop Pamplona festival with the daily *encierro* (running of the bulls) as its centrepiece (www.bullrunpamplona. com). The antibullfighting event, the Running of the Nudes (www.runningofthe nudes.com), takes place two days earlier.

✳ Bastille Day, France

Fireworks, balls, processions and – of course – good food and wine, for France's national day on 14 July, celebrated in every French town and city.

August

Everybody's going someplace as half of Europe shuts down to enjoy the traditional month of holiday with the other half.

✳ Amsterdam Gay Pride, the Netherlands

Held at the beginning of August, this is one of Europe's best GLBT events (www. amsterdamgaypride.nl). It's more about freedom and diversity than protest.

✳ Notting Hill Carnival, Great Britain

Europe's largest – and London's most vibrant – outdoor carnival is a two-day event where London's Caribbean community shows the city how to party (www. thelondonnottinghillcarnival.com).

☆ Sziget Music Festival, Hungary

A week-long, great-value world-music festival (www.sziget.hu) held all over Budapest. Sziget features bands from around the world playing at more than 60 venues.

September

Maybe the best time to visit: the weather's still good and the crowds have thinned.

☆ Venice International Film Festival, Italy

Italy's top film fest is a celebration of mainstream and indie moviemaking (www. labiennale.org). The judging here is seen as an early indication of what to look for at the next year's Oscars.

✳ Festes de la Mercè, Spain

The city's biggest celebration (around 24 September) has four days of concerts, dancing, *castellers* (human-castle builders), fireworks and *correfoc* – a parade of fireworks-spitting dragons and devils.

November

Leaves have fallen, and snow is about to, in much of Europe. Even in the temperate zones around the Med it can get chilly, rainy and blustery.

✳ Guy Fawkes Night, Great Britain

Bonfires and fireworks erupt across Britain on 5 November, recalling the foiling of a plot to blow up the Houses of Parliament in the 1600s. Go to high ground in London to see glowing explosions erupt everywhere.

☆ Iceland Airwaves, Iceland

Roll on up to Reykjavík for Iceland Airwaves, a great music festival featuring both Icelandic and international acts (www.icelandair waves.is).

December

Despite freezing temperatures this is a magical time to visit, with Christmas markets and decorations brightening Europe's dark streets. Prices remain surprisingly low provided you avoid Christmas and New Year's Eve.

✳ Natale, Italy

Italian churches set up an intricate crib or a *presepe* (nativity scene) in the lead-up to Christmas. Some are quite famous, most are works of art, and many date back hundreds of years and are venerated for their spiritual ties.

Plan Your Trip
Get Inspired

ELENA ROSTUNOVA / SHUTTERSTOCK ©

Read

Neither Here Nor There: Travels in Europe Bill Bryson retraces a youthful European backpacking trip with hilarious observations.

Europe: A History Professor Norman Davies' sweeping overview of European history.

In Europe: Travels through the Twentieth Century Fascinating account of journalist Geert Mak's travels.

Fifty Years of Europe: An Album A lifetime of travel around the continent, distilled by British travel writer Jan Morris.

The Imperfectionists Tom Rachman's novel charts the fortunes of an English-language newspaper based in Rome.

Watch

The Third Man (1949) Classic tale of wartime espionage in old Vienna, starring Orson Welles and that zither theme.

Notting Hill (1999) Superstar Julia Roberts falls for bookshop-owner Hugh Grant in this London-based rom-com.

Amélie (2001) Endearing tale following the quirky adventures of Parisian do-gooder Amélie Poulain.

Vicky Christina Barcelona (2008) Woody Allen–directed drama about the amorous adventures of two young American women in Spain.

Victoria (2016) Thriller set on the streets of Berlin that plays out in one continuous 138-minute camera shot.

Listen

The Original Three Tenors: 20th Anniversary Edition Operatic classics courtesy of Pavarotti, Carreras and Domingo.

The Best of Edith Piaf The sound of France, including a selection of the Little Sparrow's greatest hits.

Chambao Feel-good flamenco fused with electronica from Spain's deep south.

London Calling A post-punk classic from The Clash that incorporates a host of musical influences.

Fado Tradicional A return to basics from Mariza, a top contemporary exponent of Portugal's fado style of music.

Festival performance outside Shakespeare's Globe (p78), London

Plan Your Trip
Five-Day Itineraries

Iberian Excursion

For a short European break, with a bright burst of sunshine whatever the time of year, Portugal and Spain can't be beaten. This quartet of destinations also provides wonderful art, architecture and delicious food.

San Sebastián (p323) Enjoy a day of grazing on delicious *pintxos* (Basque tapas) in this idyllic seaside town.
🚆 1½ hrs to Barcelona

Bilbao (p316) Devote a day to the monumental contemporary art installations in Bilbao's shimmering Museo Guggenheim.
🚆 1 hr to San Sebastián

Barcelona (p268) Ramble along La Rambla; get lost in the medieval streets of the Barri Gòtic; and marvel at La Sagrada Família.

Lisbon (p330) Spend two days exploring this enchanting city from the cobbled lanes of Alfama to seaside Belem. ✈2 hrs to Bilbao

FROM LEFT: ALEXANDER SPATARI; JOSE MANUEL AZCONA / GETTY IMAGES ©

Eastern Europe to Berlin

Known as the grim, grey 'Eastern Bloc' until the early 1990s, today this half of Europe is one of the continent's most dynamic and fascinating to visit. The four cities on this itinerary each have a distinct character and charm.

Berlin (p486) Enjoy high-brow, alternative culture and the frisson of recent history in Germany's once-divided capital. **4**

Prague (p524) Wander this romantic city for a day, ending up on the iconic Charles Bridge at dusk. 🚆 5 hrs to Berlin **3**

Vienna (p564) Allow two days for Austria's capital; it's packed with palaces, museums and splendid art galleries. 🚆 4 hrs to Prague **2**

Budapest (p546) Spend a day in Hungary's capital with its architectural gems and soothing thermal baths. 🚆 2 ¾ hrs to Vienna **1**

4

1

Plan Your Trip
Five-Day Itineraries

Italy & the Adriatic Coast

This whistle-stop itinerary gives a taste of the glories of Italy starting in its ancient capital Rome. Next, the Renaissance crucible of Florence and the floating wonder of Venice, before heading down the Adriatic Coast to historic Dubrovnik in Croatia.

Venice (p400) Hop in a gondola and sail the canals – before the day is out you'll be in love with Venice.
✈ 1½ hrs to Dubrovnik

Florence (p418) You'll need to move at a pace to cram in the art and architecture of this Renaissance beauty in a day. 🚆 2 hrs to Venice

Rome (p352) Allow a couple of days in the Eternal City, home to the Vatican and Colosseum.
🚆 1½ hrs to Florence

Dubrovnik (p470) One of the world's most magnificent walled cities has a pedestrian-only old town and sublime sea views.

Canals & Castles

With only five days, you'll need to fly most of the way between Amsterdam's World Heritage–listed canals and the Schloss Neushwanstein, a classic European castle. Make stops for an injection of Nordic cool in Copenhagen and nightclubbing in Berlin.

Copenhagen (p136) Home to the Tivoli Gardens, palaces, the nonconformist enclave of Christiania and the Little Mermaid.
✈ 1 hr to Berlin

Berlin (p486) With no curfew Berlin parties through the night. Start the evening off in Prater, a historic beer garden. ✈ 1 hr to Munich

Amsterdam (p154) Rent a bike to cycle around this city beside canals, stopping off at art museums and coffeeshops.
✈ 1 ½ hrs to Copenhagen

Schloss Neuschwanstein (p520) Ludwig II's fantasy castle, two hours southwest of Munich, was a model for the one in Disney's *Sleeping Beauty*.

FROM LEFT: PHOTO.UA, RUDY BALASKO / SHUTTERSTOCK ©

Plan Your Trip
10-Day Itinerary

Iceland to Ireland

This 1500km journey around northern Europe is one of the continent's most scenic, from the bubbling hot springs outside Reykjavík to the gentle Georgian architecture of Dublin, via the grand Scottish Highlands and the history, culture and fashion of London.

Reykjavík (p176) Allot two days for the city's excellent museums, shops and cafes, as well as its vibrant nightlife.
✈ 4 hrs to London

Inverness (p104) This is your three-day base for explorations around the splendid Scottish Highlands.
✈ 1¼ hrs to Dublin

Dublin (p114) Encounter the Dublin of James Joyce as you meander between the literary haunts, museums and pubs of Ireland's capital.

London (p50) You'll be amazed how much of London you can pack into three days if you try.
✈ 1½ hrs to Inverness

Plan Your Trip
10-Day Itinerary

Southern Mediterranean

Hire a car in Avignon, a great base for touring the hilltop villages and Roman ruins of France's beautiful Provence. Devote a day to travelling the cliffside roads of the Cote d'Azur towards Italy – one of the world's great drives.

1

Avignon (p260) A couple of days is sufficient to see the sights in and around this ancient fortress town.
🚗 7 ¾ hrs to Siena

S BORISOV / SHUTTERSTOCK ©

Florence (p418) Take in the city's
Renaissance splendour from the
cupola of its landmark Duomo.
🚃 1½ hrs to Rome

3

2

Siena (p452) Spend a day exploring
one of Italy's most enchanting
medieval settlements.
🚗 1 hr to Florence

4

Rome (p352) Linger on the Spanish
steps, beside the Trevi Fountain and in
the Piazza Navona.
🚃 2 ¾ hrs to Pompeii

5

Pompeii (p462) The Unesco-listed
ruins provide a remarkable model of a
working Roman city, including baths,
taverns and a brothel.

4

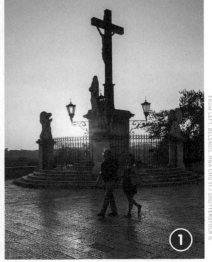

1

Plan Your Trip
Two-Week Itinerary

Classic Europe

Eight countries in 14 days may sound like squeezing too much in, but Europe's extensive network of budget flights and trains makes this itinerary easy. It's a great introduction to the continent's infinite variety of cultures and terrain.

London (p50) Spend a couple of days in this endlessly intriguing city, one of history's great survivors. 🚆 2¼ hrs to Paris

Paris (p202) Swoon for two days over the beautiful boulevards and romantic alleys of the City of Light. 🚆 3½ hrs to Amsterdam

Zermatt (p592) Spend a day gawping in awe at the Matterhorn, the Alps' most famous peak. 🚆 4 hrs to Geneva, then 1 hr to Barcelona

Barcelona (p268) Wrap up your tour on the balmy shores of the Mediterranean in a city that's both a visual treat and a foodie heaven.

ANASTASIA GALKINA / SHUTTERSTOCK ©

Amsterdam (p154) Chill out for a day cruising the canals and art galleries and enjoying the liberal atmosphere.
✈ 1½ hrs to Prague

Prague (p524) Devote a day to the town's two big attractions - the castle and the Old Town Square. 🚆 4½ hrs to Vienna

4

5

Vienna (p564) Allow two days for the grandeur of the former capital of the Austro-Hungarian empire. ✈ 1 hr to Venice

6

Venice (p400) Surrender to the haunting beauty of La Serenissima's watery world of piazza, domes, canals and bridges. 🚆 6 hrs to Zermatt

4

5

FROM LEFT: RC PHOTOGRAPHY; RADU BERCAN / SHUTTERSTOCK ©

Plan Your Trip
Family Travel

ANASTASIA PELIKH / SHUTTERSTOCK ©

Getting Around

In general, Europe is an incredibly family-friendly place to travel, but distances can be long, so it's a good idea to break up the trip with things to see and do en route.

Traffic is at its worst during holiday seasons, especially between June and August, and journey times are likely to be much longer during this period.

Trains can be a great option for family travel – kids will have more space to move around, and you can pack books, puzzles and computer games to keep them entertained.

Children and young people qualify for cheap travel on most public transport in Europe (usually around 50% of the adult fare). Look out for railcards and passes that open up extra discounts – many cities offer passes that combine entry to sights and attractions with travel on public transport.

Sights & Attractions

Most attractions offer discounted entry for children (generally for 12 years and under, although this varies). If you can, try to mix up educational activities with fun excursions they're guaranteed to enjoy – balance that visit to the Tate Modern or the Louvre with a trip to the London Aquarium or a day at Disneyland Paris, for example. The number-one rule is to avoid packing too much in – you'll get tired, the kids will get irritable and tantrums are sure to follow. Plan carefully and you'll enjoy your time much more.

Hotels & Restaurants

It's always worth asking in advance whether hotels are happy to accept kids. Many are fully geared for family travel, with children's activities, child-minding services and the like, but others may impose a minimum age limit to deter guests with kids. Family-friendly hotels will usually be

able to offer a large room with two or three beds to accommodate families, or at least neighbouring rooms with an adjoining door. Dining out en famille is generally great fun, but again, it's always worth checking to see whether kids are welcome – generally the posher or more prestigious the establishment, the less kid-friendly they're likely to be. Many restaurants offer cheaper children's menus, usually based around simple staples such as steak, pasta, burgers and chicken. Most will also offer smaller portions of adult meals. If your kids are fussy, buying your own ingredients at a local market can encourage them to experiment – they can choose their own food while simultaneously practising the local lingo.

Need to Know

Changing facilities Found at most supermarkets and major attractions.

Cots and highchairs Available in many restaurants and hotels, but ask ahead.

★ Best Cities for Kids

Paris (p202)

London (p50)

Barcelona (p268)

Copenhagen (p136)

Vienna (p564)

Health Generally good, but pack your own first-aid kit to avoid language difficulties.

Kids' menus Widely available.

Nappies (diapers) Sold everywhere, including pharmacies and supermarkets.

Strollers It's easiest to bring your own.

Transport Children usually qualify for discounts; young kids often travel free.

From left: Carousel in the Tivoli Gardens (p138), Copenhagen; Children in Paris (p202)

GREAT BRITAIN & IRELAND

In This Chapter

Westminster Abbey 52
British Museum 58
Buckingham Palace........................... 62
Tower of London 66
Sights 74
Tours 85
Shopping 86
Eating...87
Drinking & Nightlife.......................... 90
Entertainment 92
Information... 94
Getting There & Away 94
Getting Around 94

London, Great Britain

One of the world's most visited cities, London has something for everyone: from history and culture to fine food and good times. Britain may have voted for Brexit (although the majority of Londoners didn't), but for now London remains one of the world's most cosmopolitan cities, and diversity infuses daily life, food, music and fashion. It even penetrates intrinsically British institutions; the British Museum and Victoria & Albert Museum have collections as varied as they are magnificent, while the flavours at centuries-old Borough Market run the full global gourmet spectrum.

London in Two Days

First stop, **Westminster Abbey** (p52) for an easy intro to the city's (and nation's) history and then to **Buckingham Palace** (p63). Walk up the Mall to **Trafalgar Square** (p75) for its architectural grandeur and photo-op views of **Big Ben** (p74). Art lovers will make a beeline for the **National Gallery** (p74) and and **Tate Britain** (p75).

On day two, visit the **British Museum** (p59) and explore **Soho** (p75), followed by dinner at **Claridge's Foyer & Reading Room** (p90).

London in Four Days

Have a royally good time checking out the Crown Jewels at the **Tower of London** (p67), followed by some retail therapy at **Leadenhall Market** (p70) and a visit to **St Paul's Cathedral** (p78).

Dedicate the fourth day to the **V&A** (p79), **Natural History Museum** (p78) and **Science Museum** (p79). End the day with a show at **Royal Albert Hall** (p93).

After London catch the Eurostar to Paris (p202) or Amsterdam (p154).

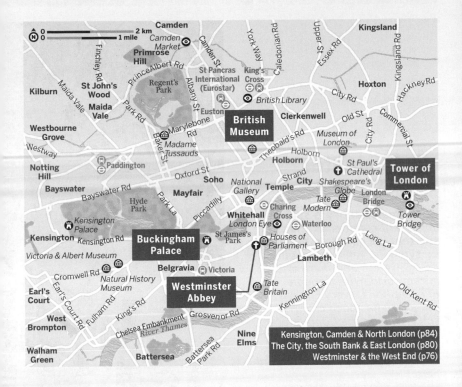

Arriving in London

Heathrow Airport Trains, the tube and buses head to central London from just after 5am to before midnight (night buses run later and 24-hour tube runs Friday and Saturday) £5.70–21.50; taxi £46–87. From 2018, express trains will run to central London and beyond along the Elizabeth Line (Crossrail).

Gatwick Airport Trains to central London from 4.30am to 1.35am cost £10–20; hourly buses to central London run around the clock, from £5; taxi £100.

St Pancras International Train Station In Central London and connected by many underground lines to other parts of the city.

Where to Stay

Hanging your hat in London can be painfully expensive, and you'll need to book well in advance. Decent hostels are easy to find, but aren't as cheap as you might hope for. Hotels range from no-frills chains through to ultra-ritzy establishments, such as the Ritz itself. B&Bs are often better value and more atmospheric than hotels.

For information on what each London neighbourhood has to offer, see the table on p95.

Westminster Abbey

Westminster Abbey is such an important commemoration site that it's hard to overstate its symbolic value or imagine its equivalent anywhere else in the world. With a couple of exceptions, every English sovereign has been crowned here since William the Conqueror in 1066, and most of the monarchs from Henry III (died 1272) to George II (died 1760) are buried here.

Great For...

ⓘ Need to Know

Map p76; ☎020-7222 5152; www.westminster-abbey.org; 20 Dean's Yard, SW1; adult/child £20/9, cloister & gardens free; ⊙9.30am-4.30pm Mon, Tue, Thu & Fri, to 7pm Wed, to 2.30pm Sat; ⊖Westminster

★ **Top Tip**
The abbey gets incredibly busy, even at opening, so come armed with patience.

There is an extraordinary amount to see at the Abbey. The interior is chock-a-block with ornate chapels, elaborate tombs of monarchs and grandiose monuments to sundry luminaries throughout the ages. First and foremost, however, it is a sacred place of worship.

A Regal History

Though a mixture of architectural styles, the Abbey is considered the finest example of Early English Gothic (1190–1300). The original church was built in the 11th century by King (later St) Edward the Confessor, who is buried in the chapel behind the sanctuary and main altar. Henry III (r 1216–72) began work on the new building, but didn't complete it; the French Gothic nave was finished by Richard II in 1388. Henry VII's huge and magnificent Lady Chapel was added in 1519.

The Abbey was initially a monastery for Benedictine monks, and many of the building's features attest to this collegial past (the octagonal Chapter House, the Quire and four cloisters). In 1536 Henry VIII separated the Church of England from the Roman Catholic Church and dissolved the monastery. The king became head of the Church of England and the Abbey acquired its 'royal peculiar' status, meaning it is administered directly by the Crown and exempt from any ecclesiastical jurisdiction.

North Transept, Sanctuary & Quire

Entrance to the Abbey is via the Great North Door. The North Transept is often referred to as Statesmen's Aisle: politicians

Quire

and eminent public figures are commemorated by large marble statues and imposing marble plaques.

At the heart of the Abbey is the beautifully tiled **sanctuary** (or sacrarium), a stage for coronations, royal weddings and funerals. George Gilbert Scott designed the ornate **high altar** in 1873. In front of the altar is the **Cosmati marble pavement** dating back to 1268. It has intricate designs of small pieces of marble inlaid into plain marble, which predicts the end of the world in AD 19,693! At the entrance to the lovely

Chapel of St John the Baptist is a sublime Virgin and Child bathed in candlelight.

The **Quire**, a magnificent structure of gold, blue and red Victorian Gothic by Edward Blore, dates back to the mid-19th century. It sits where the original choir for the monks' worship would have been, but bears no resemblance to the original. Nowadays, the Quire is still used for singing, but its regular occupants are the Westminster Choir – 22 boys and 12 'lay vicars' (men) who sing the daily services.

Chapels & Chair

The sanctuary is surrounded by chapels. **Henry VII's Lady Chapel**, in the eastern-most part of the Abbey, is the most spectacular, with its fan vaulting on the ceiling, colourful banners of the Order of the Bath and dramatic oak stalls. Behind the chapel's altar is the elaborate sarcophagus of Henry VII and his queen, Elizabeth of York.

Beyond the chapel's altar is the **Royal Air Force Chapel**, with a stained-glass window commemorating the force's finest hour, the Battle of Britain (1940), and the 1500 RAF pilots who died. A stone plaque on the floor marks the spot where Oliver Cromwell's body lay for two years (1658) until the Restoration, when it was disinterred, hanged and beheaded. Two bodies, believed to be those of the child princes allegedly murdered in the Tower of London in 1483, were buried here almost two centuries later in 1674.

There are two small chapels either side of Lady Chapel with the tombs of famous monarchs: on the left (north) is where **Elizabeth I** and her half-sister **Mary I** (aka

---

☑ **Don't Miss**

Poet's Corner, the Coronation Chair, the 14th-century cloisters, the oldest door in the UK, a 900-year-old garden, the royal sarcophagi and much, much more.

NEIL HOLMES/GETTY IMAGES ©

✖ **Take a Break**

Part of the original 14th-century Benedictine monastery, **Cellarium** (Map p76; ☎020-7222 0516; www.benugo.com/restaurants/cellarium-cafe-terrace; Westminster Abbey, 20 Dean's Yard, SW1; mains £9.50-15; ⏰8am-6pm Mon, Tue, Thu & Fri, to 9pm Wed, 9am-5pm Sat, 10am-4pm Sun; ⊕Westminster) has stunning views of the Abbey's architectural details.

Bloody Mary) rest. On the right (south) is the tomb of **Mary Queen of Scots**, beheaded on the orders of her cousin Elizabeth.

The vestibule of the Lady Chapel is the usual place for the rather ordinary-looking **Coronation Chair**, upon which every monarch since the early 14th century has been crowned.

Shrine of St Edward the Confessor

The most sacred spot in the Abbey lies behind the high altar; access is generally restricted to protect the 13th-century flooring. St Edward was the founder of the Abbey and the original building was consecrated a few weeks before his death. His tomb was slightly altered after the original was destroyed during the Reformation, but still contains Edward's remains – the only complete saint's body in Britain. Ninety-minute **verger-led tours** (£5 plus admission) of the Abbey include a visit to the shrine.

South Transept & Nave

The south transept contains **Poets' Corner**, where many of England's finest writers are buried and/or commemorated by monuments or memorials.

In the nave's north aisle is **Scientists' Corner**, where you will find **Sir Isaac Newton's tomb** (note the putto holding a prism to the sky while another feeds material into a smelting oven). Just ahead of it is the north aisle of the Quire, known as **Musicians' Aisle**, where baroque composers Henry Purcell and John Blow are buried, as well as more modern music-makers such as Benjamin Britten and Edward Elgar.

The two towers above the west door are the ones through which you exit. These were designed by Nicholas Hawksmoor and completed in 1745. Just above the door, perched in 15th-century niches, are the additions to the Abbey unveiled in 1998: 10 stone statues of international 20th-century martyrs who died for their Christian faith. These include American pacifist Dr Martin Luther King, the Polish priest St Maximilian Kolbe, who was murdered by the Nazis at Auschwitz, and

Wang Zhiming, publicly executed during the Chinese Cultural Revolution.

Outer Buildings & Gardens

The oldest part of the cloister is the **East Cloister** (or East Walk), dating from the 13th century. Off the cloister is the octagonal **Chapter House**, with one of Europe's best-preserved medieval tile floors and religious murals on the walls. It was used as a meeting place by the House of Commons in the second half of the 14th century. To the right of the entrance to Chapter House is what is claimed to be the **oldest door in Britain** – it's been there for 950 years.

The adjacent **Pyx Chamber** is one of the few remaining relics of the original Abbey, including the 10th-century **Altar of St Dunstan**. The chamber contains the pyx, a chest with standard gold and silver pieces

Statues above the west door

for testing coinage weights in a ceremony called the Trial of the Pyx, which nowadays takes place in Goldsmiths' Hall in the City of London.

To reach the 900-year-old **College Garden** (Map p76; ⏱10am-6pm Tue-Thu Apr-Sep, to 4pm Oct-Mar), enter Dean's Yard and the Little Cloisters off Great College St.

New Museum for 2018

Scheduled for completion in 2018 are the **Queen's Diamond Jubilee Galleries**, a new museum and gallery space located in the medieval triforium, the arched gallery above the nave. Its exhibits will include the death masks of generations of royalty, wax effigies representing Charles II and William III (who is on a stool to make him as tall as his wife, Mary II), armour and stained glass. Highlights are the graffiti-inscribed Mary

Chair (used for the coronation of Mary II) and the Westminster Retable, England's oldest altarpiece, from the 13th century.

✕ Take a Break

Not far from the Abbey, the (student-staffed) **Vincent Rooms** (Map p76; ☎020-7802 8391; www.westking.ac.uk/about-us/vincent-rooms-restaurant; Westminster Kingsway College, Vincent Sq, SW1; mains £9-13; ⏱noon-3pm Mon-Fri, 6-9pm Tue-Thu; ⊖Victoria) is great for top-notch mod European cuisine at rock-bottom prices.

★ Top Tip

By joining a tour of the Abbey (usually two hours) led by an accredited Blue Badge Tourist Guide you can enter via the Dean's Yard and be fast-tracked inside.

Great Court

SONGQUAN DENG/SHUTTERSTOCK ©

British Museum

Britain's most visited attraction – founded in 1753 when royal physician Hans Sloane sold his 'cabinet of curiosities'– is an exhaustive and exhilarating stampede through 7000 years of human civilisation.

The British Museum offers a stupendous selection of tours, many of them free. There are 15 free 30- to 40-minute eyeOpener tours of individual galleries per day. The museum also has free daily gallery talks, a highlights tour (adult/child £12/free, 11.30am and 2pm Friday, Saturday and Sunday) and excellent multimedia iPad tours (adult/child £5/3.50), offering six themed one-hour tours, and a choice of 35-minute children's trails.

Great For...

☑ Don't Miss

The Rosetta Stone, the Mummy of Katebet and the marble Parthenon sculptures.

Great Court

Covered with a spectacular glass-and-steel roof designed by Norman Foster in 2000, the Great Court is the largest covered public square in Europe. In its centre is the world-famous **Reading Room**, formerly the British Library, which has been frequented by all the big brains of history, from Mahatma Gandhi to Karl Marx. It is currently used for temporary exhibits.

Parthenon marble frieze

FLIKR47/SHUTTERSTOCK ©

ⓘ Need to Know

Map p76; ☎020-7323 8299; www.british museum.org; Great Russell St & Montague Pl, WC1; ⊙10am-5.30pm Sat-Thu, to 8.30pm Fri; ⊜Russell Sq, Tottenham Court Rd `FREE`

✕ Take a Break

Just around the corner from the museum in a quiet, picturesque square is one of London's most atmospheric pubs, the **Queen's Larder** (Map p84; ☎020-7837 5627; www.queenslarder.co.uk; 1 Queen Sq, WC1; ⊙11.30am-11pm Mon-Fri, noon-11pm Sat, noon-10.30pm Sun; ⊜Russell Sq).

★ Top Tip

The museum is huge, so pick your interests and consider the free tours.

Ancient Egypt, Middle East & Greece

The star of the show here is the Ancient Egypt collection. It comprises sculptures, fine jewellery, papyrus texts, coffins and mummies, including the beautiful and intriguing **Mummy of Katebet** (room 63). The most prized item in the collection (and the most popular postcard in the shop) is the **Rosetta Stone** (room 4), the key to deciphering Egyptian hieroglyphics. In the same gallery is the enormous bust of the pharaoh **Ramesses the Great** (room 4).

Assyrian treasures from ancient Mesopotamia include the 16-tonne **Winged Bulls from Khorsabad** (room 10), the heaviest object in the museum. Behind it are the exquisite **Lion Hunt Reliefs from Ninevah** (room 10) from the 7th century BC, which influenced Greek sculpture. Such antiquities

are all the more significant after the Islamic State's bulldozing of Nimrud in 2015.

A major highlight of the museum is the **Parthenon sculptures** (room 18). The marble frieze is thought to be the Great Panathenaea, a blow-out version of an annual festival in honour of Athena.

Roman & Medieval Britain

Upstairs are finds from Britain and the rest of Europe (rooms 40 to 51). Many items go back to Roman times, when the empire spread across much of the continent, including the **Mildenhall Treasure** (room 49), a collection of pieces of 4th-century Roman silverware from Suffolk with both pagan and early-Christian motifs.

Lindow Man (room 50) is the well-preserved remains of a 1st-century man (comically dubbed Pete Marsh) discovered in a bog near Manchester in northern England in 1984. Equally fascinating are artefacts from the **Sutton Hoo Ship-Burial** (room 41), an elaborate Anglo-Saxon burial site from Suffolk dating back to the 7th century.

Perennial favourites are the lovely **Lewis Chessmen** (room 40), 12th-century game pieces carved from walrus tusk and whale teeth that were found on a remote Scottish island in the early 19th century. They served as models for the game of Wizard Chess in the first Harry Potter film.

Enlightenment Galleries

Formerly known as the King's Library, this stunning neoclassical space (room 1) was built between 1823 and 1827 and was the first part of the new museum building as it is seen today. The collection traces how disciplines such as biology, archaeology, linguistics and geography emerged during the Enlightenment of the 18th century.

What's Nearby?

Sir John Soane's Museum   Museum
(Map p76; ☎020-7405 2107; www.soane.org; 12 Lincoln's Inn Fields, WC2; ☉10am-5pm Tue-Sat, plus 6-9pm 1st Tue of month; ◉Holborn) **FREE** This little museum is one of the most atmospheric and fascinating in London. The building is the beautiful, bewitching home of architect Sir John Soane (1753–1837), which he left brimming with surprising personal effects and curiosities, and the museum represents his exquisite and eccentric taste.

Soane, a country bricklayer's son, is most famous for designing the Bank of England.

The heritage-listed house is largely as it was when Soane died and is itself a main part of the attraction. It has a canopy dome that brings light right down to the crypt, a colonnade filled with statuary and a picture

Buildings along Gordon Square

gallery where paintings are stowed behind each other on folding wooden panes. This is where Soane's choicest artwork is displayed, including *Riva degli Schiavoni, Looking West* by Canaletto, architectural drawings by Christopher Wren and Robert Adam, and the original *Rake's Progress,* William Hogarth's set of satirical cartoons of late-8th-century London lowlife. Among Soane's more unusual acquisitions are an Egyptian hieroglyphic sarcophagus, a mock-up of a monk's cell and slaves' chains.

> ★ **Top Tip**
>
> Check out the outstanding *A History of the World in 100 Objects* radio series (www.bbc.co.uk/podcasts/series/ahow), which retraces two million years of history through 100 objects from the museum's collections.

Charles Dickens Museum   Museum

(Map p84; ☏020-7405 2127; www.dickens museum.com; 48 Doughty St, WC1; adult/child £9/4; ◐10am-5pm Tue-Sun; ◉Chancery Lane, Russell Sq) A £3.5 million renovation has made this museum – located in a handsome four-storey house that was the great Victorian novelist's sole surviving residence in London – bigger and better than ever. The museum showcases the family drawing room (restored to its original condition), a period kitchen and a dozen rooms containing various memorabilia.

The Squares of Bloomsbury

The Bloomsbury Group, they used to say, lived in squares, moved in circles and loved in triangles. **Russell Square** (Map p84; ◉Russell Square) sits at the very heart of the district. Originally laid out in 1800, a striking facelift at the start of the new millennium spruced it up and gave the square a 10m-high fountain. The centre of literary Bloomsbury was **Gordon Square** (Map p84; ◉Russell Sq, Euston Sq), where some of the buildings are marked with blue plaques. Lovely **Bedford Square** (Map p76; ◉Tottenham Court Rd) is the only completely Georgian square still surviving in Bloomsbury.

Tavistock Square (Map p84; ◉Russell Sq, Euston Sq), the 'square of peace', has a statue of Mahatma Gandhi, a memorial to wartime conscientious objectors and a cherry tree recalling the WWII bombings of Hiroshima and Nagasaki.

Many writers and artists made their home in Gordon Square, including Bertrand Russell (No 57), Lytton Strachey (No 51) and Vanessa and Clive Bell, Maynard Keynes and the Woolf family (No 46). Strachey, Dora Carrington and Lydia Lopokova (the future wife of Maynard Keynes) all took turns living at No 41.

> ★ **Did You Know?**
>
> Charles Dickens only spent 2½ years in the house that is now the Charles Dickens Museum, but it was here that he wrote many of his most famous works.

Buckingham Palace

The palace has been the Royal Family's London lodgings since 1837, when Queen Victoria moved in from Kensington Palace as St James's Palace was deemed too old-fashioned.

Great For...

☑ Don't Miss

Peering through the gates, going on a tour of the interior (summer only) or catching the Changing of the Guard at 11.30am.

The State Rooms are only open in August and September, when Her Majesty is holidaying in Scotland. The Queen's Gallery and the Royal Mews are open year-round, however.

State Rooms

The tour starts in the **Grand Hall** at the foot of the monumental **Grand Staircase**, commissioned by George IV in 1828. It takes in John Nash's Italianate **Green Drawing Room**, the **State Dining Room** (all red damask and Regency furnishings), the **Blue Drawing Room** (which has a gorgeous fluted ceiling by Nash) and the **White Drawing Room**, where foreign ambassadors are received.

The **Ballroom**, where official receptions and state banquets are held, was built between 1853 and 1855 and opened with

ZSOLT BICZO/SHUTTERSTOCK ©

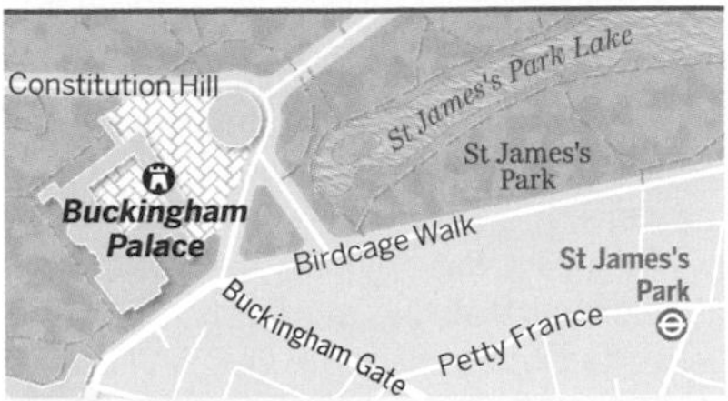
Constitution Hill
St James's Park Lake
St James's Park
Buckingham Palace
Birdcage Walk
St James's Park
Buckingham Gate
Petty France

Need to Know

Map p76; ☎0303 123 7300; www.royalcollection.org.uk/visit/the-state-rooms-buckingham-palace; Buckingham Palace Rd, SW1; adult/child/under 5yr £23/13/free, evening tour £80; 5.30pm & 6pm late Mar-Apr, 9.30am-7.30pm late Jul-Aug, to 6.30pm Sep; Green Park or St James's Park

Take a Break

During the summer months, you can enjoy light refreshments in the **Garden Café** on the Palace's West Terrace.

★ Top Tip

Come early for front-row views of the Changing of the Guard.

a ball a year later to celebrate the end of the Crimean War. The **Throne Room** is rather anticlimactic, with his-and-hers pink chairs initialled 'ER' and 'P', sitting under a curtained theatre arch.

Picture Gallery & Garden

The most interesting part of the tour is the 47m-long Picture Gallery, featuring splendid works by such artists as Van Dyck, Rembrandt, Canaletto, Poussin, Claude Lorrain, Rubens, Canova and Vermeer.

Wandering the 18 hectares of gardens is another highlight – as well as admiring some of the 350 or so species of flowers and plants and listening to the many birds, you'll get beautiful views of the palace and a peek of its famous lake.

Changing of the Guard

At 11.30am daily from April to July (on alternate days, weather permitting, for the rest of the year), the old guard (Foot Guards of the Household Regiment) comes off duty to be replaced by the new guard on the forecourt of Buckingham Palace.

Crowds come to watch the carefully choreographed marching and shouting of the guards in their bright-red uniforms and bearskin hats. It lasts about 40 minutes and is very popular, so arrive early if you want to get a good **spot** (Map p76; http://changing-guard.com).

Queen's Gallery

Since the reign of Charles I, the Royal Family has amassed a priceless collection of paintings, sculpture, ceramics, furniture and jewellery. The splendid **Queen's Gallery** (Map p76; www.royalcollection.

org.uk/visit/the-queens-gallery-buckingham-palace; adult/child £10.30/5.30, incl Royal Mews £17.70/9.70; ☉10am-5.30pm) showcases some of the palace's treasures on a rotating basis.

The gallery was originally designed as a conservatory by John Nash. It was converted into a chapel for Queen Victoria in 1843, destroyed in a 1940 air raid and reopened as a gallery in 1962. A £20-million renovation for Elizabeth II's Golden Jubilee in 2002 added three times as much display space.

Royal Mews

Southwest of the palace, the **Royal Mews** (Map p76; www.royalcollection.org.uk/visit/royalmews; Buckingham Palace Rd, SW1; adult/child £10/5.80, incl Queen's Gallery £17.70/9.70; ☉10am-5pm Apr-Oct, to 4pm Mon-Sat Feb, Mar & Nov; ⊖Victoria) started life as a falconry, but is now a working stable looking after the royals' three dozen immaculately groomed horses, along with the opulent vehicles – motorised and horse-driven – the monarch uses for transport. The Queen is well known for her passion for horses; she names every horse that resides at the mews.

Nash's 1820 stables are stunning. Highlights of the collection include the enormous and opulent Gold State Coach of 1762, which has been used for every coronation since that of George III; the 1911 Glass Coach used for royal weddings and the Diamond Jubilee in 2012; Queen Alexandra's State Coach (1893), used to transport the Imperial State Crown to the official opening of Parliament; and a Rolls-Royce Phantom VI from the royal fleet.

St James's Park

What's Nearby?

St James's Park Park

(Map p76; www.royalparks.org.uk/parks/
st-jamess-park; The Mall, SW1; ⊙5am-mid-
night; ⊖St James's Park, Green Park) At just
23 hectares, St James's is one of the
smallest but best-groomed of London's
royal parks.

It has brilliant views of the London Eye,
Westminster, St James's Palace, Carlton
Tce and the Horse Guards Parade; the sight
of Buckingham Palace from the footbridge
spanning the central lake is photo-perfect
and the best you'll find.

★ **Did You Know?**

The State Rooms represent a mere 19
of the palace's 775 rooms.

WILL RODRIGUES/SHUTTERSTOCK ©

Royal Academy of Arts Gallery

(Map p76; ☑020-7300 8000; www.royalacad
emy.org.uk; Burlington House, Piccadilly, W1;
adult/child from £13.50/free, exhibition prices
vary; ⊙10am-6pm Sat-Thu, to 10pm Fri; ⊖Green
Park) Britain's oldest society devoted to
fine arts was founded in 1768, moving
to Burlington House exactly a century
later. The collection contains drawings,
paintings, architectural designs, photographs and sculptures by past and present
Academicians such as Joshua Reynolds,
John Constable, Thomas Gainsborough,
JMW Turner, David Hockney and Norman
Foster.

The famous **Summer Exhibition** (adult/
child £14/free; ⊙10am-6pm mid-Jun–mid-Aug),
which has showcased contemporary art
for sale by unknown as well as established
artists for nearly 250 years, is the Academy's biggest annual event.

Horse Guards Parade Historic Site

(Map p76; http://changing-guard.com/
queens-life-guard.html; Horse Guards Parade,
off Whitehall, SW1; ⊙11am Mon-Sat, 10am Sun;
⊖Westminster, Charing Cross, Embankment) In
a more accessible version of Buckingham
Palace's **Changing of the Guard** (p63)
the mounted troops of the Household
Cavalry change guard here daily, at the
official vehicular entrance to the royal
palaces. A slightly less pompous version
takes place at 4pm when the dismount-
ed guards are changed. On the Queen's
official birthday in June, the Trooping of the
Colour is staged here.

★ **Local Knowledge**

At the centre of Royal Family life is the
Music Room, where four royal babies
have been christened – the Prince of
Wales (Prince Charles), the Princess
Royal (Princess Anne), the Duke of
York (Prince Andrew) and the Duke
of Cambridge (Prince William) – with
water brought from the River Jordan.

Waterloo Barracks

LITTLENY/GETTY IMAGES ©

Tower of London

With a history as bleak as it is fascinating, the Tower of London is now one of the city's top attractions, thanks in part to the Crown Jewels.

Great For...

☑ Don't Miss

The colourful Yeoman Warders (or Beefeaters), the spectacular Crown Jewels, the soothsaying ravens, and armour fit for a king.

Begun during the reign of William the Conqueror (1066–87), the Tower is in fact a castle containing 22 towers.

Tower Green

The buildings to the west and the south of this verdant patch have always accommodated Tower officials. Indeed, the current constable has a flat in Queen's House built in 1540. But what looks at first glance like a peaceful, almost village-like slice of the Tower's inner ward is actually one of its bloodiest.

Scaffold Site & Beauchamp Tower

Those 'lucky' enough to meet their fate here (rather than suffering the embarrassment of execution on Tower Hill, observed by tens of thousands of jeering and cheering onlookers) numbered but a handful

View from the Thames

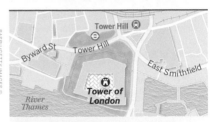

❶ Need to Know

Map p80; ☎0844 482 7777; www.hrp.org. uk/ toweroflondon; Petty Wales, EC3; adult/ child £25/12, audio guide £4/3; ◷9.30am- 5pm; ⊖Tower Hill

✕ Take a Break

The **Wine Library** (Map p80; ☎020- 7481 0415; www.winelibrary.co.uk; 43 Trinity Sq, EC3; buffet £18; ◷buffet noon-3.30pm, shop 10am-6pm Mon, to 8pm Tue-Fri) is a great place for a light but boozy lunch opposite the Tower.

★ Top Tip
Book online for cheaper rates for the Tower.

Crown Jewels

To the east of the chapel and north of the White Tower is **Waterloo Barracks**, the home of the Crown Jewels, said to be worth up to £20 billion, but in a very real sense priceless. Here, you file past film clips of the jewels and their role through history, and of Queen Elizabeth II's coronation in 1953, before you reach the vault itself.

Once inside you'll be greeted by lavishly bejewelled sceptres, church plate, orbs and, naturally, crowns. A moving walkway takes you past the dozen or so crowns and other coronation regalia, including the platinum crown of the late Queen Mother, Elizabeth, which is set with the 106-carat Koh-i-Noor (Mountain of Light) diamond, and the State Sceptre with Cross topped with the 530-carat First Star of Africa (or Cullinan I) diamond. A bit further on, exhibited on its own, is the centrepiece: the Imperial State Crown, set with 2868 diamonds (including

and included two of Henry VIII's wives (and alleged adulterers), Anne Boleyn and Catherine Howard; 16-year-old Lady Jane Grey, who fell foul of Henry's daughter Mary I by attempting to have herself crowned queen; and Robert Devereux, Earl of Essex, once a favourite of Elizabeth I.

Just west of the scaffold site is brick-faced Beauchamp Tower, where high-ranking prisoners left behind unhappy inscriptions and other graffiti.

Chapel Royal of St Peter ad Vincula

Just north of the scaffold site is the 16th-century Chapel Royal of St Peter ad Vincula (St Peter in Chains), a rare example of ecclesiastical Tudor architecture. The church can be visited on a Yeoman Warder tour, or during the first and last hour of normal opening times.

the 317-carat Second Star of Africa, or Cullinan II), sapphires, emeralds, rubies and pearls. It's worn by the Queen at the State Opening of Parliament in May/June.

White Tower

Built in stone as a fortress in 1078, this was the original 'Tower' of London – its name arose after Henry III whitewashed it in the 13th century. Standing just 30m high, it's not exactly a skyscraper by modern standards, but in the Middle Ages it would have dwarfed the wooden huts surrounding the castle walls and intimidated the peasantry.

Most of its interior is given over to a **Royal Armouries** collection of cannon, guns, and suits of mail and armour for men and horses. Among the most remarkable exhibits on the entrance floor are Henry VIII's two suits of armour, one made for him

Queen's House and Tower Green (p66)

when he was a dashing 24-year-old and the other when he was a bloated 50-year-old with a waist measuring 129cm. You won't miss the oversize codpiece. Also here is the fabulous **Line of Kings**, a late-17th-century parade of carved wooden horses and heads of historic kings. On the 1st floor, check out the 2m suit of armour once thought to have been made for the giant like John of Gaunt and, alongside it, a tiny child's suit of armour designed for James I's young son, the future Charles I. Up on the 2nd floor you'll find the block and axe used to execute Simon Fraser at the last public execution on Tower Hill in 1747.

Medieval Palace & the Bloody Tower

The Medieval Palace is composed of three towers: St Thomas's, Wakefield and

Langthorn. Inside **St Thomas's Tower** (1279) you can look at what the hall and bedchamber of Edward I might once have been like. Here archaeologists have peeled back the layers of newer buildings to find what went before. Opposite St Thomas's Tower is **Wakefield Tower**, built by Edward's father, Henry III, between 1220 and 1240. Its upper floor is entered from St Thomas's Tower and has been even more enticingly furnished with a replica throne and other decor to give an impression of

KIEV.VICTOR/SHUTTERSTOCK ©

how an anteroom in a medieval palace might have looked. During the 15th-century Wars of the Roses between the Houses of York and Lancaster, King Henry VI was murdered as (it is said) he knelt in prayer in this tower. A plaque on the chapel floor commemorates this Lancastrian king. The **Langthorn Tower**, residence of medieval queens, is to the east.

Below St Thomas's Tower along Water Lane is the famous **Traitors' Gate**, the portal through which prisoners transported by boat entered the Tower. Opposite Traitors' Gate is the huge portcullis of the Bloody Tower, taking its nickname from the 'princes in the Tower' – Edward V and his younger brother, Richard – who were held here 'for their own safety' and later murdered to annul their claims to the throne. An exhibition inside looks at the life and times of Elizabethan adventurer Sir Walter Raleigh, who was imprisoned here three times by the capricious Elizabeth I and her successor James I.

East Wall Walk

The huge inner wall of the Tower was added to the fortress in 1220 by Henry III to improve the castle's defences. It is 36m wide and is dotted with towers along its length. The East Wall Walk allows you to climb up and tour its eastern edge, beginning in the 13th-century **Salt Tower**, probably used to store saltpetre for gunpowder. The walk also takes in **Broad Arrow Tower** and **Constable Tower**, each containing small exhibits. It ends at the **Martin Tower**, which houses an exhibition about the original coronation regalia. Here you can see some of the older crowns, with their precious stones removed. It was from this tower that Colonel Thomas Blood attempted to steal the Crown Jewels in 1671 disguised as a clergyman. He was caught but – surprisingly – Charles II gave him a full pardon.

Yeoman Warders

A true icon of the Tower, the Yeoman Warders have been guarding the fortress since at least the early 16th century. There can be up to 40 – they number 37 at present – and, in order to qualify for the job, they must have served a minimum of 22 years in any branch of the British Armed Forces. They all live within the Tower walls and are known affectionately as 'Beefeaters', a nickname they dislike.

There is currently just one female Yeoman Warder, Moira Cameron, who in 2007 became the first woman to be given the post. While officially they guard the Tower and Crown Jewels at night, their main role is as tour guides. Free tours leave from the bridge near the entrance every 30 minutes; the last tour is an hour before closing.

What's Nearby?

All Hallows by the Tower   Church

(Map p80; ☎020-7481 2928; www.ahbtt.org.uk; Byward St, EC3; ⊙8am-5pm Mon-Fri, 10am-5pm Sat & Sun; ⊜Tower Hill) All Hallows (meaning 'all saints'), which dates from AD 675, survived virtually unscathed by the Great Fire, only to be hit by German bombs in 1940. Come to see the church itself, by all means, but the best bits are in the atmospheric undercroft (crypt), where you'll the discover a pavement of 2nd-century Roman tiles and the walls of the 7th-century Saxon church.

Monument   Tower

(Map p80; ☎020-7403 3761; www.themonument.org.uk; Fish St Hill, EC3; adult/child £5/2.50, incl Tower Bridge Exhibition £12/5.50; ⊙9.30am-5.30pm; ⊜Monument) Sir Christopher Wren's 1677 column, known simply as the Monument, is a memorial to the Great Fire of London of 1666, whose impact on London's history cannot be overstated. An immense Doric column made of Portland stone, the Monument is 4.5m wide and 60.6m tall – the exact distance it stands

from the bakery in Pudding Lane where the fire is thought to have started.

The Monument is topped with a gilded bronze urn of flames that some think looks like a big gold pincushion. Although Lilliputian by today's standards, the Monument would have been gigantic when built, towering over London.

Climbing up the column's 311 spiral steps rewards you with some of the best 360-degree views over London (due to its central location as much as to its height). And after your descent, you'll also be the proud owner of a certificate that commemorates your achievement.

Leadenhall Market   Market

(Map p80; www.cityoflondon.gov.uk/things-to-do/leadenhall-market; Whittington Ave, EC3; ⊙public areas 24hr; ⊜Bank) A visit to this

'The Gherkin', 30 St Mary Axe

covered mall off Gracechurch St is a step back in time. There's been a market on this site since the Roman era, but the architecture that survives is all cobblestones and late-19th-century Victorian ironwork. Leadenhall Market appears as Diagon Alley in *Harry Potter and the Philosopher's Stone* and an optician's shop was used for the entrance to the Leaky Cauldron wizarding pub in *Harry Potter and the Goblet of Fire*.

30 St Mary Axe   Notable Building

(Map p80; www.30stmaryaxe.info; 30 St Mary Axe, EC3; ⊖Aldgate) Nicknamed 'the Gherkin' for its unusual shape, 30 St Mary Axe is arguably the City's most distinctive skyscraper, dominating the skyline despite actually being slightly smaller than the neighbouring NatWest Tower. Built in 2003 by award-winning architect Norman Foster, the Gherkin's futuristic exterior has become an emblem of modern London – as recognisable as Big Ben and the London Eye.

The building is closed to the public, though in the past it has opened its doors over the **Open House London** (☏020-7383 2131; www.openhouselondon.org.uk) weekend in September.

ⓘ Local Knowledge

Common ravens, which once feasted on the corpses of beheaded traitors, have been here for centuries. Nowadays, they feed on raw beef and biscuits.

★ **Did You Know?**

Yeoman Warders are nicknamed Beefeaters. It's thought to be due to the rations of beef – then a luxury food – given to them in the past.

A Northern Point of View

This walk takes in North London's most interesting locales, including celebrity-infested Primrose Hill and chaotic Camden Town, home to loud guitar bands and the last of London's cartoon punks.
Start ⊖ Chalk Farm
Distance 2.5 miles
Duration Two hours

Classic Photo: of London's skyline from atop Primrose Hill.

2 In **Primrose Hill**, walk to the top of the park where you'll find a classic view of central London's skyline.

1 Affluent **Regent's Park Rd** is home to many darlings of the celebrity mags, so keep your eyes peeled for famous faces.

3 Walk downhill to Regent's Canal, where you'll pass the large aviary at **London Zoo**, quaint boats, superb mansions and converted industrial buildings.

START
Chalk Farm ⊖
Adelaide Rd
King Henry's Rd
Gloucester Ave
Regent's Park Rd
Primrose Hill Rd
PRIMROSE HILL
Primrose Hill
Regent's Park Rd
Prince Albert Rd
Regent's Canal
ZSL London Zoo

4 At **Camden Lock** turn left into buzzing Lock Market, with its original fashion, ethnic art and food stalls.

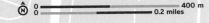

5 Exit onto **Camden High St** and turn right onto bar-lined Inverness St, which hosts its own little market.

6 At **Gloucester Cres** turn left and walk past the glorious Georgian townhouses.

Take a Break... Enjoy excellent fresh fish and seaweed-salted chips at Hook Camden Town (p87).

7 Head towards Delancey St and make a beeline for the **Edinboro Castle** (p92), where this walk ends with a well-deserved drink!

◎ SIGHTS
◎ The West End

Big Ben Landmark

(Map p76; ⊖Westminster) The most famous feature of the Palace of Westminster (Houses of Parliament) is Elizabeth Tower, more commonly known as Big Ben. To add to the confusion, Big Ben is actually the 13.5-tonne bell hanging inside the 315ft-hight tower and is thought to be named after Benjamin Hall, the commissioner of works when the tower was completed in 1858.

National Gallery Gallery

(Map p76; ☑020-7747 2885; www.national gallery.org.uk; Trafalgar Sq, WC2; ⊙10am-6pm Sat-Thu, to 9pm Fri; ⊖Charing Cross) **FREE** With some 2300 European paintings on display, this is one of the world's great art collections, with seminal works from every important epoch in the history of art – from the mid-13th to the early 20th century, including masterpieces by Leonardo da Vinci, Michelangelo, Titian, Van Gogh and Renoir.

Many visitors flock to the East Wing (1700–1900), where works by 18th-century British artists such as Gainsborough, Constable and Turner, and seminal Impressionist and post-Impressionist masterpieces by Van Gogh, Renoir and Monet await.

National Portrait Gallery Gallery

(Map p76; ☑020-7321 0055; www.npg.org. uk; St Martin's Pl, WC2; ⊙10am-6pm Sat-Wed, to 9pm Thu & Fri; ⊖Charing Cross, Leicester Sq) **FREE** What makes the National Portrait Gallery so compelling is its familiarity; in many cases, you'll have heard of the subject (royals, scientists, politicians, celebrities) or the artist (Andy Warhol, Annie Leibovitz, Lucian Freud) but not necessarily recognise the face. Highlights include the famous 'Chandos portrait' of William Shakespeare, the first artwork the gallery acquired (in 1856) and believed to be the only likeness made during the playwright's lifetime, and a touching sketch of novelist Jane Austen by her sister.

Houses of Parliament Historic Building

(Palace of Westminster; Map p76; www.parlia ment.uk; Parliament Sq, SW1; ⊖Westminster)

Staircase in the Tate Britain

FREE A visit here is a journey to the heart of UK democracy. Officially called the Palace of Westminster, the Houses of Parliament's oldest part is 11th-century **Westminster Hall**, one of only a few sections that survived a catastrophic fire in 1834. Its roof, added between 1394 and 1401, is the earliest known example of a hammerbeam roof. The rest is mostly a neo-Gothic confection built by Charles Barry and Augustus Pugin for 20 years from 1840. The palace's most famous feature is its clock tower, officially the Elizabeth Tower but better known as Big Ben.

Trafalgar Square   Square

(Map p76; 🚇Charing Cross) Trafalgar Square is the true centre of London, where rallies and marches take place, tens of thousands of revellers usher in the New Year and locals congregate for anything from communal open-air cinema and Christmas celebrations to political protests. It is dominated by the 52m-high **Nelson's Column** and ringed by many splendid buildings, including the National Gallery and the church of **St Martin-in-the-Fields**.

Tate Britain   Gallery

(Map p76; ✆020-7887 8888; www.tate.org.uk/visit/tate-britain; Millbank, SW1; ⊙10am-6pm, to 10pm on selected Fri; 🚇Pimlico) **FREE** The older and more venerable of the two Tate siblings celebrates British art from 1500 to the present, with works from Blake, Hogarth, Gainsborough, Hepworth, Whistler, Constable and Turner, as well as vibrant modern and contemporary pieces from Lucian Freud, Francis Bacon and Henry Moore.

Madame Tussauds   Museum

(Map p84; ✆0870 400 3000; www.madame-tussauds.com/london; Marylebone Rd, NW1; adult/child 4-15yr £35/30; ⊙10am-6pm; 🚇Baker St) It may be kitschy and pricey (book online for much cheaper rates), but Madame Tussauds makes for a fun-filled day. There are photo ops with your chosen celebrity (be it Daniel Craig, Lady Gaga, Benedict Cumberbatch, Audrey Hepburn or the Beckhams), the Bollywood gathering (sparring studs Hrithik Roshan and Salman

Churchill War Rooms

Winston Churchill helped coordinate the Allied resistance against Nazi Germany on a Bakelite telephone from this **underground complex** (Map p76; www.iwm.org.uk/visits/churchill-war-rooms; Clive Steps, King Charles St, SW1; adult/child £17.25/8.60; ⊙9.30am-6pm; 🚇Westminster) during WWII. The Cabinet War Rooms remain much as they were when the lights were switched off in 1945, capturing the drama and dogged spirit of the time, while the multimedia Churchill Museum affords intriguing insights into the life and times of the resolute, cigar-smoking wartime leader.

BASPHOTO/SHUTTERSTOCK ©

Khan) and the Royal Appointment (the Queen, Harry, William and Kate).

Covent Garden Piazza   Square

(Map p76; ✆020-7836 5221; 🚇Covent Garden) London's fruit-and-vegetable wholesale market until 1974 is now mostly the preserve of visitors, who flock here to shop among the quaint old arcades, eat and drink in any of the myriad of cafes and restaurants, browse through eclectic market stalls, toss coins at street performers pretending to be statues and traipse through the fun **London Transport Museum**. On the square's western side is handsome **St Paul's Church**, built in 1633.

Soho   Area

(Map p76; 🚇Tottenham Court Rd, Leicester Sq) In a district that was once pastureland, the name Soho is thought to have evolved

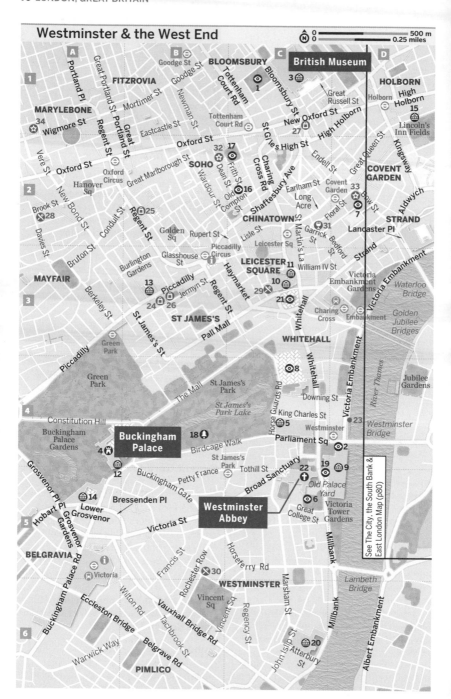

Westminster & the West End

Ⓝ 0 / 0 — 500 m / 0.25 miles

BLOOMSBURY

British Museum

HOLBORN

Goodge St

FITZROVIA

MARYLEBONE

Tottenham Court Rd

Bloomsbury St

Great Russell St

Holborn High Holborn

15

Lincoln's Inn Fields

Wigmore St

34

New Oxford St

High Holborn

Tottenham Court Rd

27

St Giles High St

Endell St

Great Queen St

COVENT GARDEN

Oxford St

SOHO

32 17

Charing Cross Rd

Earlham St

Covent Garden

33

Bow St

Oxford St

Hanover Sq

Oxford Circus

Dean St

Frith St

Old Compton St

16

Shaftesbury Ave

Long Acre

Floral St

7

STRAND

28

Regent St

25

CHINATOWN

Garrick St

31

Lancaster Pl

Golden Sq

Rupert St

Lisle St

Leicester Sq

Bedford St

Strand

MAYFAIR

Glasshouse St

Piccadilly Circus

LEICESTER SQUARE

11

William IV St

Victoria Embankment Gardens

Waterloo Bridge

13

Piccadilly

Jermyn St

Haymarket

10

29

21

Charing Cross

Embankment

Golden Jubilee Bridges

24 26

ST JAMES'S

Regent St

Whitehall

Pall Mall

WHITEHALL

Jubilee Gardens

Green Park

The Mall

St James's Park

8

Whitehall

River Thames

Piccadilly

Green Park

St James's Park Lake

Downing St

Constitution Hill

Horse Guards Rd

King Charles St

23

Westminster Bridge

Buckingham Palace Gardens

4

Buckingham Palace

18

Birdcage Walk

5

Westminster

Parliament Sq

2

12

Buckingham Gate

Petty France

St James's Park

Tothill St

19

9

14

Bressenden Pl

Lower Grosvenor

22

Old Palace Yard

Westminster Abbey

Broad Sanctuary

Hobart Pl

Grosvenor Gardens

Victoria St

Great College St

6

Victoria Tower Gardens

See The City, the South Bank & East London Map (p80)

BELGRAVIA

Buckingham Palace Rd

Victoria

Eccleston Bridge

Wilton Rd

Francis St

Rochester Row

30

Horseferry Rd

WESTMINSTER

Lambeth Bridge

Vincent Sq

Marsham St

Vauxhall Bridge Rd

Regency St

Albert Embankment

Warwick Way

Belgrave Rd

Tachbrook St

John Islip St

Atterbury St

20

PIMLICO

Westminster & the West End

◎ **Sights**
1 Bedford Square...C1
2 Big Ben..D4
3 British Museum..C1
4 Buckingham Palace......................................A4
Changing of the Guard.........................(see 4)
5 Churchill War Rooms C4
6 College Garden...C5
7 Covent Garden Piazza..................................D2
8 Horse Guards Parade...................................C4
House of Commons.................................(see 9)
House of Lords.......................................(see 9)
9 Houses of Parliament...................................D4
10 National Gallery..C3
11 National Portrait Gallery...............................C3
12 Queen's Gallery..A4
13 Royal Academy of Arts B3
14 Royal Mews..A5
15 Sir John Soane's Museum.............................D1
16 Soho...C2
17 Soho Square...C2
18 St James's Park..B4
19 St Stephen's Entrance..................................C5
20 Tate Britain..C6
21 Trafalgar Square..C3
22 Westminster Abbey......................................C5

● **Activities, Courses & Tours**
23 City Cruises..D4
Houses of Parliament Guided
Tour..(see 9)

◎ **Shopping**
24 Fortnum & Mason...B3
25 Hamleys...B2
26 Hatchards...B3
27 James Smith & Sons C1

✖ **Eating**
Cellarium .... (see 22)
28 Claridge's Foyer & Reading Room............A2
29 National Dining Rooms.................................C3
Portrait ....(see 11)
30 Vincent Rooms...B5

◎ **Drinking & Nightlife**
31 Lamb & Flag...C2

◎ **Entertainment**
32 Pizza Express Jazz Club...............................B2
33 Royal Opera House.......................................D2
34 Wigmore Hall...A1

from a hunting cry. While the centre of London nightlife has shifted east, and Soho has recently seen landmark clubs and music venues shut down, the neighbourhood definitely comes into its own in the evenings and remains a proud gay district. During the day you'll be charmed by the area's bohemian side and its sheer vitality.

◎ The City

Tower Bridge   Bridge

(Map p80; ◉Tower Hill) One of London's most recognisable sights, familiar from dozens of movies, Tower Bridge doesn't disappoint in real life. Its neo-Gothic towers and sky-blue suspension struts add extraordinary elegance to what is a supremely functional structure. London was a thriving port in 1894 when it was built as a much-needed crossing point in the east, equipped with a then-revolutionary steam-driven bascule (counter-balance) mechanism that could raise the roadway to make way for oncoming ships in just three minutes.

Museum of London   Museum

(Map p80; ✎020-7001 9844; www.museumof london.org.uk; 150 London Wall, EC2; ◎10am-6pm; ◉Barbican) **FREE** As entertaining as it is educational, the Museum of London meanders through the various incarnations of the city, stopping off in Roman Londinium and Saxon Ludenwic before eventually ending up in the 21st-century metropolis. Interesting objects and interactive displays work together to bring each era to life, without ever getting too whizz-bang, making this one of the capital's best museums. Free themed tours take place throughout the day; check the signs by the entrance for times.

◎ The South Bank

Tate Modern   Museum

(Map p80; www.tate.org.uk; Bankside, SE1; ◎10am-6pm Sun-Thu, to 10pm Fri & Sat; ◉; ◉Blackfriars, Southwark or London Bridge) **FREE** One of London's most amazing attractions, this outstanding modern- and contemporary-art gallery is housed in

 ## St Paul's Cathedral

Towering over diminutive Ludgate Hill in a superb position that's been a place of Christian worship for over 1400 years (and pagan before that), **St Paul's** (Map p80; ☑020-7246 8357; www.stpauls. co.uk; St Paul's Churchyard, EC4; adult/child £18/8; ⊘8.30am-4.30pm Mon-Sat; ⊖St Paul's) is one of London's most magnificent buildings. For Londoners, the vast dome is a symbol of resilience and pride, standing tall for more than 300 years. Viewing Sir Christopher Wren's masterpiece from the inside and climbing to the top for sweeping views of the capital is an exhilarating experience.

CLAUDIO DIVIZIA/SHUTTERSTOCK ©

the creatively revamped Bankside Power Station south of the Millennium Bridge. A spellbinding synthesis of modern art and capacious industrial brick design, Tate Modern has been extraordinarily successful in bringing challenging work to the masses, both through its free permanent collection and fee-paying big-name temporary exhibitions. The stunning Switch House extension opened in 2016, increasing the available exhibition space by 60%.

London Eye   Viewpoint
(Map p80; ☑0871-222 4002; www.londoneye. com; adult/child £23.45/18.95; ⊘11am-6pm Sep-May, 10am-8.30pm Jun-Aug; ⊖Waterloo or Westminster) Standing 135m high in a fairly flat city, the London Eye affords views 25 miles in every direction, weather permitting. Interactive tablets provide great infor-

mation (in six languages) about landmarks as they appear in the skyline. Each rotation – or 'flight' – takes a gracefully slow 30 minutes. At peak times (July, August and school holidays) it can feel like you'll spend more time in the queue than in the capsule; book premium fast-track tickets to jump the queue.

Shakespeare's Globe   Historic Building
(Map p80; www.shakespearesglobe.com; 21 New Globe Walk, SE1; adult/child £16/9; ⊘9am-5pm; ▮; ⊖Blackfriars or London Bridge) Unlike other venues for Shakespearean plays, the new Globe was designed to resemble the original as closely as possible, which means having the arena open to the fickle London skies, leaving the 700 'groundlings' (standing spectators) to weather London's spectacular downpours. Visits to the Globe include tours of the theatre (half-hourly) as well as access to the exhibition space, which has fascinating exhibits on Shakespeare and theatre in the 17th century. Or you can of course take in a **play** (☑020-7401 9919; seats £20-45, standing £5).

Borough Market   Market
(Map p80; www.boroughmarket.org.uk; 8 Southwark St, SE1; ⊘10am-5pm Wed & Thu, 10am-6pm Fri, 8am-5pm Sat; ⊖London Bridge) Located in this spot in some form or another since the 13th century (possibly since 1014), 'London's Larder' has enjoyed an astonishing renaissance in the past 15 years. Always overflowing with food lovers, inveterate gastronomes, wide-eyed visitors and Londoners in search of inspiration for their dinner party, this fantastic market has become firmly established as a sight in its own right. The market specialises in high-end fresh products; there are also plenty of takeaway stalls and an almost unreasonable number of cake stalls.

◎ Kensington & Hyde Park

Natural History Museum   Museum
(Map p84; www.nhm.ac.uk; Cromwell Rd, SW7; ⊘10am-5.50pm; ⊖South Kensington) **FREE** This colossal and magnificent-looking

London Eye and the Thames

building is infused with the irrepressible Victorian spirit of collecting, cataloguing and interpreting the natural world. The **Dinosaurs Gallery** (Blue Zone) is a must for children, who gawp at the animatronic T-Rex, fossils and excellent displays. Adults for their part will love the intriguing Treasures exhibition in the **Cadogan Gallery** (Green Zone), which houses a host of unrelated objects each telling its own unique story, from a chunk of moon rock to a dodo skeleton.

Victoria & Albert Museum   Museum

(V&A; Map p84; ☑020-7942 2000; www. vam.ac.uk; Cromwell Rd, SW7; ⊘10am-5.40pm Sat-Thu, to 10pm Fri; ⊖South Kensington) **FREE** The Museum of Manufactures, as the V&A was known when it opened in 1852, was part of Prince Albert's legacy to the nation in the aftermath of the successful Great Exhibition of 1851. It houses the world's largest collection of decorative arts, from Asian ceramics to Middle Eastern rugs, Chinese paintings, Western furniture, fashion from all ages, and modern-day domestic appliances. The (ticketed) temporary

exhibitions are another highlight, covering anything from retrospectives of David Bowie and designer Alexander McQueen to special materials and trends.

Science Museum   Museum

(Map p84; www.sciencemuseum.org.uk; Exhibition Rd, SW7; ⊘10am-6pm; ⊖South Kensington) **FREE** With seven floors of interactive and educational exhibits, this scientifically spellbinding museum will mesmerise adults and children alike, covering everything from early technology to space travel. A perennial favourite is **Exploring Space**, a gallery featuring genuine rockets and satellites and a full-size replica of the 'Eagle', the lander that took Neil Armstrong and Buzz Aldrin to the moon in 1969. The **Making the Modern World Gallery** next door is a visual feast of locomotives, planes, cars and other revolutionary inventions.

Hyde Park   Park

(Map p84; www.royalparks.org.uk/parks/ hyde-park; ⊘5am-midnight; ⊖Marble Arch, Hyde Park Corner or Queensway) At 145 hectares, Hyde Park is central London's

The City, the South Bank & East London

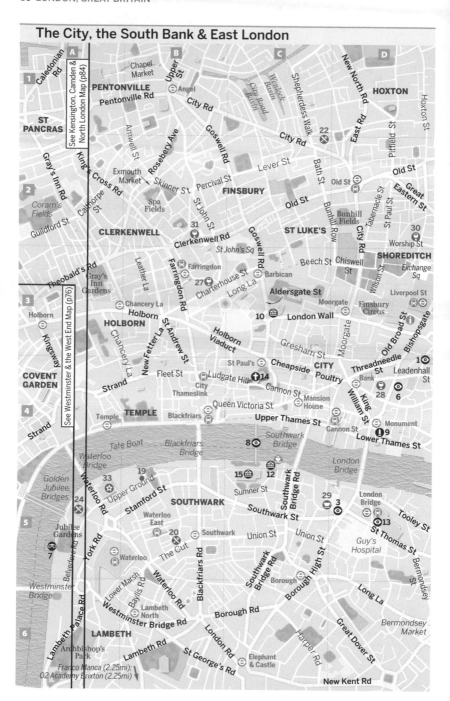

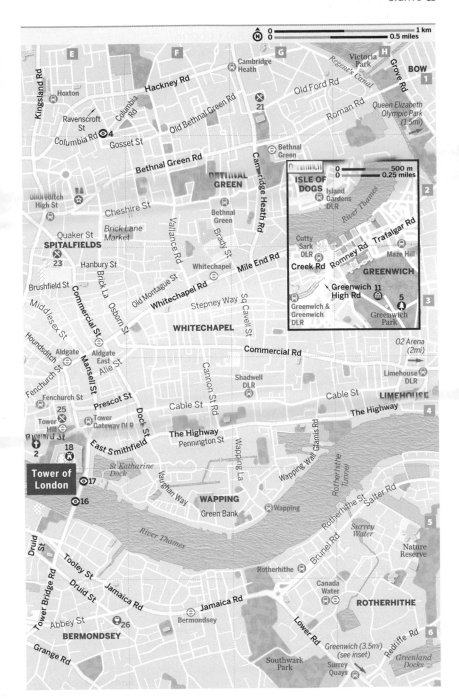

The City, the South Bank & East London

⊙ **Sights**
1 30 St Mary Axe...............................D4
2 All Hallows by the Tower.....................E4
3 Borough Market..............................D5
4 Columbia Road Flower Market E1
5 Greenwich Park..............................H3
6 Leadenhall Market..........................D4
7 London Eye..................................A5
8 Millennium Bridge...........................C4
9 Monument D4
10 Museum of London..........................C3
11 Royal Observatory..........................H3
12 Shakespeare's Globe C4
13 Shard......................................D5
14 St Paul's Cathedral........................C4
15 Tate Modern................................C5
16 Tower Bridge...............................E5
17 Tower Bridge Exhibition....................E5
18 Tower of London............................E4

⊕ **Activities, Courses & Tours**
19 London Bicycle Tour B5

⊗ **Eating**
20 Anchor & Hope.............................B5
   Arabica Bar & Kitchen...................(see 29)
21 Corner Room...............................G1
22 Fifteen...................................C2
23 Hawksmoor.................................E3
24 Skylon....................................A5
25 Wine Library..............................E4

⊖ **Drinking & Nightlife**
26 Brew By Numbers...........................E6
27 Fabric....................................B3
28 Jamaica Wine House D4
29 Monmouth Coffee Company..................C5
   Oblix..................................(see 13)
30 Queen of Hoxton...........................D2
31 Zetter Townhouse Cocktail
   Lounge....................................B2

⊕ **Entertainment**
32 Electric Cinema E2
33 National Theatre A5
   Shakespeare's Globe....................(see 12)

largest open space, expropriated from the Church in 1536 by Henry VIII and turned into a hunting ground and later a venue for duels, executions and horse racing. The 1851 Great Exhibition was held here, and during WWII the park became an enormous potato field. These days, there's boating on the **Serpentine**, summer concerts (Bruce Springsteen, Florence + The Machine, Patti Smith), film nights and other warm-weather events.

Kensington Palace   Palace

(Map p84; www.hrp.org.uk/kensingtonpalace; Kensington Gardens, W8; adult/child £19/free; ⊙10am-6pm Mar-Oct, to 4pm Nov-Feb; ⊖High St Kensington) Built in 1605, the palace became the favourite royal residence under William and Mary of Orange in 1689, and remained so until George III became king and moved out. Today, it is still a royal residence, with the likes of the Duke and Duchess of Cambridge (Prince William and his wife Catherine) and Prince Harry living there. A large part of the palace is open to the public, however, including the King's and Queen's State Apartments.

⊙ East London

Columbia Road Flower Market   Market

(Map p80; www.columbiaroad.info; Columbia Rd, E2; ⊙8am-3pm Sun; ⊖Hoxton) A wonderful explosion of colour and life, this weekly market sells a beautiful array of flowers, pot plants, bulbs, seeds and everything you might need for the garden. It's a lot of fun and the best place to hear proper Cockney barrow-boy banter ('We got flowers cheap enough for ya muvver-in-law's grave' etc). It gets really packed, so go as early as you can, or later on, when the vendors sell off the cut flowers cheaply.

Queen Elizabeth Olympic Park   Park

(www.queenelizabetholympicpark.co.uk; E20; ⊖Stratford) The glittering centrepiece of London's 2012 Olympic Games, this vast 227-hectare expanse includes the main Olympic venues as well as playgrounds, walking and cycling trails, gardens, and a diverse mix of wetland, woodland, meadow and other wildlife habitats as an environmentally fertile legacy for the future. The main focal point is **London Stadium**, with a

Games capacity of 80,000, scaled back to 54,000 seats for its new role as the home ground for West Ham United FC.

◉ Camden & North London

Hampstead Heath   Park
(Map p84; www.cityoflondon.gov.uk; ⊖Hampstead Heath or Gospel Oak) Sprawling Hampstead Heath, with its rolling woodlands and meadows, feels a million miles away – despite being approximately four miles from the City of London. Covering 320 hectares, most of it woods, hills and meadows, it's home to about 180 bird species, 23 species of butterflies, grass snakes, bats and a rich array of flora. It's a wonderful place for a ramble, especially to the top of **Parliament Hill**, which offers expansive views across the city.

British Library   Library
(Map p84; www.bl.uk; 96 Euston Rd, NW1; ⊗galleries 9.30am-6pm Mon & Fri, to 8pm Tue-Thu, to 5pm Sat, 11am-5pm Sun; ⊖King's Cross St Pancras) **FREE** Consisting of low-slung red-brick terraces and fronted by a large plaza featuring an oversized statue of Sir Isaac Newton, Colin St John Wilson's British Library building is a love-it-or-hate-it affair (Prince Charles likened it to a secret-police academy). Completed in 1997, it's home to some of the greatest treasures of the written word, including the *Codex Sinaiticus* (the first complete text of the New Testament), Leonardo da Vinci's notebooks and a copy of the Magna Carta (1215).

Regent's Canal   Canal
(Map p84) To escape the crowded streets and enjoy a picturesque, waterside side stretch of North London, take to the canals that once played such a vital role in the transport of goods across the capital. The towpath of the Regent's Canal also makes an excellent shortcut across North London, either on foot or by bike. In full, the ribbon of water runs 9 miles from Little Venice (where it connects with the Grand Union Canal) to the Thames at Limehouse.

 Camden Market

Although – or perhaps because – it stopped being cutting-edge several thousand cheap leather jackets ago, **Camden Market** (Map p84; www.camdenmarket. com; Camden High St, NW1; ⊗10am-6pm; ⊖Camden Town or Chalk Farm) attracts millions of visitors each week and is one of London's most popular attractions. What started out as a collection of attractive craft stalls beside Camden Lock on the Regent's Canal now extends most of the way from Camden Town tube station to Chalk Farm tube station.

Abbey Road Studios   Historic Building
(Map p84; www.abbeyroad.com; 3 Abbey Rd, NW8; ⊖St John's Wood) Beatles aficionados can't possibly visit London without making a pilgrimage to this famous recording studio in St John's Wood. The studios themselves are off-limits, so you'll have to content yourself with examining the decades of fan graffiti on the fence outside. Stop-start local traffic is long accustomed to groups of tourists lining up on the zebra crossing to re-enact the cover of the fab four's 1969 masterpiece *Abbey Road*. In 2010 the crossing was rewarded with Grade II heritage status.

◉ Greenwich & South London

Greenwich Park   Park
(Map p80; ☏030-0061 2380; www.royalparks. org.uk; King George St, SE10; ⊗6am-around sunset; ®DLR Cutty Sark, ®Greenwich or Maze Hill) This is one of London's loveliest expanses of green, with a rose garden, picturesque walks, Anglo-Saxon tumuli and astonishing views from the crown of the hill near the Royal Observatory (p85) towards Canary Wharf – the financial district across the Thames. Covering 74 hectares, it's the oldest enclosed royal park and is partly the work of André Le Nôtre, the landscape architect who designed the palace gardens of

Kensington, Camden & North London

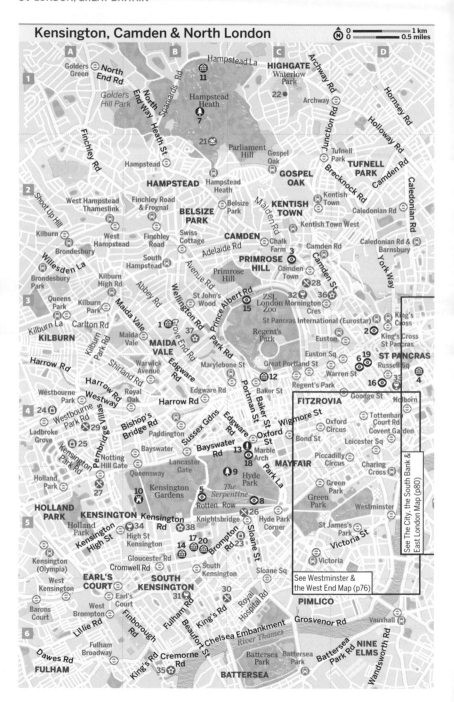

Kensington, Camden & North London

⊙ **Sights**
- 1 Abbey Road Studios B3
- 2 British Library D3
- 3 Camden Market C3
- 4 Charles Dickens Museum D4
- 5 Diana, Princess of Wales
  Memorial Fountain B5
- 6 Gordon Square D4
- 7 Hampstead Heath B1
- 8 Holocaust Memorial Garden C5
- 9 Hyde Park C5
- 10 Kensington Palace B5
- 11 Kenwood B1
- 12 Madame Tussauds C4
- 13 Marble Arch C4
- 14 Natural History Museum B5
- 15 Regent's Canal C3
- 16 Russell Square D4
- 17 Science Museum B5
  Sensational
  Butterflies .... (see 14)
- 18 Speakers' Corner C4
- 19 Tavistock Square D4
- 20 Victoria & Albert Museum B5
  Wildlife Photographer
  of the Year .... (see 14)

⊙ **Activities, Courses & Tours**
- 21 Hampstead Heath Ponds B2
- 22 Highgate Cemetery Tour C1

⊙ **Shopping**
- 23 Harrods C5
- 24 Portobello Green Arcade A4
- 25 Portobello Road Market A4

⊗ **Eating**
  Acklam Village Market .... (see 24)
- 26 Dinner by Heston Blumenthal C5
- 27 Geales A5
- 28 Hook Camden Town C3
- 29 Ledbury A4
- 30 Rabbit C6

⊙ **Drinking & Nightlife**
- 31 Anglesea Arms B6
- 32 Edinboro Castle C3
- 33 Queen's Larder D4
- 34 Roof Gardens B5

⊙ **Entertainment**
- 35 606 Club B6
- 36 KOKO D3
- 37 Lord's B3
- 38 Royal Albert Hall B5

Versailles. Greenwich Park hosted the 2012 Olympic Games equestrian events.

Royal Observatory   Historic Building

(Map p80; www.rmg.co.uk; Greenwich Park, Blackheath Ave, SE10; adult/child £9.50/5, incl Cutty Sark £18.50/8.50; ⊙10am-5pm Sep-Jun, to 6pm Jul & Aug; ⊠DLR Cutty Sark, DLR Greenwich or Greenwich) Rising south of Queen's House, idyllic Greenwich Park climbs up the hill, affording stunning views of London from the Royal Observatory, which Charles II had built in 1675 to help solve the riddle of longitude. To the north is lovely **Flamsteed House** and the **Meridian Courtyard**, where you can stand with your feet straddling the western and eastern hemispheres; admission is by ticket. The southern half contains the highly informative and free **Weller Astronomy Galleries** and the **Peter Harrison Planetarium**.

Horniman Museum   Museum

(☑020-8699 1872; www.horniman.ac.uk; 100 London Rd, Forest Hill, SE23; museum & gardens free, exhibitions are ticketed; ⊙museum 10.30am-5.30pm, gardens 7.15am-sunset Mon-Sat, 8am-sunset Sun; ⊠Forest Hill) **FREE** This museum is an extraordinary place, comprising the original collection of wealthy tea-merchant Frederick John Horniman. He had this art-nouveau building, with its clock tower and mosaics, specially designed to house his collection. Built in 1901, today it encompasses everything from a dusty walrus and voodoo altars from Haiti and Benin to a mock-up of a Fijian reef and a collection of concertinas. It's wonderful.

TOURS

City Cruises   Boating

(Map p76; ☑020-7740 0400; www.citycruises. com; adult single/return/day pass from £12.50/16.50/£6.65, child £6.25/8.25/8.35; ⊖Westminster) Ferry service departing every 30 minutes between Westminster, the London Eye, Bankside, Tower and Greenwich

A Shopping Icon

Garish and stylish in equal measures, perennially crowded **Harrods** (Map p84; ☑020-7730 1234; www.harrods.com; 87-135 Brompton Rd, SW1; ☻10am-9pm Mon-Sat, 11.30am-6pm Sun; ☻Knightsbridge) is an obligatory stop for visitors, from the cash-strapped to the big spenders. The stock is astonishing, as are many of the price tags. High on kitsch, the 'Egyptian Elevator' resembles something out of an *Indiana Jones* epic, while the memorial fountain to Dodi and Di (lower ground floor) merely adds surrealism.

FRANK GAERTNER/SHUTTERSTOCK ©

piers. A 24-hour Rover Ticket is as cheap as adult/child £10/5 online.

London Bicycle Tour   Cycling
(Map p80; ☑020-7928 6838; www.london bicycle.com; 1 Gabriel's Wharf, 56 Upper Ground, SE1; tour incl bike from adult/child £24.95/21.95, bike hire per day £20; ☻Southwark or Waterloo) Three-hour tours begin in the South Bank and take in London's highlights on both sides of the river; the classic tour is available in eight languages. A night ride is available. You can also hire traditional or speciality bikes, such as tandems and folding bikes, by the hour or day.

Highgate Cemetery Tour   Tour
(Map p84; www.highgatecemetery.org; Swain's Lane, N6; adult/child £12/6; ☻1.45pm Mon-Fri, every 30min 11am-3pm Sat & Sun Nov-Feb, to 4pm Mar-Oct; ☻Archway) The highlight of Highgate Cemetery is the overgrown West Cemetery, where a maze of winding paths

leads to the Circle of Lebanon, rings of tombs flanking a circular path and topped with a majestic cedar of Lebanon tree. Admission to the West Cemetery is by guided tour only; weekday tours must be booked in advance but weekend tours are a turn-up-and-pay affair.

🛍 SHOPPING

Fortnum & Mason   Department Store
(Map p76; ☑020-7734 8040; www.fortnum andmason.com; 181 Piccadilly, W1; ☻10am-8pm Mon-Sat, 11.30am-6pm Sun; ☻Piccadilly Circus) With its classic eau-de-Nil (pale green) colour scheme, 'the Queen's grocery store' established 1707 refuses to yield to modern times. Its staff – men and women – still wear old-fashioned tailcoats and its glamorous food hall is supplied with hampers, cut marmalade, speciality teas, superior fruitcakes and so forth. Fortnum and Mason remains the quintessential London shopping experience.

Hatchards   Books
(Map p76; ☑020-7439 9921; www.hatchards. co.uk; 187 Piccadilly, W1; ☻9.30am-8pm Mon-Sat, noon-6.30pm Sun; ☻Green Park, Piccadilly Circus) London's oldest bookshop dates drom 1797. Holding three royal warrants, it's a stupendous bookshop now in the Waterstones stable, with a solid supply of signed editions and bursting at its smart seams with very browsable stock. There's a strong selection of first editions on the ground floor and regularly scheduled literary events.

Hamleys   Toys
(Map p76; ☑0371-704 1977; www.hamleys. com; 188-196 Regent St, W1; ☻10am-9pm Mon-Fri, 9.30am-9pm Sat, noon-6pm Sun; ☻Oxford Circus) Claiming to be the world's oldest (and some say the largest) toy store, Hamleys moved to its address on Regent St in 1881. From the basement's Star Wars Collection and the ground floor where staff blow bubbles and glide foam boomerangs through the air with practised nonchalance

to Lego World and a cafe on the 5th floor, it's a rich layer cake of playthings.

James Smith & Sons
Fashion & Accessories

(Map p76; ☑020-7836 4731; www.james-smith.co.uk; 53 New Oxford St, WC1; ⊘10am-5.45pm Mon, Tue, Thu & Fri, 10.30am-5.45pm Wed, 10am-5.15pm Sat; ⊖Tottenham Court Rd) Nobody makes and stocks such elegant umbrellas (not to mention walking sticks and canes) as this place. It's been fighting the British weather from the same address since 1857 and, thanks to London's ever-present downpours, will hopefully do great business for years to come. Prices start at around £40 for a pocket umbrella.

Portobello Road Market
Clothing, Antiques

(Map p84; www.portobellomarket.org; Portobello Rd, W10; ⊘8am-6.30pm Mon-Wed, Fri & Sat, to 1pm Thu; ⊖Notting Hill Gate or Ladbroke Grove) Lovely on a warm summer's day, Portobello Road Market is an iconic London attraction with an eclectic mix of street food, fruit and veg, antiques, curios, collectables, vibrant fashion and trinkets. Although the shops along Portobello Rd open daily and the fruit and veg stalls (from Elgin Cres to Talbot Rd) only close on Sunday, the busiest day by far is Saturday, when antique dealers set up shop (from Chepstow Villas to Elgin Cres).

✪ EATING

Franco Manca
Pizza £

(www.francomanca.co.uk; 4 Market Row, SW9; pizzas £4.50-6.95; ⊘noon-5pm Mon, noon-11pm Tue-Fri, 11.30am-11pm Sat, 11.30am-10.30pm Sun; ⊖Brixton) The Brixton branch of Franco Manca remains a perennial local favourite and draws pizza enthusiasts from far and wide. The restaurant only uses its own sourdough, fired up in a wood-burning brick oven. There are no reservations, so beat the queues by arriving early, avoiding lunch hours and Saturday.

Hook Camden Town
Fish & Chips £

(Map p84; www.hookrestaurants.com; 65 Parkway, NW1; mains £8-12; ⊘noon-3pm & 5-10pm Mon-Thu, noon-10.30pm Fri & Sat, to 9pm

Portobello Road Market

WILL JONES/LONELY PLANET ©

Ledbury

Sun; 👪; ⊖Camden Town) 🖉 In addition to working entirely with sustainable small fisheries and local suppliers, Hook makes all its sauces on site and wraps its fish in recycled materials, supplying diners with extraordinarily fine-tasting morsels. Totally fresh, the fish arrives in panko breadcrumbs or tempura batter, with seaweed salted chips. Craft beers and fine wines are also to hand.

Skylon   Modern European ££
(Map p80; ☑020-7654 7800; www.skylon-restaurant.co.uk; 3rd fl, Royal Festival Hall, Southbank Centre, Belvedere Rd, SE1; 3-course menu grill/restaurant £25/30; ⊗grill noon-11pm Mon-Sat, to 10.30pm Sun, restaurant noon-2.30pm & 5.30-10.30pm Mon-Sat & noon-4pm Sun; 🛜; ⊖Waterloo) This excellent restaurant inside the Royal Festival Hall is divided into grill and fine-dining sections by a large bar. The decor is cutting-edge 1950s: muted colours and period chairs (trendy then, trendier now) while floor-to-ceiling windows bathe you in magnificent views of the Thames and the city. The six-course restaurant tasting menu costs £59. Booking is advised.

Anchor & Hope   Gastropub ££
(Map p80; www.anchorandhopepub.co.uk; 36 The Cut, SE1; mains £12-20; ⊗noon-2.30pm Tue-Sat, 6-10.30pm Mon-Sat, 12.30-3pm Sun; ⊖Southwark) A stalwart of the South Bank food scene, the Anchor & Hope is a quintessential gastropub: elegant but not formal, and utterly delicious (European fare with a British twist). The menu changes daily but think salt marsh lamb shoulder cooked for seven hours; wild rabbit with anchovies, almonds and rocket; and panna cotta with rhubarb compote.

Corner Room   Modern British ££
(Map p80; ☑020-7871 0460; www.townhall hotel.com/cornerroom; Patriot Sq, E2; mains £13-14, 2-/3-course lunch £19/23; ⊗7.30-10am, noon-3pm & 6-9.45pm; ⊖Bethnal Green) Someone put this baby in the corner, but we're certainly not complaining. Tucked away on the 1st floor of the Town Hall Hotel, this relaxed restaurant serves expertly crafted dishes with complex yet delicate flavours, highlighting the best of British seasonal produce.

Rabbit   Modern British ££

(Map p84; ☑020-3750 0172; www.rabbit-restaurant.com; 172 King's Rd, SW3; mains £6-24, set lunch £13.50; ⊘noon-midnight Tue-Sat, 6-11pm Mon, noon-6pm Sun; ☑; ⊜Sloane Sq) Three brothers grew up on a farm. One became a farmer, another a butcher, while the third worked in hospitality. So they pooled their skills and came up with Rabbit, a breath of fresh air in upmarket Chelsea. The restaurant rocks the agri-chic (yes) look and the innovative, seasonal modern British cuisine is fabulous.

Geales   Seafood ££

(Map p84; ☑020-7727 7528; www.geales.com; 2 Farmer St, W8; 2-course express lunch £9.95, mains £9-37.50; ⊘noon-3pm & 6-10.30pm Tue-Fri, noon-10.30pm Sat, noon-4pm Sun; ☎; ⊜Notting Hill Gate) Frying since 1939 – a bad year for the European restaurant trade – Geales has endured with its quiet location on the corner of Farmer St. The succulent fish in crispy batter is a fine catch, but the fish pie is also worth angling for. Look out for the good-value (two-course, one coffee) express lunch, available from Tuesday to Friday.

Portrait   Modern European £££

(Map p76; ☑020-7312 2490; www.npg.org.uk/visit/shop-eat-drink.php; 3rd fl, National Portrait Gallery, St Martin's Pl, WC2; mains £19.50-26, 2-/3-course menu £27.50/31.50; ⊘10-11am, 11.45am-3pm & 3.30-4.30pm daily, 6.30-8.30pm Thu, Fri & Sat; ☎; ⊜Charing Cross) This stunningly located restaurant above the excellent National Portrait Gallery (p74) comes with dramatic views over Trafalgar Sq and Westminster. It's a fine choice for tantalising food and the chance to relax after a morning or afternoon of picture-gazing at the gallery. The breakfast/brunch (10am to 11am) and afternoon tea (3.30pm to 4.30pm) come highly recommended. Booking is advisable.

Ledbury   French £££

(Map p84; ☑020-7792 9090; www.theledbury.com; 127 Ledbury Rd, W11; 4-course set lunch £70, 4-course dinner £115; ⊘noon-2pm Wed-Sun

🍽️ London's Celebrity Chefs

London's food renaissance was partly led by a group of telegenic chefs who built food empires around their names and their TV programs. Gordon Ramsay is the most (in)famous of the lot, but his London venues are still standard-bearers for top-quality cuisine. Other big names include Jamie Oliver, whose restaurant **Fifteen** (Map p80; ☑020-3375 1515; www.fifteen.net; 15 Westland Pl, N1; mains £22-24, 2-/3-course lunch £19/24, Sun £15-19; ⊘noon-3pm & 6-10.30pm; ☎; ⊜Old St) trains disadvantaged young people, and Heston Blumenthal, whose mad-professor-like experiments with food (molecular gastronomy, as he describes it) have earned him rave reviews at **Dinner by Heston Blumenthal** (Map p84; ☑020-7201 3833; www.dinnerby heston.com; Mandarin Oriental Hyde Park, 66 Knightsbridge, SW1; 3-course set lunch £45, mains £28-44; ⊘noon-2pm & 6-10.15pm Mon-Fri, noon-2.30pm & 6-10.30pm Sat & Sun; ☎; ⊜Knightsbridge).

Jamie Oliver's Fifteen

& 6.30-9.45pm daily; ☎; ⊜Westbourne Park or Notting Hill Gate) Two Michelin stars and swooningly elegant, Brett Graham's artful French restaurant attracts well-heeled diners in jeans with designer jackets. Dishes such as hand-dived scallops, Chinese water deer, smoked bone marrow, quince and red leaves or Herdwick lamb with salt-baked turnips, celery cream and wild garlic are triumphs. London gastronomes have the

Claridge's Foyer & Reading Room

Extend that pinkie finger to partake in afternoon tea within the classic art deco foyer and reading room of this landmark **hotel** (Map p76; ☑020-7107 8886; www.claridges.co.uk; 49-53 Brook St, W1; afternoon tea £68, with champagne £79; ☺afternoon tea 2.45-5.30pm; ☎; ⊜Bond St), where the gentle clink of fine porcelain and champagne glasses could be a defining memory of your trip to London. The setting is gorgeous and the dress code is elegant, smart casual (those in ripped jeans and baseball caps won't get served).

Claridge's Hotel
ALEX SEGRE/SHUTTERSTOCK ©

Ledbury on speed-dial, so reservations well in advance are crucial.

Hawksmoor   Steak £££
(Map p80; ☑020-7426 4850; www.the hawksmoor.com; 157 Commercial St, E1; mains £20-50; ☺noon-2.30pm & 5-10.30pm Mon-Sat, noon-9pm Sun; ☎; ⊜Liverpool St) You could easily miss discreetly signed Hawksmoor, but confirmed carnivores will find it worth seeking out. The dark wood, bare bricks and velvet curtains make for a handsome setting in which to gorge yourself on the best of British beef. The Sunday roasts (£20) are legendary.

🍷 DRINKING & NIGHTLIFE

Jamaica Wine House   Pub
(Map p80; ☑020-7929 6972; www.jamaica winehouse.co.uk; 12 St Michael's Alley, EC3; ☺11am-11pm Mon-Fri; ⊜Bank) Not a wine bar

at all, the 'Jam Pot' is a historic wood-lined pub that stands on the site of what was London's first coffee house (1652). Reached by a narrow alley, it's slightly tricky to find but well worth seeking out for the age-old ambience of its darkened rooms.

Lamb & Flag   Pub
(Map p76; ☑020-7497 9504; www.lamband flagcoventgarden.co.uk; 33 Rose St, WC2; ☺11am-11pm Mon-Sat, noon-10.30pm Sun; ⊜Covent Garden) Everybody's favourite pub in central London, pint-sized Lamb & Flag is full of charm and history, and stands on the site of a pub that dates back to at least 1772. Rain or shine, you'll have to elbow your way to the bar through the merry crowd drinking outside. Inside are brass fittings and creaky wooden floors.

Oblix   Bar
(Map p80; www.oblixrestaurant.com; 32nd fl, Shard, 31 St Thomas St, SE1; ☺noon-11pm; ⊜London Bridge) On the 32nd floor of the **Shard** (www.theviewfromtheshard.com; 32 London Bridge St, SE1; adult/child £30.95/24.95; ☺10am-10pm), Oblix offers mesmerising vistas of London. You can come for anything from a coffee (£3.50) to a cocktail (from £10) and enjoy virtually the same views as the official viewing galleries of the Shard (but at a reduced cost and with the added bonus of a drink). Live music every night from 7pm.

Fabric   Club
(Map p80; www.fabriclondon.com; 77a Charterhouse Street, EC1M; £5-25; ☺11pm-7am Fri-Sun; ⊜Farringdon or Barbican) London's leading club, Fabric's three separate dance floors in a huge converted cold store opposite Smithfield meat market draws impressive queues (buy tickets online). FabricLive (on selected Fridays) rumbles with drum and bass and dubstep, while Fabric (usually on Saturdays but also on selected Fridays) is the club's signature live DJ night. Sunday's WetYourSelf! delivers house, techno and electronica.

Outside the Lamb & Flag

Roof Gardens — Club

(Map p84; www.roofgardens.virgin.com; 99 Kensington High St, W8; club £20, gardens free; ⊙club 10pm-2am Fri & Sat, garden 9am-5pm on selected dates; ⊛; ⊜High St Kensington) Atop the former Derry and Toms building is this enchanting venue – a nightclub with 0.6 hectares of gardens and resident flamingos. The wow-factor requires £20 entry, you must register on the guest list via the website before going and drinks are £10 a pop. Open only to over-21s, the dress code is 'no effort, no entry' (leave the onesie at home).

Zetter Townhouse Cocktail Lounge — Cocktail Bar

(Map p80; ☎020-7324 4545; www.thezetter townhouse.com; 49-50 St John's Sq, EC1V; ⊙7.30am-12.45am; ⊛; ⊜Farringdon) Tucked away behind an unassuming door on St John's Sq, this ground-floor bar is decorated with plush armchairs, stuffed animal heads and a legion of lamps. The cocktail list takes its theme from the area's distilling history – recipes of yesteryear plus homemade tinctures and cordials are used

pint-sized Lamb & Flag is full of charm and history

to create interesting and unusual tipples. House cocktails are all £10.50.

Queen of Hoxton — Bar

(Map p80; www.queenofhoxton.com; 1 Curtain Rd, EC2A; ⊙4pm-midnight Mon-Wed, to 2am Thu-Sat; ⊛; ⊜Liverpool St) This industrial-chic bar has a games room, basement and varied music nights (including oddballs such as dance lessons and ukulele jamming sessions), but the real drawcard is the vast rooftop bar, decked out with flowers, fairy lights and even a wigwam. It has fantastic views across the city.

Netil360 — Rooftop Bar

(www.netil360.com; 1 Westgate St, E8; ⊙10am-10pm Wed-Fri, noon-11pm Sat & Sun Apr-Nov; ⊛; ⊜London Fields) Perched atop Netil House, this uber-hip rooftop cafe/bar offers incredible views over London, with brass telescopes enabling you to get better acquainted with workers in the Gherkin. In between drinks you can knock out a game of croquet on the AstroTurf, or perhaps book a hot tub for you and your mates to stew in.

Brew By Numbers   Microbrewery

(Map p80; www.brewbynumbers.com; 79 Enid St, SE1; ⊗6-10pm Fri, 11am-8pm Sat; ⊖Bermondsey) This microbrewery's raison d'être is experimentation. Everything from its 'scientific' branding (the numbers refer to the type of beer – porter, pale ale etc – and recipe) to its enthusiasm for exploring new beer styles and refashioning old ones (*saisons* for instance, an old Belgian beer drunk by farm workers) is about broadening the definition of beer.

Glory   Gay & Lesbian

(☎020-7684 0794; www.theglory.co; 281 Kingsland Rd E2; ⊗5pm-midnight Mon-Thu, to 2am Fri & Sat, 1-11pm Sun; ⊠Haggerston) A charming cast has taken over this cosy corner pub, transforming it into one of London's most legendary queer cabaret venues. Order a Twink in Pink or a Schlong Island Iced Tea from the cocktail list and brace yourself for whatever wackiness is on offer. All genders welcome.

Edinboro Castle   Pub

(Map p84; www.edinborocastlepub.co.uk; 57 Mornington Tce, NW1; ⊗11am-11pm; ☎; ⊖Camden Town) Large and relaxed Edinboro offers a refined atmosphere, gorgeous furniture perfect for slumping into, a fine bar and a full menu. The highlight, however, is the huge beer garden, complete with warm-weather BBQs and lit up with coloured lights on long summer evenings. Patio heaters come out in winter.

✪ ENTERTAINMENT

Wigmore Hall   Classical Music

(Map p76; www.wigmore-hall.org.uk; 36 Wigmore St, W1; ⊖Bond St) This is one of the best and most active (more than 400 concerts a year) classical-music venues in town, not only because of its fantastic acoustics, beautiful art nouveau hall and great variety of concerts and recitals, but also because of the sheer standard of the performances.

Royal Opera House

Built in 1901, it has remained one of the world's top places for chamber music.

Royal Opera House   Opera
(Map p76; ☑020-7304 4000; www.roh.org.uk; Bow St, WC2; tickets £4-270; ☻Covent Garden) Classic opera in London has a fantastic setting on Covent Garden Piazza and coming here for a night is a sumptuous – if pricey – affair. Although the program has been fluffed up by modern influences, the main attractions are still the opera and classical ballet – all are wonderful productions and feature world-class performers.

National Theatre   Theatre
(Royal National Theatre; Map p80; ☑020-7452 3000; www.nationaltheatre.org.uk; South Bank, SE1; ☻Waterloo) England's flagship theatre showcases a mix of classic and contemporary plays performed by excellent casts in three theatres (Olivier, Lyttelton and Dorfman). Artistic director Rufus Norris, who started in April 2015, made headlines in 2016 for announcing plans to stage a Brexit-based drama.

606 Club   Blues, Jazz
(Map p84; ☑020-7352 5953; www.606club. co.uk; 90 Lots Rd, SW10; ☻7-11.15pm Sun-Thu, 8pm-12.30am Fri & Sat; ☒Imperial Wharf) Named after its old address on the King's Rd that cast a spell over Jazz lovers London-wide back in the '80s, this fantastic, tucked-away basement jazz club and restaurant gives centre stage to contemporary British-based jazz musicians nightly. The club can only serve alcohol to nonmembers who are dining, and it is highly advisable to book to get a table.

Royal Albert Hall   Concert Venue
(Map p84; ☑0845 401 5034; www.royalalbert hall.com; Kensington Gore, SW7; ☻South Kensington) This splendid Victorian concert hall hosts classical-music, rock and other performances, but is most famously the venue for the BBC-sponsored Proms. Booking is possible, but from mid-July to mid-September Proms punters queue for £5 standing (or 'promenading') tickets that go on sale one hour before curtain-up. Otherwise, the box

 Anglesea Arms

Seasoned with age and decades of ale-quaffing patrons (including Charles Dickens, who lived on the same road, and DH Lawrence), this old-school **pub** (Map p84; ☑020-7373 7960; www.anglese aarms.com; 15 Selwood Tce, SW7; ☻11am-11pm Mon-Sat, noon-10.30pm Sun; ☻South Kensington) boasts considerable character and a strong showing of brews, while the terrace out front swarms with punters in warmer months. Arch-criminal Bruce Reynolds masterminded the Great Train Robbery over drinks here.

office and prepaid-ticket collection counter are through door 12 (south side of the hall).

Electric Cinema   Cinema
(Map p80; ☑020-3350 3490; www.electric cinema.co.uk; 64-66 Redchurch St, E2; tickets £11-19; ☻Shoreditch High St) Run by Shoreditch House, an uber-fashionable private member's club, this is cinema-going that will impress a date, with space for an intimate 48 on the comfy armchairs. There's a full bar and restaurant in the complex, and you can take your purchases in with you. Tickets go like crazy, so book ahead.

Lord's   Spectator Sport
(Map p84; ☑020-7432 1000; www.lords.org; St John's Wood Rd, NW8; ☎; ☻St John's Wood) For cricket devotees a trip to Lord's is often as much a pilgrimage as anything else. As well as being home to Marylebone Cricket Club, the ground hosts Test matches, one-day internationals and domestic cricket

finals. International matches are usually booked months in advance, but tickets for county cricket fixtures are reasonably easy to come by.

Pizza Express Jazz Club   Jazz

(Map p76; ☐020-7439 4962; www.pizzaex presslive.com/venues/soho-jazz-club; 10 Dean St, W1; admission £15-40; ☉Tottenham Court Rd) Pizza Express has been one of the best jazz venues in London since opening in 1969. It may be a strange arrangement, in a basement beneath a branch of the chain restaurant, but it's highly popular. Lots of big names perform here and promising artists such as Norah Jones, Gregory Porter and the late Amy Winehouse played here in their early days.

O2 Arena   Live Music

(www.theo2.co.uk; Peninsula Sq, SE10; ☎; ☉North Greenwich) One of the city's major concert venues, hosting all the biggies – the Rolling Stones, Paul Simon and Sting, One Direction, Ed Sheeran and many others – inside the 20,000-capacity arena. It's also a popular venue for sporting events and you can even climb the roof for ranging views with **Up at the O2**.

KOKO   Live Music

(Map p84; www.koko.uk.com; 1a Camden High St, NW1; ☉Mornington Cres) Once the legendary Camden Palace, where Charlie Chaplin, the Goons and the Sex Pistols performed, and where Prince played surprise gigs, KOKO is maintaining its reputation as one of London's better gig venues. The theatre has a dance floor and decadent balconies, and attracts an indie crowd. There are live bands most nights and hugely popular club nights on Saturdays.

ⓘ INFORMATION

Visit London (www.visitlondon.com) Visit London can fill you in on everything from tourist attractions and events (such as the Changing of the Guard and Chinese New Year parade) to river trips and tours, accommodation, eating, theatre, shopping, children's London, and gay and lesbian

venues. There are helpful kiosks at **Heathrow Airport** (Terminal 1, 2 & 3 Underground station concourse; ☉7.30am-8.30pm), **King's Cross St Pancras Station** (Western Ticket Hall, Euston Rd N1; ☉8am-6pm), **Liverpool Street Station** (Map p80; ☉8am-6pm), **Piccadilly Circus Underground Station** (Map p76; ☉9.30am-4pm), The City, Greenwich and **Victoria Station** (Map p76; ☉7.15am-9.15pm Mon-Sat, 8.15am-8.15pm Sun).

ⓘ GETTING THERE & AWAY

AIR

The city has five airports: Heathrow, which is the largest, to the west; Gatwick to the south; Stansted to the northeast; Luton to the northwest; and London City in the Docklands.

RAIL

Main national rail routes are served by a variety of private train-operating companies. Tickets are not cheap, but trains between cities are usually quite punctual. Check National Rail (www.nation alrail.co.uk) for timetables and fares.

EUROSTAR

Eurostar (☐03432 186186; www.eurostar.com) The high-speed passenger rail service links St Pancras International Station with Gare du Nord in Paris (or Bruxelles Midi in Brussels), with between 14 and 16 daily departures. Fares vary wildly, from £69 to £300.

ⓘ GETTING AROUND

Public transport in London is managed by Transport for London (www.tfl.gov.uk). It is extensive, often excellent and always pricey.

The cheapest way to get around is with an Oyster Card or a UK contactless card. Paper tickets still exist, but will work out substantially more expensive than using an Oyster.

The tube, DLR and Overground network are ideal for zooming across more distant parts of the city; buses and the **Santander Cycles** (☐0343 222 6666; www.tfl.gov.uk/modes/cycling/santander-cycles) ('Boris Bikes') are great for shorter journeys.

Where to Stay

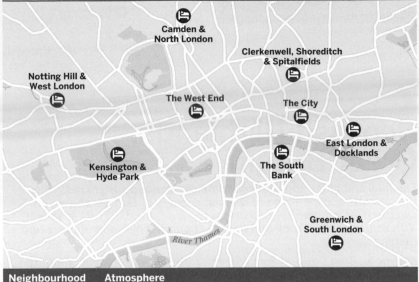

Neighbourhood	Atmosphere
The West End	Close to main sights; great transport links; wide accommodation range but expensive; good restaurants; busy tourist areas.
The City	St Paul's and Tower of London; good transport links; handy central location; quality hotels; some cheaper weekend rates; very quiet at weekends; a business district so high prices during week.
The South Bank	Cheaper than West End; excellent pubs and views; many chain hotels; choice and transport limited.
Kensington & Hyde Park	Great accommodation range; stylish area; good transport; quite expensive; drinking and nightlife options limited.
Clerkenwell, Shoreditch & Spitalfields	Trendy area with great bars and nightlife; excellent for boutique hotels; few top sights; transport options somewhat limited.
East London & Docklands	Markets; multicultural feel; great restaurants and traditional pubs; limited sleeping options; some areas less safe at night.
Camden & North London	Leafy; vibrant nightlife; excellent boutique hotels and hostels; quiet during the week; non-central and away from main sights.
Notting Hill & West London	Cool cachet; great shopping, markets and pubs; excellent boutique hotels; good transport; pricey; light on top sights.
Greenwich & South London	Great boutique options; leafy escapes; near top Greenwich sights; sights spread out beyond Greenwich; transport limited.
Richmond, Kew & Hampton Court	Smart riverside hotels; semi-rural pockets; quiet; fantastic riverside pubs; sights spread out; a long way from central London.

In This Chapter

On the Whisky Trail.............................. 98
Loch Ness... 100
Inverness.. 104
Fort William.. 111

Scottish Highlands, Great Britain

The hills and glens and wild coastline of Scotland's Highlands offer the ultimate escape – one of the last corners of Europe where you can discover genuine solitude. Here the landscape is at its grandest, with soaring hills of rock and heather bounded by wooded glens and rushing waterfalls.

Aviemore, Glen Coe and Fort William draw hill walkers and climbers in summer, and skiers, snowboarders and ice climbers in winter. Inverness, the Highland capital, provides urban rest and relaxation, while nearby Loch Ness and its elusive monster add a hint of mystery.

Two Days in the Scottish Highlands

Cruise Royal Deeside on day one, taking in the Queen's estate, **Balmoral** (p108) and nearby **Braemar Castle** (p108). On day two it's time to go Loch Ness Monster-hunting on a **boat trip** (p102). Next up, tour iconic **Urquhart Castle** (p102), before exploring the loch's quieter eastern shore, including a meal at the lovely **Dores Inn** (p103).

Four Days in the Scottish Highlands

Spend day three exploring **Inverness** (p104) or take a dolphin-watching **tour** (p106). Finish up with a drive southwest to **Glen Coe** (p112), stopping en route in Fort William to ride a **steam train** (p111) and tour a **distillery** (p99).

Finished with the Highlands? Take a 13-hour overnight train to London (p50).

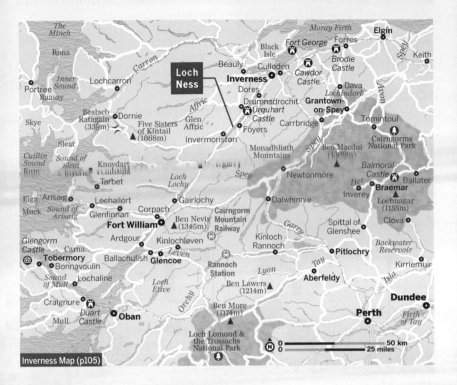

Inverness Map (p105)

Arriving in the Scottish Highlands

Air Inverness Airport at Dalcross has scheduled domestic and some international flights.

Bus There are regular bus services along the Great Glen between Inverness and Fort William.

Train Inverness is connected by train to Glasgow, Edinburgh and London.

Where to Stay

Inverness, Aviemore and Fort William are the main centres for accommodation, but most reasonably sized towns will also have a couple of hotels and a dozen or more B&Bs – many set in superb Victorian villas, farmhouses and manses (former church ministers' houses). Camping is a popular way to enjoy the great outdoors, and there's no shortage of official campsites. Wild camping is also widely practised.

Edradour Distillery

On the Whisky Trail

Scotland's national drink – in Gaelic uisge bagh, *meaning 'water of life' – has been distilled here for more than 500 years. Over 100 distilleries are still in business, producing hundreds of varieties of single malt, with new operations opening every year.*

Great For...

☑ Don't Miss

Fèis Ìle (Islay Festival), which celebrates traditional Scottish music and whisky in May.

Whisky has been distilled in Scotland at least since the 15th century and probably much longer. Learning to distinguish the smoky, peaty whiskies of Islay from, say, the flowery, sherried malts of Speyside has become a hugely popular pastime.

Whisky Central

The Speyside region, around Dufftown and Glenlivet, is the epicentre of the whisky industry. More than 50 distilleries open their doors during the twice yearly **Spirit of Speyside Festival** (www.spiritofspeyside. com), and many are open all year long.

Some pubs in the region have become known as whisky bars, because of their staggering range of single malt whiskies – the famous Quaich bar in the **Craigellachie Hotel** (☏01340-881204; www.craigellachie

JAG_CZ/SHUTTERSTOCK ©

ⓘ Need to Know

Scotch whisky (always spelt without an 'e' – 'whiskey' is Irish or American) is Scotland's biggest export. The standard measure in pubs is either 25ml or 35ml.

✘ Take a Break

Offering Highland comfort food, Pit-lochry's **Moulin Hotel** (☎01796-472196; www.moulinhotel.co.uk; Kirkmichael Rd; mains £9-16; 🅿 🛜 🛗) is within striking distance of both Edradour and Blair Athol Distilleries.

★ Top Tip

Don't ask for 'Scotch' in a bar or pub – what else would you be served in Scotland?

hotel.co.uk; Craigellachie), established in 1894, offers more than 800 different varieties.

Visiting a Distillery

Many distilleries offer guided tours, rounded off with a tasting session. Trying local varieties is a great way to explore the whisky-making regions, but while visiting a distillery can be a memorable experience, only hardcore malt-hounds will want to go to more than one or two. The following are good options for a day trip from Inverness.

Edradour Distillery   Distillery
(☎01796-472095; www.edradour.co.uk; Moulin Rd; tour adult/child £7.50/2.50; ⊗10am-5pm Mon-Sat late Apr-late Oct; 🅿🛗) This is proudly Scotland's smallest and most picturesque distillery and one of the best to visit: you

can see the whole process, easily ex-plained, in one building. It's 2.5 miles east of Pitlochry by car, along the Moulin road, or a pleasant 1-mile walk.

Blair Athol Distillery   Distillery
(☎01796-482003; www.discovering-distilleries.com; Perth Rd; standard tour £7; ⊗10am-5pm Apr-Oct, to 4pm Nov-Mar) Tours here focus on whisky making and the blending of this well-known dram. More detailed private tours give you greater insights and superior tastings.

Ben Nevis Distillery   Distillery
(☎01397-702476; www.bennevisdistillery.com; Lochy Bridge; guided tour adult/child £5/2.50; ⊗9am-5pm Mon-Fri year-round, 10am-4pm Sat Easter-Sep, noon-4pm Sun Jul & Aug; 🅿) A tour of this distillery makes for a warming rainy-day alternative to exploring the hills.

Urquhart Castle (p102)

Loch Ness

Deep, dark and narrow, the bitterly cold waters of Loch Ness have long drawn waves of people hunting Nessie, the elusive Loch Ness Monster. Despite the crowds, it's still possible to find tranquillity and gorgeous views. Add a highly photogenic castle and some superb hiking and you have a loch with bags of appeal.

Great For...

ⓘ Need to Know

A complete circuit of the loch is about 70 miles; travel anticlockwise for the best views.

★ **Top Tip**

Fancy a spot of Nessie hunting? Check out the latest at www.lochness sightings.com.

Tales of the Loch Ness Monster truly took off in the 1930s, when reported sightings led to a press furore and a string of high-profile photographs. Reports have tailed off recently, but the bizarre mini-industry that's grown up around Nessie is a spectacle in itself.

Drumnadrochit

Seized by monster madness, its gift shops bulging with Nessie cuddly toys, Drumnadrochit is a hotbed of beastie fever, with Nessie attractions battling it out for the tourist dollar.

The **Loch Ness Centre & Exhibition** (01456-450573; www.lochness.com; adult/child £7.95/4.95; 9.30am-6pm Jul & Aug, to 5pm Easter-Jun, Sep & Oct, 10am-3.30pm Nov-Easter; P) adopts a scientific approach that allows you to weigh the ev-

idence for yourself. Exhibits include those on hoaxes and optical illusions and some original equipment – sonar survey vessels, miniature submarines, cameras and sediment coring tools – used in various monster hunts, as well as original photographs and film footage of reported sightings.

To head out yourself, **Nessie Hunter** (01456-450395; www.lochness-cruises.com; adult/child £15/10; Easter-Oct) offers one-hour monster-hunting cruises, complete with sonar and underwater cameras. Cruises depart from Drumnadrochit hourly (except 1pm) from 9am to 6pm daily.

Urquhart Castle

Commanding a superb location 1.5 miles east of Drumnadrochit, with outstanding views, **Urquhart Castle** (HS; 01456-450551; adult/child £8.50/5.10; 9.30am-6pm

Loch Ness

Apr-Sep, to 5pm Oct, to 4.30pm Nov-Mar; P) is a popular Nessie-hunting hotspot. A huge visitor centre (most of which is beneath ground level) includes a video theatre and displays of medieval items discovered in the castle.

The castle has been repeatedly sacked and rebuilt over the centuries; in 1692 it was blown up to prevent the Jacobites from using it. The five-storey tower house at the northern point is the most impressive remaining fragment and offers fine views across the water.

☑ Don't Miss

Climbing to the battlements of the iconic tower of Urquhart Castle, for grandstand views from the rocky headland, up and down Loch Ness.

VISITBRITAIN/JOE CORNISH/GETTY IMAGES ©

Loch Ness' East Side

While tour coaches pour down the west side of Loch Ness to the hotspots of Drumnadrochit and Urquhart Castle, the narrow B862 road along the eastern shore is relatively peaceful. It leads to the village of Foyers, where you can enjoy a pleasant hike to the Falls of Foyers.

It's also worth making the trip just for the **Dores Inn** (01463-751203; www.thedoresinn.co.uk; Dores; mains £11-24; pub 10am-11pm, food served noon-2pm & 6-9pm; P), a beautifully restored country pub adorned with recycled furniture, local landscape paintings and fresh flowers. The menu specialises in quality Scottish produce, from haggis, turnips and *tatties* (potatoes), and haddock and chips, to steaks, scallops and seafood platters. The pub garden has stunning Loch Ness views and a dedicated monster-spotting vantage point.

Hiking at Loch Ness

The South Loch Ness Trail (www.visitinvernesslochness.com) links a series of footpaths and minor roads along the less-frequented southern side of the loch. The 28 miles from Loch Tarff near Fort Augustus to Torbreck on the fringes of Inverness can be done on foot, by bike or on horseback.

The climb to the summit of Meallfuarvonie (699m), on the northwestern shore of Loch Ness, makes an excellent short hill walk: the views along the Great Glen from the top are superb. It's a 6-mile round trip, so allow about three hours. Start from the car park at the end of the minor road leading south from Drumnadrochit to Bunloit.

Take a Break

Drumnadrochit has cafes and restaurants aplenty, but they can get very busy. To avoid the crowds, head for the Dores Inn on the east side.

The Battle of Culloden

The Battle of Culloden in 1746 – the last pitched battle ever fought on British soil – saw the defeat of Bonnie Prince Charlie and the end of the Jacobite dream when 1200 Highlanders were slaughtered by government forces in a 68-minute rout. The Duke of Cumberland, son of the reigning King George II and leader of the Hanoverian army, earned the nickname 'Butcher' for his brutal treatment of the defeated Jacobite forces. The battle sounded the death knell for the old clan system, and the horrors of the Clearances soon followed. The sombre moor where the conflict took place has scarcely changed in the ensuing 260 years.

The impressive **Culloden Visitor Centre** (NTS; www.nts.org.uk/culloden; adult/child £11/8.50; ⊙9am-6pm Jun-Aug, to 5.30pm Apr, May, Sep & Oct, 10am-4pm Nov-Mar; P) boasts an innovative film that puts you on the battlefield in the middle of the mayhem, along with a wealth of other audio presentations. The admission fee includes an audio guide for a self-guided tour of the battlefield site.

Thatched cottage on the battlefield site
MATTHI/SHUTTERSTOCK ©

Inverness

Inverness, one of the fastest growing towns in Britain, is the capital of the Highlands. Inverness is a transport hub and jumping-off point for the central, western and northern Highlands, the Moray Firth coast and the Great Glen.

The Great Glen is a geological fault, running in an arrow-straight line across Scotland from Fort William to Inverness. The glaciers of the last ice age eroded a deep trough along the fault line, which is now filled by a series of lochs – Linnhe, Lochy, Oich and Ness.

Inverness was probably founded by King David in the 12th century, but thanks to its often violent history, few buildings of real age or historical significance have survived – much of the older part of the city dates from the period following the completion of the Caledonian Canal in 1822. The broad and shallow River Ness, famed for its salmon fishing, runs through the heart of the city.

◎ SIGHTS

Ness Islands   Park
The main attraction in Inverness is a leisurely stroll along the river to the Ness Islands. Planted with mature Scots pine, fir, beech and sycamore, and linked to the river banks and each other by elegant Victorian footbridges, the islands make an appealing picnic spot. They're a 20-minute walk south of the castle – head upstream on either side of the river (the start of the Great Glen Way), and return on the opposite bank.

Inverness Museum & Art Gallery   Museum
(☎01463-237114; www.inverness.highland.museum; Castle Wynd; ⊙10am-5pm Tue-Sat Apr-Oct, noon-4pm Thu-Sat Nov-Mar) FREE Inverness Museum & Art Gallery has wildlife dioramas, geological displays, period rooms with historic weapons, Pictish stones and exhibitions of contemporary Highland arts and crafts.

Cawdor Castle   Castle
(☎01667-404615; www.cawdorcastle.com; Cawdor; adult/child £10.70/6.70; ⊙10am-5.30pm May-Sep; P) This castle, 5 miles southwest of Nairn, was once the seat of the Thane of Cawdor, one of the titles bestowed on Shakespeare's *Macbeth*. The real Macbeth – an ancient Scottish king – couldn't have lived here though, since he died in 1057, 300

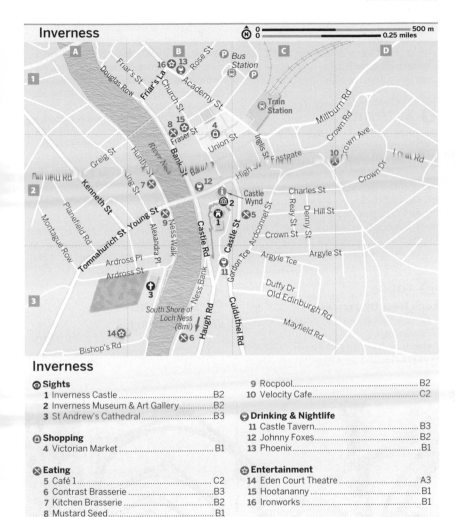

Inverness

⊚ Sights
1 Inverness Castle B2
2 Inverness Museum & Art Gallery..............B2
3 St Andrew's Cathedral B3

⊕ Shopping
4 Victorian Market B1

✖ Eating
5 Café 1...C2
6 Contrast Brasserie B3
7 Kitchen Brasserie B2
8 Mustard Seed..B1

9 Rocpool..B2
10 Velocity Cafe..C2

⊕ Drinking & Nightlife
11 Castle Tavern B3
12 Johnny Foxes..B2
13 Phoenix...B1

⊕ Entertainment
14 Eden Court Theatre A3
15 Hootananny B1
16 Ironworks B1

years before the castle was begun. Nevertheless the tour gives a fascinating insight into the lives of the Scottish aristocracy.

Brodie Castle   Castle
(NTS; ☏01309-641371; www.nts.org.uk; Brodie; adult/child £10.50/7.50; ◷10.30am-5pm daily Jul & Aug, 10.30am-4.30pm Sat-Wed Apr-Jun & Sep-Oct; P) Set in 70 hectares of parkland, Brodie Castle has a library with more than 6000 peeling, dusty volumes, wonderful clocks, a huge Victorian kitchen and

a 17th-century dining room with wildly extravagant moulded plaster ceilings depicting mythological scenes. The Brodies have been living here since 1160, but the present structure dates mostly from 1567, with many additions over the years. The castle is 4 miles west of Forres.

Inverness Castle   Castle
(Castle St) The hill above the city centre is topped by the picturesque Baronial turrets of Inverness Castle, a pink-sandstone

confection dating from 1847 that replaced a medieval castle blown up by the Jacobites in 1746; it serves today as the Sheriff's Court. It's not open to the public, but there are good views from the surrounding gardens.

🏃 ACTIVITIES

Dolphin Spirit · Wildlife Watching
(07544-800620; www.dolphinspirit.co.uk; Inverness Marina, Longman Dr; adult/child £16/10; Easter-Oct) Four times a day in season, this outfit runs cruises from Inverness into the Moray Firth to spot the UK's largest pod of bottlenose dolphins – around 130 animals. The dolphins feed on salmon heading for the rivers at the head of the firth, and can often be seen leaping and bow-surfing.

🔄 TOURS

Loch Ness by Jacobite · Boating
(01463-233999; www.jacobite.co.uk; Glenurquhart Rd; adult/child £33/26) From June to September, boats depart from Tomnahurich Bridge twice daily for a three-hour cruise along the Caledonian Canal to Loch Ness and back, with a live commentary on local history and wildlife. You can buy tickets at the tourist office and catch a free minibus to the boat. Other cruises and combined cruise/coach tours, from one to 6½ hours, are also available, some year-round.

Happy Tours · Walking
(07828-154683; www.happy-tours.biz; £10) Offers 1¼-hour guided walks exploring the town's history and legends, starting at 7pm (must be booked in advance).

Inverness Taxis · Tours
(01463-222900; www.inverness-taxis.com) Wide range of day tours to Urquhart Castle, Loch Ness, Culloden and even Skye. Fares per car (up to four people) range from £60 (two hours) to £240 (all day).

🛍 SHOPPING

Victorian Market · Market
(Academy St; 9am-5pm Mon-Sat) If the rain comes down, you could opt for a spot of retail therapy in the Victorian Market, a

Victorian Market

shopping mall that dates from the 1890s and has rather more charm than its modern equivalents.

 EATING

Inverness has some of the best – and the best-value – restaurants in the Scottish Highlands.

Velocity Cafe
Cafe £
(~~01463-419956; http://velocitylove.co.uk; 1~~ Crown Ave; mains £4-7; ⊙9am-5pm Mon, Wed, Fri & Sat, 9am-9pm Thu, 11am-5pm Sun; 🛜✏️🚼) ✎ This cyclists' cafe serves soups, sandwiches and salads prepared with organic, locally sourced produce, as well as yummy cakes and coffee. There's also a workshop where you can repair your bike or book a session with a mechanic.

Café 1
Bistro ££
(✐01463-226200; www.cafe1.net; 75 Castle St; mains £13-25; ⊙noon-2.30pm & 5-9.30pm Mon-Fri, noon-2.30pm & 6-9.30pm Sat; 🚼) ✎ Café 1 is a friendly, appealing bistro with candlelit tables amid elegant blonde-wood and wrought-iron decor. There is an international menu based on quality Scottish produce, from Aberdeen Angus steaks to crisp pan-fried sea bass and meltingly tender pork belly. The set lunch menu (two courses for £12) is served noon to 2.30pm Monday to Saturday.

Contrast Brasserie
Brasserie ££
(✐01463-223777; www.glenmoristontownhouse. com; 20 Ness Bank; mains £14-21; ⊙noon-2.30pm & 5-10pm) Book early for what we think is one of the best-value restaurants in Inverness – a dining room that drips designer style, with smiling professional staff and truly delicious food prepared using fresh Scottish produce. The two-/three-course lunch menu (£11/14) and three-course early-bird menu (£16, 5pm to 6.30pm) are bargains.

Mustard Seed
Bistro ££
(✐01463-220220; www.mustardseedrestaurant. co.uk; 16 Fraser St; mains £13-21; ⊙noon-3pm & 5.30-10pm) ✎ The menu at this bright and bustling bistro changes weekly, but focuses

 Fort George

One of the finest artillery fortifications in Europe, **Fort George** (HS; ✐01667-462777; adult/child £8.50/5.10; ⊙9.30am-5.30pm Apr-Sep, 10am-4pm Oct-Mar; 🅿) was established in 1748 in the aftermath of the Battle of Culloden, as a base for George II's army of occupation in the Highlands. By the time of its completion in 1769 it had cost the equivalent of around £1 billion in today's money. It still functions as a military barracks; public areas have exhibitions on 18th-century soldiery, and the mile-plus walk around the ramparts offers fine views out to sea and back to the Great Glen.

Given its size, you'll need at least two hours to do the place justice. The fort is off the A96 about 11 miles northeast of Inverness; there is no public transport.

JEFF J MITCHELL/GETTY IMAGES ©

on Scottish and French cuisine with a modern twist. Grab a table on the upstairs balcony if you can – it's the best outdoor lunch spot in Inverness, with a great view across the river. And a two-course lunch for £9 – yes, that's right – is hard to beat.

Kitchen Brasserie
Modern Scottish ££
(✐01463-259119; www.kitchenrestaurant. co.uk; 15 Huntly St; mains £9-20; ⊙noon-3pm & 5-10pm; 🛜🚼) This spectacular glass-fronted restaurant offers a great menu of top Scottish produce with a Mediterranean or Asian touch, and a view over the River Ness – try to get a table upstairs. Great-value

Royal Deeside

The upper valley of the River Dee stretches west from Aboyne and Ballater to Braemar, closely paralleled by the A93 road. Made famous by its long association with the monarchy, the region is often called Royal Deeside.

Built for Queen Victoria in 1855 as a private residence for the royal family, **Balmoral Castle** (☏01339-742534; www.balmoralcastle.com; Crathie; adult/child £11.50/5; ⏰10am-5pm Apr-Jul, last admission 4.30pm; 🅿) kicked off the revival of the Scottish Baronial style of architecture that characterises so many of Scotland's 19th-century country houses. The admission fee includes an interesting and well-thought-out audioguide, but the tour is very much an outdoor one through gardens and grounds.

Just north of Braemar village, turreted **Braemar Castle** (www.braemarcastle.co.uk; adult/child £8/4; ⏰10am-4pm daily Jul & Aug, Wed-Sun Apr-Jun, Sep & Oct; 🅿) dates from 1628 and served as a government garrison after the 1745 Jacobite rebellion. It was taken over by the local community in 2007, and now offers guided tours of the historic castle apartments. There's a short walk from the car park to the castle.

Balmoral Castle

two-course lunch (£9, noon to 3pm) and early-bird menu (£13, 5pm to 7pm).

Rocpool   Mediterranean £££
(☏01463-717274; www.rocpoolrestaurant.com; 1 Ness Walk; mains £13-23; ⏰noon-2.30pm & 5.45-10pm Mon-Sat) 🍴 Lots of polished wood, crisp white linen and leather booths and banquettes lend a nautical air to this relaxing bistro, which offers a Mediterranean-influenced menu that makes the most of quality Scottish produce, especially seafood. The two-course lunch is £16.

🔵 DRINKING & NIGHTLIFE

As the 'capital city' of the Highlands, Inverness has the liveliest nightlife in the area. As well as dozens of pubs, clubs and music venues, there's the Eden Court Theatre, the main cultural focus of the region.

Clachnaharry Inn   Pub
(☏01463-239806; www.clachnaharryinn.co.uk; 17-19 High St, Clachnaharry; ⏰11am-11pm Mon-Thu, 11am-1am Fri & Sat, noon-11pm Sun; 🐾) Just over a mile northwest of the city centre, on the bank of the Caledonian Canal just off the A862, this is a delightful old coaching inn (with beer garden out the back) serving an excellent range of real ales and good pub grub.

Phoenix   Pub
(☏01463-233685; 108 Academy St; ⏰11am-1am Mon-Sat, noon-midnight Sun) Beautifully refurbished, this is the most traditional of the pubs in the city centre, with a mahogany horseshoe bar and several real ales on tap, including beers from the Cairngorm, Cromarty and Isle of Skye breweries.

Castle Tavern   Pub
(☏01463-718718; www.castletavern.net; 1-2 View Pl; ⏰11am-11pm) Offering a tempting selection of craft beers, this pub has a wee suntrap of a terrace out the front. It's a great place for a pint on a summer afternoon.

Johnny Foxes   Bar
(☏01463-236577; www.johnnyfoxes.co.uk; 26 Bank St; ⏰11am-3am) Stuck beneath the ugliest building on the riverfront, Johnny Foxes is a big and boisterous Irish bar with a wide range of food served all day and live music nightly. Part of the premises, the **Den** is a smart cocktail bar and late-night club.

✪ ENTERTAINMENT

Hootananny
Live Music

(☎01463-233651; www.hootanannyinverness.co.uk; 67 Church St) Hootananny is the city's best live-music venue, with traditional folk- and/or rock-music sessions nightly, including big-name bands from all over Scotland (and, indeed, the world). The bar is well stocked with a range of beers from the local Black Isle Brewery.

Ironworks
Live Music, Comedy

(☎0871-789 4173; www.ironworksvenue.com; 122 Academy St) With live bands (rock, pop, tribute) and comedy shows two or three times a week, the Ironworks is the town's main venue for big-name acts.

Eden Court Theatre
Theatre

(☎01463-234234; www.eden-court.co.uk; Bishop's Rd; 🛜) The Highlands' main cultural venue – with theatre, art-house cinema and a conference centre – Eden Court stages a busy program of drama, dance, comedy, music, film and children's events, and has a good bar and restaurant. Pick up a program from the foyer or check the website.

ℹ INFORMATION

Inverness Tourist Office (☎01463-252401; www.visithighlands.com; Castle Wynd; internet access per 20min £1; ⊗9am-5pm Mon-Sat, 10am-3pm Sun, longer hours Mar-Oct) Bureau de change and accommodation booking service; also sells tickets for tours and cruises.

ℹ GETTING THERE & AWAY

AIR

Inverness Airport (INV; ☎01667-464000; www.hial.co.uk/inverness-airport) At Dalcross, 10 miles east of the city, off the A96 towards Aberdeen. There are scheduled flights to Amsterdam, London, Manchester, Dublin, Orkney, Shetland and the Outer Hebrides, as well as other places in the UK.

Stagecoach bus 11/11A runs from the airport to Inverness bus station (£4, 20 minutes, every 30 minutes).

BUS

Services depart from **Inverness bus station** (Margaret St). Most intercity routes are served

Highland dancing

LUKASSEK/SHUTTERSTOCK ©

Jacobite Steam Train on the Glenfinnan Viaduct

one of the great railway journeys of the world

by **Scottish Citylink** (0871-266 3333; www. citylink.co.uk).

If you book far enough in advance, **Megabus** (0141-352 4444; www.megabus.com) offers fares from as little as £1 for buses from Inverness to Glasgow and Edinburgh, and £10 to London.

TRAIN

Inverness is connected by train to Edinburgh (£50, 3½ hours, every two hours) and London (£120, eight to nine hours, one daily direct).

ⓘ GETTING AROUND

BICYCLE

Ticket to Ride (01463-419160; www.ticketto ridehighlands.co.uk; Bellfield Park; per day from £25; 9am-6pm Apr-Oct) Hires out mountain bikes, hybrids and tandems. Will deliver bikes free to local hotels and B&Bs, and bikes can be dropped off in Fort William.

BUS

City services and buses to places around Inverness, including Nairn, Forres, the Culloden Battlefield, Beauly, Dingwall and Lairg, are operated by **Stagecoach** (01463-233371; www. stagecoachbus.com).

An Inverness City Dayrider ticket costs £3.50 and gives unlimited travel for a day on buses throughout the city.

CAR

Focus Vehicle Rental (01463-709517; www. focusvehiclerental.co.uk; 6 Harbour Rd) The big boys charge from around £50 to £65 per day, but Focus has cheaper rates starting at £40 per day.

TAXI

Inverness Taxis (01463-222222; www. inverness-taxis.com) There's a taxi rank outside the train station.

Fort William

Basking on the shores of Loch Linnhe amid magnificent mountain scenery, Fort William has one of the most enviable settings in the whole of Scotland. It's a good place to base yourself for exploring the surrounding mountains and glens.

SIGHTS

West Highland Museum   Museum
(☑01397-702169; www.westhighlandmuseum. org.uk; Cameron Sq; ☺10am-5pm Mon-Sat Apr-Oct, to 4pm Mar & Nov-Dec, closed Jan & Feb) FREE This small but fascinating museum is packed with all manner of Highland memorabilia. Look out for the secret portrait of Bonnie Prince Charlie – after the Jacobite rebellions, all things Highland were banned, including pictures of the exiled leader, and this tiny painting looks like nothing more than a smear of paint until viewed in a cylindrical mirror, which reflects a credible likeness of the prince.

ACTIVITIES

Crannog Cruises   Wildlife
(☑01397-700714; www.crannog.net/cruises; adult/child £15/7.50; ☺11am, 1pm & 3pm daily Easter-Oct) Operates 1½ hour wildlife cruises on Loch Linnhe, visiting a seal colony and a salmon farm.

EATING

Lime Tree   Scottish ££
(☑01397-701806; www.limetreefortwilliam.co.uk; Achintore Rd; mains £16-20; ☺6.30-9.30pm; P ☺) ✐ Fort William is not over-endowed with great places to eat, but the restaurant at this small hotel and art gallery has put the UK's Outdoor Capital on the gastronomic map. The chef turns out delicious dishes built around fresh Scottish produce, ranging from Loch Fyne oysters to Loch Awe trout and Ardnamurchan venison.

Crannog Seafood Restaurant   Seafood ££
(☑01397-705589; www.crannog.net; Town Pier; mains £15-23; ☺noon-2.30pm & 6-9pm) ✐ The Crannog wins the prize for the best location in town – perched on the Town Pier, giving

Jacobite Steam Train

The **Jacobite Steam Train** (☑0844 850 4685; www.westcoastrailways.co.uk; day return adult/child £34/19; ☺daily Jul & Aug, Mon-Fri mid-May–Jun, Sep & Oct), hauled by a former LNER K1 or LMS Class 5MT locomotive, travels the scenic two-hour run between Fort William and Mallaig. Classed as one of the great railway journeys of the world, the route crosses the historic Glenfinnan Viaduct, made famous in the Harry Potter films – the Jacobite's owners supplied the steam locomotive and rolling stock used in the film.

Trains depart from Fort William train station in the morning and return from Mallaig in the afternoon. There's a brief stop at Glenfinnan station, and you get 1½ hours in Mallaig.

PHILIP BIRD LRPS CPAGB/SHUTTERSTOCK ©

window-table diners an uninterrupted view down Loch Linnhe. Informal and unfussy, it specialises in fresh local fish – there are three or four daily fish specials plus the main menu – though there are lamb, venison and vegetarian dishes, too. Two/three-course lunch £15/19.

Bayleaf   Scottish ££
(Cameron Sq; mains lunch £5-11, dinner £13-20; 🚻) ✐ A great new addition to the town's restaurant scene, this place combines crisp, modern decor, friendly service (the chef often comes out to chat with customers) and the best of Scottish beef, lamb and seafood freshly and simply

Glen Coe

Scotland's most famous glen is also one of its grandest. It was written into history in 1692 when the resident MacDonalds were murdered by Campbell soldiers in a notorious massacre. Soldiers largely from Campbell clan territory, on government orders, turned on their MacDonald hosts killing 38; another 40 MacDonalds perished having fled into snow-covered hills.

There are several short, pleasant walks around Glencoe Lochan, near the village. To get there, turn left off the minor road to the youth hostel, just beyond the bridge over the River Coe. There are three walks (40 minutes to an hour), all detailed on a signboard at the car park. A more strenuous hike, but well worth the effort on a fine day, is the climb to the Lost Valley, a magical mountain sanctuary still said to be haunted by the ghosts of MacDonalds.

HELEN HOTSON/SHUTTERSTOCK ©

prepared. If Scotland's national dish hasn't appealed, try a haggis fritter with Drambuie mayonnaise!

🍸 DRINKING & NIGHTLIFE

Ben Nevis Bar   Pub
(☑01397-702295; 105 High St; ⊙11am-11pm; 🛜) The lounge here enjoys a good view over the loch, and the bar exudes a relaxed, jovial atmosphere where climbers and tourists can work off leftover energy jigging to live music (Thursday and Friday nights).

Grog & Gruel   Pub
(☑01397-705078; www.grogandgruel.co.uk; 66 High St; ⊙noon-midnight; 🛜) The Grog & Gruel is a traditional-style, wood-panelled pub with an excellent range of cask ales from regional Scottish and English microbreweries.

ℹ️ INFORMATION

Fort William Tourist Office (☑01397-701801; www.visithighlands.com; 15 High St; internet per 20min £1; ⊙9am-5pm Mon-Sat, 10am-3pm Sun, longer hrs Jun-Aug) Has internet access.

ℹ️ GETTING THERE & AWAY

The bus and train stations are next to the huge Morrisons supermarket, reached from the town centre via an underpass next to the Nevisport shop.

BUS

Scottish Citylink (☑0871-266 3333; www.citylink.co.uk) buses link Fort William with other major towns and cities, including Edinburgh (£35, five hours, seven daily with a change at Glasgow; via Glencoe and Crianlarich), Glasgow (£24, three hours, eight daily) and Inverness (£11.60, two hours, six daily).

Shiel Buses (☑01397-700700; www.shielbuses.co.uk) service 500 runs to Mallaig (£6.10, 1½ hours, three daily Monday to Friday, plus one daily weekends April to September) via Glenfinnan (£3.30, 30 minutes) and Arisaig (£5.60, one hour).

CAR

Easydrive Car Hire (☑01397-701616; www.easydrivescotland.co.uk; North Rd) Hires out small cars from £36/165 a day/week, including tax and unlimited mileage, but not Collision Damage Waiver (CDW).

TRAIN

The spectacular West Highland line runs from Glasgow to Mallaig via Fort William. The overnight **Caledonian Sleeper** (www.sleeper.scot) service connects Fort William and London Euston (from £125 sharing a twin-berth cabin, 13 hours).

Lighthouse near Fort William

Edinburgh £35, five hours; change at Glasgow's Queen St station, three daily, two on Sunday

Glasgow £26, 3¾ hours, three daily, two on Sunday

Mallaig £12.20, 1½ hours, four daily, three on Sunday

 **GETTING AROUND**

BICYCLE

Nevis Cycles (☏01397-705555; www.nevis cycles.com; cnr Montrose Ave & Locheil Rd, Inverlochy; per day from £25; ◷9am-5.30pm) Located a half-mile northeast of the town centre, this place rents everything from hybrid bikes and mountain bikes to full-suspension downhill racers. Bikes can be hired here and dropped off in Inverness.

BUS

A Zone 2 Dayrider ticket (£8.60) gives unlimited travel for one day on Stagecoach bus services in the Fort William area, as far as Glencoe and Fort Augustus. Buy from the bus driver.

In This Chapter

Trinity College 116
Guinness Storehouse 118
Sights 120
Tours 125
Shopping 125
Eating 128
Drinking & Nightlife 129
Entertainment 131
Information 132
Getting There & Away 132
Getting Around 132

Dublin, Ireland

A small capital with a huge reputation, Dublin's mix of heritage and hedonism will not disappoint. There are fascinating museums, mouth-watering restaurants and the best range of entertainment available anywhere in Ireland – and that's not including the pub, the ubiquitous centre of the city's social life and an absolute must for any visitor. Dubliners at their ease are the greatest hosts of all, a charismatic bunch whose soul and sociability are so compelling and infectious that you mightn't ever want to leave.

Dublin in Two Days

Stroll through the grounds of **Trinity College** (p117), visiting the Long Room and the Book of Kells, before ambling up Grafton St to **St Stephen's Green** (p124). For more beautiful books and artefacts, drop into the **Chester Beatty Library** (p120) on day two. On your way, you can indulge in a spot of retail therapy in **Powerscourt Townhouse Shopping Centre** (p125) or in the many boutiques west of Grafton St.

Dublin in Four Days

After walking the length of **O'Connell St**, and pausing to inspect the bullet holes in the **General Post Office** (p121), explore the collection of the **Dublin City Gallery – Hugh Lane** (p120), including Francis Bacon's reconstructed studio. Begin day four learning some Irish history at **Kilmainham Gaol** (p121). Spend the afternoon at the seven-floor **Guinness Storehouse** (p119), finishing with a pint of the famous black stuff in its Gravity Bar.

Next stop: Lisbon (p330) or the Scottish Highlands (p96).

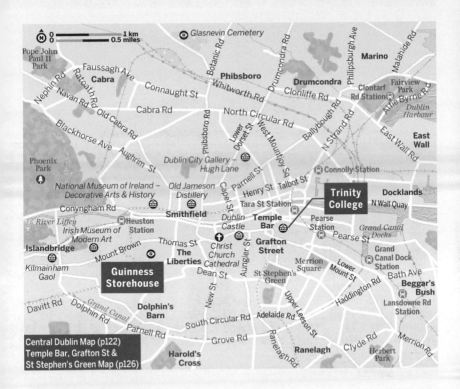

Central Dublin Map (p122)
Temple Bar, Grafton St &
St Stephen's Green Map (p126)

Arriving in Dublin

Dublin Airport Frequent buses to the city centre run from 6am to midnight; taxis (€25) take around 45 minutes.

Dun Laoghaire ferry terminal DART (€3.25) to Pearse Station (for south Dublin) or Connolly Station (for north Dublin); bus 46A to St Stephen's Green, or bus 7, 7A or 8 to Burgh Quay.

Dublin Port terminal Buses (€3) are timed to coincide with arrivals and departures.

Where to Stay

There has only been a handful of hotel openings in Dublin in the last few years, which means that hotel prices in the city are higher than they were during the boom years of the Celtic Tiger.

There are good midrange options north of the Liffey, but the biggest spread of accommodation is south of the river.

For information on what each Dublin neighbourhood has to offer, see the table on p133.

DAVID SOANES PHOTOGRAPHY/GETTY IMAGES ©

Trinity College

The student body has diversified since those days when a university education was the preserve of a small elite, but Trinity's bucolic charms persist and on a summer's evening it's one of the city's most delightful places to be: a calm retreat from the bustle of contemporary Dublin.

Great For...

☑ Don't Miss

The Long Room, which starred as the Jedi Archive in the movie *Star Wars Episode II: Attack of the Clones.*

The college was established by Elizabeth I in 1592 on land confiscated from an Augustinian priory in an effort to stop the brain drain of young Protestant Dubliners, who were skipping across to continental Europe for an education and becoming 'infected with popery'. Trinity went on to become one of Europe's most outstanding universities, producing a host of notable graduates – how about Jonathan Swift, Oscar Wilde and Samuel Beckett at the same alumni dinner?

It remained completely Protestant until 1793, but even when the university relented and began to admit Catholics, the Catholic Church held firm; until 1970, any Catholic who enrolled here could consider themselves excommunicated.

The campus is a masterpiece of architecture and landscaping beautifully preserved in Georgian aspic. Most of the

The Long Room

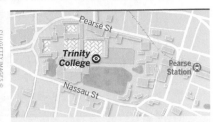

❶ Need to Know

M ᵭ ᵱ ᵽ ᵲ ᵾ; ☐ᵶᵷᵵ ᵶ ᵷᵵ ᵶᵵᵵᵶᵵ ᵾᵾᵾᵾᵾᵵᵵᵵ;
College Green; ☺8am-10pm; 🖥all city centre)
FREE

✗ Take a Break

Fade Street Social (p129) is an
excellent lunch spot just a few blocks
southwest.

★ Top Tip

Go online and buy a fast-track ticket
(adult/student/family €14/12/28)
to the Old Library, which gives timed
admission to the exhibition and allows
visitors to skip the queue.

---

buildings and statues date from the 18th
and 19th centuries, each elegantly laid out
on a cobbled or grassy square. The newer
bits include the 1978 Arts & Social Science
Building, which backs on to Nassau St and
forms the alternative entrance to the college. Like the college's Berkeley Library, it
was designed by Paul Koralek; it houses the
Douglas Hyde Gallery of Modern Art.

To the south of Library Sq is the **Old
Library** (Map p126; adult/student/family
€11/9.50/22, fast-track adult/student/family
€14/12/28; ☺8.30am-5pm Mon-Sat, 9.30am-
5pm Sun May-Sep, 9.30am-5pm Mon-Sat, noon-
4.30pm Sun Oct-Apr), built in a severe style by
Thomas Burgh between 1712 and 1732. It is
one of five copyright libraries across Ireland
and the UK, which means it's entitled to a
copy of every book published in these islands – around five million books, of which

only a fraction are stored here. You can visit
the library as part of a tour, taking in the
Long Room and the famous Book of Kells.

The **Book of Kells** is a breathtaking
illuminated manuscript of the four Gospels
of the New Testament, created around AD
800 by monks on the Scottish island of
Iona. Trinity's other great treasures are kept
in the Old Library's stunning 65m **Long
Room**, which houses about 200,000 of the
library's oldest volumes. Displays include
a rare copy of the Proclamation of the Irish
Republic, which was read out by Pádraig
(Patrick) Pearse at the beginning of the
Easter Rising in 1916.

Also here is the so-called harp of Brian
Ború, which was definitely not in use when
the army of this early Irish hero defeated
the Danes at the Battle of Clontarf in 1014.
It does, however, date from around 1400,
making it one of the oldest harps in Ireland.
Your entry ticket also includes admission
to temporary exhibitions on display in the
East Pavilion.

Guinness Storehouse

More than any beer produced anywhere in the world, Guinness is more than just a brand – for many devotees it's a substance with near spiritual qualities. This beer-lover's Disneyland is a multimedia homage to Ireland's most famous export.

Great For...

☑ Don't Miss

Enjoying the view from the Gravity Bar with your free pint of Guinness (price included with admission).

The mythology of Guinness is remarkably durable: it doesn't travel well; its distinctive flavour comes from Liffey water; and it is good for you – not to mention the generally held belief that you will never understand the Irish until you develop a taste for the black stuff. It's all absolutely true, of course, so it should be no surprise that the Guinness Storehouse, in the heart of the St James's Gate Brewery, is the city's most visited tourist attraction, an all-singing, all-dancing extravaganza that combines sophisticated exhibits, spectacular design and a thick, creamy head of marketing hype.

Grain Storehouse & Brewery

The old grain storehouse, the only part of the massive, 26-hectare St James's Gate Brewery open to the public, is a suitable

Pint of Guinness

ISLAVICEK/SHUTTERSTOCK ©

ⓘ Need to Know

Map p122; www.guinness-storehouse.com;
St James's Gate, South Market St; adult/
child €18/16.50, connoisseur experience
€48; ☺9.30am-5pm Sep-Jun, to 6pm Jul &
Aug; ☒21A, 51B, 78, 78A, 123 from Fleet St,
☒James's

✕ Take a Break

Gilroy's Bar on the 5th floor of the building serves up a delicious Irish stew.

★ Top Tip

Avoid the queues (and save €2) by
buying your ticket online in advance.

cathedral in which to worship the black
gold: shaped like a giant pint of Guinness, it
rises seven impressive storeys high around
a stunning central atrium. At the top is the
head, represented by the Gravity Bar, with a
panoramic view of Dublin.

Immediately below it is the brewery itself,
founded in 1759 by Arthur Guinness and
once the employer of over 5000 people;
the gradual shift to greater automation has
reduced the workforce to around 300.

The Perfect Pour

As you work your way to the top and your
prize of arguably the nicest Guinness you
could drink anywhere, you'll explore the
various elements that made the beer the
brand that it is and perhaps understand a
little better the efforts made by the company to ensure its quasi-mythical status.

From the (copy of) the original 9000-year
lease (in a glass box embedded in the
ground floor) to the near-scientific lesson
in how to pour the perfect pint, everything
about this place is designed to make you
understand that Guinness isn't just any
other beer.

Arthur Guinness

One fun fact you will learn is that genius
can be inadvertent: at some point in the
18th century, a London brewer accidentally burnt his hops while brewing ale, and
so created the dark beer we know today.
It's name of 'porter' came because the
dark beer was very popular with London
porters. In the 1770s, Arthur Guinness,
who had until then only brewed ale, started
brewing the dark stuff to get a jump on all
other Irish brewers. By 1799 he decided
to concentrate all his efforts on this single
brew. He died four years later, aged 83, but
the foundations for world domination were
already in place.

⊙ SIGHTS

National Museum of Ireland – Decorative Arts & History
Museum

(Map p122; www.museum.ie; Benburb St; ☺10am-5pm Tue-Sat, 2-5pm Sun; ☐25, 66, 67, 90 from city centre, ☐Museum) **FREE** Once the world's largest military barracks, this splendid early neoclassical grey-stone building on the Liffey's northern banks was completed in 1704 according to the design of Thomas Burgh (he of Trinity College's Old Library). It is now home to the Decorative Arts & History collection of the National Museum of Ireland, with a range of superb permanent exhibits ranging from a history of the Easter Rising to the work of iconic Irish designer Eileen Gray (1878-1976).

Chester Beatty Library
Museum

(Map p126; ☏01-407 0750; www.cbl.ie; Dublin Castle; ☺10am-5pm Mon-Fri, 11am-5pm Sat, 1-5pm Sun year-round, closed Mon Nov-Feb, free tours 1pm Wed, 2pm Sat & 3pm Sun; ☐all city centre) **FREE** This world-famous library, in the grounds of Dublin Castle (p121), houses the collection of mining engineer Sir Alfred Chester Beatty (1875–1968), bequeathed to the Irish State on his death. Spread over two floors, the breathtaking collection includes more than 20,000 manuscripts, rare books, miniature paintings, clay tablets, costumes and other objects of artistic, historical and aesthetic importance.

Dublin City Gallery – Hugh Lane
Gallery

(Map p122; ☏01-222 5550; www.hughlane.ie; 22 N Parnell Sq; ☺9.45am-6pm Tue-Thu, to 5pm Fri & Sat, 11am-5pm Sun; ☐7, 11, 13, 16, 38, 40, 46A, 123 from city centre) **FREE** Whatever reputation Dublin has as a repository of world-class art has a lot to do with the simply stunning collection at this exquisite gallery, housed in the equally impressive Charlemont House, designed by William Chambers in 1763. Within its walls you'll find the best of contemporary Irish art, a handful of impressionist classics and the relocated Francis Bacon's studio.

splendid early neoclassical grey-stone building

National Museum of Ireland – Decorative Arts & History

CARSO80/SHUTTERSTOCK ©

General Post Office Historic Building

(Map p122; ☏01-705 7000; www.anpost.ie; Lower O'Connell St; ⊘8am-8pm Mon-Sat; ⬚all city centre, ⬚Abbey) It's not just the country's main post office, or an eye-catching neoclassical building: the General Post Office is at the heart of Ireland's struggle for independence. The GPO served as command HQ for the rebels during the Easter Rising of 1916 and as a result has become the focal point for all kinds of protests, parades and remembrances, and is home to an interactive visitor centre.

Dublin Castle Historic Building

(Map p126; ☏01-677 7129; www.dublincastle. ie; Dame St; guided tours adult/child €10/4, self-guided tours adult/child €7/3; ⊘9.45am-5.45pm, last admission 5.15pm; ⬚all city centre) If you're looking for a turreted castle straight out of central casting you'll be disappointed: the stronghold of British power in Ireland for 700 years is principally an 18th-century creation that is more hotchpotch palace than medieval castle. Only the Record Tower, completed in 1258, survives from the original Anglo-Norman fortress commissioned by King John from 1204.

Glasnevin Cemetery Museum Museum

(www.glasnevintrust.ie; Finglas Rd; museum €4.50, museum & tour €10; ⊘10am-6pm Mon-Fri; ⬚40, 40A, 40B from Parnell St) The history of Glasnevin Cemetery is told in wonderful, award-winning detail in this museum, which relates the social and political story of Ireland through the lives of the people, known and unknown, buried here. The City of the Dead covers the burial practice and religious beliefs of the roughly 1½ million people whose final resting place this is, while the Milestone Gallery features a 10m-long digitally interactive timeline outlining the lives of the cemetery's most famous residents.

Christ Church Cathedral Church

(Church of the Holy Trinity; Map p126; www. christchurchcathedral.ie; Christ Church Pl; adult/student/child €6.50/4/2.50, with

 Gaelic Games

Easily reachable from the city centre, **Experience Gaelic Games** (☏01-254 4292; www.experiencegaelicgames.com; Saint Mobhi Rd; €25-35; ⊘Mon-Sat Mar-Oct, Fri & Sat Nov- Feb; ⬚4, 9 from O'Connell St) is the only place in Dublin to encounter the unique trio of Gaelic contests: hurling, Gaelic football and handball. The staff have an enormous passion for the sports, and their pride and delight at showing visitors is infectious. You can join one of the open sessions or groups of six or more can book a private session.

Hurleys and helmets
ANNEMARIE MCCARTHY/LONELY PLANET ©

Dublinia €14.50/12/7.50; ⊘9am-5pm Mon-Sat, 12.30-2.30pm Sun year-round, longer hours Mar-Oct; ⬚50, 50A, 56A from Aston Quay, 54, 54A from Burgh Quay) Its hilltop location and eye-catching flying buttresses make this the most photogenic of Dublin's cathedrals. It was founded in 1030 and rebuilt from 1172, mostly under the impetus of Richard de Clare, Earl of Pembroke (better known as Strongbow), the Anglo-Norman noble who invaded Ireland in 1170 and whose monument has pride of place inside.

Guided tours (⊘12.10pm, 2pm & 4pm Mon-Fri, 2pm, 3pm & 4pm Sat) include the belfry, where a campanologist explains the art of bell-ringing and you can even have a go.

Kilmainham Gaol Museum

(Map p122; ☏01-453 2037; http://kilmainham gaolmuseum.ie; Inchicore Rd; adult/child €8/4; ⊘9.30am-6.45pm Jul & Aug, to 5.30pm rest

Central Dublin

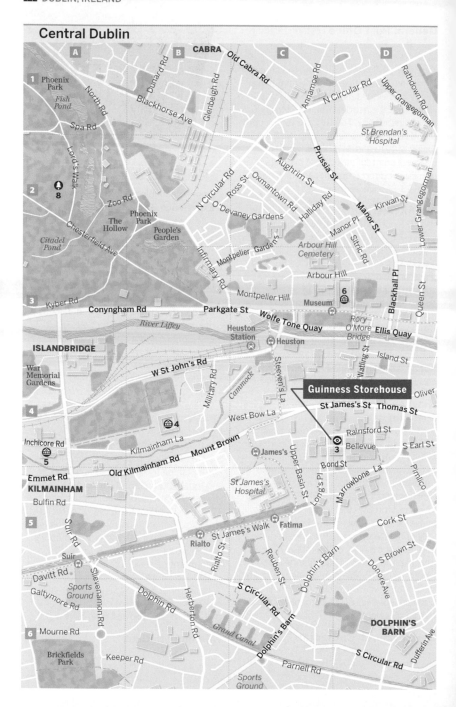

Guinness Storehouse

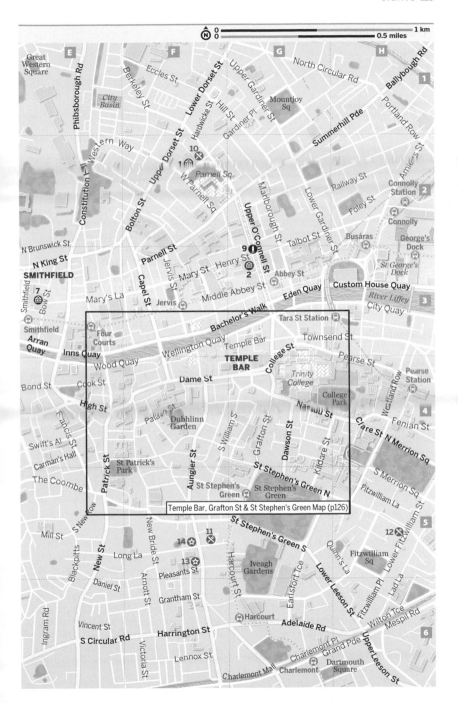

Central Dublin

◎ **Sights**
1 Dublin City Gallery – Hugh
   Lane..F2
2 General Post Office..........................G3
3 Guinness Storehouse.....................D4
4 Irish Museum of Modern Art.............B4
5 Kilmainham Gaol..............................A4
6 National Museum of Ireland –
   Decorative Arts & History.................D3
7 Old Jameson Distillery E3
8 Phoenix Park A2

9 Spire...G3

✖ **Eating**
   1837 Bar & Brasserie........................(see 3)
10 Chapter One.....................................F2
11 Gerry's F5
12 L'Ecrivain..H5

✪ **Entertainment**
13 Devitt's...F5
14 Whelan's...F5

of year; 🚌69, 79 from Aston Quay, 13, 40 from O'Connell St) If you have *any* desire to understand Irish history – especially the juicy bits about resistance to British rule – then a visit to this former prison is an absolute must. This threatening grey building, built between 1792 and 1795, played a role in virtually every act of Ireland's painful path to independence, and even today, despite closing in 1924, it still has the power to chill.

St Stephen's Green   Park
(Map p126; ☉dawn-dusk; 🚌all city centre, 🚊St Stephen's Green) As you watch the assorted groups of friends, lovers and individuals splaying themselves across the nine elegantly landscaped hectares of Dublin's most popular green lung, St Stephen's Green, consider that those same hectares once formed a common for public whippings, burnings and hangings. These days, the harshest treatment you'll get is the warden chucking you off the grass for playing football or Frisbee.

Molly Malone Statue   Statue
(Map p126; Suffolk St; 🚌all city centre) Dublin's most famous statue is that of fictional fishmonger (and lady of dubious morals) Molly Malone, she of the song alive, alive-o. Pending the ongoing expansion of the Luas tram system, she's been moved from the bottom of Grafton St to Suffolk St, but that doesn't halt the never-ending procession of visitors looking for a selfie with her.

Ha'penny Bridge   Bridge
(Map p126; 🚌all city centre) The Ha'penny Bridge – officially known as the Liffey Bridge – was built in 1816 and remains one of the world's oldest cast-iron bridges. It was built to replace the seven ferries that plied a busy route between the two banks of the river and it gets its name from the ha'penny toll that was charged until 1919 (for a time the toll was one and a half pence, and so it was called the Penny Ha'penny Bridge).

Old Jameson Distillery   Museum
(Map p122; www.jamesonwhiskey.com; Bow St; adult/student/child €18/15/9, masterclasses €55; ☉10am-5pm Mon-Sat, 10.30am-5pm Sun; 🚌25, 66, 67, 90 from city centre, 🚊Smithfield) Smithfield's biggest draw is devoted to *uisce beatha* (ish-kuh ba-ha, 'the water of life'); that's Irish for whiskey. The museum (occupying part of the old distillery that stopped production in 1971) shepherds visitors through a compulsory tour of the recreated factory (the tasting at the end is a lot of fun) and into the inevitable gift shop.

Phoenix Park   Park
(Map p122; www.phoenixpark.ie; ☉24hr; 🚌10 from O'Connell St, 25 & 26 from Middle Abbey St) FREE Measuring 709 glorious hectares, Phoenix Park is one of the world's largest city parks; you'll find MP3-rigged joggers, grannies pushing buggies, ladies walking poodles, gardens, lakes, a sporting oval, and 300 deer. There are also cricket and polo grounds, a motor-racing track and some fine 18th-century residences, including those of the Irish president and the US ambassador.

Irish Museum of
Modern Art   Museum

(IMMA; Map p122; www.imma.ie; Military
Rd; ⊙11.30am-5.30pm Tue-Fri, 10am-5.30pm
Sat, noon-5.30pm Sun, tours 1.15pm Wed &
2.30pm Sat & Sun; 🚌51, 51D, 51X, 69, 78, 79
from Aston Quay, 🚆Heuston) **FREE** Ireland's
most important collection of modern and
contemporary Irish and international art is
housed in the elegant, airy expanse of the
Royal Hospital Kilmainham, designed by Sir
William Robinson and built between 1684
and 1687 as a retirement home for soldiers.
It fulfilled this role until 1928, after which it
languished for nearly 50 years until a 1980s
restoration saw it come back to life as this
wonderful repository of art.

Little Museum of Dublin   Museum

(Map p126; 📞01-661 1000; www.littlemuseum.
ie; 15 St Stephen's Green N; adult/student €8/6;
⊙9.30am-5pm Mon-Wed & Fri, to 8pm Thu; 🚇all
city centre, 🚆St Stephen's Green) The idea
is ingeniously simple: a museum, spread
across two rooms of an elegant Georgian
building, devoted to the history of Dublin in
the 20th century, made up of memorabilia
contributed by the general public. Visits are
by guided tour and everyone is presented
with a handsome booklet on the history of
the city.

⊙ TOURS

Dublin Literary Pub Crawl   Walking

(Map p126; 📞01-670 5602; www.dublinpub
crawl.com; 9 Duke St; adult/student €13/11;
⊙7.30pm daily Apr-Oct, 7.30pm Thu-Sun Nov-
Mar; 🚇all city centre) A tour of pubs associated with famous Dublin writers is a sure-fire
recipe for success, and this 2½-hour
tour-performance by two actors is a riotous
laugh. There's plenty of drink taken, which
makes it all the more popular. It leaves from
the Duke on Duke St; get there by 7pm to
reserve a spot for the evening tour.

1916 Rebellion
Walking Tour   Walking

(Map p126; 📞086 858 3847; www.1916rising.
com; 23 Wicklow St; €13; ⊙11.30am Mon-Sat,

1pm Sun Mar-Oct; 🚇all city centre) Superb two-
hour tour starting in the International Bar
on Wicklow St. Lots of information, humour
and irreverence to boot. The guides – all
Trinity graduates – are uniformly excellent
and will not say no to the offer of a pint
back in the International at tour's end. The
also have a tour based around Michael
Collins, hero of the War of Independence.

🛍 SHOPPING

Ulysses Rare Books   Books

(Map p126; 📞01-671 8676; www.rarebooks.
ie; 10 Duke St; ⊙9.30am-5.45pm Mon-Sat; 🚇all
city centre) Our favourite bookshop in the
city stocks a rich and remarkable collection
of Irish-interest books, with a particular
emphasis on 20th-century literature and
a large selection of first editions, including
rare ones by the big guns: Joyce, Yeats,
Beckett and Wilde.

George's Street Arcade   Market

(Map p126; www.georgesstreetarcade.ie; btwn
S Great George's & Drury Sts; ⊙9am-6pm
Mon-Wed, to 7pm Thu-Sat, noon-6pm Sun; 🚇all
city centre) Dublin's best nonfood market is
sheltered within an elegant Victorian Gothic
arcade. Apart from shops and stalls selling
new and old clothes, secondhand books,
hats, posters, jewellery and records, there's
a fortune teller, some gourmet nibbles, and
a fish and chipper that does a roaring trade.

Avoca Handweavers   Arts & Crafts

(Map p126; 📞01-677 4215; www.avoca.ie; 11-13
Suffolk St; ⊙9.30am-6pm Mon-Wed & Sat, to 7pm
Thu & Fri, 11am-6pm Sun; 🚇all city centre) Combining clothing, homewares, a basement
food hall and an excellent top-floor cafe,
Avoca promotes a stylish but homey brand
of modern Irish life – and is one of the best
places to find an original present. Many of
the garments are woven, knitted and naturally dyed at its Wicklow factory. There's a
terrific kids' section.

Powerscourt Townhouse
Shopping Centre   Shopping Centre

(Map p126; 📞01-679 4144; 59 S William
St; ⊙10am-6pm Mon-Wed & Fri, to 8pm Thu,

Temple Bar, Grafton St & St Stephen's Green

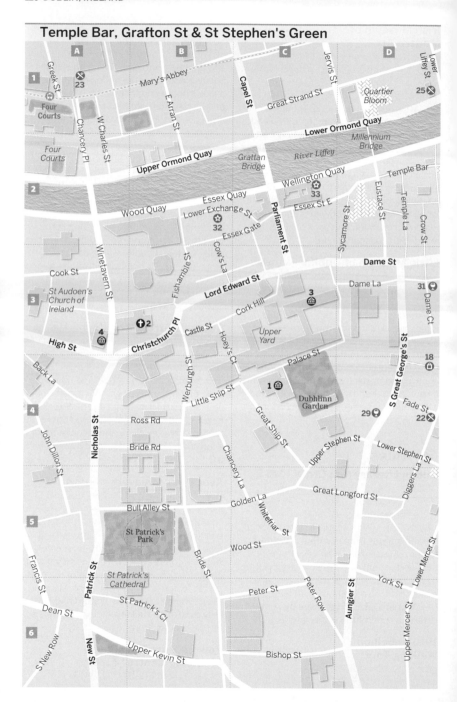

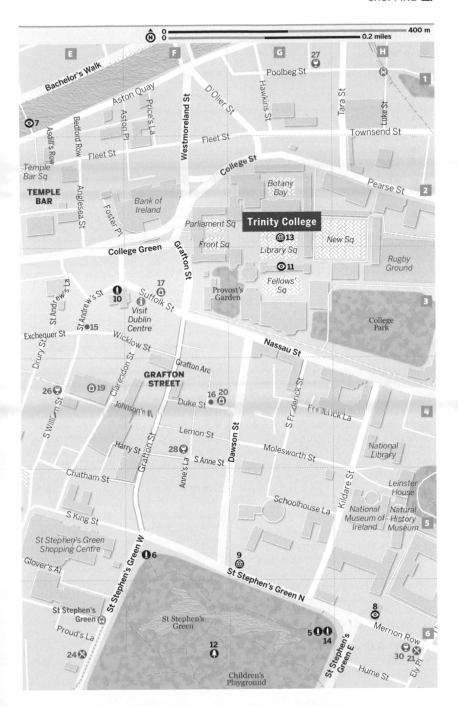

Temple Bar, Grafton St & St Stephen's Green

⊙ Sights
1 Chester Beatty Library.............................C4
2 Christ Church Cathedral...........................B3
3 Dublin Castle C3
4 Dublinia: Experience Viking
& Medieval Dublin...............................A3
5 Famine Victims Memorial........................G6
6 Fusiliers' Arch..F5
7 Ha'penny Bridge E1
8 Huguenot Cemetery.................................H6
9 Little Museum of Dublin...........................G5
10 Molly Malone Statue.................................E3
11 Old Library & Book of Kells......................G3
12 St Stephen's Green F6
13 Trinity College...G2
14 Wolfe Tone Monument G6

⊙ Activities, Courses & Tours
15 1916 Rebellion Walking
Tour..E3
16 Dublin Literary Pub Crawl........................F4

⊙ Shopping
17 Avoca Handweavers...................................F3
18 George's Street Arcade D4

19 Powerscourt Townhouse
Shopping Centre...................................E4
20 Ulysses Rare Books..................................F4

⊗ Eating
21 Etto...H6
22 Fade Street Social....................................D4
23 K Chido Mexico..A1
24 Shanahan's on the Green.........................E6
Silk Road Café ....(see 1)
25 Winding Stair...D1

⊙ Drinking & Nightlife
26 Grogan's Castle Lounge...........................E4
27 John Mulligan's...G1
28 Kehoe's...F4
29 Long Hall..D4
30 O'Donoghue's..H6
31 Stag's Head...D3

⊙ Entertainment
32 Smock Alley Theatre B2
33 Workman's Club...C2

9am-6pm Sat, noon-6pm Sun; 🚇all city centre)
This absolutely gorgeous and stylish centre
is in a carefully refurbished Georgian
townhouse, built between 1741 and 1744.
These days it's best known for its cafes
and restaurants, but it also does a top-end,
selective trade in high fashion, art, exquisite
handicrafts and other chichi sundries.

⊗ EATING

K Chido Mexico   Mexican €
(Map p126; www.kchidomexico.com; 18 Chan-
cery St; tacos €8; ⊙8am-5pm Mon-Fri, 11am-6pm
Sat & Sun; 🚇Four Courts) If you've a craving
for authentic Mexican food, try this food
truck tucked inside a garage. It's a huge
hit with nearby office workers, and seats
can be tough to find weekday lunchtimes,
but for early risers, the breakfast burrito
is great fuel for your sightseeing. The best
Mexican food in the city, no contest.

1837 Bar & Brasserie   Brasserie €
(Map p122; ☎01-471 4602; www.guinness-
storehouse.com; Guinness Storehouse, St

James's Gate; mains €9-14; ⊙noon-3pm; 🚌21A,
51B, 78, 78A, 123 from Fleet St, 🚇James's) This
lunchtime brasserie serves up tasty dishes
from really fresh oysters to an insanely
good Guinness burger, with skin-on fries
and red onion chutney. The drinks menu
features a range of Guinness variants like
West Indian porter and Golden Ale. Highly
recommended for lunch if you're visiting
the museum.

Gerry's   Cafe €
(Map p122; 6 Montague St; Irish fry €6.50;
⊙8am-2pm Mon-Fri, to 2.30pm Sat; 🚌14, 15, 65,
83) A no-nonsense, old-school 'caff' (the
British Isles' equivalent of the greasy-
spoon) is rarer than hen's teeth in the city
centre these days, which makes Gerry's
something of a treasure. You won't find a
more authentic spot to enjoy a traditional
Irish fry-up – and if you want healthy, it
always does porridge, but what's the point?

Etto   Italian €€
(Map p126; ☎01-678 8872; www.etto.ie; 18
Merrion Row; mains €18-23; ⊙noon-10pm
Mon-Fri, 12.30-10pm Sat; 🚇all city centre)

Award-winning restaurant and wine bar that does contemporary versions of classic Italian cuisine. All the ingredients are fresh, the presentation is exquisite and the service is just right. Portions are small, but the food is so rich you won't leave hungry. The only downside is the relatively quick turnover; lingering over the excellent wine would be nice. Book ahead.

Fade Street Social   Modern Irish €€

(Map p126; ☎01-604 0066; www.fadestreetso cial.com; 4-6 Fade St; mains €18-32, tapas €5-12; ⏰12.30-10.30pm Mon-Fri, 5-10.30pm Sat & Sun; 🛜; 🚊all city centre) 🍴 Two eateries in one, courtesy of renowned chef Dylan McGrath: at the front, the buzzy tapas bar, which serves up gourmet bites from a beautiful open kitchen. At the back, the more muted restaurant specialises in Irish cuts of meat – from veal to rabbit – served with home-grown, organic vegetables. There's a bar upstairs too. Reservations suggested.

Winding Stair   Modern Irish €€

(Map p126; ☎01-873 7320; www.winding-stair. com; 40 Lower Ormond Quay; 2-course lunch €21.95, mains €22-28; ⏰noon-5pm & 5.30-10.30pm; 🚊all city centre) In a beautiful Georgian building that once housed the city's most beloved bookshop (the ground floor still is one), the Winding Stair's conversion to elegant restaurant has been faultless. The wonderful Irish menu – creamy fish pie, bacon and organic cabbage, steamed mussels, and Irish farmyard cheeses – coupled with an excellent wine list makes for a memorable meal.

Chapter One   Modern Irish €€€

(Map p122; ☎01-873 2266; www.chapterone restaurant.com; 18 N Parnell Sq; 2-course lunch €32.50, 4-course dinner €75; ⏰12.30-2pm Tue-Fri, 7.30-10.30pm Tue-Sat; 🚊3, 10, 11, 13, 16, 19, 22 from city centre) Flawless haute cuisine and a relaxed, welcoming atmosphere make this Michelin-starred restaurant in the basement of the Dublin Writers Museum our choice for best dinner experience in town. The food is French-inspired contemporary Irish, the menus change regularly

and the service is top-notch. The three-course pretheatre menu (€39.50) is great.

L'Ecrivain   French €€€

(Map p122; ☎01-661 1919; www.lecrivain.com; 109a Lower Baggot St; 3-course lunch menus €45, 8-course tasting menus €90, mains €45; ⏰12.30-2pm Wed-Fri, 6.30-10pm Mon-Sat; 🚊38, 39 from city centre) Head chef Derry Clarke is considered a gourmet god for the exquisite simplicity of his creations, which put the emphasis on flavour and the best local ingredients – all given the French once over and turned into something that approaches divine dining. The Michelin people like it too and awarded it one of their stars.

Shanahan's on the Green   Steak €€€

(Map p126; ☎01-407 0939; www.shanahans. ie; 119 St Stephen's Green W; mains €42-49; ⏰6-10pm Sat-Thu, noon-10pm Fri; 🚊all city centre, 🚊St Stephen's Green) You could order seafood or a plate of vegetables, but you'd be missing the point of this supremely elegant steakhouse: the finest cuts of juicy and tender Irish Angus beef you'll find anywhere. The ambience is upmarket Americana – the bar downstairs is called the Oval Office and pride of place goes to a rocking chair once owned by JFK.

⊖ DRINKING & NIGHTLIFE

John Mulligan's   Pub

(Map p126; www.mulligans.ie; 8 Poolbeg St; ⏰10.30am-11.30pm Mon-Thu, to 12.30am Fri & Sat, noon-11pm Sun; 🚊all city centre) This brilliant old boozer is a cultural institution. Established in 1782 and in this location since 1854, a drink (or more) here is like attending liquid services at a most sacred, secular shrine. John F Kennedy paid his respects in 1945, where he joined a cast of regulars that seems barely to have changed since.

Long Hall   Pub

(Map p126; 51 S Great George's St; ⏰10.30am-11.30pm Mon-Thu, to 12.30am Fri & Sat, noon-11pm Sun; 🚊all city centre) A Victorian

Live Music

The best place to hear traditional music is in the pub, where the 'session' – improvised or scheduled – is still best attended by foreign visitors who appreciate the form far more than most Dubs and will relish any opportunity to drink and toe-tap to some extraordinary virtuoso performances.

Whelan's (Map p122; ☎01-478 0766; www.whelanslive.com; 25 Wexford St; ☐16, 122 from city centre) Perhaps the city's most beloved live-music venue is this midsized room attached to a traditional bar. This is the singer-songwriter's spiritual home: when they're done pouring out the contents of their hearts on stage, you can find them filling up in the bar along with their fans.

O'Donoghue's (Map p126; www. odonoghues.ie; 15 Merrion Row; ⊗10.30am-11.30pm Mon-Thu, to 12.30am Fri & Sat, noon-11pm Sun; ☐all city centre) The pub where traditional music stalwarts The Dubliners made their name in the 1960s still hosts live music nightly, but the crowds would gather anyway – for the excellent pints and superb ambience in the old bar or the covered coach yard next to it.

ANDREW MONTGOMERY/LONELY PLANET ©

classic that is one of the city's most beautiful and best-loved pubs. Check out the ornate carvings in the woodwork behind the bar and the elegant chandeliers. The bartenders are experts at their craft, an increasingly rare attribute in Dublin these days.

Grogan's Castle Lounge   Pub
(Map p126; www.groganspub.ie; 15 S William St; ⊗10.30am-11.30pm Mon-Thu, to 12.30am Fri & Sat, 12.30-11pm Sun; ☐all city centre) This place, known simply as Grogan's (after the original owner), is a city-centre institution. It has long been a favourite haunt of Dublin's writers and painters, as well as others from the alternative bohemian set, who enjoy a fine Guinness while they wait for that inevitable moment when they're discovered.

Kehoe's   Pub
(Map p126; 9 S Anne St; ⊗10.30am-11.30pm Mon-Thu, to 12.30am Fri & Sat, noon-11pm Sun; ☐all city centre) This classic bar is the very exemplar of a traditional Dublin pub. The beautiful Victorian bar, wonderful snug, and side room have been popular for Dubliners and visitors for generations, so much so that the publican's living quarters upstairs have since been converted into an extension – simply by taking out the furniture and adding a bar.

John Kavanagh's   Pub
(Gravediggers; ☎01-830 7978; 1 Prospect Sq; ☐13, 19, 19A from O'Connell St) The gravediggers from the adjacent **Glasnevin Cemetery** (Prospect Cemetery; www.glasnevintrust.ie; Finglas Rd; tours €10; ⊗10am-5pm, tours hourly 10.30am-3.30pm; ☐40, 40A, 40B from Parnell St) **FREE** had a secret serving hatch so that they could drink on the job – hence the pub's nickname. Founded in 1833 by one John Kavanagh and still in the family, this pub is one of the best in Ireland, virtually unchanged in 150 years.

Stag's Head   Pub
(Map p126; www.louisfitzgerald.com/stags head; 1 Dame Ct; ⊗10.30am-1am Mon-Sat, to midnight Sun; ☐all city centre) The Stag's Head was built in 1770, remodelled in 1895 and has thankfully not changed a bit since then. It's a superb pub: so picturesque that it often appears in films, and also featured

Smock Alley Theatre

in a postage-stamp series on Irish bars. A bloody great pub, no doubt.

⭐ ENTERTAINMENT

Devitt's   Live Music

(Map p122; ☎01-475 3414; www.devittspub.ie; 78 Lower Camden St; ⊙from 9pm Thu-Sat; ☒14, 15, 65, 83) Devitt's – aka the Cusack Stand – is one of the favourite places for the city's talented musicians to display their wares, with sessions as good as any you'll hear in the city centre. Highly recommended.

Smock Alley Theatre   Theatre

(Map p126; ☎01-677 0014; www.smockalley. com; 6-7 Exchange St) One of the city's most diverse theatres is hidden in this beautifully restored 17th-century building. It boasts a diverse program of events (expect anything from opera to murder mystery nights, puppet shows and Shakespeare) and many events also come with a dinner option.

The theatre was built in 1622 and was the only Theatre Royal to ever be built outside London. It's been reinvented as a warehouse and a Catholic church and was lovingly restored in 2012 to become a creative hub once again.

Workman's Club   Live Music

(Map p126; ☎01-670 6692; www.theworkmans club.com; 10 Wellington Quay; free-€20; ⊙5pm-3am; ☒all city centre) A 300-capacity venue and bar in the former workingmen's club of Dublin, the emphasis here is on keeping away from the mainstream, which means everything from singer-songwriters to electronic cabaret. When the live music at the Workman's Club is over, DJs take to the stage, playing rockabilly, hip hop, indie, house and more.

Bord Gáis Energy Theatre   Theatre

(☎01-677 7999; www.grandcanaltheatre.ie; Grand Canal Sq; ☒Grand Canal Dock) Forget the uninviting sponsored name: Daniel Libeskind's masterful design is a three-tiered, 2100-capacity auditorium where you're as likely to be entertained by the Bolshoi or a touring state opera as you are to see *Disney on Ice* or Barbra Streisand. It's a magnificent venue – designed for classical, paid for by the classics.

Dublinbikes

ℹ INFORMATION

Visit Dublin Centre (Map p126; www.
visitdublin.com; 25 Suffolk St; ⊗9am-5.30pm
Mon-Sat, 10.30am-3pm Sun; ⊒all city centre) The
main tourist information centre, with free maps,
guides and itinerary planning, plus booking
services for accommodation, attractions and
events.

ℹ GETTING THERE & AWAY

Ireland's capital and biggest city is the most
important point of entry and departure for the
country – almost all airlines fly in and out of
Dublin Airport (🖉01-814 1111; www.dublinair
port.com). The city has two ferry ports: the **Dun
Laoghaire ferry terminal** (🖉01-280 1905; Dun
Laoghaire; ⊒7A or 8 from Burgh Quay, 46A from
Trinity College, ⊠Dun Laoghaire) and the **Dublin**

Port terminal (🖉01-855 2222; Alexandra Rd;
⊒53 from Talbot St).

ℹ GETTING AROUND

Bus Useful for getting to the west side of the city
and the suburbs.

Bicycle The city's rent-and-ride Dublinbikes
scheme is the ideal way to cover ground quickly.

DART Suburban rail network that runs along the
eastern edge of the city along Dublin Bay.

Luas A two-line light-rail transport system that
links the city centre with southern suburbs.

Taxi Easily recognised by light-green-and-blue
'Taxi' sign on door; can be hailed or picked up at
ranks in the city centre.

Walking Dublin's city centre is compact, flat and
eminently walkable – it's less than 2km from one
end of the city centre to the other.

Where to Stay

Like most cities, the closer to the city centre you want to stay, the more you'll pay – and the room sizes get smaller accordingly. Prices soar during summer and festivals; be sure to book in advance.

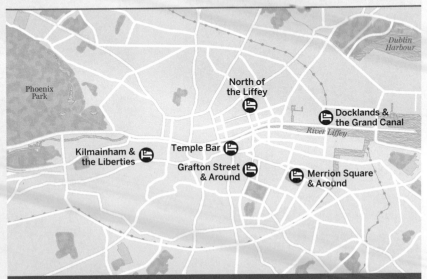

Neighbourhood	Atmosphere
Grafton Street & Around	Close to sights, nightlife and pretty much everything; a good choice of midrange and top-end hotels; generally more expensive than elsewhere; not always good value for money and rooms tend to be smaller
Merrion Square & Around	Lovely neighbourhood, elegant hotels and townhouse accommodation; some of the best restaurants in town are also in the area; not a lot of choice; virtually no budget accommodation; relatively quiet after dark
Temple Bar	In the heart of the action; close to everything, especially the party; noisy and touristy; not especially good value for money; rooms are very small and often less than pristine
Kilmainham & the Liberties	Close to the old city and the sights of west Dublin; no recommended accommodation; only a small selection of restaurants
North of the Liffey	Good range of choices; within walking distance of sights and nightlife; budget accommodation not always good quality; some locations not especially comfortable after dark
Docklands & the Grand Canal	Excellent contemporary hotels with good service, including some top-end choices; isolated in neighbourhood that doesn't have a lot of life after dark; reliant on taxis or public transport to get to city centre

SCANDINAVIA & NORTHERN EUROPE

In This Chapter

Tivoli Gardens...............................138
Designmuseum Danmark.............. 140
Sights 142
Tours 146
Shopping 147
Eating..148
Drinking & Nightlife.......................150
Entertainment 152
Information 152
Getting There & Away 153
Getting Around...............................153

Copenhagen, Denmark

Copenhagen is not only the coolest kid on the Nordic block, but it also gets constantly ranked as the happiest city in the world. Ask a dozen locals why and they would probably all zone in on the hygge, which generally means cosiness but encompasses far more. It is this laid-back contentment that helps give the Danish capital the X factor. The backdrop is pretty cool as well: its cobbled, bike-friendly streets are an enticing concoction of sherbet-hued town houses, craft studios and candlelit cafes. Add to this its compact size and it is possibly Europe's most seamless urban experience.

Two Days in Copenhagen

Get your bearings with a canal and harbour tour, wander **Nyhavn** (p142) then seek out a classic smørrebrød (Danish open sandwich), washed down with bracing akvavit (alcoholic spirit, commonly made with potatoes and spiced with caraway). Stroll through the Latin Quarter and the **Nationalmuseet** (p142) and while away the evening at **Tivoli Gardens** (p138).

On day two, walk in royal footsteps at **Rosenborg Slot** (p143)and **Kongens Have** (p143). Lunch at **Designmuseum Danmark** (p140) before exploring its extensive collection. Splurge on New Nordic cuisine at **Geranium** (p150).

Four Days in Copenhagen

If you have a third day, take a trip to **Louisiana** (p148), an easy train ride north of central Copenhagen. Back in the city, dine in Vesterbro's hip Kødbyen (the 'Meatpacking District'), an industrial area turned buzzing hub.

On day four, explore **Statens Museum for Kunst** (p143) and delve into **Torvehallerne KBH** (p148), the city's celebrated food market, and spend the afternoon exploring **Christiania** (p151).

Next up is Berlin (p486), a 7½-hour bus ride away.

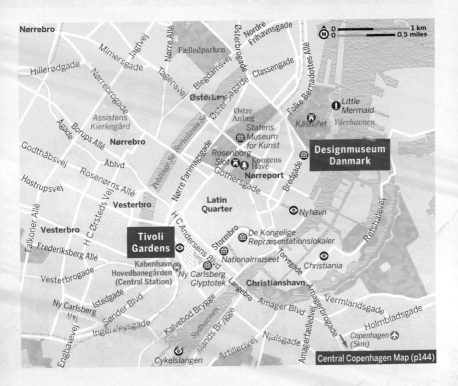

Central Copenhagen Map (p144)

Arriving in Copenhagen

Copenhagen Airport is Scandinavia's busiest hub, with direct flights to cities in Europe, North America and Asia, as well as a handful of Danish cities. Located in Kastrup, 9km southeast of Copenhagen's city centre, it has good eating, retail and information facilities.

All long-distance trains arrive at and depart from **Københavns Hovedbanegård** (Central Station), a 19th-century, wooden-beamed hall with numerous facilities, including currency exchange, a post office, left-luggage facilities and food outlets.

Where to Stay

Copenhagen's accommodation options range from higher-end Danish design establishments to excellent budget hotels and hostels, which are mainly centred on the western side of the Central Station. It's a good idea to reserve rooms in advance, especially hostels, during the busy summer season.

The **Copenhagen Visitors Centre** (p153) can book rooms in private homes. Depending on availability, it also books unfilled hotel rooms at discounted rates.

Tivoli Gardens during Christmas

MAREMAGNUM/GETTY IMAGES ©

Tivoli Gardens

The country's top-ranking tourist draw, tasteful Tivoli Gardens has been eliciting gleeful shrills since 1843. Whatever your idea of fun – hair-raising rides, twinkling pavilions, open-air stage shows or al fresco pantomime and beer – this old-timer has you covered.

Great For...

☑ Don't Miss

The city views – taken at 70km/h – from the Star Flyer, one of the world's tallest carousels.

Roller Coasters

The Rutschebanen is the best loved of Tivoli's roller coasters, rollicking its way through and around a faux 'mountain' and reaching speeds of 60km/h. Built in 1914 it claims to be the world's oldest operating wooden roller coaster. If you're after something a little more hardcore, the Dæmonen (Demon) is a 21st-century beast with faster speeds and a trio of hair-raising loops.

The Grounds

Beyond the carousels and side stalls is a Tivoli of landscaped gardens, tranquil nooks and eclectic architecture. Lower the adrenaline under beautiful old chestnut and elm trees, and amble around Tivoli Lake. Formed out of the old city moat, the lake is a top spot to snap pictures of Tivoli's commanding Chinese Tower, built in 1900.

LEPNEVA IRINA/SHUTTERSTOCK ©

ℹ **Need to Know**

www.tivoli.dk; Vesterbrogade 3, Vesterbro; adult/child under 8yr Mon-Thu Dkr110/free, Fri-Sun Dkr120/free; ⊙11am-11pm Sun-Thu, to midnight Fri & Sat Apr-Sep, reduced hours rest of year; 🛗; ⛁2A, 5A, 9A, 12, 26, 250S, 350S, ⛁S-train København H

✕ **Take a Break**

Jolly **Grøften** (🖉33 75 06 75; www.groef ten.dk; smørrebrød Dkr69-135, mains Dkr145-385; ⊙noon-10pm daily Apr-Sep, reduced hours rest of year; 🛜) is a local institution.

★ **Top Tip**
Amusement rides cost Dkr25 to Dkr75; consider purchasing a multi-ride ticket for Dkr220.

Illuminations & Fireworks

Throughout the summer season, Tivoli Lake wows the crowds with its nightly laser and water spectacular. The Saturday evening fireworks are a summer-season must, repeated again from December 26 to 30 for Tivoli's annual Fireworks Festival.

Live Performances

The indoor **Tivolis Koncertsal** (Concert Hall) hosts mainly classical music, with the odd musical and big-name pop or rock act. All tickets are sold at the **Tivoli Billetcenter** (🖉33 15 10 12; ⊙10am-8pm Mon-Fri, 11am-5pm Sat & Sun) or online through the Tivoli website.

Pantomime Theatre

Each night during the summer this criminally charming theatre presents silent

plays in the tradition of Italy's Commedia dell'Arte. Many of the performers also work at the esteemed Royal Ballet.

When to Go

After dusk Tivoli is at its most enchanting when the park's fairy lights and lanterns are switched on.

Friday evenings From early April to mid-September, the open-air Plænen stage hosts free rock concerts from 10pm – go early if it's a big-name act.

Halloween Tivoli opens for around three weeks. See the website for details.

Christmas From mid-November to early January, Tivoli hosts a large **market**. Entertainment includes costumed staff and theatre shows. Fewer rides are operational but the *gløgg* (mulled wine) and *æbleskiver* (small doughnuts) are ample compensation.

Designmuseum Danmark

Don't know your Egg from your Swan? What about your PH4 from your PH5? For a crash course in Denmark's incredible design heritage, make an elegant beeline for Designmuseum Danmark.

Housed in a converted 18th-century hospital, the museum is a must for fans of the applied arts and industrial design. Its booty includes Danish silver and porcelain, textiles and the iconic design pieces of modern innovators such as Kaare Klint, Poul Henningsen, Arne Jacobsen and Verner Panton.

20th-Century Crafts & Design

The museum's main permanent exhibition explores 20th-century industrial design and crafts in the context of social, economic, technological and theoretical changes. The collection displays celebrated furniture and applied arts from both Denmark and abroad.

Great For...

☑ **Don't Miss**

The vintage poster collection, including the iconic 1959 'Wonderful Copenhagen' poster.

PERNILLE KLEMP/DESIGNMUSEUM DANMARK'S ©

ℹ Need to Know

www.designmuseum.dk; Bredgade 68, Østerport; adult/child Dkr100/free; ⊘11am–5pm Tue & Thu-Sun, to 9pm Wed; 🚌1A, 15, Ⓜ Kongens Nytorv

✕ Take a Break

The museum's Klint Cafe, located just off the lobby, serves Danish classics and has a fine outdoor courtyard.

★ Top Tip

The museum shop is one of the city's best places to pick up savvy gifts and easy-to-carry souvenirs.

The Danish Chair

An ode to the humble chair and an explo ration of what goes into making a 'good' one, this permanent exhibition displays more than 100 beautifully designed chairs, including some international guests. Standing room only.

Porcelain

This detailed exhibition celebrates European porcelain and its journey from initial attempts through to the current day.

Danish Design Now

Showcasing contemporary fashion, furniture and products, this captivating exhibition focuses on 21st-century Danish design and innovation.

Fashion & Fabric

This permanent exhibition showcases around 350 objects from the museum's rich textile and fashion collections. Spanning four centuries, the collection's treasures include French and Italian silks, ikat and batik weaving, and two extraordinary mid-20th-century tapestries based on cartoons by Henri Matisse. As would you expect, Danish textiles and fashion feature prominently, including Danish *hedebo* embroidery from the 18th to 20th centuries, and Erik Mortensen's collection of haute couture frocks from French fashion houses Balmain and Jean-Louis Scherrer.

◎ SIGHTS

One of the great things about Copenhagen is its size. Virtually all of Copenhagen's major sightseeing attractions are in or close to the medieval city centre. Only the perennially disappointing **Little Mermaid** (Den Lille Havfrue; Langelinie, Østerport; 🚆1A, 🚢Nordre Toldbod) lies outside of the city proper, on the harbourfront.

Nyhavn   Canal
There are few nicer places to be on a sunny day than sitting at the outdoor tables of a cafe on the quayside of the Nyhavn canal. The canal was built to connect Kongens Nytorv to the harbour and was long a haunt for sailors and writers, including Hans Christian Andersen, who lived there for most of his life at, variously, numbers 20, 18 and 67.

Nationalmuseet   Museum
(National Museum; www.natmus.dk; Ny Vester-gade 10, Slotsholmen; adult/child Dkr75/60; ⊙10am-5pm Tue-Sun; 👥; 🚆1A, 2A, 11A, 33, 40, 66, 🚉S-train København H) For a crash course in Danish history and culture, spend an afternoon at Denmark's National Museum. It has first claims on virtually every antiquity uncovered on Danish soil, including Stone Age tools, Viking weaponry, rune stones and medieval jewellery. Among the many highlights is a finely crafted 3500-year-old Sun Chariot, as well as bronze *lurs* (horns), some of which date back 3000 years and are still capable of blowing a tune.

Ny Carlsberg Glyptotek   Museum
(www.glyptoteket.dk; Dantes Plads 7, Vesterbro, HC Andersens Blvd; adult/child Dkr95/free, Tue free; ⊙11am-6pm Tue-Sun, until 10pm Thu; 🚆1A, 2A, 11A, 33, 40, 66, 🚉S-train København H) Fin de siècle architecture dallies with an eclectic mix of art at Ny Carlsberg Glyptotek. The collection is divided into two parts: Northern Europe's largest trove of antiquities and an elegant collection of 19th-century Danish and French art. The latter includes the largest collection of Rodin sculptures outside of France and no fewer than 47 Gauguin paintings. These are displayed along with works by greats like Cézanne, Van Gogh, Pissarro, Monet and Renoir.

Nyhavn

An added treat for visitors is the August/September Summer Concert Series (admission around Dkr75). Classical music is performed in the museum's concert hall, which is evocatively lined by life-size statues of Roman patricians.

De Kongelige Repræsenta-tionslokaler   Historic Building

(Royal Reception Rooms at Christiansborg Slot; www.christiansborg.dk; Slotsholmen; adult/child Dkr90/45; ☺10am-5pm May-Sep, closed Mon Oct-Apr, guided tours in Danish/English 11am/3pm; ◫1A, 2A, 9A, 11A, 26, 40, 66) The grandest part of Christiansborg Slot is De Kongelige Repræsentationslokaler, an ornate Renaissance hall where the queen holds royal banquets and entertains heads of state. Don't miss the beautifully sewn and colourful wall tapestries depicting Danish history from Viking times to today. Created by tapestry designer Bjørn Nørgaard over a decade, the works were completed in 2000. Look for the Adam and Eve–style representation of the queen and her husband (albeit clothed) in a Danish Garden of Eden.

Rosenborg Slot   Castle

(www.kongernessamling.dk/en/rosenborg; Øster Voldgade 4A, Nørreport; adult/child Dkr105/free, incl Amalienborg Slot Dkr145/free; ☺10am-5pm Jun-Aug, to 4pm May, Sep & Oct, reduced hours rest of year; ◫6A, 11A, 42, 150S, 173E, 184, 185, 350S, Ⓜ Nørreport) A 'once-upon-a-time' combo of turrets, gables and moat, the early-17th-century Rosenborg Slot was built in Dutch Renaissance style between 1606 and 1633 by King Christian IV to serve as his summer home. Today, the castle's 24 upper rooms are chronologically arranged, housing the furnishings and portraits of each monarch from Christian IV to Frederik VII. The pièce de résistance is the basement Treasury, home to the dazzling crown jewels.

Statens Museum for Kunst   Museum

(www.smk.dk; Sølvgade 48-50, Østerport; adult/child Dkk110/free; ☺11am-5pm Tue & Thu-Sun, to 8pm Wed; ◫6A, 26, 42, 173E, 184, 185) **FREE** Denmark's National Gallery straddles two contrasting, interconnected buildings: a

Changing of the Guard

The Royal Life Guard is charged with protecting the Danish royal family and their city residence, Amalienborg Palace. Every day of the year, these soldiers march from their barracks through the streets of Copenhagen to perform the **Changing of the Guard** (www.kongehuset.dk/en/changing-of-the-guard-at-amalienborg; Amalienborg Slotsplads; ☺noon daily; ◫1A) **FREE**. Clad in 19th-century tunics and bearskin helmets, their performance of intricate manoeuvres is an impressive sight. If Queen Margrethe is in residence, the ceremony is even more grandiose, with the addition of a full marching band.

If you miss out on the noon ceremony, a smaller-scale shift change is performed every two hours thereafter.

BIRUTE VIJEIKIENE/SHUTTERSTOCK ©

late-19th-century 'palazzo' and a sharply minimalist extension. The museum houses medieval and Renaissance works and impressive collections of Dutch and Flemish artists including Rubens, Breughel and Rembrandt. It claims the world's finest collection of 19th-century Danish 'Golden Age' artists, among them Eckersberg and Hammershøi, foreign greats like Matisse and Picasso, and modern Danish heavy-weights including Per Kirkeby.

Kongens Have   Park

(King's Gardens; http://parkmuseerne.dk/kongens-have/; Øster Voldgade, Nørreport; ☺8.30am-6pm; ◫6A, 11A, 42, 150S, 173E, 184, 185, 350S, Ⓜ Nørreport) **FREE** The oldest park in Copenhagen was laid out in the early

Central Copenhagen (København)

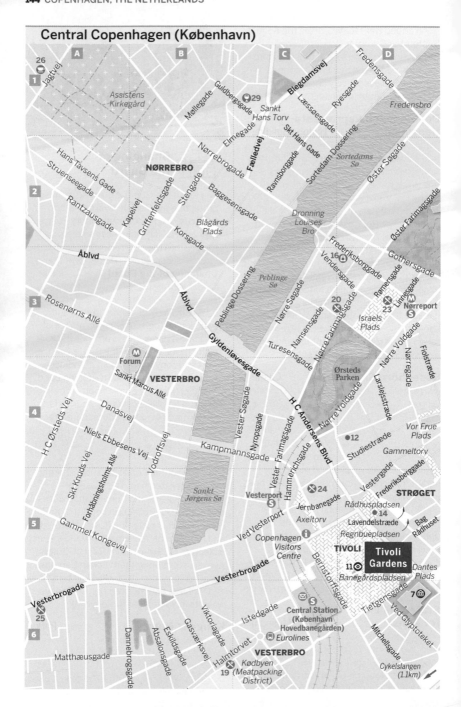

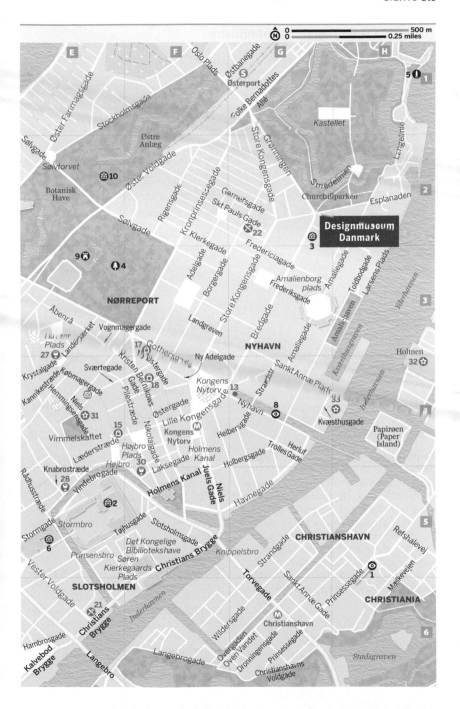

Central Copenhagen (København)

⊙ Sights
1 Christiania...................................H5
2 De Kongelige
  Repræsentationslokaler E5
3 Designmuseum Danmark.....................G2
4 Kongens Have E3
5 Little Mermaid....................................H1
6 Nationalmuseet..................................E5
7 Ny Carlsberg Glyptotek D6
8 Nyhavn..G4
9 Rosenborg Slot E3
10 Statens Museum for Kunst E2
11 Tivoli Gardens D5

⊙ Activities, Courses & Tours
12 Bike Copenhagen with Mike.............D4
13 Canal Tours Copenhagen.................G4
14 Copenhagen Free Walking
   Tours D5

⊙ Shopping
  Bornholmer Butikken........................(see 23)
15 Hay House..E4
16 Maduro D3
17 Posterland F3
18 Wood Wood F4

⊗ Eating
19 Chicky Grill B6
  Grøften ....(see 11)
20 Höst...D3
21 Lillian's Smørrebrød E6
22 Nyboders Køkken..............................G2
23 Torvehallerne KBH............................D3
24 Uformel..C5
25 WestMarket A6

⊙ Drinking & Nightlife
26 Coffee Collective Nørrebro...............A1
27 Lo-Jo's Social....................................E3
28 Ruby...E5
29 Rust..C1
30 Ved Stranden 10................................F5

⊙ Entertainment
31 Jazzhouse E4
32 Operaen...H4
33 Skuespilhuset...................................H4
  Tivoli Koncertsal...............................(see 11)

17th century by Christian IV, who used it as his vegetable patch. These days it has a little more to offer, including immaculate flower beds, romantic garden paths and a marionette theatre with free performances during the summer season (2pm and 3pm Tuesday to Sunday).

Superkilen
Park

(Nørrebrogade 210; 🚌5A, 66, Ⓢ Nørrebro) This fascinating one-kilometre-long park showcases objects sourced from around the globe with the aim of celebrating diversity and uniting the community. Items include a tiled fountain from Morocco, bollards from Ghana and swing chairs from Baghdad, as well as neon signs from Russia and China. Even the benches, manhole covers and rubbish bins hail from foreign lands.

⊙ TOURS

You can't visit Copenhagen and *not* take a canal boat trip. Not only is it a fantastic way to see the city, but you also see a side of it that landlubbers never see. Be aware that in most boats you are totally exposed to the elements (even during summer).

Bike Copenhagen with Mike
Cycling

(📞26 39 56 88; www.bikecopenhagenwithmike. dk; Sankt Peders Stræde 47, Strøget; per person Dkr299) If you don't fancy walking, Bike Mike runs three-hour cycling tours of the city, departing Sankt Peders Stræde 47 in the city centre, just east of Ørstedsparken (which is southwest of Nørreport station). Mike is a great character and will really give you the insider's scoop on the city. Book online.

Copenhagen Free Walking Tours
Walking

(www.copenhagenfreewalkingtours.dk; Rådhus (City Hall), Strøget, H C Andersens Blvd; ⊙noon) **FREE** Departing daily at noon from outside Rådhus (City Hall), these free, three-hour walking tours take in famous landmarks and include interesting anecdotes. Tours are in English and require a minimum of five people. Free 90-minute tours of Christianshavn depart at 4pm Friday to Monday from the base of the Bishop Absalon statue on Højbro Plads. A tip is expected.

Canal Tours Copenhagen · Boating

(☑32 66 00 00; www.stromma.dk; Nyhavn; adult/child Dkr80/40; ◷9.30am-9pm late Jun-late Aug, reduced hours rest of year; ♿; Ⓜ Kongens Nytorv) Canal Tours Copenhagen runs one-hour cruises of the city's canals and harbour, taking in numerous major sights, including Christiansborg Slot, Christianshavn, the Royal Library, Opera House, Amalienborg Palace and *The Little Mermaid*. Embark at Nyhavn or Ved Stranden. Boats depart up to six times per hour from late June to late August, with reduced frequency the rest of the year.

🔒 SHOPPING

Most of the big retail names and home-grown heavyweights are centred on the main pedestrian shopping strip, Strøget. The streets running parallel are dotted with intersecting jewellery and antique stores while, to the north, the so-called Latin Quarter is worth a wander for books and clothing. Arty Nørrebro is home to Elmegade and Jægersborggade, two streets lined with interesting shops.

Bornholmer Butikken · Food & Drinks

(☑30 72 00 07; www.bornholmerbutikken.dk; Frederiksborggade 21; ◷10am-7pm Mon-Thu, to 8pm Fri, to 6pm Sat, 11am-5pm Sun) The Bornholm Store in Torvehallerne Market offers a range of tasty take-home specialities from the Danish island of Bornholm, which is famed for its incredible local products. Tasty treats to bring home include honeys, relishes and jams, Johan Bulow liquorice, salamis, cheeses, herring, liquors, and beers.

Maduro · Homewares

(☑33 93 28 33; www.maduro.dk; Frederiksborggade 39; ◷11am-6pm Mon-Fri, 10am-4pm Sat) The motto of Maduro owner Jeppe Maduro Hirsch is that 'good style is more than decor and design'. His small shop is an

Copenhagen's Cykelslangen

Two of the Danes' greatest passions – design and cycling – meet in spectacular fashion with **Cykelslangen**, or Cycle Snake. Designed by local architects Dissing + Weitling, the 235-metre-long cycling path evokes a slender orange ribbon, its gently curving form contrasting dramatically with the area's block-like architecture. The elevated path winds its way from Bryggebro (Brygge Bridge) west to Fisketorvet Shopping Centre, weaving its way over the harbour and delivering a cycling experience that's nothing short of whimsical. To reach the path on public transport, catch bus 30 to Fisketorvet Shopping Centre. The best way to reach it, however, is on a bike, as Cykelslangen is only accessible to cyclists.

eclectic mix of lovely products, including ceramics, posters and jewellery. The style ranges from sleek to traditional to quirky, and the selection of children's items is especially charming.

Posterland · Arts

(☑33 11 28 21; www.posterland.dk; Gothersgade 45; ◷9:30am-6pm Mon-Thu, to 7pm Fri, to 5pm Sat) Posterland is Northern Europe's biggest poster company, and is the perfect place to find something to spruce up your walls. The wide selection of posters includes art, travel and vintage posters, as well Copenhagen posters of every description including Danish icons Hans Christian Andersen, Tivoli Gardens and the Carlsberg Brewery. You can also pick up souvenirs like postcards, maps, calendars and magnets.

Hay House · Design

(www.hay.dk; Østergade 61; ◷10am-6pm Mon-Fri, to 5pm Sat; ♿11A) Rolf Hay's fabulous interior design store sells its own coveted line of furniture, textiles and design objects, as well as those of other fresh, innovative Danish designers. Easy-to-pack

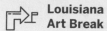

Louisiana Art Break

Even if you don't have a consuming passion for modern art, Denmark's outstanding **Louisiana** (www.louisiana.dk; Gammel Strandvej 13, Humlebæk; adult/child Dkr115/free; ⊗11am-10pm Tue-Fri, to 6pm Sat & Sun) should be high on your 'to do' list. It's a striking modernist gallery, made up of four huge wings, which stretch across a sculpture-filled park, burrowing down into the hillside and nosing out again to wink at the sea (and Sweden). The collection itself is stellar, covering everything from constructivism, CoBrA movement artists and minimalist art to abstract expressionism, pop art and photography.

Louisiana is in the leafy town of **Humlebæk**, 30km north of Copenhagen. From Humlebæk train station, the museum is a 1.5km signposted walk northeast. Trains to Humlebæk run at least twice hourly from Copenhagen (Dkr115, 35 minutes). If day-tripping from Copenhagen, the 24-hour ticket (adult/child Dkr130/65) is much better value.

---

gifts include anything from notebooks and ceramic cups to building blocks for style-savvy kids. There's a second branch at Pilestræde 29-31.

Wood Wood   Fashion & Accessories

(www.woodwood.dk; Grønnegade 1; ⊗10.30am-6pm Mon-Thu, to 7pm Fri, to 5pm Sat, noon-4pm Sun; ☑11A, ⓂKongens Nytorv) Unisex Wood Wood's flagship store is a veritable who's who of cognoscenti street-chic labels. Top of the heap are Wood Wood's own hipster-chic creations, made with superlative fabrics and attention to detail. The supporting cast includes solid knits from classic Danish brand SNS Herning, wallets from Comme des Garçons and sunglasses from Kaibosh.

 EATING

Copenhagen remains one of the hottest culinary destinations in Europe, with more Michelin stars than any other Scandinavian city. **Copenhagen Cooking** (www.copenhagencooking.dk), Scandinavia's largest food festival, serves up a gut-rumbling program twice a year.

Lillian's Smørrebrød   Danish €

(www.facebook.com/lillianssmorrebrod; Vester Voldgade 108, Slotsholmen; smørrebrød Dkr17-50; ⊗6am-1.30pm Mon-Thu, to 1am Fri; ☑1A, 2A, 9A) One of the best, the oldest (dating from 1978) and least costly smørrebrød places in the city, but word is out so you may have to opt for a takeaway as there are just a handful of tables inside and out. The piled-high, open-face sandwiches are classic and include marinated herring, chicken salad and roast beef with remoulade.

Chicky Grill   Danish €

(☑33 22 66 96; Halmtorvet 21, Vesterbro; mains from Dkr75; ⊗11am-8pm Mon-Sat; ⛟; ☑10,14, ⓂCentral Station) Blend in with the locals at this perennially popular bar and grill in hip Kødbyen (the 'Meatpacking District'). It has decor that is more diner than 'dining out', but prices are low and portions are huge with a menu of predominantly grilled meats, fried chicken, burgers and that all-time popular Danish speciality, *flæskesteg* (roast pork).

Torvehallerne KBH   Market €

(www.torvehallernekbh.dk; Israels Plads, Nørreport; snacks from Dkr80; ⊗10am-7pm Mon-Thu, to 8pm Fri, to 6pm Sat, 11am-5pm Sun; ⓂNørreport) Food market Torvehallerne KBH is an essential stop on the Copenhagen foodie trail. A delicious ode to the fresh, the tasty and the artisanal, the market's beautiful stalls peddle everything from seasonal herbs and berries to smoked meats, seafood and cheeses, smørrebrød, fresh pasta and hand-brewed coffee. You could easily spend an hour or more exploring its twin halls.

Smørrebrød, Torvehallerne KBH

WestMarket   Market €

(www.westmarket.dk; Vesterbrogade 97; ⓢbak-
eries & coffee shops 6am-7pm, food stalls 10am-
10pm; 🚌6A) Copenhagen's newest foodie
hotspot, WestMarket is both a traditional
market and a hip street food emporium.
The range of cuisines is impressive: visitors
can sample offerings from all over the
world, from Danish smørrebrød at Selma
to Ugandan egg wraps at Ugood. Try bear
sausage at Kød & Bajer for something unusual, or treat yourself to sinfully delicious
desserts at Guilty.

Nyboders Køkken   Danish €€

(📞22 88 64 14; www.nyboderskoekken.dk;
Borgergade 134, Nyhavn; mains Dkr128-185;
ⓢ5-11.30pm Mon-Fri, noon-3pm Sat & Sun; 📶;
🚌11A, 26, Ⓜ Kongens Nytorv) Located in an
affluent neighbourhood with a fashionably
chic feel, Nyboders Køkken's menu is
purposefully deeply traditional; if you are
Danish, grandma's kitchen may come to
mind. Think apple charlotte, classic wiener
schnitzel, prawn cocktail and Danish junket
with cream. Among the mains, the roasted

slices of pork with parsley sauce has had
local food critics swooning.

Höst   New Nordic €€€

(📞89 30 94 09; www.hostvakst.dk; Nørre
Farimagsgade 41, Nørrebrø; mains Dkr205-245,
5-course set menu Dkr395; ⓢ5.30pm-midnight,
last order 9.30pm; 🚌40, Ⓜ Nørrebro) Höst's
phenomenal popularity is a no-brainer:
warm, award-winning interiors and New
Nordic food that's equally as fabulous and
filling. The set menu is superb, with three
smaller 'surprise dishes' thrown in and
evocative creations like beef tenderloin
from Grambogaard with onion compote,
gherkins, cress and smoked cheese. The
'deluxe' wine menu is significantly better
than the standard option. Book ahead,
especially later in the week.

Uformel   New Nordic €€€

(📞70 99 91 11; www.uformel.dk/en/; Studiestræde 69; dishes Dkr110; ⓢ5.30-10pm Sun-Thu,
to 11pm Fri & Sat; 🚌5A, 6A, 9A, 10, 12, 14, 31,
Ⓢ Vesterport) The edgier younger brother
of Michelin-starred restaurant Formel B,
Uformel ('Informal') offers a more casual

EUGENE ANBALL/500PX ©

take on New Nordic cuisine. The restaurant serves up an ever-changing menu featuring local, seasonal ingredients to create its mouth-watering dishes. Diners can choose several small plates to create their own tasting menu, or opt for the set menu of four courses (Dkr775).

Geranium New Nordic €€€

(☑69 96 00 20; geranium.dk; Per Henrik Lings Allé 4, Østerbro; lunch/dinner tasting menu Dkr1250/1550, lighter lunch tasting menu Dkr950; ☺lunch noon-1pm Wed-Sat, dinner 6.30-9pm Wed-Sat; ☑) ✿ Perched on the 8th floor of Parken football stadium, Geranium is the only restaurant in town sporting three Michelin stars. At the helm is Bocuse d'Or prize-winning chef Rasmus Kofoed, who transforms local ingredients into edible Nordic artworks like venison with smoked lard and beetroot, or king crab with lemon balm and cloudberries.

Kronor-conscious foodies can opt for the slightly cheaper lunch menus, while those not wanting to sample the (swoon-inducing) wines can opt for enlightened juice pairings. Book ahead.

🍷 DRINKING & NIGHTLIFE

Copenhagen is packed with a diverse range of drinking options. Vibrant drinking areas include Kødbyen (the 'Meatpacking District') and Istedgade in Vesterbro; Ravnsborggade, Elmegade and Sankt Hans Torv in Nørrebro; and especially gay-friendly Studiestræde.

Coffee Collective Nørrebro Cafe

(www.coffeecollective.dk; Jægersborggade 10, Nørrebro; ☺7am-7pm Mon-Fri, 8am-7pm Sat & Sun; ☑18, 12, 66) In a city where lacklustre coffee is as common as perfect cheekbones, this microroastery peddles the good stuff – we're talking rich, complex cups of caffeinated magic. The baristas are passionate about their beans and the cafe itself sits on creative Jægersborggade in Nørrebro. There are two other outlets, at food market Torvehallerne KBH (p148) and in **Frederiksberg** (Godthåbsvej 34b; ☺7.30am-9pm Mon-Fri, from 9am Sat, from 10am Sun).

Ved Stranden 10 Wine Bar

(www.vedstranden10.dk; Ved Stranden 10; ☺noon-10pm Mon-Sat; 🛜; ☑1A, 2A, 26, 40, 66)

Politicians and well-versed oenophiles make a beeline for this canalside wine bar, its enviable cellar stocked with classic European vintages, biodynamic wines and more obscure drops. Adorned with modernist Danish design and friendly, clued-in staff, its string of rooms lends the place an intimate, civilised air that's perfect for grown-up conversation plus vino-friendly nibbles like cheeses and smoked meats.

Ruby   Cocktail Bar

(www.rby.dk; Nybrogade 10, Strøget; ⏰4pm-2am Mon-Sat, from 6pm Sun; 🛜; 🚌1A, 2A, 11A, 26, 40, 66) Cocktail connoisseurs raise their glasses to high-achieving Ruby. Here, hipster-geek mixologists whip up near-flawless libations such as the Green & White (vodka, dill, white chocolate and liquorice root) and a lively crowd spills into a labyrinth of cosy, decadent rooms. For a gentlemen's club vibe, head downstairs into a world of Chesterfields, oil paintings and wooden cabinets lined with spirits.

Lo-Jo's Social   Bar

(📞53 88 64 65; www.lojossocial.com; Landemærket 7; ⏰bar 11:30am late Mon-Sat, kitchen to 10pm) It's all in the name: colourful Lo-Jo's is a place to be social, with a range of tasty cocktails available for sharing for up to five people. Wines are largely organic or bio-dynamic, and for something a bit different, there is a bubbly Spritz menu and a refreshing Apple Press menu, using fresh apple juice as a base.

Mikkeller & Friends   Microbrewery

(📞35 83 10 20; www.mikkeller.dk/location/mikkeller-friends; Stefansgade 35; ⏰2pm-midnight Sun-Wed, to 2am Thu & Fri, from noon Sat; 🚌5A, 8A) This uniquely designed beer geek hotspot offers 40 kinds of artisan draught beers from local microbreweries and 200 varieties of bottled beers ciders, and soft drinks. Patrons can snack on gourmet sausages and cheese while enjoying their beer.

Rust   Club

(📞35 24 52 00; www.rust.dk; Guldbergsgade 8, Nørrebro; ⏰hours vary, club usually 11pm-5am Fri & Sat; 🛜; 🚌3A, 5A, 350S) A smashing

 Freetown Christiania

Escape the capitalist crunch at Freetown **Christiania** (Prinsessegade, Christianshavn; 🚌9A, 2A, 40, 350S, Ⓜ Christianshavn), a free-spirited, eco-oriented commune. Explore beyond the settlement's infamous 'Pusher St' and you'll stumble upon a semibucolic wonderland of whimsical DIY homes, cosy gardens and craft shops, eateries, beer gardens and music venues.

Before its development as an alternative enclave, the site was an abandoned 41-hectare military camp. When squatters took over in 1971, police tried to clear the area. They failed. Bowing to public pressure, the government allowed the community to continue as a social experiment. Self-governing, ecology-oriented and generally tolerant, Christiania residents did, in time, find it necessary to modify their 'anything goes' approach. A new policy was established that outlawed hard drugs and the heroin and cocaine pushers were expelled.

The main entrance into Christiania is on Prinsessegade, 200m northeast of its intersection with Bådsmandsstræde. From late June to the end of August, 60- to 90-minute guided tours (Dkr40) of Christiania run daily at 3pm (weekends only September to late June). Tours commence just inside Christiania's main entrance on Prinsessegade.

History at the Frilandsmuseet

The main sight of interest in the Lyngby area is **Frilandsmuseet** (📞41 20 64 55; www.natmus.dk; Kongevejen 100, Lyngby; ⊙10am-5pm Tue-Sun Jul-Aug, shorter hrs rest of yr) **FREE**, a sprawling open-air museum of old countryside dwellings that have been gathered from sites around Denmark. Its 100-plus historic buildings are arranged in groupings that provide a sense of Danish rural life as it was in various regions and across different social strata.

Frilandsmuseet is a 10-minute sign-posted walk from Sorgenfri station, 25 minutes from Central Station on S-train line B. You can also take bus 184 or 194, both of which stop at the entrance.

Danish farmhouse and windmill
OLIVER FOERSTNER/SHUTTERSTOCK ©

place attracting one of the largest, coolest crowds in Copenhagen. Live acts focus on alternative or upcoming indie rock, hip hop or electronica, while the club churns out hip hop, dancehall and electro on Wednesdays and house, electro and rock on Fridays and Saturdays. From 11pm Friday and Saturday, entrance is only to over 20s.

✪ ENTERTAINMENT

Copenhagen is home to thriving live-music and club scenes that range from intimate jazz and blues clubs to mega rock venues. Blockbuster cultural venues such as **Operaen** (Copenhagen Opera House; 🎫box office 33 69 69 69; www.kglteater.dk; Ekvipagemestervej 10; 🚌9A, 🚢Opera) and **Skuespilhuset**

(Royal Danish Playhouse; 📞33 69 69 69; kglteater.dk; Sankt Anne Plads 36; 🚌11A, Ⓜ Kongens Nytorv) deliver top-tier opera and theatre. The **Copenhagen Jazz Festival** (www.jazz.dk), the largest jazz festival in northern Europe, hits the city over 10 days in early July.

Jazzhouse
Jazz

(📞33 15 47 00; www.jazzhouse.dk; Niels Hemmingsensgade 10, Strøget; 🛜; 🚌11A) Copenhagen's leading jazz joint serves up top Danish and visiting talent, with music styles running the gamut from bebop to fusion jazz. Doors usually open at 7pm, with concerts starting at 8pm. On Friday and Saturday, late-night concerts (from 11pm) are also offered. Check the website for details and consider booking big-name acts in advance.

ℹ️ INFORMATION

EMERGENCY & IMPORTANT NUMBERS

Dial 112 to contact police, ambulance or fire services; the call can be made free from public phones.

DISCOUNT CARDS

The **Copenhagen Card** (www.copenhagencard. com; adult/child 10-15yr 24hr Dkr379/199, 48hr Dkr529/269, 72hr Dkr629/319, 120hr Dkr839/419), available at the Copenhagen Visitors Centre or online, gives you free access to 72 museums and attractions in the city and surrounding area, as well as free travel for all S-train, metro and bus journeys within the seven travel zones.

MONEY

Banks are plentiful, especially in central Copenhagen. Most are open from 10am to 4pm weekdays (to 5.30pm on Thursday). Most banks in Copenhagen have ATMs that are accessible 24 hours per day.

POST

Post Office (Købmagergade 33; ⊙10am-6pm Mon-Fri, to 2pm Sat) A handy post office near Strøget and the Latin Quarter.

København H Post Office (Central Station; 9am-7pm Mon-Fri, noon-4pm Sat) Post office in Central Station.

TOURIST INFORMATION

Copenhagen Visitors Centre (70 22 24 42; www.visitcopenhagen.com; Vesterbrogade 4A, Vesterbro; 9am-8pm Jul-Sep, to 5pm Mon-Fri, to 2pm Sat Oct-Feb, to 5pm Mon-Fri, to 4pm Sat & Sun Mar-Jun; ; 2A, 5A, 9A, 12, 26, 250S, 350S, S-train København H) Copenhagen's excellent and informative information centre has a superb cafe and lounge with free wi-fi; it also sells the Copenhagen Card.

GETTING THERE & AWAY

AIR

If you're waiting for a flight at **Copenhagen Airport** (www.cph.dk; Lufthavnsboulevarden 6, Kastrup), note that this is a 'silent' airport and there are no boarding calls, although there are numerous monitor screens throughout the terminal.

BUS

Eurolines (33 88 70 00; www.eurolines.dk; Halmtorvet 5) operates buses to several European cities. The ticket office is behind Central Station. Long-distance buses leave from opposite the DGI-byen sports complex on Ingerslevsgade, just southwest of København H (Central Station). Destinations include Berlin (Dkr329, 7½ hours) and Paris (Dkr699, 19 to 22¼ hours).

TRAIN

DSB Billetsalg (DSB Ticket Office; 70 13 14 15; www.dsb.dk; Copenhagen Central Station, Bernstorffsgade 16-22; 7am-8pm Mon-Fri, 8am-6pm Sat & Sun) is best for reservations and for purchasing international train tickets.

GETTING AROUND

TO/FROM THE AIRPORT

The 24-hour metro (www.m.dk) runs every four to 20 minutes between the airport arrival terminal (the station is called Lufthavnen) and the eastern side of the city centre. It does not stop at København H (Central Station) but is handy for Christianshavn and Nyhavn (get off at Kongens Nytorv for Nyhavn). Journey time to Kongens Nytorv is 14 minutes (Dkr36).

By taxi, it's about 20 minutes between the airport and the city centre, depending on traffic. Expect to pay between Dkr250 and Dkr300.

Trains (www.dsb.dk) connect the airport arrival terminal to Copenhagen Central Station (København Hovedbanegården, commonly known as København H) around every 12 minutes. Journey time is 14 minutes (Dkr36). Check schedules at www.rejseplanen.dk.

BICYCLE

Copenhagen vies with Amsterdam as the world's most bike-friendly city. The superb, city-wide rental system is **Bycyklen** (City Bikes; www.bycyklen.dk). Visit the Bycyklen website for more information.

CAR & MOTORCYCLE

Except for the weekday-morning rush hour, when traffic can bottleneck coming into the city (and vice versa around 5pm), traffic in Copenhagen is generally manageable. Getting around by car is not problematic, except for the usual challenge of finding an empty parking space in the most popular places.

PUBLIC TRANSPORT

Copenhagen has an extensive public transit system consisting of a metro, rail, bus and ferry network. All tickets are valid for travel on the metro, buses and S-tog (S-train or local train) even though they look slightly different, depending on where you buy them. The free Copenhagen city maps that are distributed by the tourist office show bus routes (with numbers) and are very useful for finding your way around the city. Online, click onto the very handy www.rejseplanen.dk for all routes and schedules.

WALKING

The best way to see Copenhagen is on foot. There are few main sights or shopping quarters more than a 20-minute walk from the city centre.

In This Chapter

Van Gogh Museum 156
Anne Frank Huis 158
Sights 160
Activities 165
Tours 166
Shopping 166
Eating 167
Drinking & Nightlife 170
Entertainment 172
Information 173
Getting There & Away 174
Getting Around 174

Amsterdam, the Netherlands

Amsterdam works its fairy-tale magic in many ways: via the gabled, Golden Age buildings; glinting, boat-filled canals; and especially the cosy, centuries-old bruin cafés (traditional pubs), where candles burn low and beers froth high. Add in mega art museums and cool street markets, and it's easy to see why this atmospheric city is one of Europe's most popular getaways.

Two Days in Amsterdam

Ogle the masterpieces at the **Van Gogh Museum** (p157) and **Rijksmuseum** (p160) in the Old South and spend the afternoon in the city centre at the Begijnhof or Royal Palace. At night venture into the eye-popping Red Light District, then sip in a brown *café* such as **In 't Aepjen** (p170).

Start the next day at the **Albert Cuypmarkt** (p160) then head to the Southern Canal Ring for a canal boat tour. At night party at hyperactive **Leidseplein** (p164).

Four Days in Amsterdam

On day three head to the haunting **Anne Frank Huis** (p159) and spend the evening in the Jordaan for dinner and canalside drinks.

Begin your fourth day at **Museum het Rembrandthuis** (p161) or cycling around **Vondelpark** (p161), then mosey over to organic brewery **Brouwerij 't IJ** (p172), at the foot of a windmill.

After Amsterdam, hop on a train to Paris (p202), a mere 3¼ hours away, or fly just over an hour to Copenhagen (p136).

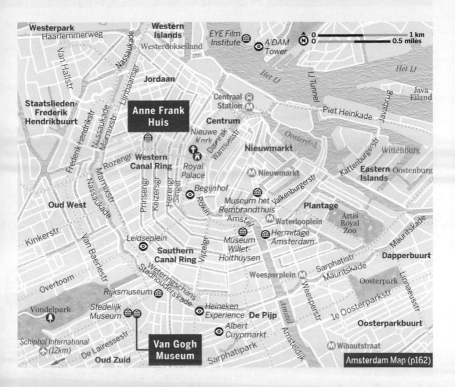

Amsterdam Map (p162)

Arriving in Amsterdam

Schiphol Airport Trains to Centraal Station depart every 10 minutes or so from 6am to 12.30am. The trip takes 17 minutes and costs €5.10; taxis cost €47.

Centraal Station Located in central Amsterdam. Most tram lines connect it to the rest of the city. Taxis queue near the front entrance.

Duivendrecht station Eurolines buses arrive here, south of the centre. Easy links to Centraal Station.

Where to Stay

Amsterdam has loads of accommodation in wild and wonderful spaces: inspired architects have breathed new life into old buildings, from converted schools and industrial lofts to entire rows of canal houses joined at the hip.

Hostels are plentiful, with most geared to youthful party animals. Hotels typically are small and ramble over several floors in charming old buildings.

For information on which neighbourhoods to stay in, see p176.

JEAFISH PING/SHUTTERSTOCK ©

Van Gogh Museum

The world's largest Van Gogh collection is a superb line-up of masterworks. Opened in 1973 to house the collection of Vincent's younger brother, Theo, the museum comprises some 200 paintings and 500 drawings by Vincent and his contemporaries.

Great For...

☑ Don't Miss

The Potato Eaters, The Yellow House, Wheatfield with Crows and *Sunflowers*.

Entrance & Set-Up

In 2015, a swish new extension and entrance hall added 800 sq metres of space to the museum, which now spreads over four levels, moving chronologically from Floor 0 (aka the ground floor) to Floor 3. It's still a manageable size; allow a couple of hours or so to browse the galleries. Seminal works to look for include the following.

Potato Eaters

Van Gogh's earliest works – shadowy and crude – are from his time in the Dutch countryside and in Antwerp between 1883 and 1885. He was particularly obsessed with peasants. *The Potato Eaters* (1885) is his most famous painting from this period.

Bible & Skeleton

Still Life with Bible (1885) is another early work, and it shows Van Gogh's religious

ⓘ Need to Know

📞 020-570 52 00; www.vangoghmuseum.
com; Museumplein 6; adult/child €17/free,
audio guide €5; ⊙9am-7pm Sun-Thu, to 9pm
Sat mid-Jul–Aug, to 6pm Sat-Thu Sep–mid-Jul,
to 5pm Jan-Mar, to 10pm Fri; 🚊2/3/5/12 Van
Baerlestraat

✖ Take a Break

Nibble on quiche and sip wine at the
museum cafe. Window tables overlook
the Museumplein.

★ Top Tip

Entrance queues can be long. Try
waiting until after 3pm or buy tickets
online and skip the queue.

inclination. The burnt-out candle is said to
represent the recent death of his father,
who was a Protestant minister. *Skeleton
with Burning Cigarette* (1886) was painted
when Van Gogh was a student at Antwerp's
Royal Academy of Fine Arts.

Self-Portraits

In 1886 Van Gogh moved to Paris, where his
brother, Theo, was working as an art dealer.
Vincent wanted to master the art of portraiture, but was too poor to pay for models.
Several self-portraits resulted. You can see
his palette begin to brighten as he comes
under the influence of the impressionists
in the city.

Sketchbooks & Letters

Intriguing displays enhance what's on
the walls. For instance, you might see Van
Gogh's actual sketchbook alongside an interactive kiosk that lets you page through a
reproduction of it. The museum has catego-
rised all of Van Gogh's letters online at www.
vangoghletters.org. Use the museum's free
wi-fi to access them with your smartphone.

Other Artists

Thanks to Theo van Gogh's prescient collecting and that of the museum's curators,
you'll also see works by Vincent's contemporaries, including Paul Gauguin, Claude
Monet and Henri de Toulouse-Lautrec.

Extras

The museum has multiple listening stations
for diverse recordings of Van Gogh's letters,
mainly to and from his closest brother
Theo, who championed his work. There
are daily workshops (for adults and kids)
where, suitably inspired, you can create
your own works of art.

Anne Frank Huis

It is one of the 20th century's most compelling stories: a young Jewish girl forced into hiding with her family and their friends to escape deportation by the Nazis. Walking through the bookcase-door is stepping back into a time that seems both distant and tragically real.

Great For...

☑ Don't Miss

Details including Anne's red-plaid diary, WWII news reels and a video of Anne's schoolmate Hanneli Gosler.

Background

It seems impossible now, but it's true: it took the German army just five days to occupy all of the Netherlands, along with Belgium and much of France. And once Hitler's forces had swept across the country, many Jews – like Anne Frank – eventually went into hiding. Anne's diary describes how restrictions were gradually imposed on Dutch Jews: from being forbidden to ride streetcars to being forced to turn in their bicycles and not being allowed to visit Christian friends.

The Franks moved into the upper floors of the specially prepared rear of the building, along with another couple, the Van Pels (called the Van Daans in Anne's diary), and their son Peter. Four months later Fritz Pfeffer (called Mr Dussel in the diary) joined the household. Here they survived until they were discovered by the Gestapo in August 1944.

Anne Frank sculpture by Mari S Andriessen

GIANNIS PAPANIKOS/SHUTTERSTOCK ©

ⓘ Need to Know

📱020-556 71 05; www.annefrank.org;
Prinsengracht 263-267; adult/child €9/4.50;
🕑9am-10pm Apr-Oct, 9am-7pm Sun-Fri, to
9pm Sat Nov-Mar; 🚋13/14/17 Westermarkt

✕ Take a Break

For pancakes and 18th-century atmosphere aplenty, stroll over to **'t Smalle**
(www.t-smalle.nl; Egelantiersgracht 12;
🕑10am-1am Sun-Thu, to 2am Fri & Sat).

★ Top Tip

Buying timed-entry tickets in advance
allows you to skip the queue entirely
and enter via a separate door (left of
the main entrance).

Ground Floor

After several renovations, the house itself
is now contained within a modern, square
shell that attempts to retain the original
feel of the building (it was used during
WWII as offices and a warehouse).

Offices & Warehouse

The building originally held Otto Frank's
pectin (a substance used in jelly-making)
business. On the lower floors you'll see the
former offices of Victor Kugler, Otto's business partner; and the desks of Miep Gies,
Bep Voskuijl and Jo Kleiman, all of whom
worked in the office and provided food,
clothing and other goods for the household.

Secret Annexe

The upper floors in the *achterhuis* (rear
house) contain the Secret Annexe, where
the living quarters have been preserved in

powerful austerity. As you enter Anne's small
bedroom, you can still sense the remnants
of a young girl's dreams: view the photos of
Hollywood stars and postcards of the Dutch
royal family that she pasted on the wall.

The Diary

More haunting exhibits and videos await after you return to the front house – including
Anne's red-plaid diary itself, sitting alone in
a glass case. Watch the video of Anne's old
schoolmate Hanneli Gosler, who describes
encountering Anne at Bergen-Belsen. Read
heartbreaking letters from Otto, the only
Secret Annexe occupant to survive the
concentration camps.

Renovations

In early 2017 a major renewal project began
at the museum, which will take two years.
The renovations include an expansion to allow more space for school groups and visitor facilities, as well as new displays. Anne
Frank Huis will remain open throughout.

⊙ SIGHTS

Rijksmuseum
Museum

(National Museum; ☑020-674 70 00; www.
rijksmuseum.nl; Museumstraat 1; adult/child
€17.50/free; ⊙9am-5pm; ☐2/5 Rijksmuseum)
The Rijksmuseum is the Netherlands'
premier art trove, splashing Rembrandts,
Vermeers and 7500 other masterpieces
over 1.5km of galleries. To avoid the biggest
crowds, come after 3pm. Or prebook tickets online, which provides fast-track entry.

The Golden Age works are the highlight.
Feast your eyes on still lifes, gentlemen in
ruffled collars and landscapes bathed in
pale yellow light. Rembrandt's *The Night
Watch* (1642) takes pride of place.

Heineken Experience
Brewery

(☑020-523 92 22; https://tickets.heineken
experience.com; Stadhouderskade 78; adult/child
self-guided tour €18/12.50, VIP guided tour €49,
Rock the City ticket €25; ⊙10.30am-7.30pm Mon-
Thu, to 9pm Fri-Sun; ☐16/24 Stadhouderskade)
On the site of the company's old brewery,
the crowning glory of this self-guided
'Experience' (samples aside) is a multimedia exhibit where you 'become' a beer by
getting shaken up, sprayed with water and
subjected to heat. True beer connoisseurs
will shudder, but it's a lot of fun. Admission
includes a 15-minute shuttle boat ride to
the Heineken Brand Store near Rembrandtplein. Prebooking tickets online saves you
€2 on the entry fee and allows you to skip
the ticket queues.

Albert Cuypmarkt
Market

(http://albertcuyp-markt.amsterdam; Albert
Cuypstraat, btwn Ferdinand Bolstraat & Van
Woustraat; ⊙9.30am-5pm Mon-Sat; ☐16/24
Albert Cuypstraat) The best place to marvel
at De Pijp's colourful scene is the Albert
Cuypmarkt, Amsterdam's largest and
busiest market. Vendors loudly tout their
odd gadgets and their arrays of fruit, vegetables, herbs and spices. They sell clothes
and other general goods too, often cheaper
than anywhere else. Snack vendors tempt
passers-by with herring sandwiches, egg
rolls, doughnuts and caramel-syrup-filled
stroopwafels. If you have room after all that,
the surrounding area teems with cosy cafes
and eateries.

Cyclists at the Rijksmuseum

MARINADA/SHUTTERSTOCK ©

Vondelpark   Park

(www.hetvondelpark.net; 🚊2/5 Hobbemastraat)
The lush urban idyll of the Vondelpark is
one of Amsterdam's most magical places
– sprawling, English-style gardens, with
ponds, lawns, footbridges and winding footpaths. On a sunny day, an open-air party
atmosphere ensues when tourists, lovers,
cyclists, in-line skaters, pram-pushing
parents, cartwheeling children, football-
kicking teenagers, spliff-sharing friends
and champagne-swilling picnickers all
come out to play.

Museum het
Rembrandthuis   Museum

(Rembrandt House Museum; 📞020-520 04 00;
www.rembrandthuis.nl; Jodenbreestraat 4; adult/
child €13/4; ⊘10am-6pm; 🚊9/14 Waterlooplein)
You almost expect to find the master
himself at the Museum het Rembrandthuis, where Rembrandt van Rijn ran the
Netherlands' largest painting studio, only to
lose the lot when profligacy set in, enemies
swooped and bankruptcy came a-knocking.
The museum has scores of etchings and
sketches. Ask for the free audio guide at
the entrance. You can buy advance tickets
online, though it's not as vital here as at
some of the other big museums.

Royal Palace   Palace

(Koninklijk Paleis; 📞020-522 61 61; www.
paleisamsterdam.nl; Dam; adult/child €10/free;
⊘10am-5pm; 🚊4/9/16/24 Dam) Opened as
a town hall in 1655, this building became
a palace in the 19th century. The interiors
gleam, especially the marble work – at
its best in a floor inlaid with maps of the
world in the great *burgerzaal* (citizens' hall),
which occupies the heart of the building.
Pick up a free audio tour at the desk after
you enter; it will explain everything you see
in vivid detail. King Willem-Alexander uses
the palace only for ceremonies; check the
website for periodic closures.

EYE Film Institute   Museum, Cinema

(📞589 14 00; www.eyefilm.nl; IJpromenade 1;
⊘10am-7pm Sat-Thu, to 9pm Fri; Ⓜ Amsterdam
Central) A modernist architectural triumph,

Exploring
the Jordaan

Though gentrified today, the Jordaan
was once a rough, densely populated
volksbuurt (district for the common
people) until the mid-20th century. That
history still shows amid the cosy pubs,
galleries and markets now squashed
into its grid of tiny lanes.

    The area doesn't have many tradi-
tional sights, but that's not the point.
It's the little things that are appealing
here – the narrow lanes, the old facades,
the funny little shops. The Jordaan is
about taking your time wandering and
not worrying if you get lost; nothing is
more quintessentially Amsterdam than
losing yourself in the labyrinth of narrow
streets and charming canals before
spending the evening in the neighbourhood's atmospheric brown *cafés*
(traditional pubs).

VERONIKA GALKINA/SHUTTERSTOCK ©

seeming to balance on its edge on the
banks of the river IJ (also pronounced
'eye'), movies from the 40,000-title archive
screen in four theatres, sometimes with
live music. Exhibits (admission €9 to €15)
of costumes, digital art and other cinephile
amusements run in conjunction with what's
playing. A view-tastic bar-restaurant with
a fabulously sunny terrace (when the sun
makes an appearance) is a popular hang-
out on this side of the river.

A'DAM Tower   Notable Building

(www.adamtoren.nl; Overhoeksplein 1; Lookout
adult/child €12.50/6.50, family ticket min 3

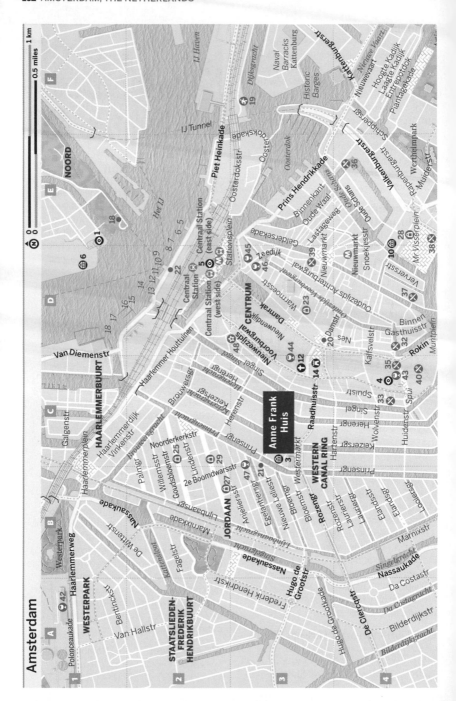

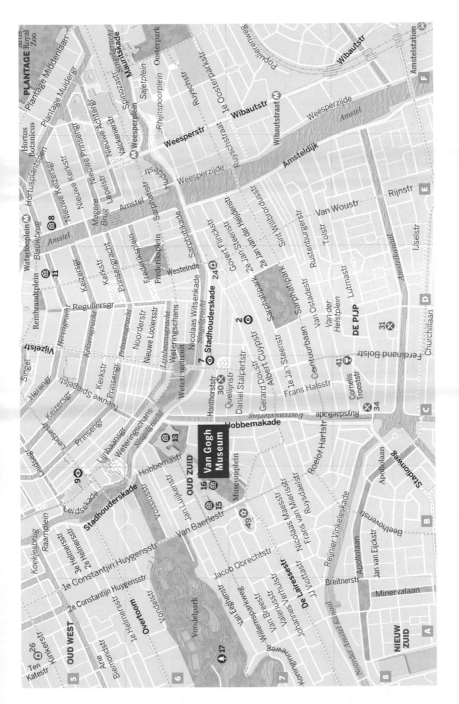

Amsterdam

◎ **Sights**
1 A'DAM Tower..E1
2 Albert Cuypmarkt.................................D7
3 Anne Frank Huis...................................... C3
4 Begijnhof.. C4
5 Centraal Station......................................D2
6 EYE Film Institute...................................D1
7 Heineken Experience............................. C6
8 Hermitage Amsterdam..........................E5
9 Leidseplein..B5
10 Museum het Rembrandthuis.................E4
11 Museum Willet-Holthuysen...................D5
12 Nieuwe Kerk.. C3
13 Rijksmuseum... C6
14 Royal Palace.. C3
15 Stedelijk Museum................................... B6
16 Van Gogh Museum................................. B6
17 Vondelpark...A6

⊕ **Activities, Courses & Tours**
18 Orangebike.. E1
19 Rederji Lampedusa..................................F3
20 Sandeman's New Amsterdam
    Tours.. D3
21 Those Dam Boat Guys C3
22 Wetlands Safari.......................................D2

🛍 **Shopping**
23 Condomerie Het Gulden Vlies.................D3
24 Hutspot D6
25 Lindengracht Market...............................C2

26 Local Goods Store...................................A5
27 Moooi Gallery.. B2
28 Waterlooplein Flea Market.....................E4
29 Westermarkt..C2

⊗ **Eating**
30 Bakers & Roasters C6
31 Ciel Bleu...D8
32 De Laatste Kruimel D4
33 D'Vijff Vlieghen C4
34 Fat Dog C8
35 Gartine... C4
36 Greetje... E4
37 Sterk Staaltje...D4
38 Tokoman E4
39 Tokoman D3
40 Vleminckx.. C4

◎ **Drinking & Nightlife**
41 Brouwerij Troost C8
42 Brouwerij Troost Westergas...................A1
43 Café de Dokter...C4
44 De Drie Fleschjes..................................... C3
45 In 't Aepjen D3
46 Proeflokaal de Ooievaar..........................D3
47 't Smalle... C3
    Twenty Third Bar.............................(see 31)

◎ **Entertainment**
48 Bitterzoet D3
49 Concertgebouw..B7

people from €20; ⏰Lookout 10am-10pm; 🚇Bad-
huiskade) The 22-storey building next to the
EYE Film Institute used to be Royal Dutch
Shell oil company offices. The oil people
would be hard pressed to recognise it now.
Take the trippy lift up to the large rooftop
for awe-inspiring views in all directions,
with large Fat Boy cushions on which
to lounge, a red model horse for surreal
photoshoots, and a giant four-person swing
that kicks out right over the edge for those
who have a head for heights (you're very
well secured and strapped in). There's a
swish bar for drinks and light meals and the
Moon revolving restaurant (book ahead)
on the 19th floor. There are also two dance
clubs (one up high, and one in the basement) and a funky hotel.

Hermitage Amsterdam   Museum
(📞530 74 88; www.hermitage.nl; Amstel 51;
adult/child incl audio guide €17.50/free, €25

combined ticket (all exhibitions) €2.50 with
Museum Card; ⏰10am-5pm; Ⓜ Waterlooplein,
🚋9/14 Waterlooplein) There have long been
links between Russia and the Netherlands
– Czar Peter the Great learned shipbuilding
here in 1697 – hence this local branch of
St Petersburg's State Hermitage Museum.
There are no permanent displays: huge
temporary exhibitions show work from the
Hermitage's vast treasure trove, such as
blockbuster shows on the Dutch Golden
Age. Come before 11am to avoid the length-
iest queues. Photography isn't permitted.

Leidseplein   Square
(🚋1/2/5/7/10 Leidseplein) Historic architecture, beer, plenty of tourists and an inordi-
nate number of steakhouses – welcome to
Leidseplein. Always busy, but coming into
its own after dark, this hyperactive square is
a major hub both for nightlife and for trams.
There are countless pubs and clubs, an aro-

ma of roasted meat, and masses of restaurants. Pavement cafes at the northern end are perfect for watching the human traffic, which gets crazier as the night goes on.

Museum
Willet-Holthuysen   Museum

(📞523 18 22; www.willetholthuysen.nl; Herengracht 605; adult/child €9/4.50, audioguide €1; ⏰10am-5pm Mon-Fri, from 11am Sat & Sun; Ⓜ️Waterlooplein, 🚊4/9/14 Rembrandtplein) This exquisite canal house was built in 1685 for Amsterdam mayor Jacob Hop, then remodelled in 1739. It's named after Louisa Willet-Holthuysen who inherited the house from her coal- and glass-merchant father, and lived a bohemian life here with her husband Abraham. She bequeathed the property to the city in 1895. It's a fascinating window into the world of the 18th-century super rich, with displays including part of the family's 275-piece Meissen table service, and the immaculate French-style garden.

Stedelijk Museum   Museum

(📞020-573 29 11; www.stedelijk.nl; Museumplein 10; adult/child €18.75/free; ⏰10am-6pm Sat-Thu, to 10pm Fri; 🚊2/3/5/12 Van Baerlestraat) This fabulous museum houses the collection amassed by postwar curator Willem Sandberg that makes up the National Museum of Modern Art. Displays rotate but you'll see an amazing selection featuring works by Picasso, Matisse, Mondrian, Van Gogh and more, plus great temporary exhibitions. The building was originally a bank, built in 1895 to a neo-Renaissance design by AM Weissman, and the modern extension is nicknamed 'the bathtub' for reasons obvious when you see it.

Nieuwe Kerk   Church

(New Church; 📞020-638 69 09; www.nieuwekerk.nl; Dam; €8-16; ⏰10am-6pm; 🚊1/2/5/13/14/17 Dam) This 15th-century, late-Gothic basilica – a historic stage for Dutch coronations – is only 'new' in relation to the Oude Kerk. A few monumental items dominate the otherwise spartan interior – a magnificent carved oak chancel, a bronze choir screen, a massive organ and enormous stained-glass windows. The building is now used for exhibitions and organ concerts. Opening times and admission fees can vary, depending on what's going on.

Begijnhof   Courtyard

(www.nicolaas-parochie.nl; off Gedempte Begijnsloot; ⏰9am-5pm; 🚊1/2/5 Spui) **FREE** This enclosed former convent dates from the early 14th century. It's a surreal oasis of peace, with tiny houses and postage-stamp gardens around a well-kept courtyard. The Beguines were a Catholic order of unmarried or widowed women who cared for the elderly and lived a religious life without taking monastic vows. The last true Beguine died in 1971.

❸ ACTIVITIES

Amsterdam has more canals than Venice and getting on the water is one of the best ways to feel the pulse of the city. You could catch the vibe by sitting canalside and watching boats glide by: myriad *cafés* seem purpose-built for this sport. Or you could stroll alongside the canals and check out some of the city's 2500 houseboats. Better yet, hop on a tour boat and cruise the curved passages.

There are more bicycles in Amsterdam than cars. Everyone rides: young, old, club-goers in high heels, cops on duty, bankers in suits with ties flapping in the breeze. Pedal power is what moves the masses to work, to shop and to socialise at the *cafés*. Renting a bike not only puts you shoulder to shoulder with locals but it gives you easy access to the city's outer neighbourhoods and their cool architecture and museums, as well the windmill-dotted countryside and its time-warped villages.

Rederji Lampedusa   Boating

(www.rederjilampedusa.nl; 1-2hr canal tour €17, VIP tours by donation; ⏰canal tours weekends, VIP tours Friday fortnightly May-Sept) Take a canal boat tour or a sunset trip around Amsterdam harbour in former refugee boats, brought from Lampedusa by Dutch founder Tuen. The tours are full of heart and offer a

Celebrating King's Day

A celebration of the House of Orange, **King's Day** (Koningsdag) sees more than 400,000 orange-clad people filling Amsterdam's streets for drinking and dancing. The city also becomes one big flea market, as people sell off all their unwanted junk.

For decades it was Queen's Day, but there's a new monarch in the house. So now it's King's Day, celebrated on King Willem-Alexander's birthday of April 27 (unless it falls on a Sunday, in which case it's celebrated the day before). Whatever the name, whatever the date, it's really just an excuse for a gigantic drinking fest and for everyone to wear ridiculous orange outfits, the country's national colour. There's also a free market citywide (where anyone can sell anything) and rollicking free concerts.

fascinating insight, not only into stories of contemporary migration, but also of how immigration shaped Amsterdam's history – especially the canal tour. Both leave from next to Mediamatic.

Wetlands Safari   Boating

(☑️06 5355 2669; www.wetlandssafari.nl; adult/child incl transport & picnic €59/33; ⊙9.30am Mon-Fri, 10am Sat & Sun early-Apr–late Sep) For a change from Amsterdam's canals, book an exceptional five-hour wetlands boat trip. Participants take a bus to just north of the centre, then canoe through boggy, froggy wetlands and on past windmills and 17th-century villages. Departure is from behind Centraal Station at the 'G' bus stop. Four-hour sunset tours (adult/child €51/29) depart at 5pm from early May to late August.

 TOURS

The following tours provide a good introduction to Amsterdam, particularly if you're short on time:

Sandeman's New Amsterdam Tours
(www.neweuropetours.eu; by donation; ⊙up to 8 tours daily; 🚊4/9/16/24 Dam) Pay-what-you-can walking tours that cover the Medieval Centre, Red Light District and Jordaan.

Those Dam Boat Guys (☑️06 1885 5219; www.thosedamboatguys.com; €25; ⊙11am, 1pm, 3pm, 5pm & 7pm Mar-Sep; 🚊13/14/17 Westermarkt) Low-key canal tours on small, electric boats where you bring your own picnic.

Orangebike (☑️646842083; www.orange-bike.nl; Buiksloterweg 5c; tours €22.50-37.50, hire per hr/day from €5/11; ⊙9am-6pm; 🚢Buiksloterweg) Easy cycling jaunts that take in the city's sights, architecture and windmills.

 SHOPPING

During the Golden Age, Amsterdam was the world's warehouse, stuffed with riches from the far corners of the earth. The capital's cupboards are still stocked with all kinds of exotica (just look at that Red Light gear!), but the real pleasure here is finding some odd, tiny shop selling something you wouldn't find anywhere else.

Hutspot   Design

(www.hutspotamsterdam.com; Van Woustraat 4; ⊙shop & cafe 10am-7pm Mon-Sat, noon-6pm Sun; 🛜; 🚊4 Stadhouderskade) Named after the Dutch dish of boiled and mashed vegies, 'Hotchpotch' was founded with a mission to give young entrepreneurs the chance to sell their work. As a result, this concept store is an inspired mishmash of Dutch-designed furniture, furnishings, art, homewares and clothing,` plus a barber and a cool in-store cafe as well as various pop-ups.

Moooi Gallery   Design

(☑️020-528 77 60; www.moooi.com; Westerstraat 187; ⊙10am-6pm Tue-Sat; 🚊3/10 Marnixplein) Founded by Marcel Wanders, this is Dutch design at its most over-the-top, from the life-sized black horse lamp to the 'blow away vase' (a whimsical twist on the classic

Delft vase) and the 'killing of the piggy bank' ceramic pig (with a gold hammer).

Condomerie Het
Gulden Vlies   Adult

(https://condomerie.com; Warmoesstraat 141; ⊙11am-9pm Mon & Wed-Sat, 11am-6pm Tue, 1-6pm Sun; 🚊4/9/14/16/24 Dam) Perfectly positioned for the Red Light District, this boutique sells condoms in every imaginable size, colour, flavour and design (horned devils, marijuana leaves, Delftware tiles...), along with lubricants and saucy gifts. Photos aren't allowed inside the shop.

Local Goods Store   Arts & Crafts

(www.localgoodsstore.nl; Hannie Dankbaar Passage 39, De Hallen; ⊙noon-7pm Tue-Fri & Sun, 11am-7pm Sat; 🚊17 Ten Katestraat) As the name implies, everything at this concept shop inside De Hallen is created by Dutch designers. Look for Woody skateboards, I Made Gin gin production kits, Carhusa purses and handbags, Timbies wooden bow ties, Lucila Kenny hand-dyed scarves and jewellery, and Neef Louis industrial vintage homewares, as well as racks of

great Dutch-designed casual men's and women's fashion.

🍴 EATING

Amsterdam's food scene is woefully underrated. Beyond pancakes and potatoes, Dutch chefs put their spin on all kinds of regional and global dishes using ingredients plucked from local seas and farms. Wherever you go, meals are something to linger over as the candles burn low on the tabletop.

Bakers & Roasters   Cafe €

(www.bakersandroasters.com; 1e Jacob van Campenstraat 54; dishes €7.50-15.50; ⊙8.30am-4pm; 🚊16/24 Stadhouderskade) Sumptuous brunch dishes served up at Brazilian/Kiwi-owned Bakers & Roasters include banana nutbread French toast with homemade banana marmalade and crispy bacon; Navajo eggs with pulled pork, avocado, mango salsa and chipotle cream; and a smoked salmon stack with poached eggs, potato cakes and hollandaise. Wash them

Canalside cafe

From left: *Frites* (fries); Canalside dining; Shops in an Amsterdam street

down with a fiery Bloody Mary. Fantastic pies, cakes and slices, too.

De Laatste Kruimel   Cafe, Bakery €

(☎020-423 04 99; www.delaatstekruimel.nl; Langebrugsteeg 4; dishes €3.50-7.50; ⏰8am-8pm Mon-Sat, 9am-8pm Sun; 🚊4/9/14/16/24 Spui/Rokin) Decorated with vintage objects from the Noordermarkt and wooden pallets upcycled as furniture, and opening to a tiny canalside terrace, the 'Last Crumb' has glass display cases piled high with pies, quiches, breads, cakes and lemon poppy-seed scones. Grandmothers, children, couples on dates and just about everyone else crowds in for the fantastic organic sandwiches and treats.

Gartine   Cafe €

(☎020-320 41 32; www.gartine.nl; Taksteeg 7; dishes €6.50-11.50; high tea €17.50-24.75; ⏰10am-6pm Wed-Sat; 🖊; 🚊4/9/14/16/24 Spui/Rokin) 🖋 Gartine is magical, from its covert location in an alley off busy Kalverstraat to its mismatched antique tableware and its sublime breakfast pastries, sandwiches and salads (made from produce grown in its garden plot and eggs from its

chickens). The sweet-and-savoury high tea, from 2pm to 5pm, is a treat.

Fat Dog   Hot Dogs €

(www.thefatdog.nl; Ruysdaelkade 251; dishes €4.50-12; ⏰noon Wed-Sun; 🚊12 Cornelis Troostplein) Überchef Ron Blaauw, of **Ron Gastrobar** (☎020-496 19 43; www.rongastrobar.nl; Sophialaan 55; dishes €15, desserts €9; ⏰noon-2.30pm & 5.30-10.30pm; 🛜; 🚊2 Amstelveenseweg), elevates the humble hot dog to an art form. Ultra-gourmet options include Naughty Bangkok (pickled vegetables, red curry mayo and dry crispy rice); Vive La France (fried mushrooms, foie gras and truffle mayo); Gangs of New York (sauerkraut, bacon and smoked-onion marmalade) and Vega Gonzalez (vegetarian sausage, corn, guacamole, sour cream and jalapeño mayo).

Vleminckx   Fast Food €

(http://vleminckxdesausmeester.nl; Voetboogstraat 33; fries €2.30-4.50, sauces €0.70; ⏰noon-7pm Sun & Mon, 11am-7pm Tue, Wed, Fri & Sat, 11am-8pm Thu; 🚊1/2/5 Koningsplein) Frying up *frites* (fries) since 1887, Vleminckx has been based at this hole-in-the-wall

takeaway shack near the Spui since 1957. The standard is smothered in mayonnaise, though its 28 different sauces also include apple, green pepper, ketchup, peanut, sambal and mustard. Queues often stretch down the block but move fast.

Tokoman South American €

(Waterlooplein 327; sandwiches €3-4.50, dishes €6.50-13.50; ☉11am-8pm Mon-Sat; 🚋9/14 Waterlooplein) Queue with the folks getting their Surinamese spice on at Tokoman. It makes a sensational *broodje pom* (a sandwich filled with a tasty mash of chicken and a starchy Surinamese tuber). You'll want the *zuur* (pickled-cabbage relish) and *peper* (chilli) on it, plus a cold can of coconut water to wash it down.

Sterk Staaltje Deli €

(www.sterkstaaltje.com; Staalstraat 12; dishes €4-7.60; ☉8am-7pm Mon-Fri, 8am-6pm Sat, 11am-5pm Sun; 🚋4/9/14/16/24 Muntplein) With pristine fruit and veg stacked up outside, Sterk Staaltje is worth entering just to breathe in the scent of the foodstuffs, with a fine range of ready-to-eat treats: teriyaki meatballs, feta and sundried

tomato quiche, pumpkin-stuffed wraps, a soup of the day, and particularly fantastic sandwiches (roast beef, horseradish and rucola; marinated chicken with guacamole and sour cream).

Ciel Bleu Gastronomy €€€

(☎020-450 67 87; www.okura.nl; Hotel Okura Amsterdam, Ferdinand Bolstraat 333; mains €45-120, 6-course menu €160, with paired wines €255; ☉6.30-10.30pm Mon-Sat; 🚋12 Cornelius Trootsplein) Mindblowing, two-Michelin-star creations at this pinnacle of gastronomy change with the seasons; spring, for instance, might see scallops and oysters with vanilla sea salt and gin-and-tonic foam, king crab with salted lemon, beurre blanc ice cream and caviar, or saddle of lamb with star anise. Just as incomparable is the 23rd-floor setting with aerial views north across the city.

D'Vijff Vlieghen Dutch €€€

(☎020-530 40 60; http://vijffvlieghen.nl; Spuistraat 294-302; mains €23.50-29.25; ☉6-10pm; 🚋1/2/5 Spui) Spread across five 17th-century canal houses, the 'Five Flies' is a classic. Old-wood dining rooms are full

Amsterdam's Best Markets

Albert Cuypmarkt (p160) Europe's largest daily (except Sunday) street market spills over with food, fashion and bargain finds.

Waterlooplein Flea Market (www.waterlooplein.amsterdam; Waterlooplein; ☺9.30am-6pm Mon-Sat; 🚊9/14 Waterlooplein) Piles of curios, used footwear and cheap bicycle parts for treasure hunters.

Westermarkt (www.jordaanmarkten.nl; Westerstraat; ☺9am-1pm Mon; 🚊3/10 Marnixplein) Bargain-priced clothing and fabrics at 163 stalls.

Lindengracht Market (www.jordaanmarkten.nl; Lindengracht; ☺9am-4pm Sat; 🚊3 Nieuwe Willemsstraat) Wonderfully authentic local affair, with bushels of fresh produce.

IJ Hallen (www.ij-hallen.nl; Tt Neveritaweg 15; €5; ☺9am-4.30pm Sat & Sun monthly; 🚤NDSM-werf) The monthly flea market at NDSM-werf is Europe's largest.

Camera stall at Waterlooplein Flea Market
IVICA DRUSANY/SHUTTERSTOCK ©

---

of character, featuring Delft-blue tiles and original works by Rembrandt; chairs have coppers plates inscribed with the names of its famous guests (Walt Disney, Mick Jagger...). Exquisite dishes span goose breast with apple, sauerkraut and smoked butter to candied haddock with liquorice sauce.

Greetje
Dutch €€€

(☎779 74 50; www.restaurantgreetje.nl; Peperstraat 23-25; mains €23-27; ☺6-10pm Sun-Fri, to 11pm Sat; 🚊22/34/35/48 Prins Hendrikkade) 🍴

Using market-fresh, organic produce, Greetje resurrects and re-creates traditional Dutch recipes like pickled beef, braised veal with apricots and leek *stamppot* (traditional mashed potatoes and vegetables), and pork belly with Dutch mustard sauce. A good place to start is the two-person Big Beginning (€15 per person), with a sampling of hot and cold starters.

🍷 DRINKING & NIGHTLIFE

Amsterdam is one of the wildest nightlife cities in Europe and the world, and the testosterone-fuelled stag parties of young chaps roaming the Red Light District know exactly what they're doing here. Yet you can easily avoid the hardcore party scene if you choose to: Amsterdam remains a *café* (pub) society where the pursuit of pleasure centres on cosiness and charm.

For the quintessential Amsterdam experience, pull up a stool in one of the city's famed brown *cafés*. The true specimen has been in business a while and gets its name from the centuries' worth of smoke stains on the walls. Brown *cafés* have candle-topped tables, sandy wooden floors and sometimes a house cat that sidles up for a scratch. Most importantly, they induce a cosy vibe that prompts friends to linger and chat for hours over drinks – the same enchantment the *cafés* have cast for 300 years.

In 't Aepjen
Brown Cafe

(Zeedijk 1; ☺noon-1am Mon-Thu, to 3am Fri & Sat; 🚊1/2/4/5/9/13/16/17/24 Centraal Station) Candles burn even during the day in this 15th-century building – one of two remaining wooden buildings in the city – which has been a tavern since 1519: in the 16th and 17th centuries it served an inn for sailors from the Far East, who often brought *aapjes* (monkeys) to trade for lodging. Vintage jazz on the stereo enhances the time-warp feel.

Amsterdam Roest
Beer Garden

(www.amsterdamroest.nl; Jacob Bontiusplaats 1; ☺noon-1am Sun-Thu, to 3pm Fri & Sat; 🚊22 Wittenburgergracht) This is one of those 'only in

Brown *café*

Amsterdam' places, and well worth the trip to what were derelict shipyards and now host an epically cool artist collective/bar/restaurant, Amsterdam Roest (Dutch for 'Rust'), with a canalside terrace, mammoth playground of ropes and tyres, hammocks, street art, a sandy beach in summer and bonfires in winter.

It's slightly tricky to find; the most direct approach is to go along Oostenburgervoorstraat and cross the bridge at the northern end – it's 150m ahead on your left.

Pllek Bar

(www.pllek.nl; TT Neveritaweg 59; ⊙9.30am-1am Sun-Thu, to 3am Fri & Sat; ⚓NDSM-werf) Ubercool Pllek is one of the key destinations in the Noord, with hip things of all ages streaming over to hang out in its interior made out of old shipping containers, and lie out on its artificial sandy beach. It's a terrific spot for a waterfront beer or glass of wine. Locals flock here for events, too: al fresco film screenings on Tuesday nights in summer, weekend yoga classes and dance parties under the giant disco ball.

Brouwerij Troost Brewery

(☑020-760 58 20; http://brouwerijtroost.nl; Cornelis Troostplein 21; ⊙4pm-1am Mon-Thu, 4pm-3am Fri, 2pm-3am Sat, 2pm-midnight Sun; 🖭; 🚊12 Cornelis Troostplein) ⚑ Watch beer being brewed in copper vats behind a glass wall at this outstanding craft brewery. Its dozen beers include a summery blonde, smoked porter, strong tripel, and deep-red Imperial IPA; it also distils cucumber and juniper gin and serves fantastic bar food including crispy prawn tacos and humongous burgers. Book ahead on weekend evenings.

Café de Dokter Brown Cafe

(www.cafe-de-dokter.nl; Rozenboomsteeg 4; ⊙4pm-1am Wed-Sat; 🚊1/2/5 Spui) Candles flicker on the tables, old jazz records play in the background, and chandeliers and a birdcage hang from the ceiling at atmospheric Café de Dokter, which is said to be Amsterdam's smallest pub. Whiskies and smoked beef sausage are the specialities. A surgeon opened the bar in 1798, hence the name. His descendants still run it.

Vats at the Heineken Experience (p160)

Proeflokaal de Ooievaar — Distillery

(www.proeflokaaldeooievaar.nl; St Olofspoort 1; ☺noon-midnight; 🚊1/2/4/5/9/13/16/17/24 Centraal Station) Not much bigger than a vat of *jenever*, this magnificent little tasting house has been going strong since 1782. On offer are 14 *jenevers* and liqueurs (such as Bride's Tears with gold and silver leaf) from the De Ooievaar distillery, still located in the Jordaan. Despite appearances, the house has not subsided but was built leaning over.

De Drie Fleschjes — Distillery

(www.dedriefleschjes.nl; Gravenstraat 18; ☺4-8.30pm Mon-Wed, 2-8.30pm Thu-Sat, 3-7pm Sun; 🚊1/2/5/13/14/17 Dam) A treasure dating from 1650, with a wall of barrels made by master shipbuilders, the tasting room of distiller Bootz specialises in liqueurs including its signature almond-flavoured *bitterkoekje* (Dutch-style macaroon) liqueur, as well as superb *jenever* (Dutch gin). Take a peek at the collection of *kalkoentjes:* small bottles with hand-painted portraits of former mayors.

Brouwerij 't IJ — Brewery

(www.brouwerijhetij.nl; Funenkade 7; ☺brewery 2-8pm, English tour 3.30pm Fri-Sun; 🚊10 Hoogte Kadijk) ✔ Beneath the creaking sails of the 1725-built De Gooyer windmill, Amsterdam's leading organic microbrewery produces delicious (and often very potent) standard, seasonal and limited-edition brews. Pop in for a beer in the tiled tasting room, lined by an amazing bottle collection, or on the plane tree–shaded terrace. A beer is included in the 30-minute brewery tour (€5).

⊕ ENTERTAINMENT

Amsterdam supports a flourishing arts scene, with loads of big concert halls, theatres, cinemas and other performance venues filled on a regular basis. Music fans will be in their glory, as there's a fervent subculture for just about every genre, especially jazz, classical and avant-garde beats.

Concertgebouw — Classical Music

(✆671 83 45; www.concertgebouw.nl; Concertgebouwplein 10; ☺box office 1-7pm Mon-Fri, 10am-

7pm Sat & Sun; 🚊3/5/12/16/24 Museumplein)
Bernard Haitink, former conductor of the
venerable Royal Concertgebouw Orchestra,
once remarked that the world-famous
hall (built in 1888 with near-perfect
acoustics) was the orchestra's best
instrument. Free half-hour concerts take
place every Wednesday at 12.30pm from
mid-September to late June; arrive early.
Try the **Last Minute Ticket Shop** (www.
lastminuteticketshop.nl; ⊗online ticket sales
from 10am on day of performance; 🚊1/2/5/7/10
Leidseplein) for half-price seats to all other
performances.

Bitterzoet   Live Music
(☑020-421 23 18; www.bitterzoet.com; Spuistraat 2; ⊗8pm-late; 🚊1/2/5/13/17 Nieuwezijds
Kolk) Always full, always changing, this
venue with a capacity of just 350 people
is one of the friendliest venues in town,
with a diverse crowd. Music (sometimes
live, sometimes a DJ) can be funk, roots,
drum'n'bass, Latin, Afro-beat, old-school
jazz or hip-hop groove.

ℹ INFORMATION

DISCOUNT CARDS
Visitors of various professions, including artists,
journalists, museum conservators and teachers,
may get discounts at some venues if they show
accreditation.

Students regularly get a few euros off museum admission; bring ID.

Seniors over 65, and their partners of 60 or
older, benefit from reductions on public transport, museum admissions, concerts and more.
You may look younger, so bring your passport.

I Amsterdam Card (per 24/48/72 hours
€49/59/69) Provides admission to more than
30 museums (though not the Rijksmuseum), a
canal cruise, and discounts at shops, entertainment venues and restaurants. Also includes
a GVB transit pass. Useful for quick visits to
the city. Available at VVV I Amsterdam Visitor
Centres and some hotels.

Museumkaart (adult/child €55/27.50, plus for
first-time registrants €5) Free and discounted

🗨 Gezellig Culture

This particularly Dutch quality, which
is most widely found in old brown *cafés*
(traditional pubs), is one of the best reasons to visit Amsterdam. It's variously
translated as snug, friendly, cosy, informal and convivial, but *gezelligheid* – the
state of being *gezellig* – is something
more easily experienced than defined.
You can get this warm and fuzzy feeling
in many places and situations, often
while nursing a brew with friends. And
nearly any cosy establishment lit by
candles probably qualifies.

entry to some 400 museums all over the country
for one year. Purchase at participating museum
ticket counters or at Uitburo ticket shops.

Holland Pass (2/4/6 attractions €42/62/82)
Similar to the I Amsterdam Card, but without the
rush for usage; you can visit sights over a month.
Prices are based on the number of attractions,
which you pick from tiers (the most popular/
expensive sights are gold tier). Also includes a
train ticket from the airport to the city, and a
canal cruise. Available from GWK Travelex offices
and various hotels.

EMERGENCY NUMBERS
Police, fire, ambulance ☑112

LEGAL MATTERS
⊙ Technically, marijuana is illegal. However,
possession of soft drugs (eg cannabis) up to
5g is tolerated. Larger amounts are subject to
prosecution.

Dutch Etiquette

Greetings Do give a firm handshake and a double or triple cheek kiss.

Marijuana and alcohol Don't smoke dope or drink beer on the streets.

Smoking Don't smoke cigarettes in bars or restaurants.

Bluntness Don't take offence if locals give you a frank, unvarnished opinion. It's not considered impolite; rather it comes from the desire to be direct and honest.

Cycling paths Don't walk in bike lanes (which are marked by white lines and bicycle symbols), and do look both ways before crossing a bike lane.

○ Don't light up in an establishment other than a *coffeeshop* (cafe authorised to sell cannabis) without checking that it's OK to do so.

○ Never buy drugs of any kind on the street.

MONEY

ATMs are widely available. Credit cards are accepted in most hotels but not all restaurants; non-European credit cards are sometimes rejected.

TIPPING

Bars Not expected.

Hotels €1 to €2 per bag for porters; not typical for cleaning staff.

Restaurants Leave 5% to 10% for a cafe snack (if your bill comes to €9.50, you might round up to €10) and 10% or so for a restaurant meal.

Taxis Tip 5% to 10%, or round up to the nearest euro.

OPENING HOURS

Hours can vary by season. Our listings depict operating times for peak season (from around May to September). Opening hours often decrease during off-peak months.

GETTING THERE & AWAY

Schiphol International Airport (AMS; www.schiphol.nl) is among Europe's busiest airports and has copious air links worldwide, including many on low-cost European airlines. It's the hub of Dutch passenger carrier KLM.

National and international trains arrive at **Centraal Station** (Stationsplein; 🚃1/2/4/5/9/13/16/17/24 Centraal Station). There are good links with several European cities. The high-speed Thalys (www.thalys.com) runs from Paris (3¼ hours direct, 3¾ hours via Brussels) nearly every hour between 6am and 7pm. Eurostar (www.eurostar.com) runs from London (around five hours); it stops in Brussels, where you transfer onward via Thalys.

Eurolines (www.eurolines.nl; Rokin 38a; ⊙9am-5pm Mon-Sat; 🚃4/9/14/16/24 Dam) buses connect with all major European capitals. Bus travel is typically the cheapest way to get to Amsterdam.

Flights, cars and tours can be booked online at lonelyplanet.com/bookings.

GETTING AROUND

GVB passes in chip-card form are the most convenient option for public transport. Buy them at visitor centres or from tram conductors. Always wave your card at the pink machine when entering and departing.

Walking Central Amsterdam is compact and very easy to cover by foot.

Bicycle This is the locals' main mode of getting around. Rental companies are all over town; bikes cost about €11 per day.

Tram Fast, frequent and ubiquitous, operating between 6am and 12.30am.

Bus and Metro Primarily serve the outer districts; not much use in the city centre.

Ferry Free ferries depart for northern Amsterdam from docks behind Centraal Station.

Taxi Expensive and not very speedy given Amsterdam's maze of streets.

Where to Stay

Book as far in advance as possible, especially in summer and for weekends at any time of the year. Apartment rentals work well for local-life areas such as the Jordaan and De Pijp.

Neighbourhood	Atmosphere
Medieval Centre & Red Light District	In the thick of the action and close to everything. Can be noisy, touristy and seedy; not great value for money.
Nieuwmarkt, Plantage & the Eastern Islands	Nieuwmarkt is near the action, but with a slightly more laid-back vibe than the Centre. Some parts are close enough to the Red Light District to get rowdy spillover.
Western Canal Ring	Tree-lined canals within walking distance of Amsterdam's most popular sights. Rooms book out early and can be pricey.
Southern Canal Ring	Swanky hotels, not far from the restaurants of Utrechtsestraat and the antique shops of Nieuwe Spiegelstraat. Can be loud, crowded, pricey and touristy.
Jordaan & the West	Cosy cafes, quirky shops and charming village character, though sleeping options are few.
Vondelpark & the Old South	Genteel, leafy streets; walking distance to Museumplein; lots of midrange options and cool design hotels.
De Pijp	Ongoing explosion of dining/drinking cool in the area. Easy walking distance to Museumplein, Vondelpark and Leidseplein, but a hike from the Centre.
Oosterpark & South Amsterdam	Lower prices due to location (which is really just a short tram/metro ride away); a quiet area amid locals.

In This Chapter

National Museum 178
Blue Lagoon 180
Golden Circle 182
Sights 184
Activities 189
Shopping......................................190
Eating.. 191
Drinking & Nightlife.......................195
Entertainment 197
Information 197
Getting There & Away 198
Getting Around 198

Reykjavík, Iceland

Reykjavík is loaded with captivating art, rich cuisine and quirky, creative people. The music scene is epic, with excellent festivals, creative DJs gigging and any number of home-grown bands.

Even if you come for a short visit, be sure to take a trip to the countryside. Tours and services abound, and understanding Reykjavík and its people is helped by understanding the vast, raw and gorgeous land they anchor. The majority of Icelanders live in the capital, but you can guarantee their spirits also roam free across the land. Absorb what you see, hear, taste and smell – it's all part of Iceland's rich heritage.

Two Days in Reykjavík

Spend your first morning exploring historic **Old Reykjavík** (p188) and your afternoon wandering up arty **Skólavörðustígur** (p184), shopping and sightseeing. Head to **Laugavegur** (p191) for dinner, drinks and late-night dancing.

On your second day, catch a **whale-watching cruise** (p189) or explore the **Old Harbour** (p185) and its museums in the morning. While away the afternoon at **Laugardalur** (p190) and your evening at a top Icelandic restaurant, such as **Dill** (p191).

Four Days in Reykjavík

On your third day, rent a bike at the Old Harbour and ferry out to historic **Viðey** (p194). Come back in time for last-minute shopping around **Laugavegur** (p190) and **Skólavörðustígur** (p190). Sample the area's seafood before catching a show, an Icelandic movie or some live music.

On your final day take a trip to the **Golden Circle** (p182). If you haven't the time to visit the **Blue Lagoon** (p180) coming or going from the airport, go late this evening, after the crowds have dwindled.

After Reykjavík, catch a three-hour flight to London (p48) or Dublin (p114).

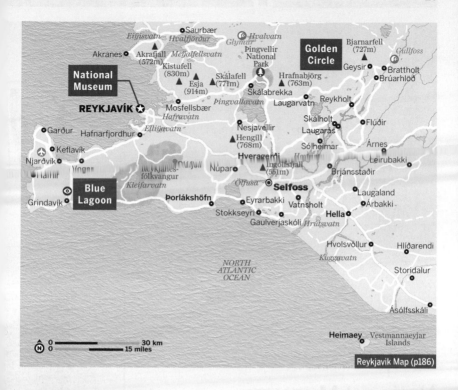

Reykjavik Map (p186)

Arriving in Reykjavík

Keflavík International Airport Iceland's primary international airport is 48km west of Reykjavík.

Reykjavík Domestic Airport Only a 2km walk into town.

Smyril Line (www.smyrilline.com) operates a pricey but well-patronised weekly car ferry from Hirsthals (Denmark) through Tórshavn (Faroe Islands) to Seyðisfjörður in East Iceland. It's possible to make a stopover in the Faroes.

Where to Stay

Reykjavík has loads of accommodation choices, with hostels, midrange guesthouses (often with shared bathrooms, kitchen and lounge) and business-class hotels galore, but top-end boutique hotels and apartments seem to be opening daily. Reservations are essential from June through August and prices are high. Plan for hostels, camping or short-term apartment rentals to save money. Most places open year-round and many offer discounts or variable pricing online.

For information on what each neighbourhood has to offer, see the table on p199.

National Museum

Iceland's premier museum is packed with artefacts and interesting displays. Exhibits give an excellent overview of the country's history and culture, and the audio guide (kr300) adds loads of detail.

The superb National Museum beautifully displays Icelandic artefacts from settlement to the modern age, providing a meaningful overview of Iceland's history and culture. Brilliantly curated exhibits lead you through the struggle to settle and organise the forbidding island, the radical changes wrought by the advent of Christianity, the lean times of domination by foreign powers and Iceland's eventual independence.

Great For...

 Don't Miss

The gaming pieces made from cod ear bones, and the wooden doll that doubled as a kitchen utensil.

Settlement Era Finds

The premier section of the museum describes the Settlement Era – including how the chieftains ruled and the introduction of Christianity – and features swords, meticulously carved **drinking horns**, and **silver hoards**. A powerful **bronze figure of Thor** is thought to date from about 1000. The priceless 13th-century **Valþjófsstaðir**

ⓘ Need to Know

Þjóðminjasafn Íslands; 530 2200; www.
nationalmuseum.is; Suðurgata 41; adult/child
kr1500/free; ⏰10am–5pm May–mid-Sep,
closed Mon mid-Sep–Apr; 🚌1, 3, 6, 12, 14

✕ Take a Break

The ground-floor **Museum Café** (snacks
kr600-1800; ⏰10am–5pm May–mid-Sep,
9am–5pm Tue-Fri, 11am–5pm Sat & Sun mid-
Sep–Apr; 🛜) offers wi-fi and a welcome
respite.

★ Top Tip

Free English tours run at 11am on
Wednesdays, Saturdays and Sundays
from May to mid-September.

---

church door is carved with the story of
a knight, his faithful lion and a passel of
dragons.

Domestic Life

Exhibits explain how the chieftains ruled
and how people survived on little, lighting
their dark homes and fashioning bog iron.
There's everything from the remains of
early *skyr* (yoghurt-like dessert) production
to intricate pendants and brooches. Look
for the Viking-era **hnefatafl game set** (a
bit like chess); this artefact's discovery in a
grave in Baldursheimar led to the founding
of the museum.

Viking Graves

Encased in the floor, you'll find Viking-era
graves, with their precious burial goods:
horse bones, a sword, pins, a ladle and
a comb. One of the tombs containing an
eight-month-old infant is the only one of its
kind ever found.

Ecclesiastical Artefacts

The section of the museum that details
the introduction of Christianity is chock-a-
block with rare art and artefacts, such as
the priceless 13th-century **Valþjófsstaðir
church door**.

The Modern Era

Upstairs, collections span from 1600 to
today and give a clear sense of how Iceland
struggled under foreign rule, finally gained
independence and went on to modernise.
Look for the **papers and belongings of
Jón Sigurðsson**, the architect of Iceland's
independence.

Blue Lagoon

In a magnificent black-lava field, this scenic spa is fed water from the futuristic Svartsengi geothermal plant. With its silver towers, roiling clouds of steam and people daubed in white silica mud, it's an other-worldly place.

Great For...

☑ Don't Miss

A bike or quad-bike tour in the lava fields.

A Good Soak

Before your dip, don't forget to practise standard Iceland pool etiquette: naked pre-pool showering.

The super-heated spa water (70% sea water, 30% fresh water) is rich in blue-green algae, mineral salts and fine silica mud, which condition and exfoliate the skin – it sounds like advertising speak, but you really do come out as soft as a baby's bum. The water is hottest near the vents where it emerges, and the surface is several degrees warmer than the bottom.

Towel or bathing-suit hire is €5.

Explore the Complex

The lagoon has been developed for visitors with an enormous, modern complex of changing rooms (with 700 lockers!),

RAYINTS/SHUTTERSTOCK ©

Need to Know

Bláa Lónið; ☎420 8800; www.bluelagoon.com; adult/child Jun-Aug from €50/free, Sep-May from €40/free; 8am-midnight Jun–mid-Aug, reduced hours mid-Aug–May

Take a Break

Try the on-site **Blue Café** (snacks kr1000-2100; 8am-midnight Jun–mid-Aug, reduced hours mid-Aug–May;) or **LAVA Restaurant** (mains lunch/dinner kr4500/5900; 11.30am-9.30pm Jun-Aug, to 8.30pm Sep-May;).

★ Top Tip

Avoid summertime between 10am and 2pm – go early or after 7pm.

restaurants and a gift shop. It is also landscaped with hot-pots, steam rooms, sauna, a silica mask station, a bar and a piping-hot waterfall that delivers a powerful hydraulic massage. A VIP section has its own interior wading space, lounge and viewing platform.

Massage

For extra relaxation, lie on a floating mattress and have a massage therapist knead your knots (30/60 minutes €75/120). Book spa treatments well in advance; look online for packages and winter rates.

Guided Tours

In addition to the spa opportunities at the Blue Lagoon, you can combine your visit with package tours, or hook up with nearby **ATV Adventures** (☎857 3001; www.atv4x4.is) for quad-bike or cycling tours (kr5900 from the Blue Lagoon through the lava fields) or bicycle rental. The company can pick you up and drop you off at the lagoon.

Planning Your Visit

Many day trips from Reykjavík tie in a visit to the lagoon, which is 47km southwest of the city. It's also seamless to visit on your journey to/from Keflavík International Airport – there's a luggage check in the car park (kr600 per bag, per day).

You should book ahead or risk being turned away. On a tour, always determine whether your ticket for the lagoon is included or if you need to book it separately.

Reykjavík Excursions (Kynnisferðir; ☎580 5400; www.re.is; BSÍ Bus Terminal, Vatnsmýrarvegur 10) and **Bustravel** (☎511 2600; www.bustravel.is) connect the lagoon with Reykjavík and the airport.

Gullfoss waterfall

F11PHOTO/SHUTTERSTOCK ©

Golden Circle

The Golden Circle is a beloved tourist circuit that takes in three popular attractions all within 100km of the capital: Þingvellir, Geysir and Gullfoss.

The Golden Circle offers the opportunity to see a meeting-point of the continental plates and the site of the ancient Icelandic parliament (Þingvellir), a spouting hot spring (Geysir) and a roaring waterfall (Gullfoss), all in one doable-in-a-day loop.

Visiting under your own steam allows you to visit at off-hours and explore exciting attractions further afield. Almost every tour company in the Reykjavík area offers a Golden Circle excursion, which can often be confined with virtually any activity from quad-biking to caving and rafting.

If you're planning to spend the night in the relatively small region, Laugarvatn is a good base with excellent dining options.

Þingvellir National Park

Þingvellir National Park (www.thingvellir. is), 40km northeast of central Reykjavík,

Great For...

☑ **Don't Miss**

The Sigríður memorial near the foot of the stairs from the Gullfoss visitors centre.

Þingvellir National Park

EINAR/GETTY IMAGES ©

ℹ Need to Know

Tours generally go from 8.30am to 6pm or from noon to 7pm. In summer there are evening trips from 7pm to midnight.

✕ Take a Break

Eateries, mini-marts and grocery stores dot the route.

★ Top Tip

To go on to West Iceland afterwards, complete the Circle backwards, finishing with Þingvellir.

very reliable **Strokkur** geyser sits alongside. You rarely have to wait more than five to 10 minutes for the hot spring to shoot an impressive 15m to 30m plume before vanishing down its enormous hole. Stand downwind only if you want a shower.

The geothermal area containing Geysir and Strokkur was free to enter at the time of writing, though there is discussion of instituting a fee.

Gullfoss

Iceland's most famous waterfall, **Gullfoss** (Golden Falls; www.gullfoss.is) FREE is a spectacular double cascade. It drops 32m, kicking up tiered walls of spray before thundering away down a narrow ravine. On sunny days the mist creates shimmering rainbows, and it's also magical in winter when the falls glitter with ice.

A tarmac path suitable for wheelchairs leads from the tourist information centre to a lookout over the falls, and stairs continue down to the edge. There is also an access road down to the falls.

is Iceland's most important historical site and a place of vivid beauty. The Vikings established the world's first democratic parliament, the Alþingi, here in AD 930. The meetings were conducted outdoors and, as with many Saga sites, there are only the stone foundations of ancient encampments. The site has a superb natural setting with rivers and waterfalls in an immense, fissured rift valley, caused by the meeting of the North American and Eurasian tectonic plates.

Geysir

One of Iceland's most famous tourist attractions, **Geysir** FREE (gay-zeer; literally 'gusher') is the original hot-water spout after which all other geysers are named. Earthquakes can stimulate activity, though eruptions are rare. Luckily for visitors, the

⊙ SIGHTS

⊙ Laugavegur & Skólavörðustígur

This district is Reykjavík's liveliest. While it's justifiably well known for its shops and pubs, it's also home to some of the city's top restaurants, local music venues and the city's top art-house cinema.

Hallgrímskirkja Church

(☑510 1000; www.hallgrimskirkja.is; Skólavörðustígur; tower adult/child kr900/100; ⊙9am-9pm Jun-Sep, to 5pm Oct-May) Reykjavík's immense white-concrete church (1945–86), star of a thousand postcards, dominates the skyline, and is visible from up to 20km away. Get an unmissable view of the city by taking an elevator trip up the 74.5m-high tower. In contrast to the high drama outside, the Lutheran church's interior is quite plain. The most eye-catching feature is the vast 5275-pipe organ installed in 1992.

> *sparkling Harpa concert hall and cultural centre is a beauty to behold*

Harpa Arts Centre

(☑box office 528 5050; www.harpa.is; Austurbakki 2; ⊙8am-midnight, box office 10am-6pm) With its ever-changing facets glistening on the water's edge, Reykjavík's sparkling Harpa concert hall and cultural centre is a beauty to behold. In addition to a season of top-notch shows (some free), it's worth stopping by to explore the shimmering interior with harbour vistas, or take one of the guided tours and visit areas not open to the general public (see website for daily times and prices).

Culture House Gallery

(Þjóðmenningarhúsið; ☑530 2210; www.culturehouse.is; Hverfisgata 15; adult/child kr1200/free; ⊙10am-5pm May–mid-Sep, closed Mon mid-Sep–Apr) This superbly curated exhibition covers the artistic and cultural heritage of Iceland from settlement to today. Priceless artefacts are arranged by theme, and highlights include 14th-century manuscripts, contemporary art and items including the skeleton of a great auk (now extinct). The renovated 1908 building is beautiful, with great views of the harbour, and a cafe on the ground floor. Check website for free guided tours.

Harpa

National Gallery of Iceland
Museum

(Listasafn Íslands; ☑515 9600; www.listasafn. is; Fríkirkjuvegur 7; adult/child kr1500/free; ☉10am-5pm mid-May–mid-Sep, 11am-5pm Tue-Sun mid-Sep–mid-May) This pretty stack of marble atriums and spacious galleries overlooking Tjörnin offers ever-changing exhibits drawn from the 10,000-piece collection. The museum can only exhibit a small sample at any time; shows range from 19th- and 20th-century paintings by Iceland's favourite sons and daughters (including Jóhannes Kjarval and Nína Sæmundsson) to sculptures by Sigurjón Ólafsson and others.

◉ Old Harbour

Largely a service harbour until recently, the **Old Harbour** (Geirsgata; ☐1, 3, 6, 11, 12, 13, 14) has blossomed into a hotspot for tourists, with several museums, volcano and Northern Lights films, and excellent restaurants. Whale-watching and puffin-viewing trips depart from the pier.

Omnom Chocolate
Factory

(☑519 5959; www.omnomchocolate.com; Hólmaslóð 4, Grandi; adult/child kr3000/1500; ☉8am-5pm Mon-Fri) Reserve ahead for a tour at this full-service chocolate factory where you'll see how cocoa beans are transformed into high-end scrumptious delights. The shop sells its bonbons and stylish bars, with specially designed labels and myriad sophisticated flavours. You'll find the bars in shops throughout Iceland.

Víkin Maritime Museum
Museum

(Víkin Sjóminjasafnið; ☑517 9400; www. maritimemuseum.is; Grandagarður 8; adult/child kr1500/free; ☉10am-5pm; ☐14) Based appropriately in a former fish-freezing plant, this museum celebrates the country's seafaring heritage, focusing on the trawlers that transformed Iceland's economy. Guided tours go aboard coastguard ship *Óðinn* (kr1200, or joint ticket with museum kr2200; check website for times).

The on-site **cafe** (snacks kr800-2200; ☉10am-5pm) offers relaxing views of the

 Reykjavík Art Museum

The excellent **Reykjavík Art Museum** (Listasafn Reykjavíkur; www.artmuseum. is; adult/child kr1600/free) is split over three well-done sites: the large, modern downtown **Hafnarhús** (☑411 6400; Tryggvagata 17; ☉10am-5pm Fri-Wed, to 10pm Thu) focusing on contemporary art; **Kjarvalsstaðir** (☑411 6420; Flókagata 24, Miklatún Park; ☉10am-5pm), in a park just east of Snorrabraut, and displaying rotating exhibits of modern art; and **Ásmundarsafn** (Ásmundur Sveinsson Museum; ☑411 6430; ☉10am-5pm May-Sep, 1-5pm Oct-Apr; ☐2, 5, 15, 17), a peaceful haven near Laugardalur for viewing sculptures by Ásmundur Sveinsson.

One ticket is good at all three sites, and if you buy after 3pm you get a 50% discount should you want a ticket the next day.

Reykjavík Art Museum
IMAGE COURTESY OF REYKJAVÍK ART MUSEUM ©

boat-filled harbour, and has a great sunny-weather terrace.

Saga Museum
Museum

(☑511 1517; www.sagamuseum.is; Grandagarður 2; adult/child kr2100/800; ☉10am-6pm; ☐14) The endearingly bloodthirsty Saga Museum is where Icelandic history is brought to life by eerie silicon models and a multilanguage soundtrack with thudding axes and hair-raising screams. Don't be surprised if you see some of the characters wandering around town, as moulds were taken from Reykjavík residents (the owner's daughters

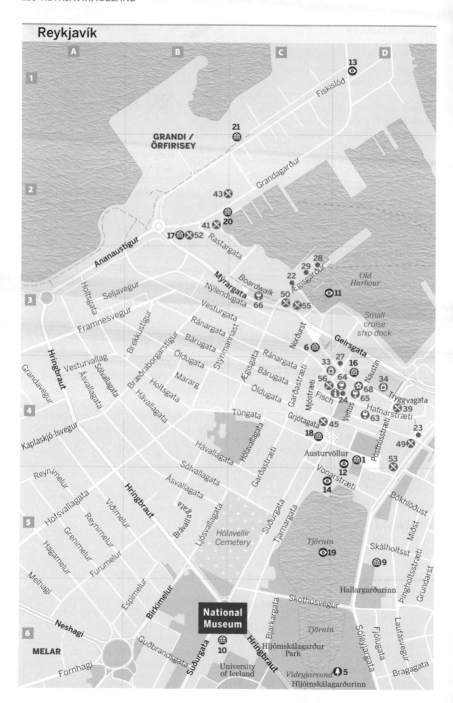

Reykjavík

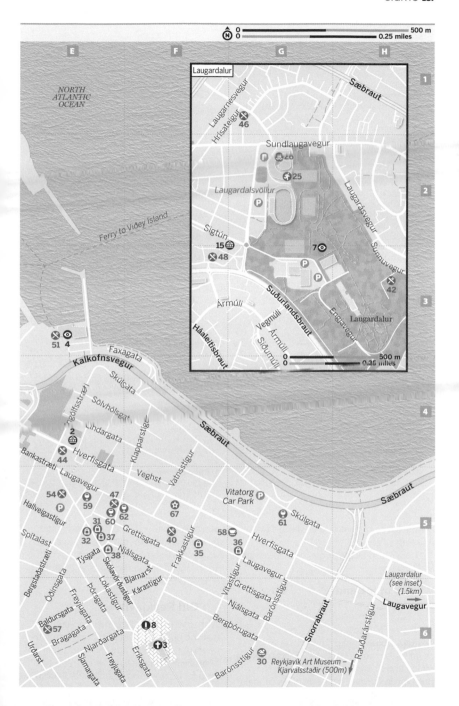

Reykjavík

◉ Sights
1 Alþingi	D4
2 Culture House	E4
3 Hallgrímskirkja	F6
4 Harpa	E3
5 Hljómskálagarður Park	D6
6 i8	C3
7 Laugardalur	G3
8 Leifur Eiríksson Statue	F6
9 National Gallery of Iceland	D5
10 National Museum	B6
11 Old Harbour	C3
12 Old Reykjavík	D4
13 Omnom Chocolate	D1
14 Ráðhús	C5
15 Reykjavík Art Museum – Ásmundarsafn	G2
16 Reykjavík Art Museum – Hafnarhús	D4
17 Saga Museum	B2
18 Settlement Exhibition	C4
19 Tjörnin	C5
20 Víkin Maritime Museum	B2
21 Whales of Iceland	C2

◕ Activities, Courses & Tours
22 Elding Adventures at Sea	C3
23 Free Walking Tour Reykjavik	D4
24 Haunted Iceland	D4
25 Laugar Spa	G2
26 Laugardalslaug	G2
27 Literary Reykjavík	D4
28 Reykjavík Bike Tours	C3
29 Reykjavík By Boat	C3
30 Sundhöllin	G6

⊟ Shopping
31 12 Tónar	E5
32 Geysir	E5
33 Kirsuberjatréð	C4
34 Kolaportið Flea Market	D4
35 Kron	F5

36 KronKron	G5
37 Orrifinn	E5
38 Skúmaskot	E5

◆ Eating
39 Bæjarins Beztu	D4
40 Bakarí Sandholt	F5
41 Bryggjan Brugghús	B2
42 Café Flóra	H3
43 Coocoo's Nest	B2
44 Dill	E4
45 Fiskmarkaðurinn	C4
46 Frú Lauga	G1
47 Gló	E5
48 Gló Street Food	F3
49 Grillmarkaðurinn	D4
50 Hamborgara Búllan	C3
51 Kolabrautin	E3
52 Matur og Drykkur	B2
53 Messinn	D4
National Museum Café	(see 10)
54 Ostabúðin	E5
55 Sægreifinn	C3
56 Stofan Kaffihús	C4
57 Þrír Frakkar	E6
Víkin Cafe	(see 20)

◔ Drinking & Nightlife
58 Kaffi Vínyl	G5
59 Kaffibarinn	E5
60 Kaldi	E5
61 KEX Bar	G5
62 Kiki	F5
63 Loftið	D4
64 Micro Bar	D4
Mikkeller & Friends	(see 44)
65 Paloma	D4
66 Slippbarinn	C3

✪ Entertainment
67 Bíó Paradís	F5
68 Húrra	D4

are the Irish princess and the little slave gnawing a fish!).

There's also a cafe and a room for posing in Viking dress.

Whales of Iceland Museum

(☎571 0077; www.whalesoficeland.is; Fiskislóð 23-25; adult/child kr2900/1500; ◷10am-6pm Jun-Aug, to 5pm Sep-May; ▢14) Ever strolled beneath a blue whale? This museum houses full-sized models of the 23 whales found off Iceland's coast. The largest museum of this type in Europe, it also displays models

of whale skeletons, and has good audio guides and multimedia screens to explain what you're seeing. It has a cafe and gift shop, online ticket discounts and family tickets (kr5800).

◉ Old Reykjavík

With a series of sights and interesting historic buildings, Old Reykjavík forms the heart of the capital, and the focal point of many historic walking tours. It's a top area for a stroll, from scenic lake Tjörnin to the old-fashioned houses surrounding Austurvöllur and Ingólfstorg squares.

Settlement Exhibition   Museum
(Landnámssýningin; ☑411 6370; www.reykjavik museum.is; Aðalstræti 16; adult/child kr1500/ free; ◷9am-6pm) This fascinating archaeological ruin/museum is based around a 10th-century **Viking longhouse** unearthed here from 2001 to 2002, and other settlement-era finds from central Reykjavík. It imaginatively combines technological wizardry and archaeology to give a glimpse into early Icelandic life.

Tjörnin   Lake
This placid lake at the centre of the city is sometimes locally called the Pond. It echoes with the honks and squawks of over 40 species of visiting birds, including swans, geese and Arctic terns; feeding the ducks is a popular pastime for the under-fives. Pretty sculpture-dotted parks like **Hljómskálagarður** FREE line the southern shores, and their paths are much used by cyclists and joggers. In winter hardy souls strap on ice skates and turn the lake into an outdoor rink.

i8   Gallery
(☑551 3666; www.i8.is; Tryggvagata 16; ◷11am-5pm Tue-Fri, 1-5pm Sat) FREE This gallery represents some of the country's top modern artists, many of whom show overseas as well.

Alþingi   Historic Building
(Parliament; ☑563 0500; www.althingi.is; Kirkjustraeti) FREE Iceland's first parliament, the Alþingi, was created at Þingvellir in AD 930. After losing its independence in the 13th century, the country gradually won back its autonomy, and the modern Alþingi moved into this current basalt building in 1881; a stylish glass-and-stone annexe was completed in 2002. Visitors can attend **sessions** (mid-September to early June; see website for details) when parliament is sitting.

On the northern shore, the postmodern **Ráðhús** (Vonarstræti; ◷8am-4pm Mon-Fri) FREE (city hall) has an interesting topo-map of Iceland inside.

⊕ ACTIVITIES

Creative Iceland   Art
(☑615 3500; www.creativeiceland.is) Get involved with graphic design, cooking, arts, crafts, music...you name it. This service hooks you up with local creative people offering workshops in their art or craft.

Literary Reykjavík   Walking
(www.bokmenntaborgin.is; Tryggvagata 15; ◷3pm Thu Jun-Aug) FREE Part of the Unesco City of Literature initiative, free literary walking tours of the city centre start at the main library and include the Dark Deeds tour focusing on crime fiction. There is also a downloadable *Culture Walks* app with several themes.

Sundhöllin   Geothermal Pool, Hot-Pot
(☑411 5350; Barónsstigur 16; adult/child kr900/140; ◷6.30am-10pm Mon-Thu, to 8pm Fri, 8am-4pm Sat, 10am-6pm Sun; ⊕) Reykjavík's oldest swimming pool (1937), designed in art deco style by architect Guðjón Samúelsson, is smack in the city centre and offers the only indoor pool within the city, plus Hallgrímskirkja views from the decks. It's been recently renovated.

Elding Adventures at Sea   Wildlife
(☑519 5000; www.whalewatching.is; Ægisgarður 5; adult/child kr9900/4950; ◷harbour kiosk 8am-9pm; ☐14) ✦ The city's most established and ecofriendly outfit, with an included whale exhibition and refreshments sold on board. Elding also offers angling (adult/child kr13,800/6900) and puffin-watching (adult/child from kr6500/3250) trips and combo tours, and runs the ferry to Viðey. Offers pick-up.

Reykjavík Bike Tours   Cycling
(Reykjavík Segway Tours; ☑bike 694 8956, segway 897 2790; www.icelandbike.com; Ægisgarður 7, Old Harbour; bike rental per 4hr from kr3500, tours from kr6500; ◷9am-5pm Jun-Aug, reduced hours Sep-May; ☐14) This outfitter rents out bikes and offers tours of Reykjavík and the countryside: Classic Reykjavík (2½ hours, 7km), Coast of Reykjavík (2½ hours, 18km), and Golden Circle and Bike (eight hours,

Laugardalur: Hot-Springs Valley

Encompassing a verdant stretch of land 4km east of the city centre, **Laugardalur** (🚌2, 5, 14, 15, 17) was once the main source of Reykjavík's hot-water supply: it translates as 'Hot-Springs Valley', and in the park's centre you'll find relics from the old wash house. The park is a favourite with locals for its huge **swimming complex** (🖉411 5100; Sundlaugavegur 30a; adult/child kr900/140, suit/towel rental kr850/570; ⏰6.30am-10pm Mon-Fri, 8am-10pm Sat & Sun; 🚼), fed by the geothermal spring, alongside a **spa** (🖉553 0000; www. laugarspa.com; Sundlaugavegur 30a; day pass kr5490; ⏰6am-11.30pm Mon-Fri, 8am-10pm Sat, to 8pm Sun), skating rink, botanical gardens, sporting and concert arenas, and a kids' zoo/entertainment park.

Stop by the sun-dappled tables of **Café Flóra** (Flóran; 🖉553 8872; www.flo ran.is; Botanic Gardens; cakes kr950, mains kr1400-3000; ⏰10am-10pm May-Sep; 🍴) 🌿 for lovely food made from wholesome local ingredients – some grown in the gardens themselves! Soups come with fantastic sourdough bread, and snacks range from cheese platters with nuts and honey to pulled-pork sandwiches. Weekend brunch, good coffee and homemade cakes round it all out.

In the surrounding residential streets you'll find **Frú Lauga farmers market** (🖉534 7165; www.frulauga.is; Laugalækur 6; ⏰11am-6pm Mon-Fri, to 4pm Sat; 🍴) 🌿 and Reykjavík Art Museum – Ásmundarsafn (p185).

25km of cycling in 1½ hours). It also offers Reykjavík Segway (kr12,500) and walking (from kr20,000) tours. Most convenient place to rent a bike before catching the ferry to Viðey island.

Reykjavík By Boat   Boating
(🖉841 2030; www.reykjavikbyboat.is; Ægisgarður 11; adult/child kr4500/2200; 🚌14) Offers a 1½-hour boat trip on a small wooden boat from the Old Harbour, around Engey islet (with a puffin colony), to Viðey and back.

Free Walking Tour Reykjavik   Walking
(www.freewalkingtour.is; ⏰noon & 2pm Jun-Aug, reduced hours winter) **FREE** One-hour, 1.5km walking tour of the city centre, starting at the little clock tower on Lækjartorg Sq.

Haunted Iceland   Walking
(www.hauntedwalk.is; adult/child kr2500/free; ⏰8pm Sat-Thu Jun-early Sep) Ninety-minute tour, including folklore and ghost spotting, departing from the Main Tourist Office.

🛍 SHOPPING

Laugavegur and Skólavörðustígur are the central streets of Reykjavík's shopping scene. You'll find them lined with everything from stereotypical souvenir shops (derisively called 'Puffin Shops' by Reykjavíkers) to design shops and galleries selling beautiful handmade Icelandic arts and crafts, couture clothing lines and cool outdoorwear.

Geysir   Clothing
(🖉519 6000; www.geysir.com; Skólavörðustígur 16; ⏰9am-10pm) For traditional Icelandic clothing and unique modern designs, Geysir boasts an elegant selection of sweaters, blankets, and men's and women's clothes, shoes and bags.

KronKron   Clothing
(🖉562 8388; www.kronkron.com; Laugavegur 63b; ⏰10am-6pm Mon-Thu, to 6.30pm Fri, to 5pm Sat) This is where Reykjavík goes high fashion, with the likes of Marc Jacobs and Vivienne Westwood. But we really enjoy its Scandinavian designers (including Kron by KronKron) offering silk dresses, knit capes, scarves and even woollen underwear. Its handmade shoes are off the charts; the shoes are also sold down the street at **Kron** (🖉551 8388; www.kron.is; Laugavegur 48; ⏰10am-6pm Mon-Thu, to 6.30pm Fri, to 5pm Sat).

Orrifinn   Jewellery
(🖉789 7616; www.facebook.com/OrrifinnJewels; Skólavörðustígur 17a; ⏰10am-6pm Mon-Fri, to

4pm Sat) Subtle, beautiful jewellery captures the natural wonder of Iceland and its Viking history. Delicate anchors, axes and pen nibs dangle from understated matte chains.

Skúmaskot
Arts & Crafts

(☑663 1013; www.facebook.com/skumaskot. art.design/; Skólavörðustígur 21a; ⊙10am-6pm Mon-Fri, to 5pm Sat, noon-4pm Sun) Ten local designers create these unique handmade porcelain items, women's and kids' clothing, paintings and cards. It's in a recently renovated large gallery beautifully showcasing their creative Icelandic crafts.

Kolaportið Flea Market
Market

(www.kolaportid.is; Tryggvagata 19; ⊙11am-5pm Sat & Sun) Held in a huge industrial building by the harbour, this weekend market is a Reykjavík institution. There's a huge tumble of secondhand clothes and old toys, plus cheap imports. There's also a food section that sells traditional eats like *rúgbrauð* (geothermally baked rye bread), *brauðterta* ('sandwich cake'; a layering of bread with mayonnaise-based fillings) and *hákarl* (fermented shark).

Kirsuberjatréð
Arts & Crafts

(Cherry Tree; ☑562 8990; www.kirs.is; Vesturgata 4; ⊙10am-7pm & 8-10pm Mon-Fri, to 5pm Sat, to 4pm Sun) This women's art-and-design collective in an interesting 1882 former bookshop sells weird and wonderful fish-skin handbags, music boxes made from string and, our favourite, beautiful coloured bowls made from radish slices.

🗙 EATING

🗙 Laugavegur & Skólavörðustígur

The area around Laugavegur and Skólavörðustígur is packed with eateries, from chilled-out old-school coffeehouses to high-concept Nordic cuisine. Places get crowded in high season, so book ahead if there's somewhere you don't want to miss.

Bakarí Sandholt
Bakery €

(☑551 3524; www.sandholt.is; Laugavegur 36; snacks kr600-1200; ⊙7am-9pm; 🛜) Reykjavík's favourite bakery is usually crammed with folks hoovering up the

KronKron

TSUGULIEV/SHUTTERSTOCK ©

Hallgrímskirkja (p184)

generous assortment of fresh baguettes, croissants, pastries and sandwiches. The soup of the day (kr1540) comes with delicious sourdough bread.

Ostabúðin   Deli €€
(Cheese Shop; ☑562 2772; www.facebook.com/
Ostabudin/; Skólavörðustígur 8; mains kr3600-
5000; ⊙restaurant 11.30am-9pm Mon-Fri,
noon-9pm Sat & Sun, deli 10am-6pm Mon-Thu, to
7pm Fri, 11am-4pm Sat) Head to this gourmet
cheese shop and deli, with a large dining
room, for the friendly owner's cheese and
meat platters (from kr1900 to kr4000),
or the catch of the day, accompanied by
homemade bread. You can pick up other
local goods, like terrines and duck confit,
on the way out.

Gló   Organic, Vegetarian €€
(☑553 1111; www.glo.is; Laugavegur 20b; mains
kr1200-2000; ⊙11am-10pm Mon-Fri, 11.30am-
10pm Sat & Sun; 🛜🍴) Join the cool cats in
this upstairs, airy restaurant serving fresh,
large daily specials loaded with Asian-
influenced herbs and spices. Though not
exclusively vegetarian, it's a wonderland

of raw and organic foods with your choice
from a broad bar of elaborate salads, from
root vegies to Greek. It also has branches
in **Laugardalur** (Engjateigur 19; ⊙11am-9pm
Mon-Fri; 🛜🍴) 🍴 and **Kópavogur** (Hæðasmári
6; ⊙11am-9pm Mon-Fri, 11.30am-9pm Sat & Sun;
🛜🍴) 🍴.

Dill   Icelandic €€€
(☑552 1522; www.dillrestaurant.is; Hverfisgata
12; 5-course meal from kr11,900; ⊙6-10pm
Wed-Sat) Top 'New Nordic' cuisine is the
major drawcard at this elegant yet simple
bistro. The focus is very much on the food –
locally sourced produce served as a parade
of courses. The owners are friends with
Copenhagen's famous Noma clan, and take
Icelandic cuisine to similarly heady heights.
Reservation is a must.

Þrír Frakkar   Icelandic, Seafood €€€
(☑552 3939; www.3frakkar.com; Baldursgata
14; mains kr4000-6000; ⊙11.30am-2.30pm &
6-10pm Mon-Fri, 6-11pm Sat & Sun) Owner-chef
Úlfar Eysteinsson has built up a consistently excellent reputation at this snug
little restaurant – apparently a favourite of

Jamie Oliver's. Specialities range throughout the aquatic world from salt cod and halibut to *plokkfiskur* (fish stew) with black bread. Non-fish items run towards guillemot, horse, lamb and whale.

Old Harbour

The Old Harbour and nearby Grandi are burgeoning with great spots to eat. Seafood restaurants line the harbour, but it's also a top neighborhood for refined Icelandic cuisine, and some of the best burgers in town.

Sægreifinn   Seafood €

(Seabaron; ☑553 1500; www.saegreifinn.is; Geirsgata 8; mains kr1350-1900; ☉11.30am-11pm mid-May–Aug, to 10pm Sep–mid-May) Sidle into this green harbourside shack for the most famous lobster soup (kr1350) in the capital, or to choose from a fridge full of fresh fish skewers to be grilled on the spot.

Hamborgara Búllan   Burgers €

(Hamborgarabúlla Tómasar; ☑511 1888; www.bullan.is; Geirsgata 1; mains kr1200-1800; ☉11.30am-9pm; 🛜🚻) The Old Harbour's outpost of burgerdom and Americana proffers savoury patties that are perennial local favourites.

Coocoo's Nest   Cafe €€

(☑552 5454; www.coocoosnest.is; Grandagarður 23; mains kr1700-4500; ☉11am-10pm Tue-Sat, to 4pm Sun; 🛜) Pop into this cool eatery tucked behind the Old Harbour for popular weekend brunches (dishes kr1700 to kr2200; 11am to 4pm Friday to Sunday) paired with decadent cocktails (kr1300). Casual, small and groovy, with mosaic plywood tables; the menu changes and there is nightly themes, but it's always scrumptious.

Matur og Drykkur   Icelandic €€

(☑571 8877; www.maturogdrykkur.is; Grandagarður 2; lunch mains kr1900-3200, dinner menus kr3000-5000; ☉11.30am-3pm Mon-Sat, 6-10.30pm Tue-Sat; 🚌14) One of Reykjavík's top high-concept restaurants, Matur Og Drykkur means 'Food and Drink', and you surely will be plied with the best of

 Reykjavík's Best Festivals

Secret Solstice (www.secretsolstice.is; ☉Jun) This excellent music festival with local and international acts coincides with the summer solstice, so there's 24-hour daylight for partying. It's held at Reykjavík's Laugardalur.

Reykjavík Culture Night (www.menningarnott.is; ☉Aug) On Menningarnótt, held mid-month, Reykjavíkers turn out in force for a day and night of art, music, dance and fireworks. Many galleries, ateliers, shops, cafes and churches stay open until late. Your chance to get sporty and sophisticated on the one day, this event is held on the same date as the city's marathon.

Reykjavík International Film Festival (www.riff.is; ☉Sep-Oct) This intimate 11-day event from late September features quirky programming that highlights independent film-making, both home-grown and international.

Iceland Airwaves (www.icelandairwaves.is; ☉Nov) You'd be forgiven for thinking Iceland is just one giant music-producing machine. Since the first edition of Iceland Airwaves was held in 1999, this fab festival has become one of the world's premier annual showcases for new music (Icelandic or otherwise).

Crowd during Secret Solstice
MATTHEW EISMAN/GETTY IMAGES ©

both. The brainchild of brilliant chef Gísli Matthías Auðunsson, who creates inventive versions of traditional Icelandic fare. Book ahead in high season and for dinner.

Day Trip to Viðey

On fine-weather days, the tiny uninhabited island of Viðey (www.reykjavik museum.is) makes a wonderful day trip. Just 1km north of Reykjavík's Sundahöfn Harbour, it feels a world away. Well-preserved historic buildings, surprising modern art, an abandoned village and great birdwatching add to its remote spell.

Iceland's oldest stone house, **Viðe-yarstofa**, is just above the harbour. Icelandic Treasurer Skúli Magnússon was given the island in 1751 and he built Viðeyarstofa as his residence. There's also an interesting 18th-century wooden **church**, the second oldest in Iceland, with some original decor and Skúli's tomb (he died here in 1794). Excavations of the old **monastery foundations** unearthed 15th-century wax tablets and a runic love letter, now in the National Museum.

Just northwest along the coast, Yoko Ono's **Imagine Peace Tower** (2007) is a 'wishing well' that blasts a dazzling column of light into the sky every night between 9 October (John Lennon's birthday) and 8 December (the anniversary of his death). Further along, **Viðeyjarnaust day-hut** has a barbecue for use if you bring all your own supplies.

There are usually free **guided walks** in summer. Check online for the current schedule.

Viðey Ferry (☑533 5055; www.videy. com; return adult/child kr1200/600; ☺from Skarfabakki hourly 10.15am-5.15pm mid-May–Sep, weekends only Oct–mid-May) takes five minutes from Skarfabakki, 4.5km east of the city centre. During summer, two boats a day start from Elding at the Old Harbour and the Harpa concert hall. Bus 16 stops closest to Skarfabakki, and it's a point on the Reykjavík hop-on-hop-off tour bus.

Bryggjan Brugghús   Pub Food €€

(☑456 4040; www.bryggjanbrugghus. is; Grandagarður 8; mains kr2300-5000; ☺11am-midnight Sun-Thu, to 1am Sat & Sun, kitchen 11.30am-11pm; ☎) This enormous, golden-lit microbrewery and bistro is a welcome pit stop for one of its home-brewed beers (start with IPA, lager and seasonal beers, from 12 taps) or for an extensive menu of seafood and meat dishes, and occasional DJs. You've also got great harbour views out the back windows.

✪ Old Reykjavík

You'll find some of the city's highest-end restaurants in the Old Reykjavík area, where you should book ahead in high season to guarantee a table. On the other hand, you'll also encounter Reykjavík's famed hot-dog stand, **Bæjarins Beztu** (www.bbp.is; Tryggvagata; hot dogs kr420; ☺10am-2am Sun-Thu, to 4.30am Fri & Sat; ♿), and other food trucks set up in Lækjartorg Sq – everything from lobster soup to fish and chips or doughnuts.

Stofan Kaffihús   Cafe €

(☑546 1842; www.facebook.com/stofan.cafe/; Vesturgata 3; dishes kr1500-1600; ☺9am-11pm Mon-Wed, to midnight Thu-Sat, 10am-10pm Sun; ☎) This laid-back cafe in an historic brick building has a warm feel with its worn wooden floors, plump couches and spacious main room. Settle in for coffee, cake or soup, and watch the world go by.

Messinn   Seafood €€

(☑546 0095; www.messinn.com; Lækjargata 6b; lunch mains kr1900-2100, dinner mains kr2500-3800; ☺11.30am-3pm & 5-10pm; ☎) Make a beeline to Messinn for the best seafood that Reykjavík has to offer. The speciality is amazing pan-fries where your pick of fish is served up in a sizzling cast-iron skillet accompanied by buttery potatoes and salad. The mood is upbeat and comfortable, and the staff friendly.

Grillmarkaðurinn   Fusion €€€

(Grill Market; ☑571 7777; www.grillmarka durinn.is; Lækjargata 2a; mains kr4600-7000;

Grillmarkaðurinn

⊘11.30am-2pm Mon-Fri, 6-10.30pm Sun-Thu, to 11.30pm Fri & Sat) From the moment you enter the glass atrium here, high-class dining is the order of the day. Service is impeccable, and locals and visitors alike rave about the food. locally sourced Icelandic ingredients prepared with culinary imagination by master chefs. The tasting menu (kr10,400) is an extravaganza of its best dishes.

Fiskmarkaðurinn   Seafood €€€

(Fishmarket; ☑578 8877; www.fiskmarkadurinn.is; Aðalstræti 12; mains kr5100-5700; ⊘6-11.30pm) This restaurant excels in infusing Icelandic seafood and local produce with unique flavours like lotus root. The tasting menu (kr11,900) is tops, and it is renowned for its excellent sushi bar (kr3600 to kr4600).

❸ DRINKING & NIGHTLIFE

🍸 Laugavegur & Skólavörðustígur

Laugavegur is the epicentre of Reykjavík's nightlife and you could begin (and end) a night here. Bar hop until the clubs light up for dancing (late), then wander home under the early-morning sun.

Kaffi Vínyl   Cafe

(☑537 1332; www.facebook.com/vinilrvk/; Hverfisgata 76; ⊘9am-11pm Mon-Fri, 10am-11pm Sat, noon-11pm Sun; 🛜) This new entry on the Reykjavík coffee, restaurant and music scene is popular for its chilled vibe, great music, and delicious vegan and vegetarian food.

Mikkeller & Friends   Craft Beer

(www.mikkeller.dk; Hverfisgata 12; ⊘5pm-1am Sun-Thu, 2pm-1am Fri & Sat; 🛜) Climb to the top floor of the building shared by excellent pizzeria Hverfisgata 12 and you'll find this Danish craft-beer pub; its 20 taps rotate through Mikkeller's own offerings and local Icelandic craft beers.

Kaffibarinn   Bar

(www.kaffibarinn.is; Bergstaðastræti 1; ⊘3pm-1am Sun-Thu, to 4.30am Fri & Sat; 🛜) This old house with the London Underground symbol over the door contains one of Reykjavík's coolest bars; it even had a starring role in the cult movie *101 Reykjavík* (2000). At weekends you'll feel like you need a famous face or a battering ram to get in. At other times it's a place for artistic types to chill with their Macs.

Kaldi Bar

(www.kaldibar.is; Laugavegur 20b; ☺noon-1am Sun-Thu, to 3am Fri & Sat) Effortlessly cool with mismatched seats and teal banquettes, plus a popular smoking courtyard, Kaldi is awesome for its full range of Kaldi microbrews, not available elsewhere. Happy hour (4pm to 7pm) gets you one for kr700. Anyone can play the in-house piano.

Kiki Gay

(www.kiki.is; Laugavegur 22; ☺9pm-1am Thu, to 4.30am Fri & Sat) Ostensibly a queer bar, Kiki is also *the* place to get your dance on (with pop and electronica the mainstays), since much of Reyjavík's nightlife centres on the booze, not the groove.

KEX Bar Bar

(www.kexhostel.is; Skúlagata 28; ☺11.30am-11pm; 🛜) Locals like this hostel bar-restaurant (mains kr1800 to kr2600) in an old cookie factory (*kex* means 'cookie') for its broad windows facing the sea, an inner courtyard and kids' play area. Happy hipsters soak up the 1920s Vegas vibe: saloon doors, old-school barber station, scuffed floors and happy chatter.

🍺 Old Reykjavík

Austurstræti is lined with big venues that pull in the drinking crowd. As the night goes on, some of the capital's best dance clubs and late-night hangs can be found around Naustin street.

Micro Bar Bar

(www.facebook.com/MicroBarIceland/; Vesturgata 2; ☺2pm-12.30am Sun-Thu, to 2am Fri & Sat) Boutique brews is the name of the game at this low-key spot in the heart of the action. Bottles of beer represent a slew of brands and countries, but more importantly you'll discover 10 local draughts on tap from the island's top microbreweries: one of the best selections in Reykjavík. Happy hour (5pm to 7pm) offers kr850 beers.

A bar in Laugavegur

ICELANDIC PHOTO AGENCY/ALAMY STOCK PHOTO ©

Loftið   Cocktail Bar

(551 9400; www.loftidbar.is; 2nd fl, Austurstræti 9; ◷2pm-1am Sun-Thu, 4pm-3am Fri & Sat)
Loftið is all about high-end cocktails and good living. Dress up to enter the fray at this airy upstairs lounge with a zinc bar, retro tailor-shop-inspired decor, vintage tiles and a swanky, older crowd. The basic booze here is the top-shelf liquor elsewhere, and jazzy bands play from time to time.

Paloma   Club

(www.facebook.com/BarPaloma/; Naustin 1-3; ◷8pm-1am Thu & Sun, to 4.30am Fri & Sat; ♿)
One of Reykjavík's best late-night dance clubs, with DJs upstairs laying down reggae, electronica and pop, and a dark deep house dance scene in the basement. Find it in the same building as the Dubliner.

Old Harbour

Slippbarinn   Cocktail Bar

(560 8080; www.slippbarinn.is; Mýrargata 2; ◷noon-midnight Sun-Thu, to 1am Fri & Sat; 🛜)
Jet setters unite at this buzzy restaurant (mains kr2900 to kr5000) and bar at the Old Harbour in the Icelandair Hotel Reykjavík Marina. It's bedecked with vintage record players and chatting locals sipping some of the best cocktails in town.

✪ ENTERTAINMENT

Bíó Paradís   Cinema

(www.bioparadis.is; Hverfisgata 54; adult kr1600; 🛜) This totally cool cinema, decked out in movie posters and vintage officeware, screens specially curated Icelandic films with English subtitles. It has a happy hour from 5pm to 7.30pm.

Húrra   Live Music

(Tryggvagata 22; ◷5pm-1am Sun-Thu, to 4.30am Fri & Sat; 🛜) Dark and raw, this large bar opens up its back room to make a concert venue, with live music or DJs most nights, and is one of the best places in town to close out the night. It's got a range of beers on tap and happy hour runs till 9pm (beer or wine kr700).

Icelandic Pop

Iceland's pop music scene is one of its great gifts to the world. Internationally famous Icelandic musicians include (of course) Björk and her former band, the Sugarcubes. Sigur Rós followed Björk to stardom; their concert movie *Heima* (2007) is a must-see. Indie-folk Of Monsters and Men stormed the US charts in 2011 with *My Head Is an Animal;* their latest album is *Beneath the Skin (2015)*. Ásgeir had a breakout hit with *In the Silence* (2014).

Reykjavík's flourishing music landscape is constantly changing – visit www.icelandmusic.is and www.grapevine.is for news and listings. Just a few examples of local groups include Seabear, an indie-folk band, which spawned top acts like Sin Fang (*Flowers;* 2013) and Sóley (*We Sink;* 2012). Árstíðir record minimalist indie-folk, and released Verloren Verleden with Anneke van Giersbergen in 2016.

Other local bands include GusGus, a pop-electronica act, FM Belfast (electronica) and múm (experimental electronica mixed with traditional instruments). Or check out Singapore Sling for straight-up rock and roll. If your visit coincides with one of Iceland's many music festivals, go!

If you can't get enough, check out **12 Tónar** (www.12tonar.is; Skolavörðustígur 15; ◷10am-6pm Mon-Sat, from noon Sun). Besides being a very cool place to hang out, this music store is responsible for launching some of Iceland's favourite bands. Drop by to listen to CDs, drink coffee and sometimes catch a live performance.

ⓘ INFORMATION

DISCOUNT CARDS

Reykjavík City Card (www.citycard.is; 24/48/72hr kr3500/4700/5500) offers admission to Reykjavík's municipal swimming/thermal pools and to most of the main galleries and museums, plus discounts on some tours, shops and entertainment. It also gives free travel on the city's Strætó buses and on the ferry to Viðey.

EMERGENCY NUMBERS

Ambulance, fire brigade & police 📞112

LUGGAGE STORAGE

BSÍ bus terminal, Reykjavík Domestic Airport and several other locations in Reykjavík have luggage lockers (www.luggagelockers.is). Many Reykjavík hotels will keep bags for you if you take off to the countryside for a few days.

MONEY

Credit cards are accepted everywhere (except municipal buses); ATMs are ubiquitous. Currency-exchange fees at hotels or private bureaus can be obscenely high.

It's not customary to tip in restaurants.

TOURIST INFORMATION

The **Main Tourist Office** (Upplýsingamiðstöð Ferðamanna; 📞590 1550; www.visitreykjavik. is; Aðalstræti 2; ⏰8am-8pm) has friendly staff and mountains of free brochures, plus maps, Reykjavík City Card and Strætó city bus tickets. It books accommodation, tours and activities.

TRAVEL AGENCIES

Icelandic Travel Market (ITM; 📞522 4979; www. icelandictravelmarket.is; Bankastræti 2; ⏰8am-9pm Jun-Aug, 9am-7pm Sep-May) Information and tour bookings.

Trip (📞433 8747; www.trip.is; Laugavegur 54; ⏰9am-9pm) Books tours as well lodging, and rents cars.

❶ GETTING THERE & AWAY

Iceland has become very accessible in recent years, with more flights from more destinations. Ferry transport makes a good alternative for people wishing to bring a car or camper from mainland Europe.

Flights, tours and rail tickets can be booked online at www.lonelyplanet.com/bookings.

❶ GETTING AROUND

The best way to see compact central Reykjavík is by foot.

TO/FROM THE AIRPORT

The journey from Keflavík International Airport to Reykjavík takes about 50 minutes. Three easy bus services connect Reykjavík and the airport and are the best transport option; kids get discounted fares.

Flybus (📞580 5400; www.re.is; 🛜) Meets all international flights. One-way tickets cost kr2200. Pay kr2800 for hotel pickup/drop off, which must be booked a day ahead. A separate service runs to the Blue Lagoon (from where you can continue to the city centre or the airport; kr3900). Flybus will also drop off/pick up in Garðabær and Hafnarfjörður, just south of Reykjavík.

Airport Express (📞540 1313; www.airport express.is; 🛜) Operated by Gray Line Tours between Keflavík International Airport and Lækjartorg Sq in central Reykjavík (kr2100) or Mjódd bus terminal, or via hotel pickup/drop off (kr2700; book ahead). Has connections to Borgarnes and points north, including Akureyri.

Airport Direct (📞497 5000; www.reykjaviksight seeing.is/airport-direct; 🛜) Minibuses operated by Reykjavík Sightseeing shuttle between hotels and the airport (kr4500, return kr8000).

Strætó (www.bus.is) bus 55 also connects the BSÍ bus terminal and the airport (kr1680, nine daily Monday to Friday in summer).

Taxis cost around kr15,000.

From the Reykjavík Domestic Airport it's a 2km walk into town; there's a taxi rank, or bus 15 stops near the Air Iceland terminal and bus 19 stops near the Eagle Air terminal. Both go to the city centre and the Hlemmur bus stop.

BUS

Strætó (www.bus.is) operates regular, easy buses in the city centre and environs, running 7am until 11pm or midnight daily (from 11am on Sunday). A limited night-bus service runs until 2am on Friday and Saturday.

Where to Stay

Demand always outstrips supply in Reykjavík. Try to book your accommodation three to six months ahead.

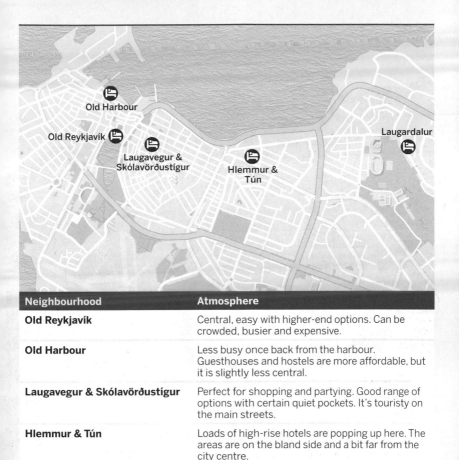

Neighbourhood	Atmosphere
Old Reykjavík	Central, easy with higher-end options. Can be crowded, busier and expensive.
Old Harbour	Less busy once back from the harbour. Guesthouses and hostels are more affordable, but it is slightly less central.
Laugavegur & Skólavörðustígur	Perfect for shopping and partying. Good range of options with certain quiet pockets. It's touristy on the main streets.
Hlemmur & Tún	Loads of high-rise hotels are popping up here. The areas are on the bland side and a bit far from the city centre.
Laugardalur	Near a large park and swimming complex. New high-rise hotels. Further from the city centre.

FRANCE, SPAIN & PORTUGAL

In This Chapter

Eiffel Tower...204
The Louvre 210
Notre Dame..216
Day Trip: Château de Versailles...... 222
Sights 228
Shopping 236
Eating... 239
Drinking & Nightlife........................... 245
Entertainment 248
Information 249
Getting There & Away 250
Getting Around 250

Paris, France

The enchanting French capital is awash with landmarks that need no introduction – the Eiffel Tower and Notre Dame among them – along with a trove of specialist museums and galleries. Creamy-stone, grey-metal-roofed buildings, lamp-lit bridges and geometrically laid-out parks are equally integral elements of the city's fabric. Dining is a quintessential part of the Parisian experience – whether it be in traditional bistros, Michelin-starred restaurants, boulangeries (bakeries) or raucous street markets. Then there's its art repository, one of the world's best. But against this iconic backdrop, Paris' real magic lies in the unexpected: hidden parks, small museums and sun-spangled cafe pavement terraces.

Two Days in Paris

Start early with **Notre Dame** (p217), the **Louvre** (p211) or the **Eiffel Tower** (p204). Afterwards, head to the Champs-Élysées to shop and climb the **Arc de Triomphe** (p229). On day two take a boat cruise along the Seine and visit your pick of **Musée d'Orsay** (p236) or **Musée National du Moyen Âge** (p235). Make soulful St-Germain your dinner date.

Four Days in Paris

Devote day three to **Montmartre** (p229). Begin the fourth day with a top sight you missed on day one. Picnic in a Parisian park and spend the afternoon scouting out treasures at the **St-Ouen flea market** (p238) or checking out famous graves in **Cimetière du Père Lachaise** (p233). By night, take in a performance at **Palais Garnier** (p248) or **Opéra Bastille** (p248), and bar crawl in Le Marais.

Not finished with France? Head south to Provence (p252).

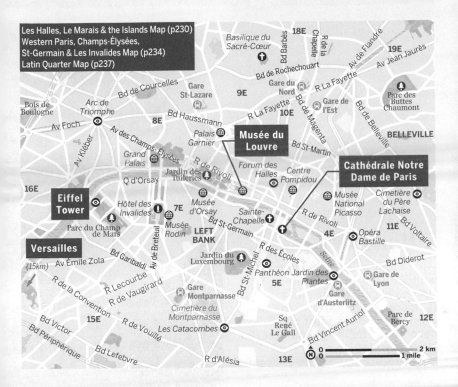

Les Halles, Le Marais & the Islands Map (p230)
Western Paris, Champs-Élysées,
St-Germain & Les Invalides Map (p234)
Latin Quarter Map (p237)

Basilique du Sacré-Cœur

18E

R de la Chapelle

Bd Barbès

19E

Av de Flandre

Av Jean Jaurès

Bd de Rochechouart

Gare St-Lazare

Bd de Courcelles

Gare du Nord

9E

R La Fayette

Parc des Buttes Chaumont

Bois de Boulogne

Arc de Triomphe

Av Foch

Av Kléber

8E

Av des Champs-Élysées

Bd Haussmann

R La Fayette

10E

Gare de l'Est

Bd de Magenta

Bd de Belleville

BELLEVILLE

Palais Garnier

Musée du Louvre

Bd St-Martin

Grand Palais

Q d'Orsay

Jardin des Tuileries

R de Rivoli

Forum des Halles

Centre Pompidou

Cathédrale Notre Dame de Paris

16E

Eiffel Tower

Hôtel des Invalides

7E

Musée d'Orsay

Sainte-Chapelle

R de Rivoli

Musée National Picasso

Cimetière du Père Lachaise

Bd Voltaire

Parc du Champ de Mars

Musée Rodin

LEFT BANK

Bd St-Germain

4E

Opéra Bastille

11E

Versailles

(15km)

Av Émile Zola

Bd Garibaldi

Av de Breteuil

Jardin du Luxembourg

R des Écoles

Bd St-Michel

Panthéon

5E

Jardin des Plantes

Gare de Lyon

Bd Diderot

R Lecourbe

R de la Convention

R de Vaugirard

15E

R de Vouillé

Gare Montparnasse

Cimetière du Montparnasse

Les Catacombes

Gare d'Austerlitz

Sq René Le Gall

Bd Vincent Auriol

Parc de Bercy

12E

Bd Victor

Bd Périphérique

Bd Lefebvre

R d'Alésia

13E

N 0   2 km
0   1 mile

Arriving in Paris

Charles de Gaulle Airport Trains (RER), buses and night buses to the city centre €6 to €17; taxi €50 to €55.

Orly Airport Trains (Orlyval then RER), buses and night buses to the city centre €8 to €12.05; T7 tram to Villejuif-Louis Aragon then metro to centre (€3.60); taxi €30 to €35.

Gare du Nord train station Within central Paris; served by metro (€1.90).

Where to Stay

Paris has a wealth of accommodation for all budgets, but it's often *complet* (full) well in advance. Reservations are recommended year-round and are essential during the warmer months (April to October) and on all public and school holidays.

Parisian hotel rooms tend to be small by international standards.

Breakfast is rarely included in hotel rates.

For information on what each Paris neighbourhood has to offer, see the table on p251.

Eiffel Tower

Paris today is unimaginable without its signature spire. Originally constructed as a temporary 1889 Exposition Universelle exhibit, it went on to become the defining fixture of the city's skyline.

Great For...

❶ Need to Know

Map p234; ☎08 92 70 12 39; www.toureiffel. paris; Champ de Mars, 5 av Anatole France, 7e; adult/child lift to top €17/8, lift to 2nd fl €11/4, stairs to 2nd fl €7/3; ⊘lifts & stairs 9am-12.45am mid-Jun–Aug, lifts 9.30am-11pm, stairs 9.30am-6.30pm Sep–mid-Jun; Ⓜ Bir Hakeim or RER Champ de Mars–Tour Eiffel

★ **Top Tip**
Head here at dusk for the best day-time vistas and glittering night-time city views.

Named after its designer, Gustave Eiffel, the Tour Eiffel was built for the 1889 Exposition Universelle (World Fair). It took 300 workers, 2.5 million rivets and two years of nonstop labour to assemble. Upon completion the tower became the tallest human-made structure in the world (324m or 1063ft) – a record held until the completion of the Chrysler Building in New York (1930). A symbol of the modern age, it faced massive opposition from Paris' artistic and literary elite, and the 'metal asparagus', as some Parisians derided it, was originally slated to be torn down in 1909. It was spared only because it proved an ideal platform for the transmitting antennas needed for the newfangled science of radio-telegraphy.

Tickets & Queues

Buying tickets in advance online usually means you avoid the monumental queues at the ticket offices. Print your ticket or show it on a smartphone screen. If you can't reserve your tickets ahead of time, expect waits of well over an hour in high season.

Stair tickets can't be reserved online. They are sold at the south pillar, where the staircase can also be accessed: the climb to the 2nd floor consists of 704 steps.

Ascend as far as the 2nd floor (either on foot or by lift), from where it is lift-only to the top floor. Prams must be folded in lifts and you are not allowed to take bags or backpacks larger than aeroplane-cabin size.

If you have reservations for either restaurant, you are granted direct access to the lifts.

1st Floor

Of the tower's three floors, the 1st (57m) has the most space, but the least impressive views. The glass-enclosed **Pavillon Ferrié** houses an immersion film along with a small cafe and souvenir shop, while the outer walkway features a discovery circuit to help visitors learn more about

---

> ### ☑ Don't Miss
>
> The view of the tower in lights – each night, every hour on the hour, the entire tower sparkles for five minutes with 20,000 6-watt lights. For the best view of the light show, head across the Seine to the Jardins du Trocadéro.

JAN-OTTO/GETTY IMAGES ©

---

the tower's ingenious design. Check out the sections of glass flooring that proffer a dizzying view of the ant-like people walking on the ground far below.

This level also hosts the **58 Tour Eiffel** (Map p234; 📞01 76 64 14 64; www.restaurants-toureiffel.com; 1st fl; menus lunch €41.50, dinner €85-180; ⊙11.30am-4.30pm & 6.30-11pm; ⚙🖫) restaurant.

Not all lifts stop at the 1st floor (check before ascending), but it's an easy walk down from the 2nd floor should you accidentally end up one floor too high.

2nd Floor

Views from the 2nd floor (115m) are the best – impressively high, but still close enough to see the details of the city below. Telescopes and panoramic maps placed around the tower pinpoint locations in Paris and beyond. Story windows give an overview of the lifts' mechanics, and the vision well allows you to gaze through glass panels to the ground. Also up here are toilets, a macaron bar and Michelin-starred restaurant **Le Jules Verne** (Map p234; 📞01 45 55 61 44; www.lejulesverne-paris.com; 2nd fl; 5-/6-course menus €190/230, 3-course lunch menu €105; ⊙noon-1.30pm & 7-9.30pm)

Top Floor

Views from the wind-buffeted top floor (276m) stretch up to 60km on a clear day, though at this height the panoramas are more sweeping than detailed. Celebrate your ascent with a glass of bubbly (€12 to €21) from the Champagne bar (open noon to 10pm). Afterwards peep into Gustave Eiffel's restored top-level office where lifelike wax models of Eiffel and his daughter Claire greet Thomas Edison.

To access the top floor, take a separate lift on the 2nd floor (closed during heavy winds).

> ### ✗ Take a Break
>
> At the tower's two restaurants, snack bars, macaron bar or top-floor Champagne bar.

What's Nearby?

Parc du Champ de Mars   Park

(Map p234; Champ de Mars, 7e; MÉcole Militaire or RER Champ de Mars–Tour Eiffel) Running southeast from the Eiffel Tower, the grassy Champ de Mars – an ideal summer picnic spot – was originally used as a parade ground for the cadets of the 18th-century **École Militaire**, the vast French-classical building at the southeastern end of the park, which counts Napoléon Bonaparte among its graduates. The steel-and-etched-glass **Wall for Peace Memorial** (Map p234; http://wallforpeace.org), erected in 2000, is by Clara Halter.

Musée du Quai Branly   Museum

(Map p234; ☎01 56 61 70 00; www.quaibranly.fr; 37 quai Branly, 7e; adult/child €10/free; ⊘11am-7pm Tue, Wed & Sun, 11am-9pm Thu-Sat; MAlma Marceau or RER Pont de l'Alma) A tribute to the diversity of human culture, Musée du Quai Branly inspires travellers, armchair anthropologists, and anyone who appreciates the beauty of traditional craftsmanship, through an overview of indigenous and folk art. Spanning four main sections – Oceania, Asia, Africa and the Americas – an impressive array of masks, carvings, weapons, jewellery and more makes up the body of the rich collection, displayed in a refreshingly unique interior without rooms or high walls. Look out for excellent temporary exhibitions and performances.

Musée Guimet des Arts Asiatiques   Gallery

(Map p234; ☎01 56 52 53 00; www.guimet.fr; 6 place d'Iéna, 16e; adult/child €7.50/free; ⊘10am-6pm Wed-Mon; MIéna) France's foremost Asian art museum has a superb collection of sculptures, paintings and religious articles that originated in the vast stretch of land between Afghanistan and Japan. Observe the gradual transmission of both Buddhism and artistic styles along the Silk Road in pieces ranging from 1st-century Gandhara Buddhas from Afghanistan and Pakistan to later Central Asian, Chinese and Japanese Buddhist sculptures and art. Part of the collection is housed in the nearby

Galeries du Panthéon Bouddhique (Map p234; 19 av d'Iéna, 16e; ⊘10am-5.45pm Wed-Mon, garden to 5pm; MIéna) with a **Japanese garden**.

Palais de Tokyo   Gallery

(Map p234; www.palaisdetokyo.com; 13 av du Président Wilson, 16e; adult/child €12/free; ⊘noon-midnight Wed-Mon; MIéna) The Tokyo Palace, created for the 1937 Exposition Internationale des Arts et Techniques dans la Vie Moderne (International Exposition of Art and Technology in Modern Life), has no permanent collection. Instead, its shell-like interior of concrete and steel is a stark backdrop to interactive contemporary-art exhibitions and installations. Its bookshop is fabulous for art and design magazines, and its eating and drinking options are magic.

View of Parc du Champ de Mars from the Eiffel Tower

Musée Marmottan Monet Gallery

(📞01 44 96 50 33; www.marmottan.fr; 2 rue Louis Boilly, 16e; adult/child €11/7.50; ⏰10am-6pm Tue, Wed & Fri-Sun, to 9pm Thu; Ⓜ La Muette) This museum showcases the world's largest collection of works by impressionist painter Claude Monet (1840–1926) – about 100. Some of the masterpieces to look out for include *La Barque* (1887), *Cathédrale de Rouen* (1892), *Londres, le Parlement* (1901) and the various *Nymphéas*.

Temporary exhibitions, included in the admission price and always excellent, are generally shown either in the basement or on the 1st floor. Also on display are paintings by Gauguin, Sisley, Pissarro, Renoir, Degas, Manet and Berthe Morisot, and an important collection of French, English, Italian and Flemish illuminations from the 13th to 16th centuries.

ℹ Did You Know?

Slapping a fresh coat of paint on the tower is no easy feat. It takes a 25-person team 18 months to complete the 60-tonnes-of-paint task, redone every seven years.

★ Man on a Wire

In 1989 tightrope artist Philippe Petit walked up an inclined 700m cable across the Seine, from Palais Chaillot to the Eiffel Tower's 2nd floor. The act, performed before an audience of 250,000 people, was held to commemorate the French Republic's bicentennial.

NEALE CLARK/ROBERTHARDING/GETTY IMAGES ©

The Louvre

The **Mona Lisa** *and the* **Venus de Milo** *are just two of the priceless treasures resplendently housed inside the fortress turned royal palace turned France's first national museum.*

Few art galleries are as prized or as daunting as the Musée du Louvre – one of the world's largest and most diverse museums. Showcasing 35,000 works of art, it would take nine months to glance at every piece, rendering advance planning essential.

Works of art from Europe form the permanent exhibition, alongside priceless collections of Mesopotamian, Egyptian, Greek, Roman and Islamic art and antiquities – a fascinating presentation of the evolution of Western art up through the mid-19th century.

Great For...

☑ Don't Miss

The museum's thematic trails – from the 'Art of Eating' to 'Love in the Louvre'. Download trail brochures in advance from the website.

Visiting

You need to queue twice to get in: once for security and then again to buy tickets. The longest queues are outside the Grande Pyramide; use the Carrousel du Louvre

Canova's Psyche Revived by Cupid's Kiss

❶ Need to Know

Map p234; ☎01 40 20 53 17; www.louvre.fr; rue de Rivoli & quai des Tuileries, 1er; adult/child €15/free; ⊙9am-6pm Mon, Thu, Sat & Sun, to 9.45pm Wed & Fri; Ⓜ Palais Royal–Musée du Louvre

✗ Take a Break

The Hall Napoléon sells sandwiches, ideal for a picnic in the Jardin des Tuileries (p233).

★ Top Tip

Tickets are valid for the whole day, meaning you can come and go.

vamped the central Hall Napoléon to vastly improve what was previously bewildering chaos.

Palais du Louvre

The Louvre today rambles over four floors and through three wings: the **Sully Wing** creates the four sides of the Cour Carrée (literally 'Square Courtyard') at the eastern end of the complex; the **Denon Wing** stretches 800m along the Seine to the south; and the northern **Richelieu Wing** skirts rue de Rivoli. The building started life as a fortress built by Philippe-Auguste in the 12th century – medieval remnants are still visible on the Lower Ground Floor (Sully). In the 16th century it became a royal residence, and after the Revolution, in 1793, it was turned into a national museum. At the time, its booty was no more than 2500 paintings and objets d'art.

Over the centuries French governments amassed the paintings, sculptures and artefacts displayed today. The 'Grand Louvre' project, inaugurated by the late

entrance at the rue de Rivoli or direct from the metro).

A Paris Museum Pass or Paris City Passport gives you priority; buying tickets in advance (on the Louvre website) will also help expedite the process.

You can rent a Nintendo 3DS multimedia guide (adult/child €5/3; ID required). More formal, English-language **guided tours** (Map p234; ☎01 40 20 52 63; adult/child €12/7; ⊙11.30am & 2pm except 1st Sun of month) depart from the Hall Napoléon. Reserve a spot up to 14 days in advance or sign up on arrival at the museum.

In late 2014, the Louvre embarked on a 30-year renovation plan, with the aim of modernising the museum to make it more accessible. Phase 1 increased the number of main entrances in order to reduce wait times to get through security. It also re-

President Mitterrand in 1989, doubled the museum's exhibition space, and both new and renovated galleries have since opened, including the state-of-the-art **Islamic art galleries** (Lower Ground Floor, Denon) in the stunningly restored Cour Visconti.

Priceless Antiquities

Whatever your plans are, don't rush by the Louvre's astonishing cache of treasures from antiquity: both Mesopotamia (ground floor, Richelieu) and Egypt (ground and 1st floors, Sully) are well represented, as seen in the *Code of Hammurabi* (Room 3, ground floor, Richelieu) and the *Seated Scribe* (Room 22, 1st floor, Sully). Room 12 (ground floor, Sackler Wing) holds impressive friezes and an enormous two-headed-bull column from the Darius Palace in ancient Iran, while an enormous seated statue of Pharaoh Ramesses II highlights the temple room (Room 12, Sully).

Also worth a look are the mosaics and figurines from the Byzantine empire (lower ground floor, Denon), and the Greek statuary collection, culminating with the world's most famous armless duo, the *Venus de Milo* (Room 16, ground floor, Sully) and the *Winged Victory of Samothrace* (top of Daru staircase, 1st floor, Denon).

French & Italian Masterpieces

The 1st floor of the Denon Wing, where the *Mona Lisa* is found, is easily the most popular part of the Louvre – and with good reason. Rooms 75 through 77 are hung with monumental French paintings, many iconic: look for the *Consecration of the Emperor Napoleon I* (David), *The Raft of the Medusa* (Géricault) and *Grande Odalisque* (Ingres).

Paintings in the Denon Wing

Rooms 1, 3, 5 and 8 are also must-visits. Filled with classic works by Renaissance masters – Raphael, Titian, Uccello, Botticini – this area culminates with the crowds around the *Mona Lisa*. But you'll find plenty else to contemplate, from Botticelli's graceful frescoes (Room 1) to the superbly detailed *Wedding Feast at Cana* (Room 6).

Mona Lisa

Easily the Louvre's most admired work (and the world's most famous painting) is Leonardo da Vinci's *La Joconde* (in French;

La Gioconda in Italian), the lady with that enigmatic smile known as *Mona Lisa* (Room 6, 1st floor, Denon).

Mona (*monna* in Italian) is a contraction of *madonna*, and Gioconda is the feminine form of the surname Giocondo. Canadian scientists used infrared technology to peer through paint layers and confirm *Mona Lisa's* identity as Lisa Gherardini (1479–1542?), wife of Florentine merchant Francesco de Giocondo. Scientists also discovered that her dress was covered in a transparent gauze veil typically worn in early 16th-century Italy by pregnant women or new mothers; it's surmised that the work was painted to commemorate the birth of her second son around 1503, when she was aged about 24.

The Pyramid Inside & Out

Almost as stunning as the masterpieces inside is the 21m-high glass pyramid designed by Chinese-born American architect IM Pei that bedecks the main entrance to the Louvre. Beneath Pei's Grande Pyramide is the **Hall Napoléon**, the main entrance area, comprising an information booth, temporary exhibition hall, bookshop, souvenir store, cafe and auditoriums. To revel in another Pei pyramid of equally dramatic dimensions, head towards the **Carrousel du Louvre** (Map p234; http://carrouseldulouvre. com; 99 rue de Rivoli, 1er; ⊗8.30am-11pm, shops 10am-8pm; 🛜), a busy shopping mall – its centrepiece is Pei's **Pyramide Inversée** (inverted glass pyramid).

★ **Italian Sculptures**

On the ground floor of the Denon Wing, take time for the Italian sculptures, including Michelangelo's *The Dying Slave* and Canova's *Psyche and Cupid* (Room 4).

★ **Behind the Smile**

Recent tests done with 'emotion recognition' computer software suggest that the smile on 'Madam Lisa' is at least 83% happy. And one other point remains unequivocally certain: she was not the lover of Leonardo, who preferred his *Vitruvian Man* to his Mona.

The Louvre

A HALF-DAY TOUR

Successfully visiting the Louvre is a fine art. Its complex labyrinth of galleries and staircases spiralling three wings and four floors renders discovery a snakes-and-ladders experience. Initiate yourself with this three-hour itinerary – a playful mix of *Mona Lisa*–obvious and up-to-the-minute unexpected.

Arriving in the newly renovated ❶**Hall Napoléon** beneath IM Pei's glass pyramid, pick up colour-coded floor plans at an information stand, then ride the escalator up to the Sully Wing and swap passport or credit card for a multimedia guide (there are limited descriptions in the galleries) at the wing entrance.

The Louvre is as much about spectacular architecture as masterful art. To appreciate this, zip up and down Sully's Escalier Henri II to admire ❷**Venus de Milo**, then up parallel Escalier Henri IV to the palatial displays in ❸**Cour Khorsabad**. Cross Room 1 to find the escalator up to the 1st floor and the opulent ❹**Napoleon III apartments**. Next traverse 25 consecutive galleries (thank you, floor plan!) to flip conventional contemplation on its head with Cy Twombly's ❺**The Ceiling**, and the hypnotic ❻**Winged Victory of Samothrace sculpture**, which brazenly insists on being admired from all angles. End with the impossibly famous ❼**The Raft of the Medusa**, ❽**Mona Lisa** and ❾**Virgin & Child**.

Napoleon III Apartments
1st Floor, Richelieu
Napoleon III's gorgeous gilt apartments were built from 1854 to 1861, featuring an over-the-top decor of gold leaf, stucco and crystal chandeliers that reaches a dizzying climax in the Grand Salon and State Dining Room.

Jardin du Carrousel

Galerie du Carrousel Entrances

Porte des Lions Entrance

TOP TIPS

➡ Don't even consider entering the Louvre's maze of galleries without a floor plan, free from the information desk in the Hall Napoléon.

➡ The Denon Wing is always packed; visit on late nights (Wednesday or Friday) or trade Denon in for the notably quieter Richelieu Wing.

➡ The 2nd floor isn't for first-timers: save its more specialist works for subsequent visits.

LOUVRE AUDITORIUM

Classical-music concerts are staged several times a week at the Louvre Auditorium (off the main entrance hall). Don't miss the Thursday lunchtime concerts featuring emerging composers and musicians. The season runs from September to April or May, depending on the concert series.

Mona Lisa
Room 6, 1st Floor, Denon
No smile is as enigmatic or bewitching as hers. Da Vinci's diminutive *La Joconde* hangs opposite the largest painting in the Louvre – sumptuous, fellow Italian Renaissance artwork *The Wedding at Cana*.

The Raft of the Medusa
Room 77, 1st Floor, Denon
Decipher the politics behind French romanticism in Théodore Géricault's *Raft of the Medusa*.

Cour Khorsabad
Ground Floor, Richelieu
Time travel with a pair of winged human-headed bulls to view some of the world's oldest Mesopotamian art. **DETOUR»** Night-lit statues in Cour Puget.

PRYZMAT/SHUTTERSTOCK ©

The Ceiling
Room 32, 1st Floor, Sully
Admire the blue shock of Cy Twombly's 400-sq-metre contemporary ceiling fresco – the Louvre's latest, daring commission. **DETOUR»** *The Braque Ceiling*, Room 33.

Rue de Rivoli Entrance

3

Cour Khorsabad

Cour Puget

Cour Marly

Cour Carrée

4

RICHELIEU WING

SULLY WING

5

Cour Napoléon

1

2

Pyramid Main Entrance

Inverted Pyramid

6

Cour Visconti

7 **8**

9

DENON WING

Pont des

Pont du Carrousel

Venus de Milo
Room 16, Ground Floor, Sully
No one knows who sculpted this seductively realistic goddess from Greek antiquity. Naked to the hips, she is a Hellenistic masterpiece.

PRYZMAT/SHUTTERSTOCK ©

Winged Victory of Samothrace
Escalier Daru, 1st Floor, Sully
Draw breath at the aggressive dynamism of this headless, handless Hellenistic goddess. **DETOUR»** The razzle-dazzle of the Apollo Gallery's crown jewels.

Virgin & Child
Grande Galerie, 1st Floor, Denon
In the spirit of artistic devotion save the Louvre's most famous gallery for last: a feast of Virgin-and-child paintings by Da Vinci, Raphael, Domenico Ghirlandaio, Giovanni Bellini and Francesco Botticini.

TUTTI/FRUTTI/SHUTTERSTOCK ©

ALDORADO/SHUTTERSTOCK ©

Notre Dame

A vision of stained-glass rose windows, flying buttresses and frightening gargoyles, Paris' glorious cathedral, on the larger of the two inner-city islands, is the city's geographic and spiritual heart.

Great For...

☑ Don't Miss

Climbing the bell towers, which brings you face to face with the cathedral's ghoulish gargoyles.

When you enter the cathedral its grand dimensions are immediately evident: the interior alone is 127m long, 48m wide and 35m high, and can accommodate some 6000 worshippers.

Architecture

Built on a site occupied by earlier churches and, a millennium prior, a Gallo-Roman temple, Notre Dame was begun in 1163 and largely completed by the early 14th century. The cathedral was badly damaged during the Revolution, prompting architect Eugène Emmanuel Viollet-le-Duc to oversee extensive renovations between 1845 and 1864. Enter the magnificent forest of ornate flying buttresses that encircle the cathedral chancel and support its walls and roof.

Notre Dame is known for its sublime balance, though if you look closely you'll see

Interior of Notre Dame

JULIAN ELLIOTT PHOTOGRAPHY/GETTY IMAGES ©

❶ Need to Know

Map p230; ☏01 42 34 56 10; www.
notredamedeparis.fr; 6 place du Parvis
Notre Dame, 4e; cathedral free, adult/child
towers €10/free, treasury €4/2; ⏱cathedral
7.45am-6.45pm Mon-Fri, to 7.15pm Sat & Sun,
towers 10am-6.30pm Sun-Thu, to 11pm Fri &
Sat Jul & Aug, 10am-6.30pm Apr-Jun & Sep,
10am-5.30pm Oct-Mar, treasury 9.30am-6pm
Apr-Sep, 10am-5.30pm Oct-Mar; MCité

✕ Take a Break

On hidden place Dauphine, **Le Caveau
du Palais** (Map p230; ☏01 43 26 04 28;
www.caveaudupalais.fr; 19 place Dauphine,
1er; mains €21-28; ⏱noon-2.30pm & 7-10pm;
MPont Neuf) serves contemporary
French fare.

★ Top Tip

Invariably huge queues get longer
throughout the day – arrive as early
as possible.

all sorts of minor asymmetrical elements introduced to avoid monotony, in accordance
with standard Gothic practice. These include
the slightly different shapes of each of the
three main portals, the statues of which
were once brightly coloured to make them
more effective as a *Biblia pauperum* (a 'Bible
of the poor' to help the illiterate faithful understand Old Testament stories, the Passion
of the Christ and the lives of the saints).

Rose Windows & Pipe Organ

The most spectacular interior features
are three rose windows, particularly the
10m-wide window over the western facade
above the organ – one of the largest in the
world, with 7800 pipes (900 of which have
historical classification), 111 stops, five
56-key manuals and a 32-key pedalboard
– and the window on the northern side of

the transept (virtually unchanged since the
13th century).

Towers

A constant queue marks the entrance to
the **Tours de Notre Dame**, the cathedral's
bell towers. Climb the 400-odd spiralling
steps to the top of the western facade of
the North Tower, where you'll find yourself
on the rooftop **Galerie des Chimères**
(Gargoyles Gallery), face to face with
frightening and fantastic gargoyles. These
grotesque statues divert rainwater from the
roof to prevent masonry damage, with the
water exiting through the elongated, open
mouth; they also, purportedly, ward off evil
spirits. Although they appear medieval,

they were installed by Eugène Viollet-le-Duc in the 19th century. From the rooftop there's a spectacular view over Paris.

In the South Tower hangs Emmanuel, the cathedral's original 13-tonne bourdon bell (all of the cathedral's bells are named). During the night of 24 August 1944, when the Île de la Cité was retaken by French, Allied and Resistance troops, the tolling of the Emmanuel announced Paris' approaching liberation.

As part of 2013's celebrations for Notre Dame's 850th anniversary since construction began, nine new bells were installed, replicating the original medieval chimes.

Treasury

In the southeastern transept, the *trésor* (treasury) contains artwork, liturgical objects and first-class relics; pay a small fee to enter. Among its religious jewels and gems is the **Ste-Couronne** (Holy Crown), purportedly the wreath of thorns placed on Jesus' head before he was crucified. It is exhibited between 3pm and 4pm on the first Friday of each month, 3pm to 4pm every Friday during Lent, and 10am to 5pm on Good Friday.

Easier to admire is the treasury's wonderful collection, **Les Camées des Papes** (Papal cameos). Sculpted with incredible finesse in shell and framed in silver, the 268-piece collection depicts every pope in miniature from St Pierre to Pope Benoit XVI. Note the different posture, hand gestures and clothes of each pope.

The Mays

Walk past the choir, with its carved wooden stalls and statues representing the Passion of the Christ, to admire the cathedral's wonderful collection of paintings in its

nave side chapels. From 1449 onwards, city goldsmiths offered to the cathedral each year on 1 May a tree strung with devotional ribbons and banners to honour the Virgin Mary – to whom Notre Dame (Our Lady) is dedicated. Fifty years later the goldsmiths' annual gift, known as a May, had become a tabernacle decorated with scenes from the Old Testament, and, from 1630, a large canvas – 3m tall – commemorating one of the Acts of the Apostles, accompanied by a poem or literary explanation. By the early 18th century, when the brotherhood of goldsmiths was dissolved, the cathedral had received 76 such monumental paintings – just 13 can be admired today.

Crypt

Under the square in front of Notre Dame lies the **Crypte Archéologique** (Archaeo-

MATTEO COLOMBO/GETTY IMAGES ©

logical Crypt; Map p230; www.crypte.paris.fr; adult/child €8/free; ⊘10am-6pm Tue-Sun), a 117m-long and 28m-wide area displaying *in situ* the remains of structures built on this site during the Gallo-Roman period, a 4th-century enclosure wall, the foundations of the medieval foundlings hospice and a few of the original sewers sunk by Haussmann.

Audioguides & Tours

Pick up an audioguide (€5) from Notre Dame's information desk, just inside the entrance. Audio guide rental includes admission to the treasury.

Free one-hour English-language tours take place at 2pm Wednesday and Thursday and 2.30pm Saturday.

Landmark Occasions

Historic events that have taken place at Notre Dame include Henry VI of England's 1431 coronation as King of France, the 1558 marriage of Mary, Queen of Scots, to the Dauphin Francis (later Francis II of France), the 1804 coronation of Napoléon I by Pope Pius VII and the 1909 beatification and 1920 canonisation of Joan of Arc.

Music at Notre Dame

Music has been a sacred part of Notre Dame's soul since birth. The best day to appreciate its musical heritage is on Sunday at a Gregorian or polyphonic Mass (10am and 6.30pm, respectively) or a free organ recital (4.30pm).

From October to June the cathedral stages evening concerts; find the program online at www.musique-sacree-notredame deparis.fr.

★ **Square Jean XXIII**

One of the best views of the cathedral's forest of flying buttresses is from square Jean XXIII, the little park behind the cathedral.

Notre Dame

TIMELINE

1160 Maurice de Sully becomes bishop of Paris. Mission: to grace growing Paris with a lofty new cathedral.

1182–90 The ❶ **choir with double ambulatory** is finished and work starts on the nave and side chapels.

1200–50 The ❷ **west façade**, with rose window, three portals and two soaring towers, goes up. Everyone is stunned.

1345 Some 180 years after the foundation stone was laid, the Cathédrale de Notre Dame is complete. It is dedicated to notre dame (our lady), the Virgin Mary.

1789 Revolutionaries smash the original ❸ **Gallery of Kings**, pillage the cathedral and melt all its bells except the great bell Emmanuel. The cathedral becomes a Temple of Reason then a warehouse.

1831 Victor Hugo's novel *The Hunchback of Notre Dame* inspires new interest in the half-ruined Gothic cathedral.

1845–64 Architect Viollet-le-Duc undertakes its restoration. Twenty-eight new kings are sculpted for the west façade. The heavily decorated ❹ **portals** and ❺ **spire** are reconstructed. The neo-Gothic ❻ **treasury** is built.

1860 The area in front of Notre Dame is cleared to create the parvis, an al fresco classroom where Parisians can learn a catechism illustrated on sculpted stone portals.

1935 A rooster bearing part of the relics of the Crown of Thorns, St Denis and Ste Geneviève is put on top of the cathedral spire to protect those who pray inside.

1991 The architectural masterpiece of Notre Dame and its Seine-side riverbanks become a Unesco World Heritage Site.

2013 Notre Dame celebrates 850 years since construction began with a bevy of new bells and restoration works.

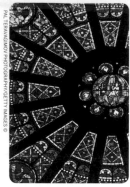

Virgin & Child
Spot all 37 artworks representing the Virgin Mary. Pilgrims have revered the pearly-cream sculpture of her in the sanctuary since the 14th century. Light a devotional candle and write some words to the *Livre de Vie* (Book of Life).

North Rose Window
See prophets, judges, kings and priests venerate Mary in vivid blue and violet glass, one of three beautiful rose blooms (1225–70), each almost 10m in diameter.

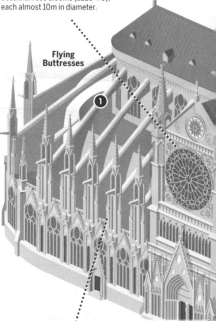

Flying Buttresses

❶

Choir Screen
No part of the cathedral weaves biblical tales more evocatively than these ornate wooden panels, carved in the 14th century after the Black Death killed half the country's population. The faintly gaudy colours were restored in the 1960s.

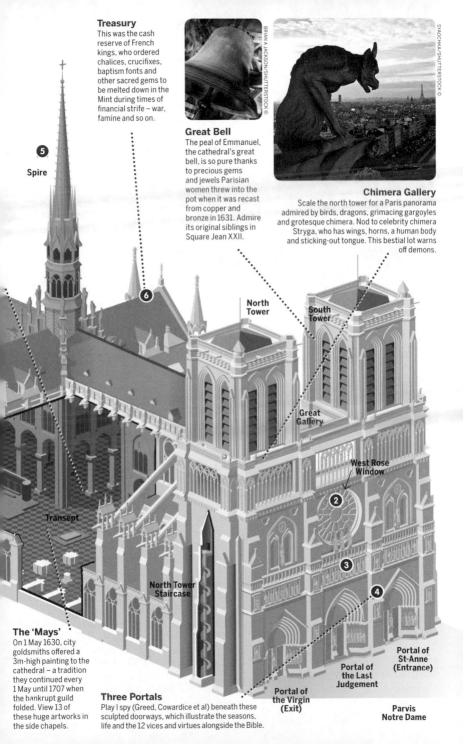

Treasury
This was the cash reserve of French kings, who ordered chalices, crucifixes, baptism fonts and other sacred gems to be melted down in the Mint during times of financial strife – war, famine and so on.

Great Bell
The peal of Emmanuel, the cathedral's great bell, is so pure thanks to precious gems and jewels Parisian women threw into the pot when it was recast from copper and bronze in 1631. Admire its original siblings in Square Jean XXII.

Chimera Gallery
Scale the north tower for a Paris panorama admired by birds, dragons, grimacing gargoyles and grotesque chimera. Nod to celebrity chimera Stryga, who has wings, horns, a human body and sticking-out tongue. This bestial lot warns off demons.

⑤ Spire

⑥

North Tower

South Tower

Great Gallery

West Rose Window

②

③

④

Transept

North Tower Staircase

The 'Mays'
On 1 May 1630, city goldsmiths offered a 3m-high painting to the cathedral – a tradition they continued every 1 May until 1707 when the bankrupt guild folded. View 13 of these huge artworks in the side chapels.

Three Portals
Play I spy (Greed, Cowardice et al) beneath these sculpted doorways, which illustrate the seasons, life and the 12 vices and virtues alongside the Bible.

Portal of the Virgin (Exit)

Portal of the Last Judgement

Portal of St-Anne (Entrance)

Parvis Notre Dame

BRIAN A JACKSON/SHUTTERSTOCK ©

SYADOCHKA/SHUTTERSTOCK ©

Day Trip: Château de Versailles

This monumental, 700-room palace and sprawling estate – with its gardens, fountains, ponds and canals – is a Unesco World Heritage–listed wonder situated an easy 40-minute train ride from central Paris.

Great For...

☑ Don't Miss

Summertime 'dancing water' displays set to music by baroque- and classical-era composers.

Amid magnificently landscaped formal gardens, this splendid and enormous palace was built in the mid-17th century during the reign of Louis XIV – the Roi Soleil (Sun King) – to project the absolute power of the French monarchy, which was then at the height of its glory. The château has undergone relatively few alterations since its construction, though almost all the interior furnishings disappeared during the Revolution and many of the rooms were rebuilt by Louis-Philippe (r 1830–48).

Some 30,000 workers and soldiers toiled on the structure, the bills for which all but emptied the kingdom's coffers.

Work began in 1661 under the guidance of architect Louis Le Vau (Jules Hardouin-Mansart took over from Le Vau in the mid-1670s), painter and interior designer Charles Le Brun, and landscape artist

SIMON TAM (TAMCHUNGMAN)/GETTY IMAGES ©

❶ Need to Know

📞01 30 83 78 00; www.chateauversailles.fr; place d'Armes; adult/child passport ticket incl estate-wide access €20/free, with musical events €27/free, palace €15/free; ⊘9am-6.30pm Tue-Sun Apr-Oct, to 5.30pm Tue-Sun Nov-Mar; Ⓜ RER Versailles-Château–Rive Gauche

✕ Take a Break

Nearby rue de Satory is lined with restaurants and cafes.

★ Top Tip

Prepurchase tickets on the château's website or at Fnac branches (p248) and head straight to the entrance.

André Le Nôtre, whose workers flattened hills, drained marshes and relocated forests as they laid out the seemingly endless **gardens** (free except during musical events; ⊘gardens 8am-8.30pm Apr-Oct, to 6pm Nov-Mar, park 7am-8.30pm Apr-Oct, 8am-6pm Nov-Mar), ponds and fountains.

Le Brun and his hundreds of artisans decorated every moulding, cornice, ceiling and door of the interior with the most luxurious and ostentatious of appointments: frescos, marble, gilt and woodcarvings, many with themes and symbols drawn from Greek and Roman mythology. The King's Suite of the Grands Appartements du Roi et de la Reine (King's and Queen's State Apartments), for example, includes rooms dedicated to Hercules, Venus, Diana, Mars and Mercury. The opulence reaches its peak in the Galerie des Glaces (Hall of Mirrors), a 75m-long ballroom with 17 huge mirrors on one side and, on the other, an equal number of windows looking out over the gardens and the setting sun.

Guided Tours

To access areas that are otherwise off-limits and to learn more about Versailles' history, prebook a 90-minute **guided tour** (📞01 30 83 77 88; tours €7, plus palace entry; ⊘English-language tours 9.30am Tue-Sun) of the Private Apartments of Louis XV and Louis XVI and the Opera House or Royal Chapel. Tours also cover the most famous parts of the palace.

Planning Your Visit

The château is situated in the leafy, bourgeois suburb of Versailles, about 22km southwest of central Paris. Take the frequent RER C5 (€4.20) from Paris' Left Bank RER stations to Versailles-Château–Rive Gauche station.

Versailles

A DAY IN COURT

Visiting Versailles – even just the State Apartments – may seem overwhelming at first, but think of it as a house where people ate, drank, worked, slept and conspired and you'll be on the right path.

Some two decades into his long reign, Louis XIV began turning his father's hunting lodge into a palace large enough to house his entire court (to keep closer tabs on the 6000-strong army of courtiers). Sparing no expense, the Sun King employed the greatest artists and craftspeople of the day and by 1682 he'd created the most extravagant dormitory in history.

The royal schedule was as accurate and predictable as a Swiss watch. By following this itinerary of rooms you can recreate the king's day, starting with the ❶ **King's Bedchamber** and the ❷ **Queen's Bedchamber**, where the royal couple was roused at about the same time. The royal procession then leads through the ❸ **Hall of Mirrors** to the ❹ **Royal Chapel** for morning Mass and returns to the ❺ **Council Chamber** for late-morning meetings with ministers. After lunch the king might ride or hunt or visit the ❻ **King's Library**. Later he could join courtesans for an 'apartment evening' starting from the ❼ **Hercules Drawing Room** or play billiards in the **Diana** ❽ **Drawing Room** before supping at 10pm.

VERSAILLES BY NUMBERS

Rooms 700 (11 hectares of roof)

Windows 2153

Staircases 67

Gardens and parks 800 hectares

Trees 200,000

Fountains 50 (with 620 nozzles)

Paintings 6300 (measuring 11km laid end to end)

Statues and sculptures 2100

Objets d'art and furnishings 5000

Visitors 5.3 million per year

Queen's Bedchamber
Chambre de la Reine
The queen's life was on constant public display and even the births of her children were watched by crowds of spectators in her own bedchamber. DETOUR » The Guardroom, with a dozen armed men at the ready.

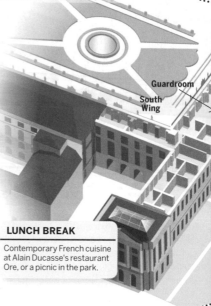

Guardroom

South Wing

LUNCH BREAK

Contemporary French cuisine at Alain Ducasse's restaurant Ore, or a picnic in the park.

Hercules Drawing Room
Salon d'Hercule
This salon, with its stunning ceiling fresco of the strong man, gave way to the State Apartments, which were open to courtiers three nights a week. DETOUR» Apollo Drawing Room, used for formal audiences and as a throne room.

Hall of Mirrors
Galerie des Glaces
The solid-silver candelabra and furnishings in this extravagant hall, devoted to Louis XIV's successes in war, were melted down in 1689 to pay for yet another conflict. DETOUR» The antithetical Peace Drawing Room, adjacent.

WALTER.G/SHUTTERSTOCK ©

King's Bedchamber
Chambre du Roi
The king's daily life was anything but private and even his *lever* (rising) at 8am and *coucher* (retiring) at 11.30pm would be witnessed by up to 150 sycophantic courtiers.

Council Chamber
Cabinet du Conseil
This chamber, with carved medallions evoking the king's work, is where the monarch met his various ministers (state, finance, religion etc) depending on the days of the week.

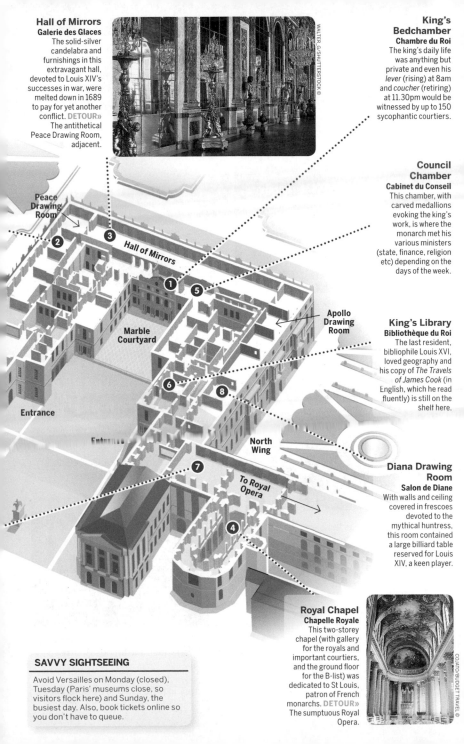

Peace Drawing Room

❷ ❸ Hall of Mirrors

❶ ❺

Marble Courtyard

Apollo Drawing Room

❻ ❽

Entrance

Entrance

North Wing

❼

To Royal Opera

❹

King's Library
Bibliothèque du Roi
The last resident, bibliophile Louis XVI, loved geography and his copy of *The Travels of James Cook* (in English, which he read fluently) is still on the shelf here.

Diana Drawing Room
Salon de Diane
With walls and ceiling covered in frescoes devoted to the mythical huntress, this room contained a large billiard table reserved for Louis XIV, a keen player.

Royal Chapel
Chapelle Royale
This two-storey chapel (with gallery for the royals and important courtiers, and the ground floor for the B-list) was dedicated to St Louis, patron of French monarchs. DETOUR» The sumptuous Royal Opera.

COATO/BUDGET TRAVEL ©

Seine-Side Meander

The world's most romantic city has no shortage of beguiling spots, but the Seine and its surrounds are Paris at its most seductive. Descend the steps along the quays wherever possible to stroll along the water's edge.
Start Place de la Concorde
Distance 7km
Duration 3 hours

3 Take the steps to **Square du Vert Galant**, before ascending to place du Pont Neuf and place Dauphine.

Classic Photo: Enjoy fountain views in this elegant 28-hectare garden.

1 After taking in the panorama at place de la Concorde, stroll through the **Jardin des Tuileries** (p233).

2 Walk through the Jardin de l'Oratoire to the **Cour Carrée** and exit at the Jardin de l'Infante.

7 End your romantic meander at the tranquil **Jardin des Plantes** (⏱7.30am–8pm early Apr–mid-Sep, shorter hours rest of year). Cruise back along the Seine by Batobus.

0 500 m
0 0.25 miles
SHAKESPEARE AND COMPANY
Jardin du Palais Royal
Palais-Royal – Musée du Louvre
R du Louvre
Louvre Rivoli
Pont Neuf
Q du Louvre
Pont Neuf
Q des Grands Augustins
Île de la Cité
Bd du Palais
Châtelet
Hôtel de Ville
4E
Q de l'Hôtel de Ville
St-Michel
Bd St-Germain
St-Michel–Notre Dame
Sq Jean XXIII
Pont St-Louis
Pont Marie
Île St-Louis
Pont de Sully
Bd St-Germain
Q Henri IV
Q St-Bernard
Seine
Jardin du Luxembourg
R Cuvier
Jardin des Plantes
FINISH
R Buffon
Place Monge
Gare d'Austerlitz

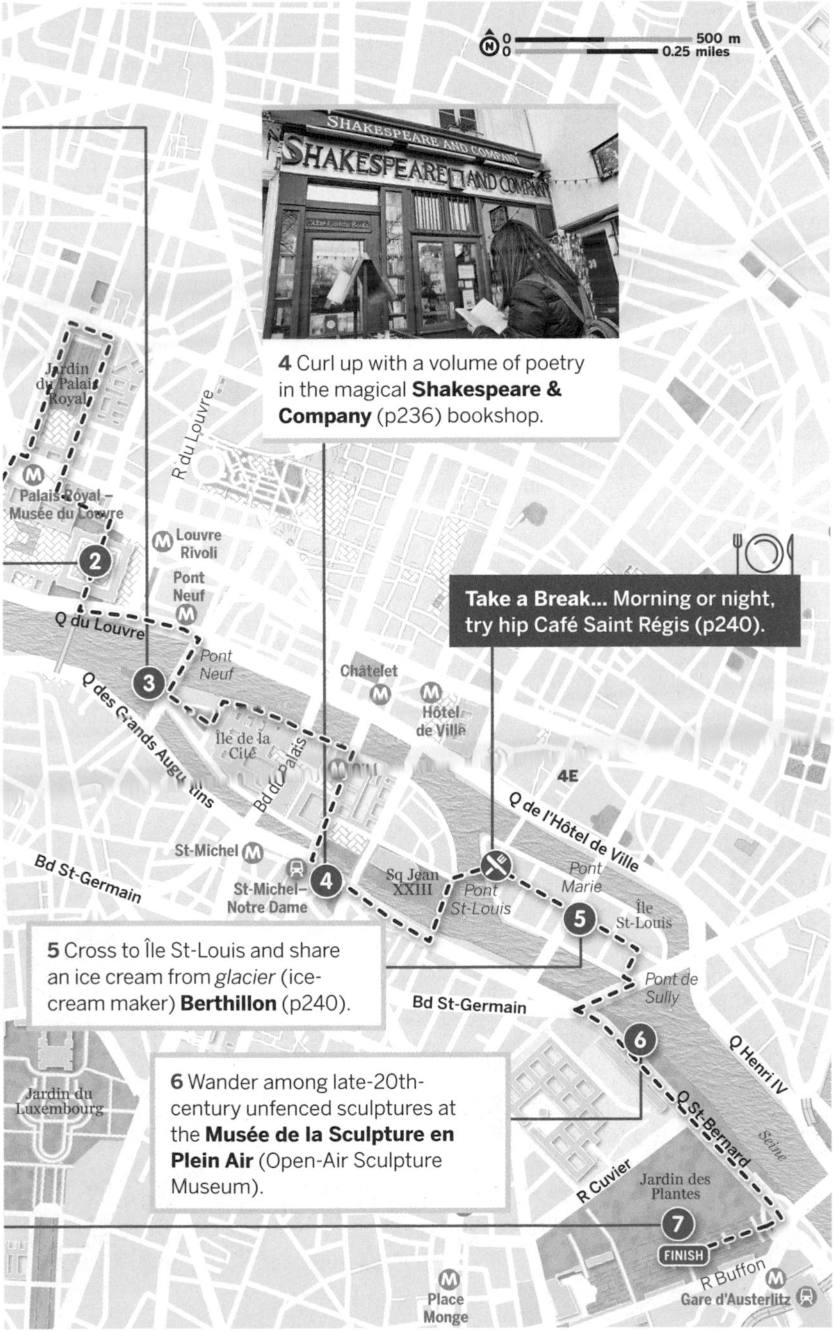

4 Curl up with a volume of poetry in the magical **Shakespeare & Company** (p236) bookshop.

Take a Break... Morning or night, try hip Café Saint Régis (p240).

5 Cross to Île St-Louis and share an ice cream from *glacier* (ice-cream maker) **Berthillon** (p240).

6 Wander among late-20th-century unfenced sculptures at the **Musée de la Sculpture en Plein Air** (Open-Air Sculpture Museum).

◉ SIGHTS

◎ Louvre & Les Halles

Centre Pompidou   Museum

(Map p230; ☎01 44 78 12 33; www.centrepom pidou.fr; place Georges Pompidou, 4e; museum, exhibitions & panorama adult/child €14/free, panorama ticket only €5; ⊙11am-10pm Wed & Fri-Mon, to 11pm Thu; ⓂRambuteau) Renowned for its radical architectural statement, the 1977-opened Centre Pompidou brings together galleries and cutting-edge exhibitions, hands-on workshops, dance performances, cinemas and other entertainment venues, with street performers and fanciful fountains outside. The **Musée National d'Art Moderne**, France's national collection of art dating from 1905 onward, is the main draw; a fraction of its 100,000-plus pieces – including fauvist, cubist and surrealist works, pop art and contemporary works – is on display. Don't miss the spectacular Parisian panorama from the rooftop.

Église St-Eustache   Church

(Map p230; www.st-eustache.org; 2 impasse St-Eustache, 1er; ⊙9.30am-7pm Mon-Fri, 9am-7pm Sat & Sun; ⓂLes Halles) Just north of the gardens adjoining the city's old marketplace, now the **Forum des Halles** (Map p230; http://forumdeshalles.com; 1 rue Pierre Lescot, 1er; ⊙shops 10am-8pm Mon-Sat, 11am-7pm Sun; ⓂChâtelet, Les Halles), is one of the most beautiful churches in Paris. Majestic, architecturally magnificent and musically outstanding, St-Eustache was constructed between 1532 and 1632. It's primarily Gothic, though a neoclassical facade was added on the western side in the mid-18th century. Highlights include a work by Rubens, Raymond Mason's colourful bas-relief of market vendors (1969) and Keith Haring's bronze triptych (1990) in the side chapels.

◎ The Islands

Sainte-Chapelle   Chapel

(Map p230; ☎01 53 40 60 80, concerts 01 42 77 65 65; www.sainte-chapelle.fr; 8 bd du Palais, 1er; adult/child €10/free, joint ticket with Conciergerie €15; ⊙9am-7pm Apr-Sep, to 5pm Oct-Mar; ⓂCité) Try to save Sainte-Chapelle for a sunny day, when Paris' oldest, finest stained glass is at its dazzling best. Enshrined within the

Champs-Élysées and the Arc de Triomphe

KIEVVICTOR/SHUTTERSTOCK ©

Palais de Justice (Law Courts), this gemlike Holy Chapel is Paris' most exquisite Gothic monument. Sainte-Chapelle was built in just six years (compared with nearly 200 years for Notre Dame) and consecrated in 1248. The chapel was conceived by Louis IX to house his personal collection of holy relics, including the famous Holy Crown (now in Notre Dame).

Champs-Élysées & Grands Boulevards

Arc de Triomphe   Landmark
(Map p234; www.paris-arc-de-triomphe.fr; place Charles de Gaulle, 8e; viewing platform adult/child €12/free; ☉10am-11pm Apr-Sep, to 10.30pm Oct-Mar; ⓂCharles de Gaulle–Étoile) If anything rivals the Eiffel Tower (p204) as the symbol of Paris, it's this magnificent 1836 monument to Napoléon's victory at Austerlitz (1805), which he commissioned the following year. The intricately sculpted triumphal arch stands sentinel in the centre of the Étoile ('Star') roundabout. From the viewing platform on top of the arch (50m up via 284 steps and well worth the climb) you can see the dozen avenues.

Grand Palais   Gallery
(Map p234; ☏01 44 13 17 17; www.grandpalais. fr; 3 av du Général Eisenhower, 8e; adult/child €11/8; ☉10am-10pm Wed & Fri-Mon, to 8pm Thu; ⓂChamps-Élysées–Clemenceau) Erected for the 1900 Exposition Universelle (World's Fair), the Grand Palais today houses several exhibition spaces beneath its huge 8.5-tonne art nouveau glass roof. Some of Paris' biggest shows (Renoir, Chagall, Turner) are held in the **Galeries Nationales**, lasting three to four months. Hours, prices and exhibition dates vary significantly for all galleries. Those listed here generally apply to the Galeries Nationales, but always check the website for exact details. Reserving a ticket online for any show is strongly advised.

Le Grand Musée
du Parfum   Museum
(Map p234; www.grandmuseeduparfum.fr; 73 rue du Faubourg St-Honoré, 8e; adult/child

Canal St-Martin

The tranquil, 4.5km-long **Canal St-Martin** (Map p230; ⓂRépublique, Jaurès, Jacques Bonsergent) was inaugurated in 1825 to provide a shipping link between the Seine and Paris' northeastern suburbs. Emerging from below ground near de la République, its towpaths take you past locks, bridges and local neighbourhoods. Come for a romantic stroll, cycle, picnic lunch or dusk-time drink. From the iron footbridge by the intersection of rue de la Grange aux Belles and quai de Jemmapes, watch the vintage road bridge swing open to let canal boats pass.

KIEV.VICTOR/T ©

€14.50/9.50; ☉10.30am-7pm Tue-Thu, Sat & Sun, to 10pm Fri; ⓂMiromesnil) History exhibits (ancient perfume bottles, interpretive French/English panels and dioramas) fill the basement of Paris' 2016-opened perfume museum, but the most engaging sections are upstairs. The 1st floor is a heady sensory guide, revealing the chemical processes while you identify scents. The 2nd floor showcases the art of fragrance creation and the 'instruments' with which professional perfumers work. Afterwards, you'll exit through the ground-floor gift shop where you can see perfume being distilled and bottles hand-painted (and stock up, too).

Montmartre & Northern Paris

Basilique du Sacré-Cœur   Basilica
(Map p230; ☏01 53 41 89 00; www.sacre-coeur-montmartre.com; Parvis du Sacré-Cœur; basilica free, dome adult/child €6/4, cash only; ☉basilica

Les Halles, Le Marais & the Islands

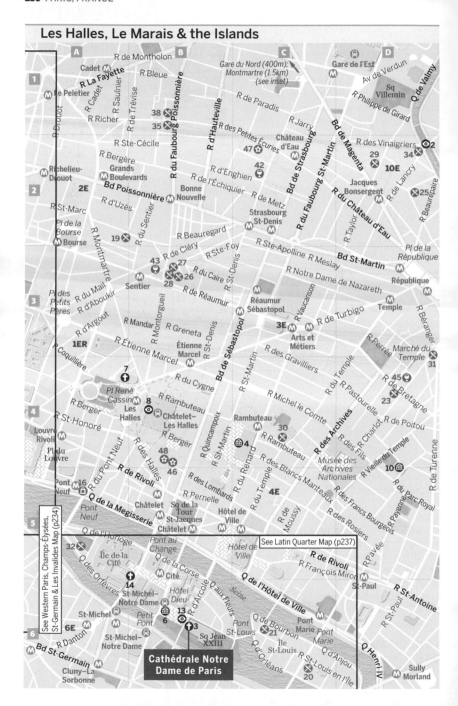

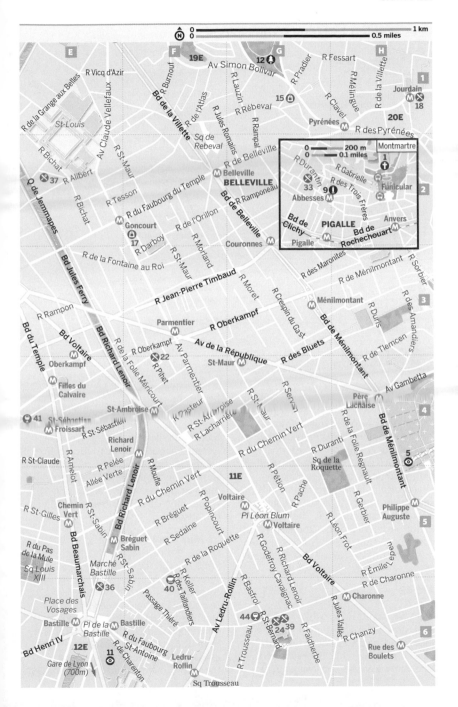

Les Halles, Le Marais & the Islands

◉ **Sights**
1 Basilique du Sacré-Cœur H2
2 Canal St-Martin..................................... D2
3 Cathédrale Notre Dame de Paris............. B6
4 Centre Pompidou.................................... C4
5 Cimetière du Père Lachaise H4
6 Crypte Archéologique.............................. B6
7 Église St-Eustache.................................. A4
8 Forum des Halles.................................... B4
9 Le Mur des je t'aime H2
10 Musée National Picasso.......................... D4
11 Opéra Bastille.. E6
12 Parc des Buttes Chaumont...................... G1
13 Point Zéro des Routes de
        France... B6
14 Sainte-Chapelle..................................... B5

⊕ **Shopping**
15 Belleville Brûlerie G1
16 Bouquinistes.. A5
17 Fromagerie Goncourt.............................. F2

✪ **Eating**
18 Au 140 .... H1
19 Bambou.. A2
20 Berthillon... C6
21 Café Saint Régis..................................... C6
22 Chambelland F4
23 Chez Alain Miam Miam D4
24 Clamato... G6

25 Du Pain et des Idées D2
26 Frenchie... B3
27 Frenchie Bar à Vins................................. B3
28 Frenchie to Go B3
29 Holybelly.. D2
30 Huré C4
31 Jacques Genin D3
32 Le Caveau du Palais................................ A5
33 Le Grenier à Pain G2
34 Le Verre Volé D2
35 L'Office.. B1
36 Marché Bastille....................................... E6
    Marché des Enfants Rouges............ (see 23)
37 Matière à. E2
38 Richer.. B1
39 Septime G6

◉ **Drinking & Nightlife**
40 Café des Anges....................................... F6
41 Le Mary Céleste...................................... E4
42 Le Syndicat C2
43 Lockwood... B3
44 Septime La Cave G6
45 Wild & the Moon..................................... D4

◉ **Entertainment**
46 Le Baiser Salé B4
47 New Morning... C2
    Opéra Bastille .... (see 11)
48 Sunset & Sunside.................................... B4

6am-10.30pm, dome 8.30am-8pm May-Sep, to 5pm Oct-Apr; Ⓜ Anvers, Abbesses) Begun in 1875 in the wake of the Franco-Prussian War and the chaos of the Paris Commune, Sacré-Cœur is a symbol of the former struggle between the conservative Catholic old guard and the secular, republican radicals. It was finally consecrated in 1919, standing in utter contrast to the bohemian lifestyle that surrounded it. The view over Paris from its parvis is breathtaking. If you don't want to walk the hill, you can use a regular metro ticket aboard the **funicular** (place St-Pierre, 18e; ⊙ 6am-12.45am).

Art 42   Gallery

(http://art42.fr; 96 bd Bessières, 17e; ⊙ tours 7-9pm Tue, 11am-3pm Sat; Ⓜ Porte de Clichy) **FREE** Street art and post-graffiti now have their own dedicated space at this 'anti-museum', with works by Banksy, Bom.K, Miss Van, Ericailcane and Invader (who's

behind the Space Invader motifs on buildings all over Paris), among other boundary-pushing urban artists. Compulsory guided tours (English generally available; confirm ahead) lead you through 4000 sq metres of subterranean rooms sheltering some 150 works. Entry's free but you need to reserve tours online (ideally several weeks in advance, although last-minute cancellations can arise).

Le Mur des je t'aime   Public Art

(Map p230; www.lesjetaime.com; Sq Jehan Rictus, place des Abbesses ,18e; ⊙ 8am-9.30pm Mon-Fri, 9am-9.30pm Sat & Sun mid-May–Aug, shorter hours Sep–mid-May; Ⓜ Abbesses) Few visitors can resist a selfie in front of Montmartre's 'I Love You' wall, a public artwork created in a small park by artists Frédéric Baron and Claire Kito in the year 2000. Made from dark-blue enamel tiles, the striking mural features the immortal phrase 'I love you' 311 times in 250 different languages (the red fragments, if joined together, would form a heart). Find a bench beneath a maple tree and brush up your language skills romantic-Paris-style.

◎ Le Marais, Ménilmontant & Belleville

Cimetière du Père Lachaise · Cemetery

(Map p230; ☎01 55 25 83 10; www.pere-lachaise.com; 16 rue du Repos & 8 bd de Ménilmontant, 20e; ⊙8am-6pm Mon-Fri, 8.30am-6pm Sat, 9am-6pm Sun mid-Mar–Oct, shorter hours Nov–mid-Mar; Ⓜ Père Lachaise, Gambetta) The world's most-visited cemetery, Père Lachaise opened in 1804. Its 70,000 ornate and ostentatious tombs of the rich and famous form a verdant, 44-hectare sculpture garden. The most visited are those of 1960s rock star Jim Morrison (division 6) and Oscar Wilde (division 89). Pick up cemetery maps at the **conservation office** (Bureaux de la Conservation; ⊙8.30am-12.30pm & 2-5pm Mon-Fri; Ⓜ Philippe Auguste, Père Lachaise) near the main bd de Ménilmontant entrance. Other notables buried here include composer Chopin; playwright Molière; poet Apollinaire; and writers Balzac, Proust, Gertrude Stein and Colette.

Musée National Picasso · Gallery

(Map p230; ☎01 85 56 00 36; www.museepicassoparis.fr; 5 rue de Thorigny, 3e; adult/child €12.50/free; ⊙10.30am-6pm Tue-Fri, 9.30am-6pm Sat & Sun; Ⓜ St-Paul, Chemin Vert) One of Paris' most beloved art collections is showcased inside the mid-17th-century Hôtel Salé, an exquisite private mansion owned by the city since 1964. The Musée National Picasso is a staggering art museum devoted to Spanish artist Pablo Picasso (1881–1973), who spent much of his life living and working in Paris. The collection includes more than 5000 drawings, engravings, paintings, ceramic works and sculptures by the *grand maître* (great master), although they're not all displayed at the same time.

Parisian Parks

Explore the city's lush green parks where Parisians stroll in style, admire art, lounge around fountains on sunchairs, bust out cheese and wine...

Jardin du Luxembourg (Map p237; www.senat.fr/visite/jardin; numerous entrances; ⊙hours vary; Ⓜ Mabillon, St-Sulpice, Rennes, Notre Dame des Champs, RER Luxembourg) Paris' most iconic swath of green, where you can stroll among the statues, play tennis, jog in style and entertain the kids.

Jardin du Palais Royal (Map p234; www.domaine-palais-royal.fr; 2 place Colette, 1er; ⊙8am-10.30pm Apr-Sep, to 8.30pm Oct-Mar; Ⓜ Palais Royal–Musée du Louvre) The perfect spot to sit, contemplate and picnic between box hedges, or shop in the trio of beautiful arcades that frame the garden.

Jardin des Tuileries (Map p234; rue de Rivoli, 1er; ⊙7am-9pm late Mar–late Sep, 7.30am-7.30pm late Sep–late Mar; ♿; Ⓜ Tuileries, Concorde) Leafy Seine-side oasis, perfect for picnics, summer carnival rides, jogging and impossibly magnificent vistas.

Parc des Buttes-Chaumont (Map p230; rue Manin & rue Botzaris, 19e; ⊙7am-10pm May-Sep, to 8pm Oct-Apr; Ⓜ Buttes Chaumont, Botzaris) Baron Haussmann's creation, this quirky local spot has a faux Greek temple, abandoned railway line, dance hall and t'ai chi vibes.

Jardin du Luxembourg
XMO/SHUTTERSTOCK ©

Western Paris, Champs-Élysées, St-Germain & Les Invalides

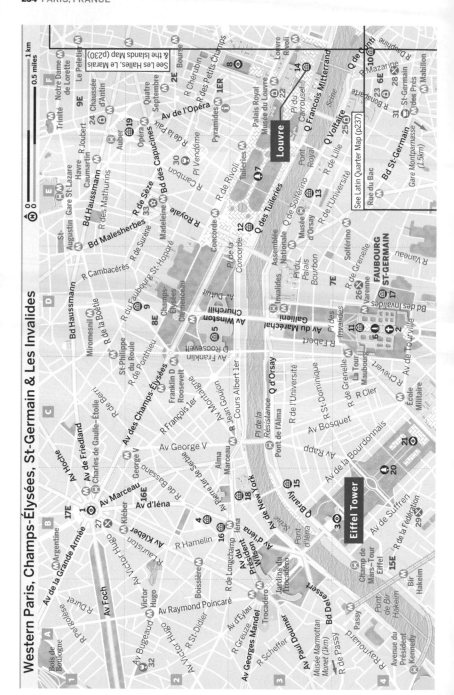

Eiffel Tower

Louvre

Western Paris, Champs-Élysées, St-Germain & Les Invalides

◎ **Sights**
1	Arc de Triomphe	B1
2	Église du Dôme	D4
3	Eiffel Tower	B4
4	Galeries du Panthéon Bouddhique	B2
5	Grand Palais	D2
6	Hôtel des Invalides	D4
7	Jardin des Tuileries	E3
8	Jardin du Palais Royal	F3
9	Le Grand Musée du Parfum	D2
10	Monnaie de Paris	F4
11	Musée de l'Armée	D4
12	Musée de l'Orangerie	E3
13	Musée d'Orsay	E3
14	Musée du Louvre	F3
15	Musée du Quai Branly	B3
16	Musée Guimet des Arts Asiatiques	B2
17	Musée Rodin	D4
18	Palais de Tokyo	B3
19	Palais Garnier	F2
20	Parc du Champ de Mars	B4
21	Wall for Peace Memorial	C4

◎ **Activities, Courses & Tours**
Louvre Guided Tours	(see 14)

◎ **Shopping**
22	Carrousel du Louvre	F3
23	Gab & Jo	F4
24	Galeries Lafayette	F1
25	Magasin Sennelier	F4

◎ **Eating**
	58 Tour Eiffel	(see 3)
26	Besnier	D4
27	Bustronome	B1
28	Goût de Brioche	F4
29	Le Casse Noix	B4
	Le Jules Verne	(see 3)
	Mini Palais	(see 5)
	Restaurant Guy Savoy	(see 10)

◎ **Drinking & Nightlife**
30	Bar Hemingway	E2
31	Les Deux Magots	F4
32	St James Paris	A2

◎ **Entertainment**
33	Kiosque Théâtre Madeleine	E2
	Palais Garnier	(see 19)
	Palais Garnier Box Office	(see 19)

◎ Latin Quarter

Panthéon   Mausoleum

(Map p237; www.paris-pantheon.fr; place du Panthéon, 5e; adult/child €9/free; ⊙10am-6.30pm Apr-Sep, to 6pm Oct-Mar; Ⓜ Maubert-Mutualité or RER Luxembourg) Overlooking the city from its Left Bank perch, the Panthéon's stately neoclassical dome is an icon of the Parisian skyline. The vast interior is an architectural masterpiece: originally a church and now a mausoleum, it has served since 1791 as the resting place of some of France's greatest thinkers, including Voltaire, Rousseau, Braille and Hugo. A copy of Foucault's pendulum, first hung from the dome in 1851 to demonstrate the rotation of the earth, takes pride of place.

Musée National du Moyen Âge   Museum

(Map p237; www.musee-moyenage.fr; 6 place Paul Painlevé, 5e; adult/child incl audioguide €8/free, during temporary exhibitions €9/free; ⊙9.15am-5.45pm Wed-Mon; Ⓜ Cluny–La Sorbonne) The National Museum of the Middle Ages holds a series of sublime treasures, from medieval statuary, stained glass and objets d'art to its celebrated series of tapestries, The Lady with the Unicorn (1500). Throw in the extant architecture – an ornate 15th-century mansion (the Hôtel de Cluny) and the frigidarium (cold room) of an enormous Roman-era bathhouse – and you have one of Paris' top small museums. Outside, four medieval gardens grace the northeastern corner; more bathhouse remains are to the west.

◎ Montparnasse & Southern Paris

Les Catacombes   Cemetery

(www.catacombes.paris.fr; 1 av Colonel Henri Roi-Tanguy, 14e; adult/child €12/free, online booking incl audioguide €27/5; ⊙10am-8pm Tue-Sun; Ⓜ Denfert Rochereau) Paris' most macabre sight is its underground tunnels lined with skulls and bones. In 1785 it was decided to rectify the hygiene problems of Paris' overflowing cemeteries by exhuming the bones and storing them in disused quarry tunnels and the Catacombes were created in 1810. After descending 20m (via

Le Jue de Boules

Don't be surprised to see groups of earnest Parisians playing *boules* (France's most popular traditional game, similar to lawn bowls) in the **Jardin du Luxembourg** (p233) and other parks and squares with suitably flat, shady patches of gravel. The **Arènes de Lutèce** (Map p237; 49 rue Monge, 5e; ⊘8am-8.30pm Apr-Oct, to 5.30pm Nov-Mar; M Place Monge) FREE *boulodrome* in a 2nd-century Roman amphitheatre in the Latin Quarter is a fabulous spot to absorb the scene. There are usually places to play at Paris Plages.

ROBERT PAUL VAN BEETS/SHUTTERSTOCK ©

130 narrow, dizzying spiral steps) below street level, you follow the dark, subterranean passages to reach the ossuary (2km in all). Exit back up 83 steps onto rue Remy Dumoncel, 14e.

◉ St-Germain & Les Invalides

Hôtel des Invalides   Monument, Museum

(Map p234; www.musee-armee.fr; 129 rue de Grenelle, 7e; adult/child €11/free; ⊘10am-6pm Apr-Oct, to 5pm Nov-Mar, hours can vary; M Varenne, La Tour Maubourg) Flanked by the 500m-long Esplanade des Invalides lawns, the Hôtel des Invalides was built in the 1670s by Louis XIV to house 4000 *invalides* (disabled war veterans). On 14 July 1789, a mob broke into the building and seized 32,000 rifles before heading on to the prison at Bastille and the start of the French Revolution.

Admission includes entry to all Hôtel des Invalides sights (temporary exhibitions cost extra). Hours for individual sites often vary – check the website for updates.

Musée d'Orsay   Museum

(Map p234; www.musee-orsay.fr; 1 rue de la Légion d'Honneur, 7e; adult/child €12/free; ⊘9.30am-6pm Tue, Wed & Fri-Sun, to 9.45pm Thu; M Assemblée Nationale, RER Musée d'Orsay) The home of France's national collection from the impressionist, post-impressionist and art-nouveau movements spanning from 1848 to 1914 is the glorious former Gare d'Orsay railway station – itself an art-nouveau showpiece – where a roll-call of masters and their world-famous works are on display.

Top of every visitor's must-see list is the museum's painting collections, centred on the world's largest collection of impressionist and post-impressionist art.

Musée Rodin   Museum, Garden

(Map p234; www.musee-rodin.fr; 79 rue de Varenne, 7e; adult/child museum incl garden €10/free, garden only €4/free; ⊘10am-5.45pm Tue-Sun; M Varenne) Sculptor, painter, sketcher, engraver and collector Auguste Rodin donated his entire collection to the French state in 1908 on the proviso that they dedicate his former workshop and showroom, the beautiful 1730 Hôtel Biron, to displaying his works. They're now installed not only in the magnificently restored mansion itself, but also in its rose-filled garden – one of the most peaceful places in central Paris and a wonderful spot to contemplate his famous work *The Thinker*.

Prepurchase tickets online to avoid queuing.

🛍 SHOPPING

Shakespeare & Company   Books

(Map p237; ☎01 43 25 40 93; www.shakespeare andcompany.com; 37 rue de la Bûcherie, 5e; ⊘10am-11pm; M St-Michel) Shakespeare's enchanting nooks and crannies overflow with new and secondhand English-language books. The original shop (12 rue l'Odéon,

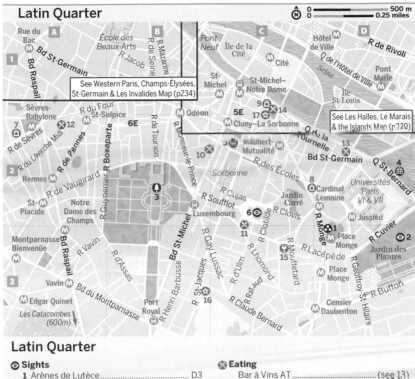

Latin Quarter

⦿ Sights
1 Arènes de Lutèce......................................D3
2 Jardin des Plantes...................................D3
3 Jardin du Luxembourg............................DL
4 Musée de la Sculpture en Plein Air..........D2
5 Musée National du Moyen Âge...............C2
6 Panthéon...C2

🔒 Shopping
7 Le Bon Marché.......................................A2
8 Le Bonbon au Palais...............................C2
9 Shakespeare & Company........................C1

✕ Eating
  Bar à Vins AT.....................................(see 13)
10 Bouillon Racine.......................................B2
11 Café de la Nouvelle Mairie.......................C2
12 Poilâne..A2
13 Restaurant AT..D2
14 Shakespeare & Company Café................C1

🍷 Drinking & Nightlife
15 Little Bastards..C3

✹ Entertainment
16 Café Universel..B3
17 Le Caveau des Oubliettes.......................C2

6e; closed by the Nazis in 1941) was run by Sylvia Beach and became the meeting point for Hemingway's 'Lost Generation'. Readings by emerging and illustrious authors take place at 7pm most Mondays. There's a wonderful **cafe** (Map p237; www. shakespeareandcompany.com; 2 rue St-Julien le Pauvre, 5e; dishes €3.50-10.50; ⊙9.30am-7pm Mon-Fri, to 8pm Sat & Sun; 🛜📥♿; MSt-Michel) 🍃 and various workshops and festivals.

La Grande Épicerie de Paris   Food & Drinks
(www.lagrandeepicerie.com; 36 rue de Sèvres, 7e; ⊙8.30am-9pm Mon-Sat, 10am-8pm Sun; MSèvres-Babylone) The magnificent food hall of department store **Le Bon Marché** (Map p237; www.bonmarche.com; 24 rue de Sèvres, 7e; ⊙10am-8pm Mon-Wed & Sat, to 8.45pm Thu & Fri, 11am-8pm Sun; MSèvres-Babylone) sells 30,000 rare and/or luxury gourmet

Cycling past *bouquinistes*

products, including 60 different types of bread baked on site and delicacies such as caviar ravioli. Its fantastical displays of chocolates, pastries, biscuits, cheeses, fresh fruit and vegetables and deli goods are a Parisian sight in themselves. Wine tastings regularly take place in the basement.

Marché aux Puces de St-Ouen Market

(www.marcheauxpuces-saintouen.com; rue des Rosiers, St-Ouen; ⊙Sat-Mon; Ⓜ Porte de Clignancourt) This vast flea market, founded in the late 19th century and said to be Europe's largest, has more than 2500 stalls grouped into 15 *marchés* (markets), each with its own speciality (eg Marché Paul Bert Serpette for 17th-century furniture, Marché Malik for casual clothing, Marché Biron for Asian art). Each market has different opening hours – check the website for details.

Le Bonbon au Palais Food

(Map p237; www.bonbonsaupalais.fr; 19 rue Monge, 5e; ⊙10.30am-7.30pm Tue-Sat; Ⓜ Cardinal Lemoine) Kids and kids-at-heart will adore this sugar-fuelled *tour de France*. The school-geography-themed boutique stocks rainbows of artisan sweets from around the country. Old-fashioned glass jars brim with treats like *calissons* (diamond-shaped, icing-sugar-topped ground fruit and almonds from Aix-en-Provence), *rigolettes* (fruit-filled pillows from Nantes), *berlingots* (striped, triangular boiled sweets from Carpentras and elsewhere) and *papalines* (herbal liqueur-filled pink-chocolate balls from Avignon).

Gab & Jo Fashion & Accessories

(Map p234; www.gabjo.fr; 28 rue Jacob, 6e; ⊙11am-7pm Mon-Sat; Ⓜ St-Germain des Prés) ✐ Forget mass-produced, imported souvenirs: for quality local gifts, browse the shelves of the country's first-ever concept store stocking only made-in-France items. Designers include La Note Parisienne (scented candles for each Parisian *arrondissement*, such as the 6e, with notes of lipstick, cognac, orange blossom, tuberose, jasmine, rose and fig), Marius Fabre (Marseille soaps), Germaine-des-Prés (lingerie), MILF (sunglasses) and Monsieur Marcel (T-shirts).

Galeries Lafayette Department Store

(Map p234; http://haussmann.galerieslafayette.
com; 40 bd Haussmann, 9e; ⊗9.30am-8.30pm
Mon-Sat, 11am-7pm Sun; 🚇; MChaussée d'Antin or
RER Auber) Grande-dame department store
Galeries Lafayette is spread across the main
store (whose magnificent stained-glass
dome is over a century old), men's store,
and homewares store with a gourmet emporium. Catch modern art in the first-floor
gallery, take in a fashion show, ascend to a
free, windswept rooftop panorama, or take a
break at one of its 24 restaurants and cafes.

Fromagerie Goncourt Cheese

(Map p230; 🖉01 43 57 91 28; 1 rue Abel Rabaud,
11e; ⊗9am-1pm & 4-8.30pm Tue-Fri, 9am-8pm
Sat; MGoncourt) Styled like a boutique,
this contemporary *fromagerie* is a must-
discover. Clément Brossault ditched a
career in banking to become a *fromager*
and his cheese selection – 70-plus types
– is superb. Cheeses flagged with a bicycle
symbol are varieties he discovered in situ
during a two-month French cheese tour he
embarked on as part of his training.

Magasin Sennelier Arts & Crafts

(Map p234; www.magasinsennelier.com; 3 quai
Voltaire, 7e; ⊗2-6.30pm Mon, 10am-12.45pm
& 2-6.30pm Tue-Sat; MSt-Germain des Prés)
Cézanne and Picasso were among the
artists who helped develop products for
this venerable 1887-founded art supplier
on the banks of the Seine, and it remains
an exceptional place to pick up canvases,
brushes, watercolours, oils, pastels, char-
coals and more. The shop's forest-green
facade with gold lettering, exquisite original
timber cabinetry and glass display cases
also fuel artistic inspiration.

EATING

🍽 Louvre & Les Halles

Bambou Southeast Asian €€

(Map p230; 🖉01 40 28 98 30; www.bambou
paris.com; 23 rue des Jeûneurs, 2e; mains €19-28;
⊗noon-2.30pm & 7-11pm, bar to midnight; 🖉;
MSentier) One of Paris' most sizzling recent
openings, this spectacular Southeast

 Bouquinistes along the Seine

With some 3km of forest-green boxes
lining the Seine – containing over
300,000 secondhand (and often out-of-
print) books, rare magazines, postcards
and old advertising posters – Paris'
bouquinistes (Map p230; quai Voltaire,
7e to quai de la Tournelle, 5e & Pont Marie, 4e
to quai du Louvre, 1er; ⊗11.30am-dusk), or
used-book sellers, are as integral to the
cityscape as Notre Dame. Many open
only from spring to autumn (and many
shut in August), but year-round you'll
still find some to browse.

The *bouquinistes* have been in
business since the 16th century, when
they were itinerant peddlers selling
their wares on Parisian bridges; back
then their sometimes subversive (eg
Protestant) materials could get them in
trouble with the authorities. By 1859 the
city had finally wised up: official licences
were issued, space was rented (10m of
railing) and eventually the permanent
green boxes were installed.

Today, *bouquinistes* (the official count
ranges from 200 to 240) are allowed
to have four boxes, only one of which
can be used to sell souvenirs. Look
hard enough and you just might find
some real treasures: old comic books,
forgotten first editions, maps, stamps,
erotica and pre-war newspapers – as in
centuries past, it's all there, waiting to
be rediscovered.

Asian restaurant occupies a 500-sq-metre
former fabric warehouse, with vintage bird-
cages and a giant metal dragon adorning
the main dining room, a downstairs billiards
room/bar, vast terrace and Zen-like garden.
Chef Antonin Bonnet's specialities include
squid with black pepper and basil, and
aromatic shrimp pad thai.

Frenchie Bistro €€€

(Map p230; 🖉01 40 39 96 19; www.frenchie-
restaurant.com; 5 rue du Nil, 2e; 4-course lunch

 Street Markets

Nowhere encapsulates Paris' village atmosphere more than its markets. Not simply places to shop, the city's street markets are social gatherings for the entire neighbourhood, and visiting one will give you a true appreciation for Parisian life. Nearly every little quarter holds its own street market at least once a week (never Monday) where tarpaulin-topped trestle tables bow beneath fresh, cooked and preserved delicacies. *Marchés biologiques* (organic markets) are increasingly sprouting up across the city. Markets in Paris' more multicultural neighbourhoods are filled with the flavours and aromas of continents beyond Europe.

The website www.paris.fr (in French) lists every market by *arrondissement* (city district), including speciality markets such as flower markets.

Marché Bastille (p244) Arguably the best open-air market in the city.

Marché d'Aligre (p244) Wonderfully chaotic market with all the staples of French cuisine.

Marché des Enfants Rouges (p241) Glorious maze of food stalls with ready-to-eat dishes from around the globe.

Marché aux Puces de St-Ouen (p238) Europe's largest flea market, with over 2500 stalls.

MATT MUNRO/LONELY PLANET ©

menu €45, 5-course dinner menu €74, with wine €175; ⊗6.30-11pm Mon-Wed, noon-2.30pm & 6.30-11pm Fri; MSentier) Tucked down an

inconspicuous alley, this tiny bistro with wooden tables and old stone walls is always packed and for good reason: excellent-value dishes are modern, market-driven and prepared with unpretentious flair by French chef Gregory Marchand. Reserve well in advance; arrive at 6.30pm and pray for a cancellation (it does happen); or head to neighbouring **Frenchie Bar à Vins** (Map p230; www.frenchie-restaurant.com; 6 rue du Nil, 2e; dishes €9-23; ⊗6.30-11pm Mon-Fri; MSentier).

✕ The Islands

Berthillon   Ice Cream €
(Map p230; www.berthillon.fr; 31 rue St-Louis en l'Île, 4e; 1/2/3 scoops take away €3/4/6.50, eat in €4.50/7.50/10.50; ⊗10am-8pm Wed-Sun, closed Aug; MPont Marie) Founded here in 1954, this esteemed *glacier* (ice-cream maker) is still run by the same family today. Its 70-plus all-natural, chemical-free flavours include fruit sorbets such as blackcurrant or pink grapefruit, and richer ice creams made from fresh milk and eggs, such as salted caramel, *marrons glacés* (candied chestnuts) and Agenaise (Armagnac and prunes), along with seasonal flavours like gingerbread.

Café Saint Régis   Cafe €
(Map p230; www.cafesaintregisparis.com; 6 rue Jean du Bellay, 4e; breakfast & snacks €3.50-14.50, mains €18-32; ⊗kitchen 8am-midnight, bar to 2am; 🛜; MPont Marie) Waiters in long white aprons, a white ceramic-tiled interior and retro vintage decor make hip Le Saint Régis (as regulars call it) a deliciously Parisian hang-out any time of day – from breakfast pastries to mid-morning pancakes, lunchtime salads and burgers and early-evening oyster platters. Come midnight it morphs into a late-night hotspot.

✕ Champs-Élysées & Grands Boulevards

Richer   Bistro €
(Map p230; www.lericher.com; 2 rue Richer, 9e; mains €18-20; ⊗noon-2.30pm and 7.30-10.30pm; MPoissonière, Bonne Nouvelle) Run by the same team as across-the-street

neighbour **L'Office** (Map p230; ☎01 47 70 67 31; www.office-resto.com; 3 rue Richer, 9e; 2-/3-course lunch menus €22/27, mains €19-32; ⌚noon-2pm & 7.30-10.30pm Mon-Fri; Ⓜ Poissonière, Bonne Nouvelle), Richer's pared-back, exposed-brick decor is a smart setting for genius creations like smoked duck breast ravioli in miso broth, and quince and lime cheesecake for dessert. It doesn't take reservations, but it serves up snacks and Chinese tea, and has a full bar (open until midnight). Fantastic value.

Montmartre & Northern Paris

Le Verre Volé Bistro €€
(Map p230; ☎01 48 03 17 34; http://leverre vole.fr; 67 rue de Lancry, 10e; 2-/3-course lunch menu €19/22, mains €16.50-26; ⌚bistro 12.30-2.30pm & 7.30-11.30pm, wine bar 10am-2am; 📶; Ⓜ Jacques Bonsergent) The tiny 'Stolen Glass' – a wine shop with a few tables – is one of the most popular wine bar–restaurants in Paris, with outstanding natural and unfiltered wines and expert advice. Unpretentious and hearty *plats du jour* are excellent. Reserve well in advance for meals, or stop by to pick up a gourmet sandwich (€7.90) and a bottle.

Matière à. Modern French €€
(Map p230; ☎09 83 07 37 85; 15 rue Marie et Louise, 10e; 2-/3-course lunch menu €21/25, 4-course dinner menu €46; ⌚12.30-2pm & 7.30pm-11pm Mon-Fri, 7.30pm-11pm Sat; Ⓜ Goncourt) The short but stunning seasonal menu changes daily at this unique space. *Table d'hôte*-style dining for up to 14 is around a shared oak table lit by dozens of naked light bulbs. In the kitchen is young chef Anthony Courteille, who prides himself on doing everything *fait maison* (homemade), including bread and butter to die for. Reservations essential.

Le Marais, Ménilmontant & Belleville

Marché des Enfants Rouges Market €
(Map p230; 39 rue de Bretagne & 33bis rue Charlot, 3e; ⌚8.30am-1pm & 4-7.30pm Tue-Fri, 4-8pm Sat, 8.30am-2pm Sun; Ⓜ Filles du Calvaire) Built in 1615, Paris' oldest covered

Parisian bistrot

market is secreted behind an inconspicuous green-metal gate. A glorious maze of 20-odd food stalls selling ready-to-eat dishes from around the globe (Moroccan couscous, Japanese bento boxes, and more), as well as produce, cheese and flower stalls, it's a great place to come for a meander and to dine with locals at communal tables. Don't miss out on a sandwich or *galette* (savoury pancake) from **Chez Alain Miam Miam** (Map p230; www.facebook.com/ ChezAlainMiamMiam; dishes €3-9.50; ⊗9am-3.30pm Wed-Fri, to 5.30pm Sat, to 3pm Sun; ✈).

Jacques Genin   Pastries €
(Map p230; ✆01 45 77 29 01; www.jacques genin.fr; 133 rue de Turenne, 3e; pastries €9; ⊗11am-7pm Tue-Sun; Ⓜ Oberkampf, Filles du Calvaire) Wildly creative *chocolatier* Jacques Genin is famed for his flavoured caramels, *pâtes de fruits* (fruit jellies) and exquisitely embossed *bonbons de chocolat* (chocolate sweets). But what completely steals the show at his elegant chocolate showroom is the *salon de dégustation* (aka tearoom), where you can order a pot of outrageously

thick hot chocolate and legendary Genin *millefeuille,* assembled to order.

❌ Latin Quarter
Café de la Nouvelle Mairie   Cafe €
(Map p237; ✆01 44 07 04 41; 19 rue des Fossés St-Jacques, 5e; mains €9-19; ⊗kitchen noon-2.30pm & 8-10.30pm Mon-Thu, 8-10pm Fri; Ⓜ Cardinal Lemoine) Shhhh...just around the corner from the Panthéon (p235) but hidden away on a small, fountained square, this narrow wine bar is a neighbourhood secret, serving blackboard-chalked natural wines by the glass and delicious seasonal bistro fare from oysters and ribs (*à la française*) to grilled lamb sausage over lentils. It takes reservations for dinner but not lunch – arrive early.

Restaurant AT   Gastronomy €€€
(Map p237; ✆01 56 81 94 08; www.atsushitana ka.com; 4 rue du Cardinal Lemoine, 5e; 6-course lunch menu €55, 12-course dinner tasting menu €95; ⊗12.15-2pm & 8-9.30pm Tue-Sat; Ⓜ Cardinal Lemoine) Trained by some of the biggest names in gastronomy (Pierre Gagnaire

Montmartre

included), chef Atsushi Tanaka showcases abstract art–like masterpieces incorporating rare ingredients (charred bamboo, kohlrabi turnip cabbage, juniper berry powder, wild purple fennel, Nepalese Timut pepper) in a blank-canvas-style dining space on stunning outsized plates. Just off the entrance, steps lead to his cellar wine bar, **Bar à Vins AT** (Map p237; dishes €12-16; ⊙7pm-2am Tue-Sun).

✖ Montparnasse & Southern Paris

Le Casse Noix Modern French €€

(Map p234; ☑01 45 66 09 01; www.le-casse noix.fr; 56 rue de la Fédération, 15e; 3-course menus €34; ⊙noon-2.30pm & 7-10.30pm Mon-Fri; Ⓜ Bir Hakeim) Proving that a location footsteps from the Eiffel Tower doesn't mean compromising on quality, quantity or authenticity, 'the nutcracker' is a neighbourhood gem with a cosy retro interior, affordable prices, and exceptional cuisine that changes by season and by the inspiration of owner-chef Pierre Olivier Lenormand, who has honed his skills in some of Paris' most fêted kitchens. Book ahead.

Holybelly International €

(Map p230; http://holybel.ly; 19 rue Lucien Sampaix, 10e; breakfast €5-11.50, lunch mains €15.50-16.50; ⊙kitchen 9am-2.15pm Thu, Fri & Mon, 10am-3.15pm Sat & Sun, cafe to 5pm; Ⓜ Jacques Bonsergent) This outstanding cafe is always rammed with a buoyant crowd, who never tire of its Belleville-roasted coffee, cuisine and exceptional service. Sarah Mouchot's breakfast pancakes (served with egg, bacon, homemade bourbon butter and maple syrup) and black-rice porridge are legendary, while her lunch menu features everything from beetroot gnocchi to almond couscous with tzatziki or beef cottage pie. No reservations.

✖ St-Germain & Les Invalides

Bouillon Racine Brasserie €€

(Map p237; ☑01 44 32 15 60; www.bouillon racine.com; 3 rue Racine, 6e; weekday 2-course lunch menu €17, menus €33-46, mains €18.50-

 Best Boulangeries (Bakeries)

Poilâne (Map p237; www.poilane.com; 8 rue du Cherche Midi, 6e; ⊙7am-8.30pm Mon-Sat; Ⓜ Sèvres-Babylone) Turning out distinctive wood-fired, rounded sourdough loaves since 1932.

Besnier (Map p234; 40 rue de Bourgogne, 7e; ⊙7am-8pm Mon-Sat, closed Aug; Ⓜ Varenne) Watch baguettes being made through the viewing window.

Du Pain et des Idées (Map p230; www. dupainetdesidees.com; 34 rue Yves Toudic, 10e; ⊙6.45am-8pm Mon-Fri; Ⓜ Jacques Bonsergent) Traditional bakery near Canal St-Martin with an exquisite 1889 interior.

Au 140 (Map p230; www.au140.com; 140 rue de Belleville, 20e; sandwiches €3-5; ⊙7am-8pm Tue-Fri, 7.30am-8pm Sat, 7am-7pm Sun; Ⓜ Jourdain) Crunchy-to-perfection baguettes and gourmet, wood-fired-oven breads.

Le Grenier à Pain (Map p230; http:// legrenierapain.com; 38 rue des Abbesses, 18e; ⊙7.30am-8pm Thu-Mon; Ⓜ Abbesses) Perfect Montmartre picnic stop.

Huré (Map p230; ☑01 42 72 32 18; www. hure-createur.fr; 18 rue Rambuteau, 3e; sandwiches €5-10; ⊙6.30am-8.30pm Tue-Sat; Ⓜ Rambuteau) Contemporary bakery with a graffitied red-brick wall.

Croissants

29; ⊙noon-11pm; 🚻; Ⓜ Cluny-La Sorbonne) Inconspicuously situated in a quiet street, this heritage-listed 1906 art-nouveau 'soup kitchen', with mirrored walls, floral motifs

Gluten-free in Paris

In a city known for its bakeries, it's only right there's **Chambelland** (Map p230; [☎]01 43 55 07 30; http://chambelland.com; 14 rue Ternaux, 11e; lunch menu €10-12; [◷]9am-8pm Tue-Sun; [Ⓜ]Parmentier) – a 100% gluten-free bakery with serious breads to die for. Using rice and buckwheat flour milled at the bakery's very own mill in southern France, this pioneering bakery creates exquisite cakes and pastries as well as sourdough loaves and brioches (sweet breads) peppered with nuts, seeds, chocolate and fruit.

ROMAN DOMBROWSKI/SHUTTERSTOCK ©

and ceramic tiling, was built in 1906 to feed market workers. Despite the magnificent interior, the food – inspired by age-old recipes – is no afterthought but superbly executed (stuffed, spit-roasted suckling pig, pork shank in Rodenbach red beer, scallops and shrimps with lobster coulis).

Restaurant Guy Savoy   Gastronomy €€€
(Map p234; [☎]01 43 80 40 61; www.guysavoy.com; Monnaie de Paris, 11 quai de Conti, 6e; lunch menu via online booking €110, 12-/18-course tasting menus €420/490; [◷]noon-2pm & 7-10.30pm Tue-Fri, 7-10.30pm Sat; [Ⓜ]Pont Neuf) If you're considering visiting a three-Michelin-star temple of gastronomy, this should certainly be on your list. The world-famous chef needs no introduction (he trained Gordon Ramsay, among others) but now his flagship, entered via a red-carpeted staircase,

is ensconced in the gorgeously refurbished neoclassical **Monnaie de Paris** (Map p234; [☎]01 40 46 56 66; www.monnaiedeparis.fr). Monumental cuisine to match includes Savoy icons like artichoke and black-truffle soup with layered brioche.

✖ Bastille & Eastern Paris
Marché Bastille   Market €
(Map p230; bd Richard Lenoir, 11e; [◷]7am-2.30pm Thu, 7am-3pm Sun; [Ⓜ]Bastille, Bréguet–Sabin) If you only get to one open-air street market in Paris, this one – stretching between the Bastille and Richard Lenoir metro stations – is among the city's very best.

Marché d'Aligre   Market €
(rue d'Aligre, 12e; [◷]8am-1pm Tue-Sun; [Ⓜ]Ledru-Rollin) A real favourite with Parisians, this chaotic street market's stalls are piled with fruit, vegetables and seasonal delicacies such as truffles. Behind them, specialist shops stock cheeses, coffee, chocolates, meat, seafood and wine. More stands are located in the adjoining covered market hall, **Marché Beauvau** (place d'Aligre, 12e; [◷]9am-1pm & 4-7.30pm Tue-Fri, 9am-1pm & 3.30-7.30pm Sat, 9am-1.30pm Sun; [Ⓜ]Ledru-Rollin). The small but bargain-filled flea market **Marché aux Puces d'Aligre** (place d'Aligre, 12e; [◷]8am-1pm Tue-Sun; [Ⓜ]Ledru-Rollin) takes place on the square.

Septime   Modern French €€€
(Map p230; [☎]01 43 67 38 29; www.septime-charonne.fr; 80 rue de Charonne, 11e; 4-course lunch menu €42, dinner menu €80, with wine €135; [◷]7.30-10pm Mon, 12.15-2pm & 7.30-10pm Tue-Fri; [Ⓜ]Charonne) The alchemists in Bertrand Grébaut's Michelin-starred kitchen produce truly beautiful creations, while blue-aproned waitstaff ensure culinary surprises are all pleasant. Each dish on the menu is a mere listing of three ingredients, while the mystery *carte blanche* dinner menu puts you in the hands of the innovative chef. Reservations require planning and perseverance – book at least three weeks in advance.

Cheese for sale at a market

🍽 Eiffel Tower & Western Paris

Bustronome Gastronomy €€€
(Map p234; ☑09 54 44 45 55; www.bustro
nome.com; 2 av Kléber, 16e; 4-course lunch
menu €65, with paired wines €85 6-course
dinner menu €100, with paired wines €130; ⏰by
reservation 12.15pm, 12.45pm, 7.45pm & 8.45pm;
☑🚻; Ⓜ Kléber, Charles de Gaulle–Étoile) A true
moveable feast, Bustronome is a voyage
into French gastronomy aboard a glass-
roofed bus, with Paris' famous monuments
– the Arc de Triomphe, Grand Palais, Palais
Garnier, Notre Dame and Eiffel Tower – gliding by as you dine on seasonal creations
prepared in the purpose-built vehicle's
lower-deck galley. Children's menus for
lunch/dinner cost €40/50; vegetarian,
vegan and gluten-free menus are available.

🍸 DRINKING & NIGHTLIFE

Bar Hemingway Cocktail Bar
(Map p234; www.ritzparis.com; Hôtel Ritz Paris,
15 place Vendôme, 1er; ⏰6pm-2am; 🛜; Ⓜ Opéra)
Black-and-white photos and memorabilia
(hunting trophies, old typewriters and

framed handwritten letters by the great
writer) fill this snug bar inside the **Ritz**
(☑01 43 16 30 30; www.ritzparis.com; 15 place
Vendôme, 1er; d from €1000, ste from €1900;
Ⓟ❄@🛜♨; Ⓜ Opéra). Head bartender Colin
Field mixes monumental cocktails, including three different Bloody Marys made
with juice from freshly squeezed seasonal
tomatoes. Legend has it that Hemingway
himself, wielding a machine gun, helped
liberate the bar during WWII.

Lockwood Cocktail Bar
(Map p230; ☑01 77 32 97 21; www.lockwood
paris.com; 73 rue d'Aboukir, 2e; ⏰6pm-2am
Mon-Fri, 10am-4pm & 6pm-2am Sat, 10am-4pm
Sun; Ⓜ Sentier) Cocktails incorporating premium spirits such as Hendrick's rose- and
cucumber-infused gin and Pierre Ferrand
Curaçao are served in Lockwood's stylish
ground-floor lounge and subterranean
candlelit cellar. It's especially buzzing on
weekends, when brunch stretches out
between 10am and 4pm, with Bloody
Marys, coffee brewed with Parisian-roasted
Belleville Brûlerie (Map p230; ☑09 83 75
60 80; http://cafesbelleville.com; 10 rue Pradier,

GLENN BEANLAND/GETTY IMAGES ©

Al fresco diners in Paris

19e; ◔11.30am-5.30pm Sat; M Pyrénées) beans and fare including eggs Benedict and Florentine (dishes €8.50 to €13).

Le Syndicat
Cocktail Bar

(Map p230; http://syndicatcocktailclub.com; 51 rue du Faubourg St-Denis, 10e; ◔6pm-2am Mon-Sat, 7pm-2am Sun; M Château d'Eau) Plastered top to bottom in peeling posters, this otherwise unmarked facade conceals one of Paris' hottest cocktail bars, but it's no fly-by-night. Le Syndicat's subtitle, Organisation de Défense des Spiritueux Français, reflects its impassioned commitment to French spirits. Ingeniously crafted (and named) cocktails include Saix en Provence (Armagnac, chilli syrup, lime and lavender).

Le Mary Céleste
Cocktail Bar

(Map p230; www.quixotic-projects.com/venue/mary-celeste; 1 rue Commines, 3e; ◔6pm-2am, kitchen 7-11.30pm; M Filles du Calvaire) Snag a stool at the central circular bar at this uberpopular brick-and-timber-floored cocktail bar or reserve one of a handful of tables (in advance online). Creative cocktails such as Ahha Kapehna (grappa, absinthe, beetroot,

fennel and Champagne) are the perfect partner to a dozen oysters (€29 to €38) or tapas-style 'small plates' to share (€7 to €14).

Wild & the Moon
Juice Bar

(Map p230; www.wildandthemoon.com; 55 rue Charlot, 3e; ◔8am-7pm Mon-Fri, 9am-7pm Sat & Sun; M Filles du Calvaire) A beautiful crowd hobnobs over nut milks, vitality shots, smoothies, cold-pressed juices and raw food in this sleek juice bar in the fashionable Haut Marais. Raw, all-vegan ingredients are fresh, seasonal and organic, and it's one of the few places in town where you can have dishes such as avocado slices on almond and rosemary crackers for breakfast.

Little Bastards
Cocktail Bar

(Map p237; 5 rue Blainville, 5e; ◔7pm-2am Mon, 6pm-2am Tue-Thu, 6pm-4am Fri & Sat; M Place Monge) Only house-creation cocktails are listed on the menu at uberhip Little Bastards – among them Fal' in Love (Beefeater gin, cranberry juice, lime, mint, guava puree, and Falernum clove, ginger and almond syrup), Be a Beet Smooth (Jameson, coriander, sherry, egg white and pepper) and Deep Throat (Absolut vodka, watermelon syrup and Pernod) – but they'll also mix up classics if you ask.

Les Deux Magots   Cafe
(Map p234; www.lesdeuxmagots.fr; 170 bd St-Germain, 6e; ⊙7.30am-1am; Ⓜ St-Germain des Prés) If ever there was a cafe that summed up St-Germain des Prés' early-20th century literary scene, it's this former hang-out of anyone who was anyone. You will spend *beaucoup* to sip a coffee in a wicker chair on the terrace shaded by dark-green awnings and geraniums spilling from window boxes, but it's an undeniable piece of Parisian history.

Coutume   Coffee
(www.coutumecafe.com; 47 rue de Babylone, 7e; ⊙8am-6pm Mon-Fri, 9am-6pm Sat & Sun; 🛜; Ⓜ St-François Xavier) ✒ The dramatic improvement in Parisian coffee in recent years is thanks in no small part to Coutume, artisan roaster of premium beans for scores of establishments around town. Its flagship cafe – a bright, light-filled, postindustrial space – is ground zero for innovative preparation methods including cold extraction and siphon brews. Fabulous organic fare and pastries are also available.

Le Baron Rouge   Wine Bar
(☎01 43 43 14 32; www.lebaronrouge.net; 1 rue Théophile Roussel, 12e; ⊙5-10pm Mon, 10am-2pm & 5-10pm Tue-Fri, 10am-10pm Sat, 10am-4pm Sun; Ⓜ Ledru-Rollin) Just about the ultimate Parisian wine-bar experience, this wonderfully unpretentious local meeting place where everyone is welcome has barrels stacked against the bottle-lined walls and serves cheese, charcuterie and oysters. It's especially busy on Sunday after the Marché d'Aligre (p244) wraps up. For a small deposit, you can fill up 1L bottles straight from the barrel for under €5.

Café des Anges   Cafe
(Map p230; ☎01 47 00 00 63; www.cafedes angesparis.com; 66 rue de la Roquette, 11e; ⊙7.30am-2am; 🛜; Ⓜ Bastille) With its pastel-

 Jazz Clubs

Café Universel (Map p237; ☎01 43 25 74 20; www.cafeuniversel.com; 267 rue St-Jacques, 5e; ⊙9pm-2am Tue-Sat; 🛜; Ⓜ Censier Daubenton or RER Port Royal) Unpretentious vibe and no cover.

New Morning (Map p230; www.newmorn ing.com; 7 & 9 rue des Petites Écuries, 10e; Ⓜ Château d'Eau) Solid and varied line-up.

Le Baiser Salé (Map p230; ☎01 42 33 37 71; www.lebaisersale.com; 58 rue des Lombards, 1er; ⊙daily; Ⓜ Châtelet) Focuses on Caribbean and Latin sounds.

Sunset & Sunside (Map p230; ☎01 40 26 46 60; www.sunset-sunside.com; 60 rue des Lombards, 1er; ⊙daily; Ⓜ Châtelet) Blues, fusion and world sounds.

Le Caveau des Oubliettes (Map p237; ☎01 46 34 23 09; www.caveau-des-oubli ettes.com; 52 rue Galande, 5e; ⊙5pm-2am Sun & Tue, to 4am Wed-Sat; Ⓜ St-Michel) Dungeon jam sessions.

shaded paintwork and locals sipping coffee beneath the terracotta-coloured awning on its busy pavement terrace, Angels Cafe lives up to the 'quintessential Paris cafe' dream. In winter wrap up beneath a blanket outside, or squeeze through the crowds at the zinc bar to snag a coveted table inside. Happy hour runs from 5pm to 9pm.

St James Paris   Bar
(Map p234; www.saint-james-paris.com; 43 av Bugeaud, 16e; ⊙7pm-1am Mon-Sat; 🛜; Ⓜ Porte Dauphine) Hidden behind a stone wall, this historic mansion-turned-hotel opens its

Buying Tickets

The most convenient place to purchase concert, theatre and other cultural and sporting-event tickets is from electronics and entertainment megashop **Fnac** (08 92 68 36 22; www.fnactickets.com), whether in person at the *billeteries* (ticket offices) or by phone or online. There are branches throughout Paris, including in the Forum des Halles. Tickets generally can't be refunded.

On the day of performance, theatre, opera and ballet tickets are sold for half price (plus €3 commission) at the central **Kiosque Théâtre Madeleine** (Map p234; www.kiosqueculture.com; opposite 15 place de la Madeleine, 8e; 12.30-7.30pm Tue-Sat, to 3.45pm Sun; Madeleine).

bar each evening to nonguests – and the setting redefines extraordinary. Winter drinks are in the wood-panelled library; in summer they're on the impossibly romantic 300-sq-metre garden terrace with giant balloon-shaped gazebos (the first hot-air balloons took flight here). There are over 70 cocktails and an adjoining Michelin-starred restaurant.

⊕ ENTERTAINMENT

Palais Garnier
Opera, Ballet

(Map p234; www.operadeparis.fr; place de l'Opéra, 9e; audio-guided tours €5; guided tours adult/child €15.50/11; audio-guided tours 10am-5pm, to 1pm on matinee performance days, guided tours by reservation Opéra) The city's original opera house is smaller than its Bastille counterpart, but has perfect acoustics. Due to its odd shape, some seats have limited or no visibility – book carefully. Ticket prices and conditions (including last-minute discounts) are available from the **box office** (Map p234; international calls 01 71 25 24 23, within France 08 25 05 44 05; 11am-6.30pm Mon-Sat). Online flash sales are held from noon on Wednesdays.

Opéra Bastille
Opera

(Map p230; international calls 01 71 25 24 23, within France 08 92 89 90 90; www.operadeparis.fr; 2-6 place de la Bastille, 12e; box office 11.30am-6.30pm Mon-Sat, 1hr prior to performances Sun; Bastille) Paris' premier opera hall, Opéra Bastille's 2745-seat main auditorium also stages ballet and classical concerts. Online tickets go on sale up to three weeks before telephone or box office sales (from noon on Wednesdays, online flash sales offer significant discounts). Standing-only tickets (*places débouts;* €5) are available 90 minutes before performances. French-language 90-minute **guided tours** (Map p230; within France 08 92 89 90 90; guided tours adult/child €15/11) take you backstage.

Point Éphémère
Live Music

(01 40 34 02 48; www.pointephemere.org; 200 quai de Valmy, 10e; 12.30pm-2am Mon-Sat, to 10pm Sun; Louis Blanc) On the banks of Canal St-Martin in a former fire station and later squat, this arts and music venue attracts an underground crowd for concerts, dance nights and art exhibitions. Its rockin' restaurant, **Animal Kitchen**, fuses gourmet cuisine with music from Animal Records (Sunday brunch from 1pm is a highlight); the rooftop bar, **Le Top**, opens in fine weather.

Le Batofar
Club

(www.batofar.fr; opposite 11 quai François Mauriac, 13e; club 11.30pm-6am Tue-Sat, bar 6-11pm Tue-Sat May-Sep, 7pm-midnight Tue-Sat Oct-Apr; Quai de la Gare, Bibliothèque) This much-loved, red-metal tugboat has a rooftop bar that's terrific in summer, and a respected restaurant, while the club underneath provides memorable underwater acoustics between its metal walls and portholes. Le Batofar is known for its edgy, experimental music policy and live performances from 7pm, mostly electro-oriented but also incorporating hip hop, new wave, rock, punk and jazz.

Food is served at the restaurant from 7.30pm to midnight Tuesday and Wednesday, and until 2am Thursday to Saturday.

ⓘ INFORMATION

DANGERS & ANNOYANCES

In general, Paris is a safe city and random street assaults are rare. The city is generally well lit and there's no reason not to use the metro until it stops running, at some time between 12.30am and just past 1am (2.15am on weekends).

Pickpocketing is typically the biggest concern. Places to be particularly careful include Montmartre (especially around Sacré Cœur); Pigalle; the areas around Forum des Halles and the Centre Pompidou; the Latin Quarter (especially the rectangle bounded by rue St-Jacques, bd St-Germain, bd St-Michel and quai St-Michel); beneath the Eiffel Tower; and on the metro during rush hour (particularly on line 4 and the western part of line 1).

MEDICAL SERVICES

Pharmacies (chemists) are marked by a large illuminated green cross outside. At least one in each neighbourhood is open for extended hours; find a complete night-owl listing at www.parisinfo.com.

American Hospital of Paris (☏01 46 41 25 25; www.american-hospital.org; 63 bd Victor Hugo, Neuilly-sur-Seine; Ⓜ Pont de Levallois) Private hospital; emergency 24-hour medical and dental care.

Hôpital Hôtel Dieu (☏01 42 34 88 19; www.aphp.fr; 1 place du Parvis Notre Dame, 4e; Ⓜ Cité) One of the city's main government-run public hospitals; after 8pm use the emergency entrance on rue de la Cité.

l 'Institut Hospitalier Franco-Britannique Hertford British Hospital (IHFB; ☏01 46 39 22 00; www.ihfb.org; 4 rue Kléber, Levallois-Perret; Ⓜ Anatole France) Less expensive, private, English-speaking option.

INTERNET ACCESS

❂ Wi-fi (pronounced '*wee*-fee' in France) is available in most Paris hotels, usually at no extra cost, and in some museums.

❂ Free wi-fi is available in some 300 public places, including parks, libraries and municipal buildings, between 7am and 11pm daily. In parks look for a purple 'Zone Wi-fi' sign near the entrance. To connect, select the 'PARIS_WI-FI_' network and connect; sessions are limited to

Palais Garnier

two hours. For complete details and a map of hotspots see www.paris.fr/wifi.

TOURIST INFORMATION

Paris Convention & Visitors Bureau (Office du Tourisme et des Congrès de Paris; Map p234; www.parisinfo.com; 25 rue des Pyramides, 1er; ☺9am-7pm May-Oct, 10am-7pm Nov-Apr; Ⓜ Pyramides) The main branch is 500m northwest of the Louvre. It sells tickets for tours and several attractions, plus museum and transport passes. Also books accommodation.

GETTING THERE & AWAY

AIR

Paris is a major air-transport hub serviced by virtually all major airlines, with three airports.

Aéroport de Charles de Gaulle (CDG; ☑01 70 36 39 50; www.parisaeroport.fr) Most international airlines fly here; it's 28km northeast of central Paris. In French, the airport is commonly called 'Roissy'.

Aéroport d'Orly (ORY; ☑01 70 36 39 50; www.parisaeroport.fr) Located 19km south of central Paris but not as frequently used by international airlines.

Aéroport de Beauvais (BVA; ☑08 92 68 20 66; www.aeroportbeauvais.com) Not really in Paris at all (75km north of Paris) but served by a few low-cost flights.

CAR

Cars are a hassle in Paris, so it's only worth bringing yours here if you're travelling further afield. To enter the city within the bd Périphérique (ring road) between 8am and 8pm Monday to Friday, cars registered after 1997 (including foreign-registered cars) need a Crit'Air Vignette (compulsory anti-pollution sticker); older vehicles are banned during these hours.

TRAIN

Paris has six major train stations serving both national and international destinations. For mainline train information, check SNCF (www.sncf-voyages.com).

Gare du Nord (rue de Dunkerque, 10e; Ⓜ Gare du Nord) Trains to/from the UK, Belgium, Germany and northern France.

Gare de l'Est (bd de Strasbourg, 10e; Ⓜ Gare de l'Est) Trains to/from Germany, Switzerland and eastern France.

Gare de Lyon (bd Diderot, 12e; Ⓜ Gare de Lyon) Trains to/from Provence, the Riviera, the Alps and Italy. Also serves Geneva.

Gare d'Austerlitz (bd de l'Hôpital, 13e; Ⓜ Gare d'Austerlitz) Trains to/from Spain and Portugal, and non-TGV trains to southwestern France.

Gare Montparnasse (av du Maine & bd de Vaugirard, 15e; Ⓜ Montparnasse Bienvenüe) Trains to/from western France (Brittany, Atlantic coast) and southwestern France.

Gare St-Lazare (Esplanade de la Gare St-Lazare, 8e; Ⓜ St-Lazare) Trains to Normandy.

GETTING AROUND

Walking is a pleasure in Paris, and the city also has one of the most efficient and inexpensive public-transport systems in the world, making getting around a breeze.

Metro & RER The fastest way to get around. Runs from about 5.30am and finishes around 12.35am or 1.15am (to around 2.15am on Friday and Saturday nights), depending on the line.

Bicycle Virtually free pick-up, drop-off **Vélib** (☑01 30 79 79 30; www.velib.paris.fr; day/week subscription €1.70/8, bike hire up to 30/60/90/120min free/€1/2/4) bikes operate across 1800 stations citywide.

Bus Good for parents with prams/strollers and people with limited mobility.

Boat The **Batobus** (www.batobus.com; adult/child 1-day pass €17/8, 2-day pass €19/10; ☺10am-9.30pm Apr-Aug, to 7pm Sep-Mar) is a handy hop-on, hop-off service stopping at nine key destinations along the Seine.

Where to Stay

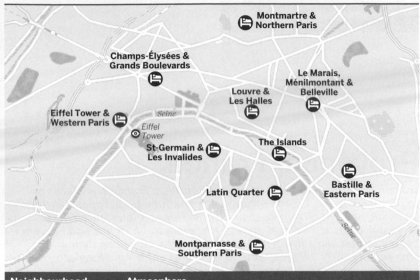

Neighbourhood	Atmosphere
Eiffel Tower & Western Paris	Close to Paris' iconic tower and museums. Upmarket area with quiet residential streets. Limited nightlife.
Champs-Élysées & Grands Boulevards	Luxury hotels, famous boutiques and department stores, gastronomic restaurants, great nightlife. Some areas extremely pricey. Nightlife hotspots can be noisy.
Louvre & Les Halles	Epicentral location, excellent transport links, major museums, shopping galore. Not many bargains. Noise can be an issue.
Montmartre & Northern Paris	Village atmosphere. Further out than some areas. Pigalle's red-light district, although well lit and safe, won't appeal to all.
Le Marais, Ménilmontant & Belleville	Buzzing nightlife, hip shopping, fantastic eating options. Lively gay and lesbian scene. Can be seriously noisy in areas where bars and clubs are concentrated.
Bastille & Eastern Paris	Few tourists, excellent markets, loads of nightlife options. Some areas slightly out of the way.
The Islands	As geographically central as it gets. No metro station on the Île St-Louis. Limited self-catering shops, minimal nightlife.
Latin Quarter	Energetic student area, stacks of eating and drinking options, late-opening bookshops. Rooms hardest to find from March to June and in October.
St-Germain & Les Invalides	Stylish, central location, proximity to the Jardin du Luxembourg. Budget accommodation is seriously short-changed.
Montparnasse & Southern Paris	Good value, few tourists, excellent links to both major airports. Some areas out of the way and/or not well served by metro.

In This Chapter
Pont du Gard 254
Hilltop Villages 256
Avignon 260
Moustiers Ste-Marie 266

Provence, France

Travelling in this sun-blessed part of southern France translates as touring scenic back roads strewn with stunning landscapes: fields of lavender, ancient olive groves and snow-tipped mountains. Factor in its prehistoric sites, medieval abbeys and elegant churches and Provence begins to feel like a living history book. Attractions can be low key: ambling in pretty villages, wine tasting and enjoying a long afternoon lunch on a panoramic terrace, or more energetic – the area is prime cycling territory, there are dozens of hiking trails and some unique spots to explore, such as the ochre quarries of Roussillon. Take your time.

Two Days in Provence

Spend day one in **Avignon** (p260), exploring the old town and the **Palais des Papes** (p260), and perhaps trying some local wine. On day two, make a day trip to either **Les Baux-de-Provence** (p258) for hilltop-village meandering or to the **Pont du Gard** (p255) for Roman history and memorable canoeing action on the River Gard.

Four Days in Provence

On day three, hop between hilltop villages – don't miss a red-rock hike in **Roussillon** (p259) or wine tasting and truffles in **Ménerbes** (p259). Aim to make it to **Gordes** (p258) for sunset. Devote the fourth day to exploring charming **Moustiers Ste-Marie** (p266).

Finished in Provence? Catch a train to Barcelona (p268) or fly to London (p50).

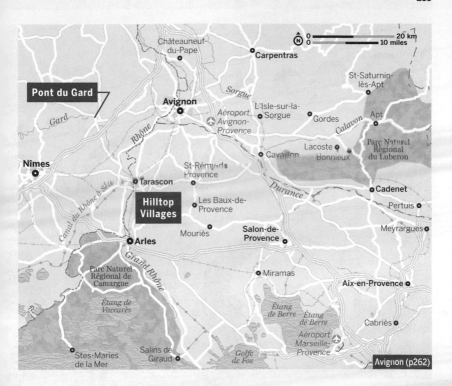

Arriving in Provence

Aéroport Marseille-Provence Buses to Aix-en-Provence every 20 minutes. Direct trains to destinations including Marseille, Arles and Avignon.

Aéroport Avignon-Provence Bus 30 (www.tcra.fr; €1.40; 30 minutes) to the post office and LER bus 22 (www.info-ler.fr; €1.50) to Avignon bus station and TGV station. Taxis about €35.

Where to Stay

Provence has perhaps the most varied range of accommodation anywhere in France, spanning the spectrum from super-luxury hotels to cosy little cottages nestled among vineyards and lavender fields. In summer, prices skyrocket and rooms are scarce. Avignon is an excellent base for Pont du Gard (a 30-minute drive); magical Moustiers Ste-Marie is a key stop for Gorge du Verdon explorers; and Apt and its rural surrounds are perfect for touring the Luberon's hilltop villages.

Pont du Gard

Southern France has some fine Roman sites, but nothing can top the Unesco World Heritage–listed Pont du Gard, a breathtaking three-tiered aqueduct 25km west of Avignon.

The extraordinary three-tiered Pont du Gard, 21km northeast of Nîmes, was once part of a 50km-long system of channels built around 19 BC to transport water from Uzès to Nîmes. The scale is huge: the bridge is 48.8m high, 275m long and graced with 52 precision-built arches. It was sturdy enough to carry up to 20,000 cu metres of water per day.

Great For...

☑ **Don't Miss**

With kids? Don't miss fun, hands-on learning in the Ludo play area.

Musée de la Romanité

Each block was carved by hand and transported from nearby quarries – no mean feat, considering the largest blocks weighed over 5 tonnes. The height of the bridge descends by 2.5cm across its length, providing just enough gradient to keep the water flowing – an amazing demonstration of the precision of Roman engineering. The Musée de la Romanité

SIGURCAMP/SHUTTERSTOCK ©

Pont du Gard

Remoulins

Avignon

Gard

Rhône

Durance

❶ Need to Know

04 66 37 50 99; www.pontdugard.fr; car & up to 5 passengers €18, after 8pm €10, by bicycle or on foot €7, after 8pm €3.50; ☉site 24hr year-round, visitor centre & museum 9am-8pm Jul & Aug, shorter hours Sep–mid-Jan & mid-Feb–Jun

✗ Take a Break

Dine at outstanding restaurant **LeTracteur** (www.lucietestud.com/letracteur) in nearby Argilliers.

★ Top Tip

Evening is a good time to visit: admission is cheaper and the bridge is illuminated.

provides background on the bridge's construction, and the Ludo play area helps kids to learn in a fun, hands-on way; both are closed from mid-January to mid-February.

Mémoires de Garrigue

You can walk across the tiers for panoramic views over the Gard River, but the best perspective on the bridge is from downstream, along the 1.4km Mémoires de Garrigue walking trail.

Canoeing on the Gard

Paddling beneath the Pont du Gard is unforgettable. The best time to do it is early spring between April and June, as winter floods and summer droughts can sometimes make the river impassable. The Gard flows from the Cévennes mountains all the way to the aqueduct, passing through the dramatic Gorges du Gardon en route.

Hire companies are in Collias, 8km from the bridge, a journey of about two hours by kayak. Depending on the season and height of the river, canoe further by being dropped upstream at Pont St-Nicholas (19km, four to five hours) or Russan (32km, six to seven hours); the latter includes a memorable paddle through the Gorges du Gardon.

There's a minimum age of six. Life jackets are always provided, but you must be a competent swimmer.

Gordes (p258)

Hilltop Villages

Impossibly perched on a rocky peak, gloriously lost in back country, fortified or château-topped: Provence's impressive portfolio of villages perchés calls for go-slow touring – on foot, by bicycle or by car. Most villages are medieval, built from golden stone and riddled with cobbled lanes, flower-filled alleys and fountain-pierced squares. Combine with a long lazy lunch for a perfect day.

Great For...

ⓘ Need to Know

Apt Tourist Office (📞04 90 74 03 18; www.luberon-apt.fr; 20 av Philippe de Girard; ⊙9.30am-1pm & 2.30-7pm Mon-Sat, 9.30am-12.30pm Sun Jul & Aug, 9.30am-12.30pm & 2-6pm Mon-Sat Sep-Jun)

★ **Top Tip**
Visit early in the morning or just before sunset for the best light and fewer people.

Les Baux-de-Provence

Clinging precariously to an ancient limestone *baou* (Provençal for 'rocky spur'), this fortified hilltop village is one of the most visited in France. It's easy to understand its popularity: narrow cobbled streets wend car-free past ancient houses, up to a splendid ruined **Château des Baux** (☎04 90 54 55 56; www.chateau-baux-provence.com; adult/child Apr-Sep €10/8, Oct-Mar €8/6; ☺9am-8pm Jul & Aug, to 7pm Apr-Jun & Sep, reduced hours Oct-Mar), whose dramatic maze-like ruins date from the 10th century. The clifftop castle was largely destroyed in 1633, during the reign of Louis XIII, and is a thrilling place to explore – climb crumbling towers for incredible views, descend into disused dungeons and flex your knightly prowess with giant medieval weapons dotting the open-air site. Medieval-themed entertainment abounds in summer.

Gordes

Like a giant wedding cake rising over the rivers Sorgue and Calavon, the tiered village of Gordes juts spectacularly out of the white-rock face of the Vaucluse plateau. Come sunset, the village glows gold.

From the central square, meander downhill along rue Baptist in Picca to **La Boulangerie de Mamie Jane** (☎04 90 72 09 34; rue Baptistin Picca; lunch menus from €6.50; ☺6.30am-1pm & 2-6pm Thu-Tue), a pocket-sized family-run bakery with outstanding bread, pastries, cakes and biscuits, including lavender-perfumed *navettes* and delicious peanut-and-almond brittle known as *écureuil* (from the French for squirrel).

Abbaye Notre-Dame de Sénanque

Roussillon

Dazzling Roussillon was once the centre of local ochre mining and is still unmistakably marked by its vivid crimson colour. Artist workshops lace its streets and the **Sentier des Ocres** (Ochre Trail; adult/child €2.50/ free; ⊙9.30am-5.30pm; 📷) plunges intrigued visitors into a mini-desert landscape of chestnut groves, pines and sunset-coloured ochre formations. Information panels along the two circular trails (30 or 50 minutes) highlight flora to spot. Wear walking shoes and avoid white clothing!

☑ **Don't Miss**

Rows of summertime lavender in bloom at **Abbaye Notre-Dame de Sénanque** (www.abbayedesenanque. com), a supremely peaceful Cistercian abbey 4km northwest of Gordes.

PROCHASSON FREDERIC/SHUTTERSTOCK ©

Ménerbes

Hilltop Ménerbes gained fame as the home of expat British author Peter Mayles, whose book *A Year in Provence* recounts his renovation of a farmhouse just outside the village in the late 1980s. Opposite the village's 12th-century church, the **Maison de la Truffe et du Vin** (House of Truffle & Wine; ☑04 90 72 38 37; www.vin-truffe-luberon. com; place de l'Horloge; ⊙10am-noon & 2.30-6pm daily Apr-Oct, Thu-Sat Nov-Mar) represents 60 local *domaines* (wine-growing estates). April to October there is free wine tasting and wine sales at bargain-basement prices. Winter brings truffle workshops.

Lacoste

Lacoste has nothing to do with the designer brand – although it does have couturier connections. In 2001 designer Pierre Cardin purchased the 9th-century **Château de Lacoste** (☑04 90 75 93 12; www.chateau-la-coste.com). The château was looted by revolutionaries in 1789, and the 45-room palace remained an eerie ruin until Cardin arrived. He created a 1000-seat theatre and opera stage adjacent, only open during July's month-long **Festival de Lacoste** (www. festivaldelacoste.com). Daytime visits are possible only by reservation.

Bonnieux

Settled during the Roman era, Bonnieux has preserved its medieval character. It's riddled with alleyways and hidden stair-cases: from place de la Liberté, 86 steps lead to a 12th-century church. The **Musée de la Boulangerie** (☑04 90 75 88 34; 12 rue de la République; adult/student/child €3.50/1.50/ free; ⊙10am-12:30pm & 2.30-6pm Wed-Mon Apr-Oct), in an old 17th-century bakery building, explores the history of bread-making. Time your visit for the lively Friday market.

🍴 **Take a Break**

The villages are the ideal place to try Provençal specialities like aïoli (a fish dish with garlicky mayo) and *daube provençale* (a rich stew).

Rue des Teinturiers

Canalside **rue des Teinturiers** (literally 'street of dyers') is a picturesque pedestrian street known for its alternative vibe in Avignon's old dyers' district. A hive of industrial activity until the 19th century, the street today is renowned for its bohemian bistros, cafes and gallery-workshops. Stone 'benches' in the shade of ancient plane trees make the perfect perch to ponder the irresistible trickle of the River Sorgue.

ANDREA PISTOLESI/GETTY IMAGES ©

Avignon

Attention, quiz fans: name the city where the pope lived during the early 14th century. Answered Rome? Bzzz: sorry, wrong answer. For 70-odd years of the early 1300s, the Provençal town of Avignon served as the centre of the Roman Catholic world, and though its stint as the seat of papal power only lasted a few decades, it's been left with an impressive legacy of ecclesiastical architecture, most notably the soaring, World Heritage–listed fortress-cum-palace known as the Palais des Papes.

Avignon is now best known for its annual arts festival, the largest in France, which draws thousands of visitors for several weeks in July. The rest of the year, it's a lovely city to explore, with boutique-lined streets, leafy squares and some excellent restaurants – as well as an impressive medieval wall that entirely encircles the old city.

⊚ SIGHTS

Palais des Papes   Palace

(Papal Palace; www.palais-des-papes.com; place du Palais; adult/child €11/9, with Pont St-Bénezet €13.50/10.50; ⊗9am-8pm Jul, to 8.30pm Aug, shorter hours Sep-Jun) The largest Gothic palace ever built, the Palais des Papes was erected by Pope Clement V, who abandoned Rome in 1309 as a result of violent disorder following his election. It served as the seat of papal power for seven decades, and its immense scale provides ample testament to the medieval might of the Roman Catholic church. Ringed by 3m-thick walls, its cavernous halls, chapels and antechambers are largely bare today, but an audioguide (€2) provides a useful backstory.

Pont St-Bénezet   Bridge

(bd du Rhône; adult/child 24hr ticket €5/4, with Palais des Papes €13.50/10.50; ⊗9am-8pm Jul, to 8.30pm Aug, shorter hours Sep-Jun) Legend says Pastor Bénezet had three saintly visions urging him to build a bridge across the Rhône. Completed in 1185, the 900m-long bridge with 20 arches linked Avignon with Villeneuve-lès-Avignon. It was rebuilt several times before all but four of its spans were washed away in the 1600s.

If you don't want to pay to visit the bridge, admire it for free from Rocher des Doms park or Pont Édouard Daladier, or on Île de la Barthelasse's chemin des Berges.

Don't be surprised if you spot someone dancing: in France, the bridge is known as Pont d'Avignon after the nursery rhyme: 'Sur le pont d'Avignon/L'on y danse, l'on y danse...' (On Avignon Bridge, all are dancing...).

Musée du Petit Palais   Museum

(☏04 90 86 44 58; www.petit-palais.org; place du Palais; adult/child €6/free; ⊗10am-1pm & 2-6pm Wed-Mon) The archbishops' palace during the 14th and 15th centuries now houses outstanding collections of 'primitive', pre-Rennaissance, 13th- to 16th-century Italian religious paintings by artists including Botticelli, Carpaccio and Giovanni di

Paolo – the most famous is Botticelli's *La Vierge et l'Enfant* (1470).

Musée Angladon · · · · · · · · · · Gallery
(☑04 90 82 29 03; www.angladon.com; 5 rue Laboureur; adult/child €8/6.50; ⊙1-6pm Tue-Sun Apr-Sep, 1-6pm Tue-Sat Oct-Mar) Tiny Musée Angladon harbours an impressive collection of impressionist treasures, including works by Cézanne, Sisley, Manet and Degas – but the star piece is Van Gogh's *Railway Wagons*, the only painting by the artist on display in Provence. Impress your friends by pointing out that the 'earth' isn't actually paint, but bare canvas.

Collection Lambert · · · · · · · · · Gallery
(☑04 90 16 56 20; www.collectionlambert. com; 5 rue Violette; adult/child €10/8; ⊙11am-6pm Tue-Sun Sep-Jun, to 7pm daily Jul & Aug) Reopened in summer 2015 after significant renovation and expansion, Avignon's contemporary-arts museum focuses on works from the 1960s to the present. Work spans from minimalist and conceptual to video and photography – in stark contrast to the classic 18th-century mansion housing it.

🏃 ACTIVITIES & TOURS

Le Carré du Palais · · · · · · · Wine Tasting
(☑04 90 27 24 00; www.carredupalaisavignon. com; 1 place du Palais) The historic Hôtel Calvet de la Palun building in central Avignon has been renovated into a wine centre promoting and serving Côtes du Rhône and Vallée du Rhône appellations. Stop in to get a taste of the local vintages.

Avignon Wine Tour · · · · · · · · · · Tours
(☑06 28 05 33 84; www.avignon-wine-tour.com; per person €80-110) Visit the region's vineyards with a knowledgeable guide, leaving you free to enjoy the wine.

🍴 EATING

Place de l'Horloge is crammed with touristy restaurants that don't offer the best cuisine or value in town. Delve instead into the pedestrian old city where ample pretty

> *the seat of papal power for seven decades*

Palais des Papes

HANS GEORG EIBEN/GETTY IMAGES ©

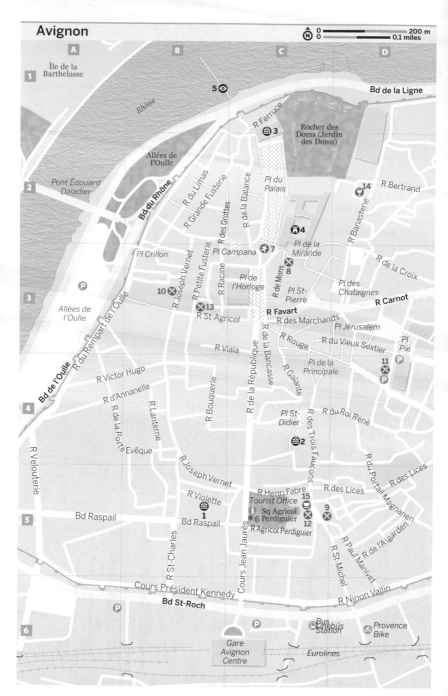

Avignon

Île de la Barthelasse

Rhône

Bd de la Ligne

R Ferruce

🏛 3

Rocher des Doms (Jardin des Doms)

Allées de l'Oulle

Bd du Rhône

R du Limas

R Grande Fusterie

R des Grottes

R de la Balance

Pl du Palais

R Bertrand

🔴 14

R Banasterie

🏛 4

R de la Croix

Pl Crillon

R Joseph Vernet

R Petite Fusterie

R Racine

Pl Campana

🔵 7

Pl de la Mirande

R de Mons

❌ 8

Pl St-Pierre

Pl des Chataignes

🅿

❌ 10

Pl de l'Horloge

R Carnot

Allées de l'Oulle

R du Rempart de l'Oulle

❌ 13

R St-Agricol

R Favart

R des Marchands

Pl Jérusalem

Bd de l'Oulle

R Viala

R de la Bancasse

R Rouge

R du Vieux Sextier

Pl Pie

🅿

❌ 11

🅿

R Victor Hugo

R Galante

Pl de la Principale

R d'Annanelle

R Bouquerie

R de la République

Pl St-Didier

R du Roi René

R de la Porte Evêque

R Lanterne

R des Trois Faucons

R du Portail Magnanen

R des Lices

R Velouterie

🏛 2

R Joseph Vernet

R Henri Fabre

R des Lices

R Violette

🏛 1

Bd Raspail

Tourist Office

ℹ 15

Sq Agricol Perdiguier

❌ 9

❌ 12

❌ 6

R Agricol Perdiguier

R St-Michel

R Paul Manivet

R de l'Aigarden

Bd Raspail

R St-Charles

Cours Jean Jaurès

Cours Président Kennedy

R Ninon Vallin

Bd St-Roch

🅿

🅿

Bus Station

🅿

Provence Bike

Gare Avignon Centre

Eurolines

N

0 — 200 m
0 — 0.1 miles

A B C D

1

2

3

4

5

6

Avignon

◎ **Sights**
1 Collection Lambert B5
2 Musée Angladon C4
3 Musée du Petit Palais C1
4 Palais des Papes C2
5 Pont St-Bénezet B1

⊕ **Activities, Courses & Tours**
6 Avignon Guided Tours C5
7 Le Carré du Palais C3

⊗ **Eating**
8 Christian Etienne C3
9 Ginette et Marcel C5
10 Les 5 Sens B3
11 Les Halles D4
12 Maison Violette C5
13 Restaurant L'Essentiel B3

⊖ **Drinking & Nightlife**
14 La Manutention D2
15 Milk Shop C5

squares tempt: place des Châtaignes and place de la Principe are two particularly beautiful restaurant-clad squares.

Restaurants open seven days during the summer festival season, when reservations become essential.

Maison Violette   Bakery €

(☏ 06 59 44 62 94; place des Corps Saints; ⊗7am-7.30pm Mon-Sat) We simply defy you not to walk into this bakery and not instantly be tempted by the stacks of baguettes, *ficelles* and *pains de campagnes* loaded up on the counter, not to mention the orderly ranks of eclairs, *millefeuilles*, fruit tarts and cookies lined up irresistibly behind the glass. Go on, a little bit of what you fancy does you good, non?

Ginette et Marcel   Cafe €

(☏ 04 90 85 58 70; 27 place des Corps Saints; tartines €4.30-6.90; ⊗11am-11pm Wed-Mon; ⊕) Set on one of Avignon's most happening plane-tree-shaded squares, this vintage cafe styled like a 1950s grocery is a charming spot to hang out and people-watch over a *tartine* (open-face sandwich), tart, salad or other light dish – equally tasty for lunch or an early-evening *apéro*. Kids adore Ginette's cherry- and violet-flavoured cordials and Marcel's glass jars of old-fashioned sweets.

Restaurant L'Essentiel   French €€

(☏ 04 90 85 87 12; www.restaurantlessentiel. com; 2 rue Petite Fusterie; menus €32-46; ⊗noon-2pm & 7-9.45pm Tue-Sat) Snug in an elegant, caramel-stone *hôtel particulier*, the Essential is one of the finest places to

eat in town – inside or in the wonderful courtyard garden. Begin with courgette flowers poached in a crayfish and truffle sauce, then continue with rabbit stuffed with candied aubergine, perhaps.

Au Jardin des Carmes   French €€

(☏ 09 54 25 10 67; 21 place des Carmes; mains €20; ⊗noon-10.30pm Tue-Sat) There's one standout reason to lunch at this lovely little restaurant, and that's the delightful courtyard garden, shaded by sails, tall bamboo and climbing plants. Starters are €10, mains €20 and desserts €9, plus the *plat du jour* at €16. The food is honest rather than *haute cuisine*, but it's prettily presented and packed with flavour

Christian Etienne   French €€€

(☏ 04 90 86 16 50; www.christian-etienne.fr; 10 rue de Mons; lunch/dinner menus from €35/75; ⊗noon-2pm & 7.30-10pm Tue-Sat) One of Avignon's top tables, this much-vaunted restaurant occupies a 12th-century palace with a leafy outdoor terrace, adjacent to Palais des Papes. Interiors feel slightly dated, but the refined Provençal cuisine remains exceptional, and the restaurant has earned a Michelin star.

Les 5 Sens   Gastronomy €€€

(☏ 04 90 85 26 51; www.restaurantles5sens. com; 18 rue Joseph Vernet; menus lunch €16-22, dinner €40-59; ⊗noon-1.30pm & 7.45-11.30pm Tue-Sat) Chef Thierry Baucher, one of France's *meilleurs ouvriers* (top chefs), reveals his southwestern origins in specialities such as *cassoulet* and foie gras, but skews contemporary-Mediterranean

Al fresco dining in Avignon

in gastronomic dishes such as butternut-squash ravioli with *escargots*. Surroundings are sleek; service is impeccable.

DRINKING & NIGHTLIFE

Chic yet laid-back Avignon is awash with gorgeous, tree-shaded pedestrian squares buzzing with cafe life. Favourite options, loaded with pavement terraces and drinking opportunities, include place Crillon, place Pie, place de l'Horloge and place des Corps Saints.

Students tend to favour the many bars dotted along the aptly named rue de la Verrerie (Glassware St).

La Manutention   Bar
(4 rue des Escaliers Ste-Anne; ⊘noon-midnight) No address better reflects Avignon's artsy soul than this bistro-bar at cultural centre La Manutention. Its leafy terrace basks in the shade of Palais des Papes' stone walls and, inside, giant conservatory-style windows open onto the funky decor of pocket-size-bar Utopia. There's a cinema too.

Milk Shop   Cafe
(⚇09 82 54 16 82; www.milkshop.fr; 26 place des Corps Saints; ⊘7.45am-7pm Mon-Fri, 9.30am-7pm Sat; ☎) Keen to mingle with Avignon students? Make a beeline for this *salon au lait* ('milk bar') where super-thick ice-cream shakes (€4.50) are slurped through extra-wide straws. Bagels (€5 to €7), cupcakes and other American snacks create a deliberate US vibe, while comfy armchairs and wi-fi encourage hanging out.

INFORMATION

Tourist Office (⚇04 32 74 32 74; www.avignon-tourisme.com; 41 cours Jean Jaurès; ⊘9am-6pm Mon-Sat, 10am-5pm Sun Apr-Oct, shorter hours Nov-Mar) Offers guided walking tours and information on other tours and activities, including boat trips on the River Rhône and wine-tasting trips to nearby vineyards. Smartphone apps too.

Tourist Office Annexe (Gare Avignon TGV; ⊘Jun-Aug) During summer, Avignon has an information booth at the TGV station.

GETTING THERE & AWAY

AIR

Aéroport Avignon-Provence (AVN; ☑04 90 81 51 51; www.avignon.aeroport.fr; Caumont) In Caumont, 8km southeast of Avignon. Currently has direct flights to London.

BUS

The **bus station** (bd St-Roch; ⏰information window 8am-7pm Mon-Fri, to 1pm Sat) is next to the central train station. Tickets are sold on board. For schedules, see www.lepilote.com, www.info-ler.fr and www.vaucluse.fr. Long-haul companies **Linebús** (☑04 90 85 30 48; www.linebus.com) and **Eurolines** (☑04 90 85 27 60; www.eurolines.com) have offices at the far end of bus platforms and serve places such as Barcelona.

Aix-en-Provence €17.40; LER Line 23; 1¼ hours; six daily Monday to Saturday, two on Sunday.

Carpentras €2; TransVaucluse Line 5.1; 45 minutes; two or three hourly Monday to Saturday, every two hours Sunday.

TRAIN

If you're arriving in Avignon from elsewhere in France, it's nearly always easier, cheaper (and in many cases faster) to take the train than fly. There are two train stations in Avignon. There is an airport 8km southeast of Avignon in Caumont.

Avignon has two train stations: **Gare Avignon Centre** (42 bd St-Roch), on the southern edge of the walled town, and **Gare Avignon TGV** (Courtine), 4km southwest in Courtine. Local shuttle trains link the two every 20 minutes (€1.60, five minutes, 6am to 11pm). Note that there is no luggage storage at the train station.

Destinations served by TGV include Paris Gare du Lyon (€35 to €80, 3½ hours), Marseille (€17.50, 35 minutes) and Nice (€31 to €40, 3¼ hours). **Eurostar** (www.eurostar.com) services operate one to five times weekly between Avignon TGV and London (from €59.50, 5¾ hours) en route to/from Marseille.

Marseille €17.50, 1¼ to two hours

Marseille airport (Vitrolles station) €14.50, one to 1½ hours

 Provençal Produce

Avignon's covered food market, **Les Halles** (www.avignon-leshalles.com; place Pie; ⏰6am-1.30pm Tue-Fri, to 2pm Sat & Sun), has over 40 food stalls showcasing seasonal Provençal ingredients. Even better, free cooking demonstrations are held at 11am Saturday. Outside on place Pie, admire Patrick Blanc's marvellous vegetal wall.

KEN SCICLUNA/GETTY IMAGES ©

GETTING AROUND

BICYCLE

Vélopop (☑08 10 45 64 56; www.velopop.fr) Shared-bicycle service, with 17 stations around town. The first half-hour is free; each additional half-hour is €1. Membership per day/week is €1/5.

Provence Bike (☑04 90 27 92 61; www.provence-bike.com; 7 av St-Ruf; bicycles per day/week from €12/65, scooters €25/150; ⏰9am-6.30pm Mon-Sat, plus 10am-1pm Sun Jul) Rents city bikes, mountain bikes, scooters and motorcycles.

CAR & MOTORCYCLE

Find car-hire agencies at both train stations (reserve ahead, especially in July). Narrow, one-way streets and impossible parking make driving within the ramparts difficult: park outside the walls. The city has 900 free spaces at **Parking de L'Ile Piot**, and 1150 at **Parking des Italiens**, both under surveillance and served by the free **TCRA shuttle bus** (Transports en Commun de la Région d'Avignon; ☑04 32 74 18 32; www.tcra.

Where to Stay in Avignon

Avignon is an excellent place to base yourself, with a wide range of hotels and B&Bs. **Avignon & Provence** (www. avignon-et-provence.com) is a local tourist site with accommodation listings. Note that parking is pretty much non-existent inside the city walls, so you'll have to drop off your luggage, leave your car at one of the large car parks on the edge of the city and walk.

fr). On directional signs at intersections, 'P' in yellow means pay car parks; 'P' in green, free car parks. Pay **Parking Gare Centre** (☑04 90 80 74 40; bd St-Roch; ☺24hr) is next to the central train station.

Moustiers Ste-Marie

Dubbed 'Étoile de Provence' (Star of Provence), jewel-box Moustiers Ste-Marie crowns towering limestone cliffs, which mark the beginning of the Alps and the end of Haute-Provence's rolling prairies. A 227m-long chain, bearing a shining gold star, is stretched high above the village – a tradition, legend has it, begun by the Knight of Blacas, who was grateful to have returned safely from the Crusades. Twice a century, the weathered chain snaps, and the star gets replaced, as happened in 1996. In summer, it's clear that Moustiers' charms are no secret.

⊙ SIGHTS

Chapelle Notre Dame de Beauvoir   Church

(guided tours adult/child €3/free) Lording over the village, beneath Moustiers' star, this 14th-century church clings to a cliff ledge like an eagle's nest. A steep trail climbs beside a waterfall to the chapel, passing 14 stations of the cross en route. On 8 September, Mass at 5am celebrates the na-

tivity of the Virgin Mary, followed by flutes, drums and breakfast on the square.

Musée de la Faïence   Museum

(☑04 92 74 61 64; rue Seigneur de la Clue; adult/student/under 16yr €3/2/free; ☺10am-12.30pm Jul & Aug, to 5pm or 6pm rest of year, closed Tue year-round) Moustiers' decorative *faïence* (glazed earthenware) once graced the dining tables of Europe's most aristocratic houses. Today each of Moustiers' 15 ateliers has its own style, from representational to abstract. Antique masterpieces are housed in this little museum, adjacent to the town hall.

ACTIVITIES

Des Guides pour l'Aventure   Outdoors

(☑06 85 94 46 61; www.guidesaventure.com) Offers activities including canyoning (from €45 per half-day), rock climbing (€40 for three hours), rafting (€45 for 2½ hours) and 'floating' (€50 for three hours) – which is like rafting, except you have a buoyancy aid instead of a boat.

✕ EATING

La Grignotière   Provencal €

(☑04 92 74 69 12; rte de Ste-Anne; mains €6-15; ☺11.30am-10pm May-Sep, to 6pm Feb–mid-May) Hidden behind the soft pink facade of Moustiers' Musée de la Faïence is this utterly gorgeous, blissfully peaceful garden restaurant. Tables sit between olive trees and the colourful, eye-catching decor – including the handmade glassware – is the handiwork of talented, dynamic owner Sandrine. Cuisine is 'picnic chic', meaning lots of creative salads, tapenades, quiches and so on.

La Treille Muscate   Provencal €€

(☑04 92 74 64 31; www.restaurant-latreillemuscate.fr; place de l'Église; lunch/dinner menus from €24/32; ☺noon-2pm Fri-Wed, 7.30-10.30pm Fri-Tue) The top place to eat in the village proper: classic Provençal cooking served with panache, either in the stone-walled

Moustiers Ste-Marie

dining room or on the terrace with valley views. Expect tasty dishes like oven-roasted lamb served with seasonal veg and rainbow trout with *sauce vierge*. Reservations recommended.

La Ferme Ste-Cécile
Gastronomy €€

(☏04 92 74 64 18; D952; menus €29-38; ⊙noon-2pm Tue-Sun, 7.30-10pm Tue-Sat) Just outside Moustiers, this wonderful *ferme auberge* (country inn) immerses you in the full Provençal dining experience, from the sun-splashed terrace and locally picked wines right through to the chef's meticulous Mediterranean cuisine. It's about 1.2km from Moustiers; look out for the signs as you drive towards Castellane.

La Bastide de Moustiers
Gastronomy €€€

(☏04 92 70 47 47; www.bastide-moustiers.com; chemin de Quinson; lunch menus €40-50, dinner menus €64-82; ⊙noon-2pm & 7.30-9.30pm May-Sep, closed Tue & Wed Oct-Apr; ❄) Legendary chef Alain Ducasse has created his own Provençal bolthole here, and it's an utter treat from start to finish, from the playful *amuses bouches* to the rich, sauce-heavy mains and indulgent desserts. The views from the terrace are dreamy too. Dress smartly and reserve ahead in high season. It's 500m down a country lane, signposted off the D952 to Ste-Croix de Verdon.

Rooms (double from €280) are spacious and luxurious, and nearly all have valley views.

ⓘ GETTING THERE & AROUND

A car makes exploring the gorges much more fun, though if you're very fit, cycling is an option too. Bus services run to Castellane and Moustiers, but there's scant transport inside the gorges.

In This Chapter

La Sagrada Família 270
La Rambla 278
Montjuïc 284
Sights 288
Tours 297
Shopping 297
Eating..298
Drinking & Nightlife........................ 301
Entertainment 304
Information 305
Getting There & Away 306
Getting Around 306

Barcelona, Spain

Barcelona is a mix of sunny Mediterranean charm and European urban style. The city bursts with art and architecture (from Gothic to Gaudí), Catalan cooking is among the country's best, summer sun seekers fill the beaches in and beyond the city, and the bars and clubs heave year-round. The city began as a middle-ranking Roman town, of which vestiges can be seen today, and its old centre constitutes one of the greatest concentrations of Gothic architecture in Europe. Beyond this core are some of the world's more bizarre buildings: surreal spectacles capped by Gaudí's church, La Sagrada Família.

Two Days in Barcelona

Start with the Barri Gòtic. After a stroll along **La Rambla** (p278), admire **La Catedral** (p288) and the **Museu d'Història de Barcelona** (p288) on historic **Plaça del Rei** (p289), then visit the **Basílica de Santa Maria del Mar** (p292), and the nearby **Museu Picasso** (p292). Round off with a meal and cocktails in El Born. On day two, experience **Park Güell** (p294) and **La Sagrada Família** (p271). Afterwards, go for dinner at **Suculent** (p299).

Four Days in Barcelona

Start the third day with more Gaudí, visiting **Casa Batlló** (p294) and **La Pedrera** (p294), followed by beachside relaxation and seafood in **Barceloneta** (p300). Day four should be dedicated to **Montjuïc** (p284), with its museums, galleries, fortress, gardens and Olympic stadium.

Looking for more Spain? Drive or catch a train to Basque Country (p308).

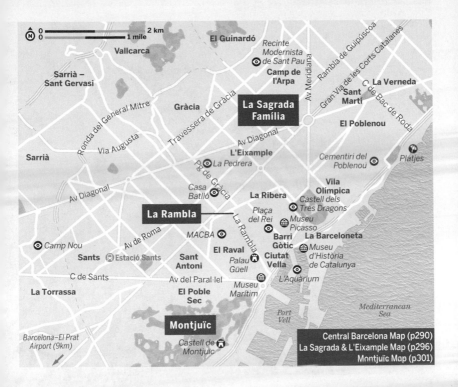

N
0 — 2 km
0 — 1 mile

Vallcarca

El Guinardó

Recinte
Modernista
de Sant Pau

Sarrià –
Sant Gervasi

Camp de
l'Arpa

La Verneda

Gràcia

**La Sagrada
Família**

Sant
Martí

El Poblenou

Ronda del General Mitre

Via Augusta

Travessera de Gràcia

Sarrià

Av Diagonal

L'Eixample

La Pedrera

Cementiri del
Poblenou

Platjes

Av Diagonal

Pg de Gràcia

Casa
Batlló

La Ribera

Vila
Olímpica

Castell dels
Tres Dragons

La Rambla

Plaça
del Rei

Museu
Picasso

Av de Roma

MACBA

La Rambla

Barri
Gòtic

La Barceloneta

El Raval

Camp Nou

Sants

Estació Sants

Sant
Antoni

Palau
Güell

Ciutat
Vella

Museu
d'Història
de Catalunya

C de Sants

Av del Paral·lel

Museu
Marítim

L'Aquàrium

La Torrassa

El Poble
Sec

Port
Vell

Mediterranean
Sea

Montjuïc

Barcelona–El Prat
Airport (9km)

Castell de
Montjuïc

Central Barcelona Map (p290)
La Sagrada & L'Eixample Map (p296)
Montjuïc Map (p301)

Arriving in Barcelona

Frequent *aerobúses* make the 35-minute run into town (€5.90) from 6am to 1am from **El Prat airport**. Taxis cost around €25. If arriving at the long-distance train station **Estació Sants** near the centre of town, there is a metro connection available to other neighbourhoods. **Estació del Nord** is Barcelona's long-haul bus station in L'Eixample, about 1.5km northeast of Plaça de Catalunya. It's a short walk from several metro stations.

Where to Stay

Barcelona has some fabulous accommodation, but never – and we repeat never – arrive in town without a reservation. Designer digs are something of a Barcelona speciality, with midrange and top-end travellers particularly well served. Apartments are also widespread and a fine alternative to hotels. Prices in Barcelona are generally higher than elsewhere in the country.

For information on what each neighbourhood has to offer, see p307.

La Sagrada Família's interior

JASON WALTMAN/500PX ©

La Sagrada Família

If you have time for only one sightseeing outing, this is it. The Sagrada Família inspires awe by its sheer verticality, inspiring use of light and Gaudí's offbeat design elements.

Great For...

☑ **Don't Miss**

The apse, the extraordinary pillars and the stained glass.

In the manner of the medieval cathedrals La Sagrada Família emulates, it's still under construction after more than 100 years. When completed, the highest tower will be more than half as high again as those that stand today.

A Holy Mission

The Temple Expiatori de la Sagrada Família (Expiatory Temple of the Holy Family) was Antoni Gaudí's all-consuming obsession. Given the commission by a conservative society that wished to build a temple as atonement for the city's sins of modernity, Gaudí saw its completion as his holy mission. As funds dried up, he contributed his own, and in the last years of his life he was never shy of pleading with anyone he thought a likely donor.

❶ Need to Know

Map p296; ☏ 93 208 04 14; www.sagrada
familia.cat; Carrer de Mallorca 401; adult/
concession/under 11yr €15/13/free; ⊙9am-
8pm Apr-Sep, to 6pm Oct-Mar; Ⓜ Sagrada
Família

✗ Take a Break

Michael Collins (Map p296; ☏ 93 459 19
64; www.michaelcollinspubs.com; Plaça de la
Sagrada Família 4; ⊙1pm-2.30am Sun-Thu,
1pm-3am Fri & Sat; ☏; Ⓜ Sagrada Família)
across the square is good for a beer.

> ★ **Top Tip**
> Buying tickets online in advance is a
> must to beat the frequently dispiriting
> queues.

Gaudí devised a temple 95m long and
60m wide, able to seat 13,000 people,
with a central tower 170m high above the
transept (representing Christ) and another
17 towers of 100m or more. The 12 along
the three facades represent the Apostles,
while the remaining five represent the
Virgin Mary and the four evangelists. With
his characteristic dislike for straight lines
(there were none in nature, he said), Gaudí
gave his towers swelling outlines inspired
by the weird peaks of the holy mountain Montserrat outside Barcelona, and
encrusted them with a tangle of sculpture
that seems an outgrowth of the stone.

At Gaudí's death, only the crypt, the apse
walls, one portal and one tower had been
finished. Three more towers were added by
1930, completing the northeast (Nativity)
facade. In 1936 anarchists burned and
smashed the interior, including workshops,
plans and models. Work began again in
1952, but controversy has always clouded
progress. Opponents of the continuation
of the project claim that the computer
models based on what little of Gaudí's
plans survived the anarchists' ire have led
to the creation of a monster that has little
to do with Gaudí's plans and style. It is a
debate that appears to have little hope of
resolution. Like or hate what is being done,
the fascination it awakens is undeniable.

Guesses on when construction might
be complete range from the 2020s to the
2040s. Even before reaching that point,
some of the oldest parts of the church, especially the apse, have required restoration
work.

The Interior & the Apse

Inside, work on roofing over the church
was completed in 2010. The roof is held up
by a forest of extraordinary angled pillars.

As the pillars soar towards the ceiling, they sprout a web of supporting branches, creating the effect of a forest canopy. The tree image is in no way fortuitous – Gaudí envisaged such an effect. Everything was thought through, including the shape and placement of windows to create the mottled effect one would see with sunlight pouring through the branches of a thick forest. The pillars are of four different types of stone. They vary in colour and load-bearing strength, from the soft Montjuïc stone pillars along the lateral aisles through to granite, dark grey basalt and finally burgundy-tinged Iranian porphyry for the key columns at the intersection of the nave and transept. The stained glass, divided in shades of red, blue, green and ochre, creates a hypnotic, magical atmosphere when the sun hits the windows. Tribunes built high above the aisles can host two choirs: the main tribune up to 1300 people and the children's tribune up to 300.

Nativity Facade

The Nativity Facade is the artistic pinnacle of the building, mostly created under Gaudí's personal supervision. You can climb high up inside some of the four towers by a combination of lifts and narrow spiral staircases – a vertiginous experience. Do not climb the stairs if you have cardiac or respiratory problems. The towers are destined to hold tubular bells capable of playing complex music at great volume. Their upper parts are decorated with mosaics spelling out 'Sanctus, Sanctus, Sanctus, Hosanna in Excelsis, Amen, Alleluia'. Asked why he lavished so much care on the tops of the spires, which

Nativity Facade

no one would see from close up, Gaudí answered: 'The angels will see them'.

Three sections of the portal represent, from left to right, Hope, Charity and Faith. Among the forest of sculpture on the Charity portal you can see, low down, the manger surrounded by an ox, an ass, the shepherds and kings, and angel musicians. Some 30 different species of plant from around Catalonia are reproduced here, and the faces of the many figures are taken from plaster casts done of local people and the occasional one made from corpses in the local morgue.

★ Did You Know?

Unfinished it may be, but La Sagrada Família attracts over 4.5 million visitors yearly and is the most visited monument in Spain.

PECOLD/SHUTTERSTOCK ©

Directly above the blue stained-glass window is the archangel Gabriel's Annunciation to Mary. At the top is a green cypress tree, a refuge in a storm for the white doves of peace dotted over it. The mosaic work at the pinnacle of the towers is made from Murano glass from Venice.

To the right of the facade is the curious Claustre del Roser, a Gothic-style mini-cloister tacked on to the outside of the church (rather than the classic square enclosure of the great Gothic church monasteries). Once inside, look back to the intricately decorated entrance. On the lower right-hand side you'll notice the sculpture of a reptilian devil handing a terrorist a bomb. Barcelona was regularly rocked by political violence, and bombings were frequent in the decades prior to the civil war. The sculpture is one of several on the 'temptations of men and women'.

Passion Facade

The southwest Passion Facade, on the theme of Christ's last days and death, was built between 1954 and 1978 based on surviving drawings by Gaudí, with four towers and a large, sculpture-bedecked portal. The sculptor, Josep Subirachs, worked on its decoration from 1986 to 2006. He did not attempt to imitate Gaudí, rather producing angular, controversial images of his own. The main series of sculptures, on three levels, are in an S-shaped sequence, starting with the Last Supper at the bottom left and ending with Christ's burial at the top right. Decorative work on the Passion Facade continues even today, as construction of the Glory Facade moves ahead.

To the right, in front of the Passion Facade, the Escoles de Gaudí is one of his simpler gems. Gaudí built this as a children's school, creating an original,

---

❶ When to Go

There are always lots of people visiting the Sagrada Família, but if you can get there when it opens, you'll find fewer people.

undulating roof of brick that continues to charm architects to this day. Inside is a recreation of Gaudí's modest office as it was when he died, and explanations of the geometric patterns and plans at the heart of his building techniques.

A Hidden Portrait

Careful observation of the Passion Facade will reveal a special tribute from sculptor Josep Subirachs to Gaudí. The central sculptural group (below Christ crucified) shows, from right to left, Christ bearing his cross, Veronica displaying the cloth with Christ's bloody image, a pair of soldiers and, watching it all, a man called the evangelist. Subirachs used a rare photo of Gaudí, taken a couple of years before his death, as the model for the evangelist's face.

Glory Facade

The Glory Facade is under construction and will, like the others, be crowned by four towers – the total of 12 representing the Twelve Apostles. Gaudí wanted it to be the most magnificent facade of the church. Inside will be the narthex, a kind of foyer made up of 16 'lanterns', a series of hyperboloid forms topped by cones. Further decoration will make the whole building a microcosmic symbol of the Christian church, with Christ represented by a massive 170m central tower above the transept, and the five remaining planned towers symbolising the Virgin Mary and the four evangelists.

Museu Gaudí

Open the same times as the church, the Museu Gaudí, below ground level, includes interesting material on Gaudí's life and other works, as well as models and photos of La Sagrada Família. You can see a good example of his plumb-line models that showed him the stresses and strains he could get away with in construction. A side hall towards the eastern end of the museum leads to a viewing point above the simple crypt in which the genius is buried. The crypt, where Masses are now held, can also be visited from the Carrer de Mallorca side of the church.

What's Nearby?

Església de les Saleses   Church

(Map p296; ☑93 458 76 67; www.parroquia concepciobcn.org; Passeig de Sant Joan 90; ⊗7.30am-1pm & 5-9pm Mon-Fri, 7.30am-2pm & 5-9pm Sun; ⓂTetuan) A singular neo-Gothic effort, this church is interesting because it was designed by Joan Martorell i Montells (1833–1906), Gaudí's architecture professor. It was raised in 1878–85 with an adjacent convent (badly damaged in the civil war and now a school), and the use of brick, mosaics and sober stained glass offers hints of what was to come with Modernisme.

Recinte Modernista de Sant Pau   Architecture

(☑93 553 78 01; www.santpaubarcelona.org; Carrer de Sant Antoni Maria Claret 167; adult/child €13/free; ⊗10am-6.30pm Mon-Sat, to

Passion facade (p273)

2.30pm Sun Apr-Oct, 10am-4.30pm Mon-Sat Nov-Mar; Ⓜ Sant Pau/Dos de Maig) Domènech i Montaner outdid himself as architect and philanthropist with the Modernista Hospital de la Santa Creu i de Sant Pau, redubbed in 2014 the 'Recinte Modernista'. It was long considered one of the city's most important hospitals and only recently repurposed, its various spaces becoming cultural centres, offices and something of a monument. The complex, including 16 pavilions, is lavishly decorated and each pavilion is unique. Together with the Palau de la Música Catalana it is a World Heritage site.

Museu del Disseny de Barcelona   Museum

(☎ 93 256 68 00; www.museudeldisseny.cat; Plaça de les Glòries Catalanes 37; permanent/temporary exhibition €6/4.40, combination ticket €8; ☺ 10am-8pm Tue-Sun; Ⓜ Glòries) Barcelona's design museum lies inside a new monolithic building with geometric facades and a rather brutalist appearance – which has already earned the nickname *la grapadora* (the stapler) by locals. Architecture aside, the museum houses a dazzling collection of ceramics, decorative arts and textiles, and is a must for anyone interested in the design world.

★ Did You Know?

Pope Benedict XVI consecrated the church in a huge ceremony in November 2010.

★ Top Tip

Audio guides – including some tailored to children – are available for an additional fee.

La Sagrada Família

A TIMELINE

1882 Construction begins on a neo-Gothic church designed by Francisco de Paula del Villar y Lozano.

1883 Antoni Gaudí takes over as chief architect and plans a far more ambitious church to hold 13,000 faithful.

1926 Gaudí dies; work continues under Domènec Sugrañes i Gras. Much of the **apse ❶** and **Nativity Facade ❷** is complete.

1930 Bell towers ❸ of the Nativity Facade completed.

1936 Construction is interrupted by Spanish Civil War; anarchists destroy Gaudí's plans.

1939–40 Architect Francesc de Paula Quintana i Vidal restores the crypt and meticulously reassembles many of Gaudí's lost models, some of which can be seen in the **museum ❹**.

1976 Passion Facade ❺ completed.

1986–2006 Sculptor Josep Subirachs adds sculptural details to the Passion Facade including the panels telling the story of Christ's last days, amid much criticism for employing a style far removed from what was thought typical of Gaudí.

2000 Central nave vault ❻ completed.

2010 Church completely roofed over; Pope Benedict XVI consecrates the church; work begins on a high-speed rail tunnel that will pass beneath the church's **Glory Facade ❼**.

2020s–40s Projected completion date.

TOP TIPS

➡ The best light through the stained-glass windows of the Passion Facade bursts into the heart of the church in the late afternoon.

➡ Visit at opening time on weekdays to avoid the worst of the crowds.

➡ Head up the Nativity Facade bell towers for the views, as long queues generally await at the Passion Facade towers.

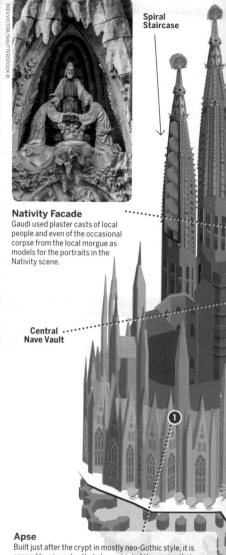

Spiral Staircase

Nativity Facade
Gaudí used plaster casts of local people and even of the occasional corpse from the local morgue as models for the portraits in the Nativity scene.

Central Nave Vault

Apse
Built just after the crypt in mostly neo-Gothic style, it is capped by pinnacles that show a hint of the genius that Gaudí would later deploy in the rest of the church.

Bell Towers
The towers of the three facades will represent the 12 Apostles. Eight are completed. Lifts whisk visitors up one tower of the Nativity and Passion Facades (the latter gets longer queues) for fine views.

Completed Church
Along with the Glory Facade and its four towers, six other towers remain to be completed. They will represent the four Evangelists, the Virgin Mary and, soaring above them all over the transept, a 170m colossus symbolising Christ.

Glory Facade
This will be the most fanciful facade of all, with a narthex boasting 16 hyperboloid lanterns topped by cones that will look something like an organ made of melting ice cream.

Museu Gaudí
Jammed with old photos, drawings and restored plaster models that bring Gaudí's ambitions to life, the museum also houses an extraordinarily complex plumb-line device he used to calculate his constructions.

Escoles de Gaudí

Crypt
The first completed part of the church, the crypt is in largely neo-Gothic style and lies under the transept. Gaudí's burial place here can be seen from the Museu Gaudí.

Passion Facade
See the story of Christ's last days from Last Supper to burial in an S-shaped sequence from bottom to top of the facade. Check out the cryptogram in which the numbers always add up to 33, Christ's age at his death.

La Rambla

Barcelona's most famous street is both tourist magnet and window into Catalan culture, with arts centres, theatres and intriguing architecture. The middle is a broad pedestrian boulevard, crowded daily with a wide cross-section of society. A stroll here is pure sensory overload, with souvenir hawkers, buskers, pavement artists and living statues part of the ever-changing street scene.

Great For...

❶ Need to Know

The **Rambla** (Map p290; Ⓜ Catalunya, Liceu, Drassanes) stroll, from Plaça de Catalunya to Plaça del Portal de la Pau, is 1.5km. To get here use the Catalunya, Liceu or Drassanes metro stations.

★ **Top Tip**

Things have improved in recent years, but pickpockets still prey on head-in-air tourists along here.

History

La Rambla takes its name from a seasonal stream (derived from the Arabic word for sand, *raml*) that once ran here. From the early Middle Ages, it was better known as the Cagalell (Stream of Shit) and lay outside the city walls until the 14th century. Monastic buildings were then built and, subsequently, mansions of the well-to-do from the 16th to the early 19th centuries. Unofficially, La Rambla is divided into five sections, which explains why many know it as Las Ramblas.

La Rambla de Canaletes

The section of La Rambla north of Plaça de Catalunya is named after the **Font de Canaletes** (Map p290; MCatalunya), an inconspicuous turn-of-the-20th-century drinking fountain, the water of which supposedly emerges from what were once known as the springs of Canaletes. It used to be said that *barcelonins* 'drank the waters of Les Canaletes'. Nowadays people claim that anyone who drinks from the fountain will return to Barcelona, which is not such a bad prospect. Delirious football fans gather here to celebrate whenever the city's principal team, FC Barcelona, wins a cup or league title.

La Rambla dels Estudis

La Rambla dels Estudis, from Carrer de la Canuda running south to Carrer de la Portaferrissa, was formerly home to a twittering bird market, which closed in 2010 after 150 years in operation.

Església de Betlem

Just north of Carrer del Carme, this **church** (Map p290; ☎93 318 38 23; www.mdbetlem. net; Carrer d'en Xuclà 2; ⊘8.30am-1.30pm &

6-9pm; MLiceu) was constructed in baroque style for the Jesuits in the late 17th and early 18th centuries to replace an earlier church destroyed by fire in 1671. Fire was a bit of a theme for this site: the church was once considered the most splendid of Barcelona's few baroque offerings, but leftist arsonists torched it in 1936.

Palau Moja

Looming over the eastern side of La Rambla, **Palau Moja** (Map p290; 933 16 27 40; https://palaumoja.com; Carrer de Portaferrissa

★ **Did You Know**
La Rambla saw plenty of action during the civil war. In *Homage to Catalonia*, George Orwell vividly described the avenue gripped by revolutionary fervour.

KARSOL/SHUTTERSTOCK ©

1; info centre/shop 10am-9pm, cafe 9am-midnight Mon-Fri, 11am-midnight Sat & Sun; MLiceu) FREE is a neoclassical building dating from the second half of the 18th century. Its clean, classical lines are best appreciated from across La Rambla. Unfortunately, interior access is limited, as it houses mostly government offices.

La Rambla de Sant Josep

From Carrer de la Portaferrissa to Plaça de la Boqueria, what is officially called La Rambla de Sant Josep (named after a now nonexistent monastery) is lined with flower stalls, which give it the alternative name La Rambla de les Flors.

Palau de la Virreina

The **Palau de la Virreina** (Map p290; La Rambla 99; MLiceu) is a grand 18th-century rococo mansion (with some neoclassical elements) that houses a municipal arts/ entertainment information and ticket office run by the Ajuntament (town hall). Built by Manuel d'Amat i de Junyent, the corrupt captain general of Chile (a Spanish colony that included the silver mines of Potosí), it is a rare example of such a postbaroque building in Barcelona. It's home to the **Centre de la Imatge** (Map p290; 93 316 10 00; www.ajuntament.barcelona.cat; Palau de la Virreina; noon-8pm Tue-Sun; MLiceu) FREE, which has rotating photography exhibits. Admission prices vary.

Mosaïc de Miró

At Plaça de la Boqueria, where four side streets meet just north of Liceu metro station, you can walk all over a Miró – the colourful **mosaic** (Map p290; Plaça de la Boqueria; MLiceu) in the pavement, with one tile signed by the artist. Miró chose this site

★ **Local Knowledge**
While there are some decent eateries in the vicinity, the vast majority of cafes and restaurants along La Rambla are expensive, mediocre tourist traps.

as it's near the house where he was born on the Passatge del Crèdit. The mosaic's bold colours and vivid swirling forms are instantly recognisable to Miró fans, though plenty of tourists stroll right over it without realising.

La Rambla dels Caputxins

La Rambla dels Caputxins, named after a former monastery, runs from Plaça de la Boqueria to Carrer dels Escudellers. The latter street is named after the potters' guild, founded in the 13th century, the members of which lived and worked here. On the western side of La Rambla is the **Gran Teatre del Liceu** (Map p290; ☏93 485 99 00; www.liceubarcelona.cat; La Rambla 51-59; tours 45/30min €9/6; ⏱45min tours hourly 2-6pm Mon-Fri, from 9.30am Sat, 30min tours 1.30pm daily; ⓜLiceu); to the southeast is the entrance to the palm-shaded Plaça Reial. Below this point La Rambla gets seedier, with the occasional strip club and peep show.

La Rambla de Santa Mònica

The final stretch of La Rambla widens out to approach the Mirador de Colom overlooking Port Vell. La Rambla here is named after the Convent de Santa Mònica, which once stood on the western flank of the street and has since been converted into a cultural centre.

What's Nearby?
Església de Santa Maria del Pi   Church
(Map p290; ☏93 318 47 43; www.basilicadelpi. com; Plaça del Pi; adult/concession/under 6yr €4/3/free; ⏱10am-6pm; ⓜLiceu) This striking 14th-century church is a classic of Catalan Gothic, with an imposing facade, a wide interior and a single nave. The simple decor in the main sanctuary contrasts with the gilded chapels and exquisite stained-glass windows that bathe the interior in ethereal light. The beautiful rose window above its entrance is one of the world's largest. Occasional concerts are staged here (clas-

sical guitar, choral groups and chamber orchestras).

Plaça Reial   Sqaure
(Map p290; ⓜLiceu) One of the most photogenic squares in Barcelona, the Plaça Reial is a delightful retreat from the traffic and pedestrian mobs on the nearby Rambla. Numerous eateries, bars and nightspots lie beneath the arcades of 19th-century neoclassical buildings, with a buzz of activity at all hours.

Via Sepulcral Romana   Archaeological Site
(Map p290; ☏93 256 21 00; www.museuhistor ia.bcn.cat; Plaça de la Vila de Madrid; adult/ concession/child €2/1.50/free; ⏱11am-2pm Tue & Thu, to 7pm Sat & Sun; ⓜCatalunya) Along Carrer de la Canuda, a block east

Plaça Reial

of the top end of La Rambla, is a sunken garden where a series of Roman tombs lies exposed. A smallish display in Spanish and Catalan by the tombs explores burial and funerary rites and customs. A few bits of pottery (including a burial amphora with the skeleton of a three-year-old Roman child) accompany the display.

Mirador de Colom   Viewpoint

(☏93 302 52 24; www.barcelonaturisme.com; Plaça del Portal de la Pau; adult/concession €6/4; ☺8.30am-8.30pm; ⓂDrassanes) High above the swirl of traffic on the roundabout below, Columbus keeps permanent watch, pointing vaguely out to the Mediterranean. Built for the Universal Exhibition in 1888, the monument allows you to zip up 60m in a lift for bird's-eye views back up La Rambla and across the ports of Barcelona.

Centre d'Art Santa Mònica   Arts Centre

(☏93 567 11 10; http://artssantamonica.gencat. cat; La Rambla 7; ☺11am-9pm Tue-Sat, 11am-5pm Sun; ⓂDrassanes) FREE The Convent de Santa Mònica, which once stood on the western flank of the street, has since been converted into the Centre d'Art Santa Mònica, a cultural centre that mostly exhibits modern multimedia installations; admission is free.

Don't Miss

Strolling the whole Rambla from end to end, keeping an eye on the architecture alongside.

★ Top Tip

Take an early morning stroll and another late at night to sample La Rambla's many moods.

Montjuïc

The Montjuïc hillside, crowned by a castle and gardens, overlooks the port with some of the city's finest art collections: the Museu Nacional d'Art de Catalunya, the Fundació Joan Miró and CaixaForum.

Great For...

☑ Don't Miss

The Romanesque frescoes in the Museu Nacional d'Art de Catalunya.

Museu Nacional d'Art de Catalunya

From across the city, the bombastic neobaroque silhouette of the **Museu Nacional d'Art de Catalunya** (MNAC; Map p301; ☑ 93 622 03 76; www.museunacional.cat; Mirador del Palau Nacional; adult/student/child €12/8.40/free, after 3pm Sat & 1st Sun of month free; ☉10am-8pm Tue-Sat, to 3pm Sun May-Sep, to 6pm Tue-Sat Oct-Apr; Ⓜ Espanya) can be seen on the slopes of Montjuïc. Built for the 1929 World Exhibition and restored in 2005, it houses a vast collection of mostly Catalan art from the early Middle Ages to the early 20th century. The high point is the collection of extraordinary Romanesque frescoes. Rescued from neglected country churches across northern Catalonia, the collection consists of 21 frescoes, woodcarvings and painted altar frontals.

Museu Nacional d'Art de Catalunya

ℹ Need to Know

The metro stops at the foot of Montjuïc; buses and funiculars go all the way

✕ Take a Break

Montjuïc eateries tend to be overpriced. The gardens surrounding Fundació Joan Miró museum are perfect for a picnic.

★ Top Tip

Ride the Transbordador Aeri from Barceloneta for a bird's-eye approach to Montjuïc.

Fundació Joan Miró

Joan Miró, the city's best-known 20th-century artistic progeny, bequeathed the **Fundació Joan Miró** (Map p301; ☑93 443 94 70; www.fmirobcn.org; Parc de Montjuïc; adult/child €12/free; ☉10am-8pm Tue-Wed & Fri, to 9pm Thu, to 3pm Sun Apr-Oct, shorter hours rest of the year; ☐55, 150, ☐Paral·lel) to his home town in 1971. Its light-filled buildings, designed by close friend and architect Josep Lluís Sert (who also built Miró's Mallorca studios), are crammed with seminal works, from Miró's earliest timid sketches to paintings from his last years. Highlights include **Sala Joan Prats**, with works spanning the early years until 1919; **Sala Pilar Juncosa**, which covers his surrealist years 1932–55; and Rooms 18 and 19, which contain masterworks of the years 1956–83.

CaixaForum

The Caixa building society prides itself on its involvement in (and ownership of) art, in particular all that is contemporary. **Caixa-Forum** (Map p301; ☑93 476 86 00; www.fundacio.lacaixa.es; Avinguda de Francesc Ferrer i Guàrdia 6-8; adult/student & child €4/free, 1st Sun of month free; ☉10am-8pm; Ⓟ; ⓂEspanya) hosts part of the bank's extensive collection from around the globe. The setting is a completely renovated former factory, the Fàbrica Casaramona, an outstanding Modernista brick structure designed by Puig i Cadafalch. On occasion portions of La Caixa's own collection goes on display, but more often than not major international exhibitions are the key draw.

Castell de Montjuïc

This forbidding *castell* (castle or fort) dominates the southeastern heights of Montjuïc and enjoys commanding views over the Mediterranean. It dates, in its present form, from the late 17th and 18th centuries. For most of its dark history, it has been used to watch over the city and as a political prison and killing ground.

Treasures in the Barri Gòtic

This scenic walk through the Barri Gòtic will take you back in time, from the early days of Roman-era Barcino through to the medieval era.

Start La Catedral
Distance 1.5km
Duration 1½ hours

Classic Photo: La Catedral

1 Before entering the cathedral, look at three Picasso friezes on the building facing the square. Next, wander through the magnificent **La Catedral** (p288).

2 Pass through the city gates; turn right into **Plaça de Sant Felip Neri**. The shrapnel-scarred church was damaged by pro-Francist bombers in 1939.

3 Head west to the looming 14th-century **Església de Santa Maria del Pi** (p282), famed for its magnificent rose window.

4 Follow the curving road to pretty **Plaça Reial** (p282). Flanking the fountain are Gaudí-designed lamp posts.

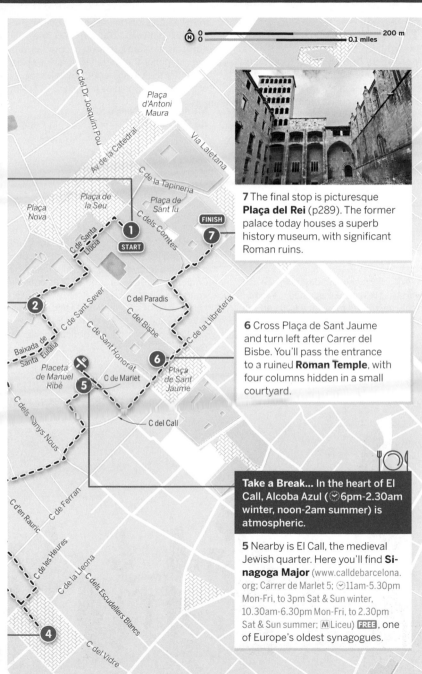

N 0 / 0   200 m / 0.1 miles

C del Dr Joaquim Pou

Plaça d'Antoni Maura

Via Laietana

Av de la Catedral

C de la Tapineria

Plaça de la Seu

Plaça de Sant Iu

Plaça Nova

C dels Comtes

C de Santa Llúcia

1 START

FINISH

7

C del Paradis

2

C de Sant Sever

C del Bisbe

C de la Llibreteria

Baixada de Santa Eulàlia

C de Sant Honorat

6

Plaça de Sant Jaume

Placeta de Manuel Ribé

C de Marlet

5

C del Call

C dels Banys Nous

C d'en Rauric

C de Ferran

C de les Heures

C de la Lleona

C dels Escudellers Blancs

4

C del Vidre

7 The final stop is picturesque **Plaça del Rei** (p289). The former palace today houses a superb history museum, with significant Roman ruins.

6 Cross Plaça de Sant Jaume and turn left after Carrer del Bisbe. You'll pass the entrance to a ruined **Roman Temple**, with four columns hidden in a small courtyard.

Take a Break... In the heart of El Call, Alcoba Azul (⏰6pm-2.30am winter, noon-2am summer) is atmospheric.

5 Nearby is El Call, the medieval Jewish quarter. Here you'll find **Sinagoga Major** (www.calldebarcelona. org; Carrer de Marlet 5; ⏰11am-5.30pm Mon-Fri, to 3pm Sat & Sun winter, 10.30am-6.30pm Mon-Fri, to 2.30pm Sat & Sun summer; MLiceu) FREE, one of Europe's oldest synagogues.

⊙ SIGHTS

◉ La Rambla & Barri Gòtic

Mercat de la Boqueria   Market
(Map p290; ☎93 412 13 15; www.boqueria.info;
La Rambla 91; ◷8am-8.30pm Mon-Sat; ⓂLiceu)
Mercat de la Boqueria is possibly La Rambla's most interesting building, not so much
for its Modernista-influenced design (it was
actually built over a long period, from 1840
to 1914, on the site of the former St Joseph
Monastery), but for the action of the food
market within.

La Catedral   Cathedral
(Map p290; ☎93 342 82 62; www.catedralbcn.
org; Plaça de la Seu; free, 'donation entrance'
€7, choir €3, roof €3; ◷8am-12.45pm & 5.15-
7.30pm Mon-Fri, 8am-8pm Sat & Sun, entry by
donation 1-5.30pm Mon, 1-5pm Sat, 2-5pm Sun;
ⓂJaume I) Barcelona's central place of
worship presents a magnificent image. The
richly decorated main facade, laced with
gargoyles and the stone intricacies you
would expect of northern European Gothic,
sets it quite apart from other churches in
Barcelona. The facade was actually added

in 1870, although the rest of the building
was built between 1298 and 1460. The
other facades are sparse in decoration, and
the octagonal, flat-roofed towers are a clear
reminder that, even here, Catalan Gothic
architectural principles prevailed.

Museu d'Història
de Barcelona   Museum
(MUHBA; Map p290; ☎93 256 21 00; www.
museuhistoria.bcn.cat; Plaça del Rei; adult/con-
cession/child €7/5/free, 3-8pm Sun & 1st Sun of
month free; ◷10am-7pm Tue-Sat, to 2pm Mon,
to 8pm Sun; ⓂJaume I) One of Barcelona's
most fascinating museums takes you back
through the centuries to the very foundations of Roman Barcino. You'll stroll over ruins of the old streets, sewers, laundries and
wine- and fish-making factories that flourished here following the town's founding by
Emperor Augustus around 10 BC. Equally
impressive is the building itself, which was
once part of the Palau Reial Major (Grand
Royal Palace) on Plaça del Rei, among the
key locations of medieval princely power in
Barcelona.

Mosaic chimneys on the roof of Palau Güell

Museu Frederic Marès   Museum

(Map p290; ☑93 256 35 00; www.museumares.
bcn.cat; Plaça de Sant lu 5; adult/concession/
child €4.20/2.40/free, after 3pm Sun & 1st Sun
of month free; ☺10am-7pm Tue-Sat, 11am-8pm
Sun; ⓂJaume I) One of the wildest collections of historical curios lies inside this vast
medieval complex, once part of the royal
palace of the counts of Barcelona. A rather
worn coat of arms on the wall indicates that
it was also, for a while, the seat of the Span
ish Inquisition in Barcelona. Frederic Marès
i Deulovol (1893–1991) was a rich sculptor,
traveller and obsessive collector, and
displays of religious art and vast varieties of
bric-a-brac litter the museum.

Plaça del Rei   Square

(Map p290; ⓂJaume I) Plaça del Rei (King's
Sq) is a picturesque plaza where Fernando
and Isabel received Columbus following his
first New World voyage. It is the courtyard
of the former Palau Reial Major. The palace
today houses a superb history museum
(p288), with significant Roman ruins
underground.

◎ El Raval

MACBA   Arts Centre

(Museu d'Art Contemporani de Barcelona; ☑93
481 33 68; www.macba.cat; Plaça dels Àngels
1; adult/concession/under 12yr €10/8/free;
☺11am-7.30pm Mon & Wed-Fri, 10am-9pm
Sat, 10am-3pm Sun & holidays; ⓂUniversitat)
Designed by Richard Meier and opened
in 1995, MACBA has become the city's
foremost contemporary art centre, with
captivating exhibitions for the serious art
lover. The permanent collection is on the
ground floor and dedicates itself to Spanish
and Catalan art from the second half of the
20th century, with works by Antoni Tàpies,
Joan Brossa and Miquel Barceló, among
others, though international artists, such as
Paul Klee, Bruce Nauman and John Cage,
are also represented.

Palau Güell   Palace

(Map p290; ☑93 472 57 75; www.palauguell.cat;
Carrer Nou de la Rambla 3-5; adult/concession/
under 10yr incl audio guide €12/9/free, 1st Sun

Gaudí: a Catholic & a Catalan

Gaudí was a devout Catholic and a
Catalan nationalist. Catalonia's great
medieval churches, in addition to nature, were a source of inspiration to him.
He took pride in utilising the building
materials of the countryside: clay, stone
and timber.

In contrast to his architecture,
Gaudí's life was simple; he was not
averse to knocking on doors, literally
begging for money to help fund construction of the cathedral. As Gaudí became more adventurous he appeared as
a lone wolf. With age he became almost
exclusively motivated by stark religious
conviction, and he devoted much of the
latter part of his life to what remains
Barcelona's call sign – the unfinished La
Sagrada Família. He died in 1926, struck
down by a streetcar while taking his
daily walk to the Sant Felip Neri church.

Wearing ragged clothes with empty
pockets – save for some orange peel
– Gaudí was initially taken for a beggar
and taken to a nearby hospital where
he was left in a pauper's ward; he died
two days later. Thousands attended his
funeral forming a half-mile procession
to La Sagrada Família, where he was
buried in the crypt.

Much like his work in progress, La
Sagrada Família, Gaudí's story is far
from over. In March 2000 the Vatican
decided to proceed with the case for
canonising him, and pilgrims already
stop by the crypt to pay him homage.
One of the key sculptors at work on the
church, the Japanese Etsuro Sotoo,
converted to Catholicism because of his
passion for Gaudí.

of month free; ☺10am-8pm Tue-Sun Apr-Oct,
to 5.30pm Nov-Mar; ⓂDrassanes) Finally reopened in its entirety in 2012 after several
years of refurbishment, this is a magnificent example of the early days of Gaudí's

Central Barcelona

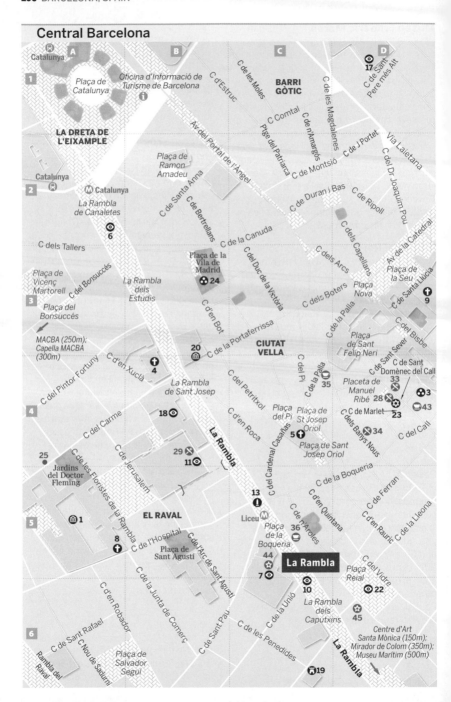

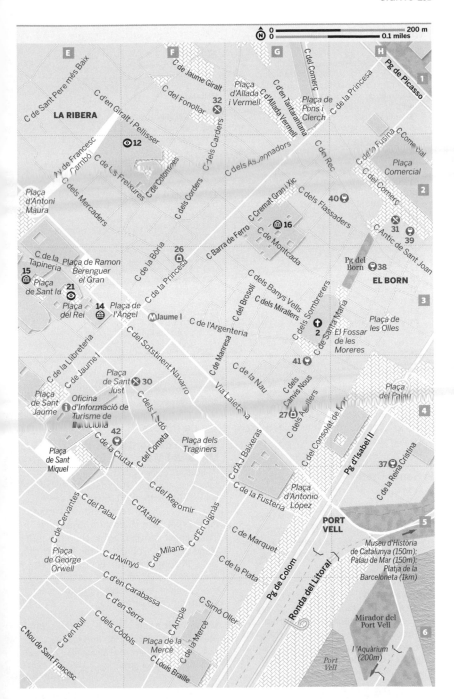

0   200 m
0   0.1 miles

E

LA RIBERA

C de Sant Pere més Baix

C d'en Giralt i Pellisser

Av de Francesc Cambó

C de Les Freixures

C de les Mercaders

Plaça
d'Antoni
Maura

⊙ 12

F

C de Jaume Giralt

C del Fonollar

C dels Colomines

C dels Carders

32 ⊗

C dels Corders

G

Plaça
d'Allada
i Vermell

C d'Allada Vermell

C d'en Tantarantana

C dels Assonadors

Plaça de
Pons i
Clerch

C del Comerç

C de la Princesa

C del Rec

H

Pg de Picasso

C de la Fusina

C Comercial

Plaça
Comercial

C del Comerç

2

C de la Tapineria

Plaça de Ramon
Berenguer
el Gran

15
🏛

Plaça
de Sant Iu

21 ⊙

Plaça
del Rei

14
🏛

Plaça de
l'Àngel

Ⓜ Jaume I

C de la Bòria

26
🔒

C de la Princesa

C Cremat Gran i Xic

C dels Flassaders

40 ⊕

C Barra de Ferro

🏛 16

C de Montcada

C dels Banys Vells

C Brosoli

C dels Mirallers

C de l'Argenteria

C dels Sombrerers

❶ 2

C de Santa Maria

31 ⊗
39 ⊕

C Antic de Sant Joan

Pg del
Born

⊕ 38

EL BORN

3

El Fossar
de les
Moreres

Plaça de
les Olles

C del Sotstinent Navarro

C de la Llibreteria

C de Jaume I

Plaça
de Sant
Jaume

Oficina
d'Informació de
Turisme de
Barcelona

42 ⊕

C de la Ciutat

Plaça
de Sant
Miquel

Plaça
de Sant
Just

30 ⊗

C dels Lledó

C del Cometa

Plaça dels
Traginers

Via Laietana

C de Manresa

C de la Nau

C dels
Canvis Nous

27 🔒

C dels Agullers

C de Santa Maria

41 ⊕

Plaça
del Palau

4

C de Consolat de Mar

Pg d'Isabel II

37 ⊕

C de la Reina Cristina

C de Cervantes

C del Palau

C d'Ataülf

C del Regomir

C d'En Gignàs

C de la Fusteria

Plaça
d'Antonio
López

PORT
VELL

5

Museu d'Història
de Catalunya (150m);
Palau de Mar (150m);
Platja de la
Barceloneta (1km)

Plaça
de George
Orwell

C d'Avinyó

C de Milans

C de Marquet

C de la Plata

Pg de Colom

Ronda del Litoral

Mirador del
Port Vell

6

C Nou de Sant Francesc

C d'en Rull

C dels Còdols

C d'en Serra

C d'en Carabassa

C Ample

C Simó Oller

Plaça de la
Mercè

C de la Mercè

C Louis Braille

Port
Vell

l'Aquàrium
(200m)

Central Barcelona

◎ Sights
1 Antic Hospital de la Santa Creu.................A5
2 Basílica de Santa Maria del Mar G3
   Centre de la Imatge.........................(see 18)
3 Domus de Sant Honorat...........................D4
4 Església de Betlem B4
5 Església de Santa Maria del Pi.................C4
6 Font de Canaletes.....................................A2
7 Gran Teatre del Liceu...............................C5
8 La Capella A5
9 La Catedral D3
10 La Rambla C6
11 Mercat de la Boqueria..............................B4
12 Mercat de Santa Caterina........................F2
13 Mosaïc de Miró...C5
14 Museu d'Història de Barcelona.................E3
15 Museu Frederic Marès..............................E3
16 Museu Picasso...G2
17 Palau de la Música Catalana D1
18 Palau de la Virreina B4
19 Palau Güell C6
20 Palau Moja B4
21 Plaça del Rei F3
22 Plaça Reial D6
23 Sinagoga Major D4
24 Via Sepulcral Romana..............................B3

⊕ Activities, Courses & Tours
25 Runner Bean Tours....................................A4

🛍 Shopping
26 El Rei de la Màgia.....................................F3
27 Vila Viniteca G4

✴ Eating
28 Alcoba Azul D4
29 Bar Pinotxo B4
30 Cafè de l'Acadèmia F4
31 Casa Delfín...H2
32 El Atril..F1
33 La Vinateria del Call D4
34 Xurreria..D4

◉ Drinking & Nightlife
35 Caelum C4
36 Cafè de l'Òpera C5
37 Can Paixano..H4
38 El Born Bar H3
39 Guzzo..H2
40 Juanra Falces..H2
41 La Vinya del Senyor G4
42 L'Ascensor E4
43 Salterio D4

🎭 Entertainment
44 Gran Teatre del Liceu C5
   Palau de la Música
   Catalana ....(see 17)
45 Sala Tarantos..D6

fevered architectural imagination. The extraordinary neo-Gothic mansion, one of the few major buildings of that era raised in Ciutat Vella, gives an insight into its maker's prodigious genius.

Antic Hospital de la Santa Creu   Historic Building

(Former Hospital of the Holy Cross; Map p290; ☑93 270 16 21; www.bcn.cat; Carrer de l'Hospital 56; ◎9am-8pm Mon-Fri, to 2pm Sat; Ⓜ Liceu) Behind La Boqueria stands the Antic Hospital de la Santa Creu, which was once the city's main hospital. Begun in 1401, it functioned until the 1930s, and was considered one of the best in Europe in its medieval heyday – it is famously the place where Antoni Gaudí died in 1926. Today it houses the **Biblioteca de Catalunya**, and the **Institut d'Estudis Catalans** (Institute for Catalan Studies). The hospital's Gothic chapel, **La Capella** (Map p290; ☑93 256 20 44; www.bcn.cat/lacapella; ◎noon-8pm Tue-Sat, 11am-2pm Sun & holidays; ◻91, 1, 120) FREE, shows temporary exhibitions.

◎ La Ribera

Basílica de Santa Maria del Mar   Church

(Map p290; ☑93 310 23 90; www.santamaria delmarbarcelona.org; Plaça de Santa Maria del Mar; €8; ◎guided tours 1.15pm, 2pm, 3pm, 5.15pm; Ⓜ Jaume I) At the southwest end of Passeig del Born stands the apse of Barcelona's finest Catalan Gothic church, Santa Maria del Mar (Our Lady of the Sea). Built in the 14th century with record-breaking alacrity for the time (it took just 54 years), the church is remarkable for its architectural harmony and simplicity.

Museu Picasso   Museum

(Map p290; ☑93 256 30 00; www.museu picasso.bcn.cat; Carrer de Montcada 15-23; adult/concession/child all collections €14/7.50/free, permanent collection €11/7/free, temporary exhibitions €4.50/3/free, 3-7pm Sun & 1st Sun of month free; ⏰9am-7pm Tue-Sun, to 9.30pm Thu; ⓂJaume I) The setting alone, in five contiguous medieval stone mansions, makes the Museu Picasso unique (and worth the probable queues). The pretty courtyards, galleries and staircases preserved in the first three of these buildings are as delightful as the collection inside.

While the collection concentrates on the artist's formative years – sometimes disappointing for those hoping for a feast of his better-known later works – there is enough material from subsequent periods to give you a thorough impression of the man's versatility and genius. Above all, you come away feeling that Picasso was the true original, always one step ahead of himself (let alone anyone else) in his search for new forms of expression.

Palau de la Música Catalana Architecture

(Map p290; ☎93 295 72 00; www.palaumusica. cat; Carrer de Palau de la Música 4-6; adult/ concession/child €18/11/free; ⏰guided tours 10am-3.30pm, to 6pm Easter, Jul & Aug; ⓂUrquinaona) This concert hall is a high point of Barcelona's Modernista architecture, a symphony in tile, brick, sculpted stone and stained glass. Built by Domènech i Muntaner between 1905 and 1908 for the Orfeó Català musical society, it was conceived as a temple for the Catalan Renaixença (Renaissance).

Mercat de Santa Caterina Market

(Map p290; ☎93 319 57 40; www.mercatsanta caterina.com; Avinguda de Francesc Cambó 16; ⏰7.30am-3.30pm Mon, Wed & Sat, to 8.30pm Tue, Thu & Fri, closed afternoons Jul & Aug; ⓂJaume I) Come shopping for your tomatoes at this extraordinary-looking produce market, designed by Enric Miralles and Benedetta Tagliabue to replace its 19th-century predecessor. Finished in 2005, it is distinguished by its kaleidoscopic and undulating roof, held up above the bustling produce stands, restaurants, cafes and bars by twisting slender branches of what look like grey steel trees.

◉ La Barceloneta & the Waterfront

Museu Marítim Museum

(☎93 342 99 20; www.mmb.cat; Avinguda de les Drassanes; adult/child €5/2.50, 3-8pm Sun free; ⏰10am-8pm; ⓂDrassanes) These mighty Gothic shipyards shelter the Museu Marítim, a remarkable relic from Barcelona's days as the seat of a seafaring empire. Highlights include a full-sized replica (made in the 1970s) of Don Juan of Austria's 16th-century flagship, fishing vessels, antique navigation charts and dioramas of the Barcelona waterfront.

Platjes Beach

(🚌36, 41; ⓂCiutadella Vila Olímpic, Bogatell, Llacuna, Selva de Mar) A series of pleasant beaches stretches northeast from the Port Olímpic marina. They are largely artificial, but this doesn't stop an estimated seven million bathers from piling in every year!

Museu d'Història de Catalunya Museum

(Museum of Catalonian History; ☎93 225 47 00; www.mhcat.net; Plaça de Pau Vila 3; adult/ child €4.50/3.50, last Tue of the month Oct-Jun free; ⏰10am-7pm Tue & Thu-Sat, to 8pm Wed, to 2.30pm Sun; ⓂBarceloneta) Inside the **Palau de Mar**, this worthwhile museum takes you from the Stone Age through to the early 1980s. It is a busy hotchpotch of dioramas, artefacts, videos, models, documents and interactive bits: all up, an entertaining exploration of 2000 years of Catalan history. Signage is in Catalan/Spanish.

L'Aquàrium Aquarium

(☎93 221 74 74; www.aquariumbcn.com; Moll d'Espanya; adult/child €20/15, dive €300; ⏰9.30am-11pm Jul & Aug, to 9pm Sep-Jun; ⓂDrassanes) It is hard not to shudder at the sight of a shark gliding above you, displaying its toothy, wide-mouthed grin. But this, the 80m shark tunnel, is the highlight of one of Europe's largest aquariums. It has the world's best Mediterranean collection and plenty of colourful fish from as far off as the Red Sea, the Caribbean and the Great Barrier Reef. All up, some 11,000 fish

Park Güell

North of Gràcia and about 4km from Plaça de Catalunya, **Park Güell** (☑93 409 18 31; www.parkguell.cat; Carrer d'Olot 7; adult/child €8/6; ◷8am-9.30pm May-Aug, to 8pm Sep-Apr; Ⓜ24, ⓂLesseps, Vallcarca) is where Gaudí turned his hand to landscape gardening. It's a strange, enchanting place where his passion for natural forms really took flight – to the point where the artificial almost seems more natural than the natural.

(including a dozen sharks) of 450 species reside here.

Platja de la Barceloneta   Beach

(ⓂBarceloneta) This beach, just east of its namesake neighbourhood, has obvious appeal, with Mediterranean delights, plus ample eating and drinking options inland from the beach when you need a bit of refreshment.

◉ L'Eixample

Casa Batlló   Architecture

(Map p296; ☑93 216 03 06; www.casabatllo. es; Passeig de Gràcia 43; adult/concession/ under 7yr €23.50/20.50/free; ◷9am-9pm, last admission 8pm; ⓂPasseig de Gràcia) One of the strangest residential buildings in Europe, this is Gaudí at his hallucinatory best. The facade, sprinkled with bits of blue, mauve and green tiles and studded with wave-shaped window frames and balconies, rises to an uneven blue-tiled roof with a solitary tower.

It is one of the three houses on the block between Carrer del Consell de Cent and Carrer d'Aragó that gave it the playful name Manzana de la Discordia, meaning 'Apple (Block) of Discord'. The others are Puig i Cadafalch's **Casa Amatller** (Map p296; ☑93 461 74 60; www.amatller.org; Passeig de Gràcia 41; adult/child 6-12yr/under 6yr 1hr tour €17/8.50/free, 30min tour €14/7/free; ◷11am-6pm) and Domènech i Montaner's

Casa Lleó Morera (Map p296; ☑93 676 27 33; www.casalleomorera.com; Passeig de Gràcia 35; guided tour adult/concession/under 12yr €15/13.50/free, express tour adult/under 12yr €12/free; ◷10am-1.30pm & 3-7pm Tue-Sun). They were all renovated between 1898 and 1906 and show how eclectic a 'style' Modernisme was.

Locals know Casa Batlló variously as the casa dels ossos (house of bones) or casa del drac (house of the dragon). It's easy enough to see why. The balconies look like the bony jaws of some strange beast and the roof represents Sant Jordi (St George) and the dragon. Even the roof was built to look like the shape of an animal's back, with shiny scales – the 'spine' changes colour as you walk around. If you stare long enough at the building, it seems almost to be a living being. Before going inside, take a look at the pavement. Each paving piece carries stylised images of an octopus and a starfish, designs that Gaudí originally cooked up for Casa Batlló.

When Gaudí was commissioned to re-fashion this building, he went to town inside and out. The internal light wells shimmer with tiles of deep sea blue. Gaudí eschewed the straight line, and so the staircase wafts you up to the 1st (main) floor, where the salon looks on to Passeig de Gràcia. Everything swirls: the ceiling is twisted into a vortex around its sunlike lamp; the doors, window and skylights are dreamy waves of wood and coloured glass. The same themes continue in the other rooms and covered terrace. The attic is characterised by Gaudí trademark hyperboloid arches. Twisting, tiled chimney pots add a surreal touch to the roof.

La Pedrera   Architecture

(Casa Milà; Map p296; ☑902 202138; www. lapedrera.com; Passeig de Gràcia 92; adult/ concession/under 13yr/under 7yr €22/16.50/11/ free; ◷9am-6.30pm & 7pm-9pm Mon-Sun; ⓂDiagonal) This undulating beast is another madcap Gaudí masterpiece, built in 1905–10 as a combined apartment and office block. Formally called Casa Milà, after the businessman who commissioned it, it

Platja de la Barceloneta

is better known as La Pedrera (the Quarry) because of its uneven grey stone facade, which ripples around the corner of Carrer de Provença.

Pere Milà had married the older and far richer Roser Guardiola, the widow of Josep Guardiola, and clearly knew how to spend his new wife's money. Milà was one of the city's first car owners and Gaudí built parking space into this building, itself a first. When commissioned to design this apartment building, Gaudí wanted to top anything else done in L'Eixample.

The Fundació Caixa Catalunya has opened the top-floor apartment, attic and roof, together called the Espai Gaudí (Gaudí Space), to visitors. The roof is the most extraordinary element, with its giant chimney pots looking like multicoloured medieval knights. Short concerts are often staged up here in summer. Gaudí wanted to put a tall statue of the Virgin up here too: when the Milà family said no, fearing it might make the building a target for anarchists, Gaudí resigned from the project in disgust.

One floor below the roof, where you can appreciate Gaudí's taste for parabolic

arches, is a modest museum dedicated to his work.

The next floor down is the apartment (El Pis de la Pedrera). It is fascinating to wander around this elegantly furnished home, done up in the style a well-to-do family might have enjoyed in the early 20th century. The sensuous curves and unexpected touches in everything from light fittings to bedsteads, from door handles to balconies, might seem admirable to us today, but not everyone thought so at the time. The story goes that one tenant, a certain Mrs Comes i Abril, had complained that there was no obvious place to put her piano in these wavy rooms. Gaudí's response was to suggest that she take up the flute.

For a few extra euros, a 'Premium' ticket means you don't have to queue.

Casa de les Punxes   Architecture
(Casa Terrades; Map p296; ☎93 016 01 28; www.casadelespunxes.com; Avinguda Diagonal 420; adult/concession/under 5yr €12.50/€11.25/free; ☺9am-8pm; Ⓜ Diagonal) Puig i Cadafalch's Casa Terrades is better known as the Casa de les Punxes (House of

La Sagrada & L'Eixample

◎ Sights

1	Casa Amatller	C3
2	Casa Batlló	C3
3	Casa de les Punxes	C2
4	Casa Lleó Morera	C3
5	Església de les Saleses	D2
6	La Pedrera	B3
7	La Sagrada Família	D1
8	Palau del Baró Quadras	B2
9	Palau Montaner	C2

⊗ Eating

10	Cerveseria Catalana	B3
11	Speakeasy	A3
12	Tapas 24	C3

⊖ Drinking & Nightlife

	Dry Martini	(see 11)
13	Les Gens Que J'Aime	C3
14	Michael Collins Pub	D1

Spikes) because of its pointed turrets. This apartment block, completed in 1905, looks like a fairy-tale castle and has the singular attribute of being the only fully detached building in L'Eixample.

Palau Montaner   Architecture

(Map p296; ☑93 317 76 52; www.fundaciotapies. org; Carrer de Mallorca 278; adult/child €7/free; ☺guided tours 11am Sat; Ⓜ Passeig de Gràcia) Interesting on the outside and made all the more enticing by its gardens, this creation by Domènech i Montaner is spectacular on the inside. Completed in 1896, its central

feature is a grand staircase beneath a broad, ornamental skylight. The interior is laden with sculptures (some by Eusebi Arnau), mosaics and fine woodwork. It is currently only open by guided tour, organised by the Fundació Tàpies and in Catalan only.

Palau del Baró Quadras   Architecture

(Map p296; ☑93 467 80 00; www.llull.cat; Avinguda Diagonal 373; ☺8am-8pm Mon-Fri; Ⓜ Diagonal) FREE Puig i Cadafalch designed Palau del Baró Quadras (built 1902–06) in an exuberant Gothic-inspired style. The main facade is its most intriguing, with a soaring, glassed-in gallery. Take a closer look at the gargoyles and reliefs – the pair of toothy fish and the sword-wielding knight clearly have the same artistic signature as the architect behind Casa Amatller. Decor inside is eclectic, but dominated by Middle Eastern and East Asian themes.

TOURS

Oficina d'Informació de Turisme de Barcelona (Map p290; 93 285 38 34; www.barcelonaturisme.com; Plaça de Catalunya 17; 9.30am-9.30pm; Catalunya) Organises a series of guided walking tours. One explores the Barri Gòtic (adult/child €16/free); another follows in Picasso's footsteps and winds up at the Museu Picasso, to which entry is included in the price (adult/child €22/7); and a third takes in the main jewels of Modernisme (adult/child €16/free). There's also a 'gourmet' tour of traditional purveyors of fine foodstuffs across the Ciutat Vella (adult/child €22/7). Stop by the tourist office or go online for the latest schedule. Tours typically last two hours and start at the tourist office.

Barcelona Metro Walks Consists of seven self-guided routes around the city, combining travel on the metro and other public transport as well as stretches on foot. Tourist information points at Plaça de Catalunya and Plaça de Sant Jaume sell the €16 package, which includes a walks guide, two-day transport pass and map.

My Favourite Things (637 265405; www.myft.net; tours from €26) Offers tours for no more than 10 participants based on numerous themes: anything from design to food. Other activities include flamenco and salsa classes, and bicycle rides in and out of Barcelona.

Runner Bean Tours (Map p290; 636 108776; www.runnerbeantours.com; Carrer del Carme 44; tours 11am year-round & 4.30pm Apr-Sep, 3pm Mar; Liceu) Has several daily thematic tours. It's a pay-what-you-wish tour, with a collection taken at the end for the guide. The Old City tour explores the Roman

and medieval history of Barcelona, visiting highlights in the Ciutat Vella. The Gaudí tour takes in the great works of Modernista Barcelona. It involves two trips on the metro. Runner Bean Tours also has ghostly evening tours and a Kids and Family Walking Tour. Check the website for departure times.

SHOPPING

If your doctor has prescribed an intense round of retail therapy to deal with the blues, then Barcelona is the place. Across Ciutat Vella (Barri Gòtic, El Raval and La Ribera), L'Eixample and Gràcia is spread a thick mantle of boutiques, historic shops, original one-off stores, gourmet corners, wine dens and more designer labels than you can shake your gold card at. You name it, you'll find it here.

El Rei de la Màgia   Magic

(Map p290; 93 319 39 20; www.elreydelamagia.com; Carrer de la Princesa 11; 10.30am-2pm & 4-7.30pm Mon-Sat; Jaume I) For more than 100 years, the people behind this box of tricks have been keeping locals both astounded and amused. Should you decide to stay in Barcelona and make a living as a magician, this is the place to buy levitation brooms, glasses of disappearing milk and decks of magic cards.

Vila Viniteca   Wine

(Map p290; 902 327777; www.vilaviniteca.es; Carrer dels Agullers 7; 8.30am-8.30pm Mon-Sat; Jaume I) One of the best wine stores in Barcelona (and there are a few...), this place has been searching out the best local and imported wines since 1932. On a couple of November evenings it organises what has become an almost riotous wine-tasting event in Carrer dels Agullers and surrounding lanes, at which cellars from around Spain present their young new wines.

Els Encants Vells   Market

(Fira de Bellcaire; 93 246 30 30; www.encantsbcn.com; Plaça de les Glòries Catalanes; 9am-8pm Mon, Wed, Fri & Sat; Glòries) In a gleaming open-sided complex near Plaça de les Glòries Catalanes, the 'Old Charms' flea

Flea market stalls

market is the biggest of its kind in Barcelona. Over 500 vendors ply their wares beneath massive mirror-like panels. It's all here, from antique furniture through to secondhand clothes. A lot of it is junk, but occasionally you'll stumble across a *ganga* (bargain).

😵 EATING

Barcelona has a celebrated food scene fuelled by a combination of world-class chefs, imaginative recipes and magnificent ingredients fresh from farms and the sea. Catalan culinary masterminds like Ferran Adrià and Carles Abellan have become international icons, reinventing the world of haute cuisine, while classic old-world Catalan recipes continue to earn accolades in dining rooms and tapas bars across the city.

😵 La Rambla & Barri Gòtic

Xurreria   Churros €
(Map p290; ☑93 318 76 91; Carrer dels Banys Nous 8; cone €1.20; ⊙7.30am-1.30pm & 3.30-8.15pm; Ⓜ Jaume I) It doesn't look much from the outside, but this brightly lit street joint is Barcelona's best spot for paper cones of piping-hot churros – long batter sticks fried and sprinkled with sugar and best enjoyed dunked in hot chocolate.

Cafè de l'Acadèmia   Catalan €€
(Map p290; ☑93 319 82 53; Carrer dels Lledó 1; mains €15-20; ⊙1-3.30pm & 8-11.30pm Mon-Fri; ☜; Ⓜ Jaume I) Expect a mix of traditional Catalan dishes with the occasional creative twist. At lunchtime, local Ajuntament (town hall) office workers pounce on the *menú del día* (€14.30). In the evening it is rather more romantic, as low lighting emphasises the intimacy of the beamed ceiling and stone walls. On warm days you can also dine on the pretty square at the front.

La Vinateria del Call   Spanish €€
(Map p290; ☑93 302 60 92; www.lavinateria delcall.com; Carrer de Sant Domènec del Call 9; raciones €7-12; ⊙7.30pm-1am; Ⓜ Jaume I) In a magical setting in the former Jewish quarter, this tiny jewel box of a restaurant (recently extended to add another dining room) serves up tasty Iberian dishes including Galician octopus, cider-cooked

chorizo and the Catalan *escalivada* (roasted peppers, aubergine and onions) with anchovies. Portions are small and made for sharing, and there's a good and affordable selection of wines.

El Raval

Mami i Teca Catalan €€

(93 441 33 35; Carrer de la Lluna 4; mains €10-12; 1-4pm & 8pm-midnight Mon, Wed-Fri & Sun, 8pm-midnight Sat; San Antoni) A tiny place with half a dozen tables, Mami i Teca is as much a lifestyle choice as a restaurant. Locals drop in and hang at the bar, and diners are treated to Catalan dishes made with locally sourced products and that adhere to Slow Food principles (such as cod fried in olive oil with garlic and red pepper, or pork ribs with chickpeas).

Suculent Catalan €€

(93 443 65 79; www.suculent.com; Rambla del Raval 43; mains €16-22; 1-4pm & 8-11.30pm Wed-Sun; Liceu) Michelin-starred chef Carles Abellan adds to his stable with this old-style bistro, which showcases the best of Catalan cuisine. From the cod brandade to the oxtail stew with truffled sweet potato, only the best ingredients are used. Be warned that the prices can mount up a bit, but this is a great place to sample regional highlights.

Bar Pinotxo Tapas €€

(Map p290; www.pinotxobar.com; Mercat de la Boqueria; mains €8-17; 7am-4pm Mon-Sat; Liceu) Bar Pinotxo is arguably La Boqueria's, and even Barcelona's, best tapas bar. It sits among the half-dozen or so informal eateries within the market, and the popular owner, Juanito, might serve up chickpeas with pine nuts and raisins, a soft mix of potato and spinach sprinkled with salt, soft baby squid with cannellini beans, or a quivering cube of caramel-sweet pork belly.

La Ribera

El Atril International €€

(Map p290; 93 310 12 20; www.atrilbarcelona.com; Carrer dels Carders 23; mains €11-15; noon-midnight; ; Jaume I) Aussie owner Brenden is influenced by culinary flavours

 Shopping Strips

Avinguda del Portal de l'Àngel This broad pedestrian avenue is lined with high-street chains, shoe shops, bookshops and more. It feeds into Carrer dels Boters and Carrer de la Portaferrissa, characterised by stores offering light-hearted costume jewellery and youth-oriented streetwear.

Avinguda Diagonal This boulevard is loaded with international fashion names and design boutiques, suitably interspersed with cafes to allow weary shoppers to take a load off.

Carrer d'Avinyó Once a fairly squalid old city street, Carrer d'Avinyó has morphed into a dynamic young fashion street.

Carrer de la Riera Baixa The place to look for a gaggle of shops flogging preloved threads.

Carrer del Petritxol Best for chocolate shops and art.

Carrer dels Banys Nous Along with nearby Carrer de la Palla, this is the place to look for antiques.

Passeig de Gràcia This is the premier shopping boulevard, chic with a capital 'C', and mostly given over to big-name international brands.

Shop on Passeig de Gràcia
JZR/SHUTTERSTOCK ©

from all over the globe, so while you'll see plenty of tapas (the *patatas bravas* are recommended for their homemade sauce), you'll also find kangaroo fillet, salmon and date rolls with mascarpone, chargrilled turkey with fried yucca, and plenty more.

Casa Delfín   Catalan €€

(Map p290; ☑93 319 50 88; www.tallerdetapas.
com; Passeig del Born 36; mains €10-15;
☺8am-midnight Sun-Thu, to 1am Fri & Sat; ☎;
MBarceloneta) One of Barcelona's culinary
delights, Casa Delfín is everything you
dream of when you think of Catalan (and
Mediterranean) cooking. Start with the
tangy and sweet *calçots* (a cross between
a leek and an onion; February and March
only) or salt-strewn *padron* peppers,
moving on to grilled sardines speckled with
parsley, then tackle the meaty monkfish
roasted in white wine and garlic.

✖ La Barceloneta
& the Waterfront

La Cova Fumada   Tapas €

(☑93 221 40 61; Carrer del Baluard 56; tapas
€4-8; ☺9am-3.20pm Mon-Wed, 9am-3.20pm &
6-8.15pm Thu & Fri, 9am-1pm Sat; MBarceloneta)
There's no sign and the setting is decidedly downmarket, but this tiny, buzzing
family-run tapas spot always packs in a
crowd. The secret? Mouthwatering *pulpo*
(octopus), *calamar, sardinias* and 15 or so
other small plates cooked to perfection
in the small open kitchen. The *bombas*
(potato croquettes served with *alioli*) and
grilled *carxofes* (artichokes) are good, and
everything is amazingly fresh.

Can Recasens   Catalan €€

(☑93 300 81 23; www.canrecasens.com; Rambla
del Poblenou 102; mains €8-15; ☺9pm-1am Mon-
Fri & 1-4pm & 9pm-1am Sat; MPoblenou) One
of Poblenou's most romantic settings,
Can Recasens hides a warren of warmly lit
rooms full of oil paintings, flickering candles,
fairy lights and baskets of fruit. The food is
outstanding, with a mix of salads, fondues,
smoked meats, cheeses, and open-faced
sandwiches piled high with delicacies like
wild mushrooms and brie, *escalivada* (grilled
vegetables) and gruyère, and spicy chorizo.

✖ L'Eixample

Tapas 24   Tapas €

(Map p296; ☑93 488 09 77; www.carlesabellan.
com; Carrer de la Diputació 269; tapas €4-9.50;

☺9am-midnight; ☎; MPasseig de Gràcia)
Carles Abellan, master of the now-defunct
Comerç 24 in La Ribera, runs this basement tapas haven known for its gourmet
versions of old faves. Specials include the
bikini (toasted ham and cheese sandwich –
here the ham is cured and the truffle makes
all the difference) and a thick black *arròs
negre de sípia* (squid-ink black rice).

Cerveseria Catalana   Tapas €€

(Map p296; ☑93 216 03 68; Carrer de Mallorca
236; tapas €4-11; ☺8am-1.30am Mon-Fri, 9am-
1.30am Sat & Sun; MPasseig de Gràcia) The 'Catalan Brewery' is good for breakfast, lunch
and dinner. Come for your morning coffee
and croissant, or enjoy the abundance of tapas and *montaditos* (canapés) at lunch. You
can sit at the bar, on the pavement terrace
or in the restaurant at the back. The variety
of hot tapas, salads and other snacks draws
a well-dressed crowd of locals and outsiders.

Disfrutar   Modern European €€€

(☑93 348 68 96; www.en.disfrutarbarcelona.
com; Carrer de Villarroel 163; tasting menus €110-
180; ☺1-2.30pm & 8-9.30pm Tue-Sat; MHospital
Clínic) In its first few months of life, Disfrutar
rose stratospherically to become the city's
finest restaurant – book now while it's still
possible to get a table. Run by alumni of
Ferran Adrià's game-changing El Bulli restaurant, it operates along similar lines.

✖ Montjuïc & Poble Sec

Quimet i Quimet   Tapas €€

(Map p301; ☑93 442 31 42; Carrer del Poeta
Cabanyes 25; tapas €4-10, montaditos around €3;
☺noon-4pm & 7-10.30pm Mon-Fri, noon-4pm Sat;
MParal·lel) Quimet i Quimet is a family-run
business that has been passed down
from generation to generation. There's
barely space to swing a *calamar* in this
bottle-lined, standing-room-only place, but
it is a treat for the palate, with *montaditos*
(tapas on a slice of bread) made to order.

Palo Cortao   Tapas €€

(Map p301; ☑93 188 90 67; www.palocortao.
es; Carrer de Nou de la Rambla 146; mains
€10-15; ☺8pm-1am Tue-Sun, 1-5pm Sat & Sun;

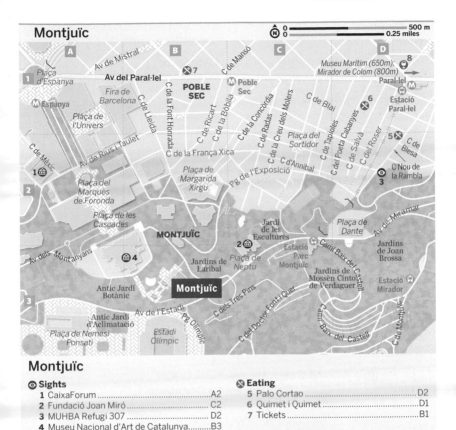

Montjuïc

◎ Sights

1 CaixaForum	A2
2 Fundació Joan Miró	C2
3 MUHBA Refugi 307	D2
4 Museu Nacional d'Art de Catalunya	B3

✖ Eating

5 Palo Cortao	D2
6 Quimet i Quimet	D1
7 Tickets	B1

◉ Drinking & Nightlife

8 La Confitería	D1

Ⓜ Paral·lel) Palo Cortao has a solid reputation for its beautifully executed seafood and meat dishes, served at fair prices. Highlights include octopus with white bean hummus, skirt steak with foie armagnac, and tuna tataki tempura. You can order half sizes of all plates – which will allow you to try more dishes.

Tickets Modern Spanish €€€

(Map p301; ☎606 225545; www.ticketsbar.es; Avinguda del Paral·lel 164; tapas €5-27; ⊙6.30-10.30pm Tue-Fri, 1-3pm & 7-10.30pm Sat, closed Aug; Ⓜ Paral·lel) This is, literally, one of the sizzling tickets in the restaurant world, a tapas bar opened by Ferran Adrià, of the legendary El Bulli, and his brother Albert. And unlike El Bulli, it's an affordable venture – if you can book a table, that is: you can only book online, and two months in advance (or call for last-minute cancellations).

◉ DRINKING & NIGHTLIFE

Barcelona is a nightlife lovers' town, with an enticing spread of candlelit wine bars, old-school taverns, stylish lounges and kaleidoscopic nightclubs where the party continues until daybreak. For something a little more sedate, the city's atmospheric cafes and teahouses make a fine retreat when the skies turn grey.

Classic Catalan Cuisine

Traditional Catalan recipes showcase the great produce of the Mediterranean: fish, prawns, cuttlefish, clams, pork, rabbit, game, first-rate olive oil, peppers and loads of garlic. Classic dishes also feature unusual pairings (seafood with meat, fruit with fowl): cuttlefish with chickpeas, cured pork with caviar, rabbit with prawns, goose with pears.

Great Catalan restaurants can be found in nearly every neighbourhood around town. The settings can be a huge part of the appeal – with candle-lit medieval chambers in the Ciutat Vella and Modernista design in L'Eixample setting the stage for a memorable feast. Although there are plenty of high-end places in this city, foodie-minded *barcelonins* aren't averse to eating at humbler, less elegant places – which sometimes cook up the best meals.

La Rambla & Barri Gòtic

Caelum
Cafe

(Map p290; ✆93 302 69 93; www.caelumbar celona.com; Carrer de la Palla 8; ⏲10am-8.30pm Mon-Thu, 10.30am-10pm Fri & Sat, to 9pm Sun; MLiceu) Centuries of heavenly gastronomic tradition from across Spain are concentrated in this exquisite medieval space in the heart of the city. The upstairs cafe is a dainty setting for decadent cakes and pastries, while descending into the underground chamber with its stone walls and flickering candles is like stepping into the Middle Ages.

Cafè de l'Òpera
Cafe

(Map p290; ✆93 317 75 85; www.cafeopera bcn.com; La Rambla 74; ⏲8.30am-2.30am; 🛜; MLiceu) Opposite the Gran Teatre del Liceu is La Rambla's most intriguing cafe. Operating since 1929, it is pleasant enough for an early evening libation or coffee and croissants. Head upstairs for an elevated seat above the busy boulevard. Can you be tempted by the *cafè de l'Òpera* (coffee with chocolate mousse)?

L'Ascensor
Cocktail Bar

(Map p290; ✆93 318 53 47; Carrer de la Bellafila 3; ⏲6pm-2.30am Sun-Thu, to 3am Fri & Sat; 🛜; MJaume I) Named after the lift (elevator) doors that serve as the front door, this elegant drinking den with its vaulted brick ceilings, vintage mirrors and marble-topped bars gathers a faithful crowd that comes for old-fashioned cocktails and lively conversation against a soundtrack of up-tempo jazz and funk.

Salterio
Cafe

(Map p290; ✆933 02 50 28; Carrer de Sant Domènec del Call 4; ⏲12.30pm-1am; 🛜; MJaume I) A wonderfully photogenic candle-lit spot tucked down a tiny lane in El Call, Salterio serves refreshing teas, Turkish coffee, authentic mint teas and snacks amid stone walls, incense and ambient Middle Eastern music. If hunger strikes, try the *sardo* (grilled flat-bread covered with pesto, cheese or other toppings).

El Raval

La Confitería
Bar

(Map p301; Carrer de Sant Pau 128; ⏲7.30pm-2.30am Mon-Thu, 6pm-3.30am Fri, 5pm-3.30am Sat, 12.45pm-2.45am Sun; MParal·lel) This is a trip into the 19th century. Until the 1980s it was a confectioner's shop, and although the original cabinets are now lined with booze, the look of the place barely changed with its conversion into a laid-back bar. A quiet enough spot for a house *vermut* (€3; add your own soda) in the early evening.

Casa Almirall
Bar

(www.casaalmirall.com; Carrer de Joaquín Costa 33; ⏲6pm-2.30am Mon-Thu, 6.30pm-3am Fri, noon-3am Sat, noon-12.30am Sun; MUniversitat) In business since the 1860s, this unchanged corner bar is dark and intriguing, with Modernista decor and a mixed clientele. There are some great original pieces in here, such as the marble counter, and the cast-iron statue of the muse of the Universal Exposition, held in Barcelona in 1888.

La Ribera

El Born Bar
Bar

(Map p290; ☑93 319 53 33; www.elbornbar. neositios.com; Passeig del Born 26; ⓢ10am-2am Mon-Thu, to 3am Fri & Sat, noon-2.30am Sun; 🛜; ⓜJaume I) El Born Bar effortlessly attracts everyone from cool thirty-somethings from all over town to locals who pass judgment on Passeig del Born's passing parade. Its staying power depends on a good selection of beers, spirits, and *empanadas*.

Guzzo
Cocktail Bar

(Map p290; ☑93 667 00 36; www.guzzoclub. es; Plaça Comercial 10; ⓢ6pm-3am Mon-Thu, to 3.30am Fri & Sat, noon-3am Sun; 🛜; ⓜBarceloneta) A swish but relaxed cocktail bar, run by much-loved Barcelona DJ Fred Guzzo, who is often to be found at the decks, spinning his delicious selection of funk, soul and rare groove. You'll also find frequent live-music acts of consistently decent quality, and a funky atmosphere at almost any time of day.

Juanra Falces
Cocktail Bar

(Map p290; ☑93 310 10 27; Carrer del Rec 24; ⓢ10am-3pm Sun-Mon, 8pm-3am Tue-Thu, 7pm-

3am Fri & Sat; ⓜJaume I) Transport yourself to a Humphrey Bogart movie in this narrow little bar, formerly (and still, at least among the locals) known as Gimlet. White-jacketed bar staff with all the appropriate aplomb will whip you up a gimlet or any other classic cocktail (around €10) that your heart desires.

La Vinya del Senyor
Wine Bar

(Map p290; ☑93 310 33 79; Plaça de Santa Maria del Mar 5; ⓢnoon-1am Mon-Thu, noon-2am Fri & Sat, noon-midnight Sun; 🛜; ⓜJaume I) Relax on the *terrassa*, which lies in the shadow of the Basílica de Santa Maria del Mar, or crowd inside at the tiny bar. The wine list is as long as *War and Peace* and there's a table upstairs for those who opt to sample by the bottle rather than the glass.

La Barceloneta
& the Waterfront

Absenta
Bar

(☑93 221 36 38; Carrer de Sant Carles 36; ⓢ7pm-1am Tue & Wed, from 11am Thu-Mon; ⓜBarceloneta) Decorated with old paintings,

Al fresco dining in the Barri Gòtic

Tickets to FC Barcelona Matches

Tickets to FC Barcelona matches are available at **Camp Nou** (📞902 189900; www.fcbarcelona.com; Carrer d'Arístides Maillol; Ⓜ Palau Reial), online (through FC Barcelona's official website: www.fcbarcelona.com) and through various city locations. Tourist offices sell them – the branch at Plaça de Catalunya is a centrally located option – as do FC Botiga stores. Tickets can cost anything from €39 to upwards of €250, depending on the seat and match. On match day the ticket windows (at gates 9 and 15) open from 9.15am until kick off. Tickets are not usually available for matches with Real Madrid.

vintage lamps and curious sculpture (including a dangling butterfly woman and face-painted TVs), this whimsical and creative drinking den takes its liquor seriously. Stop in for the house-made vermouth or for more bite try one of the many absinthes on hand. Just go easy: with an alcohol content of 50% to 90%, these spirits have kick!

Can Paixano Wine Bar
(Map p290; 📞93 310 08 39; www.canpaixano.com; Carrer de la Reina Cristina 7; ⊙9am-10.30pm Mon-Sat; Ⓜ Barceloneta) This lofty old champagne bar (also called La Xampanyeria) has long been run on a winning formula. The standard poison is bubbly rosé in elegant little glasses, combined with bite-sized *bocadillos* (filled rolls) and tapas (€3 to €7). Note that this place is usually jammed to the rafters, and elbowing your way to the bar can be a titanic struggle.

🏛 L'Eixample

Dry Martini Bar
(Map p296; 📞93 217 50 80; www.drymartiniorg.com; Carrer d'Aribau 162-166; ⊙1pm-2.30am Mon-Thu, 6pm-3am Fri & Sat, 7pm-2.30am Sun; Ⓜ Diagonal) Waiters with a discreetly knowing smile will attend to your cocktail needs

and make uncannily good suggestions, but the house drink, taken at the bar or in one of the plush green leather banquettes, is a safe bet. The gin and tonic comes in an enormous mug-sized glass – one will take you most of the night.

Monvínic Wine Bar
(📞93 272 61 87; www.monvinic.com; Carrer de la Diputació 249; ⊙1-11pm Tue-Fri, 7-11pm Mon & Sat; Ⓜ Passeig de Gràcia) Apparently considered unmissable by El Bulli's sommelier, Monvínic is an ode, a rhapsody even, to wine loving. The interactive wine list sits on the bar for you to browse, on a digital tablet similar to an iPad, and boasts more than 3000 varieties.

Les Gens Que J'Aime Bar
(Map p296; 📞93 215 68 79; www.lesgensquejaime.com; Carrer de València 286; ⊙6pm-2.30am Sun-Thu, 7pm-3am Fri & Sat; Ⓜ Passeig de Gràcia) This intimate basement relic of the 1960s follows a deceptively simple formula: chilled jazz music in the background, minimal lighting from an assortment of flea-market lamps and a cosy, cramped scattering of red-velvet-backed lounges around tiny dark tables.

⭐ ENTERTAINMENT

Palau de la Música Catalana Classical Music
(Map p290; 📞93 295 72 00; www.palaumusica.cat; Carrer de Palau de la Música 4-6; tickets from €15; ⊙box office 9.30am-9pm Mon-Sat, 10am-3pm Sun; Ⓜ Urquinaona) A feast for the eyes, this Modernista confection is also the city's most traditional venue for classical and choral music, although it has a wide-ranging program, including flamenco, pop and – particularly – jazz. Just being here for a performance is an experience. In the foyer, its tiled pillars all a-glitter, sip a pre-concert tipple.

Gran Teatre del Liceu Theatre, Live Music
(Map p290; 📞93 485 99 00; www.liceubarcelona.cat; La Rambla 51-59; ⊙box office 9.30am-8pm Mon-Fri, 9.30am-6pm Sat & Sun;

Palau de la Música Catalana

MLiceu) Barcelona's grand old opera house, restored after fire in 1994, is one of the most technologically advanced theatres in the world. To take a seat in the grand auditorium, returned to all its 19th-century glory but with the very latest in acoustics, is to be transported to another age.

Sala Tarantos — Flamenco

(Map p290; ☎93 304 12 10; www.masimas. com/tarantos; Plaça Reial 17; tickets €15; ☺shows 8.30pm, 9.30pm & 10.30pm; MLiceu) Since 1963, this basement locale has been the stage for up-and-coming flamenco groups performing in Barcelona. These days Tarantos has become a mostly tourist-centric affair, with half-hour shows held three times a night. Still, it's a good introduction to flamenco, and not a bad setting for a drink.

ℹ INFORMATION

SAFE TRAVEL

o Violent crime is rare in Barcelona, but petty crime (bag-snatching, pickpocketing) is a major problem.

o You're at your most vulnerable when dragging around luggage to or from your hotel; make sure you know your route before arriving.

o Be mindful of your belongings, particularly in crowded areas.

o Avoid walking around El Raval and the southern end of La Rambla late at night.

TOURIST INFORMATION

Several tourist offices operate in Barcelona; the main one is on Plaça de Catalunya (p297). A couple of general information telephone numbers worth bearing in mind are ☎010 and ☎012. The first is for Barcelona and the other is for all Catalonia (run by the Generalitat). You sometimes strike English speakers, although for the most part operators are Catalan/Spanish bilingual. In addition to tourist offices, information booths operate at Estació del Nord bus station and at Portal de la Pau, at the foot of the Mirador de Colom at the port end of La Rambla. Others set up at various points in the city centre in summer.

Plaça Sant Jaume (Map p290; ☎93 285 38 32; www.barcelonaturisme.com; Carrer de la Ciutat

2; ☉8.30am-8.30pm Mon-Fri, 9am-7pm Sat, 9am-2pm Sun & holidays; Ⓜ Jaume I)

Palau Robert Regional Tourist Office (Map p296; 🖉93 238 80 91; www.palaurobert.gencat. cat; Passeig de Gràcia 107; ☉10am-8pm Mon-Sat, to 2.30pm Sun; Ⓜ Diagonal) Offers a host of material on Catalonia, audiovisual resources, a bookshop and a branch of Turisme Juvenil de Catalunya (for youth travel).

GETTING THERE & AWAY

AIR

After Madrid, Barcelona is Spain's busiest international transport hub. A host of airlines fly to **El Prat Airport** (🖉902 404704; www.aena. es), including many budget carriers, from around Europe. Ryanair uses Girona and Reus airports (buses link Barcelona to both).

Most intercontinental flights require passengers to change flights in Madrid or another major European hub.

Iberia, Air Europa, Spanair and Vueling all have dense networks across the country, and while flights can be costly, you can save considerable time by flying from Barcelona to distant cities like Seville or Málaga.

BUS

Long-distance buses leave from **Estació del Nord**. A plethora of companies service different parts of Spain; many come under the umbrella of **Alsa** (🖉902 422242; www.alsa.es). For other companies, ask at the bus station. There are frequent services to Madrid, Valencia and Zaragoza (20 or more a day) and several daily departures to distant destinations such as Burgos, Santiago de Compostela and Seville.

Eurolines (www.eurolines.com), in conjunction with local carriers all over Europe, is the main international carrier; its website provides links to national operators. It runs services across Europe and to Morocco from Estació del Nord, and from **Estació d'Autobusos de Sants** (🖉93 339 73 29; www.adif.es; Carrer de Viriat; Ⓜ Estació Sants), next to Estació Sants Barcelona.

Much of the Pyrenees and the entire Costa Brava are served only by buses, as train services are limited to important railheads such as Girona, Figueres, Lleida, Ripoll and Puigcerdà.

TRAIN

○ Train is the most convenient overland option for reaching Barcelona from major Spanish centres such as Madrid and Valencia. It can be a long haul from other parts of Europe – budget flights frequently offer a saving in time and money.

○ A network of *rodalies/cercanías* serves towns around Barcelona (and the airport). Contact **Renfe** (🖉902 320320; www.renfe.es).

○ Eighteen high-speed Tren de Alta Velocidad Española (AVE) trains between Madrid and Barcelona run daily in each direction, nine of them in under three hours.

○ Most long-distance (*largo recorrido* or *Grandes Línias*) trains have 1st and 2nd classes (known as *preferente* and *turista*). After the AVE, Euromed and several other similarly modern trains, the most common long-distance trains are the slower, all-stops Talgos.

○ The main train station in Barcelona is **Estació Sants** (www.adif.es; Plaça dels Països Catalans; Ⓜ Estació Sants), located 2.5km west of La Rambla. Direct overnight trains from Paris, Geneva, Milan and Zurich arrive here.

GETTING AROUND

Barcelona has abundant options for getting around town. The excellent metro can get you most places, with buses and trams filling in the gaps. Taxis are the best option late at night.

Metro The most convenient option. Runs 5am to midnight Sunday to Thursday, till 2am on Friday and 24 hours on Saturday. Targeta T-10 (10-ride passes; €10.30) are the best value; otherwise, it's €2.15 per ride.

Bus A hop-on, hop-off **Bus Turístic** (🖉93 298 70 00; www.barcelonabusturistic.cat/en; day ticket adult/child €29/16; ☉9am-8pm), departing from Plaça de Catalunya, is handy for those wanting to see the city's highlights in one or two days.

Taxi You can hail taxis on the street (try La Rambla, Via Laietana, Plaça de Catalunya and Passeig de Gràcia) or at taxi stands.

On foot To explore the old city, all you need is a good pair of walking shoes.

Where to Stay

Barcelona has a wide range of sleeping options, from cheap hostels in the old quarter to luxury hotels overlooking the waterfront. Small-scale apartment rentals around the city are a good-value choice.

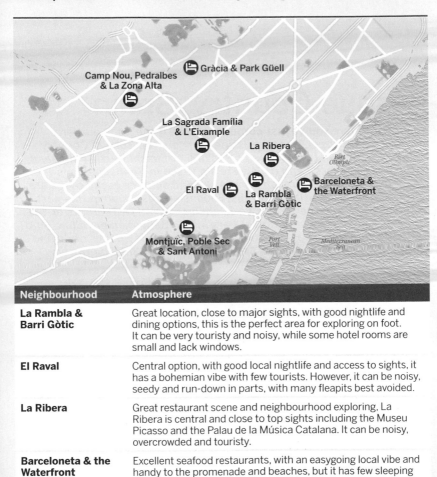

Neighbourhood	Atmosphere
La Rambla & Barri Gòtic	Great location, close to major sights, with good nightlife and dining options, this is the perfect area for exploring on foot. It can be very touristy and noisy, while some hotel rooms are small and lack windows.
El Raval	Central option, with good local nightlife and access to sights, it has a bohemian vibe with few tourists. However, it can be noisy, seedy and run-down in parts, with many fleapits best avoided.
La Ribera	Great restaurant scene and neighbourhood exploring, La Ribera is central and close to top sights including the Museu Picasso and the Palau de la Música Catalana. It can be noisy, overcrowded and touristy.
Barceloneta & the Waterfront	Excellent seafood restaurants, with an easygoing local vibe and handy to the promenade and beaches, but it has few sleeping options, and can be far from the action. Better suited to business travellers.
La Sagrada Família & L'Eixample	Offering a wide range of options for all budgets, it is close to Modernista sights, good restaurants and nightlife, and is a prime neighbourhood for the LGBT scene (in the 'Gaixample'). Can be very noisy with lots of traffic though, and is not a great area for walking as it is a little far from the old city.

308

In This Chapter

Museo Guggenheim Bilbao 310
Pintxo Bars 312
Bilbao 316
San Sebastián 323

Basque Country, Spain

No matter where you've just come from – be it the hot, southern plains of Spain or gentle and pristine France – the Basque Country is different. Known to Basques as Euskadi or Euskal Herria ('the land of Basque Speakers') and called El Pais Vasco in Spanish, this is where mountain peaks reach for the sky and sublime rocky coves are battered by mighty Atlantic swells. Food is an obsession in this part of the country, whether it's three-Michelin-starred restaurants or the fabulous pintxos (Basque tapas) bars in San Sebastián or Bilbao. And the Basque Country has reinvented itself as one of Spain's style and culture capitals, with Bilbao's Museo Guggenheim leading the way.

Two Days in Basque Spain

With so little time, you've little choice but to spend a day in **Bilbao** (p316) with the **Museo Guggenheim Bilbao** (p311) as your visit's centrepiece, followed by an afternoon of delicious *pintxos*. On day two, wander around the **Casco Viejo** (p317) and enjoy some shopping – take in the market if you happen to be visiting on a Sunday. Round out the day with some live music.

Four Days in Basque Spain

Spend days three and four in **San Sebastián** (p323), sampling some of the best food Europe has to offer and wandering along the sublime **Playa de la Concha** (p325).

Next stop: Lisbon (p330), only a two-hour flight away from Bilbao.

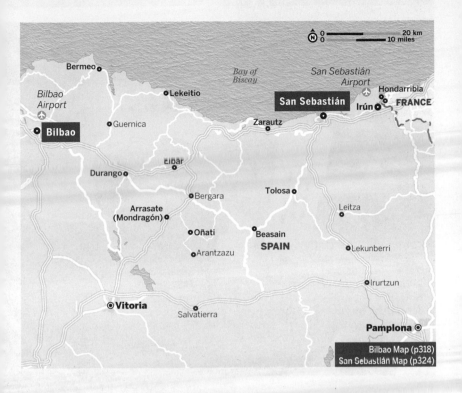

Arriving in Basque Spain

Bilbao is connected by air to numerous European and other Spanish cities; an airport bus connects the airport with the city centre. Otherwise, train and bus services connect Bilbao and San Sebastián with other Basque towns and villages, as well as to Madrid, Barcelona and other northern Spanish cities.

Where to Stay

Bilbao and San Sebastián have the largest selection of places to stay, but you'll need to book ahead at any time of the year. Apart from being fantastic destinations in their own right, these two cities make good bases for exploring the region. The Bilbao tourism authority has a very useful reservations department (p322); if you do turn up in San Sebastián without a booking, head to the tourist office (p329), which keeps a list of available rooms.

Museo Guggenheim Bilbao

Bilbao's titanium Museo Guggenheim Bilbao is one of contemporary architecture's most iconic buildings. It almost single-handedly lifted Bilbao into the international art and tourism spotlight.

Great For...

☑ Don't Miss

The atrium – the interior counterpoint to the facade's flights of fancy.

The Exterior

Some might say, probably quite rightly, that the Guggenheim is more famous for its architecture than its content. But Canadian architect Frank Gehry's inspired use of flowing canopies, cliffs, promontories, ship shapes, towers and flying fins is irresistible.

Gehry designed the Guggenheim with historical and geographical contexts in mind. The site was an industrial wasteland, part of Bilbao's wretched and decaying warehouse district on the banks of the Ría del Nervión. The city's historical industries of shipbuilding and fishing reflected Gehry's own interests, not least his engagement with industrial materials in previous works. The gleaming titanium tiles that sheathe most of the building like giant herring scales are said to have been inspired by the architect's childhood fascination with fish.

FMGB GUGGENHEIM BILBAO MUSEUM. PHOTO ERIKA BARAHONA EDE ©

❶ Need to Know

☏944 35 90 16; www.guggenheim-bilbao.es; Avenida Abandoibarra 2; adult/student/child from €13/7.50/free, depends on exhibits; ⊙10am-8pm, closed Mon Sep-Jun

✗ Take a Break

The museum has a high-class restaurant (p320).

★ Top Tip

The Artean Pass is a joint ticket for the Museo Guggenheim Bilbao and the Museo de Bellas Artes, which, at €16 for adults, offers significant savings. It's available from either museum.

Beyond Gehry

Other artists have added their touch to the Guggenheim as well. Lying between the glass buttresses of the central atrium and the Ría del Nervión is a simple pool of water that emits a mist installation by Fuyiko Nakaya. Near the riverbank is Louise Bourgeois' *Maman,* a skeletal spider-like canopy said to symbolise a protective embrace. In the open area west of the museum, the fountain sculpture randomly fires off jets of water. Jeff Koons' kitsch whimsy *Puppy,* a 12m-tall Highland Terrier made up of thousands of begonias, is on the city side of the museum.

The Interior

The interior of the Guggenheim is purposefully vast. The cathedral-like atrium is more than 45m high, with light pouring in through the glass cliffs. Permanent exhibits till the ground floor and include such wonders as mazes of metal and phrases of light reaching for the skies.

For most people, though, it is the temporary exhibitions – from the life work of Yoko Ono to the extraordinary sculptures of Brazilian Ernesto Neto – that are the main attraction.

Guggenheim Essentials

Admission prices vary depending on special exhibitions and the time of year. The last ticket sales are half an hour before closing. Free guided tours in Spanish take place at 12.30pm and 5pm. Tours can be conducted in other languages, but you must ask at the information desk beforehand. Excellent self-guided audiotours in various languages are free with admission and there is also a special children's audio guide. Entry queues can be horrendous, with wet summer days and Easter almost guaranteeing you a wait of over an hour. The museum is wheelchair accessible.

Pintxo bar

Pintxo Bars

San Sebastián stands atop a pedestal as one of the planet's culinary capitals. The city overflows with bars, almost all of which have bar tops weighed down under a mountain of Spain's best pintxos.

Great For...

☑ Don't Miss

Bar Border Berri – the essence of *pintxos* San Sebastián style.

The Art of Eating Pintxos

Just rolling the word *pintxo* around your tongue defines the essence of this cheerful, cheeky little slice of Basque cuisine. The perfect *pintxo* should have exquisite taste, texture and appearance and should be savoured in two elegant bites. The Basque version of a tapa, the *pintxo* transcends the commonplace by the sheer panache of its culinary campiness. In San Sebastián especially, Basque chefs have refined the *pintxo* to an art form.

Many *pintxos* are bedded on small pieces of bread or on tiny half-baguettes, upon which towering creations are constructed, often melded with flavoursome mayonnaise and then pinned in place by large tooth-picks. Some bars specialise in seafood, with much use of marinated anchovies, prawns and strips of squid, all topped with anything

ℹ Need to Know

Tell the barman what you want first; never just help yourself!

✗ Take a Break

Go for a stroll along Playa de la Concha to compensate for over-eating.

★ Top Tip

Pace yourself: try the speciality in each bar then move on to the next.

from chopped crab to pâté. Others deal in pepper or mushroom delicacies, or simply offer a mix of everything. And the choice isn't normally limited to what's on the bar top in front of you: many of the best *pintxos* are the hot ones you need to order. These are normally chalked up on a blackboard on the wall somewhere.

San Sebastián's Pintxo Bars

La Cuchara de San Telmo (☏043 44 16 55; www.lacucharadesantelmo.com; Calle de 31 de Agosto 28; pintxos from €2.50; ⊙7.30-11pm Tue, noon-3.30pm & 7.30-11pm Wed-Sun) This un-fussy, hard-to-find bar offers miniature *nueva cocina vasca* (Basque nouvelle cuisine) from a supremely creative kitchen.

Bar Borda Berri (☏943 43 03 42; www.bordaberri.com; Calle Fermín Calbetón 12; pintxos from €2.50; ⊙noon-midnight) This mustard-

yellow *pintxo* bar really stands out. The house specials are pig's ears served in garlic soup (much better than it sounds!), braised veal cheeks in wine, and a mushroom and *idiazabal* (a local cheese) risotto.

Astelena (☏943 42 58 67; www.restaurante astelena.com; Calle de Iñigo 1; pintxos from €2.50; ⊙1-4.30pm & 8-11pm Tue & Thu-Sat, 1-4.30pm Wed) The *pintxos* draped across the counter in this bar, tucked into the corner of Plaza de la Constitución, stand out. Many are a fusion of Basque and Asian inspirations. The great positioning means that prices are slightly elevated.

Bodega Donostiarra (☏943 42 58 67; www.bodegadonostiarra.com; Calle de Peña y Goñi 13; pintxos from €2.50, mains from €11; ⊙9.30am-midnight Mon-Sat) The stone walls, potted plants and window ornaments give Bodega Donostiarra a real old-fashioned French bistro look, but at the same time it feels very up to date and modern. It's best known for humble *jamón*, chorizo and, most of all, tortilla.

Bar Goiz-Argi (Calle de Fermín Calbetón 4; pintxos from €2.50; ⊙9.30am-3.30pm & 6.30-11.30pm Wed-Sun, 9.30-3.30pm Mon) *Gambas a la plancha* (prawns cooked on a hotplate) are the house speciality. Sounds simple, we know, but never have we tasted prawns cooked quite as perfectly as this.

La Mejíllonera (Calle del Puerto 15; pintxos from €2.50; ⊙11.30am-3pm & 6-11pm) If you thought mussels only came with garlic sauce, come here to discover mussels by the thousand in all their glorious forms.

Mussels not for you? Opt for the calamari and *patatas bravas* (fried potatoes with a spicy tomato and mayo sauce).

Bar Martinez (☏943 42 49 65; www.barmar tinezdonosti.com; Calle 31 de Agosto 13; pintxos from €2.50; ☺9.30am-11pm Tue-Sun, Fri & Sat open late) This small bar, with dusty bottles of wine stacked up, has won awards for its *morros de bacalao* (delicate slices of cod balanced atop a piece of bread) and is one of the more character-laden places to dip into some *pintxos*.

Bar Diz (Calle Zabaleta 17; pintxos from €2.50; ☺8am-late) In beach-blessed Gros, tiny Bar Diz has massively good *pintxos* (and the breakfast isn't bad either), and other foreign tourists are rare, so it's a totally local affair. If you're hungry opt for a *ración* (plate).

Bergara Bar (www.pinchosbergara.es; General Artetxe 8; pintxos from €2.50; ☺9am-11pm) The Bergara Bar, which sits on the edge of a busy square, is one of the most highly regarded *pintxo* bars in Gros, a growing powerhouse in the *pintxo*-bar stakes, and has a mouth-watering array of delights piled onto the bar counter as well as others chalked up on the board.

Bilbao's Pintxo Bars

Although it lacks San Sebastián's stellar reputation for *pintxos,* prices are generally slightly lower in Bilbao and the quality is about equal. There are literally hundreds of *pintxo* bars throughout Bilbao, but the Plaza Nueva on the edge of the Casco Viejo offers especially rich pickings, as do Calle de Perro and Calle Jardines. Some of

Pintxos on display, Bilbao

the city's standouts, in no particular order include:

Bar Gure Toki (Plaza Nueva 12; pintxos from €2.50) Has a subtle but simple line in creative *pintxos* including some made with ostrich.

Sorginzulo (Plaza Nueva 12; pintxos from €2.50; ☻9.30am-12.30am) A matchbox-sized bar with an exemplary spread of *pintxos*. The house special is calamari but it's only served on weekends.

Berton Sasibil (Calle Jardines 8; pintxos from €2.50; ☻8.30am-midnight Mon-Sat, 10am-4pm Sun) Here you can watch informative films on the crafting of the same superb *pintxos* that you're munching on.

Claudio: La Feria del Jamón (Calle Iparragirre 9-18; pintxos from €2.50; ☻10am-2pm & 5-9pm Mon-Fri, 10am-2pm & 6-9.30pm Sat) A creaky old place full of ancient furnishings. As you'll guess from the name and the dozens of legs of ham hanging from the ceiling, it's all about pigs.

La Viña del Ensanche (☏944 15 56 15; www.lavinadelensanche.com; Calle de la Diputación 10; pintxos from €1.35, menú €30; ☻8.30am-11.30pm Mon-Fri, noon-1am Sat) Hundreds of bottles of wine line the walls of this outstanding *pintxo* bar. And when we say outstanding, we mean that it could well be the best place to eat *pintxos* in the city.

Museo del Vino (Calle de Ledesma 10; pintxos from €2.50; ☻1-5pm & 8-11pm Mon-Fri) Tiled white interior, Gaudiesque windows, delicious octopus *pintxos* and an excellent wine selection (as you'd hope with a name like this). This place makes us smile.

Bitoque de Albia (www.bitoque.net; Alameda Mazarredo 6; pintxos from €2.50; ☻1.30-4pm Mon-Wed, 1.30-4pm & 8.30-11.15pm Thu-Sat) Award-winning modern *pintxo* bar serving such unclassic dishes as miniature red tuna burgers, salmon sushi and clams with wild mushrooms. It also offers a *pintxos* tasting menu (€12).

Mugi (www.mugiardotxoko.es; Licenciado Poza 55; pintxos from €2.50; ☻7am-midnight Mon-Sat, noon-midnight Sun) Widely regarded *pintxo* bar. It can get so busy that you might have to stand outside.

CULTURA EXCLUSIVE/RUSS ROHDE/GETTY IMAGES ©

---

❶ The Price of Pintxos

Most of the San Sebastián bars listed here charge between €2.50 and €3.50 for one *pintxo*. Not so bad if you just take one, but is one ever enough?

Bilbao

Bilbao isn't the kind of city that knocks you out with its physical beauty – head on over to San Sebastián for that particular pleasure – but it's a city that slowly wins you over. Bilbao, after all, has had a tough upbringing. Surrounded for years by an environment of heavy industry and industrial wastelands, its riverfront landscapes and quirky architecture were hardly recognised or appreciated by travellers on their way to more pleasant destinations. But Bilbao's graft paid off when a few wise investments left it with a shimmering titanium landmark, the Museo Guggenheim – and a horde of art world types from around the world started coming to see what all the fuss was about.

The *Botxo* (Hole), as it's fondly known to its inhabitants, has now matured into its role of major European art centre. But at heart it remains a hard-working town, and one that has real character. It's this down-to-earth soul, rather than its plethora of art galleries, that is the real attraction of the vital, exciting and cultured city of Bilbao.

SIGHTS

Many first-time visitors associate Bilbao with its world-famous art museum, the Museo Guggenheim. But there's a wide variety of interesting sights around town, from architectural highlights to landmark bridges, and from bustling plazas to the winding streets of the Casco Viejo (historic centre).

Museo de Bellas Artes   Gallery
(944 39 60 60; www.museobilbao.com; Plaza del Museo 2; adult/student/child €9/7/free, Wed free; 10am-8pm Wed-Mon) The Museo de Bellas Artes houses a compelling collection that includes everything from Gothic sculptures to 20th-century pop art. There are three main subcollections: classical art, with works by Murillo, Zurbarán, El Greco, Goya and van Dyck; contemporary art, featuring works by Gauguin, Francis Bacon and Anthony Caro; and Basque art, with works of the great sculptors Jorge de Oteiza and Eduardo Chillida, and strong paintings by the likes of Ignacio Zuloago and Juan de Echevarria.

Zubizuri

Casco Viejo   Old Town

The compact Casco Viejo, Bilbao's atmospheric old quarter, is full of charming streets, boisterous bars and plenty of quirky and independent shops. At the heart of the Casco are Bilbao's original seven streets, Las Siete Calles, which date from the 1400s.

The 14th-century Gothic **Catedral de Santiago** (www.bilbaoturismo.net; Plaza de Santiago; ☺10am-1pm & 5-7.30pm Tue-Sat, 10am-1pm Sun & holidays) has a splendid Renaissance portico and a pretty little cloister. Further north, the 19th-century arcaded **Plaza Nueva** is a rewarding *pintxo* (Basque tapas) haunt. There's a lively Sunday-morning **flea market** here, which is full of secondhand book and record stalls, and pet 'shops' selling chirpy birds (some kept in old-fashioned wooden cages), fluffy mice and tiny baby terrapins. Elsewhere in the market, children and adults alike swap and barter football cards and old stamps; in between weave street performers and waiters with trays piled high. The market is much more subdued in winter. A sweeter-smelling **flower market** takes place on Sunday mornings in the nearby Plaza del Arenal.

Basilica de Begoña   Basilica

(Calle Virgen de Begoña; ☺8.30am-1.30pm & 5-8.30pm Mon-Sat, 9am-2pm & 5-9pm Sun) This 16th-century basilica towers over the Casco Viejo from atop a nearby hill. It's mainly Gothic in look, although Renaissance touches, such as the arched main entrance, crept in during its century-long construction. The austere vaulted interior is brightened by a gold altarpiece that contains a statue of the Virgin Begoña, the patron saint of Biscay who's venerated locally as Amatxu (Mother).

Euskal Museoa   Museum

(Museo Vasco; ☎944 15 54 23; www.euskal-museoa.org/es/hasiera; Plaza Miguel Unamuno 4; adult/child €3/free, Thu free; ☺10am-7pm Mon & Wed-Fri, 10am-1.30pm & 4-7pm Sat, 10am-2pm Sun) This is probably the most complete museum of Basque culture and history in all of Spain. The story begins in prehistory;

Las Siete Calles

Forming the heart of Bilbao's Casco Viejo are seven streets known as Las Siete Calles (Basque: Zazpi Kaleak). These dark, atmospheric lanes – Barrenkale Barrena, Barrenkale, Carnicería Vieja, Belostikale, Tendería, Artekale and Somera – date from the 1400s when the east bank of the Ría del Nervión was first developed. They originally constituted the city's commercial centre and river port; these days they teem with lively cafes, *pintxo* bars and boutiques.

Casco Viejo
AYHAN ALTUN/GETTY IMAGES ©

from this murky period the displays bound rapidly into the modern age, in the process explaining just how long the Basques have called this corner of the world home.

Alas, unless you read Spanish (or perhaps you studied Euskara at school?), it's all a little meaningless as there are no English translations.

The museum is housed in a fine old building, at the centre of which is a peaceful cloister that was part of an original 17th-century Jesuit college. In the cloister is the Mikeldi Idol, a powerful pre-Christian symbolic figure, possibly from the Iron Age.

Zubizuri   Bridge

The most striking of the modern bridges that span the Ría del Nervión, the Zubizuri (Basque for 'White Bridge') has become an iconic feature of Bilbao's cityscape since its completion in 1997. Designed by Spanish architect Santiago Calatrava, it has a curved walkway suspended under a flowing

Bilbao

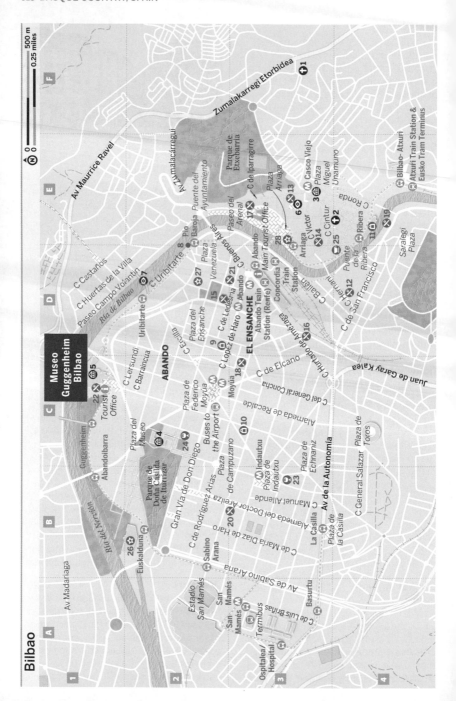

Museo Guggenheim Bilbao

Bilbao

⊙ Sights
1 Basilica de Begoña F3
2 Catedral de Santiago E4
3 Euskal Museoa E3
4 Museo de Bellas Artes C2
5 Museo Guggenheim Bilbao C1
6 Plaza Nueva E3
7 Zubizuri D2

⊙ Activities, Courses & Tours
8 Bilboats D2

🛍 Shopping
9 Arrese D2
10 Chocolates de Mendaro C3
11 Mercado de la Ribera E4

🍴 Eating
12 Agape Restaurante D4
13 Bar Gure Toki E3

14 Berton Sasibil E3
15 Bitoque de Albia D2
16 Casa Rufo D3
17 Claudio: La Feria del Jamón E3
18 La Viña del Ensanche C3
19 Mina Restaurante E4
20 Mugi B3
21 Museo del Vino D3
22 Nerua Guggenheim Bilbao C1
   Sorginzulo .... (see 13)

⊙ Drinking & Nightlife
23 Cotton Club B3
24 Geo Cocktail Lounge C2
25 Lamiak D4

⊙ Entertainment
26 Euskalduna Palace B2
27 Kafe Antzokia D2
28 Teatro Arriaga E3

white arch to which it's attached by a series of steel spokes.

🎫 TOURS

Bilbao tourist office (p322) organises 1½-hour walking tours covering either the old town or the architecture in the newer parts of town. At busy times tours can run with more frequency.

Bilboats (94U 42 41 57; www.bilboats. com; Plaza Pío Baroja; adult/child from €12/7) runs boat cruises along the Nervión several times a day.

One of the more original, and interesting, ways to see the city and get to know a local is through the **Bilbao Greeters** (www. bilbaogreeters.com; adult €12) organisation. Essentially a local person gives you a tour of the city showing you their favourite sights, places to hang out and, of course, *pintxos* (Basque tapas) bars. You need to reserve through the website at least a fortnight in advance.

🛍 SHOPPING

For major department stores and big-name fashion labels trawl the streets of El Ensanche. For more one-of-a-kind, independent boutiques, Casco Viejo is the place to look (although even here the chain shops are increasingly making their presence felt). Bilbao is also a great place for food shopping (of course!).

Mercado de la Ribera   Market
(Calle de la Ribera) Overlooking the river, the Mercado de la Ribera is supposedly one of the longest covered food markets in Spain. It's had a recent makeover, which has sanitised it somewhat, but many of the city's top chefs still come here to select fresh produce each morning.

Arrese   Food
(www.arrese.biz; Calle Lopez de Haro 24; ⊙9am-9pm Mon-Sat, 9am-3pm & 5-9pm Sun) With 160 years of baking experience you'd hope the cakes at this little patissiere would taste divine, but frankly, they're even better than expected.

Chocolates de Mendaro   Food
(www.chocolatesdemendaro.com; Calle de Licenciado Poza 16; ⊙10am-2pm & 4-8pm Mon-Sat) This old-time chocolate shop created its first chocolate treats way back in 1850 and is hands down the best place to ruin a diet in Bilbao.

EATING

In the world of trade and commerce, the Basques are an outward-looking lot, but when it comes to food they refuse to believe that any other people could possibly match their culinary skills (and they may well have a point). This means that eating out in Bilbao is generally a choice of Basque, Basque or Basque food. Still, life could be worse and there are some terrific places to eat.

The porticoed Plaza Nueva is a good spot for coffee and people-watching, especially in summer.

Agape Restaurante   Basque €€

(☏944 16 05 06; www.restauranteagape.com; Calle de Hernani 13; menú del día €12.90, menús €21-36; ⏱1-4pm Sun-Wed, 1-4pm & 8.30-11.30pm Thu-Sat; 🛜) With a solid reputation among locals for good-value meals that don't sacrifice quality, this is a great place for a slice of real Bilbao culinary life. It's well away from the standard tourist circuit, but is worth the short walk. The lunch menu, at €12.20, is exceptional value, comprising starters such as mushroom risotto and mains like fried anchovies with sweet ratatouille. Book ahead.

Casa Rufo   Basque €€

(☏944 43 21 72; www.casarufo.com; Hurtado de Amézaga 5; mains €10-15; ⏱1.30-4pm & 8.30-11pm Mon-Sat) Despite the emergence of numerous glitzy restaurants that are temples to haute cuisine, this resolutely old-fashioned place, with its shelves full of dusty bottles of top-quality olive oil and wine, still stands out as one of the best places to eat traditional Basque food in Bilbao. The house special is steak – lovingly cooked over hot coals.

Mina Restaurante   Basque €€€

(☏944 79 59 38; www.restaurantemina.es; Muelle Marzana; tasting menu €60-110; ⏱2-3.30pm & 9-10.30pm Wed-Sat, 2-3.30pm Sun & Tue) Offering unexpected sophistication and fine dining in an otherwise fairly grimy neighbourhood, this riverside restaurant has some critics citing it as the current *número uno* in Bilbao. Expect serious culinary creativity: think along the lines of spider crab with passion fruit or frozen 'seawater' with seaweed and lemon sorbet. Reservations are essential.

Nerua Guggenheim Bilbao   Basque €€€

(☏944 00 04 30; www.neruaguggenheimbilbao.com; tasting menu from €65, mains €30-35; ⏱1-3pm & 8.30-9.30pm Thu-Sat, 1-3pm Tue, Wed & Sun) The Guggenheim's modernist, chic and very white restaurant is under the direction of Michelin-starred chef Josean Alija (a disciple of Ferran Adria). Needless to say, the *nueva cocina vasca* (Basque nouvelle cuisine) is breathtaking – even the olives are vintage classics: all come from 1000-year-old olive trees! Reservations are essential.

🍷 DRINKING & NIGHTLIFE

In the Casco Viejo, around Calles Barrenkale, Ronda and de Somera, there are plenty of terrific hole-in-the-wall, no-nonsense bars with a generally youthful crowd.

Across the river, in the web of streets around Muelle Marzana and Bilbao la Vieja, are scores more little bars and clubs. This is gritty Bilbao as it used to be in the days before the arty makeover. It's both a Basque heartland and the centre of the city's ethnic community. The many bars around here are normally welcoming, but one or two can be a bit seedy. It's not a great idea for women to walk here alone at night.

Lamiak   Cafe

(Calle Pelota 8; ⏱4pm-midnight Sun-Thu, 3.30pm-2.30am Fri & Sat) Lamiak, a long-standing Casco Viejo favourite, is a buzzing cafe with a cavernous red and black hall, cast iron columns and upstairs seating on a mezzanine floor. Good for coffees and cocktails, it exudes an arty, laid-back vibe and pulls in a cool weekend crowd.

Lunchtime crowd in a Bilbao restaurant

Geo Cocktail Lounge   Cocktail Bar

(☑944 66 84 42; Calle Maximo Aguirre 12; ⊙3pm-1.30am Tue-Sun) For a refined post-dinner cocktail, search out this lounge bar in the area south of the Guggenheim. Expect subdued lighting, low-key tunes and expertly crafted cocktails.

Cotton Club   Club

(☑944 10 49 51; www.cottonclubbilbao.es; Calle de Gregorio de la Revilla 25; ⊙8.30pm-3am Tue & Wed, to 5am Thu, to 6.30am Fri & Sat, 7pm-1.30am Sun) A historic Bilbao nightspot, the Cotton Club draws a mixed crowd to its DJ-stoked nights and regular gigs – mainly blues, jazz and rock. It's a tiny place so prepare to get up close with your fellow revellers.

⊕ ENTERTAINMENT

There are plenty of clubs and live venues in Bilbao, and the vibe is friendly and generally easy-going. Venue websites usually have details of upcoming gigs.

Kafe Antzokia   Live Music

(☑944 24 46 25; www.kafeantzokia.com; Calle San Vicente 2) This is the vibrant heart of contemporary Basque Bilbao, featuring international rock, blues and reggae, as well as the cream of Basque rock-pop. Weekend concerts run from 10pm to 1am, followed by DJs until 5am. During the day it's a cafe, restaurant and cultural centre all rolled into one and has frequent exciting events on.

Euskalduna Palace   Live Music

(☑944 03 50 00; www.euskalduna.net; Avenida Abandoibarra) About 600m downriver from the Guggenheim is this modernist gem, built on the riverbank in a style that echoes the great shipbuilding works of the 19th century. The Euskalduna is home to the Bilbao Symphony Orchestra and the Basque Symphony Orchestra, and hosts a wide array of events.

Teatro Arriaga   Theatre

(☑944 79 20 36; www.teatroarriaga.com; Plaza Arriaga) The baroque facade of this venue commands the open spaces of El Arenal between the Casco Viejo and the river.

It stages theatrical performances and classical-music concerts.

ℹ INFORMATION

Friendly staff at Bilbao's tourist office are extremely helpful, well informed and, above all, enthusiastic about their city. At all offices ask for the free bimonthly *Bilbao Guía,* which has entertainment listings plus tips on restaurants, bars and nightlife.

At the newly opened, state-of-the-art **main tourist office** (☑944 79 57 60; www.bilbao turismo.net; Plaza Circular 1; ☉9am-9pm; 🛜), there's free wi-fi access, a bank of touch-screen information computers and, best of all, some humans to help answer questions. There are also branches at the **airport** (☑944 71 03 01; www. bilbaoturismo.net; Bilbao Airport; ☉9am-9pm Mon-Sat, 9am-3pm Sun) and the **Guggenheim** (www.bilbaoturismo.net; Alameda Mazarredo 66; ☉10am-7pm daily, to 3pm Sun Sep-Jun).

The Bilbao tourism authority has a very useful **reservations service** (☑902 87 72 98; www. bilbaoreservas.com).

ℹ GETTING THERE & AWAY

AIR

Bilbao's **airport** (BIO; ☑902 404 704; www.aena. es) is near Sondika, to the northeast of the city. A number of European flag carriers serve the city. Of the budget airlines, EasyJet (www.easyjet. com) and Vueling (www.vueling.com) cover the widest range of destinations.

BUS

Bilbao's main bus station, **Termibus** (☑944 39 50 77; www.termibus.es; Gurtubay 1, San Mamés), is west of the centre.

Bizkaibus travels to destinations throughout the rural Basque Country, including coastal communities such as Mundaka and Guernica (€2.50). Euskotren buses serve Lekeitio (€6.65).

TRAIN

The Abando train station is just across the river from Plaza Arriaga and the Casco Viejo. There are frequent trains to Barcelona (from €19.60, 6¾ hours), Burgos (from €7, three hours), Madrid (from €20, five hours) and Valladolid (from €12.55, four hours).

Casco Viejo (p317)

STEFANO POLITI MARKOVINA/GETTY IMAGES ©

Nearby is the **Concordia train station**, with its art-nouveau facade of wrought iron and tiles. It is used by the **FEVE** (www.renfe.com/viajeros/feve), a formerly private rail company that was recently purchased by RENFE. It has trains running west into Cantabria. There are three daily trains to Santander (from €12.55, three hours) where you can change for stations in Asturias.

The **Atxuri train station** is just upriver from Casco Viejo. From here, **Eusko Tren/Ferrocarril Vasco** (www.euskotren.es) operates services every half-hour to Bermeo (€3.70, 1½ hours), Guernica (€3.70, one hour) and Mundaka (€3.70, 1½ hours).

GETTING AROUND

TO/FROM THE AIRPORT

The **airport bus** (Bizkaibus A3247; €1.45) departs from a stand on the extreme right as you leave arrivals. It runs through the northwestern section of the city, passing the Museo Guggenheim, stopping at Plaza de Federico Moyúa and terminating at the Termibus (bus station). It runs from the airport every 20 minutes in summer and every 30 minutes in winter from 6.20am to midnight. There is also a direct hourly bus from the airport to San Sebastián (€16.85, 1¼ hours). It runs from 7.45am to 11.15pm.

Taxis from the airport to the Casco Viejo cost about €23 to €30, depending on traffic.

METRO

There are metro stations at all the main focal points of El Ensanche and at Casco Viejo. Tickets start at €1.65. The metro runs to the north coast from a number of stations on both sides of the river and makes it easy to get to the beaches closest to Bilbao.

TRAM

Bilbao's Eusko Tren tramline is a boon to locals and visitors alike. It runs to and fro between Basurtu, in the southwest of the city, and the Atxuri train station. Stops include the Termibus station, the Guggenheim and Teatro Arriaga by the Casco Viejo. Tickets cost €1.50 and need to be validated in the machine next to the ticket dispenser before boarding.

 Basque Language

Victor Hugo described the Basque language as a 'country', and it would be a rare Basque who'd disagree with him. The language, known as *Euskara*, is the oldest in Europe and has no known connection to any Indo-European languages. Suppressed by Franco, Basque was subsequently recognised as one of Spain's official languages, and it has become the language of choice among a growing number of young Basques.

MONKEY BUSINESS IMAGES/GETTY IMAGES ©

San Sebastián

It's impossible to lay eyes on stunning San Sebastián (Basque: Donostia) and not fall madly in love. This city is cool and happening by night, charming and well mannered by day. It's a city filled with people that love to indulge – and with Michelin stars apparently falling from the heavens onto its restaurants, not to mention *pintxo* (tapas) culture almost unmatched anywhere else in Spain, San Sebastián frequently tops lists of the world's best places to eat.

San Sebastián has four main centres of action. The lively Parte Vieja (old town) lies across the neck of Monte Urgull, the bay's eastern headland, and is where the most popular *pintxo* bars and many of the cheap lodgings are to be found. South of the Parte Vieja is the commercial and shopping district, the Área Romántica, its handsome grid of late-19th-century buildings extending from behind Playa de la Concha to the banks of Río Urumea. On the eastern side

San Sebastián

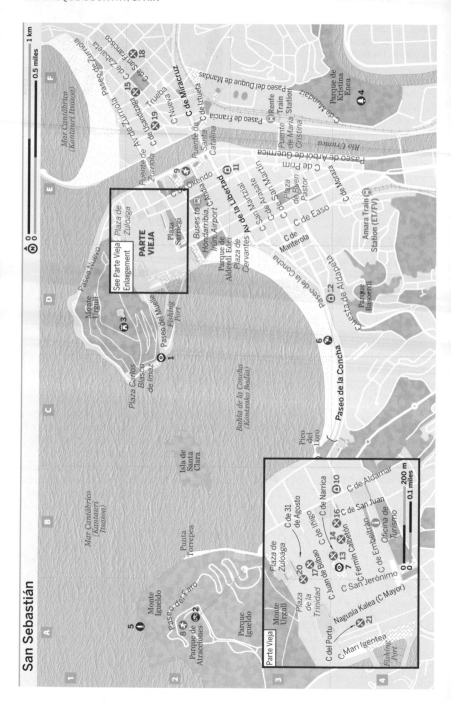

0.5 miles
1 km

F
Mar Cantábrico
(Kantauri Itsasoa)

× 18
C de San Francisco
Paseo de Zurriola
× 15
C de Usandizaga
C de Zabaleta
× 19 Trueba
C Nueva
C de Miracruz
C de Iztueta
Paseo del Duque de Mandas
Puente de Santa Catalina
Paseo de Francia
Renfe Train Station
Puente de María Cristina
Paseo del Duque de Mandas
Río Urumea
Paseo de Árbol de Guernica
C de Prim
C de Mundaiz
Parque de Kristina Enea
× 4

E
Paseo Nuevo
Plaza de Zuloaga
Plaza de Zuloaga
PARTE VIEJA
See Parte Vieja Enlargement
Plaza Sarriegi
C de Okendo
C de Okendo
Buses to Hondarribia, Irún, Airport,
C Aldia
× 9
AV de la Libertad
11
San Martín
C de San Martín
C de Arasate
Plaza de Buen Pastor
C de Moraza
C de Easo

D
Monte Urgull
M 3
Paseo del Muelle
Fishing Port
Parque de Alderdi Eder
Plaza de Cervantes
C de Manterola
Paseo de la Concha
2
Parque Basoerdi
Amara Train Station (ET/FV)
C de Aldapeta

C
Plaza Carlos Blasco de Imaz
1
Bahía de la Concha
(Kontxako Badia)
6
Paseo de la Concha
Pico del Loro

B
Mar Cantábrico
(Kantauri Itsasoa)
Punta Torrepea
Isla de Santa Clara
Parque Igueldo

A
Monte Igueldo
5
Paseo del Faro
× 2
Parque de Atracciones
8
Parque Igueldo

N
0

Parte Vieja
Monte Urgull
Plaza de la Trinidad
Plaza de Zuloaga
C de 31 de Agosto
× 20
17
C de Iñigo
C de Narrica
14 16
× 13
7
C de San Juan
10
C de Aldamar
C Fermín Calbetón
C de Embeltrán
Oficina de Turismo
C del Portu
C San Jerónimo
Nagusia Kalea (C Mayor)
× 21
C Mari Igentea
Fishing Port
200 m
0.1 miles

1
2
3
4

San Sebastián

⊙ Sights
1 Aquarium C2
2 Monte Igueldo A2
3 Monte Urgull D1
4 Parque de Cristina Enea F4
5 Peine del Viento A2
6 Playa de la Concha D3
7 Plaza de la Constitución B4

⊕ Activities, Courses & Tours
8 Parque de Atracciones A2
9 San Sebastián Food E2

⊕ Shopping
10 Aitor Lasa B4

11 Chocolates de Mendaro E2
12 Follow Me San Sebastián D3

⊗ Eating
13 Astelena... B4
14 Bar Borda Berri B4
15 Bar Diz F2
16 Bar Goiz-Argi B4
17 Bar Martinez B3
18 Bergara Bar F2
19 Bodega Donostiarra.............................. F2
20 La Cuchara de San Telmo....................... A3
21 La Fábrica... A4
  La Mejíllonera .... (see 21)

of the river is the district of Gros, a pleasant enclave that, with its relaxed ambience and the surfing beach of Playa de Gros, makes a cheerful alternative to the honeypots on the western side of the river. Right at the opposite, western end of the city is Playa de Ondarreta (essentially a continuation of Playa de la Concha), a very upmarket district known as a millionaires' belt on account of its lavish holiday homes.

◎ SIGHTS

San Sebastián is more about the beautiful beach – and the world-famous *pintxo* bars, and the quaint streets of the historic quarter – than it is about specific sights and attractions. Still, there's plenty to keep visitors busy here when you tire of sun and sand.

Aquarium　　　　Aquarium
(www.aquariumss.com; Plaza Carlos Blasco de Imaz 1; adult/child €13/6.50; ☉10am-9pm Jul & Aug, 10am-8pm Mon-Fri, 10am-9pm Sat & Sun Easter-Jun & Sep, shorter hours rest of year) Fear for your life as huge sharks bear down behind glass panes, or gaze in disbelief at tripped-out fluoro jellyfish. The highlights of a visit to the city's excellent aquarium are the cinema-screen-sized deep-ocean and coral-reef exhibits and the long tunnel, around which swim monsters of the deep. The aquarium also contains a maritime

museum section. Allow at least 1½ hours for a visit.

Parque de Cristina Enea　　Park
(Paseo Duque de Manda) Created by the Duke of Mandas in honour of his wife, the Parque de Cristina Enea is a favourite escape for locals. This formal park, the most attractive in the city, contains ornamental plants, ducks and peacocks, and open lawns.

Playa de la Concha　　　Beach
(Paseo de la Concha) Fulfilling almost every idea of how a perfect city beach should be formed, Playa de la Concha (and its westerly extension, Playa de Ondarreta) is easily among the best city beaches in Europe. Throughout the long summer months a fiesta atmosphere prevails, with thousands of tanned and toned bodies spread across the sands. The swimming is almost always safe.

Plaza de la Constitución　　Plaza
(Plaza de la Constitución) One of the most attractive city squares in the Basque country, the Plaza de la Constitución sits at the heart of the old town. The square dates from 1813 but sits on the site of an older square. It was once used as a bullring; the balconies of the fringing houses were rented to spectators.

Peine del Viento　　　Sculpture
A symbol of the city, the *Peine del Viento* (Wind Comb) sculpture, which sits at the

far western end of the Bahía de la Concha, below Monte Igueldo, is the work of the famous Basque sculptor Eduardo Chillida and architect Luis Peña Ganchegui.

Monte Igueldo — Viewpoint

(www.monteigueldo.es; ⊙10am-10pm Jun-Sep, shorter hours rest of year) The views from the summit of Monte Igueldo, just west of town, will make you feel like a circling hawk staring down over the vast panorama of the Bahía de la Concha and the surrounding coastline and mountains. The best way to get there is via the old-world **funicular railway** (www.monteigueldo.es; Plaza del Funicular; return adult/child €3.15/2.35; ⊙10am-9pm Jun-Aug, shorter hours rest of year) to the **Parque de Atracciones** (⌨943 21 35 25; www.monteigueldo.es; Paseo de Igeldo; adult/child €3.15/2.35; ⊙11am-2pm & 4-8.30pm Mon-Fri, to 9pm Sat & Sun Jul-Sep, shorter hours rest of year), a slightly tacky theme park at the top of the hill.

Monte Urgull — Castle

You can walk to the summit of Monte Urgull, topped by the low castle walls of the Castillo de la Mota and a grand statue of Christ, by taking a path from Plaza de Zuloaga or from behind the aquarium. The views are breathtaking and the shady parkland on the way up is a peaceful retreat from the city.

⊙ TOURS

The tourist office (p329) runs several different city tours (including a cinema tour) starting at €10.

Sabores de San Sebastián — Tours

(Flavours of San Sebastián; ⌨902 44 34 42; www.sansebastianreservas.com; tour €18; ⊙11.30am Tue & Thu Jul & Aug) The tourist office runs the Sabores de San Sebastián, a two-hour tour (in Spanish and English; French tours are available on request) of some of the city's *pintxo* haunts. Tours are also held with less frequency outside high season – contact the tourist office for dates.

San Sebastián Food — Food

(⌨943 42 11 43; www.sansebastianfood.com; Hotel Maria Cristina, Paseo de la República Argentina 4) The highly recommended San

From left: Playa de Ondarreta (p325) and Monte Igueldo; San Sebastián's Parte Vieja (Old Town); Bahía de la Concha

Sebastián Food runs an array of *pintxo* tasting tours (from €95) and cookery courses (from €145) in and around the city, as well as wine tastings (from €45). The shop/booking office also sells an array of high-quality local food and drink products.

🔒 SHOPPING

The Parte Vieja is awash with small independent boutiques, while the Área Romántica has all your brand-name and chain-store favourites.

Aitor Lasa   Food
(www.aitorlasa.com; Calle de Aldamar 12) This high-quality deli is the place to stock up on ingredients for a gourmet picnic you'll never forget. It specialises in cheeses, mushrooms and seasonal products.

Follow Me
San Sebastián   Food & Drinks
(www.justfollowme.com; Calle de Zubieta 7; ☺10am-2pm & 4-8pm Mon-Sat) A small selection of top-quality regional wine and foodstuffs. You can also learn all about their products on one of the gastronomic tours.

Chocolates de Mendaro   Food
(www.chocolatesdemendaro.com; Calle de Echaide 6; ☺10am-2pm & 4-8pm) We dare you to walk past this fabulous old chocolate shop and resist the temptation to walk inside.

❌ EATING

With 16 Michelin stars (including three restaurants with the coveted three stars), San Sebastián stands atop a pedestal as one of the culinary capitals of the planet. As if that alone weren't enough, the city is overflowing with bars – almost all of which have bar tops weighed down under a mountain of *pintxos* (p312) that almost every Spaniard will (sometimes grudgingly) tell you are the best in country. These statistics alone make San Sebastián look pretty impressive. But it's not just us who thinks this: a raft of the world's best chefs, including such luminaries as Catalan super-chef Ferran Adrià, have said that San Sebastián is quite

GONZALO AZUMENDI/GETTY IMAGES ©

ASIFE/SHUTTERSTOCK ©

Seafood *paella*

San Sebastián stands atop a pedestal as one of the culinary capitals of the planet

possibly the best place on the entire planet to eat.

La Fábrica   Basque €€
(☎943 98 05 81; www.restaurantelafabrica.es; Calle del Puerto 17; mains €15-20, menús from €28; ☺12.30-4pm & 7.30-11.30pm Mon-Fri, 1-4pm & 8-11pm Sat-Sun) The red-brick interior walls and white tablecloths lend an air of class to this restaurant, whose modern takes on Basque classics have been making waves with San Sebastián locals over the last couple of years. At just €25, the multi-dish tasting *menú* is about the best-value deal in the city. Advance reservations are essential.

Arzak   Basque €€€
(☎943 27 84 65; www.arzak.info; Avenida Alcalde Jose Elosegui 273; meals around €195; ☺Tue-Sat, closed Nov & late Jun) With three shining Michelin stars, acclaimed chef Juan Mari

Arzak is king when it comes to *nueva cocina vasca* and his restaurant is considered one of the best in the world. Arzak is now assisted by his daughter Elena, and they never cease to innovate. Reservations, well in advance, are obligatory.

The restaurant is located just east of San Sebastián.

Martín Berasategui
Restaurant   Basque €€€
(☎943 36 64 71; www.martinberasategui. com; Calle Loidi 4, Lasarte-Oria; tasting menu €195; ☺Wed-Sun lunch) This superlative restaurant, about 9km southwest of San Sebastián, is considered by foodies to be one of the best restaurants in the world. The chef, Martín Berasategui, approaches cuisine as a science and the results are tastes you never knew existed. Reserve well ahead.

Akelaŕe   Basque €€€
(☎943 31 12 09; www.akelarre.net; Paseo Padre Orcolaga 56; tasting menu €170; ☺1-3.30pm & 8.30-11pm Tue-Sat Jul-Dec, Wed-Sat Jan-Jun) This is where chef Pedro Subijana creates

cuisine that is a feast for all five senses. As with most of the region's top *nueva cocina vasca* restaurants, the emphasis here is on using fresh, local produce and turning it into something totally unexpected. It's in the suburb of Igeldo just west of the city.

DRINKING & NIGHTLIFE

It would be hard to imagine a town with more bars than San Sebastián. Most of the city's bars mutate through the day from calm morning-coffee hang-outs to *pintxo*-laden delights, before finally finishing up as noisy bars full of writhing, sweaty bodies. Nights in San Sebastián start late and go on until well into the wee hours.

INFORMATION

Oficina de Turismo (943 48 11 66; www.sansebastianturismo.com; Alameda del Boulevard 8; 9am-8pm Mon-Sat, 10am-7pm Sun Jul-Sep, shorter hours rest of year) This friendly office offers comprehensive information on the city and the Basque Country in general.

GETTING THERE & AWAY

AIR

The city's **airport** (free call 902 404704; www.aena.es) is 22km out of town, near Hondarribia. There are regular flights to Madrid and Barcelona and occasional charters to other major European cities. Biarritz, just over the border in France, is served by Ryanair and EasyJet, among various other budget airlines, and is generally much cheaper to fly into.

BUS

The main bus stop is a 20-minute walk south of the Parte Vieja, between Plaza de Pío XII and the river. Local buses 28 and 26 connect the bus station with Alameda del Boulevard (€1.65, 10 minutes), but it's also a pleasant stroll into the historic center from here, especially if you walk along the river. There's no real station here, but all the bus companies have offices and ticket booths near the bus stop.

TRAIN

The main **Renfe train station** (Paseo de Francia) is just across Río Urumea, on a line linking Paris to Madrid. There are several services daily to Madrid (from €27, 5½ hours) and two to Barcelona (from €19.25, six hours).

GETTING AROUND

Buses to Hondarribia (€2.35, 45 minutes) and the airport (€2.35, 45 minutes) depart from Plaza de Gipuzkoa.

In This Chapter

Mosteiro dos Jerónimos 332
Lisbon's Trams 334
Sights 336
Activities 341
Tours 342
Shopping 343
Eating 344
Drinking & Nightlife 346
Entertainment 347
Information 348
Getting There & Away 348
Getting Around 348

Lisbon, Portugal

Spread across steep hillsides that overlook the Rio Tejo, Lisbon has captivated visitors for centuries. Windswept vistas reveal the city in all its beauty: Roman and Moorish ruins, white-domed cathedrals, grand plazas. However, the real delight of discovery is delving into the narrow cobblestone lanes.

As yellow trams clatter through tree-lined streets, lisboêtas stroll through lamp-lit old quarters. Gossip is exchanged over wine at tiny restaurants as fado singers perform in the background. In other neighbourhoods, Lisbon reveals her youthful alter ego at bohemian bars and late-night street parties.

Lisbon in Two Days

Explore Lisbon's old town – the **Alfama** (p336) – on day one, perhaps taking a ride on **tram 28** (p335) part of the way. Round off with a **fado performance** (p347) in the evening. On day two explore **Belém** (p341) and the **Mosteiro dos Jerónimos** (p332). In the evening sample some of Lisbon's famous **night-life** (p346).

Lisbon in Four Days

On day three hit the museums – Lisbon has plenty dedicated to a range of subjects, but one highlight is the **Museu Nacional do Azulejo** (p337) packed with traditional tiles. On day four seek out a a picnic lunch at the **Mercado da Ribeira** (p344) and laze the day away at the **Jardim da Cerca da Graça** (p337).

Finished in Lisbon? Fly to Copenhagen (p136) or Prague (p524).

Central Lisbon Map (p338)

Arriving in Lisbon

Aeroporto de Lisboa Direct flights to major international hubs including London, New York, Paris and Frankfurt.

Sete Rios bus station The main long-distance bus terminal.

Gare do Oriente bus station Bus services to the north and Spain.

Gare do Oriente train station Lisbon's largest train station.

Where to Stay

Lisbon has an array of boutique hotels, upmarket hostels and both modern and old-fashioned guesthouses. Be sure to book ahead for high season (July to September). A word to those with weak knees and/or heavy bags: many guesthouses lack lifts, meaning you'll have to haul your luggage up three flights or more. If this disconcerts, be sure to book a place with a lift.

For information on what each Lisbon neighbourhood has to offer, see the table on p349.

Mosteiro dos Jerónimos

One of Lisbon's top attractions is this Unesco-listed monastery, an outstanding example of the elaborate Manueline style.

Great For...

☑ Don't Miss

The rows of seats in the church are Portugal's first Renaissance woodcarvings.

The Monastery's Story

Belém's undisputed heart-stealer is the stuff of pure fantasy: a fusion of Diogo de Boitaca's creative vision and the spice-and-pepper dosh of Manuel I, who commissioned it to trumpet Vasco da Gama's discovery of a sea route to India in 1498. The building embodies the golden age of Portuguese discoveries and was funded using the profits from the spices da Gama brought back from the subcontinent. Building began in 1502 but was not completed for almost a century. Wrought for the glory of God, Jerónimos was once populated by monks of the Order of St Jerome, whose spiritual job for four centuries was to comfort sailors and pray for the king's soul. The monastery withstood the 1755 earthquake but fell into disrepair when the order was dissolved in 1833. It was later used as a

The cloisters

TAKASHI IMAGES/SHUTTERSTOCK ©

❶ Need to Know

www.mosteirojeronimos.pt; Praça do Império; adult/child €10/5, 1st Sun of month free; ⊘10am-6.30pm Tue-Sun, to 5.30pm Oct-May

✗ Take a Break

Pão Pão Queijo Queijo (☎213 626 369; Rua de Belém 124; mains €4-8; ⊘10am-midnight Mon-Sat, to 8pm Sun; 🛜🅿) is a popular fast-food stop selling sandwiches and snacks.

★ Top Tip

A €12 admission pass is valid for both the monastery and the nearby Torre de Belém.

school and orphanage until about 1940. In 2007 the now much-discussed Treaty of Lisbon was signed here.

Vasco da Gama

Born in Alentejo in the 1460s, Vasco da Gama was the first European explorer to reach India by ship. This was a key moment in Portuguese history as it opened up trading links to Asia and established Portugal's maritime empire, the wealth from which made the country into a world superpower. Da Gama died from malaria on his third voyage to India in 1524.

The Church

Entering the church through the western portal, you'll notice tree-trunk-like columns that seem to grow into the ceiling, which is itself a spiderweb of stone. Windows cast a

soft golden light over the church. Superstar Vasco da Gama is interred in the lower chancel, just left of the entrance, opposite venerated 16th-century poet Luís Vaz de Camões. From the upper choir, there's a superb view of the church.

The Cloisters

There's nothing like the moment you walk into the honey-stone Manueline cloisters, dripping with organic detail in their delicately scalloped arches, twisting auger-shell turrets and columns intertwined with leaves, vines and knots. It will simply wow. Keep an eye out for symbols of the age such as the armillary sphere and the cross of the Military Order, plus gargoyles and fantastical beasties on the upper balustrade.

JORGE CASAIS/SHUTTERSTOCK ©

Lisbon's Trams

Quintessentially Lisbon, a ride on one of the city's typical yellow trams should be on your to-do list. Tram 28 climbs through the Alfama and is a must for every visitor.

Great For...

☑ Don't Miss

In addition to tram 28, other city-centre tram routes are 12, 15, 18 and 25.

Lisbon's Old Trams

Lisbon's old yellow streetcars are a nostalgic throwback to the early days of urban public transport and would have long since been pensioned off to a transport museum in most other European countries. They have survived largely because they were specially designed for a specific task – to trundle up and down central Lisbon's steep gradients (just like their San Francisco cousins) and would be much too expensive to replace. These roller-coaster vintage trams date from the 1930s and are called *remodelados* (remodelled). The name comes from the fact the cars were slightly upgraded in the 1990s to include such luxuries as late 20th-century brakes. There were once 27 lines in the city, but the construction of the metro put the system

PETER ADAMS/GETTY IMAGES ©

Tram 28

The famous tram 28, Lisbon's longest tram
route, is extremely popular with tourists as
it heads through Baixa, Graça, Alfama and
Estrela, climbing the steep hill from Baixa
to the castle and Alfama as well as three of
the city's seven other hills en route. There
are 34 stops between Campo Ourique
in the west of the city centre to Martim
Monique, though the most interesting section is between Estrela and Graça. Trams
depart every 11 minutes, though the last
leaves fairly early (before 10pm, depending on the day). The experience on the
museum-piece tram can be an uncomfort-
able one for some, with varnished wooden
benches, steps and crowds of tourists
getting in each other's way. But it's worth it
for the ride – there's no cheaper way to see
the city and it's a great option to take when
the weather is not playing ball.

into decline. Today there are only five lines
left – *remodelados* run on all of them.

Tram Stops & Fares

Lisbon's tram stops are marked by a small
yellow *paragem* (stop) sign hanging from a
lamp post or from the overhead wires. You'll
pay more for a tram ride if you buy your
ticket on board rather than purchasing a
prepaid card. On-board one-way prices are
€2.90, but a day pass costs just €6.15 and
is valid on all of the city's public transport
for 24 hours.

Pickpockets

With groups of tourists crammed into a
small space, sadly tram 28 is a happy hunting ground for pickpockets. Take the usual
precautions to avoid being parted from
your possessions.

◉ SIGHTS

At the riverfront is the grand Praça do Comércio. Behind it march the pedestrian-filled streets of Baixa (lower) district, up to Praça da Figueira and Praça Dom Pedro IV (aka Rossio). From Baixa it's a steep climb west, through swanky shopping district Chiado, into the narrow streets of night-life-haven Bairro Alto. Eastwards from the Baixa it's another climb to Castelo de São Jorge and the Moorish, labyrinthine Alfama district around it. The World Heritage Sites of Belém lie further west along the river – an easy tram ride from Praça do Comércio.

◉ Alfama, Castelo & Graça

Castelo de São Jorge　　　Castle
(www.castelodesaojorge.pt; adult/student/child €8.50/5/free; ⊙9am-9pm Mar-Oct, to 6pm Nov-Feb) Towering dramatically above Lisbon, the mid-11th-century hilltop fortifications of Castelo de São Jorge sneak into almost

the anachronous feeling of stepping back in time

every snapshot. Roam its snaking ramparts and pine-shaded courtyards for superlative views over the city's red rooftops to the river. Three guided tours daily (Portuguese, English and Spanish) at 1pm and 5pm are included in the admission price.

These smooth cobbles have seen it all – Visigoths in the 5th century, Moors in the 9th century, Christians in the 12th century, royals from the 14th to 16th centuries, and convicts in every century.

Inside the **Ulysses Tower**, a camera obscura offers a unique 360-degree angle on Lisbon, with demos every 20 minutes. There are also a few galleries displaying relics from past centuries, including traces of the Moorish neighbourhood dating from the 11th century at the **Archaeological Site**. But the standout attraction is the view – as well as the anachronous feeling of stepping back in time amid fortified courtyards and towering walls. There are a few cafes and restaurants to while away time in as well.

Bus 737 from Sé or Praça da Figueira goes right to the gate. Tram 28 also passes nearby.

Castelo de São Jorge

MANFRED GOTTSCHALK/GETTY IMAGES ©

Miradouro do Castelo de São Jorge — Viewpoint

One of Lisbon's privileged views is on offer from this outstanding lookout point on the grounds of the Castelo.

Jardim da Cerca da Graça — Park

(Calçada Do Monte 46;) Closed for centuries, this 1.7-hectare green space debuted in 2015 and clocks in as Lisbon's second-biggest park, offering a lush transition between the neighbourhoods of Graça and Mouraria. There are superb city and castle views from several points and a shady picnic park along with a playground, an orchard and a peaceful kiosk with a terrace.

Load up on wine and cheese and call it an afternoon!

Museu do Fado — Museum

(www.museudofado.pt; Largo do Chafariz de Dentro; adult/child €5/3; ⏰10am-6pm Tue-Sun) Fado (traditional Portuguese melancholic song) was born in the Alfama. Immerse yourself in its bittersweet symphonies at the Museu do Fado. This engaging museum traces fado's history from its working-class roots to international stardom.

Museu de Artes Decorativas — Museum

(Museum of Decorative Arts; www.fress.pt; Largo das Portas do Sol 2; adult/child €4/free; ⏰10am-5pm Wed-Mon) Set in a petite 17th-century palace, the Museu de Artes Decorativas creaks under the weight of treasures including blingy French silverware, priceless Qing vases and Indo-Chinese furniture, a collection amassed by a wealthy Portuguese banker from the age of 16. It's worth a visit alone to admire the lavish apartments, embellished with baroque *azulejos*, frescoes and chandeliers.

It's a particularly atmospheric spot for live **fado** on Wednesday at 6pm.

Mosteiro de São Vicente de Fora — Church

(Largo de São Vicente; adult/child €5/free; ⏰10am-6pm Tue-Sun) Graça's Mosteiro de São Vicente de Fora was founded in 1147

When to Go to Lisbon

The peak summer season (June to August) serves up hot weather and is the best time for open-air festivals, beach days and al fresco dining. However, the perfect season for exploring may be spring (March to May) – it has milder but often sunny days, and accommodation is still reasonably priced.

and revamped by Italian architect Felipe Terzi in the late 16th century. Since the adjacent church took the brunt of the 1755 earthquake (the church's dome crashed through the ceiling of the **sacristy**, but emerged otherwise unscathed), elaborate blue-and-white *azulejos* dance across almost every wall, echoing the building's architectural curves.

Museu Nacional do Azulejo — Museum

(www.museudoazulejo.pt; Rua Madre de Deus 4; adult/child €5/2.50, free 1st Sun of the month; ⏰10am-6pm Tue-Sun) Housed in a sublime 16th-century convent, Lisbon's Museu Nacional do Azulejo covers the entire *azulejo* (hand-painted tile) spectrum. Star exhibits feature a 36m-long panel depicting pre-earthquake Lisbon, a Manueline cloister with web-like vaulting and exquisite blue-and-white *azulejos,* and a gold-smothered baroque chapel.

Here you'll find every kind of *azulejo* imaginable, from early Ottoman geometry to zinging altars, scenes of lords a-hunting and Goan intricacies. Bedecked with food-inspired *azulejos* – ducks, pigs and the like – the **restaurant** opens onto a vine-clad courtyard.

Sé de Lisboa — Cathedral

(Largo de Sé; ⏰9am-7pm Tue-Sat, to 5pm Mon & Sun) **FREE** One of Lisbon's icons is the fortress-like Sé de Lisboa, built in 1150 on the site of a mosque soon after Christians recaptured the city from the Moors.

Central Lisbon

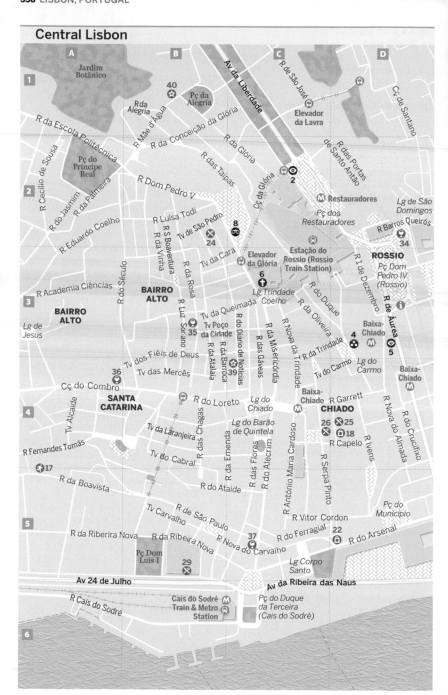

Jardim Botânico

A **B** **C** **D**

1

Av da Liberdade

R de São José

Cç de Santano

40

Pç da Alegria

R da Alegria

R Mãe d'Água

R da Conceição da Glória

R da Glória

Elevador da Lavra

Cç de Santano

R da Escola Politécnica

2

R Cecílio de Sousa

Pç do Príncipe Real

R do Jasmim

R da Palmeira

R Eduardo Coelho

R Dom Pedro V

R das Taipas

R das Portas de Santo Antão

M Restauradores

Lg de São Domingos

R Barros Queirós

34

R Luísa Todi

R S Boaventura

R da Vinha

Tv de São Pedro

24 8

R da Cara

Pç dos Restauradores

3

BAIRRO ALTO

R Academia Ciências

R do Século

BAIRRO ALTO

Lg de Jesus

R da Rosa

R Luz Soriano

Tv da Cara

Elevador da Glória

6

Lg Trindade Coelho

Estação do Rossio (Rossio Train Station)

R 1 de Dezembro

ROSSIO

Pç Dom Pedro IV (Rossio)

R de Áurea

Tv da Queimada

Tv Poço da Cidade

35

R da Atalaia

R da Barroca

39

R do Diário de Notícias

R das Gáveas

R da Misericórdia

R Nova da Trindade

R da Trindade

R da Oliveira

R do Duque

Baixa-Chiado

4 M

5

Baixa-Chiado M

Lg do Carmo

Tv do Carmo

36

Cç do Combro

Tv dos Fiéis de Deus

Tv das Mercês

SANTA CATARINA

R do Loreto

Lg do Chiado

Lg do Barão de Quintela

Baixa-Chiado M

CHIADO

R Garrett

26 25

18

R Capelo

R Ivens

R Nova do Almada

R do Crucifixo

4

Tv Alcaide

Tv da Laranjeira

R das Chagas

R da Emenda

R das Flores

R do Alecrim

R António Maria Cardoso

R Serpa Pinto

R Fernandes Tomás

17

R da Boavista

Tv do Cabral

R do Ataíde

Pç do Município

5

Tv Carvalho

R de São Paulo

R Nova do Carvalho

37

R Vitor Cordon

R do Ferragial

22

R do Arsenal

R da Ribeira Nova

R da Ribeira Nova

Pç Dom Luís I

29

Lg Corpo Santo

Av 24 de Julho

Av da Ribeira das Naus

R Cais do Sodré

Cais do Sodré Train & Metro Station M

Pç do Duque da Terceira (Cais do Sodré)

6

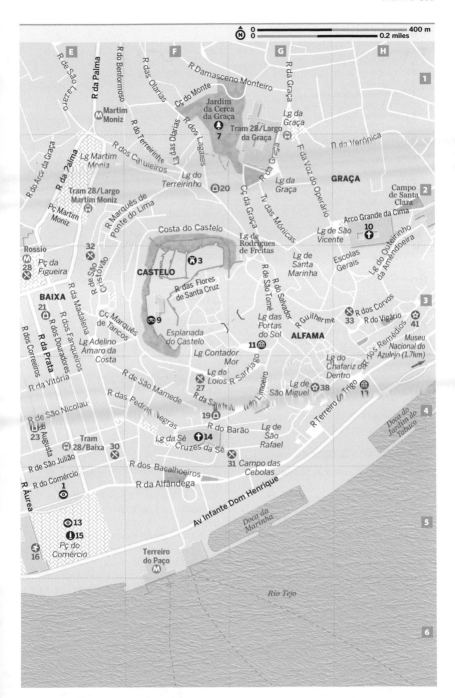

N

0   400 m
0   0.2 miles

Central Lisbon

◎ **Sights**
1 Arco da Rua Augusta...................................E5
2 Ascensor da Glória.......................................C2
3 Castelo de São Jorge F3
4 Convento do Carmo & Museu
    Arqueológico...D3
5 Elevador de Santa Justa.........................D3
    Gothic Cloister.................................(see 14)
6 Igreja & Museu São Roque.....................C3
7 Jardim da Cerca da Graça........................F1
8 Miradouro de São Pedro de
    Alcântara...C2
9 Miradouro do Castelo de São Jorge........F3
10 Mosteiro de São Vicente de Fora H2
11 Museu de Artes Decorativas.................G3
12 Museu do Fado..H4
13 Praça do Comércio..................................E5
14 Sé de Lisboa..F4
15 Statue of Dom José I..............................E5
    Treasury..(see 14)

◑ **Activities, Courses & Tours**
16 ViniPortugal...E5
17 Zeev...A5

▣ **Shopping**
18 A Vida Portuguesa..................................D4
19 Arte da Terra...F4

20 Cortiço & Netos.......................................F2
21 Garrafeira Nacional................................E3
22 Loja das Conservas.................................D5
23 Typographia...E4

⊗ **Eating**
24 100 Maneiras...B2
25 Alma...D4
26 Belcanto..C4
27 Chapitô à Mesa.......................................F4
28 Mercado da Baixa....................................E3
29 Mercado da Ribeira.................................B5
30 Nova Pombalina.......................................E4
31 Pois Café..G4
32 Tasca Zé dos Cornos...............................E3
33 Ti-Natércia...H3

◎ **Drinking & Nightlife**
34 A Ginjinha..D2
35 BA Wine Bar do Bairro Alto....................B3
36 Park..A4
37 Pensão Amor..C5

◎ **Entertainment**
38 A Baîuca...G4
39 A Tasco do Chico.....................................C4
40 Hot Clube de Portugal.............................B1
41 Senhor Fado..H3

It was sensitively restored in the 1930s. Despite the masses outside, the rib-vaulted interior, lit by a rose window, is calm. Stroll around the cathedral to spy leering gargoyles peeking above the orange trees.

◎ Bairro Alto & Chiado

Convento do Carmo & Museu Arqueológico   Ruins

(Largo do Carmo; adult/child €3.50/free; ⊙10am-7pm Mon-Sat, to 6pm Oct-May) Soaring above Lisbon, the skeletal Convento do Carmo was all but devoured by the 1755 earthquake and that's precisely what makes it so captivating. Its shattered pillars and wishbone-like arches are completely exposed to the elements. The Museu Arqueológico shelters archaeological treasures, such as 4th-century sarcophagi, griffin-covered column fragments, 16th-century azulejo (hand-painted tile) panels and two gruesome 16th-century Peruvian mummies.

Igreja & Museu São Roque   Church, Museum

(www.museu-saoroque.com; Largo Trindade Coelho; church free, museum adult/child €2.50/free, free 10am-2pm Sun; ⊙2-7pm Mon, 10am-7pm Tue-Wed & Fri-Sun, 10am-8pm Thu) The plain facade of 16th-century Jesuit Igreja de São Roque belies its dazzling interior of gold, marble and Florentine azulejos – bankrolled by Brazilian riches. Its star attraction is **Capela de São João Baptista**, a lavish confection of amethyst, alabaster, lapis lazuli and Carrara marble. The **museum** adjoining the church is packed with elaborate sacred art and holy relics.

Free guided tours are offered in four languages. For English, arrive on Thursdays (3pm), Fridays (11.30am and 4.30pm), Saturdays (10am) and Sundays (3pm).

Miradouro de São Pedro de Alcântara   Viewpoint

(Rua São Pedro de Alcântara; ⊙viewpoint 24hr, kiosk 10am-midnight Mon-Wed, to 2am Thu-

Sun) Hitch a ride on vintage **Ascensor da Glória** (www.transporteslisboa.pt; return €3.60; ⊙7am-midnight Mon-Thu, 7am-12.30pm Fri, 8.30am-12.30am Sat, 9am-midnight Sun) from Praça dos Restauradores, or huff your way up steep Calçada da Glória to this terrific hilltop viewpoint. Fountains and Greek busts add a regal air to the surroundings, and the open-air kiosk doles out wine, beer and snacks, which you can enjoy while taking in the castle views and live music.

Elevador de Santa Justa — Elevator

(www.transporteslisboa.pt; cnr Rua de Santa Justa & Largo do Carmo; return trip €5; ⊙7am-11pm, to 10pm Oct-May) If the lanky, wrought-iron Elevador de Santa Justa seems uncannily familiar, it's probably because the neo-Gothic marvel is the handiwork of Raul Mésnier, Gustave Eiffel's apprentice. It's Lisbon's only vertical street lift, built in 1902 and steam-powered until 1907. Get there early to beat the crowds and zoom to the top for sweeping views over the city's skyline.

Bear in mind, however, some call the €5 fee Santa Injusta! You can save €3.50 by entering the platform from the top (behind Convento do Carmo) and paying just €1.50 to access the viewing platform.

⊙ Baixa & Rossio

Praça do Comércio — Plaza

(Terreiro do Paço) With its grand 18th-century arcades, lemon-meringue facades and mosaic cobbles, the riverfront Praça do Comércio is a square to out-pomp them all. Everyone arriving by boat used to disembark here, and it still feels like the gateway to Lisbon, thronging with activity and rattling trams.

At its centre rises the dashing equestrian **statue of Dom José I**, hinting at the square's royal roots as the pre-earthquake site of Palácio da Ribeira. In 1908, the square witnessed the fall of the monarchy, when anarchists assassinated Dom Carlos I and his son. The biggest crowd-puller is Verissimo da Costa's triumphal **Arco da Rua Augusta** (Rua Augusta 2-10; €2.50; ⊙9am-7pm), crowned with bigwigs such

as 15th-century explorer Vasco da Gama; come at dusk to see the arch glow gold.

⊙ Belém

Torre de Belém — Tower

(www.torrebelem.pt; adult/child €6/3, 1st Sun of month free; ⊙10am-6.30pm Tue-Sun, to 5.30pm Oct-Apr) Jutting out onto the Rio Tejo, this Unesco World Heritage–listed fortress epitomises the Age of Discoveries. You'll need to breathe in to climb the narrow spiral staircase to the tower, which affords sublime views over Belém and the river.

Francisco de Arruda designed the pearly-grey chess piece in 1515 to defend Lisbon's harbour and nowhere else is the lure of the Atlantic more powerful. The Manueline show-off flaunts filigree stonework, meringue-like cupolas and – just below the western tower – a stone rhinoceros.

The ungulate depicts the one Manuel I sent Pope Leo X in 1515, which inspired Dürer's famous woodcut. Crowds can be intense on weekends (especially Sunday) – a warning to claustrophobes.

Museu Colecção Berardo — Museum

(www.museuberardo.pt; Praça do Império; ⊙10am-7pm) Hordes of culture fiends get their contemporary-art fix for free at Museu Colecção Berardo, the star of the Centro Cultural de Belém. The ultrawhite, minimalist gallery displays millionaire José Berardo's eye-popping collection of abstract, surrealist and pop art, including Hockney, Lichtenstein, Warhol and Pollack originals.

Temporary exhibitions are among the best in Portugal. Also in the complex is a cafe-restaurant that faces a grassy lawn, a bookshop and a crafty museum store.

⊕ ACTIVITIES

Sipping away summer on numerous hilltop and waterfront *esplanadas* (terraces) and plaza kiosks is a quintessential Lisbon experience. Fancy some football? Two of Portugal's big three clubs, Benfica and Sporting, call Lisbon home. Guided tours are extremely popular and, for certified beach

Torre de Belém (p341)

bums, idyllic sands at Carcavelos, Parede, Estoril and Cascais are easy train rides away.

ViniPortugal
Wine

(www.winesofportugal.info; Praça do Comércio; ⊙11am-7pm Tue-Sat) Under the arcades on Praça do Comércio, this viticultural organisation offers €6 themed wine tastings, if booked in advance. Otherwise, pop in and grab a €3 enocard, which allows you to taste between two and four Portuguese wines, from Alentejo whites to full-bodied Douro reds.

Kiss the Cook
Cooking

(☑968 119 652; www.kissthecook.pt; Rua Rodrigues Faria 103, LX Factory; classes €65; ⊙noon-3pm) If you're into Portuguese food in a big way and fancy picking up a few tips and tricks from the experts, why not pass by Kiss the Cook? Here you can prepare (and devour) traditional dishes. The cookery classes are totally hands-on and the price includes lunch and wine.

Teleférico
Cable Car

(Telecabine Lisboa; www.telecabinelisboa.pt; Passeio do Tejo; 1-way adult/child €3.95/2;

⊙10.30am-8pm, 11am-7pm low season) Hitch a ride on this 20m-high cable car, linking Torre Vasco da Gama to the Oceanário. The ride affords bird's-eye views across Parque das Nações' skyline and the glittering Tejo that will have you burning up the pixels on your camera.

Zeev
Cycling

(☑915 100 242; www.rent.zeev.pt; Rua da Boavista 166; bike hire per 3/8/24hr €16/22/30; ⊙9am-7pm Mon-Sat) 🚲 Rents electric bikes (you'll appreciate the pedal-assist on Lisbon's hills), Renault Twizy electric two-person buggies, and full-size electric cars. Charging is free as is parking for electric vehicles within Lisbon city limits.

🎫 TOURS

Culinary Backstreets
Food & Drink

(☑963 472 188; www.culinarybackstreets.com/culinary-walks/lisbon; 3/6hr tours €85/118) *Eat Portugal* co-author Célia Pedroso leads epic culinary walks through Lisbon, a fantastic way to take in some of the best treats in town. Try *ginjinha* (cherry liqueur) followed by *pastel de nata* (custard tarts) and *porco preto* (Iberian black pork), paired with killer local wines. Tours are available Monday to Saturday. Expect tantalising multiple food-gasms followed by a debilitating food coma.

Lisbon Explorer   Walking

(☑213 629 263; www.lisbonexplorer.com; tour per person/group from €60/150) Top-notch English-speaking guides peel back the many layers of Lisbon's history during the three-hour walking tours offered by this highly rated outfit. Fees do not include admissions but often include public-transport costs during the tour. Tours typically depart from Praça do Comércio or other central locations. You'll receive the meeting point upon booking.

🛍 SHOPPING

Bairro Alto attracts vinyl lovers and vintage devotees to its cluster of late-opening boutiques. Alfama, Baixa and Rossio have frozen-in-time stores dealing exclusively in buttons and kid gloves, tawny port and tinned fish. Elegant Chiado is the go-to place for high-street and couture shopping to the backbeat of buskers.

Arte da Terra   Gifts & Souvenirs

(www.aarteloterra.pt; Rua Augusto Rosa 40; ⊙11am-8pm) In the stables of a centuries-old bishop's palace, Arte da Terra brims with authentic Portuguese crafts including Castello Branco embroideries, nativity figurines, hand-painted *azulejos,* fado CDs and quality goods (umbrellas, aprons, writing journals) made from cork. Some items are beautifully lit in former troughs.

Cortiço & Netos   Homewares

(www.corticoenetos.com; Calçada de Santo André 66; ⊙10am-1pm & 2-7pm Mon-Sat) A wonder wall of fabulous *azulejos* greets you as you enter this very special space. It's the vision of brothers Pedro, João, Ricardo and Tiago Cortiço, whose grandfather dedicated more than 30 years to gathering, storing and selling discontinued Portuguese industrial tiles. Reviving the family trade, they are

experts on the *azulejo* and how it can be interpreted today.

Garrafeira Nacional   Wine

(www.garrafeiranacional.com; Rua de Santa Justa 18; ⊙9.30am-7.30pm Mon-Fri, to 7.30pm Sat) This Lisbon landmark has been slinging Portuguese juice since 1927 and is easily the best spot to pick up a bevy of local wines and spirits. It is especially helpful and will steer you towards lesser-known boutique wines and vintage ports in addition to the usual suspects. The small museum features vintages dating to the 18th century.

There is a second, smaller outlet in the Mercado da Ribeira.

Typographia   Clothing

(www.typographia.com; Rua Augusta 93; T-shirts €16-24; ⊙10am-9pm) With shops in Porto and Madrid as well, this high-design T-shirt shop is one of Europe's best. It features a select, monthly-changing array of clever and artsy, locally designed T-shirts, which everyone else won't be wearing once you get back home.

A Vida Portuguesa Gifts & Souvenirs

(www.avidaportuguesa.com; Rua Anchieta 11; ⊙10am-8pm Mon-Sat, from 11am Sun) A flashback to the late 19th century with its high ceilings and polished cabinets, this former warehouse and perfume factory lures nostalgics with all-Portuguese products from retro-wrapped Tricona sardines to Claus Porto soaps, heart-embellished Viana do Castelo embroideries and Bordallo Pinheiro porcelain swallows. Also in Intendente.

Loja das Conservas   Food

(www.facebook.com/lojadasconservas; Rua do Arsenal 130; ⊙10am-9pm Mon-Sat, noon-8pm Sun) What appears to be a gallery is on closer inspection a fascinating temple to tinned fish (or *conservas* as the Portuguese say), the result of an industry on its deathbed revived by a savvy marketing about-face and new generations of hipsters. The retro-wrapped tins, displayed along with the history of each canning factory, are the artworks.

Craft Beer

Lisboêtas have finally been released from the decades-long suds purgatory imposed on them by commoner lagers Super Bock and Sagres. IPAs, stouts, porters, *saisons* and sours are booming – keep an eye out for an ever-expanding list of local standouts that includes Dois Corvos, Oitava Colina, Passarola, Mean Sardine, Amnesia and Musa. Drink in the local scene at several new craft-beer bars and brewpubs. The hops revolution has begun!

AFRICA STUDIO/SHUTTERSTOCK ©

 EATING

Mercado da Baixa   Market €
(www.adbaixapombalina.pt; Praça da Figueira; ⊙10am-10pm Fri-Sun) This tented market/ glorious food court on Praça da Figueira has been slinging cheese, wine, smoked sausages and other gourmet goodies since 1855. It takes place on the last weekend of each month and it is fantastic fun to stroll the stalls eating and drinking yourself into a gluttonous mess.

Nova Pombalina   Portuguese €
(www.facebook.com/anovapombalina; Rua do Comércio 2; sandwiches €2.20-4; ⊙7am-7.30pm, closed Sun) The reason this bustling traditional restaurant is always packed around midday is its delicious *leitão* (suckling pig) sandwich, served on freshly baked bread in 60 seconds or less by the lightning-fast crew behind the counter.

Ti-Natércia   Portuguese €
(☑218 862 133; Rua Escola Gerais 54; mains €5-12; ⊙7pm-midnight Mon-Fri, noon-3pm & 7pm-midnight Sat) A decade in and a legend in the making, 'Aunt' Natércia and her downright delicious Portuguese home cooking is a tough ticket: there are but a mere six tables and they fill up fast. She'll talk your ear off (and doesn't mince words!) while you devour her excellent take on the classics. Reservations essential (and cash only).

If you do manage to get a seat, you're in for a treat, especially with the *bacalhau com natas* (shredded codfish with bechamal, served au gratin) or *à Brás* (shredded codfish with eggs and potatoes) or, well, anything you else you might order. President Marcelo Rebelo de Sousa approved – his photo is on the wall.

Pois Café   Cafe €
(www.poiscafe.com; Rua de São João da Praça 93; mains €7-10; ⊙noon-11pm Mon, 10am-11pm Tue-Sun; ⌨) Boasting a laid-back vibe under dominant stone arches, atmospheric Pois Café has creative salads, sandwiches and fresh juices, plus a handful of heartier daily specials (salmon quiche, sirloin steak). Its sofas invite lazy afternoons spent reading novels and sipping coffee, but you'll fight for space with the laptop brigade.

Mercado da Ribeira   Market €
(www.timeoutmarket.com; Av 24 de Julho; ⊙10am-midnight Sun-Wed, to 2am Thu-Sat; ⌨) Doing trade in fresh fruit and veg, fish and flowers since 1892, this oriental-dome-topped market hall is the word on everyone's lips since *Time Out* transformed half of it into a gourmet food court in 2014. Now it's like Lisbon in microcosm, with everything from Garrafeira Nacional wines to Conserveira de Lisboa fish, Arcádia chocolate and Santini gelato.

Follow the lead of locals and come for a browse in the morning followed by lunch at one of 35 kiosks – there's everything from Café de São Bento's famous steak and fries to a stand by top chef Henrique Sá Pessoa. Do not miss it.

Dona Quitéria
Portuguese €

(☏213 951 521; Travessa de São José 1; small plates €5-12; ⊙7pm-midnight Tue-Sun) Locals do their best to keep this quaint corner *petiscaria* (small plates restaurant), a former grocery store from 1870, all to themselves – no such luck. Pleasant palette surprises such as tuna *pica-pau* instead of steak, or a pumpkin-laced cream-cheese mousse for dessert, put tasty creative spins on tradition. It's warm, welcoming and oh so tiny – so reserve ahead.

Chapitô à Mesa
Portuguese €€

(☏218 875 077; www.facebook.com/chapito amesa; Rua Costa do Castelo 7; mains €18-21; ⊙noon-11pm Mon-Fri, 7.30-11pm Sat-Sun; ☈) Up a spiral iron staircase from this circus school's casual cafe, the decidedly creative menu of Chef Bertílio Gomes is served alongside views worth writing home about. His modern takes include classic dishes (*bacalhau à Brás,* stewed veal cheeks, suckling pig), plus daring ones (rooster testicles – goes swimmingly with a drop of Quinta da Silveira Reserva).

Tasca Zé dos Cornos
Portuguese €€

(☏218 869 641; www.facebook.com/ZeCornos; Beco Surradores 5; mains €10-15; ⊙8am-11pm Mon-Sat) This family-owned tavern welcomes regulars and first-timers with the same undivided attention. Lunchtime is particularly busy but the service is whirlwind quick and effective. Space is tight so sharing tables is the norm. The menu is typical Portuguese cuisine with emphasis on pork and *bacalhau* (salted cod) grilled on the spot, served in very generous portions.

Alma
Contemporary, Portuguese €€€

(☏213 470 650; www.almalisboa.pt; Rua Anchieta 15; mains €25-29, tasting menus €60-80; ⊙noon-3pm & 7-11pm Tue-Sun; ☈) Henrique Sá Pessoa, one of Portugal's most talented chefs, moved his flagship Alma from Santos to more fitting digs in Chiado in 2015. The casual space exudes understated style amid its original stone flooring and gorgeous hardwood tables, but it's Pessoa's outrageously good nouveau Portuguese cuisine that draws the foodie flock from far and wide.

Mercado da Ribeira

100 Maneiras   Fusion €€€

(📱910 307 575; www.restaurante100maneiras.
com; Rua do Teixeira 35; tasting menu €58,
with classic/premium wine pairing €93/118;
⊘7.30pm-2am; 📶) How do we love 100
Maneiras? Let us count the 100 ways... The
nine-course tasting menu changes twice
yearly and features imaginative, delicately
prepared dishes. The courses are all a
surprise – part of the charm – though
somewhat disappointingly, the chef will
only budge so far to accommodate special
diets and food allergies. Reservations are
essential for the elegant and small space.

Belcanto   Portuguese €€€

(📱213 420 607; www.belcanto.pt; Largo de São
Carlos 10; mains €45, tasting menu €125-145,
with 5/7 wines €50/60; ⊘12.30-3pm & 7.30-
11pm Tue-Sat; 📶) Fresh off a 2016 intimacy
upgrade, José Avillez' two-Michelin-starred
cathedral of cookery wows diners with
painstaking creativity, polished service and
first-rate sommelier. Standouts among
Lisbon's culinary adventure of a lifetime
include suckling pig with orange purée,
sea bass with seaweed and bivalves and

a stunning roasted butternut squash with
miso; paired wines sometimes date to the
'70s! Reservations essential.

🍸 DRINKING & NIGHTLIFE

Park   Bar

(www.facebook.com/00park; Calçada do Combro
58; cocktails €6.50-8; ⊘1pm-2am Tue-Sat, 1-8pm
Sun; 📶) If only all multistorey car parks
were like this... Take the elevator to the 5th
floor, and head up and around to the top,
which has been transformed into one of
Lisbon's hippest rooftop bars, with sweeping views reaching right down to the Tejo
and over the bell towers of Santa Catarina
Church.

Pensão Amor   Bar

(www.pensaoamor.pt; Rua do Alecrim 19;
cocktails €5.50-13; ⊘noon-3am Mon-Wed, to
4am Thu-Sat, to 3am Sun) Set inside a former
brothel, this cheeky bar pays homage to
its passion-filled past with colourful wall
murals, a library of erotic-tinged works, and
a small stage where you can sometimes
catch burlesque shows. The Museu Erótico

Fado performer

de Lisboa (MEL) was on the way at time of research.

BA Wine Bar
do Bairro Alto
Wine Bar

(☏213 461 182; bawinebar@gmail.com; Rua da Rosa 107; wines from €3, tapas from €12; ⊘6-11pm Tue-Sun; 🛜) Reserve ahead unless you want to get shut out of Bairro Alto's best wine bar, where the genuinely welcoming staff will offer you three fantastic choices to taste based on your wine proclivities. The cheeses (from small artisanal producers) and charcuterie (melt-in-your-mouth black-pork *presuntos*) are not to be missed, either. You could spend the night here.

A Ginjinha
Bar

(Largo de Saõ Domingos 8; ⊘9am-10pm) Hipsters, old men in flat caps, office workers and tourists all meet at this microscopic *ginjinha* (cherry liqueur) bar for that moment of cherry-licking, pip-spitting pleasure (€1.40 a shot).

Watch the owner line 'em up at the bar under the beady watch of the drink's 19th-century inventor, Espinheira. It's less about the grog, more about the event.

Lux-Frágil
Club

(www.luxfragil.com; Av Infante Dom Henrique, Armazém A - Cais de Pedra, Santo Apolónia; ⊘11pm-6am Thu-Sat) Lisbon's ice-cool, must-see club, Lux hosts big-name DJs spinning electro and house. It's run by ex-Frágil maestro Marcel Reis and part-owned by John Malkovich. Grab a spot on the terrace to see the sun rise over the Tejo; or chill like a king on the throne-like giant interior chairs.

Style policing is heartwarmingly lax but arrive after 4am at weekends and you might have trouble getting in because of the crowds.

⭐ ENTERTAINMENT

Infused by Moorish song and the ditties of homesick sailors, bluesy, bittersweet fado encapsulates the Lisbon psyche like nothing else. There's usually a minimum cover

Lisbon Online

Lonely Planet (www.lonelyplanet.com/lisbon) Destination information, hotel bookings, traveller forum and more.

Visit Lisboa (www.visitlisboa.com) Comprehensive tourist office website.

Lisbon Lux (www.lisbonlux.com) Trendy city guide.

Spotted by Locals (www.spottedbylocals.com/lisbon) Insider tips.

Go Lisbon (www.golisbon.com) Dining, drinking and nightlife insight.

of €15 to €25. Book ahead at weekends. If you prefer a spontaneous approach, seek out *fado vadio* where anyone can – and does – have a warble.

Hot Clube de Portugal
Jazz

(☏213 460 305; www.hcp.pt; Praça da Alegria 48; ⊘10pm-2am Tue-Sat) As hot as its name suggests, this small, poster-plastered cellar (and newly added garden) has staged top-drawer jazz acts since the 1940s. It's considered one of Europe's best.

A Baîuca
Fado

(☏218 867 284; Rua de São Miguel 20; ⊘8pm-midnight Thu-Mon) On a good night, walking into A Baîuca is like gatecrashing a family party. It's a special place with *fado vadio,* where locals take a turn and spectators hiss if anyone dares to chat during the singing. There's a €25 minimum spend, which is as tough to swallow as the food, though the fado is spectacular. Reserve ahead.

A Tasco do Chico
Fado

(☏961 339 696; www.facebook.com/atasca.dochico; Rua Diário de Notícias 39; ⊘noon-2am, to 3am Fri-Sat) This crowded dive (reserve ahead), full of soccer banners and spilling over with people of all ilk is a fado free-for-all. It's not uncommon for taxi drivers to roll up, hum a few bars, and hop right back into their cabs, speeding off into the night.

Portugal's most famous fado singer, Mariza, brought us here in 2005. It's legit.

Senhor Fado
Fado

(218 874 298; www.sr-fado.com; Rua dos Remédios 176; ☺8pm-2am Wed-Sat) Small and lantern-lit, this is a cosy spot for *fado vadio* (street fado). *Fadista* Ana Marina and guitarist Duarte Santos make a great double act.

ℹ INFORMATION

The largest and most helpful tourist office in the city, **Ask Me Lisboa** (☑213 463 314; www.askme lisboa.com; Praça dos Restauradores, Palácio Foz; ☺9am-8pm) faces Praça dos Restauradaures inside the Palácio Foz. Staff dole out maps and information, book accommodation and reserve rental cars.

Ask Me Lisboa runs several information kiosks, which are handy places for maps and quick information:

Airport (☑218 450 660; Aeroporto de Lisboa, Arrivals Hall; ☺7.30am-9.30am Tue-Sat)

Belém (☑213 658 435; Largo dos Jernónimos; ☺10am-1pm & 2-6pm Tue-Sat)

Santa Apolónia (☑910 517 982; Door 48, Santa Apolónia train station; ☺7.30am-9.30pm Tue-Sat)

Rossio Square (☑910 517 914; Praça Dom Pedro IV; ☺10am-1pm & 2-6pm)

Parque das Nações (☑910 518 028; Alameda dos Oceanos; ☺10am-1pm & 2-7pm Apr-Sep, to 6pm Oct-Mar)

ℹ GETTING THERE & AWAY

AIR

Situated around 6km north of the centre, the ultramodern **Aeroporto de Lisboa** (Lisbon Airport; 218 413 700; www.ana.pt; Alameda das Comunidades Portuguesas) operates direct flights to major international hubs including London, New York, Paris and Frankfurt. Several low-cost carriers (easyJet, Ryanair, Transavia, Norwegian etc) leave from the less-efficient terminal 2 – you'll

need to factor in extra time for the shuttle ride if arriving at the airport on the metro.

BUS

Lisbon's main long-distance bus terminal is **Rodoviário de Sete Rios** (Praça General Humberto Delgado, Rua das Laranjeiras), adjacent to both Jardim Zoológico metro station and Sete Rios train station. The big carriers, **Rede Expressos** (☑707 223 344; www.rede-expressos.pt) and **Eva** (☑707 223 344; www.eva-bus.com), run frequent services to almost every major town. You can buy your ticket up to seven days in advance.

TRAIN

Lisbon is linked by train to other major cities. Check the **Comboios de Portugal** (☑707 210 220; www.cp.pt) website for schedules.

ℹ GETTING AROUND

BUS, TRAM & FUNICULAR

Companhia Carris de Ferro de Lisboa (Carris; ☑213 500 115; http://carris.transporteslisboa. pt) operates all transport in Lisbon proper except the metro. Its buses and trams run from about 5am or 6am to about 10pm or 11pm; there are some night bus and tram services.

Pick up a transport map, *Rede de Transportes de Lisboa,* from tourist offices. The Carris website has timetables and route details.

METRO

The **metro** (www.metro.transporteslisboa.pt; single/day ticket €1.40/6; ☺6.30am-1am) is useful for short hops, and to reach the stations.

Buy tickets from metro ticket machines, which have English-language menus. The Lisboa Card is also valid.

Entrances are marked by a big red 'M'. Useful signs include *correspondência* (transfer between lines) and *saída* (exit to the street).

TICKETS & PASSES

On-board one-way prices are €1.80 for buses, €2.85 for trams and €3.60 (return) for funicular rides (one-way tickets not available). A day pass for all public transport is €6.

Where to Stay

You're spoilt for choice in the Portuguese capital when it comes to places to unpack your duffle bag. Room rates tend to be lower than in most of Western Europe.

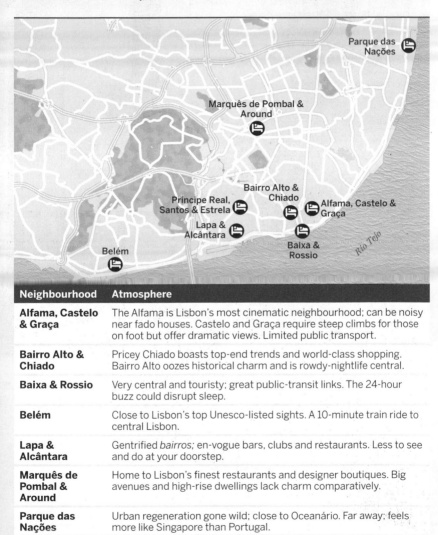

Neighbourhood	Atmosphere
Alfama, Castelo & Graça	The Alfama is Lisbon's most cinematic neighbourhood; can be noisy near fado houses. Castelo and Graça require steep climbs for those on foot but offer dramatic views. Limited public transport.
Bairro Alto & Chiado	Pricey Chiado boasts top-end trends and world-class shopping. Bairro Alto oozes historical charm and is rowdy-nightlife central.
Baixa & Rossio	Very central and touristy; great public-transit links. The 24-hour buzz could disrupt sleep.
Belém	Close to Lisbon's top Unesco-listed sights. A 10-minute train ride to central Lisbon.
Lapa & Alcântara	Gentrified *bairros;* en-vogue bars, clubs and restaurants. Less to see and do at your doorstep.
Marquês de Pombal & Around	Home to Lisbon's finest restaurants and designer boutiques. Big avenues and high-rise dwellings lack charm comparatively.
Parque das Nações	Urban regeneration gone wild; close to Oceanário. Far away; feels more like Singapore than Portugal.
Príncipe Real, Santos & Estrela	Bohemian Príncipe Real is tops for cutting-edge local fashion, shopping, restaurants and the LGBT community; Santos and Estrela are ideal for escapists who prefer pin-drop peace to central bustle.

ITALY & CROATIA

In This Chapter

Colosseum 354
Pantheon 358
St Peter's Basilica 362
Vatican Museums 366
Roman Forum 372
Sights 380
Shopping 390
Eating 391
Drinking & Nightlife 394
Entertainment 395
Information 396
Getting There & Away 397
Getting Around 397

Rome, Italy

A heady mix of haunting ruins, breathtaking art, vibrant street life and incredible food, Italy's hot-blooded capital is one of the world's most romantic and inspiring cities. Ancient icons such as the Colosseum, Roman Forum and Pantheon recall the city's golden age as caput mundi (capital of the world), while monumental basilicas testify to the role that great popes have played in its history. And Rome's astonishing artistic heritage is almost unrivalled. A walk around the centre will have you encountering masterpieces by the giants of Western art: sculptures by Michelangelo, canvases by Caravaggio, frescoes by Raphael and fountains by Bernini.

Rome in Two Days

Start early at the **Colosseum** (p354), then visit the **Palatino** (p380) and **Roman Forum** (p372). Spend the afternoon in the *centro storico* (historic centre) exploring **Piazza Navona** (p381) and the **Pantheon** (p358).
On day two, hit the **Vatican Museums** (p367) and **St Peter's Basilica** (p363). Afterwards, check out the **Spanish Steps** (p387) and **Trevi Fountain** (p387). Round the day off in the **Campo de' Fiori** (p383).

Rome in Four Days

Spend day three investigating **Villa Borghese** (p389) – make sure to book for the **Museo e Galleria Borghese** (p389) – and **Piazza del Popolo** (p387). End the day with dinner in Trastevere. Next day, admire classical art at the **Capitoline Museums** (p380) before checking out the basilicas on the Esquiline.

Next up? Catch the train to Florence (p418) or step back in time at Pompeii (p462).

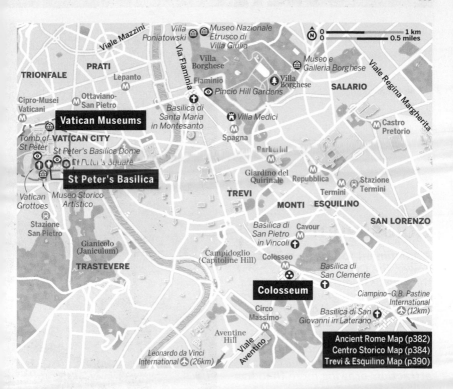

Arriving in Rome

Leonardo da Vinci (Fiumicino) Airport
Half-hourly Leonardo Express trains run to Stazione Termini (€14, 30 minutes). A taxi to the centre is €48.

Ciampino Airport Arrival point for Ryanair flights to Rome. SIT Bus and Terravision run regular services to Via Marsala outside Termini (from €5, 45 minutes). Taxi fare is €30.

Stazione Termini Rome's principal train station.

Where to Stay

Rome has many boutique-style guesthouses offering chic accommodation at midrange to top-end prices. Alternatively, try a *pensione* (a small family-run hotel with simple rooms, most with private bathroom). Some religious institutions also offer good-value rooms, though many have strict curfews and the rooms are no-frills.

For information on what each Roman neighbourhood has to offer, see the table on p399.

Colosseum

A monument to raw, merciless power, the Colosseum is the most thrilling of Rome's ancient sights. It was here that gladiators met in mortal combat and condemned prisoners fought off wild beasts in front of baying, bloodthirsty crowds. Two thousand years on and it's Italy's top tourist attraction, drawing more than five million visitors a year.

Great For...

ⓘ Need to Know

Colosseo; ☎06 3996 7700; www.coopculture.
it; Piazza del Colosseo; adult/reduced incl Roman Forum & Palatino €12/7.50; ⊙8.30am-1hr before sunset; Ⓜ Colosseo

★ **Top Tip**
Beat the queues by buying your
ticket at the Palatino (Via di San
Gregorio 30).

Built by Vespasian (r AD 69–79) in the grounds of Nero's vast Domus Aurea complex, the arena was inaugurated in AD 80, eight years after it had been commissioned. To mark the occasion, Vespasian's son and successor Titus (r 79–81) staged games that lasted 100 days and nights, during which 5000 animals were slaughtered. Trajan (r 98–117) later topped this, holding a marathon 117-day killing spree involving 9000 gladiators and 10,000 animals.

The 50,000-seat arena was originally known as the Flavian Amphitheatre, and although it was Rome's most fearsome arena it wasn't the biggest – the Circo Massimo could hold up to 250,000 people. The name Colosseum, when introduced in medieval times, was a reference not to its size but to the Colosso di Nerone, a giant statue of Nero that stood nearby.

With the fall of the Roman Empire in the 5th century, the Colosseum was abandoned and gradually became overgrown. In the Middle Ages it served as a fortress for two of the city's warrior families, the Frangipani and the Annibaldi. Later, during the Renaissance and baroque periods, it was plundered of its precious travertine, and the marble stripped from it was used to make huge palaces such as Palazzo Venezia, Palazzo Barberini and Palazzo Cancelleria.

More recently, pollution and vibrations caused by traffic and the metro have taken their toll, but the first stage of a €25 million clean-up, the first in its 2000-year history, has once again revealed the creamy hues of the Colosseum walls.

Exterior

The outer walls have three levels of arches, framed by Ionic, Doric and Corinthian columns. These were originally covered in travertine, and marble statues filled the niches on the 2nd and 3rd storeys. The upper level, punctuated with windows and slender Corinthian pilasters, had supports for 240 masts that held up a huge canvas awning over the arena, shielding spectators from sun and rain. The 80 entrance arches, known as *vomitoria*, allowed the spectators to enter and be seated in a matter of minutes.

> ☑ **Don't Miss**
>
> The hypogeum's network of dank tunnels beneath the main arena. Visits require advance booking and cost an extra €9.

GEORGY KURYATOV/SHUTTERSTOCK ©

Arena

The arena originally had a wooden floor covered in sand to prevent the combatants from slipping and to soak up the blood. It could also be flooded for mock sea battles. Trapdoors led down to the hypogeum, a subterranean complex of corridors, cages and lifts beneath the arena floor.

Stands

The *cavea,* for spectator seating, was divided into three tiers: magistrates and senior officials sat in the lowest tier, wealthy citizens in the middle, and the plebeians in the highest tier. Women (except for vestal virgins) were relegated to the cheapest sections at the top. As in modern stadiums, tickets were numbered and spectators assigned a seat in a specific sector – in 2015, restorers uncovered traces of red numerals on the arches, indicating how the sectors were numbered. The podium, a broad terrace in front of the tiers of seats, was reserved for the emperor, senators and VIPs.

Hypogeum

The hypogeum served as the stadium's backstage area. Sets for the various battle scenes were prepared here and hoisted up to the arena by a complicated system of pulleys. Caged animals were kept here and gladiators would gather here before showtime, having come in through an underground corridor from the nearby Ludus Magnus (gladiator school).

✗ Take a Break

Cafè Cafè (✆06 700 87 43; www.cafe cafebistrot.it; Via dei Santi Quattro 44; meals €15-20; ◷9.30am-8.50pm; 🚇Via di San Giovanni in Laterano) is the perfect venue for a post-arena break, for tea and cake or a light meal.

Pantheon

A striking 2000-year-old temple that's now a church, the Pantheon is Rome's best-preserved ancient monument and one of the most influential buildings in the Western world. Its greying, pockmarked exterior may look its age, but inside it's a different story. It's a unique and exhilarating experience to pass through the vast bronze doors and gaze up at the largest unreinforced concrete dome ever built.

Great For...

Piazza della Rotonda

⦿ *Pantheon*

Via della Rotonda — Via della Minerva

Corso Vittorio Emanuele II — Largo di Torre Argentina — Via del Plebiscito

ⓘ Need to Know

Map p384; www.pantheonroma.com; Piazza della Rotonda; 🕗8.30am-7.15pm Mon-Sat, 9am-5.45pm Sun; 🚊Largo di Torre Argentina
FREE

★ **Top Tip**

Mass is celebrated at the Pantheon at 5pm on Saturday and 10.30am on Sunday.

In its current form the Pantheon dates from around AD 125. The original temple, built by Marcus Agrippa in 27 BC, burnt down in AD 80, and although it was rebuilt by Domitian, it was struck by lightning and destroyed for a second time in 110. The emperor Hadrian had it reconstructed between 118 and 125, and it's this version that you see today.

Hadrian's temple was dedicated to the classical gods – hence the name Pantheon, a derivation of the Greek words *pan* (all) and *theos* (god) – but in 608 it was consecrated as a Christian church. It's now officially known as the Basilica di Santa Maria ad Martyres.

Thanks to this consecration, it was spared the worst of the medieval plundering that reduced many of Rome's ancient buildings to near dereliction. But it didn't escape entirely unscathed – its gilded-bronze roof

tiles were removed and bronze from the portico was used by Bernini for the *baldachino* at St Peter's Basilica.

Exterior

The dark-grey pitted exterior faces onto busy, cafe-lined Piazza della Rotonda. And while its facade is somewhat the worse for wear, it's still an imposing sight. The monumental entrance **portico** consists of 16 Corinthian columns, each 13m high and made of Egyptian granite, supporting a triangular **pediment**. Behind the columns, two 20-tonne **bronze doors** – 16th-century restorations of the original portal – give onto the central rotunda. Rivets and holes in the building's brickwork indicate where marble-veneer panels were originally placed.

The oculus

Inscription

For centuries the inscription under the pediment – M:AGRIPPA.L.F.COS.TERTIUM. FECIT or 'Marcus Agrippa, son of Lucius, consul for the third time built this' – led scholars to think that the current building was Agrippa's original temple. However, 19th-century excavations revealed traces of an earlier temple and historians realised that Hadrian had simply kept Agrippa's original inscription.

Interior

Although impressive from outside, it's only when you get inside that you can really

> ### ☑ Don't Miss
> The 7m-high bronze doors, which provide a suitably grand entrance to your visit.

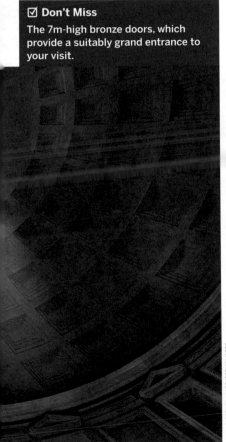

appreciate the Pantheon's full size. With light streaming in through the **oculus** (the 8.7m-diameter hole in the centre of the dome), the cylindrical marble-clad interior seems vast.

Opposite the entrance is the church's main **altar**, over which hangs a 7th-century icon of the *Madonna col Bambino* (Madonna and Child). To the left are the tombs of the artist Raphael, King Umberto I and Margherita of Savoy. Over on the opposite side of the rotunda is the tomb of King Vittorio Emanuele II.

Dome

The Pantheon's dome, considered to be the Romans' most important architectural achievement, was the largest dome in the world until Brunelleschi beat it with his Florentine cupola. Its harmonious appearance is due to a precisely calibrated symmetry – its diameter is exactly equal to the building's interior height of 43.3m. At its centre, the oculus, which symbolically connected the temple with the gods, plays a vital structural role by absorbing and re-distributing the dome's huge tensile forces.

What's Nearby?
Basilica di Santa Maria Sopra Minerva   Basilica
(Map p384; www.santamariasopraminerva.it; Piazza della Minerva 42; ⊗6.40am-7pm Mon-Fri, 6.40am-12.30pm & 3.30-7pm Sat, 8am-12.30pm & 3.30-7pm Sun; ⊇Largo di Torre Argentina) Built on the site of three pagan temples, including one to the goddess Minerva, the Dominican Basilica di Santa Maria Sopra Minerva is Rome's only Gothic church. However, little remains of the original 13th-century structure and these days the main drawcard is a minor Michelangelo sculpture and the colourful, art-rich interior.

> ### ✕ Take a Break
> Get caffeinated at Caffè Sant'Eustachio (p394), known to serve some of the best coffee in town.

St Peter's Basilica

In this city of outstanding churches, none can hold a candle to St Peter's, Italy's largest, richest and most spectacular basilica.

Great For...

☑ Don't Miss

Climbing the (numerous, steep and tiring, but worth it) steps of the dome for views over Rome.

The original church was commissioned by the emperor Constantine and built around 349 on the site where St Peter is said to have been buried between AD 64 and 67. But like many medieval churches, it eventually fell into disrepair. It wasn't until the mid-15th century that efforts were made to restore it, first by Pope Nicholas V and then, rather more successfully, by Julius II.

In 1506 construction began on a design by Bramante, but ground to a halt when the architect died in 1514. In 1547 Michelangelo stepped in to take on the project. He simplified Bramante's plans and drew up designs for what was to become his greatest architectural achievement: the dome. He didn't live to see it built, though, and it was left to Giacomo della Porta, Domenico Fontana and Carlo Maderno to complete the basilica, which was finally consecrated in 1626.

St Peter's Basilica and the Tiber River

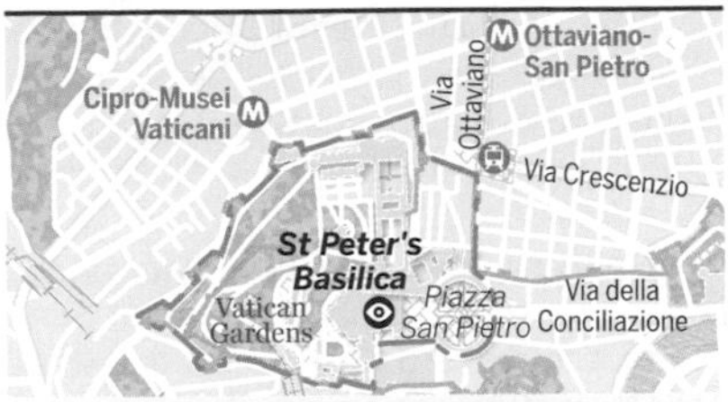

Need to Know

Basilica di San Pietro; 06 6988 5518; www.vatican.va; St Peter's Square; 7am-7pm summer, to 6.30pm winter; Piazza del Risorgimento, M Ottaviano-San Pietro FREE

Take a Break

With more than 200 teas to choose from, you'll find the perfect cuppa at **Makasar Bistrot** (06 687 46 02; www.makasar.it; Via Plauto 33; noon-midnight Mon-Thu, to 2am Fri & Sat, 5pm-midnight Sun; Piazza del Risorgimento).

★ Top Tip

Strict dress codes are enforced, which means no shorts, miniskirts or bare shoulders.

Facade

Built between 1608 and 1612, Maderno's immense facade is 48m high and 118.6m wide. Eight 27m-high columns support the upper attic on which 13 statues stand representing Christ the Redeemer, St John the Baptist and the 11 apostles. The central balcony, the **Loggia della Benedizione**, is where the pope stands to deliver his *Urbi et Orbi* blessing at Christmas and Easter.

Interior

At the beginning of the right aisle is Michelangelo's hauntingly beautiful **Pietà**. Sculpted when the artist was 25 (in 1499), it's the only work he ever signed; his signature is etched into the sash across the Madonna's breast.

On a pillar just beyond the *Pietà*, Carlo Fontana's gilt and bronze **monument to Queen Christina of Sweden** commemorates the far-from-holy Swedish monarch who converted to Catholicism in 1655.

Moving on, you'll come to the **Cappella di San Sebastiano**, home of Pope John Paul II's tomb, and the **Cappella del Santissimo Sacramento**, a sumptuously decorated baroque chapel.

Dominating the centre of the basilica is Bernini's 29m-high **baldachin**. Supported by four spiral columns and made with bronze taken from the Pantheon, it stands over the **high altar**, which itself sits on the site of St Peter's grave.

Above the baldachin, Michelangelo's **dome** soars to a height of 119m. Based on Brunelleschi's cupola in Florence, it's supported by four massive stone piers named after the saints whose statues adorn the Bernini-designed niches – Longinus, Helena, Veronica and Andrew.

At the base of the **Pier of St Longinus** is Arnolfo di Cambio's much-loved 13th-century bronze **statue of St Peter**, whose right foot has been worn down by centuries of caresses.

Dominating the tribune behind the altar is Bernini's extraordinary **Cattedra di San Pietro**, centred on a wooden seat that was once thought to have been St Peter's, but in fact dates from the 9th century.

To the right of the throne, Bernini's **monument to Urban VIII** depicts the pope flanked by the figures of Charity and Justice.

Near the head of the left aisle are the so-called **Stuart monuments**. On the right is the monument to Clementina Sobieska, wife of James Stuart, by Filippo Barigioni, and on the left is Canova's vaguely erotic monument to the last three members of the Stuart clan, the pretenders to the English throne who died in exile in Rome.

Dome

From the **dome** (with/without lift €8/6; ◎8am-6pm summer, to 5pm winter) entrance on the right of the basilica's main portico, you can walk the 551 steps to the top or take a small lift halfway and then follow on foot for the last 320 steps. Either way, it's a long, steep climb and not recommended for anyone who suffers from claustrophobia or vertigo. Make it to the top, though, and you're rewarded with stunning views.

Museo Storico Artistico

Accessed from the left nave, the **Museo Storico Artistico** (Tesoro, Treasury; adult/reduced €7/5; ◎8am-6.50pm summer, to 5.50pm winter) sparkles with sacred relics.

Top of St Peter's Square and the basilica

Highlights include a tabernacle by Donatello and the 6th-century *Crux Vaticana* (Vatican Cross).

Vatican Grottoes

Extending beneath the basilica, the **Vatican Grottoes** (⊙8am-6pm summer, to 5.30pm winter) **FREE** contain the tombs and sarcophagi of numerous popes, as well as several columns from the original 4th-century basilica. The entrance is in the Pier of St Andrew.

★ **Free Tours**

Between October and late May, free English-language tours of the basilica are run by seminarians from the Pontifical North American College, usually departing 2.15pm Monday to Friday from Centro Servizi Pellegrini e Turisti.

MARIIA GOLOVIANKO/SHUTTERSTOCK ©

St Peter's Tomb

Excavations beneath the basilica have uncovered part of the original church and what archaeologists believe is the **Tomb of St Peter** (✆06 6988 5318; www.scavi.va; €13, over 15s only).

The excavations can only be visited by guided tour. To book a spot, email the Ufficio Scavi (scavi@fsp.va) as far in advance as possible.

What's Nearby?

St Peter's Square   Piazza

(Piazza San Pietro; Ⓜ Ottaviano-San Pietro) Overlooked by St Peter's Basilica, the Vatican's central square was laid out between 1656 and 1667 to a design by Gian Lorenzo Bernini. Seen from above, it resembles a giant keyhole with two semicircular colonnades, each consisting of four rows of Doric columns, encircling a giant ellipse that straightens out to funnel believers into the basilica. The effect was deliberate – Bernini described the colonnades as representing 'the motherly arms of the church'.

Castel Sant'Angelo   Museum, Castle

(Map p384; ✆06 681 91 11; www.castelsant angelo.beniculturali.it; Lungotevere Castello 50; adult/reduced €10/5; ⊙9am-7.30pm, ticket office to 6.30pm; ☐ Piazza Pia) With its chunky round keep, this castle is an instantly recognisable landmark. Built as a mausoleum for the emperor Hadrian, it was converted into a papal fortress in the 6th century and named after an angelic vision that Pope Gregory the Great had in 590. Nowadays it houses the **Museo Nazionale di Castel Sant'Angelo** and its eclectic collection of paintings, sculpture, military memorabilia and medieval firearms.

★ **Local Knowledge**

Near the main entrance, a red floor disc marks the spot where Charlemagne and later Holy Roman Emperors were crowned by the pope.

Spiral staircase

GIORGIO ART/SHUTTERSTOCK ©

Vatican Museums

Founded in the 16th century, the Vatican Museums boast one of the world's greatest art collections. Highlights include spectacular classical statuary, rooms frescoed by Raphael, and the Michelangelo-decorated Sistine Chapel.

Great For...

☑ Don't Miss

The Museo Gregoriano Egizio's fascinating 3rd-century linen 'Shroud of the Lady of the Vatican'.

Housing the museums are the lavishly decorated halls and galleries of the Palazzo Apostolico Vaticano. This vast 5.5-hectare complex consists of two palaces – the Vatican palace (nearer to St Peter's) and the Belvedere Palace – joined by two long galleries. Inside are three courtyards: the Cortile della Pigna, the Cortile della Biblioteca and, to the south, the Cortile del Belvedere. You'll never cover it all in one day, so it pays to be selective.

Pinacoteca

Often overlooked by visitors, the papal picture gallery contains Raphael's last work, *La Trasfigurazione* (Transfiguration; 1517–20), and paintings by Giotto, Fra Angelico, Filippo Lippi, Perugino, Titian, Guido Reni, Guercino, Pietro da Cortona, Caravaggio and Leonardo da Vinci, whose

Gallery in the Vatican Museums

🛈 Need to Know

Musei Vaticani; 📞06 6988 4676; www.musei vaticani.va; Viale Vaticano; adult/reduced €16/8, last Sun of month free; ⊘9am-6pm Mon-Sat, 9am-2pm last Sun of month, last entry 2hr before close; 🚇Piazza del Risorgimento, ⓂOttaviano-San Pietro

✕ Take a Break

Snack on a scissor-cut square of pizza or a rice croquette from Pizzarium (p392).

> ### ★ Top Tip
> Avoid queues by booking tickets online (http://biglietteriamusei.vatican.va/musei/tickets/do); the booking fee is €4.

haunting *San Gerolamo* (St Jerome; c 1480) was never finished.

Museo Chiaramonti & Braccio Nuovo

The Museo Chiaramonti is effectively the long corridor that runs down the eastern side of the Belvedere Palace. Its walls are lined with thousands of statues and busts representing everything from immortal gods to playful cherubs and unattractive Roman patricians. Near the end of the hall, off to the right, is the Braccio Nuovo (New Wing), which contains a famous statue of the Nile as a reclining god covered by 16 babies.

Museo Pio-Clementino

This stunning museum contains some of the Vatican Museums' finest classical statu-ary, including the peerless *Apollo Belvedere* and the 1st-century *Laocoön,* both in the **Cortile Ottagono** (Octagonal Courtyard). Before you go into the courtyard, take a moment to admire the 1st-century *Apoxyomenos,* one of the earliest known sculptures to depict a figure with a raised arm.

To the left as you enter the courtyard, the *Apollo Belvedere* is a 2nd-century Roman copy of a 4th-century-BC Greek bronze. A beautifully proportioned representation of the sun god Apollo, it's considered one of the great masterpieces of classical sculpture. Nearby, the *Laocoön* depicts a muscular Trojan priest and his two sons in mortal struggle with two sea serpents.

Back inside, the **Sala degli Animali** is filled with sculpted creatures and some magnificent 4th-century mosaics. Continuing on, you come to the **Sala delle Muse**, centred on the *Torso Belvedere,* another of the museum's must-sees. A fragment of a muscular 1st-century-BC Greek sculpture, it was found in Campo de' Fiori and used by Michelangelo as a model for his *ignudi* (male nudes) in the Sistine Chapel. It's currently undergoing restoration.

The next room, the **Sala Rotonda**, contains a number of colossal statues, including a gilded-bronze *Ercole* (Hercules) and an exquisite floor mosaic. The enormous basin in the centre of the room was found at Nero's Domus Aurea and is made out of a single piece of red porphyry stone.

Museo Gregoriano Egizio

Founded by Gregory XVI in 1839, this museum contains pieces taken from Egypt in Roman times. The collection is small, but there are fascinating exhibits including the *Trono di Ramses II* (part of a statue of the seated king), vividly painted sarcophagi dating from around 1000 BC, and some macabre mummies.

Museo Gregoriano Etrusco

At the top of the 18th-century Simonetti staircase, the Museo Gregoriano Etrusco contains artefacts unearthed in the Etruscan tombs of northern Lazio, as well as a superb collection of vases and Roman antiquities. Of particular interest is the *Marte di Todi* (Mars of Todi), a black bronze of a warrior dating from the late 5th century BC.

Galleria delle Carte Geografiche & Sala Sobieski

The last of three galleries – the other two are the **Galleria dei Candelabri** (Gallery of the Candelabra) and the **Galleria degli**

Cortile della Pigna

Arazzi (Tapestry Gallery) – this 120m-long corridor is hung with 40 huge topographical maps. These were created between 1580 and 1583 for Pope Gregory XIII based on drafts by Ignazio Danti, one of the leading cartographers of his day.

Beyond the gallery, the **Sala Sobieski** is named after an enormous 19th-century painting depicting the victory of the Polish king John III Sobieski over the Turks in 1683.

★ **Local Knowledge**

Tuesdays and Thursdays are the quietest days to visit, Wednesday mornings are also good, and afternoons are better than mornings. Avoid Mondays, when many other museums are closed.

GUZEL STUDIO/SHUTTERSTOCK ©

Stanze di Raffaello

These four frescoed chambers, currently undergoing partial restoration, were part of Pope Julius II's private apartments. Raphael himself painted the Stanza della Segnatura (1508–11) and the Stanza d'Eliodoro (1512–14), while the Stanza dell'Incendio (1514–17) and Sala di Costantino (1517–24) were decorated by students following his designs

The first room you come to is the **Sala di Costantino**, which features a huge fresco depicting Constantine's defeat of Maxentius at the battle of Milvian Bridge.

The **Stanza d'Eliodoro**, which was used for private audiences, takes its name from the *Cacciata d'Eliodoro* (Expulsion of Heliodorus from the Temple), an allegorical work reflecting Pope Julius II's policy of forcing foreign powers off Church lands. To its right, the *Messa di Bolsena* (Mass of Bolsena) shows Julius paying homage to the relic of a 13th-century miracle at the lakeside town of Bolsena. Next is the *Incontro di Leone Magno con Attila* (Encounter of Leo the Great with Attila) by Raphael and his school, and, on the fourth wall, the *Liberazione di San Pietro* (Liberation of St Peter), a brilliant work illustrating Raphael's masterful ability to depict light.

The **Stanza della Segnatura**, Julius' study and library, was the first room that Raphael painted, and it's here that you'll find his great masterpiece, *La Scuola di Atene* (The School of Athens), featuring philosophers and scholars gathered around Plato and Aristotle. The seated figure in front of the steps is believed to be Michelangelo, while the figure of Plato is said to be a portrait of Leonardo da Vinci, and Euclide (the bald man bending over) is Bramante. Raphael also included a self-portrait in the

---

★ **Top Tip**

Most exhibits are not well labelled. Consider hiring an audio guide (€7) or buying the excellent *Guide to the Vatican Museums and City* (€14).

lower right corner – he's the second figure from the right.

The most famous work in the **Stanza dell'Incendio di Borgo** is the *Incendio di Borgo* (Fire in the Borgo), which depicts Pope Leo IV extinguishing a fire by making the sign of the cross. The ceiling was painted by Raphael's master, Perugino.

Sistine Chapel

The jewel in the Vatican's crown, the Sistine Chapel (Cappella Sistina) is home to two of the world's most famous works of art: Michelangelo's ceiling frescoes and his *Giudizio Universale* (Last Judgment).

The chapel was originally built for Pope Sixtus IV, after whom it's named, and was consecrated on 15 August 1483. However, apart from the wall frescoes and floor, little remains of the original decor, which was sacrificed to make way for Michelangelo's two masterpieces. The first, the ceiling, was commissioned by Pope Julius II and painted between 1508 and 1512; the second, the spectacular *Giudizio Universale,* was painted between 1535 and 1541.

Michelangelo's ceiling design, which is best viewed from the chapel's main entrance in the far east wall, covers the entire 800-sq-m surface. With painted architectural features and a cast of colourful biblical characters, it's centred on nine panels depicting scenes from the Creation, the story of Adam and Eve, the Fall, and the plight of Noah.

As you look up from the east wall, the first panel is the *Drunkenness of Noah,* followed by *The Flood* and the *Sacrifice of Noah.* Next, *Original Sin and Banishment from the Garden of Eden* famously depicts Adam and Eve being sent packing after accepting the forbidden fruit from Satan, represented by a snake with the body of a woman coiled around a tree. The *Creation of Eve* is then followed by the *Creation of Adam.* This, one of the most famous images in Western art, shows a bearded God pointing his finger at Adam, thus bringing him to life. Completing the sequence are the *Separation of Land from Sea;* the *Creation*

of the *Sun, Moon and Plants;* and the *Separation of Light from Darkness,* featuring a fearsome God reaching out to touch the sun. Set around the central panels are 20 athletic male nudes, known as *ignudi.*

Opposite, on the west wall, is Michelangelo's mesmeric *Giudizio Universale,* showing Christ – in the centre near the top – passing sentence over the souls of the dead as they are torn from their graves to face him. The saved get to stay in heaven (in the upper right); the damned are sent down to face the demons in hell (in the bottom right).

Near the bottom, on the right, you'll see a man with donkey ears and a snake wrapped around him. This is Biagio de Cesena, the papal master of ceremonies, who was a fierce critic of Michelangelo's composition. Another famous figure is St

Raphael's Stanza della Segnatura

Bartholomew, just beneath Christ, holding his own flayed skin. The face in the skin is said to be a self-portrait of Michelangelo, its anguished look reflecting the artist's tormented faith.

The chapel's walls also boast superb frescoes. Painted between 1481 and 1482 by a crack team of Renaissance artists, including Botticelli, Ghirlandaio, Pinturicchio, Perugino and Luca Signorelli, they represent events in the lives of Moses (to the left looking at the *Giudizio Universale*) and Christ (to the right). Highlights include Botticelli's *Temptations of Christ* and Perugino's *Handing over of the Keys*.

As well as providing a showcase for priceless art, the Sistine Chapel serves an important religious function as the place where the conclave meets to elect a new pope.

✗ Take a Break

For something quick and delicious, stop by **Fa-Bìo** (☑06 6452 5810; www. fa-bio.com; Via Germanico 43; sandwiches €5; ◷10.30am-5.30pm Mon-Fri, to 4pm Sat; ☐Piazza del Risorgimento, ⓂOttaviano-San Pietro) ✿ for a healthy salad or a tasty sandwich.

★ Did You Know

A popular Sistine Chapel myth is that Michelangelo painted the ceilings lying down. In fact, he designed a curved scaffolding that allowed him to work standing up.

VVOE/SHUTTERSTOCK ©

Tempio di Saturno (Temple of Saturn: p374)

Roman Forum

The Roman Forum was ancient Rome's showpiece centre, a grandiose district of temples, basilicas and vibrant public spaces. Nowadays, it's a collection of impressive, if badly labelled, ruins that can leave you drained and confused. But if you can get your imagination going, there's something wonderfully compelling about walking in the footsteps of Julius Caesar and other legendary figures of Roman history.

Great For...

❶ Need to Know

Foro Romano; Map p382; ☎06 3996 7700; www.coopculture.it; Largo della Salara Vecchia, Piazza di Santa Maria Nova; adult/ reduced incl Colosseum & Palatino €12/7.50; ☉8.30am-1hr before sunset; ☒Via dei Fori Imperiali

★ **Top Tip**
Get grandstand views of the
Roman Forum from the Palatino and
Campidoglio.

Originally an Etruscan burial ground, the Forum was first developed in the 7th century BC, growing over time to become the social, political and commercial hub of the Roman Empire. In the Middle Ages it was reduced to pasture land and extensively plundered for its marble. The area was systematically excavated in the 18th and 19th centuries and work continues to this day.

Via Sacra Towards Campidoglio

Entering the Forum from Largo della Salara Vecchia, you'll see the **Tempio di Antonino e Faustina** ahead to your left. Erected in AD 141, this was transformed into a church in the 8th century, the **Chiesa di San Lorenzo in Miranda**. To your right, is the 179 BC **Basilica Fulvia Aemilia**.

At the end of the path, you'll come to **Via Sacra**, the Forum's main thoroughfare,

and the **Tempio di Giulio Cesare**, which stands on the spot where Julius Caesar was cremated.

Heading right brings you to the **Curia**, the original seat of the Roman Senate, though what you see today is a reconstruction of how it looked in the reign of Diocletian (r 284–305).

At the end of Via Sacra, the **Arco di Settimio Severo** (Arch of Septimius Severus) is dedicated to the eponymous emperor and his sons, Caracalla and Geta. Close by the **Colonna di Foca** (Column of Phocus) rises above what was once the Forum's main square, Piazza del Foro.

The eight granite columns that rise behind the Colonna are all that survive of the **Tempio di Saturno** (Temple of Saturn), an important temple that doubled as the state treasury.

Basilica di Massenzio

Tempio di Castore e Polluce & Casa delle Vestali

From the path that runs parallel to Via Sacra, you'll pass the stubby ruins of the **Basilica Giulia**, which was begun by Caesar and finished by Augustus. At the end of the basilica, three columns remain from the 5th-century BC **Tempio di Castore e Polluce** (Temple of Castor and Pollux). Nearby, the 6th-century **Chiesa di Santa Maria Antiqua** (⊘currently closed) is the oldest Christian church in the Forum.

Back towards Via Sacra is the **Casa delle Vestali** (House of the Vestal Virgins), home of the virgins who tended the flame in the adjoining **Tempio di Vesta**.

Via Sacra Towards the Colosseum

Heading up Via Sacra past the **Tempio di Romolo** (Temple of Romulus), you'll come to the **Basilica di Massenzio** (Basilica di Costantino; Piazza di Santa Maria Nova), the largest building on the forum.

Beyond the basilica, the **Arco di Tito** (Arch of Titus; Piazza di Santa Maria Nova) was built in AD 81 to celebrate Vespasian and Titus' victories against rebels in Jerusalem.

What's Nearby?

Imperial Forums   Archaeological Site
(Fori Imperiali; Via dei Fori Imperiali; Map p382; 🚇Via dei Fori Imperiali) The forums of Trajan, Augustus, Nerva and Caesar are known collectively as the Imperial Forums. These were largely buried when Mussolini bulldozed Via dei Fori Imperiali through the area in 1933, but excavations have since unearthed much of them. The standout sights are the **Mercati di Traiano** (Trajan's Markets), accessible through the Museo dei Fori Imperiali, and the landmark **Colonna di Traiano**.

Mercati di Traiano Museo dei Fori Imperiali   Museum
(Map p382; 🕿06 06 08; www.mercatiditraiano.it; Via IV Novembre 94; adult/reduced €11.50/9.50; ⊘9.30am-7.30pm, last admission 6.30pm; 🚇Via IV Novembre) This striking museum brings to life the **Mercati di Traiano**, emperor Trajan's great 2nd-century complex, while also providing a fascinating introduction to the Imperial Forums with multimedia displays, explanatory panels and a smattering of archaeological artefacts.

> ☑ **Don't Miss**
> The Basilica di Massenzio, to get some idea of the scale of ancient Rome's mammoth buildings.

VIACHESLAV LOPATIN/SHUTTERSTOCK ©

> ✕ **Take a Break**
> Continue up to the Capitoline Museums (p380) to enjoy inspiring views and coffee at the Caffè Capitolino.

Roman Forum

A HISTORICAL TOUR

In ancient times, a forum was a market place, civic centre and religious complex all rolled into one, and the greatest of all was the Roman Forum (Foro Romano). Situated between the Palatino (Palatine Hill), ancient Rome's most exclusive neighbourhood, and the Campidoglio (Capitole Hill), it was the city's busy, bustling centre. On any given day it teemed with activity. Senators debated affairs of state in the ❶ **Curia**, shoppers thronged the squares and traffic-free streets and crowds gathered under the ❷ **Colonna di Foca** to listen to politicians holding forth from the ❷ **Rostrum**. Elsewhere, lawyers worked the courts in basilicas including the ❸ **Basilica di Massenzio**, while the Vestal Virgins quietly went about their business in the ❹ **Casa delle Vestali**.

Special occasions were also celebrated in the Forum: religious holidays were marked with ceremonies at temples such as ❺ **Tempio di Saturno** and ❻ **Tempio di Castore e Polluce**, and military victories were honoured with dramatic processions up Via Sacra and the building of monumental arches like ❼ **Arco di Settimio Severo** and ❽ **Arco di Tito**.

The ruins you see today are impressive but they can be confusing without a clear picture of what the Forum once looked like. This spread shows the Forum in its heyday, complete with temples, civic buildings and towering monuments to heroes of the Roman Empire.

TOP TIPS

➡ Get grandstand views of the Forum from the Palatino and Campidoglio.

➡ Visit first thing in the morning or late afternoon; crowds are worst between 11am and 2pm.

➡ In summer it gets hot in the Forum and there's little shade, so take a hat and plenty of water.

Colonna di Foca & Rostrum

Campidoglio (Capitoline Hill)

The free-standing, 13.5m-high Column of Phocus is the Forum's youngest monument, dating to AD 608. Behind it, the Rostrum provided a suitably grandiose platform for pontificating public speakers.

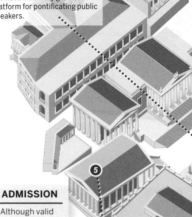

ADMISSION

Although valid for two days, admission tickets only allow for one entry into the Forum, Colosseum and Palatino.

Tempio di Saturno

Ancient Rome's Fort Knox, the Temple of Saturn was the city treasury. In Caesar's day it housed 13 tonnes of gold, 114 tonnes of silver and 30 million sestertii worth of silver coins.

IASCIC/SHUTTERSTOCK ©

VIACHESLAV LOPATIN/SHUTTERSTOCK ©

Tempio di Castore e Polluce

Only three columns of the Temple of Castor and Pollux remain. The temple was dedicated to the Heavenly Twins after they supposedly led the Romans to victory over the Latin League in 496 BC.

Arco di Settimio Severo

One of the Forum's signature monuments, this imposing triumphal arch commemorates the military victories of Septimius Severus. Relief panels depict his campaigns against the Parthians.

Curia

This big barn-like building was the official seat of the Roman Senate. Most of what you see is a reconstruction, but the interior marble floor dates to the 3rd-century reign of Diocletian.

Basilica di Massenzio

Marvel at the scale of this vast 4th-century basilica. In its original form the central hall was divided into enormous naves; now only part of the northern nave survives.

JULIUS CAESAR

Julius Caesar was cremated on the site where the Tempio di Giulio Cesare now stands.

Via Sacra

Tempio di Giulio Cesare

Arco di Tito

Said to be the inspiration for the Arc de Triomphe in Paris, the well-preserved Arch of Titus was built by the emperor Domitian to honour his elder brother Titus.

Casa delle Vestali

White statues line the grassy atrium of what was once the luxurious 50-room home of the Vestal Virgins. The virgins played an important role in Roman religion, serving the goddess Vesta.

Centro Storico Piazzas

Rome's *centro storico* boasts some of the city's most celebrated piazzas, and several lovely but lesser-known squares. Each has its own character, but together they encapsulate much of the city's beauty, history and drama.

Start Piazza Colonna
Distance 1.5km
Duration 3½ hours

Classic Photo: Piazza della Rotonda with the Pantheon in the background.

4 It's a short walk along Via del Seminario to Piazza della Rotonda, where the **Pantheon** (p358) needs no introduction.

5 Piazza Navona (p381) is Rome's geat showpiece square, where you can compare the two giants of Roman baroque – Gian Lorenzo Bernini and Francesco Borromini.

Take a Break... Those in the know head to Forno di Campo de' Fiori (p391) for some of Rome's best *pizza bianca* (white pizza with olive oil and salt).

7 Just beyond the Campo, the more sober **Piazza Farnese** is overshadowed by the austere façade of the Renaissance **Palazzo Farnese** (p383).

1 Piazza Colonna is dominated by the 30m-high Colonna di Marco Aurelio and flanked by Palazzo Chigi, the official residence of the Italian PM.

2 Follow Via dei Bergamaschi to **Piazza di Pietra**, a refined space overlooked by the 2nd-century Tempio di Adriano.

3 Continue down Via de' Burro to **Piazza di Sant'Ignazio Loyola**, a small piazza with a church boasting celebrated *trompe l'œil* frescoes.

Piazza di Montecitorio

START

Via di Pietra

Via dei Pastini

Via del Seminario

Via del Caravita

Via di Sant'Ignazio

Via della Minerva

6 On the other side of Corso Vittorio Emanuele II, **Campo de' Fiori** (p383) hosts a noisy market and boisterous drinking scene.

⊙ SIGHTS

◉ Ancient Rome

Palatino   Archaeological Site

(Palatine Hill; Map p382; ☎06 3996 7700; www.
coopculture.it; Via di San Gregorio 30, Piazza di
Santa Maria Nova; adult/reduced incl Colosseum
& Roman Forum €12/7.50; ☺8.30am-1hr before
sunset; ⓜColosseo) Sandwiched between the
Roman Forum and the Circo Massimo, the
Palatino (Palatine Hill) is an atmospheric
area of towering pine trees, majestic ruins
and memorable views. It was here that
Romulus supposedly founded the city in 753
BC and Rome's emperors lived in unabashed
luxury. Look out for the **stadio** (stadium), the
ruins of the **Domus Flavia** (imperial palace),
and grandstand views over the Roman
Forum from the **Orti Farnesiani**.

Capitoline Museums   Museum

(Musei Capitolini; Map p382; ☎06 06 08; www.
museicapitolini.org; Piazza del Campidoglio 1;

> *atmospheric area of towering
> pine trees, majestic ruins
> and memorable views*

Stadio in the Palatino

adult/reduced €11.50/9.50; ☺9.30am-7.30pm,
last admission 6.30pm; ⓠPiazza Venezia) Dating
from 1471, the Capitoline Museums are the
world's oldest public museums. Their collection of classical sculpture is one of Italy's
finest, including crowd-pleasers such as
the iconic *Lupa capitolina* (Capitoline Wolf),
a sculpture of Romulus and Remus under a
wolf, and the *Galata morente* (Dying Gaul),
a moving depiction of a dying Gaul warrior.
There's also a formidable picture gallery
with masterpieces by the likes of Titian,
Tintoretto, Rubens and Caravaggio.

Ticket prices increase when there's a
temporary exhibition on.

Vittoriano   Monument

(Victor Emmanuel Monument; Map p382;
Piazza Venezia; ☺9.30am-5.30pm summer, to
4.30pm winter; ⓠPiazza Venezia) FREE Love it
or loathe it, as many Romans do, you can't
ignore the Vittoriano (aka the Altare della
Patria, Altar of the Fatherland), the massive
mountain of white marble that towers over
Piazza Venezia. Begun in 1885 to honour
Italy's first king, Victor Emmanuel II – who's
immortalised in its vast equestrian statue

VIACHESLAV LOPATIN/SHUTTERSTOCK ©

– it incorporates the **Museo Centrale del Risorgimento** (06 679 35 98; www.risorgimento.it; adult/reduced €5/2.50; 9.30am-6.30pm), a small museum documenting Italian unification, and the **Tomb of the Unknown Soldier**.

For Rome's best 360-degree views, take the **Roma dal Cielo** (adult/reduced €7/3.50; 9.30am-7.30pm, last admission 7pm) lift to the top.

Bocca della Verità   Monument

(Mouth of Truth; Map p382; Piazza Bocca della Verità 18; 9.30am-5.50pm; Piazza Bocca della Verità) A bearded face carved into a giant marble disc, the *Bocca della Verità* is one of Rome's most popular curiosities. Legend has it that if you put your hand in the mouth and tell a lie, the Bocca will slam shut and bite your hand off.

The mouth, which was originally part of a fountain, or possibly an ancient manhole cover, now lives in the portico of the **Chiesa di Santa Maria in Cosmedin**, a handsome medieval church.

◎ Centro Storico

Piazza Navona   Piazza

(Map p384; Corso del Rinascimento) With its showy fountains, baroque *palazzi* (mansions) and colourful cast of street artists, hawkers and tourists, Piazza Navona is central Rome's elegant showcase square. Built over the 1st-century **Stadio di Domiziano** (Domitian's Stadium; 06 4568 6100; www.stadiodomiziano.com; Via di Tor Sanguigna 3; adult/reduced €8/6; 10am-7pm Sun-Fri, to 8pm Sat; Corso del Rinascimento), it was paved over in the 15th century and for almost 300 years hosted the city's main market. Its grand centrepiece is Bernini's **Fontana dei Quattro Fiumi** (Fountain of the Four Rivers), a flamboyant fountain featuring an Egyptian obelisk and muscular personifications of the rivers Nile, Ganges, Danube and Plate.

Galleria Doria Pamphilj   Gallery

(Map p384; 06 679 73 23; www.doriapamphilj.it; Via del Corso 305; adult/reduced €12/8; 9am-7pm, last admission 6pm; Via del Corso) Hidden behind the grimy grey exterior of

 Via Appia Antica

Completed in 190 BC, the Appian Way connected Rome with Brindisi on Italy's Adriatic coast. It's now a picturesque area of ancient ruins, grassy fields and towering pine trees. But it has a dark history – this is where Spartacus and 6000 of his slave rebels were crucified in 71 BC, and where the ancients buried their dead. Well-to-do Romans built elaborate mausoleums, while the early Christians went underground, creating a 300km network of subterranean burial chambers – the catacombs.

Highlights include the **Catacombe di San Sebastiano** (06 785 03 50; www.catacombe.org; Via Appia Antica 136; adult/reduced €8/5; 10am-5pm Mon-Sat Jan-Nov; Via Appia Antica) and the nearby **Catacombe di San Callisto** (06 513 01 51; www.catacombe.roma.it; Via Appia Antica 110-126; adult/reduced €8/5; 9am-noon & 2-5pm Thu-Tue Mar-Jan; Via Appia Antica).

To get to the Via, take bus 660 from Colli Albani metro station (line A) or bus 118 from Circo Massimo (line B).

Palazzo Doria Pamphilj, this wonderful gallery boasts one of Rome's richest private art collections, with works by Raphael, Tintoretto, Titian, Caravaggio, Bernini and Velázquez, as well as several Flemish masters. Masterpieces abound, but the undisputed star is Velázquez' portrait of an implacable Pope Innocent X, who grumbled that the depiction was 'too real'. For a comparison, check out Gian Lorenzo

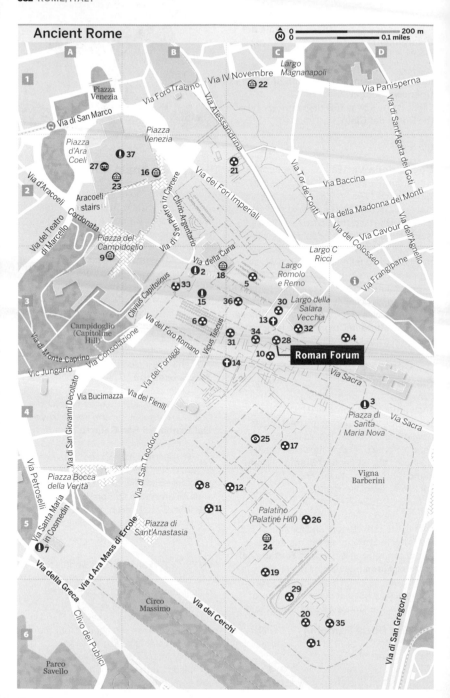

Ancient Rome

Ancient Rome

◎ Sights
1 Arcate Severiane...C6
2 Arco di Settimio Severo B3
3 Arco di Tito...D4
4 Basilica di Massenzio................................D3
5 Basilica Fulvia Aemilia C3
6 Basilica Giulia..B3
7 Bocca della Verità A5
8 Capanne Romulee......................................B5
9 Capitoline Museums..................................A3
10 Casa delle Vestali......................................C3
11 Casa di Augusto B5
12 Casa di Livia...C5
13 Chiesa di San Lorenzo in Miranda C3
14 Chiesa di Santa Maria Antiqua.................C4
15 Colonna di Foca...B3
16 Complesso del Vittoriano B2
17 Criptoportico Neroniano...........................C4
18 Curia..B3
19 Domus Augustana C5

20 Domus Severiana C6
21 Imperial Forums C2
22 Mercati di Traiano Museo dei Fori
    Imperiali C1
23 Museo Centrale del Risorgimento.............A2
24 Museo Palatino C5
25 Orti Farnesiani C4
26 Palatino...C5
27 Roma dal Cielo...A2
28 Roman Forum...C3
29 Stadio..C6
30 Tempio di Antonino e Faustina.................C3
31 Tempio di Castore e Polluce C3
32 Tempio di Romolo C3
33 Tempio di Saturno......................................B3
34 Tempio di Vesta..C3
35 Terme di Settimio Severo D6
36 Via Sacra..C3
37 Vittoriano...A2

Bernini's sculptural interpretation of the same subject.

Chiesa del Gesù   Church

(Map p384; ☑06 69 70 01; www.chiesadelgesu. org; Piazza del Gesù; ☉7am-12.30pm & 4-7.45pm, St Ignatius rooms 4-6pm Mon-Sat, 10am-noon Sun; ☐Largo di Torre Argentina) An imposing example of Counter-Reformation architecture, Rome's most important Jesuit church is a fabulous treasure trove of baroque art. Headline works include a swirling vault fresco by Giovanni Battista Gaulli (aka Il Baciccia), and Andrea del Pozzo's opulent tomb for Ignatius Loyola, the Spanish soldier and saint who founded the Jesuits in 1540. St Ignatius lived in the church from 1544 until his death in 1556 and you can visit his private rooms to the right of the main building in the Cappella di Sant'Ignazio.

Palazzo Farnese   Historic Building

(Map p384; www.inventerrome.com; Piazza Farnese; €9; ☉guided tours 3pm, 4pm & 5pm Mon, Wed & Fri; ☐Corso Vittorio Emanuele II) Home of the French Embassy, this formidable Renaissance *palazzo*, one of Rome's finest, was started in 1514 by Antonio da Sangallo the Younger, continued by Michelangelo and finished by Giacomo della Porta. Inside it boasts a series of frescoes by Annibale and Agostino Carracci that are said by some to rival Michelangelo's in the Sistine Chapel. The highlight, painted between 1597 and 1608, is the monumental ceiling fresco *Amori degli Dei* (The Loves of the Gods) in the Galleria dei Carracci.

Campo de' Fiori   Piazza

(Map p384; ☐Corso Vittorio Emanuele II) Noisy, colourful 'Il Campo' is a major focus of Roman life: by day it hosts one of Rome's best-known markets, while at night it morphs into a raucous open-air pub as drinkers spill out from its many bars and eateries. For centuries the square was the site of public executions, and it was here that philosopher Giordano Bruno was burned for heresy in 1600. The spot is marked by a sinister statue of the hooded monk, which was created by Ettore Ferrari in 1889.

Elefantino   Monument

(Map p384; Piazza della Minerva; ☐Largo di Torre Argentina) Just south of the Pantheon, the Elefantino is a curious and much-loved statue of a puzzled-looking elephant carrying a 6th-century-BC Egyptian obelisk. Commissioned by Pope Alexander VII and completed in 1667, the elephant, symbolising strength and wisdom, was sculpted by Ercole Ferrata to a design by Gian Lorenzo

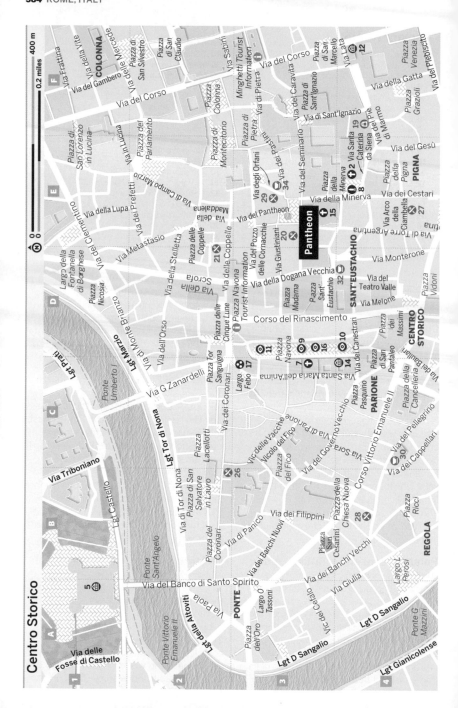

Centro Storico

0.2 miles
400 m

Pantheon

COLONNA

PIGNA

SANT'EUSTACHIO

CENTRO
STORICO

PARIONE

REGOLA

PONTE

Via delle
Fosse di Castello

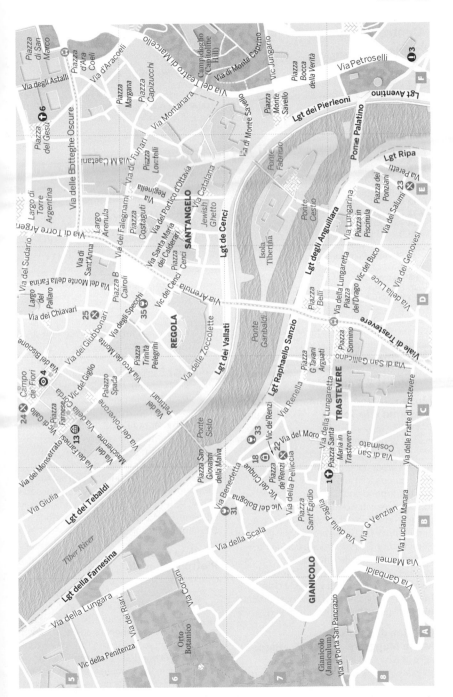

Centro Storico

◎ Sights
1 Basilica di Santa Maria in
  Trastevere.................................B7
2 Basilica di Santa Maria Sopra
  Minerva....................................E4
3 Bocca della Verità.........................F8
4 Campo de' Fiori.............................C5
5 Castel Sant'Angelo......................A1
6 Chiesa del Gesù............................F5
7 Chiesa di Sant'Agnese in Agone.............C3
8 Elefantino....................................E4
9 Fontana dei Quattro Fiumi........................D3
10 Fontana del Moro.......................D4
11 Fontana del Nettuno....................D3
12 Galleria Doria Pamphilj..................F4
13 Palazzo Farnese...........................C5
14 Palazzo Pamphilj..........................C4
15 Pantheon......................................E3
16 Piazza Navona..............................D3
17 Stadio di Domiziano.....................C3

◎ Shopping
18 Benheart.......................................C7
19 Confetteria Moriondo & Gariglio...............F4

◎ Eating
20 Armando al Pantheon...................E3
21 Casa Coppelle..............................D2
22 Da Augusto..................................C7
23 Da Enzo.......................................E8
24 Forno di Campo de' Fiori...............C5
25 Forno Roscioli..............................D5
26 Gelateria del Teatro......................B2
27 La Ciambella................................E4
28 Supplizio.......................................B4
29 Venchi..E3

◎ Drinking & Nightlife
30 Barnum Cafe................................C4
31 Bir & Fud.....................................B6
32 Caffè Sant'Eustachio....................D4
33 Freni e Frizioni.............................C7
34 La Casa del Caffè Tazza d'Oro.................E3
35 Open Baladin................................D6

Bernini. The obelisk was taken from the nearby Basilica di Santa Maria Sopra Minerva (p361).

◎ Monti & Esquilino

Museo Nazionale Romano: Palazzo Massimo alle Terme   Museum

(Map p390; ☑06 3996 7700; www.coopculture.it; Largo di Villa Peretti 1; adult/reduced €7/3.50; ◷9am-7.45pm Tue-Sun; ⓂTermini) One of Rome's great unheralded museums, this is a fabulous treasure trove of classical art. The ground and 1st floors are devoted to sculpture with some breathtaking pieces – check out the *Pugile* (Boxer), a 2nd-century-BC Greek bronze; the graceful 2nd-century-BC *Ermafrodite dormiente* (Sleeping Hermaphrodite); and the idealised *Il discobolo* (Discus Thrower). It's the magnificent and vibrantly coloured frescoes on the 2nd floor, however, that are the undisputed highlight.

Basilica di Santa Maria Maggiore   Basilica

(Map p390; ☑06 6988 6800; Piazza Santa Maria Maggiore; basilica free, museum adult/reduced €3/2, museum & loggia €5/4; ◷7am-7pm, loggia guided tours 9.30am-5.45pm; ⌨Piazza Santa Maria Maggiore) One of Rome's four patriarchal basilicas, this monumental 5th-century church stands on the summit of the Esquiline Hill, on the spot where snow is said to have miraculously fallen in the summer of AD 358. To commemorate the event, every year on 5 August thousands of white petals are released from the basilica's coffered ceiling. Much altered over the centuries, it's an architectural hybrid with 14th-century Romanesque belfry, 18th-century baroque facade, largely baroque interior and a series of glorious 5th-century mosaics.

Basilica di San Pietro in Vincoli   Basilica

(Piazza di San Pietro in Vincoli 4a; ◷8am-12.30pm & 3-7pm summer, to 6pm winter; ⓂCavour) Pilgrims and art lovers flock to this 5th-century basilica for two reasons: to marvel at Michelangelo's colossal *Moses* (1505) sculpture and to see the chains that supposedly bound St Peter when he was imprisoned in the Carcere Mamertino (near the Roman Forum). Access to the church is via a flight of steps through a low arch that leads up from Via Cavour.

⊙ Tridente & Trevi

Trevi Fountain   Fountain
(Fontana di Trevi; Map p390; Piazza di Trevi; ⓂBarberini) The Fontana di Trevi, scene of Anita Ekberg's dip in La Dolce Vita, is a flamboyant baroque ensemble of mythical figures and wild horses taking up the entire side of the 17th-century Palazzo Poli. After a Fendi-sponsored restoration finished in 2015, the fountain gleams brighter than it has for years. The tradition is to toss a coin into the water, thus ensuring that you'll return to Rome – on average about €3000 is thrown in every day.

Palazzo Barberini   Gallery
(Galleria Nazionale d'Arte Antica; Map p390; ☑06 481 45 91; www.barberinicorsini.org; Via delle Quattro Fontane 13; adult/reduced €5/2.50, incl Palazzo Corsini €10/5; ⊗8.30am-7pm Tue-Sun; ⓂBarberini) Commissioned to celebrate the Barberini family's rise to papal power, Palazzo Barberini is a sumptuous baroque palace that impresses even before you clap eyes on the breathtaking art. Many high-profile architects worked on it, including rivals Bernini and Borromini: the former contributed a large squared staircase, the latter a helicoidal one. Amid the masterpieces, don't miss Pietro da Cortona's Il Trionfo della Divina Provvidenza (Triumph of Divine Providence; 1632–39), the most spectacular of the palazzo's ceiling frescoes in the 1st-floor main salon.

Piazza di Spagna & the Spanish Steps   Piazza
(Map p390; ⓂSpagna) A magnet for visitors since the 18th century, the Spanish Steps (Scalinata della Trinità dei Monti) provide a perfect people-watching perch. The 135 steps, gleaming after a recent clean-up, rise from Piazza di Spagna to the landmark **Chiesa della Trinità dei Monti** (Map p390; ☑06 679 41 79; Piazza Trinità dei Monti 3; ⊗7.30am-8pm Tue-Fri, 10am-5pm Sat & Sun).

Piazza di Spagna was named after the Spanish Embassy to the Holy See, although

the staircase, designed by the Italian Francesco de Sanctis, was built in 1725 with money bequeathed by a French diplomat.

Piazza del Popolo   Piazza
(ⓂFlaminio) This dazzling piazza was laid out in 1538 to provide a grandiose entrance to what was then Rome's main northern gateway. It has since been remodelled several times, most recently by Giuseppe Valadier in 1823. Guarding its southern approach are Carlo Rainaldi's twin 17th-century churches, **Chiesa di Santa Maria dei Miracoli** (Via del Corso 528; ⊗6.45am-12.30pm & 4.30-7.30pm Mon-Sat, 8am-1.15pm & 4.30-7.45 Sun) and **Chiesa di Santa Maria in Montesanto** (Chiesa degli Artisti; www.chiesadegliartisti.it; Via del Babuino 198; ⊗5.30-8pm Mon-Fri, 11am-1.30pm Sun). In the centre, the 36m-high **obelisk** (Piazza del Popolo) was brought by Augustus from ancient Egypt; it originally stood in Circo Massimo.

Villa Medici   Palace
(☑06 676 13 11; www.villamedici.it; Viale Trinità dei Monti 1; 1½hr guided tour adult/reduced €12/6; ⊗10am-7pm Tue-Sun; ⓂSpagna) This sumptuous Renaissance palace was built for Cardinal Ricci da Montepulciano in 1540, but Ferdinando dei Medici bought it in 1576. It remained in Medici hands until 1801, when Napoleon acquired it for the French Academy. Guided tours take in the wonderful landscaped gardens, cardinal's painted apartments, and incredible views over Rome – tours in English depart at noon. Note the pieces of ancient Roman sculpture from the Ara Pacis embedded in the villa's walls.

Keats-Shelley House   Museum
(Map p390; ☑06 678 42 35; www.keats-shelley-house.org; Piazza di Spagna 26; adult/reduced €5/4; ⊗10am-1pm & 2-6pm Mon-Sat; ⓂSpagna) The Keats-Shelley House is where Romantic poet John Keats died of TB at the age of 25, in February 1821. Keats came to Rome in 1820 to try to improve his health in the Italian climate, and rented two rooms on the 3rd floor of a townhouse next to the Spanish Steps, with painter companion Joseph Severn (1793–1879). Watch a film

From left: Temple and lake in Villa Borghese ; A pizzeria in Trastevere; Trevi Fountain (p387)

on the 1st floor about the Romantics, then head upstairs to see where Keats and Severn lived and worked.

◉ Trastevere

Trastevere is one of central Rome's most vivacious neighbourhoods, a tightly packed warren of ochre *palazzi,* ivy-clad facades and photogenic lanes. Originally working class, it's now a trendy hang-out full of bars and restaurants.

Basilica di Santa Maria in Trastevere   Basilica

(Map p384; ☑06 581 4802; Piazza Santa Maria in Trastevere; ⊙7.30am-9pm Sep-Jul, 8am-noon & 4-9pm Aug; ☐Viale di Trastevere, ☐Viale di Trastevere) Nestled in a quiet corner of Trastevere's focal square, this is said to be the oldest church dedicated to the Virgin Mary in Rome. In its original form, it dates from the early 3rd century, but a major 12th-century makeover saw the addition of a Romanesque bell tower and glittering facade. The portico came later, added by Carlo Fontana in 1702. Inside, the 12th-century mosaics are the headline feature.

◉ San Giovanni & Testaccio

Basilica di San Giovanni in Laterano   Basilica

(Piazza di San Giovanni in Laterano 4; basilica/ cloister free/€5 with audio guide; ⊙7am-6.30pm, cloister 9am-6pm; Ⓜ San Giovanni) For a thousand years this monumental cathedral was the most important church in Christendom. Commissioned by Constantine and consecrated in AD 324, it was the first Christian basilica built in the city and, until the late 14th century, was the pope's main place of worship. It's still Rome's official cathedral and the pope's seat as the bishop of Rome.

The basilica has been revamped several times, most notably by Borromini in the 17th century, and by Alessandro Galilei, who added the immense white facade in 1735.

Basilica di San Clemente   Basilica

(www.basilicasanclemente.com; Piazza San Clemente; excavations adult/reduced €10/5; ⊙9am-12.30pm & 3-6pm Mon-Sat, 12.15-6pm Sun; ☐Via Labicana) Nowhere better illustrates the various stages of Rome's turbulent past than this fascinating multilayered church. The ground-level 12th-century basilica sits

⟩

NINELLE/GETTY SHUTTERSTOCK ©

atop a 4th-century church, which, in turn, stands over a 2nd-century pagan temple and a 1st-century Roman house. Beneath everything are foundations dating from the Roman Republic.

👁 Villa Borghese

Accessible from Piazzale Flaminio, Pincio Hill and the top of Via Vittorio Veneto, **Villa Borghese** (www.sovraintendenzaroma.it; entrances at Piazzale San Paolo del Brasile, Piazzale Flaminio, Via Pinciana, Via Raimondo, Largo Pablo Picasso; ☉sunrise-sunset; ☒Via Pinciana) is Rome's best-known park.

Museo e Galleria Borghese   Museum

(☎06 3 28 10; www.galleriaborghese.it; Piazzale del Museo Borghese 5; adult/reduced €15/8.50; ☉9am-7pm Tue-Sun; ☒Via Pinciana) If you only have the time (or inclination) for one art gallery in Rome, make it this one. Housing what's often referred to as the 'queen of all private art collections', it boasts paintings by Caravaggio, Raphael and Titian, as well as some sensational sculptures by Bernini. Highlights abound, but look out

for Bernini's *Ratto di Proserpina* (Rape of Proserpina) and Canova's *Venere vincitrice* (Venus Victrix).

To limit numbers, visitors are admitted at two-hourly intervals, so you'll need to pre-book your ticket and get an entry time.

Museo Nazionale Etrusco di Villa Giulia   Museum

(☎06 322 65 71; www.villagiulia.beniculturali.it; Piazzale di Villa Giulia; adult/reduced €8/4; ☉8.30am-7.30pm Tue-Sun; ☒Via delle Belle Arti) Pope Julius III's 16th-century villa provides the charming setting for Italy's finest collection of Etruscan and pre-Roman treasures. Exhibits, many of which came from tombs in the surrounding Lazio region, range from bronze figurines and black *bucchero* tableware to temple decorations, terracotta vases and a dazzling display of sophisticated jewellery.

Must-sees include a polychrome terracotta statue of Apollo from a temple in Veio and the 6th-century-BC *Sarcofago degli Sposi* (Sarcophagus of the Betrothed), found in 1881 in Cerveteri.

Trevi & Esquilino

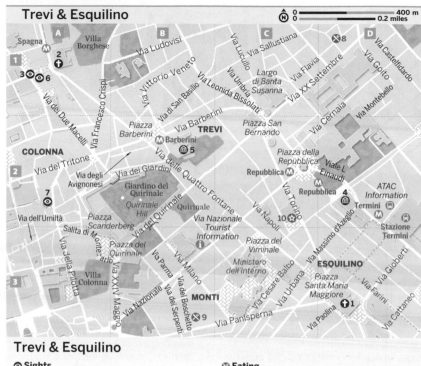

Trevi & Esquilino

◎ Sights
1 Basilica di Santa Maria Maggiore D3
2 Chiesa della Trinità dei Monti A1
3 Fontana della Barcaccia A1
  Keats-Shelley House .... (see 6)
4 Museo Nazionale Romano: Palazzo
  Massimo alle Terme D2
5 Palazzo Barberini B2
6 Piazza di Spagna & the Spanish
  Steps A1
7 Trevi Fountain A2

✕ Eating
8 I Caruso D1
9 L'Asino d'Oro B3

⊙ Entertainment
10 Teatro dell'Opera di Roma C2

🔒 SHOPPING

Rome boasts the usual cast of flagship chain stores and glitzy designer outlets, but what makes shopping here fun is its legion of small, independent shops: family-run delis, small-label fashion boutiques, artisans' studios and neighbourhood markets.

Antica Caciara
Trasteverina   Food & Drinks

(📱06 581 28 15; www.anticacaciara.it; Via San Francesco a Ripa 140; ⊙7am-?pm & 4-8pm Mon-Sat; 🚊Viale di Trastevere, 🚊Viale di Trastevere) The fresh ricotta is a prized possession at this century-old deli, and it's all usually snapped up by lunchtime. If you're too late, take solace in the to-die-for *ricotta infornata* (oven-baked ricotta), 35kg wheels of famous, black-waxed *pecorino romano DOP* (€16.50 per kilo), and aromatic garlands of *guanciale* (pig's jowl) begging to be chopped up, pan-fried and thrown into the perfect carbonara.

Benheart   Fashion & Accessories

(Map p384; ☑06 5832 0801; www.benheart.it;
Via del Moro 47; ◷11am-11pm; ▣Piazza Triussa)
From the colourful resin floor papered with
children's drawings to the vintage typewrit-
er, dial-up telephone and old-fashioned tools
decorating the interior, everything about this
artisanal leather boutique is achingly cool.
Benheart, a young Florentine designer, is
one of Italy's savviest talents and his fashionable handmade shoes (from €190) and
jackets for men and women are glorious

Confetteria Moriondo
& Gariglio   Chocolate

(Map p384; ☑06 699 0856; Via del Piè di
Marmo 21-22; ◷9am-7.30pm Mon-Sat; ▣Via
del Corso) Roman poet Trilussa was so
smitten with this historic chocolate shop
– established by the Torinese confectioners to the royal house of Savoy – that he
was moved to mention it in verse. And we
agree: it's a gem. Decorated like an elegant
tearoom with crimson walls, tables and
glass cabinets, it specialises in delicious
handmade chocolates, many prepared
according to original 19th-century recipes.

Re(f)use   Design

(☑06 6813 6975; www.carminacampus.com; Via
della Fontanelle di Borghese 40; ◷11am-7pm;
▣Via del Corso) Fascinating to browse, this
clever boutique showcases unique Carmina
Campus pieces – primarily bags and jewellery – made from upcycled objects and recycled fabrics. The brand is the love child of
Rome-born designer Ilaria Venturini Fendi
(of *the* Fendi family), a passionate advocate
of ethical fashion, who crafts contemporary
bracelets from beer and soft drink cans,
and bold bags from recycled materials.

Porta Portese Market   Market

(Piazza Porta Portese; ◷6am-2pm Sun; ▣Viale
di Trastevere, ▣Viale di Trastevere) To see another side of Rome, head to this mammoth
flea market. With thousands of stalls selling
everything from rare books and fell-off-
a-lorry bikes to Peruvian shawls and MP3
players, it's crazily busy and a lot of fun.
Keep your valuables safe and wear your
haggling hat.

EATING

The most atmospheric neighbourhoods to
dine in are the *centro storico* and Trastevere. There are also excellent choices in
boho Monti and Testaccio. Watch out for
overpriced tourist traps around Termini and
the Vatican.

Centro Storico

Supplizio   Fast Food €

(Map p384; ☑06 8987 1920; www.facebook.
com/suppliziroma; Via dei Banchi Vecchi 143;
supplì €3-7; ◷noon-8pm Mon-Thu, noon-3.30pm
& 6.30-10.30pm Fri & Sat; ▣Corso Vittorio Emanuele II) Rome's favourite snack, the *supplì*
(a fried croquette filled with rice, tomato
sauce and mozzarella), gets a gourmet
makeover at this elegant street food joint.
Sit back on the vintage leather sofa and dig
into a crispy classic or push the boat out
and try something different, maybe a little
fish number stuffed with fresh anchovies,
cheese, bread and raisins.

Forno Roscioli   Pizza, Bakery €

(Map p384; ☑06 686 4045; www.anticoforno
roscioli.it; Via dei Chiavari 34; pizza slices from
€2, snacks €2; ◷6am-8pm Mon-Sat, 9am-7pm
Sun; ▣Via Arenula) This is one of Rome's top
bakeries, much loved by lunching locals
who crowd here for luscious sliced pizza,
prized pastries and hunger-sating *supplì*
(risotto balls). The *pizza margherita* is
superb, if messy to eat, and there's also a
counter serving hot pastas and vegetable
side dishes.

Forno di
Campo de' Fiori   Pizza, Bakery €

(Map p384; www.fornocampodefiori.com; Campo de' Fiori 22; pizza slices around €3; ◷7.30am-
2.30pm & 4.45-8pm Mon-Sat, closed Sat dinner
Jul & Aug; ▣Corso Vittorio Emanuele II) This
buzzing bakery on Campo de' Fiori, divided
into two adjacent shops, does a roaring
trade in *panini* and delicious fresh-from-
the-oven *pizza al taglio* (pizza by the slice).
Aficionados swear by the *pizza bianca*
('white' pizza with olive oil, rosemary and
salt), but the *panini* and *pizza rossa* ('red'

pizza, with olive oil, tomato and oregano) taste plenty good too.

La Ciambella   Italian €€

(Map p384; ☑06 683 2930; www.la-ciambella. it; Via dell'Arco della Ciambella 20; meals €35-45; ☺bar 7.30am-midnight, wine bar & restaurant noon-11pm Tue-Sun; ☐Largo di Torre Argentina) Central but largely undiscovered by the tourist hordes, this friendly wine-bar-cum-restaurant beats much of the neighbourhood competition. Its spacious, light-filled interior is set over the ruins of the Terme di Agrippa, visible through transparent floor panels, and its kitchen sends out some excellent food, from tartares and chickpea pancakes to slow-cooked beef and traditional Roman pasta.

Armando al Pantheon   Roman €€

(Map p384; ☑06 6880 3034; www.armandoalpantheon.it; Salita dei Crescenzi 31; meals €40; ☺12.30-3pm Mon-Sat & 7-11pm Mon-Fri; ☐Largo di Torre Argentina) With its cosy wooden interior and unwavering dedication to old-school Roman cuisine, Armando al Pantheon is a regular go-to for local foodies. It's

been trading for more than 50 years and has served its fair share of celebs, but it hasn't let fame go to its head and it remains as popular as ever. Reservations essential.

Casa Coppelle   Ristorante €€€

(Map p384; ☑06 6889 1707; www.casacoppelle. it; Piazza delle Coppelle 49; meals €65, tasting menu €85; ☺noon-3.30pm & 6.30-11.30pm; ☐Corso del Rinascimento) Boasting an enviable setting near the Pantheon and a plush, theatrical look – think velvet drapes, black lacquer tables and bookshelves – Casa Coppelle sets a romantic stage for high end Roman-French cuisine. Gallic trademarks like snails and onion soup feature alongside updated Roman favourites such as pasta *amatriciana* (with tomato sauce and pancetta) and *cacio e pepe* (pecorino and black pepper), here re invented as a risotto with prawns.

✖ Vatican City, Borgo & Prati

Pizzarium   Pizza €

(☑06 3974 5416; Via della Meloria 43; pizza slices €5; ☺11am-10pm; ⋈Cipro-Musei Vaticani) When a pizza joint is packed on a wet

Market on Campo de' Fiori (p383)

KEN WELSH/GETTY IMAGES ©

winter lunchtime, you know it's something special. Pizzarium, the takeaway of Gabriele Bonci, Rome's acclaimed pizza king, serves Rome's best sliced pizza, bar none. Scissor-cut squares of soft, springy base are topped with original combinations of seasonal ingredients and served on paper trays for immediate consumption. Also worth trying are the freshly fried *supplì* (crunchy rice croquettes).

Monti & Esquilino

L'Asino d'Oro   Italian €€

(Map p390; ☑06 4891 3832; www.facebook. com/asinodoro; Via del Boschetto 73; weekday lunch menu €16, meals €45; ☺12.30-2.30pm & 7.30-11pm Tue-Sat; Ⓜ Cavour) This fabulous restaurant was transplanted from Orvieto, and its Umbrian origins resonate in Lucio Sforza's exceptional cooking. Unfussy yet innovative dishes feature bags of flavourful contrasts, like lamb meatballs with pear and blue cheese. Save room for the equally amazing desserts. Intimate, informal and classy, this is one of Rome's best deals – its lunch menu is a steal.

Trastevere

Da Augusto   Trattoria €

(Map p384; ☑06 580 37 98; Piazza de' Renzi 15; meals €25; ☺12.30-3pm & 8-11pm; 🚊 Viale di Trastevere, 🚋 Viale di Trastevere) Bag one of Augusto's rickety tables outside and tuck into some truly fabulous mamma-style cooking on one of Trastevere's prettiest piazza terraces. Hearty portions of all the Roman classics are dished up here as well as lots of rabbit, veal, hare and *pajata* (calf intestines). Winter dining is around vintage formica tables in a bare-bones interior, unchanged for decades. Be prepared to queue. Cash only.

Da Enzo   Trattoria €

(Map p384; ☑06 581 22 60; www.daenzoal29. com; Via dei Vascellari 29; meals €30; ☺12.30-3pm & 7-11pm Mon-Sat; 🚊 Viale di Trastevere, 🚋 Viale di Trastevere) Vintage buttermilk walls, red chequered tablecloths and a traditional menu featuring all the Roman classics: what

Rome's Best Gelato

Fatamorgana (☑06 3265 2238; www. gelateriafatamorgana.com; Via Laurina 10; 2/3/4/5 scoops €2.50/3.50/4.50/5; ☺noon-11pm; Ⓜ Flaminio) Superb artisanal flavours at multiple central locations.

Gelateria del Teatro (Map p384; ☑06 4547 4880; www.gelateriadelteatro.it; Via dei Coronari 65; gelato €2.50-5; ☺10.30am-8pm winter, 10am-10.30pm summer; 🚊 Via Zanardelli) Seasonal fruit and spicy chocolate flavours, all made on site.

I Caruso (Map p390; ☑06 4201 6420; Via Collina 13-15; cones & tubs from €2.50; ☺noon-midnight; Ⓜ Repubblica) A small but perfect selection of creamy flavours.

Venchi (Map p384; ☑06 6992 5423; www. venchi.com; Via degli Orfani 87; gelato €2.50-5; ☺10.30am-11pm Sun-Thu, to midnight Fri & Sat summer, 10am-10pm Sun-Thu, to 11pm Fri & Sat winter; 🚊 Via del Corso) Nirvana for chocoholics.

makes this staunchly traditional trattoria exceptional is its careful sourcing of local, quality products, many from nearby farms in Lazio. The seasonal, deep-fried Jewish artichokes and the *pasta cacio e pepe* (cheese and black pepper pasta) in particular are among the best in Rome.

San Giovanni & Testaccio

Sbanco   Pizza €€

(☑06 78 93 18; Via Siria 1; pizzas €7.50-12.50; ☺7.30pm-midnight; 🚊 Piazza Zama) With its informal warehouse vibe and buzzing

Rome for Free

Some of Rome's most famous sights are free, including all state museums and monuments on the first Sunday of the month, and all of Rome's churches. **Vatican Museums** (p367) Free on the last Sunday of the month.

Trevi Fountain (p387)
Spanish Steps (p387)
Pantheon (p358)
St Peter's Basilica (p363)

---

atmosphere, Sbanco is one of the capital's hottest pizzerias. Since opening in 2016, it has quickly made a name for itself with its creative, wood-fired pizzas and sumptuous fried starters – try the carbonara *supplì* (risotto balls). To top things off, it serves some deliciously drinkable craft beer.

🍷 DRINKING & NIGHTLIFE

Much of the drinking action is in the *centro storico*: Campo de' Fiori is popular with students, while the area around Piazza Navona hosts a more upmarket scene. Over the river, Trastevere is another favoured spot with dozens of bars and pubs.

Rome's clubbing scene is centred on Testaccio and the Ostiense area, although you'll also find places in Trastevere and the *centro storico*. Admission to clubs is often free, but drinks are expensive.

Il Tiaso   Bar

(📞06 4547 4625; www.iltiaso.com; Via Ascoli Piceno 25; ⏰6pm-2am; 🛜; 🚆Circonvallazione Casilina) Think living room with zebra-print chairs, walls of indie art, Lou Reed biographies wedged between wine bottles, and 30-something owner Gabriele playing a New York Dolls album to neo-beatnik chicks, corduroy-clad professors and the odd neighbourhood dog. Expect well-priced wine, an intimate chilled vibe, regular live music and lovely pavement terrace.

Barnum Cafe   Cafe

(Map p384; 📞06 6476 0483; www.barnumcafe.com; Via del Pellegrino 87; ⏰9am-10pm Mon. to 2am Tue-Sat; 🛜; 🚆Corso Vittorio Emanuele II) A laid-back *Friends*-style cafe, evergreen Barnum is the sort of place you could quickly get used to. With its shabby-chic vintage furniture and white bare-brick walls, it's a relaxed spot for a breakfast cappuccino, a light lunch or a late afternoon drink. Come evening, a coolly dressed-down crowd sips seriously good cocktails.

Caffè Sant'Eustachio   Coffee

(Map p384; www.santeustachioilcaffe.it; Piazza Sant'Eustachio 82; ⏰8.30am-1am Sun-Thu, to 1.30am Fri, to 2am Sat; 🚆Corso del Rinascimento) This small, unassuming cafe, generally three deep at the bar, is reckoned by many to serve the best coffee in town. To make it, the bartenders sneakily beat the first drops of an espresso with several teaspoons of sugar to create a frothy paste to which they add the rest of the coffee. It's superbly smooth and guaranteed to put some zing into your sightseeing.

Open Baladin   Bar

(Map p384; 📞06 683 8989; www.openbaladinroma.it; Via degli Specchi 6; ⏰noon-2am; 🛜; 🚆Via Arenula) For some years, this cool, modern pub near Campo de' Fiori has been a leading light in Rome's craft beer scene, and it's still a top place for a pint with more than 40 beers on tap and up to 100 bottled brews, many from Italian artisanal microbreweries. There's also a decent food menu with *panini*, gourmet burgers and daily specials.

La Casa del Caffè
Tazza d'Oro   Coffee

(Map p384; 📞06 678 9792; www.tazzadorocoffeeshop.com; Via degli Orfani 84-86; ⏰7am-8pm Mon-Sat, 10.30am-7.30pm Sun; 🚆Via del Corso) A busy, stand-up affair with burnished 1940s fittings, this is one of Rome's best coffee houses. Its espresso hits the mark nicely and there's a range of delicious coffee concoctions, including a cooling *granita di caffè*, a crushed-ice coffee drink served with whipped cream. There's also a small shop and, outside, a coffee *bancomat* for those out-of-hours caffeine emergencies.

Bir & Fud Craft Beer

(Map p384; ☑06 589 40 16; www.birandfud.it; Via Benedetta 23; ☺noon-2am; ☐Piazza Trilussa) On a narrow street lined with raucous drinking holes, this brick-vaulted bar-pizzeria wins plaudits for its outstanding collection of craft *bir* (beer), many on tap, and equally tasty *fud* (food) for when late-night munchies strike. Its Neapolitan-style wood-fired pizzas are particularly excellent.

Freni e Frizioni Bar

(Map p384; ☑06 4549 7499; www.freniefrizioni. com; Via del Politeama 4-6; ☺7pm-2am; ☐Piazza Trilussa) This perennially cool Trastevere bar is housed in an old mechanic's workshop – hence its name ('brakes and clutches') and tatty facade. It draws a young *spritz*-loving crowd that swells onto the small piazza outside to sip superbly mixed cocktails (€10) and seasonal punches, and fill up on its lavish early-evening *aperitivo* buffet (7pm to 10pm). Table reservations are essential on Friday and Saturday evenings.

⭐ ENTERTAINMENT

Rome has a thriving cultural scene, with a year-round calendar of concerts, performances and festivals. Upcoming events are also listed on www.turismoroma.it and www.inromenow.com.

Auditorium Parco della Musica Concert Venue

(☑06 8024 1281; www.auditorium.com; Viale Pietro de Coubertin; ☐Viale Tiziano) The hub of Rome's thriving cultural scene, the Auditorium is the capital's premier concert venue. Its three concert halls offer superb acoustics, and together with a 3000-seat open-air arena, stage everything from classical music concerts to jazz gigs, public lectures and film screenings.

The Auditorium is also home to Rome's world-class **Orchestra dell'Accademia Nazionale di Santa Cecilia** (www.santa cecilia.it).

Alexanderplatz Jazz

(☑06 8377 5604; www.facebook.com/alex ander.platz.37; Via Ostia 9; ☺8.30pm-1.30am;

Restaurants in Trastevere

Teatro dell'Opera di Roma

MOttaviano-San Pietro) Intimate, underground, and hard to find – look for the discreet black door – Rome's most celebrated jazz club draws top Italian and international performers and a respectful cosmopolitan crowd. Book a table for the best stage views or to dine here, although note that it's the music that's the star act not the food.

Teatro dell'Opera di Roma
Opera, Ballet

(Map p390; ✆06 48 16 01; www.operaroma.it; Piazza Beniamino Gigli 1; ⊙box office 10am-6pm Mon-Sat, 9am-1.30pm Sun; MRepubblica) Rome's premier opera house boasts a plush gilt interior, a Fascist 1920s exterior and an impressive history: it premiered Puccini's *Tosca,* and Maria Callas once sang here. Opera and ballet performances are staged between September and June.

ℹ INFORMATION

DANGERS & ANNOYANCES

Rome is not a dangerous city, but petty theft can be a problem. Watch out for pickpockets around the big tourist sites, at Stazione Termini and on crowded public transport – the 64 Vatican bus is notorious.

MEDICAL SERVICES

Policlinico Umberto I (✆06 4 99 71; www.policlinicoumberto1.it; Viale del Policlinico 155; MPoliclinico, Castro Pretorio) Rome's largest hospital is located near Stazione Termini.

TOURIST INFORMATION

For phone enquiries, there's a **tourist information line** (✆06 06 08; www.060608.it; ⊙9am-9pm), and for information about the Vatican, contact the **Centro Servizi Pellegrini e Turisti** (✆06 6988 1662; St Peter's Square; ⊙8.30am-6.30pm Mon-Sat; ⟐Piazza del Risorgimento, MOttaviano-San Pietro).

There are tourist information points at **Fiumicino** (Fiumicino Airport; International Arrivals, Terminal 3; ⊙8am-8.45pm) and **Ciampino** (Arrivals Hall; ⊙8.30am-6pm) airports, and at locations across town.

Fori Imperiali Tourist Information (Via dei Fori Imperiali; ⊙9.30am-7pm; ⟐Via dei Fori Imperiali)

Has a useful panel illustrating the Roman and Imperial Forums.

Minghetti Tourist Information (06 06 08; www.turismoroma.it; Via Marco Minghetti; ☉9.30am-7pm; 🚇Via del Corso) Info kiosk between Via del Corso and the Trevi Fountain.

Piazza Navona Tourist Information (Piazza delle Cinque Lune; ☉9.30am-7pm; 🚇Corso del Rinascimento) Located just off Piazza Navona.

Stazione Termini Tourist Information (⏰06 06 08; www.turismoroma.it; Via Giovanni Giolitti 34; ☉9am-5pm; Ⓜ Termini) Located inside the station next to the Mercato Centrale, not far from the car rental and left luggage desk. Pick up city maps and reserve city tours.

Via Nazionale Tourist Information (⏰06 06 08; www.turismoroma.it; Via Nazionale 184; ☉9.30am-7pm; 🚇Via Nazionale) In front of Palazzo delle Esposizioni.

ⓘ GETTING THERE & AWAY

AIR

Rome's main international airport, **Leonardo da Vinci** (Fiumicino; ⏰06 6 59 51; www.adr.it/fiumicino), better known as Fiumicino, is on the coast 30km west of the city.

The much smaller **Ciampino Airport** (www.ciampino-airport.info), 15km southeast of the city centre, is the hub for European low-cost carrier Ryanair.

BOAT

The nearest port to Rome is at Civitavecchia, about 80km north. Ferries sail here from Spain, Tunisia, Sicily and Sardinia. Book tickets at travel agents or online at www.traghettiweb.it. You can also buy directly at the port.

Half-hourly trains connect Civitavecchia and Termini (€5 to €15.50, 40 minutes to 1¼ hours).

BUS

Long-distance national and international buses use the **Autostazione Tiburtina** (Tibus; Largo Guido Mazzoni; Ⓜ Tiburtina). Get tickets at the bus station or at travel agencies.

Roma Pass

A cumulative sightseeing and transport card, available online or from tourist information points and participating museums, the Roma Pass (www.roma pass.it) comes in two forms:

72 hours (€38.50) Provides free admission to two museums or sites, as well as reduced entry to extra sites, unlimited city transport, and discounted entry to other exhibitions and events.

48 hours (€28) Gives free admission to one museum or site, and then as per the 72-hour pass.

CAR & MOTORCYCLE

Rome is circled by the Grande Raccordo Anulare (GRA), to which all autostrade (motorways) connect, including the main A1 north–south artery, and the A12, which runs to Civitavecchia and Fiumicino airport.

Car hire is available at the airport and Stazione Termini.

TRAIN

Rome's main station is **Stazione Termini** (www.romatermini.com; Piazza dei Cinquecento; Ⓜ Termini). It has regular connections to other European countries, all major Italian cities and many smaller towns. **Left luggage** (Stazione Termini; 1st 5hr €6, 6-12hr per hour €0.90, 13hr & over per hour €0.40; ☉6am-11pm; Ⓜ Termini) is in the wing on the Via Giolitti side of the station, near the tourist office.

Rome's other principal train stations are Stazione Tiburtina and Stazione Roma-Ostiense.

ⓘ GETTING AROUND

TO/FROM THE AIRPORTS

FIUMICINO

The easiest way to get to/from Fiumicino is by train, but there are also bus services. The set taxi fare to the city centre is €48 (valid for up to four people with luggage).

Leonardo Express Train (one way €14) Runs to/from Stazione Termini. Departures from Fiumicino airport every 30 minutes between 6.23am and 11.23pm; from Termini between 5.35am and 10.35pm. Journey time is 30 minutes.

FL1 Train (one way €8) Connects to Trastevere, Ostiense and Tiburtina stations, but not Termini. Departures from Fiumicino airport every 15 minutes (half-hourly on Sundays and public holidays) between 5.57am and 10.42pm; from Tiburtina every 15 minutes between 5.01am and 7.31pm, then half-hourly to 10.01pm.

CIAMPINO

The best option from Ciampino is to take one of the regular bus services into the city centre. The set taxi fare to the centre is €30.

SIT Bus – Ciampino (✆06 591 68 26; www.sit busshuttle.com; from/to airport €5/6, return €9) Regular departures from the airport to Via Marsala outside Stazione Termini between 7.45am and 11.15pm; from Termini between 4.30am and 9.30pm. Get tickets on the bus. Journey time is 45 minutes.

Schiaffini Rome Airport Bus – Ciampino (✆06 713 05 31; www.romeairportbus.com; Via Giolitti; one way/return €4.90/7.90) Regular departures to/from Via Giolitti outside Stazione Termini. From the airport, services are between 4am and 10.50pm; from Via Giolitti, buses run from 4.50am to midnight. Buy tickets onboard, online, at the airport, or at the bus stop. Journey time is approximately 40 minutes.

PUBLIC TRANSPORT

Rome's public transport system includes buses, trams, a metro and a suburban train network.

Tickets are valid on all forms of public transport, except for routes to Fiumicino airport. Buy tickets at *tabacchi,* newsstands or from vending machines. They come in various forms:

BIT (€1.50) Valid for 100 minutes and one metro ride.

Roma 24h (€7) Valid for 24 hours.

Roma 48h (€12.50) Valid for 48 hours.

Roma 72h (€18) Valid for 72 hours.

BUS

o Rome's buses and trams are run by **ATAC** (✆06 5 70 03; www.atac.roma.it).

o The main bus station is in front of Stazione Termini on Piazza dei Cinquecento, where there's an **information booth** (Piazza dei Cinquecento; ☺8am-8pm; Ⓜ Termini).

o Other important hubs are at Largo di Torre Argentina and Piazza Venezia.

o Buses run from about 5.30am to midnight, with limited services throughout the night.

METRO

o Rome has two main metro lines, A (orange) and B (blue), which cross at Termini.

o Trains run from 5.30am to 11.30pm (to 1.30am on Fridays and Saturdays).

TAXI

o Official licensed taxis are white with an ID number and *Roma Capitale* on the sides.

o Always go with the metered fare, never an arranged price (the set fares to and from the airports are exceptions).

Where to Stay

Accommodation in Rome is expensive, and with the city busy year-round, you'll want to book as far ahead as you can to secure the best deal.

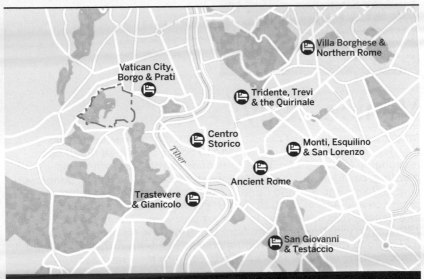

Neighbourhood	Atmosphere
Ancient Rome	Close to major sights such as the Colosseum and Roman Forum; quiet at night; not cheap; restaurants are touristy.
Centro Storico	Atmospheric area with everything on your doorstep – Pantheon, Piazza Navona, restaurants, bars, shops; most expensive part of town; can be noisy.
Tridente, Trevi & the Quirinale	Good for Spanish Steps, Trevi Fountain and designer shopping; excellent midrange to top-end options; good transport links.
Vatican City, Borgo & Prati	Near St Peter's Basilica; decent range of accommodation; some excellent shops and restaurants; on the metro; not much nightlife; sells out quickly for religious holidays.
Monti, Esquilino & San Lorenzo	Lots of budget accommodation around Stazione Termini; top eating in Monti and good nightlife in San Lorenzo; good transport links; some dodgy streets near Termini.
Trastevere & Gianicolo	Gorgeous, atmospheric area; party vibe with hundreds of bars, cafes and restaurants; expensive; noisy, particularly in summer.
San Giovanni & Testaccio	Authentic atmosphere with good eating and drinking options; Testaccio is a top food and nightlife district; not many big sights.
Villa Borghese & Northern Rome	Largely residential area good for the Auditorium and Stadio Olimpico; some top museums; generally quiet after dark.

In This Chapter

Grand Canal 402
Basilica di San Marco 404
Palazzo Ducale 406
Sights 410
Activities 411
Shopping 414
Eating 414
Drinking & Nightlife 416
Entertainment 416
Information 417
Getting There & Away 417
Getting Around 417

Venice, Italy

Imagine the audacity of deciding to build a city of marble palaces on a lagoon. Instead of surrendering to acque alte (high tides) like reasonable folk might do, Venetians flooded the world with vivid painting, baroque music, modern opera, spice-route cuisine, bohemian-chic fashions and a Grand Canal's worth of spritz: the signature prosecco and Aperol cocktail. Today, cutting-edge architects and billionaire benefactors are spicing up the art scene, musicians are rocking out 18th-century instruments and backstreet osterie (taverns) are winning a Slow Food following. Your timing couldn't be better: the people who made walking on water look easy are well into their next act.

Venice in Two Days

Spend your first day in Venice cruising the **Grand Canal** (p402), hopping on and off *vaporetti* as the mood takes you.

On the second day rise early to get to **Basilica di San Marco** (p405) and **Palazzo Ducale** (p407), then revive your spirits (but not your wallet!) at **Caffè Florian** (p416). Glimpse gorgeous **La Fenice** (p416), and make sure you don't leave Venice without indulging in an evening **gondola trip**.

Venice in Four Days

Explore **Ca' Rezzonico** (p410), then choose between the **Gallerie dell'Accademia** (p410) and the **Peggy Guggenheim** (p410) before finishing at the **Basilica di Santa Maria della Salute** (p411). On day four begin at the **Rialto Market** (p411), then wander to Gothic **I Frari** (p411). Once admired, slip into **Scuola Grande di San Rocco** (p410) for prime-time-drama Tintorettos.

After Venice hop on the train to Rome (p352) or glam out in the Swiss Alps (p586).

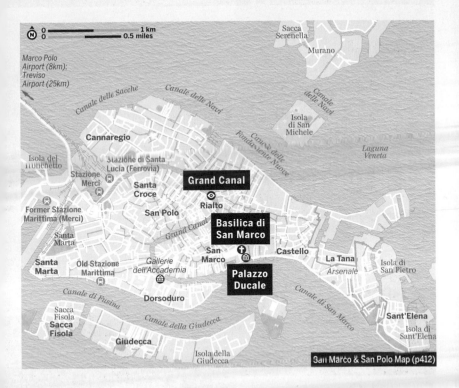

Map labels: Marco Polo Airport (8km); Treviso Airport (25km) · Canale delle Sacche · Canale delle Navi · Sacca Serenella · Murano · Canale delle Navi · Cannaregio · Isola di San Michele · Laguna Veneta · Isola del Tronchetto · Stazione di Santa Lucia (Ferrovia) · Stazione Merci · Santa Croce · **Grand Canal** · Former Stazione Marittima (Merci) · San Polo · **Rialto** · Santa Marta · Grand Canal · **Basilica di San Marco** · Santa Marta · Old Stazione Marittima · Gallerie dell'Accademia · San Marco · Castello · **La Tana** · Isola di San Pietro · Arsenale · **Palazzo Ducale** · Canale di Fusina · Dorsoduro · Canale di San Marco · Sant'Elena · Sacca Fisola · **Sacca Fisola** · Canale della Giudecca · **Giudecca** · Isola della Giudecca · Isola di Sant'Elena · San Marco & San Polo Map (p412)

Arriving in Venice

Marco Polo airport Located on the mainland 12km from Venice. Alilaguna operates a ferry service (€15) to Venice from the airport ferry dock. Water taxis cost from €110. Half-hourly buses (€6) connect with Piazzale Roma.

Stazione Santa Lucia Venice's train station. *Vaporetti* (small passenger boats) depart from Ferrovia (Station) docks.

Stazione Venezia Mestre The mainland train station; transfer here to Stazione Santa Lucia.

Where to Stay

With many Venetians opening their homes to visitors, you can become a local overnight. Venice was once known for charmingly decrepit hotels where English poets quietly expired, but new design-literate boutique hotels are glamming up historic palaces. In peak seasons quality hotels fill up fast. In summer, many people decamp to the Lido where prices are more reasonable.

Grand Canal

Never was a thoroughfare so aptly named as the Grand Canal. Snaking through the heart of the city, Venice's signature waterway is flanked by a magnificent array of Gothic, Moorish, Renaissance and Rococo palaces.

Great For...

☑ Don't Miss

The Ponte di Rialto, the Palazzo Grassi and the iconic Basilica di Santa Maria della Salute.

For most people, a trip down the Canal starts near the train station, near the Ponte di Calatrava. Officially known as the Ponte della Costituzione (Constitution Bridge), this contemporary bridge, designed by avant-garde Spanish architect Santiago Calatrava in 2008, is one of the few modern structures you'll see in central Venice.

To the Rialto

Leaving the bridge in your wake, one of the first landmarks you'll pass is the arcaded Gothic facade of the **Ca' d'Oro** (⏹041 520 03 45; www.cadoro.org; Calle di Ca' d'Oro 3932; adult/reduced €8.50/4.25; ◷8.15am-2pm Mon, to 7.15pm Tue-Sun; 🚤Ca' d'Oro), a 15th-century palazzo that now houses an art museum.

Ponte di Rialto & Around

A short way on, the Ponte di Rialto (p411) is the oldest of the four bridges that cross

Grand Canal ⦿

Canale di
San Marco

❶ Need to Know

Tuke *Vaporetti* 1 or 2 from the Ferrovia; it takes 35 to 40 minutes to Piazza San Marco.

✕ Take a Break

Jump off at Rialto and search out **Cantina Do Spade** (☎041 521 05 83; www.cantinadospade.com; Calle delle Do Spade 860, San Polo; ☺10am-3pm & 6-10pm; 🛜; 🛳Rialto-Mercato) for a cosy drink.

★ Top Tip

Avoid the crowds and tour the canal in the early evening or at night.

fairy-tale architecture. For an art gallery interlude, head to the nearby Gallerie dell'Accademia (p410) or the Peggy Guggenheim (p410).

the canal. Nearby, local chappels crowd to the Rialto Market (p411) and Pescaria fish market (p411).

Palazzo Grassi

The clean, geometric form of **Palazzo Grassi** (☎041 200 10 57; www.palazzograssi.it; Campo San Samuele 3231; adult/reduced incl Punta della Dogana €18/15; ☺10am-7pm Wed-Mon mid-Apr–Nov; 🛳San Samuele) comes into view on the first bend after the Rialto. A noble 18th-century palace, it now provides the neo-classical setting for show-stopping contemporary art. Over the water, spy out the sumptuous Ca' Rezzonico (p410).

Ponte dell'Accademia & Around

A couple of ferry stops further down and you arrive at the wooden Ponte dell'Accademia, a bridge whose simple design seems strangely out of place amid Venice's

Basilica di Santa Maria della Salute

The imperious dome of the Basilica di Santa Maria della Salute (p411) has been overlooking the canal's entrance since the 17th century. Beyond the basilica, the **Punta della Dogana** (☎041 271 90 39; www.palazzograssi.it; Fondamente della Dogana alla Salute 2, Dorsoduro; adult/reduced €15/10, incl Palazzo Grassi €18/15; ☺10am-7pm Wed-Mon Apr-Nov; 🛳Salute) is a former customs warehouse that now stages contemporary art exhibitions.

St Marks & Palazzo Ducale

You're now at the mouth of the canal, where you can disembark for Piazza San Marco. Dominating the waterside here is Palazzo Ducale (p407), the historic residence of the Venetian Doges.

CLAUDIO STOCCO/SHUTTERSTOCK ©

Basilica di San Marco

With its profusion of spires and domes, lavish marble-work and 8500 sq metres of luminous mosaics, the Basilica di San Marco, Venice's signature basilica, is an unforgettable sight.

Great For...

☑ Don't Miss

Loggia dei Cavalli, where reproductions of the four bronze horses gallop off the balcony over Piazza San Marco.

The basilica was founded in the 9th century to house the corpse of St Mark after wily Venetian merchants smuggled it out of Egypt in a barrel of pork fat. When the original burnt down in 932 Venice rebuilt the basilica in its own cosmopolitan image, with Byzantine domes, a Greek cross layout and walls clad in marble from Syria, Egypt and Palestine.

Exterior & Portals

The front of St Mark's ripples and crests like a wave, its five niched portals capped with shimmering mosaics and frothy stone-work arches. The oldest mosaic on the facade (1270) is in the lunette above the far-left portal, depicting St Mark's stolen body arriving at the basilica. The theme is echoed in three of the other lunettes,

Gold-leaf mosaics inside Basilica di San Marco

ℹ Need to Know

St Mark's Basilica; ☏041 270 83 11; www.
basilicasanmarco.it; Piazza San Marco;
⊙9.45am-5pm Mon-Sat, 2-5pm Sun summer,
to 4pm Sun winter; ⛴San Marco FREE

✕ Take a Break

Treat yourself to a *bellini* at world-
famous **Harry's Bar** (☏041 528 57 77;
www.harrysbarvenezia.com; Calle Vallaresso
1323; ⊙10.30am-11pm).

★ Top Tip

There's no charge to enter the church
and wander around the roped-off
central circuit, although you'll need
to dress modestly, with knees and
shoulders covered.

---

including one showing turbaned officials
recoiling from the hamper of pork fat containing the sainted corpse.

Mosaics

Blinking is natural upon your first glimpse
of the basilica's glittering ceiling mosaics,
many made with 24-carat gold leaf. Just
inside the vestibule are the basilica's oldest
mosaics: Apostles with the Madonna,
standing sentry by the main door for more
than 950 years. Inside the church proper,
three golden domes vie for your attention.
The Pentecost Cupola shows the Holy Spirit, represented by a dove, shooting tongues
of flame onto the heads of the surrounding
saints. In the central 13th-century Ascension Cupola, angels swirl around the central
figure of Christ hovering among the stars.

Pala d'Oro

Tucked behind the main altar (€2), this
stupendous golden screen is studded with
2000 emeralds, amethysts, sapphires,
rubies, pearls and other gemstones. But
the most priceless treasures here are
biblical figures in vibrant cloisonné, begun
in Constantinople in AD 976 and elaborated
by Venetian goldsmiths in 1209.

Tesoro & Museum

Holy bones and booty from the Crusades
fill the Tesoro (Treasury; €3); while ducal
treasures on show in the **museum** (adult/
reduced €5/2.50; ⊙9.45am-4.45pm) would
put a king's ransom to shame. A highlight is
the Quadriga of St Mark's, a group of four
bronze horses originally plundered from
Constantinople and later carted off to Paris
by Napoleon before being returned to the
basilica and installed in the 1st-floor gallery.

CGE2010/SHUTTERSTOCK ©

Palazzo Ducale

Gothic Palazzo Ducale was the doge's official residence and the seat of the Venetian Republic's government (and location of its prisons) for over seven centuries.

Although the ducal palace probably moved to this site in the 10th century, the current complex only started to take shape in around 1340. In 1424 the wing facing Piazzetta San Marco was added and the palace assumed its final form, give or take a few major fires and refurbishments.

First Floor

The doge's suite of private 1st-floor rooms is now used to house temporary art exhibitions, which are ticketed separately (around €10 extra). The doge lived like a caged lion in his gilded suite in the palace, which he could not leave without permission. The most intriguing room is the Sala dello Scudo (Shield Room), covered with world maps that reveal the extent of Venetian power (and the limits of its cartographers).

Great For...

☑ Don't Miss

The face of a grimacing man with his mouth agape at the top of the Scala d'Oro; this was a post box for secret accusations.

ANSHARPHOTO/SHUTTERSTOCK ©

🛈 Need to Know

Ducal Palace; 📞041 271 59 11; www.palazzo ducale.visitmuve.it; Piazzetta San Marco 1; adult/reduced incl Museo Correr €19/12, or with Museum Pass; 🕘8.30am-7pm Apr-Oct, to 5.30pm Nov-Mar; 🚢San Zaccaria

✖ Take a Break

Continue the rarefied vibe within the jewellery-box interior of Caffè Florian (p416).

> ### ★ Top Tip
> Check www.palazzoducale.visitmuve. it for details of Secret Itineraries tours and special openings.

Second Floor

Ascend Sansovino's 24-carat gilt stuccowork Scala d'Oro (Golden Staircase) and emerge into 2nd-floor rooms covered with gorgeous propaganda. In the Palladio-designed Sala delle Quattro Porte (Hall of the Four Doors), ambassadors awaited ducal audiences under a lavish display of Venice's virtues by Giovanni Cambi, Titian and Tiepolo.

Few were granted an audience in the Palladio-designed Collegio (Council Room), where Veronese's 1575–78 *Virtues of the Republic* ceiling shows Venice as a bewitching blonde waving her sceptre like a wand over Justice and Peace. Father-son team Jacopo and Domenico Tintoretto attempt similar flattery, showing Venice keeping company with Apollo, Mars and Mercury in their *Triumph of Venice* ceiling for the Sala del Senato (Senate Hall).

Government cover-ups were never so appealing as in the Sala Consiglio dei Dieci (Trial Chambers of the Council of Ten), where Venice's star chamber plotted under Veronese's *Juno Bestowing Her Gifts on Venice*. Arcing over the Sala della Bussola (Compass Room) is his *St Mark in Glory* ceiling.

Sala del Maggior Consiglio

The cavernous 1419 Sala del Maggior Consiglio (Grand Council Hall) provides the setting for Domenico Tintoretto's swirling *Paradise,* a work that's more politically correct than pretty: heaven is crammed with 500 prominent Venetians, including several Tintoretto patrons. Veronese's political posturing is more elegant in his oval *Apotheosis of Venice* ceiling, where gods marvel at Venice's coronation by angels, with foreign dignitaries and Venetian blondes rubbernecking on the balcony below.

Venice Gourmet Crawl

From market discoveries to delectable gelato, Venice is a gourmand's paradise waiting to be explored.

Start Rialto Market
Distance 2.9km
Duration Two hours

7 Finish with a wine or a cocktail at a bar such as **Al Prosecco** (p416),

6 Savour a sinful scoop of organic gelato at standout **Gelato di Natura** (www.gelatodinatura.com; Calle Larga 1628).

5 Impress your dinner guests with for to-die-for menu cards or invitations printed at **Veneziastampa** (www.veneziastampa.com; Campo Santa Maria Mater Domini 2173; ⊘8.30am-7.30pm Mon-Fri, 9am-12.30pm Sat).

FINISH 7

Campo San Giacomo dell'Orio 6

Campo Santa Maria Mater Domini 5

Rio di Ca' Foni
C del Tentor
Saliz di San Stae
C del Ravano
Saliz Carminati
C d'Chiesa
C Lunga
C Filosi
C del Scaleter
C Larga
C del Tentor

SAN POLO

Rio dei Frari
Rio di San Polo
Rio della Madonnetta

0 — 200 m
0 — 0.1 miles
Ⓝ

Classic Photo: Colourful produce at the Rialto Market.

2 At **Drogheria Mascari** (www. imascari.com; Ruga degli Spezieri 381; ⊙8am-1pm & 4-7.30pm Mon, Tue & Thu-Sat, 8am-1pm Wed) glimpse the fragrant spices and trade-route treasures that made Venice's fortune.

1 A trip through gourmet history starts at the **Rialto Market** (p411), where fishmongers artfully arrange the day's catch.

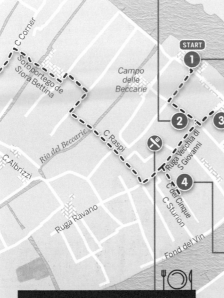

START
1

Rio dei Santi Apostoli

C Corner

Sotoportego de Siora Bettina

Campo delle Beccarie

2

3

Rio del Beccarie

C. Raspi

C Albrizzi

Ruga Vecchia di S Giovanni

4

Ruga Ravano

C. dei Cinque

C Sturion

Fond del Vin

Ponte di Rialto

3 Casa del Parmigiano (www. aliani-casadelparmigiano.it; Campo Cesare Battisti 214; ⊙8am-1.30pm Mon-Wed, to 7.30pm Thu-Sat) is a historic deli laden with hard-to-find cheeses and mouth-watering cured meats.

4 Stop for an aromatic espresso at specialist coffee pedlar **Caffè del Doge** (www.caffedeldoge.com; Calle dei Cinque 609; ⊙7am-7pm).

Take a Break... Duck into All'Arco (p414) for some of the city's best *cicheti*.

SAN MARCO

Rio di San Salvador

⊙ SIGHTS

Gallerie dell'Accademia   Gallery

(🖉041 520 03 45; www.gallerieaccademia.
org; Campo della Carità 1050, Dorsoduro; adult/
reduced €12/6, 1st Sun of month free; ⊘8.15am-
2pm Mon, to 7.15pm Tue-Sun; 🚊Accademia) Venice's historic gallery traces the development
of Venetian art from the 14th to 18th centuries, with works by Bellini, Titian, Tintoretto,
Veronese and Canaletto, among others. The
former Santa Maria della Carità convent
complex housing the collection maintained
its serene composure for centuries until
Napoleon installed his haul of Venetian art
trophies here in 1807. Since then there's
been nonstop visual drama on its walls.

Peggy Guggenheim
Collection   Museum

(🖉041 240 54 11; www.guggenheim-venice.it;
Palazzo Venier dei Leoni 704, Dorsoduro; adult/
reduced €15/9; ⊘10am-6pm Wed-Mon; 🚊Acca-
demia) After losing her father on the *Titanic,*
heiress Peggy Guggenheim became one
of the great collectors of the 20th century.
Her palatial canalside home, Palazzo Venier
dei Leoni, showcases her stockpile of surrealist, futurist and abstract expressionist art
with works by up to 200 artists, including
her ex-husband Max Ernst, Jackson Pollock
(among her many rumoured lovers), Picasso and Salvador Dalí.

Ca' Rezzonico   Museum

(Museum of the 18th Century; 🖉041 241 01
00; www.visitmuve.it; Fondamenta Rezzonico
3136, Dorsoduro; adult/reduced €10/7.50;
⊘10am-6pm Wed-Mon summer, to 5pm winter;
🚊Ca' Rezzonico) Baroque dreams come
true at Baldassare Longhena's Grand
Canal palace, where a marble staircase
leads to gilded ballrooms, frescoed salons
and sumptuous boudoirs. Giambattista
Tiepolo's Throne Room ceiling is a masterpiece of elegant social climbing, showing
gorgeous Merit ascending to the Temple of
Glory clutching the Golden Book of Venetian nobles' names – including Tiepolo's
patrons, the Rezzonico family.

Scuola Grande
di San Rocco   Museum

(🖉041 523 48 64; www.scuolagrandesanrocco.it;
Campo San Rocco 3052, San Polo; adult/reduced
€10/8; ⊘9.30am-5.30pm; 🚊San Tomà) Every-

Gondola ride past Basilica di Santa Maria della Salute

one wanted the commission to paint this building dedicated to the patron saint of the plague-stricken, St Roch, so Tintoretto cheated: instead of producing sketches like rival Veronese, he gifted a splendid ceiling panel of St Roch, knowing it couldn't be refused, or matched by other artists. The artist documents Mary's life story in the assembly hall, and both Old and New Testament scenes in the Sala Grande Superiore upstairs.

Ponte di Rialto   Bridge

(⬚Rialto-Mercato) A superb feat of engineering, Antonio da Ponte's 1592 Istrian stone span took three years and 250,000 gold ducats to construct. Adorned with stone reliefs depicting St Mark, St Theodore and the Annunciation, the bridge crosses the Grand Canal at its narrowest point, connecting the neighbourhoods of San Polo and San Marco.

When crowds of shutterbugs clear out around sunset, the bridge's southern side offers a romantic view of black gondolas pulling up to golden Grand Canal *palazzi*.

Basilica di Santa Maria della Salute   Basilica

(La Salute; www.basilicasalutevenezia.it; Campo della Salute 1b, Dorsoduro; basilica free, sacristy adult/reduced €4/2; ☺basilica 9.30am-noon & 3-5.30pm, sacristy 10am-noon & 3-5pm Mon-Sat, 3-5pm Sun; ⬚Salute) Guarding the entrance to the Grand Canal, this 17th-century domed church was commissioned by Venice's plague survivors as thanks for their salvation. Baldassare Longhena's uplifting design is an engineering feat that defies simple logic; in fact, the church is said to have mystical curative properties. Titian eluded the plague until age 94, leaving 12 key paintings in the basilica's art-slung sacristy.

Rialto Market   Market

(⬚041 296 06 58; San Polo; ☺7am-2pm; ⬚Rialto-Mercato) Venice's Rialto Market has been whetting appetites for seven centuries. To see it at its best arrive in the morning with trolley-totting shoppers

 Top Tours

See Venice (⬚349 084 8303; www.seevenice.it; tours per hr €75) Intimate and insightful cultural tours with a Venetian native.
Monica Caserato (www.monicacaserato.com; tours €35) A whirlwind of cultural, social and epicurean information punctuated by generous pours of wine and excellent food.

and you'll be rewarded by pyramids of colourful seasonal produce like Sant'Erasmo *castraure* (baby artichokes), *radicchio trevisano* (bitter red chicory) and thick, succulent white asparagus. If you're in the market for picnic provisions, vendors may offer you samples. The **Pescaria** (Fish Market; Rialto, San Polo; ☺7am-2pm Tue-Sun; ⬚Rialto-Mercato) is closed Monday.

I Frari   Church

(Basilica di Santa Maria Gloriosa dei Frari; ⬚041 272 86 18; www.basilicadeifrari.it; Campo dei Frari 3072, San Polo; adult/reduced €3/1.50; ☺9am-6pm Mon-Sat, 1-6pm Sun; ⬚San Tomà) A soaring Gothic church, I Frari's assets include marquetry choir stalls, Canova's pyramid mausoleum, Bellini's achingly sweet *Madonna with Child* triptych in the sacristy, and Longhena's creepy Doge Pesaro funereal monument. Upstaging them all, however, is the small altarpiece. This is Titian's 1518 *Assunta* (Assumption), in which a radiant red-cloaked Madonna reaches heavenward, steps onto a cloud and escapes this mortal coil. Titian himself – lost to the plague in 1576 at the age 94 – is buried near his celebrated masterpiece.

⊕ ACTIVITIES

Row Venice   Boating

(⬚347 7250637; www.rowvenice.org; Fondamenta Gasparo Contarini; 90min lessons 1-2 people €85, 3/4 people €120/140; ⬚Orto) The next best thing to walking on water: rowing

San Marco & San Polo

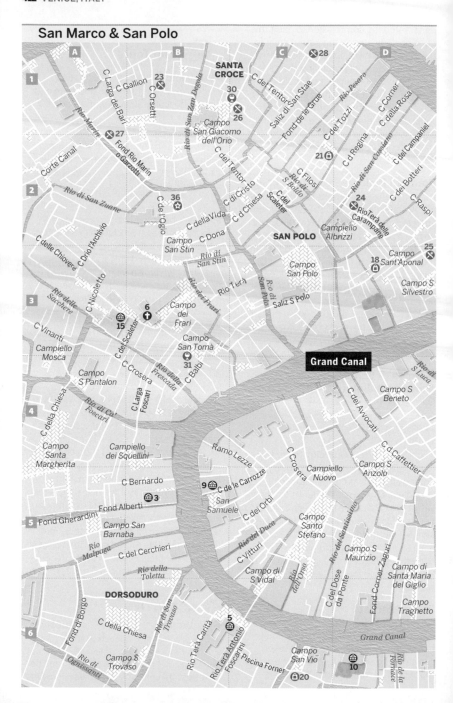

SANTA CROCE

SAN POLO

Grand Canal

DORSODURO

C Larga dei Bari
C Gallion
C Orsetti
Rio di San Zan Degola
C del Tentor/San Stae
Saliz di San Stae
Fond de le Grue
Rio Pesaro
C Corner
C della Rosa
C Campaniel
Fond Rio Marin o Garzotti
Corte Canal
Campo San Giacomo dell'Orio
C del Tentor
C del Tozzi
C d Regina
Rio di Sant Cassiano
C dei Botteri
C Raspi
Rio di San Zuane
C del l'Ogio
C della Vida
C di Cristo
C d Chiesa
C del Scaleter
C del S Boldo
Rio di S Filosi
Campiello Albrizzi
RioTerà delle Carampane
Campo San Stin
Campo Dona
Rio di San Stin
Campo San Polo
Campo Sant'Aponal
Campo Silvestro
C delle Chiovere
C Drio l'Archivio
C Nicoleto
Rio dei Frari
Rio Terà
Saliz S Polo
Rio delle Sacchere
C Vinanti
Campiello Mosca
C del Scaleter
Campo dei Frari
Campo San Tomà
Rio della Frescada
C Balbi
Campo S Pantalon
C Crosera
C Larga Foscari
Rio di Ca' Foscari
Campiello dei Squellini
Ramo Lezze
C de le Carrozze
C Crosera
Campiello Nuovo
Campo S Beneto
C dei Avvocati
C d Caffettier
Campo S Anzolo
C della Chiesa
Campo Santa Margherita
C Bernardo
Fond Alberti
Fond Gherardini
Campo San Barnaba
San Samuele
C dei Orbi
Campo Santo Stefano
Rio del Santissimo
Campo S Maurizio
Campo di Santa Maria del Giglio
Rio Malpaga
C del Cerchieri
Rio della Toletta
San Vidal
C Vitturi
Rio del Duca
Campo di S Vidal
Rio dell'Orso
C del Dose da Ponte
Fond Corner Zaguri
Campo Traghetto
Fond di Borgo
C della Chiesa
Rio di San Trovaso
Rio Terà Carità
Rio Terà Antonio Foscarini
Piscina Forner
Campo San Vio
Grand Canal
Rio di Ognissanti
Campo S Trovaso
Rio di S Luca
Grand Canal
Rio de la Fornase

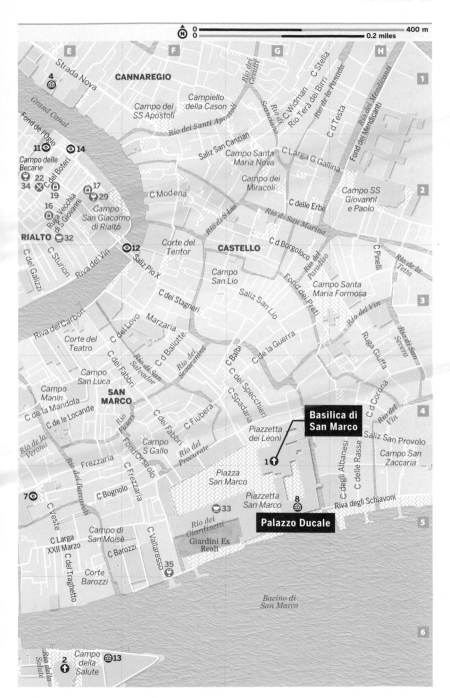

San Marco & San Polo

⊙ **Sights**
1 Basilica di San Marco G4
2 Basilica di Santa Maria della
  Salute E6
3 Ca' Rezzonico B5
4 Galleria Giorgio Franchetti alla
  Ca' d'Oro E1
5 Gallerie dell'Accademia C6
6 I Frari B3
7 La Fenice E5
  Museo di San Marco .... (see 1)
8 Palazzo Ducale G5
9 Palazzo Grassi B5
10 Peggy Guggenheim Collection D6
11 Pescaria E2
12 Ponte di Rialto F3
13 Punta della Dogana E6
14 Rialto Market E2
15 Scuola Grande di San Rocco A3

🛍 **Shopping**
16 Alberto Sarria E2
17 Casa del Parmigiano E2
18 Damocle Edizioni D3

19 Drogheria Mascari E2
20 Marina e Susanna Sent C6
21 Veneziastampa C2

❌ **Eating**
22 All'Arco E2
23 Antica Besseta B1
24 Antiche Carampane D2
25 Dai Zemei D3
26 Gelato di Natura C1
27 Osteria Trefanti A1
28 Ristorante Glam C1

🍷 **Drinking & Nightlife**
29 Al Mercà E2
30 Al Prosecco C1
31 Basegò B4
32 Caffè del Doge E2
33 Caffè Florian F5
34 Cantina Do Spade E2
35 Harry's Bar F5

🎭 **Entertainment**
36 Palazzetto Bru Zane B2

a traditional *batellina coda di gambero* (shrimp-tailed boat) standing up like gondoliers do. Tours must be pre-booked and commence at the wooden gate of the Sacca Misericordia boat marina.

🛍 SHOPPING

Marina e Susanna Sent   Glass

(⌨041 520 81 36; www.marinaesusannasent. com; Campo San Vio 669, Dorsoduro; ☺10am-1pm & 1.30-6.30pm; ☵Accademia) Wearable waterfalls and soap-bubble necklaces are Venice style signatures, thanks to the Murano-born Sent sisters. Defying centuries-old beliefs that women can't handle molten glass, their minimalist art-glass statement jewellery is featured in museum stores worldwide, from Palazzo Grassi to MoMA.

Alberto Sarria   Arts & Crafts

(⌨041 520 72 78; www.masksvenice.com; San Polo 777, San Polo; ☺10am-7pm; ☵San Stae) Go Gaga or channel Casanova at this atelier, dedicated to the art of masquerade for over 30 years. Sarria's *commedia dell'arte*

masks are worn by theatre companies from Argentina to Osaka – ominous burnished black leather for dramatic leads, harlequin-chequered *cartapesta* (papier-mâché) for comic foils, starting from around €20. Beyond the masks is a cast of one-of-a-kind marionettes.

Damocle Edizioni   Books

(⌨346 8345720; www.edizionidamocle.com; Calle Perdon 1311, San Polo; ☺10am-1pm & 3-7pm Mon-Fri, 10am-1pm Sat; ☵San Silvestro) Pocket-sized Damocle is both a bookshop and publisher, translating literary greats and showcasing emerging writing talent. Most of Damocle's creations feature beautiful artwork created through collaborations with local and foreign artists.

❌ EATING

All'Arco   Venetian €

(⌨041 520 56 66; Calle dell'Ochialer 436, San Polo; cicheti from €2; ☺8am-2.30pm Mon, Tue & Sat, to 7pm Wed-Fri summer, 8am-2.30pm Mon-Sat winter; ☵Rialto-Mercato) Search out this authentic neighbourhood *osteria* (casual tavern) for the best *cicheti* (bar snacks) in town. Armed with ingredients from the nearby Rialto Market, father-son team Francesco and Matteo serve miniature masterpieces such as *cannocchia* (mantis shrimp) with pumpkin and roe, and *otrega crudo* (raw butterfish) with mint-and-olive-oil marinade. Even with copious *prosecco*, hardly any meal here tops €20.

Dai Zemei   Venetian, Cicheti €

(☎041 520 85 96; www.ostariadaizemei.it; Ruga Vecchia San Giovanni 1045, San Polo; cicheti from €1.50; ⊗8.30am-8.30pm Mon-Sat, 9am-7pm Sun; ⚊San Silvestro) Running this closet-sized *cicheti* counter are *zemei* (twins) Franco and Giovanni, who serve loyal regulars small meals with plenty of imagination. A gourmet bargain for inspired bites and impeccable wines – try a crisp *nosiola* or invigorating *prosecco* brut.

Osteria Trefanti   Venetian €€

(☎041 520 17 89; www.osteriatrefanti.it; Fondamenta Garzotti 888, Santa Croce; meals €40; ⊗noon-2.30pm & 7-10.30pm Tue-Sun; ⚇; ⚊Riva de Biasio) 🍴 La Serenissima's spice trade lives on at simple, elegant Trefanti, where a dish of marinated prawns, hazelnuts, berries and caramel might get an intriguing kick from garam masala. Sip a small, beautifully curated selection of local and organic wines served among old pews and recycled copper lamps.

Antica Besseta   Venetian €€

(☎041 72 16 87; www.anticabesseta.it; Salizada de Cà Zusto 1395, Santa Croce; meals €35; ⊗6.30-10pm Mon, Wed & Thu, noon-2pm & 6.30-10.30pm Fri-Sun; ⚇; ⚊Riva de Biasio) Wood panelling and fresh flowers set the scene at this veteran trattoria, known for giving contemporary verve to regional classics. The *delizie di pesce dell'Adriatico* – a tasting plate which might see seared scallops served with a brandy and asparagus salsa – makes for a stimulating prologue to dishes like almond-crusted turbot with artichokes and cherry tomatoes.

♡ Gondola Rides

Cheesy or the ultimate romance? You choose. Daytime rates run to €80 for 30 minutes (six passengers maximum) or €100 for 35 minutes from 7pm to 8am, not including songs (negotiated separately) or tips.

CANADASTOCK/SHUTTERSTOCK ©

Antiche Carampane   Venetian €€€

(☎041 524 01 65; www.antichecarampane.com; Rio Terà delle Carampane 1911, San Polo; meals €50; ⊗12.45-2.30pm & 7.30-10.30pm Tue-Sat; ⚊San Stae) Hidden in the once-shady lanes behind Ponte delle Tette, this culinary indulgence is a trick to find. Once you do, say goodbye to soggy lasagne and hello to a market-driven menu of silky *crudi* (raw fish/seafood), surprisingly light *fritto misto* (fried seafood) and *caramote* prawn salad with seasonal vegetables. Never short of a smart, convivial crowd, it's a good idea to book ahead.

Riviera   Venetian €€€

(☎041 522 76 21; www.ristoranteriviera.it; Fondamenta Zattere al Ponte Lungo 1473, Dorsoduro; meals €70-85; ⊗12.30-3pm & 7-10.30pm Fri-Tue; ⚊Zattere) Seafood connoisseurs concur that dining at GP Cremonini's restaurant is a Venetian highlight. A former rock musician, GP now focuses his considerable talents on delivering perfectly balanced octopus stew, feather-light gnocchi with lagoon crab, and risotto with langoustine and hop shoots. The setting, overlooking the Giudecca Canal, is similarly spectacular,

 Opera at La Fenice

From January to July and September to October, opera season is in full swing at **La Fenice** (☏041 78 66 75; www.teatrolafenice.it; Campo San Fantin 1977; audioguide adult/reduced €10/7; ☉9.30am-6pm; 🚇Giglio), Venice's gorgeous gilt opera house. If you can't attend a performance, it's possible to explore the theatre with an audio guide.

PISAPHOTOGRAPHY/SHUTTERSTOCK ©

encompassing views of Venetian domes backed by hot pink sunsets.

Ristorante Glam · Venetian €€€
(Palazzo Venart; ☏041 523 56 76; www.enrico bartolini.net/i-ristoranti/glam; Calle Tron 1961, Santa Croce; tasting menu €90-110; ☉12.30-2.30pm & 7.30-10.30pm; 🚇San Stae) Step out of your water taxi into the canalside garden of Enrico Bartolini's new Venetian restaurant in the Venart Hotel. The tasting menus focus on local ingredients, pepping up Veneto favourites with unusual spices that would once have graced the tables of this trade route city.

DRINKING & NIGHTLIFE

Al Mercà · Wine Bar
(☏346 8340660; Campo Cesare Battisti 213, San Polo; ☉10am-2.30pm & 6-8pm Mon-Thu, to 9.30pm Fri & Sat; 🚇Rialto-Mercato) Discerning drinkers throng to this cupboard-sized counter on a Rialto Market square to sip on top-notch *prosecco* and DOC wines by the glass (from €3). Edibles usually include meatballs and mini *panini* (€1.50), proudly made using super-fresh ingredients.

Al Prosecco · Wine Bar
(☏041 524 02 22; www.alprosecco.com; Campo San Giacomo dell'Orio 1503, Santa Croce; ☉10am-8pm Mon-Fri, to 5pm Sat Nov-Mar, to 10.30pm Apr-Oct; 🚇San Stae) 🍷 The urge to toast sunsets in Venice's loveliest *campo* is only natural – and so is the wine at Al Prosecco. This forward-thinking bar specialises in *vini naturi* (natural-process wines) – organic, biodynamic, wild-yeast fermented – from enlightened Italian winemakers like Cinque Campi and Azienda Agricola Barichel. So order a glass of unfiltered 'cloudy' *prosecco* and toast the good things in life.

Caffè Florian · Cafe
(☏041 520 56 41; www.caffeflorian.com; Piazza San Marco 57; ☉9am-11pm; 🚇San Marco) The oldest still-operating cafe in Europe and one of the first to welcome women, Florian maintains rituals (if not prices) established in 1720: be-suited waiters serve cappuccino on silver trays, lovers canoodle in plush banquettes and the orchestra strikes up as the sunset illuminates San Marco's mosaics. Piazza seating during concerts costs €6 extra, but dreamy-eyed romantics hardly notice.

Basegò · Bar
(☏041 850 02 99; www.basego.it; Campo San Tomá, San Polo; ☉9am-11pm; 🚇San Tomà) Focusing on three essential ingredients – good food, good wine and good music – newly opened Basegò has rapidly formed a dedicated group of drinkers. Indulge in a *cicheti* feast of lagoon seafood, Norcia prosciutto, smoked tuna and Lombard cheeses.

✪ ENTERTAINMENT

Palazzetto Bru Zane · Classical Music
(Centre du Musique Romantique Française; ☏041 521 10 05; www.bru-zane.com; Palazzetto Bru Zane 2368, San Polo; adult/reduced €15/5; ☉box office 2.30-5.30pm Mon-Fri, closed late Jul–mid-Aug; 🚇San Tomà) Pleasure palaces don't get

more romantic than Palazetto Bru Zane on concert nights, when exquisite harmonies tickle Sebastiano Ricci angels tumbling across stucco-frosted ceilings. Multi-year restorations returned the 1695–97 Casino Zane's 100-seat music room to its original function, attracting world-class musicians to enjoy its acoustics from late September to mid-May.

INFORMATION

Vènezia Unica (041 24 24; www.veneziaunica. it) runs all tourist information services and offices in Venice. It provides information on sights, itineraries, day trips, transport, special events, shows and temporary exhibitions. Discount passes can be pre-booked on its website.

GETTING THERE & AWAY

AIR

Most flights to Venice fly into **Marco Polo Airport** (flight information 041 260 92 60; www. veniceairport.it; Via Galileo Gallilei 30/1, Tessera), 12km outside Venice, east of Mestre. Ryanair and some other budget airlines also use **Treviso Airport** (042 231 51 11; www.trevisoairport.it; Via Noalese 63), about 4km southwest of Treviso and a 26km, one-hour drive from Venice.

BOAT

Venice has regular ferry connections with Greece, Croatia and Slovenia. However, remember that long-haul ferries and cruise ships have an outsized environmental impact on tiny Venice and its fragile lagoon aquaculture. Consider the lower-impact train instead – Venice will be grateful.

CAR

If you drive to Venice, you have to park at the western end of the city and then walk or take a *vaporetto*.

You'll find car parks in Piazzale Roma or on Isola del Tronchetto. Prices in Venice start at €3.50 per hour and rise to €32 for five to 24 hours. At peak times, many car parks become completely full. However, you can book a parking place ahead of time at www.veneziaunica.it. To make the most of the cheaper car parks, consider parking in Mestre, and take the bus or train into Venice instead.

For a range of parking options in Venice and Mestre, including prices and directions, head to www.avmspa.it.

TRAIN

Direct intercity services operate out of Venice to most major Italian cities, as well as to points in France, Germany, Austria, Switzerland, Slovenia and Croatia.

GETTING AROUND

Vaporetto (small passenger ferry) Venice's main public transport. Single rides cost €7.50; for frequent use, get a timed pass for unlimited travel within a set period (1-/2-/3-/7-day passes cost €20/30/40/60). Tickets and passes are available dockside from ACTV ticket booths and ticket vending machines, or from tobacconists.

Traghetto Locals use this daytime public gondola service (€2) to cross the Grand Canal between bridges.

Water taxi Sleek teak boats offer taxi services for €15 plus €2 per minute, plus €5 for pre-booked services and extra for night-time, luggage and large groups.

In This Chapter

Duomo 420
Galleria dell'Accademia..................424
Galleria degli Uffizi.........................426
Sights 432
Shopping 438
Eating..440
Drinking & Nightlife........................442
Information 442
Getting There & Away 443
Getting Around 443

Florence, Italy

Cradle of the Renaissance – romantic, enchanting and utterly irre-
sistible – Florence (Firenze) is a place to feast on world-class art and
gourmet Tuscan cuisine. Few cities are so compact in size or so packed
with extraordinary art and architecture at every turn. The urban
fabric of this small city, on the banks of the Arno river in northeastern
Tuscany, has hardly changed since the Renaissance and its narrow
cobbled streets are a cinematic feast of elegant 15th- and 16th-century
palazzi (mansions), medieval chapels, fresco-decorated churches,
marble basilicas and world-class art museums. Unsurprisingly, the
entire city centre is a Unesco World Heritage Site.

Florence in Two Days

Start with a coffee on **Piazza della Repubblica** (p433) before hitting the **Uffizi** (p427). After lunch visit the **Duomo** (p420), **Baptistry** (p433) and **Grande Museo del Duomo** (p432). Set aside day two to explore the **Galleria dell'Accademia** (p425) and **Museo di San Marco** (p433). In the evening, venture across to the Oltrarno, stopping en route to admire sunset views from **Ponte Vecchio** (p436) and **Piazzale Michelangelo** (p437).

Florence in Four Days

On day three, explore **Palazzo Pitti** (p436) and the **Giardino di Boboli** (p437) or visit the city's major basilicas – **San Lorenzo** (p437), **Santa Croce** (p437) and **Santa Maria Novella** (p437). Stop by **Il Teatro del Sale** (p440) for dinner and a show. On day four, take a guided tour of **Palazzo Vecchio** (p432) and explore the city's artisanal shops.

Where next? The Tuscan countryside (p444) and Rome (p352) are both waiting.

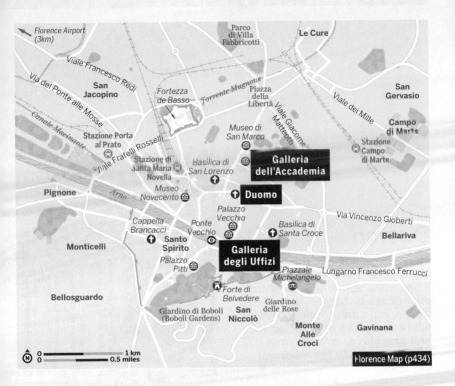

Florence Map (p434)

Arriving in Florence

Pisa International Airport Tuscany's main international airport. There are regular buses to Stazione di Santa Maria Novella (€5). Buy tickets online, on board or at the information desk in the arrivals hall.

Florence Airport ATAF operates a half-hourly Volainbus shuttle (€6) to Florence bus station. A taxi costs €20.

Stazione di Santa Maria Novella A 10-minute walk from the historic centre, Florence's main train station is on the Rome–Milan line.

Where to Stay

Advance reservations are essential between Easter and September, while winter ushers in some great deals for visitors – room rates are practically halved. Many top-end boutique options hide in courtyards or behind the inconspicuous door of a *residenza d'epoca* (historical residence) – not listed as hotel or graced with any stars, making such addresses all the more atmospheric and oh-so-Florentine.

Duomo

Florence's Duomo is the city's most iconic landmark. Capped by Filippo Brunelleschi's red-tiled cupola, it's a staggering construction, and its breathtaking pink, white and green marble facade and graceful campanile (bell tower) dominate the medieval cityscape.

Great For...

Stazione di Santa Maria Novella

Via del Panzani

Via de' Cerretani

Duomo

❶ Need to Know

Cattedrale di Santa Maria del Fiore; ☎055 230 28 85; www.ilgrandemuseodelduomo. it; Piazza del Duomo; ⊙10am-5pm Mon-Wed & Fri, to 4.30pm Thu, to 4.45pm Sat, 1.30-4.45pm Sun **FREE**

★ **Top Tip**

Reservations are required to climb the dome. Book online or at the ticket office at Piazza San Giovanni 7, opposite the Baptistry's northern entrance.

Sienese architect Arnolfo di Cambio began work on the Duomo in 1296, but construction took almost 150 years and it wasn't consecrated until 1436.

Facade

The neo-Gothic facade was designed in the 19th century by architect Emilio de Fabris to replace the uncompleted original, torn down in the 16th century. The oldest and most clearly Gothic part of the cathedral is its south flank, pierced by the Porta dei Canonici (Canons' Door), a mid-14th-century High Gothic creation (you enter here to climb up inside the dome).

Dome

One of the finest masterpieces of the Renaissance, the **cupola** (Brunelleschi's Dome; adult/reduced incl cupola, baptistry, campanile,

crypt & museum €15/3; ☺8.30am-7pm Mon-Fri, to 5pm Sat, 1-4pm Sun) is a feat of engineering that cannot be fully appreciated without climbing its 463 interior stone steps. It was built between 1420 and 1436 to a design by Filippo Brunelleschi, and is a staggering 91m high and 45.5m wide.

Taking his inspiration from Rome's Pantheon, Brunelleschi arrived at an innovative engineering solution of a distinctive octagonal shape of inner and outer concentric domes resting on the drum of the cathedral rather than the roof itself, allowing artisans to build from the ground up without needing a wooden support frame. Over four million bricks were used in the construction, all of them laid in consecutive rings in horizontal courses using a vertical herringbone pattern.

The climb up the spiral staircase is relatively steep. Make sure to pause when

The Duomo is the city's most iconic landmark

you reach the balustrade at the base of the dome, which gives an aerial view of the octagonal *coro* (choir) in the cathedral below and the seven round stained-glass windows (by Donatello, Andrea del Castagno, Paolo Uccello and Lorenzo Ghiberti) that pierce the octagonal drum.

Interior

After the visual wham-bam of the facade, the sparse decoration of the cathedral's vast interior, 155m long and 90m wide, comes as a surprise – most of its artistic treasures have been removed over the centuries according to the vagaries of ecclesiastical fashion, and many are on show

---

☑ Don't Miss

The flamboyant dome frescoes by Giorgio Vasari and Federico Zuccari.

ROSSHELEN/SHUTTERSTOCK ©

in the Grande Museo del Duomo (p432). The interior is also unexpectedly secular in places (a reflection of the sizeable chunk of the cathedral not paid for by the church): down the left aisle two immense frescoes of equestrian statues portray two *condottieri* (mercenaries) – on the left Niccolò da Tolentino by Andrea del Castagno (1456), and on the right Sir John Hawkwood (who fought in the service of Florence in the 14th century) by Uccello (1436).

Between the left (north) arm of the transept and the apse is the Sagrestia delle Messe (Mass Sacristy), its panelling a marvel of inlaid wood carved by Benedetto and Giuliano da Maiano. The fine bronze doors were executed by Luca della Robbia – his only known work in the material. Above the doorway is his glazed terracotta *Resurrezione* (Resurrection).

A stairway near the main entrance of the cathedral leads down to the Cripta Santa Reparata (crypt), where excavations between 1965 and 1974 unearthed parts of the 5th-century Chiesa di Santa Reparata that originally stood on the site.

Campanile

The 414-step climb up the cathedral's 85m-tall **campanile** (Bell Tower; ☑ adult/ reduced incl campanile, baptistry, cupola, crypt & museum €15/3; ⏱8.15am-8pm), begun by Giotto in 1334, rewards with a staggering city panorama. The first tier of bas-reliefs around the base of its elaborate Gothic facade are copies of those carved by Pisano depicting the Creation of Man and the *attività umane* (arts and industries). Those on the second tier depict the planets, the cardinal virtues, the arts and the seven sacraments. The sculpted Prophets and Sibyls in the upper-storey niches are copies of works by Donatello and others.

✗ Take a Break

Take time out over a taste of Tuscan wine at stylish **Coquinarius** (www.coquin arius.com; Via delle Oche 11r; ⏱12.30-3pm & 6.30-10.30pm Wed-Mon).

SYLVAIN SONNET/GETTY IMAGES ©

Galleria dell'Accademia

A lengthy queue marks the door to the Galleria dell'Accademia, the late 18th-century gallery that's home to one of the Renaissance's most iconic masterpieces, Michelangelo's David.

Great For...

☑ Don't Miss

David – look for the two pale lines visible on his lower left arm where it was broken in 1527.

David

Fortunately, the world's most famous statue is worth the wait. Standing at over 5m tall and weighing in at 19 tonnes, *David* is a formidable sight. But it's not just its scale that impresses, it's also the subtle detail – the veins in his sinewy arms, the muscles in his legs, the change in expression as you move around him. Carved from a single block of marble, Michelangelo's most famous work was also his most challenging – he didn't choose the marble himself, it was veined, and its larger-than-life dimensions were already decided.

When the statue of the boy-warrior, depicted for the first time as a man in the prime of life rather than a young boy, assumed its pedestal in front of Palazzo Vecchio on Piazza della Signoria in 1504,

Michelangelo's *David*

MARVIN E. NEWMAN/GETTY IMAGES ©

ⓘ Need to Know

www.firenzemusei.it; Via Ricasoli 60; adult/reduced €8/4, incl temporary exhibition €12.50/6.25; ⊘8.15am-6.50pm Tue-Sun

✕ Take a Break

Grab a pizza slice at the much-loved **Pugi** (☑055 28 09 81; www.focacceria-pugi.it; Piazza San Marco 9b; per kg €15-24; ⊘7.45am-8pm Mon-Sat, closed 2 weeks mid-Aug), a stone's throw from the Galleria.

> ★ **Top Tip**
> Cut queuing time by booking tickets in advance at www.firenzemusei.it; the reservation fee is €4.

Florentines immediately adopted it as a powerful emblem of Florentine power, liberty and civic pride. It stayed in the piazza until 1873 when it was moved to its current purpose-built tribune in the Galleria.

Other Works

Michelangelo was also the master behind the unfinished *San Matteo* (St Matthew; 1504–08) and four *Prigioni* ('Prisoners' or 'Slaves'; 1521–30), also displayed in the gallery. The prisoners seem to be writhing and struggling to free themselves from the marble; they were meant for the tomb of Pope Julius II, itself never completed.

Adjacent rooms contain paintings by Andrea Orcagna, Taddeo Gaddi, Domenico Ghirlandaio, Filippino Lippi and Sandro Botticelli.

What's Nearby?

To the east of the Galleria, Giambologna's equestrian statue of Grand Duke Ferdinando I de' Medici lords it over **Piazza della Santissima Annunziata**, a majestic square dominated by the facades of the **Chiesa della Santissima Annunziata**, built in 1250, then rebuilt by Michelozzo et al in the mid-15th century, and the **Ospedale degli Innocenti** (Hospital of the Innocents), Europe's first orphanage founded in 1421. Look up to admire Brunelleschi's classically influenced portico, decorated by Andrea della Robbia (1435–1525) with terracotta medallions of babies in swaddling clothes.

About 200m southeast of the piazza is the **Museo Archeologico** (☑055 23 57; www.archeotoscana.beniculturali.it; Piazza della SS Annunziata 9b; adult/reduced €4/2; ⊘8.30am-7pm Tue-Fri, to 2pm Sat-Mon). Its rich collection of finds, including most of the Medici hoard of antiquities, plunges you deep into the past and offers an alternative to Renaissance splendour.

Galleria degli Uffizi

An art lover's paradise, the Galleria degli Uffizi houses the world's finest collection of Renaissance paintings, including masterpieces by Giotto, Botticelli, Michelangelo, da Vinci, Raphael, Titian and Caravaggio, in a magnificent 16th-century palazzo.

Great For...

☑ Don't Miss

The reverse side of *The Duke and Duchess of Urbino*, depicting the duke and duchess accompanied by the Virtues.

The gallery is undergoing a €65 million refurbishment (the Nuovi Uffizi project) that will eventually see the doubling of exhibition space. Work is pretty much complete on the permanent collection, which has grown over the years from 45 to 101 revamped rooms split across two floors; but there is much to be done still on areas earmarked for temporary exhibitions. Until the project is completed (date unknown) expect some halls to be closed and the contents of others changed.

Tuscan Masters: 13th to 14th Centuries

Starting in the Primo Corridoio (First Corridor) on the 2nd floor, Rooms 2 to 7 are dedicated to pre- and early Renaissance Tuscan art. Among the 13th-century Sienese works displayed in Room 2 are

JULIAN ELLIOTT PHOTOGRAPHY/GETTY IMAGES ©

ℹ Need to Know

Uffizi Gallery; ☏055 29 48 83; www.uffizi. beniculturali.it; Piazzale degli Uffizi 6; adult/ reduced €8/4, incl temporary exhibition €12.50/6.25; ⏲8.15am-6.50pm Tue-Sun

✖ Take a Break

To clear your head of art overload, stop by the gallery's rooftop cafe, for fresh air and fabulous views.

★ Top Tip

Save money and visit on the first Sunday of the month – admission is free.

three large altarpieces by Duccio di Buoninsegna, Cimabue and Giotto. These clearly reflect the transition from the Gothic to the nascent Renaissance style.

The highlight in Room 3 is Simone Martini's shimmering *Annunciazione* (1333), painted with Lippo Memmi and setting the Madonna in a sea of gold.

In Room 4 savour the realism of the *Lamentation over the Dead Christ* (1360–65) by gifted Giotto pupil, Giottino.

Renaissance Pioneers

Florence's victory over the Sienese at the Battle of San Romano, near Pisa, in 1432, is brought to life with outstanding realism and increased use of perspective in Paolo Uccello's magnificent *Battaglia di San Romano* (1435–40) in Room 8. In the same room, don't miss the exquisite *Madonna*

con bambino e due angeli (Madonna and Child with Two Angels; 1460–65) by Fra' Filippo Lippi.

In Room 9, Piero della Francesca's famous profile portraits (1465) of the crooked-nosed, red-robed duke and duchess of Urbino are wholly humanist in spirit: the former painted from the left side as he'd lost his right eye in a jousting accident, and the latter painted a deathly stone-white, reflecting the fact the portrait was painted posthumously.

In the same room, the seven cardinal and theological values of 15th-century Florence by brothers Antonio and Piero del Pollaiolo – commissioned for the merchant's tribunal in Piazza della Signoria – radiate energy. The only canvas in the theological and cardinal virtues series not to be painted by the Pollaiolos is *Fortitude* (1470), the first documented work by Botticelli.

Botticelli Room

The spectacular Sala del Botticelli, numbered as Rooms 10 to 14, is one of the

Uffizi's hot spots and is always packed. Of the 18 Botticelli works displayed in the Uffizi in all, the iconic *La nascita di Venere* (The Birth of Venus; c 1485), *Primavera* (Spring; c 1482) and *Madonna del Magnificat* (Madonna of the Magnificat; 1483) are the best known by the Renaissance master known for his ethereal figures. Take time to study the lesser-known *Annunciazione* (Annunciation), a 6m-wide fresco painted by Botticelli in 1481 for the San Martino hospital in Florence.

True aficionados rate his twin set of miniatures depicting a sword-bearing Judith returning from the camp of Holofernes and the discovery of the decapitated Holofernes in his tent (1495–1500) as being among his finest works.

La Tribuna

The Medici clan stashed away their most precious masterpieces in this octagonal-shaped treasure trove (Room 18). Perfectly restored to its original exquisite state, a small collection of classical statues and paintings adorn its crimson silk walls and 6000 mother-of-pearl shells painted with crimson varnish encrust the domed ceiling.

Elsewhere in Italy: 15th Century

In Rooms 19 to 23, the ornate vaulted ceilings – frescoed in the 16th and 17th centuries with military objects, allegories, battles and festivals held on piazzas in Florence – are as compelling as the art strung on the walls.

Sculptures in the Primo Corridoio (First Corridor; p426)

High Renaissance to Mannerism

Passing through the loggia or Secondo Corridoio (Second Corridor), visitors enjoy wonderful views of Florence before entering the Terzo Corridoio (Third Corridor).

Michelangelo dazzles with the *Doni Tondo,* a depiction of the Holy Family that steals the High Renaissance show in Room 35. The composition is unusual – Joseph holding an exuberant Jesus on his muscled mother's shoulder as she twists round to gaze at him, the colours as vibrant as when they were first applied in 1506–08.

★ **Did You Know**

The Uffizi Gallery presents works in chronological order, giving viewers the opportunity to see the whole panoply of Renaissance art in the manner it developed.

First-Floor Galleries

Head downstairs to the 1st-floor galleries where Rooms 46 to 55 display 16th- to 18th-century works by foreign artists, including Rembrandt (Room 49), and Rubens and Van Dyck (who share Room 55). In Room 66, Raphael's *Madonna del cardellino* (Madonna of the Goldfinch; 1505–06) steals the show

Room 65 is dedicated to Medici portrait artist, Agnolo Bronzino (1503–72), who worked at the court of Cosimo I from 1539 until 1555. His 1545 portraits of the Grand Duchess Eleonora of Toleto and her son Giovanni together, and the 18-month-old Giovanni alone holding a goldfinch – symbolising his calling into the church – are considered masterpieces of 16th-century European portraiture.

As part of the seemingly endless New Uffizi expansion project, four early Florentine works by Leonardo da Vinci are currently displayed in Room 79. His *Annunciazione* (Annunciation; 1472) was deliberately painted to be admired, not face on (from where Mary's arm appears too long, her face too light, the angle of buildings not quite right), but rather from the lower right-hand side of the painting.

Room 90, with its canary-yellow walls, features works by Caravaggio, deemed vulgar at the time for his direct interpretation of reality. *The Head of Medusa* (1598–99) is supposedly a self-portrait of the young artist who died at the age of 39. The biblical drama of an angel steadying the hand of Abraham as he holds a knife to his son Isaac's throat in Caravaggio's *Sacrifice of Isaac* (1601–02) is glorious in its intensity.

★ **Local Knowledge**

In 1966 flood waters threatened to destroy the Uffizi Gallery. Locals and tourists rushed to the gallery to help rescue the artworks, and these saviours became known as 'mud angels'.

Heart of the City

Every visitor to Florence spends time navigating the cobbled medieval lanes that run between Via de' Tornabuoni and Via del Proconsolo, but few explore them thoroughly.
Start Piazza della Repubblica
Distance 2km
Duration Two hours

4 Head past the market and along Via Porta Rossa to **Palazzo Davanzati** with its magnificent studded doors and fascinating museum.

FINISH **6**

6 Wander down the narrow **Via del Parione** to spy out old mansions and artisans workshops.

5 Hidden behind the unassuming facade of the **Chiesa di Santa Trinìta** are some of the city's finest 15th-century frescoes.

Via Parioncino
Via del Parione
Via de' Tornabuoni
Via Monalda

5 Piazza Santa Trinita

Lungarno Corsini

Piazza del Limbo

Classic Photo: The Arno river and Ponte Vecchio.

7 Finish with a sundowner and spectacular Ponte Vecchio views at **La Terrazza Lounge Bar** (p442).

0 — 100 m
0 — 0.05 miles

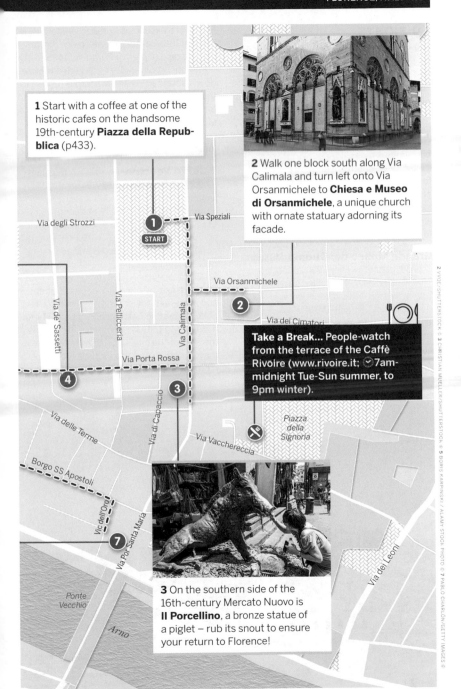

1 Start with a coffee at one of the historic cafes on the handsome 19th-century **Piazza della Repubblica** (p433).

2 Walk one block south along Via Calimala and turn left onto Via Orsanmichele to **Chiesa e Museo di Orsanmichele**, a unique church with ornate statuary adorning its facade.

Via degli Strozzi

Via Speziali

START

Via Orsanmichele

Via de' Sassetti

Via Pellicceria

Via Calimala

Via Porta Rossa

Via dei Cimatori

Take a Break... People-watch from the terrace of the Caffè Rivoire (www.rivoire.it; ⏱7am–midnight Tue-Sun summer, to 9pm winter).

Via delle Terme

Via di Capaccio

Via Vaccherreccia

Piazza della Signoria

Borgo SS Apostoli

Vic dell'Oro

Via Por Santa Maria

Ponte Vecchio

Arno

Via dei Leoni

3 On the southern side of the 16th-century Mercato Nuovo is **Il Porcellino**, a bronze statue of a piglet – rub its snout to ensure your return to Florence!

2 VVOE/SHUTTERSTOCK © 3 CHRISTIAN MUELLER/SHUTTERSTOCK © 5 BORIS KARPINSKY / ALAMY STOCK PHOTO © 7 PABLO CHARLON/GETTY IMAGES ©

◉ SIGHTS

Florence's wealth of museums and galleries house many of the world's most exquisite examples of Renaissance art, and its architecture is unrivalled. Yet don't feel pressured to see everything: combine your personal pick of sights with ample meandering through the city's warren of narrow streets broken by cafe and *enoteca* (wine bar) stops.

Churches enforce a strict dress code for visitors: no shorts, sleeveless shirts or plunging necklines. Photography with no flash is allowed in museums, but leave the selfie stick at home – they are officially forbidden.

Grande Museo del Duomo Museum

(Cathedral Museum; ☑055 230 28 85; www. ilgrandemuseodelduomo.it; Piazza del Duomo 9; adult/reduced incl cathedral bell tower, cupola, baptistry & crypt €15/3; ⊙9am-7.30pm) This awe-inspiring museum tells the magnificent story of how the Duomo and its cupola was built through art and short films. Among its many sacred and liturgical treasures is Lorenzo Ghiberti's original 15th-century masterpiece, *Porta del paradiso* (Gates of Paradise; 1425–52) – gloriously golden, 16m-tall gilded bronze doors designed for the eastern entrance to the Baptistry – as well as those he sculpted for the northern entrance (1403–24). Michelangelo's achingly beautiful *La pietà*, sculpted when he was almost 80 and intended for his own tomb, is also here.

Palazzo Vecchio Museum

(☑055 276 85 58, 055 27 68 22; www.muse-firenze.it; Piazza della Signoria; adult/reduced museum €10/8, tower €10/8, museum & tower €14/12, archaeological tour €4, combination ticket €18/16; ⊙museum 9am-11pm Fri-Wed, to 2pm Thu Apr-Sep, 9am-7pm Fri-Wed, to 2pm Thu Oct-Mar, tower 9am-9pm Fri-Wed, to 2pm Thu Apr-Sep, 10am-5pm Fri-Wed, to 2pm Thu Oct-Mar) This fortress palace, with its crenellations and 94m-high tower, was designed by Arnolfo di Cambio between 1298 and 1314 for the *signoria* (city government). It remains the seat of the city's power, home to the mayor's office and the municipal council. From the top of the **Torre d'Arnolfo** (tow-

Palazzo Vecchio

QQ7/SHUTTERSTOCK ©

er), you can revel in unforgettable rooftop views. Inside, Michelangelo's *Genio della vittoria* (Genius of Victory) sculpture graces the Salone dei Cinquecento, a magnificent painted hall created for the city's 15th-century ruling Consiglio dei Cinquecento (Council of 500).

Battistero di San Giovanni   Landmark

(Baptistry; ☎056 230 00 0? ᴜᴜᴜᴜ.ᴵgʳᴀ∩ᴅᴇᴍᴜ⁰ seodelduomo.it; Piazza di San Giovanni; adult/reduced incl baptistry, campanile, cupola, crypt & museum €15/3; ⊗8.15am-10.15am & 11.15am-7.30pm Mon-Fri, 8.15am-6.30pm Sat, 8.15am-1.30pm Sun) This 11th-century baptistry is a Romanesque, octagonal-striped structure of white-and-green marble with three sets of doors conceived as panels illustrating the story of humanity and the Redemption. Most celebrated are Lorenzo Ghiberti's gilded bronze doors at the eastern entrance, the *Porta del paradiso* (Gates of Paradise). What you see today are copies – the originals are in the Grande Museo del Duomo. Buy tickets online or at the ticket office at Piazza di San Giovanni 7, opposite the main baptistry entrance.

Piazza della Signoria   Piazza

Florentines flock to this square, the hub of local life since the 13th century, to meet friends and chat over early-evening *aperitivi* at historic cafes. Presiding over everything is Palazzo Vecchio (p432), Florence's city hall, and the 14th-century **Loggia dei Lanzi** `FREE`, an open-air gallery showcasing Renaissance sculptures, including Giambologna's *Rape of the Sabine Women* (c 1583), Benvenuto Cellini's bronze *Perseus* (1554) and Agnolo Gaddi's *Seven Virtues* (1384–89).

Piazza della Repubblica   Piazza

The site of a Roman forum and heart of medieval Florence, this busy civic space was created in the 1880s as part of a controversial plan of 'civic improvements' involving the demolition of the old market, Jewish ghetto and slums, and the relocation of nearly 6000 residents. Vasari's lovely *Log-

 Florence by Fiat

Hook up with Florence's **500 Touring Club** (☎346 8262324; www.500touringclub.com; Via Gherardo Silvani 149a) for a guided tour in a vintage motor – with you behind the wheel! Every car has a name in this outfit's fleet of gorgeous vintage Fiat 500s from the 1960s. Motoring tours are guided – hop in your car and follow the leader – and themed – families love the picnic trip, couples the wine tasting.

ALEXSTEPANOV/GETTY IMAGES ©

gia del Pesce (Fish Market) was saved and re-erected on Via Pietrapiana.

Museo delle Cappelle Medicee   Mausoleum

(Medici Chapels; www.firenzemusei.it; Piazza Madonna degli Aldobrandini 6; adult/reduced €8/4; ⊗8.15am-1.50pm, closed 1st, 3rd & 5th Mon, 2nd & 4th Sun of month) Nowhere is Medici conceit expressed so explicitly as in the Medici Chapels. Adorned with granite, marble, semi-precious stones and some of Michelangelo's most beautiful sculptures, it is the burial place of 49 dynasty members. Francesco I lies in the dark, imposing **Cappella dei Principi** (Princes' Chapel) alongside Ferdinando I and II and Cosimo I, II and III. Lorenzo il Magnifico is buried in the graceful **Sagrestia Nuova** (New Sacristy), which was Michelangelo's first architectural work.

Museo di San Marco   Museum

(☎055 238 86 08; Piazza San Marco 3; adult/reduced €4/2; ⊗8.15am-1.50pm Mon-Fri,

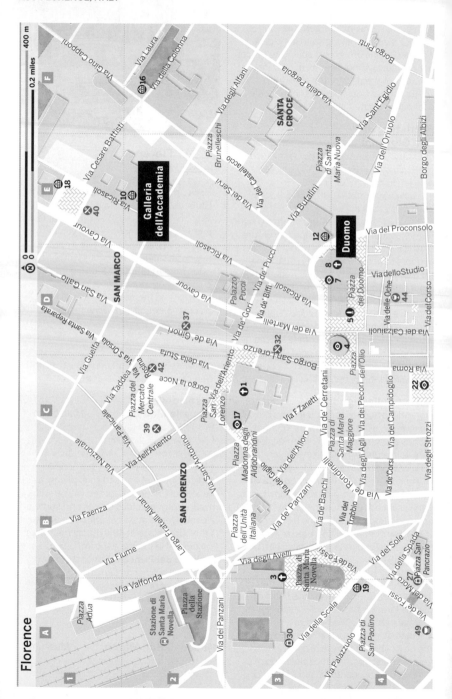

Florence

400 m

0.2 miles

Galleria dell'Accademia

Duomo

SAN MARCO

SAN LORENZO

SANTA CROCE

Via Gino Capponi
Via Laura
Via della Colonna
Via Cesare Battisti
Via Ricasoli
Via San Gallo
Via Santa Reparata
Via Guelfa
Via S. Orsola
Via della Stufa
Via de' Ginori
Via Cavour
Via Cavour
Via Panicale
Via Nazionale
Via Faenza
Via Fiume
Via Valfonda
Via del Panzani
Largo Fratelli Alinari
Via Sant'Antonino
Via dell'Ariento
Via Taddea
Via Rosina
Borgo la Noce
Borgo San Lorenzo
Via de' Martelli
Via de' Gori
Via de' Pucci
Via de' Biffi
Via Ricasoli
Via degli Alfani
Via della Pergola
Via dei Servi
Via del Castellaccio
Via Bufalini
Via Sant'Egidio
Via dell'Oriuolo
Borgo degli Albizi
Borgo Pinti
Via del Proconsolo
Via dello Studio
Via del Corso
Via dell'Oche
Via dei Calzaiuoli
Via Roma
Via de' Cerretani
Via de' Pecori
Via de' Tosinghi
Via degli Agli
Via de' Banchi
Via de' Rondinelli
Via del Trebbio
Via del Moro
Via de' Fossi
Via del Sole
Via della Spada
Via del Campidoglio
Via de' Corsi
Via degli Strozzi
Via del Giglio
Via dell'Alloro
Via de' Panzani
Via F Zanetti
Via dell'Ariento
Via Sant'Antonino

Piazza Adua
Stazione di Santa Maria Novella
Piazza della Stazione
Piazza dell'Unità Italiana
Piazza di Santa Maria Novella
Piazza di San Paolino
Piazza San Pancrazio
Piazza Madonna degli Aldobrandini
Piazza San Lorenzo
Piazza del Mercato Centrale
Palazzo Pucci
Palazzo della
Piazza di Santa Maria Maggiore
Piazza dell'Olio
Piazza del Duomo
Piazza di Santa Maria Nuova
Piazza Brunelleschi
Piazza della Scala
Via Palazzuolo
Via delle Scala

16
18
40
10
12
8
7
5
4
1
17
37
32
42
39
22
44
3
30
19
27
49

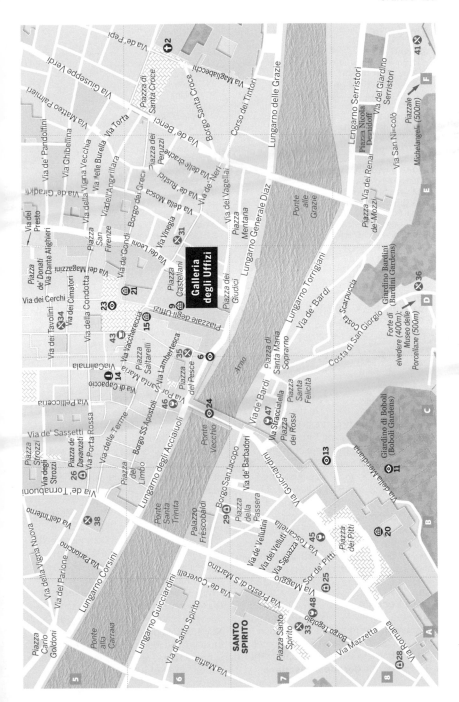

Galleria
degli Uffizi

Florence

⊙ **Sights**
1 Basilica di San Lorenzo..............................C3
2 Basilica di Santa Croce............................F6
3 Basilica di Santa Maria
   Novella...B3
4 Battistero di San Giovanni.......................D4
5 Campanile..D4
6 Corridoio Vasariano C6
7 Cupola del Brunelleschi...........................D3
8 Duomo..D4
9 Galleria degli Uffizi....................................D6
10 Galleria dell'Accademia E2
11 Giardino di Boboli B8
12 Grande Museo del Duomo........................E3
13 Grotta del Buontalenti..............................C7
14 Il Porcellino...C5
15 Loggia dei Lanzi D6
16 Museo Archeologico..................................F2
17 Museo delle Cappelle
   Medicee..C3
18 Museo di San Marco.................................. E1
19 Museo Novecento.......................................A4
20 Palazzo Pitti... B8
21 Palazzo Vecchio...D6
22 Piazza della Repubblica C4
23 Piazza della Signoria.................................D5
24 Ponte Vecchio C6

⊚ **Shopping**
25 &Co..A7

26 Il Papiro..B5
27 La Bottega Della Frutta A4
28 Lorenzo Perrone A8
29 Obsequium..B6
30 Officina Profumo-
   Farmaceutica di Santa
   Maria Novella.. A3

⊗ **Eating**
31 All'Antico Vinaio E6
32 Dal Barone...D3
33 Gustapanino.. A7
34 I Due Fratellini..D5
35 'Ino..D6
36 La Leggenda dei Frati D8
37 La Ménagère D2
38 Mariano..B5
39 Mercato Centrale C2
40 Pugi... E1
41 San Niccolò 39..F8
42 Trattoria Mario C2

⊙ **Drinking & Nightlife**
43 Caffè Rivoire D5
44 Coquinarius...D4
45 Enoteca Pitti Gola e Cantina.................. B7
46 La Terrazza Lounge Bar............................C6
47 Le Volpi e l'Uva C7
48 Rasputin...A7
49 Todo Modo..A4

8.15am-4.50pm Sat & Sun, closed 1st, 3rd & 5th Sun, 2nd & 4th Mon of month) At the heart of Florence's university area sits **Chiesa di San Marco** and adjoining 15th-century Dominican monastery where both gifted painter Fra' Angelico (c 1395–1455) and the sharp-tongued Savonarola piously served God. Today the monastery, aka one of Florence's most spiritually uplifting museums, showcases the work of Fra' Angelico. After centuries of being known as 'Il Beato Angelico' (literally 'The Blessed Angelic One') or simply 'Il Beato' (The Blessed), the Renaissance's most blessed religious painter was made a saint by Pope John Paul II in 1984.

Ponte Vecchio   Bridge
Dating to 1345, Ponte Vecchio was the only Florentine bridge to survive destruction at the hands of retreating German forces in 1944. Above the jewellers' shops on the eastern side, the **Corridoio Vasariano**

(Vasarian Corridor; ⊙by guided tour; 🚍B) is a 16th-century passageway between the Uffizi and Palazzo Pitti that runs around, rather than through, the medieval **Torre dei Mannelli** at the bridge's southern end. The first documentation of a stone bridge here, at the narrowest crossing point along the entire length of the Arno, dates from 972.

Palazzo Pitti   Museum
(www.uffizi.beniculturali.it; Piazza dei Pitti; ⊙8.15am-6.50pm Tue-Sun) Commissioned by banker Luca Pitta and designed by Brunelleschi in 1457, this vast Renaissance palace was later bought by the Medici family. Over the centuries, it served as the residence of the city's rulers until the Savoys donated it to the state in 1919. Nowadays it houses an impressive silver museum, a couple of art museums and a series of rooms recreating life in the palace during House of Savoy times.

Giardino di Boboli   Gardens

(☑055 29 48 83; www.polomuseale.firenze.it;
Palazzo Pitti, Piazza dei Pitti; adult/reduced incl
Tesoro del Granduchi, Museo delle Porcellane
& Museo della Moda e del Costume €7/3.50,
during temporary exhibition €10/5; ☺8.15am-
7.30pm summer, reduced hours winter, closed
1st & last Mon of month) Behind Palazzo Pitti,
the Boboli Gardens were laid out in the
mid-16th century to a design by architect
Niccolò Pericoli. At the upper, southern
limit, beyond the box-hedged rose garden
and **Museo delle Porcellane** (Porcelain
Museum), beautiful views over the Florentine
countryside unfold. Within the lower reaches of the gardens, don't miss the fantastical
shell- and gem-encrusted **Grotta del
Buontalenti**, a decorative grotto built by
Bernardo Buontalenti between 1583 and
1593 for Francesco I de' Medici.

Basilica di San Lorenzo   Basilica

(www.operamedicealaurenziana.org; Piazza San
Lorenzo; €6, with Biblioteca Medicea Laurenziana
€8.50; ☺10am-5pm Mon-Sat, plus 1.30-5pm
Sun Mar-Oct) Considered one of Florence's
most harmonious examples of Renaissance
architecture, this unfinished basilica was
the Medici parish church and mausoleum.
It was designed by Brunelleschi in 1425 for
Cosimo the Elder and built over an earlier
4th-century church. In the solemn interior,
look for Brunelleschi's austerely beautiful
Sagrestia Vecchia (Old Sacristy) with its
sculptural decoration by Donatello. Michelangelo was commissioned to design the
facade in 1518, but his design in white Carrara marble was never executed, hence the
building's rough unfinished appearance.

Basilica di Santa Maria Novella   Church

(☑055 21 92 57; www.smn.it; Piazza di Santa
Maria Novella 18; adult/reduced €5/3.50;
☺9am-7pm Mon-Thu, 11am-7pm Fri, 9am-6.30pm
Sat, noon-6.30pm Sun summer, shorter hours
winter) The striking green-and-white marble
facade of 13th- to 15th-century Basilica
di Santa Maria Novella fronts an entire
monastical complex, comprising romantic
church cloisters and a frescoed chapel. The
basilica itself is a treasure chest of artistic
masterpieces, climaxing with frescoes by
Domenico Ghirlandaio. The lower section
of the basilica's striped marbled facade is
transitional from Romanesque to Gothic;
the upper section and the main doorway
(1456–70) were designed by Leon Battista
Alberti. Book tickets in advance online to
cut queuing time.

Museo Novecento   Museum

(Museum of the 20th Century; ☑055 28 61 32;
www.museonovecento.it; Piazza di Santa Maria
Novella 10; adult/reduced €8.50/4; ☺9am-7pm
Mon-Wed, Sat & Sun, to 2pm Thu, to 11pm Fri
summer, 9am-6pm Fri-Wed, to 2pm Thu winter)
Don't allow the Renaissance to distract
from Florence's fantastic modern art museum, in a 13th-century *palazzo* previously
used as a pilgrim shelter, hospital and
school. A well-articulated itinerary guides
visitors through modern Italian painting
and sculpture from the early 20th century
to the late 1980s. Installation art makes
effective use of the outside space on the
1st-floor loggia. Fashion and theatre get a
nod on the 2nd floor, and the itinerary ends
with a 20-minute cinematic montage of the
best films set in Florence.

Basilica di Santa Croce   Church, Museum

(☑055 246 61 05; www.santacroceopera.it; Piazza
di Santa Croce; adult/reduced €8/4; ☺9.30am-
5.30pm Mon-Sat, 2-5.30pm Sun) The austere
interior of this Franciscan basilica is a shock
after the magnificent neo-Gothic facade
enlivened by varying shades of coloured
marble. Most visitors come to see the tombs
of Michelangelo, Galileo and Ghiberti inside
this church, but frescoes by Giotto in the
chapels right of the altar are the real highlights. The basilica was designed by Arnolfo
di Cambio between 1294 and 1385 and
owes its name to a splinter of the Holy Cross
donated by King Louis of France in 1258.

Piazzale Michelangelo   Viewpoint

(☐13) Turn your back on the bevy of
ticky-tacky souvenir stalls flogging *David*
statues and boxer shorts and take in the

 Florence's Best Panini

Semel (Piazza Ghiberti 44r; panini €3.50-5; ⊙11.30am-3pm Mon-Sat) Irresistibly creative sandwiches to go in Sant'Ambrogio.

'Ino (✐055 21 45 14; www.inofirenze. com; Via dei Georgofili 3r-7r; bruschette/panini €6/8; ⊙noon-4.30pm) 🍴 Made-to-measure, gourmet *panini* by the Galleria degli Uffizi.

Mariano (✐055 21 40 67; Via del Parione 19r; panini €3.50; ⊙8am-3pm & 5-7.30pm Mon-Fri, 8am-3pm Sat) Local neighbourhood cafe serving super-fresh *panini* to boot.

Gustapanino (www.facebook.com/pages/Gustapanino; Piazza Santa Spirito; focacce from €3.50; ⊙11am-8pm Mon-Sat, noon-5pm Sun) Hole-in-the-wall *enopaninoteca* (wine and sandwich stop) in Santa Croce.

Dal Barone (✐366 1479432; https://dalbarone.jimdo.com; Borgo San Lorenzo 30; sandwiches €5-10; ⊙11am-8pm) Hot and gooey *panini* to go by San Lorenzo market.

I Due Fratellini (✐055 239 60 96; www. iduefratellini.com; Via dei Cimatori 38r; panini €4; ⊙10am-7pm) Memorable vintage kid on the block, around since 1875.

spectacular city panorama from this vast square, pierced by one of Florence's two *David* copies. Sunset here is particularly dramatic. It's a 10-minute uphill walk along the serpentine road, paths and steps that scale the hillside from the Arno and Piazza Giuseppe Poggi; from Piazza San Niccolò walk uphill and bear left up the long flight of steps signposted Viale Michelangelo. Or take bus 13 from Stazione di Santa Maria Novella.

🛍 SHOPPING

Officina Profumo-Farmaceutica di Santa Maria Novella
Beauty, Gifts

(✐055 21 62 76; www.smnovella.it; Via della Scala 16; ⊙9.30am-8pm) In business since 1612, this exquisite perfumery-pharmacy began life when Santa Maria Novella's Dominican friars began to concoct cures and sweet-smelling unguents using medicinal herbs cultivated in the monastery garden. The shop, with interior from 1848, sells fragrances, skincare products, ancient herbal remedies and preparations for everything from relief of heavy legs to improving skin elasticity, memory and mental energy

It also sells teas, herbal infusions, liqueurs and scented candles. A real treasure, the shop has touchscreen catalogues and a state-of-the-art payment system, yet still manages to ooze vintage charm. After a day battling crowds at the Uffizi or Accademia, you might just want to come here for a cup of carefully prepared tea in its **Tisaneria** (Tearoom) or to buy a bottle of Aqua di Santa Maria Novella, one of the pharmacy's oldest herbal concoctions, taken to cure hysterics since 1614.

La Bottega Della Frutta
Food & Drinks

(✐055 239 85 90; Via dei Federighi 31r; ⊙8.30am-7.30pm Mon-Sat, closed Aug) Follow the trail of knowing Florentines, past the flower- and veg-laden bicycle parked outside, into this enticing food shop bursting with boutique cheeses, organic fruit and veg, biscuits, chocolates, conserved produce, excellent-value wine et al. Mozzarella oozing raw milk arrives fresh from Eboli in Sicily every Tuesday, and if you're looking to buy olive oil, this is the place to taste. Simply ask Elisabeta or husband Francesco.

Piazza Santa Trinita

&Co   Arts & Crafts
(And Company; ☑055 21 99 73; www.andcom-
panyshop.com; Via Maggio 51r; ☉10.30am-1pm
& 3-7pm Mon-Sat) Souvenir shopping at
its best! This Pandora's box of beautiful
objects is the love child of Florence-born,
British-raised callligrapher and graphic
designer Betty Soldi and her vintage-
loving husband, Matteo Perduca. Their
extraordinary boutique showcases Betty's
customised cards, decorative paper products, upcycled homewares and custom
fragrances alongside work by other designers (including super-chic leather-printed
accessories by Danish design company
Edition Poshette).

Obsequium   Wine
(☑055 21 68 49; www.obsequium.it; Borgo San
Jacopo 17/39; ☉10am-10pm Mon, to 9pm Tue &
Wed, to midnight Thu-Sat, noon-midnight Sun)
Tuscan wines, wine accessories and gourmet foods, including truffles, in one of the
city's finest wine shops – on the ground
floor of one of Florence's best-preserved
medieval towers to boot. Not sure which
wine to buy? Linger over a glass or indulge
in a three-wine tasting with (€20 to €40)
or without (€15 to €30) an accompanying *taglieri* (board) of mixed cheese and
salami.

Lorenzo Perrone   Art
(☑340 274402; www.libribianchi.info; Borgo
Tegolaio 59r; ☉hours vary) Every book tells a
different story in this absolutely fascinating artist's workshop, home to Milan-born
Lorenzo Perrone who creates snow-white
Libri bianchi (White Books) – aka sublime
book sculptures – out of plaster, glue,
acrylic and various upcycled objects. His
working hours are somewhat predictably
erratic; call ahead.

Il Papiro   Gifts & Souvenirs
(☑055 21 65 93; http://ilpapirofirenze.eu/
en/; Via Porta Rosso 76; ☉10am-7pm) One of
several branches around town, this elegant
boutique specialises in books, journals,
writing paper, cards and other stationery
made from Florence's signature, hand-
decorated marbled paper.

A terrace cafe

🍴 EATING

Mercato Centrale   Food Hall €

(📞055 239 97 98; www.mercatocentrale.it; Piazza del Mercato Centrale 4; dishes €7-15; 🕙10am-midnight; 🛜) Meander the maze of stalls rammed with fresh produce at Florence's oldest and largest food market, on the ground floor of a fantastic iron-and-glass structure designed by architect Giuseppe Mengoni in 1874. Head to the 1st floor's buzzing, thoroughly contemporary food hall with dedicated bookshop, cookery school and artisan stalls cooking steaks, burgers, tripe *panini,* vegetarian dishes, pizza, gelato, pastries and pasta.

Load up and find a free table.

Trattoria Mario   Tuscan €

(📞055 21 85 50; www.trattoria-mario.com; Via Rosina 2; meals €25; 🕙noon-3.30pm Mon-Sat, closed 3 weeks Aug; ❄) Arrive by noon to ensure a stool around a shared table at this noisy, busy, brilliant trattoria – a legend that retains its soul (and allure with locals) despite being in every guidebook. Charming Fabio, whose grandfather opened the

place in 1953, is front of house while big brother Romeo and nephew Francesco cook with speed in the kitchen. No advance reservations; no credit cards.

All'Antico Vinaio   Osteria €

(📞055 238 27 23; www.allanticovinaio.com; Via de' Neri 65r; tasting platters €10-30; 🕙10am-4pm & 6-11pm Tue-Sat, noon-3.30pm Sun) The crowd spills out the door of this noisy Florentine thoroughbred. Push your way to the tables at the back to taste cheese and salami in situ (advance reservations recommended). Or join the queue at the deli counter for a well-stuffed foccacia wrapped in waxed paper to take away – quality is outstanding. Pour yourself a glass of wine while you wait.

Il Teatro del Sale   Tuscan €€

(📞055 200 14 92; www.teatrodelsale.com; Via dei Macci 111r; lunch/dinner/weekend brunch €15/35/20; 🕙11am-3pm & 7.30-11pm Tue-Sat, 11am-3pm Sun, closed Aug) Florentine chef Fabio Picchi is one of Florence's living treasures who steals the Sant' Ambrogio show with this eccentric, good-value members-only club (everyone welcome; membership €7) inside an old theatre. He cooks up weekend brunch, lunch and dinner, culminating at 9.30pm in a live performance of drama, music or comedy arranged by his wife, artistic director and comic actress Maria Cassi.

Dinners are hectic: grab a chair, serve yourself water, wine and antipasti and wait for the chef to yell out what's about to be served before queuing at the glass hatch for your *primo* (first course) and *secondo* (second course).

San Niccolò 39   Seafood €€

(☑055 200 13 97; www.sanniccolo39.com; Via di San Niccolò 39; meals €40; ⓘ7-10.30pm Tue, 12.30-2.30pm & 7-10.30pm Wed-Sat; 🗟) With street terrace in front and hidden summer garden out the back, this contemporary address in quaint San Niccolò is a gem. Fish – both raw and cooked – is the house speciality, with chef Vanni cooking up a storm with his creative salted-cod burgers, swordfish steak with radicchio, and famous linguine with squid ink and Cetara anchovy oil.

Essenziale   Tuscan €€

(☑055.247 69 56; http://essenziale.me; Piazza di Cestello 3r; 3-/5-/7-course tasting menu €35/55/75, brunch €28; ⓘ7-10pm Tue-Sat, 11am-4pm Sun; 🗟) There's no finer showcase for modern Tuscan cuisine than this loft-style restaurant in a 19th-century warehouse. Preparing dishes at the kitchen bar, in rolled-up shirt sleeves and navy butcher's apron, is dazzling young chef Simone Cipriani. Order one of his tasting menus to sample the full range of his inventive, thoroughly modern cuisine inspired by classic Tuscan dishes.

La Ménagère   International €€

(☑055 075 06 00; www.lamenagere.it; Via de' Ginori 8r; meals €15-70; ⓘ7am-2am; 🗟) Be it breakfast, lunch, dinner, good coffee or cocktails after dark, this bright industrial-styled space lures Florence's hip brigade. A concept store, the Housewife is a fashionable one-stop shop for chic china and tableware, designer kitchen gear and fresh flowers. For daytime dining and drinking,

🍷 Aperitivo Time

No ritual is more sacrosanct than *aperitivo* or 'Happy Hour' as many bars call it in English when friends gather for pre-dinner drinks accompanied by gourmet tapas or a banquet of savoury snacks. Be it a perfectly mixed cocktail at **Mad Souls & Spirits** (☑055 627 16 21; www.facebook.com/madsoulsandspirits; Borgo San Frediano 38r; ⓘ6pm-2am Thu-Sun, to midnight Mon & Wed; 🗟), or a glass of Tuscan wine paired with cured meats at **Enoteca Pitti Gola e Cantina** (p442) or **Le Volpi e l'Uva** (p442), *aperitivo* is a cherished Florentine tradition that should be embraced with gusto when in town.

Aperol spritz
DALLAS STRIBLEY/GETTY IMAGES ©

pick from retro sofas in the boutique area, or banquet seating and bar stools in the jam-packed bistro.

La Leggenda dei Frati   Tuscan €€€

(☑055 068 05 45; www.laleggendadeifrati.it; Villa Bardini, Costa di San Giorgio 6a; menus €60 & €75, meals €70; ⓘ12.30-2pm & 7.30-10pm Tue-Sun; 🗟) Summertime's hottest address. At home in the grounds of historic Villa Bardini, Michelin-starred Legend of Friars enjoys the most romantic terrace with view in Florence. Veggies are plucked fresh from the vegetable patch, tucked between waterfalls and ornamental beds in Giardino Bardini, and contemporary art jazzes up the classically chic interior. Cuisine is Tuscan, gastronomic and well worth the vital advance reservation.

Florence Online

The Florentine (www.theflorentine.net) English-language newspaper.

Girl in Florence (www.girlinflorence. com) Inside musings, practical tips and smart drinking and dining recommendations from an American gal called Georgette, at home in Florence.

Lost in Florence (www.lostinflorence. it) Great for 'hipster chic' boutique openings in the city.

Art Trav (www.arttrav.com) Florence-based art historian's museum and sightseeing recommendations.

Emiko Davies (www.emikodavies.com) Exceptional, Florence-based food blogger, cookbook writer and photographer; author of *Florentine: Food and Stories from the Renaissance City* (2016).

🍸 DRINKING & NIGHTLIFE

Le Volpi e l'Uva   Wine Bar

(055 239 81 32; www.levolpieluva.com; Piazza dei Rossi 1; 11am-9pm Mon-Sat) This unassuming wine bar hidden away by Chiesa di Santa Felicità remains as appealing as the day it opened over a decade ago. Its food and wine pairings are first class – taste and buy boutique wines by small producers from all over Italy, matched perfectly with cheeses, cold meats and the best crostini in town. Wine-tasting classes too.

Rasputin   Cocktail Bar

(055 28 03 99; www.facebook.com/rasputin firenze; Borgo Tegolaio 21r; 8pm-2am) The 'secret' speakeasy everyone knows about. It has no sign outside and is disguised as a chapel of sorts; look for the tiny entrance with two-seat wooden pew, crucifix on the wall, vintage pics and tea lights flickering in the doorway. Inside, it's back to the 1930s with period furnishings, an exclusive vibe and barmen mixing prohibition-era cocktails. Reservations (phone or Facebook page) recommended.

Todo Modo   Cafe

(055 239 91 10; www.todomodo.org; Via dei Fossi 15r; 10am-8pm Tue-Sun) This contemporary bookshop with hip cafe and pocket theatre at the back makes a refreshing change from the usual offerings. A salvaged mix of vintage tables and chairs sits between book- and bottle-lined shelves in the relaxed cafe, actually called 'UqBar' after the fictional place of the same name in a short story by Argentinian writer Jorges Luis Borges.

Its weekend lunches are particularly popular: think healthy salads, a couple of homemade mains chalked on the board, and delicious muffins and cakes.

La Terrazza Lounge Bar   Bar

(055 272 659 87; www.lungarnocollection. com; Vicolo dell' Oro 6r; 2.30-11.30pm Apr-Sep) This rooftop bar with wooden-decking terrace accessible from the 5th floor of the 1950s-styled, design Hotel Continentale is as chic as one would expect of a fashion-house hotel. Its *aperitivo* buffet is a modest affair, but who cares with that fabulous, drop-dead-gorgeous panorama of one of Europe's most beautiful cities. Dress the part or feel out of place. Count on €19 for a cocktail.

Santarosa Bistrot   Bar

(055 230 90 57; www.facebook.com/santa rosa.bistrot; Lungarno di Santarosa; 8am-midnight;) The living is easy at this hipster garden bistro-bar, snug against a chunk of ancient city wall in the flowery Santarosa gardens. Comfy cushioned sofas built from recycled wooden crates sit beneath trees al fresco; the food is superb (meals €30); and mixologists behind the bar complement an excellent wine list curated by **Enoteca Pitti Gola e Cantina** (055 21 27 04; www.pittigo-laecantina.com; Piazza dei Pitti 16; 1pm-midnight Wed-Mon) with serious craft cocktails.

ℹ️ INFORMATION

There are several places in the city to get information, including the following:

Airport tourist office (055 31 58 74; www. firenzeturismo.it; Florence Airport, Via del Termine 11; 9am-7pm Mon-Sat, to 2pm Sun)

GIORGIO COSULICH/GETTY IMAGES ©

Wine bar

Central tourist office (055 29 08 32; www.
firenzeturismo.it; Via Cavour 1r; ⊗9am-1pm
Mon-Fri)

Infopoint Bigallo (☑055 28 84 96; www.firen-
zeturismo.it; Piazza San Giovanni 1; ⊗9am-7pm
Mon-Sat, to 2pm Sun)

Infopoint Stazione (☑055 21 22 45; www.
firenzeturismo.it; Piazza della Stazione 4; ⊗9am-
6.30pm Mon-Sat, to 1.30pm Sun)

🛈 GETTING THERE & AWAY

Most people arrive one of two ways: by air from
international airports in Florence and Pisa, or by
train to Stazione Campo di Marte or **Stazione
di Santa Maria Novella** (Piazza della Stazione),
both in central Florence. Florence is on the
Rome–Milan train line.

🛈 GETTING AROUND

Florence itself is small and best navigated on
foot; most major sights are within easy walking
distance.

Bicycle Rent city bikes from in front of Stazione
di Santa Maria Novella and elsewhere in the city.

Car & Motorcycle Nonresident traffic is banned
from the historic centre; parking is an absolute
headache and best avoided.

Public Transport There's an efficient network of
buses and trams, most handy for visiting Fiesole
and getting up the hill to Piazzale Michelangelo.

Taxi Cabs can't be hailed on the street; find
ranks at the train and bus stations or call ☑055
42 42 or ☑055 43 90.

In This Chapter

Towers of San Gimignano 446
Leaning Tower of Pisa 448
Siena 452
Arezzo 455
Montepulciano 458
Montalcino 460

Tuscany, Italy

With its lyrical landscapes, superlative art and superb cucina contadina *(food from the farmer's kitchen), Tuscany offers a splendid array of treats for travellers. No land is more caught up with the fruits of its fertile earth than Tuscany, a gourmet destination where locality, seasonality and sustainability are revered. And oh, the art! During the medieval and Renaissance periods, Tuscany's painters, sculptors and architects created world-class masterpieces. Squirrelled away and safeguarded today in churches, museums and galleries all over the region, Tuscan art is truly unmatched.*

Tuscany in Two Days

Base yourself in **Siena** (p452), and spend your first day exploring this charming town, including a visit to the Duomo and the Museo Civico. On day two, head northwest to San Gimignano's famed **towers** (p446), or east to **Arezzo** (p455) for churches, museums and, if the timing is right, antiques.

Tuscany in Four Days

With an additional two days, head southwest to **Montepulciano** and **Montalcino** on day three, and over to Pisa and its famous **tower** (p448) on day four. Or, for a little luxury, spend some time in a local **spa** (p457).

After leaving Tuscany, Rome (p352) and Venice (p400) are ideal next stops.

Parco Regionale delle Alpi Apuane

Pistoia
Prato
Viareggio
Lucca
Leaning Tower of Pisa
Pisa
Pontedera

Florence

EMILIA-ROMAGNA

0 — 40 km
0 — 20 miles

Chianti

San Gimignano
Towers of San Gimignano
Poggibonsi
Montevarchi
Arezzo

Livorno

Volterra
TUSCANY

Cecina
Siena

Riserva Naturale Alto Merse

MEDITERRANEAN SEA

Massa Marittima
Montalcino
Pienza
Val D'Orcia
Montepulciano

UMBRIA

Siena Map (p453)

Arriving in Tuscany

Pisa International Airport Tuscany's principal international gateway; from here, buses run to Pisa, Florence and Siena.

Florence Airport This smaller airport serves flights from Italian and European destinations.

Stazione di Santa Maria Novella Florence's station is the region's biggest and busiest; it's served by regular fast trains on the main Rome–Milan line.

Where to Stay

An *agriturismo* (rural accommodation on a working farm, winery or agricultural domain) is an idyllic five-star way of experiencing country life in Tuscany. It's perfect for those with a car, and usually highly practical for those travelling with children. Tuscany also abounds in *palazzo* hotels: these historic 'palace' hotels, designer in vibe, are the boutique option for those in towns and cities with a midrange to top-end budget.

Towers of San Gimignano

A mecca for day trippers, San Gimignano lies deep in the Tuscan countryside northwest of Siena. Known as the 'medieval Manhattan', it features 15 11th-century towers that soar above its hilltop centro storico (historic centre).

Great For...

☑ Don't Miss

The town's **Galleria Continua** (☎0577 94 31 34; www.galleriacontinua.com; Via del Castello 11; ☺10am-1pm & 2-7pm) **FREE**.

Originally an Etruscan village, the town was named after the bishop of Modena, San Gimignano, who is said to have saved it from Attila the Hun. It became a *comune* in 1199 and quickly flourished, thanks in no small part to its position on the Via Francigena. Up to 72 towers were built as the town's prosperous burghers sought to outdo their neighbours and flaunt their wealth.

Collegiata

San Gimignano's Romanesque cathedral, the **Collegiata** (Duomo; Basilica di Santa Maria Assunta; ☎0577 94 01 52; www.duomosangimignano.it; Piazza del Duomo; adult/reduced €4/2; ☺10am-7pm Mon-Sat, to 4.30pm winter), is named after the college of priests who originally managed it. Parts of the building

CANADASTOCK/SHUTTERSTOCK ©

❶ Need to Know

Frequent buses run to/from Florence
(€6.80, 1¼ to two hours) and Siena (€6,
one to 1½ hours).

✖ Take a Break

Stop by for some earthy local fare at
Locanda Sant'Agostino (📞0577 94 31
41; Piazza Sant'Agost; m meals €33, pizzas
€8-10; ⊙noon-3pm & 7-10pm Thu-Tue).

★ Top Tip

San Gimignano's helpful tourist office
(📞0577 94 00 08; www.sangimignano.com;
Piazza del Duomo 1; ⊙10am-1pm & 3-7pm
summer, 10am-1pm & 2-6pm winter) **organises a range of English-language tours.**

Palazzo Comunale

The 12th-century **Palazzo Comunale**
(📞0577 99 03 12; www.sangimignanomusei.it;
Piazza del Duomo 2; combined Civic Museums
ticket adult/reduced €9/7; ⊙10am-7.30pm
summer, 11am-5.30pm winter) has always been
the centre of local government – its Sala di
Dante is where the great poet addressed
the town's council in 1299, urging it to
support the Guelph cause. The room (also
known as the Sala del Consiglio) is home to
Lippo Memmi's early 14th-century *Maestà*,
which portrays the enthroned Virgin and
Child surrounded by angels, saints and
local dignitaries.

Upstairs, the pinacoteca has a charming
collection of paintings from the Sienese
and Florentine schools of the 12th to 15th
centuries.

In the Camera del Podestà is a meticulously restored cycle of frescoes by
Memmo di Filippuccio, illustrating a moral
history – the rewards of marriage are
shown in the scenes of a husband and wife
naked in a bath and in bed.

After you've enjoyed the art, be sure
to climb the 218 steps of the palazzo's
54m-tall Torre Grossa for spectacular views
of the town and surrounding countryside.

were built in the second half of the 11th
century, but its remarkably vivid frescoes
date from the 14th century.

Entry is via the side stairs and through
a loggia that originally functioned as the
baptistry. Once in the main space, face
the altar and look to your left (north). On
the wall are scenes from Genesis and the
Old Testament by Bartolo di Fredi, dating
from around 1367. On the right (south)
wall are scenes from the New Testament
by the workshop of Simone Martini, which
were completed in 1336. On the inside
of the front facade is Taddeo di Bartolo's
striking depiction of the *Last Judgment* –
on the upper-left side is a fresco depicting
Paradiso (Heaven) and on the upper-right
Inferno (Hell).

Leaning Tower of Pisa

One of Italy's signature sights, Pisa's stunning Torre Pendente (Leaning Tower) truly lives up to its name, leaning a startling 3.9 degrees off the vertical. Visit Pisa as a day trip from Florence or one of the charming Tuscan towns further south.

Great For...

☑ Don't Miss

Planning an enchanting after-dark visit: if you're in Pisa from mid-June to late August, doors don't close till 10pm.

The 56m-high tower, officially the Duomo's *campanile* (bell tower), took almost 200 years to build, but was already listing when it was unveiled in 1372. Over time, the tilt, caused by a layer of weak subsoil, steadily worsened until it was finally halted by a major stabilisation project in the 1990s.

Planning Your Visit

Access to the Leaning Tower is limited to 40 people at a time – children under eight are not allowed in and those aged eight to 10 years must hold an adult's hand.

Visits last 35 minutes and involve a steep climb up 251 occasionally slippery steps. All bags, handbags included, must be deposited at the free left-luggage desk next to the central ticket office – cameras are about the only thing you can take up.

The Duomo and the Leaning Tower

JAVEN/SHUTTERSTOCK ©

Need to Know

Torre Pendente; 📞050 83 50 11; www.opa-pisa.it; Piazza dei Miracoli; €18; ⊗8am-8pm Apr-Sep, 9am-7pm Oct, to 6pm Mar, 10am-5pm Nov-Feb

✕ Take a Break

Grab a huge gourmet *panino* from **L'Ostellino** (Piazza Cavallotti 1; panini €3.50-7; ⊗noon-4.30pm Mon-Fri, to 6pm Sat & Sun) for a picnic beside the tower.

> ### ★ Top Tip
> With two million visitors every year, crowds are the norm. Visit between November and March for shorter queues.

Tower & Combo Tickets

To guarantee your visit and cut the long high-season queue, buy tickets in advance online (maximum 20 days before visiting), or go straight to a ticket office when you arrive in Pisa to book a slot for later in the day.

Buy tickets from the main **ticket office** (⊗8.30am-7.30pm summer, to 5.30pm winter) behind the tower or the smaller office inside Museo delle Sinopie (on Piazza dei Miracoli). Ticket offices in Pisa also sell combination tickets for other city sights.

What's Nearby?

Pisa's medieval heart lies north of the water; from **Piazza Cairoli**, with its evening bevy of bars and gelato shops, meander along **Via Cavour**. A daily fresh-produce market fills **Piazza delle Vettovaglie**.

Duomo   Cathedral

(Duomo di Santa Maria Assunta; 📞050 83 50 11; www.opapisa.it; Piazza dei Miracoli; ⊗10am-8pm Apr-Sep, to 7pm Oct, to 6pm Nov-Mar) FREE The Romanesque Duomo was begun in 1064 and consecrated in 1118. Admission is free, but you'll need an entrance coupon from the ticket office or a ticket from one of the other Piazza dei Miracoli sights.

Battistero   Christian Site

(Battistero di San Giovanni; 📞050 83 50 11; www.opapisa.it; Piazza dei Miracoli; €5, combination ticket with Camposanto or Museo delle Sinopie €7, Camposanto & Museo €8; ⊗8am-8pm Apr-Sep, 9am-7pm Oct, to 6pm Mar, 10am-5pm Nov-Feb) This unusual round baptistry (1395) has one dome piled on top of another, each roofed half in lead, half in tiles, and topped by a gilt bronze John the Baptist.

Tuscan Road Trip

Taking in Tuscany's two great medieval rivals, Florence and Siena, Chianti's wine-rich hills, and the Unesco-listed Val d'Orcia, this drive offers artistic masterpieces, soul-stirring scenery and captivating Renaissance towns.

Start Florence
Distance 185km
Duration Four days

1 Start your journey in the cradle of the Renaissance, **Florence**. Admire Brunelleschi's Duomo dome, wander around the Galleria degli Uffizi, and greet Michelangelo's *David* at the Galleria dell'Accademia.

START ❶

SR222

RA3

Badia a Passignano ❷

Take a Break... Enjoy a meal at Osteria di Passignano (www. osteriadipassignano.com; Via di Passignano 33; ⏱12.15-2.15pm & 7.30-10pm Mon-Sat) in Badia a Passignano, about 20 minutes from Greve.

❸

Riserva Naturale Alto Merse

SR2

3 The medieval cityscape of **Siena** is one of Italy's most captivating. Be inspired by the Duomo's intricate facade, bustling Piazza del Campo, and fine art in the Museo Civico.

SS223

❹

4 Take the SR2 (Via Cassia) to **Montalcino**, known to wine buffs around the world for its celebrated local drop, Brunello.

San
Godenzo

Parco Nazionale
delle Foreste
Casentinesi, Monte
Falterona e Campigna

Monte
Falterona

40 km

20 miles

? Pick up the SR222 (Via Chianti-
giana) and head south to Chianti
wine country. Stop off in the
centuries-old wine centre of **Greve**,
then continue south to Siena.

Classic Photo: The stunning Val
d'Orcia offers open views of undulating fields, stone farmhouses
and rows of elegant cypresses.

5 Head east to the Val d'Orcia
and pretty **Pienza**. Check out the
magnificent Renaissance buildings
in and around Piazza Pio II, which
went up in just four years in the
15th century and haven't been
remodelled since.

5   **6**
      FINISH

SR2

6 Steeply stacked **Montepulciano**
harbours a wealth of *palazzi* and
fine buildings, plus grandstand
views over the Val di Chiana and
Val d'Orcia. Round off your trip
with a glass or two of the local Vino
Nobile.

Siena

Siena is one of Italy's most enchanting medieval towns. Its walled centre is a beautifully preserved warren of dark lanes punctuated with Gothic *palazzi,* and at its heart, Piazza del Campo, the sloping square that is the venue for the city's famous annual horse race, Il Palio.

◎ SIGHTS

Piazza del Campo   Square
This sloping piazza, popularly known as Il Campo, has been Siena's civic and social centre since being staked out by the ruling Consiglio dei Nove in the mid-12th century. It was built on the site of a Roman marketplace, and its pie-piece paving design is divided into nine sectors to represent the number of members of that ruling council.

Palazzo Pubblico   Historic Building
(Palazzo Comunale; Piazza del Campo) The restrained, 14th-century Palazzo Comunale serves as the grand centrepiece of the square in which it sits – notice how its concave facade mirrors the opposing convex curve. From the *palazzo* soars a graceful bell tower, the **Torre del Mangia** (⌖0577 29 23 43; www.enjoysiena.it; €10; ⊙10am-6.15pm summer, to 3.15pm winter), 102m high and with 500-odd steps. The views from the top are magnificent.

Museo Civico   Museum
(Civic Museum; ⌖0577 29 22 32; Palazzo Pubblico, Piazza del Campo 1; adult/reduced €9/8; ⊙10am-6.15pm summer, to 5.15pm winter) Siena's most famous museum occupies rooms richly frescoed by artists of the Sienese school. Commissioned by the governing body of the city, rather than by the Church, many – unusually – depict secular subjects. The highlight is Simone Martini's celebrated *Maestà* (Virgin Mary in Majesty; 1315) in the **Sala del Mappamondo** (Hall of the World Map). It features the Madonna beneath a canopy surrounded by saints and angels, and is Martini's first known work.

Duomo   Cathedral
(Cattedrale di Santa Maria Assunta; ⌖0577 28 63 00; www.operaduomo.siena.it; Piazza Duomo; summer/winter €4/free, when floor displayed €7; ⊙10.30am-7pm Mon-Sat, 1.30-6pm Sun summer, to 5.30pm winter) Siena's cathedral is one of Italy's most awe-inspiring churches. Construction started in 1215 and over the centuries many of Italy's top artists have contributed: Giovanni Pisano designed the intricate white, green and red marble facade; Nicola Pisano carved the elaborate pulpit; Pinturicchio painted some of the frescoes; Michelangelo, Donatello and Gian Lorenzo Bernini all produced sculptures. Buy tickets from the **duomo ticket office** (Santa Maria della Scala, Piazza del Duomo; ⊙10am-6.30pm summer, to 5pm winter).

Museale Santa Maria della Scala   Museum
(⌖0577 53 45 71, 0577 53 45 11; www.santamariadellascala.com; Piazza Duomo 1; adult/reduced €9/7; ⊙10am-5pm Mon, Wed & Thu, to 8pm Fri, to 7pm Sat & Sun, extended hours in summer) This former hospital, parts of which date from the 13th century, was built as a hospice for pilgrims travelling the Via Francigena pilgrimage trail. Its highlight is the upstairs Pellegrinaio (Pilgrim's Hall), with vivid 15th-century frescoes by Lorenzo Vecchietta, Priamo della Quercia and Domenico di Bartolo lauding the good works of the hospital and its patrons.

Pinacoteca Nazionale   Gallery
(⌖0577 28 11 61; http://pinacotecanazionale.siena.it; Via San Pietro 29; adult/reduced €4/2; ⊙8.15am-7.15pm Tue-Sat, 9am-1pm Sun & Mon) An extraordinary collection of Gothic masterpieces from the Sienese school sits inside the once grand but now sadly dishevelled 14th-century Palazzo Buonsignori. The pick of the collection is on the 2nd floor, including magnificent works by Duccio di Buoninsegna, Simone Martini, Niccolò di Segna, Lippo Memmi, Ambrogio and Pietro Lorenzetti, Bartolo di Fredi and Taddeo di Bartolo.

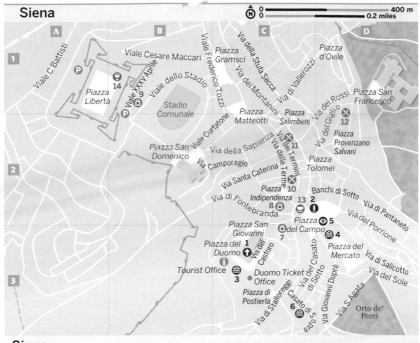

Siena

◎ Sights
1 Duomo C3
2 Fonte Gaia C2
3 Museale Santa Maria della Scala C3
4 Museo Civico D3
   Palazzo Pubblico .... (see 4)
5 Piazza del Campo D2
6 Pinacoteca Nazionale C3
   Torre del Mangia .... (see 4)

ⓐ Shopping
7 Il Magnifico C3
8 Il Pellicano C2
9 Wednesday Market B1

◎ Eating
10 Enoteca I Terzi C2
11 Morbidi C2
12 Tre Cristi D1

◎ Drinking & Nightlife
13 Caffè Fiorella C2
14 Enoteca Italiana B1

ⓐ SHOPPING

Il Magnifico   Food
(☐0577 28 11 06; www.ilmagnifico.siena.it; Via dei Pellegrini 27; ⏱7.30am-7.30pm Mon-Sat) Lorenzo Rossi is Siena's best baker, and his *panforte*, *ricciarelli* (sugar-dusted chewy almond biscuits) and *cavallucci* (almond biscuits made with Tuscan millefiori honey) are a weekly purchase for most local households. Try them at his bakery and shop behind the *duomo*, and you'll understand why.

Il Pellicano   Ceramics
(☐0577 24 79 14; www.siena-ilpellicano.it; Via Diaccetto 17a; ⏱10.30am-7pm summer, hours vary in winter) Elisabetta Ricci has been making traditional hand-painted Sienese ceramics for over 30 years. She shapes,

Celebrating Il Palio

Dating from the Middle Ages, Il Palio is a spectacular annual event in July and August that includes a series of colourful pageants and a wild horse race in Piazza del Campo. Ten of Siena's 17 *contrade* (town districts) compete for the coveted *palio* (silk banner). Each *contrada* has its own traditions, symbol and colours, plus its own church and *palio* museum.

LONGJON/SHUTTERSTOCK ©

fires and paints her creations, often using Renaissance-era styles or typical *contrade* designs. Elisabetta also conducts lessons in traditional ceramic techniques.

Wednesday Market   Market

(⊙7.30am-2pm) Spreading around Fortezza Medicea and towards the Stadio Comunale, this is one of Tuscany's largest markets and is great for cheap clothing; some food is also sold. An antiques market is held here on the third Sunday of each month.

⊗ EATING & DRINKING

Morbidi   Deli €

(📞0577 28 02 68; www.morbidi.com; Via Banchi di Sopra 75; lunch €12, aperitivo buffet from €7; ⊙8am-8pm Mon-Thu, to 10pm Fri & Sat) Possibly the classiest cheap feed in Siena: set in the stylish basement of Morbidi's deli, the lunch buffet on offer here is excellent. For a mere €12, you can join the well-dressed locals sampling antipasti, salads, risottos, pastas and a dessert of the day. Bottled water is supplied; wine and coffee cost extra.

Buy your ticket upstairs before heading down.

Enoteca I Terzi   Tuscan €€

(📞0577 4 43 29; www.enotecaiterzi.it; Via dei Termini 7; meals €35; ⊙11am-3pm & 6.30pm-1am Mon-Sat, shorter hrs in winter) A favourite for many locals who head to this historic *enoteca* (wine bar)to linger over lunches, *aperitivi* and casual dinners featuring top-notch Tuscan *salumi* (cured meats), delicate handmade pasta and wonderful wines.

Tre Cristi   Seafood €€€

(📞0577 28 06 08; www.trecristi.com; Vicolo di Provenzano 1-7; meals €45, tasting menus €40-65; ⊙12.30-2.30pm & 7.30-10pm Mon-Sat) Seafood restaurants are thin on the ground in this meat-obsessed region, so the long existence of Tre Cristi (it's been around since 1830) should be heartily celebrated. The menu here is as elegant as the decor, and touches such as a complimentary glass of *prosecco* (dry sparkling wine) at the start of the meal add to the experience.

Enoteca Italiana   Wine Bar

(📞0577 22 88 43; www.enoteca-italiana.it; Fortezza Medicea, Piazza Libertà 1; ⊙noon-7.30pm Mon & Tue, to midnight Wed-Sat) The former munitions cellar and dungeon of this Medici fortress has been artfully transformed into a classy *enoteca* that carries more than 1500 Italian labels. You can take a bottle with you, ship a case home or just enjoy a glass in the attractive courtyard or vaulted interior. There's usually food available, too.

Caffè Fiorella   Cafe

(Torrefazione Fiorella; www.torrefazionefiorella.it; Via di Città 13; ⊙7am-6pm Mon-Sat) Squeeze into this tiny, heart-of-the-action space to enjoy some of Siena's best coffee. In summer, the coffee granita with a dollop of cream is a wonderful indulgence.

ℹ INFORMATION

Tourist Office (📞0577 28 05 51; www.enjoysiena.it; Piazza Duomo 1, Santa Maria della Scala; ⊙9am-6pm summer, to 5pm winter)

Siena's Duomo (p452)

ℹ️ GETTING THERE & AWAY

Bus service **Siena Mobilità** (800 922984; www.sienamobilita.it) links Siena with Florence (€7.80, 1¼ hours, at least hourly) and San Gimignano (€6, 1¼ hours, 10 daily Monday to Saturday).

Arezzo

Arezzo may not be a Tuscan centrefold, but those parts of its historic centre that survived merciless WWII bombings are as compelling as any destination in the region – the city's central square is as beautiful as it appears in Roberto Benigni's classic film *La vita è bella* (Life is Beautiful).

Today, the city is known for its churches, museums and fabulously sloping Piazza Grande, across which a huge antiques fair spills during the first weekend of each month. Come dusk, Arentini (locals of Arezzo) spill along the length of shop-clad Corso Italia for the ritual *passeggiata* (evening stroll).

> *Siena's cathedral is one of Italy's most awe-inspiring churches*

◎ SIGHTS

Cappella Bacci   Church
(📞0575 35 27 27; www.pierodellafrancesca. it; Piazza San Francesco; adult/reduced €8/5; ⏰9am-6pm Mon-Fri, to 5.30pm Sat, 1-5.30pm Sun) This chapel, in the apse of 14th-century **Basilica di San Francesco**, safeguards one of Italian art's greatest works: Piero della Francesca's fresco cycle of the *Legend of the True Cross*. Painted between 1452 and 1466, it relates the story of the cross on which Christ was crucified. Only 25 people are allowed in every half-hour, making advance booking (by telephone or email) essential in high season. The ticket office is down the stairs by the basilica's entrance.

Chiesa di Santa
Maria della Pieve   Church
(Corso Italia 7; ⏰8am-12.30pm & 3-6.30pm) `FREE` This 12th-century church – Arezzo's

oldest – has an exotic Romanesque arcaded facade adorned with carved columns, each uniquely decorated. Above the central doorway are 13th-century carved reliefs called *Cyclo dei mesi* representing each month of the year. The plain interior's highlight – removed for restoration work at the time of writing – is Pietro Lorenzetti's polyptych *Madonna and Saints* (1320–24), beneath the semidome of the apse. Below the altar is a 14th-century silver bust reliquary of the city's patron saint, San Donato.

Duomo di Arezzo — Cathedral

(Cattedrale di SS Donato e Pietro; Piazza del Duomo; ☉7am-12.30pm & 3.30-6.30pm) **FREE** Construction started in the 13th century but Arezzo's cathedral wasn't completed until the 15th century. In the northeast corner, left of the intricately carved main altar, is an exquisite fresco of *Mary Magdalene* (c 1459) by Piero della Francesca. Also notable are five glazed terracottas by Andrea della Robbia and his studio. Behind the cathedral is the pentagonal **Fortezza Medicea** (1502) atop the crest of one of Arezzo's two hills – the *duomo* was built on the crest of the other.

Museo Archeologico Nazionale 'Gaio Cilnio Mecenate' — Museum

(Gaius Cilnius Maecenas Archeological Museum; ☏0575 2 08 82; www.facebook.com/archeologicoarezzo; Via Margaritone 10; adult/reduced €6/3; ☉8.30am-7.30pm, to 1.30pm Nov) Overlooking the remains of a Roman amphitheatre that once seated up to 10,000 spectators, this museum in a 14th-century convent building exhibits Etruscan and Roman artefacts. The highlight is the *Cratere di Euphronios,* a 6th-century BC Etruscan vase decorated with vivid scenes showing Hercules in battle. Also of note is an exquisite tiny portrait of a bearded man from the second half of the 3rd century AD, executed in chrysography whereby a fine sheet of gold is engraved then encased between two glass panes.

✖ EATING & DRINKING

Antica Osteria Agania — Tuscan €

(☏0575 29 53 81; www.agania.com; Via G Mazzini 10; meals €20; ☉noon-3pm & 6-10.30pm Tue-Sun) Agania has been around for years and her fare is die-hard traditional – the tripe

Cobblestone alley

and *grifi con polenta* (lambs' cheeks with polenta) are sensational. But it is timeless, welcoming addresses like this, potted fresh herbs on the doorstep, that remain the cornerstone of Tuscan dining. Begin with *antipasto misto* (mixed appetisers) followed by your choice combo of six pastas and eight sauces.

Arrive by 1pm to beat the crowd of regulars.

Osteria dell'Acquolina   Tuscan €€

(📞 055 97 74 97; www.acquolina.it; Via Setteponti Levante 26, Terranuova Bracciolini; meals €30; ☻noon-4pm & 7-11pm Tue-Sun) Heading east from Florence to Arezzo, this vivid pink villa in an olive grove is the perfect lunch stop, especially in summer when the dining action spills out onto the terracotta-brick terrace with 360-degree view of olive trees, vines and hills beyond. Cuisine is Tuscan and there's no written menu – the chef cooks different dishes every day.

Take the Valdarno exit off the A1 and follow signs for 'Terranuova Bracciolini' and 'Arezzo' until you pick up 'Osteria dell'Acquolina' signs.

Trattoria del Leone   Tuscan €€

(📞 0575 35 79 27; www.trattoriadelleone.it; Piazza del Popolo 11; meals €30; ☻noon-2.30pm Tue-Sun, 7.30-10pm Tue-Sat, closed Aug) A perfect example of the trattoria model that is trending in Tuscany today, del Leone is found in a slightly obscure location on some stairs leading down into Piazza del Popolo. The food is delicious – smallish portions of beautifully prepared modern riffs on Tuscan classics, with homemade pasta, bruschetta and salads.

Caffè dei Costanti   Cafe

(📞 0575 182 40 75; www.caffedeicostanti.it; Piazza San Francesco 19-20; ☻7.30am-2am summer, to 9.30pm Wed-Sun winter) Arezzo's oldest and most atmospheric cafe is located directly opposite the Basilica di San Francesco, so it's a perfect coffee stop before or after a visit to the Cappella Bacci. The coffee is excellent, as are the home-baked pastries. The outdoor tables are popular with the *aperitivo* set.

Thermal Spas

Tuscany is one of Italy's thermal activity hotspots, with the province of Siena particularly rich in mineral-packed waters. Ranging from swish indoor spas to natural woodland pools, tracking them down – and trying them out – is a delight.

Terme di Saturnia (📞 0564 60 01 11; www.termedisaturnia.it; day pass €25, after 2pm €20; ☻9.30am-7pm summer, to 5pm winter) A stunning, cascading cluster of open-air pools near Pitigliano.

Bagni di Lucca Terme (📞 0583 8 72 21; www.termebagnidilucca.it; Piazza San Martino 11) Thermal swims and massage treatments in a northwestern spa town.

Bagni San Filippo (☻24hr) FREE Free, alfresco backwoods bathing at its best in the Val d'Orcia, about 15km south of Bagno Vignoni along the SR2.

Calidario Terme Etrusche (📞 0565 85 15 04; www.calidario.it; Via del Bottaccio 40, Venturina; pool entry per day adult/child €20/10, spa package per person €29-55; ☻1-4pm & 4.30-7.30pm Mon-Fri, 9.30am-12.30pm, 1-4pm & 4.30-7.30pm Sat & Sun, closed early Jan–early Mar & weekends Jul & Aug) Spa treatments and atmospheric outdoor swims on the Etruscan coast.

Bagni San Filippo
BUS/GETTY IMAGES ©

ℹ INFORMATION

Tourist Office (📞 0575 40 19 45; Piazza della Libertà; ☻2-4pm) Find another **branch** (📞 0575 2 68 50; Piazza della Repubblica 22-23;

Talking to Locals

Many locals in towns and cities speak at least one language other than Italian – usually English or French. But in the Tuscan countryside you'll need that Italian phrasebook. Region-wide, many traditional places to eat have no written menu or only a menu penned in Italian in spidery handwriting.

ZERO CREATIVES/GETTY IMAGES ©

⊘10.30am-12.30pm) to the right as you exit the train station.

Una Vetrina per Arezzo e Le Sue Vallate (✍0575 182 27 70; www.arezzoturismo.it; Emiciclo Giovanni Paolo II, Scale Mobili di Arezzo; ⊘9am-6pm Mon-Fri, to 7pm Sat & Sun) Private tourist office on the *scala mobile* (escalator) leading up to Piazza del Duomo; it has toilet facilities (€0.50).

❶ GETTING THERE & AWAY

To drive here from Florence, take the A1. Parking at the train station costs €2 per hour. By train, Arezzo is on the Florence–Rome line.

Montepulciano

Exploring this reclaimed narrow ridge of volcanic rock will push your quadriceps to failure point. When this happens, self-medicate with a generous pour of the highly reputed Vino Nobile while drinking in the spectacular views over the Val di Chiana and Val d'Orcia.

◉ SIGHTS

Il Corso Street
Montepulciano's main street – called in stages Via di Gracciano, Via di Voltaia, Via dell'Opio and Via d'Poliziano – climbs up the eastern ridge of the town from **Porta al Prato** and loops to meet Via di Collazzi on the western ridge. To reach the centre of town (Piazza Grande) take a dog-leg turn into Via del Teatro.

In Piazza Savonarola, up from the Porta al Prato, is the **Colonna del Marzocca**, erected in 1511 to confirm Montepulciano's allegiance to Florence. The splendid stone lion, squat as a pussycat atop this column is, in fact, a copy; the original is in the town's Museo Civico.

Notable buildings further along the street include the late-Renaissance **Palazzo Avignonesi** (Via di Gracciano nel Corso 91); **Palazzo di Bucelli** (Via di Gracciano nel Corso 73) – look for the recycled Etruscan and Latin inscriptions and reliefs on the lower facade; and **Palazzo Cocconi** (Via di Gracciano nel Corso 70).

Continuing uphill, you'll find Michelozzo's **Chiesa di Sant'Agostino** (www.montepulcianochiusipienza.it; Piazza Michelozzo; ⊘9am-noon & 3-6pm), with its lunette above the entrance holding a terracotta Madonna and Child, John the Baptist and St Augustine. Opposite, the **Torre di Pulcinella**, a medieval tower house, is topped by the town clock and the hunched figure of Pulcinella (Punch of Punch and Judy fame), which strikes the hours. After passing historic **Caffè Poliziano** (✍0578 75 86 15; www.caffepoliziano.it; Via di Voltaia 27; ⊘7am-8pm Mon-Fri, to 11pm Sat, to 9pm Sun; 🛜), the Corso continues straight ahead and Via del Teatro veers off to the right.

Museo Civico & Pinocoteca Crociani Gallery, Museum
(✍0578 71 73 00; www.museocivicomontepulciano.it; Via Ricci 10; adult/reduced €5/3; ⊘10.30am-6.30pm Wed-Mon summer, reduced hours winter) Montepulciano's modest museum and pinacoteca have recently had a curatorial dream come true: a painting in

their collections has been attributed to Caravaggio. The masterpiece is a characteristic *Portrait of a Gentleman*. Worth the entrance fee alone, it's accompanied by high-tech, touchscreen interpretation, which allows you to explore details of the painting, its restoration and diagnostic attribution.

Palazzo Comunale   Palace

(Piazza Grande; terrace & tower adult/child incl €3/2.50, terrace only €2.50; ☉10am-6pm) Built in the 14th-century in Gothic style and remodelled in the 15th century by Michelozzo, the Palazzo Comunale still functions as the town hall. The main reason to head inside is to drink in the extraordinary views from the panoramic terrace and the tower – from the latter you can see as far as Pienza, Montalcino and even, on a clear day, Siena.

🟢 EATING & DRINKING

Osteria Acquacheta   Tuscan €€

(☏0578 71 70 86; www.acquacheta.eu; Via del Teatro 22; meals €25-30; ☉12.30-3pm & 7.30-10.30pm Wed-Mon mid-Apr–Dec) Hugely

popular with locals and tourists alike, this bustling *osteria* (tavern) specialises in *bistecca alla fiorentina* (chargrilled T-bone steak), which comes to the table in huge, lightly seared and exceptionally flavoursome slabs (don't even *think* of asking for it to be served otherwise). Book ahead; no email reservations.

La Grotta   Ristorante €€€

(☏0578 75 74 79; www.lagrottamontepulciano.it; Via di San Biagio 15; meals €40; ☉12.30-2pm & 7.30-10pm Thu-Tue, closed mid-Jan–mid-Mar) The ingredients, and sometimes dishes, may be traditional, but the presentation is full of refined flourishes – artfully arranged Parmesan shavings and sprigs of herbs crown delicate towers of pasta, vegetables and meat. The service is exemplary and the courtyard garden divine. It's just outside town on the road to Chiusi. Booking recommended.

E Lucevan Le Stelle   Wine Bar

(☏0578 75 87 25; www.lucevanlestelle.it; Piazza San Francesco 5; ☉11.30am-11.30pm mid-Mar–Dec; 🛜) The decked terrace here is

Al fresco diners in Montalcino (p460)

A wine bar in Montalcino

the top spot in Montepulciano to watch the sun go down. Inside squishy sofas, modern art and jazz on the sound system give the place a chilled-out vibe. Dishes (antipasto plates €4.50 to €8; *piadinas* €6; pastas €6.50 to €9) are simple but tasty, and there's Montepulciano Nobile by the glass (€5 to €7).

Or opt for a tasting flight featuring three wines (€15); choose from Tuscany (Chianti, Montepulciano Nobile and Brunello) or Montepulciano (Rosso, Nobile and Nobile Riserva).

ℹ️ INFORMATION

Tourist Office (📞0578 75 73 41; www.prolocomontepulciano.it; Piazza Don Minzoni 1; ⊙9am-1pm)

ℹ️ GETTING THERE & AWAY

If driving from Florence, take the Valdichiana exit off the A1 (direction Bettolle-Sinalunga) and then follow the signs. From Siena, take the Siena–Bettolle–Perugia Super Strada.

Siena Mobilità runs four buses daily between Siena and Montepulciano (€6.60, one hour) stopping at Pienza (€2.50) en route. There are three services per day to/from Florence (€11.20, 1½ hours).

Montalcino

Known globally as the home of one of the world's great wines, Brunello di Montalcino, the attractive hilltop town of Montalcino has number of *enoteche* lining its medieval streets, and is surrounded by hugely picturesque vineyards. There's history to explore, too; the town's efforts to hold out against Florence even after Siena had fallen earned it the title 'the Republic of Siena in Montalcino'.

✖️ EATING & DRINKING

Poggio Antico   Wine €€

(📞0577 84 80 44, restaurant 0577 84 92 00; www.poggioantico.com; Località Poggio Antico, off SP14; ⊙cantina 10am-6pm, restaurant noon-2.30pm & 7-9.30pm Tue-Sun, closed Sun evening winter) Located 5km outside Montalcino on the road to Grosseto, Poggio Antico is a superb foodie one-stop-shop. It makes award-winning wines (try its Brunello Altero or Riserva), conducts free cellar tours in Italian, English and German, offers tastings (approximately €25 depending on wines) and has an on-site restaurant (meals €40). Book tours in advance.

Il Leccio   Tuscan €€

(📞0577 84 41 75; www.illeccio.net; Via Costa Castellare 1/3, Sant'Angelo in Colle; meals €30, 4-course set menu €36; ⏰noon-2.30pm & 7-9pm Thu-Tue; 🖉) Watching the chef make his way between his stove and kitchen garden to gather produce for each order puts a whole new spin on the word 'fresh', and both the results and the house Brunello are spectacular.

Sant'Angelo in Colle is 10km southwest of Montalcino along Via del Sole (and 10km west of the Abbazia di Sant'Antimo) along an unsealed but signed road through vineyards.

Enoteca Osteria Osticoio   Wine Bar

(📞0577 84 82 71; www.osticcio.it; Via Giacomo Matteotti 23; antipasto & cheese plates €7-17, meals €40; ⏰noon-4pm & 7-11pm Fri-Wed, plus noon-7pm Thu summer) In a town overflowing with *enoteche*, this is definitely one of the best. A huge selection of Brunello and its more modest sibling Rosso di Montalcino accompanies tempting dishes such as marinated anchovies, *cinta senese* (Tuscan pork) crostini, and pasta with pumpkin and *pecorino* (sheep's milk cheese). The panoramic view, meanwhile, almost upstages it all.

Caffè Fiaschetteria Italiana 1888   Cafe

(📞0577 84 90 43; Piazza del Popolo 6; ⏰7.30am-11pm, closed Thu winter) You could take a seat in the slender square outside this atmosphere-laden *enoteca*-cafe, but then you'd miss its remarkable 19th-century decor – all brass, mirrors and ornate lights. It's been serving coffee and glasses of Brunello to locals since 1888 (hence the name) and is still chock-full of charm.

ℹ INFORMATION

The **Tourist Office** (📞0577 84 93 31; www.prolocomontalcino.com; Costa del Municipio 1; ⏰10am-1pm & 2-5.50pm, closed Mon winter) is just off the main square. It can book cellar-door visits and accommodation.

ℹ GETTING THERE & AWAY

If driving from Siena, take the SS2 (Via Cassia); after Buonconvento, turn off onto the SP45. There's plenty of parking around the *fortezza* (€1.50 per hour 8am to 8pm).

By bus, Siena Mobilità buses (€5, 1½ hours, six daily Monday to Saturday) run to/from Siena.

Teatro Grande (p465)

Ruins of Pompeii

Around 30 minutes by train from Naples, you'll find Europe's most compelling archaeological site: the ruins of Pompeii. Sprawling and haunting, the site is a remarkably well-preserved slice of ancient life. Here you can walk down Roman streets and snoop around millennia-old houses, temples, shops, cafes, amphitheatres and even a brothel.

Great For...

❶ Need to Know

📞 081 857 53 47; www.pompeiisites.org; entrances at Porta Marina, Piazza Esedra & Piazza Anfiteatro; adult/reduced €13/7.50, incl Herculaneum €22/12; ⊘9am-7.30pm, last entry 6pm Apr-Oct, to 5pm, last entry 3.30pm Nov-Mar

★ **Top Tip**

The ruins are not well labelled, so pick up a free booklet or an audio guide (€6.50) to enhance your visit.

Visiting the Site

Much of the site's value lies in the fact that the city wasn't blown away by Vesuvius in AD 79, but buried beneath a layer of lapilli (burning fragments of pumice stone). The remains first came to light in 1594, but systematic exploration didn't begin until 1748. Since then 44 of Pompeii's original 66 hectares have been excavated.

Remember that you'll need sustenance for your explorations. You'll find an on-site cafeteria at the ruins, and no shortage of touristy, mediocre eateries directly outside the site. The modern town is home to a few better-quality options, or bring your own snacks and beverages.

Before entering the site through **Porta Marina**, the gate that originally connected the town with the near by harbour,

duck into the **Terme Suburbane**. This 1st-century-BC bathhouse is famous for several erotic frescoes that scandalised the Vatican when they were revealed in 2001. The panels decorate what was once the *apodyterium* (changing room). The room leading to the colourfully frescoed *frigidarium* (cold-water bath) features fragments of stucco-work, as well as one of the few original roofs to survive at Pompeii.

Done in the Terme, continue through the city walls to the main part of the site. Highlights to look out for here include:

Foro

A huge grassy rectangle flanked by limestone columns, the **foro** (forum) was ancient Pompeii's main piazza, as well as the site of gladiatorial battles before the

Impluvium (rain tank) in a Pompeii house

Anfiteatro was constructed. The buildings surrounding the forum are testament to its role as the city's hub of civic, commercial, political and religious activity.

Lupanare

Ancient Pompeii's only dedicated brothel, **Lupanare** is a tiny two-storey building with five rooms on each floor. Its collection of raunchy frescoes was a menu of sorts for clients. The walls in the rooms are carved with graffiti – including declarations of love and hope written by the brothel workers – in various languages.

> ★ **Top Tip**
>
> On the first Sunday of the month, all tickets are free; see www.pompeii sites.org.

Teatro Grande

The 2nd-century-BC **Teatro Grande** was a huge 5000-seat theatre carved into the lava mass on which Pompeii was originally built.

Anfiteatro

Gladiatorial battles thrilled up to 20,000 spectators at the grassy **anfiteatro** (Amphitheatre). Built in 70 BC, it's the oldest known Roman amphitheatre in existence.

Casa del Fauno

Covering an entire *insula* (city block) and boasting two atria at its front end (humbler homes had one), Pompeii's largest **private house** (House of the Faun) is named after the delicate bronze statue in the *impluvium* (rain tank). It was here that early excavators found Pompeii's greatest mosaics, most of which are now in Naples' **Museo Archeologico Nazionale** (🖉848 80 02 88, from mobile 06 399 67050; www.museoarcheologiconapoli.it; Piazza Museo Nazionale 19; adult/reduced €12/6; ⊙9am-7.30pm Wed-Mon; Ⓜ Museo, Piazza Cavour). Valuable on-site survivors include a beautiful, geometrically patterned marble floor.

Villa dei Misteri

This recently restored, 90-room **villa** is one of the most complete structures left standing in Pompeii. The dionysiac frieze, the most important fresco still on site, spans the walls of the large dining room. One of the biggest and most arresting paintings from the ancient world, it depicts the initiation of a bride-to-be into the cult of Dionysus, the Greek god of wine.

> ✗ **Take a Break**
>
> For a memorable bite in Pompeii town, head to Michelin-starred **President** (🖉081 850 72 45; www.ristorantepresident.it; Piazza Schettini 12; meals from €40, tasting menus €65-90; ⊙noon-3.30pm & 7pm-late Tue-Sun; Ⓡ FS to Pompei, Ⓡ Circumvesuviana to Pompei Scavi-Villa dei Misteri), where you can try bread made to ancient Roman recipes and sweet slow-cooked snapper.

DE AGOSTINI / L. ROMANO/GETTY IMAGES ©

A farm for much of its life, the villa has a vino-making area that is still visible at the northern end.

Follow Via Consolare out of the town through **Porta Ercolano**. Continue past **Villa di Diomede**, turn right, and you'll come to Villa dei Misteri.

Body Casts

One of the most haunting sights at Pompeii are the body casts in the **Granai del Foro** (Forum Granary). These were made in the late 19th century by pouring plaster into the hollows left by disintegrated bodies. Among the casts is a pregnant slave; the belt around her waist would have displayed the name of her owner.

Tours

You'll almost certainly be approached by a guide outside the *scavi* (excavations) ticket office: note that authorised guides wear identification tags. If considering a guided tour of the ruins, reputable tour operators include **Yellow Sudmarine** (329 1010328; www.yellowsudmarine.com; 2½hr Pompeii guided tour €135, plus entrance fee) and **Walks of Italy** (www.walksofitaly.com; 3hr Pompeii guided tour per person €59), both of which also offer excursions to other areas of Campania.

Getting to Pompeii

Circumvesuviana trains run to Pompei-Scavi-Villa dei Misteri station from Naples (€3.20, 36 minutes) and Sorrento (€2.80, 30 minutes). By car, take the A3 from Naples, then use the Pompeii exit and follow signs to Pompeii Scavi. Car parks (approximately €5 per hour) are clearly marked and vigorously touted.

What's Nearby?

If you have time for further exploration in the area, check out these ancient sites.

Ruins of
Herculaneum   Archaeological Site

(081 857 53 47; www.pompeiisites.org; Corso Resina 187, Ercolano; adult/reduced €11/5.50, incl Pompeii €22/12; 8.30am-7.30pm Apr-

Oct, to 5pm Nov-Mar; Circumvesuviana to Ercolano-Scavi) Upstaged by its larger rival, Pompeii, Herculaneum harbours a wealth of archaeological finds, from ancient advertisements and stylish mosaics to carbonised furniture and terror-struck skeletons. This superbly conserved Roman fishing town is easier to navigate than Pompeii, and can be explored in a half-day with a map and audio guide (€6.50).

From the site's main gateway on Corso Resina, head down the walkway to the ticket office (at the bottom on your left). Ticket purchased, follow the walkway to the actual entrance to the ruins.

MAV   Museum

(Museo Archeologico Virtuale; 081 1777 6843; www.museomav.com; Via IV Novembre 44; adult/reduced €7.50/6, with 3D documentary

€11.50/10; ⏱9am-5.30pm daily Mar-May, 10am-6.30pm daily Jun-Sep, 10am-4pm Tue-Sun Oct-Feb; 🛜♿; 🚆Circumvesuviana to Ercolano-Scavi) Using high-tech holograms and computer-generated recreations, this 'virtual archaeological museum' brings ancient ruins alive; it's especially fun for kids. The museum is on the main street linking Ercolano-Scavi train station to the ruins of Herculaneum.

Mt Vesuvius

Towering loftily over Naples and its environs, 1281m Mt Vesuvius (Vesuvio) is the only active volcano on the European mainland. From the summit car park, an 860m path leads up to the volcano's **crater** (Vesuvius National Park; www.epnv.it).

From Ercolano, **Vesuvio Express** (📞081 739 36 66; www.vesuvioexpress.it; Piazzale Stazi-

one Circumvesuviana, Ercolano; return incl admission to summit €20; ⏱every 40min, 9.30am to 4pm) runs shuttle buses from outside the train station up to the summit car park. The journey time is 20 minutes each way.

From Pompeii, **Busvia del Vesuvio** (📞081 878 21 03; www.busviadelvesuvio.com; Via Villa dei Misteri, Pompeii; return incl entry to summit adult/reduced €22/7; ⏱hourly from 9am-5pm) runs hourly shuttle services between Pompei-Scavi-Villa dei Misteri train station (steps away from the ruins of Pompeii) and Boscoreale Terminal Interchange, from where a bus continues the journey up the slope to the summit car park.

> ★ **Top Tip**
>
> For the Mt Vesuvius climb, take water, sunscreen and a hat. You'll also need sturdy shoes, as the path can have loose stones.

DE AGOSTINI / L. ROMANO/GETTY IMAGES ©

Tragedy in Pompeii

24 AUGUST AD 79

8am Buildings including the **❶ Terme Suburbane** and the **❷ Foro** are still undergoing repair after an earthquake in AD 63 caused significant damage to the city. Despite violent earth tremors overnight, residents have little idea of the catastrophe that lies ahead.

Midday Peckish locals pour into the **❸ Thermopolium di Vetutius Placidus**. The lustful slip into the **❹ Lupanare**, and gladiators practise for the evening's planned games at the **❺ Anfiteatro**. A massive boom heralds the eruption. Shocked onlookers witness a dark cloud of volcanic matter shoot some 14km above the crater.

3pm–5pm Lapilli (burning pumice stone) rains down on Pompeii. Terrified locals begin to flee; others take shelter. Within two hours, the plume is 25km high and the sky has darkened. Roofs collapse under the weight of the debris, burying those inside.

25 AUGUST AD 79

Midnight Mudflows bury the town of Herculaneum. Lapilli and ash continue to rain down on Pompeii, bursting through buildings and suffocating those taking refuge within.

4am–8am Ash and gas avalanches hit Herculaneum. Subsequent surges smother Pompeii, killing all remaining residents, including those in the **❻ Orto dei Fuggiaschi**. The volcanic 'blanket' will safeguard frescoed treasures like the **❼ Casa del Menandro** and **❽ Villa dei Misteri** for almost two millennia.

TOP TIPS

➡ Visit in the afternoon.
➡ Allow three hours.
➡ Wear comfortable shoes and a hat.
➡ Bring drinking water.
➡ Don't use flash photography.

Terme Suburbane
The *laconicum* (sauna), *caldarium* (hot bath) and large, heated swimming pool weren't the only sources of heat here; scan the walls of this suburban bathhouse for some of the city's raunchiest frescoes.

Villa di Diomede

❽

Casa del Poeta Tragico

Porta Ercolano

Casa del Fauno

Tempio di Apollo

Basilica

Porta Marina

❶

Terme del Foro

❷

❹

Macellum

Teatro Grande

Quadriportico dei Teatri

Porta di Stabia

Teatro Piccolo

Foro
An ancient Times Square of sorts, the forum sits at the intersection of Pompeii's main streets and was closed to traffic in the 1st century AD. The plinths on the southern edge featured statues of the imperial family.

Villa dei Misteri
Home to the world-famous *Dionysiac Frieze* fresco. Other highlights at this villa include *trompe l'oeil* wall decorations in the *cubiculum* (bedroom) and Egyptian-themed artwork in the *tablinum* (reception).

Lupanare
The prostitutes at this brothel were often slaves of Greek or Asian origin. Mattresses once covered the stone beds and the names engraved in the walls are possibly those of the workers and their clients.

Thermopolium di Vetutiu Placidu
The counter at this ancient snack bar once held urns filled with hot food. The *lararium* (household shrine) on the back wall depicts Dionysus (the god of wine) and Mercury (the god of profit and commerce).

Casa dei Vettii

Porta del Vesuvio

Porta di Nola

Casa della Venere in Conchiglia

Porta di Sarno

EYEWITNESS ACCOUNT

Pliny the Younger (AD 61–c 112) gives a gripping, first-hand account of the catastrophe in his letters to Tacitus (AD 56–117).

---

③

⑦

⑥

Grande Palestra

⑤

Tempio di Iside

Orto dei Fuggiaschi
The Garden of the Fugitives showcases the plaster moulds of 13 locals seeking refuge during Vesuvius' eruption – the largest number of victims found in any one area. The huddled bodies make for a moving scene.

Anfiteatro
Magistrates, local senators and the games' sponsors and organisers enjoyed front-row seating at this veteran amphitheatre, home to gladiatorial battles and the odd riot. The parapet circling the stadium featured paintings of combat, victory celebrations and hunting scenes.

Casa del Menandro
This dwelling most likely belonged to the family of Poppaea Sabina, Nero's second wife. A room to the left of the atrium features Trojan War paintings and a polychrome mosaic of pygmies rowing down the Nile.

In This Chapter

City Walls & Forts 472
Game of Thrones Locations 474
Sights 476
Activities 479
Tours 480
Shopping 480
Eating 480
Drinking & Nightlife 482
Information 482
Getting There & Away 483
Getting Around 483

Dubrovnik, Croatia

Regardless of whether you are visiting Croatia's Dubrovnik for the first time or the hundredth, the sense of awe never fails to descend when you set eyes on the beauty of the old town. Indeed it's hard to imagine anyone becoming jaded by the city's marble streets, baroque buildings and the endless shimmer of the Adriatic, or failing to be inspired by a walk along the ancient city walls that protected a civilised, sophisticated republic for centuries.

Although the shelling of Dubrovnik in 1991 horrified the world, the city has bounced back with vigour to enchant visitors again.

Two Days in Dubrovnik

Start early with a walk along the **city walls** (p473), before it's too hot, then wander the marbled streets and call into whichever church, palace or museum takes your fancy.

On day two, take the **cable car** (p479) up Mt Srđ and visit the exhibition **Dubrovnik During the Homeland War** (p477). Afterwards, continue exploring the old town. When it starts to bake, wander along to **Banje Beach** (p479).

Four Days in Dubrovnik

With another couple of days you'll have the luxury of confining your old-town explorations to the evenings, when it's quieter. On day three, visit the island of **Lokrum** (p477). On your final day, jump on a boat to **Cavtat** (p480), allowing a couple of hours to stroll around the historic town.

Moving on from Dubrovnik? It's a short flight to Rome (p352) or Venice (p400).

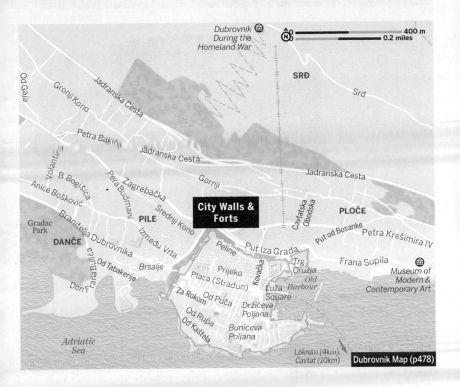

Arriving in Dubrovnik

Dubrovnik Airport In Čilipi, 19km southeast of Dubrovnik. Allow up to 280KN for a taxi, or Atlas runs the airport bus service (40KN, 30 minutes), which stops at the Pile Gate and the bus station.

Dubrovnik Bus Station Times are detailed at www.libertasdubrovnik.hr.

Where to Stay

There's limited accommodation in the compact old town itself. You should book well in advance, especially in summer.

Private accommodation can be a good, well-priced alternative; contact local travel agencies or the tourist office for options.

Minčeta Tower (p475) along the city walls

ANSHARPHOTO/SHUTTERSTOCK ©

City Walls & Forts

No visit to Dubrovnik would be complete without a walk around the spectacular city walls – the finest in the world and the city's main claim to fame.

Great For...

☑ Don't Miss

The sublime view over the old town and the shimmering Adriatic from the top of the walls.

Walking the Walls

There are entrances to the walls from near the Pile Gate (p476), the **Ploče Gate** (Vrata od Ploča) and the **Maritime Museum** (Pomorski muzej; www.dumus.hr). The Pile Gate entrance tends to be the busiest, and entering from the Ploče side has the added advantage of getting the steepest climbs out of the way first (you're required to walk in an anticlockwise direction).

The round Minčeta Tower protects the landward edge of the city from attack, while Fort Revelin and Fort St John guard the eastern approach and the Old Harbour.

The Bokar Tower and Fort Lawrence look west and out to sea. St Blaise gazes down from the walls of **Fort Lawrence** (Tvrđava Lovrjenac; admission 30KN; ⊘8am-7.30pm), a large free-standing fortress. There's

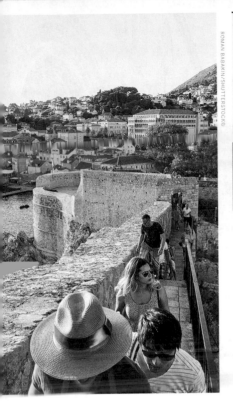

ROMAN BABAKIN/SHUTTERSTOCK©

❶ Need to Know

Gradske zidine; adult/child 150/50KN; ⊘8am-7.30pm Apr-Oct, 9am-3pm Nov-Mar

✕ Take a Break

Bring your own snacks, and especially your own drinks: the few vendors selling water on the route tend to be overpriced.

★ Top Tip

Don't underestimate how strenuous the wall walk can be, particularly on a hot day.

Recent History

Caught in the cross-hairs of the war that ravaged the former Yugoslavia, Dubrovnik was pummelled with some 2000 shells in 1991 and 1992, suffering considerable damage. There were 111 strikes on the walls.

The walls themselves and all of the damaged buildings have since been restored, but you can get a good handle on the extent of the shelling damage by gazing over the rooftops as you walk the walls: those sporting bright new terracotta suffered damage and had to be replaced.

Guided Tours

Dubrovnik Walks (⌖095 80 64 526; www. dubrovnikwalks.com; Brsalje bb; ⊘Apr-Nov) runs excellent English-language guided walks departing from near the Pile Gate. The two-hour 'Walls & Wars' tour is 190KN. No reservations necessary.

not a lot inside, but the battlements offer wonderful views over the old town and its large courtyard is often used as a venue for summer theatre and concerts.

History of the Walls

The first set of walls to enclose the city was built in the 9th century. In the middle of the 14th century the 1.5m-thick defences were fortified with 15 square forts. The threat of attacks from the Turks in the 15th century prompted the city to strengthen the existing forts and add new ones, so that the entire old town was contained within a stone barrier 2km long and up to 25m high. The walls are thicker on the land side – up to 6m – and range from 1.5m to 3m on the sea side.

Rector's Palace

ROMAN BABAKIN/SHUTTERSTOCK ©

Game of Thrones Locations

Dubrovnik is like a fantasy world for many, but fans of Game of Thrones have more reason to indulge in flights of fancy than most, as much of the immensely popular TV series was filmed here.

Great For...

☑ Don't Miss

The city walls, which have often featured in the TV series, particularly during the siege of King's Landing.

City Walls & Fort Lawrence

Tyrion Lannister commanded the defence of King's Landing from the seaward-facing walls (p473) during the Battle of the Blackwater. Fort Lawrence (p472) is King's Landing's famous Red Keep and both the interior and the exterior will be familiar. Cersei farewelled her daughter Myrcella from the little harbour beneath the fort.

Rector's Palace

The grand atrium of the **Rector's Palace** (Knežev dvor; ☎020-321 422; www.dumus.hr; Pred Dvorom 3; adult/child multimuseum pass 100/25KN; ⊙9am-6pm Apr-Oct, to 4pm Nov-Mar) featured as the palace of the Spice King of Qarth – they didn't even bother moving the statue! Built in the late 15th century for the elected rector who governed Dubrovnik,

Fort Lawrence

SABINE LUBENOW/GETTY IMAGES ©

rus orchards, a maze, a fine palm collection and a gorgeous pond. To get to Trsteno, catch local bus 12, 15, 22 or 35 from Dubrovnik's bus station.

Other Notable Spots

Minčeta Tower (Tvrđava Minčeta; City Walls) The exterior of Qarth's House of Undying.

Uz Jezuite The stairs connecting the St Ignatius of Loyola Church to Gundulić Sq were the starting point for Cersei Lannister's memorable naked penitential walk. The walk continued down Stradun.

Gradac Park The site of the Purple Wedding feast, where King Joffrey finally got his comeuppance.

Sv Dominika street The street and staircase outside the Dominican Monastery (p479) were used for various King's Landing market scenes.

Ethnographic Museum (Etnografski muzej; www.dumus.hr; Od Rupa 3; adult/child multimuseum pass 100/25KN; ⊙9am-4pm Wed-Mon) Littlefinger's brothel.

Lokrum (p477) The reception for Daenerys in Qarth was held in the monastery cloister.

this Gothic-Renaissance palace contains the rector's office, his private chambers, public halls, administrative offices and a dungeon. Today the palace has been turned into the Cultural History Museum, with artfully restored rooms, portraits, coats of arms and coins, evoking the glorious history of Dubrovnik.

Trsteno Arboretum

The Red Keep gardens, where the Tyrells chatted and plotted endlessly during seasons three and four, are at the **Trsteno Arboretum** (☑020-751 019; adult/child 45/25KN; ⊙8am-7pm Jun-Sep, to 4pm Oct-May). These leafy gardens, 14km northwest of Dubrovnik, are the oldest of their kind in Croatia and well worth a visit. There is a Renaissance layout, with a set of geometric shapes made with plants and bushes, cit-

◎ SIGHTS

Today Dubrovnik is the most prosperous, elegant and expensive city in Croatia. In many ways it still feels like a city state, isolated from the rest of the nation by geography and history. It's become such a tourism magnet that there's even talk of having to limit visitor numbers in the car-free old town – the main thoroughfares can get impossibly crowded, especially when multiple cruise ships disgorge passengers at the same time.

Pile Gate   Gate

(Gradska vrata Pile) The natural starting point to any visit to Dubrovnik, this fabulous city gate was built in 1537. While crossing the drawbridge, imagine that this was once lifted every evening, the gate closed and the key handed to the rector. Notice the statue of St Blaise, the city's patron saint, set in a niche over the Renaissance arch.

After passing through the outer gate you'll come to an inner gate dating from 1460, and soon after you'll be struck by the gorgeous view of the main street, Placa, or as it's commonly known, Stradun, Dubrovnik's pedestrian promenade.

Onofrio Fountain   Fountain

(Velika Onofrijeva fontana; Placa bb) One of Dubrovnik's most famous landmarks, this large fountain was built in 1438 as part of a water-supply system that involved bringing water from a well 12km away. Originally the fountain was adorned with sculpture, but it was heavily damaged in the 1667 earthquake and only 16 carved masks remain, with water dribbling from their mouths into a drainage pool.

War Photo Limited   Gallery

(☏020-322 166; www.warphotoltd.com; Antuninska 6; adult/child 50/40KN; ◷10am-10pm daily May-Sep, 10am-4pm Wed-Mon Apr & Oct) An immensely powerful experience, this gallery features intensely compelling exhibitions curated by New Zealand photojournalist Wade Goddard, who worked in the Balkans in the 1990s. Its declared intention is to 'expose the myth of war...to let people see war as it is, raw, venal, frightening, by focusing on how war inflicts injustices on innocents

Onofrio Fountain

and combatants alike'. There's a permanent exhibition on the upper floor devoted to the wars in Yugoslavia, but the changing exhibitions cover a multitude of conflicts.

Lokrum   Island

(www.lokrum.hr; adult/child incl boat 100/20KN; ☺Apr-Nov) Lush Lokrum is a beautiful, forested island full of holm oaks, black ash, pines and olive trees, and an ideal escape from urban Dubrovnik. It's a popular swimming spot, although the beaches are rocky. To reach the nudist beach, head left from the ferry and follow the signs marked FKK; the rocks at the far end are Dubrovnik's de facto gay beach. Also popular is the small saltwater lake known as the **Dead Sea**.

The island's main hub is its large medieval **Benedictine monastery**, which houses a restaurant and a display on the island's history and the TV show *Game of Thrones*, which was partly filmed in Dubrovnik. This is your chance to pose imperiously in a reproduction of the Iron Throne. The monastery has a pretty cloister garden and a significant botanical garden, featuring giant agaves and palms from South Africa and Brazil.

Lokrum is only a 10-minute ferry ride from Dubrovnik's Old Harbour. Boats leave roughly hourly in summer (half-hourly in July and August). Make sure you check what time the last boat to the mainland departs. Note that no one can stay overnight and smoking is not permitted anywhere on the island.

Dubrovnik During
the Homeland War   Museum

(Dubrovnik u domovinskom ratu; Fort Imperial, Srd; adult/child 30/15KN; ☺8am-10pm) Set inside a Napoleonic fort near the cable-car terminus, this permanent exhibition is dedicated to the siege of Dubrovnik during the 'Homeland War', as the 1990s war is dubbed in Croatia. The local defenders stationed inside this fort ensured the city wasn't captured. If the displays are understandably one-sided, they still provide in-depth coverage of the events, including plenty of video footage.

 ### Deconstruction &
Reconstruction

From late 1991 to May 1992, images of the shelling of Dubrovnik dominated the news worldwide. While memories may have faded for those who watched it from afar, those who suffered through it will never forget, and the city of Dubrovnik is determined that visitors don't either. You'll see reminders of it on several plaques throughout the old town, especially at the main gates.

Shells struck 68% of the 824 buildings in the old town, leaving holes in two out of three tiled roofs. Building facades and the paving stones of streets and squares suffered 314 direct hits and there were 111 strikes on the great wall. Nine historic palaces were completely gutted by fire, while the Sponza Palace, Rector's Palace, St Blaise's Church, Franciscan Monastery and the carved fountains Amerling and Onofrio all sustained serious damage. It was quickly decided that the repairs and rebuilding would be done with traditional techniques, using original materials whenever feasible.

Dubrovnik has since regained most of its original grandeur. The town walls are once again intact, the gleaming marble streets are smoothly paved and famous monuments have been lovingly restored, with the help of an international brigade of specially trained stonemasons.

Museum of Modern &
Contemporary Art   Museum

(Umjetnička galerija; ☎020-426 590; www.ug-dubrovnik.hr; Frana Supila 23; adult/child multi-museum pass 100/25KN; ☺9am-8pm Tue-Sun) Spread over three floors of a significant modernist building east of the old town, this excellent gallery showcases Croatian artists, particularly painter Vlaho Bukovac from nearby Cavtat. Head up to the sculpture terrace for excellent views.

Dubrovnik

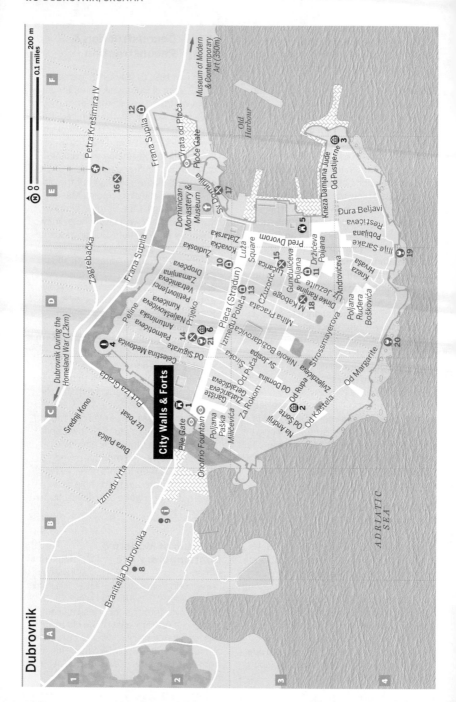

200 m
0.1 miles

City Walls & Forts

Pile Gate
Onofrio Fountain
Poljana Paška Miličevića

Braniteja Dubrovnika

Srednji Kono
Uz posat
Put iza Grada
Đura Pulića
Između Vrta

Zagrebačka
Frana Supila
Petra Krešimira IV
Frana Supila

Dominican Monastery & Museum
Sv Dominika
Vrata od Ploča
Ploče Gate
Museum of Modern & Contemporary Art (350m)
Old Harbour

Celestina Medovića
Palmotićeva
Peline
Antuninska
Kunićeva
Peljskovićeva
Nalješkovićeva
Veljanićeva
Zamanjina
Đropčeva
Prijeko
Žudioska
Kovačka
Zlatarska

Od Sigurate
Placa (Stradun)
Između Polača
Lučarica
Od Puča
Stross
Luža Square
Gundulićeva Poljana
Pred Dvorom
Držićeva Poljana

Miha Pracata
Strossmayerova
Androvićeva
Od Domina
Nikole Božidarevića
Zvijezdičeva
Od Rupa
Za Rokom
Od Domina
Zlatarićeva Getaldićeva
Garište
Sv Josipa
Široka

Na Andriji
Od Sorte
Od Kaštela
Od Margarite
Poljana Rudera Boškovića

Kneza Hvaša
Ilije Sarake Pobljana
Restićeva
Đura Beljavi
Kneza Damjana Jude
Od Pustijerne

M Kaboge
Dinke Ranjine
Sv Jezuite

ADRIATIC SEA

Dubrovnik During the Homeland War (1.2km)

Dubrovnik

◎ **Sights**
1 City Walls & Forts C2
2 Ethnographic Museum C3
3 Maritime Museum E3
4 Minčeta Tower D1
5 Rector's Palace E3
6 War Photo Limited D2

◎ **Activities, Courses & Tours**
7 Cable Car E1
8 Dubrovnik Shore Tours B2
9 Dubrovnik Walks B2

◎ **Shopping**
10 Algoritam D2
11 Gundulić Square Market D3

12 KAWA F2
13 Uje D3

◎ **Eating**
14 Nishta D2
15 Oliva Pizzeria D3
16 Pizzeria Tabasco E1
17 Restaurant 360° E2
18 Restaurant Dubrovnik D3

◎ **Drinking & Nightlife**
19 Bard D4
20 Buža D4
21 D'vino D2

Dominican Monastery & Museum   Christian Monastery

(Muzej Dominikanskog samostana; Sv Dominika 4; 30KN; ◎9am-5pm) This imposing structure is an architectural highlight, built in a transitional Gothic-Renaissance style, and containing an impressive art collection. Constructed around the same time as the city walls in the 14th century, the stark exterior resembles a fortress more than a religious complex. The interior contains a graceful 15th-century **cloister** constructed by local artisans after the designs of the Florentine architect Maso di Bartolomeo.

◎ ACTIVITIES

Cable Car   Cable Car

(Žičara; ☑020-414 355; www.dubrovnikcable car.com; Petra Krešimira IV bb; return adult/child 120/50KN; ◎9am-5pm Nov-Mar, to 9pm Apr, May, Sep & Oct, to midnight Jun-Aug) Dubrovnik's cable car whisks you from just north of the city walls to Mt Srđ in under four minutes. At the end of the line there's a stupendous perspective of the city from a lofty 405m, taking in the terracotta-tiled rooftops of the old town and the island of Lokrum, with the Adriatic and distant Elafiti Islands filling the horizon.

Banje Beach   Swimming

(www.banjebeach.eu; Frana Supila 10) Banje Beach is the closest beach to the old town,

just beyond the 17th-century Lazareti (a former quarantine station) outside Ploče Gate. Although many people rent lounge chairs and parasols from the beach club, there's no problem with just flinging a towel on the beach if you can find a space.

Bellevue Beach   Swimming

The nicest beach within an easy walk of the old town is below the Hotel Bellevue. This pebbly cove is sheltered by high cliffs, which provide a platform for daredevil cliff divers but also cast a shadow over the beach by late afternoon – a boon on a scorching day. Public access is via a steep staircase off Kotorska street.

Way of the Cross Walking Trail   Hiking

(Križni Put; Jadranska) Filled with jaw-dropping views of the entire town and art reliefs illustrating the Stations of the Cross, the hike up the 418m Mt Srđ takes roughly an hour. This free alternative to the cable-car ride starts nearby the eastern entrance to the Adriatic Motorway and runs up to the Fort Imperial on top. It's best done early in the morning or at sunset.

Keep in mind there is no shade along the way, so pack ample water, a hat and sunscreen, and skip the hike altogether in peak summer heat. On the top, consider descending straight to the old town with a one-way cable-car ticket.

Detour: Cavtat

Without Cavtat, there'd be no Dubrovnik, as it was refugees from the original Cavtat town who established the city of Dubrovnik in 614. But Cavtat is interesting in itself. A lot more 'local' than Dubrovnik – read, not flooded by tourists on a daily basis – it has its own charm. Wrapped around a very pretty harbour that's bordered by beaches and backed by a curtain of imposing hills, the setting is lovely.

Cavtat's most famous personality is the painter Vlaho Bukovac (1855–1922), one of the foremost exponents of Croatian modernism. His paintings are liberally distributed around the town's main sights.

From June to September there are 11 sailings a day between Dubrovnik's Old Harbour and Cavtat (one-way/return 50/80KN, 45 minutes). For the rest of the year this reduces to three to five a day, weather dependent.

LUKASZIMILENA/SHUTTERSTOCK ©

🕒 TOURS

Dubrovnik Shore Tours　　Tours

(☏095 80 33 587; www.dubrovnikshoretours.net; Branitelja Dubrovnika 15) Offers tailored small-group tours; popular options include a trip to Mt Srđ and Cavtat followed by a guided walk in the old town (four hours), or to the Pelješac Peninsula for wine and oysters (four hours).

Dubrovnik Day Tours　　Tours

(☏091 44 55 846; www.dubrovnikdaytours.net) Private day trips led by licensed guides to as far away as Korčula, Split, Kotor, Mostar and Sarajevo, as well as sightseeing and *Game of Thrones* tours around Dubrovnik.

🔒 SHOPPING

Gundulić Square Market　　Market

(Gundulićeva poljana; ◷6am-1pm Mon-Sat) Stallholders sell mainly produce, local artisanal products and craft at this open-air market.

Algoritam　　Books

(www.algoritam.hr; Placa 8; ◷9am-9pm Mon-Sat, 10am-1pm Sun) A good bookshop with a wide range of English-language books and a variety of guides on Dubrovnik and Croatia.

Uje　　Food & Drinks

(www.uje.hr; Placa 5; ◷9am-11pm) Uje specialises in olive oils – among the best is Brachia, from the island of Brač – along with a wide range of other locally produced epicurean delights, including some excellent jams (the lemon spread is divine), pickled capers, local herbs and spices, honey, figs in honey, chocolate, wine and *rakija* (grappa).

KAWA　　Gifts & Souvenirs

(☏091 89 67 509; www.kawa.life; Hvarska 2; ◷10am-midnight) Selling 'wonderful items made by Croatians', KAWA combines an inviting, smart interior with a heartfelt appreciation of Croatian artisans and culture. From wines and craft beers to jewellery, clothing, homewares and even its own line of products under the Happy Čevapi label, KAWA's selection reflects a refined taste and great passion. Superb service rounds off the experience.

⊗ EATING

Pizzeria Tabasco　　Pizza €

(☏020-429 595; www.pizzeriatabasco.hr; Hvarska 48; pizzas 55-120KN; ◷9.30am-midnight;) Positioned right above the old town and just underneath the cable-car station, Tabasco is a tasty stopover between the two attractions and a local's fave. Wood-fired pizzas with an ample variety of toppings, plus shaded terraces and a maze-like interior definitely compensate for a seemingly unsexy location at the end of a parking lot.

Oliva Pizzeria   Pizza €

(☑020-324 594; www.pizza-oliva.com; Lučarica 5; mains 41-86KN; ⊗10am-midnight) There are a few token pasta dishes on the menu, but this attractive little place is really all about pizza. And the pizza is worthy of the attention. Grab a seat on the street and tuck in.

Pantarul   Modern European €€

(☑020-333 486; www.pantarul.com; Kralja Tomislava 1; mains 70-128KN; ⊗noon-4pm & 6pm-midnight) This breezy bistro serves exceptional homemade bread, pasta and risotto, alongside the likes of pork belly, steaks, ox cheeks, burgers and a variety of fish dishes. There's a fresh modern touch to most dishes but chef Ana-Marija Bujić knows her way around traditional

Dalmatian cuisine too – she's got her own cookbook to prove it.

Nishta   Vegetarian €€

(☑020-322 088; www.nishtarestaurant.com; Prijeko 29; mains 77-85KN; ⊗11.30am-11.30pm; �'✎) The popularity of this tiny old-town eatery (expect to queue) is testament not just to the paucity of options for vegetarians and vegans in Croatia but to the excellent, imaginative food produced within. Alongside the expected curries, pastas and vegie burgers, the menu delivers more unusual delicious options such as eggplant tartare, 'tempehritos' and pasta-free zucchini 'spaghetti'.

Shizuku   Japanese €€

(☑020-311 493; www.facebook.com/Shizuku Dubrovnik; Kneza Domagoja 1f; mains 65-99KN; ⊗noon-midnight Tue-Sun; ⚑) Tucked away in a residential area between the harbour and Lapad Bay, this charming little restaurant has an appealing front terrace and an interior decorated with silky draperies, paper lampshades and colourful umbrellas. The Japanese owners will be in the kitchen,

Al fresco dining

preparing authentic sushi, sashimi, udon and gyoza. Wash it all down with Japanese beer or sake.

Restaurant 360° Modern European €€€

(☑020-322 222; www.360dubrovnik.com; Sv Dominika bb; mains 240-290KN, 5-course degustation 780KN; ☺6.30-11pm) Dubrovnik's glitziest restaurant offers fine dining at its finest, with flavoursome, beautifully presented, creative cuisine, and slick, professional service. The setting is unrivalled, on top of the city walls with tables positioned so you can peer through the battlements over the harbour.

Amfora International €€€

(☑020-419 419; www.amforadubrovnik.com; Obala Stjepana Radića 26; mains 145-185KN; ☺noon-4pm & 7-11pm) From the street, Amfora looks like just another local cafe-bar, but the real magic happens at the six-table restaurant at the rear. Dalmatian favourites such as *pašticada* (stew with gnocchi) and black risotto sit alongside fusion dishes such as swordfish sashimi, veal kofte, and miso fish soup.

Restaurant Dubrovnik European €€€

(☑020-324 810; www.restorandubrovnik.com; Marojice Kaboge 5; mains 105-210KN; ☺noon-midnight) One of Dubrovnik's most upmarket restaurants has a wonderfully unstuffy setting, occupying a covered rooftop terrace hidden among the venerable stone buildings of the old town. A strong French influence pervades a menu full of decadent and rich dishes, such as confit duck and plump Adriatic lobster tail served on homemade pasta.

🍷 DRINKING & NIGHTLIFE

Bard Bar

(off Ilije Sarake; ☺9am-3am) The more upmarket and slick of two cliff bars pressed up against the seaward side of the city walls, this one is lower on the rocks and has a shaded terrace where you can lose a day

quite happily, mesmerised by the Adriatic vistas. At night the surrounding stone is lit in ever-changing colours.

Cave Bar More Bar

(www.hotel-more.hr; Hotel More, Šetalište Nika i Meda Pucića; ☺10am-midnight) This little beach bar serves coffee, snacks and cocktails to bathers reclining by the dazzlingly clear waters of Lapad Bay, but that's not the half of it – the main bar is set in an actual cave. Cool off beneath the stalactites in the side chamber, where a glass floor exposes a water-filled cavern.

D'vino Wine Bar

(☑020-321 130; www.dvino.net; Palmotićeva 4a; ☺10am-late; 🛜) If you're interested in sampling top-notch Croatian wine, this upmarket little bar is the place to go. As well as a large and varied wine list, it offers themed tasting flights (multiple wine tastings; three wines for 50KN) accompanied by a thorough description by the knowledgable staff.

Buža Bar

(off Od Margarite; ☺8am-2am) Finding this ramshackle bar-on-a-cliff feels like a real discovery as you duck and dive around the city walls and finally see the entrance tunnel. However, Buža's no secret – it gets insanely busy, especially around sunset. Wait for a space on one of the concrete platforms, grab a cool drink in a plastic cup and enjoy the vibe and views.

ℹ️ INFORMATION

Dubrovnik Tourist Board Has offices in **Pile** (☑020-312 011; www.tzdubrovnik.hr; Brsalje 5; ☺8am-9pm Jun-Sep, 8am-7pm Mon-Sat, 9am-3pm Sun Oct-May), **Gruž** (☑020-417 983; Obala Pape Ivana Pavla II 1; ☺8am-9pm Jun-Sep, to 3pm Mon-Sat Oct-May) and **Lapad** (☑020-437 460; Kralja Tomislava 7; ☺8am-8pm Mon-Fri, 9am-noon & 5-8pm Sat & Sun Jun-Sep).

Dubrovnik General Hospital (Opća bolnica Dubrovnik; ☑020-431 777; www.bolnica-du.hr; Dr Roka Mišetića 2; ☺emergency department 24hr) On the southern edge of the Lapad peninsula.

Travel Corner (020-492 313; Obala Stjepana Radića 40; internet per hr 25KN, left luggage 2hr 10KN then per hr 4KN, per day 40KN; ☺9am-8pm Mon-Sat, 9am-4.30pm Sun) This handy one-stop shop has a left-luggage service and internet terminals, dispenses tourist information, books excursions and sells Kapetan Luka ferry tickets.

 GETTING THERE & AWAY

Dubrovnik Airport (DBV, Zračna luka Dubrovnik; 020-773 100; www.airport-dubrovnik.hr) is in Čilipi, 19km southeast of Dubrovnik. Both Croatia Airlines and British Airways fly to Dubrovnik year-round. In summer they're joined by dozens of other airlines flying seasonal routes and charter flights.

Croatia Airlines has domestic flights from Zagreb (year-round), Split and Osijek (both May to October only).

A taxi to the old town costs up to 280KN.

 GETTING AROUND

BUS

Dubrovnik has a superb bus service, buses run frequently and generally on time. The key tourist routes run until after 2am in summer. The fare is 15KN if you buy from the driver, and 12KN if you buy a ticket at a *tisak* (news-stand). Timetables are available at www.libertasdubrovnik.hr.

To get to the old town from the bus station, take buses 1a, 1b, 3 or 8.

CAR

The entire old town is a pedestrian area, public transport is good and parking is expensive, so you're better off not hiring a car until you're

 Where to Stay

Croatia is traditionally seen as a summer destination and good places book out well in advance in July and August. It's also very busy in June and September.

Accommodation in Dubrovnik's old town is limited. Private accommodation is a good alternative but beware the scramble of private owners at the bus station and ferry terminal. Some provide what they say they offer, others are scamming – try to pin down the location in advance if you want to be able to walk to the old town. Note that if you stay in unlicensed accommodation you are unprotected in case of a problem; all registered places should have a blue *'sobe'* (rooms available) sign.

Dubrovnik's Old Town
IHOR PASTERNAK/SHUTTERSTOCK ©

ready to leave the city. All of the street parking surrounding the old town is metered from May to October (40KN per hour). Further out it drops to 20KN or 10KN per hour.

All of the usual car-hire companies are represented at the airport and most also have city branches.

GERMANY & EASTERN EUROPE

In This Chapter

The Berlin Wall 488
The Reichstag 492
Berlin Nightlife 494
Historical Highlights 496
Sights 498
Tours 508
Shopping 509
Eating 509
Drinking & Nightlife 513
Entertainment 516
Information 517
Getting There & Away 517
Getting Around 518

Berlin, Germany

Berlin's combo of glamour and grit is bound to mesmerise anyone keen to explore its vibrant culture, cutting-edge architecture, fabulous food, intense parties and tangible history.

It's a city that staged a revolution, was headquartered by Nazis, bombed to bits, divided in two and finally reunited – and that was just in the 20th century! Berlin is a big multicultural metropolis, but deep down it maintains the unpretentious charm of an international village.

Two Days in Berlin

Start your first day at the **Reichstag** (p493), then stroll over to the iconic **Brandenburger Tor** (p498). Next, head west along Strasse des 17 Juli, passing the Soviet War memorial before you reach the **Siegessäule** (p505). Take the steps to the top to view the beautiful **Tiergarten** (p504), before getting lost in the park itself. Dedicate your second day to exploring the museums and galleries at **Museumsinsel** (p503).

Four Days in Berlin

Start your third day at the vast **Holocaust Memorial** (p498). Stroll through nearby **Potsdamer Platz** (p504) and then on to the **Topographie des Terrors** (p504) documentation centre and **Checkpoint Charlie** (p499). Use day four to visit the **Gedenkstätte Berliner Mauer** (p489) before heading to the **East Side Gallery** (p489), the longest surviving piece of the Berlin Wall.

Next stop: **Schloss Neuschwanstein** (p520) or beautiful Prague (p524).

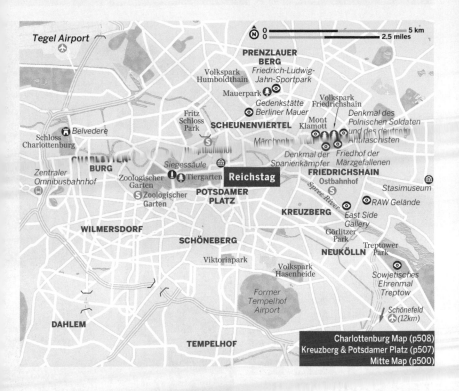

Arriving in Berlin

Tegel & Schönefeld Airports Handle domestic and international flights. Tegel is served directly only by bus and taxi. From Schönefeld, take the S-Bahn or a regional train to the city centre.

Hauptbahnhof Main train station in the city centre; served by S-Bahn, U-Bahn, tram, bus and taxi.

Zentraler Omnibusbahnhof (ZOB) Point of arrival for most long-haul buses.

Where to Stay

Berlin has over 137,000 hotel rooms, but the most desirable properties book up quickly, especially in summer and around major holidays; prices soar and reservations are essential. Otherwise, rates are low by Western capital standards. Options range from chain hotels and Old Berlin–style B&Bs to happening hostels, handy self-catering apartments and trendy boutique hotels.

For information on what each Berlin neighbourhood has to offer, see the table on p519.

The Berlin Wall

For 28 years the Berlin Wall was the most potent symbol of the Cold War. Surprisingly very few of its reinforced concrete slabs remain in today's reunited Berlin.

Construction

Shortly after midnight on 13 August 1961 East German soldiers and police began rolling out miles of barbed wire that would soon be replaced with prefab concrete slabs. The wall was a desperate measure taken by the German Democratic Republic (GDR) government to stop the sustained brain and brawn drain it had experienced since its 1949 founding. Around 3.6 million people had already left for the West, putting the GDR on the verge of economic and political collapse.

Demise

The Wall's demise in 1989 came as unexpectedly as its construction. Once again the GDR was losing its people in droves, this time via Hungary, which had opened its borders with Austria. Something had to give. It did on 9 November 1989 when a GDR

Great For...

☑ **Don't Miss**

The open-air mural collection of the East Side Gallery.

Mural by Thierry Noir on the Wall

⊚ **Gedenkstätte Berliner Mauer**

Ⓢ Nordbahnhof

❶ Need to Know

A double row of cobblestones guides you along 5.7km of the Wall's course. Track down remaining fragments of the Wall using Memorial Landscape Berlin Wall (www.berlin-wall-map.com).

✗ Take a Break

Not far from the Berlin Wall Memorial is the famous Konnopke's Imbiss (p510).

★ Top Tip

There's a great view from the Documentation Centre's viewing platform.

Eberswalder Strasse) **FREE** extends for 1.4km along Bernauer Strasse and integrates an original section of Wall, vestiges of the border installations and escape tunnels, a chapel and a monument. Multimedia stations, panels, excavations and a Documentation Centre provide context and explain what the border fortifications looked like and how they shaped the everyday lives of people on both sides of it.

spokesperson (mistakenly, it later turned out) announced during a press conference that all travel restrictions to the West would be lifted. When asked when, he said simply 'Immediately'. Amid scenes of wild partying, the two Berlins came together again.

In the course of 1990 the Wall almost disappeared from Berlin, some bits smashed up and flogged to tourists, other sections carted off to museums, parks, embassies, exhibitions and even private gardens across the globe. The longest section to survive intact is the East Side Gallery.

Gedenkstätte Berliner Mauer

The outdoor **Berlin Wall Memorial** (☏030-467 986 666; www.berliner-mauer-gedenkstaette. de; Bernauer Strasse, btwn Schwedter Strasse & Gartenstrasse; ☺visitor & documentation centre 10am-6pm Tue-Sun, open-air exhibit 8am-10pm daily; ⓢNordbahnhof, Bernauer Strasse,

East Side Gallery

The year was 1989. After 28 years, the Berlin Wall, that grim and grey divider of humanity, finally met its maker. Most of it was quickly dismantled, but along Mühlenstrasse, paralleling the Spree, a 1.3km stretch became the **East Side Gallery** (www.eastsidegallery-berlin. de; Mühlenstrasse btwn Oberbaumbrücke & Ostbahnhof; ☺24hr; ⓤWarschauer Strasse, ⓢOstbahnhof, Warschauer Strasse) **FREE**, the world's largest open-air mural collection. In more than 100 paintings, dozens of international artists translated the era's global euphoria and optimism into a mix of political statements, drug-induced musings and truly artistic visions.

The Berlin Wall

The construction of the Berlin Wall was a unique event in human history, not only for physically bisecting a city but by becoming a dividing line between competing ideologies and political systems. It's this global impact and universal legacy that continue to fascinate people more than a quarter century after its triumphant tear-down. Fortunately, plenty of original Wall segments and other vestiges remain, along with museums and memorials, to help fathom the realities and challenges of daily life in Berlin during the Cold War.

Our illustration points out the top highlights you can visit to learn about different aspects of these often tense decades. The best place to start is the ❶ **Gedenkstätte Berliner Mauer**, for an excellent introduction to what the inner-city border really looked liked and what it meant to live in its shadow. Reflect upon what you've learned while relaxing along the former death strip, now the ❷ **Mauerpark**, before heading to the emotionally charged exhibit at the ❸ **Tränenpalast**, an actual border-crossing pavilion. Relive the euphoria of the

Brandenburg Tor
People around the world cheered as East and West Berliners partied together atop the Berlin Wall in front of the iconic city gate, which today is a photogenic symbol of united Germany.

Potsdamer Platz
Nowhere was the death strip as wide as on the former no-man's-land around Potsdamer Platz from which sprouted a new postmodern city quarter in the 1990s. A tiny section of the Berlin Wall serves as a reminder.

Checkpoint Charlie
Only diplomats and foreigners were allowed to use this border crossing. Weeks after the Wall was built, US and Soviet tanks faced off here in one of the hottest moments of the Cold War.

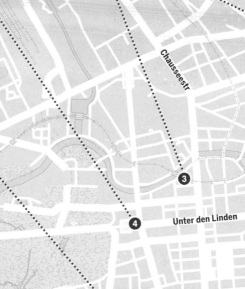

Tränenpalast
This modernist 1962 glass-and-steel border pavilion was dubbed 'Palace of Tears' because of the many tearful farewells that took place outside the building as East Germans and their western visitors had to say goodbye.

Bernauer Strasse

Chausseestr

Unter den Linden

Leipziger Str

Wall's demise at the ❹ **Brandenburg Tor**, then marvel at the revival of ❺ **Potsdamer Platz**, which was nothing but death-strip wasteland until the 1990s. The Wall's geopolitical significance is the focus at ❻ **Checkpoint Charlie**, which saw some of the tensest moments of the Cold War. Wrap up with finding your favourite mural motif at the ❼ **East Side Gallery**.

It's possible to explore these sights by using a combination of walking and public transport, but a bike ride is the best method for gaining a sense of the former Wall's erratic flow through the central city.

FAST FACTS

Beginning of construction 13 August 1961
Total length 155km
Height 3.6m
Weight of each segment 2.6 tonnes
Number of watchtowers 300

❷ ....
Remnants of the Wall →

Mauerpark
Famous for its flea market and karaoke, this popular park actually occupies a converted section of death strip. A 30m segment of surviving Wall is now an official practice ground for budding graffiti artists.

LINNA A ODOM/GETTY IMAGES ©

Gedenkstätte Berliner Mauer
Germany's central memorial to the Berlin Wall and its victims exposes the complexity and barbaric nature of the border installation along a 1.4km stretch of the barrier's course.

Alexanderplatz

Alexanderstr

East Side Gallery
Paralleling the Spree for 1.3km, this is the longest Wall vestige. After its collapse, more than a hundred international artists expressed their feelings about this historic moment in a series of colourful murals.

EWAIS/SHUTTERSTOCK ©

❼

HENRYK SADURA/GETTY IMAGES ©

The Reichstag

Reinstated as the home of the German parliament in 1999, the late 19th-century Reichstag is one of Berlin's most iconic buildings.

Great For...

☑ Don't Miss

Free auto-activated audioguides provide info on the building, landmarks and the workings of parliament.

The Reichstag's Beginnings

It's been burned, bombed, rebuilt, buttressed by the Wall, wrapped in plastic and finally brought back from the dead by Norman Foster: 'turbulent history' just doesn't do it when describing the life this most famous of Berlin's landmarks has endured. This neo-baroque edifice was finished in 1894 to house the German Imperial Diet and served its purpose until 1933 when it was badly damaged by fire in an arson attack carried out by Marinus van der Lubbe, a young Dutch communist. This shocking event conveniently gave Hitler a pretext to tighten his grip on the German state. In 1945 the building was a major target for the Red Army who raised the red flag from the Reichstag, an act that became a symbol of the Soviet defeat of the Nazis.

TRENT ZUM MALLEN/EYEEM/GETTY IMAGES ©

ⓘ Need to Know

Map p500; www.bundestag.de; Platz der Republik 1, Visitors' Service, Scheidemann-strasse; ⊙lift ride 8am-midnight, last entry 10pm, Visitors' Service 8am-8pm Apr-Oct, to 6pm Nov-Mar; 🚌100, ⑤Brandenburger Tor, Hauptbahnhof, Ⓤ Brandenburger Tor, Bundestag **FREE**

✕ Take a Break

For quick feeds, the tourist-geared, self-service **Berlin Pavillon** (Map p500; 📞030-2065 4737; www.berlin-pavillon. de; Scheidemannstrasse 1; mains €3.50-9; ⊙8am-9pm) comes in handy.

★ Top Tip

For guaranteed access, make free ticket reservations online before you leave home. Note that all visitors must show ID to enter the building.

The Cold War Years

Although in West Berlin, the Reichstag found itself very near the dividing line between East and West Berlin and from the early 1960s, the Berlin Wall. With the German government sitting safely in faraway Bonn, this grand facade lost its purpose and in the 1950s some in West Berlin thought it should be demolished. However, the wrecking balls never got their day and the Reichstag was restored, albeit without a lot of the decoration which had adorned the old building.

Reunification & Norman Foster

Almost a year after the Wall came down, the official reunification ceremony was symbolically held at the Reichstag which, it was later decided, would become the seat of the German Bundestag (parliament)

once again. Before Norman Foster began his reconstruction work, the entire Reichstag was spectacularly wrapped in plastic sheeting by the Bulgarian-American artist Christo in the summer of 1995. The following four years saw the erection of Norman Foster's now famous glittering glass copula, the centrepiece of the visitor experience today. It is the Reichstag's most distinctive feature, serviced by lift and providing fabulous 360-degree city views and the opportunity to peer down into the parliament chamber. To reach the top, follow the ramp spiralling up around the dome's mirror-clad central cone. The cupola was a spanking new feature, but Foster's brief also stipulated that some parts of the building were to be preserved. One example is the Cyrillic graffiti left by Soviet soldiers in 1945.

MAREMAGNUM/GETTY IMAGES ©

Berlin Nightlife

With its well-deserved reputation as one of Europe's primo party capitals, Berlin offers a thousand-and-one scenarios for getting your cocktails and kicks (or wine or beer, for that matter).

Great For...

☑ Don't Miss

Café am Neuen See (p514), generally regarded as Berlin's best beer garden.

Bars & Cafes

Berlin is a notoriously late city: bars stay packed from dusk to dawn and beyond, and some clubs don't hit their stride until 4am. The lack of a curfew never created a tradition of binge drinking.

Edgier, more underground venues cluster in Kreuzberg, Friedrichshain, Neukölln and up-and-coming outer boroughs like Wedding (north of Mitte) and Lichtenberg (past Friedrichshain). Places in Charlottenburg, Mitte and Prenzlauer Berg tend to be quieter and close earlier. Some proprietors have gone to extraordinary lengths to come up with special design concepts.

The line between cafe and bar is often blurred, with many changing stripes as the hands move around the clock. Alcohol, however, is served pretty much all day. Cocktail bars are booming in Berlin and

Beach bars along the Spree River

several new arrivals have measurably elevated the 'liquid art' scene. Dedicated drinking dens tend to be elegant cocoons with mellow lighting and low sound levels. A good cocktail will set you back between €10 and €15.

Beaches & Outdoor Drinking

Berliners are sun cravers and as soon as the first rays spray their way into spring, outdoor tables show up faster than you can pour a pint of beer. The most traditional places for outdoor chilling are, of course, the beer gardens with long wooden benches set up beneath leafy old chestnuts and with cold beer and bratwurst on the menu. In 2002, Berlin also jumped on the 'sandwagon' with the opening of its first beach bar, Strandbar Mitte (p513), in a prime location on the Spree River. Many

that followed have since been displaced by development, which has partly fuelled the latest trend: rooftop bars.

Clubbing

Over the past 25 years, Berlin's club culture has put the city firmly on the map of hedonists. With more than 200 venues, finding one to match your mood isn't difficult. Electronic music in its infinite varieties continues to define Berlin's after-dark action but other sounds like hip-hop, dancehall, rock, swing and funk have also made inroads. The edgiest clubs have taken up residence in power plants, transformer stations, abandoned apartment buildings and other repurposed locations. The scene is in constant flux as experienced club owners look for new challenges and a younger generation of promoters enters the scene with new ideas and impetus.

Historical Highlights

This walk checks off Berlin's blockbuster landmarks as it cuts right through the historic city centre, Mitte (literally 'Middle'). This is the birthplace and glamorous heart of Berlin, a high-octane cocktail of culture, architecture and commerce.
Start Reichstag
Distance 3.5km
Duration Three hours

Classic Photo: The iconic Brandenburger Tor is now a symbol of German reunification.

2 The **Brandenburger Tor** (p498) became an involuntary neighbour of the Berlin Wall during the Cold War.

3 Unter den Linden has been Berlin's showpiece road since the 18th century.

Take a Break... Stop in at Augustiner am Gendarmenmarkt (p509) for some German fare.

1 The sparkling glass dome of the **Reichstag** (p493) has become a shining beacon of unified Berlin.

5 The northern half of Spree island is **Museumsinsel** (p503), a Unesco-recognised treasure chest of art, sculpture and objects.

7 Pompous and majestic inside and out, the **Berliner Dom** (p503) is a symbol of Prussian imperial power.

6 Opposite Museumsinsel, the massive **Humboldt Forum** is taking shape. Its facade will mimic the old Prussian city palace when completed.

4 Berlin's most beautiful square, **Gendarmenmarkt** (p499) is bookended by domed cathedrals with the famous Konzerthaus (Concert Hall) in between.

◉ SIGHTS
◎ Mitte

With the mother lode of sights clustered within a walkable area, the most historic part of Berlin is a prime port of call for visitors.

Deutsches Historisches Museum   Museum

(Map p500; German Historical Museum; ☎030-203 040; www.dhm.de; Unter den Linden 2; adult/concession/under 18 €8/4/free; ◷10am-6pm; 🚌100, 200, Ⓤ Hausvogteiplatz, Ⓢ Hackescher Markt) If you're wondering what the Germans have been up to for the past two millennia, take a spin around this engaging museum in the baroque Zeughaus, formerly the Prussian arsenal and now home of the German Historical Museum. Upstairs, displays concentrate on the period from the 1st century AD to the end of WWI in 1918, while the ground floor tracks the 20th century all the way through to German reunification.

> *sarcophagi-like concrete columns rising in sombre silence*

Holocaust Memorial

Brandenburger Tor   Landmark

(Brandenburger Gate; Map p500; Pariser Platz; Ⓢ Brandenburger Tor, Ⓤ Brandenburger Tor) A symbol of division during the Cold War, the landmark Brandenburg Gate now epitomises German reunification. Carl Gotthard Langhans found inspiration in Athens' Acropolis for the elegant triumphal arch, completed in 1791 as the royal city gate. It stands sentinel over Pariser Platz, a harmoniously proportioned square once again framed by banks, a hotel and the US, British and French embassies, just as it was during its 19th-century heyday.

Holocaust Memorial   Memorial

(Memorial to the Murdered Jews of Europe; Map p500; ☎030-2639 4336; www.stiftung-denkmal.de; Cora-Berliner-Strasse 1; ◷24hr; Ⓢ Brandenburger Tor, Ⓤ Brandenburger Tor) 🆓 Inaugurated in 2005, this football-field-sized memorial by American architect Peter Eisenman consists of 2711 sarcophagi-like concrete columns rising in sombre silence from undulating ground. You're free to access this maze at any point and make your individual journey through it. For context

ANTON HAVELAAR/SHUTTERSTOCK ©

visit the subterranean **Ort der Information** (Information Centre; Map p500; ☑030-7407 2929; www.holocaust-mahnmal.de; audio guide adult/concession €4/2; ☺10am-8pm Tue-Sun Apr-Sep, to 7pm Oct-Mar, last admission 45min before closing) **FREE** whose exhibits will leave no one untouched. Audioguides and audio translations of exhibit panels are available.

Gendarmenmarkt Square

(Map p500; ⓤFranzösische Strasse, Stadtmitte) The Gendarmenmarkt area is Berlin at its ritziest, dappled with luxury hotels, fancy restaurants and bars. The graceful square is bookended by the domed 18th-century German and French cathedrals and punctuated by a grandly porticoed concert hall, the **Konzerthaus** (Map p500; ☑030-203 092 333; www.konzerthaus.de; tours €3). It was named for the Gens d'Armes, an 18th-century Prussian regiment consisting of French Huguenot refugees whose story is chronicled in a museum inside the **Französischer Dome** (French Cathedral; Map p500; www.franzoesischer-dom.de; church free, museum adult/concession €3.50/2, tower adult/child €3/1; ☺church & museum noon-5pm Tue-Sun, tower 10am-7pm Apr-Oct, noon-5pm Jan-Mar, last entry 1hr before closing). Climb the tower here for grand views of historic Berlin.

Checkpoint Charlie   Historic Site
(Map p507; cnr Zimmerstrasse & Friedrichstrasse; ☺24hr; ⓤKochstrasse) **FREE** Checkpoint Charlie was the principal gateway for foreigners and diplomats between the two Berlins from 1961 to 1990. Unfortunately, this potent symbol of the Cold War has degenerated into a tacky tourist trap, though a free open-air exhibit that illustrates milestones in Cold War history is one redeeming aspect.

◎ Scheunenviertel
Hackesche Höfe   Historic Site
(Map p500; ☑030-2809 8010; www.hackesche-hoefe.com; enter from Rosenthaler Strasse 40/41 or Sophienstrasse 6; ☐M1, ⓢHackescher Markt, ⓤWeinmeisterstrasse) **FREE** The Hackesche Höfe is the largest and most famous of the

 Treptower Park & the Soviet Memorial

The former East Berlin district of Treptow gets its character from the Spree River and two parks: Treptower Park and Plänterwald. Both are vast sweeps of expansive lawns, shady woods and tranquil riverfront and are popular for strolling, jogging and picnicking.

Treptower Park's main sight is the gargantuan **Sowjetisches Ehrenmal Treptow** (Soviet War Memorial; ☺24hr; ☐Treptower Park) **FREE**, which stands above the graves of 5000 Soviet soldiers killed in the 1945 Battle of Berlin. Inaugurated in 1949, it's a bombastic and sobering testament to the immensity of Russia's wartime losses. Coming from the S-Bahn station, you'll first be greeted by a **statue of Mother Russia** grieving for her dead children. Beyond, two mighty walls fronted by soldiers kneeling in sorrow flank the gateway to the memorial itself; the red marble used here was supposedly scavenged from Hitler's ruined chancellery. Views open up to an enormous sunken lawn lined by **sarcophagi** representing the then 16 Soviet republics, each decorated with war scenes and Stalin quotations. The epic dramaturgy reaches a crescendo at the **mausoleum**, topped by a 13m statue of a Russian soldier clutching a child, his sword resting melodramatically on a shattered swastika. The socialist-realism mosaic within the plinth shows grateful Soviets honouring the fallen.

Sowjetisches Ehrenmal Treptow
CAROL.ANNE/SHUTTERSTOCK ©

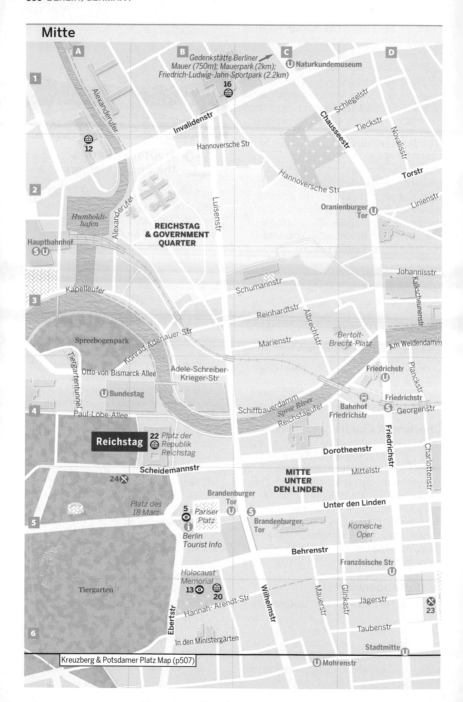

Mitte

Gedenkstätte Berliner
Mauer (750m); Mauerpark (2km);
Friedrich-Ludwig-Jahn-Sportpark (2.2km)

Naturkundemuseum

16

12

Invalidenstr

Hannoversche Str

Schlegelstr

Tieckstr

Chausseestr

Novalisstr

Hannoversche Str

Torstr

Oranienburger
Tor

Linienstr

Alexanderufer

Luisenstr

**REICHSTAG
& GOVERNMENT
QUARTER**

Humboldt-
hafen

Johannisstr

Hauptbahnhof

Alexanderufer

Kapelleufer

Schumannstr

Reinhardtstr

Albrechtstr

Bertolt-
Brecht-Platz

Am Weidendamm

Kalkscheunenstr

Spreebogenpark

Konrad-Adenauer-Str

Otto-von-Bismarck-Allee

Adele-Schreiber-
Krieger-Str

Marienstr

Friedrichstr

Planckstr

Tiergartentunnel

Bundestag

Schiffbauerdamm

Spree River
Reichstagufer

Bahnhof
Friedrichstr

Friedrichstr

Georgenstr

Paul-Löbe-Allee

Reichstag

22
Republik
Reichstag

Platz der

Dorotheenstr

Friedrichstr

Charlottenstr

24

Scheidemannstr

Mittelstr

**MITTE
UNTER
DEN LINDEN**

Platz des
18 März

Brandenburger
Tor

5
Pariser
Platz

Brandenburger
Tor

Unter den Linden

Berlin
Tourist Info

Behrenstr

Komische
Oper

Tiergarten

Holocaust
Memorial
13

20

Hannah- Arendt-Str

Wilhelmstr

Mauerstr

Glinkastr

Französische Str

Jägerstr

23

Ebertstr

Taubenstr

In den Ministergärten

Stadtmitte

Kreuzberg & Potsdamer Platz Map (p507)

Mohrenstr

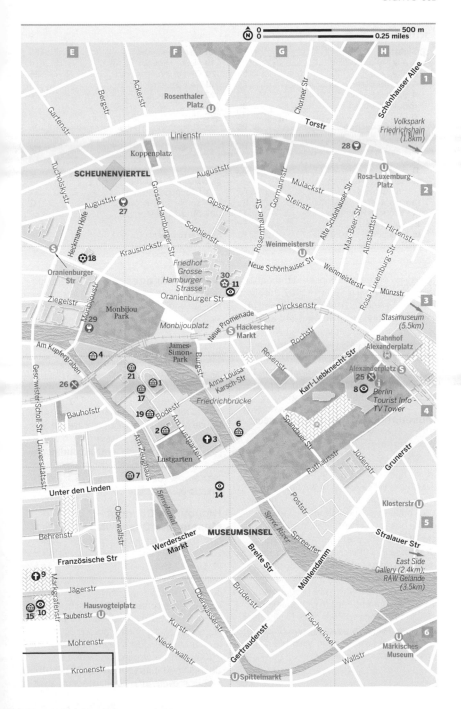

Mitte

⦿ Sights
1 Alte Nationalgalerie F4
2 Altes Museum...F4
3 Berliner Dom..F4
4 Bode-Museum E3
5 Brandenburger Tor B5
6 DDR Museum..G4
7 Deutsches Historisches Museum.............F5
8 Fernsehturm..H4
9 Französischer Dom....................................E5
10 Gendarmenmarkt E6
11 Hackesche Höfe G3
12 Hamburger Bahnhof – Museum
    für Gegenwart..A2
13 Holocaust Memorial B6
14 Humboldt Forum..F5
15 Konzerthaus E6
16 Museum für Naturkunde...........................B1
17 Museumsinsel..F4

18 Neue Synagoge..E3
19 Neues Museum..F4
20 Ort der Information B6
21 Pergamonmuseum F4
22 Reichstag...B4

⊗ Eating
23 Augustiner am Gendarmenmarkt.............D6
24 Berlin Pavillon A5
25 Sphere..H4
26 Zwölf Apostel E4

⊙ Drinking & Nightlife
27 Clärchens Ballhaus E2
28 Kaffee Burger...H2
29 Strandbar Mitte E3

⊗ Entertainment
30 Chamäleon Varieté......................................F3

courtyard ensembles peppered throughout the Scheunenviertel. Built in 1907, the eight interlinked *Höfe* (courtyards) reopened in 1996 with a congenial mix of cafes, galleries, boutiques and entertainment venues. The main entrance on Rosenthaler Strasse leads to **Court I**, prettily festooned with art nouveau tiles, while Court VII segues to the romantic **Rosenhöfe** with a sunken rose garden and tendril-like balustrades.

Museum für Naturkunde Museum

(Museum of Natural History; Map p500; ☏030-2093 8591; www.naturkundemuseum.berlin; Invalidenstrasse 43; adult/concession incl audioguide €8/5; ⊙9.30am-6pm Tue-Fri, 10am-6pm Sat & Sun; ᴍM5, M8, M10, 12, ᴜNaturkundemuseum) Fossils and minerals don't quicken your pulse? Well, how about Tristan, one of the best-preserved *Tyrannosaurus rex* skeletons in the world, or the 12m-high *Brachiosaurus branchai,* the world's largest mounted dino skeleton? These Jurassic superstars are joined by a dozen other buddies, some of which are brought to virtual flesh-and-bone life with the help of clever 'Juraskopes'. Other crowd favourites in this excellent museum include Knut, the world's most famous dead polar bear, and an ultrarare archaeopteryx.

Neue Synagoge Synagogue

(Map p500; ☏030-8802 8300; www.centrumju daicum.de; Oranienburger Strasse 28-30; adult/ concession €5/4; ⊙10am-6pm Mon-Fri, to 7pm Sun, closes 3pm Fri & 6pm Sun Oct-Mar; ᴍM1, ᴜOranienburger Tor, ꜱOranienburger Strasse) The gleaming gold dome of the Neue Synagoge is the most visible symbol of Berlin's revitalised Jewish community. The 1866 original was Germany's largest synagogue but its modern incarnation is not so much a house of worship (although prayer services do take place), as a museum and place of remembrance called **Centrum Judaicum**. The dome can be climbed from April to September (adult/concession €3/2.50). An audioguide costs €3.

Hamburger Bahnhof – Museum für Gegenwart Museum

(Contemporary Art Museum; Map p500; ☏030-266 424 242; www.smb.museum; Invalidenstrasse 50-51; adult/concession €14/7; ⊙10am-6pm Tue, Wed & Fri, 10am-8pm Thu, 11am-6pm Sat & Sun; ᴍM5, M8, M10, ꜱHauptbahnhof, ᴜHauptbahnhof) Berlin's contemporary art showcase opened in 1996 in an old railway station, whose loft and grandeur are a great backdrop for this Aladdin's cave of paintings, installations, sculptures and video art. Changing exhibits span the arc of post-1950 artistic movements – from conceptual art and pop art to minimal art and Fluxus – and include seminal works by such major players as Andy Warhol, Cy Twombly, Joseph Beuys and Robert Rauschenberg.

⊙ Alexanderplatz

It's practically impossible to visit Berlin without spending time in this area, which packs some of Berlin's must-see sights into a very compact frame.

Museumsinsel   Museum

(Museum Island; Map p500; ☎030-266 424 242; www.smb.museum; day tickets for all 5 museums adult/concession/under 18 €18/9/free; ☺varies by museum; ☒100, 200, TXL, ⓤHackescher Markt, Friedrichstrasse) Walk through ancient Babylon, meet an Egyptian queen, clamber up a Greek altar or be mesmerised by Monet's ethereal landscapes. Welcome to Museumsinsel (Museum Island), Berlin's most important treasure trove, spanning 6000 years' worth of art, artefacts, sculpture and architecture from Europe and beyond. Spread across five grand museums built between 1830 and 1930, the complex takes up the entire northern half of the little Spree Island where Berlin's settlement began in the 13th century.

The first repository to open was the **Altes Museum** (Old Museum; Map p500; Am Lustgarten; adult/concession €10/5; ☺10am-6pm Tue, Wed & Fri-Sun, to 8pm Thu), which presents Greek, Etruscan and Roman antiquities. Behind it, the **Neues Museum** (New Museum; Map p500; Bodestrasse 1-3; adult/concession €12/6; ☺10am-6pm, to 8pm Thu) showcases the Egyptian collection, most famously the bust of Queen Nefertiti, and also houses the Museum of Pre- and Early History. The temple-like **Alte Nationalgalerie** (Old National Gallery; Map p500; Bodestrasse 1-3; adult/concession €12/6; ☺10am-6pm Tue, Wed & Fri-Sun, to 8pm Thu) trains the focus on 19th-century European art. The island's top draw is the **Pergamonmuseum** (Map p500; Bodestrasse 1-3; adult/concession €12/6; ☺10am-6pm Fri-Wed, to 8pm Thu), with its monumental architecture from ancient worlds, including the namesake Pergamonaltar. The **Bode-Museum** (Map p500; cnr Am Kupfergraben & Monbijoubrücke; adult/concession €12/6; ☺10am-6pm Tue, Wed & Fri-Sun, to 8pm Thu), at the island's northern tip, is famous for its medieval sculptures.

DDR Museum   Museum

(GDR Museum; Map p500; ☎030-847 123 731; www.ddr-museum.de; Karl-Liebknecht-Strasse 1; adult/concession €9.50/6; ☺10am-8pm Sun-Fri, to 10pm Sat; ☒100, 200, TXL, ⓢHackescher Markt) This interactive museum does an entertaining job of pulling back the iron curtain on an extinct society. You'll learn how, under communism, kids were put through collective potty training, engineers earned little more than farmers, and everyone, it seems, went on nudist holidays. A highlight is a simulated ride in a Trabi (an East German car).

Fernsehturm   Landmark

(TV Tower; Map p500; ☎030-247 575 875; www.tv-turm.de; Panoramastrasse 1a; adult/child €13/8.50, premium ticket €19.50/12; ☺9am-midnight Mar-Oct, 10am-midnight Nov-Feb, last ascent 11.30pm; ☒100, 200, TXL, ⓤAlexanderplatz, ⓢAlexanderplatz) Germany's tallest structure, the TV Tower has been soaring 368m high since 1969 and is as iconic to Berlin as the Eiffel Tower is to Paris. On clear days, views are stunning from the panorama level at 203m or from the upstairs **restaurant** (☎030-247 5750; www.tv-turm.de/en/bar-restaurant; mains lunch €9.50-18.50, dinner €14.50-28.50; ☺10am-midnight), which makes one revolution per hour. To shorten the wait, buy a timed ticket online.

Berliner Dom   Church

(Berlin Cathedral; Map p500; ☎030-2026 9136; www.berlinerdom.de; Am Lustgarten; adult/concession/under 18 €7/5/free; ☺9am-8pm Apr-Oct, to 7pm Nov-Mar; ☒100, 200, TXL, ⓢHackescher Markt) Pompous yet majestic, the Italian Renaissance–style former royal court church (1905) does triple duty as house of worship, museum and concert hall. Inside it's gilt to the hilt and outfitted with a lavish marble-and-onyx altar, a 7269-pipe Sauer organ and elaborate royal sarcophagi. Climb up the 267 steps to the gallery for glorious city views.

◎ Potsdamer Platz & Tiergarten

Potsdamer Platz   Area

(Map p507; Alte Potsdamer Strasse; 🚌200,
⑤ Potsdamer Platz, Ⓤ Potsdamer Platz) The
rebirth of the historic Potsdamer Platz
was Europe's biggest building project of
the 1990s, a showcase of urban renewal
masterminded by such top international
architects as Renzo Piano and Helmut
Jahn. An entire city quarter sprouted on
terrain once bifurcated by the Berlin Wall
and today houses offices, theatres and
cinemas, hotels, apartments and museums. Highlights include the glass-tented
Sony Center (Map p507; Potsdamer Strasse)
and the **Panoramapunkt** (Map p507; 🖉030-
2593 7080; www.panoramapunkt.de; Potsdamer
Platz 1; adult/concession €6.50/5, without wait
€10.50/8; ⊙10am-8pm Apr-Oct, to 6pm Nov-
Mar) observation deck.

Topographie des Terrors   Museum

(Topography of Terror; Map p507; 🖉030-2548
0950; www.topographie.de; Niederkirchner
Strasse 8; ⊙10am-8pm, grounds close at
dusk or 8pm at the latest; ⑤ Potsdamer Platz,
Ⓤ Potsdamer Platz) FREE In the same spot
where the most feared institutions of Nazi
Germany (including the Gestapo headquarters and the SS central command) once
stood, this compelling exhibit chronicles
the stages of terror and persecution, puts
a face on the perpetrators and details the
impact these brutal institutions had on all
of Europe. A second exhibit outside zeroes
in on how life changed for Berlin and its
people after the Nazis made it their capital.

Tiergarten   Park

(Map p507; Strasse des 17 Juni; 🚌100, 200,
⑤ Potsdamer Platz, Brandenburger Tor,
Ⓤ Brandenburger Tor) FREE Berlin's rulers
used to hunt boar and pheasants in the
rambling Tiergarten until garden architect
Peter Lenné landscaped the grounds in the
18th century. Today it's one of the world's
largest urban parks, popular for strolling,
jogging, picnicking, Frisbee tossing and,
yes, nude sunbathing and gay cruising
(especially around the Löwenbrücke). It
is bisected by a major artery, the Strasse
des 17 Juni. Walking across the entire park
takes about an hour, but even a shorter
stroll has its rewards.

DE VISU/SHUTTERSTOCK ©

Gemäldegalerie Gallery

(Gallery of Old Masters; Map p507; ☏030-266 424 242; www.smb.museum/gg; Matthäikirchplatz; adult/concession €10/5; ☉10am-6pm Tue, Wed & Fri, 10am-8pm Thu, 11am-6pm Sat & Sun; ⛟; ☐M29, M48, M85, 200, Ⓢ Potsdamer Platz, Ⓤ Potsdamer Platz) This museum ranks among the world's finest and most comprehensive collections of European art ⫸⫸⫸⫸⫸ ⫸⫸ 1600 paintings spanning the arc of artistic vision from the 13th to the 18th century. Wear comfy shoes when exploring the 72 galleries: a walk past masterpieces by Titian, Dürer, Hals, Vermeer, Gainsborough and many more Old Masters covers almost 2km. Don't miss the Rembrandt Room (Room X).

Siegessäule Monument

(Victory Column; Grosser Stern; adult/concession €3/2.50; ☉9.30am-6.30pm Mon-Fri, to 7pm Sat & Sun Apr-Oct, 10am-5pm Mon-Fri, to 5.30pm Sat & Sun Nov-Mar; ☐100, 200, Ⓤ Hansaplatz, Ⓢ Bellevue) Like arms of a starfish, five roads merge into the Grosser Stern roundabout at the heart of the huge Tiergarten park. The Victory Column at its centre is crowned by a gilded statue of the goddess Victoria

in celebration of 19th-century Prussian military triumphs. Today it is also a symbol of Berlin's gay community. Climb 285 steps for sweeping views of the park.

Bauhaus Archiv Museum

(Map p507; ☏030-254 0020; www.bauhaus. de; Klingelhöferstrasse 14; adult/concession/ under 18 incl audioguide Wed-Fri €7/4 (free, Sat-Mon €8/5/free; ☉10am-5pm Wed-Mon; ☐100, Ⓤ Nollendorfplatz) Founded in 1919, the Bauhaus was a seminal school of avant-garde architecture, design and art. This avant-garde building, designed by Bauhaus' founder Walter Gropius, presents paintings, drawings, sculptures, models and other objects and documents by such famous artist-teachers as Klee, Feininger and Kandinsky. There's a decent cafe and good gift shop. A building expansion by Berlin architect Volker Staab is planned to open in 2021.

 Prenzlauer Berg

Prenzlauer Berg doesn't have any blockbuster sights, and most of what it does have is concentrated in the pretty southern section around Kollwitzplatz.

> ★ **Top Five Historical Sites**
> **Gedenkstätte Berliner Mauer (p489)**
> **Topographie des Terrors (p504)**
> **Jüdisches Museum (p506)**
> **Sachsenhausen (p514)**
> **Deutsches Historisches Museum (p498)**

From left: Sony Center, Potsdamer Platz; Bauhaus Archiv; Goddess Victoria on top of the Siegessäule

The neighbourhood does include the city's most important exhibit on the Berlin Wall, the Gedenkstätte Berliner Mauer (p489), which begins in Wedding and stretches for 1.4km all the way into Prenzlauer Berg.

Mauerpark Park

(www.mauerpark.info; btwn Bernauer Strasse, Schwedter Strasse & Gleimstrasse; ⍾M1, M10, 12, UEberswalder Strasse) With its wimpy trees and anaemic lawn, Mauerpark is hardly your typical leafy oasis, especially given that it was forged from a section of Cold War–era death strip (a short stretch of Berlin Wall survives). It's this mystique combined with an unassuming vibe and a hugely popular Sunday flea market and karaoke show that has endeared the place to locals and visitors alike.

◎ **Kreuzberg**

Jüdisches Museum Museum

(Jewish Museum; Map p507; ☑030-2599 3300; www.jmberlin.de; Lindenstrasse 9-14; adult/concession €8/3, audioguide €3; ◷10am-8pm Tue-Sun, to 10pm Mon, last entry 1hr before closing; UHallesches Tor, Kochstrasse) In a landmark building by American-Polish architect Daniel Libeskind, Berlin's Jewish Museum offers a chronicle of the trials and triumphs in 2000 years of Jewish life in Germany. The exhibit smoothly navigates all major periods, from the Middle Ages via the Enlightenment to the community's post-1990 renaissance. Find out about Jewish cultural contributions, holiday traditions, the difficult road to emancipation and outstanding individuals (eg Moses Mendelssohn, Levi Strauss) and the fates of ordinary people.

Deutsches Technikmuseum Museum

(German Museum of Technology; Map p507; ☑030-902 540; www.sdtb.de; Trebbiner Strasse 9; adult/concession/under 18 €8/4/after 3pm free, audioguide adult/concession €2/1; ◷9am-5.30pm Tue-Fri, 10am-6pm Sat & Sun; P🚼; UGleisdreieck, Möckernbrücke) A roof-mounted 'candy bomber' (the plane used in the 1948 Berlin airlift) is merely the over-ture to this enormous and hugely engaging shrine to technology. Fantastic for kids, the giant museum counts the world's first computer, an entire hall of vintage locomotives and extensive exhibits on aerospace and navigation among its top attractions. At the adjacent **Science Center Spectrum** (enter Möckernstrasse 26; same ticket) kids can participate in hands-on experiments.

◎ **Friedrichshain**

This notorious party district also has a serious side, especially when it comes to blockbuster vestiges of the GDR era such as the East Side Gallery (p489), Karl-Marx-Allee and the Stasi HQ. Alas, the key sights are all pretty spread out and best reached by public transport.

Volkspark Friedrichshain Park

(bounded by Am Friedrichshain, Friedenstrasse, Danziger Strasse & Landsberger Allee; P; 🚌142, 200, ⍾M5, M6, M8, M10, USchillingstrasse) Berlin's oldest public park has provided relief from urbanity since 1840, but has been hilly only since the late 1940s when wartime debris was piled up here to create two 'mountains' – the taller one, **Mont Klamott** (◷24hr) FREE, rises 78m high. Diversions include expansive lawns for lazing, tennis courts, a halfpipe for skaters, a couple of handily placed beer gardens and an outdoor cinema.

◎ **Charlottenburg**

Schloss Charlottenburg Palace

(Map p508; ☑030-320 910; www.spsg.de; Spandauer Damm 10-22; day passes to all 4 buildings adult/concession €12/9; ◷hours vary by building; P; 🚌M45, 109, 309, URichard-Wagner-Platz, Sophie-Charlotte-Platz) Charlotten-burg Palace is one of the few sites in Berlin that still reflects the one-time grandeur of the Hohenzollern clan that ruled the region from 1415 to 1918. Originally a petite summer retreat, it grew into an exquisite baroque pile with opulent private apartments, richly festooned festival halls, collections of precious porcelain and paintings by French 18th-century masters. It's lovely

Kreuzberg & Potsdamer Platz

◎ Sights

1 Bauhaus Archiv A1
2 Checkpoint Charlie D1
3 Deutsches Technikmuseum C2
4 Gemäldegalerie B1
5 Jüdisches Museum D2
6 Panoramapunkt C1
7 Potsdamer Platz C1
8 Sony Center B1
9 Tiergarten A1
10 Topographie des Terrors C1

ⓐ Shopping

11 LP12 Mall of Berlin C1

⊗ Eating

12 Curry 36 .... D3
13 Restaurant Tim Raue D1

⊖ Drinking & Nightlife

14 Fragrances C1

⊛ Entertainment

15 Berliner Philharmonie B1

in fine weather when you can fold a stroll in the palace park into a day of peeking at royal treasures.

Kaiser-Wilhelm-Gedächtniskirche
Church

(Kaiser Wilhelm Memorial Church; Map p508; ☎030-218 5023; www.gedaechtniskirche.com; Breitscheidplatz; ⊗church 9am-7pm, memorial hall 10am-6pm Mon-Fri, 10am-5.30pm Sat, noon-5.30pm Sun; ☐100, 200, ⓤZoologischer Garten, Kurfürstendamm, ⓢZoologischer Garten) FREE

Allied bombing in 1943 left only the husk of the west tower of this once magnificent neo-Romanesque church standing. Now an antiwar memorial, it stands quiet and dignified amid the roaring traffic. Historic photographs displayed in the **Gedenkhalle** (Hall of Remembrance), at the bottom of the tower, help you visualise the former grandeur of this 1895 church. The adjacent octagonal hall of worship, added in 1961, has glowing midnight-blue glass walls and a giant 'floating' Jesus.

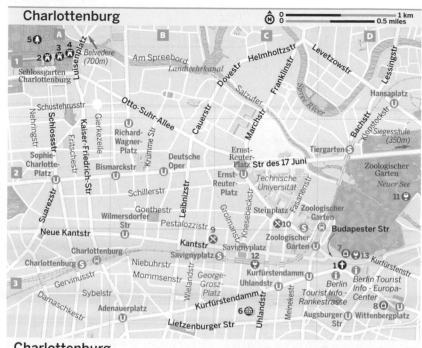

Charlottenburg

◎ Sights
1 Kaiser-Wilhelm-Gedächtniskirche	D3
2 Schloss Charlottenburg	A1
Schloss Charlottenburg - Altes Schloss	(see 2)
3 Schloss Charlottenburg - Neuer Flügel	A1
4 Schloss Charlottenburg - Neuer Pavillon	A1
5 Schlossgarten Charlottenburg	A1
6 Story of Berlin	C3

🛍 Shopping
7 Bikini Berlin	D3
8 KaDeWe	D3

🍴 Eating
9 Good Friends	B3
10 Restaurant am Steinplatz	C2

🍷 Drinking & Nightlife
Bar am Steinplatz	(see 10)
11 Café am Neuen See	D2
12 Diener Tattersall	C3
13 Monkey Bar	D3

Story of Berlin   Museum

(Map p508; ☎030-8872 0100; www.story-of-berlin.de; Kurfürstendamm 207-208, enter via Ku'damm Karree mall; adult/concession €12/9; ☉10am-8pm, last admission 6pm; ☐X9, X10, 109, 110, M19, M29, TXL, ⓊUhlandstrasse) This engaging museum breaks 800 years of Berlin history down into bite-size chunks that are easy to swallow but substantial enough to be satisfying. Each of the 23 rooms uses sound, light, technology and original objects to zero in on a specific theme or epoch in the city's history, from its founding in 1237 to the fall of the Berlin Wall. The creepily fascinating climax is a tour (in English) of a still-functional atomic bunker beneath the building.

🅖 TOURS

Berliner Unterwelten   Tours

(☎030-4991 0517; www.berliner-unterwelten.de; Brunnenstrasse 105; adult/concession €11/9;

⊗Dark Worlds tours in English 1pm Mon & 11am Thu-Mon year-round, 11am Wed Mar-Nov, 3pm Wed-Mon & 1pm Wed-Sun Apr-Oct; Ⓢ Gesundbrunnen, Ⓤ Gesundbrunnen) After you've checked off the Brandenburg Gate and the TV Tower, why not explore Berlin's dark and dank underbelly? Join Berliner Unterwelten on its 'Dark Worlds' tour of a WWII underground bunker (available in English) and pick your way through a warren of claustrophobic rooms, past heavy steel doors, hospital beds, helmets, guns, boots and lots of other wartime artefacts.

Berlin on Bike — Cycling

(☎030-4373 9999; www.berlinonbike.de; Knaackstrasse 97, Kulturbrauerei, Court 4; tours incl bike adult/concession €21/18; ⊗8am-8pm mid-Mar–mid-Nov, 10am-4pm Mon-Sat mid-Nov–mid-Mar; ◻M1, Ⓤ Eberswalder Strasse) This well-established company has a busy schedule of insightful and fun bike tours led by locals. There are daily English-language city tours (Berlin's Best) and Berlin Wall tours as well as an Alternative Berlin tour three times weekly. Other tours (eg street art, night tours) run in German or in English on request.

Original Berlin Walks — Walking

(☎030-301 9194; www.berlinwalks.de; adult/concession from €14/12) Berlin's longest-running English-language walking tour company has a large roster of general and themed tours (eg Hitler's Germany, Jewish Life, Berlin Wall), as well as trips out to Sachsenhausen concentration camp, Potsdam and Wittenberg. The website has details on timings and meeting points.

🅐 SHOPPING

KaDeWe — Department Store

(Map p508; ☎030-212 10; www.kadewe.de; Tauentzienstrasse 21-24; ⊗10am-8pm Mon-Thu, 10am-9pm Fri, 9.30am-8pm Sat; Ⓤ Wittenbergplatz) Every day some 180,000 shoppers invade continental Europe's largest department store. Going strong since 1907, it boasts an assortment so vast that a pirate-style campaign is the best way to

plunder its bounty. If pushed for time, at least hurry up to the legendary 6th-floor gourmet food hall. The name, by the way, stands for *Kaufhaus des Westens* (department store of the West).

LP12 Mall of Berlin — Mall

(Map p507; www.mallofberlin.de; Leipziger Platz 12; ⊗10am-9pm Mon-Sat; 🛜; ◻200, Ⓤ Potsdamer Platz, Ⓢ Potsdamer Platz) This spanking new retail quarter is tailor-made for black-belt mall rats. More than 270 shops vie for your shopping euros, including flagship stores by Karl Lagerfeld, Hugo Boss, Liebeskind, Marc Cain, Muji and other international high-end brands alongside the usual high-street chains like Mango and H&M. Free mobile-phone recharge station on the 2nd floor.

Bikini Berlin — Mall

(Map p508; www.bikiniberlin.de; Budapester Strasse 38-50; ⊗shops 10am-8pm Mon-Sat, building 9am-9pm Mon-Sat, 1-6pm Sun; 🛜; ◻100, 200, Ⓤ Zoologischer Garten, Ⓢ Zoologischer Garten) Germany's first concept mall opened in 2014 in a spectacularly rehabilitated 1950s architectural icon nicknamed 'Bikini' because of its design: 200m-long upper and lower sections separated by an open floor, now chastely covered by a glass facade. Inside are three floors of urban indie boutiques and short-lease pop-up 'boxes' that offer a platform for up-and-coming designers.

EATING

🅧 Mitte

Augustiner am Gendarmenmarkt — German €€

(Map p500; ☎030-2045 4020; www.augustiner-braeu-berlin.de; Charlottenstrasse 55; mains €6.50-26.50; ⊗10am-2am; Ⓤ Französische Strasse) Tourists, concert-goers and hearty-food lovers rub shoulders at rustic tables in this authentic Bavarian beer hall. Soak up the down-to-earth vibe right along with a mug of full-bodied Augustiner brew. Sausages, roast pork and pretzels provide rib-sticking sustenance, but there's also plenty of lighter (even meat-free) fare as well as good-value lunch specials.

Flea Markets

Berlin's numerous flea markets set up on weekends (usually Sunday) year-round – rain or shine – and are also the purview of fledgling local fashion designers and jewellery makers.

Flohmarkt im Mauerpark (www.flohmarktimmauerpark.de; Bernauer Strasse 63-64; ⏲9am-6pm Sun; 🚋M1, M10, 12, U Eberswalder Strasse) Join the throngs of thrifty trinket hunters, bleary-eyed clubbers and excited tourists sifting for treasure at this always busy flea market with cult status, running right where the Berlin Wall once ran. Source new faves among retro threads, local-designer T-shirts, vintage vinyl and offbeat stuff. Street-food stands and beer gardens, including **Mauersegler** (☎030-9788 0904; www.mauersegler-berlin.de; ⏲2pm-2am May-Oct; 📶), provide sustenance.

Nowkoelln Flowmarkt (www.nowkoelln.de; Maybachufer; ⏲10am-6pm 2nd & 4th Sun of month Mar-Oct or later; U Kottbusser Tor, Schönleinstrasse) This hipster-heavy flea market sets up twice-monthly along the scenic Landwehrkanal and delivers secondhand bargains galore along with handmade threads and jewellery.

RAW Flohmarkt (www.raw-flohmarkt-berlin.de; Revaler Strasse 99, RAW Gelände; ⏲9am-7pm Sun; 🚋M10, M13, S Warschauer Strasse, U Warschauer Strasse) Bargains abound at this smallish flea market right on the grounds of **RAW Gelände** (www.raw-tempel.de), a former train repair station turned party village. It's wonderfully free of professional sellers, meaning you'll find everything from the proverbial kitchen sink to 1970s go-go boots. Bargains are plentiful, and food, a beer garden and cafes are nearby.

Zwölf Apostel — Italian **€€**

(Map p500; www.12-apostel.de; Georgenstrasse 2; pizza €10-15, mains €16.50-22.50; 🚋M1, S Friedrichstrasse, U Friedrichstrasse) A pleasant pit stop between museums, this place beneath the railway arches has over-the-top religious decor and tasty thin-crust pizzas named after the 12 apostles, plus good-value lunch specials.

Restaurant Tim Raue — Asian **€€€**

(Map p507; ☎030-2593 7930; www.tim-raue.com; Rudi-Dutschke-Strasse 26; 3-/4-course lunch €48/58, 8-course dinner €198, mains €55-66; ⏲noon-3pm & 7pm-midnight Wed-Sat; U Kochstrasse) Now here's a two-Michelin-starred restaurant we can get our mind around. Unstuffy ambience and a reduced design with walnut and Vitra chairs perfectly juxtapose with Raue's brilliant Asian-inspired plates that each shine the spotlight on a few choice ingredients. His interpretation of Peking duck is a perennial bestseller. Popular at lunchtime too.

Prenzlauer Berg

Kanaan — Middle Eastern **€**

(☎0176 2258 6673; www.facebook.com/kanaanrestaurantberlin; Kopenhagener Strasse 17; dishes €4-7; ⏲noon-4pm Mon-Fri, to 10pm Sat & Sun; 📶🌱; 🚋M1, U Schönhauser Allee, S Schönhauser Allee) In this feel-good venture, an Israeli biz whiz and a Palestinian chef have teamed up to bring a progressive blend of Middle Eastern fare to Berlin. Top menu picks are hummus, *shakshuka* and *sabich*. For now, weekday lunch is served from a rakishly ramshackle hut, while on weekends a bigger menu is dished up across the street at Kohlenquelle, a funky bar in a former coal cellar.

Konnopke's Imbiss — German **€**

(☎030-442 7765; www.konnopke-imbiss.de; Schönhauser Allee 44a; sausages €1.30-2; ⏲9am-8pm Mon-Fri, 11.30am-8pm Sat; 🚋M1, M10, U Eberswalder Strasse) Brave the inevitable queue at this famous sausage kitchen, ensconced in the same spot below the elevated U-Bahn tracks since 1930, but now equipped with a heated pavilion and an English menu. The 'secret' sauce topping its classic *Currywurst* comes in a four-tier heat scale from mild to wild.

Outdoor cafe

Umami   Vietnamese €€

(☑030-2886 0626; www.umami-restaurant.de;
Knaackstrasse 16-18; mains €7.50-15; ⊙noon-
11.30pm; 🛜🐾; 🚊M2, ⓊSenefelderplatz) A
mellow 1950s lounge-vibe and an inspired
menu of Indochine home cooking divided
into 'regular' and 'vegetarian' choices are
the main draws of this restaurant with large
pavement terrace. Leave room for the green-
tea apple pie or a Vietnamese cupcake
called 'popcake'. The six-course family meal
is a steal at €20 (€9 per additional person).

Bird   American €€

(☑030-5105 3283; www.thebirdinberlin.com;
Am Falkplatz 5; burgers €9.50-14, steaks from
€22.50; ⊙6pm-midnight Mon-Thu, 4pm-midnight
Fri, noon-midnight Sat & Sun; 🛜; 🚊M1, ⓊSchön-
hauser Allee, ⓈSchönhauser Allee) New York
meets Berlin at this expat favourite whose
dry-aged steaks, burgers and hand-cut
fries might just justify the hype. Sink your
teeth into a dripping half-pounder made
from freshly ground premium German beef
trapped between a toasted English muffin
(yes, it's messy – that's what the kitchen
paper is for!).

🟢 Kreuzberg

Curry 36   German €

(Map p507; ☑030-2580 088 336; www.curry36.
de; Mehringdamm 36; snacks €2-6; ⊙9am-5am;
ⓊMehringdamm) Day after day, night after
night, a motley crowd – cops, cabbies,
queens, office jockeys, savvy tourists etc –
wait their turn at this top-ranked *Currywurst* snack shop that's been frying 'em up
since 1981.

Cafe Jacques   International €€

(☑030-694 1048; Maybachufer 14; mains €12-20;
⊙6pm-late; ⓊSchönleinstrasse) A favourite
with off-duty chefs and loyal foodies,
Jacques infallibly charms with flattering
candlelight, arty-elegant decor and fantastic wine. It's the perfect date spot but, quite
frankly, you only have to be in love with good
food to appreciate the French- and North
African–inspired blackboard menu. Fish
and meat are always tops and the pasta is
homemade. Reservations essential.

Restaurant Richard   French €€€

(☑030-4920 7242; www.restaurant-richard.de;
Köpenicker Strasse 174; 4-course dinner €58,

Berlin nightlife

additional courses €10; ⊘7pm-midnight Tue-Sat; Ⓤ Schlesisches Tor) A venue where Nazis partied in the 1930s and leftists debated in the '70s has been reborn as a fine-dining shrine solidly rooted in the French tradition and, since 2015, endowed with a Michelin star. With its coffered ceiling, bubble chandeliers and risqué canvases, the decor is as luscious as the fancy food while the vibe remains charmingly relaxed.

✖ Charlottenburg

Good Friends   Chinese €€

(Map p508; ☏030-313 2659; www.goodfriends-berlin.de; Kantstrasse 30; 2-course lunches €7, dinner mains €7-20; ⊘noon-1am; Ⓢ Savignyplatz) Good Friends is widely considered Berlin's best Cantonese restaurant. The ducks dangling in the window are merely an overture to a menu long enough to confuse Confucius, including plenty of authentic homestyle dishes. If sea cucumber with fish belly proves too challenging, you can always fall back on sweet-and-sour pork or fried rice with shrimp.

Lucky Leek   Vegan €€

(☏030-6640 8710; www.lucky-leek.de; Kollwitzstrasse 54; mains €14-20, 3-/5-course dinners €33/55; ⊘6-10pm Wed-Sun; ✔; Ⓤ Senefelderplatz) Josita Hartanto has a knack for coaxing maximum flavour out of the vegetable kingdom and for boldly combining ingredients in unexpected ways. Hers is one of the best vegan restaurants in town and is especially lovely in the summer, when seating expands to a leafy pavement terrace. No à la carte on Fridays and Saturdays.

Restaurant am Steinplatz   German €€€

(Map p508; ☏030-5544 447 053; www.hotelsteinplatz.com; Steinplatz 4; mains €18-38, 4-/5-course dinners €56/65; ⊘noon-2.30pm & 6.30-10.30pm; Ⓟ; ⊞M45, Ⓤ Ernst-Reuter-Platz, Zoologischer Garten, Ⓢ Zoologischer Garten) The 1920s get a 21st-century makeover at this stylish outpost with an open kitchen where Marcus Zimmer feeds regional products into classic German and Berlin recipes. Even rustic beer-hall dishes such as *Eisbein* (boiled pork knuckle) are imaginatively reinterpreted and beautifully plated. A perennial favourite is the Königsberger Klopse (veal dumplings with capers, beetroot and mashed potatoes).

🍷 DRINKING & NIGHTLIFE
🍷 Mitte

Clärchens Ballhaus Club

(Map p500; 030-282 9295; www.ballhaus.de; Auguststrasse 24; 11am-late; M1, S Oranienburger Strasse) Yesteryear is right now at this late, great 19th-century dance hall where groovers and grannies hoof it across the parquet without even a touch of irony. There are different sounds nightly – salsa to swing, tango to disco – and a live band on Saturday. Dancing kicks off from 9pm or 9.30pm. Easy door but often packed, so book a table.

Strandbar Mitte Bar

(Map p500; 030-2838 5588; www.strandbar-mitte.de; Monbijoustrasse 3; dancing €4; 10am-late May-Sep; M1, S Oranienburger Strasse) With a full-on view of the Bode-Museum, palm trees and a relaxed ambience, Germany's first beach bar (since 2002) is great for balancing a surfeit of sightseeing stimulus with a reviving drink and thin-crust pizza. At night, there's dancing under the stars with tango, cha-cha, swing and salsa, often preceded by dance lessons.

Kaffee Burger Club

(Map p500; www.kaffeeburger.de; Torstrasse 60; from 9pm Mon-Thu, from 10pm Fri-Sun; U Rosa-Luxemburg-Platz) Nothing to do with either coffee or meat patties, this sweaty cult club with lovingly faded Communist-era decor is a fun-for-all concert and party pen. The sound policy swings from indie and electro to klezmer punk without missing a beat. Also has readings and poetry slams.

🍷 Potsdamer Platz & Tiergarten

Fragrances Cocktail Bar

(Map p507; 030-337 777; www.ritzcarlton. com; Ritz-Carlton, Potsdamer Platz 3; from 7pm Wed-Sat; 🐾; 200, S Potsdamer Platz, U Potsdamer Platz) Berlin cocktail maven Arnd

 ### East Berlin's Stasi Museum

The **Stasimuseum** (030-553 6854; www.stasimuseum.de; Haus 1, Ruschestrasse 103; adult/concession €6/4.50; 10am-6pm Mon-Fri, 11am-6pm Sat & Sun; U Magdalenenstrasse) provides an overview of the structure, methods and impact of the Ministry of State Security (Stasi), the secret police of former East Germany, inside the feared institution's fortress-like headquarters. At its peak, more than 8000 people worked in this compound alone; the scale model in the entrance foyer will help you grasp its vast dimensions. Other rooms introduce the ideology, rituals and institutions of East German society. You can marvel at cunningly low-tech surveillance devices (hidden in watering cans, rocks, even neckties), a prisoner transport van with tiny, lightless cells, and the stuffy offices of Stasi chief Erich Mielke. There's also background on the SED party and on the role of the youth organisation Junge Pioneere (Young Pioneers). Panelling is partly in English, and there are free English tours at 3pm Saturday and Sunday.

The museum is in the eastern district of Lichtenberg, just north of U-Bahn station Magdalenenstrasse.

Conference room in the Stasi headquarters
ULLSTEIN BILD/CONTRIBUTOR/GETTY IMAGES ©

Heissen's newest baby is the world's first 'perfume bar', a libation station where he mixes potable potions mimicking famous scents. The black-mirrored space in the Ritz-Carlton is like a 3D menu where adventurous drinkers sniff out their favourite

 Sachsenhausen Concentration Camp

About 35km north of Berlin, **Sachsenhausen** (Memorial & Museum Sachsenhausen; ☑03301-200 200; www.stiftung-bg.de; Strasse der Nationen 22, Oranienburg; ☺8.30am-6pm mid-Mar–mid-Oct, to 4.30pm mid-Oct–mid-Mar, museums closed Mon mid-Oct–mid-Mar; Ⓟ; Ⓢ Oranienburg) **FREE** was built by prisoners and opened in 1936 as a prototype for other concentration camps. By 1945, some 200,000 people had passed through its sinister gates, most of them political opponents, Jews, Roma people and, after 1939, POWs. Tens of thousands died here from hunger, exhaustion, illness, exposure, medical experiments and executions. Thousands more succumbed during the death march of April 1945, when the Nazis evacuated the camp in advance of the Red Army.

A tour of the memorial site with its remaining buildings and exhibits will leave no one untouched.

The S1 makes the trip thrice hourly from central Berlin (eg Friedrichstrasse station) to Oranienburg (€3.30, 45 minutes). Hourly regional RE5 and RB12 trains leaving from Hauptbahnhof are faster (€3.30, 25 minutes). The camp is about 2km from the Oranienburg train station.

from among a row of perfume bottles, then settle back into flocked couches to enjoy exotic blends served in unusual vessels, including a birdhouse.

Café am Neuen See   Beer Garden

(Map p508; ☑030-254 4930; www.cafeamneuensee.de; Lichtensteinallee 2; ☺restaurant 9am-11pm, beer garden 11am-late Mon-Fri, 10am-late Sat & Sun; ♣; ☐200, Ⓤ Zoologischer Garten, Ⓢ Zoologischer Garten, Tiergarten) Next to an idyllic pond in Tiergarten, this restaurant gets jammed year-round for its sumptuous breakfast and seasonal fare, but it really comes into its own during beer garden season. Enjoy a microvacation over a cold one and a pretzel or pizza, then take your sweetie for a spin in a rowing boat.

Prenzlauer Berg

Prater Biergarten   Beer Garden

(☑030-448 5688; www.pratergarten.de; Kastanienallee 7-9; snacks €2.50-6; ☺noon-late Apr-Sep, weather permitting; Ⓤ Eberswalder Strasse) Berlin's oldest beer garden has seen beer-soaked nights since 1837 and is still a charismatic spot for guzzling a custom-brewed Prater Pilsner beneath the ancient chestnut trees (self-service). Kids can romp around the small play area.

Weinerei Forum   Wine Bar

(☑030-440 6983; www.weinerei.com; Fehrbelliner Strasse 57; ☺10am-midnight; 🛜; ☐M1, Ⓤ Rosenthaler Platz) After 8pm, this living-room-style cafe turns into a wine bar that works on the honour principle: you 'rent' a wine glass for €2, then help yourself to as much vino as you like and in the end decide what you want to pay. Please be fair to keep this fantastic concept going.

Zum Starken August   Pub

(☑030-2520 9020; www.zumstarkenaugust.de; Schönhauser Allee 56; ☺11am-1am Sun & Mon, to 2am Tue, to 3am Wed, to 4am Thu, to 5am Fri & Sat; ☐M1, M10, Ⓤ Eberswalder Strasse) Part circus, part burlesque bar, this vibrant venue dressed in Victorian-era exuberance is a fun and friendly addition to the Prenzlauer Berg pub culture. Join the unpretentious, international crowd over cocktails and craft beers while being entertained with drag-hosted bingo, burlesque divas, wicked cabaret or the hilarious 'porno karaoke'.

Kreuzberg

Schwarze Traube   Cocktail Bar
(☏030-2313 5569; www.schwarzetraube.de; Wrangelstrasse 24; ☺7pm-2am Sun-Thu, to 5am Fri & Sat; Ⓤ Görlitzer Bahnhof) Mixologist Atalay Aktas was Germany's Best Bartender of 2013 and this pint-sized drinking parlour is where he and his staff create their magic potions. Since there's no menu, each drink is calibrated to the taste and mood of each patron using premium spirits, expertise and a dash of psychology.

Friedrichshain

Berghain/Panorama Bar   Club
(www.berghain.de; Am Wriezener Bahnhof; ☺midnight Fri-Mon morning; Ⓢ Ostbahnhof) Only world-class spinmasters heat up this hedonistic bass-junkie hellhole inside a labyrinthine ex–power plant. Hard-edged minimal techno dominates the ex–turbine hall (Berghain) while house dominates at Panorama Bar, one floor up. Strict door; no cameras. Check the website for midweek concerts and record-release parties at the main venue and the adjacent **Kantine am**

Berghain (☏030-2936 0210; admission varies; ☺hours vary).

Briefmarken Weine   Wine Bar
(☏030-4202 5292; www.briefmarkenweine.de; Karl-Marx-Allee 99; ☺7pm-midnight; Ⓤ Weberwiese) For *dolce vita* right on socialist Karl-Marx-Allee, head to this charmingly nostalgic Italian wine bar ensconced in a former stamp shop. The original wooden cabinets cradle a hand-picked selection of Italian bottles that complement a snack menu of yummy cheeses, prosciutto and salami, plus a pasta dish of the day.

Hops & Barley   Pub
(☏030-2936 7534; www.hopsandbarley-berlin. de; Wühlischstrasse 22/23; ☺from 5pm Mon-Fri, from 3pm Sat & Sun; ☒M13, Ⓤ Warschauer Strasse, Ⓢ Warschauer Strasse) Conversation flows as freely as the unfiltered Pilsner, malty *Dunkel* (dark) and fruity *Weizen* (wheat) produced right here at one of Berlin's oldest craft breweries. The pub is inside a former butcher's shop and still has the tiled walls to prove it. Two projectors show football (soccer) games.

Cocktail bar in Kreuzberg

🍷 Charlottenburg

Bar am Steinplatz   Bar

(Map p508; ☎030-554 4440; www.hotelam
steinplatz.com; Steinplatz 4; ⊙4pm-late; ☒M45,
245, ⓊErnst-Reuter-Platz) Christian Gen-
temann's liquid playground may reside at
art deco Hotel am Steinplatz, but it hardly
whispers 'stuffy hotel bar'. The classic and
creative drinks (how about a Red Beet Old
Fashioned?) often showcase regionally produced spirits and ingredients, and even the
draught beer hails from the Berlin-based
Rollberg brewery. Inventive bar bites complement the drinks.

Diener Tattersall   Pub

(Map p508; ☎030-881 5329; www.diener-berlin.
de; Grolmanstrasse 47; ⊙6pm-2am; ⓈSavigny-
platz) In business for over a century, this
Old Berlin haunt was taken over by German
heavyweight champion Franz Diener in
the 1950s and has since been one of West
Berlin's pre-eminent artist pubs. From Billy
Wilder to Harry Belafonte, they all came for
beer and *Bulette* (meat patties), and left
behind signed black-and-white photographs that grace Diener's walls to this day.

Monkey Bar   Bar

(Map p508; ☎030-120 221 210; www.25hours-
hotel.com; Budapester Strasse 40; ⊙noon-1am
Sun-Thu, to 2am Fri & Sat; 🛜; ☒100, 200,
Ⓢ Zoologischer Garten, Ⓤ Zoologischer Garten)
On the 10th floor of the 25hours Hotel Bikini
Berlin, this 'urban jungle' hot spot delivers
fabulous views of the city and the Berlin Zoo.
On balmy days, the sweeping terrace is a
handy perch for sunset drinks selected from
a menu that gives prominent nods to tiki
concoctions (including the original Trader
Vic's Mai Tai) and gin-based cocktail sorcery.

⭐ ENTERTAINMENT

Berliner
Philharmonie   Classical Music

(☎tickets 030-254 888 999; www.berliner-
philharmoniker.de; Herbert-von-Karajan-Strasse 1;
tickets €30-100; ☒M29, M48, M85, 200, ⓈPots-

*supreme acoustics and not
a bad seat in the house*

Berliner Philharmonie

MATO/SHUTTERSTOCK ©

damer Platz, U Potsdamer Platz) This world-famous concert hall has supreme acoustics and, thanks to Hans Scharoun's terraced vineyard configuration, not a bad seat in the house. It's the home turf of the Berliner Philharmoniker, who will be led by Sir Simon Rattle until 2018. One year later, Russia-born Kirill Petrenko will pick up the baton as music director.

Chamäleon Varieté Cabaret
(⤵030-400 0590; www.chamaeleonberlin. com; Rosenthaler Strasse 40/41; tickets €29-69; ⛱M1, S Hackescher Markt) A marriage of art nouveau charms and high-tech theatre trappings, this intimate 1920s-style venue in an old ballroom hosts classy variety shows – comedy, juggling acts and singing – often in sassy, sexy and unconventional fashion.

ⓘ INFORMATION

Visit Berlin (⤵030-2500 25; www.visitberlin. de), the Berlin tourist board, operates five walk-in offices, info desks at the airports, and a call centre (⤵030-2500 2333; ⊙9am-7pm Mon-Fri, 10am-6pm Sat, 10am-2pm Sun) whose multilingual staff field general questions and make hotel and ticket bookings.

Brandenburger Tor (South Wing, Pariser Platz; ⊙9.30am-7pm Apr-Oct, to 6pm Nov-Mar; S Brandenburger Tor, U Brandenburger Tor)

Hauptbahnhof (Europaplatz entrance, ground fl; ⊙8am-10pm; S Hauptbahnhof, ⍯Hauptbahnhof)

Europa-Center (Tauentzienstrasse 9, ground fl; ⊙10am-8pm Mon-Sat; ⛱100, 200, U Kurfürstendamm)

Rankestrasse (cnr Rankestrasse & Kurfürstendamm; ⊙10am-6pm Apr-Oct, to 4pm Nov-Mar; ⛱100, 200, U Kurfürstendamm)

TV Tower (Panoramastrasse 1a, ground fl; ⊙10am-6pm Apr-Oct, to 4pm Nov-Mar; ⛱100, 200, TXL, U Alexanderplatz, S Alexanderplatz)

ⓘ GETTING THERE & AWAY

AIR

Most visitors arrive in Berlin by air. Berlin's new central airport, about 24km southeast of the

⚤ LGBT Berlin

Berlin's legendary liberalism has spawned one of the world's biggest, most divine and diverse GLBT playgrounds. Anything goes in 'Homopolis' (and we do mean anything!), from the highbrow to the hands-on, the bourgeois to the bizarre, the mainstream to the flamboyant. Except for the most hardcore places, gay spots get their share of opposite-sex and straight patrons.

Generally speaking, Berlin's gayscape runs the entire spectrum from mellow cafes, campy bars and cinemas to saunas, cruising areas, clubs with darkrooms and all-out sex venues. In fact, sex and sexuality are entirely everyday matters to the unshockable city folks and there are very few, if any, itches that can't be quite openly and legally scratched. As elsewhere, gay men have more options for having fun, but grrrrls of all stripes won't feel left out either.

city centre, is under construction. Check www. berlin-airport.de for the latest. In the meantime, flights continue to land at the city's **Tegel** (TXL; ⤵030-6091 1150; www.berlin-airport.de; ⛱Tegel Flughafen) and **Schönefeld** (SXF; ⤵030-6091 1150; www.berlin-airport.de; ⍯Airport-Express, RE7 & RB14) airports.

BUS

Most long-haul buses arrive at the **Zentraler Omnibusbahnhof** (ZOB; ⤵030-3010 0175; www.iob-berlin.de; Masurenallee 4-6; S Messe/

ICC Nord, U Kaiserdamm) near the trade fair-grounds on the western city edge. Some stop at Alexanderplatz or other points in town. The closest U-Bahn station to ZOB is Kaiserdamm, about 400m north and served by the U2 line, which travels to Zoologischer Garten in about eight minutes and to Alexanderplatz in 28 minutes.

TRAIN

Berlin's **Hauptbahnhof** (Main Train Station; www.berliner-hbf.de; Europaplatz, Washingtonplatz; S Hauptbahnhof, U Hauptbahnhof) is in the heart of the city, just north of the Government Quarter and within walking distance of major sights and hotels. From here, the U-Bahn, the S-Bahn, trams and buses provide links to all parts of town. Taxi ranks are located outside the north exit (Europaplatz) and the south exit (Washingtonplatz).

GETTING AROUND

Berlin's extensive and efficient public transport system is operated by BVG (www.bvg.de) and consists of the U-Bahn (underground, or subway), the S-Bahn (light rail), buses and trams.

For trip planning and general information, call the 24-hour hotline (📞030-194 49) or check the website.

U-Bahn Most efficient way to travel; operates 4am to 12.30am and all night Friday, Saturday and public holidays. From Sunday to Thursday, half-hourly night buses take over in the interim.

S-Bahn Less frequent than U-Bahn trains, but with fewer stops, and thus useful for longer distances. Same operating hours as the U-Bahn.

Bus Slow but useful for sightseeing on the cheap. Run frequently 4.30am to 12.30am; half-hourly night buses in the interim. Metro-Buses (designated eg M1, M19) operate 24/7.

Tram Only in the eastern districts; MetroTrams (designated eg M1, M2) run 24/7.

Cycling Bike lanes and rental stations abound; bikes allowed in specially marked U-Bahn and S-Bahn carriages.

Taxi Can be hailed; fairly inexpensive; avoid during daytime rush hour.

Uber The only Uber option is uberTaxi. Prices are identical to regular taxis, including a surcharge of €1.50 for cash-free payments.

Where to Stay

Berlin offers the full gamut of places to unpack your suitcase – you can even sleep in a former bank, boat or factory, in the home of a silent-movie diva or in a 'flying bed'.

Neighbourhood	Atmosphere
Mitte	Close to major sights such as the Reichstag and Brandenburger Tor; great transport links; mostly high-end hotels; top restaurants; touristy, expensive, pretty dead at night.
Scheunenviertel	Hipster quarter; trendy, historic, central; brims with boutique and designer hotels; strong cafe scene; top galleries and plenty of great street art; pricey, busy, noisy, no parking, bit touristy.
Museumsinsel & Alexanderplatz	Supercentral sightseeing quarter; easy transport access; close to blockbuster sights and mainstream shopping; noisy, busy and dusty thanks to lots of major construction; hardly any nightlife.
Potsdamer Platz & Tiergarten	Urban flair in Berlin's newest quarter; cutting-edge architecture; high-end hotels; top museums; limited eating options; pricey.
Prenzlauer Berg	Charming residential area; lively cafe and restaurant scene; indie boutiques and Mauerpark flea market; limited late-night action.
Friedrichshain	Student and young family quarter; bubbling nightlife; limited sleeping options; not so central; transport difficult in some areas
Kreuzberg & Northern Neukölln	Best for bar-hopping and clubbing; lots of hostels; great foodie scene; excellent street art; gritty, noisy and busy.
City West & Charlottenburg	Great shopping; 'Old Berlin' bars and top restaurants; best range of good-value lodging; historic B&Bs; far from key sights and nightlife.

Schloss Neuschwanstein

Appearing through the mountainous forest like a mirage, Schloss Neuschwanstein was the model for Disney's Sleeping Beauty *castle.*

Great For...

Schloss Neuschwanstein ◎

Hohenschwangau Village

Alpsee

❶ Need to Know

☎tickets 08362-930 830; www.neuschwan stein.de; Neuschwansteinstrasse 20; adult/ concession €12/11, incl Hohenschwangau €23/21; ◷9am-6pm Apr–mid-Oct, 10am-4pm mid-Oct–Mar

★ **Top Tip**
Arrive as early as 8am to make sure you bag a ticket for that day.

Ludwig II, the Fairy-Tale King

King Ludwig II drew the blueprints for this fairy-tale pile himself. He envisioned it as a giant stage on which to re-create the world of Germanic mythology, inspired by the operatic works of Wagner. His obsession with French culture and the Sun King, Louis XIV, further inspired the fantastical design.

Ludwig was an enthusiastic leader initially, but Bavaria's days as a sovereign state were numbered, and he became a puppet king after the creation of the German Reich in 1871. Ludwig withdrew completely to drink, draw up castle plans and view concerts and operas in private.

In January 1886, several ministers and relatives arranged a hasty psychiatric test that diagnosed Ludwig as mentally unfit to rule. That June, he was removed to Schloss Berg on Lake Starnberg. A few days later the dejected bachelor and his doctor took a Sunday-evening lakeside walk and were found several hours later, drowned in just a few feet of water. No one knows with certainty what happened that night, and conspiracy theories abound. That summer the authorities opened Neuschwanstein to the public to help pay off Ludwig's huge debts. King Ludwig II was dead, but the myth was just being born.

Construction

Built as a romantic medieval castle, the grey-white granite pile was begun in 1869 but was an anachronism from the start: at the time of Ludwig's death in 1886, the first high-rises had pierced New York's skyline. However, despite his love for the old-fashioned look, the palace had plenty of high-tech features, including a hot-air

Schloss Hohenschwangau

heating system and running water. Like so many of the king's grand schemes, Neuschwanstein was never finished. For all the coffer-depleting sums spent on it, the king spent just over 170 days in residence.

The Interior

The most impressive room is the **Sänger-saal** (Minstrels' Hall), whose frescoes depict scenes from Wagner's opera *Tannhäuser*. Other completed sections include Ludwig's *Tristan and Isolde*–themed

> ☑ **Don't Miss**
>
> The excellent **Museum der Bayerischen Könige** (www.museumderbayerischenkoenige.de; Alpseestrasse 27; adult/concession €9.50/8; ⊙10am-6pm) is a short walk from the castle ticket office.

MESPILIA/SHUTTERSTOCK ©

bedroom, dominated by a huge Gothic-style bed crowned with intricately carved cathedral-like spires; a gaudy artificial grotto (another allusion to the *Tannhäuser*); and the Byzantine-style **Thronsaal** (Throne Room) with an incredible mosaic floor containing over two million stones. The painting opposite the (throneless) throne platform depicts another castle imagined up by Ludwig that was never built.

Schloss Hohenschwangau

King Ludwig II grew up at the sun-yellow **Schloss Hohenschwangau** (☏08362-930 830; www.hohenschwangau.de; Alpseestrasse 30; adult/concession €12/11, incl Neuschwanstein €23/21; ⊙8am-5pm Apr–mid-Oct, 9am-3.30pm mid-Oct–Mar) and later enjoyed summers here until his death in 1886. His father, Maximilian II, built this palace in a neo-Gothic style atop 12th-century ruins left by Schwangau knights. Far less showy than Neuschwanstein, Hohenschwangau has a distinctly lived-in feel where every piece of furniture is a used original. After his father died, Ludwig's main alteration was having stars, illuminated with hidden oil lamps, painted on the ceiling of his bedroom.

Castle Tickets & Tours

Schloss Neuschwanstein and Hohenschwangau can only be visited on guided tours (in German or English), which last about 35 minutes each (Hohenschwangau is first). Strictly timed tickets are available from the **Ticket Centre** (☏08362-930 830; www.hohenschwangau.de; Alpenseestrasse 12; ⊙8am-5pm Apr–mid-Oct, 9am-3.30pm mid-Oct–Mar) at the foot of the castles.

Enough time is left between tours for the steep 30- to 40-minute walk between the castles. All Munich's tour companies run day excursions out to the castles.

> ★ **Classic Image**
>
> For the postcard view of Neuschwanstein, walk 10 minutes up to Marienbrücke (Mary's Bridge).

In This Chapter

Prague Castle 526
Prague River Stroll 530
Sights 532
Tours 539
Shopping 539
Eating 540
Drinking & Nightlife 542
Entertainment 543
Information 544
Getting There & Away 544
Getting Around 545

Prague, Czech Republic

Everyone who visits the Czech Republic starts with Prague, the cradle of Czech culture and one of Europe's most fascinating cities. Prague offers a near-intact medieval core of Gothic architecture that can transport you back 500 years – the 14th-century Charles Bridge, connecting two historic neighbourhoods across the Vltava River, with the castle ramparts and the spires of St Vitus Cathedral rising above, is one of the classic sights of world travel. But the city is not just about history, it's also a vital urban centre with a rich array of cultural offerings and a newly emerging foodie scene.

Two Days in Prague

Start the day wandering through the courtyards of **Prague Castle** (p527) before the main sights open, then spend the afternoon visiting the baroque beauty of **St Nicholas Church** (p532). End the day with dinner at **Augustine** (p541). Spend the morning of day two in the **Old Town Square** (p532), before visiting the half-dozen monuments that comprise the **Prague Jewish Museum** (p532).

Four Days in Prague

Explore the passages and arcades around **Wenceslas Square** (p535) on day three, then take in the historical and artistic treasures of the **Prague City Museum** (p535). On the final day take a metro ride out to Vyšehrad and explore Prague's other castle, the **Vyšehrad Citadel** (p538), with its gorgeous views along the Vltava. In the evening catch a performance at the **National Theatre** (p543) or the **Palác Akropolis** (p543).

After Prague travel to Budapest (p546) or Vienna (p564).

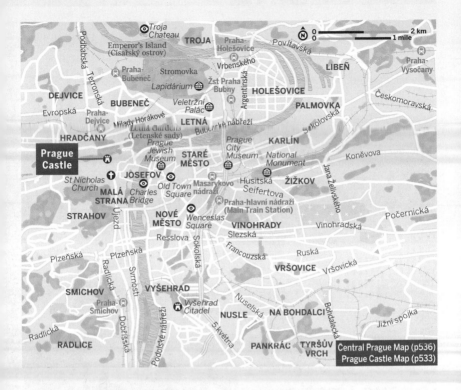

Central Prague Map (p536)
Prague Castle Map (p533)

Arriving in Prague

Václav Havel Airport Buses to metro stops Nádraží Veleslavín (service No 119) and Zličín (No 100) depart every 10 minutes from 4am to midnight, from stops just outside the arrivals terminal (32Kč). A taxi to the centre costs 500Kč.

Praha hlavní nádraží Prague's main train station is in the city centre and is accessible by metro line C (red); all international rail connections arrive here.

Florenc bus station International buses arrive here, just east of Prague centre, with metro and tram links to the rest of the city.

Where to Stay

Gone are the days when Prague was a cheap destination. The Czech capital now ranks alongside most Western European cities when it comes to the quality, range and price of hotels. Accommodation ranges from cosy, romantic hotels set in historic townhouses to the new generation of funky design hotels and hostels. Book as far in advance as possible (especially during festival season in May, and at Easter and Christmas/New Year).

St Vitus Cathedral (p528) surrounded by Prague Castle

PVTYSHUTTERSTOCK ©

Prague Castle

Prague Castle – Pražský hrad, or just hrad to Czechs – is Prague's most popular attraction. Looming above the Vltava's left bank, its serried ranks of spires, towers and palaces dominate the city centre like a fairy-tale fortress.

Great For...

☑ Don't Miss

The tiny, colourful 16th-century cottages on Golden Lane, or the Princely Collections at Lobkowicz Palace.

Within the castle walls lies a varied and fascinating collection of historic buildings, museums and galleries that are home to some of the Czech Republic's greatest artistic and cultural treasures.

First Courtyard

The First Courtyard lies within the castle's main gate on Hradčany Square (Hradčanské náměstí), flanked by huge, baroque statues of battling **Titans** (1767–70) that dwarf the castle guards standing beneath them. After the fall of communism in 1989, then-president Václav Havel hired his old pal Theodor Pistek, the costume designer on the film *Amadeus* (1984), to replace the guards' communist-era khaki uniforms with the stylish pale-blue kit they now wear, which harks back to the army of the first Czechoslovak Republic of 1918 to 1938.

Titans battle on the main gate

❶ Need to Know

Pražský hrad; Map p533; 📞224 372 423; www.hrad.cz; Hradčanské náměstí 1; grounds free, sights adult/concession Tour A & C 350/175Kč, Tour B 250/125Kč; ☺grounds 6am-11pm year-round, gardens 10am-6pm Apr-Oct, closed Nov-Mar, historic buildings 9am-5pm Apr-Oct, to 4pm Nov-Mar; Ⓜ Malostranská, 🚊22

✘ Take a Break

Stop by **Lobkowicz Palace Café** (Map p533; 📞233 312 925; Jiřská 3; mains 200-300Kč; ☺10am-6pm; 📶♿; 🚊22) for great goulash and superb city views.

★ Top Tip

To avoid the worst of the crowds, try to visit the castle early or late – before 10.30am or after 3.30pm – and on a weekday if possible.

The **changing of the guard** takes place every hour on the hour, but the longest and most impressive display is at noon, when banners are exchanged while a brass band plays a fanfare from the windows of the Plečnik Hall, which overlooks the First Courtyard.

Second Courtyard

Beyond the Matthias Gate lies the Second Courtyard, centred on a baroque fountain and a 17th-century well with lovely Renaissance latticework.

On the right, the Chapel of the Holy Cross (1763) houses the **St Vitus Treasury** (Svatovítský poklad; Map p533; 📞224 373 442; adult/child 300/150Kč, admission incl with Prague Castle Tour C ticket; ☺10am-6pm Apr-Oct, to 5pm Nov-Mar), a spectacular collection of ecclesiastical bling that was founded by

Charles IV in the 14th century. The oldest items include a reliquary arm of St Vitus dating from the early 10th century, while the most impressive treasures include a gold coronation cross of Charles IV (1370) and a diamond-studded baroque monstrance from 1708.

The **Prague Castle Picture Gallery** (Map p533; adult/child 100/50Kč, admission incl with Prague Castle Tour C ticket; ☺9am-5pm Apr-Oct, to 4pm Nov-Mar), in the castle's beautiful Renaissance stables, houses an exhibition of 16th- to 18th-century European art, based on the Habsburg collection that was begun in 1650 to replace stolen paintings; it includes works by Cranach, Holbein, Rubens, Tintoretto and Titian

Third Courtyard

As you pass through the passage on the eastern side of the Second Courtyard, the huge western facade of St Vitus Cathedral soars directly above you; to its south (to the right as you enter) lies the Third Courtyard. At its entrance you'll see a 16m-tall **granite monolith** dedicated to the victims of WWI, designed by Jože Plečnik in 1928, and a copy of a 14th-century bronze figure of **St George** slaying the dragon; the original is on display in the **Story of Prague Castle** (adult/child 140/70Kč, admission incl with Prague Castle Tour A ticket; ☺9am-5pm Apr-Oct, to 4pm Nov-Mar) exhibition.

The **Old Royal Palace** (Starý královský palác; Map p533; admission incl with Prague Castle tour A & B tickets; ☺9am-5pm Apr-Oct, to 4pm Nov-Mar) at the courtyard's eastern end is one of the oldest parts of the castle, dating from 1135. It was originally used only by Czech princesses, but from the 13th to the 16th centuries it was the king's own palace.

The courtyard is dominated by the southern facade of **St Vitus Cathedral** (Katedrála sv Víta; Map p533; ☎257 531 622; www.katedralasvatehovita.cz; admission incl with Prague Castle Tour A & B tickets; ☺9am-5pm Mon-Sat, noon-5pm Sun Apr-Oct, to 4pm Nov-Mar), one of the most richly endowed cathedrals in central Europe, and pivotal to the religious and cultural life of the Czech Republic. It houses treasures that range from the 14th-century mosaic of the Last Judgement and the tombs of St Wenceslas and Charles IV, to the baroque silver tomb of St John of Nepomuck, the ornate Chapel of St Wenceslas, and art nouveau stained glass by Alfons Mucha.

Golden Lane

St George Square

St George Sq (Jiřské náměstí), the plaza to the east of St Vitus Cathedral, lies at the heart of the castle complex.

The striking, brick-red, early-baroque facade that dominates the square conceals the **Basilica of St George** (Bazilika sv Jiří; Jiřské náměstí; Map p533; admission incl with Prague Castle tour A & B tickets, ⏰9am–5pm Apr-Oct, to 4pm Nov-Mar), the Czech Republic's best-preserved Romanesque basilica, established in the 10th century by Vratislav I (the father of St Wenceslas). What you see today is mostly the result of restorations made between 1887 and 1908.

George Street

George Street (Jiřská) runs from the Basilica of St George to the castle's eastern gate.

The picturesque alley known as **Golden Lane** (Zlatá ulička; Map p533; admission incl with Prague Castle tour A & B tickets; ⏰9am–5pm Apr-Oct, to 4pm Nov-Mar) runs along the northern wall of the castle. Its tiny, colourful cottages were built in the 16th century for the sharpshooters of the castle guard, but were later used by goldsmiths. In the 19th and early 20th centuries they were occupied by artists, including the writer Franz Kafka (who frequently visited his sister's house at No 22 from 1916 to 1917).

Sixteenth-century **Lobkowicz Palace** (Lobkovický palác; Map p533; ☎233 312 925; www.lobkowicz.com; Jiřská 3; adult/concession/family 275/200/690Kč; ⏰10am-6pm) houses a private museum known as the **Princely Collections**, which includes priceless paintings, furniture and musical memorabilia. Your tour includes an audio guide dictated by owner William Lobkowicz and his family – this personal connection really brings the displays to life, and makes the palace one of the castle's most interesting attractions.

> ★ **A World Record**
>
> According to the *Guinness World Records*, Prague Castle is the largest ancient castle in the world – 570m long, an average of 128m wide and occupying 7.28 hectares.

DESPERADO/GETTY IMAGES ©

> ★ **South Gardens**
>
> At the castle's eastern gate, you can take a sharp right and wander back to Hradčany Square through the **South Gardens** (Zahrada na valech; Map p533; ⏰10am-6pm Apr-Oct, closed Nov-Mar) `FREE`. The terrace garden offers superb views across the rooftops of Malá Strana.

Prague River Stroll

The Vltava River runs through the heart of Prague and served as muse for composer Bedřich Smetana in writing his moving 'Vltava' (Moldau) symphony. But you don't need to be a musician to enjoy the river's breathtaking bridges and backdrops on this extended walk along the waterway.
Start Convent of St Agnes
Distance 8km
Duration Three hours

2 Amble around **Letná Gardens** (p542) and take in the view of the Old Town and Malá Strana below.

Classic Photo: Photogenic Prague Castle from any angle.

3 Enjoy views over the Vltava and the red roofs of Malá Strana from the ramparts of **Prague Castle** (p527) or from the beautifully manicured royal gardens.

6 The whimsical yet elegant **Dancing House**, by architects Vlado Milunić and Frank Gehry, surprisingly fits in with its ageing neighbours.

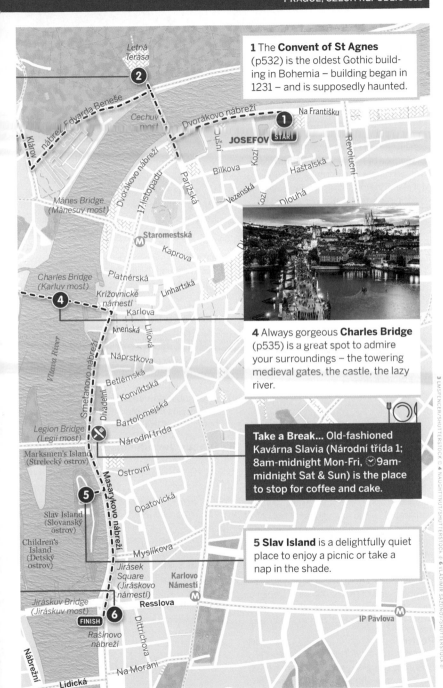

1 The **Convent of St Agnes** (p532) is the oldest Gothic building – building began in 1231 – and is supposedly haunted.

4 Always gorgeous **Charles Bridge** (p535) is a great spot to admire your surroundings – the towering medieval gates, the castle, the lazy river.

Take a Break... Old-fashioned Kavárna Slavia (Národní třída 1; 8am-midnight Mon-Fri, ⊙9am-midnight Sat & Sun) is the place to stop for coffee and cake.

5 Slav Island is a delightfully quiet place to enjoy a picnic or take a nap in the shade.

◉ SIGHTS

◎ Hradčany

Loreta   Church

(📞220 516 740; www.loreta.cz; Loretánské náměstí 7; adult/child/family 150/80/310Kč, photography permit 100Kč; ⊘9am-5pm Apr-Oct, 9.30am-4pm Nov-Mar; 🚋22) The Loreta is a baroque place of pilgrimage founded by Benigna Kateřina Lobkowicz in 1626, designed as a replica of the supposed Santa Casa (Sacred House; the home of the Virgin Mary) in the Holy Land. Legend says that the original Santa Casa was carried by angels to the Italian town of Loreto as the Turks were advancing on Nazareth.

Strahov Library   Historic Building

(Strahovská knihovna; 📞233 107 718; www.strahovskyklaster.cz; Strahovské nádvoří 1; adult/child 100/50Kč; ⊘9am-noon & 1-5pm; 🚋22) Strahov Library is the largest monastic library in the country, with two magnificent baroque halls dating from the 17th and 18th centuries. You can peek through the doors but, sadly, you can't go into the halls themselves – it was found that fluctuations in humidity caused by visitors' breath was endangering the frescoes. There's also a display of historical curiosities.

◎ Malá Strana

St Nicholas Church   Church

(Kostel sv Mikuláše; Map p533; 📞257 534 215; www.stnicholas.cz; Malostranské náměstí 38; adult/child 70/50Kč; ⊘9am-5pm Mar-Oct, to 4pm Nov-Feb; 🚋12, 15, 20, 22) Malá Strana is dominated by the huge green cupola of St Nicholas Church, one of Central Europe's finest baroque buildings. (Don't confuse it with the other Church of St Nicholas on the Old Town Square.) On the ceiling, Johann Kracker's 1770 *Apotheosis of St Nicholas* is Europe's largest fresco (clever *trompe l'œil* technique has made the painting merge almost seamlessly with the architecture).

Petřín   Hill

(🚋Nebozízek, Petřín) This 318m-high hill is one of Prague's largest green spaces. It's great for quiet, tree-shaded walks and fine views over the 'City of a Hundred Spires'. Most of the attractions atop the hill, including a lookout tower and mirror maze, were built in the late 19th to early 20th century, lending the place an old-fashioned, fun-fair atmosphere.

◎ Staré Město

Convent of St Agnes   Gallery

(Klášter sv Anežky; Map p536; 📞224 810 628; www.ngprague.cz; U Milosrdných 17; incl admission to all National Gallery venues adult/child 300/150Kč; ⊘10am-6pm Tue-Sun; 🚋6, 8, 15, 26) In the northeastern corner of Staré Město is the former Convent of St Agnes, Prague's oldest surviving Gothic building. The 1st-floor rooms hold the National Gallery's permanent collection of medieval and early Renaissance art (1200–1550) from Bohemia and Central Europe, a treasure house of glowing Gothic altar paintings and polychrome religious sculptures.

Old Town Square   Square

(Staroměstské náměstí; Map p536; MStaroměstská) One of Europe's biggest and most beautiful urban spaces, the Old Town Square (Staroměstské náměstí, or Staromák for short) has been Prague's principal public square since the 10th century, and was its main marketplace until the beginning of the 20th century.

Prague Jewish Museum   Museum

(Židovské muzeum Praha; Map p536; 📞222 749 211; www.jewishmuseum.cz; Reservation Centre, Maiselova 15; ordinary ticket adult/child 300/200Kč, combined ticket incl entry to Old-New Synagogue 480/320Kč; ⊘9am-6pm Sun-Fri Apr-Oct, to 4.30pm Nov-Mar; MStaroměstská) This museum consists of six Jewish monuments clustered together in Josefov: the **Maisel Synagogue** (Maiselova synagóga; Map p536; Maiselova 10); the **Pinkas Synagogue** (Pinkasova synagóga; Map p536; Široká 3); the **Spanish Synagogue** (Španělská synagóga; Map p536; Vězeňská 1); the **Klaus Synagogue** (Klauzová synagóga; Map p536; U starého hřbitova 1; 🚋17); the **Ceremonial Hall** (Obřadní síň; Map p536; Old Jewish Cemetery; 🚋17); and the **Old Jewish Cemetery** (Starý židovský hřbitov; Map p536; Pinkas Synagogue,

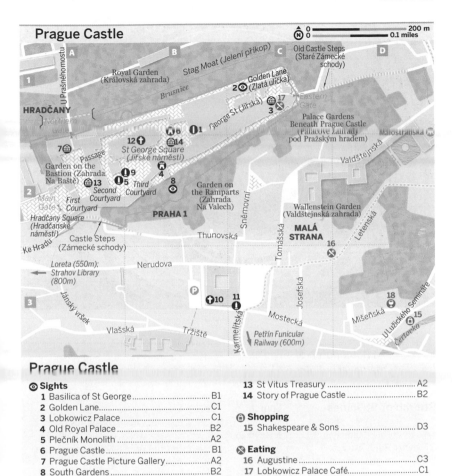

Prague Castle

⊙ **Sights**

1 Basilica of St George	B1
2 Golden Lane	C1
3 Lobkowicz Palace	C1
4 Old Royal Palace	B2
5 Plečník Monolith	A2
6 Prague Castle	B1
7 Prague Castle Picture Gallery	A2
8 South Gardens	B2
9 St George Slaying the Dragon	B2
10 St Nicholas Church	B3
11 St Nicholas Church Bell Tower	C3
12 St Vitus Cathedral	B2
13 St Vitus Treasury	A2
14 Story of Prague Castle	B2

ⓐ **Shopping**

15 Shakespeare & Sons	D3

⊗ **Eating**

16 Augustine	C3
17 Lobkowicz Palace Café	C1

ⓖ **Drinking & Nightlife**

18 Vinograf	D3

Široká 3), Europe's oldest surviving Jewish graveyard. There is also the **Old-New Synagogue** (Staronová synagóga; Map p536; Červená 2; adult/child 200/140Kč; 🚊17), which is still used for religious services, and requires a separate ticket or additional fee.

Church of Our Lady Before Týn
Church

(Kostel Panny Marie před Týnem; Map p536; 🕿222 318 186; www.tyn.cz; Staroměstské náměstí; suggested donation 25Kč; ⊙10am-1pm & 3-5pm Tue-Sat, 10am-noon Sun Mar-Dec; Ⓜ Staroměstská) Its distinctive twin Gothic spires make the Týn Church an unmistakable Old Town landmark. Like something out of a 15th-century – and probably slightly cruel – fairy tale, they loom over the Old Town Square, decorated with a golden image of the Virgin Mary made in the 1620s from the melted-down Hussite chalice that previously adorned the church.

Astronomical Clock

*a hotchpotch of
medieval buildings*

Church of St James — Church

(Kostel sv Jakuba; Map p536; http://praha.
minorite.cz; Malá Štupartská 6; ⊗9.30am-noon &
2-4pm Tue-Sat, 2-4pm Sun; ⅿNáměstí Republiky)
FREE The great Gothic mass of the Church
of St James began in the 14th century as a
Minorite monastery church, and was given
a beautiful baroque facelift in the early 18th
century. But in the midst of the gilt and
stucco is a grisly memento: on the inside of
the western wall (look up to the right as you
enter) hangs a shrivelled human arm.

Municipal House — Historic Building

(Obecní dům; Map p536; ☑222 002 101; www.
obecnidum.cz; náměstí Republiky 5; guided tours
adult/concession/child under 10yr 290/240Kč/
free; ⊗public areas 7.30am-11pm, information
centre 10am-8pm; ⅿNáměstí Republiky, ☐6, 8,
15, 26) Restored in the 1990s after decades
of neglect, Prague's most exuberantly art
nouveau building is a labour of love, every

detail of its design and decoration carefully
considered, every painting and sculpture
loaded with symbolism. The **restaurant**
(☑222 002 770; www.francouzskarestaurace.cz;
mains 695Kč; ⊗noon-11pm) and **cafe** (☑222
002 763; www.kavarnaod.cz; ⊗7.30am-11pm;
🛜) here are like walk-in museums of art
nouveau design, while upstairs there are
half a dozen sumptuously decorated halls
that you can visit by guided tour.

Old Town Hall — Historic Building

(Staroměstská radnice; Map p536; ☑236
002 629; www.staromestskaradnicepraha.cz;
Staroměstské náměstí 1; guided tours adult/child
100/70Kč, incl tower 180Kč; ⊗11am-6pm Mon,
9am-6pm Tue-Sun; ⅿStaroměstská) Prague's
Old Town Hall, founded in 1338, is a
hotchpotch of medieval buildings acquired
piecemeal over the centuries, presided
over by a tall Gothic tower with a splendid
Astronomical Clock (Map p536; ⊗chimes
on the hour 9am-9pm). As well as housing
the Old Town's main tourist information
office, the town hall has several historic
attractions, and hosts art exhibitions on the
ground floor and 2nd floor.

The town hall's best feature is the view across the Old Town Square from its 60m-tall **clock tower** (Věž radnice; Map p536; adult/child 130/80Kč, incl Old Town Hall tour 180Kč; ⊙11am-10pm Mon, 9am-10pm Tue-Sun). It's well worth the climb up the modern, beautifully designed steel spiral staircase; there's also a lift.

⊚ Nové Město

Wenceslas Square   Square

(Václavské náměstí; Map p536; M Můstek, Muzeum) More a broad boulevard than a typical city square, Wenceslas Square has witnessed a great deal of Czech history – a giant Mass was held here during the revolutionary upheavals of 1848; in 1918 the creation of the new Czechoslovak Republic was celebrated here; and it was here in 1989 that the fall of communism was announced. Originally a medieval horse market, the square was named after Bohemia's patron saint during the nationalist revival of the mid-19th century.

Mucha Museum   Gallery

(Muchovo muzeum; Map p000; ☎001 161 333; www.mucha.cz; Panská 7; adult/child 240/160Kč; ⊙10am-6pm; ☐3, 5, 6, 9, 14, 24) This fascinating (and busy) museum features the sensuous art nouveau posters, paintings and decorative panels of Alfons Mucha (1860–1939), as well as many sketches, photographs and other memorabilia. The exhibits include countless artworks showing Mucha's trademark Slavic maidens with flowing hair and piercing blue eyes, bearing symbolic garlands and linden boughs.

National Memorial to the Heroes of the Heydrich Terror   Museum

(Národní památník hrdinů Heydrichiády; ☎224 916 100; www.pamatnik-heydrichiady.cz; Resslova 9; ⊙9am-5pm Tue-Sun Mar-Oct, 9am-5pm Tue-Sat Nov-Feb; M Karlovo Náměstí) FREE The Church of Sts Cyril & Methodius houses a moving memorial to the seven Czech paratroopers who were involved in the assassination of Reichsprotektor Reinhard Heydrich in 1942, with an exhibit and video about Nazi persecution of the Czechs. The

Charles Bridge

Strolling across **Charles Bridge** (Karlův most; Map p536; ⊙24hr; ☐2, 17, 18 to Karlovy lázně, 12, 15, 20, 22 to Malostranské náměstí) – browsing the stalls of hawkers and caricaturists and listening to buskers beneath the impassive gaze of the baroque statues that line the parapets – is everybody's favourite Prague activity. Don't forget to look at the bridge itself (the bridge towers have great views) and at the grand vistas up and down the river.

church appeared in the 2016 movie based on the assassination, *Anthropoid*.

Prague City Museum   Museum

(Muzeum hlavního města Prahy; Map p536; ☎224 816 773; www.muzeumprahy.cz; Na Poříčí 52; adult/child 120/50Kč; ⊙9am-6pm Tue-Sun; M Florenc) This excellent museum, opened in 1898, is devoted to the history of Prague from prehistoric times to the 20th century (labels are in English as well as Czech). Among the many intriguing exhibits are an astonishing scale model of Prague, and the Astronomical Clock's original 1866 calendar wheel with Josef Mánes' beautiful painted panels representing the months – that's January at the top, toasting his toes by the fire, and August near the bottom, sickle in hand, harvesting the corn.

⊚ Holešovice

Veletržní Palác   Museum

(Trade Fair Palace; ☎224 301 111; www.ngprague. cz; Dukelských hrdinů 47; incl admission to all

Central Prague

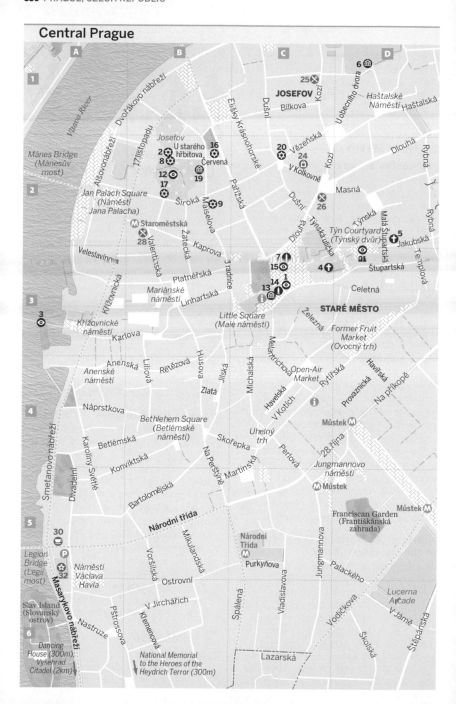

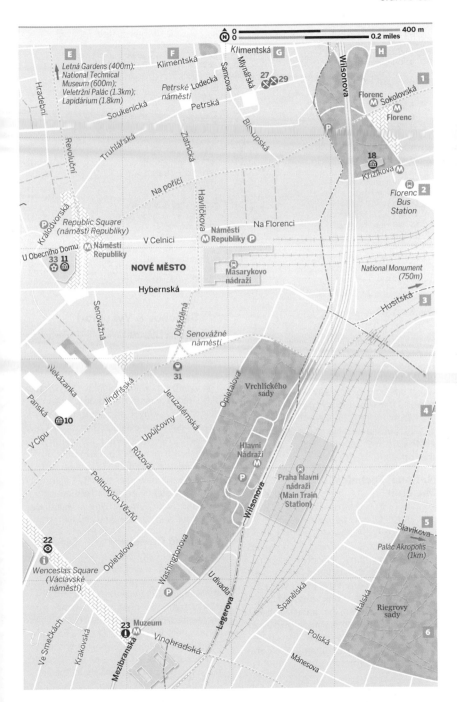

Central Prague

◎ **Sights**

1	Astronomical Clock	C3
2	Ceremonial Hall	B2
3	Charles Bridge	A3
4	Church of Our Lady Before Týn	C3
5	Church of St James	D2
6	Convent of St Agnes	D1
7	Jan Hus Statue	C3
8	Klaus Synagogue	B2
9	Maisel Synagogue	B2
10	Mucha Museum	E4
11	Municipal House	E3
12	Old Jewish Cemetery	B2
13	Old Town Hall	C3
14	Old Town Hall Tower	C3
15	Old Town Square	C3
16	Old-New Synagogue	B2
17	Pinkas Synagogue	B2
18	Prague City Museum	H2
19	Prague Jewish Museum	B2
20	Spanish Synagogue	C2
21	Týn Courtyard	D3
22	Wenceslas Square	E5
23	Wenceslas Statue	E6

🛍 **Shopping**

24	TEG1	C2

🍴 **Eating**

25	Field	C1
	Francouzská Restaurace	(see 11)
26	Kalina	C2
27	Maso a Kobliha	G1
28	Mistral Café	B2
29	Sansho	G1

🍷 **Drinking & Nightlife**

	Kavárna Obecní Dům	(see 11)
30	Kavárna Slavia	A5
31	Vinograf	F4

🎭 **Entertainment**

32	National Theatre	A5
33	Smetana Hall	E3

National Gallery venues; adult/child 300/150Kč; ⊙10am-6pm Tue-Sun; Ⓜ Vltavská, 🚋1, 6, 8, 12, 17, 25, 26) The National Gallery's collection of 'Art of the 19th, 20th and 21st Centuries' is spread out over four floors and is a strong contender for Prague's best museum. It has an unexpectedly rich collection of world masters, including works from Van Gogh, Picasso, Schiele, Klimt and on and on, but the holdings of Czech interwar abstract, surrealist and cubist art are worth the trip alone.

National Technical
Museum   Museum

(Národní Technické Muzeum; 🕿220 399 111; www.ntm.cz; Kostelní 42; adult/concession 190/90Kč; ⊙9am-5.30pm Tue-Fri, 10am-6pm Sat & Sun; 👶; 🚋1, 8, 12, 25, 26 to Letenské náměstí) Prague's most family-friendly museum got a high-tech renovation in 2012 and is a dazzling presentation of the country's industrial heritage. If that sounds dull, it's anything but. Start in the main hall, filled to the rafters with historic planes, trains and automobiles. There are separate halls devoted to exhibits on astronomy, photography, printing and architecture.

◎ Smíchov & Vyšehrad

Vyšehrad Citadel   Fortress

(🕿261 225 304; www.praha-vysehrad.cz; information centre at V pevnosti 159/5b; admission to grounds free; ⊙grounds 24hr; Ⓜ Vyšehrad) **FREE** The Vyšehrad Citadel refers to the complex of buildings and structures atop Vyšehrad Hill that have played an important role in Czech history for over 1000 years as a royal residence, religious centre and military fortress. While most of the surviving structures date from the 18th century, the citadel is still viewed as the city's spiritual home. The sights are spread out over a wide area, with commanding views out over the Vltava and surrounding city.

Vyšehrad Cemetery   Cemetery

(Vyšehradský hřbitov; 🕿274 774 835; www.praha-vysehrad.cz; K Rotundě 10, Vyšehrad; ⊙8am-7pm May-Sep, shorter hours Oct-Apr; Ⓜ Vyšehrad) **FREE** Vyšehrad Cemetery is a main attraction for many visitors, being the final resting place for dozens of Czech luminaries, including Antonín Dvořák, Bedřich Smetana and Alfons Mucha. Many tombs and headstones are works of art – Dvořák's is a sculpture by Ladislav Šaloun, the art nouveau sculptor who created the Jan Hus monument in the Old Town Square.

◎ Žižkov & Karlín

National Monument · Museum

(Národní Památník na Vítkově; ☑224 497 600; www.nm.oz; U Památníku 1900, Žižkov; adult/ child exhibition only 80/60Kč, roof terrace 80/50Kč, combined ticket 120/80Kč; ◎10am-6pm Wed-Sun Apr-Oct, Thu-Sun Nov-Mar; ⊒133, 175, 207) While this monument's massive functionalist structure has all the elegance of a nuclear power station, the interior is a spectacular extravaganza of polished art-deco marble, gilt and mosaics, and is home to a fascinating museum of 20th-century Czechoslovak history.

⊕ TOURS

Taste of Prague · Food & Drink

(☑775 577 275; www.tasteofprague.com; per person 2700Kč) Locals Jan and Zuzi are passionate about Prague's restaurant scene. They lead four-hour foodie tours of the city, tasting trad and modern Czech dishes and drinks in a variety of venues, with intriguing asides on Czech history and culture along the way. Private one- or two-day tasting tours of Moravian vineyards can also be arranged.

AlenaGuide · Tours

(☑724 129 201; www.alenaguide.com; tours from 2300Kč) Alena Vopalkova is a graduate of La Salle University in Philadelphia, USA, who has returned to Prague to lead private, customised tours of her home city. Subjects range from general sightseeing to more specialised tours covering the Jewish Museum, food or shopping, and from three-hour walking tours to day trips exploring off-the-beaten-track spots such as the scenic Český raj (Bohemian Paradise).

Biko Adventures Prague · Cycling

(☑733 750 990; www.bikoadventures.com; Vratislavova 3, Vyšehrad; standard rental per day 450Kč, group tours per person from 1250Kč; ◎9am-6pm Apr-Oct; ⊒2, 3, 7, 17, 21) Italian owner Fillippo Mari loves to cycle, ski and hike and has created this small outfit dedicated to outdoor pursuits of all kinds. From April to October Biko rents bikes and offers day-long guided cycling trips for riders of all levels, as well as hiking and skiing tours. Rental bikes include standard mountain bikes and high-end hardtails from Giant.

⊟ SHOPPING

Shakespeare & Sons · Books

(Map p533; ☑257 531 894; www.shakes.cz; U Lužického semináře 10; ◎11am-9pm; ⊒12, 15, 20, 22) Though its shelves groan with a formidable range of literature in English, French and German, this is more than just a bookshop (with Prague's best range of titles on Eastern European history) – it's a congenial literary hang-out with knowledgeable staff, occasional author events, and a cool downstairs space for sitting and reading.

Wine Food Market · Food

(☑733 338 650; www.winemarket.cz; Strakonická 1, Smíchov; ◎7am-11pm Mon-Sat, 8am-11pm Sun; 🚇; ⓂSmíchovské Nádraží) This rather unpromising, industrial corner in a forgotten Smíchov neighbourhood holds arguably the city's best Italian market, with all manner of breads, cheeses, meats, and Italian goodies such as marinated mushrooms and peppers. It's the perfect spot to assemble a picnic lunch. There's a dining room in the back where you can treat yourself to the spoils. A real treasure.

TEG1 · Fashion & Accessories

(Map p536; ☑222 327 358; www.timoure.cz; V Kolkovně 6; ◎10am-7pm Mon-Fri, 11am-5pm Sat; ⓂStaroměstská) TEG (Timoure et Group) is the design team created by Alexandra Pavalová and Ivana Šafránková, two of Prague's most respected fashion designers. This boutique showcases their quarterly collections, which feature a sharp, imaginative look that adds zest and sophistication to everyday, wearable clothes.

Obchod s Uměním · Art, Antiques

(☑224 252 779; Korunní 34, Vinohrady; ◎11am-5pm Mon-Fri; ⓂNáměstí Míru, ⊒10, 16)

Náplavka Farmers Market

Stretching along the embankment from Trojická to Výton, the weekly **Náplavka Farmers Market** (www.farmarsketrziste. cz; Rašínovo nábřeží; ⊙8am-2pm Sat; ☐2, 3, 7, 17, 21) ✔ makes the most of its riverside setting with live music and outdoor tables scattered among stalls selling freshly baked bread, organic locally grown vegetables, homemade cakes and pastries, wild mushrooms (in season), herbs, flowers, wild honey, hot food, Czech cider, coffee and a range of arts and crafts.

The 'Shop with Art' specialises in original paintings, prints and sculpture from 1900 to 1940, when Czech artists were at the forefront in movements such as constructivism, surrealism and cubism. Naturally, these artworks now fetch astronomical prices, but it's still fun to drop by and browse.

EATING

Restaurace U Veverky   Czech €
(☑603 781 997; www.uveverky.com; Eliášova 14, Dejvice; mains 140-240Kč; ⊙11am-11pm; MHradčanská) This highly rated traditional pub has some of the best-tasting and best-value lunches in the city and is worth a detour. The set-up is classic, with a drinking room out the front and two big dining rooms in the back. The restaurant is filled with the welcoming smell of grilled onions and beer. Reserve in advance.

Mistral Café   Bistro €
(Map p536; ☑222 317 737; www.mistralcafe. cz; Valentinská 11; mains 130-250Kč; ⊙10am-11pm; ☎📶; MStaroměstská) Is this the coolest bistro in the Old Town? Pale stone, bleached birchwood and potted shrubs make for a clean, crisp, modern look, and the clientele of local students and office workers clearly appreciate the competi-

tively priced, well-prepared food. Fish and chips in crumpled brown paper with lemon and black-pepper mayo – yum!

Můj Šálek Kávy   Cafe €
(☑725 556 944; www.mujsalekkavy.cz; Křižíkova 105, Karlín; mains 80-160Kč; ⊙9am-10pm Mon-Sat, 10am-6pm Sun; ☎📶; MKřižíkova) A symbol of Karlín's up-and-coming, neighbourhood-to-watch status, 'My Cup of Coffee' uses Direct Trade beans prepared by expert baristas, and serves what is probably the city's best caffeine hit. Add on a friendly, laid-back atmosphere and superb breakfast and lunch dishes, and you can see why it's often full – reservations are recommended at weekends.

Café Savoy   European €€
(☑257 311 562; http://cafesavoy.ambi.cz; Vítězná 5; mains 200-400Kč; ⊙8am-10.30pm Mon-Fri, 9am-10.30pm Sat & Sun; ☎; ☐9, 12, 15, 20, 22) The Savoy is a beautifully restored belle époque cafe, with smart, suited waiting staff and a Viennese-style menu of hearty soups, salads, roast meats and schnitzels. There's also a 'gourmet menu' (mains 400Kč to 700Kč) where the star of the show is Parisian steak tartare mixed at your table, and a superb wine list (ask the staff for recommendations).

Sansho   Asian, Fusion €€
(Map p536; ☑222 317 425; www.sansho.cz; Petrská 25; lunch mains 190-245Kč, 6-course dinner 900-1200Kč; ⊙11.30am-2pm Tue-Fri, 6-11pm Tue-Sat, last orders 10pm; ☑; ☐3, 8, 14, 24) ✔ 'Friendly and informal' best describes the atmosphere at this ground-breaking restaurant where British chef Paul Day champions Czech farmers by sourcing all his meat and vegetables locally. There's no menu as such – the waitstaff will explain what dishes are available, depending on market produce. Typical dishes include curried rabbit, pork belly with watermelon and hoisin, and 12-hour beef rendang. Reservations recommended.

Nejen Bistro   Bistro €€
(☑222 960 515; www.nejenbistro.cz; Křižíkova 24, Karlín; mains 200-380Kč; ⊙10am-11pm;

🚌3, 8, 24) 🥢 Nejen (Not Only) is emblematic of the new breed of restaurant that is transforming Karlín into one of Prague's hottest neighbourhoods, its quirky interior nominated for a slew of design awards. But just as much attention is lavished on the food, which makes the most of the kitchen's fancy Josper grill, turning out superb steaks, beef ribs and Nejen's signature Black Angus burger.

Augustine   Czech, European €€€

(Map p533; 🖉266 112 280; www.augustine-restaurant.cz; Letenská 12, Augustine Hotel; mains 350-590Kč, 4-course tasting menu 1350Kč; ☺7am-11pm; 🛜; 🚋12, 15, 20, 22) Hidden away in the historic Augustine Hotel (check out the ceiling fresco in the bar), this sophisticated yet relaxed restaurant is well worth seeking out. The menu ranges from down-to-earth but delicious dishes such as pork cheeks braised in the hotel's own St Thomas beer, to inventive dishes built around fresh Czech produce. The two-course business lunch costs 380Kč

Field   Czech €€€

(Map p536; 🖉222 316 999; www.fieldrestau rant.cz; U Milosrdných 12; mains 590-620Kč, 6-course tasting menu 2800Kč; ☺11am-2.30pm & 6-10.30pm Mon-Fri, noon-3pm & 6-10.30pm Sat, noon-3pm & 6-10pm Sun; 🚋17) 🥢 Prague's third Michelin-starred restaurant is its least formal and most fun. The decor is an amusing art-meets-agriculture blend of farmyard implements and minimalist chic, while the chef creates painterly presentations from the finest of local produce along with freshly foraged herbs and edible flowers. You'll have to book at least a couple of weeks in advance to have a chance of a table.

Kalina   French €€€

(Map p536; 🖉222 317 715; www.kalinarestau rant.cz; Dlouhá 12; mains 500-900Kč; ☺noon-3pm & 6-11.30pm; 🛜; 🚋6, 8, 15, 26) Setting a trend for taking the best of fresh Czech produce and giving it the French gourmet treatment, this smart but unfailingly friendly little restaurant offers dishes such as Prague snails with beef marrow and parsley purée, and roast sweetbreads with glazed

Drinks beside a Bedřich Smetana statue and the Vltava River

FRANCESCO IACOBELLI/GETTY IMAGES ©

salsify and black truffles. Weekday lunch specials are good value at 150Kč to 300Kč.

🍷 DRINKING & NIGHTLIFE

Beer Geek   Pub

(https://beergeek.cz; Vinohradská 62, Vinohrady; ⊙3pm-2am; 🛜; Ⓜ Jiřího z Poděbrad) One of the most successful of a new generation of multi-tap pubs in Prague to offer the best beers from local Czech producers as well as brewers from around the world. They have 32 taps in all, and regularly rotate in obscure and hard-to-find labels. The 'geek' part of the name extends to the cool, lab-like presentation of the pub.

Cross Club   Club

(🕽736 535 010; www.crossclub.cz; Plynární 23; admission free-200Kč; ⊙cafe noon-2am, club 6pm-4am; 🛜; Ⓜ Nádraží Holešovice) An industrial club in every sense of the word: the setting in an industrial zone; the thumping music (both DJs and live acts); and the interior, an absolute must-see jumble of gadgets, shafts, cranks and pipes, many of which move and pulsate with light to the music. The program includes occasional live music, theatre performances and art happenings.

Letná Beer Garden   Beer Garden

(🕽233 378 208; www.letenskyzamecek.cz; Letenské sady 341; ⊙11am-11pm May-Sep; 🚋1, 8, 12, 25, 26) No accounting of watering holes in the neighbourhood would be complete without a nod toward the city's best beer garden, with an amazing panorama, situated at the eastern end of the **Letná Gardens** (Letenské sady; ⊙24hr; 🚻). Buy a takeaway beer from a small kiosk and grab a picnic table, or sit on a small terrace where you can order beer by the glass and decent pizza.

Vinograf   Wine Bar

(Map p536; 🕽214 214 681; www.vinograf.cz; Senovážné náměstí 23; ⊙11.30am-midnight Mon-Sat, 5pm-midnight Sun; 🛜; 🚋3, 5, 6, 9, 14, 24) With knowledgeable staff, a relaxed atmosphere and an off-the-beaten-track feel, this appealingly modern wine bar is a great place to discover Moravian wines. There's good finger food to accompany

Cross Club

RADIOKAFKA/SHUTTERSTOCK ©

your wine, mostly cheese and charcuterie, with food and wine menus (in Czech and English) on big blackboards behind the bar. Very busy at weekends, when it's worth booking a table.

There's another branch in **Malá Strana** (Map p533; ☎604 705 730; Míšeňská 8; ⏲4pm-midnight Mon-Sat, 2-10pm Sun; 📶; 🚋12, 15, 20, 22).

Pivovarský Klub Pub

(☎222 315 777; www.pivovarskyklub.com; Křižíkova 17, Karlín; ⏲11.30am-11.30pm; Ⓜ Florenc) This bar is to beer what the Bodleian Library is to books – wall-to-wall shelves lined with more than 200 varieties of bottled beer from all over the world, and six guest beers on tap. Perch on a bar stool or head downstairs to the snug cellar and order some of the pub's excellent grub, such as authentic *guláš* (goulash) with bacon dumplings, to soak up the beer.

U Slovanské Lípy Pub

(☎734 743 094; www.uslovanskelipy.cz; Tachovské náměstí 6, Žižkov; ⏲11am-midnight; 📶 👪; 🚌133, 175, 207) A classic Žižkov pub, plain and unassuming in and out, 'At the Linden Trees' (the linden is a Czech and Slovak national emblem) is something of a place of pilgrimage for beer lovers. The reason is its range of artisan brews (from 28Kč for 0.5L), such as those from the Kocour brewery, including its superb Sumeček 11° (Catfish pale ale).

✪ ENTERTAINMENT

Palác Akropolis Live Music

(☎296 330 913; www.palacakropolis.cz; Kubelíkova 27, Žižkov; tickets free-250Kč; ⏲club 6.30pm-5am; 📶; 🚋5, 9, 15, 26) The Akropolis is a Prague institution, a smoky, labyrinthine, sticky-floored shrine to alternative music and drama. Its various performance spaces host a smorgasbord of musical and cultural events, from DJs to string quartets to Macedonian Roma bands to local rock gods to visiting talent – Marianne Faithfull, the Flaming Lips and the Strokes have all played here.

Czech Beer

There are two main varieties of beer: *světlé* (light) and *tmavy* or *černé* (dark). The *světlé* is a pale amber or golden lager-style beer with a crisp, refreshing, hoppy flavour. Dark beers are sweeter and more full-bodied, with a rich, malty or fruity flavour.

Czechs like their beer served at cellar temperature (around 6°C to 10°C) with a tall, creamy head (known as *pěna*, meaning 'foam'). Americans and Australians may find it a bit warm, but this improves the flavour. Most draught beer is sold in *půl-litr* (0.5L) glasses; if you prefer a small beer, ask for a *malé pivo* (0.3L). Some bars confuse the issue by using 0.4L glasses, while others offer a German-style 1L mug known as a *tuplák*.

Prague pubs traditionally offered just three beers on tap, all from one large brewery such as Pilsner Urquell; some pioneering bar owners added a *čtvrtá pípa* ('fourth pipe') to allow them to offer a rotating range of guest beers from various independent regional breweries. Many now have five, six or even more pipes.

National Theatre Opera, Ballet

(Národní divadlo; Map p536; ☎224 901 448; www.narodni-divadlo.cz; Národní třída 2; tickets 100-1290Kč; ⏲box offices 10am-6pm; 🚋2, 9, 18, 22) The much-loved National Theatre provides a stage for traditional opera, drama and ballet by the likes of Smetana, Shakespeare and Tchaikovsky, sharing the

 Troja
Chateau

Troja Chateau (Zámek Troja; ☑283 851
614; www.ghmp.cz; U Trojského Zámku 1,
Troja; adult/concession 120/60Kč; ☺10am-
6pm Tue-Sun, from 1pm Fri Apr-Oct, closed
Nov-Mar; ⌨112, Ⓜ Nádraží Holešovice) is a
17th-century baroque palace that was
built for the Šternberk family, inspired
by Roman country villas seen by the
architect on a visit to Italy. A visit to the
chateau can easily be combined with
a trip to **Prague Zoo** (Zoo Praha; ☑296
112 230; www.zoopraha.cz; U Trojského
zámku 120, Troja; adult/concession/family
200/150/600Kč; ☺9am-7pm Jun-Aug, to
6pm Apr, May, Sep & Oct, to 5pm Mar, to 4pm
Nov-Feb; 🎡; ⌨112, Ⓜ Nádraží Holešovice), as
the two are side by side. It's a pleasant
20-minute walk from Stromovka park,
including crossing a dramatic footbridge
over the Vltava.

The sumptuously decorated palace
now houses collections of the Prague
City Gallery and exhibits explaining the
sculptures and frescoes that adorn the
palace itself. There's free admission to
the grounds, where you can wander in
the beautiful French gardens.

Troja Chateau
MILONK/SHUTTERSTOCK ©

program alongside more modern works by
composers and playwrights such as Philip
Glass and John Osborne. The box offices
are in the Nový síň building next door, in
the Kolowrat Palace (opposite the Estates
Theatre) and at the State Opera.

La Fabrika Theatre, Performing Arts
(☑box office 774 417 644; www.lafabrika.cz; Ko-
munardů 30; admission 200-400Kč; ☺box office
2-7.30pm Mon-Fri; ⌨1, 6, 12, 14, 25) The name
refers to a 'factory', but this is actually a former paint warehouse that's been converted
into an experimental performance space.
Depending on the night, come here to
catch live music (jazz or cabaret), theatre,
dance or film. Consult the website for the
latest program. Try to reserve in advance as
shows typically sell out.

 INFORMATION

Prague City Tourism (☑221 714 714; www.
prague.eu) branches are scattered around town
at the **Old Town Hall** (Staroměstské náměstí
5; ☺9am-7pm; Ⓜ Staroměstská), in **Staré
Město** (Rytířská 12; ☺9am-7pm; Ⓜ Můstek)
and at **Wenceslas Square** (Václavské náměstí
42; ☺10am-6pm; Ⓜ Můstek, Muzeum), and at
both airport arrivals terminals at **Václav Havel
Airport Prague** (Terminals 1 & 2; ☺8am-8pm;
⌨100, 119). Offices are good sources of maps
and general information; they also sell Prague
Card discount cards and can book guides and
tours.

 GETTING THERE & AWAY

AIR

Václav Havel Airport Prague (Prague Ruzyně International Airport; ☑220 111 888; www.prg.aero;
K letišti 6, Ruzyně; 🛜; ⌨100, 119), 17km west of
the city centre, is the main international gateway
to the Czech Republic and the hub for the national carrier Czech Airlines, which operates direct
flights to Prague from many European cities.
There are also direct flights from North America
(from April to October) as well as to select cities
in the Middle East and Asia.

BUS

Several bus companies offer long-distance
coach service connecting Prague to cities
around Europe. Nearly all international buses
(and most domestic services) use the renovated
and user-friendly **Florenc bus station** (ÚAN

Praha Florenc; ☑900 144 444; www.florenc.cz; Křižíkova 2110/2b, Karlín; ⊙5am-midnight; 🛜; MFlorenc).

CAR

Prague lies at the nexus of several European four-lane highways and is a relatively easy drive from many major regional cities, including Berlin (four hours), Vienna (four hours) and Budapest (five hours).

TRAIN

Prague is well integrated into European rail networks. **České dráhy** (ČD, Czech Rail; ☑221 111 122; www.cd.cz), the Czech state rail operator, sells tickets for international destinations. Train travel makes the most sense if coming from Berlin or from Vienna and Budapest in the east and south.

Most domestic and international trains arrive at **Praha hlavní nádraží** (Prague Main Train Station; ☑840 112 113; www.cd.cz; Wilsonova 8, Nové Město; ⊙3.30am-12.30am; MHlavní nádraží). Some international trains, particularly those travelling to or coming from Berlin, also stop at a smaller station, **Praha-Holešovice** (Nádraží Holešovice; ☑040 112 113; www.od.ozi Vrbenského, Holešovice; MNádraží Holešovice), north of the centre. Both stations have stops on metro line C (red).

❶ GETTING AROUND

Central Prague is easily managed on foot (though be sure to wear comfortable shoes). For longer trips, the city has a reliable public-transport system of metros, trams and buses operated by the **Prague Public Transport**

Authority (DPP; ☑296 191 817; www.dpp.cz; ⊙7am-9pm). The system is integrated, meaning that the same tickets are valid on all types of transport, and for transfers between them.

METRO

Prague's excellent metro operates daily from 5am to midnight. The metro has three lines:

Line A (shown on transport maps in green) Links the airport bus to Malá Strana, Old Town Square, Wenceslas Square and Vinohrady.

Line B (Yellow) Cross-river route from Smichov in southwest to central Náměstí Republiky and Florenc bus station.

Line C (Red) Links main train station to Florenc bus station, Wenceslas Square and Vyšehrad.

BUS & TRAM

To supplement the metro, there is a comprehensive system of trams (streetcars) and buses that reach virtually every nook and cranny in the city. The DPP website has a handy 'Journey Planner' tab in English to allow you to plan your route.

❍ Trams are convenient for crossing the river and moving between neighbourhoods.

◼ Buses are less useful for visitors and normally connect far-flung residential neighbourhoods to nearby metro stations or the centre.

❍ Always validate an unstamped ticket on entering the tram or bus.

❍ Trams and buses run from around 5am to midnight daily. After the system shuts down, a smaller fleet of night trams (51 to 59) and night buses rumble across the city about every 40 minutes (only full-price 32Kč tickets are valid on these services).

In This Chapter

Royal Palace 548
Thermal Baths & Spas 550
Sights 552
Shopping 558
Eating 559
Drinking & Nightlife 561
Entertainment 562
Information 562
Getting There & Away 563
Getting Around 563

Budapest, Hungary

Budapest is paradise for explorers. Architecturally, the city is a treasure trove, with enough baroque, neoclassical and art nouveau buildings to satisfy everyone. Amid these splendid edifices, history waits around every corner, with bullet holes and shrapnel pockmarks poignant reminders of past conflicts. And to buoy the traveller on their explorations, the city generously supplies delicious Magyar cuisine (among an array of other top eats), excellent wines, rip-roaring nightlife and an abundance of hot springs to soak the day's aches away.

Two Days in Budapest

Spend most of the first day on **Castle Hill** (p557), taking in the views and visiting the **Royal Palace** (p549) and a museum or two. In the afternoon, ride the **Sikló** (p557) down to Clark Ádám tér and make your way to the **Gellért Baths** (p551). In the evening, head to Erzsébetváros and the Jewish Quarter. On the second day take a walk up Andrássy út, stopping off at the **House of Terror** (p552). In the afternoon, take the waters at the **Széchenyi Baths** (p551).

Four Days in Budapest

The next day, concentrate on the two icons of Hungarian nationhood and the places that house them: the Crown of St Stephen in **Parliament** (p553) and the saint-king's mortal remains in the **Basilica of St Stephen** (p553). In the evening, go for drinks at a **ruin pub** (p561). On day four visit the **Great Synagogue** (p552) and in the afternoon cross over to idyllic **Margaret Island** (p553). Spend the rest of the afternoon at **Veli Bej Bath** (p551).

Next waltz on to Vienna (p564), 2½ hours by train or 5½ to 6½ hours by boat.

Budapest Map (p554)

Arriving in Budapest

Ferenc Liszt International Airport
Minibuses, buses and trains to central Budapest run from 4am to midnight. A taxi will cost from 6500Ft.

Keleti, Nyugati & Déli Train Stations
All three are connected to metro lines of the same name and night buses call when the metro is closed.

Stadion & Népliget Bus Stations Both are on metro lines and are served by trams.

Where to Stay

Accommodation in Budapest runs the gamut from hostels in converted flats and private rooms in far-flung housing estates to luxury guesthouses in the Buda Hills and five-star properties charging upwards of €350 a night.

Because of the changing value of the forint, many midrange and top-end hotels quote their rates in euros.

CGE2010/SHUTTERSTOCK ©

Royal Palace

The enormous Royal Palace (Királyi Palota) has been razed and rebuilt six times over the past seven centuries. Today it contains two museums, the national library and an abundance of statues and monuments. It is the focal point of Buda's Castle Hill and the city's most visited sight.

Great For...

☑ Don't Miss

Late Gothic altarpieces, Gothic statues and heads, and the Renaissance door frame.

Hungarian National Gallery

The **Hungarian National Gallery** (Nemzeti Galéria; ☎1-201 9082; www.mng.hu; Bldgs A-D; adult/concession 1800/900Ft, audio guide 1000Ft; ⊘10am-6pm Tue-Sun) boasts an overwhelming collection that traces Hungarian art from the 11th century to the present day. The largest collections include medieval and Renaissance stonework, Gothic wooden sculptures and panel paintings, late Gothic winged altars and late Renaissance and baroque art. The museum also has an important collection of Hungarian paintings and sculpture from the 19th and 20th centuries. Much of the gallery was closed for renovations at the time of writing, and by 2019 the collection is due to move to a purpose-built gallery in City Park.

/GETTY IMAGES ®

Royal Palace

ⓘ Need to Know

Királyi Palota; I Szent György tér; 🚌16, 16A, 116

✖ Take a Break

If you need something hot and/or sweet after your visit, head for **Ruszwurm Cukrászda** (☏1-375 5284; www.ruszwurm. hu; I Szentháromság utca 7; ⊘10am-7pm Mon-Fri, to 6pm Sat & Sun; 🚌16, 16A, 116).

> ★ **Top Tip**
> Exiting through the museum's back courtyard door will take you straight down to I Szarvas tér in the Tabán.

Castle Museum

Part of the multibranched Budapest History Museum, the **Castle Museum** (Vármúzeum; ☏1-487 8800; www.btm.hu; Bldg E; adult/concession 2000/1000Ft; ⊘10am-6pm Tue-Sun Mar-Oct, to 4pm Nov-Feb) explores the city's 2000-year history over three floors. Restored palace rooms dating from the 15th century can be entered from the basement, where there are three vaulted halls. One of the halls features a magnificent Renaissance door frame in red marble, leading to the Gothic and Renaissance Halls, the Royal Cellar and the vaulted Tower Chapel (1320) dedicated to St Stephen.

On the ground floor, exhibits showcase Budapest during the Middle Ages, with dozens of important Gothic statues, heads and fragments of courtiers, squires and saints, discovered during excavations in 1974.

A wonderful exhibit on the 1st floor called '1000 Years of a Capital' traces the history of Budapest from the arrival of the Magyars and the Turkish occupation to modern times, taking an interesting look at housing, ethnic diversity, religion and other such issues over the centuries. The excellent audioguide is 1200Ft.

National Széchenyi Library

The **National Széchenyi Library** (Országos Széchenyi Könyvtár; ☏1-224 3700; www.oszk. hu; Bldg F; ⊘9am-8pm, stacks to 7pm Tue-Sat) contains codices and manuscripts, a large collection of foreign newspapers and a copy of everything published in Hungary or the Hungarian language. It was founded in 1802 by Count Ferenc Széchenyi, father of the heroic István, who endowed it with 15,000 books and 2000 manuscripts.

Széchenyi Baths

UNGVARI ATTILA/SHUTTERSTOCK ©

Thermal Baths & Spas

Budapest sits on a crazy quilt of almost 125 thermal springs, and 'taking the waters' is very much a part of everyday life here. Some baths date from Turkish times, others are art nouveau marvels and still others are chic modern spas boasting all the mod cons.

Great For...

☑ Don't Miss

The sight of locals playing chess on floating boards (regardless of the weather) at Széchenyi Baths.

History of a Spa City

The remains of two sets of baths found at Aquincum – for the public and the garrisons – indicate that the Romans took advantage of Budapest's thermal waters almost two millennia ago. But it wasn't until the Turkish occupation of the 16th and 17th centuries that bathing became an integral part of everyday Budapest life. In the late 18th century, Habsburg Empress Maria Theresa ordered that Budapest's mineral waters be analysed/recorded in a list at the Treasury's expense. By the 1930s Budapest had become a fashionable spa resort.

Healing Waters

Of course, not everyone goes to the baths for fun and relaxation. The warm, mineral-rich waters are also believed to relieve a number of specific complaints, ranging from

Gellért Baths

MARTCHAN/SHUTTERSTOCK ©

cupola and eight massive pillars. They're mostly men-only during the week, but turn into a real zoo on mixed weekend nights.

Gellért Baths (Gellért gyógyfürdő; ☎1-466 6166; www.gellertbath.hu; XI Kelenhegyi út 4, Danubius Hotel Gellért; with locker/cabin Mon-Fri 5100/5500Ft, Sat & Sun 5300/5700Ft; ⊗6am-8pm; 🚊7, 86, Ⓜ M4 Szent Gellért tér, 🚊18, 19, 47, 49) Soaking in these art nouveau baths, now open to both men and women at all times, has been likened to taking a bath in a cathedral.

Széchenyi Baths (Széchenyi Gyógyfürdő; ☎1-363 3210; www.szechenyibath.hu; XIV Állatkerti körút 9-11; tickets incl locker/cabin Mon-Fri 4700/5200Ft, Sat & Sun 4900/5400Ft; ⊗6am-10pm; Ⓜ M1 Széchenyi fürdő) The gigantic 'wedding-cake' building in City Park houses these baths, which are unusual for three reasons: their immensity (a dozen thermal baths and three outdoor swimming pools); the bright, clean atmosphere; and the high temperature of the water (up to 40°C).

Veli Bej Baths (Veli Bej Fürdője; ☎1-438 8500; www.irgalmas.hu/veli-bej-furdo; II Árpád fejedelem útja 7 & Frankel Leó út 54; 6am-noon 2240Ft, 3-7pm 2800Ft, after 7pm 2000Ft; ⊗6am-noon & 3-9pm; 🚊9, 109, 🚊4, 6, 17, 19) This venerable (1575) Turkish bath in Buda has got a new lease of life after having been forgotten for centuries.

arthritis and muscle pain to poor blood circulation and post-traumatic stress. They are also a miracle cure for that most unpleasant of afflictions: the dreaded hangover.

Choosing a Bath

The choice of bathhouses today is legion, and which one you choose is a matter of taste and what exactly you're looking for – be it fun, a hangover cure, or relief for something more serious.

Rudas Baths (Rudas Gyógyfürdő; ☎1-356 1322; www.rudasfurdo.hu; I Döbrentei tér 9; with cabin Mon-Fri/Sat & Sun 3200/3500Ft, morning/night ticket 2500/4600Ft; ⊗men 6am-8pm Mon & Wed-Fri, women 6am-8pm Tue, mixed 10pm-4am Fri, 6am-8pm & 10pm-4am Sat, 6am-8pm Sun; 🚊7, 86, 🚊18, 19) These renovated baths are the most Turkish of all in Budapest, built in 1566, with an octagonal pool, domed

⊙ SIGHTS

Budapest's most important museums are found on Castle Hill, in City Park, along Andrássy út in Erzsébetváros, and in Southern Pest. The area surrounding the splendid Parliament building is also home to Budapest's most iconic church; both Parliament and Belváros feature some of the city's best art nouveau architecture. Margaret Island and City Park are the city's most appealing green spaces, while the Buda Hills is a veritable playground for hikers, cavers and bikers. Óbuda is home to extensive Roman ruins and quirky museums, and Gellért Hill gives you some of the best views of the city.

Great Synagogue   Synagogue

(Nagy Zsinagóga; ☎1-462 0477; www.dohany-zsinagoga.hu; VII Dohány utca 2; adult/concession incl museum 3000/2000Ft; ⊙10am-6pm Sun-Thu, to 4pm Fri Mar-Oct, 10am-4pm Sun-Thu, to 2pm Fri Nov-Feb; Ⓜ M2 Astoria, ☐47, 49) Budapest's stunning Great Synagogue is the largest Jewish house of worship in the world outside New York City. Built in 1859, the synagogue has both Romantic and Moorish architectural elements. Inside, the **Hungarian Jewish Museum & Archives** (Magyar Zsidó Múzeum és Levéltár; ☎1-343 6756; www.milev.hu) contains objects relating to both religious and everyday life. On the synagogue's north side, the **Holocaust Tree of Life Memorial** (Raoul Wallenberg Memorial Park, opp VII Wesselényi utca 6) presides over the mass graves of those murdered by the Nazis.

House of Terror   Museum

(Terror Háza; ☎1-374 2600; www.terrorhaza. hu; VI Andrássy út 60; adult/concession 2000/1000Ft, audioguide 1500Ft; ⊙10am-6pm Tue-Sun; Ⓜ M1 Oktogon) The headquarters of the dreaded secret police is now the startling House of Terror, focusing on the crimes and atrocities of Hungary's fascist and Stalinist regimes in a permanent exhibition called Double Occupation. But the years after WWII leading up to the 1956 Uprising get the lion's share of the exhibition space (almost three-dozen spaces on three levels). The reconstructed prison cells in the basement and the Perpetrators' Gallery, featuring photographs of the turncoats, spies and torturers, are chilling.

Holocaust Tree of Life Memorial

JENNIFER WALKER/LONELY PLANET ©

Liberty Monument Monument

(Szabadság-szobor; 🚌27) The Liberty Monument, the lovely lady with the palm frond proclaiming freedom throughout the city, is to the east of the Citadella. Some 14m high, she was raised in 1947 in tribute to the Soviet soldiers who died liberating Budapest in 1945. The victims' names in Cyrillic letters on the plinth and the soldiers' statues were removed in 1992 and sent to Memento Park. The inscription reads: 'To those who gave up their lives for Hungary's independence, freedom and prosperity'.

Memento Park Historic Site

(🚗1-424 7500; www.mementopark.hu; XXII Balatoni út & Szabadkai utca; adult/student 1500/1000Ft; ⊙10am-dusk; 🚌101, 150) Home to more than 40 statues, busts and plaques of Lenin, Marx, Béla Kun and others whose likenesses have ended up on rubbish heaps elsewhere, Memento Park, 10km southwest of the city centre, is truly a mind-blowing place to visit. Ogle the socialist realism and try to imagine that some of these relics were erected as recently as the late 1980s.

Basilica of St Stephen Cathedral

(Szent István Bazilika; 🚗06 30 703 6599, 1-311 0839; www.basilica.hu; V Szent István tér; requested donation 200Ft; ⊙9am-7pm Mon-Sat, 7.45am-7pm Sun; ⓂM3 Arany János utca) Budapest's neoclassical cathedral was built over half a century and completed in 1905. Much of the interruption during construction had to do with a fiasco in 1868 when the dome collapsed during a storm, and the structure had to be demolished and then rebuilt from the ground up. The basilica is rather dark and gloomy inside, but take a trip to the top of the dome for incredible views.

Hungarian State
Opera House Notable Building

(Magyar Állami Operaház; 🚗1-332 8197; www.operavisit.hu; VI Andrássy út 22; adult/concession 2990/1990Ft; ⊙tours in English 2pm, 3pm & 4pm; ⓂM1 Opera) The neo-Renaissance Hungarian State Opera House was designed by Miklós Ybl in 1884 and is among the most beautiful buildings in Budapest. Its facade is decorated with statues of muses and

 Margaret Island

Situated in the middle of the Danube, leafy Margaret Island is neither Buda nor Pest, but its shaded walkways, large swimming complexes, thermal spa and gardens offer refuge to the denizens of both sides of the river. The island was always the domain of one religious order or another until the Turks turned it into a harem, and it remains studded with picturesque ruins.

The island is bigger than you think, so rent a bicycle or other wheeled equipment from **Bringóhintó** (🚗1-329 2073; www.bringohinto.hu; per 30/60min mountain bikes 690/990Ft, pedal coaches for 4 people 2280/3680Ft; ⊙8am-dusk; 🚌26) at the refreshment stand near the Japanese Garden in the northern part of the island, then work your way south. The island is at its best during the day, though you can also check out the on-site club, **Holdudvar** (🚗1-236 0155; www.facebook.com/holdudvaroldal; XIII Margitsziget; ⊙11am-2am Sun-Wed, to 4am Thu, to 5am Fri & Sat; 🚌4, 6), in the evening.

Church ruins
GASCHWALD/SHUTTERSTOCK ©

opera greats such as Puccini, Mozart, Liszt and Verdi, while its interior dazzles with marble columns, gilded vaulted ceilings, chandeliers and near-perfect acoustics. If you cannot attend a performance, join one of the three daily tours. Tickets are available from the souvenir shop inside the lobby.

Parliament Historic Building

(Országház; 🚗1-441 4904; www.hungarianparliament.com; V Kossuth Lajos tér 1-3; adult/

Budapest

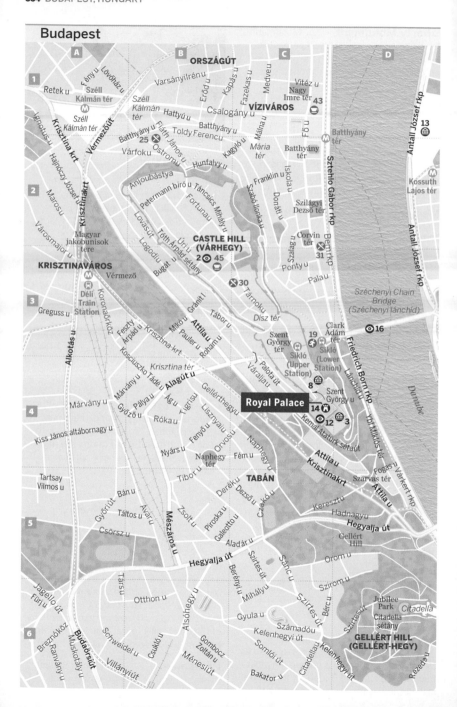

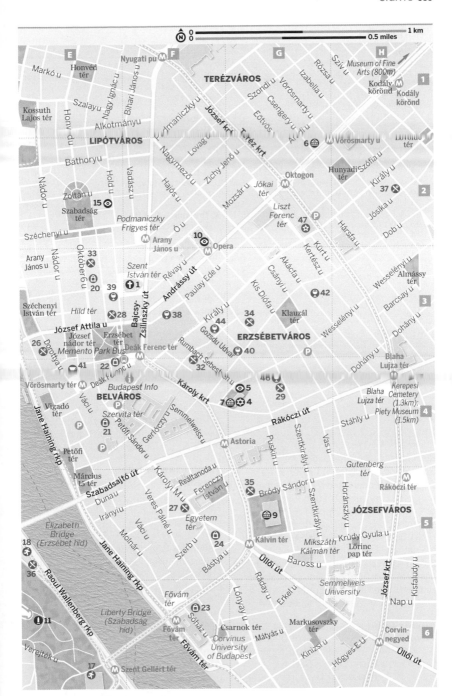

Budapest

◎ **Sights**
1 Basilica of St Stephen	F3
Basilica of St Stephen Treasury	(see 1)
2 Castle Hill	B3
3 Castle Museum	D4
4 Great Synagogue	G4
5 Holocaust Tree of Life Memorial	G4
6 House of Terror	G2
7 Hungarian Jewish Museum & Archives	G4
8 Hungarian National Gallery	C4
9 Hungarian National Museum	G5
10 Hungarian State Opera House	F2
11 Liberty Monument	E6
12 National Széchenyi Library	C4
13 Parliament	D1
14 Royal Palace	C4
15 Royal Postal Savings Bank	E2
16 Széchenyi Chain Bridge	D3

◎ **Activities, Courses & Tours**
17 Gellért Baths	E6
18 Rudas Baths	E5
19 Sikló	C3

🏬 **Shopping**
20 Bestsellers	E3
21 Bomo Art	E4
22 Le Parfum Croisette	E4
23 Nagycsarnok	F6
24 Rózsavölgyi Csokoládé	F5

🍴 **Eating**
25 Arany Kaviár Étterem	B2
26 Baraka	E3
27 Belvárosi Disznótoros	F5
28 Borkonyha	E3
29 Bors Gasztro Bár	G4
30 Budavári Rétesvár	C3
31 Horgásztanya Vendéglő	C2
32 Igen	F4
33 Kisharang	E3
34 Kőleves	G3
35 Múzeum	G5
36 Rudas Restaurant & Bar	E5
37 Zeller Bistro	H2

🍷 **Drinking & Nightlife**
38 Boutiq' Bar	F3
39 DiVino Borbár	E3
40 Doblo	G3
41 Gerbeaud	E4
42 Instant	G3
43 Kávé Műhely	C1
44 Léhűtő	F3
45 Ruszwurm Cukrászda	B3
46 Szimpla Kert	G4

🎭 **Entertainment**
Hungarian State Opera House	(see 10)
47 Liszt Music Academy	G2

student EU citizen 2200/1200Ft, non-EU citizen 5400/2800Ft; ⊙8am-6pm Mon-Fri, to 4pm Sat, to 2pm Sun; Ⓜ️M2 Kossuth Lajos tér, 🚋2) The Eclectic-style Parliament, designed by Imre Steindl and completed in 1902, has 691 sumptuously decorated rooms, but you'll only get to see several of these and other features on a guided tour of the North Wing: the Golden Staircase; the Domed Hall, where the **Crown of St Stephen**, the nation's most important national icon, is on display; the Grand Staircase and its wonderful landing; Loge Hall; and Congress Hall, where the House of Lords of the one-time bicameral assembly sat until 1944.

Royal Postal Savings Bank
Notable Building

(V Hold utca 4; 🚋15) East of Szabadság tér, the former Royal Postal Savings Bank is a Secessionist extravaganza of colourful tiles and folk motifs, built by Ödön Lechner in 1901. One of the most beautiful buildings in Pest, it is now part of the National Bank of Hungary.

Hungarian National Museum
Museum

(Magyar Nemzeti Múzeum; 🖉1-338 2122; www. hnm.hu; VIII Múzeum körút 14-16; adult/concession 1600/800Ft; ⊙10am-6pm Tue-Sun; 🚋47, 49, Ⓜ️M3/4 Kálvin tér) The Hungarian National Museum houses the nation's most important collection of historical relics in an impressive neoclassical building, purpose built in 1847. Exhibits trace the history of the Carpathian Basin from earliest times to the end of the Avar period, and the ongoing story of the Magyar people from the conquest of the basin to the end of communism. Don't miss King Stephen's crimson silk coronation mantle and the Broadwood piano, used by both Beethoven and Liszt.

Kerepesi Cemetery Cemetery

(Kerepesi temető; 📞06 30 331 8822; www.
nemzetisirkert.hu; VIII Fiumei út 16; ⊗7am-8pm
May-Jul, to 7pm Apr & Aug, to 6pm Sep, to 5pm
Mar & Oct, 7.30am-5pm Nov-Feb; Ⓜ M2/4 Keleti
train station, 🚃24) **FREE** Budapest's equivalent of London's Highgate or Père Lachaise
in Paris, this 56-hectare necropolis was
established in 1847 and holds some 3000
gravestones and mausoleums, including
those of statesmen and national heroes
Lajos Kossuth, Ferenc Deák and Lajos
Batthyány. Maps indicating the location of
noteworthy graves are available free at the
entrance. Plot 21 contains the graves of
many who died in the 1956 Uprising.

Castle Hill Hill

(Várhegy; 🚃16, 16A, 116, Ⓜ M2 Batthyány tér,
Széll Kálmán tér, 🚋19, 41;) Castle Hill is a
kilometre-long limestone plateau towering
170m above the Danube. It contains some
of Budapest's most important medieval
monuments and museums, and is a Unesco
World Heritage Site. Below it is a 28km-long
network of caves formed by thermal springs.

The walled area consists of two distinct
parts: the Old Town, where commoners
once lived, and the Royal Palace, the original site of the castle built by Béla IV in the
13th century and reserved for the nobility.

The easiest way to reach Castle Hill from
Pest is to take bus 16 from Deák Ferenc tér
to Dísz tér, more or less the central point
between the Old Town and the Royal Palace.
Much more fun, though, is to stroll across
Széchenyi Chain Bridge and board the **Sikló**
(www.bkv.hu; I Szent György tér; one way/return
adult 1200/1800Ft, 3-14yr 700/1100Ft; ⊗7.30am-
10pm, closed 1st & 3rd Mon of month; 🚃16, 16A,
🚋19, 41), a funicular railway built in 1870 that
ascends steeply from Clark Ádám tér to
Szent György tér near the Royal Palace.

Alternatively, you can walk up the Király
lépcső (Royal Steps) leading northwest off
Clark Ádám tér.

Another option is to take metro M2 to
Széll Kálmán tér, go up the stairs in the
southeastern part of the square and walk
up Várfok utca to Vienna Gate. This medieval entrance to the Old Town was rebuilt in

Budapest's Flea Markets

Jostling with locals shopping for bargains
at **Ecseri Piac** (Ecseri Market; www.piacon-
line.hu; XIX Nagykőrösi út 156; ⊗8am-4pm
Mon-Fri, 5am-3pm Sat, 8am-1pm Sun; 🚃54,
84E, 89E 94E), one of Central Europe's
largest flea markets, is a fabulous way to
spend a Saturday morning. Lose yourself
amid a cornucopia of gramophones,
rocking horses, uniforms, violins and
even suits of armour. If you can't make
it here, the smaller **PECSA Bolhapiac**
(www.bolhapiac.com; XIV Zichy Mihály utca
14; admission 150Ft; ⊗7am-2pm Sat & Sun;
🚎trolleybus 72, 74, 🚋1) offers a less impressive jumble of vintage knick-knacks.

Old radios and TVs for sale at Ecseri Piac
WESTEND61 PREMIUM/SHUTTERSTOCK ©

1936 to mark the 250th anniversary of the
castle being taken back from the Turks. Bus
16A follows the same route from the start
of Várfok utca.

Museum of Fine Arts Museum

(Szépművészeti Múzeum; 📞1-469 7100; www.
mfab.hu; XIV Dózsa György út 41; Ⓜ M1 Hősök
tere) Housed in a grand neoclassical
building, the Museum of Fine Arts is home
to the city's most outstanding collection of
foreign works of art, ranging from articles
from ancient Egypt and ancient Mediterranean cultures to stellar collections of
Spanish, Flemish, Italian and German art.
The private collection of Count Miklós
Esterházy, purchased by the state in 1870,
forms the nucleus of this collection. At
research time, the museum was closed for
renovation until March 2018.

The Danube and Its Bridges

Budapest's dustless highway is ever present, neatly dividing the city and still serving as an important means of transport. The Danube bridges (all eight of them, not counting train bridges), at once landmarks and vantage points over the river, are the stitches that have bound Buda and Pest together since well before the two were linked politically in 1873. The four bridges in the centre stand head and shoulders above the rest: Margaret Bridge, wonderful **Széchenyi Chain Bridge** (Széchenyi lánchíd; 🚌16, 🚋19, 41), Elizabeth Bridge and Liberty Bridge.

Széchenyi Chain Bridge
PAOLO PARADISO/SHUTTERSTOCK ©

Aquincum — Archaeological Site

(📞1-250 1650; www.aquincum.hu; III Szentendrei út 133-135; adult/concession museum & park 1600/800Ft, park only 1000/500Ft; ⊗museum 10am-6pm Tue-Sun Apr-Oct, to 4pm Nov-Mar, park 9am-6pm Tue-Sun Apr-Oct; 🚌34, 106, 🚆HÉV to Aquincum) The most complete Roman civilian town in Hungary was built around AD 100 and became the seat of the Roman province of Pannonia Inferior in AD 106. Visitors can explore its houses, baths, courtyards, fountains and sophisticated underfloor heating systems, as well as a recreation of a Roman painter's dwelling. Alight at the Aquincum stop.

The purpose-built Aquincum Museum, just inside the entrance, puts the ruins in perspective, with a vast collection of Roman daily life objects and wall paintings.

🛍 SHOPPING

Nagycsarnok — Market

(Great Market Hall; 📞1-366 3300; www.piacon line.hu; IX Vámház körút 1-3; ⊗6am-5pm Mon, to 6pm Tue-Fri, to 3pm Sat; Ⓜ M4 Fővám tér) This is Budapest's biggest market, though it has become a tourist magnet since its renovation for the millecentenary celebrations in 1996. Still, plenty of locals come here for fruit, vegetables, deli items, fish and meat. Head up to the 1st floor for Hungarian folk costumes, dolls, painted eggs, embroidered tablecloths, carved hunting knives and other souvenirs.

Bestsellers — Books

(📞1-312 1295; www.bestsellers.hu; V Október 6 utca 11; ⊗9am-6.30pm Mon-Fri, 11am-6pm Sat, noon-6pm Sun; Ⓜ M1/2/3 Deák Ferenc tér) Our favourite English-language bookshop in town, with fiction, travel guides and lots of Hungarica, as well as a large selection of newspapers and magazines overseen by master bookseller Tony Láng. Helpful staff are at hand to advise and recommend.

Le Parfum Croisette — Perfume

(📞06 30 405 0668; www.leparfum.hu; V Deák Ferenc utca 18; ⊗10am-7pm Mon-Fri, to 5pm Sat & Sun; Ⓜ M1/2/3 Deák Ferenc tér, 🚋47, 48, 49) 🖊 Hungary's only *parfumier*, Zsolt Zólyomi, creates scents at his atelier-shop, as well as selling cutting-edge, animal-friendly perfumes from around the globe, such as Romano Ricci's Juliette Has a Gun range of cognac scents, whose recipes go back 750 years. Zólyomi, who foresees a renaissance in the once-great Hungarian perfume industry, holds perfume-making workshops here too.

Rózsavölgyi Csokoládé — Chocolate

(📞06 30 814 8929; www.rozsavolgyi.com; V Királyi Pál utca 6; ⊗10.30am-1pm & 1.30-6.30pm Mon-Fri, noon-6pm Sat; Ⓜ M3/4 Kálvin tér) A tiny, low-lit boutique selling delicious and artfully packaged, award-winning bean-to-bar chocolate. The range of handmade chocolates includes such interesting flavours as coffee and balsamic vinegar, and star anise with red peppercorn.

Bomo Art — Arts & Crafts
(1-318 7280; www.bomoart.hu; V Régi Posta utca 14; ⏱10am-6.30pm Mon-Fri, to 6pm Sat; Ⓜ M3 Ferenciek tere) This tiny shop just off Váci utca sells some of the finest paper and paper goods in Budapest, including leather-bound notebooks, photo albums and address books.

🍴 EATING

Budavári Rétesvár — Hungarian €
(Strudel Castle; ☎06 70 408 8696; www. budavariretesvar.hu; I Balta köz 4; strudel 310Ft; ⏱8am-7pm; 🚌16, 16A, 116) Strudel in all its permutations – from poppyseed with sour cherry to dill with cheese and cabbage – is available at this hole-in-the wall dispensary in a narrow alley of the Castle District.

Bors Gasztro Bár — Sandwiches €
(www.facebook.com/BorsGasztroBar; VII Kazinczy utca 10; soups 600Ft, baguettes 670-890Ft; ⏱11.30am-midnight; 🖌; Ⓜ M2 Astoria) We love this thimble-sized place, not just for its hearty, imaginative soups (how about sweet potato with coconut or tiramisu?) but also for its equally good grilled baguettes: try 'Bors Dog' (spicy sausage and cheese) or 'Brain Dead' (pig's brains are the main ingredient). It's not a sit-down kind of place; most chow down on the pavement outside.

Zeller Bistro — Hungarian €€
(☎06 30 651 0880, 1-321 7879; VII Izabella utca 38; mains 2900-5400Ft; ⏱noon-3pm & 6-11pm Tue-Sat; Ⓜ M1 Vörösmarty utca, 🚌4, 6) You'll receive a very warm welcome at this lovely candlelit cellar where the attentive staff serve food sourced largely from the owner's family and friends in the Lake Balaton area. The Hungarian home cooking includes some first-rate dishes such as grey beef, duck leg, oxtail and lamb's knuckle. Superb desserts, too. Popular with both locals and expats; reservations are essential.

Borkonyha — Hungarian €€
(Wine Kitchen; ☎1-266 0835; www.borkonyha. hu; V Sas utca 3; mains 3150-7950Ft; ⏱noon-4pm & 6pm-midnight Mon-Sat; 🚌15, 115, Ⓜ M1 Bajcsy-Zsilinszky út) Chef Ákos Sárközi's approach to Hungarian cuisine at this

Outdoor dining

Gerbeaud

Michelin-starred restaurant is contemporary, and the menu changes every week or two. Go for the signature foie gras appetiser wrapped in strudel pastry and a glass of sweet Tokaj wine. If *mangalica* (a special type of Hungarian pork) is on the menu, try it with a glass of dry *furmint*.

Kőleves   Jewish €€
(📞06 20 213 5999; www.kolevesvendeglo.hu; VII Kazinczy utca 37-41; mains 2120-4920Ft; 🕙8am-1am Mon-Fri, 9am-1am Sat & Sun; 🛜🍴; MM1/2/3 Deák Ferenc tér) Always buzzy and lots of fun, the 'Stone Soup' attracts a young crowd with its Jewish-inspired (but not kosher) menu, lively decor, great service and reasonable prices. Good vegetarian choices. Breakfast (890Ft to 1250Ft) is served from 8am to 11.30am. The daily lunch is just 1250Ft, or 1100Ft for the vegetarian version.

Gerbeaud   Cafe €€
(📞1-429 9001; www.gerbeaud.hu; V Vörösmarty tér 7-8; 🕙noon-10pm; MM1 Vörösmarty tér) Founded on the northern side of Pest's busiest square in 1858, Gerbeaud has been the most fashionable meeting place for the city's elite since 1870. Along with exquisitely prepared cakes and pastries, it serves continental/full breakfast and a smattering of nicely presented Hungarian dishes with international touches. A visit is mandatory.

Baraka   Fusion €€€
(📞1-200 0817; www.barakarestaurant.hu; V Dorottya utca 6; mains 7200-17,500Ft, 3-course lunches 6900Ft, 7-course tasting menus 27,000Ft; 🕙11am-3pm & 6-11.30pm Mon-Sat; 🛜; MM1 Vörösmarty tér) If you only eat in one fine-dining establishment while in Budapest, make it Baraka. You're ushered into the monochrome dining room, where chef Norbert Bíró works his magic in the half-open kitchen. Seafood features heavily, with French, Asian and Hungarian elements in the beautifully presented dishes. The bar, with its vast array of Japanese whiskies and pan-Asian tapas, is a treat.

Múzeum   Hungarian €€€
(📞1-267 0375; www.muzeumkavehaz.hu; VIII Múzeum körút 12; mains 3600-7200Ft; 🕙6pm-midnight Mon-Sat, noon-3pm Sun;

M M3/4 Kálvin tér) This cafe-restaurant is the place to come if you like to dine in old-world style with a piano softly tinkling in the background. It's still going strong after 130 years at the same location. The goose-liver parfait (3400Ft) is to die for, the goose leg and cabbage (3900Ft) iconic. There's also a good selection of Hungarian wines.

DRINKING & NIGHTLIFE

In recent years Budapest has justifiably gained a reputation as one of Europe's top nightlife destinations. Alongside its age-old cafe culture, it offers a magical blend of unique drinking holes, fantastic wine, home-grown firewaters and emerging craft beers, all served up with a warm Hungarian welcome and a wonderful sense of fun. The website www.wheretraveler.com/budapest is useful for nightlife listings.

Doblo   Wine Bar

(www.budapestwine.com; VII Dob utca 20; ⊙1pm-2am Sun-Wed, to 4am Thu-Sat; M M1/2/3 Deák Ferenc tér) Brick-lined and candlelit, Doblo is where you go to taste Hungarian wines with scores available by the 1.5cL (15mL) glass for 900Ft to 2150Ft. There's food too, such as meat and cheese platters.

Léhűtő   Bar

(☑06 30 731 0430; www.facebook.com/lehuto.kezmuvessorozo; VII Holló utca 12-14; ⊙4pm-midnight Mon, to 2am Tue-Thu, to 4am Fri & Sat; ⏃; M M1/2/3 Deák Ferenc tér) Drop into this very friendly basement bar if you fancy a craft beer, of which it has a large Hungarian and international range, with staff willing to advise and let you try before you buy. Coffee-based craft beer? Yep. There's also above-ground seating amid an often-buzzing crowd that gathers at this crossroads on warm nights.

DiVino Borbár   Wine Bar

(☑06 70 935 3980; www.divinoborbar.hu; V Szent István tér 3; ⊙4pm-midnight Sun-Wed, to 2am Thu-Sat; M M1 Bajcsy-Zsilinszky út) Central and always heaving, DiVino is Budapest's most popular wine bar, as the crowds

🍷 Ruin Pubs

Romkocsmák (ruin pubs) began to appear in the city from the early 2000s, when entrepreneurial free thinkers took over abandoned buildings and turned them into pop-up bars. At first a very word-of-mouth scene, the ruin bars' popularity grew exponentially and many have transformed from ramshackle, temporary sites full of flea-market furniture to more slick, year-round fixtures with covered areas to protect patrons from the winter elements. Budapest's first *romkocsmá*, **Szimpla Kert** (☑06 20 261 8669; www.szimpla.hu; VII Kazinczy utca 14; ⊙noon-4am Mon-Thu & Sat, 10am-1am Fri, 9am-5am Sun; M M2 Astoria) is firmly on the drinking-tourists' trail, but remains a landmark place for a beverage.

Szimpla Kert

spilling out onto the square in front of the Basilica of St Stephen in the warm weather attest. Choose from more than 140 wines produced by 36 winemakers under the age of 35, but be careful: those 0.15dL (15mL) glasses (650Ft to 3500Ft) go down quickly. The glass deposit is 500Ft.

Instant   Club

(☑06 30 830 8747, 1-311 0704; www.instant.co.hu; VII Akácfa utca 51; ⊙4pm-6am; M M1 Opera) We still love this 'ruin pub' on one of Pest's most vibrant nightlife strips and so do all our friends. It has 26 rooms, seven bars, seven stages and two gardens with underground DJs and dance parties. It's always heaving.

Where to Stay

In general, accommodation is more limited in the Buda neighbourhoods than on the other side of the Danube River in Pest. The districts of Erzsébetváros and Terézváros have the lion's share of Budapest's accommodation, though the area can be very noisy at night. Options on Castle Hill tend to be somewhat limited and in the upper price bracket. Belváros is close to just about everything, especially drinking and entertainment options, while Parliament is a great area to lay your hat as it's central but still just that little bit away from the noise. Accommodation in Óbuda and Buda Hills is thin on the ground.

Szatyor Bár és Galéria   Bar
(Carrier Bag Bar & Gallery; ☑1-279 0290; www.szatyorbar.com; XIII Bartók Béla út 36-38; ☺noon-1am; Ⓜ M4 Móricz Zsigmond körtér, ☐18, 19, 47, 49) Sharing the same building as the cafe **Hadik Kávéház** (☑1-279 0291; www.hadikkavehaz.com; XIII Bartók Béla út 36; ☺noon-1am) and separated by just a door, the Szatyor is the funkier of the twins, with cocktails, street art on the walls and a Lada driven by the poet Endre Ady. Cool or what? There's food here, too (mains 1900Ft to 2400Ft).

Double Shot   Coffee
(☑06 70 674 4893; www.facebook.com/doubleshotspecialtycoffee; XIII Pozsonyi út 16; ☺7am-8pm Mon-Thu, to 9pm Fri, 8am-9pm Sat, 8am-7pm Sun; ☐4, 6) With an unfinished, grungy look, and break-your-neck stairs to the small seating area upstairs, this thimble-sized coffee shop is the brainchild of two expats. The artisan coffee from around the globe is excellent.

Kávé Műhely   Coffee
(☑06 30 852 8517; www.facebook.com/kavemuhely; II Fő utca 49; ☺7.30am-6.30pm Mon-Fri, 9am-5pm Sat & Sun; Ⓜ M2 Batthyány tér, ☐19, 41) This tiny coffee shop is one of the best

in the city. These guys roast their own beans, and their cakes and sandwiches are fantastic. Too hot for coffee? They've got craft beers and homemade lemonades, too. The attached gallery stages vibrant contemporary art exhibitions.

ⓧ ENTERTAINMENT

Hungarian State Opera House   Opera
(Magyar Állami Operaház; ☑1-814 7100, box office 1-353 0170; www.opera.hu; VI Andrássy út 22; ☺box office 10am-8pm; Ⓜ M1 Opera) The gorgeous neo-Renaissance opera house is worth a visit as much to admire the incredibly rich decoration inside as to view a performance and hear the perfect acoustics.

Liszt Music Academy   Classical Music
(Liszt Zeneakadémia; ☑1-462 4600, box office 1-321 0690; www.zeneakademia.hu; VI Liszt Ferenc tér 8; ☺box office 10am-6pm; Ⓜ M1 Oktogon, ☐4, 6) Performances at Budapest's most important concert hall are usually booked up at least a week in advance, but more expensive (though still affordable) last-minute tickets can sometimes be available. It's always worth checking.

Palace of Arts   Concert Venue
(Művészetek Palotája; ☑1-555 3300; www.mupa.hu; IX Komor Marcell utca 1; ☺box office 10am-6pm; ☎; ☐2, 24, ℞HÉV 7 Közvágóhíd) The two concert halls at this palatial arts centre by the Danube are the 1700-seat **Béla Bartók National Concert Hall** (Bartók Béla Nemzeti Hangversenyterem) and the smaller **Festival Theatre** (Fesztivál Színház), accommodating up to 450 people. Both are purported to have near-perfect acoustics. Students can pay 500Ft one hour before all performances for a standing-only ticket.

ⓘ INFORMATION

Budapest Info (☑1-438 8080; www.budapestinfo.hu; V Sütő utca 2; ☺8am-8pm; Ⓜ M1/2/3

POSZTOS/SHUTTERSTOCK©

Hungarian State Opera House

Deák Ferenc tér) is the main tourist office; there is another **branch** (Olof Palme sétány 5, City Ice Rink; ☺9am-7pm; Ⓜ M1 Hősök tere) in City Park and info desks in the arrivals sections of Ferenc Liszt International Airport's Terminals 2A and 2B.

ⓘ GETTING THERE & AWAY

AIR

Budapest's **Ferenc Liszt International Airport** (BUD; ☏1-296 7000; www.bud.hu) has two modern terminals side by side 24km southeast of the city centre.

TRAIN

Keleti Train Station (Keleti pályaudvar; VIII Kerepesi út 2-6; Ⓜ M2/M4 Keleti pályaudvar) Most international trains (and domestic traffic to/from the north and northeast) arrive here. **MÁV** (Magyar Államvasutak, Hungarian State Railways; ☏1-349 4949; www.mavcsoport.hu) links up with the European rail network in all directions.

Nyugati Train Station (Western Train Station; VI Nyugati tér) Trains from some international destinations (eg Romania) and from the Danube Bend and Great Plain.

Déli Train Station (Déli pályaudvar; I Krisztina körút 37; Ⓜ M2 Déli pályaudvar) Trains from some destinations in the south, eg Osijek in Croatia and Sarajevo in Bosnia, as well as some trains from Vienna.

ⓘ GETTING AROUND

Travel passes valid for one day to one month are valid on all trams, buses, trolleybuses, HÉV suburban trains (within city limits) and metro lines.

Metro The quickest but least scenic way to get around. Runs from 4am to about 11.15pm.

Bus Extensive network of regular buses runs from around 4.15am to between 9pm and 11.30pm; from 11.30pm to just after 4am a network of 41 night buses (three digits beginning with '9') kicks in.

Tram Faster and more pleasant for sightseeing than buses; a network of 30 lines. Tram 6 runs overnight.

Trolleybus Mostly useful for getting to and around City Park in Pest.

In This Chapter

Schloss Schönbrunn 566
Kunsthistorisches
Museum Vienna 568
Sights 570
Activities 578
Shopping 578
Eating 580
Drinking & Nightlife 583
Entertainment 584
Information 585
Getting There & Away 585
Getting Around 585

Vienna, Austria

Few cities in the world waltz so effortlessly between the present and the past like Vienna. Its splendid historical face is easily recognised: grand imperial palaces and bombastic baroque interiors, revered opera houses and magnificent squares. But Vienna is also one of Europe's most dynamic urban spaces. A stone's throw from the Hofburg (Imperial Palace), the MuseumsQuartier houses provocative and high-profile contemporary art behind a striking basalt facade. In the Innere Stadt (Inner City), up-to-the-minute design stores sidle up to old-world confectioners, and Austro-Asian fusion restaurants stand alongside traditional Beisl (small taverns).

Two Days in Vienna

Start your day at Vienna's heart, the **Stephansdom** (p575), being awed by the cathedral's cavernous interior. Soak up the grandeur of the **Hofburg** (p570), a Habsburg architectural masterpiece, before ending the day with a craft beer at **Brickmakers Pub & Kitchen** (p583). Spend the morning of the second day in the **Kunsthistorisches Museum** (p569) and the afternoon in at least one of the museums in the **MuseumsQuartier** (p574).

Four Days in Vienna

Divide your morning between **Schloss Belvedere** (p576) and its magnificently landscaped French-style formal **gardens** (p577). Make your way to the **Prater** (p571), Vienna's playground of woods, meadows and sideshow attractions. Dedicate your final day to **Schloss Schönbrunn** (p567). If there's any time left check out **Karlskirche** (p576) or **Secession** (p576).

Looking for more castles? Take a train to Schloss Neuschwanstein (p520) or fly to Dubrovnik (p470).

Vienna Map (p572)

Arriving in Vienna

Vienna International Airport The frequent City Airport Train (CAT; €11, 15 minutes) runs from 6am to 11.30pm. There's also a cheaper but slower S7 suburban train (€4.40, 25 minutes) from the airport to Wien-Mitte. A taxi costs €25 to €50.

Wien Hauptbahnhof Situated 3km south of Stephansdom, Vienna's main train station handles all international trains. It's linked to the centre by U-Bahn line 1, trams D and O, and buses 13A and 69A. A taxi to the centre costs about €10.

Where to Stay

Vienna's lodgings cover it all, from inexpensive youth hostels to luxury establishments where chandeliers, antique furniture and original 19th-century oil paintings abound. In between are homey, often family-run *Pensionen* (guesthouses), many traditional, and less ostentatious hotels, plus a smart range of apartments. It's wise to book ahead at all times; for the best value, especially in the centre, at least a few weeks in advance is advisable.

Schloss Schönbrunn

The Habsburg Empire is revealed in all its frescoed, gilded, chandelier-lit glory in the wondrously ornate apartments of Schloss Schönbrunn, which are among Europe's best-preserved baroque interiors.

Great For...

☑ Don't Miss

The Great Gallery, Neptunbrunnen, Gloriette and Wagenburg.

State Apartments

The frescoed **Blue Staircase** makes a regal ascent to the palace's upper level. First up are the 19th-century apartments of Emperor Franz Josef I and his beloved wife Elisabeth. The tour whisks you through lavishly stuccoed, chandelier-lit apartments such as the **Billiard Room**, where army officials would pot a few balls while waiting to attend an audience, and Franz Josef's **study**, where the emperor worked tirelessly from 5am.

In the exquisite white-and-gold **Mirror Room**, a six-year-old Mozart performed for a rapturous Maria Theresia in 1762. Fairest of all, however, is the 40m-long **Great Gallery**, where the Habsburgs threw balls and banquets, a frothy vision of stucco and chandeliers, topped with a fresco by Italian artist Gregorio Guglielmi showing the glorification of Maria Theresia's reign. Decor

Schönbrunn Palace Main Courtyard with fountain

SCHLOSS SCHÖNBRUNN KULTUR- UND BETRIEBSGESMBH PHOTOGRAPHER ALEXANDER E. KOLLER ©

ℹ Need to Know

www.schoenbrunn.at; 13, Schönbrunner Schlossstrasse 47; adult/child Imperial Tour €13.30/9.80, Grand Tour €16.40/10.80, Grand Tour with guide €19.40/12.30; ⊙8.30am-6.30pm Jul & Aug, to 5.30pm Sep, Oct & Apr-Jun, to 5pm Nov-Mar; Ⓤ Hietzing

✕ Take a Break

Head to **Waldemar** (www.waldemar-tagesbar.at; 13, Altgasse 6; lunch mains €4.30-6.90; ⊙7.30am-8pm Mon-Fri, 9am-8pm Sat & Sun) for bolstering coffee and cake or a superhealthy lunch.

★ Top Tip

If you plan to see several sights at Schönbrunn, it's worth buying one of the combined tickets, which can be purchased in advance online.

aside, this was where the historic meeting between John F Kennedy and Soviet leader Nikita Khrushchev took place in 1961.

If you have a Grand Tour ticket, you can continue through to the palace's **east wing**. Franz Stephan's apartments begin in the sublime **Blue Chinese Salon**, where the intricate floral wall paintings are done on Chinese rice paper. The negotiations that led to the collapse of the Austro-Hungarian Empire in 1918 were held here.

Schloss Schönbrunn Gardens

The beautifully tended formal **gardens** (⊙6.30am-dusk) FREE of the palace, arranged in the French style, are appealing whatever the season: a symphony of colour in the summer and a wash of greys and browns in winter. The grounds, which were opened to the public by Joseph II in 1779,

hide a number of attractions in the tree-lined avenues (arranged according to a grid and star-shaped system between 1750 and 1755), including the 1781 **Neptunbrunnen** (Neptune Fountain; adult/child €3.60/2.80), a riotous ensemble from Greek mythology, and the crowning glory, the 1775 **Gloriette** (adult/child €3.60/2.80; ⊙9am-6pm, closed early Nov–mid-Mar).

Wagenburg

The **Wagenburg** (Imperial Coach Collection; www.kaiserliche-wagenburg.at; adult/child €8/free; ⊙9am-5pm mid-Mar–Nov, 10am-4pm Dec–mid-Mar) is *Pimp My Ride* imperial style. On display is a vast array of carriages, including Emperor Franz Stephan's coronation carriage, with its ornate gold plating, Venetian glass panes and painted cherubs. The whole thing weighs an astonishing 4000kg.

ANDREI RYBACHUK/GETTY IMAGES ©

Kunsthistorisches Museum Vienna

Occupying a neoclassical building as sumptuous as the art it contains, this museum takes you on a time-travel treasure hunt – from classical Rome to Egypt and the Renaissance.

Great For...

☑ Don't Miss

Dutch Golden Age paintings, the Kunstkammer and the Offering Chapel of Ka-ni-nisut.

Picture Gallery

The vast Picture Gallery is by far and away the most impressive of the museum's collections. First up is the German Renaissance, where the key focus is the prized Dürer collection, followed by the Flemish baroque, epitomised by Rubens, Van Dyck and Pieter Bruegel the Elder.

In the 16th- and 17th-century Dutch Golden Age paintings, the desire to faithfully represent reality is captured in works by Rembrandt, Ruisdael and Vermeer.

High on your artistic agenda in the 16th-century Venetian rooms should be Titian's *Nymph and Shepherd* (1570), Veronese's dramatic *Lucretia* (1583) and Tintoretto's *Susanna at her Bath* (1556).

Devotion is central to Raphael's *Madonna of the Meadow* (1506), one of the true masterpieces of the High Renaissance, just as it is to the *Madonna of the Rosary* (1601),

Museum interior

🛈 Need to Know

KHM, Museum of Art History; www.khm.at; 01, Maria-Theresien-Platz; adult/child incl Neue Burg museums €15/free; ⏱10am-6pm Fri-Wed, to 9pm Thu Jun-Aug, closed Mon Sep-May; Ⓤ Museumsquartier, Volkstheater

✕ Take a Break

Head to hip **Said the Butcher to the Cow** (www.butcher-cow.at; 01, Opernring 11; mains €10.80-31.90; ⏱kitchen 5-11pm Tue-Sat, bar 5pm-1am Tue & Wed, 5pm-2am Thu-Sat; 🚋D, 1, 2, 71 Kärntner Ring/Oper, Ⓤ Karlsplatz) for a post-museum burger.

★ Top Tip

If your time's limited, skip straight to the Old Master paintings in the Picture Gallery.

a stirring Counter-Reformation altarpiece by Italian baroque artist Caravaggio.

Of the artists represented in the final rooms dedicated to Spanish, French and English painting, the undoubted star is Spanish court painter Velázquez.

Kunstkammer

The Habsburgs filled their Kunstkammer (cabinet of art and curiosities) with an encyclopaedic collection of the rare and the precious: from narwhal-tusk cups to table holders encrusted with fossilised shark teeth. Its 20 themed rooms containing 2200 artworks open a fascinating window on the obsession with collecting curios in royal circles in Renaissance and baroque times.

Egyptian & Near Eastern Art

Decipher the mysteries of Egyptian civil-isations with a chronological romp through this miniature Giza of a collection. Here the **Offering Chapel of Ka-ni-nisut** spells out the life of the high-ranking 5th-dynasty official in reliefs and hieroglyphs.

In the Near Eastern collection, the representation of a prowling lion from Babylon's triumphal Ishtar Gate (604–562 BC) is the big attraction.

Greek & Roman Antiquities

This rich Greek and Roman repository reveals the imperial scope for collecting classical antiquities, with 2500 objects traversing three millennia from the Cypriot Bronze Age to early medieval times.

Among the Greek art is a fragment from the Parthenon's northern frieze, while the sizeable Roman stash includes the 4th-century AD *Theseus Mosaic* from Salzburg and the captivating 3rd-century AD *Lion Hunt* relief.

◉ SIGHTS
◉ The Hofburg & Around

Hofburg   Palace
(Imperial Palace; www.hofburg-wien.at; 01,
Michaelerkuppel; 🚌1A, 2A Michaelerplatz, 🚋D,
1, 2, 46, 49, 71 Burgring, Ⓤ Herrengasse) **FREE**
Nothing symbolises Austria's resplendent
cultural heritage more than its Hofburg,
home base of the Habsburgs from 1273 to
1918. The oldest section is the 13th-century
Schweizerhof (Swiss Courtyard), named
after the Swiss guards who used to protect
its precincts. The Renaissance **Swiss gate**
dates from 1553. The courtyard adjoins
a larger courtyard, **In der Burg**, with a
monument to Emperor Franz II adorning its
centre. The palace now houses the Austrian
president's offices and a raft of museums.

Kaiserappartements   Palace
(Imperial Apartments; 📞01-533 75 70; www.
hofburg-wien.at; 01, Michaelerplatz; adult/
child €12.90/7.70, incl guided tour €15.90/9.20;
⊙9am-6pm Jul & Aug, to 5.30pm Sep-Jun; Ⓤ Herrengasse) The Kaiserappartements, once
the official living quarters of Franz Josef I
and Empress Elisabeth, are dazzling in their
chandelier-lit opulence. The highlight is the
Sisi Museum, devoted to Austria's most
beloved empress, which has a strong focus
on the clothing and jewellery of Austria's
monarch. Multilingual audio guides are included in the admission price. Guided tours
take in the Kaiserappartements, the Sisi
Museum and the **Silberkammer** (Silver
Depot), whose largest silver service caters
to 140 dinner guests.

Kaiserliche
Schatzkammer   Museum
(Imperial Treasury; www.kaiserliche-schatz
kammer.at; 01, Schweizerhof; adult/child €12/free;
⊙9am-5.30pm Wed-Mon; Ⓤ Herrengasse) The
Kaiserliche Schatzkammer contains secular
and ecclesiastical treasures, including
devotional images and altars, particularly
from the baroque era, of priceless value and
splendour – the sheer wealth of this collection of crown jewels is staggering. As you
walk through the rooms you see magnificent
treasures such as a golden rose, diamond-
studded Turkish sabres, a 2680-carat

Sisi Museum, Imperial Apartments and Silver Collection, Hofburg

Colombian emerald and, the highlight of the treasury, the imperial crown.

Spanish Riding School
Performing Arts

(Spanische Hofreitschule; ☎01-533 90 31; www.srs.at; 01, Michaelerplatz 1; performances €25-217; ⊙hours vary; ☒1A, 2A Michaelerplatz, ⓤHerrengasse) The world-famous Spanish Riding School is a Viennese institution truly reminiscent of the imperial Habsburg era. This unequalled equestrian show is performed by Lipizzaner stallions formerly kept at an imperial stud established at Lipizza (hence the name). These graceful stallions perform an equine ballet to a program of classical music while the audience watches from pillared balconies – or from a cheaper standing-room area – and the chandeliers shimmer above.

Albertina
Gallery

(www.albertina.at; 01, Albertinaplatz 3; adult/child €12.90/free; ⊙10am-6pm Thu-Tue, to 9pm Wed; ☒D, 1, 2, 71 Kärntner Ring/Oper, ⓤKarlsplatz, Stephansplatz) Once used as the Habsburgs' imperial apartments for guests, the Albertina is now a repository for what's regularly touted as the greatest collection of graphic art in the world. The permanent Batliner Collection – with over 100 paintings covering the period from Monet to Picasso – and the high quality of changing exhibitions really make the Albertina worthwhile.

Multilingual audio guides (€4) cover all exhibition sections and tell the story behind the apartments and the works on display.

Neue Burg Museums
Museum

(☎01-525 240; www.khm.at; 01, Heldenplatz; adult/child €15/free; ⊙10am-6pm Wed-Sun; ☒D, 1, 2, 71 Burgring, ⓤHerrengasse, Museumsquartier) The Neue Burg is home to the three Neue Burg Museums. The **Sammlung Alter Musik Instrumente** (Collection of Ancient Musical Instruments) contains a wonderfully diverse array of instruments. The **Ephesos Museum** features artefacts unearthed during Austrian archaeologists' excavations at Ephesus in Turkey

Prater & the Riesenrad

Spread across 60 sq km, central Vienna's largest **park** (www.wiener-prater.at; ⓘ; ⓤPraterstern) comprises woodlands of poplar and chestnut, meadows, and tree-lined boulevards, as well as children's playgrounds, a swimming pool, a golf course and a race track. Fringed by statuesque chestnut trees that are ablaze with russet and gold in autumn and frilly with white blossom in spring, the central Hauptallee avenue is the main vein. It runs straight as an arrow from the Praterstern to the **Lusthaus** (☎01-728 95 65; 02, Freudenau 254, mains €11-19; ⊙noon-10pm Mon-Fri, to 6pm Sat & Sun, shorter hours winter; ☎; ☒77A), a former 16th-century Habsburg hunting lodge that today shelters a chandelier-lit cafe and restaurant serving classic Viennese fare.

Twirling above the **Würstelprater** amusement park is one of the city's most visible icons, the **Riesenrad** (www.wienerriesenrad.com; 02, Prater 90; adult/child €9.50/4; ⊙9am-11.45pm, shorter hours winter; ⓘ; ⓤPraterstern). It's top of every Prater wish-list; at least for anyone of an age to recall Orson Welles' cuckoo clock speech in British film noir The Third Man (1949), set in a shadowy postwar Vienna. Built in 1897 by Englishman Walter B Basset, the Ferris wheel rises to 65m and takes about 20 minutes to rotate its 430-tonne weight one complete circle – giving you ample time to snap some fantastic shots of the city spread out below.

Riesenrad Ferris wheel and the Prater

Vienna

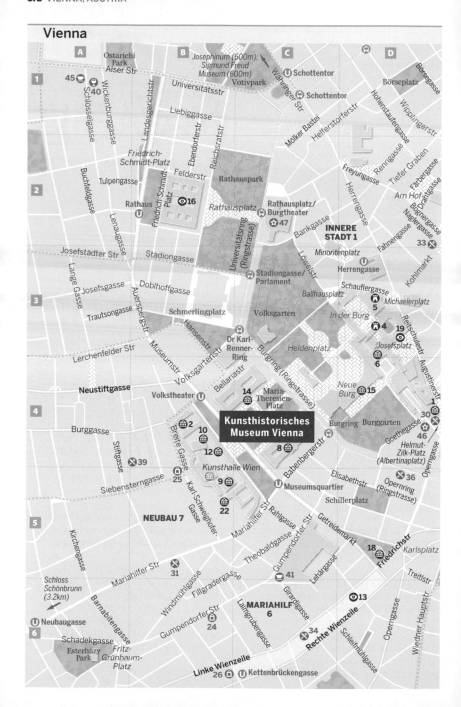

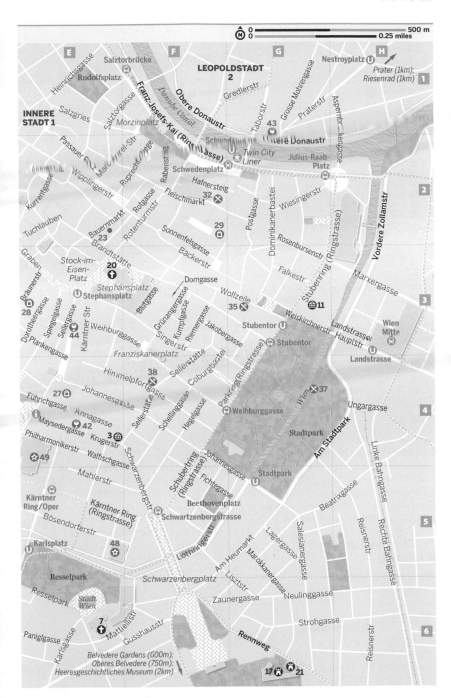

Vienna

◎ Sights
1 Albertina	D4
2 Architekturzentrum Wien	B4
3 Haus der Musik	E4
4 Hofburg	D3
5 Kaiserappartements	D3
6 Kaiserliche Schatzkammer	D3
7 Karlskirche	E6
8 Kunsthistorisches Museum Vienna	C4
9 Leopold Museum	B5
10 MUMOK	B4
11 Museum für Angewandte Kunst	G3
12 MuseumsQuartier	B4
13 Naschmarkt	D6
14 Naturhistorisches Museum	C4
15 Neue Burg Museums	D4
16 Rathaus	B2
17 Schloss Belvedere	G6
18 Secession	D5
Silberkammer	(see 5)
Sisi Museum	(see 5)
19 Spanish Riding School	D3
20 Stephansdom	E3
21 Unteres Belvedere	G6
22 Zoom	B5

❹ Activities, Courses & Tours
23 Wrenkh Cookery School	E2

ⓐ Shopping
24 Beer Lovers	B6
25 Die Werkbank	B5
26 Flohmarkt	B6
27 J&L Lobmeyr Vienna	E4
Meinl am Graben	(see 33)

28 Steiff	E3
29 Wiener Rosenmanufaktur	F2

⊗ Eating
30 Bitzinger Würstelstand am Albertinaplatz	D4
31 Eis Greissler	B5
32 Griechenbeisl	F2
33 Meinl's Restaurant	D2
34 Naschmarkt Deli	C6
35 Plachutta	G3
36 Said the Butcher to the Cow	D5
37 Steirereck im Stadtpark	G4
38 Tian	F4
39 Tian Bistro	B4
Wrenkh	(see 23)

❻ Drinking & Nightlife
40 Achtundzwanzig	A1
Café Leopold	(see 9)
41 Café Sperl	C5
42 Kruger's American Bar	E4
43 Le Loft	G1
44 Loos American Bar	E3
Meinl's Weinbar	(see 33)
45 POC Cafe	A1

❻ Entertainment
46 Bundestheaterkassen	D4
47 Burgtheater	C2
48 Musikverein	E5
Österreichisches Filmmuseum	(see 1)
49 Staatsoper	E4

between 1895 and 1906. The **Hofjägd und Rüstkammer** (Arms and Armour) museum contains ancient armour dating mainly from the 15th and 16th centuries. Admission includes the Kunsthistorisches Museum (p568) and all three Neue Burg museums. An audio guide costs €4.

◎ The Museum District & Neubau

MuseumsQuartier Museum
(Museum Quarter; MQ; www.mqw.at; 07, Museumsplatz; ⊗information & ticket centre 10am-7pm; ⓤMuseumsquartier, Volkstheater) The MuseumsQuartier is a remarkable ensemble of museums, cafes, restaurants and bars inside former imperial stables designed by Fischer von Erlach. This breeding ground of Viennese cultural life

is the perfect place to hang out and watch or meet people on warm evenings. With over 60,000 sq metres of exhibition space – including the Leopold Museum (p575), MUMOK (p575), **Kunsthalle** (Arts Hall; ☑01-521 890; www.kunsthallewien.at; both halls adult/child €12/free; ⊗11am-7pm Fri-Wed, to 9pm Thu), **Architekturzentrum** (Vienna Architecture Centre; ☑01-522 31 15; www.azw. at; exhibition prices vary, library admission free; ⊗architecture centre 10am-7pm, library 10am-5.30pm Mon, Wed & Fri, to 7pm Sat & Sun, closed Thu; ⓠ49 Volkstheater, ⓤVolkstheater, Museumsquartier) and **Zoom** (☑01-524 79 08; www.kindermuseum.at; exhibition adult/child €4/ free, activities child €4-6, accompanying adult free; ⊗12.45-5pm Tue-Sun Jul & Aug, 8.30am-4pm Tue-Fri, 9.45am-4pm Sat & Sun Sep-Jun, activity times vary) – the complex is one of the world's most ambitious cultural hubs.

Leopold Museum   Museum

(www.leopoldmuseum.org; 07, Museumsplatz 1; adult/child €13/8; 🕙10am-6pm Fri-Wed, to 9pm Thu Jun-Aug, 10am-6pm Wed & Fri-Mon, to 9pm Thu Sep-May; Ⓤ Volkstheater, Museumsquartier) Part of the MuseumsQuartier, the Leopold Museum is named after ophthalmologist Rudolf Leopold, who, after buying his first Egon Schiele for a song as a young student in 1950, amassed a huge private collection of mainly 19th-century and modernist Austrian artworks. In 1994 he sold the lot – 5266 paintings – to the Austrian government for €160 million (individually, the paintings would have made him €574 million), and the Leopold Museum was born. **Café Leopold** (www.cafe-leopold.at; 🕙10am-midnight Sun-Wed, to 4am Thu, to 6am Fri & Sat; 🛜) is located on the top floor.

MUMOK   Gallery

(Museum Moderner Kunst; Museum of Modern Art; www.mumok.at; 07, Museumsplatz 1; adult/child €11/free; 🕙2-7pm Mon, 10am-7pm Tue, Wed & Fri-Sun, 10am-9pm Thu; 🚌49 Volkstheater, Ⓤ Volkstheater, Museumsquartier) The dark basalt edifice and sharp corners of the Museum Moderner Kunst are a complete contrast to the MuseumsQuartier's historical sleeve. Inside, MUMOK contains Vienna's finest collection of 20th-century art, centred on fluxus, nouveau realism, pop art and photo-realism. The best of expressionism, cubism, minimal art and Viennese Actionism is represented in a collection of 9000 works that are rotated and exhibited by theme – but note that sometimes all this Actionism is packed away to make room for temporary exhibitions.

Naturhistorisches Museum   Museum

(Museum of Natural History; www.nhm-wien.ac.at; 01, Maria-Theresien-Platz; adult/child €10/free, rooftop tours €8; 🕙9am-6.30pm Thu-Mon, to 9pm Wed, rooftop tours in English 3pm Fri, Sat & Sun; Ⓤ Museumsquartier, Volkstheater) Vienna's astounding Naturhistorisches Museum covers four billion years of natural history in a blink. With its exquisitely stuccoed, frescoed halls and eye-catching cupola, this late 19th-century building is the identical twin of the Kunsthistorisches Museum which sits opposite. Among its minerals, fossils and dinosaur bones are one-of-a-kind finds like the minuscule 25,000-year-old Venus von Willendorf and a peerless 1100-piece meteorite collection. Panoramic rooftop tours take you onto the building's roof to view the ornate architecture up-close; children under 12 aren't allowed.

Rathaus   Landmark

(City Hall; www.wien.gv.at; 01, Rathausplatz 1; 🕙tours 1pm Mon, Wed & Fri Sep-Jun, 1pm Mon-Fri Jul & Aug; 🚋D, 1, 2 Rathaus, Ⓤ Rathaus) **FREE** The crowning glory of the Ringstrasse boulevard's 19th-century architectural ensemble, Vienna's neo-Gothic City Hall was completed in 1883 by Friedrich von Schmidt of Cologne Cathedral fame and modelled on Flemish city halls. From the fountain-filled **Rathauspark**, where Josef Lanner and Johann Strauss I, fathers of the Viennese waltz, are immortalised in bronze, you get the full effect of its facade of lacy stonework, pointed-arch windows and spindly turrets. One-hour guided tours are in German; multilingual audio guides are free.

⊙ Stephansdom & the Historic Centre

Stephansdom   Cathedral

(St Stephen's Cathedral; 📞tours 01-515 323 054; www.stephanskirche.at; 01, Stephansplatz; main nave adult & one child €6, additional child €1.50; 🕙public visits 9-11.30am & 1-4.30pm Mon-Sat, 1-4.30pm Sun; Ⓤ Stephansplatz) Vienna's Gothic masterpiece, Stephansdom – or Steffl (Little Stephan), as it's ironically nicknamed – is Vienna's pride and joy. A church has stood here since the 12th century, and reminders of this are the Romanesque **Riesentor** (Giant Gate) and **Heidentürme**. From the exterior, the first thing that will strike you is the glorious tiled **roof**, with its dazzling row of chevrons and Austrian eagles. Inside, the magnificent Gothic stone **pulpit** presides over the main nave, fashioned in 1515 by Anton Pilgrim.

Haus der Musik   Museum

(www.hausdermusik.com; 01, Seilerstätte 30; adult/child €13/6, with Mozarthaus Vienna €18/8; ⊙10am-10pm; ⎕D, 1, 2, 71 to Kärntner Ring/Oper, Ⓤ Karlsplatz) The Haus der Musik explains the world of sound and music to adults and children alike in an amusing and interactive way (in English and German). Exhibits are spread over four floors and cover everything from how sound is created, from Vienna's Philharmonic Orchestra to street noises. The staircase between floors acts as a piano, and the glassed-in ground-floor courtyard hosts musical events. Admission is discounted after 8pm.

⊚ Alsergrund & the University District

Sigmund Freud Museum   Museum, House

(www.freud-museum.at; 09, Berggasse 19; adult/child €10/4; ⊙10am-6pm; ⎕D, Ⓤ Schottentor, Schottenring) Sigmund Freud is a bit like the telephone – once he happened, there was no going back. This is where Freud spent his most prolific years and developed the most significant of his ground-breaking theories; he moved here with his family in 1891 and stayed until forced into exile by the Nazis in 1938.

Josephinum   Museum

(www.josephinum.meduniwien.ac.at; 09, Währinger Strasse 25; adult/child €8/free, guided tours €4; ⊙4-8pm Wed, 10am-6pm Fri-Sat, guided tours 11am Fri; ⛟; Ⓤ Währinger Strasse/Volksoper) Architecture fans sometimes visit this Enlightenment-era complex for its superb 1785 neo-classical structures alone, although Joseph II's purpose-built medical academy for army surgeons does, in fact, house the city's most unusual museum. The highlight is its large collection of 200-year-old anatomical and obstetric models made of wax: while designed as visual aids for teaching, they were also intended for public viewing and to this day are exhibited in their original display cases, made of rosewood and Venetian glass.

⊙ Karlsplatz & Around

Naschmarkt

Secession   Museum

(www.secession.at; 01, Friedrichstrasse 12; adult/child €9/5.50; ⊙10am-6pm Tue-Sun; Ⓤ Karlsplatz) In 1897, 19 progressive artists swam away from the mainstream Künstlerhaus artistic establishment to form the *Wiener Secession* (Vienna Secession). Among their number were Klimt, Josef Hoffman, Kolo Moser and Joseph M Olbrich. Olbrich designed the new exhibition centre of the Secessionists, which combined sparse functionality with stylistic motifs. Its biggest draw is Klimt's exquisitely gilded *Beethoven Frieze*. Guided tours in English (€3) lasting one hour take place at 11am Saturday. An audio guide costs €3.

Karlskirche   Church

(St Charles Church; www.karlskirche.at; 04, Karlsplatz; adult/child €8/free; ⊙9am-6pm Mon-Sat, noon-7pm Sun; Ⓤ Karlsplatz) Built between 1716 and 1739, after a vow by Karl VI at the end of the 1713 plague, Vienna's finest baroque church rises at the southeast corner of Resselpark. It was designed and commenced by Johann Bernhard Fischer von Erlach and completed by his son Joseph. The huge elliptical copper **dome** reaches 72m; the highlight is the lift (elevator) to the cupola (included in admission) for a close-up view of the intricate frescoes by Johann Michael Rottmayr. Audio guides cost €2.

⊙ Schloss Belvedere to the Canal

Schloss Belvedere   Palace

(www.belvedere.at; adult/child Oberes Belvedere €14/free, Unteres Belvedere €12/free, combined ticket €20/free; ⊙10am-6pm; ⎕D, 71 Schwarzenbergplatz, Ⓤ Taubstummengasse, Südtiroler Platz) A masterpiece of total art, Schloss Belvedere is one of the world's finest baroque palaces. Designed by Johann Lukas von Hildebrandt (1668–1745), it was built for the brilliant military strategist Prince Eugene of Savoy, conqueror of the Turks in 1718. What giddy romance is evoked in its

Karlskirche

sumptuously frescoed halls, replete with artworks by Klimt, Schiele and Kokoschka; what stories are conjured in its landscaped **gardens** (03, Rennweg/Prinz-Eugen-Strasse; ☺6.30am-8pm, shorter hours in winter; 🚊D), which drop like the fall of a theatre curtain to reveal Vienna's skyline.

The first of the palace's two buildings is the **Oberes Belvedere** (Upper Belvedere; 03, Prinz-Eugen-Strasse 27; adult/child €14/free; ☺10am-6pm), showcasing Gustav Klimt's *The Kiss* (1908), the perfect embodiment of Viennese art nouveau, alongside other late 19th- to early 20th-century Austrian works. The lavish **Unteres Belvedere** (Lower Belvedere; 03, Rennweg 6; adult/child €12/free; ☺10am-6pm Thu-Tue, to 9pm Wed; 🚊D), with its richly frescoed Marmorsaal (Marble Hall), sits at the end of sculpture-dotted gardens.

Heeresgeschichtliches Museum Museum

(Museum of Military History; www.hgm.or.at; 03, Arsenal; adult/under 19yr €6/free, 1st Sun of month free; ☺9am-5pm; Ⓤ Südtiroler Platz) The superb Heeresgeschichtliches Museum is housed in the Arsenal, a large neo-Byzantine barracks and munitions depot. Spread over two floors, the museum works its way from the Thirty Years' War (1618–48) to WWII, taking in the Hungarian Uprising and the Austro-Prussian War (ending in 1866), the Napoleonic and Turkish Wars, and WWI. Highlights on the 1st floor include the Great Seal of Mustafa Pasha, which fell to Prince Eugene of Savoy in the Battle of Zenta in 1697.

Museum für Angewandte Kunst Museum

(MAK, Museum of Applied Arts; www.mak.at; 01, Stubenring 5; adult/under 19yr €9.90/free, 6-10pm Tue free, tours €2; ☺10am-6pm Wed-Sun, to 10pm Tue, English tours noon Sun; 🚊2 Stubentor, Ⓤ Stubentor) MAK is devoted to craftsmanship and art forms in everyday life. Each exhibition room showcases a different style, which includes Renaissance, baroque, orientalism, historicism, empire, art deco and the distinctive metalwork of the Wiener Werkstätte. Contemporary artists were invited to present the rooms in ways they felt were appropriate, resulting in eye-catching and unique displays. The

J&L Lobmeyr Vienna

20th-century design and architecture room is one of the most fascinating, and Frank Gehry's cardboard chair is a gem.

🌀 ACTIVITIES

Wrenkh Cookery School   Cooking
(📞01-533 15 26; www.wrenkh-wien.at; 01, Bauermarkt 10; ⏱per person from €48; Ⓤ Stephansplatz) This cookery school based in its eponymous **restaurant** (mains €8-25; ⏱11am-11pm Mon-Sat; 🖊) has classes in English and German covering Austrian classics such as schnitzels, *Tafelspitz* (boiled beef), fresh-water fish, and apple strudel, along with international cuisines (Indian, Thai etc) and vegetarian and vegan cuisine. Look out for foraging expeditions, too. Courses start from €48 for 2½ hours to €130 for 6 hours. Check programs online.

Donauinsel   Island
(Danube Island; Ⓤ Donauinsel) The svelte Danube Island stretches some 21.5km from opposite Klosterneuburg in the north to the Nationalpark Donau-Auen in the south and splits the Danube in two, creating a sepa-rate arm known as the Neue Donau (New Danube). Created in 1970, it is Vienna's aquatic playground, with sections of beach (don't expect much sand) for swimming, boating and a little waterskiing.

🔒 SHOPPING

Beer Lovers   Drinks
(www.beerlovers.at; 06, Gumpendorfer Strasse 35; ⏱11am-8pm Mon-Fri, 10am-5pm Sat; Ⓤ Kettenbrückengasse) A wonderland of craft beers, this emporium stocks over 1000 labels from over 125 different breweries in over 70 styles, with more being sourced every day. Tastings are offered regularly, and cold beers are available in the walk-in glass fridge and in refillable growlers. It also stocks craft ciders, small-batch liqueurs and boutique nonalcoholic drinks such as ginger beers.

Meinl am Graben   Food & Drinks
(www.meinlamgraben.at; 01, Graben 19; ⏱8am-7.30pm Mon-Fri, 9am-6pm Sat; Ⓤ Stephansplatz) Vienna's most prestigious providore brims with quality European foodstuffs.

MONYSAS/GETTY IMAGES ©

Chocolate and confectionery dominate the ground floor, and impressive cheese and cold meats are tantalisingly displayed upstairs. The basement stocks European and Austrian wine and fruit liqueurs and has a classy on-site wine bar; there's also an exceptional on-site restaurant (p583).

Wiener Rosenmanufaktur Food, Cosmetics

(www.wienerrosenmanufaktur.at; 01, Schönlaterngasse 7; ⊙3-7pm Mon-Fri, 11am-5pm Sat Jul & Aug, 1-6.30pm Mon-Fri, 11am-6.30pm Sat, 2-5pm Sun Sep-Jun; Ⓤ Schwedenplatz) Roses grown by Ingrid Maria Heldstab in her garden in Vienna's 23rd district are used in an incredible array of products, from jams (including spicy versions with ginger), jellies and liqueurs – which you can taste in store – to soaps, aromatic oils and other cosmetics. The tiny shop occupies one of Vienna's oldest buildings, the Basiliskenhaus, which dates from 1212.

J&L Lobmeyr Vienna   Homewares

(www.lobmeyr.at; 01, Kärntner Strasse 26; ⊙10am-7pm Mon-Fri, to 6pm Sat; Ⓤ Stephansplatz) Reached by a beautifully ornate wrought iron staircase, this is one of Vienna's most lavish retail experiences. The collection of Biedermeier pieces, Loos-designed sets, fine/arty glassware and porcelain on display here glitters from the lights of the chandelier-festooned atrium. Lobmeyr has been in business since 1823, when it exclusively supplied the imperial court.

Steiff   Toys

(www.steiff-galerie-wien.at; 01, Bräunerstrasse 3; ⊙10am-12.30pm & 1.30-6pm Mon-Fri, 10am-12.30pm & 1.30-5pm Sat; Ⓤ Stephansplatz) Founded in Germany in the late 19th century, Steiff is widely regarded as the original creator of the teddy bear, which it presented at the Leipzig Toy Fair in 1903: an American businessman bought 3000 and sold them under the name 'teddy bear' after US president Theodore ('Teddy') Roosevelt. Today its flagship Austrian shop is

 ## Naschmarkt & Flohmarkt

Vienna's famous **market** (www.wiener naschmarkt.eu; 06, Linke & Rechte Wienzeile; ⊙6am-7.30pm Mon-Fri, to 6pm Sat; Ⓤ Kettenbrückengasse) and **eating strip** (www.naschmarkt-deli.at; 04, Naschmarkt stand 421-436; dishes €6.50-16.50; ⊙7am-midnight Mon-Sat; Ⓤ Kettenbrückengasse) began life as a farmers market in the 18th century, when the fruit market on Freyung was moved here.

The fruits of the Orient poured in, the predecessors of the modern-day sausage stand were erected, and sections were set aside for coal, wood and furniture finds and machines. Officially, it became known as Naschmarkt ('munch market') in 1905, a few years after Otto Wagner bedded the Wien River down in its open-topped stone and concrete sarcophagus. This Otto Wagnerian horror was a blessing for Naschmarkt, because it created space to expand. Today the Naschmarkt is not only the place to shop for food, but also has the weekly Flohmarkt antique market.

One of the best flea markets in Europe, and a Vienna institution, **Flohmarkt** (Flea Market; 05, Linke Wienzeile; ⊙6.30am-6pm Sat; Ⓤ Kettenbrückengasse) brims with antiques and *Altwaren* (old wares). Stalls hawking books, clothes, records, ancient electrical goods, old postcards, ornaments and carpets stretch for several blocks. Arrive early, as it gets increasingly crammed as the morning wears on, and be prepared to haggle.

Naschmarkt

 Viennese Specialities

Vienna has a strong repertoire of traditional dishes. One or two are variations on dishes from other regions. Classics include the following:

Schnitzel *Wiener Schnitzel* should always be crumbed veal, but pork is gaining ground in some places.

Goulash *Rindsgulasch* (beef goulash) is everywhere in Vienna. Originating in Hungary, the Austrian version is often served with *Semmelknoedel* (bread dumplings).

Tafelspitz Traditionally this boiled prime beef swims in the juices of locally produced *Suppengrün* (fresh soup vegetables), before being served with *Kren* (horseradish) sauce.

Beuschel Offal, usually sliced lung and heart, with a slightly creamy sauce.

Backhendl Fried, breaded chicken, often called *steirischer Backhendl* (Styrian fried chicken).

Zwiebelrostbraten Slices of roast beef smothered in gravy and fried onions.

Schinkenfleckerln Oven-baked ham and noodle casserole.

Bauernschmaus Platter of cold meats.

The undeniable monarchs of all desserts are *Kaiserschmarrn* (sweet pancake with raisins) and *Apfelstrudel* (apple strudel), but also look out for *Marillenknödel* (apricot dumplings) in summer.

Wiener Schnitzel
CARLY HULLS/LONELY PLANET ©

filled with adorable bears, along with other premium quality cuddly toys.

Die Werkbank Design
(www.werkbank.cc; 07, Breite Gasse 1; ⊘noon-6.30pm Tue-Fri, 11am-5pm Sat; ⓤVolkstheater) Furniture, lamps, rugs, vases, jewellery, watches, graphic art, bags, even bicycles are among the creations you might find on display at 'The Workbench', an all-white space that operates as a design collective, where some of Vienna's most innovative designers showcase their works.

Dirndlherz Clothing
(www.dirndlherz.at; 07, Lerchenfelder Strasse 50; ⊘11am-6pm Thu & Fri, to 4pm Sat; ⓤVolkstheater) Putting her own spin on alpine fashion, Austrian designer Gabriela Urabl creates one-of-a-kind, high-fashion *Dirndls* (women's traditional dress), from sassy purple-velvet bosom-lifters to 1950s-style gingham numbers and *Dirndls* emblazoned with quirky motifs like pop-art and punk-like conical metal studs. T-shirts with taglines like *'Mei Dirndl is in da Wäsch'* ('My *Dirndl* is in the wash') are also available.

⊗ EATING

Mamamon Thai €
(☏01-942 31 55; www.mamamonthaikitchen.com; 08, Albertgasse 15; mains €7-9.50; ⊘11.30am-9.30pm Mon-Fri, noon-9.30pm Sat; ⓤJosefstädter Strasse, Rathaus) Owner Piano, who named her restaurant for her mum Mon, has spiced up Vienna's burgeoning Southeast Asian food scene with a menu of southern Thai flavours, street-style decor and an indie soundtrack. On mild nights, a young, happy crowd spills out into the courtyard, while single diners pull up a stool at the large communal table or window seats within.

Bitzinger Würstelstand am Albertinaplatz Street Food €
(www.bitzinger-wien.at; 01, Albertinaplatz; sausages €3.40-4.40; ⊘8am-4am; ☒Kärntner Ring/Oper, ⓤKarlsplatz, Stephansplatz) Behind

the Staatsoper, Vienna's best sausage stand has cult status. Bitzinger offers the contrasting spectacle of ladies and gents dressed to the nines, sipping beer, wine (from €2.30) or Joseph Perrier Champagne (€19.90 for 0.2L) while tucking into sausages at outdoor tables or the heated counter after performances. Mustard (€0.40) comes in *süss* (sweet; io mild) or *scharf* (fiercely hot).

Eis Greissler   Ice Cream €

(www.eis-greissler.at; 06, Mariahilfer Strasse 33; 1/2/3/4/5 scoops €1.50/2.80/3.80/4.80/5.30; ⊙11am-10pm; Ⓤ Museumsquartier) ✔ The inevitable queue makes Eis Greissler easy to spot. Locals flock here whatever the weather for ice cream made from organic milk, yoghurt and cream from its own farm in Lower Austria, and vegans are well catered for with soy and oat milk varieties. All-natural flavours vary seasonally but might include cinnamon, pear, strawberry, raspberry, chocolate, hazelnut or butter caramel.

Lingenhel   Modern European €€

(⌖ 01-710 15 66; www.lingenhel.com; 03, Landstrasser Hauptstrasse 74; mains €19-24; ⊙ shop 8am-8pm, restaurant 8am-10pm Mon-Sat; Ⓤ Rochusgasse) One of Vienna's most exciting gastro newcomers, Lingenhel is an ultra-slick deli-shop-bar-restaurant, lodged in a 200-year-old house. Salamis, wines and own-dairy cheeses tempt in the shop, while much-lauded chef Daniel Hoffmeister helms the kitchen in the pared-back, whitewashed restaurant. The season-inflected food – simple as char with kohlrabi and pork belly with aubergines – tastes profoundly of what it ought to.

Punks   Modern European €€

(⌖ 0664 275 70 72; www.punks.wien; 08, Florianigasse 50; small plates €4.50) The name might be a giveaway, but this guerilla-style restaurant *is* indeed shaking up an otherwise genteel neighbourhood. Patrick Müller, Anna Schwab and René Steindachner have 'occupied' a former wine bar and eschewed the usual refit or any form of interior decoration; the focus is, quite literally, on

Griechenbeisl (p582)

the kitchen, with a menu of inventive small dishes prepared behind the bar.

Griechenbeisl
Bistro €€

(☏01-533 19 77; www.griechenbeisl.at; 01, Fleischmarkt 11; mains €15-28; ☺11.30am-11.30pm; ✦; 🚋1, 2, Ⓤ Schwedenplatz) Dating from 1447 and frequented by Beethoven, Brahms, Schubert and Strauss among other luminaries, Vienna's oldest restaurant has vaulted rooms, wood panelling and a figure of Augustin trapped at the bottom of a well inside the front door. Every classic Viennese dish is on the menu, along with three daily vegetarian options. In summer, head to the plant-fringed front garden.

Tian Bistro
Vegetarian €€

(☏01-890 466 532; www.tian-bistro.com; 07, Schrankgasse 4; mains €10-18; ☺11.30am-10pm Mon-Fri, 9am-10pm Sat & Sun; ✦; 🚋49 Siebensterngasse/Stiftgasse, Ⓤ Volkstheater) Colourful tables set up on the cobbled laneway outside Tian Bistro in summer, while indoors, a glass roof floods the atrium-style, greenery-filled dining room in light. It's the cheaper, more relaxed offspring of Michelin-starred vegetarian restaurant **Tian** (☏01-890 46 65-2; www. taste-tian.com; 01, Himmelpfortgasse 23; 2-/3-course lunch menus €29/34, 4-/6-course dinner menus €93/108; ☺noon-2pm & 5.45-9pm Tue-Sat; ✦; 🚋2, Ⓤ Stephansplatz) ✦, and serves sublime vegetarian and vegan dishes such as black truffle risotto with Piedmont hazelnuts, as well as breakfast until 2pm on weekends.

Steirereck
im Stadtpark
Gastronomy €€€

(☏01-713 31 68; www.steirereck.at; 03, Am Heumarkt 2a; mains €48-52, 6-/7-course menus €142/152; ☺11.30am-2.30pm & 6.30pm-midnight Mon-Fri; Ⓤ Stadtpark) Heinz Reitbauer is at the culinary helm of this two-starred Michelin restaurant, beautifully lodged in a 20th-century former dairy building in the leafy Stadtpark. His tasting menus are an exuberant feast, fizzing with natural, integral flavours that speak of a chef with exacting standards. Wine pairing is an additional €79/89 (six/seven courses).

Café Sperl

Meinl's
Restaurant International €€€

(☏01-532 33 34 6000; www.meinlamgraben. at; 01, Graben 19; mains €16-39, 4-/5-course menus €67/85; ☺noon-midnight Mon-Sat; 🛜🍴; Ⓤ Stephansplatz) Meinl's combines cuisine of superlative quality with an unrivalled wine list and views of Graben. Creations at its high ꞏnꞏꞏ ꞏꞏꞏꞏ ꞏꞏꞏ ꞏꞏꞏ ꞏꞏꞏꞏ calamari and white-truffle risotto, and apple-schnapps-marinated pork fillet with green beans and chanterelles. Its on-site providore (p578) has a cafe and sushi bar, and its cellar **wine bar** (☺11am-midnight Mon-Sat) serves great-value lunch menus.

Plachutta Austrian €€€

(☏01-512 15 77; www.plachutta.at; 01, Wollzeile 38; mains €16.50-27.20; ☺11.30am-11.15pm; Ⓤ Stubentor) If you're keen to taste *Tafelspitz,* you can't beat this specialist wood-panelled, white-tableclothed restaurant. It serves no fewer than 13 varieties from different cuts of Austrian-reared beef, such as *Mageres Meisel* (lean, juicy shoulder meat), *Beinfleisch* (larded rib meat) and *Lueger Topf* (shoulder meat with beef tongue and calf's head). Save room for the Austrian cheese plate.

🍷 DRINKING & NIGHTLIFE

Le Loft Bar

(02, Praterstrasse 1; ☺10am-2am; 🚋2 Gredlerstrasse, Ⓤ Schwedenplatz) Wow, what a view! Take the lift to Le Loft on the Sofitel's 18th floor to reduce Vienna to toy-town scale in an instant. From this slinky, glass-walled lounge, you can pick out landmarks such as the Stephansdom and the Hofburg over a pomegranate martini or mojito. By night, the backlit ceiling swirls with an impressionist painter's palette of colours.

Brickmakers
Pub & Kitchen Craft Beer

(☏01-997 44 14; www.brickmakers.at; 07, Zieglergasse 42; ☺4pm-2am Mon-Fri, 10am-2am Sat, 10am-1am Sun; Ⓤ Zieglergasse) British racing-green metro tiles, a mosaic floor and

a soundtrack of disco, hip-hop, funk and soul set the scene for brilliant craft beers and ciders: there are 30 on tap at any one time and over 150 by the bottle. Pop-ups take over the kitchen, and at lunch and dinner guest chefs cook anything from gourmet fish and chips to BBQ-smoked beef brisket.

Loos American Bar Cocktail Bar

(www.loosbar.at; 01, Kärntner Durchgang 10; ☺noon-5am Thu-Sat, to 4am Sun-Wed; Ⓤ Stephansplatz) Loos is *the* spot in the Innere Stadt for a classic cocktail such as its signature dry martini, expertly whipped up by talented mixologists. Designed by Adolf Loos in 1908, this tiny 27-sq-metre box (seating just 20-or-so patrons) is bedecked from head to toe in onyx and polished brass, with mirrored walls that make it appear far larger.

POC Cafe Coffee

(www.poccafe.com; 08, Schlösselgasse 21; ☺8am-5pm Mon-Fri; 🚋5, 43, 44 to Lange Gasse, Ⓤ Schottentor) Friendly Robert Gruber is one of Vienna's coffee legends and his infectious passion ripples through this beautifully rambling, lab-like space. POC stands for 'People on Caffeine'; while filter, espresso-style or a summertime iced coldbrew are definitely this place's raison d'être, it's also known for moreish sweets like killer poppy-seed cake, cheesecake or seasonal fruit tarts.

Café Sperl Coffee

(www.cafesperl.at; 06, Gumpendorfer Strasse 11; ☺7am-11pm Mon-Sat, 11am-8pm Sun; 🛜; Ⓤ Museumsquartier, Kettenbrückengasse) With its gorgeous *Jugendstil* (art nouveau) fittings, grand dimensions, cosy booths and unhurried air, 1880-opened Sperl is one of the finest coffee houses in Vienna. The must-try is *Sperl Torte,* an almond-and-chocolate-cream dream. Grab a slice and a newspaper (over 10 daily in English, French and German), order a coffee (from 34 types), and join the rest of the people-watching patrons.

Opera & Classical Music

The glorious **Staatsoper** (☑01-514 44 7880; www.wiener-staatsoper.at; 01, Opernring 2; tickets €10-208, standing room €3-4; 🚋D, 1, 2, 71 to Kärntner Ring/Oper, Ⓤ Karlsplatz) is Vienna's premiere opera and classical-music venue. Productions are lavish, formal affairs, where people dress up accordingly. In the interval, wander the foyer and refreshment rooms to fully appreciate the gold and crystal interior. Opera is not performed here in July and August (tours still take place). Tickets can be purchased from the **state ticket office** (☑01-514 44 7810; www.bundestheater.at; 01, Operngasse 2; ☺8am-6pm Mon-Fri, 9am-noon Sat & Sun; Ⓤ Stephansplatz) up to two months in advance.

Tickets to the annual **Opernball** (www.wiener-staatsoper.at; ☺Jan/Feb) range from €490 to an eye-watering €21,000 and sell out years in advance.

Staatsoper
IZIM M. GULCUK/SHUTTERSTOCK ©

Kruger's American Bar   Bar
(www.krugers.at; 01, Krugerstrasse 5; ☺6pm-4am Mon-Sat, 7pm-4am Sun; 🚋D, 1, 2, 71 to Kärntner Ring/Oper, Ⓤ Stephansplatz) Retaining some of its original decor from the 1920s and '30s, this dimly lit, wood-panelled American-style bar is a legend in Vienna, furnished with leather Chesterfield sofas and playing a soundtrack of Frank Sinatra, Dean Martin and the like. The drinks list runs to 71 pages; there's a separate cigar and smoker's lounge.

Achtundzwanzig   Wine Bar
(www.achtundzwanzig.at; 08, Schlösslegasse 28; ☺4pm-1am Mon-Thu, to 2am Fri, 7pm-2am Sat; 🚋5, 43, 44, Ⓤ Schottentor) Austrian wine fans with a rock-and-roll sensibility will feel like they've found heaven at this black-daubed *vinothek* (wine bar) that vibes casual but takes its wines super seriously. Wines by the glass are all sourced from small producers – many of them are organic or minimal-intervention and friends of the owners – and are well priced at under €4 a glass.

🟢 ENTERTAINMENT

Burgtheater   Theatre
(National Theatre; ☑01-514 44 4440; www.burgtheater.at; 01, Universitätsring 2; seats €7.50-61, standing room €3.50, students €9; ☺box office 9am-5pm Mon-Fri; 🚋D, 1, 2 to Rathaus, Ⓤ Rathaus) The Burgtheater hasn't lost its touch over the years – this is one of the foremost theatres in the German-speaking world, staging some 800 performances a year, which reach from Shakespeare to Woody Allen plays. The theatre also runs the 500-seater Akademietheater, which was built between 1911 and 1913.

Musikverein   Concert Venue
(☑01-505 81 90; www.musikverein.at; 01, Musikvereinsplatz 1; tickets €24-95, standing room €4-6; ☺box office 9am-8pm Mon-Fri, to 1pm Sat Sep-Jun, 9am-noon Mon-Fri Jul & Aug; Ⓤ Karlsplatz) The opulent Musikverein holds the proud title of the best acoustics of any concert hall in Austria, which the Vienna Philharmonic Orchestra embraces. The lavish interior can be visited by 45-minute guided tour (in English and German; adult/child €6.50/4) at 10am, 11am and noon Monday to Saturday. Smaller-scale performances are held in the Brahms Saal. There are no student tickets.

MuTh   Concert Venue
(☑01-347 80 80; www.muth.at; 02, Obere Augartenstrasse 1e; Vienna Boys' Choir Fri performance €39-89; ☺4-6pm Mon-Fri & 1 hour before performances; Ⓤ Taborstrasse) Opened to much

acclaim in December 2012, this striking baroque meets contemporary concert hall is the new home of the Wiener Sängerknaben (Vienna Boys' Choir), who previously only performed at the Hofburg. Besides Friday afternoon choral sessions with the angelic-voiced lads, the venue also stages a top-drawer roster of dance, drama, opera, classical, rock and jazz performances.

INFORMATION

Tourist Info Wien (☎01-245 55; www.wien.info; 01, Albertinaplatz; ⊙9am-7pm; ☎; ☒D, 1, 2, 71 to Kärntner Ring/Oper, ⓊStephansplatz) Vienna's main tourist office, with a ticket agency, hotel booking service, free maps and every brochure under the sun.

GETTING THERE & AWAY

Vienna sits at the crossroads of Western and Eastern Europe, and has excellent air, road and rail connections to both regions, as well as services further afield.

AIR

Located 15km southwest of the city centre, **Vienna International Airport** (VIE; ☎01-700 722 233; www.viennaairport.com; ☎) operates services worldwide. Facilities include restaurants and bars, banks and ATMs, money-exchange counters, supermarkets, a post office, car-hire agencies and two left-luggage counters open 5.30am to 11pm (€4 to €8 per 24 hours; maximum six-month storage). Bike boxes (€35) and baggage wrapping (€12 per item) are available.

BOAT

The Danube is a traffic-free access route for arrivals and departures from Vienna. Eastern Europe is the main destination; **Twin City Liner** (☎01-904 88 80; www.twincityliner.com; 01, Schwedenplatz; one-way adult €20-35; ☒1, 2, ⓊSchwedenplatz) connects Vienna with Bratislava in 1½ hours, while its sister company **DDSG Blue Danube Schiffahrt** (☎01-588 80; www.ddsg-blue-danube.at; 02, Handelskai 265, Reichsbrücke; one-way €99-109, return €125; ⊙9am-5pm Mon-Fri, 10am-4pm Sat & Sun, closed Sat & Sun Nov-Feb) links Budapest with Vienna from mid-May to September, departing Vienna Wednesday, Friday and Sunday, departing Budapest Tuesday, Thursday and Saturday. DDSG tickets may also be obtained or picked up at Twin City Liner.

CAR & MOTORCYCLE

Bordering eight countries, Austria is easily reached by road. If you're bringing your own vehicle, you'll need a Motorway Vingette (toll sticker). For 10 days/two months it costs €8.80/25.70 per car; €5.50/12.90 per motorcycle. Buy it at petrol stations in neighbouring countries before entering Austria. More information is available at www.austria.info.

TRAIN

Vienna's main train station, the Wien Hauptbahnhof, 3km south of Stephansdom, handles all international trains as well as trains from all of Austria's provincial capitals, and many local and regional trains.

GETTING AROUND

Tickets and passes for **Wiener Linien** (☎01-7909-100; www.wienerlinien.at) services can be purchased at U-Bahn stations, on trams and buses, or in a *Tabakladen* (*Trafik*; tobacco kiosk), as well as from a few staffed ticket offices. Tickets should be validated prior to boarding (U-Bahn) or on boarding (tram and bus).

U-Bahn Fast, comfortable and safe. Trains run from 5am to midnight Monday to Thursday and continuously from 5am Friday through to midnight Sunday.

Tram Slower but more enjoyable. Depending on route, trams run from around 5.15am to about 11.45pm. Tickets bought from the driver are more expensive.

Bus Reliable and punctual, with several very useful routes for visitors. Most run from 5am to midnight; services can be sporadic or nonexistent on weekends.

Night Bus Especially useful for outer areas; runs every 30 minutes from 12.30am to 5am. Main stops are located at Schwedenplatz, Schottentor and Kärntner Ring/Oper.

In This Chapter

Matterhorn 588
Glacier Express 590
Zermatt 592

Swiss Alps, Switzerland

You can sense the anticipation on the train from Täsch: couples gaze wistfully out of the window, kids fidget, folk rummage for their cameras. And then, as they arrive in Zermatt, all give little whoops of joy at the pop-up-book effect of the Matterhorn, the hypnotically beautiful, one-of-a-kind peak that rises like a shark's fin above town.

Since the mid-19th century, Zermatt has starred among Switzerland's glitziest resorts. Today skiers cruise along well-kept pistes, spellbound by the scenery, while style-conscious darlings flash designer threads in the town's swish lounge bars. But all are smitten with the Matterhorn, an unfathomable monolith you can't quite stop looking at.

Two Days in the Swiss Alps

Get up high with Europe's highest-altitude **cable car** (p589) or **cogwheel railway** (p589) and walk or ski down – never taking your eyes off the pyramid-perfect, bewitching Matterhorn. Dedicate day two to exploring **Zermatt** (p592) and gorging yourself on delicious **raclette** or **fondue** (p596).

Four Days in the Swiss Alps

Spend the morning hiking the Matterhorn **Glacier Trail** (p594) for more stunning views before taking to the **slopes** (p593) for the rest of the day. On the fourth day, hop aboard the **Glacier Express** (p591) in Zermatt, sit back and enjoy a spectacular train journey to St Moritz.

At the end of your trip, take a train to Florence (p418) or Provence (p252).

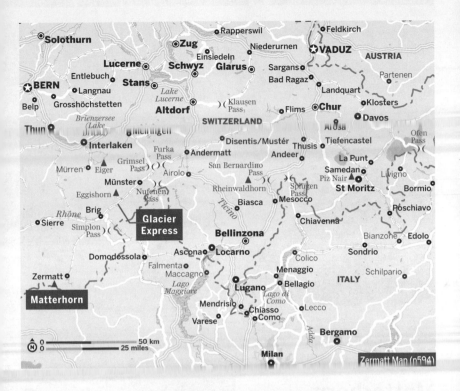

Arriving in the Swiss Alps

Train Direct trains to Zermatt depart hourly from Brig (Sfr38, 1½ hours), stopping at Visp en route. Zermatt is also the start/end point of the **Glacier Express** (p591) to/from St Moritz.

Car Zermatt is car-free. Motorists have to park in the Matterhorn Terminal Täsch (www.matterhornterminal.ch; Sfr15.50 per 24 hours) in Täsch and ride the Zermatt Shuttle train (return adult/child Sfr16.80/8.40, 12 minutes) the last 5km up to Zermatt.

Where to Stay

Book well ahead in winter, and bear in mind that nearly everywhere closes from May to mid- or late June and mid-October to November or early December. With advance warning, many places will pick you and your bags up at the station in an electro-shuttle. Check when you book.

Sleeping choices in Zermatt run from hostel beds to ultra-chic designer digs, with plenty of chalet-style midrange options in between.

JAKL LUBOS/SHUTTERSTOCK ©

Matterhorn

No mountain has so much pulling power and natural magnetism or – is so easy to become obsessed with – as this charismatic peak.

Great For...

☑ Don't Miss

Visiting the Matterhorn Museum (p592) to learn about the first successful ascent of the peak.

Beautiful Matterhorn demands to be admired, ogled and repeatedly photographed at sunrise and sunset, in different seasons, and from every last infuriating angle.

Climbing Matterhorn

Some 3000 alpinists summit Europe's most photographed, 4478m-high peak each year. You don't need to be superhuman to do it, but you do need to be a skilled climber (with crampons), be in tiptop physical shape (12-hours-endurance performance) and have a week in hand to acclimatise beforehand to make the iconic ascent up sheer rock and ice.

No one attempts the Matterhorn without local know-how: mountain guides at the Snow & Alpine Center (p593) charge Sfr1790 per person for the eight-hour return climb, including cable car from

Matterhorn Glacier Paradise cable car

ⓘ Need to Know

Mid-July to mid-September is the best time of year to attempt the ascent.

✕ Take a Break

There are restaurants at Riffelalp (2211m) and Riffelberg (2582m) along the Gornergratbahn path.

★ Top Tip

For outstanding views of the Matterhorn, jump aboard the *Sunnegga Express* funicular (p592) to the top of Sunnegga.

and an ice slide to swoosh down bum first. End with some exhilarating **snow tubing** outside in the snowy surrounds.

Gornergratbahn

Europe's highest **cogwheel railway** (www.gornergrat.ch; Bahnhofplatz 7; adult/child return trip Sfr94/47; ⊘7am-7.15pm) has climbed through picture-postcard scenery to **Gornergrat** (3089m) – a 30-minute journey – since 1898. On the way up, sit on the right-hand side of the little red train to goggle at the Matterhorn. Tickets allow you to get on and off en route at stops including Riffelalp (2211m) and Riffelberg (2582m). In summer an extra train runs once a week at sunrise and sunset – the most spectacular trips of all.

Zermatt to Schwarzee and half-board accommodation in a mountain hut. Client:guide ratios are 1:1. You'll probably be required to do training climbs first, just to prove you really are 100% up to it. The Matterhorn claims more than a few lives each year.

Matterhorn Glacier Paradise

Views from Zermatt's cable cars are all remarkable, but the **Matterhorn Glacier Paradise** (www.matterhornparadise.ch; adult/child return Sfr100/50; ⊘8.30am-4.20pm) is the icing on the cake. Ride Europe's highest-altitude cable car to 3883m and gawp at 14 glaciers and 38 mountain peaks over 4000m from the **Panoramic Platform** (only open in good weather). Don't miss the **Glacier Palace**, an ice palace complete with glittering ice sculptures

Glacier Express

The Glacier Express is one of Europe's mythical train journeys. It starts and ends in two of Switzerland's oldest, glitziest mountain resorts – Zermatt and St Moritz – and the Alpine scenery is magnificent in parts.

Hop aboard the red train with floor-to-ceiling windows in St Moritz or Zermatt, and savour shot after cinematic shot of green peaks, glistening Alpine lakes, glacial ravines and other hallucinatory natural landscapes. Pulled by steam engine when it first puffed out of the station in 1930, the Glacier Express traverses 191 tunnels and 291 bridges on its famous 290km journey.

Highlights include the one-hour ride from Disentis to Andermatt, across the Oberalp Pass (2033m) – the highest point of the journey in every way; and the celebrity six-arch, 65m-high Landwasser Viaduct, pictured on almost every feature advertising the Glacier Express, that dazzles passengers during the 50km leg between Chur and Filisur.

Great For...

☑ Don't Miss

The ride from Disentis to Andermatt and the Landwasser Viaduct.

🚇 Need to Know

www.glacierexpress.ch; adult/child one way St Moritz–Zermatt Sfr153/76.50, obligatory seat reservation summer/winter Sfr33/13, on-board 3-course lunch Sfr45; ⊘3 trains daily May–Oct, 1 train daily mid-Dec–Feb

✕ Take a Break

Have lunch in the vintage restaurant car or bring your own Champagne picnic.

> ### ★ Top Tip
> **Check the weather forecast before committing: a blue sky is essential for the eight-hour train ride to be worthwhile.**

or film. If photography/video is the reason you're aboard, ditch the direct glamour train for regional express SBB trains along the same route – cheaper, no reservations required, with windows that open and the chance to stretch your legs when changing trains.

○ The southern side of the train is said to have the best views.

○ Children aged under six travel free (buy an extra seat reservation if you don't fancy a young child on your lap for eight hours), and children aged six to 16 years pay half-price plus a seat reservation fee.

A ticket is not cheap, and to avoid disappointment it pays to know the nuts and bolts of this long mountain train ride.

○ Don't asume it is hard-core mountain porn for the duration of the journey: the views in the tunnels the train passes through are not particularly wonderful, for starters.

○ The complete trip takes almost eight hours. If you're travelling with children or can't bear the thought of sitting all day watching mountain scenery that risks becoming monotonous, opt for just a section of the journey: the best bit is the one-hour ride from Disentis to Andermatt.

○ Windows in the stylish panoramic carriages are sealed and can't be opened, making it tricky to take good photographs

Zermatt

◉ SIGHTS

Meander main-strip **Bahnhofstrasse** with its flashy boutiques and stream of horse-drawn sleds or carriages and electric taxis, then head downhill towards the noisy Vispa river along **Hinterdorfstrasse**. This old-world street is crammed with 16th-century pig stalls and archetypal Valaisian timber granaries propped up on stone discs and stilts to keep out pesky rats; look for the **fountain** commemorating Ulrich Inderbinen (1900–2004), a Zermatt-born mountaineer who climbed the Matterhorn 370 times, the last time at age 90. Nicknamed the King of the Alps, he was the oldest active mountain guide in the world when he retired at the ripe old age of 95.

Matterhorn Museum   Museum
(☎027 967 41 00; www.zermatt.ch/museum; Kirchplatz; adult/child Sfr10/5; ⊘11am-6pm Jul-Sep, 3-6pm Oct–mid-Dec, 3-7pm mid-Dec–Mar, 2-6pm Apr-Jun) This crystalline, state-of-the-art museum provides fascinating insight into Valaisian village life, mountaineering,

the dawn of tourism in Zermatt and the lives the Matterhorn has claimed. Short films portray the first successful ascent of the Matterhorn on 13 July 1865 led by Edward Whymper, a feat marred by tragedy on the descent when four team members crashed to their deaths in a 1200m fall. The infamous rope that broke is exhibited.

Gornerschlucht   Gorge
(☎027 967 20 96; www.gornergorge.ch; adult/child Sfr5/2.50; ⊘9.15am-5.45pm Jun–mid-Oct) It is a 20-minute walk from town along the river to this dramatic gorge, carved out of green serpentinite rock and accessed by a series of wooden staircases and walkways. Good fun for families.

Sunnegga   Funicular
(www.matterhornparadise.ch; adult/child one way Sfr12/6, return Sfr24/12) Take the *Sunnegga Express* 'tunnel funicular' up to Sunnegga (2288m) for amazing views of the Matterhorn. This is a top spot for families – take the Leisee Shuttle (free) down to the lake for beginner ski slopes at Wolli's Park in winter, and a children's playground plus splashing around in the lake in summer. A

From left: Zermatt and the Matterhorn; Mountaineers' Cemetery; Skiing in the Swiss Alps

marmot-watching station is a few minutes' walk from Sunnegga. It's a relatively easy downhill walk back to Zermatt via Findeln in about 1½ hours.

Ricola Herb Garden
Gardens

(www.ricola.com; Blatten; ☺Jun-Sep) **FREE** The Ricola Herb Garden in the pretty mountain hamlet of Blatten bristles with aromatic herbs that end up in Ricola sweets; and there's a family fun 'touch and smell' quiz.

Mountaineers' Cemetery
Cemetery

(Kirchstrasse) A walk in Zermatt's twinset of cemeteries – the Mountaineers' Cemetery in the garden of Zermatt's **St Mauritius Church** (Kirchplatz) and the main cemetery across the road – is a sobering experience. Numerous gravestones tell of untimely deaths on Monte Rosa, the Matterhorn and Breithorn.

🟢 ACTIVITIES

An essential stop in activity planning is the **Snow & Alpine Center** (☏027 966 24 60; www.alpincenter-zermatt.ch; Bahnhofstrasse 58; ☺9am-noon & 3-7pm Mon-Fri, 4-7pm Sat & Sun Dec-Apr, 9am-noon & 3-7pm Jul-Sep), home to Zermatt's ski school and mountain guides. In winter buy lift passes here (Sfr79/430 for a one-day/one-week pass excluding Cervinia; Sfr92/494 including Cervinia).

🟢 Skiing

Zermatt is cruising heaven, with mostly long, scenic red runs, plus a smattering of blues for ski virgins and knuckle-whitening blacks for experts. The main skiing areas in winter are **Rothorn**, **Stockhorn** and **Klein Matterhorn** – 360km of ski runs in all with a link from Klein Matterhorn to the Italian resort of **Cervinia** and a freestyle park with half-pipe for snowboarders.

Summer skiing (20km of runs) and boarding (gravity park at Plateau Rosa on the Theodul glacier) is Europe's most extensive. Count on Sfr84/125 for a one-/two-day summer ski pass.

🟢 Hiking

Zermatt is a hiker's paradise, with 400km of summer trails through some of the most incredible scenery in the Alps – the

OLIVER FOERSTNER/SHUTTERSTOCK ©

Zermatt

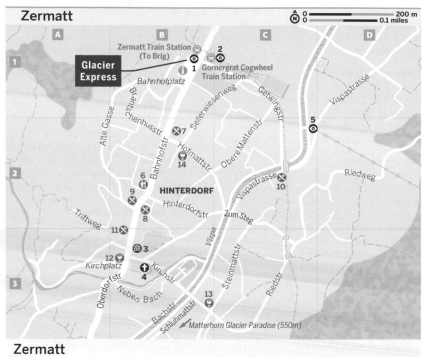

Zermatt

◉ Sights
1 Glacier Express	B1
2 Gornergratbahn	C1
3 Matterhorn Museum	B3
Mountaineers' Cemetery	(see 4)
4 St Mauritius Church	B3
5 Sunnegga	C2

⊕ Activities, Courses & Tours
6 Snow & Alpine Center	B2

⊗ Eating
7 Bayard Metzgerei	B2
8 Brown Cow Pub	B2
9 Le Gitan – Zermatterstübli	B2
10 Snowboat Bar & Yacht Club	C2
11 Whymper Stube	B3

⊖ Drinking & Nightlife
12 Elsie Bar	B3
13 Papperla Pub	B3
14 Vernissage Bar Club	B2

tourist office has trail maps. For Matterhorn close-ups, nothing beats the highly dramatic **Matterhorn Glacier Trail** (two hours, 6.5km) from Trockener Steg to Schwarzsee; 23 information panels en route tell you everything you could possibly need to know about glaciers and glacial life.

For those doing lots of walking, local excursion passes offer a convenient way to get into the high country. A **Peak Pass** – offering unlimited use of the Schwarzsee, Rothorn and Matterhorn Glacier Paradise (p589) cable cars plus the Gornergrat-bahn (p589) cog railway – costs Sfr220 for three days or Sfr315 for a week. To find your perfect walk, search by duration, distance and difficulty on the hiking page of the excellent tourist office website.

⊗ EATING

You won't go hungry in Zermatt. The entire town centre is packed with restaurants, with the greatest concentration along busy Bahnhofstrasse.

Snowboat Bar & Yacht Club
International €

(☑027 967 43 33; www.zermattsnowboat.com; Vispastrasse 20; mains Sfr22-39; ⊙noon-midnight) This hybrid eating-drinking, riverside address, with deckchairs sprawled across its rooftop sun terrace, is a blessing. When fondue tires, head here for barbecue-sizzled burgers (not just beef, but crab and veggie burgers too), creative salads (the Omega 3 buster is a favourite) and great cocktails. The vibe? 100% friendly, fun and funky.

Klein Matterhorn
Pizza €

(☑027 967 01 42; www.kleinmatterhorn-zermatt.com; Schluhmattstrasse 50; pizza Sfr17-22; ⊙8am-midnight, kitchen 11.30am-10pm) For first-rate Italian pizza in the sun with a Matterhorn view, this simple pizzeria and cafe-bar opposite the Matterhorn Glacier Express cable car station is the address.

Bayard Metzgerei
Swiss €

(☑027 967 22 66; www.metzgerei-bayard.ch; Bahnhofstrasse 9; sausage Sfr6; ⊙noon-6.30pm Jul-Sep, 4-6.30pm Dec-Mar) Join the line for a street-grilled sausage (pork, veal or beef) and chunk of bread to down with a beer on the hop – or at a bar stool with the sparrows in the alley by this first-class butcher's shop.

Chez Vrony
Swiss €€

(☑027 967 25 52; www.chezvrony.ch; Findeln; breakfast Sfr15-28, mains Sfr25-45; ⊙9.15am-5pm Dec-Apr & mid-Jun–mid-Oct) Ride the Sunnegga Express funicular (p592) to 2288m, then ski down or summer-hike 15 minutes to Zermatt's tastiest slope-side address in the Findeln hamlet. Delicious dried meats, homemade cheese and sausage come from Vrony's own cows that graze away the summer on the high alpine pastures (2100m) surrounding it, and the Vrony burger (Sfr31) is legendary. Advance reservations essential in winter.

Le Gitan – Zermatterstübli
Swiss €€

(☑027 968 19 40; www.legitan.ch; Bahnhofstrasse 64; mains Sfr23-39; ⊙noon-3pm &

Hiking with Kids

Try out these short-walk favourites for families with younger children.

● Take the *Sunnegga Express* up to Sunnegga then the Leisee Shuttle (or walk the 10 minutes) downhill to **Leisee**, a lake made for bracing summer dips with bijou pebble beach and old-fashioned wooden raft for children to tug themselves across the water pirate-style.

● In town, embark on the 20-minute walk along the river to the Gornerschlucht (p592), a dramatic gorge carved out of green serpentinite rock and accessed by a series of wooden staircases and walkways.

● The easy circular walk around the Ricola Herb Garden (p593), in the pretty mountain hamlet of Blatten (signposted from Gornergratschlucht).

● The 1¼-hour circular walk (2.9km) in **Füri** takes in the Glatschergarten Dossen (Dossen Glacier Garden) with its bizarre glacial rock formations, a picnic area with stone-built barbecues to cook up lunch, and the dizzying 90m-high, 100m-long steel suspension bridge above the Gornerschlucht Gorge.

7-10pm) Le Gitan stands out for its elegant chalet-style interior and extra-tasty cuisine. Plump for a feisty pork or veal sausage with onion sauce and rösti, or dip into a cheese fondue – with Champagne (yes!), or, if you're feeling outrageously indulgent, Champagne and fresh truffles. End with coffee ice cream doused in kirsch, or apricot sorbet with abricotine (local Valais apricot liqueur).

Whymper Stube
Swiss €€

(☑027 967 22 96; www.whymper-stube.ch; Bahnhofstrasse 80; raclette Sfr9, fondue Sfr25-48; ⊙11am-11pm Nov-Apr & Jun–mid-Oct) This cosy bistro, attached to the Monte Rosa

A Feast of a Meal: Fondue & Raclette

It is hard to leave Switzerland without dipping into a fondue. A pot of gooey melted cheese is placed in the centre of the table and kept on a slow burn while diners dip in cubes of crusty bread using slender two-pronged fondue forks. Traditionally a winter dish, the Swiss tend to eat it mostly if there's snow around or they're at a suitable altitude – unlike tourists who tuck in year-round and wherever they find it.

The classic fondue mix in Switzerland is equal amounts of emmental and gruyère cheese, grated and melted with white wine and a shot of kirsch (cherry-flavoured liquor), then thickened slightly with potato or corn flour. It is served with a basket of bread slices (which are soon torn into small morsels) and most people order a side platter of cold meats and tiny gherkins to accompany it.

Switzerland's other signature alpine cheese dish is raclette. Unlike fondue, raclette – both the name of the dish and the cheese at its gooey heart – is eaten year-round. A half-crescent slab of the cheese is screwed onto a specially designed 'rack oven' that melts the top flat side. As it melts, cheese is scraped onto plates for immediate consumption with boiled potatoes, cold meats and pickled onions or gherkins.

Fondue
SILKENPHOTOGRAPHY/GETTY IMAGES ©

Hotel that Whymper left from to climb the Matterhorn in 1865, is legendary for its excellent raclette and fondues. The icing on the cake is a segmented pot bubbling with three different cheese fondues. Service is relaxed and friendly, tables are packed tightly together, and the place – all inside – buzzes come dusk.

Brown Cow Pub   Pub Food
(☎027 967 19 31; www.hotelpost.ch; Bahnhofstrasse 41; ☺9am-2am, kitchen 9am-10.30pm) Dozens of dining joints line Bahnhofstrasse, including this busier-than-busy pub, one of several eating spots inside the legendary Hotel Post. The Brown Cow serves pub grub (hot dogs from Sfr9, burgers from Sfr16) all day.

🍷 DRINKING & NIGHTLIFE
Still fizzing with energy after hurtling down the slopes? Zermatt pulses in party-mad après-ski huts, suave lounge bars and Brit-style pubs. Most close (and some melt) in low season.

Elsie Bar   Wine Bar
(☎027 967 24 31; www.elsiebar.ch; Kirchplatz 16; ☺4pm-1am) In a building originally erected in 1879, this elegant, old-world wine bar with wood-panelled walls, across from the church, has been known as Elsie's since 1961. Oysters, caviar and snails are on the winter menu, along with a top selection of wine and whisky.

Hennu Stall   Bar
(☎027 966 35 10; www.facebook.com/ HennustallZermatt; Klein Matterhorn; ☺2-10pm Dec-Apr) Last one down to this snowbound 'chicken run' is a rotten egg. Hennu is the wildest après-ski shack on Klein Matterhorn. Order a caramel vodka and take your ski boots grooving to live music on the terrace. A metre-long 'ski' of shots will make you cluck all the way down to Zermatt. Below Furi on the way to Zermatt.

Vernissage Bar Club   Bar
(☎027 966 69 70; www.backstagehotel.ch; Hofmattstrasse 4; ☺5pm-midnight Sun-Wed, to 2am Thu-Sat) The ultimate après-ski antithesis, Vernissage at the Backstage Hotel exudes

Al fresco restaurant with Matterhorn views

grown-up sophistication. Local artist Heinz Julen has created a theatrical space with flowing velvet drapes, film-reel chandeliers and candlelit booths. Catch an exhibition, watch a movie, or pose in the lounge bar.

Papperla Pub
Pub

(www.julen.ch; Steinmattstrasse 34; ⊙2pm-2am; 🛜) Rammed with sloshed skiers in winter and happy hikers in summer, this buzzing pub with red director chairs on its pavement terrace blends pulsating music with lethal Jägermeister bombs, good vibes and pub grub (from 5pm). Its downstairs **Schneewittli club** rocks until dawn in season.

ⓘ INFORMATION

Make the Swiss tourist board, **Switzerland Tourism** (www.myswitzerland.com), your first port of call. For detailed information, contact the local **tourist office** (⌕027 966 81 00; www.zermatt.ch; Bahnhofplatz 5; ⊙8.30am-6pm; 🛜). Information and maps are free and somebody invariably speaks English. In German-speaking Switzerland tourist offices are called Verkehrsbüro, or Kurverein in some resorts.

ⓘ GETTING AROUND

Dinky electro-taxis zip around town transporting goods and the weary (and taking pedestrians perilously by surprise – watch out!). Pick one up at the main rank in front of the train station on Bahnhofstrasse.

Parliament building (p553). Budapest

In Focus

Europe Today 600
The UK is on the way out, but other countries are lining up to join the EU.

History 602
For centuries, emperors and royal dynasties shaped the destiny of a continent where democracy now rules.

Arts & Architecture 609
So many of the world's artistic treasures and architectural styles were born of European creativity.

Food & Drink 614
It's no time to go on a diet – a fabulous culinary feast awaits as you travel across Europe.

German train station

Europe Today

These are challenging times for Europe. Economically, many countries are still struggling, while politically, pro- and anti- European Union (EU) forces are engaged in a titanic struggle. The UK public narrowly voted for 'Brexit' – leaving the EU – and that process is now underway. Across the Channel, voters in France and the Netherlands have backed candidates and parties that favour a stronger, united Europe.

State of the Union

Where Europe should be headed as a political entity remains a burning question for EU nations, especially those hostile to relinquishing further powers to the EU parliament. In 2016 a referendum in the UK over the issue saw voters opt by a slim majority for 'Brexit'. The Conservative government went on to trigger Article 50 of the Treaty of Lisbon at the end of March 2017 setting the UK on course to leave the EU by 2019.

EU membership also raises questions about democratic representation: in exchange for their financial bailouts, financially strapped countries have been forced to follow the political will of Brussels, often in direct contradiction to the wishes of their own constituents and, in some cases, the platforms on which their governments were elected. Despite the unease over this, the French presidential election in 2017 saw a decisive victory for

belief systems
(% of population)

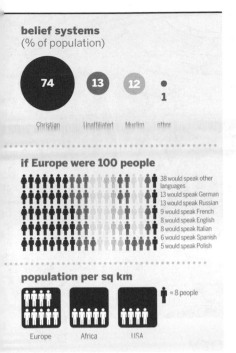

74 Christian

13 Unaffiliated

12 Muslim

1 other

if Europe were 100 people

38 would speak other languages
13 would speak German
13 would speak Russian
9 would speak French
8 would speak English
8 would speak Italian
6 would speak Spanish
5 would speak Polish

population per sq km

≈ 8 people

Europe   Africa   USA

the pro-EU centrist candidate Emmanuel Macron, over the far right Front National leader Marine Le Pen.

Refugee Crisis

It was a similar story in the Netherlands. In the March 2017 general election the centre-right VVD party prevailed over the right-wing Partij voor de Vrijheid (PVV) led by Geert Wilders, an anti-EU politician advocating a ban on immigration from Muslim countries and closing down mosques.

Such hostility to Muslims has been on the rise in the wake of the worst refugee crisis to hit Europe since the end of WWII. Since 2015 over one million refugees and migrants have arrived in the EU, the majority of them fleeing from war and terror in Syria and other troubled countries. The response has ranged from some countries in the EU's Schengen Area closing previously open borders to Germany's open arms policy of accepting refugees.

Greener Europe

On a brighter note, many European countries are stepping up efforts to combat climate change. Increasingly, high-speed rail services provide an ecofriendly alternative to short-haul flights, green spaces flourish in urban areas, share-bicycle schemes are becoming prevalent in cities and towns, and vehicle emissions are being reduced with more electric and hybrid engines and biofuels. London mayor Sadiq Khan has added a £10 charge for motorists driving older, more polluting vehicles on top of the congestion charge that already exists for central London. The mayors of Paris, Madrid and Athens also plan to to take diesel cars and vans off their roads by 2025.

The Eurovision Issue

On a lighter note, every May Europe plops down on the sofa to enjoy the Eurovision Song Contest. This one-of-a-kind musical marathon has been screened every year since 1956, making it the longest-running television show of its kind.

Created to symbolise Euro harmony, the contest has also developed into a reflection of Euro discord. Is the voting system rigged? Should acts sing in English or in their own language? Is that kitschy pop song some kind of coded political statement?

Each country enters one song, and then votes for their favourites among the competitors. Inevitably this leads to accusations of 'block voting' (neighbouring countries tending to vote for each other, for example). Confusingly, too, several non-European countries are allowed to enter. The host city, with a few exceptions, is in the winner country of the previous year, with cities competing domestically for the honour and associated tourism boost.

Ceiling at Széchenyi Baths (p551), Budapest

VIDALGO/SHUTTERSTOCK ©

History

Understanding Europe's long and often troubled history is a crucial part of figuring out what makes this continent tick. Fragments of that history can be encountered in the tumbledown remains of Roman ampitheatres and bathhouses, in the fabulously ostentatious architecture of French chateaux and German castles, and in the winding streets, broad boulevards and governing institutions of its many stately cities.

4500–2500 BC

Neolithic tribes build burial tombs, barrows, stone circles and alignments across Europe.

1st century BC–AD 4

The Romans conquer much of Europe. The Roman Empire flourishes under Augustus and his successors.

410

The sacking of Rome by the Goths brings an end to Roman dominance.

Roman Forum (p372), Rome

Prehistory

The first settlers arrived in Europe around two million years ago, but it wasn't until the end of the last major ice age between 12,000 BC and 8000 BC that humans really took hold. As the glaciers and ice sheets retreated, hunter-gatherer tribes extended their reach northwards in search of new land. Some of Europe's earliest human settlements were left behind by Neolithic tribes.

Greeks & Romans

The civilisation of ancient Greece emerged around 2000 BC and made huge leaps forward in science, technology, architecture, philosophy and democratic principles. Many of the writers, thinkers and mathematicians of ancient Greece, from Pythagoras to Plato, exert a profound influence to this day. Then came the Romans, who set about conquering most of Europe and devised the world's first republic. At its height, Roman power extended all the

1066
William the Conqueror defeats the English King Harold at the Battle of Hastings.

1340s–1350s
The Black Death reaches its peak in Europe, killing between 30% and 60% of Europe's population.

15th century
The Italian Renaissance brings about a revolution in art, architecture and science.

Trinity College entrance, Dublin

AITORMMFOTO/SHUTTERSTOCK ©

★ **Best Historical Buildings**

Colosseum (p354), Rome

Pompeii (p462), Italy

City Walls & Forts (p473), Dubrovnik

Tower of London (p67), London

Prague Castle (p527), Prague

Trinity College (p117), Dublin

way from Celtic Britain to ancient Persia (Iran). The Romans' myriad achievements are almost too numerous to mention: they founded cities, raised aqueducts, constructed roads, laid sewers and built baths all over the continent, and produced a string of brilliant writers, orators, politicians, philosophers and military leaders.

Dark Ages to Middle Ages

Rome's empire-building ambitions eventually proved too much, and a series of political troubles and military disasters resulted in the sacking of Rome (in 410) by the Goths. Although Roman emperors clung onto their eastern Byzantine empire for another thousand years, founding a new capital at Constantinople (modern day Istanbul), Rome's dominance over Western Europe was over. A new era, the Dark Ages, had begun.

The next few centuries were marked by a series of conflicts in which the various kingdoms of the European mainland sought to gain political and strategic control. In AD 711, the Moors – Arabs and Berbers who had converted to the Islamic religion prevailing throughout northern Africa – crossed the Straits of Gibraltar, defeating the Visigothic army. They went on to rule the Iberian Peninsula for almost 800 years, until the fall of Granada in 1492, leaving behind a flourishing architectural, scientific and academic legacy.

Meanwhile, in the late 8th century Charlemagne, King of the Franks, brought together much of Western Europe under what would become known as the Holy Roman Empire. This alliance of Christian nations sent troops to reclaim the Holy Land from Islamic control in a series of campaigns known as the Crusades.

The Renaissance

Europe's troubles rumbled on into the 14th and 15th centuries. In the wake of further conflicts and political upheavals, as well as the devastating outbreak of the Black Death (estimated to have wiped out somewhere between 30% to 60% of Europe's population), control over the Holy Roman Empire passed into the hands of the Austrian Habsburgs, a

1517	**1789**	**1815**
Martin Luther nails his demands to the church door in Wittenburg, sparking the Reformation.	France becomes a republic following the French Revolution. Numerous aristocrats are executed by guillotine.	France's defeat at the Battle of Waterloo ends First French Empire and military career of Napoleon Bonaparte.

political dynasty that became one of the continent's dominant powers.

The Italian city-states of Genoa, Venice, Pisa and Amalfi consolidated their control over the Mediterranean, establishing trading links with much of the rest of Europe and the Far East, and embarking on some of the first journeys in search of the New World.

In the mid-15th century, a new age of artistic and philosophical development broke out across the continent. The Renaissance encouraged writers, artists and thinkers to challenge the accepted doctrines of theology, philosophy, architecture and art. The centre of this artistic tsunami was Florence, Italy, where such inspirational figures as Michelangelo and Leonardo da Vinci made great strides in art and architecture. Another epoch-changing development was under way in Germany, thanks to the invention of the printing press by Johannes Gutenburg in around 1440. The advent of 'movable type' made printed books available to the masses for the first time.

The Reformation

While the Renaissance challenged artistic ideas, the Reformation dealt with questions of religion. Challenging Catholic 'corruption' and the divine authority of the Pope, the German theologian Martin Luther established his own breakaway branch of the Church, to which he gave the name 'Protestantism', in 1517. Luther's stance was soon echoed by the English monarch Henry VIII, who cut ties with Rome in 1534 and went on to found his own (Protestant) Church of England, sowing the seeds for centuries of conflict between Catholics and Protestants.

The New World

The schisms of the Church weren't the only source of tension. The discovery of the 'New World' in the mid-16th century led to a colonial arms race between the major European nations, in which each country battled to lay claim to the newly discovered lands – often enslaving or killing the local populace in the process.

More trouble followed during the Thirty Years' War (1618–48), which began as a conflict between Catholics and Protestants and eventually sucked in most of Europe's principal powers. The war was ended by the Peace of Westphalia in 1648, and Europe entered a period of comparative stability.

The Enlightenment

The Enlightenment (sometimes known as 'The Age of Reason') is the name given to a philosophical movement that spread throughout European society during the mid- to late-17th century. It emphasised the importance of logic, reason and science over the doctrines of religion. Key figures included the philosophers Baruch Spinoza, John Locke, Immanuel Kant and Voltaire, as well as scientists such as Isaac Newton.

19th century	**1914**	**1939–45**
The Industrial Revolution transforms European society; with railways and factories bringing in the modern age.	The assassination of Archduke Franz Ferdinand leads to the outbreak of WWI (1914–18).	WWII rages across Europe, devastating many cities. After peace is declared, much of Eastern Europe falls under communist rule.

The Enlightenment also questioned the political status quo. Since the Middle Ages, the majority of Europe's wealth and power had been concentrated in the hands of an all-powerful elite, largely made up of monarchs and aristocrats. This stood in direct contradiction to one of the core values of the Enlightenment – equality. Many thinkers believed it was an impasse that could only be solved by revolution.

Revolution

Things came to a head in 1789 when armed mobs stormed the Bastille prison in Paris, thus kick-starting the French Revolution. The Revolution began with high ideals, inspired by its iconic slogan of *liberté, egalité, fraternité* (liberty, equality, brotherhood). Before long things turned sour and heads began to roll. Hard-line republicans seized control and demanded retribution for centuries of oppression. Scores of aristocrats met their end under the guillotine's blade, including the French monarch Louis XVI, who was publicly executed in January 1793 in Paris' Place de la Concorde, and his queen, Marie-Antoinette, killed in October that year.

The Reign of Terror between September 1793 and July 1794 saw religious freedoms revoked, churches closed, cathedrals turned into 'Temples of Reason' and thousands beheaded. In the chaos, a dashing young Corsican general named Napoleon Bonaparte (1769– 1821) seized his chance.

Napoleon assumed power in 1799 and in 1804 was crowned Emperor. He fought a series of campaigns across Europe and conquered vast swathes of territory for the French empire but, following a disastrous campaign to conquer Russia in 1812, his grip on power faltered and he was defeated by a coalition of British and Prussian forces at the Battle of Waterloo in 1815.

Industry, Empire & WWI

Having vanquished Napoleon, Britain emerged as Europe's predominant power. With such innovations as the steam engine, the railway and the factory, Britain unleashed the Industrial Revolution and, like many of Europe's major powers (including France, Spain, Belgium and the Austro-Hungarian empire), set about developing its colonies across much of Africa, Australasia and the Middle and Far East.

Before long these competing empires clashed again, with predictably catastrophic consequences. The assassination of the heir to the Austro-Hungarian Empire Franz Ferdinand in 1914 led to the outbreak of the Great War, or WWI, as it came to be known. By the end of hostilities in 1918, huge tracts of northern France and Belgium had been razed and over 16 million people across Europe had been killed.

In the Treaty of Versailles, the defeated powers of Austro-Hungary and Germany lost large areas of territory and found themselves saddled with a massive bill for reparations,

1957
The European Economic Community (EEC) is formed by a collection of Western European countries.

1989
The fall of the Berlin Wall heralds the downfall of oppressive regimes across much of Eastern Europe.

1993
The Maastricht Treaty leads to the formation of the European Union (EU).

sowing seeds of discontent that would be exploited a decade later by a fanatical Austrian painter by the name of Adolf Hitler.

Rise of Fascism

Hitler's rise to power was astonishingly swift. By 1933 he had become Chancellor and, as the head of the Nazi Party, assumed total control of Germany. Having spent much of the 1930s building up a formidable war machine, assisting General Franco's nationalist forces during the Spanish Civil War, Hitler annexed Austria and engineered the occupation of Czechoslovakia, before extending his reach onwards into Poland in 1939.

The occupation of Poland proved the final straw. Britain, France and its Commonwealth allies declared war on Germany, which had formed its own alliance of convenience with the Axis powers of Italy (led by the fascist dictator Mussolini) and Japan.

WWII

Having done a secret deal with Stalin over the Soviet Union's spheres of influence to the east, Hitler unleashed his blitzkrieg on an unsuspecting western Europe, and within a few short months had conquered huge areas of territory, forcing the French into submission and driving the British forces to a humiliating retreat at Dunkirk. Europe was to remain under Nazi occupation for the next six years.

The Axis retained the upper hand until the Japanese attack on Pearl Harbor forced a reluctant USA into the war in 1941. Hitler's subsequent decision to invade the Soviet Union in 1941 proved to be a catastrophic error, resulting in devastating German losses that opened the door for the Allied invasion of Normandy in June 1944.

After several months of bitter fighting, Hitler's remaining forces were pushed back towards Berlin. Hitler committed suicide on 30 April 1945 and the Russians took the city, crushing the last pockets of German resistance. By 8 May Germany and Italy had unconditionally surrendered to the Allied powers, bringing the war in Europe to an end.

The Iron Curtain

Differences of opinion between the Western powers and the communist Soviet Union soon led to a stand-off. The USSR closed off its assigned sectors, including East Berlin, East Germany and much of Eastern Europe, which heralded the descent of the Iron Curtain and the beginning of the Cold War. This period of political tension and social division in Europe lasted for 40 years and saw popular uprisings in Prague and Budapest put down by Communist forces.

By the late 1980s the Soviet Union's grip on Eastern Europe was weakening as the former superpower's economic feet of clay crumbled. The Cold War era came to an end in 1989 with the fall of the Berlin Wall. Germany was reunified in 1990; a year later the

2002	2009	2014
Twelve member states of the EU ditch their national currencies in favour of the euro.	Europe is rocked by a series of financial crises, leading to costly bailouts for Ireland, Greece, Portugal and Spain.	Scotland votes on and rejects becoming a fully independent nation and so remains part of the United Kingdom.

USSR was dissolved. Shortly afterwards Romania, Bulgaria, Poland, Hungary and Albania had implemented multiparty democracy. In Czechoslovakia (now the Czech Republic and Slovakia), the so-called Velvet Revolution brought about the downfall of the communist government through mass demonstrations and other nonviolent means.

Europe United

The process of political and economic integration across Europe continued apace after the end of WWII. The formation of the European Economic Community (EEC) in 1957 began as a loose trade alliance between six nations. By 1992 this alliance had evolved into the European Union (EU) and when the Treaty of Maastricht came into effect in 1993 its core membership had expanded to 28 countries. Even though the UK is in the process of leaving the EU, five other candidates – Turkey, Macedonia, Montenego, Albania and Serbia – are on the books for future membership. All except Albania and Macedonia have started negotiations for entry.

Another key development was the implementation of the Schengen Agreement in 1995, which abolished border checks across much of mainland Europe and allowed EU citizens to travel freely throughout member states (with the notable exceptions of the UK and Ireland).

Even more momentous was the adoption of the single currency of the euro on 1 January 1999 as a cashless accounting currency; euro banknotes and coins have been used since 1 January 2002. To date, 19 countries have joined the Eurozone, while the UK, Denmark and Sweden have chosen to retain their national currencies. In future any new states joining the EU will be required to adopt the euro as a condition of entry. It's a hot topic, especially since the financial crash in countries including Greece and Spain, which has required richer nations (principally France and Germany) being called on to bail out several of their more indebted European neighbours.

Economic Challenges

Since the 2009 European debt crisis, growth throughout the EU has been sluggish, with many countries dipping in and out of recession. Unemployment figures across many European nations remain high, especially in Spain and Greece.

Although the euro stabilised after a series of multi billion-euro rescue packages for Greece, Ireland, Portugal and Spain, the currency is still subject to uncertainty. In 2015 an extension of Greece's bailout was granted in the hope of keeping the country within the Eurozone, to avoid a Greek exit (aka 'Grexit'), and to avoid other debt-saddled countries following suit. And the European Central Bank launched massive quantitative easing measures involving money printing and bond buying, pumping over €1 trillion into the economy in an effort to resuscitate it.

2015
Greece defaults on loan payments. Bailout proposals with tough conditions trigger riots and Greek banks close.

2016
Some EU borders are shut as millions of refugees and other unofficial migrants attempt to reach save European havens.

2017
Following a referendum in favour of quitting the EU, the UK triggers Article 50 setting in motion 'Brexit'.

La Pedrera (p294), Barcelona

MAKS ERSHOV/SHUTTERSTOCK ©

Arts & Architecture

For millennia great art and architecture has sprung forth from Europe. The continent's museums and galleries are repositories of all kinds of creative treasures. Caesars, royal families and wealthy elites served as patrons to artists of the stature of Michelangelo, Rembrandt and Monet. Modernist and contemporary architects such as Antonio Gaudí and Richard Rogers have designed buildings that are mammoth works of art in their own right.

Arts

Ancient Art

Art was a crucial part of everyday life for ancient civilisations: decorative objects were a sign of status and prestige, while statues were used to venerate and honour the dead, and monuments and temples lavishly decorated in an attempt to appease the gods.

You'll find sculptures and artefacts from early civilisations in all Europe's top art museums, including the British Museum, the Louvre in Paris and the Pergamonmuseum in Berlin. Perhaps the most famous ancient artwork is the *Venus de Milo* at the Louvre, thought to have been created between 130 BC and 100 BC by the master sculptor Alexandros of Antioch.

Tate Modern, London

★ **Best Modern Art Galleries**

Tate Modern (p77), London

Museu Picasso (p292), Barcelona

Centre Pompidou (p228), Paris

Museo Guggenheim (p311), Bilbao

Designmuseum Danmark (p141), Copenhagen

Medieval Art

During the Middle Ages, the power of the Church and its importance as an artistic patron meant that the majority of medieval art dealt with religious subjects. The Old Testament, the crucifixion, the apostles and the Last Judgment were common topics. Some of the finest medieval artworks are actually woven into the fabric of Europe's churches in the form of frescoes painted onto panels or walls.

Flemish and German painting produced several important figures during the period, including Jan van Eyck (c 1390–1441) and Hans Memling (c 1430–94), known for their lifelike oils, and Hieronymus Bosch (1450–1516), known for his use of fantastic imagery and allegorical concepts.

The Renaissance

The Renaissance marked Europe's golden age of art. Artists such as Leonardo da Vinci (1452–1519), Michelangelo (1475–1564), Raphael (1483–1520), Titian (c 1488/90–1576) and Botticelli (1445–1510) introduced new techniques, colours and forms into the artistic lexicon, drawing inspiration from the sculptors and artists of the classical world.

Landscape and the human form gained increasing importance during the Renaissance. Michelangelo's masterpiece, *David*, is often cited as the perfect representation of the human figure (despite the fact that the artist deliberately distorted its proportions to make it more pleasing to the eye). The sculpture is now displayed at the Galleria dell'Accademia in Florence. Florence's Galleria degli Uffizi contains the greatest collection of Italian Renaissance art.

In the wake of the Renaissance came the great names of the baroque period, epitomised by the Italian artist Caravaggio (1571–1610) and the Dutch artists Rembrandt (1606–69), Rubens (1577–1640) and Johannes Vermeer (1632–75). The baroque artists employed light and shadow (*chiaroscuro*) to heighten the drama of a scene and give their work a photographic intensity.

Romanticism & Impressionism

During the 18th century, Romantic artists such as Caspar David Friedrich (1774–1840) and JMW Turner (1775–1851) explored the drama of the natural landscape – cloudcapped mountains, lonely hilltops, peaceful meadows and moody sunsets. Other artists, such as Théodore Géricault (1791–1824) and Eugène Delacroix (1798–1863), drew inspiration from French history and prominent people of the day. One of Spain's most important artists, Francisco Goya (1746–1828), covered everything from royal portraits to war scenes, bullfight etchings and tapestry designs.

During the late 19th century, artists such as Claude Monet (1840–1926), Edgar Degas (1834–1917), Camille Pissarro (1830–1903), Edouard Manet (1832–83) and Pierre-

Auguste Renoir (1841–1919) aimed to capture the general 'impression' of a scene rather than its naturalistic representation (hence the name of their movement, 'Impressionism').

Their bold experiments with light, colour and form segued into that of their successors, the post-Impressionists such as Paul Cézanne (1839–1906), Vincent van Gogh (1853–90) and Paul Gauguin (1848–1903).

From Fauvism to Conceptual Art

The upheavals of the 20th century inspired many new artistic movements. The fauvists were fascinated by colour, typified by Henri Matisse (1869–1954), while the cubists, such as Georges Braque (1882–1963) and Pablo Picasso (1881–1973), broke their work down into abstract forms, taking inspiration from everything from primitive art to psychoanalysis.

The dadaists and surrealists took these ideas to their illogical extreme, exploring dreams and the subconscious: key figures include René Magritte (1898–1967) from Belgium, Max Ernst (1891–1976) from Germany, and Joan Miró (1893–1983) and Salvador Dalí (1904–89) from Spain.

Conceptual art, which stresses the importance of the idea behind a work rather than purely its aesthetic value, also got its start in the early 20th century with the works of Marcel Duchamp (1887-1968) having a seminal influence on the movement.

European Cinema

Europe is the birthplace of cinema. It was in Paris that Antoine Lumière debuted his Cinematograph in 1885 and Georges Méliès set up the world's first movie studio two years later. Germany was also an early country to the cinematic party with classics such as Fritz Lang's *Metropolis* (1927).

France has gone on to produce some of cinema's greatest talents, including François Truffaut (1932-84) and Jean-Luc Godard (1930–). It also hosts the Cannes film festival, one of Europe's top-three annual movie jamborees along with Venice and Berlin.

The 1940s were the golden age of British cinema with classics including David Lean's *Brief Encounter*, Carol Reed's *The Third Man* and Powell and Pressburger's *The Red Shoes*. In the 1960s, Britain gave the world James Bond and, in recent times, the Harry Potter series.

Modern & Contemporary Art

After 1945 abstract art became a mainstay of the European scene, with key figures such as Joseph Beuys (1921–86) and Anselm Kiefer (1945–) from Germany and the Dutch-American Willem de Kooning (1904–97).

The late 20th century and 21st century to date have introduced many more artistic movements: abstract expressionism, neoplasticism, minimalism, formalism and pop art, to name a few.

Britain has a particularly vibrant contemporary art scene: key names such as Tracey Emin (1963–), Dinos (1962–) and Jake (1966–) Chapman (known as the Chapman Brothers), Rachel Whiteread (1963–), Mark Wallinger (1959–) and Damien Hirst (1965–), famous for his pickled shark and diamond-encrusted skull, continue to provoke controversy.

Architecture

The Ancient World

Europe's oldest examples of architecture are the many hundreds of stone circles, henges, barrows, burial chambers and alignments built by Neolithic people between 4500 BC and 1500 BC. The most impressive examples of these ancient structures are at Carnac in Brittany and, of course, Stonehenge in the southwest of England.

No one is quite sure what the purpose of these structures was, although theories abound. Some say they could be celestial calendars, burial monuments or tribal meeting places, although it's generally agreed these days that they served some sort of religious function.

Greek & Roman Architecture

Several ancient cultures have left their mark around the shores of the Mediterranean, including the Etruscans (in present-day Tuscany) and the ancient Greeks and Romans. Athens is the best place to appreciate Greece's golden age: the dramatic monuments of the Acropolis illustrate the ancient Greeks' sophisticated understanding of geometry, shape and form, and set the blueprint for many of the architectural principles that have endured to the present day

The Romans were even more ambitious, and built a host of monumental structures designed to project the might and majesty of the Roman Empire. Roman architecture was driven by a combination of form and function – structures such as the Pont du Gard in southern France show how the Romans valued architecture that looked beautiful but also served a practical purpose. Rome has the greatest concentration of architectural treasures, including the famous Colosseum, but remains of Roman buildings are scattered all over the continent.

Romanesque & Gothic Architecture

The solidity and elegance of ancient Roman architecture echoed through the 10th and 11th centuries in buildings constructed during the Romanesque period. Many of Europe's earliest churches are classic examples of Romanesque construction, using rounded arches, vaulted roofs, and massive columns and walls.

Even more influential was the development of Gothic architecture, which gave rise to many of Europe's most spectacular cathedrals. Tell-tale characteristics include the use of pointed arches, ribbed vaulting, great showpiece windows and flying buttresses. Notre-Dame in Paris is an ideal place to see Gothic architecture in action.

Renaissance & Baroque Architecture

The Renaissance led to a huge range of architectural experiments. Pioneering Italian architects such as Brunelleschi, Michelangelo and Palladio shifted the emphasis away from Gothic austerity towards a more human approach. They combined elements of classical architecture with new building materials, and specially commissioned sculptures and decorative artworks. Florence and Venice are particularly rich in Renaissance buildings, but the movement's influence can be felt right across Europe.

Architectural showiness reached its zenith during the baroque period, when architects pulled out all the stops to show off the wealth and prestige of their clients. Baroque buildings are all about creating drama, and architects often employed swathes of craftsmen and used the most expensive materials available to create the desired effect. Paris' Hôtel des Invalides is a good example of the ostentation and expense that underpinned baroque architecture.

The Industrial Age

The 19th century was the great age of urban planning, when the chaotic streets and squalid slums of many of Europe's cities were swept away in favour of grand squares and ruler-straight boulevards. This was partly driven by an attempt to clean up the urban environment, but it also allowed architects to redesign the urban landscape to suit the industrial age, merging factories, public buildings, museums and residential suburbs into a seamless whole. One of the most obvious examples of urban remodelling was Baron Haussmann's reinvention of Paris during the late 19th century, which resulted in the construction of the city's great boulevards and many of its landmark buildings.

Nineteenth-century architects began to move away from the showiness of the baroque and rococo periods in favour of new materials such as brick, iron and glass. Neo-Gothic architecture was designed to emphasise permanence, solidity and power, reflecting the confidence of the industrial age. It was an era that gave rise to many of Europe's great public buildings, including many landmark museums, libraries, town halls and train stations.

Top Musical Destinations

Vienna The Staatsoper is the premier venue in a city synonymous with opera and classical music.

Berlin Everything from the world's most acclaimed techno venue to the Berlin Philharmonic can be seen in Germany's music-obsessed capital.

Dublin The Irish have music in their blood and it takes little to get them singing, particularly down the pub.

Lisbon Portuguese love the melancholic and nostalgic songs of fado; hear it in the city's Alfama district.

Reykjavík Iceland's capital has a vibrant live-music scene producing famous pop talents such as Björk and Sigur Rós.

The 20th Century

By the turn of the 20th century, the worlds of art and architecture had both begun to experiment with new approaches to shape and form. The flowing shapes and natural forms of art nouveau had a profound influence on the work of Charles Rennie Mackintosh in Glasgow, the Belgian architect Victor Horta and the Modernista buildings of Spanish visionary Antonio Gaudí. Meanwhile, other architects stripped their buildings back to the bare essentials, emphasising strict function over form: Le Corbusier, Ludwig Mies van der Rohe and Walter Gropius are among the most influential figures of the period.

Functional architecture continued to dominate much of mid-20th-century architecture, especially in the rush to reconstruct Europe's shattered cities in the wake of two world wars, although the 'concrete box' style of architecture has largely fallen out of fashion over recent decades. Europeans may have something of a love-hate relationship with modern architecture, but the best buildings eventually find their place – a good example is the inside-out Centre Pompidou in Paris (designed by the architectural team of Richard Rogers, Renzo Piano and Gianfranco Franchini), which initially drew howls of protest but is now considered one of the icons of 20th-century architecture.

Contemporary Architecture

Regardless of whether you approve of the more recent additions to Europe's architectural landscape, one thing's for sure – you won't find them boring.

The fashion for sky-high skyscrapers seems to have caught on in several European cities, especially London, where a rash of multistorey buildings have recently been completed, all with their own nickname (the Walkie Talkie, the Cheesegrater and so on). The official name for the Norman Foster–designed 'Gerkin' buildling is 30 St Mary Axe. Topping them all is the Shard, which became the EU's highest building at 309.6m when it was completed in 2013.

A quirky peacock among Rome's classical architecture is the Maxxi, a contemporary art museum designed by the late Zaha Hadid. Norman Foster's Reichstag is a icon of modern, unified Germany, while Frank Gehry's Museo Guggenheim is a silvery masterpiece that is perhaps Europe's most dazzling piece of modern architecture.

Macarons, France

ABELENA/SHUTTERSTOCK ©

Food & Drink

Europe is united by its passion for eating and drinking
with gusto. Every country has its own flavours, incor-
porating olive oils and sun-ripened vegetables in the hot
south, rich cream and butter in cooler areas, fresh-off-
the-boat seafood along the coast, delicate river and lake
fish, and meat from fertile mountains and pastures. Each
country has its own tipples, too, spanning renowned
wines, beers, stouts and ciders, and feistier firewater.

Great Britain & Ireland

Great Britain might not have a distinctive cuisine, but it does have a thriving food culture, with a host of celebrity chefs and big-name restaurants. Great Britain's colonial legacy has also left it with a taste for curry – a recent poll suggested the nation's favourite food was chicken tikka masala.

The Brits love a good roast, traditionally eaten on a Sunday and accompanied by roast potatoes, vegetables and gravy. The classic is roast beef with Yorkshire pudding (a crisp batter puff), but lamb, pork and chicken are equally popular. 'Bangers and mash' (sausages and mashed potato) and fish and chips (battered cod or haddock served with thick-cut fried potatoes) are also old favourites.

Specialities in Scotland include haggis served with 'tatties and neeps' (potato and turnip).

Ireland's traditional dishes reflect the country's rustic past: look out for colcannon (mashed potato with cabbage), coddle (sliced sausages with bacon, potato and onion) and boxty (potato pancake), plus classic Irish stew (usually made with lamb or mutton).

The traditional British brew is ale, served at room temperature and flat, in order to bring out the hoppy flavours. It's an acquired taste, especially if you're used to cold, fizzy lagers.

Ireland's trademark ale is stout – usually Guinness, but you can also sample those produced by Murphy's or Beamish.

Scotland and Ireland are both known for whisky-making, with many distilleries open for tours and tasting sessions. Note that in Scotland it's always spelt 'whisky'; only in Ireland do you add the 'e'.

The Netherlands

The Netherlands' colonial legacy has given the Dutch a taste for Indonesian and Surinamese-inspired meals like *rijsttafel* (rice table): an array of spicy dishes such as braised beef, pork satay and ribs, all served with white rice.

Other Dutch dishes to look out for are *erwertensoep* (pea soup with onions, carrots, sausage and bacon), *krokotten* (filled dough balls that are crumbed and deep-fried) and, of course, *friet* (fries). Here they're thin, crispy and eaten with mayonnaise rather than ketchup (tomato sauce).

Beer is the tipple of choice. Small Dutch brewers like Gulpen, Haarlem's Jopen, Bavaria, Drie Ringen and Leeuw are all excellent. Jenever (gin) is also a favourite in the Netherlands.

Sweet Treats

From pralines to puddings, Europe specialises in foods that are sweet, sticky and sinful. Germans and Austrians have a particularly sweet tooth – treats include *Salzburger nockerl* (a fluffy soufflé) and *Schwarzwalder kirschtorte* (Black Forest cherry cake), plus many types of *apfeltasche* (apple pastry) and *strudel* (filled filo pastry).

The Brits are another big cake-eating nation – a slice of cake or a dunked biscuit is an essential teatime ritual. The Italians are famous for their *gelaterie* (ice-cream stalls; the best will be labelled *produzione propria*, indicating that it's handmade on the premises). In Lisbon don't miss out on the deliciously cream egg custard tarts known as *pastel de nata*.

But it's the French who have really turned dessert into a fine art. Stroll past the window of any *boulangerie* (bakery) or patisserie and you'll be assaulted by temptations from creamy *éclairs* (filled choux buns) and crunchy *macarons* (meringue-based biscuits with a ganache filling) to fluffy *madeleines* (shell-shaped sponge cakes) and wicked *gâteaux* (cakes).

Go on – you know you want to.

France

Each French region has its distinctive dishes. Broadly, the hot south favours dishes based on olive oil, garlic and tomatoes, while the cooler north tends towards root vegetables, earthy flavours and creamy or buttery sauces. The French are famously unfussy about which bits of the animal they eat – kidney, liver, cheek and tongue are as much of a delicacy as a fillet steak or a prime rib.

Bouillabaisse, a saffron-scented fish stew, is a signature southern dish. It is served with spicy rouille sauce, gruyère cheese and croutons.

The Alps are the place to try fondue: hunks of toasted bread dipped into cheese sauces. Brittany and Normandy are big on seafood, especially mussels and oysters.

Outdoor restaurant, Rome

★ **Best Foodie Experiences**

Sunday roast in a British pub

A light-as-air macaron in Paris

Pintxos in Basque country, Spain

Crispy pizza in a real Roman pizzeria

Coffee and cake in a Viennese cafe

ALEXANDER MAZURKEVICH /SHUTTERSTOCK ©

Central France prides itself on its hearty cuisine, including *foie gras* (goose liver), *boeuf bourguignon* (beef cooked in red wine), *confit de canard* (duck cooked in preserved fat) and black truffles.

France is Europe's biggest wine producer. The principal regions are Alsace, Bordeaux, Burgundy, Languedoc, the Loire and the Rhône, all of which produce reds, whites and rosés. Then, of course, there's Champagne – home to the world's favourite bubbly, aged in centuries-old cellars beneath Reims and Épernay.

Spain

Spain's cuisine is typical of the flavours of Mediterranean cooking, making extensive use of herbs, tomatoes, onions, garlic and lashings of olive oil.

The nation's signature dish is *paella*, consisting of rice and chicken, meat or seafood, simmered with saffron in a large pan. Valencia is considered the spiritual home of *paella*.

Spain also prides itself on its ham and spicy sausages (including *chorizo*, *lomo* and *salchichón*). These are often used in making the bite-size Spanish dishes known as tapas (or *pintxos* in the Basque region). Tapas is usually a snack, but it can also be a main meal – three or four dishes is generally enough for one person.

Spain boasts the largest area (1.2 million hectares) of wine cultivation in the world. La Rioja and Ribera del Duero are the principal wine-growing regions.

Portugal

The Portuguese take pride in simple but flavourful dishes honed to perfection over the centuries. Bread remains integral to every meal, and it even turns up in some main courses. Be on the lookout for *açorda* (bread stew, often served with shellfish), *migas* (bread pieces prepared as a side dish) and *ensopados* (stews with toasted or deep-fried bread).

Seafood stews are superb, particularly *caldeirada*, which is a mix of fish and shellfish in a rich broth, not unlike a *bouillabaisse*. *Bacalhau* (dried salt-cod) is bound up in myth, history and tradition, and is excellent in baked dishes. Classic meat dishes include *porco preto* (sweet 'black' pork), *cabrito assado* (roast kid) and *arroz de pato* (duck risotto).

Portuguese wines are also well worth sampling such as fortified port and reds from the Douro valley and *alvarinho* and *vinho verde* (crisp, semi-sparkling wine) from the Minho.

Italy

Italian cuisine is dominated by the twin staples of pizza and pasta, which have been eaten in Italy since Roman times. A full meal comprises an *antipasto* (starter), *primo* (pasta or rice dish), *secondo* (usually meat or fish), *contorno* (vegetable side dish or salad), *dolce* (dessert) and coffee. When eating out it's OK to mix and match any combination.

Italian pasta comes in numerous shapes, from bow-shaped *farfalle* to twisty *fusilli*, ribbed *rigatoni* and long *pappardelle*. Italian pasta is made with durum flour, which gives it a distinctive *al dente* bite; the type of pasta used is usually dictated by the type of dish being served (ribbed or shaped pastas hold sauce better, for example).

Italian pizza comes in two varieties: the Roman pizza with a thin crispy base, and the Neapolitan pizza, which has a higher, doughier base. The best are always prepared in a *forno a legna* (wood-fired oven). Flavours are generally kept simple – the best pizza restaurants often serve only a couple of toppings, such as *margherita* (tomato and mozzarella) and *marinara* (tomato, garlic and oregano).

Italy's wines run the gamut from big-bodied reds such as Piedmont's Barolo, to light white wines from Sardinia and sparkling *prosecco* from the Veneto.

Europe's Favourite Cheeses

Britain Cheddar is tops but also try Wensleydale, Red Leicester and Stilton.

Netherlands Edam and Gouda, sometimes served as bar snacks with mustard.

France The big names are camembert, Brie, Livarot, Pont l'Évêque and Époisses (all soft cheeses); Roquefort and Bleu d'Auvergne (blue cheeses); and Comté, cantal and gruyère (hard cheeses).

Spain Manchego, a semi-hard sheep's cheese with a buttery flavour, is often used in tapas.

Italy Prestigious varieties include Parmesan, ricotta and mozzarella.

Switzerland Emmental and Gruyère are the best-known Swiss cheeses.

Germany Sample hard cheeses, especially Allgäu Emmentaler and Bergkäse (mountain cheese).

Germany, Austria & Switzerland

The Germanic nations are all about big flavours and big portions. *Wurst* (sausage) comes in hundreds of forms, and is often served with *Sauerkraut* (fermented cabbage).

The most common types of *Wurst* include *Bratwurst* (roast sausage), *Weisswurst* (veal sausage) and *Currywurst* (sliced sausage topped with ketchup and curry powder). Austria's signature dish is *Wiener Schnitzel* (breaded veal cutlet) but schnitzel in general (usually featuring pork) are also popular in Germany.

Other popular mains include *Rippenspeer* (spare ribs), *Rotwurst* (black pudding), *Rostbrätl* (grilled meat) and *Putenbrust* (turkey breast). Potatoes are served as *Bratkartoffeln* (fried), *Kartoffelpüree* (mashed), Swiss-style *Rösti* (grated then fried) or *Pommes Frites* (French fries).

The Swiss are known for their love of fondue and the similar dish *Raclette* (melted cheese with potatoes).

Beer is the national beverage. *Pils* is the crisp pilsner Germany is famous for, which is often slightly bitter. *Weizenbier* is made with wheat instead of barley malt and served in a tall, 500mL glass. *Helles Bier* means light beer, while *dunkles* means dark.

Germany is principally known for white wines – inexpensive, light and intensely fruity. The Rhine and Moselle Valleys are the largest wine-growing regions.

Czech Republic

Like many nations in Eastern Europe, Czech cuisine revolves around meat, potatoes and root vegetables, dished up in stews, goulashes and casseroles. *Pečená kachna* (roast duck

Vegetarians & Vegans

Vegetarians will have a tough time in many areas of Europe – eating meat is still the norm, and fish is often seen as a vegetarian option. However, you'll usually find something meat-free on most menus, though don't expect much choice. Vegans will have an even tougher time – cheese, cream and milk are integral ingredients of most European cuisines.

Vegetable-based *antipasti* (starters), tapas, meze, pastas, side dishes and salads are good options for a meat-free meal. Shopping for yourself in markets is an ideal way of trying local flavours without having to compromise your principles.

is the quintessential Czech restaurant dish, while *klobása* (sausage) is a common beer snack. A common side dish is *knedliky*, boiled dumplings made from wheat or potato flour.

The Czechs have a big beer culture, with some of Europe's best *pivo* (beer), usually lager style. The Moravian region is the up-and-coming area for Czech wines.

Denmark & Iceland

In Copenhagen you can sample creations inspired by the New Nordic culinary movement that has got foodies the world over talking. Simpler but no less tasty are *smørrebrød*, slices of rye bread topped with anything from beef tartar to egg and prawns.

The caraway-spiced schnapps *akvavit* is Denmark's best loved spirit – drink it as a shot followed by a chaser of *øl* (beer). Speaking of which, Denmark is also the home of Carlsberg as well as a battalion of microbreweries including Mikkeller and Grauballe.

Traditional Icelandic dishes reflect a historical need to eat every scrap and make it last through winter. Fish, seafood, lamb, bread and simple vegetables still form the typical Icelandic diet. A popular snack is Harðfiskur – dried strips of haddock eaten with butter. More challenging dishes include *svið* (singed sheep's head, complete with eyes, sawn in two, boiled and eaten fresh or pickled) and the famous stomach churner *hákarl* – Greenland shark, an animal so inedible it has to rot away underground for six months before humans can even digest it.

Wash it all down with the traditional alcoholic brew *brennivin* (schnapps made from potatoes and caraway seeds), a drink fondly known as 'black death'. If that's not to your taste, there are plenty of craft beers.

Skiing near the Matterhorn (p588), Swiss Alps

GORILLAIMAGES/SHUTTERSTOCK ©

Survival Guide

DIRECTORY A–Z   620

Accommodation 620
Customs Regulations 621
Climate 621
Electricity 622
Food 622
Gay & Lesbian
Travellers 622
Health 622
Insurance 623

Internet Access 624
Legal Matters 624
Maps 624
Money 624
Opening Hours 626
Post 626
Public Holidays 626
Safe Travel 626
Telephone 627
Time 628
Toilets 628

Tourist Information 628
Travellers with
Disabilities 628
Visas 629
Women Travellers 629
Getting There & Away 630

TRANSPORT   630

Getting There & Away 630
Getting Around 631

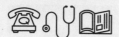

Directory A–Z

Accommodation

Reservations

During peak holiday periods, particularly Easter, summer and Christmas – and any time of year in popular destinations such as London, Paris and Rome – it's wise to book ahead. Most places can be reserved online. Always try to book directly with the establishment; this means you're paying just for your room, with no surcharge going to a hostel- or hotel-booking website.

B&Bs & Guest Houses

Guesthouses (pension, gasthaus, chambre d'hôte etc) and B&Bs (bed and breakfasts) offer greater

Book Your Stay Online

For more accommodation reviews by Lonely Planet authors, check out http://hotels.lonely planet.com/europe. You'll find independent reviews, as well as recommendations on the best places to stay. Best of all, you can book online.

comfort than hostels for a marginally higher price. Most are simple affairs, normally with shared bathrooms.

In some destinations, particularly in Eastern Europe, locals wait in train stations touting rented rooms. Just be sure such accommodation isn't in a far-flung suburb that requires an expensive taxi ride to and from town. Confirm the price before agreeing to rent a room and remember that it's unwise to leave valuables in your room when you go out.

B&Bs in the UK and Ireland often aren't really budget accommodation – even the lowliest tend to have midrange prices and there is a new generation of 'designer' B&Bs that are positively top end.

Camping

Most camping grounds are some distance from city centres. National tourist offices provide lists of camping grounds and camping organisations. Also see www.coolcamping.co.uk for details on prime campsites across Europe.

Homestays & Farmstays

You needn't volunteer on a farm to sleep on it. In Switzerland and Germany, there's the opportunity to sleep in barns or 'hay hotels'. Farmers provide cotton undersheets (to avoid straw pricks) and woolly blankets for extra warmth, but guests

need their own sleeping bag and torch. For further details, visit Abenteuer im Stroh (www.schlaf-im-stroh.ch).

Italy has a similar and increasingly popular network of farmstays called *agriturismi*. Participating farms must grow at least one of their own crops. Otherwise, accommodation runs the gamut from small rustic hideaways to grand country estates. See www.agriturismo.it for more details.

Hostels

There's a vast variation in hostel standards across Europe.

HI Hostels (those affiliated to Hostelling International; www.hihostels.com), usually offer the cheapest (secure) roof over your head in Europe and you don't have to be particularly young to use them. That said, if you're over 26 you'll frequently pay a small surcharge (usually about €3) to stay in an official hostel.

Hostel rules vary per facility and country, but some ask that guests vacate the rooms for cleaning purposes or impose a curfew. Most offer a complimentary breakfast, although the quality varies. Hostels are also great places to meet other travellers and pick up all kinds of information on the region you are visiting. They often usurp tourist offices in this respect.

You need to be a YHA or HI member to use HI-affiliated hostels, but nonmembers can stay by paying a few extra euros,

Price Ranges

Rates in our reviews are for high season and often drop outside high season by as much as 50%. High season in ski resorts is usually between Christmas and New Year and around the February to March winter holidays. Price categories are broken down differently for individual countries – see each country for full details.

which will be set against future membership. After sufficient nights (usually six), you automatically become a member. To join, ask at any hostel or contact your national hostelling office, which you'll find on the HI website – where you can also make online bookings.

Europe has many private hostelling organisations and hundreds of unaffiliated backpacker hostels. These have fewer rules, more self-catering kitchens and fewer large, noisy school groups. Dorms in many private hostels can be mixed sex. If you aren't happy to share mixed dorms, be sure to ask when you book.

Hotels

Hotels are usually the most expensive accommodation option, though at their lower end there is little to differentiate them from guesthouses or even hostels.

Cheap hotels around bus and train stations can be convenient for late-night or early-morning arrivals and departures, but some are also unofficial brothels or just downright sleazy. Check the room beforehand and make sure you're clear on the price and what it covers.

Discounts for longer stays are usually possible and hotel owners in southern Europe *might* be open to a little bargaining if times are slack. In many countries it's common for business hotels (usually more than two stars) to slash their rates by up to 40% on Friday and Saturday nights.

Customs Regulations

The European Union (EU) has a two-tier customs system: one for goods bought duty-free to import to or export from the EU, and one for goods bought in another EU country where taxes and duties have been paid.

❍ Entering or leaving the EU, you are allowed to carry duty-free: 200 cigarettes, 50 cigars or 250g of tobacco; 2L of still wine plus 1L of spirits over 22% alcohol or another

Climate

London

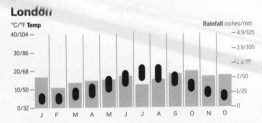

Paris

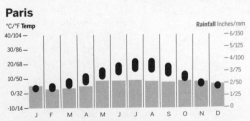

Rome

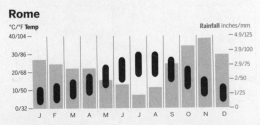

4L of wine (sparkling or otherwise); 50g of perfume, 250cc of eau de toilette.

o Travelling from one EU country to another, the duty-paid limits are: 800 cigarettes, 200 cigars, 1kg of tobacco, 10L of spirits, 20L of fortified wine, 90L of wine (of which not more than 60L is sparkling) and 110L of beer.

o Non-EU countries often have different regulations and many countries forbid the export of antiquities and cultural treasures.

Electricity

Europe generally runs on 220V, 50Hz AC, but there are exceptions. The UK runs on 230/240V AC, and some old buildings in Italy and Spain have 125V (or even 110V in Spain). The continent is moving towards a 230V standard. If your home country has a vastly different voltage you will need a transformer for delicate and important appliances.

The UK and Ireland use three-pin square plugs (Type G) . Most of Europe uses a 'europlug' with two round pins. Greece, Italy and Switzerland use a third round pin in a way that the two-pin plug usually (but not always in Italy and Switzerland) fits. Buy an adapter before leaving home; those on sale in Europe generally go the other way, but ones for visitors to Europe are also available.

Food

Rates in our reviews are based on the price of a main meal. Price categories are broken down differently for individual countries – see each country for full details.

Gay & Lesbian Travellers

Across Western Europe you'll find very liberal attitudes towards homosexuality. London, Paris, Berlin, Amsterdam and Lisbon have thriving gay communities and pride events.

Eastern Europe tends to be far less progressive. Outside the big cities, attitudes become more conservative and discretion is advised.

Health

Before You Go
Recommended Vaccinations

No jabs are necessary for Europe. However, the World Health Organization

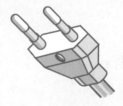

Type C
220V/50Hz

Type F
230V/50Hz

Type G
230V/50Hz

(WHO) recommends that all travellers be covered for diphtheria, tetanus, measles, mumps, rubella and polio, regardless of their destination. Since most vaccines don't produce immunity until at least two weeks after they're given, visit a physician at least six weeks before departure.

Health Insurance

It is unwise to travel anywhere in the world without travel insurance. A good policy should include comprehensive health insurance including medical care and emergency evacuation. If you are engaging in hazardous sports, you may need to pay for extra cover.

If you're an EU citizen, the free EHIC (European Health Insurance Card) covers you for most medical care in the 28 EU member states, including maternity care and care for chronic illnesses such as diabetes (though not for emergency repatriation). However, you will normally have to pay for medicine bought from pharmacies, even if prescribed, and perhaps for some tests and procedures. The EHIC does not cover private medical consultations and treatment out of your home country; this includes nearly all dentists, and some of the better clinics and surgeries. In the UK, you can apply for an EHIC online, by telephone, or by filling out a form available at post offices.

Non-EU citizens should find out if there is a recip-rocal arrangement for free medical care between their country and the EU country they are visiting.

Websites

The **World Health Organization** (www.who.int/ith/en) publishes the annually revised, free online book *International Travel and Health*. **MD Travel Health** (www.mdtravelhealth.com) provides up-to-date travel-health recommendations for every country.

It's usually a good idea to consult your government's website before departure, if one is available:
Australia (www.smartraveller.gov.au)
Canada (www.phac-aspc.gc.ca)
UK (www.gov.uk/foreign-travel-advice)
USA (www.cdc.gov/travel)

In Europe

Good health care is readily available in Western Europe and, for minor illnesses, pharmacists can give valuable advice and sell over-the-counter medication. They can also advise if you need specialised help and point you in the right direction. The standard of dental care is usually good.

While the situation in Eastern Europe is improving since the EU accession of many countries, quality medical care is not always readily available outside major cities, but embassies, consulates and five-star hotels can usually recommend doctors or clinics.

Tap Water

Tap water is generally safe to drink in Western Europe. However, bottled water is recommended in most of Eastern Europe, and a must in some countries where the giardia parasite can be a problem. Do not drink water from rivers or lakes as it may contain bacteria or viruses.

Condoms are widely available in Europe, however emergency contraception may not be, so take the necessary precautions.

Insurance

It's foolhardy to travel without insurance to cover theft loss and medical problems. There are a wide variety of policies, so check the small print.

Some policies specifically exclude 'dangerous activities', which can include scuba diving, motorcycling, winter sports, adventure sports or even hiking.

Check that the policy covers ambulances or an emergency flight home.

Worldwide travel insurance is available online at www.lonelyplanet.com/travel-insurance. You can buy, extend and claim online anytime – even if you're already on the road.

Internet Access

Internet access varies enormously across Europe. In most places, you'll be able to find wireless (wi-fi, also called WLAN in some countries), although whether it's free varies greatly.

Where the wi-fi icon appears, it means that the establishment offers free wi-fi that you can access immediately, or by asking for the access code from staff.

Access is generally straightforward, although a few tips are in order. If you can't find the @ symbol on a keyboard, try Alt Gr + 2, or Alt Gr + Q. Watch out for German keyboards, which reverse the Z and the Y positions. Using a French keyboard is an art unto itself.

Where necessary in relevant countries, click on the language prompt in the bottom right-hand corner of the screen or hit Ctrl + Shift to switch between the Cyrillic and Latin alphabets.

Legal Matters

You can generally purchase alcohol (beer and wine) from between 16 and 18 years (usually 18 for spirits), but if in doubt, ask. Although you can drive at 17 or 18, you might not be able to hire a ─ until you're 25.

─ Drugs are often quite ─ only available in Europe,

but that doesn't mean they're legal. The Netherlands is most famed for its liberal attitudes, with *coffeeshops* openly selling cannabis even though the drug is *not* technically legal. However, a blind eye is generally turned to the trade as the possession and purchase of small amounts (5g) of 'soft drugs' (ie marijuana and hashish) is allowed and users won't be prosecuted for smoking or carrying this amount. Don't take this relaxed attitude as an invitation to buy harder drugs; if you get caught, you'll be punished. Since 2008 magic mushrooms have been banned in the Netherlands.

Spain also has pretty liberal laws regarding marijuana although its use is usually reserved for private 'cannabis clubs'.

Switzerland, Portugal, Austria and the Czech Republic have decriminalised possession of marijuana; however, selling remains illegal.

Getting caught with drugs in some parts of Europe can lead to imprisonment. If in any doubt, err on the side of caution, and don't even think about taking drugs across international borders.

Maps

Tourist offices usually provide free but fairly basic maps.

Road atlases are essential if you're driving or cycling. Leading brands are Freytag & Berndt, Hallwag, Kümmerly + Frey and Michelin.

Maps published by European automobile associations, such as Britain's **AA** (www.theaa.co.uk) and Germany's **ADAC** (www.adac.de), are usually excellent and sometimes free if membership of your local association gives you reciprocal rights.

Money

ATMs

Across major European towns and cities international ATMs are common, but you should always have a back-up option, as there can be glitches. In some remote areas, ATMs might be scarce.

Much of Western Europe now uses a chip-and-pin system for added security. You will have problems if you don't have a four-digit PIN number and might have difficulties if your card doesn't have a metallic chip. Check with your bank.

Always cover the keypad when entering your PIN and make sure there are no unusual devices attached to the machine, which can copy your card's details or cause it to stick in the machine. If your card disappears and the screen goes blank before you've even entered your PIN, don't enter it –

especially a 'helpful' by-stander tells you to *jump*. If you can't retrieve your card, call your bank's emergency number, if you can, before leaving the ATM.

Cash

It's a good idea to bring some local currency in cash, if only to cover yourself until you get to an exchange facility or find an ATM. The equivalent of €150 should usually be enough. Some extra cash in an easily exchanged currency is also a good idea, especially in Eastern Europe.

Credit Cards

Visa and MasterCard/Eurocard are more widely accepted in Europe than Amex and Diners Club; Visa (sometimes called Carte Bleue) is particularly strong in France and Spain.

There are, however, regional differences in the general acceptability of credit cards; in Germany, for example, it's rare for restaurants to take credit cards. Cards are not widely accepted once you're off the beaten track.

To reduce the risk of fraud, always keep your card in view when making transactions; for example, in restaurants that do accept cards, pay as you leave, following your card to the till. Keep transaction records and either check your statements when you return home, or check your account online while still on the road.

Letting your credit-card company know roughly where you're going lessens the chance of fraud – or of your bank cutting off the card when it sees (your) unusual spending.

Currency

Apart from Denmark, Switzerland and the UK (which have their own currencies), all the countries covered in this guide use the euro, which is made up of 100 cents. Notes come in denominations of €5, €10, €20, €50, €100, €200 and €500 euros, though any notes above €50 are rarely used on a daily basis. Coins come in 1c, 2c, 5c, 10c, 20c, 50c, €1 and €2.

Debit Cards

It's always worthwhile having a Maestro-compatible debit card, which differs from a credit card in deducting money straight from your bank account. Check with your bank or Master-Card (Maestro's parent) for compatibility.

Exchanging Money

Euros, US dollars and UK pounds are the easiest currencies to exchange. You may have trouble exchanging some lesser-known ones at small banks.

Importing or exporting some currencies is restricted or banned, so try to get rid of any local currency before you leave. Get rid of Scottish pounds before leaving the UK; nobody outside Britain will touch them.

Most airports, central train stations, big hotels and many border posts have banking facilities outside regular business hours, at times on a 24-hour basis. Post offices in Europe often perform banking tasks, tend to open longer hours and outnumber banks in remote places. While they always exchange cash, they might balk at handling travellers cheques not in the local currency.

The best exchange rates are usually at banks. *Bureaux de change* usually – but not always – offer worse rates or charge higher commissions. Hotels and airports are almost always the worst places to change money.

International Transfers

International bank transfers are good for secure one-off movements of large amounts of money, but they might take three to five days and there will be a fee (about £25 in the UK, for example). Be sure to specify the name of the bank, plus the sort code and address of the branch where you'd like to pick up your money.

In an emergency it's quicker but more costly to have money wired via an Amex office (www.american express.com), Western Union (www.westernunion. com) or MoneyGram (www. moneygram.com).

Taxes & Refunds

When non-EU residents spend more than a certai

amount (around €75, but amounts vary from country to country), they can usually reclaim any sales tax when leaving the country.

Making a tax-back claim is straightforward. First, make sure the shop offers duty-free sales (often a sign will be displayed reading 'Tax-Free Shopping'). When making your purchase, ask the shop attendant for a tax-refund voucher, filled in with the correct amount and the date. This can be used to claim a refund directly at international airports, or stamped at ferry ports or border crossings and mailed back for a refund.

Tipping

○ 'Service charges' are increasingly added to bills. In theory this means you're not obliged to tip. In practice that money often doesn't go to the server. Don't pay twice. If the service charge is optional, remove it and pay a tip. If it's not optional, don't tip.

○ Tipping isn't such a big deal in Europe as it is say in North America. If you tip, 5% to 10% will usually suffice.

Travellers Cheques

It's become more difficult to find places that cash travellers cheques. In parts of Eastern Europe only a few banks handle them, and the process can be quite bureaucratic and costly.

That said, having a few cheques is a good back-up. If they're stolen you can claim a refund, provided you

have a separate record of cheque numbers.

Amex and Thomas Cook are reliable brands of travellers cheques, while cheques in US dollars, euros or British pounds are the easiest to cash. When changing them ask about fees and commissions as well as the exchange rate.

Opening Hours

Opening times vary significantly between countries. The following is a general overview.

Shops & Businesses 9am–6pm Monday to Friday, to 1pm or 5pm Saturday. In smaller towns there may be a one- to two-hour closure for lunch. Some shops close on Sunday. Businesses also close on national holidays and local feast days.

Banks 9am to between 3pm and 5pm Monday to Friday. Occasionally shut for lunch.

Restaurants noon to midnight

Bars 6pm to midnight or later.

Museums close Monday or (less commonly) Tuesday.

Post

From major European centres, airmail typically takes about five days to North America and about a week to Australasian destinations.

Courier services such as DHL are best for essential deliveries.

Public Holidays

There are large variations in statutory holidays in Europe. The following are the most common across the board:

New Year's Day 1 January

Good Friday March/April

Easter Sunday March/April

May Day 1 May

Pentecost/Whitsun May/June

Christmas Day 25 December

Safe Travel

Travelling in Europe is usually very safe.

Discrimination

In some parts of Europe travellers of African, Arab or Asian descent might encounter unpleasant attitudes that are unrelated to them personally. In rural areas travellers whose skin colour marks them out as foreigners might experience unwanted attention.

Attitudes vary from country to country. People tend to be more accepting in cities than in the country.

Druggings

Although rare, some drugging of travellers does occur in Europe. Travellers are especially vulnerable on trains and buses where a new 'friend' may offer you food or a drink that will knock you out, giving them *(uuu to* steal your belongings.

Gassings have also been reported on a handful of overnight international trains. The best protection is to lock the door of your compartment (use your own lock if there isn't one) and to lock your bags to luggage racks, preferably with a sturdy combination cable.

If you can help it, never sleep alone in a train compartment.

Pickpockets & Thieves

Theft is definitely a problem in parts of Europe and you have to be aware of unscrupulous fellow travellers. The key is to be sensible with your possessions.

○ Don't store valuables in train-station lockers or luggage-storage counters and be careful about people who offer to help you operate a locker. Also be vigilant if someone offers to carry your luggage: they might carry it away altogether.

○ Don't leave valuables in your car, on train seats or in your room. When going out, don't flaunt cameras,

laptops and other expensive electronic goods.

○ Carry a small day pack, as shoulder bags are an open invitation for snatch-thieves. Consider using small zipper locks on your packs.

○ Pickpockets are most active in dense crowds, especially in busy train stations and on public transport during peak hours. Be careful in these situations.

○ Spread valuables, cash and cards around your body or in different bags.

○ A money belt with your essentials (passport, cash, credit cards, airline tickets) is usually a good idea. However, so you needn't delve into it in public, carry a wallet with a day's worth of cash.

○ Having your passport stolen is less of a disaster if you've recorded the number and issue date or, even better, photocopied the relevant data pages. You can also scan them and email them to yourself. If you lose your passport, notify the police immediately to get a statement and contact your nearest consulate.

○ Carry photocopies of your credit cards, airline tickets and other travel documents.

Unrest & Terrorism

Civil unrest and terrorist bombings are relatively rare in Europe, all things considered, but they do occur. Attacks by Muslim extremists in the UK, France and Germany have occurred in recent years. Keep an eye

on the news and avoid areas where any flare-up seems likely.

Telephone

Mobile Phones

If your mobile phone is European, it's often perfectly feasible to use it on roaming throughout the Continent.

If you're coming from outside Europe, it's usually worth buying a prepaid local SIM in one European country. Even if you're not staying there long, calls across Europe will still be cheaper if they're not routed via your home country and the prepaid card will enable you to keep a limit on your spending. In several countries you need your passport to buy a SIM card.

In order to use other SIM cards in your phone, you'll need to have your handset unlocked by your home provider. Even if your phone is locked, you can use apps such as 'whatsapp' to send free text messages internationally wherever you have wi-fi access, or Skype to make free international calls whenever you're online.

Europe uses the GSM 900 network, which also covers Australia and New Zealand, but is not compatible with the North American GSM 1900 or the totally different system in Japan and South Korea. If you have a GSM phone, check with your service provider a...

using it in Europe. You'll need international roaming, but this is usually free to enable.

You can call abroad from almost any phone box in Europe. Public telephones accepting phonecards (available from post offices, telephone centres, news stands or retail outlets) are virtually the norm now; coin-operated phones are rare if not impossible to find.

Without a phonecard, you can ring from a telephone booth inside a post office or telephone centre and settle your bill at the counter. Reverse-charge (collect) calls are often possible. From many countries the Country Direct system lets you phone home by billing the long-distance carrier you use at home. These numbers can often be dialled from public phones without even inserting a phonecard.

Time

Europe is divided into four time zones. The countries covered in this guide fall into the following zones:

UTC (Coordinated Universal Time; Britain, Ireland, Portugal) the same as GMT (GMT+1 in summer)

ET (Central European Time; the majority of European countries) GMT+1 (GMT+2 in summer)

At 9am in Britain it's 1am (GMT/UTC minus eight hours) on the US west coast, 4am (GMT/UTC minus five hours) on the US east coast, 10am in Paris and Prague, 11am in Athens, midday in Moscow and 7pm (GMT/UTC plus 10 hours) in Sydney.

Nearly all of Europe, with several exceptions (including Iceland), observes daylight saving time on synchronised dates in late March (clocks go forward an hour) and late October (clocks go back an hour).

Toilets

Many public toilets require a small fee either deposited in a box or given to the attendant. Sit-down toilets are the rule in the vast majority of places. Squat toilets can still be found in rural areas, although they are definitely a dying breed.

Public-toilet provision is changeable from city to city. If you can't find one, simply drop into a hotel or restaurant and ask to use theirs.

Tourist Information

Unless otherwise indicated, tourist offices are common and widespread, although their usefulness varies enormously.

Travellers with Disabilities

Cobbled medieval streets, 'classic' hotels, congested inner cities and underground subway systems make Europe a tricky destination for people with mobility impairments. However, the train facilities are good and some destinations boast new tram services or lifts to platforms. Download Lonely Planet's free Accessible Travel guide from http://lptravel.to/AccessibleTravel. The following websites can help with specific details:

Accessible Europe (www.accessibleurope.com) Specialist European tours with van transport.

Mobility International Schweiz (www.mis-ch.ch) Good site (only partly in English) listing 'barrier-free' destinations in Switzerland and abroad, plus wheelchair-accessible hotels in Switzerland.

Mobility International USA (www.miusa.org) Publishes guides and advises travellers with disabilities on mobility issues.

DisabledGo.com (www.disabledgo.com) Detailed access information on thousands of venues across the UK and Ireland.

Society for Accessible Travel & Hospitality (SATH; www.sath.org) Reams of information for travellers with disabilities.

The Schengen Area

Twenty-six European countries are signatories to the Schengen Agreement, which has effectively dismantled internal border controls between them. They are Austria, Belgium, Czech Republic, Denmark, Estonia, Finland, France, Germany, Greece, Iceland, Italy, Hungary, Latvia, Liechtenstein, Lithuania, Luxembourg, Malta, the Netherlands, Norway, Poland, Portugal, Slovenia, Slovakia, Spain, Sweden and Switzerland.

The UK and Ireland, as well as much of Eastern Europe, are not part of the Schengen Agreement. Visitors from non-EU countries will have to apply for visas to these countries separately.

Citizens of the US, Australia, New Zealand, Canada and the UK only need a valid passport to enter Schengen countries (as well as the UK and Ireland). However, other nationals, including South Africans, can apply for a single visa – a Schengen visa – when travelling throughout this region.

Non-EU visitors (with or without a Schengen visa) should expect to be questioned, however perfunctorily, when first entering the region. However, later travel within the zone is much like a domestic trip, with no border controls.

If you need a Schengen visa, you must apply at the consulate or embassy of the country that's your main destination, or your point of entry. You may then stay up to a maximum of 90 days in the entire Schengen area within a six-month period. Once your visa has expired, you must leave the zone and may only re-enter after three months abroad. Shop around when choosing your point of entry, as visa prices may differ from country to country.

If you're a citizen of the US, Australia, New Zealand or Canada, you may stay visa-free a total of 90 days, during six months, within the entire Schengen region.

For up-to-date details see www.schengenvisainfo.com.

Visas

◦ Citizens of the USA, Canada, Australia, New Zealand and the UK need only a valid passport to enter nearly all countries in Europe, including the entire EU.

◦ Transit visas are usually cheaper than tourist or business visas but they allow only a very short stay (one to five days) and can be difficult to extend.

◦ All visas have a 'use-by' date and you'll be refused entry afterwards. In some cases it's easier to get visas as you go along, rather than arranging them all beforehand. Carry spare passport photos (you may need from one to four every time you apply for a visa).

◦ Visas to neighbouring countries are usually issued immediately by consulates in Eastern Europe, although some may levy a hefty surcharge for 'express service'.

◦ Consulates are generally open weekday mornings (if there's both an embassy and a consulate, you want the consulate).

◦ Because regulations can change, double-check with the relevant embassy or consulate before travelling.

Women Travellers

◦ Women might attract unwanted attention in rural Spain and southern Italy where many men view whistling and catcalling as flattery. Conservative dress can help to deter lascivious gazes and wolf whistles; dark sunglasses help avoid unwanted eye contact.

◦ Marriage is highly respected in southern Europe, and a wedding ring can help along with talk about 'my husband'.

◦ Hitchhiking alone is not recommended anywher

○ **Journeywoman** (www.journeywoman.com) maintains an online newsletter about solo female travels all over the world.

Transport

Getting There & Away

Europe is one of the world's major destinations; sporting many of its busiest airports with routes fanning out to the far corners of the globe. More adventurous travellers can enter from Asia on some epic long-distance train routes. Numerous ferries jockey across the Mediterranean between Europe and Africa.

Flights, cars and tours can be booked online at lonelyplanet.com/bookings.

Air

Airports & Airlines

To save money, it's best to travel off-season. This means, if possible, avoid mid-June to early September, Easter, Christmas and school holidays.

Regardless of your ultimate destination, it's sometimes better to pick a recognised transport 'hub' as your initial port of entry, where high traffic volumes help keep prices down. Long-haul airfares to Eastern Europe are rarely a bargain; you're usually better flying to a Western European hub and taking an onward budget-airline flight or train. The main hubs in Eastern Europe are Budapest and Prague.

Gateway cities such as London and Paris are also well serviced by low-cost carriers that fly to other parts of Europe.

Land

It's possible to reach Europe by various different train routes from Asia. Most common is the Trans-Siberian Railway, connecting Moscow to Siberia, the Russian Far East, Mongolia and China. See www.seat61.com for more information about these adventurous routes.

Border Crossings

Border formalities have been relaxed in most of the EU, but still exist in all their original bureaucratic glory in the more far-flung parts of Eastern Europe.

In line with the Schengen Agreement (p629), there are officially no passport controls at the borders between 26 European states. Sometimes, however, there are spot checks on trains crossing borders, so always have your passport. The UK maintains border controls over traffic from other EU countries (except Ireland, with which it shares an open border), although there is no customs control. For up-to-date details see www.schengenvisainfo.com.

Sea

There are numerous ferry routes between Europe and Africa, including links from Spain to Morocco, Italy to Tunisia, France to Morocco and France to Tunisia. Check out www.traghettiweb.it for comprehensive information on all Mediterranean ferries. Ferries are often filled to capacity in summer, especially to and from Tunisia, so book well in advance if you're taking a vehicle across.

Climate Change & Travel

Every form of transport that relies on carbon-based fuel generates CO_2, the main cause of human-induced climate change. Modern travel is dependent on aeroplanes, which might use less fuel per kilometre per person than most cars but travel much greater distances. The altitude at which aircraft emit gases (including CO_2) and particles also contributes to their climate change impact. Many websites offer 'carbon calculators' that allow people to estimate the carbon emissions generated by their journey and, for those who wish to do so, to offset the impact of the greenhouse gases emitted with contributions to portfolios of climate-friendly initiatives throughout the world. Lonely Planet offsets the carbon footprint of all staff and author travel.

Passenger freig//(u//.
(typically carrying up to 12
passengers) aren't nearly
as competitively priced
as airlines. Journeys also
take a long time. However,
if you have your heart set
on a transatlantic journey,
**TravLtips Cruise and
Freighter** (www.travltips.
com) has information on
freighter cruises.

Getting Around

Air

Airlines

Low-cost carriers have
revolutionised European
transport. Most airlines,
budget or otherwise, have
a similar pricing system –
namely that ticket prices
rise with the number of
seats sold on each flight, so
book as early as possible to
get a decent fare.

Some low-cost carriers
– Ryanair being the prime
example – have made a
habit of flying to smaller,
less convenient airports
on the outskirts of their
destination city, or even to
the airports of nearby cities,
so check the exact location
of the departure and arrival
airports before you book.
Many flights also leave at
the crack of dawn or arrive
inconveniently late at night.

Departure and other tax-
es (including booking fees,
checked-baggage fees and
other surcharges) soon add
up and are included in the
final price by the end of the

online booking process –
//(u/)ally a lot more than you
we/e b//(//ing to pay – but
with careful U//(//cing and
advance booking y(u (///(/
get great deals.

For a comprehensive
overview of which low-cost
carriers fly to or from which
European cities, check
out the excellent www.
flycheapo.com.

Air Passes

Various travel agencies and
airlines offer air passes
including the three main
airline alliances: **Oneworld**
(www.oneworld.com), **Star
Alliance** (www.staralliance.
com) and **SkyTeam** (www.
Jryteam.com). Check with
you(H A/p/ agent for current
promotions.

Bicycle

Much of Europe is ideally
suited to cycling. It's easy to
hire bikes throughout most
of Europe but, for major
cycling trips, it's best to have
a bike you're familiar with, so
consider bringing your own
rather than buying on arrival.
If coming from outside Europe, ask about the airline's
policy on transporting bikes
before buying your ticket

A primary consideration
on a cycling trip is to travel
light, but you should take a
few tools and spare parts,
including a puncture-repair
kit and a extra inner tube.
Panniers are essential to
balance your possessions on
either side of the bike frame.
Wearing a helmet is not compulsory in most countries,
but is certainly sensible.

Seasoned cyclists can
average 80km a day, but
it depends on what you're
carrying and your level of
fitness.

(/r/ists' Touring Club (CTC;
www.U/o //(/(g/)k) The national
cycling assoc/u/(/(/ of the UK
runs organised trips to C(//(/
nental Europe.

European Cyclists' Federation
(www.ecf.com) Has details of
'EuroVelo', the European cycle
network of 12 pan-European
cycle routes, plus tips for other
tours.

SwitzerlandMobility (www.
veloland.ch/en/cycling-in-
switzerland.html) Details of
Swiss national routes and more.

Boat

Several different ferry
companies compete on the
main ferry routes, resulting in
a w/(/(prehensive but complicated se/ w//(/. The same ferry
company can ha(/u //(//(st of
different prices for the sa(/(/
route, depending on the time
of day or year, validity of the
ticket and length of your vehicle. Vehicle tickets usually
include the driver and often
up to five passengers free of
charge.

It's worth booking ahead
where possible as there
may be special reductions
on off-peak crossings
and advance-purchase
tickets. On English Channel
routes, apart from one-day
or short-term excursion
returns, there is little price
advantage in buying a ret(/
ticket versus two singles

Rail-pass holders are
entitled to discounts o(
travel on some lines. F

on ferries is often expensive (and lousy), so it is worth bringing your own. Also be aware that if you take your vehicle on board, you are usually denied access to it during the voyage.

Lake and river ferry services operate in many countries, Austria and Switzerland being just two. Some of these are very scenic.

Bus

International Buses

Europe's biggest organisation of international buses operates under the name **Eurolines** (www.eurolines. com), comprised of various national companies. A **Eurolines Pass** (www.eurolines. com/en/eurolines-pass) is offered for extensive travel, allowing passengers to visit a choice of 53 cities across Europe over 15 or 30 days. In the high season (mid-June to mid-September) the pass costs €315/405 for those aged under 26, or €375/490 for those 26 and over. It's cheaper in other periods.

Busabout (www. busabout.com) offers a 'hop-on, hop-off' service around Europe, stopping at major cities. Buses are often oversubscribed, so book each sector to avoid being stranded. It departs every two days from May to the end of October.

ational Buses

mestic buses provide a le alternative to trains in countries. Again, they ually slightly cheaper newhat slower.

Buses are generally best for short hops, such as getting around cities and reaching remote villages, and they are often the only option in mountainous regions.

Reservations are rarely necessary. On many city buses you usually buy your ticket in advance from a kiosk or machine and validate it on entering the bus.

Car & Motorcycle

Travelling with your own vehicle gives flexibility and is the best way to reach remote places. However, the independence does sometimes isolate you from local life. Also, cars can be a target for theft and are often impractical in city centres, where traffic jams, parking problems and getting thoroughly lost can make it well worth ditching your vehicle and using public transport. Various car-carrying trains can help you avoid long, tiring drives.

Campervan

One popular way to tour Europe is for a group of three or four people to band together and buy or rent a campervan. London is the usual embarkation point. Look at the ads in London's free magazine *TNT* (www. tntmagazine.com) if you wish to form or join a group. *TNT* is also a good source for purchasing a van, as is Loot (www.loot.com).

Some secondhand dealers offer a 'buy-back' scheme for when you return from the Continent, but check the small print

before signing anything and remember that if an offer is too good to be true, it probably is. Buying and reselling privately should be more advantageous if you have time. In the UK, DUInsure (www.duinsure.com) offers a campervan policy.

Motorcycle Touring

Europe is made for motorcycle touring, with quality winding roads, stunning scenery and an active motorcycling scene. Just make sure your wet-weather motorcycling gear is up to scratch.

o Rider and passenger crash helmets are compulsory everywhere in Europe.

o Austria, France, Germany, Portugal and Spain require that motorcyclists use headlights during the day; in other countries it is recommended.

o On ferries, motorcyclists rarely have to book ahead as they can generally be squeezed on board.

o Take note of the local custom about parking motorcycles on pavements (sidewalks). Though this is illegal in some countries, the police often turn a blind eye provided the vehicle doesn't obstruct pedestrians.

Fuel

o Fuel prices can vary enormously (though fuel is always more expensive than in North America or Australia).

o Unleaded petrol only is available throughout

Europe. Diesel is usually cheaper, though the difference is marginal in Britain, Ireland and Switzerland.

○ Ireland's Automobile Association maintains a webpage of European fuel prices at www.theaa.ie/aa/motoring-advice/petrol-prices.aspx.

Insurance

○ Third-party motor insurance is compulsory. Most UK policies automatically provide this for EU countries. Get your insurer to issue a Green Card (which may cost extra), an internationally recognised proof of insurance, and check that it lists every country you intend to visit. You'll need this in the event of an accident outside the country where the vehicle is insured.

○ Ask your insurer for a European Accident Statement form, which can simplify things if worst comes to worst. Never sign statements that you can't read or understand – insist on a translation and sign that only if it's acceptable.

○ For non-EU countries, check the requirements with your insurer. Travellers from the UK can obtain additional advice and information from the **Association of British Insurers** (www.abi.org.uk).

○ Take out a European motoring assistance policy. Non-Europeans might find it cheaper to arrange international coverage with their national motoring organisation before leaving

home. Ask your motoring organisation for details about the free services offered by affiliated organisations around Europe.

○ Residents of the UK should contact the **RAC** (www.rac.co.uk) or the **AA** (www.theaa.co.uk) for more information. Residents of the US, contact **AAA** (www.aaa.com).

Rental

○ Renting a car is ideal for people who will need cars for 16 days or less. Anything longer, it's better to lease.

○ Big international rental firms will give you reliable service and good vehicles. National or local firms can often undercut the big companies by up to 40%.

○ Usually you will have the option of returning the car to a different outlet at the end of the rental period, but there's normally a charge for this and it can be very steep if it's a long way from your point of origin.

○ Book early for the lowest rates and make sure you compare rates in different cities. Taxes range from 15% to 20% and surcharges apply if rented from an airport.

○ If you rent a car in the EU you might not be able to take it outside the EU, and if you rent the car outside the EU, you will only be able to drive within the EU for eight days. Ask at the rental agencies for other such regulations.

○ Make sure you understand what is included

in the price (unlimited or paid kilometres, tax, injury insurance, collision damage waiver etc) and what your liabilities are. We recommend taking the collision damage waiver, though you can probably skip the injury insurance if you and your passengers have decent travel insurance.

○ The minimum rental age is usually 21 years and sometimes 25. You'll need a credit card and to have held your licence for at least a year.

○ Motorcycle and moped rental is common in some countries, such as Italy, Spain, Greece and southern France.

Road Conditions & Road Rules

○ Conditions and types of roads vary across Europe. The fastest roads are generally four- or six-lane highways known locally as motorways, autoroutes, autostrade, autobahnen etc. These tend to skirt cities and plough through the countryside in straight lines, often avoiding the most scenic bits.

○ Some highways incur tolls, which are often quite hefty (especially in Italy, France and Spain), but there will always be an alternative route. Motorways and other primary routes are generally in good condition.

○ Road surfaces on minor routes are unreliable in some countries (eg parts of eastern Europe and Ireland), although normally they will be more than adequate.

○ Except in Britain and Ireland, you should drive on the right. Vehicles brought to the continent from any of these locales should have their headlights adjusted to avoid blinding oncoming traffic (a simple solution on older headlight lenses is to cover up a triangular section of the lens with tape). Priority is often given to traffic approaching from the right in countries that drive on the right-hand side.

○ Speed limits vary from country to country. You may be surprised at the apparent disregard for traffic regulations in some places (particularly in Italy and Greece), but as a visitor it is always best to be cautious. Many driving infringements are subject to an on-the-spot fine. Always ask for a receipt.

○ European drink-driving laws are particularly strict. The blood-alcohol concentration (BAC) limit when driving is usually between 0.05% and 0.08%, but in certain areas it can be zero.

○ Always carry proof of ownership of your vehicle (Vehicle Registration Document for British-registered cars). An EU driving licence is acceptable for those driving through Europe. If you have any other type of licence, you should obtain an International Driving Permit (IDP) from your motoring organisation. Check what type of licence is required in your destination prior to departure.

○ Every vehicle that travels across an international border should display a sticker indicating its country of registration. A warning triangle, to be used in the event of breakdown, is compulsory almost everywhere.

○ Some recommended accessories include a first-aid kit (compulsory in Austria and Croatia), a spare bulb kit (compulsory in Spain), a reflective jacket for every person in the car (compulsory in France, Italy and Spain) and a fire extinguisher.

Local Transport

European towns and cities have excellent local-transport systems, often encompassing trams as well as buses and underground-rail networks.

Most travellers will find areas of interest in European cities can be easily traversed by foot or bicycle. A growing number of European cities have bike-sharing schemes where you can casually borrow a bike from a docking station for short hops around the city for a small cost.

In Italy travellers sometimes rent mopeds and motorcycles for scooting around a city or island.

Taxi

Taxis in Europe are metered and rates are usually high. There might also be supplements for things such as luggage, time of day, location of pick-up and extra passengers.

Good bus, rail and under-ground-railway networks often render taxis unnecessary, but if you need one in a hurry, they can be found idling near train stations or outside big hotels. Lower fares make taxis more viable in some countries such as Spain and Portugal.

Train

Comfortable, frequent and reliable, trains are the way to get around Europe.

○ Many state railways have interactive websites publishing their timetables and fares, including www.bahn.de (Germany) and www.sbb.ch (Switzerland), which both have pages in English. **Eurail** (www.eurail.com) links to 28 European train companies.

○ **The Man in Seat 61** (www.seat61.com) is very comprehensive and a gem, while the US-based **Budget Europe Travel Service** (www.budgeteuropetravel.com) can also help with tips.

○ European trains sometimes split en route to service two destinations, so even if you're on the right train, make sure you're also in the correct carriage.

○ A train journey to almost every station in Europe can be booked via Voyages-sncf.com (http://uk.voyages-sncf.com/en), which also sells InterRail and other passes.

Language

Don't let the language barrier get in the way of your travel experience. This section offers basic phrases and pronunciation guides to help you negotiate your way around Europe. Note that in our pronunciation guides, the stressed syllables in words are indicated with italics.

To enhance your trip with a phrasebook (covering all of these languages in much greater detail), visit **lonelyplanet.com**.

Czech

Hello.	*Ahoj.*	uh·hoy
Goodbye.		
Na shledanou.	nuh·skhle·duh·roh	
Yes./No.	*Ano./Ne.*	uh·no/ne
Please.	*Prosím.*	pro·seem
Thank you.	*Děkuji.*	dye·ku·yi
Excuse me.	*Promiňte.*	pro·min'·te
Help!	*Pomoc!*	po·mots

Do you speak English?
Mluvíte anglicky? mlu·vee·te uhn·glits·ki
I don't understand.
Nerozumím. ne·ro·zu·meem
How much is this?
Kolik to stojí? ko·lik to sto·yee
I'd like ..., please.
Chtěl/Chtěla bych ..., khtyel/khtye·luh bikh ...
prosím. (m/f) pro·seem
Where's (the toilet)?
Kde je (záchod)? gde ye (za·khod)
I'm lost.
Zabloudil/ zuh·bloh·dyil/
Zabloudila jsem. (m/f) zuh·bloh·dyi·luh ysem

Dutch

Hello.	*Dag.*	dakh
Goodbye.	*Dag.*	dakh
Yes.	*Ja.*	yaa
No.	*Nee.*	ney
Please.	*Alstublieft.*	al·stew·*bleeft*
Thank you.	*Dank u.*	dangk ew
Excuse me.	*Excuseer mij.*	eks·kew·*zeyr* mey
Help!	*Help!*	help

Do you speak English?
Spreekt u Engels? spreykt ew eng·uhls
I don't understand.
Ik begrijp het niet. ik buh·*khreyp* huht neet
How much is this?
Hoeveel kost het? hoo·*veyl* kost huht
I'd like ..., please.
Ik wil graag ... ik wil khraakh ...
Where's (the toilet)?
Waar zijn waar zeyn
(de toiletten)? (duh twa·*le*·tuhn)
I'm lost.
Ik ben verdwaald. ik ben vuhr·*dwaalt*

French

Hello.	*Bonjour.*	bon·zhoor
Goodbye.	*Au revoir.*	o·rer·vwa
Yes.	*Oui.*	wee
No.	*Non.*	noh
Please.	*S'il vous*	seel voo
	plaît.	play
Thank you.	*Merci.*	mair·see
Excuse me.	*Excusez-moi.*	
	ek·skew·zay·mwa	
Help!	*Au secours!*	o skoor

Do you speak English?
Parlez-vous anglais? par·lay·voo ong·glay
I don't understand.
Je ne comprends pas. zher ner kom·pron pa
How much is this?
C'est combien? say kom·byun
I'd like ..., please.
Je voudrais ..., zher voo·dray ...
s'il vous plaît. seel voo play
Where's (the toilet)?
Où sont oo son
(les toilettes)? (lay twa·let)
I'm lost.
Je suis perdu(e). (m/f) zhe swee·pair·dew

German

Hello.	*Guten Tag.*	goo·ten taak
Goodbye.	*Auf Wiedersehen.*	owf vee·der·zey·en
Yes.	*Ja.*	yaa
No.	*Nein.*	nain
Please.	*Bitte.*	bi·te
Thank you.	*Danke.*	dang·ke
Excuse me.	*Entschuldigung.*	ent·shul·di·gung
Help!	*Hilfe!*	hil·fe

Do you speak English?
Sprechen Sie Englisch? shpre·khen zee eng·lish
I don't understand.
Ich verstehe nicht. ikh fer·shtey·e nikht
How much is this?
Was kostet das? vas kos·tet das
I'd like ..., please.
Ich hätte gern ..., bitte. ikh he·te gern ... bi·te
Where's (the toilet)?
Wo ist (die Toilette)? vaw ist (dee to·a·le·te)
I'm lost.
Ich habe mich verirrt. ikh haa·be mikh fer·irt

Icelandic

Hello.	*Halló.*	ha·loh
Goodbye.	*Bless.*	bles
Yes.	*Já.*	yow
No.	*Nei.*	nay
Thank you.	*Takk./ Takk fyrir.*	tak/ tak fi·rir
Excuse me.	*Afsakið.*	af·sa·kidh
Help!	*Hjálp!*	hyowlp

Do you speak English?
Talar þú ensku? ta·lar thoo ens·ku
I don't understand.
Ég skil ekki. yekh skil e·ki
How much is this?
Hvað kostar þetta? kvadh kos·tar the·ta
I'd like a/the..., please.
...fengið..., takk get yekh fen·gidh..., tak
Where's (the toilet)?
...vrtingin? kvar er snir·tin·gin
I'm lost.
...illt. (m/f) yekh er vil·tur/vilt

Italian

Hello.	*Buongiorno.*	bwon·jor·no
Goodbye.	*Arrivederci.*	a·ree·ve·der·chee
Yes.	*Sì.*	see
No.	*No.*	no
Please.	*Per favore.*	per fa·vo·re
Thank you.	*Grazie.*	gra·tsye
Excuse me.	*Mi scusi.*	mee skoo·zee
Help!	*Aiuto!*	a·yoo·to

Do you speak English?
Parla inglese? par·la een·gle·ze
I don't understand.
Non capisco. non ka·pee·sko
How much is this?
Quanto costa? kwan·to ko·sta
I'd like ..., please.
Vorrei ..., per favore. vo·ray ... per fa·vo·re
Where's (the toilet)?
Dove sono (i gabinetti)? do·ve so·no (ee ga·bee·ne·ti)
I'm lost.
Mi sono perso/a. (m/f) mee so·no per·so/a

Spanish

Hello.	*Hola.*	o·la
Goodbye.	*Adiós.*	a·dyos
Yes.	*Sí.*	see
No.	*No.*	no
Please.	*Por favor.*	por fa·vor
Thank you.	*Gracias.*	gra·thyas
Excuse me.	*Disculpe.*	dees·kool·pe
Help!	*¡Socorro!*	so·ko·ro

Do you speak English?
¿Habla inglés? a·bla een·gles
I don't understand.
No entiendo. no en·tyen·do
How much is this?
¿Cuánto cuesta? kwan·to kwes·ta
I'd like ..., please.
Quisiera ..., por favor. kee·sye·ra ... por fa·vor
Where's (the toilet)?
¿Dónde están (los servicios)? don·de es·tan (los ser·vee·thyos)
I'm lost.
Estoy perdido/a. (m/f) es·toy per·dee·do/a

Behind the Scenes

Acknowledgements

Climate map data adapted from Peel MC, Finlayson BL & McMahon TA (2007) 'Updated World Map of the Köppen-Geiger Climate Classification', Hydrology and Earth System Sciences, 11, 1633–44.

Illustrations pp214–15, pp220–1, 224–5, pp276–7, pp376–7 and pp468–9 by Javier Zarracina.

This Book

This guidebook was researched and written by Alexis Averbuck, Mark Baker, Oliver Berry, Abigail Blasi, Cristian Bonetto, Kerry Christiani, Fionn Davenport, Sally Davies, Peter Dragicevich, Steve Fallon, Emilie Filou, Duncan Garwood, Bridget Gleeson, Paula Hardy, Damian Harper, Anna Kaminski, Catherine Le Nevez, Virginia Maxwell, Craig McLachlan, Josephine Quintero, Kevin Raub, Andrea Schulte-Peevers, Regis St Louis, Nicola Williams, Neil Wilson. This guidebook was produced by the following:

Curators Simon Richmond, Kate Chapman, Sasha Drew, Liz Heynes, Sandie Kestell, Anne Mason, Martine Power, Kathryn Rowan, Jessica Ryan, Tracy Whitney

Destination Editors Daniel Fahey, Gemma Graham, James Smart, Tom Stainer, Anna Tyler, Brana Vladisavljevic

Product Editors Kathryn Rowan, Martine Power

Senior Cartographer Mark Griffiths

Book Designer Katherine Marsh

Assisting Editors Pete Cruttenden, Victoria Harrison, Kate Mathews, Gabrielle Stefanos, Saralinda Turner

Assisting Cartographers Julie Dodkins, Julie Sheridan

Assisting Book Designer Meri Blazevski

Cover Researcher Naomi Parker

Thanks to Carolyn Boicos, Hannah Cartmel, Kate Chapman, Clara Monitto, Jenna Myers, Catherine Naghten, Susan Paterson, Mazzy Prinsep, Kirsten Rawlings, Wibowo Rusli, Tony Wheeler

Send Us Your Feedback

We love to hear from travellers – your comments keep us on our toes and help make our books better. Our well-travelled team reads every word on what you loved or loathed about this book. Although we cannot reply individually to postal submissions, we always guarantee that your feedback goes straight to the appropriate authors, in time for the next edition. Each person who sends us information is thanked in the next edition, the most useful submissions are rewarded with a selection of digital PDF chapters.

Visit lonelyplanet.com/contact to submit your updates and suggestions or to ask for help. Our award-winning website also features inspirational travel stories, news and discussions.

Note: We may edit, reproduce and incorporate your comments in Lonely Planet products such as guidebooks, websites and digital products, so let us know if you don't want your comments reproduced or your name acknowledged. For a copy of our privacy policy visit lonelyplanet.com/privacy.

A–Z

Index

A

Abbey Road Studios 83
accommodation 27, 620-1, see also individual locations
activities 30
air passes 631
air travel 630, 631
airlines 631
Amsterdam 15, 154-75, **155, 162-3, 175**
  accommodation 155, 175
  activities 165-6
  discount cards 173
  drinking & nightlife 170-2
  emergency numbers 173
  entertainment 172-3
  food 167-70
  itineraries 154
  legal matters 173-4
  shopping 166-7
  sights 160-5
  tours 166
  travel to/from 155, 174
  travel within 174
Anglesea Arms 93
Anne Frank Huis 158-9
architecture 29, 609-13
  20th-century 613
  ancient world, the 611-12
  baroque 612
  contemporary 613
  Gaudí, Antoni 270-7, 289, 292, 294-5
  Gothic 612
  Greek 612
  Industrial Age, the 612-13
  Renaissance 612

Roman 612
Romanesque 612
Arezzo 455-8
arts 29, 609-13
  ancient art 609
  cinema 611
  conceptual art 611
  contemporary art 611
  Fauvism 611
  impressionism 610-11
  medieval art 610
  modern 611
  Renaissance, the 610
  romanticism 610-11
ATMs 624-5
Austria 564-85
Avignon 260, **262**

B

Balmoral Castle 108
Barcelona 16, 268-307, **269, 286-7, 290-1, 296, 307**
  accommodation 269, 307
  drinking & nightlife 301-4
  entertainment 304-5
  food 298-301
  itineraries 268
  safety 305
  shopping 297-8, 299
  tourist information 305-6
  tours 297
  travel to/from 269, 306
  travel within 306
  walking tour 286-7, **286-7**
Basilica di San Marco 404-5
Basilique du Sacré-Cœur 229, 232
Basque Country, Spain 22, **309**
  accommodation 309
  itineraries 308
  travel to/from 309
Battle of Culloden 104

beaches
  Berlin 495
  Dubrovnik 479
  Platja de la Barceloneta 294
  Playa de la Concha 325
beer 344, 543
Berlin 11, 486-519, **487, 496-7, 500-1, 507, 508, 519**
  accommodation 487, 519
  drinking 513-16
  entertainment 516-17
  food 509-13
  gay travellers 517
  itineraries 486
  lesbian travellers 517
  nightlife 494-5, 513-16
  shopping 509
  sights 498-508
  tourist information 517
  tours 508-9
  travel to/from 487, 517-18
  travel within 518
  walking tour 496-7, **496-7**
Berlin Wall 488-91, **490-1**
bicycle travel, see cycling
Bilbao 316-23, **318**
Blue Lagoon 180-1
boat travel 630-1, 631-2
Bonaparte, Napoleon 606
Bonnieux 259
books 35
border crossings 630
boulangeries 243
boules 236
bouquinistes 239
Brandenburger Tor 498
breweries
  Brouwerij 't IJ 172
  Brouwerij Troost 171
  Guinness Storehouse 118-9
  Heineken Experience 160
Brexit 600

British Museum 58-61
Buckingham Palace 62-5
Budapest 16, 546-63, **547**, **554-5**
  accommodation 547, 562
  drinking & nightlife 561
  entertainment 562
  food 559-61
  itineraries 546
  shopping 558-9
  sights 552-8
  spas 550-1
  tourist information 562-3
  travel to/from 547, 563
  travel within 563
bus travel 632
business hours 626

C

Canal St-Martin 229
car travel 632-4
  Florence 433
  insurance 633
cash 625
castles & palaces
  Balmoral Castle 108
  Braemar Castle 108
  Brodie Castle 105
  Buckingham Palace 62-5
  Castell de Montjuïc 285
  Castelo de São Jorge 336
  Cawdor Castle 104-5
  Château de Versailles 222-5, **224-5**
  Hofburg 570
  Inverness Castle 105-6
  Kaiserappartements 570
  Monte Urgull 326
  Palau Güell 289, 292
  Palazzo Comunale 459
  Palazzo Ducale 406-7
  Prague Castle 526-9, **533**
  Rosenborg Slot 143
  Royal Palace (Amsterdam) 161
  Royal Palace (Budapest) 548-9

Schloss Belvedere 576-7
Schloss Charlottenburg 506-7
Schloss Hohenschwangau 523
Schloss Neuschwanstein 520-3
Schloss Schönbrunn 566-7
Troja Chateau 544
Urquhart Castle 102-3
Villa Medici 387
cathedrals, see churches & cathedrals
Cavtat 480
celebrity chefs 89
cell phones 26, 627-8
Centro Storico 378-9
Changing of the Guard
  Amalienborg Palace 143
  Buckingham Palace 63
  Prague Castle 527
Charles Bridge 535
Château de Versailles 222-5, **224-5**
cheese 617
Checkpoint Charlie 499
children, travel with 46-7
Christiania 151
churches & cathedrals
  Basilica de Begoña 317
  Basílica de Santa Maria del Mar 292
  Basilica di San Clemente 388
  Basilica di San Giovanni in Laterano 388
  Basilica di San Lorenzo 437
  Basilica di San Marco 404-5
  Basilica di San Pietro in Vincoli 386
  Basilica di Santa Croce 437
  Basilica di Santa Maria della Salute 411
  Basilica di Santa Maria in Trastevere 388
  Basilica di Santa Maria Maggiore 386
  Basilica di Santa Maria Novella 437

Basilica of St Stephen 553
Basilique du Sacré-Cœur 229-32
Berliner Dom 503
Cappella Bacci 455
Chapelle Notre Dame de Beauvoir 266
Chiesa del Gesù 383
Chiesa di Santa Maria della Pieve 455
Christ Church Cathedral 121
Church of Our Lady Before Týn 533
Church of St James 534
Duomo (Florence) 420-3
Duomo (Siena) 452
Duomo di Arezzo 456
Église St-Eustache 228
Església de Santa Maria del Pi 282
Hallgrímskirkja 184
I Frari 411
Igreja & Museu São Roque 340
Kaiser Wilhelm-Gedächtniskirche 507
Karlskirche 576
La Catedral (Barcelona) 288
La Sagrada Família 270-7, **276-7**
Loreta 532
Mosteiro de São Vicente de Fora 337
Nieuwe Kerk 165
Notre Dame 216-21, **220-1**
Sainte-Chapelle 228-9
Sé de Lisboa 337-40
Stephansdom 575
St Nicholas Church 532
St Paul's Cathedral 78
St Peter's Basilica 362-5
St Vitus Cathedral 528
Westminster Abbey 52-7
Churchill War Rooms 75
Claridge's Foyer & Reading Room 90
climate 26, 621

Colosseum 354-7
Copenhagen 24, 136-53, **137**, **144-5**
  accommodation 137
  discount cards 152
  drinking & nightlife 150
  emergency numbers 152
  entertainment 152
  food 148-50
  itineraries 136
  money 152
  postal services 152-3
  shopping 147-8
  sights 142-6
  tourist information 153
  tours 146-7
  travel to/from 137, 153
  travel within 153
costs 27
credit cards 625
Croatia 470-83
currency 625
customs regulations 621-2
cycling 147, 631
Czech Republic 524-45
  language 635

D

dangers, *see* safety
Danube bridges 558
debit cards 625
Denmark 136-53
Designmuseum Danmark 140-1
disabilities, travellers with 628
discrimination 626
distilleries 98-9
drinking 31
drinks 29, 614-18
  Austria 617
  Czech Republic 617-18
  Denmark 618
  France 615-16

Germany 617
Great Britain 614-15
Iceland 618
Ireland 614-15
Italy 616-17
Netherlands, the 615
Portugal 616
Spain 616
Switzerland 617
driving, *see* car travel
druggings 626-7
Drumnadrochit 102
Dublin 19, 114-33, **115**, **122-3**, **126-7**, **133**
  accommodation 115, 133
  drinking & nightlife 129-31
  entertainment 131
  food 128-9
  itineraries 114
  shopping 125-8
  sights 120-5
  tourist information 132
  tours 125
  travel to/from 115, 132
  travel within 132
Dubrovnik 12, 470-83, **471**, **478**
  accommodation 471, 483
  activities 479
  drinking & nightlife 482
  food 480-2
  itineraries 470
  shopping 480
  sights 476-9
  tourist information 482
  tours 480
  travel to/from 471, 483
  travel within 483
Dubrovnik bombing 477
Dubrovnik City Walls 472-3
Duomo (Florence) 420-3

E

Eiffel Tower 204-9
electricity 622

emergencies 627
entertainment 30
etiquette 174
Eurovision Song Contest 601
events, *see* festivals & events
exchanging money 625

F

Ferdinand, Franz 606
festivals & events 32-4
  Il Palio 454
  King's Day 166
  Reykjavík 193
films 35
Florence 25, 418-43, **419**, **430-1**, **434-5**
  accommodation 419
  drinking & nightlife 442
  food 440-1
  internet resources 442
  itineraries 418
  shopping 438-9
  sights 432-8
  tourist information 443
  travel to/from 419, 443
  travel within 443
  walking tour 430-1, **430-1**
fondue 596
food 29, 30-1, 614-18, 622, *see also* celebrity chefs
  Austrian 617
  British 614-15
  Catalan 302
  cheese 617
  Czech 617-18
  Danish 618
  Dutch 615
  fondue 596
  French 615-16
  German 617
  gluten free 244
  Icelandic 618
  Irish 614-15
  Italian 616-17

pintxo bars 312
Portuguese 616
raclette 596
Spanish 616
sweet treats 615
Swiss 617
vegan 618
vegetarian 618
Viennese 580
football 304
Fort George 107
Fort William 110-13
France 202-51, 252-67
   language 635
Frilandsmuseet 152

G

Galleria degli Uffizi 426-9
Galleria dell'Accademia 424-5
Game of Thrones locations
   474-5, 477
   tours 480
gardens, *see* parks & gardens
Gaudí, Antoni 289
   Casa Batlló 294
   La Pedrera 294-5
   La Sagrada Família 270-7
   Palau Güell 289, 292
   Park Güell 294
gay travellers 622
gelato 393
Gellért Baths 551
Germany 486-519, 520-3
   language 636
Glacier Express 590-7
Glen Coe 112
gluten-free food 244
Golden Circle 182-3
gondolas 415
Gordes 258
Gornergratbahn 589
Grand Canal 402-3
Great Britain 50-95, 96-113
Guinness Storehouse 118-19

H

Harrods 86
health 622-3
hiking
   Loch Ness 103
   Zermatt 593-4, 595
historic sites 28
history 602-8
   Battle of Culloden 104
   Dark Ages 604
   economy 608
   empires 606-7
   Enlightenment, the 605-6
   fascism 607
   Greeks 603-4
   Iron Curtain, the 607-8
   Middle Ages 604
   New World, the 605
   prehistory 603
   Reformation, the 605
   Renaissance, the 604-5
   Revolution 606
   Romans 603-4
   unifcation 608
   WWI 606-7
   WWII 607
Hitler, Adolf 607
holidays 626
Holocaust Memorial 498
hot springs, *see* spas
Hungary 546-63

I

Iceland 176-99
   language 636
Il Palio 454
insurance 623
international transfers 625
internet access 624
internet resources 27
   health 623
Inverness 104-10, **105**
Ireland 114-33

Italy 352-99, 400-17, 418-43,
   444-61, 462-9
   language 636
   itineraries 36-45, **36**, **37**, **38**,
   39, **40**, **42-3**, **44-5**

J

Jacobite Steam Train 111
jazz clubs 247
Jordaan 161

K

King's Day 166
Kunsthistorisches Museum
   Vienna 568-9

L

Lacoste 259
land travel 630
languages 458, 635-6
La Pedrera 294-5
La Rambla 278-83
La Sagrada Família 270-7, **276-7**
Las Siete Calles 317
Laugardalur 190
Leaning Tower of Pisa 448-9
legal matters 624
Les Baux-de-Provence 258
lesbian travellers 622
Lisbon 17, 330-49, **331**, **338-9**,
   349
   accommodation 349
   activities 341-2
   drinking & nightlife 346-7
   entertainment 347-8
   food 344-6
   internet resources 347
   itineraries 330
   shopping 343
   sights 336-41
   tourist information 348
   tours 342-3
   travel to/from 331, 348
   travel within 348

live music 130
local transport 634
Loch Ness 100-3
London 6, 50-95, **51**, **72-3**, **76**,
  80-1, **84**, **95**
  accommodation 51, 95
  drinking & nightlife 90-2
  entertainment 92-4
  food 87-90
  itineraries 50
  shopping 86-7
  sights 74-85
  tourist information 94
  tours 85-6
  travel to/from 51, 94
  travel within 94
  walking tour 72-3, **72-3**
Louisiana 148
Louvre, the 210-15, **214-15**

M

maps 624
Margaret Island 553
markets
  Albert Cuypmarkt 160
  Amsterdam 170
  Beriln 510
  Borough Market 78
  Budapest 557
  Camden Market 83
  Colombia Road Flower
    Market 82
  George's Street Arcade 125
  Kolaportið Flea Market 191
  Leadenhall Market 70
  Les Halles 265
  Lisbon 344
  Marché aux Puces de St-Ouen
    238
  Mercado de la Ribera 319
  Mercat de la Boqueria 288
  Mercat de Santa Caterina 293

Nagycsarnok 558
  Paris 240
  Porta Portese Market 391
  Portobello Road Market 87
  Prague 540
  Rialto Market 411
  Vienna 579
  WestMarket 149
Matterhorn 25, 588-9
Ménerbes 259
mobile phones 26, 627-8
Mona Lisa 213
Monet, Claude 209
money 26, 624-5
Montalcino 460
Montepulciano 458-60
Montjuïc 284-5
Mosteiro dos Jerónimos 332-3
motorcycle travel 632-4
Moustiers Ste-Marie 266-7
Mt Vesuvius 467
Museo Guggenheim Bilbao
  310-11
museums & galleries
  Albertina 571
  Alte Nationalgalerie 503
  Art 42 232
  Bauhaus Archiv 505
  Bode-Museum 503
  British Museum 58-61
  Ca' Rezzonico 410
  Capitoline Museums 380
  Castle Museum 549
  Centre Pompidou 228
  Chester Beatty Library 120
  Collection Lambert 261
  Convent of St Agnes 532
  Culture House 184
  DDR Museum 503
  Designmuseum Danmark
    140-1
  Deutsches Historisches
    Museum 498
  Deutsches Technikmuseum
    506

Dublin City Gallery – Hugh
  Lane 120
Dubrovnik During the
  Homeland War 477
Euskal Museoa 317
Frilandsmuseet 152
Fundació Joan Miró 285
Galleria degli Uffizi 426-9
Galleria dell'Accademia 424-5
Galleria Doria Pamphilj 381-3
Gallerie dell'Accademia 410
Gemäldegalerie 505
Glasnevin Cemetery Museum
  121
Grand Palais 229
Grande Museo del Duomo 432
Hamburger Bahnhof –
  Museum für Gegenwart
  502-3
Haus der Musik 576
Heeresgeschichtliches
  Museum 577
Hermitage Amsterdam 164
Hôtel des Invalides 236
House of Terror 552
Hungarian National Gallery
  548
Hungarian National Museum
  556
i8 189
Inverness Museum & Art
  Gallery 104
Irish Museum of Modern Art
  125
Josephinum 576
Jüdisches Museum 506
Kaiserliche Schatzkammer
  570-1
Keats-Shelley House 387
Kunsthistorisches Museum
  Vienna 568-9
Le Grand Musée du Parfum
  229
Leopold Museum 575
Little Museum of Dublin 125
Louisiana 148

Louvre, the 210-15, **214-15**
Matterhorn Museum 592
Mucha Museum 535
MOMOW 575
Museale Santa Maria della
    Scala 452
Musée Angladon 261
Musée d'Orsay 236
Musée du Petit Palais 260-1
Musée du Quai Branly 208
Musée Guimet des Arts
    Asiatiques 208
Musée Marmottan Monet
    209
Musée National du Moyen
    Âge 235
Musée National Picasso 233
Musée Rodin 236
Museo Archeologico Nazion-
    ale 'Gaio Cilnio Mecenate'
    456
Museo Civico 452
Museo Civico & Pinocoteca
    Crociani 458
Museo de Bellas Artes 316
Museo di San Marco 433-6
Museo e Galleria Borghese
    389
Museo Guggenheim Bilbao
    310-11
Museo Nazionale Etrusco di
    Villa Giulia 389-90
Museo Nazionale Romano:
    Palazzo Massimo alle Terme
    386
Museo Novecento 437
Museu Colecção Berardo 341
Museu de Artes Decorativas
    337
Museu d'Història de
    Barcelona 288
Museu d'Història de
    Catalunya 293
Museu do Fado 337
Museu Frederic Marès 289
Museu Marítim 293

Museu Nacional d'Art de
    Catalunya 284
Museu Nacional do Azulejo
    337
Museu Picasso 292-3
Museum für Angewandte
    Kunst 577
Museum für Naturkunde 502
Museum het Rembrandthuis
    161
Museum of Fine Arts 557
Museum of London 77
Museum of Modern &
    Contemporary Art 477
Museum Willet-Holthuysen
    165
Museumsinsel 503
MuseumsQuartier 574
National Gallery 74
National Gallery of Iceland
    185
National Memorial to the
    Heroes of the Heydrich
    Terror 533
National Monument 539
National Museum 178-9
National Museum of Ireland
    – Decorative Arts & History
    120
National Portrait Gallery 74
National Technical Museum
    538
Nationalmuseet 142
Naturhistorisches Museum
    575
Neue Burg Museums 571-4
Neues Museum 503
Ny Carlsberg Glyptotek 142-3
Old Jameson Distillery 124
Palais de Tokyo 208
Palazzo Barberini 387
Palazzo Pitti 436
Palazzo Vecchio 432-3
Peggy Guggenheim Collection
    410
Pergamonmuseum 503

Pinacoteca Nazionale 452-3
Prague City Museum 535
Prague Jewish Museum 532-3
Reykjavik Art Museum 185
Rijksmuseum 160
Sachsenhausen
    Concentration Camp 514
Saga Museum 184
Science Museum 79
Scuola Grande di San Rocco
    410
Secession 576
Settlement Exhibition 189
Sigmund Freud Museum 576
Stasimuseum 513
Statens Museum for Kunst
    143
Stedelijk Museum 165
Story of Berlin 508
Tate Britain 75
Tate Modern 77-8
Topographie des Terrors 504
Van Gogh Museum 156-7
Vatican Museums 366-71
Veletržní Palác 536-8
Victoria & Albert Museum 79
Víkin Maritime Museum 185
War Photo Limited 476-7
West Highland Museum 111
Whales of Iceland 188
Museumsinsel 503
music 35, 613
    Iceland 197

N

National Museum 178-9
natural wonders 28
Netherlands, the 154-75
    language 635
nightlife 31
Notre Dame 216-21, **220-1**

O

opening hours 626

P

palaces, see castles & palaces
Palazzo Ducale 406-7
panini 438
Pantheon 358-61
Paris 10, 202-51, **203**, **226-7**, **230-1**, **234**, **237**, **251**
    accommodation 203, 251
    drinking & nightlife 245-8
    entertainment 248-9
    food 239-45
    internet access 249-50
    itineraries 202
    medical services 249
    safety 249
    shopping 236-9
    sights 228-36
    ticketing 248
    tourist information 250
    travel to/from 203, 250
    travel within 250
    walking tour 226-7, **226-7**
parks & gardens
    Giardino di Boboli 437
    Jardim da Cerca da Graça 337
    Jardin des Tuileries 233
    Jardin du Luxembourg 233
    Jardin du Palais Royal 233
    Kongens Have 143-6
    Mauerpark 506
    Parc des Buttes-Chaumont 233
    Parc du Champ de Mars 208
    Paris 233
    Park Güell 294
    Parque de Cristina Enea 325
    Prater 571
    Ricola Herb Garden 593
    Superkilen 146
    Tiergarten 504
    Treptower Park 499
    Volkspark Friedrichshain 506

Vondelpark 161
pickpockets 627
pintxo bars 312-15
planning
    budgeting 27
    calendar of events 32-4
    children 46-7
    itineraries 36-45, **36**, **37**, **38**, **39**, **40**, **42-3**, **44-5**
    travel seasons 26
politics 600-1
Pompeii 20, 462-9
Pont du Gard 254-5
Portugal 268-307
postal services 626
Potsdamer Platz 504
Prague 12, 524-45, **525**, **530-1**, **533**, **536-7**
    accommodation 525
    drinking & nightlife 542-3
    entertainment 543-4
    food 540-2
    itineraries 524
    shopping 539-40
    sights 532-9
    tourist information 544
    tours 539
    travel to/from 525, 544
    travel within 545
    walking tour 530-1, **530-1**
Prague Castle 526-9, **533**
Provence 252-67, **253**
    accommodation 253
    activities 261
    food 261-4
    itineraries 252
    sights 260-1
    tours 261
    travel to/from 253
public holidays 626

R

raclette 596
refunds 625-6

Reichstag 492-3
Reykjavík 23, 176-99, **177**, **186-7**, **199**
    accommodation 177, 199
    activities 189-90
    discount cards 197
    drinking & nightlife 195-7
    emergency numbers 198
    entertainment 197
    food 191-5
    itineraries 176
    luggage 198
    money 198
    shopping 190-1
    sights 184-9
    tourist information 198
    travel agencies 198
    travel to/from 177, 198
    travel within 198
Riesenrad 571
Roman Forum 372-7, **376-7**
Rome 9, 352-99, **353**, **378-9**, **382**, **384-5**, **390**, **399**
    accommodation 353, 399
    discount passes 397
    drinking & nightlife 394-5
    entertainment 395-6
    food 391-4
    free attractions 394
    itineraries 352
    medical services 396
    safety 396
    shopping 390-1
    sights 380-9
    tourist information 396-7
    travel to/from 353, 397
    travel within 397
    walking tour 378-9, **378-9**
Roussillon 259
Royal Deeside 108
Royal Palace (Budapest) 548-9
Rudas Baths 551
rue des Teinturiers 260
ruin pubs 561

000 Map pages

S

Sachsenhausen Concentration
  Camp 514
safety 626-7
San Gimignano 446-7
San Sebastián 323-9, **324**
scenic railways
  Glacier Express 590
  Gornergratbahn 589
  Jacobite Steam Train 111
Schengen area 629
Schloss Neuschwanstein 520-3
Schloss Schönbrunn 566-7
Scottish Highlands 18, 96-113,
  97, 105
  accommodation 97
  itineraries 96
  travel to/from 97
secondhand books 239
shopping 30
Siena 452-5 **453**
skiing
  Zermatt 593
Spain 268-307, 308-29
  language 636
spas 190
  Budapest 550-1
  Laugardalur 190
  Tuscany 457
St Paul's Cathedral 78
St Peter's Basilica 362-5
Staatsoper 584
Stasimuseum 513
Swiss Alps 586-97, **587**
  accommodation 587
  itineraries 586
  travel to/from 587
  trave within 587
Switzerland 586-97
synagogues
  Great Synagogue 552
  Neue Synagoge 502
Széchenyi Baths 551

T

tap water 623
taxes 625-6
telephone services 627-8
terrorism 627
time 20, 680
tipping 626
Tivoli Gardens 138-9
toilets 628
tourist information 628
Tower of London 66-71
Towers of San Gimignano 446-7
train travel 634, see also scenic
  railways
trams 334-5
transport 630-4
travellers cheques 626
travel seasons 26, 32
travel to/from Europe 27, 630-1
travel within Europe 27, 631-4
Treptower Park 499
Trinity College 116-17
Troja Chateau 544
Tuscany 20, 444-61, **445**
  accommodation 445
  driving tour 450-1, **450-1**
  itineraries 444, 450-1, **450-1**
  travel to/from 445

U

used-book sellers 239

V

vacations 626
vaccinations 622-3
Van Gogh Museum 156-7
Vatican Museums 366-71
Veli Bej Baths 551
Venice 8, 400-17, **401**, **408-9**,
  412-13
  accommodation 401
  activities 411-14
  drinking & nightlife 416
  entertainment 416-17
  food 414-16
  itineraries 400
  shopping 414
  sights 410-11
  tourist information 417
  travel to/from 401, 417
  travel within 417
  walking tour 408-9
Versailles 222-5, **224-5**
Via Appia Antica 381
Viðey 194
Vienna 14, 564-85, **565**, **572-3**
  accommodation 565
  activities 578
  drinking & nightlife 583-4
  entertainment 584
  food 580-3
  itineraries 564
  shopping 578-80
  sights 570-8
  tourist information 585
  travel to/from 565, 585
  travel within 585
  villages 256-9
visas 26, 629

W

weather 26
Westminster Abbey 52-7
whisky 98-9
women travellers 629-30

Z

Zermatt 592-7, **594**
  activities 593-4
  drinking & nightlife 596-7
  food 594-6
  sights 592-3
  tourist information 597
  travel within 597

Symbols & Map Key

Look for these symbols to quickly identify listings:

- ⊙ Sights
- ✪ Activities
- ⊖ Courses
- ⊙ Tours
- ✪ Festivals & Events
- ✪ Eating
- ⊙ Drinking
- ✪ Entertainment
- ⊙ Shopping
- ❶ Information & Transport

These symbols and abbreviations give vital information for each listing:

🌿 Sustainable or green recommendation

FREE No payment required

- ☎ Telephone number
- ⊗ Opening hours
- Ⓟ Parking
- ⊖ Nonsmoking
- ❄ Air-conditioning
- @ Internet access
- 📶 Wi-fi access
- 🏊 Swimming pool
- 🚌 Bus
- ⛴ Ferry
- 🚊 Tram
- 🚆 Train
- 📖 English-language menu
- 🥗 Vegetarian selection
- 👪 Family-friendly

Find your best experiences with these Great For... icons.

 Art & Culture
Beaches
💳 Budget
☕ Cafe/Coffee
🚲 Cycling
 Detour
🍷 Drinking
 Entertainment
✨ Events
👨‍👩‍👧 Family Travel
🍴 Food & Drink

📖 History
💬 Local Life
🐦 Nature & Wildlife
📷 Photo Op
🔭 Scenery
🛍 Shopping
Short Trip
🏀 Sport
🚶 Walking
❄ Winter Travel

Sights

- 🏖 Beach
- 🐦 Bird Sanctuary
- Buddhist
- 🏰 Castle/Palace
- ✝ Christian
- Confucian
- 🕉 Hindu
- ☪ Islamic
- Jain
- ✡ Jewish
- 🗿 Monument
- 🏛 Museum/Gallery/ Historic Building
- Ruin
- ⛩ Shinto
- Sikh
- ☯ Taoist
- 🍷 Winery/Vineyard
- 🦁 Zoo/Wildlife Sanctuary
- ⊙ Other Sight

Points of Interest

- Bodysurfing
- ⛺ Camping
- ☕ Cafe
- 🛶 Canoeing/Kayaking
- • Course/Tour
- 🤿 Diving
- 🍸 Drinking & Nightlife
- ✪ Eating
- 🎭 Entertainment
- ♨ Sento Hot Baths/ Onsen
- 🛍 Shopping
- ⛷ Skiing
- 😴 Sleeping
- 🤿 Snorkelling
- 🏄 Surfing
- 🏊 Swimming/Pool
- 🚶 Walking
- 🏄 Windsurfing
- ✪ Other Activity

Information

- 🏦 Bank
- Embassy/Consulate
- ✚ Hospital/Medical
- Internet
- Police
- ✉ Post Office
- ☎ Telephone
- 🚻 Toilet
- ❶ Tourist Information
- • Other Information

Geographic

- 🏖 Beach
- ⊣ Gate
- ⛺ Hut/Shelter
- Lighthouse
- Lookout
- ▲ Mountain/Volcano
- Oasis
- Park
-)(Pass
- Picnic Area
- Waterfall

Transport

- ✈ Airport
- Ⓑ BART station
- ⊗ Border crossing
- Ⓣ Boston T station
- 🚌 Bus
- Cable car/Funicular
- Cycling
- ⛴ Ferry
- Ⓜ Metro/MRT station
- Monorail
- Ⓟ Parking
- Petrol station
- Ⓢ Subway/S-Bahn/ Skytrain station
- 🚕 Taxi
- Train station/Railway
- Tram
- Ⓤ Tube Station
- Ⓤ Underground/ U-Bahn station
- • Other Transport

Kevin Raub

Atlanta native Kevin Raub started his career as a music journalist in New York, working for *Men's Journal* and *Rolling Stone* magazines. He ditched the rock 'n' roll lifestyle for travel writing and has written nearly 50 Lonely Planet guides, focused mainly on Brazil, Chile, Colombia, USA, India, the Caribbean and Portugal. Raub also contributes to a variety of travel magazines in both the USA and UK. Along the way, the self-confessed hophead is in constant search of wildly high IBUs in local beers. Follow him on Twitter and Instagram (@ RaubOnTheRoad).

Andrea Schulte-Peevers

Born and raised in Germany and educated in London and at UCLA, Andrea has travelled the distance to the moon and back in her visits to some 75 countries. She has earned her living as a professional travel writer for over two decades and authored or contributed to nearly 100 Lonely Planet titles as well as to newspapers, magazines and websites around the world. She also works as a travel consultant, translator and editor. Andrea's destination expertise is especially strong when it comes to Germany, Dubai and the UAE, Crete and the Caribbean Islands. She makes her home in Berlin.

Regis St Louis

Regis grew up in a small town in the American Midwest—the kind of place that fuels big dreams of travel—and he developed an early fascination with foreign dialects and world cultures. He spent his formative years learning Russian and a handful of Romance languages, which served him well on journeys across much of the globe. Regis has contributed to more than 50 Lonely Planet titles, covering destinations across six continents. His travels have taken him from the mountains of Kamchatka to remote island villages in Melanesia, and to many grand urban landscapes. When not on the road, he lives in New Orleans. Follow him on www. instagram.com/regisstlouis.

Nicola Williams

Border-hopping is way of life for British writer, runner, foodie, art aficionado and mum-of-three Nicola Williams who has lived in a French village on the southern side of Lake Geneva for more than a decade. Nicola has authored more than 50 guidebooks on Paris, Provence, Rome, Tuscany, France, Italy and Switzerland for Lonely Planet and covers France as a destination expert for the *Telegraph*. She also writes for the *Independent*, *Guardian*, lonelyplanet.com, Lonely Planet Magazine, French Magazine, Cool Camping France and others. Catch her on the road on Twitter and Instagram at @tripalong.

Neil Wilson

Neil was born in Scotland and has lived there most of his life. Based in Perthshire, he has been a full-time writer since 1988, working on more than 80 guidebooks for various publishers, including the Lonely Planet guides to Scotland, England, Ireland and Portugal. An avid lover and enthusiast since childhood, Neil is an active hill-walker, mountain-biker, sailor, snowboarder, fly-fisher and rock-climber, and has climbed and tramped in four continents, including ascents of Jebel Toubkal in Morocco, Mount Kinabalu in Borneo, the Old Man of Hoy in Scotland's Orkney Islands and the Northwest Face of Half Dome in California's Yosemite Valley.

Duncan Garwood

From facing fast bowlers in Barbados to sidestepping hungry pigs in Goa, Duncan's travels have thrown up many unique experiences. These days he largely dedicates himself to Italy, his adopted homeland where he's been living since 1997. From his base in the Castelli Romani hills outside Rome, he's clocked up endless kilometres exploring the country's well-known destinations and far-flung reaches, working on guides to *Rome, Sardinia, Sicily, Piedmont* and *Naples & the Amalfi Coast*. Other LP titles include *Italy's Best Trips,* the *Food Lover's Guide to the World* and *Pocket Bilbao & San Sebastian*. He also writes on Italy for newspapers, websites and magazines.

Bridget Gleeson

Bridget has written and taken photos for a variety of web and print publications including Lonely Planet, BBC Travel, BBC Culture, The Guardian, Budget Travel, Afar, Wine Enthusiast, Mr & Mrs Smith, Jetsetter, Tablet Hotels, The Independent, Delta Sky, Continental, LAN Airlines and Korean Air, and she's lived in Italy, the Czech Republic, Nicaragua and Argentina.

Paula Hardy

Paula Hardy is an independent travel writer and editorial consultant, whose work for Lonely Planet and other flagship publications has taken her from nomadic camps in the Danakil Depression to Seychellois beach huts and the jewel-like bar at the Gritti Palace on the Grand Canal. Over two decades, she has authored more than 30 Lonely Planet guidebooks and spent five years as commissioning editor of Lonely Planet's bestselling Italian list. These days you'll find her hunting down new hotels, hip bars and up-and-coming artisans primarily in Milan, Venice and Marrakech. Get in touch at www. paulahardy.com.

Damian Harper

Damian has been working largely full time as a travel writer (and translator) since 1997 and has also written for *National Geographic Traveler*, the *Guardian*, the *Daily Telegraph*, Abbeville Press (*Celestial Realm: The Yellow Mountains of China*), Lexean, Frequent Traveller, China Ethos and various other magazines and newspapers.

Anna Kaminski

Soviet-born, Anna finds a lot to appreciate about Hungary, a country she first visited as a dental tourist in the early 2000s and has been drawn back to since – from the familiar relics of Communism to the world's best poppyseed strudel. The latest

research stint took her from the art galleries and palaces along the Danube and Lake Balaton's shores to Budapest's graveyards; she trawled the latter for her great-uncle who died during the Siege of Budapest.

Catherine Le Nevez

Catherine's wanderlust kicked in when she roadtripped across Europe from her Parisian base aged four, and she's been hitting the road at every opportunity since, travelling to around 60 countries and completing her Doctorate of Creative Arts in Writing, Masters in Professional Writing, and postgrad qualifications in Editing and Publishing along the way. Over the past dozen-plus years she's written scores of Lonely Planet guides and articles covering Paris, France, Europe and far beyond. Her work has also appeared in numerous online and print publications. Topping Catherine's list of travel tips is to travel without any expectations.

Virginia Maxwell

Although based in Australia, Virginia spends at least half of her year updating Lonely Planet destination coverage in Europe and the Middle East. The Mediterranean is her favourite place to travel, and she has covered Spain, Italy, Turkey, Syria, Lebanon, Israel, Egypt and Morocco for LP guidebooks – there are only eight more countries to go! Virginia also writes about Armenia, Iran and Australia. Follow her @maxwellvirginia on Instagram and Twitter.

Craig McLachlan

Craig has covered destinations all over the globe for Lonely Planet for two decades. Based in Queenstown, New Zealand for half the year, he runs an outdoor activities company and a sake brewery, then moonlights overseas for the other half, leading tours and writing for Lonely Planet. Craig has completed a number of adventures in Japan and his books are available on Amazon. Describing himself as a 'freelance anything', Craig has an MBA from the University of Hawai'i and is also a Japanese interpreter, pilot, photographer, hiking guide, tour leader, karate instructor and budding novelist. Check out www.craigmclachlan.com

Josephine Quintero

Josephine first got her taste of not-so-serious travel when she slung a guitar on her back and travelled in Europe in the early '70s. She eventually reached Greece and caught a ferry to Israel where she embraced kibbutz life and the Mexican-American she was to subsequently wed. Josephine primarily covers Spain and Italy for Lonely Planet.

Oliver Berry

Oliver is a writer and photographer from Cornwall. He has worked for Lonely Planet for more than a decade, covering destinations from Cornwall to the Cook Islands, and has worked on more than 30 guidebooks. He is also a regular contributor to many newspapers and magazines, including *Lonely Planet Traveller*. His writing has won a host of awards, including The Guardian Young Travel Writer of the Year and the TNT Magazine People's Choice Award. His latest work is published at www.oliverberry.com.

Abigail Blasi

A freelance travel writer, Abigail has lived and worked in London, Rome, Hong Kong, and Copenhagen. Lonely Planet have sent her to India, Egypt, Tunisia, Mauritania, Mali, Italy, Portugal, Malta and around Britain. She writes regularly for newspapers and magazines, such as the *Independent*, the *Telegraph* and *Lonely Planet Traveller*. She has three children and they often come along for the ride. Twitter/Instagram: @abiwhere

Cristian Bonetto

Cristian has contributed to over 30 Lonely Planet guides to date, including *New York City, Italy, Venice & the Veneto, Naples & the Amalfi Coast, Denmark, Copenhagen, Sweden* and *Singapore*. Lonely Planet work aside, his musings on travel, food, culture and design appear in numerous publications around the world, including *The Telegraph* (UK) and *Corriere del Mezzogiorno* (Italy). When not on the road, you'll find the reformed playwright and TV scriptwriter slurping espresso in his beloved hometown, Melbourne. Instagram: rexcat75.

Kerry Christiani

Kerry is an award-winning travel writer, photographer and Lonely Planet author, specialising in Central and Southern Europe. Based in Wales, she has authored/co-authored more than a dozen Lonely Planet titles. An adventure addict, she loves mountains, cold places and true wilderness. She features her latest work at https://its-a-small-world.com and tweets @kerrychristiani.

Fionn Davenport

Irish by birth and conviction, Fionn has been writing about his native country for more than two decades. He's come and gone over the years, pushed to travel in order to escape Dublin's comfortable stasis and by the promise of adventure, but it has cemented his belief that Ireland remains his favourite place to visit, if not always live in. These days, he has a weekly commute home to Dublin from Manchester, where he lives with his partner Laura and their car Trevor. In Dublin he presents Inside Culture on RTE Radio 1 and writes travel features for a host of publications, including *The Irish Times*.

Sally Davies

Sally landed in Seville in 1992 with a suitcase full of pesetas and five words of Spanish, and, despite a complete inability to communicate, promptly snared a lucrative number handing out leaflets at Expo '92. In 2001 she settled in Barcelona, where she is still incredulous that her daily grind involves researching fine restaurants, wandering about museums and finding ways to convey the beauty of this spectacular city.

Peter Dragicevich

After a successful career in niche newspaper and magazine publishing, both in his native New Zealand and in Australia, Peter finally gave into Kiwi wanderlust, giving up staff jobs to chase his diverse roots around much of Europe. Over the last decade he's written literally dozens of guidebooks for Lonely Planet on an oddly disparate collection of countries, all of which he's come to love. He once again calls Auckland, New Zealand his home – although his current nomadic existence means he's often elsewhere.

Steve Fallon

After a full 15 years living in the centre of the known universe – East London – Steve cockney-rhymes in his sleep, eats jellied eel for brekkie, drinks lager by the bucketful and dances around the occasional handbag. As always, during research he did everything the hard/fun way: walking the walks, seeing the sights, taking (some) advice from friends, colleagues and the odd taxi driver and digesting everything in sight. Steve is a qualified London Blue Badge Tourist Guide (www.steveslondon.com).

Emilie Filou

Emilie Filou is a freelance journalist specialising in business and development issues, with a particular interest in Africa. Born in France, Emilie is now based in London, UK, from where she makes regular trips to Africa. Her work has appeared in publications such as *The Economist*, *The Guardian*, the BBC, the *Africa Report* and the *Christian Science Monitor*. She has contributed to some 20 Lonely Planet guides, including *France, Provence & the Côte d'Azur, London, West Africa, Madagascar* and *Tunisia*. You can find out more on www.emiliefilou.com.

Our Story

A beat-up old car, a few dollars in the pocket and a sense of adventure. In 1972 that's all Tony and Maureen Wheeler needed for the trip of a lifetime – across Europe and Asia overland to Australia. It took several months, and at the end – broke but inspired – they sat at their kitchen table writing and stapling together their first travel guide, *Across Asia on the Cheap*. Within a week they'd sold 1500 copies. Lonely Planet was born.

Today, Lonely Planet has offices in Franklin, London, Melbourne, Oakland, Dublin, Beijing and Delhi, with more than 600 staff and writers. We share Tony's belief that 'a great guidebook should do three things: inform, educate and amuse'.

Our Writers

Simon Richmond

Journalist and photographer Simon Richmond has specialised as a travel writer since the early 1990s and first worked for Lonely Planet in 1999 on their Central Asia guide. He's long since stopped counting the number of guidebooks he's researched and written for the company, but countries covered include Australia, China, India, Iran, Japan, Korea, Malaysia, Mongolia, Myanmar (Burma), Russia, Singapore, South Africa and Turkey. For Lonely Planet's website he's penned features on topics from the world's best swimming pools to the joys of Urban Sketching – follow him on Instagram to see some of his photos and sketches. Simon contributed to the Plan and Survival Guide chapters.

Alexis Averbuck

Alexis has travelled and lived all over the world, from Sri Lanka to Ecuador, Zanzibar and Antarctica. In recent years she's been living on the Greek island of Hydra and exploring her adopted homeland; sampling oysters in Brittany and careening through hill-top villages in Provence; and adventuring along Iceland's surreal lava fields, sparkling fjords and glacier tongues. A travel writer for over two decades, Alexis has lived in Antarctica for a year, crossed the Pacific by sailboat and written books on her journeys through Asia, Europe and the Americas.

Mark Baker

Mark is a freelance travel writer with a penchant for offbeat stories and forgotten places. He's originally from the United States, but now makes his home in the Czech capital, Prague. He writes mainly on Eastern and Central Europe for Lonely Planet as well as other leading travel publishers, but finds real satisfaction in digging up stories in places that are too remote or quirky for the guides. Prior to becoming an author, he worked as a journalist for The Economist, Bloomberg News and Radio Free Europe, among other organisations. Instagram: @markbakerprague Twitter: @markbakerprague

More Writers

STAY IN TOUCH LONELYPLANET.COM/CONTACT

AUSTRALIA The Malt Store, Level 3, 551 Swanston St, Carlton, Victoria 3053 📞 03 8379 8000, fax 03 8379 8111

IRELAND Unit E, Digital Court. The Digital Hub, Rainsford St, Dublin 8, Ireland

USA 124 Linden Street, Oakland, CA 94607 📞 510 250 6400, toll free 800 275 8555, fax 510 893 8572

UK 240 Blackfriars Road, London SE1 8NW 📞 020 3771 5100, fax 020 3771 5101

 twitter.com/ lonelyplanet

 facebook.com/ lonelyplanet

 instagram.com/ lonelyplanet

 youtube.com/ lonelyplanet

 lonelyplanet.com/ newsletter

The PROPHETS STILL SPEAK

MESSIAH IN BOTH TESTAMENTS

The
PROPHETS
STILL SPEAK

MESSIAH IN BOTH
TESTAMENTS

by
Fred John Meldau

1988 Edition Edited by
Donald A. Hoglin
Amy L. Julian

FOREWARD

Some years ago I came across an exceptional book. It was called *Messiah in Both Testaments*. And through the years I have repeatedly gone back to it for rereading. Recently a friend called to say that he had just finished the book and found it to be a veritable reservoir of spiritual insight and blessing.

As a result, I was very attentive when one of my administrators came into my office recently to inform me that this very book was out of print but that we could receive permission to republish it.

The book you now hold in your hand is the result of those events. Happily, with minimal editing, a modernized format and a new cover, the classic work, *Messiah in Both Testaments* by Fred John Meldau, will continue to touch multitudes under a new title, *The Prophets Still Speak*.

My sincere thanks to Donald A. Hoglin, director of the Christian Victory Publishing Company, who gave us permission to publish the book; and to my co-workers, Ray Oram, Amy Julian, Josephine Bak, Barbara Alber and Marjorie Hall, who faithfully saw the project through to completion.

Marvin J. Rosenthal
Executive Director
THE FRIENDS OF ISRAEL
GOSPEL MINISTRY, INC.

TABLE OF CONTENTS

CHAPTER ONE
AMAZING DRAMA 1

CHAPTER TWO
**PROPHECIES ESTABLISHING THE CREDENTIALS
OF THE MESSIAH** 15

CHAPTER THREE
**PROPHECIES CONCERNING THE LIFE AND MINISTRY
OF THE MESSIAH** 29

CHAPTER FOUR
**PROPHECIES CONCERNING THE
PROPHETIC PARADOXES** 37

CHAPTER FIVE
**PROPHECIES CONCERNING THE SUFFERING, DEATH
AND RESURRECTION OF THE MESSIAH** 51

CHAPTER SIX
**PROPHECIES DESCRIBING THE MESSIANIC OFFICES
OF CHRIST** 69

CHAPTER SEVEN
**PROPHECIES PROVING THAT THE MESSIAH
IS GOD** 79

CHAPTER EIGHT
**PROPHECIES FROM THE OLD TESTAMENT
FULFILLED IN CHRIST** 87

CONCLUSION 91

AMAZING DRAMA

To him give all the prophets witness (Acts 10:43).
In the volume of the book it is written of me
(Ps. 40:7; Heb. 10:7).

"The most amazing drama that ever was presented to the mind of man — a drama written in prophecy in the Old Testament and in biography in the four Gospels of the New Testament — is the narrative of Jesus the Christ. One outstanding fact, among many, completely isolates Him. It is this: that one man only in the history of the world has had explicit details given beforehand of His birth, life, death and resurrection; that these details are in documents given to the public centuries before He appeared, and that no one challenges, or can challenge, that these documents were widely circulated long before His birth; and that anyone and everyone can compare for himself/herself the actual records of His life with those ancient documents, and find that they match one another perfectly. The challenge of this pure miracle is that it happened concerning one man in the whole history of the world" (D. M. Panton).

Scores of other Bible students have called attention to this same amazing fact. We quote from one more, Canon Dyson Hague. He says: "Centuries before Christ was born His birth and career, His sufferings and glory, were all described in outline and detail in the Old Testament. Christ is the only person ever born into this world whose ancestry, birth time, forerunner, birthplace, birth manner, infancy, manhood, teaching, character, career, preaching, reception, rejection, death, burial, resurrection and ascension were all prewritten in the most marvelous manner centuries before He was born.

1

"Who could draw a picture of a man not yet born? Surely God, and God alone. Nobody knew 500 years ago that Shakespeare was going to be born; or 250 years ago that Napoleon was to be born. Yet here in the Bible we have the most striking and unmistakable likeness of a man portrayed, not by one, but by twenty or twenty-five artists, none of whom had ever seen the man they were painting."

To focus attention on the unparalleled wonder of this literary miracle, think for a moment. Who could have prewritten the life of George Washington, Abraham Lincoln or any other character 500 years before he was born? Nowhere in any of the literature of the world, secular or religious, can one find a duplicate to the astounding miracle of the prewritten life of Christ. "The inspiration of that portrait came from the heavenly gallery, and not from the studio of an earthly artist" (A. T. Pierson). So amazing is this miracle of the prewritten life of Christ and its perfect fulfillment in the Lord Jesus that, "Nothing but divine prescience could have foreseen it, and nothing but divine power could accomplish it." As the full evidence is presented, it becomes obvious that, "the prophecy came not at any time by the will of man, but holy men of God spoke as they were moved by the Holy Spirit" (2 Pet. 1:21).

Four Great Truths Demonstrated by This Fact

With no variations or aberrations between the Old Testament predictions of the coming Messiah and the New Testament fulfillment in Jesus of Nazareth, one instinctively leaps to the conclusion that the hand that drew the image in prophecy molded the portrait in history; and the inevitable result of this miracle is fourfold.

First, it proves that the Bible is the inspired Word of God, for unaided man is neither capable of writing nor of fulfilling such a literary wonder.

Second, it proves that the God of the Bible, the only One who knows the end from the beginning, and who alone has the power to fulfill all His Word, is the true and living God.

Third, it proves that the God of the Bible is both all-knowing (able to foretell the future entwined around numberless men who are free moral agents) and all-powerful (able to bring to pass a perfect fulfillment of His Word in the midst of widespread unbelief, ignorance and rebellion on the part of men).

Fourth, it proves that Jesus, who so perfectly and completely fulfilled all the Old Testament predictions, is indeed the Messiah, the Savior of the world, the Son of the living God.

Christ is, therefore, seen to be the center of all history as well as the central reality of the Bible. "The Christ of the New Testament is the fruit of the tree of prophecy, and Christianity is the realization of a plan, the first outlines of which were sketched more than 1,500 years before" (David Baron, *Rays of Messiah's Glory*, p. 14).

Fulfilled Prophecy is Unique to the Bible

The fact of fulfilled prophecy is found in the Bible alone; hence, it presents proof of divine inspiration that is positive, conclusive and overwhelming. Here is the argument in brief.

No man, unaided by divine inspiration, foreknows the future, for it is an impenetrable wall to all mankind. Only an all-powerful and an all-knowing God can infallibly predict the future. If, then, one can find true prophecy (as one does in the Bible), with proven fulfillment, sufficient time intervening between the prediction and the fulfillment, and explicit details in the prediction to assure that the prophecies are not clever guesses, then the case is perfect. There were 400 years between the last of the messianic predictions of the Old Testament and their fulfillment in the Christ of the Gospels. Many prophecies are, of course, much older than 400 B.C. During the period of 1,100 years from the time of Moses (1500 B.C.) to that of Malachi (400 B.C.), a succession of prophets arose, messianic prediction took form, and all of them testified of the Messiah who was to come.

The perfect proof of the long period of time that elapsed between the last book of the Old Testament and the first book of the New Testament is the presence in the world of the *Septuagint*, a translation of the Old Testament into Greek. This translation was begun during the reign of Ptolemy Philadelphus in about 280 B.C. and was completed not long thereafter. With a translation of the entire Old Testament, as we now know it, made more than 200 years before Christ, it is obvious that the books of the Old Testament, from which the translation was made, are still older.

Moreover, there were no prophets in the 400-year intertestament period. In 1 Maccabees 9:27 we are told of the "great affliction in Israel, such as there was not since the day that a prophet was not seen among them." Intense regret over the lack of a prophet merged into an intense longing for the coming again of prophets, so that even in their public actions men were careful to claim validity for their legislation only until a faithful prophet should again arise (see 1 Macc. 4:46; 14:41).

So specific and so voluminous are these Old Testament predictions, and so complete is their fulfillment in the New Testament, that Dr. A. T. Pierson

3

says: "There would be no honest infidel in the world were messianic prophecy studied...nor would there be any doubting disciples if this fact of prediction and fulfillment were fully understood. And, the sad fact is, we have yet to meet the first honest skeptic or critic who has carefully studied the prophecies which center in Christ" (*Many Infallible Proofs*). Here indeed is God's rock of ages, faith's unshakable standing place.

Prophecy is God's Own Method of Proving His Truth

The teachings of the Bible are so peculiar and different from all other religions and so important — telling us that man's eternal destiny, for weal or woe, depends on his acceptance of the Christ of the Bible — that it is appropriate that we know whether the Bible is or is not a heavenly decree, the absolute and final Word of God, and whether its message is fully authorized by the Almighty. If God has given a revelation of His will in the Bible, there can be no doubt that in some unmistakable way He will show men that the Bible is indeed His revealed will; and the way He has chosen to show men that the Bible is His Word is through the giving and subsequent fulfillment of specific, detailed prophecies. This specific fulfillment is the divine seal, letting all men know that He has spoken. This seal can never be counterfeited, for His foreknowledge of the actions of free and intelligent agents — men — is one of the most "incomprehensible attributes of deity and is exclusively a divine perfection" (Alexander Keith, *Evidences of Prophecy*, p. 8).

In challenging the false gods of Isaiah's time, the true God said: "Produce your cause...bring forth your strong reasons...show us what shall happen...declare us things to come. Show the things that are to come hereafter, that we may know that ye are gods" (Isa. 41:21-23).

There are false faiths, such as Mohammedanism and Buddhism, which have tried to prop up their claims on pretended miracles, but neither of these, nor any other religious scripture in the history of the world, apart from the Bible, has ever ventured to frame prophecies.

It is the peculiar glory of the Almighty, the all-knowing God, who is "the LORD, the Creator" (Isa. 40:28) to declare "new things...before they spring forth" (Isa. 42:9) and that glory He will not share with another (Isa. 42:8). The true God alone foreknows and foretells the future, and He has chosen to confine His foretelling to the pages of Scripture.

Many have made an effort to foretell the future — not one, apart from the Bible, has ever succeeded. "The extreme difficulty of framing a prophecy which shall prove accurate may be seen in that familiar but crude rhyme known as 'Mother Shipton's Prophecy.' Some years ago it appeared as a

4

pretended relic of a remote day and claimed to have predicted the invention of the steam locomotive, the rise of D'Israeli in English politics, etc., etc....For years I tried to unearth and expose what seemed to me a huge impostor, and I succeeded. I traced the whole thing to one Charles Hindley (of England) who acknowledged himself the author of this prophetic hoax, which was written in 1862 instead of 1448, and palmed off on a credulous public. It is one of the startling proofs of human perversity that the very people who will try to cast suspicion on prophecies two thousand years old will, without straining, swallow a forgery that was first published *after* the events it predicted, and will not even look into its claim to antiquity" (Dr. A. T. Pierson, *Many Infallible Proofs*, pp. 44-45).

Although there are many other subjects of divine prophecy in the Bible (i.e., the Jews, the Gentile nations which surrounded Israel, ancient cities, the Church, the last days, etc.), the divine perfections of foreknowledge and fulfillment can be seen better in the realm of prophecies concerning Christ than in any other sphere.

Here is a clear statement that God alone, in the Bible alone, gives true prophecies:

> I am God, and there is none else; I am God, and there is none like me, declaring the end from the beginning, and from ancient times the things that are not yet done, saying, My counsel shall stand, and I will do all my pleasure (Isa. 46:9-10).

This declaration by God that He alone can give and fulfill prophecy, and that prophecy is to be found only in the Bible, is found in many other places in the Bible (see Dt. 18:21-22; Isa. 41:21-23; Jer. 28:9; Jn. 13:19; 2 Tim. 3:16: 2 Pet. 1:19-21; etc.).

Sensing the tremendous force of this fact, Justin Martyr said, "To declare a thing shall come to pass long before it is in being, and to bring it to pass, this or nothing is the work of God."

Chance Fulfillment of Prophecy is Ruled Out

Atheists and other unbelievers, seeking a way to circumvent the fact of fulfilled prophecy and its connotations, have argued that the fulfillments were *accidental, chance* or *coincidental.* But when such complete details are given, the *chance* fulfillment of prophecy is ruled out. One writer says:

> It is conceivable that a prediction, uttered at a venture and expressing what in a general way may happen to result, may seem like a genuine prophecy. But only let the prophecy give several

details of time, place and accompanying incidents, and it is evident that the possibility of a chance fulfillment, by a 'fortuitous concurrence of events,' will become extremely desperate — yea, altogether impossible. Hence, the prophecies of heathen antiquity always took good care to confine their predictions to one or two particulars and to express them in the most general and ambiguous terms. Therefore, in the whole range of history, except the prophecies of Scripture, *there is not a single instance of a prediction, expressed in unequivocal language and descending to any minuteness, which bears the slightest claim to fulfillment.* 'Suppose,' says Dr. Olinthus Gregory, 'that there were only 50 prophecies in the Old Testament (instead of 333) concerning the first advent of Christ, giving details of the coming Messiah and all meet in the person of Jesus...the probability of chance fulfillment as calculated by mathematicians according to the theory of probabilities is less than one in 1,125,000,000,000,000. Now add only two more elements to these 50 prophecies and fix the *time* and *place* at which they must happen, and the *immense improbability that they will take place by chance exceeds all the power of numbers to express* (or the mind of man to grasp). This is enough, one would think, to silence forever all pleas for *chance* as furnishing an unbeliever the least opportunity of escape from the evidence of prophecy' (Gregory's Letters) [Alexander Keith, *Evidences of Prophecy*, p.8].

Let it be further observed that many of the prophecies about the Messiah are of such a nature that only God *could* fulfill them (i.e., His virgin birth, His sinless and holy character, His resurrection and His ascension). Only God could cause Jesus "to be born of a virgin or be raised from the dead" (David Baron).

THE COMING MESSIAH

In the Old Testament there is a definite, clear and continuous teaching that the Messiah will come. Dozens of times we read such promises as, "behold, thy King cometh unto thee" (Zech. 9:9); "the Lord GOD will come" (Isa. 40:10); "the Lord, whom ye seek, shall suddenly come to his temple" (Mal. 3:1); "The LORD thy God will raise up unto thee a Prophet from the midst of thee" (Dt. 18:15-19); the "Prophet" will be the Lord's "fellow" (equal) [Zech. 13:7]. Daniel predicted the coming of "Messiah, the Prince" at a set time (Dan. 9:25-26), and Isaiah foretold the "rod out of the stem of Jesse" (Isa. 11:1) on whom the Lord would lay "the iniquity of us all" (Isa. 53:6). Prophets and seers of old often spoke of the time when "the desire of all nations" would come (Hag. 2:7; see also Gen. 3:15; 49:10, Num. 24:17; Ps. 2:5-6; 118:26; Isa. 35:4; 62:11; Jer. 23:5-6).

The coming of Christ, promised in the Old Testament and fulfilled in the New — His birth, character, work, teachings, sufferings, death and resurrection — are the grand, central themes of the Bible. Christ is the bond that ties the two Testaments together. The Old Testament is in the New revealed; the New Testament is in the Old concealed.

A. T. Pierson says:

> The most ordinary reader may examine the old curious predictions of the Messiah's person and work found in the Old Testament, follow the gradual progress of these revelations from Genesis to Malachi, and trace the prophecies as they descend into details more and more specific and minute, until at last the full figure of the coming One stands out. Then, with this image clearly fixed in his mind's eye, he may turn to the New Testament and beginning with Matthew see how the *historic* personage, Jesus of Nazareth, corresponds and coincides in every particular with the *prophetic* personage depicted by the prophets....There is not a difference or a divergence, yet there could have been no collusion or contact between the prophets of the Old Testament and the narrators of the New Testament. Observe, the reader has not gone out of the Bible itself. He has simply compared two portraits, one in the Old Testament of a mysterious coming One and another in the New of One who has actually come, and his irresistible conclusion is that these two blend in absolute unity.

A BRIEF SUMMARY OF THE PROPHECIES

Let us briefly trace a few of the outstanding points in the comparison of Old Testament prediction and New Testament fulfillment. The work of redemption was to be accomplished by one person, the central figure in both Testaments, the promised Messiah. As the *seed of the woman*, He was to bruise Satan's head (Gen. 3:15; cp. Gal. 4:4). As the *seed of Abraham* (Gen. 22:18; cp. Gal. 3:16) and the *seed of David* (Ps. 132:11; Jer. 23:5; cp. Acts 13:23), He was to come from the tribe of Judah (Gen. 49:10; cp. Heb. 7:14).

The Messiah was to come at a specific time (Gen. 49:10; Dan. 9:24-25; cp. Lk. 2:1-2) and be born of a virgin (Isa. 7:14; cp. Mt. 1:18-23) in Bethlehem of Judea (Mic. 5:2; cp. Mt. 2:1; Lk. 2:4-5). Great persons were to visit and adore Him (Ps. 72:10; cp. Mt. 2:1-11). Through the rage of a jealous king, innocent children were to be slaughtered (Jer. 31:15; cp. Mt. 2:16-18).

He was to be preceded by a forerunner, John the Baptist, before entering His public ministry (Isa. 40:3; Mal. 3:1; cp. Mt. 3:1-3; Lk. 1:17).

He was to be a prophet like Moses (Dt. 18:18; cp. Acts 3:20-22) and have a special anointing of the Holy Spirit (Ps. 45:7; Isa. 11:2; 61:1-2; cp. Mt. 3:16; Lk. 4:15-21, 43). He was to be a priest after the order of Melchizedek (Ps. 110:4; cp. Heb. 5:5-6). As the servant of the Lord, He was to be a faithful and patient Redeemer, for the Gentiles as well as the Jews (Isa. 42:1-4; cp. Mt. 12:18-21).

The Messiah's ministry was to begin in Galilee (Isa. 9:1-2; cp. Mt. 4:12-17, 23). Later He was to enter Jerusalem (Zech. 9:9; cp. Mt. 21:1-5) to bring salvation. He was also to enter the Temple (Hag. 2:7-9; Mal. 3:1; cp. Mt. 21:12).

His zeal for the Lord was to be remarkable (Ps. 69:9; cp. Jn. 2:17). His manner of teaching was to be by parables (Ps. 78:2; cp. Mt. 13:34-35), and His ministry was to be characterized by miracles (Isa. 35:5-6; cp. Mt. 11:4-6; Jn. 11:47). He was to be rejected by His brethren (Ps. 69:8; Isa. 53:3; cp. Jn. 1:11; 7:5) and be a "stone of stumbling" to the Jews and a "rock of offense" (Isa. 8:14; cp. Rom. 9:32-33; 1 Pet. 2:8).

The Messiah was to be hated without a cause (Ps. 69:4; Isa. 49:7; cp. Jn. 7:48; 15:25), rejected by the rulers (Ps. 118:22; cp. Mt. 21:42), betrayed by a friend (Ps. 41:9; 55:12-13; cp. Jn. 13:18, 21), forsaken by His disciples (Zech. 13:7; cp. Mt. 26:31, 56), sold for 30 pieces of silver (Zech. 11:12; cp. Mt. 26:15) and His price given for the potter's field (Zech. 11:13; cp. Mt. 27:3, 7). He was to be smitten on the cheek (Mic. 5:1; cp. Mt. 27:30), spat upon (Isa. 50:6; cp. Mt. 27:30), mocked (Ps. 22:7-8; cp. Mt. 27:31, 39-44) and beaten (Isa. 50:6 ff.; cp Mt. 26:67; 27:26, 30).

It is most impressive to read in parallel statements the prediction in comparison with the fulfillment. For example, compare the following Old Testament and New Testament passages.

Prophecy:
I gave my back to the smiters, and my cheeks to them that plucked off the hair; I hid not my face from shame and spitting (Isa. 50:6).

Fulfillment:
Then they spat in his face, and buffeted him; and others smote him with the palms of their hands (Mt.26:67).

The Messiah's death by crucifixion is given in detail in Psalm 22 and the meaning of His death as a substitutionary atonement is given in Isaiah 53. His hands and feet were to be pierced (Ps. 22:16; Zech. 12:10; cp. Jn. 19:18, 37; 20:25); yet not one of His bones was to be broken (Ex. 12:46; Ps. 34:20; cp. Jn. 19:33-36). He was to suffer thirst (Ps. 22:15; cp. Jn. 19:28) and be given vinegar to drink (Ps. 69:21; cp. Mt. 27:34); and He was to be numbered with transgressors (Isa. 53:12; cp. Mt. 27:38).

The Messiah's body was to be buried with the rich in His death (Isa. 53:9; cp. Mt. 27:57-60) but was not to see corruption (Ps. 16:10; Acts 2:31).

He was to be raised from the dead (Ps. 2:7; 16:10; cp. Acts 13:33) and ascend to the right hand of God (Ps. 68:18; cp. Lk. 24:51; Acts 1:9; also Ps. 110:1; cp. Heb. 1:3).

This brief sketch of Old Testament messianic prophecies with their New Testament fulfillments is, of course, far from complete; it is merely suggestive, although many of the main points have been covered. There are actually 333 predictions concerning the coming Messiah in the Old Testament!

It is valuable to gather together, as in a great museum, at least some of the prophetic masterpieces scattered throughout the realm of the entire 39 books of the Old Testament, so that one can get a view of them in one group without having to travel laboriously throughout hundreds of pages of Scripture.

THE MESSIAH WHO HAS COME

Christ's Testimony to the Fact that He Fulfilled Old Testament Prophecy

The golden milestone in the ancient city of Rome was the point in the old world at which the many roads, running from all directions in the Roman Empire, met and converged. In like manner, all lines of Old Testament messianic prophecy meet in Jesus, the Christ of the New Testament.

Not only was the life of Christ prewritten in the Old Testament, but Jesus knew it and fully witnessed to that fact in the New Testament. This is a miracle in itself and finds no parallel in the literature of the world. No other character of history — Caesar, Gladstone, Shakespeare or any other — ever dreamed of saying of the Bible or any other book, as our Lord did, "Search the scriptures; for they...testify of me" (Jn. 5:39). Nor has any false Christ ever appealed to fulfilled prophecy to vindicate his claims.

In *Rays of Messiah's Glory* (p. 46), David Baron calls attention to the fact that "More than forty false Messiahs have appeared in the history of the Jewish nation," and *not one of them* ever appealed to fulfilled prophecy to establish his claims. Rather, they bolstered their fake claims by "promises of revenge and by flatteries which gratified national vanity. And now, except to a few students of history, the remembrance of their names has perished from the earth, while Jesus of Nazareth, the true Messiah, who fulfilled all the prophecies, is worshipped by hundreds of millions."

Thus, Christianity is not a new religion unconnected to the Old Testament. It is based solidly on being the *fulfillment* of the Old Testament promises. "Christianity, with its central figure human and divine, Prophet, Priest and King, is nothing less than the translation of prophecy from the region of ardent belief to actual fact...and we see the living and organic connection between the two dispensations and recognize it is the same God who spake in both — in the first to prepare, in the second to accomplish....'Known unto God are all his works from the beginning of the age' (Acts 15:18)" [E. A. Edghill, *The Value of Prophecy*, pp. 389-390].

Jesus calmly said, "Abraham...saw...my day" (Jn. 8:56) and "Moses...wrote of me" (Jn. 5:46). To show the connection between Old Testament prediction and New Testament fulfillment, He said in His Sermon on the Mount, "Think not that I am come to destroy the law, or the prophets...but to fulfill" (Mt. 5:17).

The life of Christ was unique; all was according to the divine pattern as given in the Old Testament. He was the One sent by the Father to fulfill all His will, to accomplish His work as Redeemer, and to fulfill all the prophecies concerning Him (Jn. 3:16-17; Heb. 10:9; 1 Jn. 4:14).

In the beginning of His ministry, after reading to the people in the synagogue at Capernaum the important messianic prophecy in Isaiah 61:1-2, when all eyes were fastened on Him, He said, "This day is this scripture fulfilled in your ears" (Lk. 4:16-21). When talking to Jesus at the well, the woman of Samaria said, "I know that Messiah cometh, who is called Christ [all devout readers of the Old Testament knew that], when he is come, he will tell us all things. Jesus saith unto her, I that speak unto thee am he" (Jn. 4:25-26). When Peter confessed his faith in Jesus as the Messiah — "Thou art the Christ, the Son of the living God" (Mt. 16:16) — the Lord Jesus acknowledged the truth of what he had said by answering, "Blessed art thou,

Simon Bar-jona; for flesh and blood hath not revealed it unto thee, but my Father, who is in heaven" (Mt. 16:17).

Jesus quoted from Psalm 110 to identify Himself as the "Son of David" (a messianic title) and also to prove that David called Him "Lord" (Ps. 110:1; cp. Mt. 22:41-46). By taking the title "Son of man," He identified Himself with that messianic title used in Daniel (Dan. 7:13; cp. Mk. 14:62). By taking the title "Son of God," He identified Himself with that messianic title used in Psalm 2.

He connected the blessings of salvation given to all who trust in Him with the promises of the Old Testament, "He that believeth on me, as the scripture hath said, out of his heart shall flow rivers of living water" (Jn. 7:38). Here the Lord was speaking of the fulfillment, *through Himself,* of the type in the Feast of Tabernacles (see context, Jn. 7:37; Lev. 23:34-36; Isa. 12:3).

Almost everything Christ said or did had some connection with Old Testament prophecy. His miracles were in fulfillment of Old Testament predictions (Isa. 35:5-6); His ministry corresponded with what Isaiah had predicted concerning Him (Isa. 42:1-4; 61:1-3; cp. Mt. 12:17-21). His sufferings and death at Jerusalem were all in accordance with what had been foretold (Ps. 22, Isa. 53). When praising John the Baptist, Jesus called attention to the fact that John was His forerunner — "For this is he [John the Baptist] of whom it is written, Behold, I send my messenger before thy face, who shall prepare thy way before thee" (Mt. 11:10) — which had been predicted in Isaiah 40:3 and Malachi 3:1. The Lord was saying that not only did *John* come in fulfillment of prophecy, but that He was the One for whom John came to be a forerunner!

As He drew near to the cross, Jesus said to His disciples, "Behold, we go up to Jerusalem, and all things that are written by the prophets concerning the Son of man shall be accomplished" (Lk. 18:31). On the eve of His crucifixion He said, "this that is written must yet be accomplished in me, And he was reckoned among the transgressors; for the things concerning me have a fulfillment" (Lk. 22:37). Note the word "must."

During the crucial hours of His trial, Jesus said to Peter (who was willing to defend his Master with his sword), "Thinkest thou that I cannot now pray to my Father, and he shall presently give me more than twelve legions of angels? But how, then, shall the scriptures be fulfilled, that thus it must be?" (Mt. 26:53-54). Then, chiding the multitudes, He said, "Are ye come out as against a thief with swords and clubs to take me? I sat daily with you teaching in the temple, and ye laid no hold on me. But all this was done, that the scriptures of the prophets might be fulfilled" (Mt. 26:55-56). At His trial, when the high priest put Him under oath and asked, "Art thou the Christ, the Son of the Blessed?" Jesus answered, "I am" (Mk. 14:61-62).

Suffering on the cross, the Lord Jesus identified Himself as the One whose hands and feet were to be pierced (Ps. 22:16) and quoted Psalm 22:1, "My God, my God, why hast thou forsaken me?" Three of His seven sayings on the cross were the very words of Scripture.

After His resurrection, while talking to His two disciples on the Emmaus road, "beginning at Moses and all the prophets, he expounded unto them, in all the scriptures, the things concerning himself" (Lk. 24:27). And later, when meeting with the assembled disciples, He said, "These are the words which I spoke unto you, while I was yet with you, that all things must be fulfilled, which were written in the law of Moses, and in the prophets, and in the psalms, concerning me" (Lk. 24:44).

On various occasions, the Lord spoke of the necessity — "must" — of Old Testament prophecy being fulfilled in Him. This was necessary because the Word of God cannot fail, the God of the Word cannot lie, and the Son of God who fulfilled the Word cannot fail. "The scripture cannot be broken" (Jn. 10:35).

After His resurrection, the Lord gave His disciples the key that unlocks messianic prophecy in the Old Testament: "And [He] said unto them, Thus it is written, and thus it behooved Christ to suffer, and to rise from the dead the third day; And that repentance and remission of sins should be preached in his name among all nations" (Lk. 24:46-47). This great statement is a summary of His teachings during the 40 days He ministered to His disciples between His resurrection and ascension. The Jews of His day, and to this day, looked for a triumphant, reigning Messiah and failed to see from their own Scriptures that Christ must *suffer* for the sins of the world before entering His glory.

Peter bore the same testimony of the witness of the Holy Spirit through the prophets of the Old Testament when He testified beforehand of "the sufferings of Christ, and the glory that should follow" (1 Pet. 1:11).

The Apostles and Writers of the New Testament Also Bear Witness that Jesus the Christ Fulfilled Old Testament Prophecies

Many modern Christians have lost — or never had — an enlightened understanding of the genius of Christianity: that the New Testament is the fulfillment of the predictions and promises of the Old; that Jesus, the Christ, is the link binding the two Testaments together. The early New Testament church writers and preachers saw this clearly and constantly pointed out the New Testament fulfillment of Old Testament prophecy.

When Matthew narrated the virgin birth of Christ in Matthew 1:18-25, he said it was the fulfillment of the Old Testament prediction of Messiah's virgin birth: "Now all this was done, that it might be fulfilled which was spoken by the Lord through the prophet, saying, Behold, the virgin shall be with child, and shall bring forth a son, and they shall call his name Immanuel, which, being interpreted, is God with us" (Mt. 1:22-23; cp. Isa. 7:14).

When King Herod, in a jealous rage, slaughtered the innocent children in his vain effort to kill the Christ child, Matthew called attention to the fact that even this gruesome murder was predicted by God and then fulfilled (Mt. 2:16-18; cp. Jer. 31:15).

In dozens of places in the Gospels, the evangelists imply or state that Jesus fulfilled Old Testament prophecy. Peter expressed the convictions of the other disciples when he made his great confession, "Thou art the Christ, the Son of the living God" (Mt. 16:16; cp. Mt. 8:17; 12:17-18; etc.).

The main theme of the Gospel of John, as well as all four Gospels, is to prove that Jesus was the predicted Messiah, the Son of God, the One who was to come. "But these are written, that ye might believe that Jesus is the Christ, the Son of God; and that believing ye might have life through his name" (Jn. 20:31).

The purpose of John's Gospel is to show that Jesus has all the qualifications, the character and the works of the Messiah — Jesus fulfills all that was written of the Messiah — hence, He is the Messiah.

All of the apostles "laid great stress upon this argument from prophecy: it was not only the main, but almost the sole, argument employed in the New Testament...[They felt] it necessary to show the marvelous correspondence between the well-known *facts* [of the life, death and resurrection of Christ] with Old Testament prophecy, in order to carry conviction to every fair mind; and so this was the common method of preaching the gospel, the solid but simple base of argument upon which rested all appeal" (A. T. Pierson, *Many Infallible Proofs,* p. 187).

The backbone of Peter's sermon on the day of Pentecost was an argument from the Old Testament to prove to the Jews that Jesus of Nazareth, whom they had crucified but whom God had raised from the dead, *was the Messiah about whom David had written,* and that this God had raised Him up and made Him "both Lord and Christ" (Acts 2:22-36).

In Peter's second sermon recorded in the Book of Acts and delivered at the gate of the Temple, he proved his argument by saying: "And now, brethren, I know that through ignorance ye did it [rejected and killed Jesus, the Messiah], as did also your rulers. But those things, which God had shown by the mouth of all his prophets, that Christ should suffer, he hath so fulfilled. Repent, therefore, and be converted, that your sins may be blotted out" (Acts 3:17-19).

Even in his sermon to the assembled Gentiles in the house of Cornelius, Peter said: "To him [Jesus] give all the prophets witness, that through his name whosoever believeth in him shall receive remission of sins" (Acts 10:43).

In Paul's sermon in the synagogue at Antioch he said: "And when they had fulfilled all that was written of him, they took him down from the tree, and laid him in a sepulcher. But God raised him from the dead" (Acts 13:29-30).

Paul's method of preaching the gospel to the Jews is given in Acts 17:2-3: "And Paul, as his manner was, went in unto them, and three sabbath days reasoned with them out of the scriptures [Old Testament], Opening and alleging that Christ [Messiah] must needs have suffered, and risen again from the dead; and that this Jesus, whom I preach unto you, is Christ" (Acts 17:2-3).

When Paul defined the gospel by which people are saved, he connected the New Testament facts of the death and resurrection of Christ with Old Testament prediction and teaching: "Moreover, brethren, I declare unto you the gospel...By which also ye are saved...that Christ died for our sins according to the scriptures [Old Testament]; And that he was buried, and that he rose again the third day according to the scriptures" (1 Cor. 15:1-4).

Thus, the writers and preachers of the New Testament constantly pointed out that Jesus lived, suffered, died and rose again in fulfillment of Old Testament prophecy. Commenting on this fact, Dr. A. T. Pierson said, "No miracle which He wrought so unmistakably set on Jesus the seal of God as the convergence of the thousand lines of prophecy in Him, as in one burning focal point of dazzling glory. Every sacrifice presented, from the hour of Abel's altar fire down to the last Passover lamb of the passion week, pointed as with flaming finger to Calvary's cross. Nay, all the centuries moved as in solemn procession to lay their tributes upon Golgotha."

Looked at in more detail and divided into different categories, one can demonstrate that all messianic predictions of the Old Testament converge in Jesus of Nazareth as a "focal point of dazzling glory."

CHAPTER TWO

PROPHECIES ESTABLISHING THE CREDENTIALS OF THE MESSIAH

C redentials are testimonials, written proofs, proving the bearer to right of office or position. Our gracious Redeemer, when He came to the earth, condescended to present His *credentials* from the heavenly court. These credentials prove that Jesus is the Christ. In the first chapter of Matthew, he presents a succinct summary of His credentials, "The book of the genealogy of Jesus Christ, the son of David, the son of Abraham" (Mt 1·1).

By giving a sufficient number of definite *specifications* in the Old Testament concerning the coming Messiah, God enabled us to pick out one man from all history, from all nations, from all peoples, and be absolutely sure that one man is the Messiah! These details of His credentials, these specifications, these elements of His *address*, were given that all might know who the true Messiah is. As these prophecies are listed and explained, it soon becomes obvious that no other person in the history of the world could fulfill them all — or even a very small percentage of them — other than Jesus.

Very early on in the biblical narrative, God eliminated *half* of the human race as the immediate parent of the Messiah; and at the same time He made it clear that the Messiah would come as a man and not as an angel when He gave the promise that the coming Deliverer would be the *seed of the woman*:

> And I will put enmity between thee and the woman, and between thy seed and her seed; he shall bruise thy head, and thou shalt bruise his heel (Gen. 3:15).

This, the first of the direct messianic promises in the Bible, is "the Bible in embryo, the sum of all history and prophecy in a germ" (H. Grattan Guinness,

15

The Approaching End of the Age). Here is foretold not only the virgin birth of Christ but also His vicarious sufferings — "thou shalt bruise his heel" — and His complete, eventual victory over Satan and his works — "he [the Messiah] shall bruise thy head."

There is further remarkable evidence in Genesis 4:1 that this promise in Genesis 3:15 was well-understood by Adam and Eve, for at the birth of her first son, Eve ecstatically exclaimed, "I have obtained the man, even the Lord!" (Heb. of Gen. 4:1). When her firstborn son arrived, Eve thought the promised Deliverer had come. But she was mistaken as to the time, place and many other yet-to-be-revealed specifications. Many centuries must pass before the Messiah could come. "But, when the fullness of the time was come, God sent forth his Son, made of a woman, made under the law, To redeem them that were under the law" (Gal. 4:4-5).

Then God eliminated two-thirds of the nations by indicating that the Messiah must come through Noah's son *Shem*, not Ham or Japheth.

In the very beginning of the history of the nations, God, through His prophet Noah, identified Himself with Shem in a special way:

> Blessed be the LORD God of Shem...God shall enlarge Japheth, and he shall dwell in the tents of Shem (Gen. 9:26-27).

In the Hebrew of Genesis 9:27, there is no word corresponding to "he" as found in the King James Version; therefore, the verse correctly reads, "God will enlarge Japheth, and will dwell in the tents of Shem." The *Chaldee of Onkelos* paraphrase of the verse reads, "and will make his glory to dwell in the tabernacles of Shem." The final fulfillment of the prediction in Genesis 9:27 came when the eternal Word, who was with God and was God (Jn. 1:1), "was made flesh, and dwelt among us (and we beheld his glory, the glory as of the only begotten of the Father), full of grace and truth" (Jn. 1:14). He came to His people Israel, who are descendants of Shem, through Abraham (see Gen. 11:10-27).

Later still, another choice was made by God. All of the hundreds of nations of the world were eliminated except one, the new nation begun by God himself when He called Abraham. God divided the nations into two groups, Jews and Gentiles, and separated one small nation, the Jews, that through them the Messiah might come.

> Now the LORD had said unto Abram, Get thee out of thy country, and from thy kindred, and from thy father's house, unto a land that I will show thee; And I will make of thee a great nation, and I will bless thee, and make thy name great; and thou shalt

be a blessing. And I will bless them that bless thee, and curse him that curseth thee: and in thee shall all families of the earth be blessed...Unto thy seed will I give this land (Gen. 12:1-3, 7; cp. Gen. 17:1-8).

And the angel of the LORD called unto Abraham out of heaven the second time, And said, By myself have I sworn, saith the LORD...That in blessing I will bless thee...And in thy seed shall all the nations of the earth be blessed (Gen. 22:16-18).

Here is a phenomenon of the first magnitude, a record that goes back 1,500 years before Christ *in which the writer hazards multiple predictions* that God would bless Abraham, make him a blessing, give him the land of Canaan and bless the world through him and his "seed." A great nation was created and given a land of their own for one purpose — so that the Messiah might come to and through them to bless the world! The prediction has been in the Book of Genesis, unchanged, for thousands of years.

Its fulfillment is an age-long miracle and is as definite and complete as the original prophecy. Not only did God make of Abraham a great nation, giving Canaan to the Jews under the conquest of Joshua, but in due time the Messiah came to them, and the world has been immeasurably blessed through Abraham's seed, which is Christ. Concerning this subject, we read in the Book of Galatians:

And the scripture, foreseeing that God would justify the Gentiles through faith, preached before the gospel unto Abraham, saying, In thee shall all nations be blessed...Now to Abraham and his seed were the promises made. He saith not, And to seeds, as of many; but as of one, And to thy seed, which is Christ (Gal. 3:8, 16).

And so, the messianic story slowly unfolded in the Old Testament. The Messiah must be the *seed of the woman*, come through the *line of Shem*, and be the *seed of Abraham*. That narrowed the search for the Messiah. Men knew to look for Him in the Jewish race, as a descendant of Abraham.

Abraham, however, had several sons, including Ishmael, his firstborn, and Isaac. Another choice was therefore made, and the line narrowed still more. The Messiah would come through Isaac (Gen. 17:19; 21:12; cp. Heb. 11:18; Rom. 9:7, "in Isaac shall thy seed be called") and not through Ishmael, the progenitor of the modern Arabs.

And the LORD appeared unto him [Isaac], and said, Go not down into Egypt; dwell in the land which I shall tell thee of. Sojourn in this land, and I will be with thee, and will bless thee; for unto thee, and unto thy seed, I will give all these countries [the promised land], and I will perform the oath which I swore unto Abraham thy father; And I will make thy seed to multiply as the stars of heaven, and will give unto thy seed all these countries; and in thy seed shall all the nations of the earth be blessed (Gen. 26:2-4).

That the Messiah and the promised blessing must come through Isaac and the Jewish race, not the Arabs, is further emphasized in Deuteronomy 18:15-18, where it is specifically prophesied that the Messiah, the great Prophet yet to come, would be raised up "from the midst of thee [Israel], of thy brethren." This fact is also clearly set forth in the New Testament: "Who are Israelites...Whose are the fathers, and of whom, as concerning the flesh, Christ came, who is over all, God blessed forever" (Rom. 9:4-5).

Since Isaac had two sons, the messianic line was again narrowed through the clear prediction that the Messiah would come through Jacob, not Esau; that is, the Messiah could not be an Edomite (the descendants of Esau).

And, behold, the LORD...said, I am the LORD God of Abraham, thy father, and the God of Isaac: the land whereon thou liest, to thee will I give it, and to thy seed...and in thee and in thy seed shall all the families of the earth be blessed (Gen. 28:13-14).

I shall see him, but not now: I shall behold him, but not near: there shall come a Star out of Jacob, and a Scepter shall rise out of Israel...Out of Jacob shall he come who shall have dominion (Num. 24:17, 19).

But Jacob had twelve sons, so another choice had to be made by the Almighty. One of the twelve, *Judah*, was selected. The Messiah would come, not from the other eleven tribes of Israel, but through Judah:

The scepter shall not depart from Judah, nor a lawgiver from between his feet, until Shiloh come; and unto him shall the gathering of the people be (Gen. 49:10).

For Judah prevailed above his brethren, and of him came the prince (1 Chr. 5:2; note that the word "prince" in the original is *Nagid,* the same word applied to the Messiah in Dan. 9:25).

Moreover, he refused the tabernacle of Joseph, and chose not the tribe of Ephraim; But chose the tribe of Judah (Ps. 78:67-68).

In the New Testament we read that Jesus "sprang out of Judah" (Heb. 7:14; cp. Rev. 5:5).

Next, of the thousands of families in the tribe of Judah, the Lord made another choice: The Messiah must come from one family line, the *family of Jesse.*

And there shall come forth a rod out of the stem of Jesse, and a Branch shall grow out of his roots; And the Spirit of the LORD shall rest upon him (Isa. 11:1-2).

The word "rod" appears in only one other Old Testament passage (Prov. 14:3) and means *a twig, a shoot such as starts up from the roots of a cut-down tree stump.* Isaiah 11:1-2 is a clear statement that God will take a man with no standing — a mere *stump* of a tree cut down — and graft new life into it. Jesse was not the head of a royal family until God made him the father of a king and put him into the messianic line!

Since Jesse had eight sons, another divine choice was made. The Messiah was to be a descendant of *David,* Jesse's youngest son.

I will set up thy seed after thee, which shall proceed out of thine own body, and I will establish his kingdom. He shall build an house for my name, and I will establish the throne of his kingdom forever (2 Sam. 7:12-13; cp. 1 Chr. 17:11, 14; Ps. 89:35-37; Jer. 23:5-6).

Mark Lev, in his book *Lectures on Messianic Prophecy* (p. 125), commented on 2 Samuel 7:14, which reads, "I will be his father, and he shall be my son. If he commit iniquity, I will chasten him with the rod of men, and with the stripes of the children of men." Lev says, "This could be rendered, 'For iniquity committed [not by Him, but by men] I will chasten Him with the rod due to men, and with the stripes due to the children of men.' " This speaks of the vicarious sufferings of the Son of David and agrees with Isaiah 53:6. If the King James Version is correct, it is a reference to the backsliding and consequent chastening of Solomon, David's immediate successor.

The Lord not only made a promise to David, but He confirmed His promise by an oath: "The LORD hath sworn in truth unto David; he will not turn from it: Of the fruit of thy body will I set upon thy throne" (Ps. 132:11; cp. Heb. 6:13-18).

Again turning to the New Testament, we read: "The book of the genealogy of Jesus Christ, the son of David" (Mt. 1:11); and "Concerning his Son, Jesus Christ our Lord, who was made of the seed of David according to the flesh" (Rom. 1:3; cp. Lk. 1:30-35; Acts 2:29-30; 2 Tim. 2:8; Rev. 5:5; 22:16).

The public knew Jesus as the "Son of David" and so called Him (see Mt. 9:27; 12:22-23; 15:22; 20:30-31; 21:9, 15; Mk. 10:47-48; Lk. 18:38-39). The Pharisees also knew full well that the Messiah must be the Son of David. When Jesus asked them, "What think ye of Christ [Messiah]? Whose son is he? They say unto him, The Son of David" (Mt. 22:41-42). It is obvious that the Messiah had to be a son of David according to the flesh — and Jesus was.

During Bible times, every Jew could trace his genealogy. "So all Israel was reckoned by genealogies" (1 Chr. 9:1). These records were kept in the cities (Neh. 7:5-6; Ezra 2:1) and were public property. Each Israelite's genealogical record constitutes his title to his farm or home; therefore, he had a pecuniary interest in preserving the genealogical records of his family. These national genealogical records were carefully kept until the destruction of Jerusalem, the Temple and the Jewish state in 70 A.D. During the life of Jesus, no one offered to dispute the well-known fact that He was of the house and lineage of David, because it was in the public records to which all had access.

Since 70 A.D., when Israel's genealogical records (except those in the Bible) were destroyed or confused, no pretending Messiah can prove he is the son of David as prophecy demands. In other words, Messiah *had to come before 70 A.D.*

Of all of David's "many sons," the Messiah had to obtain His right to the throne of David through the regal line of *Solomon.*

> And of all my sons (for the LORD hath given me many sons) he hath chosen Solomon, my son, to sit upon the throne of the kingdom of the LORD over Israel (1 Chr. 28:5; cp. v. 6; 1 Chr. 29:24).

In the New Testament, Solomon is in the royal line from David to Joseph (see Mt. 1:6).

Yet another most important *credential* for the Messiah is that *He had to be born of a virgin.* Since the Messiah had to be of the fruit of David's body (Ps. 132:11), this virgin had to be a *direct* descendant of King David.

Hear ye now, O house of David...the LORD himself shall give you a sign [a *sign* in the Bible is a *wonder*, a *miracle*]; Behold, the virgin shall conceive, and bear a son, and shall call his name Immanuel [God with us] (Isa. 7:13-14).

The New Revised Standard Version of the Bible is grossly in error in translating the Hebrew word *almah* in Isaiah 7:14 as "young woman." *Almah* refers to a virgin in every instance of its use in the Old Testament (one of which is in Exodus 2:8, where it is used of a maid, a young girl, the baby Moses' sister). In the Septuagint, *almah* is translated as *parthenos*, the Greek word for virgin.

Indeed, whenever the birth of the Messiah is spoken of in the Old Testament, mention is made of His mother or the womb, but never of a human father. Consider the following references: "Thou art he who took me out of the *womb*" (Ps. 22:9); "The LORD hath called me from the *womb*" (Isa. 49:1); "And now, saith the LORD who formed me from the *womb* to be his servant" (Isa. 49:5); "The LORD hath created a new thing in the earth, A *woman* shall compass a man" (Jer. 31:22); "until the time that *she* who travaileth hath brought forth" (Mic. 5:3).

In the New Testament it is written that Jesus was indeed born of a virgin, a virgin who was a direct descendant of King David. After listing the genealogical record from Abraham to Christ, using the often repeated word "begat" to show descent by natural generation, we finally come to this striking statement:

Now the birth of Jesus Christ was in this way: When, as his mother, Mary, was espoused to Joseph, before they came together, she was found with child of the Holy Spirit ...for that which is conceived in her is of the Holy Spirit. And she shall bring forth a son, and thou shalt call his name JESUS; for he shall save his people from their sins. Now all this was done, that it might be fulfilled which was spoken by the Lord through the prophet, saying, Behold, the virgin shall be with child, and shall bring forth a son, and they shall call his name Immanuel, which, being interpreted, is God with us (Mt. 1:18, 20-23).

This much is patently clear, whoever the Almighty sent to earth via the virgin birth is the Messiah; for here is a true "sign," a wonder of heavenly origin that cannot be counterfeited. The God who gave the specification in Isaiah 7:14 fulfilled it in the virgin birth of Jesus.

This messianic chain giving the Messiah's lineage was formed through many centuries: from Eve, to David, to Isaiah, to the Prophet Micah's time. It was added to by many human agents who spoke "in diverse manners, times and places" (A. T. Pierson, *God's Living Oracles*). And every time prophecy made a particular choice, there was a new risk, humanly speaking, of selecting the wrong branch; but nothing short of *absolute accuracy* will do when God speaks.

Absolute accuracy it was, for when the Messiah came He fulfilled to the letter all the specifications of His lineage. He was indeed the *seed of the woman*, the *Son of Abraham*, the *Son of David* (Mt. 1:1). No other person in the history of the world could have met all of these qualifications.

It is easy to see that if enough characteristic details are given, identification of the Messiah is positive. The same is true of prophecy. If a sufficient number of details are given, *identification is positive.* Many details concerning the Messiah are given, and each one is exactly fulfilled in Jesus of Nazareth, so that His identification is positive.

Moreover, prophecy has given us a further specific *credential,* His *address* in terms of the town where He was to be born.

> But thou, Bethlehem Ephrathah, though thou be little among the thousands of Judah, yet out of thee shall he come forth unto me that is to be ruler in Israel, whose goings forth have been from of old, from everlasting (Mic. 5:2).

Of all the continents on earth, one was chosen — Asia; of all the states of Asia, one was chosen — Canaan; of all the provinces of Palestine, one was chosen — Judea; of all the cities of Judea, one was chosen — Bethlehem Ephrathah, a tiny village having, at that time, fewer than one thousand inhabitants. The prophet pinpointed one obscure village on the map of the world, but he spoke infallibly, for the omniscient God was behind his utterance. The prophet spoke clearly, with unequivocal certainty; for when King Herod demanded of the chief priests and scribes of the people where Christ should be born, they told him, "In Bethlehem of Judea, for thus it is written by the prophet" (Mt. 2:4-6; cp. Jn. 7:42).

Jesus was born in Bethlehem of Judea (Mt. 2:1) in a manner altogether marvelous. Until shortly before the time of His birth, Mary was living at the wrong place — wrong, that is, if her expected child was indeed the Messiah. But, we cannot ignore the intricacies of God's providence in fulfilling His Word. In 1923 at Ankara, Turkey, a Roman temple inscription was found which, when deciphered, related that in the reign of Caesar Augustus there were three great tax collections. The second was ordered *four years before the birth of Christ.*

The proud Jews resented the idea of a special tax, so they sent a commission to Rome to protest it. Quirinius, the local governor of Syria, did not have the authority to settle the problem. Those were days of slow communications and even slower travel. The commission finally failed, and the Jews had to submit to the enrollment and taxing. However, by the time the official tax collectors had worked their way eastward, town by town and province by province, and after the time-consuming delays caused by the Jewish protests, enough time elapsed that, when the enrollment was put into force in Judea, *the exact time had come for the birth of the baby Jesus!*

Neither Mary, Caesar nor the Roman tax collectors controlled the timing, nor were they in charge of affairs. The God who rules the world behind the scenes had His hand on the wheel, and He literally moved the peoples of the world and timed everything to the very day, so that Mary and Joseph arrived in Bethlehem at the precise time, and Jesus, the Messiah, was born in the right place, the place designated by the infallible finger of prophecy!

Finally, to accurately identify the Messiah, the *time* of His coming was predicted.

First, the Messiah had to come *before the tribe of Judah lost its tribal identity.*

> The scepter shall not depart from Judah, nor a lawgiver from between his feet, until Shiloh come; and unto him shall the gathering of the people be (Gen. 49:10).

The word "scepter" in this passage does not necessarily refer to a king's staff. The primary meaning of the word translated "scepter" is a *tribal staff.* "The word *shebet,* which is translated 'scepter' in the Authorized Version signifies a rod or staff, particularly the rod or staff which belonged to each tribe as an ensign of their authority. Each tribe was in possession of its own peculiar 'rod' or 'staff' with its name inscribed thereon" (Bishop Sherlock, *Discourses on Prophecy*). Hence, the "scepter" signified their identity as a tribe. The *tribal identity* of Judah would not pass away — as did that of the other tribes of Israel — "until Shiloh come."

For ages, both Jewish and Christian commentators have taken "Shiloh" to be a name of Messiah. It means *peace* or *one sent.*

Even though the tribe of Judah, during the seventy-year period of their captivity in Babylon, had been deprived of national sovereignty, they *never lost their tribal staff, their national identity;* and they always had their own lawgivers (judges), even in captivity (Ezra 1:5, 8).

At the time of Christ, although the Romans were overlords of the Jews, the Jews had a king in their own land. Moreover, they were, to a large extent, governed by their own laws, and the Sanhedrin of the nation exercised its authority. But in the span of a few years (during the year when Jesus was twelve years of age and appeared publicly in the Temple, Lk. 2:41-52), Archelaus, the king of the Jews, was dethroned and banished. Coponius was appointed Roman Procurator, and the kingdom of Judah, the last remnant of the former greatness of the nation of Israel, was formally debased into a part of the province of Syria (see Josephus' *Antiquities 17*, chapter 13:1-5). For almost another half century, the Jews retained the semblance of a provincial governmental structure; but in 70 A.D., both their city and Temple were destroyed by the armies of the Roman General Titus, and all semblance of Jewish national sovereignty disappeared. The remarkable thing is that the Messiah (Shiloh) came *before* Judah lost its tribal identity, exactly as stated in Genesis 49:10!

Twenty-two years before the Lord Jesus was crucified, the Sanhedrin lost the power of passing the death sentence (see Jn. 18:31) when Judah became a Roman province. Rabbi Rachmon said, "When the members of the Sanhedrin found themselves deprived of their right over life and death, a general consternation took possession of them; they covered their heads with ashes and their bodies with sackcloth, exclaiming, 'Woe unto us, for the scepter has departed from Judah and the Messiah has not come' " (*Chosen People*). The rabbis did not realize that the Messiah had come. From this it is apparent that they considered Genesis 49:10 a messianic passage and had a clear concept of its meaning.

Second, the Messiah had to come *while the second Temple was still standing.*

> And I will shake all nations, and the desire of all nations shall come; and I will fill this house with glory, saith the LORD of hosts...The glory of this latter house shall be greater than of the former, saith the LORD of hosts; and in this place will I give peace, saith the LORD of hosts (Hab. 2:7, 9).

Malachi confirmed Haggai's prophecy, "the Lord, whom ye seek, shall suddenly come to his temple" (Mal. 3:1). This prediction in Malachi, as well as the one in Haggai, could not be fulfilled *after* the destruction of the Temple in 70 A.D. Therefore, if the Messiah were to come, He had to come before the Temple was destroyed. Zechariah 11:13 also demands that the Messiah come before the destruction of the Jewish Temple, for that prediction speaks of "thirty pieces of silver" being "cast...unto the potter in the house of the LORD." In Psalm 118:26 the prophetic pen informs us that the people who would welcome the Messiah were to say not only, "Blessed is he that cometh in the name of the LORD," but also, "we have blessed you out of the house of the LORD." That is, from the house of the Lord (the Temple) the people would bless Him when He came.

All of this prophecy was beautifully fulfilled in the life of Jesus. When He approached Jerusalem for His triumphal entry, the people said, "Blessed is he that cometh in the name of the Lord! Hosanna in the highest!" (Mt. 21:9). We then read that Jesus healed many who were blind and lame *in the Temple* (Mt. 21:14), and there can be no doubt that those who were healed in the Temple blessed Him in the house of the Lord, even as Psalm 118:26 predicted they would!

There is another specific fulfillment to this prophecy. Matthew 21:15 informs us that the children cried out *in the Temple*, saying, "Hosanna to the Son of David!" Surely, "Out of the mouth of babes and sucklings thou hast perfected praise" (Mt. 21:16; cp. Ps. 8:2). God used *children* to fulfill His prediction given in Psalm 118:26 that the Messiah would be blessed in the house of the Lord!

Thus, at least five scriptural predictions of the coming of the Messiah *demand that He come while the Temple at Jerusalem was still standing.* This is of great significance, inasmuch as the Temple has not been rebuilt since its destruction in 70 A.D. These five Scriptures are Psalm 118:26; Haggai 2:7, 9; Zechariah 11:13 and Malachi 3:1.

Clearly, the public entry of Jesus into Jerusalem and the Temple, as reported in the New Testament, was prearranged and predicted in the Old Testament (see Mt. 21:1-16; Mk. 11:1-11; Lk. 19:29-40).

> And Jesus went into the temple of God...And the blind and the lame came to him in the temple, and he healed them...and the children crying in the temple, and saying, Hosanna to the Son of David! (Mt. 21:12-15).

Two other Scriptures bear on this: when the child Jesus was taken to the Temple by His parents, as recorded in Luke 2:25-32; and when Jesus, as a boy of twelve, was "in the temple, sitting in the midst of the teachers...And all that heard him were amazed at his understanding" (Lk. 2:46-47).

After years, even centuries, of waiting, the Messiah suddenly came to His Temple (Mal. 3:1)! A few years later, God destroyed the Temple and the city of Jerusalem, even as Jesus had warned. Clearly, the Messiah has already come. He can't come now, since there is no Temple. The Messiah had to come almost 2,000 years ago, before God had the Temple destroyed.

Jesus warned that the Temple, the heart of Jewish worship, the very heart and soul of their national existence, would be torn down, and "There shall not be left here one stone upon another" (Mt. 24:2). As Jesus, the true Prophet, said, so it came to pass — no doubt sooner than the disciples expected.

Third, Daniel said something very remarkable about the coming of Christ relative to the Temple. In giving the timetable from his time to the coming of the Messiah, Daniel made it clear that the Messiah would come and be "cut off" (die) before the "people [the Romans] of the prince that shall come shall destroy the city [Jerusalem] and the sanctuary [the Temple]" (Dan. 9:26).

Fourth, the Messiah had to come *483 years after a specific date in Daniel's time*. This definite prediction as to the exact time of the coming of the Messiah is one of the most wonderful prophecies in the entire Bible. It established the date of the Messiah's advent almost 500 years before He came.

> Know, therefore, and understand, that from the going forth of the commandment to restore and to build Jerusalem unto the Messiah, the Prince, shall be seven weeks, and threescore and two weeks; the street shall be built again, and the wall, even in troublous times. And after threescore and two weeks shall Messiah be cut off, but not for himself; and the people of the prince that shall come shall destroy the city and the sanctuary (Dan. 9:25-26).

The date of the "commandment to restore and to build Jerusalem" was the decree by Artaxerxes in 444 B.C. granting permission to the Jews to return to Palestine and rebuild the city of Jerusalem (see Neh. 2:1-8).

The Hebrew word translated "weeks" in Daniel 9:25-26 means *sevens* and is used for years (see Gen. 29:27-28; Lev. 25:8). In other words, the *seventy sevens* which are prophetically determined on Israel and the holy city with specified events (v. 24) is a *period of 490 years.* This period is divided into three sections: (1) Seven "weeks," or seven sevens of years — the 49 years the prophet allotted for the rebuilding of Jerusalem under the leadership of Nehemiah and Ezra and their associates (see the Books of Ezra and Nehemiah). History tells us it took 49 years to do this rebuilding job. (2) A second period of 62 "weeks," or 434 years, to the time of the Messiah. (3) The 70th "week," or a period of seven years sometime after the coming of the Messiah.

The period "from...the commandment to restore and to build Jerusalem unto Messiah, the Prince, is a period of 483 years. Sir Robert Anderson in his book, *The Coming Prince,*" made some calculations and gave the world his findings.

He begins with March 14, 444 B.C., the date of "the commandment to restore and to build Jerusalem"; and he ends the period with Jesus' triumphal entry into Jerusalem, which he believes was the official presentation of the Messiah as "Prince" to Israel (cp. Lk. 19:38; Zech 9:9). After careful investigation and consultation with noted astronomers, he gives these startling findings. From 444 B.C. to 32 A.D. is 476 years; 476 multiplied by 365 is 173,740 days; from March 14 to April 6 (the day of Christ's triumphal entry) is 24 days; add 116 days for leap years, and the total is 173,880 days. Since the *prophetic year* of the Bible is always 360 days, the 69 *sevens* of the prophecy in Daniel (69 multiplied by 7, multiplied by 360) equals 173,880 days. And so, the time given by Daniel from the "commandment to restore and to build Jerusalem unto the Messiah, the Prince" works out perfectly — to the very day!

This is a prophecy as detailed as a road map with not a taint of uncertainty. It is a prediction which can be conclusively proven. It points unerringly to Jesus of Nazareth who was "Messiah, the Prince" who was "cut off" by a violent death, "but not for himself." When Jesus began His public ministry, He said significantly, "The time is fulfilled, and the kingdom of God is at hand" (Mk. 1:15). Thus, with absolute certainty the exact year, the very month of a notable event in His life was foretold.

These twelve elements comprise the Messiah's credentials. They were given in the prophetic Word so that all might know the Messiah when He came. The accuracy of these predictions is minute; the fulfillments are exact. All is in perfect agreement: *Jesus of Nazareth fulfills all the specifications* foretold as to His lineage, His birthplace and the time of His birth. It is a nondebatable fact that within a generation of Christ's sufferings on the cross, the Temple was destroyed, the Jewish priesthood ceased to exist, the sacrifices were no longer offered, the Jews' genealogical records were destroyed, their city was destroyed, and the people of Israel were driven out of their land, sold into slavery and dispersed to the four corners of the earth!

CHAPTER THREE

PROPHECIES CONCERNING THE LIFE AND MINISTRY OF THE MESSIAH

The Messiah's Character and Characteristics are Clearly Delineated: He Will be the Sinless One, as Holy as God

The Messiah must be as righteous as God himself, for He will be the "righteous Branch...he shall be called, THE LORD OUR RIGHTEOUSNESS" (Jer. 23:5-6). The Messiah must be God's chosen One in whom He "delighteth" (Isa. 42:1). In Matthew 3:17 the Father says of Jesus, "This is my beloved Son, in whom I am well pleased." The Messiah, on His part, will be the obedient *servant of the Lord* who will ever "delight to do thy [God's] will" (Ps. 40:8). The Lord Jesus could testify, "My food is to do the will of him that sent me, and to finish his work" (Jn. 4:34; cp. Jn. 6:38).

The Messiah will be anointed by the Holy Spirit in a manner and degree far beyond any other man ("above" His "fellows," Ps. 45:7; cp. Heb. 1:9). Another remarkable passage, Isaiah 11:2-5, tell us:

> And the Spirit of the LORD shall rest upon him, the spirit of wisdom and understanding, the spirit of counsel and might, the spirit of knowledge and of the fear of the LORD, And shall make him of quick understanding in the fear of the LORD; and he shall not judge after the sight of his eyes, neither reprove after the hearing of his ears, But with righteousness shall he judge the poor...And righteousness shall be the girdle of his loins, and faithfulness the girdle of his waist.

In the New Testament, we read of Jesus' anointing with the Holy Spirit at the time of His baptism when the Holy Spirit descended like a dove and sat upon Him (Mt. 3:16). He bore witness that the "Spirit of the Lord" was upon Him (Lk. 4:18), which was in fulfillment of a prediction about the Messiah's character and ministry in Isaiah 61:1-3. The people "bore him [Jesus] witness, and wondered at the gracious words which proceeded out of his mouth" (Lk. 4:22).

The Messiah must be a man of perfect self-control, "He shall not cry, nor lift up, nor cause his voice [in anger or as an excited rabble-rouser] to be heard in the street" (Isa. 42:2). He will have patience with the frailties of men, "A bruised reed shall he not break, and smoking flax shall he not quench" (Isa. 42:3). The Messiah will have perseverance in the course of doing His Father's will. He will have courage and success in that goal, as well as steadfastness of purpose, "He shall not fail nor be discouraged" (Isa. 42:4). Matthew, in describing the ministry of Jesus, said that He fulfilled what Isaiah had said about Him:

> That it might be fulfilled which was spoken by Isaiah, the prophet, saying, Behold my servant, whom I have chosen; my beloved, in whom my soul is well pleased; I will put my Spirit upon him, and he shall show justice to the Gentiles. He shall not strive, nor cry; neither shall any man hear his voice in the streets. A bruised reed shall he not break, and smoking flax shall he not quench, till he send forth justice unto victory. And in his name shall the Gentiles trust (Mt. 12:17-21).

The Messiah's compassion and tenderness are revealed in an exquisite figure of touching tenderness, "He shall feed his flock like a shepherd; he shall gather the lambs with his arm, and carry them in his bosom, and shall gently lead those that are with young" (Isa. 40:11). In the New Testament, we read of the compassion of Jesus in Matthew 9:36; 14:14; 15:32 and many other places. In the tenth chapter of John, Christ is presented as the "good shepherd" who loves His sheep and cares for them, even to the point of giving His life for them (Jn. 10:11-18).

The Messiah will be "just" and "lowly" (Zech. 9:9); "fairer than the children of men" with "grace...poured into thy lips" and blessed by God forever (Ps. 45:2). He will be without "violence," indicating a blameless outward life; "neither was any deceit in his mouth," indicating an innocent inner life (Isa. 53:9; cp. 1 Pet. 2:22). He will suffer great personal wrong done to Him without complaining to God or man (Isa. 53:7; 50:6-7). In the New Testament, we learn that Jesus was "meek and lowly in heart" (Mt. 11:29); and the Father testified of Him, "Thou hast loved righteousness, and hated iniquity; therefore, God...hath anointed thee with the oil of gladness above thy fellows" (Heb. 1:9). When the Lord Jesus was crucified, He meekly suffered all the indignities, insults, blasphemies, mental torture and physical violence heaped upon Him and did not complain; in fact, He prayed for His persecutors (Mt. 27:12-14; Lk. 23:34).

As a teacher, the Messiah "shall not fail...till he have set justice in the earth," and the nations "shall wait for his law" (Isa. 42:4). Today, multitudes in our most advanced nations wait on Jesus' teaching; and when the Kingdom of God, with Christ as King, is finally set up on earth, He will indeed have "set justice in the earth."

The word "justice" is a very rich word, translated by 31 different words in the King James Version. It means to bring *law, order, salvation, truth and righteousness* to mankind. The Messiah's ministry was to bring salvation and truth (justice) to Jews and Gentiles alike (Isa. 42:6).

It was prewritten of the Messiah that He would "open [His] mouth in a parable," He will "utter dark sayings of old" (Ps. 78:2). When Jesus the great Teacher came, He taught "as one having authority, and not as the scribes" (Mt. 7:29). The scribes taught by quoting what certain rabbis had said; but when Jesus taught, He gave God's words and spoke with finality and assurance, "Verily, verily, I say unto you..." (Jn. 5:24; 6:47; etc.). Moreover, Christ's characteristic method of teaching was by the use of parables: "and without a parable spake he not unto them, That it might be fulfilled which was spoken by the prophet, saying, I will open my mouth in parables" (Mt. 13:34-35).

It is clear in the Old Testament that when the Messiah comes, He will be holier and wiser than men, even as just and righteous as God himself.

The Portrayal of the Perfect Character

As was foretold throughout the Old Testament Scriptures, when the Messiah did come, He possessed the perfect character. He was Jesus the Christ. That which is given in general terms and in an abstract way in the Old Testament, in portraying the coming perfect Messiah, became a concrete reality, in the flesh, in the person of Jesus Christ in the New Testament. In the Lord Jesus we see the One who is altogether lovely, the chief among ten thousand, the delight of the Heavenly Father.

Christ's perfectly poised character was not unbalanced by eccentricities or human foibles. His perfections were not tainted by pride, nor was His wisdom marred by an occasional bit of folly. His equity was not twisted by prejudice, nor was His justice adulterated by selfish whims. He had a becoming dignity which was happily blended with His gracious humility. He had concern for others without worry, zeal without fretfulness, patience without dilatoriness, tact without dishonesty, and frankness without rudeness. His authority was balanced and blended with gentleness and patience.

He never had to admit defeat, retract a statement, offer an apology, change His teachings, confess a sin or a mistake, or ask advice. He never lost His temper or spoke rashly. He was never bested in an argument; He always had the right answer — the will and Word of God.

He went about doing good, prayed much, gave God the glory and thanks in all things, and had no interest in the accumulation of material things. He lived and died in poverty, yet He never lacked until His time of suffering on the cross.

His miracles were all beneficent, never for vainglory. He was the perfect Teacher and lived what He taught. He was, in the truest sense, the Son of man; yet He was not one of us, for He never sinned. He was from above and not from the earth, and He was the unique Son of God. No other man was like this man.

He never made a claim to supernatural power or prerogative without performing a miracle to prove it. He who said, "I am the light of the world" (Jn. 9:5) also opened the eyes of the man born blind, so that all could see His right to the claim. He who said, "I am the resurrection, and the life" (Jn. 11:25) proved that these were sober words of truth by raising Lazarus from the dead (Jn. 11:25, 43-44). He who said, "I am the bread of life" (Jn. 6:35) gave full evidence that He was all He claimed to be by performing the miracle of feeding the five thousand from five loaves and two fish (Jn. 6:5-14).

Volumes have been written, volumes more probably will be written, on the moral glory and perfect character of the Lord Jesus. In summation, suffice it to say that He is the image of the invisible God (Heb. 1:3), the sum and substance of all good, the One in whom dwelt all the fullness of the Godhead (Col. 2:9). His holiness shone with undiminished luster; His loveliness was as pure and genuine as the glory of God. His love was as selfless and complete as the love of God, for in all the history of the world, mankind has never seen, except in the death of Christ, a perfect character dying under an unparalleled weight of unmerited agony. The mighty yet lowly royal sufferer uncomplainingly bore the weight of the sin of all humanity in His atoning death on the cross.

The Messiah's Supernatural Miracles are Clearly Foretold

The Messiah must show as His hallmarks supernatural works which prove Him to be the God-appointed, God-sent Redeemer. As His *special* work, the Messiah would offer Himself as a substitutionary sacrifice to redeem the race. The Messiah's ministry must *bless* people, as Isaiah foretold:

> The Spirit of the Lord GOD is upon me, because the LORD hath anointed me to preach good tidings unto the meek, he hath sent me to bind up the brokenhearted, to proclaim liberty to the captives, and the opening of the prison to those who are bound; To proclaim the acceptable year of the LORD...to give unto them beauty for ashes, the oil of joy for mourning, the garment of praise for the spirit of heaviness (Isa. 61:1-3).

The Messiah, as the Lord God in the midst of the people, must be the miracle worker par excellence.

> Behold, your God will come...he will come and save you. Then the eyes of the blind shall be opened, and the ears of the deaf shall be unstopped. Then shall the lame man leap as an hart, and the tongue of the dumb sing (Isa. 35:4-6).

> I, the LORD, have called thee in righteousness...and give thee for a covenant of the people, for a light of the nations, To open the blind eyes, to bring out the prisoners from the prison (Isa. 42:6-7).

The Messiah will be the worldwide Savior for "salvation unto the end of the earth" (Isa. 49:6), as a "light of the nations" (Isa. 42:6-7; 11:10) and the "Redeemer of Israel" (Isa. 49:7).

In the New Testament, Christ is revealed as the worldwide Savior, "For God so loved the world, that he gave his only begotten Son, that whosoever believeth in him should not perish, but have everlasting life" (Jn. 3:16).

The Prophet Simeon, when he saw the child Jesus in the Temple, knew that He was the Christ. He said, "Lord...mine eyes have seen thy salvation, Which thou hast prepared before the face of all people; A light to lighten the Gentiles, and the glory of thy people, Israel" (Lk. 2:29-32; cp. Lk. 1:68-79; Rom. 3:28-30; etc.).

The Messiah's *special* work would be to offer Himself, His soul and body, as a ransom, an offering, a supreme sacrifice of Himself. He will bruise Satan's head (Gen. 3:15; cp. Heb. 2:14; 1 Jn. 3:8); and by that great work of redemption, He will establish a kingdom that will last forever (Isa. 9:7; Dan. 7:14; Lk. 1:32-33; Heb. 2:9-14).

The identification of the Old Testament Messiah in the Christ of the New Testament is perfect, describing His holy character, miraculous works and sacrificial death on the cross. The miracles Jesus wrought were well-known by His generation. Peter, in his sermon on the day of Pentecost, used the reality of Christ's miracle-working ministry as *proof* of His Messiahship:

> Ye men of Israel, hear these words: Jesus of Nazareth, a man approved of God among you by miracles and wonders and signs, which God did by him in the midst of you, as ye yourselves also know...Whom God hath raised up...let all the house of Israel know assuredly, that God hath made that same Jesus...both Lord and Christ (Acts 2:22, 24, 36).

In the Gospels, Jesus blessed, saved and helped all seekers who contacted Him. He healed the sick, cleansed the lepers, opened the eyes of the blind, raised the dead, fed the hungry, walked on the Sea of Galilee and performed many other miracles (see Mk. 1:32, 34, 41-42; Jn. 6:11-13, 19-21; 9:7; 11:43-44; etc.).

John the Baptist, after his imprisonment by King Herod, sent two of his disciples to Jesus to ask Him, "Art thou he that should come [the Messiah], or do we look for another?" (Mt. 11:2-3). In essence, he was asking, *Are you the Messiah or are you not?* Jesus answered by reminding John and his disciples of His *miracle works*, thus assuring them that He was the Messiah, for only the Messiah could do those works: "Go and show John again those things which ye do hear and see: The blind receive their sight, and the lame walk, and the lepers are cleansed, and the deaf hear, the dead are raised up, and the poor have the gospel preached to them" (Mt. 11:4-5). These miracles are the very marks of the Messiah given in the Old Testament!

Finally, after His benevolent ministry of healing and blessing the people, Christ accomplished the great work for which He came into the world, the work to which He was foreordained from before the foundation of the world (see 1 Pet. 1:18-20). He died on the cross, offering Himself as a vicarious sacrifice to redeem the race: "Christ Jesus, Who gave himself a ransom for all" (1 Tim. 2:5-6); "Jesus...by the grace of God, should taste death for every man" (Heb. 2:9); "once, in the end of the ages, hath he [Christ] appeared to put away sin by the sacrifice of himself" (Heb. 9:26).

Jesus himself appealed to the people to believe on Him for the sake of the miracles He had performed:

> Believest thou not that I am in the Father, and the Father in me? The words that I speak unto you, I speak not of myself; but the Father that dwelleth in me, he doeth the works. Believe me that I am in the Father, and the Father in me; or else believe me for the very works' sake (Jn. 14:10-11).

Indeed, Jesus had this *triple seal* as proof of his genuineness: (1) a perfect character; (2) miracle works; (3) Himself as a sacrifice for the redemption of all mankind. These three requirements clearly establish the fact that Jesus is the true Messiah, for He fulfilled all three!

During the last 2,000 years, His gospel has literally been preached around the world, and millions of Gentiles, as well as multitudes of Jews, have trusted and are trusting Him. Jesus is indeed the universal Savior, the "Lamb of God, who taketh away the sin of the world" (Jn. 1:29). His love envelopes the world (Jn. 3:16); His gospel is for every creature (Mk. 16:15); His is the only "name under heaven given among men, whereby we must be saved" (Acts 4:12).

CHAPTER FOUR

PROPHECIES CONCERNING
THE PROPHETIC PARADOXES

The Old Testament presents a mysterious prophetic puzzle of strange combinations of prophecies concerning the coming Messiah which appear at times so conflicting that they seem impossible to fulfill. These seemingly contradictory and apparently irreconcilable prophecies arc called *prophetic paradoxes*. A *prophetic paradox* is made up of two or more prophecies each of which contains a *seeming contradiction* with no real absurdity involved and presenting an enigma which, without a clue to its fulfillment, seems impossible to solve. The Old Testament abounds with such prophetic paradoxes concerning the Messiah which were and still are absolute mysteries except as the New Testament solves them in Christ.

This amazing feature of many messianic predictions prevents both wicked men and overzealous disciples from purposely fulfilling them, if they could; for the prophecies, in at least some instances, were not fully understood until the fulfillment explained and made them clear (see 1 Pet. 1:10-11). Such unique prophecies absolutely prove that the God of prophecy, who designed them, and the God of providence, who fulfilled them, are one.

Another astonishing feature about these prophetic paradoxes is the perfectly normal, artless way in which they were providentially, even miraculously, fulfilled in the life of Jesus Christ in the New Testament. It is not necessary to strain or force either the facts or the predictions to make them conform.

Consider some of these *impossible* contrasts: God will come to earth to be born as a child. The Messiah will be begotten by God, yet He will be God. He will be "a son" in time, yet He is "The Everlasting Father" (Isa. 9:6). Chosen by God, elect, precious, yet despised and rejected by men, He is a "man of sorrows, and acquainted with grief" (Isa. 53:3). Coming to the Jews and being rejected by them as a nation, He will be sought by the Gentiles and will be a "light to the nations" (Isa. 49:6). He will be a man who is God, and God who is man. Sinless and having a wholly benevolent ministry, He will eventually be forsaken by both God and man. He will be abhorred, yet extolled and exalted; "cut off," yet His days will be prolonged. "Grief and glory, travail and triumph, humiliation and exaltation, cross and crown are so strongly intermingled that the ancient Jewish expositors could not reconcile these prophecies. The whole prophetic picture of the coming Messiah, with its fulfillment, is so wholly novel, so mysterious, so artless and yet so intricate, that it was and is and must forever remain the wonder of all literature" (A. T. Pierson).

Consider these few of the many prophetic paradoxes in the predictions of the coming Messiah.

The Messiah's Birth

Notice in the following predictions these striking irreconcilables: A virgin is to bear a son, something unknown in human experience. And, this child will be God, "God with us." He will be God-begotten and yet God incarnate!

Therefore the Lord himself shall give you a sign; Behold, the virgin shall conceive, and bear a son, and shall call his name Immanuel (Isa. 7:14).

For unto us a child is born, unto us a son is given, and the government shall be upon his shoulder; and his name shall be called Wonderful, Counselor, The Mighty God, The Everlasting Father, The Prince of Peace (Isa. 9:6).

To fulfill these amazing prophecies, God performed a *biological miracle*; Christ was conceived by the Holy Spirit (Lk. 1:35) and born of the virgin Mary, as recorded in Matthew 1:16-25. To fulfill these two predictions made 700 years before, God in the person of His Son came to earth, and the incarnation became a reality; "the Son of the Highest" (Lk. 1:32) became Mary's son, God manifest in the flesh (see Lk. 1:31-33; Jn. 1:1-3, 14; 1 Tim. 3:16) — and all of this although Mary knew not a man (Lk. 1:34).

Not only was the Messiah to be the God-Man, born of a virgin (Isa. 7:14; 9:6), but He was, in some mysterious way, to be all of the following as well: the seed of the woman (Gen. 3:15); "the Son of man" (Dan. 7:13); the Son of God (Ps. 2:7); the seed of Abraham (Gen. 22:18); and the "fruit" of David's body (Ps. 132:11). But how could God be a man and man be God and, at the same time, be a son of man and Son of God? How can a person be God and yet be born of God? How can one be a "Son of man" and yet have no human father? How can He be the seed of the woman when the woman knew not a man? How could one person be all of these? Wonder of wonders, Jesus was! The Lord Jesus was God (Jn. 1:1); He was man (Jn. 1:14), He was the seed of the woman (Gal. 4:4); He was the Son of man, the representative man (Lk. 19:10); He was the Son of God (Jn. 3:16); He was the seed of Abraham and the seed of David (Mt. 1:1). Here, then, we have the miracle of the ages: Christ Jesus, perfect man, yet very God; God-begotten, yet God incarnate in one indivisible, loving, matchless personality. The Apostle John explained the supreme mystery (called the "mystery of God...and of Christ," Col. 2:2; 4:3) in these words:

> In the beginning was the Word, and the Word was with God, and the Word was God. The same was in the beginning with God...And the Word was made flesh, and dwelt among us (and we beheld his glory, the glory as of the only begotten of the Father), full of grace and truth...the only begotten Son, who is in the bosom of the Father (Jn. 1:1-2, 14, 18).

The Messiah's Place of Origin

From where did He come? Bethlehem? Egypt? Nazareth? Here is another involved series of predictions. Prophecy said, "But thou, Bethlehem Ephrathah...out of thee shall he come forth...that is to be ruler in Israel" (Mic. 5:2). But another Scripture said, "I...called my son out of Egypt" (Hos. 11:1). And there was a spoken prophecy commonly known among the people of Israel as one of the predictions of the prophets, "He shall be called a Nazarene" (Mt. 2:23), possibly based on Isaiah 11:1 where the Messiah is called the "Branch" (Heb., *neh-tzer*), meaning the *separated One* or *the Nazarene*.

Are these contradictions? Not at all, after the person came who unlocked the puzzle by the course of events in His divinely ordained life. He was *born in Bethlehem*, as Micah said. Soon after His birth, He was *taken to Egypt* by Joseph and Mary, and from there God called Him back to Palestine following the death of wicked King Herod (Mt. 2:13-23). When Joseph and Mary returned to Palestine with the child Jesus, they *lived in Nazareth,* the city where the Lord was reared; hence, in His ministry He was called "Jesus of Nazareth" (Lk. 18:37; Acts 2:22; etc.).

There is an interesting historical sidelight that adds pungency to the understanding of these predictions and their fulfillments. When Joseph and

Mary returned from Egypt, Joseph was apparently about to settle near Bethlehem in Judea:

> But when he heard that Archelaus did reign in Judea in the place of his father, Herod, he was afraid to go there...he turned aside into the parts of Galilee; And he came and dwelt in a city called Nazareth, that it might be fulfilled which was spoken by the prophets, He shall be called a Nazarene (Mt. 2:22-23).

Humanly speaking, everything hinged on one peculiar fact: In a peevish fret before his death, King Herod changed his will and appointed Archelaus, the most wicked of his living sons, to rule instead of Antipas. It was this fear of Archelaus that led Joseph to look for another residence; then God led him to Nazareth. And so, God, who uses the wrath of man to praise Him, permitted the wrath of a petulant king to bring to pass a fulfillment of His Word (see Ps. 76:10).

Being of the tribe of Judah and being born in Bethlehem, Jesus was indeed a true "Nazarene," a "separated one," by living in Galilee instead of with his Judean brethren in the land of Judah. Joseph of old also was separated (*nazared*) from his brethren by his exile for so many years in Egypt (see Gen. 49:26, where the word *separate* comes from the Hebrew root *nazar*).

The historical record of the life of Jesus completely resolves these three seemingly contradictory prophecies.

How Could the Messiah be Both David's Son and David's Lord?

Christ himself raised this interesting question with the Pharisees when He asked them pointedly:

> What think ye of Christ? Whose son is he? They say unto him, The Son of David. He saith unto them, How, then, doth David, in the Spirit, call him Lord, saying, The LORD said unto my Lord, Sit thou on my right hand, till I make thine enemies thy footstool? If David, then, call him Lord, how is he his son? (Mt. 22:42-45; cp. Ps. 110:1).

It is not hard to see how Christ could be both David's son and David's Lord when we have the key to the situation in the facts as presented in the New Testament. Christ was David's son in that He was a descendant of David after the flesh (Lk. 1:32; Rom. 1:3); and He was David's Lord, for the Messiah is God, "KING OF KINGS, AND LORD OF LORDS" (Rev. 19:16). The Messiah is called "LORD" (Jehovah) in Jeremiah 23:6, "God" (Elohim) in Psalm 45:6 (cp. Heb. 1:8) and "Lord" (Adonai) in Psalm 110:1 and Malachi 3:1. All three are names and titles of deity in the Old Testament. It is clear that the Messiah is not only David's Lord, but He is *Lord of all.*

The Messiah's Right to David's Throne

Here we encounter an intricate, involved puzzle. Christ, the seed of David, must be virgin born and yet have a legal right to the throne of David, despite the fact that one of Solomon's descendants was an evil man named Jeconiah, of whom it was written, "Is this man Coniah [Jeconiah] a despised broken idol? Is he a vessel in which is no pleasure? Why are they cast out, he and his seed, and are cast into a land which they knew not?...Thus saith the LORD, Write this man childless, a man that shall not prosper in his days; for no man of his seed shall prosper, sitting upon the throne of David, and ruling any more in Judah" (Jer. 22:28, 30). Despite the fact that in Israel, *the right to the throne was transmitted only through the male line,* Christ was born of a virgin.

It is patently clear that the Messiah would inherit "the throne of David" (1 Chr. 17:11, 14; Ps. 132:11; Isa. 9:7; Jer. 33:15-17). But since He had to be born of a virgin, *how would He obtain His legal right to the throne of David?* How could the roadblock erected by Jeconiah's sin be circumvented? Who could untangle these predictions which seem hopelessly confused? The Master who devised the strange prophecies also worked out their fulfillment. The Prophet Isaiah said, "The zeal of the LORD of hosts will perform this" (Isa. 9:7).

Not only was the apparently impossible paradox resolved in Jesus the Christ, but God has given us the complete record of how He did it in the genealogies of the New Testament. Matthew records the genealogy of Christ through *Joseph.* This genealogy shows Christ to be the son of David (giving Him the right to David's throne) and also the son of Abraham (giving Him the right to the land of promise, the territorial possessions given to Abraham and his seed).

Luke traces the genealogy of Christ through Heli (Mary's father) back to Adam and God (Lk. 3:23-38), giving Christ a title deed to the whole earth as the son of Adam (see Gen. 1:27-30; Ps. 8:4-6; Heb. 2:6-9; Rev. 5:1-10) and to "all things" as the Son of God (see Heb. 1:2).

In Matthew's genealogy, Joseph is seen to be in the *regal* line of descent from King David down through *Solomon.* But Joseph was also a descendant of David through Jeconiah; hence, succession to the throne for Joseph personally is barred. Matthew's genealogical record is careful to show that

Jesus was *not*, through Joseph, the fruit of David's body (i.e., a direct descendant of David through Joseph).

Luke gives Christ's genealogy through Mary. Heli was obviously Mary's father, Joseph's father-in-law (Lk. 3:23).

It is interesting to note that in the genealogical record of Matthew, it is written that "Jacob begat Joseph" (Mt. 1:16); that is, Jacob was the actual father of Joseph. In Luke, however, it is written that "Joseph...was the son of Heli" (Lk. 3:23). The word "son" is not in the original but was supplied by the translators. The verse should read, "son-in-law" instead of "son." Obviously, Joseph could not have had two fathers; hence, he is the son-in-law of Heli, his son in the sense that he married Heli's daughter. This is in accordance with Jewish custom (see 1 Sam. 24:16).

Christ is shown to be the *literal* fruit of David's body through His mother Mary. But (and this is important), while Mary was in a *royal* line from David, she was *not* in the *regal* lineage, for she was a descendant of King David through *Nathan*; whereas the right to the throne came through *Solomon* (see 1 Chr. 28:5-6). Therefore, Joseph's marriage to Mary *before Christ was born* was an absolute necessity, and that is exactly what occurred!

> Now the birth of Jesus Christ was in this way: When, as his mother, Mary, was espoused to Joseph, before they came together, she was found with child of the Holy Spirit...behold, an angel of the Lord appeared unto him [Joseph] in a dream, saying, Joseph, thou son of David, fear not to take unto thee Mary, thy wife; for that which is conceived in her is of the Holy Spirit (Mt. 1:18, 20).

The importance of the genealogical records in the Bible should not be minimized, because they are of prime importance in proving that Jesus is the Messiah and that He has a right to the throne of David. The genealogical records in the New Testament show the importance God places on the *proof* that Jesus is David's son and indirectly show the importance of the entire argument from fulfilled prophecy.

And so, through Mary, Jesus obtained His *literal* descent from King David; and from Mary's marriage to Joseph, who was also a son of David, He obtained His *legal* right to David's throne, for Mary was Joseph's wife *before Jesus was born*, making Joseph His legal father (foster father). Additionally, the prophecy concerning Jeconiah was fulfilled as well, for Jesus is *not* the seed (a direct descendant) of Jeconiah.

The Messiah Was to be Both the Chief Cornerstone and a Stone of Stumbling or Rock of Offense

He shall be...for a stone of stumbling and for a rock of offense to both the houses of Israel (Isa. 8:14)

The stone which the builders refused is become the head of the corner (Ps. 118:22; cp. Isa. 28:16).

To unbelievers, the Messiah would be a "rock of offense" and a "stone of stumbling." Peter explained the mystery by showing that everything depends on a person's attitude toward Christ, whether of faith or unbelief:

Wherefore also it is contained in the scripture, Behold, I lay in Zion a chief cornerstone, elect, precious; and he that believeth on him shall not be confounded. Unto you, therefore, who believe he is precious, but unto them who are disobedient, the stone which the builders disallowed, the same is made the head of the corner, And a stone of stumbling, and a rock of offense, even to them who stumble at the word, being disobedient (1 Pet. 2:6-8; cp. Rom. 9:32-33).

As He did so often, the Lord Jesus called attention to the prophecy in the Old Testament, showing Himself to be the New Testament fulfillment of it: "Jesus saith unto them, Did ye never read in the scriptures, The stone which the builders rejected, the same is become the head of the corner; this is the Lord's doing, and it is marvelous in our eyes?" (Mt. 21:42). The Lord also added this significant statement: "And whosoever shall fall on this stone [seeking His mercy and grace] shall be broken [his hopes in himself completely crushed], but on whomsoever it shall fall [in judgment], it will grind him to powder [completely ruin him for time and eternity]" (Mt. 21:44).

To the believer, Christ is the *Chief Cornerstone*, and He is very precious. To the unbeliever, Christ is the *Stone of Stumbling* or *Rock of Offense*. To the one, Christ brings eternal salvation; to the other, He brings judgment. Those who stumble in unbelief over Christ reject Him and fall to their eternal destruction.

The Messiah Was to be Rejected by Israel Yet Become a Light to the Nations and Salvation to the Ends of the Earth

Racially, the Messiah would be a Jew, a "rod out of the stem of Jesse...a root of Jesse" (Isa. 11:1, 10); and yet the Gentiles would seek Him (Isa.

43

11:10), an unheard of thing, for there is and has been through the ages animosity between Jews and Gentiles. This enmity, however, is done away with in Christ (Eph. 2:14-15).

The veil over their hearts would be destroyed for multitudes of believing Gentiles (Isa. 25:7), and a veil of unbelief would form over the hearts of many Jews. Isaiah predicted this judicial blindness for Israel because they "despised and rejected" their Messiah:

> Make the heart of this people [Israel] fat, and make their ears heavy, and shut their eyes; lest they see with their eyes, and hear with their ears, and understand with their heart, and be converted, and be healed (Isa. 6:10).

> It is a light thing that thou shouldest be my servant to raise up the tribes of Jacob, and to restore the preserved of Israel; I will also give thee for a light to the nations, that thou mayest be my salvation unto the end of the earth (Isa. 49:6).

Nearly twenty centuries of history attest to the truth of these words. When Israel crucified and rejected their Messiah, a veil of unbelief settled over the nation, and although some (a remnant) believe in the Lord Jesus and are saved, blindness is still over the hearts and minds of most Israelis (2 Cor. 3:14-15).

When the Jews rejected their Messiah, the gospel was taken to the Gentiles (see Acts 28:28) and is now preached to the whole world, Jew and Gentile alike. That Gentiles should trust in a Jew for salvation is most unlikely, but true. That the very nation He came to bless turned from Him seems most unlikely, but it is also true (Jn. 1:11-12). That the Gentiles, who were not the people of God, should become the people of God through faith in the Jewish Messiah seems preposterous, but that is the plan God used to solve this prophetic paradox.

The Messiah Was to Have a Double Anointing — A Ministry of Mercy as Savior and a Ministry of Judgment as the Coming King

Since Christ, at His first advent, came to suffer for the sins of the people, we now know (although the Jews of Jesus' day found it hard to realize) that His role as Judge and King will be fulfilled at His second advent. Concerning this subject, W. G. Moorehead wrote:

> Isaiah, who describes with eloquence worthy of a prophet the glories of the Messiah's coming kingdom, also characterizes with

the accuracy of the historian the humiliation, the trials, the agony which were to precede the triumph of the Redeemer of the world, presenting on the one hand a glorious King, Himself deity, "God with us," who has all power; yet, on the other hand, One whose visage was more marred than any man, His bones out of joint and dying of thirst (Ps. 22). How can He be both the great Davidic Monarch, restoring again the glory of Solomon's house, and also be a sacrifice bearing the sins of the people? Clearly, destinies so strongly contrasted could not be accomplished simultaneously. There is only one possible answer;...in the divine purpose the mighty drama is to be in two acts (His first advent and His second advent).

The *suffering Messiah* and His ministry of mercy are often presented in the same Scripture passage with His work as Judge and King. In Isaiah 61:1-2, the last phrase only describes His work of judgment at His second advent. The preceding part of the passage applies to His first advent:

The Spirit of the Lord GOD is upon me, because the LORD hath anointed me to preach good tidings unto the meek; he hath sent me to bind up the brokenhearted, to proclaim liberty to the captives, and the opening of the prison to those who are bound; To proclaim the acceptable year of the LORD, *and the day of vengeance of our God*; to comfort all that mourn.

This same intermingling of prophecy describing the Messiah's work at both advents — *to save* and *to judge*, His humiliation and work as the Redeemer at His first advent, and His work to establish His righteous kingdom at His second advent — is seen in many other Scriptures (i.e., Zech. 9:9-10; Mic. 5:1-4; Dan. 9:24; etc.). In studying messianic prophecy, it is important to determine if the first or second advent or both advents are in view.

When Christ, while speaking in the synagogue at Capernaum, applied the words of the Prophet Isaiah (61:1-2) to Himself (Lk. 4:17-21), He stopped His reading with the words, "To preach the acceptable year of the Lord" (v. 19). Why? He will not proclaim the day of vengeance of our God until His second advent.

The ancient rabbis, studying these and similar predictions about the coming Messiah, came to the conclusion that there must be *two Messiahs*, one a suffering Messiah and the other a conquering, judging Messiah. They failed to see the great truth that there is only *one Messiah*, the Lord Jesus, who has two distinct tasks to perform, one at His first advent, "to make reconciliation for iniquity"; and the second when He returns to earth at His second advent as the mighty King "to bring in everlasting righteousness" (Dan. 9:24).

In Christ, the scores of apparently contradictory messianic prophecies referring either to His first advent or to His second advent, with their different objectives, are fully harmonized. These two advents of Christ are in contrast in such passages as Psalm 22 and Psalm 72; Psalm 69 and Psalm 89; Isaiah 53 and Isaiah 11. This same truth is fully revealed in the New Testament in such passages as 1 Peter 1:11, which speaks of "the sufferings of Christ" at His first advent and "the glory that should follow" at His second advent. Contrast also John 3:16-17 with Revelation 19:11-21; Luke 9:56 with Jude 14-15; and Luke 19:10 with 2 Thessalonians 1:7-10.

The Messiah Will be a Priest Upon His Throne

> Thus speaketh the LORD of hosts: saying, Behold, the man whose name is THE BRANCH...he shall build the temple of the LORD...and shall sit and rule upon his throne; and he shall be a priest upon his throne (Zech. 6:12-13).

In Psalm 110:4, the Messiah is called "a priest forever after the order of Melchizedek." In Jeremiah 23:5, the Messiah is called "a righteous Branch, and a King." In the history of Israel, the chosen line of kings always came from the tribe of Judah (except among the ten tribes which split off to form the northern kingdom after the death of Solomon). Priests came from the tribe of Levi. Since Christ was from the tribe of Judah (Heb. 7:14), how could He also be a priest, since He could not come from two tribes (Judah and Levi)?

God solved this enigma as well. Christ is a King from the tribe of Judah; He will sit upon His throne on earth at His second advent. Christ also is a Priest whose priesthood is *patterned after the Aaronic priesthood* in which the priests offered sacrifices for the sins of the people; thus, Christ offered Himself as the once-for-all sacrifice for sin (Heb. 9:26). But, He was *made* a priest after the *order of Melchizedek* (Heb. 5:6; Ps. 110:4), who was both a king and a priest (Heb. 7:1-2). This intriguing subject of Christ's priesthood is fully explained in Hebrews chapters 7, 8 and 9. Again, the mystery was solved in Christ!

The Messiah, the Chosen Servant of the Lord, Would be Lovely, Most Pleasing to God, Yet He Would be Abhorred by the Nation of Israel

Isaiah 40:5 says that in the Messiah, the "glory of the LORD shall be revealed, and all flesh shall see it together." Then, in complete contrast, the Messiah is spoken of as the One who would be "despised and rejected of men," the One in whom the nation will see "no beauty" that they "should desire him" (Isa. 53:1-3).

In the history of Jesus, this paradox is explained. The Father said of Jesus, "This is my beloved Son, in whom I am well pleased" (Mt. 17:5). On the other hand, the people rejected Him; and no prophecies, other than those telling of His rejection, ever had a sadder fulfillment. The pathos of the Messiah's rejection is told by Jesus himself: "O Jerusalem, Jerusalem, thou that killest the prophets, and stonest them who are sent unto thee, how often would I have gathered thy children together, even as a hen gathereth her chickens under her wings, and ye would not!" (Mt. 23:37).

Those who hated Him "without a cause" were "more than the hairs of [his] head" (Ps. 69:4; cp. Jn. 15:25). The New Testament record tells us, "He came unto his own, and his own received him not" (Jn. 1:11).

Thirty Pieces of Silver Were Either the Price of Christ or the Price of the Potter's Field

> And I said unto them, If ye think good, give me my price; and if not, forbear. So they weighed for my price thirty pieces of silver. And the LORD said unto me, Cast it unto the potter — a lordly price that I was prized at of them. And I took the thirty pieces of silver, and cast them to the potter in the house of the LORD (Zech. 11:12-13).

These are strange words which would be difficult to understand or reconcile with any specific event in history, were it not for the fulfillment as given in the New Testament. There we read that Judas covenanted with the chief priests to betray Christ and deliver Him to them, "and they bargained with him for thirty pieces of silver" (Mt. 26:15). When the heinousness of his crime dawned on him:

> Judas...brought again the thirty pieces of silver to the chief priests and elders...And he cast down the pieces of silver in the temple, and departed, and went and hanged himself. And the chief priests took the silver pieces, and said, It is not lawful to put them into the treasury, because it is the price of blood. And they took counsel, and bought with them the potter's field, to bury strangers in...Then was fulfilled that which was spoken by Jeremiah, the prophet, saying, And they took the thirty pieces of silver, the price of him that was valued...And gave them for the potter's field (Mt. 27:3, 5-7, 9-10).

Along with Judas, the nation of Israel sold Jesus and woefully underestimated Him. They sold Him for thirty pieces of silver, the price of a dead slave (Ex. 21:31). In so doing, the Jewish leaders expressed their hatred for and contempt of Him.

"No one can suppose that the perfect agreement of the Old Testament prediction with its New Testament fulfillment, centering about the exact amount of the sum of money (30 pieces of silver) could be accidental. Still less can it be conceived that the appropriation of the money to the purchase of the potter's field could have taken place without an overruling design" (*Book of Prophecy*, pp. 343-344).

In the fulfillment, all obscurity is removed, and the perfect harmony of the fulfillment with the prophecy is seen. "It was so exactly fulfilled that every one can see that the same God who spoke through the prophet had, by the secret operation of His omnipotent power, which extends even to the ungodly, so arranged matters that when Judas threw back their money and the chief priests purchased the potter's field, they [not only fulfilled prophecy, but] perpetuated the memorial of their sin against their Messiah, and called forth the vengeance of God against their nation" (David Baron, *Visions and Prophecies of Zechariah*, p. 409).

Prophecy Presents the Messiah as Rejected by Men and Forsaken by God and Describes Horrible Sufferings and Death for the One Who Perfectly Obeyed God at All Times

In Psalm 22:1, the Messiah prophetically cried out, "My God, my God, why hast thou forsaken me?" This desolate cry of the One forsaken by God and man is repeated in the New Testament, as Jesus was hanging on the cross: "And about the ninth hour Jesus cried with a loud voice, saying...My God, my God, why hast thou forsaken me?" (Mt. 27:46).

This forsaking of the righteous One in whom God delighted (Ps. 22:8) is all the more strange in that, from the beginning of human history, the fathers trusted in God and were delivered (Ps. 22:4-5); but not so in this instance. The strange enigma can only be fully understood through the explanation of the New Testament that in the sufferings and death of Jesus on the cross, God turned away from Him, for, "God made him [Christ], who knew no sin, to be sin for us, that we might be made the righteousness of God in him" (2 Cor. 5:21).

The Messiah was Wounded and Pierced, Yet Not a Bone was Broken

The Messiah was to be wounded in the house of His friends (Zech. 13:6) and have His hands and feet pierced (Ps. 22:16); yet, in some miraculous way, not one bone of the suffering Messiah was to be broken. In the Psalms, Jehovah said of the Messiah, "He keepeth all his bones; not one of them is broken" (Ps. 34:20; cp. Ex. 12:46).

At the crucifixion, when the Jews feared that the three men being crucified might linger on until death came too late to remove their bodies from the crosses before the beginning of the Sabbath, they sought permission from Pilate to break their legs, an act to hasten death so that they might be removed from the crosses sooner:

> Then came the soldiers, and broke the legs of the first, and of the other who was crucified with him. But when they came to Jesus, and saw that he was dead already, they broke not his legs; But one of the soldiers, with a spear, pierced his side, and immediately came there out blood and water. And he that saw it bore witness, and his witness is true; and he knoweth that he saith true, that ye might believe. For these things were done, that the scripture should be fulfilled, A bone of him shall not be broken. And, again, another scripture saith, They shall look on him whom they pierced (Jn. 19:32-37).

What a marvelous miracle of divine providence. They broke the legs of the two who were crucified with Him, but *not* of Jesus; for prophecy had said, "A bone of him shall not be broken." They pierced His hands, His feet and His side, and each time the weapons struck *between* the bones and did not break them.

The Messiah Was to be Cut Off and Pour Out His Soul Unto Death, Yet God Would Prolong His Days and Divide Him a Portion With the Great

The glorious facts of the Messiah's atoning death and resurrection are prophetically stated in language which is at first obscure but which becomes clear when fulfilled in one of the most thrilling prophetic paradoxes in the entire realm of Scripture.

In the New Testament we read:

> He [Jesus] humbled himself and became obedient unto death, even the death of the cross. Wherefore, God also hath highly

exalted him, and given him a name which is above every name, That at the name of Jesus every knee should bow...And that every tongue should confess that Jesus Christ is Lord, to the glory of God, the Father (Phil. 2:8-11).

Mankind despised Jesus and set Him at nought (Isa. 53:3); but in His time, God made Him "higher than the kings of the earth" (Ps. 89:27). The Old Testament prophets and their readers puzzled over this mystery, but everything was made plain when, in the New Testament, Jesus the Christ died for our sins and was raised from the dead on the third day.

PROPHECIES CONCERNING THE SUFFERINGS, DEATH AND RESURRECTION OF THE MESSIAH

(An Examination of Psalm 22 and Isaiah 53)

PSALM 22

The miracle of the 22nd Psalm is this: Crucifixion was a Roman and Grecian custom unknown to the Jews until the days of their captivity (600 B.C.). The Jews executed their criminals by stoning; and yet, written 1,000 years before the time of Christ by a man who had never seen or heard of such a method of execution, Psalm 22 gives a graphic portrayal of death by crucifixion!

The messianic nature of this Psalm is almost universally admitted by devout students. D. M. Pantone wrote:

Psalm 22, one of David's Psalms, reveals someone — Messiah — dying an awful death, under very peculiar circumstances. The ancient document says, "the assembly of the wicked have enclosed me; they pierced my hands and my feet. I may count all my bones; they look and stare upon me" (vv. 16-17). Crucifixion in David's time was unknown among the Jews; yet the piercing of hands and feet together with the partial stripping — "counting all the bones" — obviously means crucifixion: the crucified are pierced only in their hands and feet, and stripped for exposure. Would a false Messiah have chosen this passage for fulfillment? This old document (Ps. 22) holds the very crucifixion cry, for the Psalm opens with it — "My God, my God, why hast thou forsaken me?" (v. 1). Not a jot or tittle of this Psalm has miscarried:

51

exactly as in His birth and in His ministry, so also in His death — but more so — the ancient document is a photograph of the fact, fulfilled in flawless detail (*Dawn Magazine*).

The Forsaken One

Christ on the cross identified Himself with the One spoken of in this Psalm by quoting its first verse: "My God, my God, why hast thou forsaken me?" (Mt. 27:46). This Psalm has been called "The Psalm of Sobs" (Bishop Alexander, *Witness of the Psalms to Christ*).

> The Hebrew shows not one completed sentence in the opening verses, but a series of brief ejaculations, like the gasps of a dying man whose breath and strength are failing, and who can only utter a word or two at a time. "My God — My God — why forsaken me — far from helping me — words of my roaring" presenting a picture overwhelmingly pathetic: the suffering Savior, forsaken by God, gasping for life, unable to articulate one continuous sentence...The writer thus forecasts the mystery of the cross which remained unsolved for a thousand years. It was like a dark cavern at the time but when the gospel narrative portrays Jesus as the crucified One, it is like putting a lighted torch in the cavern (A. T. Pierson, *Living Oracles*, p. 107).

Periods of Light and Darkness

In verse 2 one sees alternate periods of light and darkness: "O my God, I cry in the daytime, but thou hearest not; and in the night season, and am not silent" (Ps. 22:2).

In the New Testament account of the crucifixion of Christ, we read, "Now from the sixth hour there was darkness over all the land unto the ninth hour" (Mt. 27:45).

Righteous, Yet Forsaken by God

In verses 3-5 we see a prophetic discussion of this strange anomaly: a truly righteous One forsaken by God. It had never happened before in the history of the "fathers." They trusted and were delivered; the Messiah on the cross was forsaken. Christ on the cross was forsaken by God and man.

They Mocked Him

Verses 6-8 tell of those who reproached and mocked Him: "All they who see me laugh me to scorn; they shoot out the lip, they shake the head,

saying, He trusted on the LORD that he would deliver him; let him deliver him, seeing he delighted in him" (vv. 7-8).

The New Testament relates how the people ridiculed and derided Christ on the cross, using almost the identical words which the prophet used: "Likewise also the chief priests, mocking Him...said...He trusted in God; let him deliver him now" (Mt. 27:41, 43).

His Weakness, Thirst and Exposure to Public Scorn

In the prophetic record, further startling details are given: "They gaped upon me...I am poured out like water, and all my bones are out of joint: my heart is like wax; it is melted within me. My strength is dried up like a potsherd, and my tongue cleaveth to my jaws; and thou hast brought me into the dust of death" (vv. 13-15).

The Messiah's exposure to public scorn — "they gaped upon me" (v. 13) — was fulfilled in the New Testament when, at the cross, the people "sitting down...watched him" (Mt. 27:36). His extreme weakness, perspiration and thirst under the pitiless beating of the oriental sun were predicted: "I am poured out like water...my strength is dried up like a potsherd, and my tongue cleaveth to my jaws" (vv. 14-15).

The forsaken sufferer in the New Testament expressed in one simple statement His weakness and thirst: "After this Jesus, knowing that all things were now accomplished, that the scripture might be fulfilled, saith, I thirst" (Jn. 19:28).

He Died of a Broken Heart

One weeps in heart thinking of the Messiah's horrible sufferings, the agony from dislocated bones caused by the weight of the body suspended only by the nails in the hands and feet, "all my bones are out of joint" (v. 14). Add to that the mental and spiritual torture so great that it literally broke His heart: "my heart is like wax; it is melted within me" (v. 14). At last His sufferings were ended by death, "thou hast brought me into the dust of death" (v. 15).

There is evidence from the New Testament record that Jesus died of a broken heart. When the Roman soldier "pierced his side...immediately came there out blood and water" indicating that the heart had been ruptured before it was pierced by the spear, probably from the great emotional strain Christ had suffered. The lymphatic fluid apparently had separated from the red blood, producing "blood and water." The word "lymph" comes from the Latin *lympha*, meaning *water* (cp. 1 Jn. 5:6).

The Parting of His Garments

For exquisite detail dramatically fulfilled, verse 18 is the gem of all prophecy: "They part my garments among them, and cast lots upon my vesture." The divinely inspired prophet, looking down through ten centuries of time, saw and recorded an incident connected with the crucifixion which seems so trivial and unimportant that one wonders why it is referred to at all — unless it was to inform us that the omniscient God wrote the prophecy and the omnipotent God brought it to fulfillment.

In the New Testament account of the crucifixion of Christ, when they pierced His hands and feet, that additional, *unimportant* detail about the disposition of the Messiah's garments was mentioned. Roman soldiers, ignorant of both God and prophecy and knowing nothing of the sacred importance of what they were doing, fulfilled to the letter that age-old prediction:

> Then the soldiers, when they had crucified Jesus, took his garments, and made four parts, to every soldier a part; and also his coat. Now the coat was without seam, woven from the top throughout. They said, therefore, among themselves, Let us not tear it, but cast lots for it, whose it shall be; that the scripture might be fulfilled, which saith, They parted my raiment among them, and for my vesture they did cast lots. These things, therefore, the soldiers did (Jn. 19:23-24).

And so, an obscure prophecy, hidden in the Old Testament for a thousand years, sprang forth as a witness, a living miracle, proving again that God *spoke* in the Old Testament and *fulfilled* in the New Testament. This prophecy shows that the predictions concerning the Messiah in the Old Testament were fulfilled in the Christ of the Gospels, thereby giving a satisfying demonstration of the divine origin of both Testaments.

The Resurrection of the Messiah

The Messiah, so cruelly put to death, would be helped (v. 19), delivered (v. 20) and saved from the lion's mouth (v. 21). His prayer would be answered (v. 21, "thou hast heard me"). Verse 21 is the end of a section.

Verse 22 begins a new section, and the Messiah, now gloriously delivered and resurrected, says: "I will declare thy name unto my brethren; in the midst of the congregation will I praise thee."

The New Testament abounds with evidence that although Christ died and was forsaken by God and man, still God raised Him from the dead on the third day: "ye have taken [Christ], and by wicked hands have crucified and slain; Whom God hath raised up, having loosed the pains of death, because it was not possible that he should be held by it" (Acts 2:23-24).

"The predictions concerning Christ in this chapter," wrote Moses Margoliouth, "are so numerous and so minute that they could not possibly have been dictated by any but by Him to whom all things are naked and open, and who worketh all things according to the counsel of His own will. The most *insignificant* circumstances connected with our Lord's death are set forth with as much accuracy as those which are *most important*...What could be more unlikely than that Messiah should be crucified when crucifixion was not a Jewish but a Roman punishment? And yet David in this Psalm predicted such would be the case centuries before Rome was founded" and ten centuries before the prophecy was fulfilled!

ISAIAH 53

This remarkable prophecy of the sufferings and exaltation of the Messiah was written 700 years before the time of Christ. It reads more like "an historical summary of the Gospel narrative of the sufferings of Christ and the glory that should follow, instead of a prophecy" (David Baron). With this agrees Augustine, who said, "Me thinks Isaiah writes not a prophecy but a Gospel." And another commentator said, "It reads as if it had been written beneath the cross of Golgotha. It is the deepest and the loftiest thing that Old Testament prophecy, outstripping itself, has ever achieved." A. T. Pierson wrote:

> This chapter is a bundle of paradoxes, or apparent contradictions, as numerous as the verses in the chapter. In fact, it was *designed* to present a prophetic enigma which only the person (and work) of the Christ of the New Testament can solve. He is a root out of the dry ground — yet fruitful; He has no form nor beauty — yet He is the chosen Servant of God; He is despised and rejected of men — yet He is the appointed Savior; He suffers unto death — yet He survives; He has no offspring — yet He has a numerous seed; men would make His grave with the wicked — yet He is buried with the rich; He suffers unbelievable adversity — yet He enjoys prosperity; He is triumphed over — yet He triumphs; He is condemned — yet He justifies the condemned. These paradoxes remained a problem until the cross was set up, the

sepulcher burst open, and the Son of God who came to die went up to reign (*Living Oracles*, p. 110).

The Suffering Messiah, Jehovah's Servant

Unfortunately, the chapter division comes at the wrong place. It should begin with Isaiah 52:13, which opens with the words, "Behold, my servant," and that is the subject of this entire section (Isa. 52:13-53:12).

The first question to be answered is, "of whom speaketh the prophet this? Of himself, or of some other man?" (Acts. 8:34). The only possible correct answer is, this prophecy speaks of an individual, the Messiah, and there is only one person in the history of the world who fulfills the prophecy, Jesus Christ of the New Testament. Professor James Orr observed:

> Let anyone steep his mind in the contents of this chapter and then read what is said about Jesus in the Gospels, and as he stands underneath the cross, see if there is not the most perfect correspondence between the two. In Jesus of Nazareth alone in all history, but in Him perfectly, has this prophecy found fulfillment.

Some unbelievers have sought to interpret this passage as referring to "suffering Israel," the nation, rather than to the suffering Messiah. But the following five facts prove the theme of Isaiah 53 to be the Messiah, not the Jewish people.

First, this entire prophecy speaks of an *individual*. It is "*he* shall grow up" (v. 2); "*he* is despised...a *man* of sorrows" (v. 3); "*he* was wounded" (v. 5); and so forth throughout the chapter.

Second, verse 8 is conclusive: the sufferer was stricken for the transgressions of "my people" (Israel). He is an individual who suffers vicariously *for* the people; therefore, He cannot *be* the people.

Third, He is an *innocent* sufferer (vv. 7, 9), which could never be said of the nation of Israel.

Fourth, He is a *voluntary* sufferer who willingly "poured out his soul unto death" (v. 12), again depicting the death of an individual, not a nation.

Fifth, He is an *unresisting* sufferer who "opened not his mouth" (v. 7), which could never be said of the nation of Israel.

The meaning could not be more clear: Isaiah 53 describes an *innocent, voluntary, unresisting individual who suffered vicariously for God's people, Israel.* When Jesus of Nazareth came 700 years later and died on the cross, *these predictions were fulfilled with a literalness that astonishes and an exactness that parallels mathematical certainty.*

The Messiah's Astonishing Exaltation (52:13)

> Behold, my servant shall deal prudently; he shall be exalted and extolled, and be very high.

Before the depth of the Messiah's humiliation is presented, we are at the outset assured of His final *victory* and *glory*. Franz Delitzsch called attention to the progressive nature of the words "exalted," "extolled" and "raised." He said: "From these words we obtain this chain of thought: He will rise up, He will raise Himself still higher, He will stand on high." And Stier rightly connected this with the three principal steps in the fulfillment of the prediction in Jesus after His death, namely His *resurrection,* His *ascension* and His sitting down in *exaltation* at the *right hand of God.*

Here, then, we are at once confronted with the Messiah's final end. To prepare us, as it were, for the shock of His temporary abasement, the "Servant of the Lord (after His sufferings) is seen rising from stage to stage; and at last He reaches an immeasurable height that towers above everything beside" (Delitzsch, *The Servant of the Lord,* p. 58).

The New Testament is very clear concerning the final exaltation of Christ after His sufferings and death:

> Who, being the brightness of his glory, and the express image of his person, and upholding all things by the word of his power, when he had by himself purged our sins [by His atoning death on the cross], sat down on the right hand of the Majesty on high (Heb. 1:3).

> Christ Jesus...being in the form of God, thought it not robbery to be equal with God...humbled himself and became obedient unto death, even the death of the cross. Wherefore, God also hath highly exalted him, and given him a name which is above every name (Phil. 2:5-6, 8-9).

The Messiah's Shocking Abuse (Isa. 52:14)

> As many were astounded at thee — his visage was so marred more than any man, and his form more than the sons of men.

If the Messiah's exaltation (v. 13) is astonishingly high, His sufferings are even more astonishing: "Just as many were astonished at him, for so disfigured was he that his appearance was not human, and his form was not like that of the children of men" (trans. by Delitzsch).

During the terrible hours before His crucifixion, the Lord Jesus was brutally manhandled, buffeted, scourged and abused in other ways.

The scourging itself was violent, inhuman. The scourge was usually made of leather thongs fastened to a handle. At the ends of the thongs were often fastened bits of sharpened metal or rock which cut and lacerated the flesh of the victim and turned the back into a bleeding pulp.

On the cross, the crown of thorns, the nails driven through His quivering flesh and the consequent agony of crucifixion, in which every nerve and muscle became a flame of torture, added to the excruciating mental agony and soul suffering. Jesus' features became so marred and distorted that He no longer resembled a man. This horrifying fact is clearly revealed in the Old Testament and just as clearly documented in the New Testament: "Then Pilate, therefore, took Jesus, and scourged him. And the soldiers plaited a crown of thorns, and put it on his head" (Jn. 19:1-2).

There are thorns in Bible lands having spines two to three inches long. When dried, they are very hard, pointed and sharp as needles. Such a *crown*, if pressed down on the brow, would puncture the skin in many places and cause pain and a flow of blood which resulted in matted, disheveled hair, presenting a horrible appearance:

> Then they spat in his face, and buffeted him; and others smote him with the palms of their hands...And they stripped him, and put on him a scarlet robe. And when they had plaited a crown of thorns, they put it upon his head, and a reed in his right hand...And they spat upon him, and took the reed, and smote him on the head (Mt. 26:67; 27:28-30).

God permitted and Jesus endured this horrible suffering, not only to fulfill the prophetic picture, but to suffer in our stead. Who, but the true Messiah, would want to be a Messiah like that?

In the hours before being nailed to the cross, Jesus' *face* was marred, and on the cross, His *form* was marred, thereby completely fulfilling the prediction by Isaiah. The bloody sweat, the traces of the crown of thorns, the spittle on His face and the smiting on the head all contributed to the disfigurement of His face. The scourging, the buffeting, the nails driven through His hands and feet, the weight of the body pulling it out of joint and the spear thrust through His side distorted His body. Add to all that the extreme mental anguish and grief of soul, and the result was one so marred that He no longer resembled a man. How much He loved us; how much He paid for our redemption!

As we humbly contemplate the intensity of the dreadful sufferings of the Savior, may our hearts be "bowed with shame and sorrow for the sin which was the cause of it all, and may we have a greater love and undying gratitude to Him who bore all this for us" (David Baron).

The Messiah Will Bring a Message that Will Startle Many Nations (Isa. 52:15)

So shall he sprinkle many nations, the kings shall shut their mouths at him; for that which had not been told them shall they not see, and that which they had not heard shall they consider.

God himself, in the person of His Son, suffered so violently, creating so ghastly a scene, that it has impressed all ages. The memory of Calvary startles the most dormant, pricks the most calloused, stirs the most lethargic. Men now understand both the love of God and the wisdom of God; Calvary reveals them. Men see both the grace of God and how God can bestow righteousness on sinners who believe, "For he hath made him, who knew no sin, to be sin for us, that we might be made the righteousness of God in him" (2 Cor. 5:21). The gospel will startle many into believing.

The Messiah Brings a Message that Will be Disbelieved by Israel (Isa. 53:1)

Who hath believed our report? And to whom is the arm of the LORD revealed?

Although the shocking message of a suffering Messiah startled many nations, it found few believers among the Messiah's own people, the Jews.

In the New Testament we find the fulfillment of this prediction:

But though he had done so many miracles before them, yet they believed not on him; That the saying of Isaiah, the prophet, might be fulfilled, which he spoke, Lord, who hath believed our report? And to whom hath the arm of the Lord been revealed? (Jn. 12:37-38).

The Messiah's Supernatural Birth and Spiritual Growth (Isa. 53:2a)

For he shall grow up before him like a tender plant, and like a root out of a dry ground.

The Messiah's supernatural birth is intimated in the phrase, "As a root out of a dry ground." A root growing out of dry ground is a miracle because one essential element, moisture, is missing. The Messiah's birth was to be a miracle — the miracle of the virgin birth.

Notice also another paradox. His supernatural yet natural growth. He will grow up (normally, much as other children), and yet it will be "before him." That is, the Messiah shall grow up in Jehovah's presence and under His watch care. Here too He will owe nothing to natural surroundings, for the Messiah shall be "a tender plant...out of a dry ground." That is, the Messiah will be a precious, wholesome plant in His youth, growing up before the Heavenly Father's watchful care, yet He will grow up in the midst of the universal spiritual dearth of the nation, in a desert of hardness, sin and unbelief. But it will be a normal process; He will "grow up." He will not "burst upon the world all at once, in a sudden splendour of daring and achievement: He will conform to God's slow, silent law of growth" (James Culross).

It is amazing that God foretold the manner of His coming to earth, the growth of His childhood and the spirituality of His childhood. And, when the Messiah came, everything was fulfilled exactly as had been predicted. The Messiah did not come as a full-grown King in His might, with dash and splendor; that is reserved for His second advent. In the New Testament, we read of the child Jesus, "And the child grew, and became strong in spirit, filled with wisdom; and the grace of God was upon him" (Lk. 2:40).

The Messiah's Generation Would Fail to See and Appreciate His Greatness (Isa. 53:2b)

> He hath no form nor comeliness, and when we shall see him,
> there is no beauty that we should desire him.

When the Messiah came, the people were looking for a mighty king and a political reformer and were, therefore, disappointed with Him. Men did not see His beauty — the beauty of holiness — nor did they understand His mission. He did not answer to the worldly ideal. Having misread the prophecies, they found nothing to charm or attract them in Jehovah's servant when He came. The work of the Messiah in His first advent — to make His soul an "offering for sin" — was foreign to their ideas of what the Messiah should be.

The Messiah Would be Despised and Rejected of Men (Isa. 53:3-4)

> He is despised and rejected of men, a man of sorrows, and
> acquainted with grief, and we hid as it were our faces from him;

he was despised, and we esteemed him not...we did esteem him stricken, smitten of God and afflicted.

"Rejected of men," says David Baron, "means actually 'rejected by men of high rank. ' " That is, He would have no men of high standing, no *important* men, few men of distinction to support Him and His program with their authority and influence.

This proved to be true in the life of Jesus, as the New Testament record reveals: "Then answered them the Pharisees, Are ye also deceived? Have any of the rulers or of the Pharisees believed on him?" (Jn. 7:47-48; see context).

Who but the infinite God, who knows the end from the beginning, would dare frame a prophecy like that, presenting the Messiah as being without the support of the leaders of the people? But history fully confirmed the accuracy of the prediction.

The Messiah Would be Known as a Man of Sorrows, Smitten of God, Afflicted (Isa. 53:3-4)

He is...a man of sorrows, and acquainted with grief, and we hid as it were our faces from him...we did esteem him stricken, smitten of God, and afflicted.

The point being emphasized is that the Messiah would be "a man of pains" (Heb.). He would experience sorrow of heart in all its forms.

Jesus' sorrow came not only as He compassionately suffered with the ills of humanity — a sympathetic suffering — but also when He was repelled in His efforts to bless. His sorrow was overwhelming when the people rejected Him and continued in their lost condition. His sorrows were multiplied when men of high rank and position turned from Him. Instead of considering Him precious, they "esteemed him not" — "estimated Him as nothing" (Martin Luther).

Worst of all, the people to whom He came considered Him "smitten of God": "He came unto his own, and his own received him not" (Jn. 1:11). They did not realize that He suffered to redeem them and that He permitted Himself to be "made a curse" that He might save those for whom He suffered: "Christ hath redeemed us from the curse of the law, being made a curse for us; for it is written, Cursed is everyone that hangeth on a tree" (Gal. 3:13).

The Messiah's Vicarious Sufferings (Isa. 53:4-6, 8, 10-12)

> Surely he hath borne our griefs, and carried our sorrows...he was wounded for our transgressions, he was bruised for our iniquities; the chastisement for our peace was upon him, and with his stripes we are healed...the LORD hath laid on him the iniquity of us all...for the transgression of my people was he stricken...thou shalt make his soul an offering for sin...he shall bear their iniquities...he bore the sin of many.

"The Divine Author makes it impossible for any ingenuity or learning to eliminate the doctrine of vicarious atonement from this passage by presenting it so often, and in forms so varied and still the same, that he who succeeds in expelling it in one place is compelled to meet it in another" (Dr. Alexander).

The outstanding element of this chapter is the *vicarious, substitutionary sufferings of the Messiah.* "Marvelous chapter," comments A. T. Pierson, "containing only twelve verses, yet fourteen times announcing the doctrine of the vicarious sacrifice for all human sin." The whole section (Isa. 52:13-53:12) overflows with this concept, and the mystery was never solved until the Lord Jesus was "made...sin for us" (2 Cor. 5:21) and "died for our sins" (1 Cor. 15:3).

Jehovah "hath caused to meet with overwhelming force in Him the iniquity of us all" (Heb.). The Messiah was the divine Redeemer on whom fell "all the fiery rays of judgment which would have fallen on mankind" (Baron). How wonderful is God's grace through Christ's substitutionary atonement! The cross became Christ's deepest humiliation and His highest glory — the appointed means of bringing salvation to men.

When the Lord Jesus came, He fulfilled these messianic predictions by His atoning death on the cross: "Who his own self bore our sins in his own body on the tree, that we, being dead to sins, should live unto righteousness; by whose stripes ye were healed" (1 Pet. 2:24).

The Messiah Would Suffer Willingly and Without Complaint (Isa. 53:7)

> He was oppressed, and he was afflicted, yet he opened not his mouth; he is brought as a lamb to the slaughter, and as a sheep before he shearers is dumb, so he openeth not his mouth.

Other sufferers usually register murmuring or complaining, especially when they are unjustly treated; but not so with the suffering Messiah. He voluntarily submitted Himself to His appointed task of bearing our sins and went as a lamb to the slaughter. "In sublime and magnanimous silence Messiah will endure to the uttermost, because Jehovah wills it...And here we look down into the unfathomed mystery of infinite love" (Culross).

In the New Testament, when Jesus was beaten, falsely accused, mistreated, mocked, spat upon, persecuted, manhandled, scourged and crucified, there were no flames of resentment, no incriminations against His executioners, no loud complaints, but, rather, a prayer for His persecutors.

After many false witnesses appeared against Him, Jesus "held his peace"; and the high priest, wondering about His silence, asked "Answerest thou nothing?" (see Mt. 26:59-63). Jesus' prayer, while suffering the tortures of crucifixion, was, "Father, forgive them; for they know not what they do" (Lk. 23:34).

This entire scene was so unusual, so contrary to nature and human experience, that one cannot help but be struck by both the strange prophecy and its even more remarkable fulfillment.

The Messiah Would Have No Advocate to Plead His Cause, No Friend to Declare His Innocence (Isa. 53:8)

> He was taken from prison and from judgment; and who shall declare his generation?

An alternate reading of the last phrase is, "And who [among] his generation shall declare [his innocence]?" "The Sanhedrin had the custom in 'trials for life' to call on those who knew anything in favor of the accused to come forward and declare it" (David Baron in *The Servant of Jehovah*, p. 106). This was not observed in the trial of Jesus; but, rather, the proceedings at His hasty, mock, illegal trial before the Sanhedrin were in flagrant contradiction to their own regulations and against all standards of right and fairness.

Jesus had to appear alone and undefended before the corrupt Jewish hierarchy and the representatives of the greatest Gentile power on earth at that time. *Not one person appeared to take His part.* Judas betrayed Him; Peter denied Him with oaths; and the other disciples "forsook him, and fled" (Mt. 26:56). Many of the women who had, during His ministry, ministered to Him, stood "beholding [from] afar off" when He was crucified (Mt. 27:55). In the hour of His greatest need, humanly speaking, *not one person stood by Him.* While it is true that after the weary hours of suffering had numbed His broken body, His mother Mary, a few faithful women and His beloved disciple John "stood by" at the cross; but during His trial and the early hours of His crucifixion, He was left alone — absolutely alone. Never in the history of the world has anyone been so completely forsaken by friends and loved ones as was Jesus.

Jesus was not arrested by proper officials but by a mob, the rabble, "a great multitude with swords and clubs, from the chief priests and elders of the people" (Mt. 26:47). Even Jesus himself commented on the inconsistency of their approach: "Are ye come out as against a thief with swords and clubs to take me? I sat daily with you teaching in the temple, and ye laid no hold on me. But all this was done, that the scriptures of the prophets might be fulfilled" (Mt. 26:55-56).

"False witnesses" were suborned to testify against Him, "to put him to death" (Mt. 26:59). He was tried at night, which was illegal.

In the Roman court, when Pilate sought in vain for a cause to justly condemn Him, he asked the people, "what evil hath he done?" The only answer he received was the shouting of the mob, encouraged by their leaders, "Let him be crucified" (Mt. 27:23). When Pilate saw that words of reason and justice "could prevail nothing" and that a worse "tumult" was developing (Mt. 27:24), he weakly washed his hands of the affair and turned Jesus over to them that they might crucify Him (Mt. 27:26). This was the worst miscarriage of justice in the annals of history.

But Jesus' innocence, as attested to by Pilate — "I find no fault in him" (Jn. 19:4) — fulfilled the messianic prophecy of old, "he had done no violence, neither was any deceit in his mouth" (Isa. 53:9).

The Messiah's Humiliation Would End at the Moment of Death, and Although Men Planned His Burial With the Wicked, Providence Planned It With the Rich (Isa. 53:9)

> And he made his grave with the wicked, and with the rich in his death because he had done no violence, neither was any deceit in his mouth.

Franz Delitzsch translates this passage as follows: "They [men] appointed him his grave with the wicked [but] he was a rich man after his death."

"Dying as a criminal, ordinarily His body would have been flung over the wall to be burned like offal in the fires of Topheth (west of Jerusalem); but when His vicarious sufferings were finished, no further indignity was permitted to His lifeless body" (A. T. Pierson). "And this remarkable coincidence," wrote Franz Delitizsch, "is truly wonderful if we reflect that the Jewish rulers would have given to Jesus the same dishonorable burial as that given to the two thieves, but the Roman authorities handed over

His body to Joseph the Arimathean, a 'rich man' (Mt. 27:57) who placed it in his sepulcher in his own garden. And at once we see an agreement between the gospel history and the prophetic words which could only be the work of the God of both prophecy and its fulfillment, inasmuch as no suspicion could possibly arise of there having been any human design of bringing the former into conformity with the latter."

The reason given for His honorable burial, which was so different from what had been planned for Him by His enemies, was, "because he had done no violence, neither was any deceit in his mouth" (Isa. 53:9). This is another reiteration of the absolute *innocence* of the divine sufferer.

The New Testament account of Jesus' burial records this perfect fulfillment:

> When the evening was come, there came a rich man of Arimathea, named Joseph, who also himself was Jesus' disciple; He went to Pilate, and begged the body of Jesus. Then Pilate commanded the body to be delivered. And when Joseph had taken the body, he wrapped it in a clean linen cloth, And laid it in his own new tomb, which he had hewn out in the rock (Mt. 27:57-60).

The Messiah Would Be Resurrected to See His Seed, the Fruits of His Travail (Isa. 53:10)

> When thou shalt make his soul an offering for sin, he shall see his seed, he shall prolong his days, and the pleasure of the LORD shall prosper in his hand.

After the Messiah's offering of Himself as a trespass offering, God will "prolong his days" in resurrection, and He shall "see his seed" — saved souls — as the result of His sacrifice.

The fulfillment of this paradox, as we have already seen, is in the death and resurrection of Jesus who, "died for our sins according to the scriptures; And...rose again the third day according to the scriptures" (1 Cor. 15:3-4).

The Messiah's resurrection is in harmony with other Old Testament Scriptures, such as Psalm 16:10: "For thou wilt not leave my soul in sheol, neither wilt thou permit thine Holy One to see corruption."

Moreover, the will of God will "prosper" in the Messiah's hand. The Messiah will accomplish God's will with zeal, and He will indeed bring salvation and righteousness to Israel and the nations (see Isa. 42:4).

The New Testament tells of the glorious resurrection of Christ as well as the beginning of His ministry after His resurrection, working through His disciples, by which multitudes were and are being added to the Church.

"About three thousand souls" were saved and added to the Church on one occasion (Acts 2:41); and "the number of the men was about five thousand" who were added on another occasion (Acts 4:4).

During the last nineteen centuries of Church history, untold millions have believed in Christ and been saved. He has indeed seen His seed, and the will of God is prospering in His hand. The gospel of Christ will eventually, after His second advent, come to final and complete triumph, and then "the earth shall be full of the knowledge of the LORD, as the waters cover the sea" (Isa. 11:9). Truly, the Captain of our salvation is "bringing many sons unto glory" (Heb. 2:10).

The Messiah Will Satisfy God with His Sacrifice and Through Knowing the Messiah Many Shall Be Justified (Isa. 53:11)

> He shall see of the travail of his soul, and shall be satisfied; by
> his knowledge shall my righteous servant justify many; for he
> shall bear their iniquities.

This is a forecast of the tremendous truth, so fully developed by Paul in the New Testament, of *justification by faith*, salvation by grace — because Christ died for our sins and purchased a full redemption for all. This truth of justification by faith is the grand, central truth of the New Testament: "Even the righteousness of God which is by faith of Jesus Christ unto all and upon all them that believe...Being justified freely by his grace through the redemption that is in Christ Jesus" (Rom. 3:22, 24); "For by grace are ye saved through faith" (Eph. 2:8; cp. Rom. 4:5-6; 5:15-19; Ti. 3:5; etc.).

Lest we forget that all grace bestowed upon believers is based on the Messiah's sacrifice, we again are reminded that "He shall bear their iniquities," observes Dr. Alexander, further stating that there is an "antithesis here suggesting the idea of exchange or mutual substitution; *they* shall receive His righteousness, and *He* shall bear the heavy burden of their iniquities." This, of course, is compatible with the doctrine of the New Testament: "For he [God] hath made him [Christ], who knew no sin, to be sin for us, that we might be made the righteousness of God in him" (2 Cor. 5:21).

The Messiah's Death Will Involve Strange Circumstances (Isa. 53:12)

> He was numbered with the transgressors; and he bore the sin
> of many, and made intercession for the transgressors.

Similar to the account of the disposition of the Messiah's garments in Psalm 22:18, here is a comparable incident showing true detail in prophecy which marks it as genuine.

In verse 12, the word "transgressors" does not refer to ordinary sinners but to criminals (Heb. *poshim*, meaning *criminals, open transgressors of the law of God and man*). Furthermore, Delitzsch, Hengstenberg, Baron and others translate the reflexive verb used here, "He permitted Himself, voluntarily, to be numbered or 'reckoned' with criminals," showing again the Messiah's willingness to suffer all that the Father had planned for Him.

It is of more than passing interest to recall that Christ himself quoted Isaiah 53:12 just before His own crucifixion: "This that is written must yet be accomplished in me, And he was reckoned among the transgressors" (Lk. 22:37).

And so, as Delitzsch observed, this prediction and its fulfillment become "one of those remarkable coincidences which was brought about by providence between the prophecies and our Savior's passion," that Christ should have been crucified between two thieves (lit., *robbers*) [see Lk. 23:39-43].

Much has already been said about the vicarious nature of the Messiah's sufferings as seen in Isaiah 53. In the closing verse, that fact again is stressed: "He himself bore the sin of the many" (lit. trans.).

Those familiar with the New Testament will recall many Scriptures which set forth the substitutionary nature of the death of Christ, such as:

> But now once, in the end of the ages, hath he [Christ] appeared to put away sin by the sacrifice of himself...So Christ was once offered to bear the sins of many (Heb. 9:26, 28).

> For Christ also hath once suffered for sins, the just for the unjust, that he might bring us to God (1 Pet. 3:18).

Many volumes have been written showing the wonders of the messianic prophecies in Isaiah 53 and their fulfillment in the atoning death of Jesus as described in the New Testament. By carefully examining these parallel Old Testament and New Testament passages, the faith of many will either be generated or confirmed in both the supernatural character of the prophecies and their fulfillment. This clearly shows that Scripture has upon it the stamp of its divine Author, the mark of Heaven, the imprint of eternity.

CHAPTER SIX

PROPHECIES DESCRIBING THE MESSIANIC OFFICES OF CHRIST

Christ, the Anointed One

Both the words "Christ" (Greek) and "Messiah" (Hebrew) mean *Anointed One* (for examples of the use of "anointed" in the Old Testament, see Lev. 4:3, 5; 1 Sam. 2:10; Ps. 2:2; Dan. 9:25-26; etc.). The word "anointed" occurs most frequently in Leviticus, 1 and 2 Samuel and the Psalms. The term "Messiah" (*anointed*) is applied to the high priest (Lev. 4:3, 5, 16; 6:22), who was a type or picture of Christ our High Priest. It occurs 18 times in 1 and 2 Samuel, but not always with messianic connotation. It is found ten times in the Psalms, but again, not always with messianic import. Psalms 2:2; 20:6; 28:8; 84:9; 89:51; 132:10, 17 are, we believe, messianic. Psalm 2:2 and Daniel 9:25-26 are outstanding passages referring to the coming Messiah.

Since the fall of man and his consequent separation from God (Rom. 5:12), mankind has needed a Mediator, a Redeemer who can fill man's three basic needs.

First, sin left man in spiritual darkness, ignorant of God. Because of this, man needs knowledge of the Word, the will and the ways of God. Man needs a *prophet*. Second, sin left man guilty, lost, separated from God; hence, he needs forgiveness of sin, restoration of a righteous character and restoration to divine fellowship. For this, man needs a *priest*. Third, sin, which is rebellion against God's government, left man with a rebellious nature that expresses itself in antagonism to his fellowmen. Since man is a social creature, a unit in society, he needs authoritative governmental supervision; hence, he needs a *king*.

In the Old Testament economy, God provided these basic needs of mankind through His chosen prophets, priests and kings, but all human instruments come short and fail; therefore, God planned from the beginning that He would provide the perfect *Prophet, Priest* and *King* for mankind in the perfect One, His only begotten Son.

In Old Testament times, these three classes of public servants — prophets, priests and kings — were consecrated to their offices by an anointing with oil (prophets, see 1 Ki. 19:16; priests, see Ex. 29:21; Lev. 8:12; kings, see 1 Sam. 10:1; 16:12-13).

Christ as Prophet

The Old Testament prophet represented God to the nation; he gave His words and message to the people. When the Messiah came, He was to represent God perfectly and completely in person, as well as in words, to Israel and to the world. When Jesus came, He proved to be God's perfect Prophet:

> No man hath seen God at any time; the only begotten Son, who is in the bosom of the Father, he hath declared [revealed, manifested] him (Jn. 1:18).

> Jesus saith unto him...He that hath seen me hath seen the Father...Believest thou not that I am in the Father, and the Father in me? The words that I speak unto you, I speak not of myself; but the Father that dwelleth in me, he doeth the works (Jn. 14:9-10).

As a Prophet, the coming Messiah would be like Moses:

> I will raise them up a Prophet from among their brethren, like unto thee [Moses], and will put my words in his mouth, and he shall speak unto them all that I shall command him. And it shall come to pass, that whosoever will not hearken unto my words which he shall speak in my name, I will require it of him (Dt. 18:18-19).

Moses was a remarkable character; and he was chosen, above all other prophets, to set forth in type the prophetic ministry of the coming Messiah. In these outstanding points, Christ was a prophet "like unto Moses." Moses was a *lawgiver, leader, king* (captain), *deliverer, prophet* (God's spokesman) and *intercessor* for the people — he was the one with whom God spoke face to face. Never again did there arise a prophet like Moses (cp. Dt. 34:10-12; Num. 12:6-8). He was the only man in Jewish history who exercised the functions of prophet, priest and king in one ministry.

How right the people were who, when they had witnessed the miracle of Jesus feeding 5,000 people from a few loaves and fishes, said, "This is of a truth that prophet that should come into the world" (Jn. 6:14). "That prophet" is also referred to in John 1:21.

Although Moses was great, Christ was infinitely greater. Moses as a "servant" was "faithful"; Christ as the "son" was the perfect and omniscient Prophet (cp. Heb. 3:5-6) "Who was faithful to him that appointed him" (Heb. 3:2).

Peter summed up his sermon in the Temple with these words:

> For Moses truly said unto the fathers, A prophet shall the Lord, your God, raise up unto you of your brethren, like unto me; him shall ye hear in all things, whatever he shall say unto you. And it shall come to pass that every soul, who will not hear that prophet, shall be destroyed from among the people (Acts 3:22-23).

Other references are made in both Testaments to the prophetic ministry of Christ. Isaiah 61:1 and Luke 4:18 refer to Christ's prophetic ministry, and both passages use the same words:

> The Spirit of the Lord is upon me, because he hath anointed me to preach the gospel to the poor; he hath sent me to heal the brokenhearted, to preach deliverance to the captives, and recovering of sight to the blind, to set at liberty them that are bruised (Lk. 4:18; cp. Isa. 61:1).

Christ as Priest

The Old Testament priest, chosen by God, represented the people to God and offered sacrifices for their sins. He also had a ministry of compassion for the ignorant and erring (see Heb. 5:1-4). This priesthood, of which Aaron was the first high priest, was imperfect, for the priests were sinners themselves and had to first offer sacrifice for their own sins before they could offer sacrifice for the sins of the people (Heb. 5:3; 7:27; 9:7). Moreover, their priesthood was short-lived because the priesthood of each high priest was ended by his death (Heb. 7:23). Furthermore, their offerings were merely types, "For it is not possible that the blood of bulls and of goats should take away sins" (Heb. 10:4).

But in Christ, God's anointed High Priest, we have not only the perfect High Priest who lives forever, but One who gave Himself for our sins, the perfect offering, the once-for-all, complete atonement for the sins of humanity:

> For such an high priest was fitting for us, who is holy, harmless, undefiled, separate from sinners, and made higher than the heavens; Who needeth not daily, as those high priests, to offer up sacrifice, first for his own sins and then for the people's; for this he did once, when he offered up himself. For the law maketh men high priests who have infirmity, but the word of the oath, which was since the law, maketh the Son, who is consecrated for evermore (Heb. 7:26-28).

By that one perfect offering on the cross, Christ "perfected forever" them that are saved through faith in Him (see Heb. 7:23-28; 9:25-28; 10:10-14). Most of the Book of Hebrews is devoted to the fact that in Christ Jesus, God has given us His perfect High Priest who offered the perfect offering to atone for the sins of the race, thereby giving eternal life to all who accept Him as their substitute and Savior. The Messiah gave His body and soul as an offering for sin and sinners (Isa. 53:5, 10).

In a sense, the Messiah was anointed to be *as a leper* when He bore the sins of the world. He was truly "made sin" for us (2 Cor. 5:21). Isaiah 53:4 intimates this, "we did esteem him stricken, smitten of God, and afflicted." Jerome translates the first phrase, "we thought him a leper." The word "stricken" was often used of the plague of leprosy. David Baron says of Isaiah 53:4, " 'Stricken, smitten of God, afflicted' — every one of these three expressions was used of the plague of leprosy; and the phrases are intended to describe one suffering a terrible punishment for sin." In the Messiah's case, it was for our sins, not His own, that He suffered so. Marvelous grace, that Christ actually was willing to become as a leper for us!

In this connection, it is interesting to note that the leper who was to be "cleansed" in the Old Testament economy was *anointed* (Lev. 14:15-20). One might conclude, therefore, that Christ, the Anointed of God, was not only anointed to be God's Prophet, Priest and King, but He also had an *anointing* to be the sin offering, and He literally became *sin* (*the leprous One*) for us.

Although the Aaronic priesthood continuously presented to the people their need of atonement for sins and that remission of sins could only be obtained through the shedding of blood (see Heb. 9:22), the one person chosen to picture the Messiah's eternal priesthood was not Aaron but Melchizedek (see Ps. 110:4; Heb. 5;6;7). Melchizedek, as a type of Christ, represented His eternal, unchanging priesthood; he "abideth a priest continually" (Heb. 7:3).

72

Christ as King

Yet have I set my king upon my holy hill of Zion (Ps. 2:6).

Since man is both an individual and a social unit, he needs a king (government) to supervise his community life. God, who first ruled the people of Israel through the patriarchs, later through "captains" (leaders like Moses and Joshua) and later still through "judges," finally consented to give them kings. In God's Messiah, we have the perfect King — the "KING OF KINGS, AND LORD OF LORDS" (Rev. 19:16) — who will have a wholly righteous, beneficent reign:

> Behold, the days come, saith the LORD, that I will raise unto David a righteous Branch, and a King shall reign and prosper, and shall execute justice and righteousness in the earth...and this is his name whereby he shall be called, THE LORD OUR RIGHTEOUSNESS (Jer. 23:5-6).

> And the Spirit of the LORD shall rest upon him [the Messiah] and...with righteousness shall he judge (Isa. 11:2, 4; cp. Num. 24:17; Zech. 9:9; etc.).

God selected three great men to picture the work of the Messiah as Prophet, Priest and King: Moses as prophet, Melchizedek as priest and David as king.

The term "Messiah" is found eighteen times in the Books of 1 and 2 Samuel, which narrate the life of David. Hannah, the mother of Samuel, had the honor of being the first one to use the word "Messiah" referring to the coming One, and to Christ as God's anointed King: "the LORD shall...give strength unto his king, and exalt the horn of his anointed" (1 Sam. 2:10).

The coming of the Messiah as King usually refers to His second advent, when He will establish His Kingdom reign of righteousness (see Isa. 11:1-10; Mic. 4:1-5; etc.).

Many psalms speak of the Messiah as the coming King (see Ps. 2; 45; 47; 72; etc.). In Psalm 2 we see the coronation of the Messiah as King on Mount Zion (v. 6) and His inheritance of the heathen nations (v. 8).

In Psalm 45 we see the majesty and beauty of the King and His glorious bride.

In Psalm 47 we see the Messiah as God and His coronation as King of the earth (vv. 2, 7).

Psalm 72 gives us the most complete picture in the psalms of the Messiah's coming Kingdom and His reign of righteousness:

1. The Messiah is identified as the King's Son (v. 1).
2. Messiah the King's perfect righteousness (vv. 2-4).
3. Messiah the King's wholesome reign (vv. 5-7).
4. Messiah the King's universal dominion (vv. 8-11).
5. Messiah the King's divine compassion (vv. 12-14).
6. Messiah the King's reign produces material and spiritual prosperity (vv. 15-17).
7. Messiah the King's reign produces perfect praise of the Lord God (vv. 18-19).

The Messiah is also presented as the Priest-King, "a priest upon his throne" (Zech. 6:13). This message to Joshua certainly looks beyond Joshua to the Messiah, for there are statements in the passage (Zech. 6:10-13) which can find their fulfillment only in one greater than man.

"Thus speaketh the LORD of hosts, saying, Behold, the man whose name is THE BRANCH" (v. 12) definitely identifies the message as being messianic. "He shall grow up out of his place" (v. 12) confirms that He will have a natural yet supernatural growth as a child (cp. Isa. 53:2). "And he shall build the temple of the LORD" (v. 12); Christ is doing this even now. "And he shall bear the glory" (v. 13), "the glory as of the only begotten of the Father" (Jn. 1:14). "And shall sit and rule upon his throne" (v. 13), as King and Priest, even as Melchizedek (Ps. 110:2, 4). "And the counsel of peace shall be between them both" (v. 13); as King, the Messiah will bring peace (Ps. 46:9; 72:7) and as Priest, He will bring peace through the blood of His cross (Col. 1:20).

Jeremiah 30:21 is another remarkable messianic passage giving a similar testimony. The Messiah will be the King-Priest; He will rule the people and "draw near and...approach unto God" as the perfect Mediator (cp. 1 Tim. 2:5).

Turning to the New Testament, the "Lion of the tribe of Judah, the Root of David" (Rev. 5:5) — Christ the King — is also presented as the One who "hath an unchangeable priesthood" (Heb. 7:24-28).

The New Testament Witness that Jesus is the Christ, the Anointed of God

In the New Testament, Jesus the Christ is clearly set forth as God's anointed Prophet (Jn. 17:8) who gives His people God's words; God's anointed Priest, "who through the eternal Spirit offered himself without spot to God [to] purge your conscience" (Heb. 9:14); and God's coming "KING OF KINGS, AND LORD OF LORDS" (Rev. 19:16).

In Hebrews 1:9, Christ is seen as the anointed of God: "Thou hast loved righteousness, and hated iniquity; therefore, God, even thy God, hath anointed thee with the oil of gladness above thy fellows."

In Luke 4:18, Christ stated that He was the One "anointed...to preach the gospel to the poor," the One of whom Isaiah spoke (Isa. 61:1).

In several New Testament passages, Jesus is presented as Prophet, Priest and King:

> And from Jesus Christ, who is the faithful witness [Prophet], and the first begotten of the dead, and the prince of the kings of the earth [King]. Unto him that loveth us, and washed us from our sins in his own blood [Priest] (Rev. 1:5).

> God...Hath in these last days spoken unto us by his Son [Prophet]...Who...when he had by himself purged our sins [Priest], sat down [as King] on the right hand of the Majesty on high (Heb. 1:1-3).

Behold God's Branch

Other Bible teachers have called attention to the remarkable fourfold use of the messianic name "the Branch" in the Old Testament, and the frequent use of the word "behold" in connection with God's Messiah, the Branch. "Behold" is used as God's *Ecce Homo* in the Old Testament. Taken together, the phrase *Behold the Branch* presents a beautiful summary of the Christ of the four Gospels. Here is the fourfold use of the phrase as used of the Messiah in the Old Testament.

1. As the King

   "Behold, the days come, saith the LORD, that I will raise unto David a righteous Branch, and a King shall reign and prosper" (Jer. 23:5).

   "Behold, thy King cometh unto thee" (Zech. 9:9).

   This corresponds to the Gospel of Matthew, where Christ is presented as King.

2. As the Servant of the Lord

   "Behold, I will bring forth my servant, the BRANCH" (Zech. 3:8).

   This corresponds to the Gospel of Mark, where Christ is presented as the servant of the Lord.

3. As the Son of Man

"Thus speaketh the LORD of hosts: saying, Behold, the man whose name is THE BRANCH" (Zech. 6:12).

This corresponds to the Gospel of Luke, where Christ is presented as the ideal and the representative man.

4. As the Son of God

"Behold your God!" (Isa. 40:9).

"In that day shall the branch of the LORD be beautiful and glorious" (Isa. 4:2).

This corresponds to the Gospel of John, where Christ is presented as the Son of God — God himself in the flesh.

These four uses of "the Branch" are the only four instances in the Hebrew Scriptures (with the exception of Jer. 33:15, which is a repetition of the thought in Jer. 23:5-6) where the Messiah is designated by the title, "the Branch." Several times the Messiah is introduced in the Old Testament with the word "Behold," as though to call special attention to Him.

Professor Godet writes:

Just as a gifted painter, who wished to immortalize for a family the complete likeness of the illustrious father, would avoid any attempt in combining in a single portrait the insignia of all the various offices he had filled by representing him in the same picture as general and magistrate, as a man of science and as a father of a family; but would prefer to paint four distinct portraits. So the Holy Spirit, to preserve for mankind the perfect likeness of Him who was its chosen representative, God in man, used means to impress upon the minds of the writers of the Gospels, four different images.

All of these four accounts of the life of Christ present Him as the Messiah — God's perfect Prophet, Priest, King and the Son of God — yet each has a different emphasis. In Matthew, He is *King*; in Mark, He is *the servant of Jehovah*; in Luke, He is the *Son of man*; and in John, He is the *Son of God.*

Other Names of the Messiah in the Old Testament

There are scores of names of the Messiah in the Old Testament. Following are a few.

In Isaiah, the Messiah is frequently called *the servant of the Lord* or "my servant" (see Isa. 42:1; 52:13; etc.). As the servant of the Lord (Jehovah), He is the exponent of righteousness and true humility, the teacher and Redeemer of mankind. He fulfills all of God's desires; hence, He is:

The second Adam — the perfect Man
The second Israel — the perfect Servant
The second Moses — the perfect Prophet
The second David — the perfect King
The second High Priest — the perfect High Priest

The growing purposes of God toward the whole human race, which were manifested in the creation of Adam, the election of Israel, the raising up of Moses, the appointment of Aaron and the call of David are "brought to their full completion by, in and through Christ" (Delitzsch).

Ezekiel presented the Messiah as *the Shepherd of Israel* (see Ezek. 34:23; 37:24). In Ezekiel, "David" is used as a name of the Messiah. "David" means *beloved.*

Christ, the truly beloved of the Father, took both the name and character of the true Shepherd (see Jn. 10).

The Messiah is frequently called the "angel of the LORD," God's messenger (see Jud. 2:1; 6:12-13). He is also called the "stone" or the "rock" (Isa. 8:14); the "corner" (Isa. 28:16); the "nail" (Isa. 22:21-25); the "battle bow" (Zech. 10:4); "Shiloh" (Gen. 49:10); the "star" (Num. 24:17); etc.

The Name "Jesus" in the Old Testament

In an enlightening study, *Yeshua In The Tenach (The Name Jesus in the Old Testament),* Arthur E. Glass points out the amazing fact that the name "Jesus" is actually hidden in the Old Testament; yet it "is found about one hundred times from Genesis to Habakkuk...Every time the Old Testament uses the word *salvation* (especially with the Hebrew suffix meaning 'my,' 'thy' or 'his'), with very few exceptions (when the word is used in an impersonal sense) it is identically the same word as Yeshua (Jesus) used in Matthew 1:21." According to Glass, "This is actually what the angel said to Joseph: 'And she shall bring forth a son, and thou shalt call his name Yeshua (salvation), for he shall save his people from their sins.'"

In Psalm 9:14, David said, "I will rejoice in thy salvation." What he actually said was, "I will rejoice in thy Yeshua [Jesus]." In Isaiah 12:2-3, salvation is mentioned three times, presenting three great facets of Jesus and His salvation. They are presented here (quoting Glass) as they read in the Hebrew, with Jesus as the embodiment and the personification of the word salvation:

Behold, the mighty one [or God the mighty One] is my Yeshua [a reference to Jesus in His preincarnation, eternal existence, cp. Jn. 1:1]; I will trust and not be afraid; for Jah-Jehovah is my strength and my song: He also is become my Yeshua [Jesus, the Word made flesh, Jn. 1:14]. Therefore, with joy shall ye draw water out of the wells of Yeshua [Jesus crucified, waters of salvation flowing from Calvary, cp. Jn. 7:37-39].

CHAPTER SEVEN

PROPHECIES PROVING THAT THE MESSIAH IS GOD

The Dual Nature of the Messiah

For a correct comprehension of the person of the Messiah, it is necessary to understand that He has a *dual nature* but is a single personality. He is very God and perfect man; He is the God-Man, God and man in one indivisible personality. His humanity is seen in such names and titles as Son of man, Son of David, Son of Abraham, etc. His deity is seen in such names and titles as Son of God, God, Lord, Jehovah, El, Elohim, etc. The Bible reveals the Messiah (Christ) to be God manifest in the flesh.

The Deity of Christ as Presented in Hebrews Chapter 1

In the first six verses of Hebrews chapter 1, ten characteristics are presented about Christ, all of which prove and establish the fact of His deity.

1. Christ (the Messiah) is called God's Son, in contrast to the prophets who were only men, even though they were inspired men: "God, who...spoke in time past unto the fathers by the prophets, Hath in these last days spoken unto us by his Son" (vv. 1-2).

2. Christ is "heir of all things" (v. 2). He is the Son; therefore, He is the heir.

3. The "worlds" (universe) were made through Him (Christ) [v. 2]. This not only proves His preexistence but reveals Him as the active agent in creation. A parallel passage is John 1:1-3: "all things were made by him [Christ]; and without him was not anything made that was made" (v. 3).

79

4. He is identified with the glory of God as much as the brightness of the sun is identified with the sun: "Who, being the brightness of his glory, and the express image of his person" (v. 3).

5. He is identified with the character of God as much as the impression of a seal exactly reproduces the seal: "the express image of his person" (v. 3).

6. He is the One who upholds the vast, infinite universe, which is the work of an omnipotent God: "upholding all things by the word of his power" (v. 3; cp. Col. 1:16-17, "For by him were all things created...and by him all things consist [Gr., *are held together*]").

7. Christ accomplished the redemption of all humanity alone. No sinful man, not even a perfect man, could redeem a race of billions of lost sinners. It takes an infinite sacrifice to atone for a world of sinners: "when he had by himself purged [made purification of] our sins" (v. 3).

8. He now occupies the highest position in the universe next to the Father, at God's right hand, sharing with God the Father the eternal throne: "he...sat down on the right hand of the Majesty on high" (v. 3). That Christ, the Lamb of God, shares the eternal throne is evident from Revelation 22:1: "the throne [singular] of God and of the Lamb."

9. He is much better than the angels: "Being made so much better than the angels" (v. 4).

10. Again, the Father-Son relationship of the Father and the Messiah is established. Even the angels are commanded to worship the Messiah: "let all the angels of God worship him" (v. 6). The Scriptures command that only God is to be worshipped (Mt. 4:10). "Thou art my Son...I will be to him a Father, and he shall be to me a Son" (v. 5) is the Father's testimony to the Son.

In the remainder of the first chapter of Hebrews (together with the Old Testament Scriptures from which quotations are made in this first chapter of Hebrews), the Messiah is called by three primary names and titles of God used in the Old Testament and by the two primary names of deity used in the New Testament.

In verse 8, God the Father, speaking to God the Son (the Messiah), calls Him God (Gr.,*Theos*). Verse 8 is a quotation from Psalm 45:6, where the primary name of God, *Elohim*, is used of the Messiah: "Thy throne, O God [Heb., *Elohim*], is forever and ever."

In Hebrews 1:10, God the Father, still speaking to and about the Son (the Messiah), calls Him Lord (Gr., *Kurios*). This is a quotation from Psalm 102:25-27 which refers to *Jehovah* (see Ps. 102:16, 19, 21-22). Consider this passage:

> And, Thou, Lord, in the beginning hast laid the foundation of the earth; and the heavens are the works of thine hands. They shall perish, but thou remainest; and they all shall become old as doth a garment, And as a vesture shalt thou fold them up, and they shall be changed; but thou art the same, and thy years shall not fail (Heb. 1:10-12).

Notice that in these verses the Father (as in verse 8) is still speaking to the Son; the Father says that the Son is the Creator of the universe ("the heavens are the works of thine hands," v. 10); and the Father says that the Son is eternal, unchangeable. The universe will get old as does a used garment, but of the Son (the Messiah) the Father says, "thy years shall not fail" (v. 12).

The writer of the Book of Hebrews added two additional inspired comments concerning the Messiah: "But to which of the angels said he [God the Father] at any time, Sit on my right hand" (v. 13), again showing the exalted position of the Messiah at God's right hand; and "until I make thine enemies thy footstool" (v. 13), assuring all of the Messiah's eternal victory.

Since God the Father has testified so emphatically in this chapter of the deity of Christ and has given us 15 statements that fully set forth His deity, our eternal salvation depends on our accepting this truth: "If ye believe not that I am he [the Lord Jehovah], ye shall die in your sins" (Jn. 8:24). In this passage, Christ used the words "I am," which is the meaning of the name Jehovah (see Ex. 3:14-15), thus identifying Himself as the Jehovah of the Old Testament.

Old Testament Statements Concerning the Deity of the Messiah

Turning to the Old Testament predictions and comparing them with their New Testament fulfillments, we discover that Jehovah calls the Messiah His "fellow" (equal): "Awake, O sword, against my shepherd, and against the man who is my fellow, saith the LORD of hosts" (Zech. 13:7).

In the New Testament, Christ said the same thing when He stated, "I and my Father are one" (Jn. 10:30). Paul, inspired by the Holy Spirit, testified that Christ is equal with God: "Christ Jesus...being in the form of God, thought it not robbery [a thing to be grasped] to be equal with God" (Phil. 2:6).

Isaiah 9:6 forecasts the Messiah's humanity, deity and kingship. Names of deity are bestowed on the coming Messiah which none can mistake:

> For unto us a child is born [the Messiah's humanity], unto us a son is given [His eternal Sonship in the Triunity]...and his name shall be called Wonderful, Counselor, The Mighty God [Heb., *El Gibor*], The Everlasting Father [both names of God], The Prince of Peace.

A name in Hebrew expresses that which a person is; being called something means being that thing. Therefore, when the Messiah is called by the name "The Mighty God," it means that He is the Mighty God.

The Messiah is called God (Heb., *El, Elohim*) in the Old Testament: "Say unto the cities of Judah, Behold your God [Elohim]! Behold, the Lord GOD [Elohim] will come with strong hand" (Isa. 40:9-10).

In Psalm 47:7-8, we read of the Messiah's second advent: "For God [Elohim] is the King of all the earth...God [Elohim] reigneth over the nations" (cp. 1 Cor. 15:24-25; Rev. 11:15; 19:16).

The Messiah is also called Jehovah in the Old Testament. In Zechariah 2:10, we read that the Lord (Jehovah) said, "lo, I come, and I will dwell in the midst of thee." Psalm 47:2 says, "For the LORD [Jehovah] Most High is...a great King over all the earth." The context shows that this is a messianic psalm, looking forward to the second advent of Christ.

In Jeremiah 23:6, we read that the Messiah "shall be called, THE LORD [JEHOVAH] OUR RIGHTEOUSNESS." Psalm 102:16 tells us that "The LORD [Jehovah]...shall appear in his glory." In Zechariah 14:9, we read that "the LORD [Jehovah] shall be King over all the earth."

To prove that it is Jehovah in the flesh who is the King, Zechariah 14:3-4 tells us, "Then shall the LORD [Jehovah] go forth...and his feet shall stand in that day upon the Mount of Olives."

There can be no mistaking the meaning of Zechariah 12:10: "They shall look upon me [Jehovah] whom they have pierced." This is a direct reference to the crucified Messiah.

Isaiah 40:3 is a clear prediction that the Messiah is called both Jehovah (LORD) and Elohim (God): "The voice of him that crieth in the wilderness, Prepare ye the way of the LORD [Jehovah], make straight in the desert a highway for our God [Elohim]." This Scripture is quoted in the New Testament, showing its fulfillment in Christ and in John the Baptist, His forerunner (see Mt. 3:1-3).

In Zephaniah 3:15, we learn that it is Jehovah himself, the "Holy One" of Israel, who will be in their midst: "the King of Israel, even the LORD [Jehovah], is in the midst of thee."

In the New Testament, Jesus claimed to be the great "I AM" of the Old Testament. Jehovah said of Himself in Isaiah 43:10: "Ye are my witnesses, saith the LORD [Jehovah], and my servant whom I have chosen, that ye may know and believe me, and understand that I am he."

It is, therefore, very significant that Christ made the same claim: "that...ye may believe that I am he" (Jn. 13:19; cp. Mk. 13:6; Jn. 4:26; 8:24; 13:19; etc.). Jesus frequently used the expression "I am" in connection with some special revelation of His person or work:

"I am the light of the world" (Jn. 8:12).
"I am the door" (Jn. 10:9).
"I am the good shepherd" (Jn. 10:14).
"I am the way, the truth, and the life" (Jn. 14:6).

Adonai, another name for God, is also assigned to the Messiah in the Old Testament: "Behold, I will send my messenger, and he shall prepare the way before me; and the Lord [Heb., *Adonai*], whom ye seek, shall suddenly come to his temple" (Mal. 3:1).

The "messenger" who prepared the way for the coming of the Lord (Adonai) was John the Baptist; and the Lord for whom he prepared the way was the Messiah, Jesus: "The LORD [Jehovah] said unto my Lord [Adonai], Sit thou at my right hand until I make thine enemies thy footstool" (Ps. 110:1).

On the day of Pentecost, Peter quoted this passage in his sermon to prove both the Messiahship and the deity of Christ (Acts 2:34-36). In Matthew 22:41-45, Jesus himself proved to the Pharisees that the Messiah is not only the son of David, He is also his Lord (*Adonai*).

The Old Testament teaches the preexistence of the Messiah: "his name shall be continued as long as the sun" (Ps. 72:17). The original Hebrew of this text reads: "Before the sun was, his name [was] Yinon." This is the only occurrence in Scripture of the word "Yinon," and all ancient Jewish commentators agree that it is a name of the Messiah.

In Proverbs 8:22-24, we read of the preexistence of the Messiah: "The LORD possessed me in the beginning of his way, before his works of old. I was set up from everlasting, from the beginning, or ever the earth was." That this is a description of the eternal Messiah is beyond doubt.

In perfect agreement with the Old Testament, the New Testament also teaches the preexistence of Christ, the eternal Word: "In the beginning was the Word, and the Word was with God, and the Word was God. The same was in the beginning with God" (Jn. 1:1-2).

The Old Testament presents the Messiah as "the glory of the LORD," a phrase signifying deity: "And the glory of the LORD shall be revealed, and all flesh shall see it" (Isa. 40:5; cp. vv. 3-4 which prove v. 5 to be messianic).

In the New Testament, we read of the Messiah's incarnation: "And the Word was made flesh, and dwelt among us (and we beheld his glory, the glory as of the only begotten of the Father), full of grace and truth" (Jn. 1:14).

New Testament Statements Concerning the Deity of Christ

We have seen from Hebrews chapter 1 that the New Testament teaches the deity of Christ (the Messiah). This teaching of Christ's deity pervades the entire New Testament and can be seen in scores of direct statements and hundreds of references. Some of the inferences of Christ's deity are as follows:

1. His power to forgive sin proves His deity (Mk. 2:10).

2. His right to receive worship proves His deity (Mt. 2:11; 8:2; 9:18; 14:33; etc.).

3. His supernatural powers prove His deity (see all His miracles as recorded in the Gospels, e.g., Mk. 2:11; 3:5, 10-11; etc.).

4. His sinless character proves His deity (Heb. 7:26; 1 Pet. 2:22; 1 Jn. 3:5). In Luke 18:19, the Lord taught, indirectly, that none should call Him good unless they admit He is God, for there is none good except God.

5. His atoning death proves His deity, for none but God could atone for the race (Heb. 2:9).

6. His bodily resurrection proves His deity (Rom. 1:4).

7. He gave many promises which require deity for their fulfillment (see Mt. 11:28-29; 28:19-20; Jn. 14:23).

8. Men are to trust Him even as they do the Father, thereby affirming His deity (Jn. 14:1-3).

9. He is the Creator and Sustainer of the universe, positions which could only be attributed to deity (Jn. 1:1-3; Col. 1:16-17).

10. He has all the characteristics of deity: omnipresence, omniscience, omnipotence, etc. (see Mt. 28:18, 20; Jn. 3:13; 14:23; 16:30; etc.).

Note the striking testimony of Christ's deity in Luke 1:68 and 76. See also John 20:28; Romans 9:5; 1 Corinthians 2:8; Colossians 1:14, 17; 1 Timothy 6:14-16; Titus 2:13; Hebrews 1; etc.

The Triunity

That the Messiah should be God and yet be sent by God is a mystery unravelled only in the teaching of the Triunity. God is one God existing in three persons: Father, Son (the Messiah) and Holy Spirit.

Following are some references which directly teach or intimate the doctrine of the Triunity.

In Genesis 1:1, the word "God" (*Elohim*) is in the plural and is followed by the verb "created," which is in the singular, thus intimating a plurality of persons in the Godhead who are one.

In Deuteronomy 6:4, the word for "one" (God) is *echad*, which is the word for a compound unity, not an absolute unity. "Echad" is used in Genesis 2:24, which teaches that Adam and Eve (a man and his wife) shall be "one [*echad*] flesh" — two persons as one (see also Gen. 11:5-6; Num. 13:23; Jud. 20:1-2).

There are many direct statements concerning the Triunity in the Old Testament, such as Isaiah 11:2; 42:1; 48:16-17; 61:1; 63:7-10; Zechariah 2:10; etc. In Numbers 6:24-27, note that the singular "my name" in verse 27 follows the threefold use of the name LORD in verses 24-26.

Many Scriptures intimate the Triunity, such as Genesis 1:26-27, where God says, "Let us," implying more than one person in the Godhead (see also Gen. 3:22; 11:5-7; Isa. 6:8).

The Triunity is clearly taught in the New Testament in such instances as Matthew 3:16-17; 28:19-20; John 14:16; 2 Corinthians 13:14; Ephesians 4:4-6; Hebrews 9:14; and Revelation 1:4-5).

CHAPTER EIGHT

PROPHECIES FROM THE OLD TESTAMENT FULFILLED IN CHRIST

T he Bible is unique in its *type-pictures* of the coming Messiah as well as in its distinct and definite prophecies.

The Bible is unique in at least seven ways. First, it alone, of all the books in the world, has genuine prophecy. Second, the Bible alone contains an intricate system of "types" in the Old Testament which are fulfilled in the New Testament. Third, the Bible alone contains the record of genuine, credible miracles, fully attested to by adequate witnesses. Fourth, of all the books in the world, the Bible alone presents the perfect character, the Messiah. Fifth, the Bible alone, of all national history books, portrays its characters without bias and presents them as they are, with their weaknesses and failures as well as their strong points. Sixth, the Bible alone, of all ancient books, is in agreement with all the facts of nature and true scientific discoveries to which it refers, even though it was written thousands of years before the modern scientific era. Seventh, although written by nearly 40 human authors, the Bible has a phenomenal unity which shows the superintendence of its divine Author.

A *type* is a divinely created illustration of spiritual truth. A person, place, thing, event or a series of events becomes, by divine foresight and planning, an object lesson — a *picture* with corresponding details — of its anti-type (fulfillment). God and Christ, Satan and Antichrist, believers and unbelievers, the yielded Christian life and the world are just a few subjects of biblical types. "Even where no direct prediction is found," comments A. T. Pierson, "indirect forecasts (through types) referring to Christ may be distinctly traced all through the Bible." How true! Types of Christ — prophetic pictures giving indirect forecasts — abound in the Old Testament.

The cross of Christ has perhaps more types previewing and prefiguring the sacrifice of the Son of God than anything else in the Bible. Every Passover lamb slain (with its attendant ceremonies of the sprinkling of the blood of the Lamb on the door posts, the eating of the roasted lamb, etc., see Ex. 12:1-13), every Levitical offering brought to the altar and sacrificed (see Lev. 1-6) and every other blood offering presented "from the hour of Abel's altar-fire down to the last Passover of the passion week, pointed as with flaming finger to Calvary's Cross!...And there we see the convergence of a thousand lines of prophecy (indirect forecasts)...as in one burning focal point of dazzling glory" (A. T. Pierson).

When the Passover lamb was roasted, "a spit was thrust lengthwise through its body, and another transversely from shoulder to shoulder; every Passover lamb was thus transfixed *on a cross*. In like manner, when Moses lifted up the brazen serpent (Num. 21) it was not on a pole but on a *banner staff* — i.e., *a cross*" (A. T. Pierson, *Many Infallible Proofs*, p. 204).

Pictures of Christ abound in the Old Testament

In Genesis (especially rich in prophetic forecasts of Christ), *Adam* is presented as the head of God's creation, a type of Christ as Head of the new creation (see 1 Cor. 15:45-49). The *ark* was the only means of saving people from the judgment of the flood (Gen. 6-9). Christ is the ark of salvation; all who come to Him by faith are saved from the coming flood of God's judgment against sin. The *offering of Isaac* (Gen. 22) is an especially rich type of the offering up of Jesus by His Father. The *life of Joseph* — beloved of his father but hated and rejected by his brothers (Gen. 37) — is an amazing picture, with over 100 corresponding features, of the Lord Jesus Christ, who, likewise, was beloved of His Father but hated and rejected by His brethren. Joseph was sent to the Gentiles from whom he obtained a bride and was the means of feeding multitudes and saving them from destruction (Gen. 39-47). Christ, rejected by His brethren (the Jews), has been preached to the Gentiles, and vast multitudes have been preserved and fed the bread of life by Him. Joseph finally revealed himself to his brethren and became the means of preserving them. So too Christ, in the latter days, will reveal Himself to Israel and save many of them (see Zech. 12:10; Rom. 11:25-26).

In Exodus, the *Passover lamb* and the *life and ministry of Moses* are outstanding types of Christ. Moses, a shepherd in his youth and at first rejected by his brethren, fled to a Gentile country where he married a Gentile bride. Later, when he returned to liberate Israel, he was accepted as their leader and led them out of bondage in Egypt with great victory. This type of Christ is thrilling, for it speaks of Christ's rejection at His first coming to Israel and His eventual acceptance by and leadership over Israel at His second coming (see Acts 7:22-37, especially v. 35).

The *life of David* in 1 and 2 Samuel is a similar picture of the Messiah. David was a shepherd in his youth; was rejected by Saul, who sought to kill him; and was later accepted by the nation, anointed and crowned as their king. He is a type of the greater David who at first was the "good shepherd" who gave His life for His sheep and who later will reign as King.

Aaron and *Melchizedek* picture Christ as High Priest. *Moses* and *Samuel* (and the other prophets) foreshadow Christ as the great Prophet.

Christ explained that the *brazen serpent*, uplifted before the people as a means of deliverance from the judgment of death because of their sin (see Num. 21:5-9), was a type of His work of salvation through His cross (see Jn. 3:14-18).

Jonah, swallowed by the whale, experiencing a type of death and resurrection, and then preaching to the Gentiles, is a picture of the Messiah who was "three days and three nights" in the heart of the earth and who came forth — as Jonah did — in resurrection. In Matthew 12:40, Christ used Jonah's experience to illustrate a type of His own death and resurrection.

The *Tabernacle* (Ex. 25-31; 35-40) is one of the most extensive and meaningful of all the types. Its priesthood, offerings, furniture and arrangement are all symbolic of Christ and the believer's approach to God through Christ.

1. The brazen altar stands for atonement by blood.

2. The laver of cleansing stands for sanctification through the "washing of water by the word" (Eph. 5:26).

3. The table of show bread is a type of Christ as the food and strength of His people.

4. The golden lampstand with its seven branches is a type of Christ, the light of the world.

5. The altar of incense represents prayers and supplications ascending to the throne of God (cp. Rev. 8:3).

6. The mercy seat in the holy of holies represents Christ as the only means of justification and access to the presence of God (see Lk. 18:13, where the publican's prayer, "God be merciful to me a sinner," can be paraphrased, "God, meet me at the mercy seat").

7. The ark of the covenant in the holy of holies speaks of Christ as our Representative and Mediator at the right hand of God. The ark was made of wood and covered with pure gold (Ex. 25:10-11). This speaks of the humanity (wood) and deity (pure gold) of Christ. The ark contained three things: "the golden pot that had manna, and Aaron's rod that budded, and the tables of the covenant" (Heb. 9:4). These speak in types and pictures of the Messiah as the bread that came down from Heaven, of His resurrection and of His perfect keeping of the Law. In His heart alone the Law remains unbroken.

8. The Tabernacle itself speaks of the incarnation, Christ dwelling among His people (see Jn. 1:14). The boards, sockets, curtains, coverings — everything connected with the Tabernacle and its service — are, in some way, types of Christ.

The *feasts of the Lord* set forth in Leviticus 23 are a beautiful and progressive revelation of the work of Christ for His people and the unfolding of the plan of God, through Christ, especially as it relates to Israel.

And so, the wondrous story of the types in the Old Testament unfolds, giving us vast and understandable revelations of the coming Messiah and of His person and work.

Messianic typology in the Old Testament opens a door to the fuller comprehension of the Messiah, the Christ of God. The Book of Hebrews shows clearly that these amazing types in the Old Testament are not the result of mere chance but were divinely planned to give pictures of Christ and His offering on the cross (see Heb. 5-10). Moses, when he was about to construct the Tabernacle, was "admonished of God...to make...all things according to the pattern shown to thee" (Heb. 8:5). In other words, God planned the types — lives of men, institutions such as the Tabernacle and its worship, and events in the history of Israel — to serve as illustrations.

CONCLUSION

I n conclusion, the following points are very clear. First, there is genuine prophecy in the Bible, and in the Bible alone. Second, this prophecy proves beyond all doubt that Jesus of Nazareth, the central character of the New Testament, is the predicted Messiah of the Old Testament. Third, the Messiah (Christ) is God manifested in the flesh. Fourth, the Bible is the Word of God. Fifth, the God of the Bible is the only true God. Sixth, the eternal salvation of man's soul is accomplished solely by trusting Christ and His redeeming work on the cross.

Since these great realizations of prophecy are true and provable, it is the duty of each individual to trust Christ for his own salvation, surrender to His Lordship and live for Him. Since the Bible tells us that man's eternal destiny depends on trusting Christ — "He that believeth on the Son hath everlasting life; and he that believeth not the Son shall not see life, but the wrath of God abideth on him" (Jn. 3:36) — it should be our greatest desire to witness to others of these facts and make them aware that "there is no other name under heaven given among men, whereby we must be saved" (Acts 4:12).

THESE ARE WRITTEN, THAT YE MIGHT BELIEVE THAT JESUS
IS THE CHRIST, THE SON OF GOD; AND THAT BELIEVING
YE MIGHT HAVE LIFE THROUGH HIS NAME
(JN. 20:31).

THE SECOND
TREATISE OF
GOVERNMENT

JOHN LOCKE

Edited, with an introduction, by
THOMAS P. PEARDON
Professor of Government, Columbia University

· ·

The Library of Liberal Arts

Macmillan Publishing Company
New York
Collier Macmillan Publishers
London

John Locke: 1632-1704

THE SECOND TREATISE OF GOVERNMENT was originally
published in 1690

• • • • • • • • • • • • • • • • • • •

CONTENTS
....

INTRODUCTION   vii

SELECTED BIBLIOGRAPHY   xxiii

NOTE ON THE TEXT   xxvii

THE SECOND TREATISE OF GOVERNMENT

I.   3

II.   Of the State of Nature   4

III. Of the State of War   11

IV.   Of Slavery   15

V.   Of Property   16

VI.   Of Paternal Power   30

VII. Of Political or Civil Society   44

VIII. Of the Beginning of Political Societies   54

IX.   Of the Ends of Political Society and
      Government   70

X.   Of the Forms of a Commonwealth   73

XI.   Of the Extent of the Legislative Power   75

XII. Of the Legislative, Executive, and Federative
      Power of the Commonwealth   82

XIII. Of the Subordination of the Powers of the
      Commonwealth   84

XIV. Of Prerogative   91

XV.   Of Paternal, Political, and Despotical Power
      Considered Together   96

XVI. Of Conquest   99

XVII. Of Usurpation   110

XVIII. Of Tyranny   112

XIX. Of the Dissolution of Government   119

INTRODUCTION

Locke's Life

John Locke (1632–1704) is probably the most representative thinker in the whole Anglo-American political tradition. Often called the theorist of the English Revolution of 1688, he was also a main source of the ideas of the American Revolution of 1776. This was not because Locke was original in his political ideas, but rather because he gave clear and reasonable expression to beliefs that were the product of centuries of political experience and the stock-in-trade of liberty-loving Englishmen and Americans in the seventeenth and eighteenth centuries.

Like Hobbes and Hooker, John Locke was born in the west of England. He came from a substantial middle-class family background, his father being a small landowner and an attorney. The religious leaning of the family was Puritan; its political sympathies were with Parliament, for which cause John Locke's father fought in the Civil War. It seems to have been his father to whom Locke owed his early education. He was then sent to Westminster School where he remained for about six years. In 1652 he entered Christ Church, Oxford, thus beginning an association of some thirty years with that institution. Locke was extremely critical of the education he received both at school and at the university. He was impatient with the scholastic curriculum still in force and not always respectful of his teachers. According to Anthony Wood,[1] indeed, Locke as a student was "ever prating and troublesome and paid little attention to his lecturers." However, he read a great deal, being particularly stirred at this time by the ideas of Descartes, and some years after taking his degree he was made a lecturer in the university.

It was probably Locke's liberal religious ideas that decided him against a career in the Church. Instead, he turned to medicine al-

[1] Anthony Wood (1632–1695): Author of a history of Oxford University (in Latin 1674; in English 1791–96).

though his practice of that art was never very systematic. Locke's career was to be made in other ways. He made a deep impression upon those with whom he came into contact. His personality was as pleasing as his intellect was powerful. In 1665–1666 he first visited the Continent as secretary to Sir Walter Vane on a mission to Brandenburg. About this time, too, began his close association over many years with Anthony Ashley Cooper, the first Earl of Shaftesbury and a prominent Whig politician. Locke not only acted as family physician but was tutor to Cooper's son, the second earl, who became famous in later years as one of the leading Deists. From 1675–1679 Locke was again abroad in France for his health. There, as everywhere, he made contacts with men of science and letters. Back in England, from 1679–1683 he lived in an atmosphere of political unrest and threatened civil war. His liberal notions got him into mild trouble at Oxford and, in 1683, he went to Holland as a political exile. Here he remained during the years of preparation for the descent of William of Orange on England. Following that event, Locke returned to his native land in February, 1689, in the expedition that brought Mary to join her husband on the throne. From this time until his death in 1704, Locke lived much in the country except when official duties demanded his presence in the capital. Chief among these was his position as commissioner with the Board of Trade and Plantations at a salary of £1,000 a year, a post he held from 1696 to 1700 when ill-health forced his resignation. He died on October 28, 1704.

No one who lived in seventeenth-century England could fail to be influenced by its revolutionary upheavals. "I no sooner perceived myself in the world, but I found myself in a storm which has lasted almost hitherto." [2] In this experience may be found a partial explanation of Locke's dislike of violence and extremes. It is important, however, to note that the storm was blowing itself out before Locke was out of his twenties. The year 1660 was a watershed in English political experience. The Stuarts were restored, but not the early Stuart absolutism. Trouble indeed lay ahead, but there was not so much danger of fundamental upheavals.

[2] Quoted in Thomas Fowler, *Locke* (1899), p. 2.

Locke was not disturbed like Hobbes by the fear that the fabric
of society would be torn asunder. Stability, it has been said, was
the central assumption of his thinking. And, if one can assume
that there is a deep social stability underlying and more fundamental than government, one will be unwilling to surrender almost
all rights for the benefits of political order as Hobbes was willing
to do.

It was not only the political situation that had changed by the
latter part of the century. A new intellectual climate was spreading
over Europe. There was less religious and political zealotry and
more interest in science and in economic gain. It can be felt in the
character of Locke's Christianity. Religious faith was certainly
profoundly important in his thinking. For him men were "all the
workmanship of one omnipotent and infinitely wise Maker—all the
servants of one sovereign master, sent into the world by his order,
and about his business." [3] It is impossible to comprehend Locke
without grasping the existence of this faith. Yet his was a placid
and Latitudinarian faith belonging to the Enlightenment rather
than to that twilight of the Middle Ages, the period from 1500 to
1650, or thereabouts, in which the Reformation and the religious
wars had occurred. The old era had been full of passion and competing orthodoxies. The new era was to prefer reasonableness and
simplification in dogma and the toleration of dissent. The old era
had started its reasoning from the assumption that man was naturally vicious or wicked. The new era was destined to be rather
optimistic about man's nature and potentialities.

Much of the change in intellectual climate was produced by the
work of men like Descartes, whose *Discourse on Method* inaugurated modern philosophy. But more important was the progress of
science. Newton, whose *Principia Mathematica* appeared in 1687,
seemed to unlock the secrets of nature. Locke read both Descartes
and Newton avidly. Moreover, he was a close friend of the chemist
Boyle, whom he helped in some experiments; he was brought a
good deal closer to science, especially experimental science, through
these contacts than Hobbes has been.

[3] See Section 6.

Locke's Writings

Locke's books were the product of long years of reading and reflection. As late as his fifty-fourth year he had not published anything of importance although he had written a good deal that remained in manuscript. His years in Holland (1683–89) gave him leisure to complete much that he had undertaken long before and the Revolution provided the stimulus for publication. In this respect 1690 was Locke's *annus mirabilis*. True, his *Letter on Toleration* appeared both in Latin and English in 1689. But in the next year came forth the great *Essay Concerning Human Understanding,* attacking innate ideas and tracing all knowledge to experience (sensation and reflection); and in the same year were published the *Two Treatises of Government,* which were written to justify before world opinion the Revolution of 1688 and the ascension of William to the throne of England. In the Preface he summarizes the purpose of the two *Treatises* as follows:

READER, Thou hast here the beginning and end of a discourse concerning government. What fate has otherwise disposed of the papers that should have filled up the middle, and were more than all the rest, it is not worth while to tell thee. These which remain, I hope, are sufficient to establish the throne of our great restorer, our present King William—to make good his title in the consent of the people, which, being our only one of all lawful governments, he has more fully and clearly than any other prince in Christendom; and to justify to the world the people of England, whose love of their just and natural rights, with their resolution to preserve them, saved the nation when it was on the very brink of slavery and ruin.

Locke directs his political writing against two lines of absolutist argument. The first was the patriarchal theory of divine right monarchy given by Sir Robert Filmer (d. 1653) in his *Patriarcha, or the Natural Power of Kings,* published posthumously in 1680. Here Filmer had argued that kings are or should be thought of as being direct heirs of Adam. With this contention Locke dealt sufficiently in his *First Treatise of Government.*[4] The *Second Treatise* was

---

[4] Both the *First Treatise of Government* and Filmer's *Patriarcha* are reprinted in Locke: *Two Treatises of Government,* No. 2 of the "Hafner Library of Classics." (See "Note on the Text," p. xxvii.)

directed, although without specifically saying so, against the line of argument for absolutism presented in Hobbes' *Leviathan*, 1651. Hobbes rested his despotism on consent. He assumed that without the restraints of government men would be in a constant state of war and insecurity. They are by nature so quarrelsome and competitive that only the strongest rule will restrain them. The choice is between despotism and anarchy, and this should be apparent to every thinking being.

Both Filmer and Hobbes represented departures from traditional ways of thinking. In a sense it was the mission of Locke to use the social contract approach for the restatement of ancient political ideas. He was familiar with the great medieval tradition of politics to which modern liberty owes so much—the tradition that government emanates from the community, is subordinate to law, and must seek the popular welfare. He had learned this doctrine from his reading of Richard Hooker.[5] Moreover, this tradition had been reaffirmed in seventeenth-century controversial literature, much of it seeking to answer Hobbes. Locke was familiar with much of this literature. He almost certainly owed a good deal to the Rev. George Lawson's *Examination of the Political Part of Mr. Hobbes his Leviathan* (1657) and *Politica Sacra et Civilis* (1660), and to an earlier forerunner of the Whig tradition, Philip Hunton, whose *Treatise of Monarchie* was published in 1643. From Hunton, as from Lawson, he could learn the lesson that government is a trust on behalf of the people. He had contact with Huguenot thinkers when he was in exile on the Continent.[6] His ideas on natural law, too, were surely influenced by his reading of Grotius [7] and Pufen-

[5] See note 1, p. 4.

[6] It can safely be supposed that Locke was familiar with the celebrated treatise, *Vindiciae contra tyrannos,* published anonymously in 1579 and republished in Leyden in 1648. The author is unknown, but the work is generally attributed variously to Hubert Languet and François Hotman. Based on the social contract theory, it justified rebellion against the king in case of religious oppression. An English translation was published in London in 1924 under the title: *The Defence of Liberty against Tyrants,* edited by Harold Laski.

[7] Hugo Grotius (1583–1645): His major work is *De jure belli ac pacis* (1625). It was reprinted, with an English translation, (1925) by the Carnegie Endowment for International Peace (No. 3 of "The Classics of International Law").

dorf,[8] although he did not share those writers' propensity for absolute monarchy.

The State of Nature and the Law of Nature

The political philosophy of the *Second Treatise,* like all political philosophies, rests upon an interpretation of human nature. Locke viewed man as a pretty decent fellow, far removed from the quarrelsome, competitive, selfish creatures found in Hobbes. He has more inclination to society and is more governed by reason, "the common rule and measure God has given to mankind." [9] The rationality ascribed to man by Locke is a pervasive characteristic going beyond the cunning calculation of interests upon which Hobbes depended to induce individuals in the state of nature to inaugurate society by a compact after which they must be held in society largely by force. It could be relied upon to produce a good deal of order even without the sanctions of government and to help maintain government once it was set up. This was especially so since Locke saw that man prefers stability to change. For "people are not so easily got out of their old forms as some are apt to suggest." [10]

From this interpretation of human nature, it followed rationally that the state of nature (that is, the condition in which men were before political government came into existence or would be if government did not exist) was no condition of war and anarchy as Hobbes had declared. On the contrary, "men living together according to reason, without a common superior on earth with authority to judge between them, is properly the state of nature." [11] The state of nature thus understood is prepolitical since it lacks "a common superior on earth with authority to judge." But it can hardly be called presocial. In it men live together under the guidance of the

8 Samuel von Pufendorf (1632–1694): His major works on natural law are: *De jure naturae et gentium* (1672) and *De officio hominis et civis juxta legem naturalem* (1673). The latter work has been reprinted, with an English translation, (1927) by the Carnegie Endowment for International Peace (No. 10 of "The Classics of International Law").

9 See Section 11.

10 See Section 223.

11 See Section 19.

law of nature by which their rights and responsibilities are determined.

The conception of the law of nature is fundamental in Locke and marked one of the numerous respects in which he may be said to link emerging British constitutionalism to traditional ways of thought. For him it was really an objective rule and measure emanating from God and ascertainable by human reason. It provided a test or criterion by which political institutions and behavior could be limited and judged. It was prior to and more fundamental than the positive laws enacted by the state. And it bound men to obedience to just government once inaugurated by consent. "For truth and keeping of faith belongs to men as men, and not as members of society." [12] Here was Locke's main solution to the problem of why men ought to obey.

In one very important respect, however, Locke certainly contributed to a fundamental reformulation of the law of nature. He gave it a sharp bias toward individualism. The precepts of the law of nature as stated by him are concerned mostly with individual rights rather than with individual responsibilities to society. Under the Stuarts the scales of government had been weighted heavily on the side of authority. The balance was to be more than redressed in the era whose birth was signalized by the Revolution of 1688. And so the chief lesson John Locke learned from the law of nature was that even before government existed men were free, independent, and equal in the enjoyment of inalienable rights, chief among them being life, liberty and property.

Among these rights, property receives the most attention in the *Second Treatise*. Its protection is represented as being the primary function of government. Since this is so, and since Locke's theory of property was among the most influential elements in his teaching, the student should pay special attention to the fifth chapter of the *Second Treatise*. Its ideas loomed large in the rise of middle-class notions of the functions of government. For Locke was modifying the dominant trend of previous natural law thought most strikingly when he made property a natural right preceding civil society and not created by it. By merely applying his labor to the

[12] See Section 14.

gifts of nature man creates property. He cannot be deprived of it by government which it precedes.

It should be noted, however, that Locke means more by property than is usually included under that head. He calls it a "general name" for the "lives, liberties and estates" of men in one place,[13] and in another declares: "By property I must be understood here, as in other places, to mean that property which men have in their persons as well as goods." [14] Moreover, he limits the amount of property to which a man has a natural right to "as much land as a man tills, plants, improves, cultivates, and can use the product of. . . ." [15]

These qualifications are the heritage of earlier ages when conceptions of property were somewhat less sharp and the rights of property rather less completely asserted than they would be later in the nineteenth-century noontide of bourgeois ideology. They made it possible for Locke's theory of property to be used by many different groups—among them advocates of a wide distribution of land and socialists basing a criticism of capitalism upon the labor theory of value.

The beginning of Section 123 shows that Locke was aware that some might conclude that the blessings of the state of nature were preferable to the constraints of government. He tries to destroy this position by dwelling upon the "inconveniences" (which might be summed up as a lack of security and certainty in the enjoyment of property and rights) under which man in the state of nature must live and for the elimination of which he should be willing to set up civil society.

The anarchists would argue that the cure was worse than the disease. Extreme libertarians can always derive support from Locke. But he himself believed that if government is based on consent men can still preserve that freedom, independence, and equality with which they are endowed by nature. To secure this end, of course, he resorted to the notion of the social compact. It is impossible to be sure if he believed such an original contract had actually oc-

13 See Section 123.
14 See Section 173.
15 See Section 32.

curred in history or was merely using the concept as an expository or controversial device. Locke was not very historically minded and may have believed that he was describing what had really taken place in the remote past when political society was born. He cites some examples drawn from history and from accounts of America in support of the historicity of the state of nature and the social contract.[16] But the point is not really very important. Locke based his government on consent because that seemed reasonable to him. Believing this and thinking in the seventeenth century frame of reference, it was natural for him to justify his belief by using the device of a social contract.

The Social Contract

In Locke's use of the social contract there are at least four conspicuous features. In the first place, he used it so as to preserve natural freedom as much as possible. Men surrender only the right of enforcing the law of nature. All other rights they retain as fully as before. Moreover, since men are by nature free, independent, and equal, the contract must be unanimous. Those who wish to remain in the state of nature are permitted to do so. Thus, Locke hoped, government would be both limited in its powers and based firmly on consent.

He was careful, secondly, as Hobbes had been for a different reason, to exclude rulers from the contract. The agreement is between free individuals, not between rulers and ruled. The former are merely given a "fiduciary power" or "trust" to be exercised solely for the good of the community. The conception of a trust fitted Locke's theory of the proper relations between rulers and ruled better than a contract would do. For in a contractual relationship there are rights as well as obligations on both sides. But where a trust exists the rights are all on the side of the beneficiary (the community), the duties all on the side of the trustees (the rulers). At the same time the trustees may properly be allowed a wide sphere within which they may act freely so long as they are faithful to their trusteeship.

[16] See Sections 100–103.

Now the social contract, properly speaking, can be drawn up only once. How is the consent of later generations to be obtained? To meet this difficulty, Locke thought sometimes, perhaps, of formal ceremonies reminiscent of initiation among primitive peoples and of some episodes that were to occur in the French Revolution of 1789. But he relied most on "tacit consent." This is given when individuals on reaching maturity continue to accept the protection and benefits of an organized government instead of withdrawing to other communities or to the open spaces of the New World. Plainly this is not a very realistic resolution of the difficulty. For men are not so free in their movements or loyalties as this would imply.

A fourth feature of Locke's use of the social contract was majority rule. The decisions of a going community cannot depend upon unanimity. For this reason, Locke sensibly assumed that the majority would rule once the social contract was entered upon. But in what sense are the free and equal minority really governed by consent when they must bow to the will of the majority? How are they to be protected against a tyranny of the majority? There is a difficulty here which is not resolved merely by saying that they consented to majority rule at the time of the social compact. Such consent could soon become a very unreal thing. Locke slides over this difficulty.

Some uncertainty in Locke's use of the contract arises out of the setting-up of the institutions of government. Locke was one of the first writers to recognize the distinction between society and government. Now the contract sets up a form of society (civil or political society—what we today call the state). Just when and how is government instituted? Pufendorf had resorted to two contracts to answer this question in his theory.[17] By one, society was instituted, by the other, government; and some students have argued that two contracts are implied in Locke. Others regard the setting-up of government as the first act of the new community set up by the contract. But this explanation seems to be weak; the mark of a political society *is* government. Locke says:

[17] *De Officio Hominis et Civis,* ch. 6. (The Carnegie edition of the translation, pp. 106ff.)

Those who are united into one body and have a common established law and judicature to appeal to, with authority to decide controversies between them and punish offenders, are in civil society one with another. . . .[18]

According to this, government is itself an essential part of civil or political society and the two must have come into existence together.

The difficulty is resolved if we cease to think of Locke as reasoning in historical terms. He is really concerned with the inner logic of society. He is saying that relations between men in society and between individuals and society are *as if* there had been a contract made between them whereby men surrendered certain rights in return for protection of the rest. And he is saying further that relations between rulers and ruled are or ought to be those that exist between a trustee and the trustor and the beneficiary of the trust—the last two in this case being the same, namely, the Community or the People.

The Limits to Government

The conception of government as a trust exercised on behalf of the governed is an old one. It is deeply imbedded in the European political tradition. But where the middle ages fell short of modern times was in precision of statement concerning the limits on the power of rulers and in the provision of institutions by which rulers might be held responsible. In both respects the seventeenth century made important advances. Locke's *Second Treatise* contributed to this advance in several ways. For example, it set down specific limits on government. Thus the legislature, while the supreme organ, must exercise its supremacy through laws properly promulgated and applying equally to all groups and classes. It must not raise taxes without the consent of the people or their deputies. Nor can it delegate its legislative powers. The other branches of government are still more sharply limited.

One way of limiting government is to apply the doctrine of the separation of powers. Locke holds an important place in the development of this doctrine, although he does not formulate it as clearly as Montesquieu was to do. Locke spoke of "balancing the

[18] See Section 87.

power of government by placing several parts of it in different hands." [19] He also distinguished between three different functions—legislative, executive and federative (foreign relations)—but permitted them to be combined in practice. He was willing to place the executive and federative in the same hands, made the executive a part of the legislative and asserted strongly the supremacy of the legislative (king-in-Parliament) over other branches. Thus he contributed to the formulation of the separation-of-powers doctrine, but did not give it its modern form in which the different "powers" are placed in distinct organs each equal to the other.

One reason was that institutions were always secondary to principles in Locke. So long as government was based upon consent and conducted within proper limits he was not vitally concerned about forms. His own preference clearly went to the English system after the Revolutionary Settlement. Under this the People's role in normal times was confined to the choice of a representative assembly which was then supreme. The executive power was placed in separate hands, but was also given a share in lawmaking.

The British system has always been characterized by the large measure of freedom of action left in the hands of the responsible rulers. It is important to note that although Locke set down limits to government he saw that government to be effective must have adequate power and adequate discretion in the exercise of that power. His chapter on Prerogative, with its specific references to English experience, deserves close attention. Locke knew that the law cannot provide for everything and that sometimes to observe the letter of the law may even be to act against the public good. For such situations he believed in reserve and emergency powers. They should be restricted in the case of feeble rulers, but "a good prince who is mindful of the trust put into his hands and careful of the good of his people cannot have too much prerogative." [20]

But if rulers do not exercise their trust in the interest of the governed then resistance is justifiable and a new government may be instituted. This is the last proposition in Locke's breviary of political wisdom. He was able to make it so confidently because

[19] See Section 107.
[20] See Section 164.

of the distinction he drew between government and society. In his own lifetime he had seen civil war rage and several regimes succeed each other while the bonds of society held. And so, as was pointed out earlier, he saw that men need not tolerate despotism for fear that the sole alternative was anarchy. Nor was he afraid that a doctrine of resistance would mean constant instability. For people are "more disposed to suffer than right themselves by resistance." [21] They are conservative by nature.

Yet while Locke was clear as to the existence of a right of revolution, he was never very precise as to when, how, and by whom it should be exercised. He says enough to justify the conservative upheaval, led by men of substance, by which James II was driven from the throne. He was too cautious, too much a lover of peace and order, too much a man of the comfortable upper classes, to wish to give encouragement to ordinary rebels.

Locke's Influence

The political philosophy briefly summarized above spread widely in eighteenth-century Europe. In England, the Whigs found in it a justification for their regime including, somewhat illogically perhaps, their landed oligarchy. At the same time, it provided agrarian reformers like Spence [22] and Ogilvie [23] with arguments against that system. In France, too, Locke found a wide audience. Popularized by Voltaire and others he supplied critics and reformers with exactly the kind of doctrine they needed to assail the absolute monarchy and social injustice of prerevolutionary France. But there it appeared in a more doctrinaire and revolutionary form than in the writings of Locke himself.

But it was in America that Locke met with the most resounding response. Early in the eighteenth century his books were being circulated in the colonies, while many Americans learned about them at British universities. A study of sermons and other materials shows

[21] See Section 230.
[22] Thomas Spence (1750–1814): Advocate of land nationalization.
[23] William Ogilvie (1736–1819): Author of *An Essay on the Right of Property in Land* (1781).

that he was one of the chief sources of the political ideas expounded by the New England clergy, especially after 1763. So close is the Declaration of Independence to Locke in form, phraseology, and content, that Jefferson was accused of copying the *Second Treatise*. This, of course, he did not do. But the ideas of the Declaration are those ideas of English constitutionalism to which Locke had given expression. No one has put the connection more forcefully than the late Professor Carl Becker:

The lineage is direct: Jefferson copied Locke and Locke quoted Hooker. In political theory and in political practice the American Revolution drew its inspiration from the parliamentary struggle of the seventeenth century. The philosophy of the Declaration was not taken from the French. It was not even new; but good old English doctrine newly formulated to meet a present emergency. In 1776 it was commonplace doctrine, everywhere to be met with, as Jefferson said, "whether expressed in conversation, in letters, printed essays, or the elementary books of public right." And in sermons also, he might have added.[24]

Nor was Locke's influence confined to the Declaration of Independence; it was felt in the ideas and often the phrasing of State Declarations and Constitutions. He was quoted, too, in the Federal Convention of 1787 and often referred to thereafter. Indeed there was a natural harmony between Locke's ideas and those of the nineteenth-century United States. Paschal Larkin puts it very well in saying that "Locke's individualism, his glorification of property rights and his love of conscience have been interwoven into the economic and social texture of American life."[25]

By one of those paradoxes with which the history of political ideas abounds, Locke's philosophy was seriously undermined at the time of its greatest circulation and long before its disappearance. Early in the eighteenth century Hume subjected the social contract theory to a criticism from which it never recovered. He pronounced it inadequate both empirically and logically. Primitive man, said Hume, could never rise to the conception of a formal contract; nor does history or contemporary government give ground for belief

[24] Carl Becker, *The Declaration of Independence* (1922), p. 79.
[25] Paschal Larkin, *Property in the Eighteenth Century* (1930), p. 171.

that such contract had ever occurred. The contract theory, he further argued, is inadequate logically since it does not explain why men should obey. If we ask why men should keep their promises and why they should obey, the true answer is to be found not in any promise they have given, but in utility, that is, because only thus can society and government exist.

The utilitarian analysis, although itself open to criticism, was destined to flourish for some time. Along with it in the eighteenth century went a richer appreciation of the realities of social life represented, for example, in the writings of Adam Ferguson.[26] The weaknesses in the social contract type of political analysis were revealed still more clearly with the maturing of anthropology and social psychology in the nineteenth and twentieth centuries. At the same time the increasing demands for state action and intervention to secure economic protection and social welfare have brought into prominence aspects of government other than those revealed in the *Second Treatise.*

Modern readers, indeed, are bound to observe many weaknesses in Locke's philosophy. There is an obvious inconsistency between the concept of inherent individual rights contained in the *Second Treatise* and the rejection of innate ideas which is so prominent in his general philosophy. The assertion of individual rights is made too strongly, the distinction between individual and society drawn too sharply to be in accord with the findings of scientific anthropology and psychology. Nor, as T. H. Green was to show, can we reach a satisfactory solution to the problem of freedom by starting with the conception of an individual in a presocial or prepolitical state and endowing him with liberty there. Actually, as we have already suggested, Locke does not safeguard the individual nearly as fully as his aspirations demanded. Such devices as "tacit consent" do not guarantee real consent. And no provision is made for the situation in which the individual cannot reconcile the commands of civil law with his conscience even though they are backed by a majority.

[26] Adam Ferguson (1723–1816): His principal works are: *Essay on the History of Civil Society* (1765); *Institutes of Moral Philosophy* (1769); and *Principles of Moral and Political Science* (1792).

The truth was that Locke conceived of government in ways that were too static, too mechanical, and too rational. The state pictured in the *Second Treatise* is an artificial structure made up of independent individuals joined together by rational agreement for limited purposes. But the state as it really exists is the product of many centuries of almost unconscious development. Its institutions emerge by nearly imperceptible steps in response to needs that are felt before they can be formulated clearly. The ideas which are its rational explanation and justification have themselves a long history, deep roots that go back even beyond Greece and Rome into the river valley civilization of the Tigris and Euphrates. The emotions and loyalties which are its bonds of union are woven slowly through long ages of living together. No enduring state has ever been the mechanical construction suggested by Locke; nor are men in politics nearly so rational as he and the social contract school in general assumed.

And yet when all this is said, and more, John Locke remains one of the most appealing philosophers of liberalism and even of democracy. For he had the root of the matter in him. "The end of government is the good of mankind." [27] "Whosoever uses force without right . . . puts himself into a state of war with those against whom he so uses it . . . and everyone has a right to defend himself and to resist the aggressor." [28] Locke's *Second Treatise* is an epitome of Anglo-American ideals, the distillation of a wisdom derived from centuries of struggle for liberty and justice in government.

THOMAS P. PEARDON

BARNARD COLLEGE, COLUMBIA UNIVERSITY
July, 1952

[27] See Section 229.
[28] See Section 232.

SELECTED BIBLIOGRAPHY

LOCKE'S MAJOR WORKS

Four Letters Concerning Toleration.
  First Letter (Latin, 1685; English translation, 1689).
  Second Letter (1690).
  Third Letter (1692).
  Fourth Letter (fragment, 1706).

Two Treatises of Government (1690).

An Essay Concerning Human Understanding (1690).
  4th ed., extensively revised (1700).

  Three Letters to the Lord Bishop of Worcester concerning some passages in the Essay Concerning Human Understanding (1697, 1698, 1699).

Some Considerations on the Consequences of Lowering the Rate of Interest and Raising the Value of Money (1691).

  Further Considerations concerning Raising the Value of Money (1695).

Some Thoughts concerning Education (1693) [dedicated to Clarke of Chipley].

The Reasonableness of Christianity as delivered in the Scriptures (1695).

  A Vindication of the Reasonableness of Christianity from Mr. Edwards' Reflections (1695).
  Second Vindication of the Reasonableness of Christianity (1697).

Posthumously published:

A Paraphrase and Notes on the Epistles of St. Paul to the Galatians. First and Second Corinthians, Romans, and Ephesians. To which is prefixed an Essay for the Understanding of St. Paul's Epistles by consulting St. Paul himself (1705–7).

A Discourse of Miracles (1706).

An Examination of Father Malebranche's Opinion of Seeing all Things in God (1706).

xxiii

The Conduct of the Understanding (1706).

Some Familiar Letters between Mr. Locke and several of his friends (1706).

The Fundamental Constitutions of Carolina (1720).

Remarks upon some of Mr. Norris's Books, wherein he asserts Father Malebranche's Opinion of our Seeing all Things in God (1720).

Elements of Natural Philosophy (1720).

Original Letters of Locke, Algernon Sidney, and Anthony Lord Shaftesbury (1830).

COLLATERAL READING

Aaron, R. I., *John Locke*. Oxford, 1937.

Becker, Carl, *The Declaration of Independence*. New York, 1922.

Bourne, H. R. Fox, *The Life of John Locke*. 2 vols. New York, 1876

Bowle, John, *Hobbes and His Critics: A Study in Seventeenth Century Constitutionalism*. London, 1951.

Curti, Merle Eugene, "The Great Mr. Locke, America's Philosopher, 1783–1861." *Huntington Library Bulletin*, No. 11, April, 1937.

Czajkowski, Casimir J., *The Theory of Private Property in John Locke's Political Philosophy*. Ann Arbor, Michigan, 1941.

Driver, C. H., "John Locke," in Hearnshaw, F. J. C. (ed.), *The Social and Political Ideas of Some English Thinkers of the Augustan Age, A.D. 1650–1750*. London, 1928.

Fowler, Thomas, *Locke*. "English Men of Letters" series. New York, 1899.

Fraser, Alexander C., *Locke*. London, 1890.

Gough, John Wiedhofft, *John Locke's Political Philosophy. Eight Studies*. Oxford, 1950.

——— *The Social Contract: A Critical Study of its Development*. Oxford, 1936.

Kendall, Willmoore, *John Locke and the Doctrine of Majority Rule*. Urbana, Illinois, 1941.

King, Lord, *The Life of John Locke with Extracts from his Correspondence, Journals, and Commonplace Books*. 2 vols. (New edition with considerable additions.) London, 1830.

Lamprecht, Sterling Power, *The Moral and Political Philosophy of John Locke*. New York, 1918.

Larkin, Paschal, *Property in the Eighteenth Century, with Special References to England and Locke*. Cork, 1930.

Laski, Harold J., *Political Thought in England from Locke to Bentham*. New York, 1920.

—— *The Rise of European Liberalism*. New York, 1936.

John Locke, Tercentenary Addresses. London, 1933.
   Ryle, Gilbert, "Locke on the Human Understanding."
   Stocks, J. L., "Locke's Contribution to Political Theory."

Ogden, Henry V., "The State of Nature and the Decline of Lockian Political Theory in England, 1760–1800." *American Historical Review*, vol. XLVI, October, 1940.

Pollock, Sir Frederick, "Locke's Theory of the State." *British Academy Proceedings*, 1903–1904. Reprinted, with an Appendix: "The Social Contract in Hobbes and Locke," in Pollock: *Essays in the Law*. London, 1922, pp. 8off.

Sabine, G. H., *A History of Political Theory*. Revised edition, New York, 1950.

Vaughan, C. E., *Studies in the History of Political Philosophy Before and After Rousseau*. 2 vols., Manchester, 1925.

NOTE ON THE TEXT

The essay, *Of Civil Government,* which is here reprinted, is the second of two essays on government which were published anonymously in 1690 under the title:

TWO TREATISES OF GOVERNMENT

In the Former
The False Principles and Foundation
of Sir Robert Filmer and his Followers
Are Detected and Overthrown

The Latter
Is an Essay Concerning
The True Original, Extent, and End
Of Civil Government

The work was republished, with the author's name, in 1694 and 1698, each edition containing a number of corrections. As stated in his will, however, Locke remained dissatisfied with the text and prepared a number of additional changes, which were incorporated in subsequent editions published after his death. The alterations received a final editorial check in the sixth edition, published in 1764, which contained the following "advertisement":

The present edition of this book has not only been collated with the first three editions which were published during the author's life, but also has the advantage of his last corrections and improvements, from a copy delivered to him by Mr. Peter Coste, communicated to the editor and now lodged in Christ College, Cambridge.

The text of 1764 has now been accepted as the author's final version and has consequently been followed here, except for spelling and punctuation, which have been revised to conform to present day American usage. For the convenience of the reader the editorial staff of the publishers has contributed a few notes, marked by brackets, which supply information on authors and literature referred to by Locke.

Both *Treatises,* together with Sir Robert Filmer's *Patriarcha,* with an Introduction by Thomas I. Cook, have been reprinted in "The Hafner Library of Classics," published by the Hafner Publishing Company, New York. That edition, too, is based on the sixth edition and contains, therefore, the final version of the *First Treatise* also.

O. P.

THE SECOND TREATISE
OF GOVERNMENT

AN ESSAY CONCERNING
THE TRUE ORIGINAL, EXTENT, AND END
OF CIVIL GOVERNMENT

CHAPTER I

1. IT HAVING been shown in the foregoing discourse:[1]

(*1*) That Adam had not, either by natural right of fatherhood or by positive donation from God, any such authority over his children or dominion over the world as is pretended.

(*2*) That if he had, his heirs yet had no right to it.

(*3*) That if his heirs had, there being no law of nature nor positive law of God that determines which is the right heir in all cases that may arise, the right of succession, and consequently of bearing rule, could not have been certainly determined.

(*4*) That if even that had been determined, yet the knowledge of which is the eldest line of Adam's posterity being so long since utterly lost that in the races of mankind and families of the world there remains not to one above another the least pretense to be the eldest house, and to have the right of inheritance.

All these premises having, as I think, been clearly made out, it is impossible that the rulers now on earth should make any benefit or derive any the least shadow of authority from that which is held to be the fountain of all power: Adam's private dominion and paternal jurisdiction; so that he that will not give just occasion to think that all government in the world is the product only of force and violence, and that men live together by no other rules but that of beasts, where the strongest carries it, and so lay a foundation for perpetual disorder and mischief, tumult, sedition, and rebellion—things that the followers of that hypothesis so loudly cry out against—must of necessity find out another rise of government, another original of political power, and another way of designing and knowing the persons that have it than what Sir Robert Filmer has taught us.[2]

2. To this purpose, I think it may not be amiss to set down what I take to be political power; that the power of a magistrate

[1] [Locke refers here to the *First Treatise of Government*. (See Note on the Text.)]

[2] [See Introduction, page x.]

3

over a subject may be distinguished from that of a father over his children, a master over his servants, a husband over his wife, and a lord over his slave. All which distinct powers happening sometimes together in the same man, if he be considered under these different relations, it may help us to distinguish these powers one from another, and show the difference betwixt a ruler of a commonwealth, a father of a family, and a captain of a galley.

3. Political power, then, I take to be a right of making laws with penalties of death and, consequently, all less penalties for the regulating and preserving of property, and of employing the force of the community in the execution of such laws and in the defense of the commonwealth from foreign injury; and all this only for the public good.

—

CHAPTER II

OF THE STATE OF NATURE

4. To UNDERSTAND political power right and derive it from its original, we must consider what state all men are naturally in, and that is a state of perfect freedom to order their actions and dispose of their possessions and persons as they think fit, within the bounds of the law of nature, without asking leave or depending upon the will of any other man.

A state also of equality, wherein all the power and jurisdiction is reciprocal, no one having more than another; there being nothing more evident than that creatures of the same species and rank, promiscuously born to all the same advantages of nature and the use of the same faculties, should also be equal one amongst another without subordination or subjection; unless the lord and master of them all should, by any manifest declaration of his will, set one above another, and confer on him by an evident and clear appointment an undoubted right to dominion and sovereignty.

5. This equality of men by nature the judicious Hooker [1] looks

1 [Richard Hooker (1554?–1600): Author of *The Laws of Ecclesiastical Polity,* which was one of the most influential works in the development of

upon as so evident in itself and beyond all question that he makes it the foundation of that obligation to mutual love amongst men on which he builds the duties we owe one another, and from whence he derives the great maxims of justice and charity. His words are:

The like natural inducement hath brought men to know that it is no less their duty to love others than themselves; for seeing those things which are equal must needs all have one measure; if I cannot but wish to receive good, even as much at every man's hands as any man can wish unto his own soul, how should I look to have any part of my desire herein satisfied unless myself be careful to satisfy the like desire, which is undoubtedly in other men, being of one and the same nature? To have anything offered them repugnant to this desire must needs in all respects grieve them as much as me; so that, if I do harm, I must look to suffer, there being no reason that others should show greater measure of love to me than they have by me showed unto them; my desire therefore to be loved of my equals in nature, as much as possibly may be, imposeth upon me a natural duty of bearing to them-ward fully the like affection; from which relation of equality between ourselves and them that are as ourselves, what several rules and canons natural reason hath drawn, for direction of life, no man is ignorant. (*Eccl. Pol.* lib. i.).

6. But though this be a state of liberty, yet it is not a state of license; though man in that state have an uncontrollable liberty to dispose of his person or possessions, yet he has not liberty to destroy himself, or so much as any creature in his possession, but where some nobler use than its bare preservation calls for it. The state of nature has a law of nature to govern it, which obliges every one; and reason, which is that law, teaches all mankind who will but consult it that, being all equal and independent, no one ought to harm another in his life, health, liberty, or possessions; for men being all the workmanship of one omnipotent and infinitely wise Maker—all the servants of one sovereign master, sent into the world by his order, and about his business—they are his

---

political theory from medieval thought to the natural rights concept. It had a profound influence on Locke, as can be seen from his many quotations from Hooker. The work consists of eight books; Books I-IV were published in 1594, Book V in 1597, and Books VI-VIII posthumously in 1648.]

property whose workmanship they are, made to last during his, not one another's, pleasure; and being furnished with like faculties, sharing all in one community of nature, there cannot be supposed any such subordination among us that may authorize us to destroy another, as if we were made for one another's uses as the inferior ranks of creatures are for ours. Every one, as he is bound to preserve himself and not to quit his station wilfully, so by the like reason, when his own preservation comes not in competition, ought he, as much as he can, to preserve the rest of mankind, and may not, unless it be to do justice to an offender, take away or impair the life, or what tends to the preservation of the life, the liberty, health, limb, or goods of another.

7. And that all men may be restrained from invading others' rights and from doing hurt to one another, and the law of nature be observed, which wills the peace and preservation of all mankind, the execution of the law of nature is, in that state, put into every man's hands, whereby everyone has a right to punish the transgressors of that law to such a degree as may hinder its violation; for the law of nature would, as all other laws that concern men in this world, be in vain if there were nobody that in that state of nature had a power to execute that law and thereby preserve the innocent and restrain offenders. And if anyone in the state of nature may punish another for any evil he has done, everyone may do so; for in that state of perfect equality, where naturally there is no superiority or jurisdiction of one over another, what any may do in prosecution of that law, everyone must needs have a right to do.

8. And thus in the state of nature one man comes by a power over another; but yet no absolute or arbitrary power to use a criminal, when he has got him in his hands, according to the passionate heats or boundless extravagance of his own will; but only to retribute to him, so far as calm reason and conscience dictate, what is proportionate to his transgression, which is so much as may serve for reparation and restraint; for these two are the only reasons why one man may lawfully do harm to another, which is that we call punishment. In transgressing the law of nature, the offender declares himself to live by another rule than that of reason and

common equity, which is that measure God has set to the actions of men for their mutual security; and so he becomes dangerous to mankind, the tie which is to secure them from injury and violence being slighted and broken by him. Which being a trespass against the whole species and the peace and safety of it provided for by the law of nature, every man upon this score, by the right he has to preserve mankind in general, may restrain, or, where it is necessary, destroy things noxious to them, and so may bring such evil on any one who has transgressed that law, as may make him repent the doing of it and thereby deter him, and by his example others, from doing the like mischief. And in this case, and upon this ground, *every man has a right to punish the offender and be executioner of the law of nature.*

9. I doubt not but this will seem a very strange doctrine to some men; but before they condemn it, I desire them to resolve me by what right any prince or state can put to death or punish any alien for any crime he commits in their country. It is certain their laws, by virtue of any sanction they receive from the promulgated will of the legislative, reach not a stranger; they speak not to him, nor, if they did, is he bound to hearken to them. The legislative authority, by which they are in force over the subjects of that commonwealth, has no power over him. Those who have the supreme power of making laws in England, France, or Holland, are to an Indian but like the rest of the world—men without authority; and therefore, if by the law of nature every man has not a power to punish offenses against it as he soberly judges the case to require, I see not how the magistrates of any community can punish an alien of another country, since, in reference to him, they can have no more power than what every man naturally may have over another.

10. Besides the crime which consists in violating the law and varying from the right rule of reason, whereby a man so far becomes degenerate and declares himself to quit the principles of human nature and to be a noxious creature, there is commonly injury done to some person or other, and some other man receives damage by his transgression; in which case he who has received any damage has, besides the right of punishment common to him

with other men, a particular right to seek reparation from him that has done it; and any other person, who finds it just, may also join with him that is injured and assist him in recovering from the offender so much as may make satisfaction for the harm he has suffered.

11. From these two distinct rights—the one of punishing the crime for restraint and preventing the like offense, which right of punishing is in everybody; the other of taking reparation, which belongs only to the injured party—comes it to pass that the magistrate, who by being magistrate has the common right of punishing put into his hands, can often, where the public good demands not the execution of the law, remit the punishment of criminal offenses by his own authority, but yet cannot remit the satisfaction due to any private man for the damage he has received. That he who has suffered the damage has a right to demand in his own name, and he alone can remit; the damnified person has this power of appropriating to himself the goods or service of the offender by right of self-preservation, as every man has a power to punish the crime to prevent its being committed again, by the right he has of preserving all mankind and doing all reasonable things he can in order to that end; and thus it is that every man, in the state of nature, has a power to kill a murderer, both to deter others from doing the like injury, which no reparation can compensate, by the example of the punishment that attends it from everybody, and also to secure men from the attempts of a criminal who, having renounced reason—the common rule and measure God has given to mankind —has, by the unjust violence and slaughter he has committed upon one, declared war against all mankind, and therefore may be destroyed as a lion or a tiger, one of those wild savage beasts with whom men can have no society nor security. And upon this is grounded that great law of nature, "Whoso sheddeth man's blood, by man shall his blood be shed." And Cain was so fully convinced that every one had a right to destroy such a criminal that, after the murder of his brother, he cries out, "Every one that findeth me, shall slay me"; so plain was it written in the hearts of mankind.

12. By the same reason may a man in the state of nature pun-

ish the lesser breaches of that law. It will perhaps be demanded: with death? I answer: Each transgression may be punished to that degree and with so much severity as will suffice to make it an ill bargain to the offender, give him cause to repent, and terrify others from doing the like. Every offense that can be committed in the state of nature may in the state of nature be also punished equally, and as far forth as it may in a commonwealth; for though it would be beside my present purpose to enter here into the particulars of the law of nature, or its measures of punishment, yet it is certain there is such a law, and that, too, as intelligible and plain to a rational creature and a studier of that law as the positive laws of commonwealths, nay, possibly plainer, as much as reason is easier to be understood than the fancies and intricate contrivances of men, following contrary and hidden interests put into words; for so truly are a great part of the municipal laws of countries, which are only so far right as they are founded on the law of nature, by which they are to be regulated and interpreted

13. To this strange doctrine viz., that in the state of nature every one has the executive power of the law of nature—I doubt not but it will be objected that it is unreasonable for men to be judges in their own cases, that self-love will make men partial to themselves and their friends, and, on the other side, that ill-nature, passion, and revenge will carry them too far in punishing others, and hence nothing but confusion and disorder will follow; and that therefore God has certainly appointed government to restrain the partiality and violence of men. I easily grant that civil government is the proper remedy for the inconveniences of the state of nature, which must certainly be great where men may be judges in their own case; since it is easy to be imagined that he who was so unjust as to do his brother an injury will scarce be so just as to condemn himself for it; but I shall desire those who make this objection to remember that absolute monarchs are but men, and if government is to be the remedy of those evils which necessarily follow from men's being judges in their own cases, and the state of nature is therefore not to be endured, I desire to know what kind of government that is, and how much better it is than the state of nature, where one man commanding a multitude has

the liberty to be judge in his own case, and may do to all his subjects whatever he pleases, without the least liberty to any one to question or control those who execute his pleasure, and in whatsoever he does, whether led by reason, mistake, or passion, must be submitted to? Much better it is in the state of nature, wherein men are not bound to submit to the unjust will of another; and if he that judges, judges amiss in his own or any other case, he is answerable for it to the rest of mankind.

14. It is often asked as a mighty objection, "Where are or ever were there any men in such a state of nature?" To which it may suffice as an answer at present that since all princes and rulers of independent governments all through the world are in a state of nature, it is plain the world never was, nor ever will be, without numbers of men in that state. I have named all governors of independent communities, whether they are, or are not, in league with others; for it is not every compact that puts an end to the state of nature between men, but only this one of agreeing together mutually to enter into one community and make one body politic; other promises and compacts men may make one with another and yet still be in the state of nature. The promises and bargains for truck, etc., between the two men in the desert island, mentioned by Garcilasso de la Vega, in his history of Peru,[2] or between a Swiss and an Indian in the woods of America, are binding to them, though they are perfectly in a state of nature in reference to one another; for truth and keeping of faith belongs to men as men, and not as members of society.

15. To those that say there were never any men in the state of nature, I will not only oppose the authority of the judicious Hooker, *Eccl. Pol.*, lib. i., sect. 10, where he says,

The laws which have been hitherto mentioned (i.e., the laws of nature) do bind men absolutely, even as they are men, although they have never any settled fellowship, never any solemn agree-

[2] [Garcilasso de la Vega (1539?–1616): Called *El Inca*. A Peruvian historian whose works include: *La Florida del Inca: Historia del Adelantado Hernando de Soto* (1605) and *Comentarios Reales Que Tratan del Origen de los Incas*—Part I, a history of the Incas, published in 1609; and Part II, the conquest of Peru, published posthumously in 1617.]

ment amongst themselves what to do, or not to do; but forasmuch as we are not by ourselves sufficient to furnish ourselves with competent store of things needful for such a life as our nature doth desire, a life fit for the dignity of man; therefore to supply those defects and imperfections which are in us, as living singly and solely by ourselves, we are naturally induced to seek communion and fellowship with others. This was the cause of men's uniting themselves at first in politic societies.

But I, moreover, affirm that all men are naturally in that state and remain so till by their own consents they make themselves members of some politic society; and I doubt not in the sequel of this discourse to make it very clear.

CHAPTER III

OF THE STATE OF WAR

16. THE STATE of war is a state of enmity and destruction; and, therefore, declaring by word or action, not a passionate and hasty but a sedate, settled design upon another man's life, puts him in a state of war with him against whom he has declared such an intention, and so has exposed his life to the other's power to be taken away by him or anyone that joins with him in his defense and espouses his quarrel; it being reasonable and just I should have a right to destroy that which threatens me with destruction; for, by the fundamental law of nature, man being to be preserved as much as possible when all cannot be preserved, the safety of the innocent is to be preferred; and one may destroy a man who makes war upon him, or has discovered an enmity to his being, for the same reason that he may kill a wolf or a lion, because such men are not under the ties of the common law of reason, have no other rule but that of force and violence, and so may be treated as beasts of prey, those dangerous and noxious creatures that will be sure to destroy him whenever he falls into their power.

17. And hence it is that he who attempts to get another man

into his absolute power does thereby put himself into a state of war with him, it being to be understood as a declaration of a design upon his life; for I have reason to conclude that he who would get me into his power without my consent would use me as he pleased when he got me there, and destroy me, too, when he had a fancy to it; for nobody can desire to have me in his absolute power unless it be to compel me by force to that which is against the right of my freedom, i.e., make me a slave. To be free from such force is the only security of my preservation; and reason bids me look on him as an enemy to my preservation who would take away that freedom which is the fence to it; so that he who makes an attempt to enslave me thereby puts himself into a state of war with me. He that, in the state of nature, would take away the freedom that belongs to any one in that state must necessarily be supposed to have a design to take away everything else, that freedom being the foundation of all the rest; as he that, in the state of society, would take away the freedom belonging to those of that society or commonwealth must be supposed to design to take away from them everything else, and so be looked on as in a state of war.

18. This makes it lawful for a man to kill a thief who has not in the least hurt him, nor declared any design upon his life any farther than, by the use of force, so to get him in his power as to take away his money, or what he pleases, from him; because using force where he has no right to get me into his power, let his pretense be what it will, I have no reason to suppose that he who would take away my liberty would not, when he had me in his power, take away everything else. And therefore it is lawful for me to treat him as one who has put himself into a state of war with me, i. e., kill him if I can; for to that hazard does he justly expose himself whoever introduces a state of war and is aggressor in it.

19. And here we have the plain difference between the state of nature and the state of war which, however some men have confounded,[1] are as far distant as a state of peace, good-will, mutual

---

[1] [Locke's reference here is probably to Hobbes' concept of the state of nature as being identical with the state of war. (See Introduction, page xii and *passim*.)]

superior = arbitrator

assistance, and preservation, and a state of enmity, malice, violence, and mutual destruction are one from another. Men living together according to reason, without a common superior on earth with authority to judge between them, is properly the state of nature. But force, or a declared design of force, upon the person of another, where there is no common superior on earth to appeal to for relief, is the state of war; and it is the want of such an appeal [that] gives a man the right of war even against an aggressor, though he be in society and a fellow subject. Thus a thief, whom I cannot harm but by appeal to the law for having stolen all that I am worth, I may kill when he sets on me to rob me but of my horse or coat; because the law, which was made for my preservation, where it cannot interpose to secure my life from present force, which, if lost, is capable of no reparation, permits me my own defense and the right of war, a liberty to kill the aggressor, because the aggressor allows not time to appeal to our common judge, nor the decision of the law, for remedy in a case where the mischief may be irreparable. Want of a common judge with authority puts all men in a state of nature; force without right upon a man's person makes a state of war both where there is and is not a common judge.

20. But when the actual force is over, the state of war ceases between those that are in society and are equally on both sides subjected to the fair determination of the law, because then there lies open the remedy of appeal for the past injury and to prevent future harm. But where no such appeal is, as in the state of nature, for want of positive laws and judges with authority to appeal to, the state of war once begun continues with a right to the innocent party to destroy the other whenever he can, until the aggressor offers peace and desires reconciliation on such terms as may repair any wrongs he has already done and secure the innocent for the future; nay, where an appeal to the law and constituted judges lies open, but the remedy is denied by a manifest perverting of justice and a barefaced wresting of the laws to protect or indemnify the violence or injuries of some men, or party of men, there it is hard to imagine anything but a state of war; for wherever violence is used and injury done, though by hands

appointed to administer justice, it is still violence and injury, however colored with the name, pretenses, or forms of law, the end whereof being to protect and redress the innocent by an un-biased application of it to all who are under it; wherever that is not bona fide done, war is made upon the sufferers, who having no appeal on earth to right them, they are left to the only remedy in such cases—an appeal to heaven.

21. To avoid this state of war—wherein there is no appeal but to heaven, and wherein every the least difference is apt to end, where there is no authority to decide between the contenders—is one great reason of men's putting themselves into society and quitting the state of nature; for where there is an authority, a power on earth from which relief can be had by appeal, there the continuance of the state of war is excluded, and the controversy is decided by that power. Had there been any such court, any superior jurisdiction on earth, to determine the right between Jephthah and the Ammonites, they had never come to a state of war; but we see he was forced to appeal to heaven: "The Lord the Judge," says he, "be judge this day between the children of Israel and the children of Ammon" (Judges xi. 27.), and then prosecuting and relying on his appeal, he leads out his army to battle. And, therefore, in such controversies where the question is put, "Who shall be judge?" it cannot be meant, "who shall decide the controversy"; every one knows what Jephthah here tells us, that "the Lord the Judge" shall judge. Where there is no judge on earth, the appeal lies to God in heaven. That question then cannot mean: who shall judge whether another has put himself in a state of war with me, and whether I may, as Jephthah did, appeal to heaven in it? Of that I myself can only be judge in my own conscience, as I will answer it, at the great day, to the su-preme Judge of all men.

CHAPTER IV

OF SLAVERY

22. THE NATURAL liberty of man is to be free from any superior power on earth, and not to be under the will or legislative authority of man, but to have only the law of nature for his rule. The liberty of man in society is to be under no other legislative power but that established by consent in the commonwealth, nor under the dominion of any will or restraint of any law but what that legislative shall enact according to the trust put in it. Freedom then is not what Sir Robert Filmer tells us "a liberty for every one to do what he lists, to live as he pleases, and not to be tied by any laws"; [1] but freedom of men under government is to have a standing rule to live by, common to every one of that society and made by the legislative power erected in it, a liberty to follow my own will in all things where the rule prescribes not, and not to be subject to the inconstant, uncertain, unknown, arbitrary will of another man; as freedom of nature is to be under no other restraint but the law of nature.

23. This freedom from absolute, arbitrary power is so necessary to, and closely joined with, a man's preservation that he cannot part with it but by what forfeits his preservation and life together; for a man not having the power of his own life cannot by compact or his own consent enslave himself to any one, nor put himself under the absolute arbitrary power of another to take away his life when he pleases. Nobody can give more power than he has himself; and he that cannot take away his own life cannot give another power over it. Indeed, having by his fault forfeited his own life by some act that deserves death, he to whom he has forfeited it may, when he has him in his power, delay to take it and make use of him to his own service; and he does him no injury by it, for whenever he finds the hardship of his slavery

[1] [*Observations upon Aristotle's Politiques Touching Forms of Government* (1652), p. 55.]

outweigh the value of his life, it is in his power, by resisting the will of his master, to draw on himself the death he desires.

24. This is the perfect condition of slavery, which is nothing else but "the state of war continued between a lawful conqueror and a captive"; for if once compact enter between them and make an agreement for a limited power on the one side and obedience on the other, the state of war and slavery ceases as long as the compact endures; for, as has been said, no man can by agreement pass over to another that which he has not in himself—a power over his own life.

I confess we find among the Jews, as well as other nations, that men did sell themselves; but it is plain this was only to drudgery, not to slavery; for it is evident the person sold was not under an absolute, arbitrary, despotical power; for the master could not have power to kill him at any time whom, at a certain time, he was obliged to let go free out of his service; and the master of such a servant was so far from having an arbitrary power over his life that he could not, at pleasure, so much as maim him, but the loss of an eye or tooth set him free (Exod. xxi).

CHAPTER V

OF PROPERTY

25. WHETHER we consider natural reason, which tells us that men, being once born, have a right to their preservation, and consequently to meat and drink and such other things as nature affords for their subsistence; or revelation, which gives us an account of those grants God made of the world to Adam, and to Noah and his sons; it is very clear that God, as King David says (Psalm cxv. 16), "has given the earth to the children of men," given it to mankind in common. But this being supposed, it seems to some a very great difficulty how any one should ever come to have a property in anything. I will not content myself to answer that if it be difficult to make out property upon a supposition

that God gave the world to Adam and his posterity in common, it is impossible that any man but one universal monarch should have any property upon a supposition that God gave the world to Adam and his heirs in succession, exclusive of all the rest of his posterity. But I shall endeavor to show how men might come to have a property in several parts of that which God gave to mankind in common, and that without any express compact of all the commoners.

26. God, who has given the world to men in common, has also given them reason to make use of it to the best advantage of life and convenience. The earth and all that is therein is given to men for the support and comfort of their being. And though all the fruits it naturally produces and beasts it feeds belong to mankind in common, as they are produced by the spontaneous hand of nature; and nobody has originally a private dominion exclusive of the rest of mankind in any of them, as they are thus in their natural state; yet, being given for the use of men, there must of necessity be a means to appropriate them some way or other before they can be of any use or at all beneficial to any particular man. The fruit or venison which nourishes the wild Indian, who knows no enclosure and is still a tenant in common, must be his, and so his, i. e., a part of him, that another can no longer have any right to it before it can do him any good for the support of his life.

27. Though the earth and all inferior creatures be common to all men, yet every man has a property in his own person; this nobody has any right to but himself. The labor of his body and the work of his hands, we may say, are properly his. Whatsoever then he removes out of the state that nature has provided and left it in, he has mixed his labor with, and joined to it something that is his own, and thereby makes it his property. It being by him removed from the common state nature has placed it in, it has by this labor something annexed to it that excludes the common right of other men. For this labor being the unquestionable property of the laborer, no man but he can have a right to what that is once joined to, at least where there is enough and as good left in common for others.

Supremacy of the individual

28. He that is nourished by the acorns he picked up under an oak, or the apples he gathered from the trees in the wood, has certainly appropriated them to himself. Nobody can deny but the nourishment is his. I ask, then, When did they begin to be his? When he digested or when he ate or when he boiled or when he brought them home? Or when he picked them up? And it is plain, if the first gathering made them not his, nothing else could. That labor put a distinction between them and common; that added something to them more than nature, the common mother of all, had done; and so they became his private right. And will anyone say he had no right to those acorns or apples he thus appropriated because he had not the consent of all mankind to make them his? Was it a robbery thus to assume to himself what belonged to all in common? If such a consent as that was necessary, man had starved, notwithstanding the plenty God had given him. We see in commons, which remain so by compact, that it is the taking any part of what is common and removing it out of the state nature leaves it in which begins the property, without which the common is of no use. And the taking of this or that part does not depend on the express consent of all the commoners. Thus the grass my horse has bit, the turfs my servant has cut, and the ore I have digged in any place where I have a right to them in com-mon with others, become my property without the assignation or consent of anybody. The labor that was mine, removing them out of that common state they were in, has fixed my property in them.

29. By making an explicit consent of every commoner neces-sary to any one's appropriating to himself any part of what is given in common, children or servants could not cut the meat which their father or master had provided for them in common without assigning to every one his peculiar part. Though the water running in the fountain be every one's, yet who can doubt but that in the pitcher is his only who drew it out? His labor has taken it out of the hands of nature where it was common and belonged equally to all her children, and has thereby appropriated it to himself.

30. Thus this law of reason makes the deer that Indian's who has killed it; it is allowed to be his goods who has bestowed his

labor upon it, though before it was the common right of every one. And amongst those who are counted the civilized part of mankind, who have made and multiplied positive laws to determine property, this original law of nature, for the beginning of property in what was before common, still takes place; and by virtue thereof what fish any one catches in the ocean, that great and still remaining common of mankind, or what ambergris any one takes up here, is, by the labor that removes it out of that common state nature left it in, made his property who takes that pains about it. And even amongst us, the hare that anyone is hunting is thought his who pursues her during the chase; for, being a beast that is still looked upon as common and no man's private possession, whoever has employed so much labor about any of that kind as to find and pursue her has thereby removed her from the state of nature wherein she was common, and has begun a property.

31. It will perhaps be objected to this that "if gathering the acorns, or other fruits of the earth, etc., makes a right to them, then any one may engross as much as he will." To which I answer: not so. The same law of nature that does by this means give us property does also bound that property, too. "God has given us all things richly" (1 Tim. vi. 17), is the voice of reason confirmed by inspiration. But how far has he given it us? To enjoy. As much as any one can make use of to any advantage of life before it spoils, so much he may by his labor fix a property in; whatever is beyond this is more than his share and belongs to others. Nothing was made by God for man to spoil or destroy. And thus considering the plenty of natural provisions there was a long time in the world, and the few spenders, and to how small a part of that provision the industry of one man could extend itself and engross it to the prejudice of others, especially keeping within the bounds set by reason of what might serve for his use, there could be then little room for quarrels or contentions about property so established.

32. But the chief matter of property being now not the fruits of the earth and the beasts that subsist on it, but the earth itself, as that which takes in and carries with it all the rest, I think it is

plain that property in that, too, is acquired as the former. As much land as a man tills, plants, improves, cultivates, and can use the product of, so much is his property. He by his labor does, as it were, enclose it from the common. Nor will it invalidate his right to say everybody else has an equal title to it, and therefore he cannot appropriate, he cannot enclose, without the consent of all his fellow commoners—all mankind. God, when he gave the world in common to all mankind, commanded man also to labor, and the penury of his condition required it of him. God and his reason commanded him to subdue the earth, i. e., improve it for the benefit of life, and therein lay out something upon it that was his own, his labor. He that in obedience to this command of God subdued, tilled, and sowed any part of it, thereby annexed to it something that was his property, which another had no title to, nor could without injury take from him.

33. Nor was this appropriation of any parcel of land by improving it any prejudice to any other man, since there was still enough and as good left, and more than the yet unprovided could use. So that, in effect, there was never the less left for others because of his enclosure for himself; for he that leaves as much as another can make use of does as good as take nothing at all. Nobody could think himself injured by the drinking of another man, though he took a good draught, who had a whole river of the same water left him to quench his thirst; and the case of land and water, where there is enough for both, is perfectly the same.

34. God gave the world to men in common; but since he gave it them for their benefit and the greatest conveniences of life they were capable to draw from it, it cannot be supposed he meant it should always remain common and uncultivated. He gave it to the use of the industrious and rational—and labor was to be his title to it—not to the fancy or covetousness of the quarrelsome and contentious. He that had as good left for his improvement as was already taken up needed not complain, ought not to meddle with what was already improved by another's labor; if he did, it is plain he desired the benefit of another's pains which he had no right to, and not the ground which God had given him in common with others to labor on, and whereof there was as good left as

that already possessed, and more than he knew what to do with, or his industry could reach to.

35. It is true, in land that is common in England or any other country where there are plenty of people under government who have money and commerce, no one can enclose or appropriate any part without the consent of all his fellow commoners; because this is left common by compact, i.e., by the law of the land, which is not to be violated. And though it be common in respect of some men, it is not so to all mankind, but is the joint property of this country or this parish. Besides, the remainder after such enclosure would not be as good to the rest of the commoners as the whole was when they could all make use of the whole; whereas in the beginning and first peopling of the great common of the world it was quite otherwise. The law man was under was rather for appropriating. God commanded, and his wants forced, him to labor. That was his property which could not be taken from him wherever he had fixed it. And hence subduing or cultivating the earth and having dominion, we see, are joined together. The one gave title to the other. So that God, by commanding to subdue, gave authority so far to appropriate; and the condition of human life which requires labor and material to work on necessarily introduces private possessions.

36. The measure of property nature has well set by the extent of men's labor and the conveniences of life. No man's labor could subdue or appropriate all, nor could his enjoyment consume more than a small part, so that it was impossible for any man, this way, to entrench upon the right of another, or acquire to himself a property to the prejudice of his neighbor, who would still have room for as good and as large a possession—after the other had taken out his—as before it was appropriated. This measure did confine every man's possession to a very moderate proportion, and such as he might appropriate to himself without injury to anybody, in the first ages of the world, when men were more in danger to be lost by wandering from their company in the then vast wilderness of the earth than to be straitened for want of room to plant in. And the same measure may be allowed still without prejudice to anybody, as full as the world seems; for supposing a

man or family in the state they were at first peopling of the world
by the children of Adam or Noah, let him plant in some inland,
vacant places of America; we shall find that the possessions he
could make himself, upon the measures we have given, would
not be very large, nor, even to this day, prejudice the rest of
mankind, or give them reason to complain or think themselves
injured by this man's encroachment, though the race of men have
now spread themselves to all the corners of the world and do
infinitely exceed the small number which was at the beginning.
Nay, the extent of ground is of so little value without labor that
I have heard it affirmed that in Spain itself a man may be permitted to plough, sow, and reap, without being disturbed, upon
land he has no other title to but only his making use of it. But,
on the contrary, the inhabitants think themselves beholden to him
who by his industry on neglected and consequently waste land
has increased the stock of corn which they wanted. But be this
as it will, which I lay no stress on, this I dare boldly affirm—that
the same rule of property, viz., that every man should have as
much as he could make use of, would hold still in the world
without straitening anybody, since there is land enough in the
world to suffice double the inhabitants, had not the invention of
money and the tacit agreement of men to put a value on it introduced—by consent—larger possessions and a right to them; which,
how it has done, I shall by-and-by show more at large.

37. This is certain, that in the beginning, before the desire of
having more than man needed had altered the intrinsic value of
things which depends only on their usefulness to the life of man,
or had agreed that a little piece of yellow metal which would keep
without wasting or decay should be worth a great piece of flesh or
a whole heap of corn, though men had a right to appropriate, by
their labor, each one to himself as much of the things of nature
as he could use, yet this could not be much, nor to the prejudice
of others, where the same plenty was still left to those who would
use the same industry. To which let me add that he who appro-
priates land to himself by his labor does not lessen but increase
the common stock of mankind; for the provisions serving to the
support of human life produced by one acre of enclosed and culti-

vated land are—to speak much within compass—ten times more than those which are yielded by an acre of land of an equal richness lying waste in common. And therefore he that encloses land, and has a greater plenty of the conveniences of life from ten acres than he could have from a hundred left to nature, may truly be said to give ninety acres to mankind; for his labor now supplies him with provisions out of ten acres which were by the product of a hundred lying in common. I have here rated the improved land very low in making its product but as ten to one, when it is much nearer a hundred to one; for I ask whether in the wild woods and uncultivated waste of America, left to nature, without any improvement, tillage, or husbandry, a thousand acres yield the needy and wretched inhabitants as many conveniences of life as ten acres of equally fertile land do in Devonshire, where they are well cultivated.

Before the appropriation of land, he who gathered as much of the wild fruit, killed, caught, or tamed as many of the beasts as he could; he that so employed his pains about any of the spontaneous products of nature as any way to alter them from the state which nature put them in, by placing any of his labor on them, did thereby acquire a propriety in them; but, if they perished in his possession without their due use, if the fruits rotted or the venison putrified before he could spend it, he offended against the common law of nature and was liable to be punished; he invaded his neighbor's share, for he had no right further than his use called for any of them and they might serve to afford him conveniences of life.

38. The same measures governed the possession of land, too: whatsoever he tilled and reaped, laid up and made use of before it spoiled, that was his peculiar right; whatsoever he enclosed and could feed and make use of, the cattle and product was also his. But if either the grass of his enclosure rotted on the ground, or the fruit of his planting perished without gathering and laying up, this part of the earth, notwithstanding his enclosure, was still to be looked on as waste and might be the possession of any other. Thus, at the beginning, Cain might take as much ground as he could till and make it his own land, and yet leave enough to Abel's

sheep to feed on; a few acres would serve for both their possessions. But as families increased and industry enlarged their stocks,
their possessions enlarged with the need of them; but yet it was
commonly without any fixed property in the ground they made
use of till they incorporated, settled themselves together, and
built cities; and then, by consent, they came in time to set out the
bounds of their distinct territories, and agree on limits between
them and their neighbors, and by laws within themselves settled
the properties of those of the same society; for we see that in that
part of the world which was first inhabited, and therefore like
to be best peopled, even as low down as Abraham's time they
wandered with their flocks and their herds, which was their substance, freely up and down; and this Abraham did in a country
where he was a stranger. Whence it is plain that at least a great
part of the land lay in common, that the inhabitants valued it not,
nor claimed property in any more than they made use of. But
when there was not room enough in the same place for their
herds to feed together, they, by consent, as Abraham and Lot did
(Gen. xiii. 5), separated and enlarged their pasture where it best
liked them. And for the same reason Esau went from his father and
his brother and planted in Mount Seir (Gen. xxxvi. 6).

39. And thus, without supposing any private dominion and
property in Adam over all the world exclusive of all other men,
which can in no way be proven, nor any one's property be made
out from it; but supposing the world given, as it was, to the children of men in common, we see how labor could make men distinct
titles to several parcels of it for their private uses, wherein there
could be no doubt of right, no room for quarrel.

40. Nor is it so strange, as perhaps before consideration it may
appear, that the property of labor should be able to overbalance
the community of land; for it is labor indeed that put the difference of value on everything; and let anyone consider what the
difference is between an acre of land planted with tobacco or
sugar, sown with wheat or barley, and an acre of the same land
lying in common without any husbandry upon it, and he will
find that the improvement of labor makes the far greater part of
the value. I think it will be but a very modest computation to say

that, of the products of the earth useful to the life of man, nine-tenths are the effects of labor; nay, if we will rightly estimate things as they come to our use and cast up the several expenses about them, what in them is purely owing to nature, and what to labor, we shall find that in most of them ninety-nine hundredths are wholly to be put on the account of labor.

41. There cannot be a clearer demonstration of anything than several nations of the Americans are of this, who are rich in land and poor in all the comforts of life; whom nature having furnished as liberally as any other people with the materials of plenty, i. e., a fruitful soil, apt to produce in abundance what might serve for food, raiment, and delight, yet for want of improving it by labor have not one-hundredth part of the conveniences we enjoy. And a king of a large and fruitful territory there feeds, lodges, and is clad worse than a day-laborer in England.

42. To make this a little clear, let us but trace some of the ordinary provisions of life through their several progresses before they come to our use and see how much of their value they receive from human industry. Bread, wine, and cloth are things of daily use and great plenty; yet, notwithstanding, acorns, water, and leaves, or skins must be our bread, drink, and clothing, did not labor furnish us with these more useful commodities; for whatever bread is more worth than acorns, wine than water, and cloth or silk than leaves, skins, or moss, that is wholly owing to labor and industry. the one of these being the food and raiment which unassisted nature furnishes us with; the other, provisions which our industry and pains prepare for us, which how much they exceed the other in value when anyone has computed, he will then see how much labor makes the far greatest part of the value of things we enjoy in this world. And the ground which produces the materials is scarce to be reckoned in as any, or at most but a very small, part of it; so little that even amongst us land that is left wholly to nature, that has no improvement of pasturage, tillage, or planting, is called, as indeed it is, 'waste'; and we shall find the benefit of it amount to little more than nothing.

This shows how much numbers of men are to be preferred to largeness of dominions; and that the increase of lands and the right employing of them is the great art of government; and that prince who shall be so wise and godlike as by established laws of liberty to secure protection and encouragement to the honest industry of mankind, against the oppression of power and narrowness of party, will quickly be too hard for his neighbors; but this by the bye.

To return to the argument in hand.

43. An acre of land that bears here twenty bushels of wheat, and another in America which with the same husbandry would do the like, are, without doubt, of the same natural intrinsic value; but yet the benefit mankind receives from the one in a year is worth £5, and from the other possibly not worth a penny if all the profit an Indian received from it were to be valued and sold here; at least, I may truly say, not one-thousandth. It is labor, then, which puts the greatest part of the value upon land, without which it would scarcely be worth anything; it is to that we owe the greatest part of all its useful products; for all that the straw, bran, bread of that acre of wheat is more worth than the product of an acre of as good land which lies waste is all the effect of labor. For it is not barely the ploughman's pains, the reaper's and thresher's toil, and the baker's sweat [that] is to be counted into the bread we eat; the labor of those who broke the oxen, who digged and wrought the iron and stones, who felled and framed the timber employed about the plough, mill, oven, or any other utensils, which are a vast number requisite to this corn, from its being seed to be sown to its being made bread, must all be charged on the account of labor, and received as an effect of that; nature and the earth furnished only the almost worthless materials as in themselves. It would be a strange "catalogue of things that industry provided and made use of, about every loaf of bread" before it came to our use, if we could trace them: iron, wood, leather, bark, timber, stone, bricks, coals, lime, cloth, dyeing drugs, pitch, tar, masts, ropes, and all the materials made use of in the ship that brought any of the commodities used by any of the workmen to any part of the work; all which it would be almost impossible, at least too long, to reckon up.

44. From all which it is evident that, though the things of

nature are given in common, yet man, by being master of himself and proprietor of his own person and the actions or labor of it, had still in himself the great foundation of property; and that which made up the greater part of what he applied to the support or comfort of his being, when invention and arts had improved the conveniences of life, was perfectly his own and did not belong in common to others.

45. Thus labor, in the beginning, gave a right of property wherever anyone was pleased to employ it upon what was common, which remained a long while the far greater part and is yet more than mankind makes use of. Men, at first, for the most part contented themselves with what unassisted nature offered to their necessities; and though afterwards, in some parts of the world—where the increase of people and stock, with the use of money, had made land scarce and so of some value—the several communities settled the bounds of their distinct territories and, by laws within themselves, regulated the properties of the private men of their society, and so, by compact and agreement, settled the property which labor and industry began. And the leagues that have been made between several states and kingdoms either expressly or tacitly disowning all claim and right to the land in the others' possession have, by common consent, given up their pretenses to their natural common right which originally they had to those countries, and so have, by positive agreement, settled a property amongst themselves in distinct parts and parcels of the earth; yet there are still great tracts of ground to be found which—the inhabitants thereof not having joined with the rest of mankind in the consent of the use of their common money—lie waste, and are more than the people who dwell on it do or can make use of, and so still lie in common; though this can scarce happen amongst that part of mankind that have consented to the use of money.

46. The greatest part of things really useful to the life of man, and such as the necessity of subsisting made the first commoners of the world look after, as it does the Americans now, are generally things of short duration, such as, if they are not consumed by use, will decay and perish of themselves; gold, silver, and diamonds are things that fancy or agreement has put the value on,

more than real use and the necessary support of life. Now of those good things which nature has provided in common, every one had a right, as has been said, to as much as he could use, and property in all that he could effect with his labor; all that his industry could extend to, to alter from the state nature had put it in, was his. He that gathered a hundred bushels of acorns or apples had thereby a property in them; they were his goods as soon as gathered. He was only to look that he used them before they spoiled, else he took more than his share and robbed others. And indeed it was a foolish thing, as well as dishonest, to hoard up more than he could make use of. If he gave away a part to anybody else so that it perished not uselessly in his possession, these he also made use of. And if he also bartered away plums that would have rotted in a week for nuts that would last good for his eating a whole year, he did no injury; he wasted not the common stock, destroyed no part of the portion of the goods that belonged to others, so long as nothing perished uselessly in his hands. Again, if he would give his nuts for a piece of metal, pleased with its color, or exchange his sheep for shells, or wool for a sparkling pebble or a diamond, and keep those by him all his life, he invaded not the right of others; he might heap as much of these durable things as he pleased; the exceeding of the bounds of his just property not lying in the largeness of his possession, but the perishing of anything uselessly in it.

47. And thus came in the use of money—some lasting thing that men might keep without spoiling, and that by mutual consent men would take in exchange for the truly useful but perishable supports of life.

48. And as different degrees of industry were apt to give men possessions in different proportions, so this invention of money gave them the opportunity to continue and enlarge them; for supposing an island, separate from all possible commerce with the rest of the world, wherein there were but a hundred families, but there were sheep, horses, and cows, with other useful animals, wholesome fruits, and land enough for corn for a hundred thousand times as many, but nothing in the island, either because of its commonness or perishableness, fit to supply the place of money; what

reason could anyone have there to enlarge his possessions beyond the use of his family and a plentiful supply to its consumption, either in what their own industry produced or they could barter for like perishable, useful commodities with others? Where there is not something both lasting and scarce, and so valuable to be hoarded up, there men will not be apt to enlarge their possessions of land were it ever so rich, ever so free for them to take. For, I ask, what would a man value ten thousand or a hundred thousand acres of excellent land, ready cultivated and well stocked, too, with cattle, in the middle of the inland parts of America where he had no hopes of commerce with other parts of the world to draw money to him by the sale of the product? It would not be worth the enclosing, and we should see him give up again to the wild common of nature whatever was more than would supply the conveniences of life to be had there for him and his family.

49. Thus in the beginning all the world was America, and more so than that is now; for no such thing as money was anywhere known. Find out something that has the use and value of money amongst his neighbors, you shall see the same man will begin presently to enlarge his possessions.

50. But since gold and silver, being little useful to the life of man in proportion to food, raiment, and carriage, has its value only from the consent of men, whereof labor yet makes, in great part, the measure, it is plain that men have agreed to a disproportionate and unequal possession of the earth, they having, by a tacit and voluntary consent, found out a way how a man may fairly possess more land than he himself can use the product of, by receiving in exchange for the overplus gold and silver which may be hoarded up without injury to any one, these metals not spoiling or decaying in the hands of the possessor. This partage of things in an inequality of private possessions men have made practicable out of the bounds of society and without compact, only by putting a value on gold and silver, and tacitly agreeing in the use of money; for, in governments, the laws regulate the right of property, and the possession of land is determined by positive constitutions.

51. And thus, I think, it is very easy to conceive how labor

could at first begin a title of property in the common things of nature, and how the spending it upon our uses bounded it. So that there could then be no reason of quarreling about title, nor any doubt about the largeness of possession it gave. Right and convenience went together; for as a man had a right to all he could employ his labor upon, so he had no temptation to labor for more than he could make use of. This left no room for controversy about the title, nor for encroachment on the right of others; what portion a man carved to himself was easily seen, and it was useless, as well as dishonest, to carve himself too much or take more than he needed.

CHAPTER VI

OF PATERNAL POWER

52. It may perhaps be censured as an impertinent criticism, in a discourse of this nature, to find fault with words and names that have obtained in the world; and yet possibly it may not be amiss to offer new ones when the old are apt to lead men into mistakes, as this of 'paternal power' probably has done, which seems so to place the power of parents over their children wholly in the father, as if the mother had no share in it; whereas, if we consult reason or revelation, we shall find she has an equal title. This may give one reason to ask whether this might not be more properly called 'parental power,' for whatever obligation nature and the right of generation lays on children, it must certainly bind them equally to both concurrent causes of it. And accordingly we see the positive law of God everywhere joins them together without distinction when it commands the obedience of children: "Honour thy father and thy mother" (Exod. xx. 12); "Whosoever curseth his father or his mother" (Lev. xx. 9); "Ye shall fear every man his mother and his father" (Lev. xix. 5); "Children, obey your parents," etc. (Eph. vi. 1), is the style of the Old and New Testament.

53. Had but this one thing been well considered, without look-ing any deeper into the matter, it might perhaps have kept men from running into those gross mistakes they have made about this power of parents, which, however it might without any great harshness bear the name of absolute dominion and regal authority, when under the title of 'paternal power' it seemed appropriated to the father, would yet have sounded but oddly and in the very name shown the absurdity if this supposed absolute power over children had been called 'parental,' and thereby have discovered that it belonged to the mother, too; for it will but very ill serve the turn of those men who contend so much for the absolute power and authority of the fatherhood, as they call it, that the mother should have any share in it; and it would have but ill supported the monarchy they contend for, when by the very name it appeared that that fundamental authority from whence they would derive their government of a single person only was not placed in one but two persons jointly. But to let this of names pass.

54. Though I have said above (Chap. II) that all men by nature are equal, I cannot be supposed to understand all sorts of equality. Age or virtue may give men a just precedence; excel-lence of parts and merit may place others above the common level; birth may subject some, and alliance or benefits others, to pay an observance to those whom nature, gratitude, or other respects may have made it due; and yet all this consists with the equality which all men are in, in respect of jurisdiction or dominion one over another, which was the equality I there spoke of as proper to the business in hand, being that equal right that every man has to his natural freedom, without being subjected to the will or authority of any other man.

55. Children, I confess, are not born in this state of equality, though they are born to it. Their parents have a sort of rule and jurisdiction over them when they come into the world, and for some time after, but it is but a temporary one. The bonds of this subjection are like the swaddling clothes they are wrapped up in and supported by in the weakness of their infancy; age and rea-

son, as they grow up, loosen them, till at length they drop quite off and leave a man at his own free disposal.

56. Adam was created a perfect man, his body and mind in full possession of their strength and reason, and so was capable from the first instant of his being to provide for his own support and preservation and govern his actions according to the dictates of the law of reason which God had implanted in him. From him the world is peopled with his descendants who are all born infants, weak and helpless, without knowledge or understanding; but to supply the defects of this imperfect state till the improvement of growth and age has removed them, Adam and Eve, and after them all parents, were, by the law of nature, "under an obligation to preserve, nourish, and educate the children" they had begotten; not as their own workmanship, but the workmanship of their own Maker, the Almighty, to whom they were to be accountable for them.

57. The law that was to govern Adam was the same that was to govern all his posterity—the law of reason. But his offspring having another way of entrance into the world, different from him, by a natural birth that produced them ignorant and without the use of reason, they were not presently under the law; for nobody can be under a law which is not promulgated to him; and this law being promulgated or made known by reason only, he that is not come to the use of his reason cannot be said to be under this law; and Adam's children, being not presently as soon as born under this law of reason, were not presently free; for law, in its true notion, is not so much the limitation as the direction of a free and intelligent agent to his proper interest, and prescribes no further than is for the general good of those under that law. Could they be happier without it, the law, as a useless thing, would of itself vanish; and that ill deserves the name of confinement which hedges us in only from bogs and precipices. So that, however it may be mistaken, the end of law is not to abolish or restrain but to preserve and enlarge freedom; for in all the states of created beings capable of laws, where there is no law, there is no freedom. For liberty is to be free from restraint and violence from others, which cannot be where there is not law; but freedom is

not, as we are told: a liberty for every man to do what he lists—
for who could be free, when every other man's humor might domi-
neer over him?—but a liberty to dispose and order as he lists his
person, actions, possessions, and his whole property, within the
allowance of those laws under which he is, and therein not to be
subject to the arbitrary will of another, but freely follow his own.

58. The power, then, that parents have over their children
arises from that duty which is incumbent on them—to take care
of their offspring during the imperfect state of childhood. To
inform the mind and govern the actions of their yet ignorant
nonage till reason shall take its place and ease them of that trouble
is what the children want and the parents are bound to; for God,
having given man an understanding to direct his actions, has
allowed him a freedom of will and liberty of acting as properly
belonging thereunto, within the bounds of that law he is under.
But while he is in an estate wherein he has not understanding of
his own to direct his will, he is not to have any will of his own to
follow; he that understands for him must will for him, too; he
must prescribe to his will and regulate his actions; but when he
comes to the estate that made his father a freeman, the son is a
freeman, too.

59. This holds in all the laws a man is under, whether natural
or civil. Is a man under the law of nature? What made him free
of that law? What gave him a free disposing of his property, according to his own will, within the compass of that law? I answer,
a state of maturity wherein he might be supposed capable to
know that law, that so he might keep his actions within the
bounds of it. When he has acquired that state, he is presumed to
know how far that law is to be his guide, and how far he may
make use of his freedom, and so comes to have it; till then somebody
else must guide him who is presumed to know how far the law
allows a liberty. If such a state of reason, such an age of discretion, made him free, the same shall make his son free, too. Is a
man under the law of England? What made him free of that law,
that is, to have the liberty to dispose of his actions and possessions according to his own will, within the permission of that
law? A capacity of knowing that law; which is supposed by that

law at the age of twenty-one, and in some cases sooner. If this made the father free, it shall make the son free, too. Till then we see the law allows the son to have no will, but he is to be guided by the will of his father or guardian who is to understand for him. And if the father die and fail to substitute a deputy in his trust, if he has not provided a tutor to govern his son during his minority, during his want of understanding the law takes care to do it. Some other must govern him and be a will to him, till he has attained to a state of freedom and his understanding be fit to take the government of his will. But after that the father and son are equally free as much as tutor and pupil after nonage; equally subjects of the same law together, without any dominion left in the father over the life, liberty, or estate of his son, whether they be only in the state and under the law of nature, or under the positive laws of an established government.

60. But if, through defects that may happen out of the ordinary course of nature, anyone comes not to such a degree of reason wherein he might be supposed capable of knowing the law and so living within the rules of it, he is never capable of being a free man, he is never let loose to the disposure of his own will (because he knows no bounds to it, has not understanding, its proper guide), but is continued under the tuition and government of others all the time his own understanding is incapable of that charge. And so lunatics and idiots are never set free from the government of their parents.

Children, who are not as yet come unto those years whereat they may have; and innocents which are excluded by a natural defect from ever having; thirdly, madmen which for the present cannot possibly have the use of right reason to guide themselves; have for their guide the reason that guides other men which are tutors over them to seek and procure their good for them,

says Hooker (*Eccl. Pol.* lib., i. sect. 7). All which seems no more than that duty which God and nature has laid on man as well as other creatures—to preserve their offspring till they can be able to shift for themselves—and will scarce amount to an instance or proof of parents' regal authority.

61. Thus we are born free as we are born rational, not that we

have actually the exercise of either; age that brings one brings with it the other, too. And thus we see how natural freedom and subjection to parents may consist together and are both founded on the same principle. A child is free by his father's title, by his father's understanding which is to govern him till he has it of his own. The freedom of a man at years of discretion and the subjection of a child to his parents while yet short of that age are so consistent and so distinguishable that the most blinded contenders for monarchy by 'right of fatherhood' cannot miss this difference, the most obstinate cannot but allow their consistency. For were their doctrine all true, were the right heir of Adam now known and by that title settled a monarch in his throne, invested with all the absolute unlimited power Sir Robert Filmer talks of; if he should die as soon as his heir were born, must not the child, notwithstanding he were ever so free, ever so much sovereign, be in subjection to his mother and nurse, to tutors and governors, till age and education brought him reason and ability to govern himself and others? The necessities of his life, the health of his body, and the information of his mind would require him to be directed by the will of others and not his own; and yet will anyone think that this restraint and subjection were inconsistent with, or spoiled him of, that liberty or sovereignty he had a right to, or gave away his empire to those who had the government of his nonage? This government over him only prepared him the better and sooner for it. If anybody should ask me when my son is of age to be free, I shall answer, Just when his monarch is of age to govern. "But at what time," says the judicious Hooker (*Eccl. Pol.* lib. i. sect. 6), "a man may be said to have attained so far forth the use of reason as sufficeth to make him capable of those laws whereby he is then bound to guide his actions, this is a great deal more easy for sense to discern than for any one by skill and learning to determine."

62. Commonwealths themselves take notice of and allow that there is a time when men are to begin to act like freemen, and therefore till that time require not oaths of fealty, or allegiance, or other public owning of, or submission to, the government of their countries.

63. The freedom then of man, and liberty of acting according to his own will, is grounded on his having reason which is able to instruct him in that law he is to govern himself by, and make him know how far he is left to the freedom of his own will. To turn him loose to an unrestrained liberty before he has reason to guide him is not the allowing him the privilege of his nature to be free, but to thrust him out amongst brutes and abandon him to a state as wretched and as much beneath that of a man as theirs. This is that which puts the authority into the parents' hands to govern the minority of their children. God has made it their business to employ this care on their offspring, and has placed in them suitable inclinations of tenderness and concern to temper this power, to apply it, as his wisdom designed it, to the children's good as long as they should need to be under it.

64. But what reason can hence advance this care of the parents due to their offspring into an absolute arbitrary dominion of the father, whose power reaches no farther than, by such a discipline as he finds most effectual, to give such strength and health to their bodies, such vigor and rectitude to their minds, as may best fit his children to be most useful to themselves and others; and, if it be necessary to his condition, to make them work, when they are able, for their own subsistence? But in this power the mother, too, has her share with the father.

65. Nay, this power so little belongs to the father by any peculiar right of nature, but only as he is guardian of his children, that when he quits his care of them he loses his power over them which goes along with their nourishment and education to which it is inseparably annexed; and it belongs as much to the foster father of an exposed child as to the natural father of another; so little power does the bare act of begetting give a man over his issue, if all his care ends there and this be all the title he has to the name and authority of a father. And what will become of this paternal power in that part of the world where one woman has more than one husband at a time, or in those parts of America where, when the husband and wife part, which happens frequently, the children are all left to the mother, follow her, and are wholly under her care and provision? If the father die while the children

are young, do they not naturally everywhere owe the same obedience to their mother during their minority as to their father were he alive? And will anyone say that the mother has a legislative power over her children, that she can make standing rules, which shall be of perpetual obligation, by which they ought to regulate all the concerns of their property and bound their liberty all the course of their lives? Or can she enforce the observation of them with capital punishments? For this is the proper power of the magistrate, of which the father has not so much as the shadow. His command over his children is but temporary and reaches not their life or property; it is but a help to the weakness and imperfection of their nonage, a discipline necessary to their education; and though a father may dispose of his own possessions as he pleases when his children are out of danger of perishing for want, yet his power extends not to the lives or goods which either their own industry or another's bounty has made theirs; nor to their liberty neither when they are once arrived to the enfranchisement of the years of discretion. The father's empire then ceases, and he can from thenceforward no more dispose of the liberty of his son than that of any other man; and it must be far from an absolute or perpetual jurisdiction from which a man may withdraw himself, having license from divine authority to "leave father and mother and cleave to his wife."

66. But though there be a time when a child comes to be as free from subjection to the will and command of his father as the father himself is free from subjection to the will of anybody else, and they are each under no other restraint but that which is common to them both, whether it be the law of nature or municipal law of their country, yet this freedom exempts not a son from that honor which he ought, by the law of God and nature, to pay his parents. God having made the parents instruments in his great design of continuing the race of mankind and the occasions of life to their children, as he has laid on them an obligation to nourish, preserve, and bring up their offspring, so he has laid on the children a perpetual obligation of honoring their parents, which, containing in it an inward esteem and reverence to be shown by all outward expressions, ties up the child from anything that may

ever injure or affront, disturb, or endanger the happiness or life of those from whom he received his, and engages him in all actions of defense, relief, assistance, and comfort of those by whose means he entered into being, and has been made capable of any enjoyments of life. From this obligation no state, no freedom can absolve children. But this is very far from giving parents a power of command over their children, or an authority to make laws and dispose as they please of their lives and liberties. It is one thing to owe honor, respect, gratitude, and assistance; another to require an absolute obedience and submission. The honor due to parents, a monarch in his throne owes his mother, and yet this lessens not his authority, nor subjects him to her government.

67. The subjection of a minor places in the father a temporary government which terminates with the minority of the child; and the honor due from a child places in the parents a perpetual right to respect, reverence, support, and compliance, too, more or less as the father's care, cost, and kindness in his education have been more or less. This ends not with minority, but holds in all parts and conditions of a man's life. The want of distinguishing these two powers—viz., that which the father has in the right of tuition, during minority, and the right of honor all his life—may perhaps have caused a great part of the mistakes about this matter; for, to speak properly of them, the first of these is rather the privilege of children and duty of parents than any prerogative of paternal power. The nourishment and education of their children is a charge so incumbent on parents for their children's good that nothing can absolve them from taking care of it. And though the power of commanding and chastising them go along with it, yet God has woven into the principles of human nature such a tenderness for their offspring that there is little fear that parents should use their power with too much rigor; the excess is seldom on the severe side, the strong bias of nature drawing the other way. And therefore God Almighty, when he would express his gentle dealing with the Israelites, he tells them that, though he chastened them, "he chastened them as a man chastens his son" (Deut. viii. 5)— i. e., with tenderness and affection, and kept them under no severer discipline than what was absolutely best for them, and had been

less kindness to have slackened. This is that power to which children are commanded obedience, that the pains and care of their parents may not be increased or ill rewarded.

68. On the other side, honor and support, all that which gratitude requires to return for the benefits received by and from them, is the indispensable duty of the child and the proper privilege of the parents. This is intended for the parents' advantage as the other is for the child's; though education, the parents' duty, seems to have most power because the ignorance and infirmities of childhood stand in need of restraint and correction, which is a visible exercise of rule and a kind of dominion. And that duty which is comprehended in the word 'honor' requires less obedience, though the obligation be stronger on grown than younger children; for who can think the command, "Children obey your parents," requires in a man that has children of his own the same submission to his father as it does in his yet young children to him, and that by this precept he were bound to obey all his father's commands, if out of a conceit of authority he should have the indiscretion to treat him still as a boy.

69. The first part then of paternal power, or rather duty, which is education, belongs so to the father that it terminates at a certain season; when the business of education is over, it ceases of itself and is also alienable before, for a man may put the tuition of his son in other hands; and he that has made his son an apprentice to another has discharged him during that time of a great part of his obedience both to himself and to his mother. But all the duty of honor, the other part, remains nevertheless entire to them; nothing can cancel that; it is so inseparable from them both that the father's authority cannot dispossess the mother of this right, nor can any man discharge his son from honoring her that bore him. But both these are very far from a power to make laws and enforcing them with penalties that may reach estate, liberty, limbs, and life. The power of commanding ends with nonage; and although, after that, honor and respect, support and defense, and whatsoever gratitude can oblige a man to, for the highest benefits he is naturally capable of, be always due from a son to his parents, yet all this puts no scepter into the father's

hand, no sovereign power of commanding. He has no dominion over his son's property or actions, nor any right that his will should prescribe to his son's in all things, however it may become his son in many things not very inconvenient to him and his family to pay a deference to it.

70. A man may owe honor and respect to an ancient or wise man, defense to his child or friend, relief and support to the distressed, and gratitude to a benefactor, to such a degree that all he has, all he can do, cannot sufficiently pay it; but all these give no authority, no right to anyone, of making laws over him from whom they are owing. And it is plain all this is due not only to the bare title of father, not only because, as has been said, it is owing to the mother, too, but because these obligations to parents and the degrees of what is required of children may be varied by the different care and kindness, trouble and expense, which are often employed upon one child more than another.

71. This shows the reason how it comes to pass that parents in societies, where they themselves are subjects, retain a power over their children, and have as much right to their subjection as those who are in the state of nature. Which could not possibly be if all political power were only paternal, and that, in truth, they were one and the same thing; for then, all paternal power being in the prince, the subject could naturally have none of it. But these two powers, political and paternal, are so perfectly distinct and separate, are built upon so different foundations, and given to so much different ends, that every subject that is a father has as much a paternal power over his children as the prince has over his, and every prince that has parents owes them as much filial duty and obedience as the meanest of his subjects do theirs, and cannot therefore contain any part or degree of that kind of dominion which a prince or magistrate has over his subjects.

72. Though the obligation on the parents to bring up their children, and the obligation on children to honor their parents, contain all the power on the one hand, and submission on the other, which are proper to this relation, yet there is another power ordinary in the father whereby he has a tie on the obedience of his children; which, though it be common to him with other men,

yet, the occasions of showing it almost constantly happening to fathers in their private families, and the instances of it elsewhere being rare and less taken notice of, it passes in the world for a part of paternal jurisdiction. And this is the power men generally have to bestow their estates on those who please them best; the possession of the father being the expectation and inheritance of the children, ordinarily in certain proportions according to the law and custom of each country, yet it is commonly in the father's power to bestow it with a more sparing or liberal hand, according as the behavior of this or that child has comported with his will and humor.

73. This is no small tie on the obedience of children; and there being always annexed to the enjoyment of land a submission to the government of the country of which that land is a part, it has been commonly supposed that a father could oblige his posterity to that government of which he himself was a subject, and that his compact held them; whereas it, being only a necessary condition annexed to the land and the inheritance of an estate which is under that government, reaches only those who will take it on that condition, and so is no natural tie or engagement but a voluntary submission; for every man's children, being by nature as free as himself or any of his ancestors ever were, may, while they are in that freedom, choose what society they will join themselves to, what commonwealth they will put themselves under. But if they will enjoy the inheritance of their ancestors, they must take it on the same terms their ancestors had it and submit to all the conditions annexed to such a possession. By this power, indeed, fathers oblige their children to obedience to themselves even when they are past minority, and most commonly, too, subject them to this or that political power; but neither of these by any peculiar right of fatherhood, but by the reward they have in their hands to enforce and recompense such a compliance; and is no more power than what a Frenchman has over an Englishman, who, by the hopes of an estate he will leave him, will certainly have a strong tie on his obedience. And if, when it is left to him, he will enjoy it, he must certainly take it upon the conditions

annexed to the possession of land in that country where it lies, whether it be France or England.

74. To conclude, then: though the father's power of commanding extends no farther than the minority of his children, and to a degree only fit for the discipline and government of that age; and though that honor and respect, and all that which the Latins called 'piety,' which they indispensably owe to their parents all their lifetime and in all estates, with all that support and defense which is due to them, gives the father no power of governing—i. e., making laws and enacting penalties on his children; though by all this he has no dominion over the property or actions of his son, yet it is obvious to conceive how easy it was, in the first ages of the world, and in places still where the thinness of people gives families leave to separate into unpossessed quarters, and they have room to remove or plant themselves in yet vacant habitations, for the father of the family to become the prince [1] of it. He had been a ruler from the beginning of the infancy of his children; and, since without some government it would be hard for them to live together, it was likeliest it should, by the express or tacit consent of the children when they were grown up, be in the father where it seemed without any change barely to continue; when indeed nothing more was required to it than the permitting the father to exercise alone, in his family, that executive power of the law of nature which every free man naturally has, and by that permission resigning up to him a monarchical power while they remained

[1] "It is no improbable opinion, therefore, which the arch-philosopher was of, that the chief person in every household was always, as it were, a king: so when numbers of households joined themselves in civil societies together, kings were the first kind of governors amongst them, which is also, as it seems, the reason why the name of fathers continued still in them, who, of fathers, were made rulers; as also the ancient custom of governors to do as Melchizedeck and, being kings, to exercise the office of priests, which fathers did at the first, grew perhaps by the same occasion. Howbeit, this is not the only kind of regiment that has been received in the world. The inconveniencies of one kind have caused sundry others to be devised; so that, in a word, all public regiment, of what kind soever, seems evidently to have risen from the deliberate advice, consultation, and composition between men, judging it convenient and behoveful; there being no impossibility in nature considered by itself but that man might have lived without any public regiment" (Hooker's *Eccl. Pol.* lib. i. sect. 10).

in it. But that this was not by any paternal right but only by the consent of his children is evident from hence—that nobody doubts. But if a stranger whom chance or business had brought to his family had there killed any of his children or committed any other fact, he might condemn and put him to death, or otherwise punish him as well as any of his children, which it was impossible he should do by virtue of any paternal authority over one who was not his child, but by virtue of that executive power of the law of nature which, as a man, he had a right to; and he alone could punish him in his family, where the respect of his children had laid by the exercise of such a power to give way to the dignity and authority they were willing should remain in him, above the rest of his family.

75. Thus it was easy and almost natural for children, by a tacit and scarce avoidable consent, to make way for the father's authority and government. They had been accustomed in their childhood to follow his direction and to refer their little differences to him; and when they were men, who fitter to rule them? Their little properties, and less covetousness, seldom afforded greater controversies; and when any should arise, where could they have a fitter umpire than he by whose care they had every one been sustained and brought up and who had a tenderness for them all? It is no wonder that they made no distinction betwixt minority and full age, nor looked after twenty-one or any other age that might make them the free disposers of themselves and fortunes, when they could have no desire to be out of their pupilage; the government they had been under during it continued still to be more their protection than restraint, and they could nowhere find a greater security to their peace, liberties, and fortunes than in the rule of a father.

76. Thus the natural fathers of families by an insensible change became the politic monarchs of them too; and, as they chanced to live long, and leave able worthy heirs for several successions, or otherwise, so they laid the foundations of hereditary or elective kingdoms under several constitutions and manners, according as chance, contrivance, or occasions happened to mold them. But if princes have their titles in their father's right, and it be a suf-

ficient proof of the natural right of fathers to political authority because they commonly were those in whose hands we find, *de facto*, the exercise of government—I say, if this argument be good, it will as strongly prove that all princes, nay, princes only, ought to be priests, since it is as certain that in the beginning the father of the family was priest, as that he was ruler in his own household.

CHAPTER VII

OF POLITICAL OR CIVIL SOCIETY

77. GOD, HAVING made man such a creature that in his own judgment it was not good for him to be alone, put him under strong obligations of necessity, convenience, and inclination to drive him into society, as well as fitted him with understanding and language to continue and enjoy it. The first society was between man and wife, which gave beginning to that between parents and children; to which, in time, that between master and servant came to be added; and though all these might, and commonly did, meet together and make up but one family wherein the master or mistress of it had some sort of rule proper to a family—each of these, or all together, came short of political society, as we shall see if we consider the different ends, ties, and bounds of each of these.

78. Conjugal society is made by a voluntary compact between man and woman; and though it consist chiefly in such a communion and right in one another's bodies as is necessary to its chief end, procreation, yet it draws with it mutual support and assistance, and a communion of interests, too, as necessary not only to unite their care and affection, but also necessary to their common offspring, who have a right to be nourished and maintained by them till they are able to provide for themselves.

79. For the end of conjunction between male and female being not barely procreation but the continuation of the species, this conjunction betwixt male and female ought to last, even after

procreation, so long as is necessary to the nourishment and support of the young ones who are to be sustained by those that got them till they are able to shift and provide for themselves. This rule, which the infinite wise Maker has set to the works of his hands, we find the inferior creatures steadily obey. In those viviparous animals which feed on grass, the conjunction between male and female lasts no longer than the very act of copulation, because the teat of the dam being sufficient to nourish the young till it be able to feed on grass, the male only begets, but concerns not himself for the female or young to whose sustenance he can contribute nothing. But in beasts of prey the conjunction lasts longer because, the dam not being able well to subsist herself and nourish her numerous offspring by her own prey alone, a more laborious as well as more dangerous way of living than by feeding on grass, the assistance of the male is necessary to the maintenance of their common family, which cannot subsist till they are able to prey for themselves but by the joint care of male and female. The same is to be observed in all birds—except some domestic ones, where plenty of food excuses the cock from feeding and taking care of the young brood—whose young needing food in the nest, the cock and hen continue mates till the young are able to use their wing and provide for themselves.

80. And herein, I think, lies the chief, if not the only, reason why the male and female in mankind are tied to a longer conjunction than other creatures, viz., because the female is capable of conceiving, and *de facto* is commonly with child again and brings forth, too, a new birth long before the former is out of a dependency for support on his parents' help and able to shift for himself and has all the assistance that is due to him from his parents; whereby the father, who is bound to take care for those he has begot, is under an obligation to continue in conjugal society with the same woman longer than other creatures whose young being able to subsist of themselves before the time of procreation returns again, the conjugal bond dissolves of itself, and they are at liberty, till Hymen at his usual anniversary season summons them again to choose new mates. Wherein one cannot but admire the wisdom of the great Creator, who, having given to man foresight and an

ability to lay up for the future as well as to supply the present necessity, has made it necessary that society of man and wife should be more lasting than of male and female amongst other creatures, that so their industry might be encouraged and their interest better united to make provision and lay up goods for their common issue, which uncertain mixture or easy and frequent solutions of conjugal society would mightily disturb.

81. But though these are ties upon mankind which make the conjugal bonds more firm and lasting in man than the other species of animals, yet it would give one reason to inquire why this compact, where procreation and education are secured and inheritance taken care for, may not be made determinable, either by consent, or at a certain time, or upon certain conditions, as well as any other voluntary compacts, there being no necessity in the nature of the thing nor to the ends of it that it should always be for life; I mean, to such as are under no restraint of any positive law which ordains all such contracts to be perpetual.

82. But the husband and wife, though they have but one common concern, yet having different understandings, will unavoidably sometimes have different wills, too; it therefore being necessary that the last determination—i.e., the rule—should be placed somewhere, it naturally falls to the man's share, as the abler and the stronger. But this, reaching but to the things of their common interest and property, leaves the wife in the full and free possession of what by contract is her peculiar right, and gives the husband no more power over her life than she has over his; the power of the husband being so far from that of an absolute monarch that the wife has in many cases a liberty to separate from him where natural right or their contract allows it, whether that contract be made by themselves in the state of nature, or by the customs or laws of the country they live in; and the children upon such separation fall to the father's or mother's lot, as such contract does determine.

83. For all the ends of marriage being to be obtained under politic government as well as in the state of nature, the civil magistrate does not abridge the right or power of either naturally necessary to those ends, viz., procreation and mutual support and

assistance while they are together, but only decides any contro-versy that may arise between man and wife about them. If it were otherwise, and that absolute sovereignty and power of life and death naturally belonged to the husband and were necessary to the society between man and wife, there could be no matrimony in any of those countries where the husband is allowed no such absolute authority. But the ends of matrimony requiring no such power in the husband, the condition of conjugal society put it not in him, it being not at all necessary to that state. Conjugal society could subsist and attain its ends without it; nay, community of goods and the power over them, mutual assistance and mainte-nance, and other things belonging to conjugal society, might be varied and regulated by that contract which unites man and wife in that society as far as may consist with procreation and the bringing up of children till they could shift for themselves, noth-ing being necessary to any society that is not necessary to the ends for which it is made.

84. The society betwixt parents and children, and the distinct rights and powers belonging respectively to them, I have treated of so largely in the foregoing chapter that I shall not here need to say anything of it. And I think it is plain that it is far differ-ent from a politic society.

85. Master and servant are names as old as history, but given to those of far different condition; for a freeman makes himself a servant to another by selling him, for a certain time, the service he undertakes to do in exchange for wages he is to receive; and though this commonly puts him into the family of his master and under the ordinary discipline thereof, yet it gives the master but a temporary power over him and no greater than what is contained in the contract between them. But there is another sort of serv-ants which by a peculiar name we call slaves, who, being captives taken in a just war, are by the right of nature subjected to the absolute dominion and arbitrary power of their masters. These men, having, as I say, forfeited their lives and with it their liber-ties, and lost their estates, and being in the state of slavery not capable of any property, cannot in that state be considered as

any part of civil society, the chief end whereof is the preservation of property.

86. Let us therefore consider a master of a family with all these subordinate relations of wife, children, servants, and slaves, united under the domestic rule of a family; which, what resemblance soever it may have in its order, offices, and number, too, with a little commonwealth, yet is very far from it, both in its constitution, power, and end; or, if it must be thought a monarchy, and the paterfamilias the absolute monarch in it, absolute monarchy will have but a very shattered and short power when it is plain, by what has been said before, that the master of the family has a very distinct and differently limited power both as to time and extent over those several persons that are in it; for excepting the slave—and the family is as much a family, and his power as paterfamilias as great, whether there be any slaves in his family or no—he has no legislative power of life and death over any of them, and none, too, but what a mistress of a family may have as well as he. And he certainly can have no absolute power over the whole family who has but a very limited one over every individual in it. But how a family or any other society of men differ from that which is properly political society, we shall best see by considering wherein political society itself consists.

87. Man, being born, as has been proved, with a title to perfect freedom and uncontrolled enjoyment of all the rights and privileges of the law of nature equally with any other man or number of men in the world, has by nature a power not only to preserve his property—that is, his life, liberty, and estate—against the injuries and attempts of other men, but to judge of and punish the breaches of that law in others as he is persuaded the offense deserves, even with death itself in crimes where the heinousness of the fact in his opinion requires it. But because no political society can be, nor subsist, without having in itself the power to preserve the property and, in order thereunto, punish the offenses of all those of that society, there and there only is political society where every one of the members has quitted his natural power, resigned it up into the hands of the community in all cases that exclude him not from appealing for protection

to the law established by it. And thus all private judgment of every particular member being excluded, the community comes to be umpire by settled standing rules, indifferent and the same to all parties, and by men having authority from the community for the execution of those rules decides all the differences that may happen between any members of that society concerning any matter of right, and punishes those offenses which any member has committed against the society with such penalties as the law has established; whereby it is easy to discern who are, and who are not, in political society together. Those who are united into one body and have a common established law and judicature to appeal to, with authority to decide controversies between them and punish offenders, are in civil society one with another; but those who have no such common appeal, I mean on earth, are still in the state of nature, each being, where there is no other, judge for himself and executioner, which is, as I have before shown it, the perfect state of nature.

88. And thus the commonwealth comes by a power to set down what punishment shall belong to the several transgressions which they think worthy of it committed amongst the members of that society—which is the power of making laws—as well as it has the power to punish any injury done unto any of its members by any one that is not of it—which is the power of war and peace—and all this for the preservation of the property of all the members of that society as far as is possible. But though every man who has entered into civil society and is become a member of any commonwealth has thereby quitted his power to punish offenses against the law of nature in prosecution of his own private judgment, yet, with the judgment of offenses which he has given up to the legislative in all cases where he can appeal to the magistrate, he has given a right to the commonwealth to employ his force for the execution of the judgments of the commonwealth, whenever he shall be called to it; which, indeed, are his own judgments, they being made by himself or his representative. And herein we have the original of the legislative and executive power of civil society, which is to judge by standing laws how far offenses are to be punished when committed within the commonweath, and also to

determine, by occasional judgments founded on the present circumstances of the fact, how far injuries from without are to be vindicated; and in both these to employ all the force of all the members when there shall be need.

(89.) Whenever, therefore, any number of men are so united into one society as to quit every one his executive power of the law of nature and to resign it to the public, there and there only is a political or civil society. And this is done wherever any number of men, in the state of nature, enter into society to make one people, one body politic, under one supreme government, or else when any one joins himself to, and incorporates with, any government already made; for hereby he authorizes the society or, which is all one, the legislative thereof to make laws for him as the public good of the society shall require, to the execution whereof his own assistance, as to his own decrees, is due. And this puts men out of a state of nature into that of a commonwealth by setting up a judge on earth, with authority to determine all the controversies and redress the injuries that may happen to any member of the commonwealth; which judge is the legislative, or magistrates appointed by it. And wherever there are any number of men, however associated, that have no such decisive power to appeal to, there they are still in the state of nature.

90. Hence it is evident that absolute monarchy, which by some men is counted the only government in the world, is indeed inconsistent with civil society, and so can be no form of civil government at all; for the end of civil society being to avoid and remedy these inconveniences of the state of nature which necessarily follow from every man being judge in his own case, by setting up a known authority to which everyone of that society may appeal upon any injury received or controversy that may arise, and which everyone of the society ought to obey.[1] Wherever any persons are who have not such an authority to appeal to for the decision of any difference between them, there those persons are still in the

[1] "The public power of all society is above every soul contained in the same society; and the principal use of that power is to give laws unto all that are under it which laws in such cases we must obey, unless there be reason showed which may, necessarily enforce that the law of reason, or of God, doth enjoin the contrary" (Hooker's *Eccl. Pol.* lib. i. sect. 16).

state of nature; and so is every absolute prince, in respect of those who are under his dominion.

91. For he being supposed to have all, both legislative and executive, power in himself alone, there is no judge to be found, no appeal lies open to any one who may fairly and indifferently and with authority decide, and from whose decision relief and redress may be expected of any injury or inconvenience that may be suffered from the prince or by his order; so that such a man, however entitled, 'czar,' or 'grand seignior,' or how you please, is as much in the state of nature with all under his dominion as he is with the rest of mankind; for wherever any two men are who have no standing rule and common judge to appeal to on earth for the determination of controversies of right betwixt them, there they are still in the state of nature,[2] and under all the inconveniences of it, with only this woeful difference to the subject, or rather slave, of an absolute prince: that, whereas in the ordinary state of nature he has a liberty to judge of his right and, according to the best of his power to maintain it; now, whenever his property is invaded by the will and order of his monarch, he has not only no appeal as those in society ought to have but, as if he were degraded from the common state of rational creatures, is denied a liberty to judge of or to defend his right; and so is exposed to all the misery and inconveniences that a man can fear from one

[2] "To take away all such mutual grievances, injuries and wrongs," i.e., such as attend men in the state of nature, "there was no way but only by growing into composition and agreement amongst themselves by ordaining some kind of government public, and by yielding themselves subject thereunto, that unto whom they granted authority to rule and govern, by them the peace, tranquillity, and happy state of the rest might be procured. Men always knew that where force and injury was offered, they might be defenders of themselves; they knew that however men may seek their own commodity, yet if this were done with injury unto others, it was not to be suffered, but by all men and all good means to be withstood. Finally, they knew that no man might in reason take upon him to determine his own right, and according to his own determination proceed in maintenance thereof, inasmuch as every man is towards himself, and them whom he greatly affects, partial; and therefore that strifes and troubles would be endless except they gave their common consent all to be ordered by some whom they should agree upon, without which consent there would be no reason that one man should take upon him to be lord or judge over another" (Hooker's *Eccl. Pol.* lib. i. sect. 10).

who, being in the unrestrained state of nature, is yet corrupted
with flattery and armed with power.

92. For he that thinks absolute power purifies men's blood and
corrects the baseness of human nature need read but the history
of this or any other age to be convinced of the contrary. He that
would have been so insolent and injurious in the woods of America would not probably be much better in a throne, where perhaps
learning and religion shall be found out to justify all that he shall
do to his subjects, and the sword presently silence all those that
dare question it; for what the protection of absolute monarchy is,
what kind of fathers of their countries it makes princes to be,
and to what a degree of happiness and security it carries civil
society, where this sort of government is grown to perfection, he
that will look into the late relation of Ceylon may easily see.

93. In absolute monarchies, indeed, as well as other governments of the world, the subjects have an appeal to the law and
judges to decide any controversies and restrain any violence that
may happen betwixt the subjects themselves, one amongst another. This everyone thinks necessary, and believes he deserves to
be thought a declared enemy to society and mankind who should
go about to take it away. But whether this be from a true love of
mankind and society, and such a charity as we all owe one to
another, there is reason to doubt; for this is no more than what
every man who loves his own power, profit, or greatness may and
naturally must do—keep those animals from hurting or destroying one another who labor and drudge only for his pleasure and
advantage; and so are taken care of, not out of any love the
master has for them, but love of himself and the profit they bring
him; for if it be asked, what security, what fence is there, in such
a state, against the violence and oppression of this absolute ruler,
the very question can scarce be borne. They are ready to tell you
that it deserves death only to ask after safety. Betwixt subject and
subject, they will grant, there must be measures, laws, and judges,
for their mutual peace and security; but as for the ruler, he ought
to be absolute and is above all such circumstances; because he
has power to do more hurt and wrong, it is right when he does it.
To ask how you may be guarded from harm or injury on that side

where the strongest hand is to do it, is presently the voice of faction and rebellion, as if when men, quitting the state of nature, entered into society, they agreed that all of them but one should be under the restraint of laws, but that he should still retain all the liberty of the state of nature, increased with power and made licentious by impunity. This is to think that men are so foolish that they take care to avoid what mischiefs may be done them by polecats or foxes, but are content, nay, think it safety, to be devoured by lions.

94. But whatever flatterers may talk to amuse people's understandings, it hinders not men from feeling; and when they perceive that any man, in what station soever, is out of the bounds of the civil society which they are of, and that they have no appeal on earth against any harm they may receive from him, they are apt to think themselves in the state of nature in respect of him whom they find to be so, and to take care, as soon as they can, to have that safety and security in civil society for which it was instituted, and for which only they entered into it. And therefore, though perhaps at first (as shall be shown more at large hereafter in the following part of this discourse), some one good and excellent man, having got a pre-eminence amongst the rest, had this deference paid to his goodness and virtue as to a kind of natural authority, that the chief rule, with arbitration of their differences, by a tacit consent devolved into his hands, without any other caution but the assurance they had of his uprightness and wisdom; yet when time, giving authority and (as some men would persuade us) sacredness to customs which the negligent and unforeseeing innocence of the first ages began, had brought in successors of another stamp, the people, finding their properties not secure under the government as then it was [3]—whereas government has

[3] "At the first, when some certain kind of regiment was once appointed, it may be that nothing was then farther thought upon for the manner of governing, but all permitted unto their wisdom and discretion which were to rule, till by experience they found this for all parts very inconvenient, so as the thing which they had devised for a remedy did indeed but increase the sore which it should have cured. They saw, that to live by one man's will became the cause of all men's misery. This constrained them to come into laws wherein all men might see their duty beforehand and know the penalties of transgressing them" (Hooker's *Eccl. Pol.* lib. i. sect. 10).

no other end but the preservation of property—could never be safe nor at rest nor think themselves in civil society till the legislature was placed in collective bodies of men, call them 'senate,' 'parliament,' or what you please. By which means every single person became subject, equally with other the meanest men, to those laws which he himself, as part of the legislative, had established; nor could any one, by his own authority, avoid the force of the law when once made, nor by any pretense of superiority plead exemption, thereby to license his own or the miscarriages of any of his dependents. No man in civil society can be exempted from the laws of it;[4] for if any man may do what he thinks fit, and there be no appeal on earth for redress or security against any harm he shall do, I ask whether he be not perfectly still in the state of nature, and so can be no part or member of that civil society; unless any one will say the state of nature and civil society are one and the same thing, which I have never yet found any one so great a patron of anarchy as to affirm.

CHAPTER VIII

OF THE BEGINNING OF POLITICAL SOCIETIES

95. MEN BEING, as has been said, by nature all free, equal, and independent, no one can be put out of this estate and subjected to the political power of another without his own consent. The only way whereby any one divests himself of his natural liberty and puts on the bonds of civil society is by agreeing with other men to join and unite into a community for their comfortable, safe, and peaceable living one amongst another, in a secure enjoyment of their properties and a greater security against any that are not of it. This any number of men may do, because it injures not the freedom of the rest; they are left as they were in the liberty of the state of nature. When any number of men have so consented to

---

[4] "Civil law, being the act of the whole body politic, doth therefore overrule each several part of the same body" (Hooker, *Ibid.*).

make one <u>community or government</u>, they are thereby presently incorporated and <u>make one</u> body politic wherein <u>the majority have a right to act and</u> conclude the rest.

96. For when any number of men have, by the consent of every individual, made a community, they have thereby made that community one body, with a power to act as one body, which is only by the will and determination of the majority; for that which acts any community being only the consent of the individuals of it, and it being necessary to that which is one body to move one way, it is necessary the body should move that way whither the greater force carries it, which is the consent of the majority; or else it is impossible it should act or continue one body, one community, which the consent of every individual that united into it agreed that it should; and so every one is bound by that consent to be concluded by the majority. And therefore we see that in assemblies impowered to act by positive laws, where no number is set by that positive law which impowers them, the act of the majority passes for the act of the whole and, of course, determines, as having by the law of nature and reason the power of the whole.

97. And thus every man, by consenting with others to make one body politic under one government, puts himself under an obligation to every one of that society to submit to the determination of the majority and to be concluded by it; or else this original compact, whereby he with others incorporates into one society, would signify nothing, and be no compact, if he be left free and under no other ties than he was in before in the state of nature. For what appearance would there be of any compact? What new engagement if he were no further tied by any decrees of the society than he himself thought fit and did actually consent to? This would be still as great a liberty as he himself had before his compact, or any one else in the state of nature has who may submit himself and consent to any acts of it if he thinks fit.

98. For if the consent of the majority shall not in reason be received as the act of the whole and conclude every individual, nothing but the consent of every individual can make anything to be the act of the whole; but such a consent is next to impossible ever

to be had if we consider the infirmities of health and avocations of business which in a number, though much less than that of a commonwealth, will necessarily keep many away from the public assembly. To which, if we add the variety of opinions and contrariety of interests which unavoidably happen in all collections of men, the coming into society upon such terms would be only like Cato's coming into the theatre only to go out again.[1] Such a constitution as this would make the mighty leviathan of a shorter duration than the feeblest creatures, and not let it outlast the day it was born in; which cannot be supposed till we can think that rational creatures should desire and constitute societies only to be dissolved; for where the majority cannot conclude the rest, there they cannot act as one body, and consequently will be immediately dissolved again.

99. Whosoever, therefore, out of a state of nature unite into a community must be understood to give up all the power necessary to the ends for which they unite into society to the majority of the community, unless they expressly agreed in any number greater than the majority. And this is done by barely agreeing to unite into one political society, which is all the compact that is, or needs be, between the individuals that enter into or make up a commonwealth. And thus that which begins and actually constitutes any political society is nothing but the consent of any number of freemen capable of a majority to unite and incorporate into such a society. And this is that, and that only, which did or could give beginning to any lawful government in the world.

100. To this I find two objections made:

First, That there are no instances to be found in story of a company of men independent and equal one amongst another that met together and in this way began and set up a government.

Secondly, It is impossible of right that men should do so, because all men being born under government, they are to submit to that and are not at liberty to begin a new one.

101. To the first there is this to answer: that it is not at all to

---

[1] [Marcus Porcius Cato (234–149 B.C.): Called "Cato the Censor" and "Cato the Elder." A Roman statesman, lawyer, and writer, who tried to bring back by legislation a very stern moral standard. Locke's reference here is to Cato's disapproval of the theater.]

be wondered that history gives us but a very little account of men that lived together in the state of nature. The inconveniences of that condition, and the love and want of society, no sooner brought any number of them together, but they presently united and incorporated if they designed to continue together. And if we may not suppose men ever to have been in the state of nature, because we hear not much of them in such a state, we may as well suppose the armies of Salmanasser or Xerxes were never children because we hear little of them till they were men and embodied in armies. Government is everywhere antecedent to records, and letters seldom come in amongst a people till a long continuation of civil society has, by other more necessary arts, provided for their safety, ease, and plenty; and then they begin to look after the history of their founders and search into their original, when they have outlived the memory of it; for it is with commonwealths as with particular persons—they are commonly ignorant of their own births and infancies; and if they know anything of their original, they are beholden for it to the accidental records that others have kept of it. And those that we have of the beginning of any politics in the world, excepting that of the Jews, where God himself immediately interposed, and which favors not at all paternal dominion, are all either plain instances of such a beginning as I have mentioned, or at least have manifest footsteps of it.

102. He must show a strange inclination to deny evident matter of fact when it agrees not with his hypothesis, who will not allow that the beginnings of Rome and Venice were by the uniting together of several men free and independent one of another, amongst whom there was no natural superiority or subjection. And if Josephus Acosta's word may be taken, he tells us that in many parts of America there was no government at all.

"There are great and apparent conjectures," says he, "that these men," speaking of those of Peru, "for a long time had neither kings nor commonwealths, but lived in troops, as they do this day in Florida, the Cheriquanas, those of Brazil, and many other nations which have no certain kings, but as occasion is offered, in peace or war, they choose their captains as they please." [2]

If it be said that every man there was born subject to his father or the head of his family, that the subjection due from a child to a father took not away his freedom of uniting into what political society he thought fit has been already proved. But be that as it will, these men, it is evident, were actually free; and whatever superiority some politicians now would place in any of them, they themselves claimed it not, but by consent were all equal till by the same consent they set rulers over themselves. So that their politic societies all began from a voluntary union and the mutual agreement of men freely acting in the choice of their governors and forms of government.

103. And I hope those who went away from Sparta with Palantus, mentioned by Justin, *lib.* iii. c. 4, will be allowed to have been freemen, independent one of another, and to have set up a government over themselves by their own consent.[3] Thus I have given several examples out of history of people free and in the state of nature that, being met together, incorporated and began a commonwealth. And if the want of such instances be an argument to prove that governments were not nor could not be so begun, I suppose the contenders for paternal empire were better let it alone than urge it against natural liberty; for if they can give so many instances out of history of governments begun upon paternal right, I think—though at best an argument from what has been to what should of right be has no great force—one might, without any great danger, yield them the cause. But if I might advise them in the case, they would do well not to search too much into the original of governments as they have begun *de facto*, lest they should find at the foundation of most of them something very

[2] [Jose de Acosta (1539?–1600): A Spanish Jesuit missionary to Peru. His *Catechism* was the first book published in Peru. His most famous work was *Historia Natural y Moral de las Indias* (Seville, 1590).]

[3] [Reference here is to the exodus of a group of young Spartans who, during the first Messinian war, were born out of wedlock and, therefore, denied equal rights with other freeborn Spartans. Under their leader, Phalantus (Palantus), they reached Tarentum, conquered it, and forced the inhabitants to leave the city, thus founding a new, independent polity with Phalantus as their leader.]

little favorable to the design they promote and such a power as they contend for.

104. But to conclude, reason being plain on our side that men are naturally free, and the examples of history showing that the governments of the world that were begun in peace had their beginning laid on that foundation, and were made by the consent of the people, there can be little room for doubt either where the right is, or what has been the opinion or practice of mankind about the first erecting of governments.

105. I will not deny that, if we look back as far as history will direct us toward the original of commonwealths, we shall generally find them under the government and administration of one man. And I am also apt to believe that where a family was numerous enough to subsist by itself, and continued entire together without mixing with others, as it often happens where there is much land and few people, the government commonly began in the father; for the father, having by the law of nature the same power with every man else to punish as he thought fit any offenses against that law, might thereby punish his transgressing children even when they were men and out of their pupilage; and they were very likely to submit to his punishment and all join with him against the offender, in their turns, giving him thereby power to execute his sentence against any transgression, and so in effect make him the lawmaker and governor over all that remained in conjunction with his family. He was fittest to be trusted; paternal affection secured their property and interest under his care; and the custom of obeying him in their childhood made it easier to submit to him rather than to any other. If, therefore, they must have one to rule them, as government is hardly to be avoided amongst men that live together, who so likely to be the man as he that was their common father, unless negligence, cruelty, or any other defect of mind or body made him unfit for it? But when either the father died and left his next heir, for want of age, wisdom, courage, or any other qualities, less fit for rule, or where several families met and consented to continue together, there it is not to be doubted but they used their natural freedom to set up him whom they judged the ablest and most likely to rule well over

them. Conformable hereunto we find the people of America, who
—living out of the reach of the conquering swords and spreading
domination of the two great empires of Peru and Mexico—enjoyed their own natural freedom, though, *caeteris paribus*, they
commonly prefer the heir of their deceased king; yet, if they find
him any way weak or incapable, they pass him by and set up the
stoutest and bravest man for their ruler.

106. Thus, though looking back as far as records give us any
account of peopling the world and the history of nations, we commonly find the government to be in one hand; yet it destroys not
that which I affirm—viz., that the beginning of politic society depends upon the consent of the individuals to join into and make
one society; who, when they are thus incorporated, might set up
what form of government they thought fit. But this having given
occasion to men to mistake and think that by nature government
was monarchical and belonged to the father, it may not be amiss
here to consider why people In the beginning generally pitched
upon this form, which though perhaps the father's pre-eminence
might in the first institution of some commonwealth give rise to,
and place in the beginning the power in one hand; yet it is plain
that the reason that continued the form of government in a single
person was not any regard or respect to paternal authority, since
all petty monarchies, that is, almost all monarchies, near their
original, have been commonly, at least upon occasion, elective.

107. First, then, in the beginning of things, the father's government of the childhood of those sprung from him having accustomed them to the rule of one man and taught them that
where it was exercised with care and skill, with affection and love
to those under it, it was sufficient to procure and preserve to men
all the political happiness they sought for in society. It was no
wonder that they should pitch upon and naturally run into that
form of government which from their infancy they had been all
accustomed to and which, by experience, they had found both
easy and safe. To which, if we add that monarchy being simple
and most obvious to men whom neither experience had instructed
in forms of government, nor the ambition or insolence of empire
had taught to beware of the encroachments of prerogative or the

inconveniences of absolute power which monarchy in succession was apt to lay claim to and bring upon them, it was not at all strange that they should not much trouble themselves to think of methods of restraining any exorbitancies of those to whom they had given the authority over them, and of balancing the power of government by placing several parts of it in different hands. They had neither felt the oppression of tyrannical dominion, nor did the fashion of the age, nor their possessions, or way of living, which afforded little matter for covetousness or ambition, give them any reason to apprehend or provide against it; and therefore it is no wonder they put themselves into such a frame of government as was not only, as I said, most obvious and simple, but also best suited to their present state and condition, which stood more in need of defense against foreign invasions and injuries than of multiplicity of laws. The equality of a simple, poor way of living, confining their desires within the narrow bounds of each man's small property, made few controversies, and so no need of many laws to decide them or variety of officers to superintend the process or look after the execution of justice, where there were but few trespasses and offenders. Since, then, those who liked one another so well as to join into society cannot but be supposed to have some acquaintance and friendship together and some trust one in another, they could not but have greater apprehensions of others than of one another; and therefore their first care and thought cannot but be supposed to be how to secure themselves against foreign force. It was natural for them to put themselves under a frame of government which might best serve to that end, and choose the wisest and bravest man to conduct them in their wars and lead them out against their enemies, and in this chiefly be their ruler.

108. Thus we see that the kings of the Indians in America, which is still a pattern of the first ages in Asia and Europe, while the inhabitants were too few for the country, and want of people and money gave men no temptation to enlarge their possessions of land or contest for wider extent of ground, are little more than generals of their armies; and though they command absolutely in war, yet at home and in time of peace they exercise very little

dominion and have but a very moderate sovereignty, the resolu-
tions of peace and war being ordinarily either in the people or in
a council, though the war itself, which admits not of plurality of
governors, naturally devolves the command into the king's sole
authority.

109. And thus, in Israel itself, the chief business of their judges
and first kings seems to have been to be captains in war and leaders of their armies; which—besides what is signified by "going
out and in before the people," which was to march forth to war,
and home again at the heads of their forces—appears plainly in
the story of Jephthah. The Ammonites making war upon Israel,
the Gileadites in fear send to Jephthah, a bastard of their family
whom they had cast off, and article with him, if he will assist them
against the·Ammonites, to make him their ruler; which they do in
these words: "And the people made him head and captain over
them" (Judges xi. 11), which was, as it seems, all one as to be judge.
"And he judged Israel" (Judges xii. 7), that is, was their captain-
general, six years. So when Jotham upbraids the Shechemites with
the obligation they had to Gideon, who had been their judge and
ruler, he tells them, "He fought for you, and adventured his life
far, and delivered you out of the hands of Midian" (Judges ix.
17). Nothing is mentioned of him but what he did as a general;
and indeed that is all is found in his history, or in any of the rest
of the judges. And Abimelech particularly is called king, though at
most he was but their general. And when, being weary of the ill
conduct of Samuel's sons, the children of Israel desired a king,
"like all the nations, to judge them, and to go out before them, and
to fight their battles" (1 Sam. viii. 20), God granting their desire
says to Samuel: "I will send thee a man, and thou shalt anoint
him to be captain over my people Israel, that he may save my
people out of the hands of the Philistines" (ix. 16), as if the only
business of a king had been to lead out their armies and fight in
their defense; and, accordingly, Samuel, at his inauguration, pouring a vial of oil upon him, declares to Saul that "the Lord had
anointed him to be captain over his inheritance" (x. 1). And,
therefore, those who, after Saul's being solemnly chosen and sa-
luted king by the tribes of Mispeh, were unwilling to have him

their king, made no other objection but this: "How shall this man save us?" (vs. 27), as if they should have said, "This man is unfit to be our king, not having skill and conduct enough in war to be able to defend us." And when God resolved to transfer the government to David, it is in these words: "But now thy kingdom shall not continue. The Lord hath sought him a man after his own heart, and the Lord hath commanded him to be captain over his people" (xiii. 14), as if the whole kingly authority were nothing else but to be their general. And, therefore, the tribes who had stuck to Saul's family and opposed David's reign, when they came to Hebron with terms of submission to them, they tell him, amongst other arguments, they had to submit to him as their king; that he was in effect their king in Saul's time, and, therefore, they had no reason but to receive him as their king now. "Also," say they, "in time past, when Saul was king over us, thou wast he that leddest out and broughtest in Israel, and the Lord said unto thee, 'Thou shalt feed my people Israel and thou shalt be a captain over Israel.'"

110. Thus, whether a family by degrees grew up into a commonwealth and, the fatherly authority being continued on to the elder son, every one in his turn growing up under it tacitly submitted to it, and the easiness and equality of it not offending any one, every one acquiesced, till time seemed to have confirmed it and settled a right of succession by prescription; or whether several families, or the descendants of several families, whom chance, neighborhood, or business brought together, uniting into society, the need of a general whose conduct might defend them against their enemies in war, and the great confidence the innocence and sincerity of that poor but virtuous age—such as are almost all those which begin governments that ever come to last in the world—gave men of another, made the first beginners of commonwealths generally put the rule into one man's hand, without any other express limitation or restraint but what the nature of the thing and the end of government required. Whichever of those it was that at first put the rule into the hands of a single person, certain it is that nobody was intrusted with it but for the public good and safety, and to those ends, in the infancies of commonwealths, those who had it commonly used

it. And unless they had done so, young societies could not have subsisted; without such nursing fathers, tender and careful of the public weal, all governments would have sunk under the weakness and infirmities of their infancy, and the prince and the people had soon perished together.

111. But though the golden age—before vain ambition and *amor sceleratus habendi*, evil concupiscence, had corrupted men's minds into a mistake of true power and honor—had more virtue and, consequently, better governors, as well as less vicious subjects; and there was then no stretching prerogative on the one side to oppress the people, nor, consequently, on the other, any dispute about privilege to lessen or restrain the power of the magistrate, and so no contest betwixt rulers and people about governors or government; yet, when ambition and luxury in future ages [4] would retain and increase the power, without doing the business for which it was given, and, aided by flattery, taught princes to have distinct and separate interests from their people, men found it necessary to examine more carefully the original and rights of government, and to find out ways to restrain the exorbitancies and prevent the abuses of that power which, they having entrusted in another's hands only for their own good, they found was made use of to hurt them.

112. Thus we may see how probable it is that people that were naturally free and by their own consent either submitted to the government of their father, or united together out of different families to make a government, should generally put the rule into one man's hands and choose to be under the conduct of a single person, without so much as by express conditions limiting or regulating his power which they thought safe enough in his honesty and prudence, though they never dreamed of monarchy being

[4] "At first, when some certain kind of regiment was once approved, it may be nothing was then further thought upon for the manner of governing, but all permitted unto their wisdom and discretion, which were to rule, till by experience they found this for all parts very inconvenient, so as the thing which they had devised for a remedy did indeed but increase the sore which it should have cured. They saw that to live by one man's will became the cause of all men's misery. This constrained them to come unto laws wherein all men might see their duty beforehand, and know the penalties of transgressing them" (Hooker's *Eccl. Pol.* lib. i. sect. 10).

jure divino, which we never heard of among mankind till it was revealed to us by the divinity of this last age, nor ever allowed paternal power to have a right of dominion or to be the foundation of all government. And thus much may suffice to show that, as far as we have any light from history, we have reason to conclude that all peaceful beginnings of government have been laid in the consent of the people. I say peaceful, because I shall have occasion in another place to speak of conquest, which some esteem a way of beginning of governments.

The other objection I find urged against the beginning of politics in the way I have mentioned is this:

113. That all men being born under government, some or other, it is impossible any of them should ever be free and at liberty to unite together and begin a new one, or ever be able to erect a lawful government.

If this argument be good, I ask, how came so many lawful monarchies into the world? For if anybody, upon this supposition, can show me any one man in any age of the world free to begin a lawful monarchy, I will be bound to show him ten other free men at liberty at the same time to unite and begin a new government under a regal or any other form, it being demonstration that if any one, born under the dominion of another, may be so free as to have a right to command others in a new and distinct empire, every one that is born under the dominion of another may be so free, too, and may become a ruler or subject of a distinct separate government. And so, by this their own principle, either all men, however born, are free, or else there is but one lawful prince, one lawful government in the world. And then they have nothing to do but barely to show us which that is; which, when they have done, I doubt not but all mankind will easily agree to pay obedience to him.

114. Though it be a sufficient answer to their objection to show that it involves them in the same difficulties that it does those they use it against, yet I shall endeavor to discover the weakness of this argument a little further. "All men," say they, "are born under government, and therefore they cannot be at liberty to begin a new one. Everyone is born a subject to his father, or his prince,

and is therefore under the perpetual tie of subjection and allegiance." It is plain mankind never owned nor considered any such
natural subjection that they were born in, to one or to the other
that tied them without their own consents, to a subjection to them
and their heirs.

115. For there are no examples so frequent in history, both
sacred and profane, as those of men withdrawing themselves and
their obedience from the jurisdiction they were born under, and
the family or community they were bred up in, and setting up new
governments in other places; from whence sprang all that number
of petty commonwealths in the beginning of ages, and which
always multiplied as long as there was room enough, till the
stronger or more fortunate swallowed the weaker, and those great
ones, again breaking to pieces, dissolved into lesser dominions. All
which are so many testimonies against paternal sovereignty, and
plainly prove that it was not the natural right of the father
descending to his heirs that made governments in the beginning,
since it was impossible, upon that ground, there should have been
so many little kingdoms; all must have been but only one universal monarchy if men had not been at liberty to separate themselves from their families and the government, be it what it will,
that was set up in it, and go and make distinct commonwealths
and other governments as they thought fit.

116. This has been the practice of the world from its first beginning to this day; nor is it now any more hindrance to the freedom
of mankind that they are born under constituted and ancient
polities that have established laws and set forms of government,
than if they were born in the woods, amongst the unconfined inhabitants that run loose in them; for those who would persuade us
that "by being born under any government we are naturally subjects to it" and have no more any title or pretense to the freedom
of the state of nature, have no other reason—bating that of
paternal power, which we have already answered—to produce for
it but only because our fathers or progenitors passed away their
natural liberty, and thereby bound up themselves and their
posterity to a perpetual subjection to the government which they
themselves submitted to. It is true that, whatever engagement or

promises any one has made for himself, he is under the obligation of them, but cannot by any compact whatsoever bind his children or posterity; for his son, when a man, being altogether as free as the father, any act of the father can no more give away the liberty of the son than it can of anybody else. He may indeed annex such conditions to the land he enjoyed as a subject of any commonwealth as may oblige his son to be of that community, if he will enjoy those possessions which were his father's, because that estate, being his father's property, he may dispose or settle it as he pleases.

117. And this has generally given the occasion to mistake in this matter; because commonwealths not permitting any part of their dominions to be dismembered, nor to be enjoyed by any but those of their community, the son cannot ordinarily enjoy the possessions of his father but under the same terms his father did, by becoming a member of the society; whereby he puts himself presently under the government he finds there established as much as any other subject of that commonwealth. And thus "the consent of freemen, born under government, which only makes them members of it," being given separately in their turns, as each comes to be of age, and not in a multitude together, people take no notice of it and, thinking it not done at all, or not necessary, conclude they are naturally subjects as they are men.

118. But, it is plain, governments themselves understand it otherwise; they claim no power over the son because of that they had over the father; nor look on children as being their subjects, by their father's being so. If a subject of England have a child by an English woman in France, whose subject is he? Not the King of England's, for he must have leave to be admitted to the privileges of it; nor the King of France's, for how then has his father a liberty to bring him away and breed him as he pleases? And who ever was judged as a traitor or deserter, if he left or warred against a country, for being barely born in it of parents that were aliens there? It is plain, then, by the practice of governments themselves as well as by the law of right reason, that a child is born a subject of no country or government. He is under his father's tuition and authority till he comes to age of discretion; and then he is a

freeman, at liberty what government he will put himself under, what body politic he will unite himself to; for if an Englishman's son, born in France, be at liberty, and may do so, it is evident there is no tie upon him by his father's being a subject of this kingdom, nor is he bound up by any compact of his ancestors. And why then has not his son, by the same reason, the same liberty though he be born anywhere else? Since the power that a father has naturally over his children is the same wherever they be born, and the ties of natural obligations are not bounded by the positive limits of kingdoms and commonwealths.

119. Every man being, as has been shown, naturally free, and nothing being able to put him into subjection to any earthly power but only his own consent, it is to be considered what shall be understood to be a sufficient declaration of a man's consent to make him subject to the laws of any government. There is a common distinction of an express and a tacit consent which will concern our present case. Nobody doubts but an express consent of any man entering into any society makes him a perfect member of that society, a subject of that government. The difficulty is, what ought to be looked upon as a tacit consent, and how far it binds—i. e., how far any one shall be looked upon to have consented and thereby submitted to any government, where he has made no expressions of it at all. And to this I say that every man that has any possessions or enjoyment of any part of the dominions of any government does thereby give his tacit consent and is as far forth obliged to obedience to the laws of that government, during such enjoyment, as anyone under it; whether this his possession be of land to him and his heirs for ever, or a lodging only for a week, or whether it be barely traveling freely on the highway; and, in effect, it reaches as far as the very being of anyone within the territories of that government.

120. To understand this the better, it is fit to consider that every man, when he at first incorporates himself into any commonwealth, he, by his uniting himself thereunto, annexes also, and submits to the community, those possessions which he has or shall acquire that do not already belong to any other government; for it would be a direct contradiction for any one to enter into society

with others for the securing and regulating of property, and yet
to suppose his land, whose property is to be regulated by the laws
of the society, should be exempt from the jurisdiction of that government to which he himself, the proprietor of the land, is a subject. By the same act, therefore, whereby any one unites his
person, which was before free, to any commonwealth, by the same
he unites his possessions which were before free to it also; and
they become, both of them, person and possession, subject to the
government and dominion of that commonwealth as long as it has
a being. Whoever, therefore, from thenceforth by inheritance, purchase, permission, or otherwise, enjoys any part of the land so
annexed to, and under the government of that commonwealth,
must take it with the condition it is under—that is, of submitting
to the government of the commonwealth under whose jurisdiction
it is as far forth as any subject of it.

121. But since the government has a direct jurisdiction only
over the land, and reaches the possessor of it—before he has actually incorporated himself in the society—only as he dwells upon
and enjoys that, the obligation anyone is under by virtue of such
enjoyment, to submit to the government, begins and ends with the
enjoyment; so that whenever the owner, who has given nothing
but such a tacit consent to the government, will, by donation, sale,
or otherwise, quit the said possession, he is at liberty to go and
incorporate himself into any other commonwealth, or to agree with
others to begin a new one *in vacuis locis*, in any part of the world
they can find free and unpossessed. Whereas he that has once, by
actual agreement and any express declaration, given his consent to
be of any commonwealth is perpetually and indispensably obliged
to be and remain unalterably a subject to it, and can never be again
in the liberty of the state of nature, unless by any calamity the
government he was under comes to be dissolved, or else, by some
public act, cuts him off from being any longer a member of it.

122. But submitting to the laws of any country, living quietly
and enjoying privileges and protection under them, makes not a
man a member of that society; this is only a local protection and
homage due to and from all those who, not being in a state of war,
come within the territories belonging to any government, to all

parts whereof the force of its laws extends. But this no more makes a man a member of that society, a perpetual subject of that commonwealth, than it would make a man a subject to another in whose family he found it convenient to abide for some time, though, while he continued in it, he were obliged to comply with the laws and submit to the government he found there. And thus we see that foreigners, by living all their lives under another government and enjoying the privileges and protection of it, though they are bound, even in conscience, to submit to its administration as far forth as any denizen, yet do not thereby come to be subjects or members of that commonwealth. Nothing can make any man so but his actually entering into it by positive engagement and express promise and compact. That is that which I think concerning the beginning of political societies and that consent which makes any one a member of any commonwealth.

CHAPTER IX

OF THE ENDS OF POLITICAL SOCIETY AND GOVERNMENT

123. IF MAN in the state of nature be so free, as has been said, if he be absolute lord of his own person and possessions, equal to the greatest, and subject to nobody, why will he part with his freedom, why will he give up his empire and subject himself to the dominion and control of any other power? To which it is obvious to answer that though in the state of nature he has such a right, yet the enjoyment of it is very uncertain and constantly exposed to the invasion of others; for all being kings as much as he, every man his equal, and the greater part no strict observers of equity and justice, the enjoyment of the property he has in this state is very unsafe, very unsecure. This makes him willing to quit a condition which, however free, is full of fears and continual dangers; and it is not without reason that he seeks out and is willing to join in society with others who are already united, or have a mind to

unite, for the mutual preservation of their lives, liberties, and estates, which I call by the general name 'property.'

124. The great and chief end, therefore, of men's uniting into commonwealths and putting themselves under government is the preservation of their property. To which in the state of nature there are many things wanting:

First, there wants an established, settled, known law, received and allowed by common consent to be the standard of right and wrong and the common measure to decide all controversies between them; for though the law of nature be plain and intelligible to all rational creatures, yet men, being biased by their interest as well as ignorant for want of studying it, are not apt to allow of it as a law binding to them in the application of it to their particular cases.

125. Secondly, in the state of nature there wants a known and indifferent judge with authority to determine all differences according to the established law; for every one in that state being both judge and executioner of the law of nature, men being partial to themselves, passion and revenge is very apt to carry them too far and with too much heat in their own cases, as well as negligence and unconcernedness to make them too remiss in other men's.

126. Thirdly, in the state of nature there often wants power to back and support the sentence when right, and to give it due execution. They who by any injustice offend will seldom fail, where they are able, by force, to make good their injustice; such resistance many times makes the punishment dangerous and frequently destructive to those who attempt it.

127. Thus mankind, notwithstanding all the privileges of the state of nature, being but in an ill condition while they remain in it, are quickly driven into society. Hence it comes to pass that we seldom find any number of men live any time together in this state. The inconveniences that they are therein exposed to by the irregular and uncertain exercise of the power every man has of punishing the transgressions of others make them take sanctuary under the established laws of government and therein seek the preservation of their property. It is this makes them so willingly give up every one his single power of punishing, to be exercised

by such alone as shall be appointed to it amongst them; and by
such rules as the community, or those authorized by them to that
purpose, shall agree on. And in this we have the original right of
both the legislative and executive power, as well as of the governments and societies themselves.

128. For in the state of nature, to omit the liberty he has of
innocent delights, a man has two powers:

The first is to do whatsoever he thinks fit for the preservation of
himself and others within the permission of the law of nature, by
which law, common to them all, he and all the rest of mankind are
one community, make up one society, distinct from all other creatures. And, were it not for the corruption and viciousness of
degenerate men, there would be no need of any other, no necessity
that men should separate from this great and natural community
and by positive agreements combine into smaller and divided associations.

The other power a man has in the state of nature is the power
to punish the crimes committed against that law. Both these he
gives up when he joins in a private, if I may so call it, or particular politic society and incorporates into any commonwealth separate from the rest of mankind.

129. The first power, viz., of doing whatsoever he thought fit for
the preservation of himself and the rest of mankind, he gives up to
be regulated by laws made by the society, so far forth as the
preservation of himself and the rest of that society shall require;
which laws of the society in many things confine the liberty he
had by the law of nature.

130. Secondly, the power of punishing he wholly gives up, and
engages his natural force—which he might before employ in the
execution of the law of nature by his own single authority, as he
thought fit—to assist the executive power of the society, as the
law thereof shall require; for being now in a new state, wherein
he is to enjoy many conveniences from the labor, assistance, and
society of others in the same community as well as protection from its whole strength, he is to part also with as much
of his natural liberty, in providing for himself, as the good, prosperity, and safety of the society shall require, which is not only nec-

essary, but just, since the other members of the society do the like.

131. But though men when they enter into society give up the equality, liberty, and executive power they had in the state of nature into the hands of the society, to be so far disposed of by the legislative as the good of the society shall require, yet it being only with an intention in every one the better to preserve himself, his liberty and property—for no rational creature can be supposed to change his condition with an intention to be worse—the power of the society, or legislative constituted by them, can never be supposed to extend farther than the common good, but is obliged to secure every one's property by providing against those three defects above-mentioned that made the state of nature so unsafe and uneasy. And so whoever has the legislative or supreme power of any commonwealth is bound to govern by established standing laws, promulgated and known to the people, and not by extemporary decrees; by indifferent and upright judges who are to decide controversies by those laws; and to employ the force of the community at home only in the execution of such laws, or abroad to prevent or redress foreign injuries, and secure the community from inroads and invasion. And all this to be directed to no other end but the peace, safety, and public good of the people.

CHAPTER X

OF THE FORMS OF A COMMONWEALTH

132. THE MAJORITY, having, as has been shown, upon men's first uniting into society, the whole power of the community naturally in them, may employ all that power in making laws for the community from time to time, and executing those laws by officers of their own appointing: and then the form of the government is a perfect democracy; or else may put the power of making laws into the hands of a few select men, and their heirs or successors: and then it is an oligarchy; or else into the hands of one man: and then it is a monarchy; if to him and his heirs: it is an hereditary

monarchy; if to him only for life, but upon his death the power only of nominating a successor to return to them: an elective monarchy. And so accordingly of these the community may make compounded and mixed forms of government, as they think good. And if the legislative power be at first given by the majority to one or more persons only for their lives, or any limited time, and then the supreme power to revert to them again—when it is so reverted, the community may dispose of it again anew into what hands they please and so constitute a new form of government. For the form of government depending upon the placing of the supreme power, which is the legislative—it being impossible to conceive that an inferior power should prescribe to a superior, or any but the supreme make laws—according as the power of making laws is placed, such is the form of the commonwealth.

133. By commonwealth, I must be understood all along to mean, not a democracy or any form of government, but any independent community which the Latins signified by the word *civitas*, to which the word which best answers in our language is 'commonwealth,' and most properly expresses such a society of men, which 'community' or 'city' in English does not, for there may be subordinate communities in government; and city amongst us has quite a different notion from commonwealth; and, therefore, to avoid ambiguity, I crave leave to use the word commonwealth in that sense in which I find it used by King James the First; [1] and I take it to be its genuine signification; which if anybody dislike, I consent with him to change it for a better.

[1] [James the First (1566–1625): The only child of Mary, Queen of Scots, he ruled Scotland as James the Sixth from 1567 to 1625, and England as James the First from 1603 to 1625. Though tutored by George Buchanan (cf. note 2, p. 132), he became one of the strongest exponents of the theory of the divine right of kings. His most important work, *The True Law of Free Monarchies*, was published in Scotland in 1589 and significantly republished in London in 1603, immediately following his ascension to the British throne. His other political works include *Basilikon Doron* (1599) [Instructions to his son, Henry]; *An Apology for the Oath of Allegiance* (1607); *A Premonition to all Christian Monarchs, Free Princes and States* (1616); *A Remonstrance for the Right of Kings and the Independence of Their Crowns* (1616) [An answer to Cardinal Perron]. (Charles H. McIlwain has edited his works and contributed an excellent Introduction and an extensive bibliography: *The Political Works of James I*. Harvard University Press, Cambridge, 1918.)]

CHAPTER XI

OF THE EXTENT OF THE LEGISLATIVE POWER

134. The great end of men's entering into society being the enjoyment of their properties in peace and safety, and the great instrument and means of that being the laws established in that society, the first and fundamental positive law of all commonwealths is the establishing of the legislative power; as the first and fundamental natural law which is to govern even the legislative itself is the preservation of the society and, as far as will consist with the public good, of every person in it. This legislative is not only the supreme power of the commonwealth, but sacred and unalterable in the hands where the community have once placed it; nor can any edict of anybody else, in what form soever conceived or by what power soever backed, have the force and obligation of a law which has not its sanction from that legislative which the public has chosen and appointed; for without this the law could not have that which is absolutely necessary to its being a law: the consent of the society over whom nobody can have a power to make laws, but by their own consent and by authority received from them.[1] And therefore all the obedience, which by the most solemn ties any one can be obliged to pay, ultimately

---

[1] "The lawful power of making laws to command whole politic societies of men, belonging so properly unto the same entire societies, that for any prince or potentate of what kind soever upon earth to exercise the same of himself, and not by express commission immediately and personally received from God, or else by authority derived at the first from their consent, upon whose persons they impose laws, it is no better than mere tyranny. Laws they are not, therefore, which public approbation hath not made so" (Hooker's *Eccl. Pol.* lib. i. sect. 10).

"Of this point, therefore, we are to note, that such men naturally have no full and perfect power to command whole politic multitudes of men, therefore utterly without our consent we could in such sort be at no man's commandment living. And to be commanded we do consent, when that society whereof we be a part hath at any time before consented, without revoking the same by the like universal agreement. Laws therefore human, of what kind soever, are available by consent" (*Ibid.*).

terminates in this supreme power and is directed by those laws which it enacts; nor can any oaths to any foreign power whatsoever, or any domestic subordinate power, discharge any member of the society from his obedience to the legislative acting pursuant to their trust, nor oblige him to any obedience contrary to the laws so enacted, or farther than they do allow; it being ridiculous to imagine one can be tied ultimately to obey any power in the society which is not supreme.

135. Though the legislative, whether placed in one or more, whether it be always in being, or only by intervals, though it be the supreme power in every commonwealth; yet:

First, it is not, nor can possibly be, absolutely arbitrary over the lives and fortunes of the people; for it being but the joint power of every member of the society given up to that person or assembly which is legislator, it can be no more than those persons had in a state of nature before they entered into society and gave up to the community; for nobody can transfer to another more power than he has in himself, and nobody has an absolute arbitrary power over himself or over any other, to destroy his own life or take away the life or property of another. A man, as has been proved, cannot subject himself to the arbitrary power of another; and having in the state of nature no arbitrary power over the life, liberty, or possession of another, but only so much as the law of nature gave him for the preservation of himself and the rest of mankind, this is all he does or can give up to the commonwealth, and by it to the legislative power, so that the legislative can have no more than this. Their power, in the utmost bounds of it, is limited to the public good of the society. It is a power that has no other end but preservation, and therefore can never have a right to destroy, enslave, or designedly to impoverish the subjects.[2]

[2] "Two foundations there are which bear up public societies; the one a natural inclination whereby all men desire sociable life and fellowship; the other an order, expressly or secretly agreed upon, touching the manner of their union in living together. The latter is that which we call the law of a commonweal, the very soul of a politic body, the parts whereof are by law animated, held together, and set on work in such actions as the common good requireth. Laws politic, ordained for external order and regiment amongst men, are never framed as they should be, unless presuming the will of man to be inwardly obstinate, rebellious, and averse from all obedience to

strained and, till that moment, unknown wills, without having any measures set down which may guide and justify their actions. For all the power the government has, being only for the good of the society, as it ought not to be arbitrary and at pleasure, so it ought to be exercised by established and promulgated laws; that both the people may know their duty and be safe and secure within the limits of the law; and the rulers, too, kept within their bounds, and not be tempted by the power they have in their hands to employ it to such purposes and by such measures as they would not have known, and own not willingly.

138. Thirdly, the supreme power cannot take from any man part of his property without his own consent; for the preservation of property being the end of government and that for which men enter into society, it necessarily supposes and requires that the people should have property; without which they must be supposed to lose that, by entering into society, which was the end for which they entered into it—too gross an absurdity for any man to own. Men, therefore, in society having property, they have such right to the goods which by the law of the community are theirs, that nobody has a right to take their substance or any part of it from them without their own consent; without this, they have no property at all, for I have truly no property in that which another can by right take from me when he pleases, against my consent. Hence it is a mistake to think that the supreme or legislative power of any commonwealth can do what it will and dispose of the estates of the subject arbitrarily, or take any part of them at pleasure. This is not much to be feared in governments where the legislative consists, wholly or in part, in assemblies which are variable, whose members, upon the dissolution of the assembly, are subjects under the common laws of their country, equally with the rest. But in governments where the legislative is in one lasting assembly, always in being, or in one man, as in absolute monarchies, there is danger still that they will think themselves to have a distinct interest from the rest of the community, and so will be apt to increase their own riches and power by taking what they think fit from the people; for a man's property is not at all secure, though there be good and equitable laws

to set the bounds of it between him and his fellow subjects, if he who commands those subjects have power to take from any private man what part he pleases of his property and use and dispose of it as he thinks good.

139. But government, into whatsoever hands it is put, being, as I have before shown, entrusted with this condition, and for this end, that men might have and secure their properties, the prince, or senate, however it may have power to make laws for the regulating of property between the subjects one amongst another, yet can never have a power to take to themselves the whole or any part of the subject's property without their own consent; for this would be in effect to leave them no property at all. And to let us see that even absolute power, where it is necessary, is not arbitrary by being absolute, but is still limited by that reason and confined to those ends which required it in some cases to be absolute, we need look no farther than the common practice of martial discipline; for the preservation of the army, and in it of the whole commonwealth, requires an absolute obedience to the command of every superior officer, and it is justly death to disobey or dispute the most dangerous or unreasonable of them; but yet we see that neither the sergeant, that could command a soldier to march up to the mouth of a cannon or stand in a breach where he is almost sure to perish, can command that soldier to give him one penny of his money; nor the general, that can condemn him to death for deserting his post or for not obeying the most desperate orders, can yet, with all his absolute power of life and death, dispose of one farthing of that soldier's estate or seize one jot of his goods, whom yet he can command anything, and hang for the least disobedience. Because such a blind obedience is necessary to that end for which the commander has his power, viz., the preservation of the rest; but the disposing of his goods has nothing to do with it.

140. It is true, governments cannot be supported without great charge, and it is fit every one who enjoys his share of the protection should pay out of his estate his proportion for the maintenance of it. But still it must be with his own consent—i.e., the consent of the majority, giving it either by themselves or their

representatives chosen by them. For if any one shall claim a power to lay and levy taxes on the people, by his own authority and without such consent of the people, he thereby invades the fundamental law of property and subverts the end of government; for what property have I in that which another may by right take, when he pleases, to himself?

141. Fourthly, the legislative cannot transfer the power of making laws to any other hands; for it being but a delegated power from the people, they who have it cannot pass it over to others. The people alone can appoint the form of the commonwealth, which is by constituting the legislative and appointing in whose hands that shall be. And when the people have said, we will submit to rules and be governed by laws made by such men, and in such forms, nobody else can say other men shall make laws for them; nor can the people be bound by any laws but such as are enacted by those whom they have chosen and authorized to make laws for them. The power of the legislative, being derived from the people by a positive voluntary grant and institution, can be no other than what that positive grant conveyed, which being only to make laws, and not to make legislators, the legislative can have no power to transfer their authority of making laws and place it in other hands.

142. These are the bounds which the trust that is put in them by the society and the law of God and nature have set to the legislative power of every commonwealth, in all forms of government:

First, they are to govern by promulgated established laws, not to be varied in particular cases, but to have one rule for rich and poor, for the favorite at court and the countryman at plough.

Secondly, these laws also ought to be designed for no other end ultimately but the good of the people.

Thirdly, they must not raise taxes on the property of the people without the consent of the people, given by themselves or their deputies. And this property concerns only such governments where the legislative is always in being, or at least where the people have not reserved any part of the legislative to deputies to be from time to time chosen by themselves.

Fourthly, the legislative neither must nor can transfer the power of making laws to anybody else, or place it anywhere but where the people have.

CHAPTER XII

OF THE LEGISLATIVE, EXECUTIVE, AND FEDERATIVE POWER OF THE COMMONWEALTH

143. THE LEGISLATIVE power is that which has a right to direct how the force of the commonwealth shall be employed for preserving the community and the members of it. But because those laws which are constantly to be executed, and whose force is always to continue, may be made in a little time, therefore there is no need that the legislative should be always in being, and having always business to do. And because it may be too great a temptation to human frailty, apt to grasp at power, for the same persons who have the power of making laws to have also in their hands the power to execute them, whereby they may exempt themselves from obedience to the laws they make, and suit the law, both in its making and execution, to their own private advantage, and thereby come to have a distinct interest from the rest of the community contrary to the end of society and government; therefore, in well ordered commonwealths, where the good of the whole is so considered as it ought, the legislative power is put into the hands of diverse persons who, duly assembled, have by themselves, or jointly with others, a power to make laws; which when they have done, being separated again, they are themselves subject to the laws they have made, which is a new and near tie upon them to take care that they make them for the public good.

144. But because the laws that are at once and in a short time made have a constant and lasting force and need a perpetual execution or an attendance thereunto; therefore, it is necessary there should be a power always in being which should see to the execution of the laws that are made and remain in force. And

thus the legislative and executive power come often to be separated.

145. There is another power in every commonwealth which one may call natural, because it is that which answers to the power every man naturally had before he entered into society; for though in a commonwealth the members of it are distinct persons still in reference to one another, and as such are governed by the laws of the society, yet, in reference to the rest of mankind, they make one body which is, as every member of it before was, still in the state of nature with the rest of mankind. Hence it is that the controversies that happen between any man of the society with those that are out of it are managed by the public, and an injury done to a member of their body engages the whole in the reparation of it. So that, under this consideration, the whole community is one body in the state of nature in respect of all other states or persons out of its community.

146. This, therefore, contains the power of war and peace, leagues and alliances, and all the transactions with all persons and communities without the commonwealth, and may be called 'federative,' if anyone pleases. So the thing be understood, I am indifferent as to the name.

147. These two powers, executive and federative, though they be really distinct in themselves, yet one comprehending the execution of the municipal laws of the society within itself upon all that are parts of it, the other the management of the security and interest of the public without, with all those that it may receive benefit or damage from, yet they are always almost united. And though this federative power in the well or ill management of it be of great moment to the commonwealth, yet it is much less capable to be directed by antecedent, standing, positive laws than the executive, and so must necessarily be left to the prudence and wisdom of those whose hands it is in to be managed for the public good; for the laws that concern subjects one amongst another, being to direct their actions, may well enough precede them. But what is to be done in reference to foreigners, depending much upon their actions and the variation of designs and interests, must be left in great part to the prudence of those who have this power

committed to them, to be managed by the best of their skill for the advantage of the commonwealth.

148. Though, as I said, the executive and federative power of every community be really distinct in themselves, yet they are hardly to be separated and placed at the same time in the hands of distinct persons; for both of them requiring the force of the society for their exercise, it is almost impracticable to place the force of the commonwealth in distinct and not subordinate hands, or that the executive and federative power should be placed in persons that might act separately, whereby the force of the public would be under different commands, which would be apt some time or other to cause disorder and ruin.

CHAPTER XIII

OF THE SUBORDINATION OF THE POWERS OF THE COMMONWEALTH

149. THOUGH in a constituted commonwealth, standing upon its own basis and acting according to its own nature, that is, acting for the preservation of the community, there can be but one supreme power which is the legislative, to which all the rest are and must be subordinate, yet, the legislative being only a fiduciary power to act for certain ends, there remains still in the people a supreme power to remove or alter the legislative when they find the legislative act contrary to the trust reposed in them; for all power given with trust for the attaining an end being limited by that end; whenever that end is manifestly neglected or opposed, the trust must necessarily be forfeited and the power devolve into the hands of those that gave it, who may place it anew where they shall think best for their safety and security. And thus the community perpetually retains a supreme power of saving themselves from the attempts and designs of anybody, even of their legislators whenever they shall be so foolish or so wicked as to lay and carry on designs against the liberties and properties of the

subject; for no man or society of men having a power to deliver up their preservation, or consequently the means of it, to the absolute will and arbitrary dominion of another, whenever any one shall go about to bring them into such a slavish condition, they will always have a right to preserve what they have not a power to part with, and to rid themselves of those who invade this fundamental, sacred, and unalterable law of self-preservation for which they entered into society. And thus the community may be said in this respect to be always the supreme power, but not as considered under any form of government, because this power of the people can never take place till the government be dissolved.

150. In all cases, while the government subsists, the legislative is the supreme power; for what can give laws to another must needs be superior to him; and since the legislative is not otherwise legislative of the society but by the right it has to make laws for all the parts and for every member of the society, prescribing rules to their actions, and giving power of execution where they are transgressed, the legislative must needs be the supreme, and all other powers in any members or parts of the society derived from and subordinate to it.

151. In some commonwealths where the legislative is not always in being, and the executive is vested in a single person who has also a share in the legislative, there that single person in a very tolerable sense may also be called supreme; not that he has in himself all the supreme power, which is that of lawmaking, but because he has in him the supreme execution from whom all inferior magistrates derive all their several subordinate powers, or at least the greatest part of them. Having also no legislative superior to him, there being no law to be made without his consent which cannot be expected should ever subject him to the other part of the legislative, he is properly enough, in this sense, supreme. But yet it is to be observed that though oaths of allegiance and fealty are taken to him, it is not to him as supreme legislator, but as supreme executor of the law made by a joint power of him with others; allegiance being nothing but an obedience according to law, which, when he violates, he has no right to obedience nor

can claim it otherwise than as the public person invested with the power of the law, and so is to be considered as the image, phantom, or representative of the commonwealth, acted by the will of the society, declared in its laws; and thus he has no will, no power, but that of the law. But when he quits this representation, this public will, and acts by his own private will, he degrades himself and is but a single private person without power and without will that has no right to obedience—the members owing no obedience but to the public will of the society.

152. The executive power, placed anywhere but in a person that has also a share in the legislative, is visibly subordinate and accountable to it and may be at pleasure changed and displaced, so that it is not the supreme executive power that is exempt from subordination, but the supreme executive power vested in one who, having a share in the legislative, has no distinct superior legislative to be subordinate and accountable to, farther than he himself shall join and consent; so that he is no more subordinate than he himself shall think fit, which one may certainly conclude will be but very little. Of other ministerial and subordinate powers in a commonwealth we need not speak, they being so multiplied with infinite variety in the different customs and constitutions of distinct commonwealths that it is impossible to give a particular account of them all. Only thus much, which is necessary to our present purpose, we may take notice of concerning them, that they have no manner of authority, any of them, beyond what is by positive grant and commission delegated to them, and are all of them accountable to some other power in the commonwealth.

153. It is not necessary, no, nor so much as convenient, that the legislative should be always in being; but absolutely necessary that the executive power should, because there is not always need of new laws to be made but always need of execution of the laws that are made. When the legislative has put the execution of the laws they make into other hands, they have a power still to resume it out those hands, when they find cause, and to punish for any maladministration against the laws. The same holds also in regard of the federative power, that and the executive being both ministerial and subordinate to the legislative which, as has been shown,

in a constituted commonwealth is the supreme. The legislative also in this case being supposed to consist of several persons—for if it be a single person, it cannot but be always in being, and so will, as supreme, naturally have the supreme executive power, together with the legislative—may assemble and exercise their legislature at the times that either their original constitution or their own adjournment appoints, or when they please, if neither of these has appointed any time, or there be no other way prescribed to convoke them. For the supreme power being placed in them by the people, it is always in them, and they may exercise it when they please, unless by their original constitution they are limited to certain seasons, or by an act of their supreme power they have adjourned to a certain time; and when that time comes, they have a right to assemble and act again.

154. If the legislative, or any part of it, be made up of representatives chosen for that time by the people, which afterwards return into the ordinary state of subjects and have no share in the legislature but upon a new choice, this power of choosing must also be exercised by the people, either at certain appointed seasons, or else when they are summoned to it; and in this latter case the power of convoking the legislative is ordinarily placed in the executive, and has one of these two limitations in respect of time: that either the original constitution requires their assembling and acting at certain intervals, and then the executive power does nothing but ministerially issue directions for their electing and assembling according to due forms; or else it is left to his prudence to call them by new elections, when the occasions or exigencies of the public require the amendment of old or making of new laws, or the redress or prevention of any inconveniences that lie on or threaten the people.

155. It may be demanded here, what if the executive power, being possessed of the force of the commonwealth, shall make use of that force to hinder the meeting and acting of the legislative, when the original constitution or the public exigencies require it? I say using force upon the people without authority, and contrary to the trust put in him that does so, is a state of war with the people who have a right to reinstate their legislative in the exercise

of their power; for having erected a legislative with an intent they should exercise the power of making laws, either at certain set times or when there is need of it, when they are hindered by any force from what is so necessary to the society, and wherein the safety and preservation of the people consists, the people have a right to remove it by force. In all states and conditions, the true remedy of force without authority is to oppose force to it. The use of force without authority always puts him that uses it into a state of war, as the aggressor, and renders him liable to be treated accordingly.

156. The power of assembling and dismissing the legislative, placed in the executive, gives not the executive a superiority over it, but is a fiduciary trust placed in him for the safety of the people, in a case where the uncertainty and variableness of human affairs could not bear a steady fixed rule; for it not being possible that the first framers of the government should, by any foresight, be so much masters of future events as to be able to prefix so just periods of return and duration to the assemblies of the legislative, in all times to come, that might exactly answer all the exigencies of the commonwealth, the best remedy could be found for this defect was to trust this to the prudence of one who was always to be present and whose business it was to watch over the public good. Constant, frequent meetings of the legislative, and long continuations of their assemblies without necessary occasion, could not but be burdensome to the people and must necessarily in time produce more dangerous inconveniences, and yet the quick turn of affairs might be sometimes such as to need their present help. Any delay of their convening might endanger the public; and sometimes, too, their business might be so great that the limited time of their sitting might be too short for their work, and rob the public of that benefit which could be had only from their mature deliberation. What then could be done in this case to prevent the community from being exposed, some time or other, to eminent hazard, on one side or the other, by fixed intervals and periods set to the meeting and acting of the legislative, but to entrust it to the prudence of some who, being present and acquainted with the state of public affairs, might make use of this prerogative for the

public good? And where else could this be so well placed as in his hands who was entrusted with the execution of the laws for the same end? Thus supposing the regulation of times for the assembling and sitting of the legislative not settled by the original constitution, it naturally fell into the hands of the executive, not as an arbitrary power depending on his good pleasure but with this trust always to have it exercised only for the public weal, as the occurrences of times and change of affairs might require. Whether settled periods of their convening, or a liberty left to the prince for convoking the legislative, or perhaps a mixture of both, has the least inconvenience attending it, it is not my business here to inquire; but only to show that though the executive power may have the prerogative of convoking and dissolving such conventions of the legislative, yet it is not thereby superior to it.

157. Things of this world are in so constant a flux that nothing remains long in the same state. Thus people, riches, trade, power change their stations, flourishing mighty cities come to ruin and prove in time neglected, desolate corners, while other unfrequented places grow into populous countries, filled with wealth and inhabitants. But things not always changing equally, and private interest often keeping up customs and privileges when the reasons of them are ceased, it often comes to pass that in governments where part of the legislative consists of representatives chosen by the people, that in tract of time this representation becomes very unequal and disproportionate to the reasons it was at first established upon. To what gross absurdities the following of custom when reason has left it may lead, we may be satisfied when we see the bare name of a town of which there remains not so much as the ruins, where scarce so much housing as a sheepcote or more inhabitants than a shepherd is to be found, sends as many representatives to the grand assembly of lawmakers as a whole county numerous in people and powerful in riches. This strangers stand amazed at, and everyone must confess needs a remedy; though most think it hard to find one, because the constitution of the legislative being the original and supreme act of the society, antecedent to all positive laws in it and depending wholly on the people, no inferior power can alter it. And, therefore, the people,

when the legislative is once constituted, having in such a government as we have been speaking of no power to act as long as the government stands, this inconvenience is thought incapable of a remedy.

158. *Salus populi suprema lex* is certainly so just and fundamental a rule that he who sincerely follows it cannot dangerously err. If, therefore, the executive who has the power of convoking the legislative, observing rather the true proportion than fashion of representation, regulates, not by old custom but true reason, the number of members in all places that have a right to be distinctly represented—which no part of the people, however incorporated, can pretend to but in proportion to the assistance which it affords to the public—it cannot be judged to have set up a new legislative but to have restored the old and true one, and to have rectified the disorders which succession of time had insensibly as well as inevitably introduced. For it being the interest as well as intention of the people to have a fair and equal representative, whoever brings it nearest to that is an undoubted friend to and establisher of the government and cannot miss the consent and approbation of the community. Prerogative being nothing but a power in the hands of the prince to provide for the public good in such cases which, depending upon unforeseen and uncertain occurrences, certain and unalterable laws could not safely direct, whatsoever shall be done manifestly for the good of the people and the establishing the government upon its true foundations is, and always will be, just prerogative. The power of erecting new corporations, and therewith new representatives, carries with it a supposition that in time the measures of representation might vary, and those places have a just right to be represented which before had none; and by the same reason those cease to have a right and be too inconsiderable for such a privilege, which before had it. It is not a change from the present state, which perhaps corruption or decay has introduced, that makes an inroad upon the government, but the tendency of it to injure or oppress the people, and to set up one part or party with a distinction from, and an unequal subjection of, the rest. Whatsoever cannot but be acknowledged to be of advantage to the society and people in gen-

eral, upon just and lasting measures, will always, when done, justify itself; and whenever the people shall choose their representatives upon just and undeniably equal measures, suitable to the original frame of the government, it cannot be doubted to be the will and act of the society, whoever permitted or caused them so to do.

CHAPTER XIV

OF PREROGATIVE

159. WHERE the legislative and executive power are in distinct hands—as they are in all moderated monarchies and well-framed governments—there the good of the society requires that several things should be left to the discretion of him that has the executive power; for the legislators not being able to foresee and provide by laws for all that may be useful to the community, the executor of the laws, having the power in his hands, has by the common law of nature a right to make use of it for the good of the society, in many cases where the municipal law has given no direction, till the legislative can conveniently be assembled to provide for it. Many things there are which the law can by no means provide for; and those must necessarily be left to the discretion of him that has the executive power in his hands, to be ordered by him as the public good and advantage shall require; nay, it is fit that the laws themselves should in some cases give way to the executive power, or rather to this fundamental law of nature and government, viz., that, as much as may be, all the members of the society are to be preserved; for since many accidents may happen wherein a strict and rigid observation of the laws may do harm—as not to pull down an innocent man's house to stop the fire when the next to it is burning—and a man may come sometimes within the reach of the law, which makes no distinction of persons, by an action that may deserve reward and pardon, it is fit the ruler should have a power in many cases to mitigate the severity of the law and pardon some offenders; for the end of gov-

ernment being the preservation of all as much as may be, even the guilty are to be spared where it can prove no prejudice to the innocent.

160. This power to act according to discretion for the public good, without the prescription of the law and sometimes even against it, is that which is called 'prerogative'; for since in some governments the lawmaking power is not always in being, and is usually too numerous and so too slow for the dispatch requisite to execution, and because also it is impossible to foresee, and so by laws to provide for, all accidents and necessities that may concern the public, or to make such laws as will do no harm if they are executed with an inflexible rigor on all occasions and upon all persons that may come in their way, therefore there is a latitude left to the executive power to do many things of choice which the laws do not prescribe.

161. This power, while employed for the benefit of the community and suitably to the trust and ends of the government, is undoubted prerogative, and never is questioned; for the people are very seldom or never scrupulous or nice in the point; they are far from examining prerogative while it is in any tolerable degree employed for the use it was meant, that is, for the good of the people, and not manifestly against it. But if there comes to be a question between the executive power and the people about a thing claimed as a prerogative, the tendency of the exercise of such prerogative to the good or hurt of the people will easily decide that question.

162. It is easy to conceive that in the infancy of governments, when commonwealths differed little from families in number of people, they differed from them too but little in number of laws; and the governors, being as the fathers of them, watching over them for their good, the government was almost all prerogative. A few established laws served the turn, and the discretion and care of the ruler supplied the rest. But when mistake or flattery prevailed with weak princes to make use of this power for private ends of their own and not for the public good, the people were fain by express laws to get prerogative determined in those points wherein they found disadvantage from it; and thus declared limi-

tations of prerogative were by the people found necessary in cases which they and their ancestors had left in the utmost latitude to the wisdom of those princes who made no other but a right use of it, that is, for the good of their people.

163. And therefore they have a very wrong notion of government who say that the people have encroached upon the prerogative when they have got any part of it to be defined by positive laws; for in so doing they have not pulled from the prince anything that of right belonged to him, but only declare that that power which they indefinitely left in his or his ancestors hands to be exercised for their good was not a thing which they intended him when he used it otherwise. For the end of government being the good of the community, whatsoever alterations are made in it tending to that end cannot be an encroachment upon anybody, since nobody in government can have a right tending to any other end; and those only are encroachments which prejudice or hinder the public good. Those who say otherwise speak as if the prince had a distinct and separate interest from the good of the community and was not made for it—the root and source from which spring almost all those evils and disorders which happen in kingly governments. And, indeed, if that be so, the people under his government are not a society of rational creatures entered into a community for their mutual good, they are not such as have set rulers over themselves to guard and promote that good; but are to be looked on as a herd of inferior creatures under the dominion of a master who keeps them and works them for his own pleasure or profit. If men were so void of reason and brutish as to enter into society upon such terms, prerogative might indeed be what some men would have it: an arbitrary power to do things hurtful to the people.

164. But since a rational creature cannot be supposed, when free, to put himself into subjection to another for his own harm—though, where he finds a good and wise ruler, he may not perhaps think it either necessary or useful to set precise bounds to his power in all things—prerogative can be nothing but the people's permitting their rulers to do several things of their own free choice where the law was silent, and sometimes, too, against the direct

letter of the law, for the public good, and their acquiescing in it when so done. For as a good prince who is mindful of the trust put into his hands and careful of the good of his people cannot have too much prerogative, that is, power to do good, so a weak and ill prince, who would claim that power which his predecessors exercised without the direction of the law as a prerogative belonging to him by right of his office, which he may exercise at his pleasure to make or promote an interest distinct from that of the public, gives the people an occasion to claim their right, and limit that power which, while it was exercised for their good, they were content should be tacitly allowed.

165. And, therefore, he that will look into the history of England will find that prerogative was always largest in the hands of our wisest and best princes, because the people, observing the whole tendency of their actions to be the public good, contested not what was done without law to that end, or, if any human frailty or mistake—for princes are but men, made as others—appeared in some small declinations from that end, yet it was visible the main of their conduct tended to nothing but the care of the public. The people, therefore, finding reason to be satisfied with these princes whenever they acted without or contrary to the letter of the law, acquiesced in what they did, and without the least complaint let them enlarge their prerogative as they pleased, judging rightly that they did nothing herein to the prejudice of their laws since they acted conformably to the foundation and end of all laws—the public good.

166. Such godlike princes, indeed, had some title to arbitrary power by that argument that would prove absolute monarchy the best government, as that which God himself governs the universe by, because such kings partook of his wisdom and goodness. Upon this is founded that saying that the reigns of good princes have been always most dangerous to the liberties of their people; for when their successors, managing the government with different thoughts, would draw the actions of those good rulers into precedent and make them the standard of their prerogative, as if what had been done only for the good of the people was a right in them to do for the harm of the people if they so pleased, it has often

occasioned contest, and sometimes public disorders, before the people could recover their original right and get that to be declared not to be prerogative which truly was never so, since it is impossible that anybody in the society should ever have a right to do the people harm, though it be very possible and reasonable that the people should not go about to set any bounds to the prerogative of those kings or rulers who themselves transgressed not the bounds of the public good; for *prerogative is nothing but the power of doing public good without a rule.*

167. The power of calling parliaments in England, as to precise time, place, and duration, is certainly a prerogative of the king, but still with this trust that it shall be made use of for the good of the nation, as the exigencies of the times and variety of occasions shall require; for it being impossible to foresee which should always be the fittest place for them to assemble in, and what the best season, the choice of these was left with the executive power, as might be most subservient to the public good, and best suit the ends of parliaments.

168. The old question will be asked in this matter of prerogative: But who shall be judge when this power is made a right use of? I answer: Between an executive power in being with such a prerogative, and a legislative that depends upon his will for their convening, there can be no judge on earth; as there can be none between the legislative and the people, should either the executive or the legislative, when they have got the power in their hands, design or go about to enslave or destroy them. The people have no other remedy in this, as in all other cases where they have no judge on earth, but to appeal to heaven; for the rulers, in such attempts, exercising a power the people never put into their hands —who can never be supposed to consent that anybody should rule over them for their harm—do that which they have not a right to do. And where the body of the people, or any single man, is deprived of their right, or is under the exercise of a power without right and have no appeal on earth, then they have a liberty to appeal to heaven whenever they judge the cause of sufficient moment. And, therefore, though the people cannot be judge so as to have by the constitution of that society any superior power to

determine and give effective sentence in the case, yet they have, by a law antecedent and paramount to all positive laws of men, reserved that ultimate determination to themselves which belongs to all mankind, where there lies no appeal on earth—viz., to judge whether they have just cause to make their appeal to heaven. And this judgment they cannot part with, it being out of a man's power so to submit himself to another as to give him a liberty to destroy him, God and nature never allowing a man so to abandon himself as to neglect his own preservation; and since he cannot take away his own life, neither can he give another power to take it. Nor let anyone think this lays a perpetual foundation for disorder; for this operates not till the inconvenience is so great that the majority feel it and are weary of it and find a necessity to have it amended. But this the executive power, or wise princes, never need come in the danger of; and it is the thing, of all others, they have most need to avoid, as of all others the most perilous.

CHAPTER XV

OF PATERNAL, POLITICAL, AND DESPOTICAL
POWER CONSIDERED TOGETHER

169. THOUGH I have had occasion to speak of these separately before, yet the great mistakes of late about government having, as I suppose, arisen from confounding these distinct powers one with another, it may not, perhaps, be amiss to consider them here together.

170. First, then, paternal or parental power is nothing but that which parents have over their children to govern them for the children's good till they come to the use of reason or a state of knowledge wherein they may be supposed capable to understand that rule, whether it be the law of nature or the municipal law of their country, they are to govern themselves by—capable, I say, to know it as well as several others who live as freemen under that law. The affection and tenderness which God has planted in the

breast of parents toward their children makes it evident that this is not intended to be a severe arbitrary government, but only for the help, instruction, and preservation of their offspring. But happen it as it will, there is, as I have proved, no reason why it should be thought to extend to life and death at any time over their children more than over anybody else; neither can there be any pretense why this parental power should keep the child, when grown to a man, in subjection to the will of his parents any further than having received life and education from his parents obliges him to respect, honor, gratitude, assistance, and support all his life to both father and mother. And thus, it is true, the paternal is a natural government, but not at all extending itself to the ends and jurisdictions of that which is political. The power of the father does not reach at all to the property of the child, which is only in his own disposing.

171. Secondly, political power is that power which every man having in the state of nature has given up into the hands of the society and therein to the governors whom the society has set over itself, with this express or tacit trust that it shall be employed for their good and the preservation of their property. Now this power which every man has in the state of nature, and which he parts with to the society in all such cases where the society can secure him, is to use such means for the preserving of his own property as he thinks good and nature allows him, and to punish the breach of the law of nature in others so as, according to the best of his reason, may most conduce to the preservation of himself and the rest of mankind. So that the end and measure of this power, when in every man's hands in the state of nature, being the preservation of all of his society—that is, all mankind in general—it can have no other end or measure when in the hands of the magistrate but to preserve the members of that society in their lives, liberties, and possessions; and so cannot be an absolute arbitrary power over their lives and fortunes, which are as much as possible to be preserved, but a power to make laws, and annex such penalties to them as may tend to the preservation of the whole, by cutting off those parts, and those only, which are so corrupt that they threaten the sound and healthy, without which no severity is

lawful. And this power has its original only from compact and agreement, and the mutual consent of those who make up the community.

172. Thirdly, despotical power is an absolute, arbitrary power one man has over another to take away his life whenever he pleases. This is a power which neither nature gives—for it has made no such distinction between one man and another—nor compact can convey, for man, not having such an arbitrary power over his own life, cannot give another man such a power over it; but it is the effect only of forfeiture which the aggressor makes of his own life when he puts himself into the state of war with another. For having quitted reason, which God has given to be the rule betwixt man and man and the common bond whereby human kind is united into one fellowship and society; and having renounced the way of peace which that teaches, and made use of the force of war to compass his unjust ends upon another where he has no right, and so revolting from his own kind to that of beasts by making force, which is theirs, to be his rule of right; he renders himself liable to be destroyed by the injured person and the rest of mankind that will join with him in the execution of justice, as any other wild beast or noxious brute with whom mankind can have neither society nor security. And thus captives, taken in a just and lawful war, and such only, are subject to a despotical power, which, as it arises not from compact, so neither is it capable of any, but is the state of war continued; for what compact can be made with a man that is not master of his own life? What condition can he perform? And if he be once allowed to be master of his own life, the despotical arbitrary power of his master ceases. He that is master of himself and his own life has a right, too, to the means of preserving it; so that, as soon as compact enters, slavery ceases, and he so far quits his absolute power and puts an end to the state of war who enters into conditions with his captive.

173. Nature gives the first of these, viz., paternal power, to parents for the benefit of their children during their minority, to supply their want of ability and understanding how to manage their property. By property I must be understood here, as in other places, to mean that property which men have in their persons as

well as goods. Voluntary agreement gives the second, viz., political power, to governors for the benefit of·their subjects, to secure them in the possession and use of their properties. And forfeiture gives the third despotical power to lords, for their own benefit, over those who are stripped of all property.

174. He that shall consider the distinct rise and extent, and the different ends of these several powers, will plainly see that paternal power comes as far short of that of the magistrate as despotical exceeds it; and that absolute dominion, however placed, is so far from being one kind of civil society that it is as inconsistent with it as slavery is with property. Paternal power is only where minority makes the child incapable to manage his property; political, where men have property in their own disposal; and despotical, over such as have no property at all.

CHAPTER XVI

OF CONQUEST

175. THOUGH governments can originally have no other rise than that before-mentioned, nor politics be founded on anything but the consent of the people, yet such have been the disorders ambition has filled the world with, that in the noise of war, which makes so great a part of the history of mankind, this consent is little taken notice of; and therefore many have mistaken the force of arms for the consent of the people, and reckon conquest as one of the originals of government. But conquest is as far from setting up any government as demolishing a house is from building a new one in the place. Indeed, it often makes way for a new frame of a commonwealth by destroying the former, but, without the consent of the people, can never erect a new one.

176. That the aggressor who puts himself into the state of war with another and unjustly invades another man's right can, by such an unjust war, never come to have a right over the conquered, will be easily agreed by all men who will not think that

robbers and pirates have a right of empire over whomsoever they have force enough to master, or that men are bound by promises which unlawful force extorts from them. Should a robber break into my house and with a dagger at my throat make me seal deeds to convey my estate to him, would this give him any title? Just such a title, by his sword, has an unjust conqueror who forces me into submission. The injury and the crime are equal, whether committed by the wearer of the crown or some petty villain. The title of the offender and the number of his followers make no difference in the offense, unless it be to aggravate it. The only difference is, great robbers punish little ones to keep them in their obedience, but the great ones are rewarded with laurels and triumphs, because they are too big for the weak hands of justice in this world and have the power in their own possession which should punish offenders. What is my remedy against a robber that so broke into my house? Appeal to the law for justice. But perhaps justice is denied, or I am crippled and cannot stir, robbed and have not the means to do it. If God has taken away all means of seeking remedy, there is nothing left but patience. But my son, when able, may seek the relief of the law which I am denied; he or his son may renew his appeal till he recover his right. But the conquered, or their children, have no court, no arbitrator on earth to appeal to. Then they may appeal, as Jephthah did, to heaven, and repeat their appeal till they have recovered the native right of their ancestors, which was to have such a legislative over them as the majority should approve and freely acquiesce in. If it be objected this would cause endless trouble, I answer, no more than justice does, where she lies open to all that appeal to her. He that troubles his neighbor without a cause is punished for it by the justice of the court he appeals to; and he that appeals to heaven must be sure he has right on his side, and a right, too, that is worth the trouble and cost of the appeal, as he will answer at a tribunal that cannot be deceived and will be sure to retribute to every one according to the mischiefs he has created to his fellow subjects, that is, any part of mankind. From whence it is plain that he that conquers in an unjust war can thereby have no title to the subjection and obedience of the conquered.

177. But supposing victory favors the right side, let us consider a conqueror in a lawful war, and see what power he gets, and over whom.

First, it is plain he gets no power by his conquest over those that conquered with him. They that fought on his side cannot suffer by the conquest, but must at least be as much freemen as they were before. And most commonly they serve upon terms and on conditions to share with their leader and enjoy a part of the spoil and other advantages that attended the conquering sword, or at least have a part of the subdued country bestowed upon them. And the conquering people are not, I' hope, to be slaves by conquest and wear their laurels only to show they are sacrifices to their leader's triumph. They that found absolute monarchy upon the title of the sword make their heroes, who are the founders of such monarchies, arrant 'draw-can-sirs,' and forget they had any officers and soldiers that fought on their side in the battles they won, or assisted them in the subduing, or shared in possessing, the countries they mastered. We are told by some that the English monarchy is founded in the Norman conquest and that our princes have thereby a title to absolute dominion; which, if it were true— as by the history it appears otherwise—and that William had a right to make war on this island, yet his dominion by conquest could reach no farther than to the Saxons and Britons that were then inhabitants of this country. The Normans that came with him and helped to conquer, and all descended from them, are freemen and no subjects by conquest; let that give what dominion it will. And if I, or anybody else, shall claim freedom as derived from them, it will be very hard to prove the contrary; and, it is plain, the law that has made no distinction between the one and the other intends not there should be any difference in their freedom or privileges.

178. But supposing, which seldom happens, that the conquerors and conquered never incorporate into one people under the same laws and freedom, let us see next what power a lawful conqueror has over the subdued: and that, I say, is purely despotical. He has an absolute power over the lives of those who by an unjust war have forfeited them, but not over the lives or fortunes of those

who engaged not in the war, nor over the possessions even of those who were actually engaged in it.

179. Secondly, I say, then, the conqueror gets no power but only over those who have actually assisted, concurred, or consented to that unjust force that is used against him; for the people having given to their governors no power to do an unjust thing, such as is to make an unjust war—for they never had such a power in themselves—they ought not to be charged as guilty of the violence and injustice that is committed in an unjust war any farther than they actually abet it, no more than they are to be thought guilty of any violence or oppression their governors should use upon the people themselves or any part of their fellow subjects, they having empowered them no more to the one than to the other. Conquerors, it is true, seldom trouble themselves to make the distinction, but they willingly permit the confusion of war to sweep all together; but yet this alters not the right, for the conqueror's power over the lives of the conquered being only because they have used force to do or maintain an injustice, he can have that power only over those who have concurred in that force. All the rest are innocent, and he has no more title over the people of that country who have done him no injury, and so have made no forfeiture of their lives, than he has over any other who, without any injuries or provocations, have lived upon fair terms with him.

180. Thirdly, the power a conqueror gets over those he overcomes in a just war is perfectly despotical. He has an absolute power over the lives of those who, by putting themselves in a state of war, have forfeited them, but he has not thereby a right and title to their possessions. This I doubt not but at first sight will seem a strange doctrine, it being so quite contrary to the practice of the world; there being nothing more familiar in speaking of the dominion of countries than to say such a one conquered it, as if conquest, without any more ado, conveyed a right of possession. But when we consider that the practice of the strong and powerful, how universal soever it may be, is seldom the rule of right, however it be one part of the subjection of the conquered not to

argue against the conditions cut out to them by the conquering sword.

181. Though in all war there be usually a complication of force and damage, and the aggressor seldom fails to harm the estate when he uses force against the persons of those he makes war upon, yet it is the use of force only that puts a man into the state of war; for whether by force he begins the injury or else having quietly and by fraud done the injury, he refuses to make reparation, and by force maintains it (which is the same thing as at first to have done it by force), it is the unjust use of force that makes the war; for he that breaks open my house and violently turns me out of doors, or, having peaceably got in, by force keeps me out, does in effect the same thing. Supposing we are in such a state that we have no common judge on earth whom I may appeal to, and to whom we are both obliged to submit—for of such I am now speaking—it is the unjust use of force, then, that puts a man into the state of war with another, and thereby he that is guilty of it makes a forfeiture of his life; for, quitting reason, which is the rule given between man and man, and using force, the way of beasts, he becomes liable to be destroyed by him he uses force against, as any savage ravenous beast that is dangerous to his being.

182. But because the miscarriages of the father are no faults of the children, and they may be rational and peaceable, notwithstanding the brutishness and injustice of the father, the father, by his miscarriages and violence, can forfeit but his own life, but involves not his children in his guilt or destruction. His goods, which nature that wills the preservation of all mankind as much as is possible has made to belong to the children to keep them from perishing, do still continue to belong to his children; for supposing them not to have joined in the war, either through infancy, absence, or choice, they have done nothing to forfeit them; nor has the conqueror any right to take them away, by the bare title of having subdued him that by force attempted his destruction, though, perhaps, he may have some right to them to repair the damages he has sustained by the war and the defense of his own right, which how far it reaches to the possessions of the conquered

we shall see by and by. So that he that by conquest has a right over a man's person to destroy him if he pleases has not thereby a right over his estate to possess and enjoy it; for it is the brutal force the aggressor has used that gives his adversary a right to take away his life and destroy him if he pleases, as a noxious creature, but it is damage sustained that alone gives him title to another man's goods. For, though I may kill a thief that sets on me in the highway, yet I may not, which seems less, take away his money and let him go; this would be robbery on my side. His force and the state of war he put himself in made him forfeit his life, but gave me no title to his goods. The right, then, of conquest extends only to the lives of those who joined in the war, not to their estates, but only in order to make reparation for the damages received and the charges of the war, and that, too, with reservation of the right of the innocent wife and children.

189. Let the conqueror have as much justice on his side as could be supposed, he has no right to seize more than the vanquished could forfeit; his life is at the victor's mercy, and his service and goods he may appropriate to make himself reparation; but he cannot take the goods of his wife and children; they, too, had a title to the goods he enjoyed, and their shares in the estate he possessed. For example, I in the state of nature—and all commonwealths are in the state of nature one with another—have injured another man, and, refusing to give satisfaction, it comes to a state of war wherein my defending by force what I had gotten unjustly makes me the aggressor. I am conquered; my life, it is true, as forfeit, is at mercy, but not my wife's and children's. They made not the war nor assisted in it. I could not forfeit their lives; they were not mine to forfeit. My wife had a share in my estate; that neither could I forfeit. And my children also, being born of me, had a right to be maintained out of my labor or substance. Here then is the case: the conqueror has a title to reparation for damages received, and the children have a title to their father's estate for their subsistence. For as to the wife's share, whether her own labor or compact gave her a title to it, it is plain her husband could not forfeit what was hers. What must be done in the case? I answer: the fundamental law of nature being that all, as much

as may be, should be preserved, it follows that if there be not enough fully to satisfy both, viz., for the conqueror's losses and children's maintenance, he that has, and to spare, must remit something of his full satisfaction and give way to the pressing and preferable title of those who are in danger to perish without it.

184. But supposing the charge and damages of the war are to be made up to the conqueror to the utmost farthing, and that the children of the vanquished, spoiled of all their father's goods, are to be left to starve and perish, yet the satisfying of what shall, on this score, be due to the conqueror will scarce give him a title to any country he shall conquer; for the damages of war can scarce amount to the value of any considerable tract of land, in any part of the world, where all the land is possessed and none lies waste. And if I have not taken away the conqueror's land, which, being vanquished, it is impossible I should, scarce any other spoil I have done him can amount to the value of mine, supposing it equally cultivated and of an extent anyway coming near what I had overrun of his. The destruction of a year's product or two—for it seldom reaches four or five—is the utmost spoil that usually can be done; for as to money, and such riches and treasure taken away, these are none of nature's goods, they have but a fantastical imaginary value; nature has put no such upon them. They are of no more account by her standard than the wampompeke [1] of the Americans to a European prince, or the silver money of Europe would have been formerly to an American. And five years' product is not worth the perpetual inheritance of land, where all is possessed and none remains waste, to be taken up by him that is disseized; which will be easily granted if one do but take away the imaginary value of money, the disproportion being more than between five and five hundred; though, at the same time, half a year's product is more worth than the inheritance, where, there being more land than the inhabitants possess and make use of, any one has liberty to make use of the waste; but there conquerors take little care to possess themselves of the lands of the vanquished. No damage, therefore, that men in the state of nature—as all princes and governments are in reference to one

[1] [Wampompeke: shells used as money by the North American Indians.]

another—suffer from one another can give a conqueror power to dispossess the posterity of the vanquished and turn them out of that inheritance which ought to be the possession of them and their descendants to all generations. The conqueror, indeed, will be apt to think himself master, and it is the very condition of the subdued not to be able to dispute their right. But if that be all, it gives no other title than what bare force gives to the stronger over the weaker, and, by this reason, he that is strongest will have a right to whatever he pleases to seize on.

185. Over those, then, that joined with him in the war, and over those of the subdued country that opposed him not, and the posterity even of those that did, the conqueror, even in a just war, has by his conquest no right of dominion; they are free from any subjection to him, and if their former government be dissolved, they are at liberty to begin and erect another to themselves.

186. The conqueror, it is true, usually, by the force he has over them, compels them, with a sword at their breasts, to stoop to his conditions and submit to such a government as he pleases to afford them; but the inquiry is, what right he has to do so? If it be said they submit by their own consent, then this allows their own consent to be necessary to give the conqueror a title to rule over them. It remains only to be considered whether promises extorted by force, without right, can be thought 'consent,' and how far they bind. To which I shall say they bind not at all, because whatsoever another gets from me by force I still retain the right of, and he is obliged presently to restore. He that forces my horse from me ought presently to restore him, and I have still a right to retake him. By the same reason, he that forced a promise from me ought presently to restore it, i.e., quit me of the obligations of it, or I may resume it myself, i.e., choose whether I will perform it; for the law of nature, laying an obligation on me only by the rules she prescribes, cannot oblige me by the violation of her rules: such is the extorting anything from me by force. Nor does it at all alter the case to say, "I gave my promise," no more than it excuses the force and passes the right when I put my hand in my pocket and deliver my purse myself to a thief who demands it with a pistol at my breast.

187. From all which it follows that the government of a conqueror, imposed by force on the subdued, against whom he had no right of war, or who joined not in the war against him where he had right, has no obligation upon them.

188. But let us suppose that all the men of that community, being all members of the same body politic, may be taken to have joined in that unjust war wherein they are subdued, and so their lives are at the mercy of the conqueror.

189. I say this concerns not their children who are in their minority; for since a father has not, in himself, a power over the life or liberty of his child, no act of his can possibly forfeit it. So that the children, whatever may have happened to the fathers, are freemen, and the absolute power of the conqueror reaches no farther than the persons of the men that were subdued by him, and dies with them; and should he govern them as slaves, subjected to his absolute arbitrary power, he has no such right or dominion over their children. He can have no power over them but by their own consent, whatever he may drive them to say or do; and he has no lawful authority while force, and not choice, compels them to submission.

190. Every man is born with a double right: first, a right of freedom to his person, which no other man has a power over, but the free disposal of it lies in himself; secondly, a right, before any other man, to inherit with his brethren his father's goods.

191. By the first of these, a man is naturally free from subjection to any government, though he be born in a place under its jurisdiction; but if he disclaim the lawful government of the country he was born in, he must also quit the right that belonged to him by the laws of it and the possessions there descending to him from his ancestors if it were a government made by their consent.

192. By the second, the inhabitants of any country who are descended and derive a title to their estates from those who are subdued and had a government forced upon them against their free consents retain a right to the possession of their ancestors, though they consent not freely to the government whose hard conditions were by force imposed on the possessors of that country;

for the first conqueror never having had a title to the land of that
country, the people who are the descendants of, or claim under,
those who were forced to submit to the yoke of a government by
constraint have always a right to shake it off and free themselves
from the usurpation or tyranny which the sword has brought in
upon them, till their rulers put them under such a frame of government as they willingly and of choice consent to. Who doubts
but the Grecian Christians, descendants of the ancient possessors
of that country, may justly cast off the Turkish yoke which they
have so long groaned under, whenever they have an opportunity
to do it? For no government can have a right to obedience from
a people who have not freely consented to it; which they can
never be supposed to do till either they are put in a full state of
liberty to choose their government and governors, or at least till
they have such standing laws to which they have by themselves
or their representatives given their free consent, and also till they
are allowed their due property, which is to to be proprietors of
what they have that nobody can take away any part of it without
their own consent, without which men under any government are
not in the state of freemen but are direct slaves under the force
of war.

193. But granting that the conqueror in a just war has a right
to the estates as well as power over the persons of the conquered,
which, it is plain, he has not, nothing of absolute power will follow from hence in the continuance of the government, because the
descendants of these being all freemen, if he grants them estates
and possessions to inhabit his country—without which it would
be worth nothing. Whatsoever he grants them they have, so far
as it is granted, property in. The nature whereof is that without
a man's own consent it cannot be taken from him.

. . 194. Their persons are free by a native right, and their properties, be they more or less, are their own and at their own dispose, and not at his; or else it is no property. Supposing the conqueror gives to one man a thousand acres, to him and his heirs
for ever; to another he lets a thousand acres for his life, under
the rent of £50 or £500 per annum, has not the one of these a
right to his thousand acres for ever, and the other during his life,

paying the said rent? And has not the tenant for life a property in all that he gets over and above his rent, by his labor and industry during the said term, supposing it to be double the rent? Can any one say the king, or conqueror, after his grant, may by his power of conqueror take away all or part of the land from the heirs of one, or from the other during his life, he paying the rent? Or can he take away from either the goods or money they have got upon the said land, at his pleasure? If he can, then all free and voluntary contracts cease and are void in the world. There needs nothing to dissolve them at any time but power enough; and all the grants and promises of men in power are but mockery and collusion; for can there be anything more ridiculous than to say: "I give you and yours this for ever," and that in the surest and most solemn way of conveyance can be devised, and yet it is to be understood that I have a right, if I please, to take it away from you again tomorrow?

195. I will not dispute now whether princes are exempt from the laws of their country, but this I am sure: they owe subjection to the laws of God and nature. Nobody, no power, can exempt them from the obligations of that eternal law. Those are so great and so strong in the case of promises that Omnipotence itself can be tied by them. Grants, promises, and oaths are bonds that hold the Almighty; whatever some flatterers say to princes of the world, who altogether, with all their people joined to them, are, in comparison of the great God, but as a drop of the bucket or a dust on the balance, inconsiderable, nothing!

196. The short of the case in conquest is this: the conqueror, if he have a just cause, has a despotical right over the persons of all that actually aided and concurred in the war against him, and a right to make up his damage and cost out of their labor and estates, so he injure not the right of any other. Over the rest of the people, if there were any that consented not to the war, and over the children of the captives themselves, or the possessions of either, he has no power; and so can have, by virtue of conquest, no lawful title himself to dominion over them, or derive it to his posterity; but is an aggressor if he attempts upon their properties and thereby puts himself in a state of war against them, and has

no better a right of principality, he, nor any of his successors, than Hingar or Hubba, the Danes, had here in England,[2] or Spartacus,[3] had he conquered Italy, would have had; which is to have their yoke cast off as soon as God shall give those under their subjection courage and opportunity to do it. Thus, notwithstanding whatever title the kings of Assyria had over Judah by the sword, God assisted Hezekiah to throw off the dominion of that conquering empire. "And the Lord was with Hezekiah, and he prospered; wherefore he went forth, and he rebelled against the King of Assyria, and served him not" (2 Kings, xviii. 7). Whence it is plain that shaking off a power which force, and not right, has set over any one, though it has the name of rebellion, yet is no offense before God but is that which he allows and countenances, though even promises and covenants, when obtained by force, have intervened; for it is very probable to any one that reads the story of Ahaz and Hezekiah attentively, that the Assyrians subdued Ahaz and deposed him, and made Hezekiah king in his father's lifetime; and that Hezekiah by agreement had done him homage and paid him tribute all this time.

CHAPTER XVII

OF USURPATION

197. As CONQUEST may be called a foreign usurpation, so usurpation is a kind of domestic conquest, with this difference, that a usurper can never have right on his side, it being no usurpation but where one is got into the possession of what another has right

---

[2] [Hingar and Hubba (today more commonly known as Hengist and Horsa): Two Jutish chieftains who, according to tradition, were hired by Celtish leaders to help them in their fight against the Picts and Scots, and who afterward decided to remain in the country and settled along the Thames.]

[3] [Spartacus (d. 71 B.C.): A Roman slave and gladiator who led the rebellion against Rome in the Servile War, 73–71 B.C. His army, largely composed of slaves, defeated four Roman armies. The army was finally destroyed by M. Licinius Crassus in two battles; Spartacus died in the second.]

to. This, so far as it is usurpation, is a change only of persons, but not of the forms and rules of the government; for if the usurper extend his power beyond what of right belonged to the lawful princes or governors of the commonwealth, it is tyranny added to usurpation.

198. In all lawful governments the designation of the persons who are to bear rule is as natural and necessary a part as the form of the government itself, and is that which had its establishment originally from the people.[1] Hence all commonwealths, with the form of government established, have rules also of appointing those who are to have any share in the public authority, and settled methods of conveying the right to them; for the anarchy is much alike to have no form of government at all, or to agree that it shall be monarchical but to appoint no way to know or design the person that shall have the power and be the monarch. Whoever gets into the exercise of any part of the power by other ways than what the laws of the community have prescribed has no right to be obeyed though the form of the commonwealth be still preserved, since he is not the person the laws have appointed and, consequently, not the person the people have consented to. Nor can such a usurper, or any deriving from him, ever have a title till the people are both at liberty to consent, and have actually consented to allow and confirm in him the power he has till then usurped.

[1] [Here the following passage has been deleted: "the anarchy being much alike to have no form of government at all, or to agree that it shall be monarchical, but to appoint no way to design the person that shall have the power and be the monarch."

The posthumous editions are the only ones in which this sentence appears twice in the same section. Earlier editions had the passage in the place where it now has been omitted and where it apparently had been left only by an editor's error when the correction was made.]

CHAPTER XVIII

OF TYRANNY

199. As USURPATION is the exercise of power which another has a right to, so tyranny is the exercise of power beyond right, which nobody can have a right to. And this is making use of the power any one has in his hands, not for the good of those who are under it, but for his own private separate advantage—when the governor, however entitled, makes not the law, but his will, the rule, and his commands and actions are not directed to the preservation of the properties of his people, but the satisfaction of his own ambition, revenge, covetousness, or any other irregular passion.

200. If one can doubt this to be truth or reason because it comes from the obscure hand of a subject, I hope the authority of a king will make it pass with him. King James the First, in his speech to the parliament, 1603, tells them thus:

I will ever prefer the weal of the public and of the whole commonwealth, in making of good laws and constitutions, to any particular and private ends of mine; thinking ever the wealth and weal of the commonwealth to be my greatest weal and worldly felicity—a point wherein a lawful king doth directly differ from a tyrant; for I do acknowledge that the special and greatest point of difference that is between a rightful king and an usurping tyrant is this: that whereas the proud and ambitious tyrant doth think his kingdom and people are only ordained for satisfaction of his desires and unreasonable appetites, the righteous and just king doth by the contrary acknowledge himself to be ordained for the procuring of the wealth and property of his people.

And again, in his speech to the parliament, 1609, he has these words:

The king binds himself by a double oath to the observation of the fundamental laws of his kingdom; tacitly, as by being a king, and so bound to protect as well the people as the laws of his kingdom; and expressly, by his oath at his coronation; so as every just king, in a settled kingdom, is bound to observe that paction made to his people by his laws in framing his government agreeable thereunto, according to that paction which God made with Noah after the deluge: Hereafter seedtime and harvest, and cold and heat, and summer and winter, and day and night shall not cease while the earth remaineth. And, therefore, a king governing in a settled kingdom leaves to be a king and degenerates into a tyrant, as soon as he leaves off to rule according to his laws.

And a little after:

Therefore, all kings that are not tyrants, or perjured, will be glad to bound themselves within the limits of their laws; and they that persuade them the contrary are vipers and pests, both against them and the commonwealth.

Thus that learned king, who well understood the notions of things, makes the difference betwixt a king and a tyrant to consist only in this: that one makes the laws the bounds of his power, and the good of the public the end of his government; the other makes all give way to his own will and appetite.[1]

201. It is a mistake to think this fault is proper only to monarchies; other forms of government are liable to it as well as that. For wherever the power that is put in any hands for the government of the people and the preservation of their properties is applied to other ends, and made use of to impoverish, harass, or subdue them to the arbitrary and irregular commands of those that have it, there it presently becomes tyranny, whether those that thus use it are one or many. Thus we read of the thirty

---

[1] [The passages quoted by Locke in support of his own point of view should not be taken to mean that James was subscribing to some kind of constitutional principle. Here, as in all his writings and speeches, James argues solely against arbitrary use of the king's power for his own benefit and not against the king's absolute power of making law. The statements here quoted must be interpreted in the light of his general position that the king is above the law, and his power over the land and his subjects absolute. "And as you see it manifest that the King is overlord of the whole land, so is he master over every person that inhabits the same, having power over the life and death of every one of them; for although a just Prince will not take the life of any of his subjects without a clear law, yet the same laws whereby he takes them are made by himself or his predecessors, and so the power flows always from himself." (*The True Law of Free Monarchies*, quoted, with modern spelling and punctuation, from McIlwain, ed: *The Political Works of James I*, p. 63.) Cf. also note 1. p. 74.]

tyrants at Athens,[2] as well as one at Syracuse; [3] and the intolerable dominion of the *decemviri* [4] at Rome was nothing better.

202. Wherever law ends, tyranny begins if the law be transgressed to another's harm. And whosoever in authority exceeds the power given him by the law, and makes use of the force he has under his command to compass that upon the subject which the law allows not, ceases in that to be a magistrate and, acting without authority, may be opposed as any other man who by force invades the right of another. This is acknowledged in subordinate magistrates. He that has authority to seize my person in the street may be opposed as a thief and a robber if he endeavors to break into my house to execute a writ, notwithstanding that I know he has such a warrant and such a legal authority as will empower him to arrest me abroad. And why this should not hold in the highest as well as in the most inferior magistrate, I would gladly be informed. Is it reasonable that the eldest brother, because he has the greatest part of his father's estate, should thereby have a right to take away any of his younger brother's portions? Or that a rich man who possessed a whole country should from thence have a right to seize, when he pleased, the cottage and garden of his poor neighbor? The being rightfully possessed of great power and riches, exceedingly beyond the greatest part of the sons of Adam, is so far from being an excuse, much less a reason, for

2 [The Thirty ruled Athens in 404/403 B.C. Originally elected, with the aid of Sparta, to draft a new constitution based on the ancestral constitution, they disregarded their assignment and abused their power, killing off their opponents and confiscating the fortunes of the victims. They were defeated by a democratic group after they had invited a Spartan garrison to protect them.]

3 [Reference not clear. Probably either Dionysius (430–367 B.C.) or Agathocles (361?–289 B.C.).]

4 [Decemviri: In 451 B.C. a commission of patrician decemvirs was given temporary dictatorship to codify and make public the law which hitherto had been subject to arbitrary interpretation by the (patrician) magistrates. The commission prepared ten tables which, together with two tables drawn up by a new commission of decemvirs appointed in the following year, formed the celebrated Law of the Twelve Tables. However, these laws favored the patricians and thus laid the legal ground for the century long struggle of the plebeians to gain political equality. The second commission tried to perpetuate itself in office but was forced by a threatening revolt of the plebeians to resign.]

rapine and oppression, which the endamaging another without authority is, that it is a great aggravation of it; for the exceeding the bounds of authority is no more a right in a great than in a petty officer, no more justifiable in a king than a constable; but is so much the worse in him in that he has more trust put in him, has already a much greater share than the rest of his brethren, and is supposed, from the advantages of his education, employment, and counselors, to be more knowing in the measures of right and wrong.

203. May the commands, then, of a prince be opposed? May he be resisted as often as any one shall find himself aggrieved, and but imagine he has not right done him? This will unhinge and overturn all polities, and, instead of government and order, leave nothing but anarchy and confusion.

204. To this I answer that force is to be opposed to nothing but to unjust and unlawful force; whoever makes any opposition in any other case draws on himself a just condemnation both from God and man; and so no such danger or confusion will follow, as is often suggested. For:

205. First, as in some countries, the person of the prince by the law is sacred; and so, whatever he commands or does, his person is still free from all question or violence, not liable to force or any judicial censure or condemnation. But yet opposition may be made to the illegal acts of any inferior officer or other commissioned by him, unless he will, by actually putting himself into a state of war with his people, dissolve the government, and leave them to that defense which belongs to everyone in the state of nature; for of such things who can tell what the end will be? And a neighbor kingdom has shown the world an odd example. In all other cases the sacredness of the person exempts him from all inconveniences, whereby he is secure, while the government stands, from all violence and harm whatsoever; than which there cannot be a wiser constitution, for the harm he can do in his own person not being likely to happen often nor to extend itself far, nor being able by his single strength to subvert the laws, nor oppose the body of the people. Should any prince have so much weakness and ill nature as to be willing to do it, the inconvenience of some particular mis-

chiefs that may happen sometimes, when a heady prince comes to the throne, are well recompensed by the peace of the public and security of the government in the person of the chief magistrate thus set out of the reach of danger; it being safer for the body that some few private men should be sometimes in danger to suffer than that the head of the republic should be easily and upon slight occasions exposed.

206. Secondly, but this privilege, belonging only to the king's person, hinders not but they may be questioned, opposed, and resisted who use unjust force, though they pretend a commission from him which the law authorizes not. As is plain in the case of him that has the king's writ to arrest a man, which is a full commission from the king, and yet he that has it cannot break open a man's house to do it, nor execute this command of the king upon certain days nor in certain places, though this commission have no such exception in it; but they are the limitations of the law, which, if any one transgress, the king's commission excuses him not; for the king's authority being given him only by the law, he cannot empower any one to act against the law, or justify him by his commission in so doing. The commission or command of any magistrate, where he has no authority, being as void and insignificant as that of any private man, the difference between the one and the other being that the magistrate has some authority so far and to such ends and the private man has none at all; for it is not the commission but the authority that gives the right of acting, and against the laws there can be no authority. But notwithstanding such resistance, the king's person and authority are still both secured, and so no danger to governor or government.

207 Thirdly, supposing a government wherein the person of the chief magistrate is not thus sacred, yet this doctrine of the lawfulness of resisting all unlawful exercises of his power will not upon every slight occasion endanger him or embroil the government; for where the injured party may be relieved and his damages repaired by appeal to the law, there can be no pretense for force, which is only to be used where a man is intercepted from appealing to the law; for nothing is to be accounted hostile force but where it leaves not the remedy of such an appeal, and it is such

force alone that puts him that uses it into a state of war, and makes it lawful to resist him. A man with a sword in his hand demands my purse in the highway, when perhaps I have not twelve pence in my pocket; this man I may lawfully kill. To another I deliver £100 to hold only while I alight, which he refuses to restore me when I am got up again, but draws his sword to defend the possession of it by force if I endeavor to retake it. The mischief this man does me is a hundred or possibly a thousand times more than the other perhaps intended me—whom I killed before he really did me any—and yet I might lawfully kill the one, and cannot so much as hurt the other lawfully. The reason whereof is plain: because the one using force, which threatened my life, I could not have time to appeal to the law to secure it, and when it was gone it was too late to appeal. The law could not restore life to my dead carcass—the loss was irreparable, which to prevent, the law of nature gave me a right to destroy him who had put himself into a state of war with me and threatened my destruction. But in the other case, my life not being in danger, I may have the benefit of appealing to the law, and have reparation for my £100 that way.

208. Fourthly, but if the unlawful acts done by the magistrate be maintained—by the power he has got—and the remedy which is due by law be by the same power obstructed, yet the right of resisting, even in such manifest acts of tyranny, will not suddenly or on slight occasions disturb the government; for if it reach no farther than some private men's cases, though they have a right to defend themselves and to recover by force what by unlawful force is taken from them, yet the right to do so will not easily engage them in a contest wherein they are sure to perish; it being as impossible for one or a few oppressed men to disturb the government, where the body of the people do not think themselves concerned in it, as for a raving madman or heady malcontent to overturn a well-settled state, the people being as little apt to follow the one as the other.

209. But if either these illegal acts have extended to the majority of the people, or if the mischief and oppression has lighted only on some few, but in such cases as the precedent and consequences

seem to threaten all, and they are persuaded in their consciences
that their laws, and with them their estates, liberties, and lives are
in danger, and perhaps their religion, too, how they will be
hindered from resisting illegal force used against them I cannot
tell. This is an inconvenience, I confess, that attends all governments whatsoever, when the governors have brought it to this pass
to be generally suspected of their people; the most dangerous state
which they can possibly put themselves in, wherein they are less
to be pitied, because it is so easy to be avoided; it being as impossible for a governor, if he really means the good of his people,
and the preservation of them and their laws together, not to make
them see and feel it, as it is for the father of a family not to let
his children see he loves and takes care of them.

210. But if all the world shall observe pretenses of one kind
and actions of another, arts used to elude the law, and the trust of
prerogative—which is an arbitrary power in some things left in
the prince's hand to do good, not harm to the people—employed
contrary to the end for which it was given; if the people shall
find the ministers and subordinate magistrates chosen suitable to
such ends, and favored or laid by proportionably as they promote
or oppose them; if they see several experiments made of arbitrary
power, and that religion underhand favored, though publicly pro-
claimed against, which is readiest to introduce it, and the operators
in it supported as much as may be, and when that cannot be done,
yet approved still, and liked the better—if a long train of actions
show the councils all tending that way, how can a man any more
hinder himself from being persuaded in his own mind which way
things are going, or from casting about how to save himself, than
he could from believing the captain of the ship he was in was
carrying him and the rest of the company to Algiers, when he
found him always steering that course, though cross winds, leaks
in his ship, and want of men and provisions did often force him
to turn his course another way for some time, which he steadily
returned to again as soon as the wind, weather, and other circumstances would let him?

CHAPTER XIX

OF THE DISSOLUTION OF GOVERNMENT

211. HE THAT will with any clearness speak of the dissolution of government ought in the first place to distinguish between the dissolution of the society and the dissolution of the government. That which makes the community and brings men out of the loose state of nature into one politic society is the agreement which everybody has with the rest to incorporate and act as one body, and so be one distinct commonwealth. The usual and almost only way whereby this union is dissolved is the inroad of foreign force making a conquest upon them; for in that case, not being able to maintain and support themselves as one entire and independent body, the union belonging to that body which consisted therein must necessarily cease, and so every one return to the state he was in before, with a liberty to shift for himself and provide for his own safety, as he thinks fit, in some other society. Whenever the society is dissolved, it is certain the government of that society cannot remain. Thus conquerors' swords often cut up governments by the roots and mangle societies to pieces, separating the subdued or scattered multitude from the protection of and dependence on that society which ought to have preserved them from violence. The world is too well instructed in, and too forward to allow of, this way of dissolving of governments to need any more to be said of it; and there wants not much argument to prove that where the society is dissolved, the government cannot remain—that being as impossible as for the frame of a house to subsist when the materials of it are scattered and dissipated by a whirlwind, or jumbled into a confused heap by an earthquake.

212. Besides this overturning from without, governments are dissolved from within.

First, when the legislative is altered. Civil society being a state of peace amongst those who are of it, from whom the state of war is excluded by the umpirage which they have provided in their legislative for the ending all differences that may arise amongst any of them, it is in their legislative that the members of a commonwealth are united and combined together into one coherent living body. This is the soul that gives form, life, and unity to the commonwealth; from hence the several members have their mutual influence, sympathy, and connection; and, therefore, when the legislative is broken or dissolved, dissolution and death follows; for the essence and union of the society consisting in having one will, the legislative, when once established by the majority, has the declaring and, as it were, keeping of that will. The constitution of the legislative is the first and fundamental act of society, whereby provision is made for the continuation of their union under the direction of persons and bonds of laws made by persons authorized thereunto by the consent and appointment of the people, without which no one man or number of men amongst them can have authority of making laws that shall be binding to the rest. When any one or more shall take upon them to make laws, whom the people have not appointed so to do, they make laws without authority, which the people are not therefore bound to obey; by which means they come again to be out of subjection and may constitute to themselves a new legislative as they think best, being in full liberty to resist the force of those who without authority would impose anything upon them. Everyone is at the disposure of his own will when those who had by the delegation of the society the declaring of the public will are excluded from it, and others usurp the place who have no such authority or delegation.

213. This being usually brought about by such in the commonwealth who misuse the power they have, it is hard to consider it aright, and know at whose door to lay it, without knowing the form of government in which it happens. Let us suppose then the legislative placed in the concurrence of three distinct persons:

(1) A single hereditary person having the constant supreme executive power, and with it the power of convoking and dissolving the other two within certain periods of time.

(2) An assembly of hereditary nobility.

(3) An assembly of representatives chosen *pro tempore* by the people. Such a form of government supposed, it is evident,

214. First, that when such a single person or prince sets up his own arbitrary will in place of the laws which are the will of the society declared by the legislative, then the legislative is changed; for that being in effect the legislative whose rules and laws are put in execution and required to be obeyed. When other laws are set up, and other rules pretended and enforced than what the legislative constituted by the society have enacted, it is plain that the legislative is changed. Whoever introduces new laws, not being thereunto authorized by the fundamental appointment of the society, or subverts the old, disowns and overturns the power by which they were made, and so sets up a new legislative.

215. Secondly, when the prince hinders the legislative from assembling in its due time, or from acting freely pursuant to those ends for which it was constituted, the legislative is altered; for it is not a certain number of men, no, nor their meeting, unless they have also freedom of debating and leisure of perfecting what is for the good of the society, wherein the legislative consists. When these are taken away or altered so as to deprive the society of the due exercise of their power, the legislative is truly altered; for it is not names that constitute governments but the use and exercise of those powers that were intended to accompany them, so that he who takes away the freedom or hinders the acting of the legislative in its due seasons in effect takes away the legislative and puts an end to the government.

216. Thirdly, when, by the arbitrary power of the prince, the electors or ways of election are altered without the consent and contrary to the common interest of the people, there also the legislative is altered; for if others than those whom the society has authorized thereunto do choose, or in another way than what the society has prescribed, those chosen are not the legislative appointed by the people.

217. Fourthly, the delivery also of the people into the subjection of a foreign power, either by the prince or by the legislative, is certainly a change of the legislative, and so a dissolution of the government; for the end why people entered into society being to

be preserved one entire, free, independent society, to be governed by its own laws, this is lost whenever they are given up into the power of another.

218. Why in such a constitution as this the dissolution of the government in these cases is to be imputed to the prince is evident. Because he, having the force, treasure, and offices of the state to employ, and often persuading himself, or being flattered by others, that as supreme magistrate he is incapable of control—he alone is in a condition to make great advances toward such changes, under pretense of lawful authority, and has it in his hands to terrify or suppress opposers as factious, seditious, and enemies to the government. Whereas no other part of the legislative or people is capable by themselves to attempt any alteration of the legislative, without open and visible rebellion apt enough to be taken notice of, which, when it prevails, produces effects very little different from foreign conquest. Besides, the prince in such a form of government having the power of dissolving the other parts of the legislative, and thereby rendering them private persons, they can never in opposition to him or without his concurrence alter the legislative by a law, his consent being necessary to give any of their decrees that sanction. But yet, so far as the other parts of the legislative in any way contribute to any attempt upon the government, and do either promote or not, what lies in them, hinder such designs, they are guilty and partake in this, which is certainly the greatest crime men can be guilty of one toward another.

219. There is one way more whereby such a government may be dissolved, and that is when he who has the supreme executive power neglects and abandons that charge, so that the laws already made can no longer be put in execution. This is demonstratively to reduce all to anarchy, and so effectually to dissolve the government; for laws not being made for themselves, but to be by their execution the bonds of the society, to keep every part of the body politic in its due place and function, when that totally ceases, the government visibly ceases, and the people become a confused multitude, without order or connection. Where there is no longer the administration of justice for the securing of men's

rights, nor any remaining power within the community to direct the force to provide for the necessities of the public, there certainly is no government left. Where the laws cannot be executed, it is all one as if there were no laws; and a government without laws is, I suppose, a mystery in politics, inconceivable to human capacity and inconsistent with human society.

220. In these and the like cases, when the government is dissolved, the people are at liberty to provide for themselves by erecting a new legislative, differing from the other by the change of persons or form, or both, as they shall find it most for their safety and good; for the society can never by the fault of another lose the native and original right it has to preserve itself, which can only be done by a settled legislative, and a fair and impartial execution of the laws made by it. But the state of mankind is not so miserable that they are not capable of using this remedy till it be too late to look for any. To tell people they may provide for themselves by erecting a new legislative, when by oppression, artifice, or being delivered over to a foreign power, their old one is gone, is only to tell them they may expect relief when it is too late and the evil is past cure. This is in effect no more than to bid them first be slaves, and then to take care of their liberty; and when their chains are on, tell them they may act like freemen. This, if barely so, is rather mockery than relief, and men can never be secure from tyranny if there be no means to escape it till they are perfectly under it; and therefore it is that they have not only a right to get out of it, but to prevent it.

221. There is, therefore, secondly, another way whereby governments are dissolved, and that is when the legislative or the prince, either of them, act contrary to their trust.

First, the legislative acts against the trust reposed in them when they endeavor to invade the property of the subject, and to make themselves or any part of the community masters or arbitrary disposers of the lives, liberties, or fortunes of the people.

222. The reason why men enter into society is the preservation of their property; and the end why they choose and authorize a legislative is that there may be laws made and rules set as guards and fences to the properties of all the members of the society to

limit the power and moderate the dominion of every part and member of the society; for since it can never be supposed to be the will of the society that the legislative should have a power to destroy that which every one designs to secure by entering into society, and for which the people submitted themselves to legislators of their own making. Whenever the legislators endeavor to take away and destroy the property of the people, or to reduce them to slavery under arbitrary power, they put themselves into a state of war with the people who are thereupon absolved from any further obedience, and are left to the common refuge which God has provided for all men against force and violence. Whensoever, therefore, the legislative shall transgress this fundamental rule of society, and either by ambition, fear, folly, or corruption, endeavor to grasp themselves, or put into the hands of any other, an absolute power over the lives, liberties, and estates of the people, by this breach of trust they forfeit the power the people had put into their hands for quite contrary ends, and it devolves to the people, who have a right to resume their original liberty and, by the establishment of a new legislative, such as they shall think fit, provide for their own safety and security, which is the end for which they are in society. What I have said here concerning the legislative in general holds true also concerning the supreme executor, who having a double trust put in him—both to have a part in the legislative and the supreme execution of the law—acts against both when he goes about to set up his own arbitrary will as the law of the society. He acts also contrary to his trust when he either employs the force, treasure, and offices of the society to corrupt the representatives and gain them to his purposes, or openly pre-engages the electors and prescribes to their choice such whom he has by solicitations, threats, promises, or otherwise won to his designs, and employs them to bring in such who have promised beforehand what to vote and what to enact. Thus to regulate candidates and electors, and new-model the ways of election, what is it but to cut up the government by the roots, and poison the very fountain of public security? For the people, having reserved to themselves the choice of their representatives, as the fence to their properties, could do it for no other end but that they might always be freely chosen, and, so chosen, freely act and advise as the necessity of the commonwealth and the public good should upon examination and mature debate be judged to require. This those who give their votes before they hear the debate and have weighed the reasons on all sides are not capable of doing. To prepare such an assembly as this, and endeavor to set up the declared abettors of his own will for the true representatives of the people and the lawmakers of the society, is certainly as great a breach of trust and as perfect a declaration of a design to subvert the government as is possible to be met with. To which if one shall add rewards and punishments visibly employed to the same end, and all the arts of perverted law made use of to take off and destroy all that stand in the way of such a design, and will not comply and consent to betray the liberties of their country, it will be past doubt what is doing. What power they ought to have in the society who thus employ it contrary to the trust that went along with it in its first institution is easy to determine; and one cannot but see that he who has once attempted any such thing as this cannot any longer be trusted.

223. To this perhaps it will be said that, the people being ignorant and always discontented, to lay the foundation of government in the unsteady opinion and uncertain humor of the people is to expose it to certain ruin; and no government will be able long to subsist if the people may set up a new legislative whenever they take offense at the old one. To this I answer: Quite the contrary. People are not so easily got out of their old forms as some are apt to suggest. They are hardly to be prevailed with to amend the acknowledged faults in the frame they have been accustomed to. And if there be any original defects, or adventitious ones introduced by time or corruption, it is not an easy thing to get them changed, even when all the world sees there is an opportunity for it. This slowness and aversion in the people to quit their old constitutions has in the many revolutions which have been seen in this kingdom, in this and former ages, still kept us to, or after some interval of fruitless attempts still brought us back again to, our old legislative of king, lords, and commons; and whatever provocations have made the crown be taken from some of our

princes' heads, they never carried the people so far as to place it in another line.

224. But it will be said this hypothesis lays a ferment for frequent rebellion. To which I answer:

First, no more than any other hypothesis; for when the people are made miserable, and find themselves exposed to the ill-usage of arbitrary power, cry up their governors as much as you will for sons of Jupiter, let them be sacred or divine, descended or authorized from heaven, give them out for whom or what you please, the same will happen. The people generally ill-treated, and contrary to right, will be ready upon any occasion to ease themselves of a burden that sits heavy upon them. They will wish and seek for the opportunity, which in the change, weakness, and accidents of human affairs seldom delays long to offer itself. He must have lived but a little while in the world who has not seen examples of this in his time, and he must have read very little who cannot produce examples of it in all sorts of governments in the world.

225. Secondly, I answer, such revolutions happen not upon every little mismanagement in public affairs. Great mistakes in the ruling part, many wrong and inconvenient laws, and all the slips of human frailty will be born by the people without mutiny or murmur. But if a long train of abuses, prevarications, and artifices, all tending the same way, make the design visible to the people, and they cannot but feel what they lie under and see whither they are going, it is not to be wondered that they should then rouse themselves and endeavor to put the rule into such hands which may secure to them the ends for which government was at first erected, and without which ancient names and specious forms are so far from being better that they are much worse than the state of nature or pure anarchy—the inconveniences being all as great and as near, but the remedy farther off and more difficult.

226. Thirdly, I answer that this doctrine of a power in the people of providing for their safety anew by a new legislative, when their legislators have acted contrary to their trust by invading their property, is the best fence against rebellion, and the probablest means to hinder it; for rebellion being an opposition, not to persons, but authority which is founded only in the consti-

tutions and laws of the government, those, whoever they be, who by force break through, and by force justify their violation of them, are truly and properly rebels; for when men, by entering into society and civil government, have excluded force and introduced laws for the preservation of property, peace, and unity amongst themselves, those who set up force again in opposition to the laws do *rebellare*—that is, bring back again the state of war —and are properly rebels; which they who are in power, by the pretense they have to authority, the temptation of force they have in their hands, and the flattery of those about them, being likeliest to do, the properest way to prevent the evil is to show them the danger and injustice of it who are under the greatest temptation to run into it.

227. In both the forementioned cases, when either the legislative is changed or the legislators act contrary to the end for which they were constituted, those who are guilty are guilty of rebellion; for if any one by force takes away the established legislative of any society, and the laws of them made pursuant to their trust, he thereby takes away the umpirage which every one had consented to for a peaceable decision of all their controversies, and a bar to the state of war amongst them. They who remove or change the legislative take away this decisive power which nobody can have but by the appointment and consent of the people, and so destroying the authority which the people did, and nobody else can, set up, and introducing a power which the people has not authorized, they actually introduce a state of war which is that of force without authority; and thus by removing the legislative established by the society—in whose decisions the people acquiesced and united as to that of their own will—they untie the knot and expose the people anew to the state of war. And if those who by force take away the legislative are rebels, the legislators themselves, as has been shown, can be no less esteemed so, when they who were set up for the protection and preservation of the people, their liberties and properties, shall by force invade and endeavor to take them away; and so they putting themselves into a state of war with those who made them the protectors and guardians of

their peace, are properly, and with the greatest aggravation, *rebellantes*, rebels.

228. But if they who say "it lays a foundation for rebellion" mean that it may occasion civil wars or intestine broils, to tell the people they are absolved from obedience when illegal attempts are made upon their liberties or properties, and may oppose the unlawful violence of those who were their magistrates when they invade their properties contrary to the trust put in them, and that therefore this doctrine is not to be allowed, being so destructive to the peace of the world; they may as well say, upon the same ground, that honest men may not oppose robbers or pirates because this may occasion disorder or bloodshed. If any mischief come in such cases, it is not to be charged upon him who defends his own right, but on him that invades his neighbor's. If the innocent honest man must quietly quit all he has, for peace's sake, to him who will lay violent hands upon it, I desire it may be considered what a kind of peace there will be in the world, which consists only in violence and rapine, and which is to be maintained only for the benefit of robbers and oppressors. Who would not think it an admirable peace betwixt the mighty and the mean when the lamb without resistance yielded his throat to be torn by the imperious wolf. Polyphemus' den gives us a perfect pattern of such a peace and such a government, wherein Ulysses and his companions had nothing to do but quietly to suffer themselves to be devoured. And no doubt Ulysses, who was a prudent man, preached up passive obedience, and exhorted them to a quiet submission by representing to them of what concernment peace was to mankind, and by showing the inconveniences which might happen if they should offer to resist Polyphemus, who had now the power over them.

229. The end of government is the good of mankind. And which is best for mankind? That the people should be always exposed to the boundless will of tyranny, or that the rulers should be sometimes liable to be opposed when they grow exorbitant in the use of their power and employ it for the destruction and not the preservation of the properties of their people?

230. Nor let any one say that mischief can arise from hence.

as often as it shall please a busy head or turbulent spirit to desire the alteration of the government. It is true such men may stir whenever they please, but it will be only to their own just ruin and perdition; for till the mischief be grown general, and the ill designs of the rulers become visible, or their attempts sensible to the greater part, the people, who are more disposed to suffer than right themselves by resistance, are not apt to stir. The examples of particular injustice or oppression of here and there an unfortunate man moves them not. But if they universally have a persuasion grounded upon manifest evidence that designs are carrying on against their liberties, and the general course and tendency of things cannot but give them strong suspicions of the evil intention of their governors, who is to be blamed for it? Who can help it if they who might avoid it bring themselves into this suspicion? Are the people to be blamed if they have the sense of rational creatures and can think of things no otherwise than as they find and feel them? And is it not rather their fault who put things into such a posture that they would not have them thought to be as they are? I grant that the pride, ambition, and turbulence of private men have sometimes caused great disorders in commonwealths, and factions have been fatal to states and kingdoms. But whether the mischief has oftener begun in the people's wantonness and a desire to cast off the lawful authority of their rulers, or in the rulers' insolence and endeavors to get and exercise an arbitrary power over their people—whether oppression or disobedience gave the first rise to the disorder, I leave it to impartial history to determine. This I am sure: whoever, either ruler or subject, by force goes about to invade the rights of either prince or people and lays the foundation for overturning the constitution and frame of any just government is highly guilty of the greatest crime I think a man is capable of—being to answer for all those mischiefs of blood, rapine, and desolation, which the breaking to pieces of governments bring on a country. And he who does it is justly to be esteemed the common enemy and pest of mankind, and is to be treated accordingly.

231. That subjects or foreigners attempting by force on the properties of any people may be resisted with force, is agreed on

all hands. But that magistrates doing the same thing may be resisted has of late been denied; as if those who had the greatest
privileges and advantages by the law had thereby a power to break
those laws by which alone they were set in a better place than
their brethren; whereas their offense is thereby the greater, both
as being ungrateful for the greater share they have by the law,
and breaking also that trust which is put into their hands by their
brethren.

232. Whosoever uses force without right, as every one does in
society who does it without law, puts himself into a state of war
with those against whom he so uses it; and in that state all former
ties are canceled, all other rights cease, and every one has a right
to defend himself and to resist the aggressor. This is so evident
that Barclay himself, that great assertor of the power and sacredness of kings, is forced to confess that it is lawful for the people in
some cases to resist their king; [1] and that, too, in a chapter wherein
he pretends to show that the divine law shuts up the people from
all manner of rebellion. Whereby it is evident, even by his own
doctrine, that, since they may in some cases resist, all resisting of
princes is not rebellion. His words are these:

Quod siquis dicat, Ergone populus tyrannicae crudelitati et
furori jugulum semper praebebit? Ergone multitudo civitates suas
fame, ferro, et flammâ vastari, seque, conjuges, et liberos fortunae
ludibrio et tyranni libidini exponi, inque omnia vitae pericula

---

1 [William Barclay (1546?-1608): Scottish writer on jurisprudence and
government. He went to France in 1571, studied law first at Paris and later
at Bourges, and then taught law at Pont-a-Mousson and later at Angers.
Although a staunch defender of the theory of the divine right of kings, he
had to concede, as can be seen in the quotations given here, that under certain circumstances a rebellion against the king was justified. Locke's quotations are from his most important work: De regno et regali potestate, adversus Buchananum, Brutium, Boucherium, et relignos monarchomachos (6
books, dedicated to Henry IV of France, 1600). Books I and II refute Buchanan's arguments in De jure regni apud Scotos; Books III and IV are directed against Hubert Languet's arguments in Vindiciae contra tyrannos; and
Books V and VI against Jean Boucher's De justa Henrici III abdicatione e
Francorum regno. His other works include: In titulos pandectorum de rebus
creditus et de jure-jurando (dedicated to James I of England, 1605); and
De potestatae Papae: an et quatenus, in reges et principes seculares jus et
imperium habeat (published posthumously in 1609).]

omnesque miserias et molestias à rege deduci patientur? Num illis quod omni animantium generi est à naturâ tributum, denegari debet, ut sc. vim vi repellant, seseq; ab injuria tueantur? Huic breviter responsum sit, Populo universo negari defensionem, quae juris naturalis est, neque ultionem quae praeter naturam est adversus regem concedi debere. Quapropter si rex non in singulares tantum personas aliquot privatum odium exerceat, sed, corpus etiam reipublicae, cujus ipse caput est, i. e. totum populum, vel insignem aliquam ejus partem immani et intolerandâ saevitia seu tyrannide divexet; populo, quidem, hoc casu resistendi ac tuendi se ab injuriâ protestas competit, sed tuendi se tantum, non enim in principem invadendi: et restituendae injuriae illatae, non recedendi à debitâ reverentiâ propter acceptam injuriam. Praesentem denique impetum propulsandi non vim praeteritam ulciscenti jus habet. Horum enim alterum à naturâ est, ut vitam scilicet corpusque tueamur. Alterum vero contra naturam, ut inferior de superiori supplicium sumat. Quod itaque populus malum, antequam factum sit, impedire potest, ne fiat, id postquam factum est, in regem authorem sceleris vindicare non potest: populus igitur hoc ampliùs quam privatus quispiam habet: quod huic, vel ipsis adversariis judicibus, excepto Buchanano, nullum nisi in patentia remedium superest. Cum ille si intolerabilis tyrannus est (modicum enim ferre omnino debet) resistere cum reverentiâ possit.—Barclay, *Contra Monarchomachos, lib*. iii. c. 8.

In English thus:

233. "But if anyone should ask: Must the people then always lay themselves open to the cruelty and rage of tyranny? Must they see their cities pillaged and laid in ashes, their wives and children exposed to the tyrant's lust and fury, and themselves and families reduced by their king to ruin, and all the miseries of want and oppression, and yet sit still? Must men alone be debarred the common privilege of opposing force with force, which nature allows so freely to all other creatures for their preservation from injury? I answer: Self-defense is a part of the law of nature, nor can it be denied the community, even against the king himself; but to revenge themselves upon him must by no means

be allowed them, it being not agreeable to that law. Wherefore, if the king should show an hatred, not only to some particular persons, but sets himself against the body of the commonwealth whereof he is the head, and shall with intolerable ill-usage cruelly tyrannize over the whole or a considerable part of the people, in this case the people have a right to resist and defend themselves from injury; but it must be with this caution, that they only defend themselves, but do not attack their prince; they may repair the damages received, but must not for any provocation exceed the bounds of due reverence and respect. They may repulse the present attempt, but must not revenge past violences; for it is natural for us to defend life and limb, but that an inferior should punish a superior is against nature. The mischief which is designed them the people may prevent before it be done; but when it is done, they must not revenge it on the king, though author of the villainy. This therefore is the privilege of the people in general, above what any private person has: that particular men are allowed by our adversaries themselves—Buchanan [2] only excepted—to have no other remedy but patience, but the body of the people may with reverence resist intolerable tyranny; for when it is but moderate, they ought to endure it."

234. Thus far that great advocate of monarchical power allows of resistance.

235. It is true he has annexed two limitations to it, to no purpose:

First, he says, it must be with reverence.

Secondly, it must be without retribution or punishment; and the reason he gives is: because an inferior cannot punish a superior.

First, how to resist force without striking again, or how to strike with reverence, will need some skill to make intelligible.

[2] [George Buchanan (1506–1582); Scottish poet and humanist who spent much of his life in France. In *De Jure regni apud Scotos* (published in 1579 and acclaimed as a revolutionary work) he argued that power was derived from the people and did not lie in the king by virtue of divine right. In the same work he attempted to minimize the dependence of politics and government on religion by arguing that government arose as a result of man's social nature and was, therefore, a natural phenomenon. (Cf. note 1, p. 74.)]

He that shall oppose an assault only with a shield to receive the blows, or in any more respectful posture, without a sword in his hand, to abate the confidence and force of the assailant, will quickly be at an end of his resistance, and will find such a defense serve only to draw on himself the worst usage. This is as ridiculous a way of resisting as Juvenal [3] thought it of fighting: *ubi tu pulsas, ego vapulo tantum.* And the success of the combat will be unavoidably the same he there describes it:

Libertas pauperis haec est:
Pulsatus rogat, et pugnis concisus adorat,
Ut liceat paucis cum dentibus inde reverti.

This will always be the event of such an imaginary resistance, where men may not strike again. He, therefore, who may resist must be allowed to strike. And then let our author or anybody else join a knock on the head or a cut on the face with as much reverence and respect as he thinks fit. He that can reconcile blows and reverence may, for aught I know, deserve for his pains a civil, respectful cudgeling, wherever he can meet with it.

Secondly, as to his second: an inferior cannot punish a superior. That is true, generally speaking, while he is his superior. But to resist force with force, being the state of war that levels the parties, cancels all former relation of reverence, respect, and superiority; and then the odds that remains is that he who opposes the unjust aggressor has this superiority over him, that he has a right, when he prevails, to punish the offender both for the breach of the peace and all the evils that followed upon it. Barclay, therefore, in another place, more coherently to himself, denies it to be lawful to resist a king in any case. But he there assigns two cases whereby a king may unking himself. His words are:

Quid ergo, nulline casus incidere possunt quibus populo sese erigere atque in regem impotentius dominantem arma capere et invadere jure suo suâque authoritate liceat? Nulli certe quamdiu rex manet. Semper enim ex divinis id obstat, Regem honorificato; et qui potestati resistit, Dei ordinationi resistit: non aliàs igitur in

---

[3] [Juvenal (60?–?140 A.D.): A Roman poet who bitterly satirized the vices of Roman society.]

eum populo potestas est quam si id committat propter quod ipso jure rex esse desinat. Tunc enim se ipse principatu exuit atque in privatis constituit liber: hoc modo populus et superior efficitur, reverso ad eum sc. jure illo quod ante regem inauguratum in interregno habuit. At sunt paucorum generum commissa ejusmodi quae hunc effectum pariunt. At ego cum plurima animo perlustrem, duo tantum invenio, duos, inquam, casus quibus rex ipso facto ex rege non regem se facit et omni honore et dignitate regali atque in subditos potestate destituit; quorum etiam meminit Winzerus. Horum unus est, si regnum disperdat, quemadmodum de Nerone fertur, quod is nempe senatum populumque Romanum atque adeo urbem ipsam ferro flammaque vastare, ac novas sibi sedes quaerere decrevisset. Et de Caligula, quod palam denunciarit se neque civem neque principem senatui amplius fore, inque animo habuerit interempto utriusque ordinis electissimo quoque Alexandriam commigrare, ac ut populum uno ictu interimeret, unam ei cervicem optavit. Talia cum rex aliquis meditatur et molitur serio, omnem regnandi curam et animum ilico abjicit, ac proinde imperium in subditos amittit, ut dominus servi pro derelicto habiti dominium.

236. Alter casus est, si rex in alicujus clientelam se contulit, ac regnum quod liberum à majoribus et populo traditum accepit, alienae ditioni mancipavit. Nam tunc quamvis forte non eâ mente id agit populo plane ut incommodet: tamen quia quod praecipuum est regiae dignitatis amisit, ut summus scilicet in regno secundum Deum sit, et solo Deo inferior, atque populum etiam totum ignorantem vel invitum, cujus libertatem sartam et tectam conservare debuit, in alterius gentis ditionem et potestatem dedidit; hâc velut quadam regni ab alienatione efficit, ut nec quod ipse in regno imperium habuit retineat, nec in eum cui collatum voluit, juris quicquam transferat; atque ita eo facto liberum jam et suae potestatis populum relinquit, cujus rei exemplum unum annales Scotici suppeditant.—Barclay, *Contra Monarchomachos*, l. iii. c. 16.

Which in English runs thus:

237. "What, then, can there no case happen wherein the people may of right and by their own authority help themselves, take

arms, and set upon their king imperiously domineering over them? None at all while he remains a king. 'Honor the king,' and 'He that resists the power resists the ordinance of God,' are divine oracles that will never permit it. The people, therefore, can never come by a power over him, unless he does something that makes him cease to be a king; for then he divests himself of his crown and dignity and returns to the state of a private man, and the people become free and superior, the power which they had in the interregnum, before they crowned him king, devolving to them again. But there are but few miscarriages which bring the matter to this state. After considering it well on all sides, I can find but two. Two cases there are, I say, whereby a king, *ipso facto*, becomes no king and loses all power and regal authority over his people; which are also taken notice of by Winzerus.

"The first is, if he endeavor to overturn the government, that is, if he have a purpose and design to ruin the kingdom and commonwealth, as it is recorded of Nero, that he resolved to cut off the senate and people of Rome, lay the city waste with fire and sword, and then remove to some other place; and of Caligula, that he openly declared that he would be no longer a head to the people or senate, and that he had it in his thoughts to cut off the worthiest men of both ranks, and then retire to Alexandria, and he wished that the people had but one neck, that he might dispatch them all at a blow—such designs as these, when any king harbors in his thoughts and seriously promotes, he immediately gives up all care and thought of the commonwealth, and consequently forfeits the power of governing his subjects, as a master does the dominion over his slaves whom he has abandoned.

238. "The other case is when a king makes himself the dependent of another and subjects his kingdom, which his ancestors left him, and the people put free into his hands to the dominion of another; for however perhaps it may not be his intention to prejudice the people, yet because he has hereby lost the principal part of regal dignity, viz., to be next and immediately under God supreme in his kingdom, and also because he betrayed or forced his people, whose liberty he ought to have carefully preserved, into the power and dominion of a foreign nation. By this, as it were,

alienation of his kingdom, he himself loses the power he had in it before, without transferring any the least right to those on whom he would have bestowed it; and so by this act sets the people free, and leaves them at their own disposal. One example of this is to be found in the *Scottish Annals*."

239. In these cases Barclay, the great champion of absolute monarchy, is forced to allow that a king may be resisted and ceases to be a king. That is, in short, not to multiply cases, in whatsoever he has no authority, there he is no king and may be resisted; for wheresoever the authority ceases, the king ceases, too, and becomes like other men who have no authority. And these two cases he instances in differ little from those above-mentioned to be destructive to governments, only that he has omitted the principle from which his doctrine flows; and that is the breach of trust in not preserving the form of government agreed on, and in not intending the end of government itself, which is the public good and preservation of property. When a king has dethroned himself and put himself in a state of war with his people, what shall hinder them from prosecuting him who is no king, as they would any other man who has put himself into a state of war with them? Barclay and those of his opinion would do well to tell us. This further I desire may be taken notice of out of Barclay, that he says, "The mischief that is designed them the people may prevent before it be done," whereby he allows resistance when tyranny is but in design. "Such designs as these," says he, "when any king harbors in his thoughts and seriously promotes, he immediately gives up all care and thought of the commonwealth," so that, according to him, the neglect of the public good is to be taken as an evidence of such design, or at least for a sufficient cause of resistance. And the reason of all he gives in these words: "Because he betrayed or forced his people whose liberty he ought carefully to have preserved." What he adds—"into the power and dominion of a foreign nation"—signifies nothing, the fault and forfeiture lying in the loss of their liberty which he ought to have preserved, and not in any distinction of the persons to whose dominion they were subjected. The people's right is equally invaded and their liberty lost whether they are made slaves to any

of their own or a foreign nation; and in this lies the injury, and against this only have they the right of defense. And there are instances to be found in all countries which show that it is not the change of nations in the persons of their governors but the change of government that gives the offense. Bilson, a bishop of our church, and a great stickler for the power and prerogative of princes, does, if I mistake not, in his treatise of "Christian Subjection," acknowledge that princes may forfeit their power and their title to the obedience of their subjects; [4] and if there needed authority in a case where reason is so plain, I could send my reader to Bracton,[5] Fortescue,[6] and the author of *The Mirror*,[7] and others—writers that cannot be suspected to be ignorant of our government, or enemies to it. But I thought Hooker alone might be enough to satisfy those men who, relying on him for their ecclesiastical polity, are by a strange fate carried to deny those principles upon which he builds it. Whether they are herein made the tools of cunninger workmen to pull down their own fabric, they were best look. This I am sure: their civil policy is so

[4] [Thomas Bilson (ca. 1546–1616). Locke is here referring to *The True Difference Between Christian Subjection and Unnatural Rebellion* (1586), in which Bilson showed the necessity for the submission of English subjects to royal authority. Like Barclay, however, he found it necessary to concede that in certain cases a revolt against royal authority was justified (cf. note 1, p. 130), e.g. the revolt of the Protestants in Europe against the Catholics who were then in power.]

[5] [Henry de Bracton (d. 1268): An English lawyer and constitutional authority who, in his *De legibus et consuetudinibus Angliae* (first published in 1569), expounded the dual theory that the king must be the supreme being in his realm, but that he must be subject to law. "The king . . . ought to be subject to God and the law, since law makes the king."]

[6] [Sir John Fortescue (1394–1476): An early English constitutional lawyer, and the author of *De natura legis naturae, De laudibus legum Anglicae,* and *De Monarchia, or the Governance of England.* His works are significant because in them he developed, and applied specifically to England, the theory of *dominium regale et politicum,* i.e., the constitutional principle that neither the king nor the people could make laws without the consent of the other.]

[7] [Locke apparently refers here to William Baldwin, the author, "with diverse learned men," of *The Mirror for Magistrates.* Published in 1559, it was addressed to the "nobility and all others in office." Reciting in poetic form the tragedies of earlier rulers who, through recklessness or abuse of power, brought about their own downfalls, the author warns those currently in office against bringing upon themselves similar fates. Baldwin's Preface, in moder-

new, so dangerous, and so destructive to both rulers and people that as former ages never could bear the broaching of it, so it may be hoped those to come, redeemed from the impositions of these Egyptian under-task-masters, will abhor the memory of such servile flatterers who, while it seemed to serve their turn, resolved all government into absolute tyranny, and would have all men born to what their mean souls fitted them for—slavery.

240. Here, it is like, the common question will be made: Who shall be judge whether the prince or legislative act contrary to their trust? This, perhaps, ill-affected and factious men may spread amongst the people, when the prince only makes use of his due prerogative. To this I reply: The people shall be judge; for who shall be judge whether his trustee or deputy acts well and according to the trust reposed in him but he who deputes him and must, by having deputed him, have still a power to discard him when he fails in his trust? If this be reasonable in particular cases of private men, why should it be otherwise in that of the greatest moment where the welfare of millions is concerned, and also where the evil, if not prevented, is greater and the redress very difficult, dear, and dangerous?

241. But further, this question, Who shall be judge? cannot mean that there is no judge at all; for where there is no judicature on earth to decide controversies amongst men, God in heaven is Judge. He alone, it is true, is Judge of the right. But every man is judge for himself, as in all other cases, so in this, whether another has put himself into a state of war with him, and whether he should appeal to the Supreme Judge, as Jephthah did.

---

nized spelling, expresses it thus: "For here as in a looking glass, you shall see (if vice be in you) how the like has been punished in others heretofore, whereby admonished, I trust it will be a good occasion to move you to the sooner amendment. This is the chiefest end why it is set forth, which God grant it may attain."

The work, reprinted seven times, was very popular and had a great influence on contemporary British literature.

The original *Mirror* by Baldwin and the subsequent "Parts added" to it by John Higgins and Thomas Blenerhasset have been re-edited by Lily B. Campbell, who has also contributed excellent Introductions to the two editions: *The Mirror for Magistrates*, Cambridge University Press, 1938; *Parts Added to the Mirror for Magistrates*, Cambridge University Press, 1946.]

242. If a controversy arise betwixt a prince and some of the people in a matter where the law is silent or doubtful, and the thing be of great consequence, I should think the proper umpire in such a case should be the body of the people; for in cases where the prince has a trust reposed in him and is dispensed from the common ordinary rules of the law, there, if any men find themselves aggrieved and think the prince acts contrary to or beyond that trust, who so proper to judge as the body of the people (who, at first, lodged that trust in him) how far they meant it should extend? But if the prince, or whoever they be in the administration, decline that way of determination, the appeal then lies nowhere but to heaven; force between either persons who have no known superior on earth, or which permits no appeal to a judge on earth, being properly a state of war wherein the appeal lies only to heaven; and in that state the injured party must judge for himself when he will think fit to make use of that appeal and put himself upon it.

243. To conclude, the power that every individual gave the society when he entered into it can never revert to the individuals again as long as the society lasts, but will always remain in the community, because without this there can be no community, no commonwealth, which is contrary to the original agreement; so also when the society has placed the legislative in any assembly of men, to continue in them and their successors with direction and authority for providing such successors, the legislative can never revert to the people while that government lasts, because having provided a legislative with power to continue for ever, they have given up their political power to the legislative and cannot resume it. But if they have set limits to the duration of their legislative and made this supreme power in any person or assembly only temporary, or else when by the miscarriages of those in authority it is forfeited, upon the forfeiture, or at the determination of the time set, it reverts to the society, and the people have a right to act as supreme and continue the legislative in themselves, or erect a new form, or under the old form place it in new hands, as they think good.